CENTRAL CLAIMS UNIT

GW00686426

Munkman on
Employer's Liability

PLEASE DONATE YOUR OLD EDITION OF THIS BOOK TO THE
INTERNATIONAL LAW BOOK FACILITY

If you still have the old edition of this book, why not donate it to the
International Law Book Facility (ILBF)? This title is particularly needed by
law schools, law societies, pro bono groups and other institutions and
individuals in Africa, Asia and the Caribbean.

The ILBF is establishing itself as a charity which aims to provide key legal
texts to worthy recipients in developing jurisdictions. It is headed by a Board
and Operating Committee consisting of solicitors, barristers and legal librar-
ians, as well as by officers of Book Aid International, The Law Society, The
Bar Council, The International Bar Association, Sweet & Maxwell and
LexisNexis Butterworths. The Chairman of the Board is Lord Justice Thomas
of the Court of Appeal.

Your help is needed both in donating old editions and donating funds to cover
the costs of shipment. To make a donation, please send cheques payable to
'ILBF' to the ILBF at the following address. To donate your old edition of this
book, simply send it DX or post, to DX 149121 Canary Wharf 3 (10 Upper
Bank St, London E14 5JJ).

ISBN 1-4057-0899-9

9 781405 708999

Munkman on Employer's Liability

Fourteenth edition

General Editors
Barry Cotter *Old Square chambers*
Daniel Bennett *Old Square chambers*

Contributors
Stuart Brittendon *Old Square chambers*
Damian Brown *Old Square chambers*
Jonathan Clarke *Old Square chambers*
Corinna Ferguson *Old Square chambers*
John Hendy QC *Old Square chambers*
Andrew Hogarth QC *12 Kings Bench Walk*
Toby Kempster *Old Square chambers*
The Honourable Mr Justice Brian Langstaff
Philip Mead *Old Square chambers*
Nadia Motraghi *Old Square chambers*
Thomas Roe *3 Hare Court*
Ian Scott *Old Square chambers*
Andrew Watterson *Professor of Occupational and Environmental Health, University of Stirling*
David Wilby QC *Old Square Chambers*

LexisNexis®
Butterworths

Members of the LexisNexis Group worldwide

United Kingdom	LexisNexis Butterworths, a Division of Reed Elsevier (UK) Ltd, Halsbury House, 35 Chancery Lane, London, WC2A 1EL, and RSH, 1–3 Baxter's Place, Leith Walk Edinburgh EH1 3AF
Argentina	LexisNexis Argentina, Buenos Aires
Australia	LexisNexis Butterworths, Chatswood, New South Wales
Austria	LexisNexis Verlag ARD Orac GmbH & Co KG, Vienna
Benelux	LexisNexis Benelux, Amsterdam
Canada	LexisNexis Canada, Markham, Ontario
Chile	LexisNexis Chile Ltda, Santiago
China	LexisNexis China, Beijing and Shanghai
France	LexisNexis SA, Paris
Germany	LexisNexis Deutschland GmbH, Munster
Hong Kong	LexisNexis Hong Kong, Hong Kong
India	LexisNexis India, New Delhi
Italy	Giuffrè Editore, Milan
Japan	LexisNexis Japan, Tokyo
Malaysia	Malayan Law Journal Sdn Bhd, Kuala Lumpur
Mexico	LexisNexis Mexico, Mexico
New Zealand	LexisNexis NZ Ltd, Wellington
Poland	Wydawnictwo Prawnicze LexisNexis Sp, Warsaw
Singapore	LexisNexis Singapore, Singapore
South Africa	LexisNexis Butterworths, Durban
USA	LexisNexis, Dayton, Ohio

© Reed Elsevier (UK) Ltd 2006

Published by LexisNexis Butterworths

All rights reserved. No part of this publication may be reproduced in any material form (including photocopying or storing it in any medium by electronic means and whether or not transiently or incidentally to some other use of this publication) without the written permission of the copyright owner except in accordance with the provisions of the Copyright, Designs and Patents Act 1988 or under the terms of a licence issued by the Copyright Licensing Agency Ltd, 90 Tottenham Court Road, London, England W1T 4LP. Applications for the copyright owner's written permission to reproduce any part of this publication should be addressed to the publisher.

Warning: The doing of an unauthorised act in relation to a copyright work may result in both a civil claim for damages and criminal prosecution.

Crown copyright material is reproduced with the permission of the Controller of HMSO and the Queen's Printer for Scotland. Any European material in this work which has been reproduced from EUR-lex, the official European Communities legislation website, is European Communities copyright.

A CIP Catalogue record for this book is available from the British Library.

ISBN for this volume
ISBN 10: 1405708999
ISBN 13: 9781405708999

Typeset by Letterpart Ltd, Reigate, Surrey

Printed and bound in Great Britain by CPI Bath Press, Bath

Visit LexisNexis Butterworths at www.lexisnexis.co.uk

Preface to fourteenth edition

Employers' liability law has continued to move forward at some pace since the last edition. The development of online case reporting has resulted in the availability of many more first instance and appellate judgements. Indeed the sheer volume of appellate decisions has transformed many areas of the law and required extensive rewriting of the book. The regulations introduced since 1992 implementing European Directives on health and safety at work have now bedded down into the fabric of employers' liability such that we now feel it is appropriate to consign the chapter on the Factories Acts to history. This was of course the cornerstone of early editions of this text. Further, the radical changes introduced by statutory instruments are such that in some chapters of this book the common law of negligence has become largely irrelevant. In recognition of this, the chapter on breach of statutory duty has been elevated up the order of chapters.

The book has been reorganised and split into two parts. The first half addresses the general principles of employers' liability law whilst the second focuses on liability within specific areas. A chapter on industrial diseases was introduced for the first time in the thirteenth edition and we have extended the focus on specific types of injury, providing individual chapters on asbestos and hand-arm vibration syndrome together with a chapter focusing on the less litigated diseases.

We are extremely grateful to the authors who have contributed to this work and whose names are indicated on the contents pages and at the start of each chapter. We would also like to specifically thank Theresa Hunt for the invaluable and detailed research she conducted for many of the chapters and to Cenric Clement Evans and David Rivers who assisted in the editing of the chapters on the 'six pack'. We are also grateful to Cenric in particular for sharing his detailed knowledge of Scottish case law. Butterworths' assistance has been vital, and we thank them for their comprehensive comprehensive, speedy and informed editing of the text.

We are also greatly indebted to our learned predecessors, upon whose broad shoulders we are able to stand. The late John Munkman wrote the first 11 editions of this book, and the creation of the book's reputation by his clear, comprehensive and at times seminal analysis continues to justify the inclusion of his name in the title. We also thank John Hendy QC, whose career-long dedication to the betterment of workers' rights and seemingly limitless capacity for work has been an inspiration to both us and who, together with Michael Ford, built on the 'Munkman' reputation for comprehensive, erudite and practical coverage of the area of law known as employers' liability.

A special note of thanks is also due to Mr Justice Langstaff who, despite the increased workload brought by his elevation to the High Court bench, has produced two chapters of the very highest quality. Each is truly a tour de force.

Our only hope is that this fourteenth edition can begin to match the standards of the previous thirteen.

For one of us his involvement in health and safety law is largely due to Austin Cotter, whose work over decades in this area in the glass industry created within his son a strong interest in the law relating to worker safety.

How different the picture now is to the world of factory work that he entered when the 1937 Act was still fresh legislation.

Finally we would both like to thank wives and children for coping with the consequences of the time taken beyond that normally taken by our practices.

Barry Cotter

Daniel Bennett

June 2006

Contents

Contents

Chapter 3
Causation, Apportionment and Contribution, Remoteness of Damage, Evidence and Liability without Negligence

Chapter 4
The Employer's Duty of Care

Chapter 5
Breach of Statutory Duty

Contents

Chapter 6
Contributory Negligence, Consenting to the Risk of Injury and Unpaid
Volunteers

Chapter 7
The Liability of Third Parties to an Injured Employee

Chapter 8
The Health and Safety at Work Act 1974

Chapter 9
European Law

Chapter 10
The General Legislation: the Framework Directive, the Temporary Workers Directives, the Management of Health and Safety at Work Regulations and Working Time

Contents

Chapter 11
Reporting and Enforcement

Chapter 12
Industrial Relations

Chapter 13
Miscellaneous: Crown Liability, Transfer of Undertakings, Employers' Liability Insurance

Chapter 14
Psychiatric Injury, Stress and Harassment

Contents

Chapter 15
Dust Diseases

Chapter 16
Hand-arm Vibration Syndrome ('HAVS')

Contents

Chapter 19
Construction Sites

Chapter 20
Equipment at Work

Chapter 21
Manual Handling

Chapter 22
Statutory Control of Substances and Phenomena Hazardous to Health

Contents

Chapter 23
Shipbuilding Yards and Docks

Chapter 24
Mines and Quarries (Including Mines of Stratified Ironstone, Shale and Fireclay)

Contents

Chapter 25
Railways and Other Guided Transport Systems

Chapter 26
Agriculture and Forestry

Chapter 27
Offshore Oil, Gas and Mineral Industries and Diving Operations

Chapter 28
Foreign Accidents and Ill-health Abroad

Table of Statutes

References at the right-hand side of the column are to paragraph numbers. Where a paragraph number is in **bold** this indicates that the Act is set out in part or in full.

Table of Statutes

Table of Statutory Instruments

References at the right-hand side of the column are to paragraph numbers. Where a paragraph number is in **bold** this indicates that the Statutory Instrument is set out in part or in full.

Table of Statutory Instruments

Table of EU Legislative Material

Table of EU Legislative Material

Table of Cases

A

Table of Cases

xlviii

Table of Cases

K

M

Table of Cases

Table of Cases

Table of Cases

Table of Cases

W

Table of Cases

Table of Cases

Chapter 1

THE DEVELOPMENT OF EMPLOYER'S LIABILITY LAW

John Hendy QC

The meaning of employer's liability

1.01 Words and phrases change their meanings over time. 'Employer's liability' now conjures up thoughts of unfair dismissal law and the vast subject matter encompassed by what is today referred to as 'employment law' or, yet more broadly, as 'labour law'. When John Munkman wrote the first edition of this book in 1950, labour law had only recently become a subject for academic teaching and 'employer's liability' was an unambiguous concept referring only to the duties owed by employers to workers to take care to prevent personal injury (accident, injury and ill-health) to the latter arising in or out of their work. This book confines itself to that subject matter and retains the title.

1.02 In spite of a marked increase in the number of persons who are described as 'self-employed', most British workers are employees.[1] An employee is a person who works under a contract of employment with an employer (which may be an agency supplying the worker to another enterprise). There are also workers who are self-employed, or independent contractors. Their contracts ('for service' rather than 'of service') are to be distinguished from contracts of employment.[2] The extent of the legal obligations relating to health and safety owed by an employer to its employees are, on the whole, greater than those owed to independent contractors engaged by the 'employer'. An employer[3] also has health and safety obligations to workers employed by, or engaged as independent contractors to, other employers where those workers come onto sites occupied by the first employer or are otherwise affected by the first employer's operations. This book deals with those liabilities as well. It does not, however, attempt to deal, other than in passing, with health and safety duties to people affected not as workers but as members of the general public, eg as local inhabitants, customers, consumers, road users, and so on.

The nature of the liabilities covered derive from the common law, in particular the law of negligence, and from statute law. In addition, there are in some circumstances duties which are founded directly on European Community law.

---

[1]   In the past, employees have been referred to (in legal language) as 'servants', 'workmen' and the like. The employer has often been referred to as if 'he' were an individual. The authors have attempted a usage which reflects modern circumstances in which the employer is a company rather than a human being, and those who work are of both sexes. The term 'worker' is used in this book (except where the context shows otherwise) in broadly the sense of the very wide definition in the Trade Union and Labour Relations (Consolidation) Act 1992, s 296.

1.02 *The development of employer's liability law*

² This is an extremely difficult distinction, in legal analysis, both on the facts and in its consequences. See generally *Harvey on Industrial Relations and Employment Law*, Div A1 and paras 4.10–4.38, below.
³ And the operator of an enterprise which has no employees, or none on site.

1.03 The legal consequence of a breach of health and safety obligation by an employer will often be damages payable to the victim (or dependants). However, there are other remedies provided by law as well. Injunctions are potentially available, as is the employee's right to walk off the job in extreme circumstances. Health and Safety Executive inspectors have a number of powers, including that of serving *improvement* or *prohibition* notices. Health and safety legislation also makes provision for criminal prosecution, with penalties including fines and imprisonment.

1.04 The range of penalties draws attention to those which may be employed in respect of a breach of the law which has not caused personal injury, those which can be used only where the breach has caused personal injury, and those which may be utilised in either circumstance. The distinction between the use of the law in prevention of harm on the one hand and redress for harm on the other is fundamental, though obvious.

The beginnings of law

1.05 In the two to three million year history of hominids and the 150,000 year history of humans, law (in any modern recognisable sense) is a relatively recent social structure. Whilst rules of human conduct (articulated or not) are older than language and probably as old as humanity itself, law in the positivist sense of rules of human conduct enforced by courts probably has no more than a few thousand years of history. In this country there seems little evidence of law before the Romans 2,000 years ago. Roman law on employer's liability for death or injury at work was undeveloped. There does not seem to be evidence of any law of employer's liability between the collapse of the Roman legal system in the fifth century and the establishment of the Norman national legal system in the twelfth and thirteenth centuries.[1]

¹ A fundamental distinction between the Roman and medieval legal systems of profound importance to the contract of employment was the former's refusal to enforce informal agreements and the latter's insistence on their enforceability: see Alain Supiot 'The Dogmatic Foundations of the Market' (2000) ILJ 321 at 332–334.

1.06 While the law in the feudal period played a significant role in employment relationships,[1] it does not appear that safety at work or compensation for lack of it were matters regulated to any extent by law. This may not be surprising, since the labour laws of those times were not effected for the benefit of workers but for the advantage of employers. Furthermore, compared to the dangers of modern industry, the primitive technology of agriculture (the occupation of the overwhelming majority of working people[2]) cannot have created the numbers of casualties which were generated in later times or which gave rise to the notion that the risks of work were distinct from the risks of everyday life. It may be assumed that before the advance of capitalism,

2

in a society in which working methods and technologies changed little from generation to generation and where the worker's occupation was usually not a matter of choice but inheritance, no-one (worker, employer or judge) would have regarded the risk of accidental injury or death at work as other than part of the ordinary risks of existence itself. But it may have been customary in feudal times for the injured worker to be given by the employer ex gratia support for incapacity and to take the benefits of the extensive system of charity which played such a significant role in feudal culture and social relations.

1   Eg by the fixing of agricultural wages and standard terms of hiring, and in limiting or prohibiting combinations and industrial action—see, for example, the Statutes of Labourers after 1349: 23 Edward III; 25 Edward III st 2; 31 Edward III st 1 c 6; 34 Edward III cc 9–11, 36; Edward III cc 8, 14; 42 Edward III c 6; 2 Richard II c 8; 7 Richard II c 5; 12 Richard II cc 3–5, 7, 9; 13 Richard II c 8; 4 Henry IV c 14; 7 Henry IV c 17; 2 Henry V st 2 c 2; 2 Henry VI c 18; 6 Henry VI c 3; 8 Henry VI c 8; 23 Henry VI c 12. According to Pollock and Maitland (*The History of English Law* (1899) Vol 1, p 30) a statute of King Alfred fixed holidays for labourers working on land belonging to others.
2   Those engaged in those trades well recognised as highly dangerous, such as mining, knife grinding and the like were small in number.

1.07 It is, perhaps, more noteworthy that the rise of capitalism, the expansion of employment in industry, the fracturing (by the intervention of contractual notions) of the feudal bonds which through generations had bound employer and worker together, the intensification of methods of production and the acceleration of technological development (both of machines and substances) did not, apparently, give rise to any legal intervention in matters of work safety, health or welfare, or compensation for injury at work at any point in the transformation from feudalism towards capitalism in the sixteenth, seventeenth and eighteenth centuries.

Early legislation

1.08 In fact the common law with over seven hundred years of continuous (though erratic) development behind it, made no apparent response until 1837, and statute law intervened only 35 years earlier.[1]

1   See generally on the history of this legislation: Alfred Kydd *The History of the Factory Movement from the year 1802 to the enactment of the Ten Hours Bill in 1847* (1857); Hutchings *A History of Factory Legislation* (1st edn, 1903, several subsequent editions); Thomas *The Early Factory Legislation* (1948).

1.09 The 1802 'Act for the preservation of the Health and Morals of Apprentices and others employed in Cotton and other Mills, and Cotton and other Factories' (Geo III, c 73) was passed with little or no opposition in Parliament.[1] The Bill had been promoted by the first Sir Robert Peel, a prominent and wealthy cotton mill owner, against a background in which, at the end of the eighteenth century, the pace of the industrial revolution was accelerating. The growing concentration of labour in factories and mills, utilising powered technology and without natural limits on the hours or rate of work, had brought with it publicity about the conditions of those (particularly children) employed in such establishments. Cotton mills were at

3

the forefront of the development of the factory system, though appalling conditions of work, excessive hours and the use of cheap child labour were commonplace throughout the factory system.

1   Indeed, writing in 1816 Sir Robert Peel noted that the only real opposition was from those who wished to extend the Bill:

> 'I was desired to let that Bill operate through every cottage in the country; I deemed that so unreasonable, that I was determined to give up all management of the measure if it was not left to me; in consequence of that, the opposition which arose more from humanity than from anything else was withdrawn, and I brought in the bill in the state in which it now appears, without any opposition of any consequence being stated.' (Kydd *The History of the Factory Movement from the year 1802*...(above)).

1.10 The 1802 Act was primarily intended to protect the pauper or 'parish' children whose labour was customarily employed (under the guise of bestowing apprenticeships on them) in the cotton mills.[1] The character of the Act demonstrates that it was as much concerned with morality as with health. The Act applied to mills and factories with three or more apprentices or 20 or more employees. It restricted hours of work to 12 a day between the hours of 6am and 9pm. It provided for the abolition of night work. Each apprentice was to be provided with one complete suit of clothes each year and sleeping accommodation was to be such as to separate the sexes and provide that no more than two slept in one bed. The premises were to be given two washings with quicklime yearly, and ventilated with fresh air by means of a sufficient number of windows. The Act provided that the apprentices should be instructed in reading, writing, arithmetic and the principles of the Christian religion and that those who were members of the Church of England should be examined annually by a clergyman, and be prepared at the proper age for confirmation. At the midsummer sessions, in districts in which factories were situated, the Justices of the Peace were required to appoint two factory inspectors, one a JP, the other a clergyman, to make an annual visit to the factories and mills, and such premises in the locality were to be registered with the Clerk to the Justices.

1   See Thompson *The Making of the English Working Class* (1968) ch 10.

1.11 From at least the beginning of the nineteenth century, such was the growth of the factory system that it became increasingly evident that the accompanying demand for child labour (often with consequential adult unemployment) was not restricted to the children of the workhouses but was sucking in also children from family homes.[1] Concern at the decline in moral standards and fear of unrest amongst the working class was of course a major preoccupation of the establishment after the French Revolution. Child labour was being increasingly utilised in many workplaces other than cotton mills. Yet the JPs in the cotton districts did not enforce the 1802 Act with any vigour. Sir Robert Peel introduced a further Bill in 1815 to restrict children's hours to ten, applicable over a wider class of factories. Robert Owen (another cotton mill owner) agitated with the same object outside Parliament.[2] This time there was opposition. The Bill did not pass and Parliamentary Committees were established instead to investigate the situation. The evidence taken illustrated on the one hand the uniformity of the horror of children's working lives, and on the other, the divergence of view amongst employers to the question of legislative regulation. There was, of course, opposition from free marketeers who themselves exploited children's cheap labour. There was support for legislation from philanthropists. There was opposition on the grounds that regulation of some industries would give an unjustified privilege to manufacturers in other trades. There was support on the grounds that restriction on hours made workers more productive.

1   See, for example, Rules *Artisans and Politics in Early Nineteenth Century London* (1977).
2   See Yeo 'Robert Owen and Radical Culture' in Pollard and Salt (eds) *Robert Owen Prophet of the Poor* (1971).

1.12   In the event legislation was passed in 1819,[1] 1825 and 1831 intended to fortify the 1802 Act. The 1831 Act imposed a maximum 12-hour day for all young people in cotton mills. But the 'Ten Hours Movement' eventually resulted in the Factory Act 1833[2] which, though maintaining a 12-hour maximum day for young persons, was extended in scope to woollen and linen mills. Most significantly, in order to prevent further evasion, it provided for enforcement by government-appointed employed inspectors.[3]

Four inspectors were initially appointed.[4] The Act gave them powers of entry, power to make regulations, and the enforcement powers of the magistrates. Their impact was gravely limited by reason of their numbers.[5]

1   On which see Carpenter (ed) *The Factory Act of 1819, Six Pamphlets 1818–1819* (1972).
2   On which see Carpenter (ed) *The Factory Act of 1833, Eight Pamphlets 1833–1834* (1972). The Act followed a Royal Commission established to take the steam out of the Ten Hours Movement (which refused to co-operate with the Commission): see Henriques *The Early Factory Acts and their Enforcement* (1971).
3   On safety legislation and the inspectorate in the nineteenth century see Barhip and Fenn 'The Evolution of the Regulatory Style in the 19th Century: British Factory Inspectorate' (1983) 10 Jnl Law & Soc 201.
4   In 1893 the first women factory inspectors were appointed, becoming the Women's Branch of the Factory Inspectorate. This Branch was ultimately fused with the rest of the Factory Inspectorate in 1921: see Drake McFeely *Lady Inspectors* (1988).
5   The four inspectors were paid £1,000pa and their districts were divided into two or three each with a superintendent and, after 1844, a sub-inspector. The superintendents were paid £250pa, later £350pa.

The common law

1.13   In 1837 the landmark case of *Priestley v Fowler* (1837) 3 M & W 1[1] established that an employer owed, in common law, a personal duty of care to his employee which was actionable by the employee if breach resulted in injury. On the other hand, this case also founded what came to be described as the doctrine of common employment, by which if the cause of the injury was the negligence of a fellow employee, the employer was not to be held vicariously liable unless the employee could prove that the fellow worker was incompetent and that the employer had thereby been negligent in engaging him.[2] In that case the wheel of a butcher's van collapsed because the van was overloaded. The plaintiff was employed to ride on the van and the loading had been done by other employees. The employer was not personally concerned in the loading and was not therefore liable. The employee must be taken to have accepted the risk of negligence by a fellow employee.[3] The doctrine of vicarious liability which had been developed in English law over the previous hundred years[4] applied to protect persons outside the employer's organisation but not to protect employees.[5] These developments were against a backdrop of the 'contractualisation' of the employment relationship in the context of developing social legislation.[6]

1   On this case, the legislation and what lay behind, see Howells *'Priestley v Fowler* and the Factory Acts' (1963) MLR 367.
2   In that case, towards the end of the judgment there is an important passage, which suggests vaguely the sort of personal negligence for which a master might be held liable:

> 'In truth, the mere relation of the master and the servant never can imply an obligation on the part of the master to take more care of the servant than he may reasonably be expected to do of himself. He is, no doubt, bound to provide for the safety of his servant in the course of his employment, to the best of his judgment, information and belief.'

Here the age of laissez-faire is speaking: the 'servant' must look out for himself. But there is at least a hint of general duty resting on the employer to take reasonable care for the safety of his servants.
3   The same principle had been established in France the year before: *Cour d'Appel de Lyon* (29 December 1839), *Dalloz periodique* (1837) 2: 161 (cited in Simitis, below); but was rejected in Scotland for a heroic six years between 1852 and 1858: see *Bartonshill Coal Co v Reid* (para 1.14 below and the footnote thereto).
4   See *Boson v Sandford* (1690) 2 Salk 440.
5   In *Hutchinson v York, Newcastle and Berwick Rly Co* (1850) 5 Exch 343, Alderson B said:

> 'This principle upon which a master is in general liable to answer for accidents resulting from the negligence or unskilfulness of his servants is that the act of his servant is in truth his own act ... Equally clear it is, that though a stranger may treat the act of the servant as the act of his master, yet the servant himself, by whose negligence or want of skill the accident has occurred, cannot ... The difficulty is as to the principle applicable to the case of several servants employed by the same master, and injury resulting to one of them from the negligence of another. In such a case, however, we are of opinion that the master is not in general responsible, when he has selected persons of competent care and skill. They have both engaged in a common service, the duties of which impose a certain risk on each of them; and in case of negligence on the part of the other, the party injured knows that the negligence is that of his fellow-servant and not of his master. He knew, when he engaged in the service, that he was exposed to the risk of injury, not only from his own want of skill or care, but also from the want of it on the part of his fellow-servant; and he must be supposed to have contracted on the terms that, as between himself and his master, he would run this risk.'

This, of course, is the epitome of the doctrine of freedom of contract; on which, more generally, see Atiyah *The Rise and Fall of Freedom of Contract* (1979) and, showing the common application of the doctrine across the developing capitalist world of western Europe and the USA, Simitis 'The case of the employment relationship, elements of a comparison' in Steinmetz (ed) *Private Law and Social Inequality in the Industrial Age* (2000).
6   As to which see Deakin 'The Many Futures of the Contract of Employment' in Conaghan, Fischel and Klare (eds) *Labour Law in an Era of Globalisation* (OUP, 2002) at p 181; and Freedland *The Personal Employment Contract* Oxford Monographs on Labour Law (OUP, 2003) at p 88.

1.14 Even in large scale factory or other industrial undertakings where the employer had no personal role at all and all functions were delegated to subordinates (who, from the senior manager downwards, were in common employment), the doctrine held sway: *Bartonshill Coal Co v Reid, McGuire*

(1858) 3 Macq 266 and 300.[1] The common law as a means of regulating unsafe or unhealthy working conditions was therefore gravely limited.

[1] Scottish cases establishing a duty on the part of the employer to provide a safe system of work (*Sword v Cameron* (1839) 1 D 493), to provide safe and adequate equipment (*Brydon v Stewart* (1855) 2 Macq 30), to take reasonable care for the safety of employees (*Paterson v Wallace & Co* (1854) 1 Macq 748), and declining to follow the doctrine of common employment as foreign jurisprudence (*Dixon v Ranken* (1852) 14 D 420) were reviewed in the *Bartonshill* cases. *Sword*, *Brydon* and *Paterson* were recognised as valid but were wholly overshadowed and rendered of little value by the rejection *of Dixon* and the application of the doctrine of common employment to Scotland as well as England.

Safety legislation

1.15 In 1842 the first Report (on mines) of the Children's Employment Commission was published. Its descriptions of the sufferings of women and children working underground led to the Coal Mines Act 1842[1] which simply prohibited women and children from underground work. The radical nature of this measure undoubtedly eased the way for the milder Factories Act of 1844. The first Mines Inspector was appointed in 1843.

[1] For a discussion of the competing forces behind the Act, see Humphries 'Protective Legislation etc: the Case of the 1842 Mines Regulation Act' in Paul (ed) *On Work* (1988). Parallel struggles over child labour in French, Belgian and German coalmines are evident: Francois *Introduction au droit sociale* (1974, Liege).

1.16 It may be said that the first safety statutes, as opposed to health and welfare legislation, were the Factories Act 1844 (which required safeguarding of mill gearing and prohibited the cleaning of machinery in motion) and the Coal Mines Inspection Act 1850.[1] These Acts marked a historic episode in legal history: the doctrine of freedom of contract, only recently established in the field of employment relationships, was now subject to significant incursions by statute. It was to be the beginning of 'a growing juridification of the employment relationship'.[2] As Simitis has pointed out, in the face of the application of the doctrine of freedom of contract which sanctioned the employers' economic power to de-individualise work in the mass-productive enterprises of factory and mine; 'the legislator could no longer remain passive once it became evident that the collapse of the individual negotiating process legitimised by the expectation of a balance of interests threatened to lead to a breakdown of the societal and political order' consequent on the endangering of the physical existence of those who supplied labour as a commodity.[3] As a historical aside, it is interesting to note that it was the very success of legislative intervention into the employment relationship which led to the evolution in the British trade union movement of a requirement for a political voice (and hence to the founding of the Labour Party), though demands for freedom of association had primacy over those for health and safety protection. By the same token, the success of the health and safety legislation was part of the explanation of the minimal role which health and safety demands had in collective bargaining.

[1] These two Acts were also significant in providing for the Home Secretary to have power to award to a worker injured by a criminal breach, part of any fine imposed on an employer in respect of it. This form of compensation was not used extensively and fell into virtual disuse by the end of the century, being finally abolished in 1959.

1.16 *The development of employer's liability law*

2   Simitis 'The case of the employment relationship, elements of a comparison' in Steinmetz (ed) *Private Law and Social Inequality in the Industrial Age* (2000) at p 195.
3   Simitis above at p 194.

1.17 Between 1844 and 1856 a succession of seven factory statutes and subordinate regulations provided for the safety of children, young persons and women, including provision for the fencing of machinery, hours, mealtimes and holidays. Much of the motivation for this legislation was concern at the twin disclosures of high child mortality rates and of the neglect of very young children by reason of long hours spent in factory work by their mothers.[1] Yet pressure from factory owners was strong enough to cause the Factories Act 1856 to relax some of the requirements of the 1844 Act. The judges, dedicated adherents to the doctrine of freedom of contract, also played a role in undermining the Ten Hours Act of 1847 by legitimating children and women working in relays (*Ryder v Mills* (1850) 3 Exch 853). However, the pressure for protection proved the more powerful as the next 50 years demonstrated.

1   See the 1842 Royal Commission Report on the Sanitary Conditions of the Labouring Classes.

1.18 The Coal Mines Act 1855, extending the Coal Mines Inspection Act of 1850,[1] laid down a number of general rules to be observed in all mines: in particular, there had to be a proper system of underground ventilation to prevent the accumulation and explosion of firedamp gas. The Act of 1855, after various amendments, was followed by the Coal Mines Regulation Act 1872, a comprehensive Act imposing a series of detailed obligations to ensure the safety of the miners. This in its turn was superseded by the Coal Mines Regulation Act 1887.[2]

1   As to the very significant role of the Miners' Association in the passage of this Act see Challinor and Ripley *The Miners' Association—A Trade Union in the Age of the Chartists* (1968).
2   See generally Page-Arnot *The Miners* (1949).

1.19 In 1864 and 1867 specified non-textile factories (including pottery, matchmaking, foundries, blastfurnaces, copper mills and all manufacturing processes employing more than 50 people) and workshops were subject to some of the statutory requirements. In 1875 the Explosives Act introduced a system for the licensing and regulation of factories for the production of gunpowder and other explosives.

Common employment extended

1.20 The inadequacy of the common law in health and safety had by this time been yet further underlined. In 1862 *Clarke v Holmes* 7 H & N 937 established that an employer must provide and maintain safe machinery but *Wilson v Merry* (1868) LR 1 Sc & Div 326 (mine owners not liable for death caused by negligence of underground manager), followed by *Allen v New Gas Co* (1876) 1 Ex D 251, established that the employer could, under the doctrine of common employment, avoid the liability for defective machinery by simply delegating to a subordinate the responsibility for making and keeping it safe: employees were held to be just as much in common employment with the managing director as with employees of lesser status. Such delegation was inevitable where the company was a limited company, a form which blossomed in England after the Companies Act of 1856.[1]

[1] Consolidated by the Companies Act 1862. See Hadden *Company Law and Capitalism* (1972) ch 1.

1.21 The doctrine of common employment was thus being fortified by the judges at a time when capitalism was evolving so as to separate the management of the enterprise from its ownership, thus extending the application of the doctrine.

Statutory intervention into the common law

1.22 The Employers' Liability Act 1880 (passed partly to placate the rising tide of 'new unionism') placed some statutory limitations on the device of delegation under the doctrine of common employment so as to enable damages claims to be brought,[1] though its effect was much reduced by the provision that employers and employees could contract out of it.[2] Consequently the Departmental Committee appointed to inquire into the law relating to compensation for injuries to workmen reported in 1904 that 'the Employers' Liability Act 1880 must be considered to have been a failure'.[3]

[1] Under this Act the employee could succeed if, very broadly, he or she could prove that the accident resulted from a defect in 'the ways, works, machinery or plant', or from the negligence of some person placed in a position of superintendence or whose orders the workman had to obey, or, in the case of a railway, from the negligence of a signalman or engine-driver.
[2] See Pelling *Popular Politics and Society in Late Victorian Britain* (1968); Shannon *The Crisis of Capitalism*; Hunt *British Labour History 1825–1914* (1981).
[3] *Report of the Departmental Committee appointed to inquire into the law relating to compensation for injuries to workmen* (1904) Cmd 2208, para 8.

Comprehensive safety legislation

1.23 By 1875 the law relating to factories and workshops had come to be contained in a patchwork of statutes and regulations, each designed to meet the need (or accommodate the pressure) of the moment without regard to any general pattern of development. The law was reviewed by a Royal Commission, whose report, published in 1876, led to the passing of the Factory and Workshop Act 1878. This Act was the first attempt at comprehensive factory legislation.

However, hardly was it upon the statute book than further extensions of the law were found necessary. Additional factory statutes were passed piecemeal, in 1883, 1889, 1891, 1895 and 1897. Soon the former chaos was restored.

1.24 *The development of employer's liability law*

A step forward for the common law

1.24 In 1898 the landmark decision of *Groves v Lord Wimborne* [1898] 2 QB 402 established that an injured employee could found a claim in damages for breach of statutory duty, in that case in respect of unfenced machinery. Most significantly, it was held that the defence of common employment did not apply to actions for breach of statutory duty. Rigby LJ said in *Groves* at 413:

> 'There has been a failure in the performance of an absolute statutory duty, and there is no need for the plaintiff to allege or prove negligence on the part of anyone in order to make out his cause of action. That being so, the doctrine of common employment is out of the question.'

1.25 Damages claims henceforth became a prominent feature of health and safety law. Such claims were based on breach of statutory duty which, after *Groves*, rapidly overtook in significance common law claims, still crippled by the doctrine of common employment despite the liberalisation of the Employers' Liability Act 1880 and the rejection of the defence of volenti non fit injuria in *Smith v Baker & Sons* [1891] AC 325.[1]

[1] During the currency of the Employers' Liability Act 1880 an attempt had been made to defeat its object by introducing the doctrine of common employment under another form, through the defence of volenti non fit injuria: the claim that the worker had voluntarily assumed the risk of dangerous work, and thereby released his employer from liability. This defence was rejected, so far as actions for breach of statutory duty were concerned, in *Baddeley v Earl of Granville* (1887) 19 QBD 423, and so far as the common law was concerned (though in fact the case was brought under the special procedure of the Employers' Liability Act) in *Smith v Baker & Sons* [1891] AC 325, a case which arose out of a typical nineteenth century accident, where a gang of navvies were clearing a railway cutting. Heavy stones were being slung by crane over their place of work, and though protests were made the system was not altered. Finally one of the stones fell and injured the plaintiff. It was not enough that the plaintiff, knowing of the risk, carried on with the work; volenti did not apply unless it could be shown that the employee consented to take the risk on himself without compensation.

The Workmen's Compensation Acts

1.26 One year before *Groves*, in 1897, the first of the Workmen's Compensation Acts was passed, providing compensation for injury at work on a basis akin to social insurance. Liability did not depend on the negligence of the employer or of any of its employees. Compensation became payable whenever an employee was incapacitated by an accident 'arising out of and in the course of employment', one of the most litigated phrases in the English language. The compensation took the form of a weekly payment during incapacity, roughly representing half the wages which the employee was earning. If the employee caused the accident by misconduct, no compensation was payable and nor was it payable in respect of minor accidents, though recoverable for permanent disablement. A small lump sum was payable to dependants on death.

1.27 The Act of 1897, passed by a Conservative government, applied only to a limited group of industries; but the Liberal government of 1906 extended it by a further Act in 1906, part of their programme of social reform consequential on trade union pressure and the extension of the working class franchise. The 1906 Act covered a further six million workers by its application to all wage earners within a certain financial limit.[1] Finally, after a series of amendments, the law was consolidated in the Workmen's Compensation Act 1925. In its final form the scheme gave compensation for industrial diseases as well as for accidents.

The procedure for enforcing claims was cheap, as there was a special arbitration procedure in the county court, though an immense volume of case law grew up.

[1] The Act was largely based on the *Report of the Departmental Committee appointed to Inquire into the Law relating to Compensation for Injuries to Workmen* (1904) Cmd 2208, a report which provides a useful analysis of the Act and its operation.

1.28 The Workmen's Compensation Acts did not modify the rules of the pre-existing law, which continued to exist side by side with the new system. The employee was required to elect between a claim for damages or under the Workmen's Compensation Acts.

Further legislative protection

1.29 In 1876 the first legislative provision against 'coffin ships' gave some protection to merchant seamen.[1] The first legislative steps directed towards safety in agriculture had been taken with the passing of the Threshing Machines Act 1878, and the Chaff-Cutting Machines (Accidents) Act 1897. Despite the increasing mechanisation of the farming industry, workers in agriculture enjoyed no statutory protection save in the limited area covered by those Acts, since the Factories Acts did not apply (per Somervell LJ in *Stanger v Hendon Borough Council* [1948] 1 KB 571, CA analysing *Nash v Hollinshead* [1901] 1 KB 700, CA). From 1886 the working hours of shop workers had been regulated and in 1900 the first legislation to protect railway workers was enacted. In 1908 the Coal Mines Regulation Act established a maximum shift length of eight hours underground.

[1] The protection was little enough. The Report of the Departmental Committee (above) of 1904, Cmd 2208, App XXXII provided a table of fatal accidents at work showing that the mean annual death rate for all occupations listed in the period 1898–1902 was below 7 per ten thousand. The second most dangerous occupation was coal mining, with a rate of 12.9 per ten thousand, below which came other forms of mining and quarrying (11–12), railways (9.6) and factories (1.9). The highest rate was for seamen, with a staggering 64.5 fatalities per ten thousand.

Consolidation in the twentieth century

1.30 A fresh attempt at the rationalisation of factory legislation was made by the enactment of the Factory and Workshop Act 1901.[1] It was followed by a series *of detailed* regulations, some of which are still in force. This Act remained the principal statute for the regulation of factories until its repeal by the Factories Act 1937, and during its life it was many times extended and amended.

¹ For a history up to this Act and the demands for it see *The Case for the Factory Acts* by Mrs (Beatrice) Webb, Miss Hutchings, Miss Tuckwell, Mrs Reeves and Miss Black with an introduction by Mrs Ward (1901).

1.31 In 1911 a comprehensive Mines Act had been passed, following earlier consolidating amendments since the 1887 Act. The 1911 Act provided a novel means of enforcement, the workmen's inspectors, the forerunners of which may be found in the checkweighmen recognised in the Coal Mines Regulation Act 1872: employees' safety representatives had no statutory existence in other workplaces until 1977. The 1872 Act had also provided for imprisonment as a penal sanction, a means of enforcement continued in the subsequent mines statutes but not extended for a hundred years to other legislation which relied on fines as the sole judicial penalty.

1.32 The Factories Act 1937 had repealed and replaced the Factory and Workshop Acts 1901 to 1929, and other cognate enactments, but the subordinate legislation passed under it, including the important regulations for dangerous trades, continued in force. This Act provided, for the first time, a comprehensive code for safety, health and welfare applicable to all factories irrespective of whether they were textile or non-textile factories and whether mechanical power was used or not. Its many new requirements included such important safety provisions as those relating to lifting tackle and cranes, floors and stairs, means of access and places of work and to steam and air receivers. Electrical stations, ships under repair in harbour or wet-dock and works of engineering construction were also brought within the scope of the legislation. The 1937 Act contained a power to make regulations governing dangerous processes or plant; but owing to the wide range of such regulations made under the similar powers of the Act of 1901, it was not subsequently found necessary to make extensive use of this power, save for bringing older regulations up to date and for regulating new kinds of industry.

1.33 The Factories Act 1937 was in turn amended by the Factories Acts 1948 and 1959. These statutes, together with the Lead Paint (Protection against Poisoning) Act 1926, the Employment of Women and Young Persons Act 1936, and s 7 of the Slaughterhouses Act 1958, were repealed and replaced by the Factories Act 1961, a consolidating measure. The Factories Act 1961, like its predecessors, contained power to make regulations governing dangerous processes and plant.

The common law between the World Wars

1.34 In the transformed society of the period after the First World War, the doctrine of common employment had become an indefensible embarrassment to the common law. *Wilsons & Clyde Coal v English* [1938] AC 57 was one of several cases in the 1930s and 1940s which limited the doctrine of common employment by imposing on employers a personal, non-delegable duty to provide a safe system of work, a competent staff, and safe plant and equipment.[1] The decision in *English*'s case proved to be a more important turning point than the formal abolition of common employment ten years later; its influence on the shape of health and safety law remains to this day.[2]

[1] Thus reinstating the principles established in the Scottish cases 80 years before—see para 1.14 fn 1, above. It is notable that *English*'s case followed within six years of the landmark in negligence of *Donoghue v Stevenson* [1932] AC 562, HL.

[2] See, for example, the HSWA 1974, s 2.

1.35 These cases also ended the line of authority which began with *Smith v Baker* (see para 1.25) by holding that employees were not to be taken to have consented by virtue of an implied term in the contract of employment to the risk of the employer's negligent performance of it. On the other hand, *Caswell v Powell Duffryn Associated Collieries Ltd* [1940] AC 152 established that contributory negligence was a complete defence to an action for breach of statutory duty.[1]

[1] Though in the same case the House adopted the useful observation of Lawrence J in an earlier case:

> 'It is not for every risky thing which a workman in a factory may do in his familiarity with the machinery that a plaintiff ought to be held guilty of contributory negligence.'

The Labour government of 1945

1.36 The reforming government of 1945, as well as laying the foundations of the welfare state, made significant changes to the law on compensation for work-related injuries. The Law Reform (Contributory Negligence) Act 1945 removed contributory negligence on the part of the employee as a complete defence to a claim against an employer, reversing *Caswell*'s case. From 1945 onwards contributory negligence, if established, has been relevant only to the extent of reducing damages in proportion to the degree of contributory negligence found. In 1948 the Law Reform (Personal Injuries) Act finally put an end to what remained of the doctrine of common employment.

1.37 While *Wilsons and Clyde Coal v English* had infused fresh life into the common law by establishing that the employer's duty (in negligence) was not only to provide a competent staff of men but also adequate material, a proper system of work, and effective supervision, these two Acts cleared other obstacles to actions for breach of statutory duty and negligence.

1.38 The 1948 Act also repealed the Employers' Liability Act 1880 and the Workmen's Compensation Acts, which had been replaced in 1946 by the National Insurance (Industrial Injuries) Act,[1] with scaled benefits provided by the state and funded by contributions paid by employer and employee. The right to industrial injury benefit ran alongside the right to damages for negligence or breach of statutory duty, and the employee could exercise both.

[1] Special provision was made for pneumoconiosis by the Pneumoconiosis etc (Workers' Compensation) Act 1979.

Extending the legislation

1.39 The Gowers Committee of Enquiry on Health, Welfare and Safety in Non-Industrial Employment, reporting in 1949 (Cmd 7664), recommended that safety, health and welfare legislation should be extended over a wide field of non-industrial employment, including agriculture. The Agriculture (Poisonous Substances) Act 1952 and the Agriculture (Safety, Health and Welfare Provisions) Act 1956 were two of the results.

1.40 Two years earlier the comprehensive provisions of the Mines and Quarries Act 1954 had been enacted, imposing the most extensive safety regime in any industry. It involved not only regulation in relation to equipment, places, access, egress, processes, specific hazards and methods of working but also laid statutory duties on mine managers, required pit deputies to make inspections, gave workmen's inspectors powers of inspection, and extended the functions of the inspectors of mines.

1.41 Although shop workers' hours had been regulated since 1886 and local authorities had powers to limit the opening hours of shops since 1904, no other statutory protection extended to shop workers and none at all to office workers. The Gowers Committee had in 1949 recommended extension and in 1960 a Private Members' Bill had become the Offices Act 1960. In 1963 it was repealed and replaced by the Offices, Shops and Railway Premises Act 1963. That Act gave statutory protection to the largest remaining group of unprotected workers.

1.42 Other sections of the workforce have subsequently been covered as, for example, offshore workers under the Mineral Workings (Offshore Installations) Act 1971. In the wake of the Cullen Report (1990, Cm 1310) into the Piper Alpha oil rig disaster, the offshore industry became regulated by the Offshore Safety Act 1992, the Offshore Safety (Protection against Victimisation) Act 1992, and the Offshore Installations (Safety Case) Regulations 1992, SI 1992/2885[1] amongst other legislation. There has been further offshore safety legislation since.

[1] Revoked and replaced by the 2005 Regulations of the same name, SI 2005/3117.

1.43 From the Explosives Act 1875 (itself superseded by the Explosives Act 1923) onwards, particular industrial hazards to the public as well as to the workforce have been the subject of statutory regulation. Examples are: the Alkali etc Works Regulation Act 1906, the Petroleum (Consolidation) Act 1928, the Radioactive Substances Act 1960 and the Nuclear Installations Acts 1959, 1965 and 1969.

1.44 One hazard of very general risk is fire. The Fire Precautions Act 1971 brought together provisions in a number of unrelated pieces of legislation dealing with particular classes of premises and particular activities and were extended to all factory, office, shop and railway premises by the Fire Precautions (Factory, Offices, Shop and Railway Premises) Order 1989, SI 1989/76. The subsequent Fire Precautions (Workplace) Regulations 1997, SI 1997/1840 have now been replaced by the Regulatory Reform (Fire Safety) Order 2005, SI 2005/1541.

1.45 In 1969 two important statutes were passed. The Employers' Liability (Compulsory Insurance) Act required that all employers carry insurance to cover potential liability to employees, and the Employers' Liability (Defective Equipment) Act 1969 provided that the employer is liable in negligence for injury caused by defective equipment notwithstanding that the fault was that of a third party manufacturer or supplier.

The end of jury trials

1.46 The 1960s saw another change of importance. In *Ward v James* [1965] 1 All ER 563 (extended in *H v Ministry of Defence* [1991] 2 All ER 834) jury trials were virtually eliminated from personal injury litigation.[1] The substitution of juries by judges giving reasoned judgments clearly has contributed to the development of the law of negligence over the last 40 years—although not always in the direction of greater certainty.[2]

[1] In consequence the real value of damages in personal injury cases is significantly less than might otherwise have been expected. Compare the level of damages in cases where juries are still available, such as defamation and false imprisonment.

[2] The original author of *Munkman* heavily criticised the pervading judicially developed doctrine of reasonable foreseeability, the exercise of which he felt was 'vague, capricious and subjective' to such an extent that he felt the common law to be in the position of the seventeenth century courts of equity where 'justice varied with the length of the Chancellor's foot'. Later authors of the book have drawn attention to various principles which have evolved in recent years further extending judicial discretions.

Motives and causes

1.47 There is no doubt that a variety of factors led to the introduction of the legislation outlined above. Public outrage (informed by an increasingly mass media) at the gross exploitation of employees, particularly women and children, public horror at major industrial disasters, public distaste at a particular lacuna in the law exhibited in a widely publicised case, employer fear (in the early days) of insurrection,[1] growing trade union organisation, influence and pressure on behalf of the employees, parliamentary responses to a widening electorate, the response to the rising power of the industrialists by the aristocracy (whose wealth derived largely from agriculture, unregulated until the twentieth century), the emergence of the welfare state, pure humanitarian instincts—all played a part. It is clear that a free market in labour untrammelled by regulation on health and safety grounds was not tolerable to many sections of society, and not just workers, once capitalist methods of production intensified by the advances of technology took hold.[2]

1   'We warn legislators of the infallible result of their not carrying out the protective character of Government ... Tell the British labourer that he must fight all his own battles and make all his own conditions without help from the State, and what sort of feeling is he likely to have towards that State, towards its head and towards its aristocracy?': *The Times*, 9 May 1844, quoted and elaborated by Carson in 'Hostages to History; Some Aspects of the Occupational Health and Safety Debate in Historical Perspective' in Creighton and Cunningham (eds) *The Industrial Relations of Occupation Health and Safety* (1985).
2   See the analysis of Simitis, para 1.16, above. In fact, as many commentators have pointed out, underlying the supposed 'free market', there are always non-market regulations of sorts—in particular the legal enforcement of contractual relationships: see especially Weber *On Law in Economy and Society* (1945).

1.48 One factor in the introduction of regulation, particularly in the nineteenth century, was incontestably influential. It was the pressure from large manufacturers, sensitive to public demand for safer conditions and often able to accommodate it by their investment in more productive technology, who were determined that their smaller competitors would not undercut their production costs by working excessive hours or refusing to introduce safety measures. That factor remained highly visible until quite recently in the impetus for standardised health and safety (and other) regulation emanating from the European Union. The goal of a level playing field from which 'social dumping' is eradicated, is a concept which, but for its modern language, would have been immediately accessible to the manufacturers who supported Sir Robert Peel.[1] By the same token, resistance to the introduction in the UK of the European Working Time Directive (see chapter 10) on the grounds that it would increase labour costs and so create unemployment, that it would interfere with the employee's freedom of contract and that hours of work were unrelated to health and safety, are precisely those arguments encountered by Sir Robert Peel and the Ten Hours Movement at the beginning of the nineteenth century.[2] The retreat by the European Union from its resistance to social dumping and from its emphasis on social protection may be seen as trends which crystallised in the draft European Constitution of 18 June 2004 and which, according to some, caused the rejection of the Constitution in referenda in France and Holland.

1   The European approach, of course, encompassed many other strands not so readily comprehensible to the nineteenth century pioneers, for example, the motivation to require uniform and extensive regulation in order to reduce social costs such as health care, social security, lost tax and insurance contributions etc.
2   See eg 'A Letter to the Rt Hon Lord Ashleigh' by a Lancashire cotton spinner, 30 March 1833 in Carpenter (ed) *British Labour Struggles: Contemporary Pamphlets 1727–1850: the Factory Act of 1833* (1972).

1.49 The role of the judiciary in the development of the law, as can be seen, has oscillated between expansion and restriction of liability. It has certainly not been in congruity with the course of statutory development. The reasons for this are tangential to the text of this book.[1]

1   For a telling vignette see Howells '*Priestley v Fowler* and the Factory Acts' (1963) MLR 367 at 384–385.

Rationalisation in the 1970s

1.50 In 1974 the legislative approach to health and safety was transformed. The Labour government in 1967 published a consultative document with a view to consolidating in one Act and extending to other workplaces the Offices, Shops and Railway Premises Act 1963 and the Factories Act 1961. During 1968 and 1969 it appears that doubts arose as to the feasibility of this project.[1] In June 1970 the Secretary of State for Employment and Productivity, Barbara Castle, established a Royal Commission under the Chairmanship of Lord Robens.

[1]   See the Robens Report (below) at p 188.

1.51 The Robens Report (1972, Cmnd 5034) was the product of the first comprehensive review of 'the safety and health of persons in the course of their employment (other than transport workers ...)'. The Report quoted from Sidney Webb's 1919 preface to Hutchins and Harrison's *A History of Factory Legislation*:

'This century of experiment in factory legislation affords a typical example of English practical empiricism ... Each successive statute aimed at remedying a single ascertained evil. It was in vain the objectors urged that other evils, no more defensible, existed in other trades or amongst other classes, or with persons of ages other than those to which a particular Bill applied ...'

1.52 The Report recommended that in place of what it described as the 'haphazard mass of ill assorted and intricate detail' of the existing legislation, there should be:

'a comprehensive and orderly set of revised provisions under a new enabling Act. The new Act should contain a clear statement of the basic principles of safety responsibility. It should be supported by regulations and by non-statutory codes of practice, with emphasis on the latter. A determined effort should be made to revise, harmonise and update the existing large body of detailed statutory regulations, to simplify their style and to reduce their number ...The scope of the new legislation should extend to all employers and employees ... [and] to the self employed ...'

1.53 In fact, 25 years after the Act, the major pre-1974 Acts were still extant and the goal of unifying and extending their provisions had not been achieved. This is not to belittle the unifying and extending legislation brought in under the Act to regulate various activities and substances across industries. It remained the case, however, that, until the 1990s, the existence of the statutory requirement to fence a dangerous machine *still* depended on whether one or other of the Acts or regulations applied to the particular premises or work for which the machine was to be used.

1.54 In fact it was the European Union and its health and safety Directives which ultimately provided the impetus for the production of a 'comprehensive and orderly set of revised provisions' revised, harmonised, updated, simplified and reduced in number, rather than the 1974 Act.

1.55 The development of employer's liability law

1.55 The great achievement of the Health and Safety at Work Act 1974[1] was to unify the administration of the health and safety legislation and to give it jurisdiction over (nearly) all workers. The bringing together of the various inspectorates into the Health and Safety Executive, under the supervision of the Health and Safety Commission (appointed by the Secretary of State and upon which both sides of industry are represented) transformed regulation of health and safety at work. The enhanced powers of the inspectors, including the powers to serve improvement and prohibition notices,[2] and to prosecute with substantial penalties for serious offences, have established a formidable national policing capability (even if it does not deliver to its full potential). The model of the 1974 Act has served as inspiration in other common law jurisdictions.[3]

[1] See chapter 8. See, on the significance of Robens and the 1974 Act, Rimington *Valedictory summary of individual health and safety since the 1974 Act,* paper given to Electrical Association, 26 April 1995.
[2] See para 11.06.
[3] Eg in Ireland: Health, Safety and Welfare at Work Act 1974; in Australia: New South Wales Occupational Health and Safety Act 1983; Victoria Occupational Health and Safety Act 1985; Queensland Workplace Health and Safety Act 1989; South Australia Occupational Health, Safety and Welfare Act 1986; Western Australia Occupational Health, Safety and Welfare Act 1984; ACT Occupational Health and Safety Act 1989.

1.56 The unification of the inspectorates and the creation of the HSC also led to the creation of a world leader in research, training and information. The array of publications put out is impressive. In accessible form employers and workers are kept abreast of developing knowledge of dangers and means of overcoming them.

1.57 The creation of a single statutory source[1] for the making of regulations has also been a significant achievement. More contentious has been the allocation of protective requirements between regulations, which are enforceable, and Approved Codes of Practice (ACOPs) which are not.

[1] HSWA 1974, ss 15, 50, 80 and Sch 3.

1.58 Although they form a basis for the making of prohibition and improvement notices, and in the field of criminal law where they form the basis of charges, the statutory exposition of basic duties for employers (ss 2–6) and employees (ss 7, 8) has had negligible impact in compensation litigation, since the duties are not enforceable in civil law (s 47(1)).

1.59 The Act has also been significant in making provision for the appointment of safety representatives and safety committees, and rights to information and consultation about health and safety matters for them and workers generally.

The European revolution

1.60 The Robens Report was published in the same year that Britain joined the 'common market' by enacting the European Communities Act 1972. But few can have realised that 20 years later legislation derived from the latter was to have a far more profound impact than the legislation derived from the former.

1.61 The post-war movement towards European integration first found form in the Treaty establishing the European Coal and Steel Community in 1951. To this was added the Treaty setting up the European Atomic Energy Community and the Treaty establishing the European Economic Community both signed in Rome in 1957. The United Kingdom joined with effect from 1 January 1973 and implemented the obligations contained within the Treaties by enacting in the UK the European Communities Act 1972. This established the deference of UK law to Community law and its law-making and judicial institutions, a prerequisite of each state's membership of the European Community: *NV Algemene Transport-en Expeditie Onderneming van Gend en Loos Nederlandse v Nederlandse Belastingadministratie: 26/62* [1963] ECR 1, ECJ.[1]

[1] For the general background see Hartley *Foundations of European Community Law* (1994).

1.62 In 1986 Member States signed the Single European Act which came into effect in 1987. This Act amended the Treaty of Rome by inserting a new art 118A to the Treaty of Rome (now art 137 EC) which permitted the Community to introduce minimum standards for the health and safety of workers by a 'qualified majority' vote (rather than unanimity) of Member States. The means of standard setting was by use of Directives; these bind each Member State but leave to each the means of implementing Directives into its own law. It was the introduction of this article which enabled the European revolution in health and safety legislation.[1]

[1] See generally James *The European Community: A Positive Force for Health and Safety* (Institute of Employment Rights, 1993).

1.63 Prior to 1987 only six Directives exclusively on health and safety at work had emerged from the European Commission. Each was implemented by regulations in the UK.[1]

[1] They were: the Safety Signs Directive 77/576, implemented by the Safety Signs Regulations 1980, SI 1980/1471 soon to be overtaken by the Safety Signs Directive 92/58 in respect of which UK Regulations. The Health and Safety (Safety Signs and Signals) Regulations 1996, SI 1996/ 341, were late, since implementation was required by the Directive by 24 June 1994; the Vinyl Chloride Monomer Directive 78/610; the Chemical, Physical and Biological Agents at Work Directive 80/1107 (subsequently amended a number of times, for example by the Carcinogens Directive 90/394 and Biological Agents Directive 90/679) implemented by the Control of Substances Hazardous to Health Regulations 1988, SI 1988/1657, amended by SI 1990/2026, SI 1991/2431, SI 1992/2382, SI 1992/2966 and all replaced by the COSHH Regulations 1994 (revoked itself by SI 1999/437, since revoked by SI 2002/2677); the Lead and Ionic Compounds Directive 82/605 substantially covered by the Control of Lead at Work Regulations 1980 (revoked by SI 1998/543, since revoked by SI 2002/2676); the Asbestos Directive 83/477 (amended by the Asbestos Directive 91/382) implemented originally by the Asbestos (Prohibitions) Regulations 1985, SI 1985/910, amended by SI 1988/711, now the Asbestos (Prohibitions) Regulations 1992, SI 1992/3067, and the Control of Asbestos at Work Regulations 1987,

SI 1987/2115 and SI 1992/3068 (revoked by SI 2002/2675); the Noise at Work Directive 86/188 implemented by the Noise at Work Regulations 1989, SI 1989/1790 (partially revoked by SI 2005/1643).

1.64 The pre-1987 Directives were issued under art 100 of the Treaty of Rome (now art 94 EC) which required unanimity. That article was also the basis for other Directives where the protection of workers was incidental to their principal purpose.[1]

[1]   Such Directives included: the Classification, Labelling and Notification of Dangerous Substances Directive 67/548, which has undergone a multitude of amendments; and the Control of Major Accidents Hazards Directive 82/501, now Directive 96/82, which derives its legal base from art 175 EC (ex art 130S) on action on the environment.

1.65 In addition to Directives based on art 100 of the Treaty of Rome there continue to be Directives derived from arts 31 and 32 of the European Atomic Energy Community Treaty.[1]

[1]   Such as the Ionising Radiations Directive 80/83/Euratom, amended by Directive 84/467/ Euratom and Directive 90/641/Euratom now the Ionising Radiations Directive 96/29/Euratom.

1.66 The 1987 Single European Act established the means of implementing new health and safety at work Directives through the new art 118A (subsequently art 118 and now art 137 EC) of the Treaty establishing the European Community. This reflected a turn in European policy, the intent of which was to develop the 'social dimension' of the internal market alongside the economic and political aspects which were to culminate in the 'single market' in 1992. The social dimension was also reflected in the Social Charter and Action Programme of 1989 in which health and safety at work was particularly prominent.

Article 118A is now, since the Treaty of Amsterdam 1997, renumbered as art 137 of the Treaty Establishing the European Community and the mechanism for the passage of Directives under it has been made more flexible.

1.67 In parallel with the nineteenth century British history noted above, the factors behind the development of the EU social dimension and particularly its emphasis on health and safety, were the diverse ones of humanitarianism, union pressure, political forces and, significantly, large employers and governments determined to create 'a level playing field' without 'social dumping' (ie undercutting by competitors).

1.68 To give effect to its initiative in the health and safety at work sector of the social dimension, the European Commission proposed its Third Programme on the subject (the first two pre-dated 1987 and were not a conspicuous success, having issued only the Directives referred to above). The Third Programme included 15 new health and safety Directives. These were approved by the Council of Ministers in December 1987. More were added under the impetus of the 1989 Social Charter and Action Programme. From these initiatives came the principal Directives which culminated in the 'six pack' of new regulations in the UK (in force 1 January 1993) and a series of subsequent regulations. The European health and safety lawyer must now be *au fait* with the second, third and sometimes fourth generation of these forebears.

1.69 The first and most important of the post-1987 Directives was the Framework Directive 89/391 (see chapter 10 below). The essential strategy imposed on employers by this Directive underlies all subsequent Directives and hence the regulations implementing them. Employers are given a cascade of duties of: avoiding risks to safety and health, evaluating risks which cannot be avoided, combating risks at source, adapting the work to the individual, adapting to technical progress, replacing the dangerous by the non-dangerous or the less dangerous, developing a coherent overall prevention policy, giving collective protective measures priority over individual measures, and giving appropriate instructions to workers. The employer must ensure that the subsequent preventative measures and working and production methods assure an improvement in protection and are integrated into all the activities of the undertaking. New technology must be the subject of consultation with the workers and/or their representatives. One or more workers must be designated to carry out safety duties and given time to do so; if a sufficient level of expertise is not available in-house, then outside experts may be engaged. Workers must receive sufficient information, they (and/or their representatives) must be consulted upon all health and safety questions, and they must be trained adequately in relation to workstations used and jobs performed, both at the time of recruitment and on transfer to new work, new equipment or new technology. Arrangements must be made for first aid, fire precautions and emergency procedures.

1.70 The Framework Directive was followed (in approach and chronologically) by six numbered 'daughter' Directives, all of which (including the Framework Directive) had to be implemented by 1 January 1993. In response the UK implemented regulations supplemented by Approved Codes of Practice ('ACOPS') and Guidance Notes.[1]

[1] The Framework and six daughter Directives together with the original implementing Regulations (the first six of which were popularly known amongst practitioners as the 'six pack') were:
—Framework Directive 89/391: Management of Health and Safety at Work Regulations 1992, SI 1992/2051;
—Workplace (the First) Directive 89/654: Workplace (Health, Safety and Welfare) Regulations 1992, SI 1992/3004;
—Work Equipment (the Second) Directive 89/655: Provision and Use of Work Equipment Regulations 1992, SI 1992/2932;
—Personal Protective Equipment (the Third) Directive 89/656: Personal Protective Equipment at Work Regulations 1992, SI 1992/2966;
—Manual Handling of Heavy Loads (the Fourth) Directive 90/269: Manual Handling Operations Regulations 1992, SI 1992/2793;
—Display Screen Equipment (the Fifth) Directive 90/270: Health and Safety (Display Screen Equipment) Regulations 1992, SI 1992/2792;
—Carcinogens (the Sixth) Directive 90/394: Control of Substances Hazardous to Health Regulations 1994, SI 1994/3246; Control of Asbestos at Work (Amendment) Regulations 1992, SI 1992/3068.

Many of these, both Directive and implementing regulations, have been subsequently amended. One of the Directives has been replaced by what one supposes should be called a granddaughter Directive: the Personal Protective Equipment Directive of 1989 is now substituted by the Personal Protective Equipment Directive 1996, 96/58. Mention should also be made of the Temporary Workers Directive 91/383, partially implemented by the Management of Health and Safety at Work Regulations 1992 and 1999, above. That Directive extends equivalent health and safety protection to temporary workers and to those on fixed-term contracts. Other Directives which have implementing regulations in force, not so far mentioned, are: the Metrication Directive 89/671 implemented by the Health and Safety (Miscellaneous Provisions) (Metrication) Regulations 1992, SI 1992/1181. The Fire Precautions (Workplace) Regulations 1997, SI 1997/1840 were originally intended to be implemented on 1 April 1994 so as to put into effect (15 months late) the fire safety aspects of the Framework and Workplace Directives (89/391 and 89/654) but were delayed further until they eventually came into effect on 1 December 1997. Such procrastination has not been untypical.

1.71 The six specific daughter Directives were followed by six further Directives up to 1992. UK consequential regulations followed.[1]

[1] The seventh to twelfth daughter Directives were:
Biological Agents 90/679 and 93/88;
Construction 92/57;
Safety Signs 92/58;
Pregnant Women 92/85;
Drilling 92/91;
Mining 92/104.

1.72 Since the most productive period of the late 1980s and early 1990s, there have been many more Directives (and some European regulations). They include the following subject matter: chemical agents, dangerous substances, explosive atmospheres, fishing vessels, ionising radiation, lifts, machinery, biocidal products, major hazards, transport, work equipment, working time, temporary or mobile worksites, medical treatment on vessels, explosive atmospheres, young persons, and physical agents (including noise and vibration). Some of these cover new ground, some are amendments to existing Directives and others are consolidations of existing Directives.[1]

[1] For an up-to-date summary see the EU Occupational Health and Safety Agenciy's website: www.europe.osha.eu.int. For up-to-date news on proposed regulations to implement the Directive see the HSE website: www.hse.gov.uk/aboutus/regulations/. The year 2006 promises the implementation of regulations on Offshore Installations (Safety Cases); Control of Noise at Work; Asbestos; Construction (Design and Management); Biocidal Products; Railways and other Guided Transport Systems (Safety).

1.73 The above-mentioned Directives were brought into being under art 118A (now arts 137 EC). In addition, a few Directives have emanated from what was art 100A (now art 95 EC) of the Treaty establishing the European Community[1] which is directed to harmonisation of laws to facilitate the establishment and functioning of the internal European market.[2]

[1] As amended by the Treaty of Amsterdam.
[2] For example:
—Contained use of Genetically Modified Organisms Directive 90/219: Genetically Modified Organisms (Contained Use) Regulations 1992, SI 1992/3217 (revoked and replaced by SI 2000/2831);
—Machinery Directive 89/392 amended by 91/368: Supply of Machinery (Safety) Regulations 1992, SI 1992/3073;

—Approximation of Personal Protective Equipment Laws Directive 89/686: Personal Protective Equipment (EC Directive) Regulations 1992, SI 1992/3139 (revoked and replaced by SI 2002/1144);
—Explosive Atmosphere Directive 94/9: SI 2002/2776.

1.74 Finally, it is to be noted that there are also Directives and European 'regulations' (automatically binding as law in each Member State without requiring implementation by the State) proposed and passed dealing with issues that go wider than health and safety at work but which nonetheless have impact on this area of the law. Even to list them is beyond the scope of this edition. In addition, a European regulation (2062/94) established a European Agency for Safety and Health at Work to co-ordinate research, information etc at European level.[1]

1 Further details on the European Agency can be found on its website, www.europe.osha.e-u.int.

1.75 The breadth and depth of the innovations to UK health and safety law since the eleventh edition of *Munkman* in 1990 is apparent. The HSC Annual Report (1991/92) rightly remarked that European and international developments 'continue to set the agenda for developments in health and safety law and standards'.

1.76 Having fulfilled the object of drafting Directives on all the matters set by its Third Health and Safety Action Programme and the health and safety aspects of the Social Charter Action Programme, the Commission announced that it would not be proposing a Fourth Action Programme but would, in effect, act to consolidate by focusing on the following matters: implementation of existing Directives by Member States; achieving a high level of workplace health and safety; and improving social dialogue between employers and worker representatives, particularly through safety committees. The Commission's adoption of the Directive on Working Time (93/104) (in the teeth of UK opposition on the ground that working time is not a health and safety subject and therefore outside art 118A (now art 137 EC) which requires a majority rather than unanimity) showed that it continued to take a wide view of the matters that fall within the scope of health and safety, a stance strongly upheld by the ECJ in rejecting the UK challenge to the Working Time Directive.[1]

1 *United Kingdom v Council of the European Union* [1997] ICR 443 at 501, para 15. Note that the UK faces further infraction proceedings over its defective implementation of this Directive (over inadequacy of daily and weekly rest breaks and whether the exemption in reg 20(2) of the Working Time Regulations goes further than permitted derogation) in *Commission v United Kingdom* C-484/04, heard on 26 January 2006 and in respect of which the A-G's Opinion is awaited at the time of going to print. The government now appear to have conceded the reg 20(2), point since the Working Time (Amendment) Regulations 2006, SI 2006/99 revoke reg 20(2).

1.77 The European Council in December 2000 at Nice endorsed the European Social Agenda which defined the strategic priorities for the next five years.[1] It is an action programme and, so far as health and safety at work is concerned, it aims to develop the current strategy which is:

'— to consolidate, adapt and, where appropriate, simplify existing standards;

— to respond to new risks such as work-related stress, by initiatives on standards and exchanges of good practice;

— to promote the application of legislation in SMEs [small and medium-sized enterprises], taking into account the special constraints to which they are exposed, to apply them by means of a specific programme;

— to develop, from 2001 onwards, exchanges of good practice and collaboration between labour inspection institutions in order to satisfy the common essential requirements more effectively.'

This strategy has been further developed by the currently effective European Commission Communication (COM (2002) 118 Final) *Adapting to Change in Work and Society: a New Commission Strategy on Health and Safety at Work 2002–2006*. Amongst other things, this paper sets the following objectives for a new Community strategy on health and safety:

'The objective of the Community's policy on health and safety at work must be to bring about a continuing improvement in well-being at work, a concept which is taken to include the physical, moral and social dimensions. In addition, a number of complementary objectives must be targeted jointly by all the players.

1   *A continuing reduction in occupational accidents and illnesses.* Thought should be given to setting quantified objectives, at both Community and Member State level, particularly in sectors of activity with above-average incidence rates, and having special regard to arrangements for implementing the European employment strategy.

2   *Mainstreaming the gender dimension* into risk evaluation, preventive measures and compensation arrangements, so as to take account of the specific characteristics of women in terms of health and safety at work.

3   *Prevention of social risks.* Stress, harassment at the workplace, depression and anxiety, and risks related to dependence on alcohol, drugs and medicines, should all be the subject of specific measures but should form part of a global approach in association with health care systems.

4   *Enhanced prevention of occupational illnesses.* Priority should go to illnesses due to asbestos, hearing loss and musculo-skeletal problems.

5   *Taking account of demographic change in terms of risks, accidents and illnesses.* Preventive measures should take more account of the age factor, and should specifically target young people and ageing workers.

6   *Taking account of changes in forms of employment, work organisation arrangements and working time.* Workers in non-standard or precarious working relations constitute a sensitive group.

7   *Taking account of the size of firms.* SMEs and very small businesses, as well as self-employed workers and unpaid family helpers, should all be the subject of specific measures in terms of information, awareness and risk prevention programmes.

8   *Analysis of new or emerging risks*, with special reference to risks associated with the interaction between chemical, physical and biological agents, and those associated with the general working environment (ergonomic, psychological and social risks).'

The Communication also reiterates its philosophy of strengthening the culture of risk prevention. To this end amongst other things it states the following which is likely to have significant impact in the UK:

'Applying Community law effectively is essential if we are to improve the quality of the work environment. This in turn requires an enhanced state of awareness on the part of all concerned, and at all levels. The Commission will, in conjunction with the Advisory Committee and the social partners, be producing guides on how to apply the directives, taking account of the diverse nature of sectors of activity and companies, as suggested by the Economic and Social Committee.

For its part, the Commission will, subject to the powers bestowed on it by the Treaty, adopt a rigorous approach to ensuring that directives are properly transposed and the law is properly applied. It will also be co-operating closely with the national authorities to find ways of ensuring that Community directives are implemented correctly and equivalently. In this respect, a fundamental role will fall to the Senior Labour Inspectors Committee (SLIC) in terms of encouraging exchanges of information and experience and organising mutual co-operation and assistance. There must be practical encouragement for common inspection objectives as part of an annual action plan, the importance of which has been underlined by the European Parliament, common principles for labour inspection in the field of health and safety at work, and ways and means of evaluating national inspection systems by reference to these principles. Integrating the candidate countries' inspectorates in this committee is a matter of prime importance in terms of promoting the effective implementation of Community law.'

[1]   See para 1.97ff.

1.78 The Nice Council also adopted the EU Charter of Fundamental Rights as a declaration of rights rather than a binding instrument. Significantly modified by 'explanations' appended to it, the Charter found a place in the now disregarded 2004 draft EU Constitution. The ECJ nonetheless appears to give it some weight: see the Opinion of A-G Tizzano in *R v Secretary of State for Trade and Industry, ex p BECTU* [2001] IRLR 559[1] and other cases. The Charter declares that:

—   every worker has the right to working conditions which respect his or her health and safety;[2]

—   every worker has the right to limitation of working hours, to daily and weekly rest periods and to an annual period of paid leave;[3]

—   young people admitted to work must have working conditions appropriate to their age and be protected against ... any work likely to harm their safety, health or physical, mental, moral or social development or to interfere with their education.[4]

[1]   In his Opinion (at para 28) the A-G stated that:

'the relevant statements of the Charter cannot be ignored; in particular, we cannot ignore its clear purpose of serving, where its provisions so allow, as a substantive point of reference for all those involved—Member States, institutions, natural and legal persons—in the Community context. Accordingly, I consider that the Charter provides us with the most reliable and definitive confirmation of the fact that the right [in question] constitutes a fundamental right.'

[2]   Article 31.1.
[3]   Article 31.2.
[4]   Article 32.

1.79 Directives under art 137 (ex art 118A) EC on health and safety emanate from a department of the European Commission known as DGVd after consultation with the Advisory Committee on Safety, Hygiene and Health Protection at Work (which consists of representatives of governments, unions and employers' associations) and with the 'social partners' (ie employers and trade unions in their Europe-wide organisations).

1.80 The reformulated Treaty establishing the European Community offers other legal bases for Directives which incidentally protect health and safety at work. Thus, arts 210–212 (ex arts 71, 154–156) EC in facilitating common transport policy and networks measures offer opportunity for transport safety.[1] Article 95 (ex art 100A) EC facilitates the free movement of goods or services between Member States by removing technical barriers to trade and this has permitted some health and safety measures.[2] Article 175 (ex arts 130R, 130S and 130T) EC contains the Environment Chapter permitting action on the environment.[3] Most health and safety at work measures remain founded on what are now arts 136–145EC however.

[1]   See, for example, the High Speed Train Interoperability Directive 94/48; the Directive on Interoperability of Conventional Rail Systems COM 99/617; the Directive on Railway Safety 2004/49/EC; the amending Directives for the Carriage of Dangerous Goods by Road and Rail.

[2]   For example the Machinery Directive, 3rd amendment to 89/392; the Directives amending the Marketing and Use Directive 76/769; the adaptations to the Dangerous Preparations Directive 99/45 and to the Dangerous Substances Directive 67/548; the Biocidal Products Directive 98/8, and the Pressure Equipment Directive 97/23.

[3]   The Control of Major Accident Hazards Directive 96/82 has this as a base.

1.81 From the Commission the draft Directive goes for consultation to the European Parliament ('first reading') and to the Economic and Social Committee, thence to the Council of Ministers. If the latter reach 'common position' (ie a qualified majority), the proposal goes back to the European Parliament.[1] Thereafter, by the process of 'co-decision' making, the proposal is jointly adopted by the European Parliament and the Council of Ministers.

[1]   The European Council at Nice in December 2000 agreed changes to the European Treaty which, amongst other things, extends qualified majority voting (QMV), reweights votes and increases the size of the Commission. These changes do not affect the creation of health and safety Directives save as to the distribution of votes in the QMV mechanism. It should be noted that between 1993 and 1997, whilst the UK pursued the bizarre policy of opting out of the Social Policy Protocol (the Social Chapter) of the Maastricht Treaty, there was an alternative route to art 118A (now art 137EC)—the effect of which was simply to exclude the UK from discussion or voting on Directives in draft which were then passed by QMV. Since the UK opted into the Social Chapter in 1997, health and safety at work Directives will follow the art 137 (ex art 118A) EC route.

1.82 In the UK it is the HSE which drafts the regulatory response (and ACOPS where appropriate) for approval by the HSC and submission to Parliament.

'In bringing its influence to bear on [European] Commission proposals at the draft stage, HSE has argued consistently that Directives should be expressed as general principles, leaving detail to be decided nationally, and for better prioritisation of the proposals, proper cost justification and more thorough preparation before they were advanced to Council [of Ministers] level discussion' (HSC Annual Report 1991–92).

Both the HSC and government have further pressed the European Commission to take into account the familiar UK limitation on employers' statutory duties: 'so far as is reasonably practicable'.

1.83 The European Commission did not accept these arguments and the HSE and HSC have by and large honoured the detail of the Directives in the implementing regulations and ACOPS.[1] Furthermore, the UK implemented more Directives than most other EU States.[2] The HSC have, however, inserted the 'reasonably practicable' limitation into many of the regulations and ACOPS.

1   Although the European Trade Union Technical Bureau for Health and Safety have condemned UK implementation as 'markedly minimalist' and pointed to a number of shortcomings: Vogel *Prevention at the Workplace* (TUTB, 1994).
2   See the Annual Reports to the European Parliament on Monitoring the Application of Community Law, eg 5 February 2004, COM (2004) 62 final.

1.84 The regulations and ACOPS have been introduced under s 15 and s 16 respectively of the HSWA 1974 since the requirements of the Framework, Daughter and subsequent Directives are largely compatible with the scheme of the 1974 Act.[1] It appears that the HSE have recognised that in some respects the UK regulations do not go as far as the Directives. There is considerable doubt in legal circles as to whether the Directives are sufficiently implemented in the UK and, if not, what the consequences may be.

1   For an up to date picture of the Regulations see the HSE website: www.hse.gov.uk/aboutus/regulations/.

1.85 The European transformation of health and safety law came as a shock to practitioners of every kind and particularly to employers. In consequence the HSE enforcement policy recognised that:

'employers will need time to take sensible action when requirements are completely new. Formal enforcement measures are not likely unless the risks to health and safety are evident and immediate, or what needs to be done is not new, or employers appear deliberately unwilling to recognise their responsibilities' (HSC Annual Report 1991–92).

That time has now passed.[1]

1   See *Enforcement Policy Statement* (HSE Books, 2000).

1.86 The range of sanctions available after the European intervention remains as broad as before. It is a principle of Community law to leave enforcement to the Member States so long as they provide effective measures. The strategy outlined for 2002–2006 referred to in para 1.77 above suggests increasing Commission activity. Without any European stimulus the maximum fines under the HSWA 1974 were significantly increased in 1992 and 2000. To the extent that breach of an ACOP will not be subject, of itself, to either criminal or civil sanction, there is some doubt as to whether effective means of enforcement consistent with the requirements of European law will have been provided where implementation of a provision of a Directive is by way of a provision in an ACOP rather than a regulation. So far as the civil law is concerned, s 47(2) of the HSWA 1974 makes clear that a breach of regulations brought into effect to implement the European Directions is actionable in damages; an action for breach of the provisions of a Directive itself may well lie as an alternative or additional means of redress, but only against an emanation of the State.[1] Any judicial decisions to the contrary would doubtless fall foul of the European Court of Justice which held in *Rewe Handelsgesellschaft Nord mbH v Hauptzollamt Kiel: 158/80* [1981] ECR 1805 (and subsequent cases) that:

> 'it must be possible for every type of action provided by national law to be available before the national Courts for the purpose of ensuring observance of Community provisions having direct effect ...'[2]

1   But see *Cross v Highlands and Islands Enterprise* [2001] IRLR 336, OH.
2   And see chapter 9.

1.87 It has been suggested also that where a Directive cannot be enforced directly only because the employer is not an emanation of the State, nonetheless the standards therein contained may come to be regarded by the courts as establishing the standard of care of a reasonable employer when determining liability in negligence).

1.88 Some commentators suggested that the European derived law might stimulate claims for injunctions which, though theoretically available, have rarely if ever been used as a preventative tool in this field of law. Experience has not borne this out.

Deregulation

1.89 In the field of health and safety at work, UK governments since 1980 sought to resist the creation, content and adoption of many of the EU Directives. The UK negotiated a four year opt-out from the Young Persons Directive, challenged the legitimacy of the Working Time Directive, and applied derogations from it in the Working Time Regulations which have resulted in infraction proceedings which continue against it (see para 1.76 fn 1), and achieved exclusion from Directives made under the Social Policy Protocol of the Maastricht Treaty. The philosophy, varying in intensity, appears to be that employers should be, so far as possible, free from regulation. The EU, on the other hand, has been concerned to ensure both a humanitarian social dimension and to ensure universal application of standards so as to prevent 'social dumping' (undercutting) creating 'distortions of the internal market', though a weakening of this stance is now detectable.

1.90 The contrast in philosophy was particularly highlighted by the Deregulation and Contracting Out Act 1994, s 37 (and see ss 1–4) which gave power to the Secretary of State to repeal legislation (both primary and delegated) in the field of health and safely to remove a burden on business 'without removing any necessary protection'. Just a fortnight before the 'six pack' regulations required by the wave of European Directives took effect, the government called on the HSC to identify legislation which could be repealed when the Deregulation etc Act came into force.[1] The HSC identified 100 sets of regulations and associated primary legislation fit for repeal and proposed to move towards reducing 'by 40% the volume of health and safety law covering the generality of business. Almost all pre-1974 legislation will be removed'.[2] Contrary to fears at the time this target was achieved without any notably adverse effect on the regulatory regime, particularly against the backdrop of the European-derived regulations.

[1]   On this and the then government's policy of deregulation more generally, see Woolfson *Deregulation: the Politics of Health and Safety* (1994); Williams 'Deregulating Occupational Health and Safety' (1995) 24(2) ILJ 133.
[2]   HSC *Review of Health and Safety Regulations* (1994) p 2.

1.91 Deregulation had to some extent already started before the 1994 Act was on the statute book. The Coal Industry Act 1992 abolished the seven and a half hour maximum underground working shift for coal miners established by the Coal Mines Regulations Act 1908 (as amended). In 1993 the Management and Administration of Safety and Health at Mines Regulations 1993, SI 1993/1897 (see chapter 24) replaced parts of the Mines and Quarries Act 1954 and subsidiary legislation. On an application for judicial review to quash the 1993 Regulations on the grounds that they were ultra vires since they were not 'designed to maintain or improve the standards of health, safety and welfare established by or under' the Mines and Quarries Act 1954 as required by s 1(2) of the HSWA 1974, it was held by the Divisional Court that whether the 1993 Regulations were so designed or not was not a matter for the courts but for the Secretary of State: *R v Secretary of State for Employment, ex p NACODS* (16 December 1993, unreported Div Ct).[1]

[1]   This case contrasts with *Stark v Post Office* [2000] ICR 1013 in which the Court of Appeal held that the Work Equipment Directive's minimum standards were not permitted to substitute for higher standards in UK regulations, indeed the Directives were intended to maintain higher standards in domestic law: see para 20.26.

1.92 The strongly deregulationist agenda pursued by the Conservative governments of the 1980s and 1990s did not have any great impact on health and safety law, beyond the imposition of funding cuts on the HSC and the HSE and the adoption of a minimalist and grudging approach towards the transposition of European Directives.[1] Moreover, a weaker deregulatory approach was adopted by the Labour governments since 1997. However, an intensification of the deregulation tendency in relation to health and safety protection seems to be raising its head again.

[1]   James *The European Community: A Positive Force for Health and Safety?* (Institute of Employment Rights, 1993).

A change of course?

1.93 The advent of a Labour government has not led to the introduction of major legal changes as was envisaged by statements emanating from government.[1] The 1998 three-year Comprehensive Spending Review provided for the provision of £63 million of additional funding to the HSC/E, some £40 million of which was intended to stem from new statutory permissioning charges applying to the safety case regimes in place in the gas, offshore and railway industries.[2] More recently, there has been evidence of a reversion to the policies of the 1980s and 1990s. A Joint Memorandum by the HSC and HSE of February 2004 revealed that the spending review of 2002 set budgets for these bodies for the seven years 2001/02 to 2007/08 of £254m, £262m, £278m, £279m, £271m, £271m, and £271m. As the Memorandum states (paras 46–47):

> 'Following a period of modest increase in resources, Spending Review 2002 set a baseline which rises slightly in 2003/4, and 2004/5 and drops back in 2005/6. When rising costs are taken into account this represents a significant reduction in spending power.
>
> To meet this we have adopted a financial strategy of efficiencies and cost reductions ...'

It does not appear that these figures were significantly modified in the 2004 Spending Review. In 2000 the HSC adopted a 10-year strategy, *Revitalising Health and Safety*, which set targets to which the HSE has arguably been making progress.[3] The *2004/05 Business Plan* also set strategic goals and programmes. The HSE has modified its structure and ways of working accordingly. But neither the HSE nor the government have accepted the powerful academic arguments that both the current legal framework and the enforcement of it is fundamentally flawed.[4] In particular the inspection policy of the HSE has been severely criticised yet frequency of inspection appears to be falling.[5] The government have notoriously failed to introduce a law on corporate manslaughter despite a seven year commitment to it and proposals dating back to 2000.[6]

[1] John Prescott, when Secretary of State for the Department of the Environment, Transport and the Regions, indicated that in its second term of office the Labour government would introduce a major piece of legislation on health and safety at work: although it was unclear whether this would go so far as to repeal and replace the HSWA 1974 itself: 'New Safety Bill' (2000) 293 Health and Safety Bulletin 3. It has not happened.

[2] 'HSE to receive Cash Boost' (1999) 276 Health and Safety Bulletin 2.

[3] For criticism of this policy see P James and D Walters in *Health and Safety Revitalised or Reversed?* (Institute of Employment Rights, 2004), and P James and D Walters *Regulating Health and Safety at Work: an Agenda for Change?* (Institute of Employment Rights, 2005).

[4] See James and Walters *Regulating Health and Safety: The Way Forward* (Institute of Employment Rights, 1999); James and Walters *Regulating Health and Safety at Work: an Agenda for Change?* (Institute of Employment Rights, 2005). See also Woolfson, Foster and Beck *Paying the Piper: Capital and Labour in Britain's Offshore Oil Industry* (Mansell, 1997) ch 6. See also *The Work of the HSE* (Environment, Transport and Regional Affairs Committee, Session 1999, 4th Report, Vol 1, Report and Proceedings of the Committee, Stationery Office, 2000).

[5] See James and Walters (above) and, on the policy, see *HSE Enforcement Policy Statement* (HSE Books, 2000); *HSC Securing Health Together* (HSE Books, 2000). See also Bergman 'The Need for a Credible and Clear HSE Enforcement Policy' (2000) 292 Health and Safety Bulletin 9–12. The need for a tougher policy was identified by Lord Cullen after frank admissions as to the inadequacy of current HSE policy: *Ladbroke Grove Rail Inquiry Part 1 Report* (HSE Books, 2001) at pp 174–175. The HSE's *A Strategy for Workplace Health and Safety in Great Britain to 2010 and Beyond* (2004) emphasises its reliance on a voluntarist approach and on 'self-regulation'.

[6] *Reforming the Law of Involuntary Manslaughter: The Government's Proposals* (Home Office, 2000).

1.94 The period since the last edition has seen an incremental advance in health and safety litigation, with new sets of regulations introduced and a number of existing ones amended. With effect from 27 October 2003, the exclusion of civil liability for breach of the Management of Health and Safety at Work Regulations 1999 has been revoked. The Control of Substances Hazardous to Health (COSHH) Regulations 1999 were replaced by the 2002 Regulations of the same name, which are generally stricter and more detailed. More significantly, the Work at Height Regulations 2005 revoke and replace all prior regulations so far as they deal with falls and falling objects, imposing a far stricter and more detailed regime. The Control of Noise at Work Regulations 2005 replace the 1989 Regulations of the same name, again with a stricter regime with lower thresholds. The new Control of Vibration at Work Regulations 2005 replace the common law. At the same time, extensive appellate decision in both England and Wales and Scotland have applied the regulations strictly.

1.95 The changes made to the MHSW Regulations are, perhaps, particularly noteworthy. Thus, they, amongst other things, incorporate risk assessment and other duties relating to the employment of young people and pregnant workers, amend the previously existing duties concerning the appointment of 'competent persons', and put on a statutory footing the provisions of the EC Framework Directive which require employers to use a hierarchy of control measures that places priority on the avoidance of risks.[1]

1   Council Directive 89/391/EEC of 12 June 1989 on the introduction of measures to encourage improvements in the safety and health of workers at work, OJ L 183/29.06.89.

1.96 Virtually all these changes have been prompted by the adoption of new and amended European Directives and consequently demonstrate the continuing influence of European developments on domestic law. At the same time, it must be noted that there has been a marked slowing down of European-inspired action in the field of health and safety at work. Nonetheless, the reduction in EU health and safety activity seems likely to continue.

1.97 The European Commission's social policy agenda for the period 2000–2005 essentially set three areas of action in respect of health and safety: codifying and simplifying health and safety legislation; adapting and improving health and safety legislation to take into account ECJ case law and the changing world of work; and further developing the Community strategy on health and safety at work by issuing a Commission Communication. Strikingly, however, these broad categories of action are detailed under the broad objective of 'anticipating and managing change and adapting to the new working environment'. In doing so they are therefore located within a broader range of employment policy issues and hence are explicitly linked to wider objectives relating to employment creation and the generation of greater economic competitiveness. As a result, there seems a possibility that future health and safety policy developments will be strongly influenced by these wider objectives and a consequent danger that they will reflect a deregulationist ethos. This is particularly so given that several recent Commission-based reports have already argued that there is a need to both simplify the existing health and safety legislation and reduce any unnecessary burdens that it imposes *on* employers.[1]

1   'Will workplace health and safety be watered down in European Social Policy' (2000) 14
     Newsletter of the European Trade Union Technical Bureau for Health and Safety 1–2.

1.98 Against the backdrop of all the European inspired regulatory activity
and the controversy surrounding the performance of the HSE, the judiciary
have been active in the field of health and safety at work, as this volume
shows. In particular there is a detectable trend showing that in the field of
health and safety at work, the courts are prepared to stretch or even cast aside
the confinement of the fundamental foundation garment of employment law,
the contract of employment: see cases such *Morris v Breaveglen Ltd* [1993]
ICR 766, CA and *Hawley v Luminar Leisure etc* (2006) LTL 24/1/2006, CA
(employer liable for acts of doorman supplied by a contractor). This elasticity
has not been applied in other areas of employment law.[1]

1   See the criticism of the bilateral nature of the employment contract in relation to denial of
     entitlement to equal pay in Fredman 'Women at work: the broken promise of flexicurity'
     [2004] ILJ 299 at 316–17; or in relation to industrial action in *Dimbleby & Sons Ltd v
     NUJ* [1984] ICR 386.

1.99 Contrary to the author's belief in this chapter of the last volume, it does
not seem likely that major changes will be made to current statutory
framework for health and safety at work during the course of the next few
years.

1   See the seminal work David and Teasdale *The Costs to the British Economy of Work
     Accidents and Work-related Ill Health* (HSE, 1994).

Chapter 2

THE GENERAL PRINCIPLES OF NEGLIGENCE

David Wilby QC

2.01 Before setting out in detail the duty of an employer towards his employees— and the duties of other persons who are brought into contact with them in the course of their work—it is necessary to explain the general principles of liability for negligence, of which these duties are particular examples.

2.02 In English and Scottish law negligence or careless conduct which injures another does not automatically establish legal liability. It must first be shown that, in the circumstances of the case, there was a legal duty to take care to avoid injury to the other person. Lord Wright said in *Lochgelly Iron and Coal Co v M'Mullan* [1934] AC 1 at 25:

> '— negligence means more than heedless or careless conduct, whether in omission or commission: it properly connotes the complex concept of duty, breach of duty and damage thereby suffered by the person to whom the duty was owing'.

2.03 The tort of negligence has four elements or requirements, namely:

(1) the existence in law of a duty of care; that is, a situation in which the law attaches liability for carelessness. It is necessary that the careless infliction of the kind of damage in question on the class of person to which the claim belongs by the class of person to which the defendant belongs is recognised by the law as actionable;

(2) breach of the duty of care by the defendant; that is, where the defendant's conduct falls below the standard the law requires;

(3) a causal or causative connection between the defendant's careless conduct and the damage;

(4) that the particular kind of damage to the particular claimant is attributable because it is not so unreasonable as to be too remote.

The defendant is liable to the claimant when these four requirements are proved on the civil standard of a balance of probabilities. In practice, the courts consider these four requirements in the round and do not formalistically proceed from (1) to (4). Negligence must be carefully distinguished from other torts, for example of strict liability where it is unnecessary to prove that the injury caused was either intended by the defendant or resulted from any lack of care on his part. In torts of strict liability the claimant need only prove that his injury resulted from the kind of conduct prescribed with the relevant tort.[1]

[1] At one time an action for trespass to the person lay for any positive act which caused harm to the claimant unless a defendant was wholly without fault—which probably meant the action was beyond his control. This action has now been progressively replaced by negligence, which extends to failures to act where there is a duty so to do, with the onus being on the claimant to prove that there was fault: *Fowler v Lanning* [1959] 1 QB 426.

THE LEGAL DUTY OF CARE

2.04 The duty of care is not simply a duty not to act carelessly; it is a duty not to inflict damage carelessly, since damage is the basis of the cause of action.

The existence of a duty of care is decided by the court as a question of law, but in doing so the court will have regard to evidence of the relationship of the parties and the dangers likely to arise in given circumstances. In many kinds of relationships the existence and extent of a duty of care has been recognised by the law over a long period. Examples may be found in the duties of road users and of navigators at sea to avoid collisions, of occupiers of buildings to prevent damage from dangers on the premises, and of employers for the general safety of their workers. The duties which affect an employee in the course of employment are explained in detail in the next few chapters. Nonetheless the law of negligence is still evolving and there are recent examples where the courts have decided both the existence of a duty of care[1] or have found that a duty of care does not exist.[2]

[1] *McLoughlin v Grovers (a firm)* [2001] EWCA Civ 1743, [2002] QB 1312, [2002] 2 WLR 1279.
[2] *Gorringe v Calderdale Metropolitan Borough Council* [2004] UKHL 15, [2004] 1 WLR 1057.

2.05 A court is likely to be faced on occasions with circumstances which are not obviously in the same category as those in which a duty of care has previously been found to exist. Then the court must decide whether the defendant owes the claimant a duty of care. More accurately: did this category of defendant owe a duty to this category of claimant not to cause damage of the kind which harmed the claimant? In this context it is important to distinguish between the question of whether a notional duty of care exists, and the narrower question of whether a factual duty is owed to the claimant and whether the kind of damage is too remote. A notional duty applies to a general class of relationship and damage.[1] Once a notional duty of care has been accepted, then the question is whether the particular claimant comes within the scope of that duty so as to render the damage attributable. So it is an issue of factual duty. Specifically, does the defendant owe a factual duty of care to the particular claimant? However, it is important to note that as a general rule it is not necessary that the claimant should have been within the defendant's contemplation as an identified individual. It is sufficient if he falls within the class of persons who might foreseeably suffer the particular loss to which the duty relates.[2]

[1] See Beldam LJ in *Ancell v McDermott* [1993] 4 All ER 355 at 359.
[2] *Farrugia v Great Western Railway* [1947] 2 All ER 565.

2.06 This century has witnessed an expansion in the circumstances in which a duty of care will arise. Most famously of all, in *Donoghue v Stevenson* [1932]

AC 562 the House of Lords decided that a manufacturer could owe a duty of care to a consumer. In a well-known passage Lord Atkin, reflecting an expansionist approach to negligence and appearing to articulate an underlying principle, said:

> 'The duty which is common to all cases where liability is established must logically be based upon some element common to the cases where it is found to exist ... There must be, and is, some general conception of relations giving rise to a duty of care, of which the particular cases found in the books are but instances ... You must take reasonable care to avoid acts or omissions which you reasonably foresee would be likely to injure your neighbour. Who, then, in law is my neighbour? The answer seems to be—persons who are so closely and directly affected by my act that I ought reasonably to have them in contemplation as being so affected when I am directing my mind to the acts or omissions which are called in question.'

2.07 These words should not be, and never were, taken at face value. To the extent they were meant to be an articulation of the principle underlying the decided cases, they went too far; and the cited passage was an unreliable guide to when liability would be found in new types of case.[1] Indeed, the 'neighbour' principle was intended to place some limitation on the 'foreseeability' test, laid down in *Heaven v Pender* (1883) 11 QBD 503 at 509, through the introduction of a concept akin to 'proximity'.[2] Since Lord Atkin's conclusion on the duty issue was that:

> 'a manufacturer of products which he sells in such a form as to show that he intends them to reach the ultimate consumer in the form in which they left him, with no reasonable possibility of reasonable examination, and with the knowledge that the absence of reasonable care in the preparation or putting up of the products will result in injury to the consumer's life or property, owes a duty to the consumer to take reasonable care.'

So by these limitations of foresight and proximity he defined the scope of the notional duty owed by the manufacturer to the consumer.

[1] See Lord Reid in *Home Office v Dorset Yacht Co Ltd* [1970] AC 1004.
[2] These famous words were strictly only obiter, since Lord Atkin also decided the *Donoghue* case on the narrower ground that a manufacturer owes a purchaser a duty of care where there is no possibility of intermediate examination.

2.08 At one time, however, the courts appeared to ground liability on the application of a wide 'neighbour' principle, resulting in an expansion in the circumstances in which a duty of care would be found. This approach is illustrated by the House of Lords in *Home Office v Dorset Yacht Co Ltd* [1970] AC 1004 (see Lord Reid at 1027):

> 'The well known passage in Lord Atkin's speech should I think be regarded as a statement of principle. It is not to be treated as if it were a statutory definition. It will require clarification in new circumstances. But I think that the time has come when we can and should say that it ought to apply unless there is some justification or valid explanation for its exclusion.'

It is further exemplified by the speech of Lord Wilberforce in *Anns v Merton London Borough Council* [1978] AC 728, HL, in which he seemed to indicate that a duty of care would be presumed to exist if harm were reasonably foreseeable unless there were public policy reasons to the contrary.[1] Thus, for a time, reasonable foreseeability of harm, without more, became the touch-stone of liability, allowing the courts great freedom to expand liability for negligence. Principle, rather than precedent or policy, became the guide to the existence a duty of care.

[1]   At 757.

2.09 For a time it appeared that this expansionist tide had turned in the House of Lords and pragmatic restriction replaced principle, illustrated by the cases on nervous shock, in particular *Alcock v Chief Constable of South Yorkshire Police* [1992] 1 AC 310.[1] In *Yuen Kun Yeu v A-G of Hong Kong* [1988] AC 175, HL at 191, Lord Keith said that 'it is clear that foreseeability does not of itself, and automatically, lead to a duty of care'. However, the House of Lords then went on to reject this general principle of liability in favour of an incremental approach. A duty of care was only imposed if the factual circumstances were analogous to those giving rise to a duty in earlier cases: see *Murphy v Brentwood District Council* [1991] 1 AC 398, HL, especially Lord Keith at 461, Lord Bridge at 474, and Lord Oliver at 487. In *Caparo Industries plc v Dickman* [1990] 2 AC 605 the House of Lords, while affirming the 'traditional categorisation of distinct and recognisable situations as the guides to the existence, the scope and the limits of the varied duties of care',[2] also enunciated a three-stage test of liability, in place of the simple test of foreseeability laid down in *Anns*: first, sufficient proximity between the parties; second, that it is fair, just and reasonable to impose a duty of care; and, third, that injury to the claimant is reasonably foreseeable.[3] At 617–618 Lord Bridge explained the matter thus:

> 'in addition to foreseeability of damage, necessary ingredients in any situation giving rise to a duty of care are that there should exist between the party owing the duty and the party to whom it is owed a relationship characterised by the law as one of "proximity" or "neighbourhood" and that the situation should be one in which the court considers it fair, just and reasonable that the law should impose a duty of a given scope upon the one party for the benefit of the other. But ... the concepts of proximity and fairness embodied in these additional ingredients are not susceptible of any precise definition as would be necessary to give them utility as practical tests, but amount in effect to little more than convenient labels to attach to the features of different specific situations which, on a detailed examination of all the circumstances, the law recognises pragmatically as giving rise to a duty of care of a given scope.'

This passage has been cited in numerous subsequent decisions.[4]

[1]   See chapter 14, below.
[2]   Lord Bridge at 618.
[3]   Per Lord Bridge at 617–618, Lord Roskill at 628, Lord Oliver at 633, Lord Jauncey at 655.
[4]   Eg *Spring v Guardian Assurance plc* [1995] 2 AC 296 at 333 per Lord Slynn; *Marc Rich & Co AG v Bishop Rock Marine Co Ltd* [1996] AC 211 at 235 per Lord Slynn.

The three-stage test

2.10 The three-stage test set out in *Caparo Industries plc v Dickman* originally arose in relation to economic loss cases, but it has since been applied equally to physical damage or personal injury claims: *Marc Rich & Co AG v Bishop Rock Marine Co Ltd* [1996] AC 211, HL and *X v Bedfordshire County Council* [1995] 2 AC 633, HL. The three-stage approach was also affirmed by the House of Lords in *Spring v Guardian Assurance plc* [1995] 2 AC 296 (employer owed duty of care to an employee to take reasonable care in preparing a reference): see especially Lord Slynn at 332–334, Lord Woolf at 342 and Lord Keith (dissenting in the result) at 307–308.[1]

1   See too *Henderson v Merrett Syndicates* [1995] 2 AC 145, HL, where Lloyd's underwriting agents were held to owe a duty of care to underwriting members ('Names').

2.11 However, the decision in *X (Minors) v Bedfordshire County Council* [1995] 2 AC 633, HL (no duty of care where it was inconsistent with, or would discourage, a statutory duty) has been undermined by the decisions of the House of Lords in *Barrett v Enfield London Borough Council* [1999] 3 WLR 79 (duty of local councils to children in care) and *Phelps v London Borough of Hillingdon* [2000] 3 WLR 776 (duty of local councils in respect of children with special educational needs). Those cases appear to have been influenced by the decision of the European Court of Human Rights in *Osman v United Kingdom* (1998) 29 EHRR 245 (see in particular *Barrett,* per Lord Browne-Wilkinson at 84–85). In *Osman,* it was held that the partial immunity of police from negligence actions was a breach of art 6 of the Convention. The new approach apparent in *Osman* and also *Z v United Kingdom* [2000] 2 FCR 245 (European Commission on Human Rights: bar on actions against social services in respect of child protection decisions was a breach of art 6 of the ECHR and the 'floodgates' argument was a 'speculative factor which is only of limited weight') has led to decisions such as *W v Essex County Council* [2000] 2 WLR 601, HL (refusal to strike out psychiatric injury claim of parents whose foster child sexually abused their natural children) and *S v Gloucestershire County Council* [2000] 3 All ER 346 (refusal by Court of Appeal to strike out claims by abused foster children). Further examples of cases which might once have been thought to 'open the floodgates' are *Kent v Griffiths* [2001] QB 36 (ambulance service owed a duty of care following acceptance of a 999 call) and *Arthur JS Hall & Co v Simons* [2000] 3 WLR 543, HL (end to immunity from suit in negligence for advocates for work connected with litigation). It was originally thought that the Human Rights Act 1998 would cause a further wave of more 'expansion-ist' decisions, as immunities and exclusionary rules became harder to defend. This has not proved to be the position in practice. However, although it has been argued that the decision in *Osman* means that it is now impossible to strike out a claim as disclosing no reasonable cause of action, that is not so where the problem is absence of proximity (see para 2.13ff, below).[1]

1   See *Palmer v Tees Health Authority* [2000] PIQR P1.

2.12 The concepts governing duties of care are inevitably somewhat elusive, although they offer a concomitant flexibility. In reality, the crucial considera-tion tends to be policy, ie what is 'fair, just and reasonable'. The incremental test, of reasoning by analogy, is open-ended: any factual situation can be analysed widely or narrowly, depending upon the result to be achieved. In

White v Jones [1995] 2 AC 207 Lord Browne-Wilkinson thought the relationship of a solicitor to a potential beneficiary of a client's will was analogous to other 'special relationships' allowing recovery for economic loss; the opposite view is equally tenable. The third member of the majority in that decision appears to have founded his reasoning on the degree of proximity in the particular case including the contact at the time of the will between the solicitor and the beneficiaries.[1] *White v Jones* was followed in *Gorham v British Telecommunications plc* [2000] 1 WLR 2129, where the Court of Appeal held that an insurance company which owed a duty of care to a customer when giving insurance advice for pension and life cover also owed a duty of care to the customer's dependants where the customer clearly intended to create a benefit for them in the event of his predeceasing them. Ultimately the criteria can be considered to overlap. As stated by Steyn LJ in *Elguzoli-Daf v Commissioner of Police for the Metropolis* [1995] QB 335 at 349 those 'considerations inevitably shade into each other' and as Lord Roskill stated in *Caparo* they are 'but labels descriptive of a very different factual situation which can exist in particular cases and must be carefully examined ... before the issue can be pragmatically determined'.

1   Lord Nolan, see [1995] 2 AC 207 at 294H–295B.

The three-stage test: proximity

2.13   As part of the three-stage test, the courts require a relationship of 'proximity' between the claimant and the defendant as well as reasonable foreseeability.[1] In practice, though, the two concepts overlap: the more injury to a particular class of person is foreseeable, the more likely a member of that class will be deemed to be sufficiently proximate. The proximity of relationship is not between the defendant and claimant personally, but rather between the operations or property under the control of the defendant and the category of person—visitor, employee, or whatever—into which the claimant falls.[2]

1   See *Caparo Industries plc v Dickman* [1990] 2 AC 605; *Alcock v Chief Constable of South Yorkshire Police* [1992] 1 AC 310, especially Lord Oliver at 415; and *Marc Rich & Co AG v Bishop Rock Marine Co Ltd, The Nicholas H* [1996] AC 211.
2   See the useful South African case, *Joffe & Co Ltd v Hoskins* (1941) App D 431 at 451–452.

2.14   Proximity may generally consist of various forms of closeness: physical, circumstantial, causative or assumed. However, precisely what is meant by 'proximity' is hardly obvious; certainly, the matter is not confined to temporal or spatial closeness. Instead, it tends to revolve around vague notions such as how direct is the relationship between the defendant and the type of claimant concerned, and the degree of proximity required varies with the kind of liability. But it is established that some categories of person are sufficiently 'proximate', at least for some kinds of harm. It is beyond doubt that an employer owes a duty of care to his employees, at least as regards their physical health and safety, and that a road user owes a duty of care to other road users, depending upon where those others are in the vicinity.[1] Where one person causes physical damage to the person or property of another, proximity will usually be found,[2] especially in the case of an accident at work: see

Lord Keith in *Alcock,* above, at 396. In the context of personal injury, proximity is relatively easily established, although where the claim is based on an omission rather than a positive act this is harder. Thus in *Stovin v Wise (Norfolk County Council, third party)* [1996] AC 923, a Highway Authority was not liable to a cyclist injured by a car driver who had been partially unsighted by an obstruction on the land of a third party near the highway, since the land on which the obstruction was sited was outside the statutory duty to maintain the highway (see especially the speech of Lord Hoffmann at 943–945). Although the Highway Authority had a statutory power to make the third party remove the obstruction, they were under no duty to do so. In those circumstances the Authority were under no duty to intervene and even if they did would only be liable if they made things worse. Similarly in *Gorringe v Calderdale Metropolitan Borough Council* [2004] UKHL 15, [2004] 1 WLR 1057 the highway authority's statutory duty to improve road safety did not give rise to a specific duty of care to an individual to install signs on the road.

1   See *Wright v Lodge* [1993] 4 All ER 299 at 303.
2   See *Caparo Industries plc v Dickman* [1990] 2 AC 605 at 632–655; *B v Islington Health Authority* [1991] 1 QB 638 at 644–645; *Mobil Oil Hong Kong Ltd and Dow Chemical (Hong Kong) Ltd v Hong Kong United Dockyards Ltd, The Hua Lien* [1991] 1 Lloyd's Rep 309; and *Marc Rich & Co AG v Bishop Rock Marine Co Ltd, The Nicholas H* [1996] AC 211.

2.15 Cases involving the emergency services and other public bodies give rise to particular difficulties, especially where what is alleged is a failure to respond to a danger which they have not created.[1] Although generally these services will not owe a duty of care in respect of failure to act, this limitation does not apply where the service has created additional danger or assumed responsibility to the claimant. In such cases it is unlikely that the policy arguments will lead to the denial of a duty on grounds of justice, fairness and reasonableness.[2] However, in *Kent v Griffiths* [2001] QB 36 Lord Woolf MR stated if the claim attacked the prioritisation of the rescue or the resources allocated to it a court might reject a duty on the ground that the issues were not justiciable.

1   See *East Suffolk Rivers Catchment Board v Kent* [1941] AC 74; *Alexandrou v Oxford* [1993] 4 All ER 328 (police); *Capital and Counties plc v Hampshire County Council* [1997] QB 1004 (fire service), *OLL Ltd v Secretary of State for Transport* [1997] 3 All ER 897 (coastguards); cf *Home Office v Dorset Yacht Co* [1970] AC 1004 (borstal officers); *Kent v Griffiths* [2001] QB 36.
2   *Capital and Counties plc v Hampshire County Council* [1997] QB 1004, Stuart Smith LJ at 1043.

2.16 In cases of psychiatric harm, often described as nervous shock, a claimant can, in certain circumstances as delineated by the courts, recover in respect of a recognisable psychiatric illness suffered. Where the claimant suffers the illness as a result of a trauma of being endangered or physically injured, the claimant is referred to as a 'primary victim'.[1] A 'secondary victim' is in contrast 'no more than the passive and unwilling witness of injury caused to others'.[2] However, whether a duty of care is owed to a 'secondary victim' depends on whether psychiatric illness to the claimant was a reasonably foreseeable consequence of the defendant's negligence. This may often involve the proximity of the claimant to the event.[3] In claims by 'secondary victims', in addition to the reasonable foreseeability of psychiatric illness, such claims are subject to special restrictions on policy grounds. In *White v Chief Constable of the South Yorkshire Police* [1999] 2 AC 455 at 493 Lord Steyn explained the reasons why there was such a restrictive approach to the duty developed by the courts which were essentially policy considerations in respect of the potentially increased group of defendants who have the 'burden of liability' and 'the effect of the expansion of the availability of compensation on potential claimants who had witnessed gruesome events.' This distinction has led the courts to wish to classify claimants as 'primary victims' if at all possible, as happened in *McLoughlin v Jones* [2001] EWCA Civ 1743, [2002] QB 1312 where Hale LJ treated the claimant as a primary victim who allegedly suffered psychiatric injury as a result of imprisonment by reason of the alleged negligence of his solicitor.

1   *Alcock v Chief Constable of South Yorkshire* [1992] 1 AC 310; see chapter 14.
2   Cf rescuers who are also categorised as secondary victims.
3   Eg *Hanbrook v Stokes* [1943] AC 92.

2.17 So in this class of cases proximity is relevant but it is arguably not the primary arbiter of the existence of a duty of care. Elsewhere the proximity test has been used to restrict the kind of person who may recover for a negligent statement which causes them loss: generally the maker of the statement must intend, or know it is very likely that, a particular class of person will rely on it for a particular class of transaction, and that person must actually do so: *Caparo Industries plc v Dickman* [1990] 2 AC 605. Proximity thus operates as a pragmatic means of limiting liability, a function recognised by both Lord Oliver and Lord Bridge in *Caparo* and by Lord Oliver in *Alcock*. But proximity did not preclude the House of Lords deciding in *Spring v Guardian Assurance plc* [1995] 2 AC 296 that an employer owed a duty of care to an employee in the preparation of a reference, despite it not falling strictly within the circumstances envisaged by *Caparo*. Even the dissenting judgment of Lord Keith accepted that the relationship was sufficiently proximate.[1]

1   See too *T v Surrey County Council* [1994] 4 All ER 577: council liable in negligent misstatement to child injured by child minder when it failed to tell the boy's mother of previous suspicious incidents involving the child minder.

The three-stage test: fair, just and reasonable

2.18 The second requirement is that a duty of care will only arise if it is fair, just and reasonable to impose one in novel circumstances.[1] Although these are general considerations of policy, it is possible to identify cases where respectively the individual criteria of 'fairness', 'justice' and 'reasonableness' have assumed particular significance. Fairness is an obvious epithet for what the court considers should or should not be imposed as a duty in a particular situation and may deny it because it would be 'unfair' to do so. Justice, as Bingham LJ stated in *X v Bedfordshire County Council* [1995] 2 AC 633, HL, 'is a rule of public policy which has first claim on the loyalty of the law [is] that wrongs should be remedied'. And the reasonableness of a duty from the wider perspective of the overall coherence of the law is clearly relevant. This involves the consideration of the so-called 'public good', and a duty of care has been denied in an action against social services because it would lead to defensive policy making by social services.[2] Similar considerations have applied in respect of denials of duty of care by the police, solicitors and advocates. In *McLoughlin v O'Brien* [1983] 1 AC 410 at 421 Lord Wilberforce gave as one policy reason for restricting the duty of care in relation to nervous shock because it would be 'unfair to the defendants' because of the 'large burden ... placed on insurers.'

1   See, for example, Lord Keith in *Spring v Guardian Assurance plc* [1995] 2 AC 296.
2   *X v Bedfordshire County Council* [1995] 2 AC 633, HL.

2.19 This aspect of the three-stage test has been referred to as an exercise of judicial pragmatism which is the same as judicial policy. It may take account not only of reasonableness from the perspective of legal policy but more controversially take account of social and public policy implications of imposing a duty.[1] In practice, this concept overlaps a great deal with proximity, to the point that some judgments treat the two issues as one.[2] Reasoning backwards, courts tend to find sufficient proximity where they consider it to be fair, just and reasonable to impose a duty of care.[3] In *Caparo Industries plc v Dickman* [1990] 2 AC 605 Lord Oliver went so far as to suggest (at 633) that foreseeability, proximity and fairness, justice and reasonableness were 'merely facets of the same thing'. But the weight of authority treats this as an independent requirement: see Lord Oliver in *Caparo v Dickman* at 633; Lord Keith in *Yuen Kun Yeu v A-G of Hong Kong* [1988] AC 175 at 191 and 193; *Spring v Guardian Assurance plc,* per Lord Keith at 308, Lord Lowry at 325–326, Lord Woolf at 342–344; and Lord Browne-Wilkinson at 740 in *X (Minors) v Bedfordshire County Council* [1995] 2 AC 633.[4]

1   *Dean v Allin & Watts (a firm)* [2001] EWCA 758, [2001] PNLR 921.
2   In *Elguzouli-Daf v Metropolitan Police Comr* [1995] QB 335 Steyn LJ said (at 349) that 'it does not seem to me that these considerations can sensibly be considered separately in this case; inevitably they shade into each other'.
3   See, for example, *Spring v Guardian Assurance plc* [1995] 2 AC 296.
4   It is sometimes treated as separate from the 'public policy' head which may negative a duty of care: see para 2.32ff, below.

2.20 This test plainly allows a large discretion to the courts, especially the higher courts, to determine the limits of liability in negligence. More obviously than 'proximity', it permits the court to examine the factual consequences of imposing liability in negligence. Thus, in *X v Bedfordshire County Council* [1995] 2 AC 633, HL (above), the House of Lords refused to impose a duty of care on local authorities in relation to putting abused children into care in part because of the extraordinarily delicate nature of the duties in this field.[1] However, this was less of a concern to the court in *Barrett v Enfield London Borough Council* [1999] 3 WLR 79: see the speeches of Lord Slynn at 93–94 and Lord Hutton at 113–114 and in *Phelps v Hillingdon London Borough Council* [2001] 2 AC 619 in respect of the duty of care owed to a child in respect of the conduct of an educational psychologist employed by the authority. In *Barrett v Enfield London Borough Council* the House of Lords considered that a local authority might owe a duty of care in relation to psychiatric problems caused to a child in its care by allegedly negligent placements with unsuitable foster parents, but Lord Hutton identified that it would not be permissible to allow a child to sue his or her parents for decisions made about the child's upbringing: a clear policy issue.

1   See the leading speech of Lord Browne-Wilkinson. Lord Nolan, on the other hand, relied on public policy to deny liability.

2.21 Policy arguments were also used to deny a duty of care in *Marc Rich & Co AG v Bishop Rock Marine Co Ltd, The Nicholas H* [1996] AC 211: the House of Lords considered that finding a duty of care would have various undesirable consequences on the shipping business (although this case was distinguished in *Perrett v Collins* [1998] 2 Lloyd's Rep 255, CA, on the basis that it was inapplicable in personal injury cases). In *Mulcahy v Ministry of Defence* [1996] QB 732, the Court of Appeal held that it would not be fair, just and reasonable to impose a duty of care between soldiers in the course of battle. However, in *Kent v Griffiths* [2001] QB 36, CA, there were no policy reasons militating against a finding of negligence by an ambulance service in its response to a 999 call. At 1171, Lord Woolf MR distinguished a call to the ambulance service from calls made to the police and fire services on the basis that the potential conflict of interest between the protection of the individual and the public does not arise in the case of ambulances (except where mistakes are made as to the seriousness of injuries in cases where there are multiple injuries, but Lord Woolf doubted whether negligence would be established in such circumstances). However, as identified above,[1] this would not be so if the claim attacked the prioritisation of the resource or the resources allocated to it, which would clearly involve policy issues and the exercise of its discretion by the authority.

1   Para 2.15.

The three-stage test: foresight of harm

2.22 The next criteria is the continuing requirement of reasonable foresight that harm, of the kind which in fact occurred, might result to a class of persons which include the claimant. The defendant need not subjectively foresee harm to the particular person injured; it is sufficient that he or she ought reasonably to foresee harm to a class of persons, such as other road users near to his car, which includes the claimant, that being knowledge that someone in the defendant's position would be expected to possess. The greater the awareness of the potential for harm, the more likely it is that this criteria will be satisfied.[1] In this context, provided that the acts of the defendant and the kind of harm are defined widely, it is unlikely greatly to restrict the situations in which a duty of care will arise.[2] An example of how 'foreseeability' may be approached is to be found in the speech of Lord Reid in *Carmarthenshire County Council v Lewis* [1955] AC 549 at 564–565, where each element in the situation is taken step by step to demonstrate that the result could easily have been foreseen by a person who took the trouble to think about it. There are, however, dangers in a step by step approach: see *Smith v Littlewoods Organisation Ltd* [1987] AC 241 and in particular the speech of Lord Griffiths at 251A–B.[3]

1   This test overlaps with the test of foreseeability as a measure of recoverable damages (see para 3.52ff, below).
2   The necessity of determining, as a fact, whether an event was 'foreseeable' becomes less formidable when it is remembered that foresight must always depend on past experience, including the special experience of a particular person or undertaking. But claims failed in *Nicholls v F Austin (Leyton) Ltd* [1946] AC 493, where a piece of wood flew out of a machine because—per Lord Wright in the former case—such accidents were 'outside normal experience'.
3   'I was reminded of the fable of the prince who lost his kingdom but for the want of a nail for the shoe of his horse. A series of foreseeable possibilities were added one to another and, hey presto, there emerged the probability of a fire against which Littlewoods should have guarded. But, my Lords, that is not the common sense of this matter.'

2.23 Even a small risk is sufficient to come within the range of reasonably foreseeable damage unless a reasonable man would disregard it (see *Overseas Tankship v Miller Steamship Co Pty, The Wagon Mound (No 2)* [1967] 1 AC 617 at 642–643). Differing approaches have been taken as to the extent of the risk required. Certainly the risk does not have to be more likely than not to occur. At its highest it has been said that only if a risk is so far-fetched or fantastic that it would never occur to a reasonable man is it not foreseeable: see *Fardon v Harcourt-Rivington* [1932] All ER Rep 81, HL; and *Page v Smith* [1996] AC 155, HL. Arguably, however, there must be 'a real risk as distinct from a mere possibility of danger' see *Smith v Littlewoods Ltd* at 269B in the speech of Lord Mackay.[1]

1   See too *Koonjul v Thameslink Healthcare Services* [2000] PIQR P 123; and see para 2.68.

2.24 Where physical damage or personal injuries are likely to result from acts of the defendant, that damage is almost certainly foreseeable: see Lord Brandon in *The Hua Lien* [1991] 1 Lloyd's Rep 309 at 328–329. An example is *Pearson v Lightning* [1998] 20 LS Gaz R 33, CA, where an injury which resulted from a difficult golf shot was held to be foreseeable, despite the low risk of injury. However, in *Gillon v Chief Constable of Strathclyde* 1997 SLT 1218, it was held unforeseeable that a police officer controlling a football crowd would be injured by a player who was trying to control the ball. So too in *Bolton v Stone* [1951] AC 850, where the chances of a cricket ball hitting Miss Stone were very small and the activity being carried on was a lawful one, the accident was not reasonably foreseeable. As has been pointed out, reasonable foreseeability is not a fixed point on the scale of probability; whether avoiding the risk would involve the defendant in undue cost or require him to abstain from some otherwise lawful activity is a relevant factor here.[1]

1   *Jolley v London Borough of Sutton* [2000] 1 WLR 1082 at 1091H–1092B; and see para 2.68 below.

2.25 If physical injury is foreseeable to the primary victim of an accident, so too will be psychiatric injury—even if the claimant is in fact physically uninjured: see *Page v Smith* [1996] AC 155.[1] Nevertheless, the concept of reasonable foreseeability has been used to restrict the persons, not participants in an accident, who can recover for nervous shock. The weaker the ties of love and affection between the claimant and those he or she sees suffer injury, the less likely that injury to them is foreseeable

2.25 The general principles of negligence

1   Compare the reasoning of *Tremain v Pike* [1969] 3 All ER 1303. It is not clear if this survives *Page v Smith*.

2.26 The test is objective but takes account of the characteristics of the defendant in determining what is foreseeable: for example, a chemical manufacturer should know of the risks associated with chemicals it uses or makes: see Swanwick J in *Stokes v Guest, Keen and Nettlefold (Bolts and Nuts) Ltd* [1968] 1 WLR 1776 at 1783. If, even with such knowledge, no risk can reasonably be foreseen, no duty of care will arise. In *Wilebore v St Edmunsbury Borough Council* (24 February 1994, unreported), QBD, for example, no risk of upper limb injury was foreseeable from work—handling carcasses—not involving rapid, repetitive twisting. By contrast, a statutory authority which dug a trench in the road owed a duty of care to blind persons in the precautions it took to protect passers by against falling into the trench: *Haley v London Electricity Board* [1965] AC 778.

2.27 It is not necessary that the precise manner in which an accident happens should be foreseeable, so long as an accident of that general kind can be foreseen: see *Overseas Tankship v Mort Dock and Engineering Co, The Wagon Mound* [1961] AC 388; *Hughes v Lord Advocate* [1963] AC 837; *Doughty v Turner Manufacturing Co Ltd* [1964] 1 QB 518; *Margereson v JW Roberts Ltd* [1996] PIQR P 358 (escape of asbestos dust which children played with); *Wiszniewski v Central Manchester Health Authority* [1998] PIQR P 324 (baby suffered cerebral palsy from mistakes made by hospital during birth); *Jolley v Sutton London Borough Council* [2000] 1 WLR 1082 at 1089–1091, HL (council liable to boy injured whilst playing under an abandoned boat) and *Jebson v Ministry of Defence* [2000] ICR 1220. This is a difficult area and requires an intense focus on the circumstances of the individual case.[1] The issue is whether the accident falls within the scope of the risk created by the negligence.

1   *See Jolley* [2000] 1 WLR 1082 at 1090D–E. *Doughty v Turner Manufacturing Co* [1964] 1 QB 518 is probably close to the limits of a different kind of accident.

2.28 Even if a consequence is foreseeable it is necessary to show that it was within the scope of the duty owed. In *R v Croydon Health Authority* [1998] PIQR Q26, the Court of Appeal held that a mother could not recover the cost of bringing up a child which she claimed that she would not have had if a radiologist had not failed to report the presence of an abnormality. Applying *South Australia Asset Management Corpn v York Montague Ltd* [1997] AC 191, HL, Kennedy LJ concluded (at Q33) that the damage was not within the scope of the duty.[1] Subsequently in *MacFarlane v Tayside Health Board* [2000] 2 AC 59 the House of Lords denied a duty in similar circumstances, on the basis that the type of loss, the future cost of care of the child was not a recognised kind of harm; see para 2.32.

1   Though cf *Walkin v South Manchester Health Authority* [1995] 1 WLR 1543, CA.

2.29 Account must be taken of the possible actions of others, including the possibility that they will act negligently (see paras 2.74–2.76, below) or that children will mimic adult behaviour: *see Jolley* at 1089. In some contexts criminal acts of others are reasonably foreseeable, although, because of a reluctance to impose duties to prevent the consequences of third parties' actions, the courts tend to demand that such actions are 'very likely': per Lord Reid in *Home Office v Dorset Yacht Co Ltd* [1970] AC 1004 at 1003; Lord Mackay in *Smith v Littlewoods Organisation Ltd* [1987] AC 241 at 261 (but cf Lord Goff at 279); and see *T v Surrey County Council* [1994] 4 All ER 577.

2.30 Employers are now under a duty to conduct a full assessment of the risks arising from their work under the Management of Health and Safety at Work Regulations 1999, SI 1999/3242 (see para 10.18, below); as well as to make more specific assessments under numerous other recent regulations. It is probable that this approach should inform what is expected of an employer at common law (see para 10.19, below), so that foreseeability should extend to whatever risks would have been revealed by a proper assessment.

Application of the three-stage test

2.31 Although the three-stage test was established in cases concerned with economic loss or public services, it is equally applicable in other classes of case. In *Marc Rich & Co AG v Bishop Rock Marine Co Ltd* [1996] AC 211 the House of Lords rejected the suggestion that in cases of physical damage the only requirement was foreseeability and the three-stage test was of no application and emphasised that the test was of universal application. Two cases involving personal injury exemplify how this test is applied. In *Perrett v Collins* [1999] PNLR 77, where the claimant had suffered personal injury in the crash of an aircraft which the defendant had negligently certified as airworthy, Hobhouse LJ stated that the case fell within the recognised category of liability for personal injury and that it was not open to the defendant to avoid the existence of a duty of care and thus liability by 'appealing to some vague concept of justice and fairness.' Rather, since the defendant had involvement in the activity which, if dangerous, would cause injury to the claimant, there was sufficient foreseeability and proximity to establish a duty of care. Similarly in *Watson v Bristol Boxing Board of Control Ltd* [2001] QB 1134 the Court of Appeal held that the Board owed a duty to its members, professional boxers, to take reasonable care in making regulations imposing a duty to ensure that personal injuries sustained in a boxing match are properly treated. Lord Phillips applied the three-stage test and found that it was reasonable for the boxing members to look to the Board to look after their safety, there was proximity because of the membership and it was just, fair and reasonable to impose a duty and foreseeable that in the absence of appropriate medical precautions injury may occur. The test was applied carefully and specifically in the recent decision in *Wattleworth v Goodwood Road Racing Co Ltd* [2004] EWHC 140 (QB), [2004] All ER (D) 51 (Feb) where the Motor Sports Association were held to be under a duty to a driver killed on a racing circuit about which the Association had given safety advice. Additionally, it is important to appreciate that generally the issue of proximity may be of particular importance where the test is sought to be used to establish a novel relationship and in such circumstances it is sometimes elevated to a separate requirement of assumption of responsibility. So in *Leach v Chief Constable of Gloucestershire Constabulary* [1999] 1 WLR 1421 the Court of Appeal refused to strike out a negligence claim by a claimant against the police where he had attended a traumatic interview of a mentally disabled suspect as a voluntary worker, since the police owed a duty to provide counselling services to such volunteers because they had assumed responsibility to the volunteer.

Loss of a recognised kind

2.32 That there is no general principle of recovery for carelessness is further illustrated by another legal restriction on negligent liability: the claimant must suffer harm of a kind for which the law permits recovery in order that a duty of care may arise at all.[1] That clearly covers most kinds of tangible, physical damage, whether to the person[2] or to property. However this does not extend to all forms of injury. By way of example, pleural plaques caused by negligent exposure to asbestos were found not to support a claim in negligence, solely because they carried a risk of subsequent significant injury and gave rise to consequent anxiety and a defendant who negligently exposed a claimant to the risk of contracting a disease was not liable for free-standing psychiatric injury caused by the fear of contracting the disease: *Rothwell v Chemical & Insulating Co Ltd* [2006] EWCA Civ 27, [2006] 07 LS Gaz R 25. Further, distress and humiliation, unless actionable under statute, eg the Protection from Harassment Act 1997, are not actionable in negligence. Recent cases have also limited the circumstances in which a claimant can recover for negligently inflicted economic loss, unrelated to and not following from physical harm: see, for example, *Murphy v Brentwood District Council* [1991] 1 AC 398 and *Bellefield Computer Services Ltd v E Turner & Sons Ltd* [2000] All ER (D) 84, CA. In *McFarlane v Tayside Health Board* [2000] 2 AC 59 the House of Lords held (for a variety of reasons) there could be no liability for the costs incurred in the future cost of care of a child born because of the defendant's doctor's negligence. However, in *Parkinson v St James's and Seacroft University Hospitals NHS Trust* [2001] EWCA Civ 530, [2002] QB 266, because the child born because of the defendants' negligently performed sterilisation procedure was autistic, the additional costs attributable to that disability could be recovered. In *Rees v Darlington Memorial Hospital NHS Trust* [2003] UKHL 52, [2004] 1 AC 309, where the claimant mother had very poor eyesight, but the child born because of the negligently performed sterilisation procedure was healthy, the majority of the House of Lords rejected any liability because the additional costs of upbringing because of the mother's pre-existing disability were not a recognised loss following *McFarlane*. There is considerable difficulty in reconciling the different rationale behind the decisions in each of these cases.

---

[1] Whether a particular harm to a claimant is actionable is, therefore, a question of law.

[2] A child injured as a foetus can recover in some circumstances: see *B v Islington Health Authority* [1993] QB 204 and the Congenital Disabilities (Civil Liability) Act 1976. So may a mother for an unwanted pregnancy: *Walkin v South Manchester Health Authority* [1995] 1 WLR 1543, CA.

2.33 More significantly from the viewpoint of workers, psychiatric suffering will not permit an action for negligence unless that suffering either accompanies a physical injury or itself amounts to a recognisable psychiatric illness: see *Hicks v Chief Constable of South Yorkshire Police* [1992] 2 All ER 65, HL; *Frost v Chief Constable of South Yorkshire Police* [1999] 2 AC 455, HL, more fully discussed in chapter 14 below. A secondary victim can recover damages for mental illness caused or contributed to by the defendant's negligence, and it does not matter that the illness might also have occurred as a pathological consequence of bereavement: *Vernon v Bosley (No 1)* [1997] 1 All ER 577. Distress and humiliation is not independently actionable and so consequently deprivation of liberty is not actionable in negligence: *R v Deputy Governor of Parkhurst Prison, ex p Hague* [1992] 1 AC 58; even if accompanied by claustrophobia: *Reilly v Merseyside Regional Health Authority* [1995] 6 Med LR 246, CA. This rule applies no matter how foreseeable such suffering may be—although once a claimant has suffered a recognisable injury or suffered a physical condition for which the defendant's negligence is responsible, damages may be awarded for distress, anxiety and the like which also results from the careless acts. No such restriction applies, in principle, to physical injury. In *Gregg v Scott* [2005] UKHL 2, [2005] 2 WLR 268 where the House of Lords held that the claimant could not recover for the reduction in his chance of recovery from cancer caused by the defendant's negligent failure to diagnose because the civil standard of probability could not be established, they suggested he may be able to recover for the anguish of knowing that the disease could have been detected earlier. Similarly, although Holland J at first instance in *Grieves v FT Everard & Sons* [2005] EWHC 88 (QB) found that the claimants could recover compensation for anxiety resulting from knowledge that their exposure to asbestos through the defendant's negligence had resulted in physiological damage to lungs which made it more likely that they would suffer asbestosis, the Court of Appeal in *Rothwell v Chemical & Insulating Co Ltd* [2006] EWCA Civ 27, [2006] 07 LS Gaz R 25 reaffirmed the general principle that there is no entitlement to damages for anxiety for future incapacity alone but only where it is part of the compensation for an injury.[1]

[1]   See also para 2.32.

2.34 The point has arisen in cases involving what is loosely termed 'repetitive strain injury'[1] where an issue has arisen as to whether pain by itself permits recovery. Where there is a clinical condition, such as tenosynivitis, carpal tunnel syndrome or the like, the position is straightforward. A debate in *Smith v Baker and McKenzie* (11 April 1994, unreported), HC as to whether 'lower grade tenosynovitis' was a known medical condition was resolved in favour of the claimant. Difficulty has arisen, though, where the claimant has a diffuse non-specific condition marked by pain but without an identifiable pathology. Whether a court will accept the existence of an injury appears to depend on the judge's view of the medical evidence.[2] In *Alexander v Midland Bank plc* [2000] ICR 464, CA, it was held that where there was a clear choice between two alternative explanations of the claimants' pain, it was for the claimants to prove that the physical explanation was more probable than the psychogenic theory.[3] This is in keeping with the earlier approach of the House of Lords in *Pickford v Imperial Chemical Industries plc* [1998] ICR 673, where it was held that it was for the claimant to satisfy the court that her condition had an organic cause. Although the defendants were entitled to present evidence to refute the claimant's claim, they were not obliged to prove their alternative theory.[4]

1   On work-related upper-limb disorders see chapter 17, below.
2   In *Mughal v Reuters Ltd* [1993] IRLR 571 Judge Prosser (sitting as a deputy) held there was no such condition, as did Judge Savill (sitting as a deputy) in *Land v Volex Group plc* (1994) 10 PMILL 17, and JG Williams QC (sitting as a deputy) in *Moran v South Wales Argus* (25 November 1994, unreported). On the other hand, in *Mountenay (Hazzard) v Bernard Matthews* [1994] 5 Med LR 293, the judge permitted recovery, despite holding that what was foreseeable was the risk of one of the clinical conditions. Judge Black (sitting as a deputy) in *Bettany v Royal Doulton (UK) Ltd* (27 April 1993, transcript) also accepted potential liability for pain without pathology (though the defendants had taken all reasonable steps and were not therefore in breach of duty).
3   Stuart-Smith LJ stated at 482: 'Simply because the precise pathological/physiological explanation could not be explained by the existing techniques does not mean that these conditions were all in the mind'.
4   See, too, Langstaff 'Upper Limb Disorders: Work-related or Unrelated?' [1994] JPIL 14. And see the Australian case *of Murca v Commonwealth of Australia* (24 September 1993, unreported), Sup Ct of NSW and *Bird v Husain* (6 July 1993, unreported), High Ct.

Acts and omissions

2.35 It is important to have regard to the limitation on the imposition of a duty of care arising out of the distinction the law draws between actions and omissions (although this distinction is of more limited relevance to employers' liability). In *Smith v Littlewoods Organisation Ltd* [1987] AC 241 at 247 Lord Goff identified the fundamental principle that 'the common law does not impose liability for what are called pure omissions.' A pure omission is what is stated to be a simple failure to act, which must be distinguished from a situation where because of an earlier act the defendant is under a consequential duty to take precautions; a classic example being the person whose car breaks down in a dangerous position in the road who is under a duty to move it and if he does not do so is liable for the consequent collision: see *Lee v Lever* [1974] RTR 35. However, more generally a duty not positively to act to harm someone is more readily found than is a duty to act positively to prevent someone being harmed who will otherwise be harmed: see Lord Diplock in *Home Office v Dorset Yacht Co Ltd* [1970] AC 1004 at 1060; Lord Goff in *Smith v Littlewoods Organisation Ltd* [1987] AC 241 at 270–271; and Lord Hoffmann in *Stovin v Wise* [1996] AC 923, HL, at 943–944. Consequently, in the absence of specific reasons, neither a statutory authority nor an individual owes a duty of care to a person to attempt a rescue in an emergency. There is no duty to shout a warning to a person about to walk over a cliff (Lord Keith in *Yuen Kun Yeu v A-G for Hong Kong* [1988] AC 175 at 192). In the absence of a duty to act, the common law does not require someone to act as a good Samaritan; even if he does so he will only be liable if his own acts cause additional damage over and above that which the claimant would have suffered if the Samaritan had not intervened: see *Horslet v MacLaren, The Ogopogo* [1971] 2 Lloyd's Rep 410 and *Kent v Griffith (No 3)* [2001] QB 36. This distinction is not reconcilable with a simple test of reasonable foreseeability or proximity, but can perhaps be justified under the 'fair, just and reasonable' umbrella. It is not negligent to fail to save a drowning person, even if that could be done with little effort or risk.[1]

1   The position will be different where, as with the ambulance service, there is a duty to intervene (as in *Kent v Griffiths* [2001] QB 36).

2.36 This distinction (and consequent absence of a duty of care) does not apply where the defendant is, because of the circumstances, under a duty to act. A solicitor or other professional person who undertakes to perform a service has assumed a responsibility towards that person, so as to be liable for acts or omissions: see *Hedley Byrne & Co Ltd v Heller & Partners Ltd* [1964] AC 465, HL; *White v Jones* [1995] 2 AC 207, HL, especially Lord Goff at 262; and *Kirkham v Chief Constable of the Greater Manchester Police* [1990] 2 QB 283, CA per Lloyd LJ at 288 (police liable for failing to warn prison of danger that prisoner would commit suicide). A person whose car breaks down in a dangerous position in the road is under a duty to move it: *Wright v Lodge* [1993] 4 All ER 299; a school owes duties to its pupils;[1] and it is beyond doubt that employers are just as much liable for failures to act in accordance with the standard of care owed towards their employees as they are liable for actions causing harm, so that foreseeability alone is the general guide (see Lord Keith in *Alcock v Chief Constable of South Yorkshire Police* [1992] 1 AC 310 at 396). Underpinning these duties there may well be a principle of assumption of responsibility, a principle developed by Lord Goff in *Smith v Littlewoods Organisation Ltd* [1987] AC 241 and *White v Jones*, above. In *Barrett v Ministry of Defence* [1995] 1 WLR 1217, the Court of Appeal held that although it was fair, just and reasonable for an airman to assume responsibility for his own actions in consuming alcohol, when his colleagues took him to his bunk they assumed responsibility for him and accordingly were partly liable. In *Kirkham*, Lloyd LJ said that the existence of that duty depends upon 'whether the defendant has assumed responsibility towards the claimant and whether the claimant has relied on the assumption of that responsibility'.[2] An employer, for example, owes a duty to take reasonable care of an employee who has been injured although the employer did not itself cause the initial injury: see *Kasapis v Laimos Bros* [1959] 2 Lloyd's Rep 378. Similar considerations arise in stress at work claims where the employer is aware of the employee's vulnerability but fails to provide for the employee accordingly. So in *Walker v Northumberland County Council* [1995] ICR 702 a social worker was entitled to damages for a second nervous breakdown caused by stress at work, and in *Hatton v Sunderland* [2002] EWCA Civ 76, [2002] ICR 613 Hale LJ identified that the employer would not be liable unless 'he knows of some particular problem or vulnerability.' However, where a situation arises which necessitates action by the employer, such as the failure to provide counselling to an employee who suffered a psychiatric reaction after cutting down a suicide victim in prison, then the employer will owe a duty of care and be liable: see *Melville v The Home Office* [2005] EWCA Civ 6, [2005] ICR 782. There may be, as identified by the House of Lords in *Barber v Somerset County Council* [2004] UKHL 13, [2004] ICR 457, a positive duty to give consideration to the welfare of employees which consequently may trigger a duty of care where the individual circumstances require positive action.

1   *Chittock v Woodbridge School* [2002] EWCA Civ 915, [2003] PIQR P 6.

2   It is suggested that reliance by the claimant may not be a necessary pre-condition of liability: compare Farquharson LJ and see CA Hopkins 'Tortious Liability for Suicide' [1990] CLJ 392. In accordance with the 'assumption of responsibility' test, an undertaking may owe duties to workers who it does not employ, similar to those owed to employees by an employer: see para 4.72ff, below. The South African courts have adopted a more subtle approach: *Minister van Polisie v Ewels* 1975 3 SA 590, AD.

2.37 Whilst in the absence of special reasons there is no duty to rescue, different considerations apply where the conduct of the rescuer makes the situation worse. In *Capital & Counties plc v Hampshire County Council* [1997] QB 1004, CA, it was held that a fire brigade was not under a duty to answer a call for help or take care to do so, but where the negligence of the fire brigade actually created the danger which caused the damage, a duty of care was owed. In *OLL Ltd v Secretary of State for Transport* [1997] 3 All ER 897, May J held that the coastguard service were not liable for an alleged misdirection of Royal Navy helicopters, which delayed rescue efforts, because there was no positive act which directly caused greater injury than would have occurred if they had not intervened at all.[1] In *Kent v Griffiths* [2001] QB 36, however, once the ambulance service had accepted a call from a patient's GP requesting their immediate attendance, a duty of care was owed to the patient in respect of further injury that was caused by unexplained delay because it owed a duty based on its undertaking to respond to the emergency call. The distinctions between these cases are subtle and are apparently based on the fact that the police and fire service's and similar services' primary obligation is to the public at large rather than an individual. Further examples of where such services do owe a duty of care are based on either special relationship or more usually an assumption of responsibility. Thus in *Welsh v Chief Constable of Merseyside Police* [1993] 1 All ER 692, QBD and *Swinney v The Chief Constable of Northumbria Police* [1997] QB 464, where the service had given an undertaking to take some action, it would owe an affirmative duty to take reasonable care to honour the undertaking.

1   See also *Skinner v Secretary of State for Transport* (1995) Times, 3 January.

Public policy

2.38 Finally, even if these hurdles are overcome, the existence of a duty of care may be denied for public policy reasons. Although largely overlapping with the 'fair, just and reasonable' test above, this element is distinct,[1] although it adds to the discretion in the court. It is a final policy long-stop. But, as Lord Keith stated in *Yuen Kun Yeu v A-G of Hong Kong* [1988] AC 175 at 193 and in *Spring v Guardian Assurance plc* [1995] 2 AC 296 at 307–308, it will be a rare case in which this requirement negatives what would otherwise give rise to liability. The burden is on the defendant to establish a public policy defence: see especially Lord Lowry in *Spring* at 325–326.

1   See Lord Keith in the passage cited above in *Spring v Guardian Assurance* at 307–308.

2.39 Exceptionally, public policy has been invoked as a justification for denying a duty of care in cases involving public bodies because of the concern that it would lead to defensive decision making, for instance in policing. So it has been a ground for disallowing an action against the police for their failure to apprehend criminals: see *Hill v Chief Constable of West Yorkshire* [1989] AC 53, HL; *Alexandrou v Oxford* [1993] 4 All ER 328; and *Ancell v McDermott* [1993] 4 All ER 355. This blanket immunity of the police from suit in negligence was held to be a violation of art 6 of the European Convention on Human Rights in *Osman v United Kingdom* (1998) 29 EHRR 245. In that case no problems of proximity arose; there was a particular individual who was known to be threatened by the criminal. The decision in *Osman* appears to prohibit strike out applications on policy grounds, although in an appropriate case (eg where proximity is the issue) such applications can still succeed: see *Palmer v Tees Health Authority* [2000] PIQR P 1.

2.40 In *Leach v Chief Constable of Gloucestershire Constabulary* [1999] 1 WLR 1421, the Court of Appeal struck out substantial parts of a claim on the grounds that there were strong policy reasons why the police should not be found to owe a duty to protect a person who was acting as an 'appropriate adult' in a police interview from mental or psychological harm. They did, however, accept that there was a triable issue as to whether the police ought to have provided counselling. In *Swinney v Chief Constable of Northumbria Police Force* [1997] QB 464, the Court of Appeal resisted a strike-out application in a case concerning confidential information about a police informant, but all three judges alluded to the importance of public policy considerations: see Hirst LJ at 484, Peter Gibson LJ at 486 and Ward LJ at 487. The Crown Prosecution Service did not owe a duty to a suspect for public policy reasons in *Elguzouli-Daf v Commissioner of Police for the Metropolis* [1995] 1 All ER 833. The coastguard service was not liable for proven negligence on public policy grounds in *Skinner v Secretary of State for Transport* (1995) Times, 3 January. The Court of Appeal held that there were no public policy reasons militating against the liability of a criminal for injuries caused to a policeman pursuing him: see Stuart-Smith LJ at P321 of *Langley v Dray and MT Motor Policies at Lloyds* [1998] PIQR P 314.

2.41 It is difficult to imagine many categories of employment or work relationship where public policy will bar claims. But in *Hughes v National Union of Mineworkers* [1991] 4 All ER 278, public policy was one ground for denying recovery to members of the police injured by rioters as a result of decisions made by their senior officers. Yet even in police cases, there was never an absolute bar to recovery: *Knightley v Johns* [1982] 1 WLR 349; *Rigby v Chief Constable of Northamptonshire* [1985] 1 WLR 1242; and *Costello v Chief Constable of the Northumbria Police* [1999] ICR 752, CA (where a policeman was held to have assumed a responsibility to assist another police officer). These were cases where the negligence was clear and the injury relatively direct, as distinct from failures to investigate where a third party causes harm: see Lord Keith in *Hill* at 59 and May LJ in *Hughes v NUM* at 286–288. Since *Osman* it is no longer arguable that there is an absolute bar to recovery on policy grounds. The present attitude of the appellate courts to the relevance of public policy is evident from the speeches in the House of

Lords in *McFarlane v Tayside Health Board* [2000] 2 AC 59 at 83 and 108 where both Lord Steyn and Lord Millett were clear in their wish to avoid consideration of public policy issues.

Summary

2.42 In short, a duty of care will only be found to exist in the following circumstances: first, a relationship of sufficient proximity between the parties, analogous to other relationships in which a duty of care has been held to exist; second, it must be fair, just and reasonable to find a duty of care; third, the risk of injury must have been reasonably foreseeable; fourth, the injury must be of the sort for which the law permits recovery; and, fifth, there must be no grounds of public policy which exclude the imposition of liability. The issue is one of law, considered logically prior to the questions of what standard of care was owed by the defendant, and whether this has been breached on the facts of the particular case.

2.43 A period of bold expansionism gave way for a number of years to a much more restricted approach. It was thought that the decision in *Osman* and the advent of the HRA 1998[1] may mark a further turning of the tide towards a more expansionist approach. However, so far the speeches of Lord Hoffmann in *Wainwright v The Home Office* [2003] UKHL 53, [2004] 2 AC 406 and in *Re McKerr* [2004] UKHL 12, [2004] 1 WLR 807 suggest the contrary, although the speech of Lord Nicholls in *Campbell v MGN* [2003] UKHL 52, [2004] 1 AC 309 may suggest a more expansionist approach in specific areas of potential legal development. A relatively restrictive approach by the judiciary appears to be mirrored in other common law jurisdictions.[2]

[1] In force October 2000.
[2] See the examples cited by Lord Bridge in *Caparo Industries plc v Dickman* [1990] 2 AC 605 but compare recent decisions on privacy in Australia and New Zealand.

DUTY OF CARE IN EMPLOYMENT—GENERAL PRINCIPLES

2.44 An employer owes an employee a duty of care to safeguard his health and safety in the context of his employment as described in detail in *Wilsons & Clyde Coal Co Ltd v English* [1938] AC 57. As Lord Hoffmann stated in *White v Chief Constable of South Yorkshire Police* [1999] 2 AC 455 at 506 'the liability of an employer to his employee for negligence ... is not a separate tort with its own rules. It is an aspect of the general law of negligence.' More problematic is the extent and standard of that duty. The close relationship between employer and employee necessarily influences the nature of the duty. For instance, it is sufficient to justify an exception to the mere omission principle and justifies a duty to take care to protect the employee from harm. Difficulties arise specifically in relation to the kind of injury sustained, particularly psychiatric injury,[1] and the duties owed to other workers.[2] It is now clear that the employee's mental health comes within the scope of the duty of care owed by the employer and the law is developing in respect of the liability of an employer for psychiatric illness caused by stress at work.[3] The employer's duty is owed to each employee as an individual, so that individual weaknesses known to, or which should be known by, the employer are taken into account. Also the vulnerability of the employee may give rise to an obligation by the employer to provide for the employee's welfare.[4]

1   Dealt with in chapter 14, below.
2   See eg para 4.72ff, below.
3   *Barber v Somerset County Council* [2004] UKHL 13, [2004] ICR 457.
4   *Walker v Northumberland County Council* [1995] ICR 702.

2.45 Where the conduct of an employer's undertaking causes physical injury to a person who is not its employee, a duty of care will often be found to exist: see eg *Baker v TE Hopkins & Son Ltd* [1958] 3 All ER 147 (duty owed to doctor called to help workers overcome by fumes). More specifically, an employer may owe duties to persons working under its control who are not strictly its employees; duties will be owed to visitors by reason of an employer's occupation of a site; and duties will often be owed to third parties.[1] Thus, a duty was owed to an employee's family in respect of lead taken home on an employee's work clothes (*Hewett v Alf Brown's Transport Ltd* [1992] ICR 530), although it was held that no higher duty could be owed to the worker's wife, who seemed to be particularly susceptible to lead poisoning, than was owed to the employee.[2] The Court of Appeal came to a similar conclusion in *Maguire v Harland & Woolf plc* [2005] EWCA Civ 1, [2005] PIQR P 21 in rejecting a claim by the wife of an employee who had developed mesothelioma as a result of exposure to asbestos dust when washing her husband's dusty clothes because at the time in the early 1960s the risks of familial exposure were not recognised. However, in *Margereson and Hancock v JW Roberts Ltd* [1996] PIQR P 358 the Court of Appeal held the employer liable for mesothelioma suffered by members of the public who as children were exposed to asbestos dust allowed to escape from a factory.

1   See chapter 7, below.
2   On the facts, the duty was not breached to the employee and nor, therefore, to the wife.

2.46 The general rule is that there is no cause of action where, due to one person's negligence, pure economic loss is caused to a third party.[1] Similarly, but subject to some limited exceptions (see chapter 14, below), no duty of care is owed to a third party who suffers psychiatric injury as a consequence of injuries negligently caused to another. An employer is not liable to the relative of an injured or dead worker who suffers psychiatric illness through having to cope with that loss: see *Alcock v Chief Constable for South Yorkshire Police* [1992] 1 AC 310 at 400, per Lord Ackner (citing *Jaensch v Coffey* (1984) 155 CLR 549) and Lord Oliver at 408–409. Apart from compensating for care,[2] nor is an employer generally liable for financial loss to such a third party resulting from the employee's injuries: *Kirkham v Boughey* [1958] 2 QB 338; *Best v Samuel Fox & Co Ltd* [1952] AC 716.

1   See eg *Weller & Co v Foot and Mouth Disease Research Institute* [1966] 1 QB 569 (cattle infected: no liability to auctioneer because markets not held); *Electrochrome Ltd v Welsh Plastics Ltd* [1968] 2 All ER 205 (water supply damaged, no liability to factory for supply cut off). Contrast *White v Jones* [1995] 2 AC 207, HL.
2   The damages for which are held on trust for the carer: *Hunt v Severs* [1994] 2 AC 350, HL overruling *Donnelly v Joyce* [1974] QB 454 on this point.

2.47 The existence of a duty of care in the abstract between two parties tells little as to when that duty will be found to be breached. Not only is this because the standard of care owed varies with the circumstances (*Videan v British Transport Commission* [1963] 2 QB 650), but also because it may be unclear, particularly in relation to omissions, when one party is under a duty to act. Therefore it is necessary to examine specifically the individual circumstances in which the employer's responsibility gives rise to a duty of care.

The scope of an employer's responsibility

2.48 The employer's duty is a personal non-delegable duty of care. The employer can delegate the performance of the duties to others, whether employees or independent contractors, but remains liable for its negligent performance. However, it is not every risk to which employees are subject for which an employer is liable, even if the employer knows or should know of that risk. To fail to warn employees of the dangers of driving to work, for example, is not negligent; nor is an employer under a duty to advise an employee to take out health insurance: *Reid v Rush & Tompkins Group plc* [1990] 1 WLR 212, CA.[1] But an employer should warn an employee of inherent and specific risks of work when he or she is engaged: see *Presland v GW Padley* (29 January 1979, unreported, Tudor-Evans J): see para 2.55. The duty is sometimes said to be one to take all reasonable care for its employee's health and safety; but that is a very vague as a guide to the scope of the employer's responsibility. In practice, courts have regard to a vast array of specific duties which have been recognised in earlier cases.

[1] Although an employer may be under a contractual duty to advise an employee of lost economic benefits: see *Scally v Southern Health and Social Services Board* [1992] 1 AC 294, HL.

2.49 All the duties are connected in some sense to what happens to the employee while at work (but not necessarily while under the employer's actual control: see para 4.73, below). The duties are often analysed as a duty to provide and maintain a safe place of work and equipment; to provide competent employees; and to establish and enforce a safe system of work: see *Wilsons & Clyde Coal Co v English* [1938] AC 57 at 78, 86; *Vaughan v Ropner & Co Ltd* (1947) 80 Ll L Rep 119. Because they are aspects of the duty to take reasonable care, these categories are not exhaustive. Each duty must also be examined to ascertain its scope. An employer, for instance, must safeguard its workers against defects in its own premises, but is not usually responsible for deficiencies in the premises of others where the employee is directed to work, or the collapse of a building owned by a third party to which employees are sent in the course of their employment since the structure of such a building is not usually treated as being under the employer's control; see eg para 4.76, below. However, the employer owes a duty to provide a system of work suitable for the premises.[1] An extreme example is *Johnson v Coventry Churchill International Ltd* [1992] 3 All ER 14 where the employer, an agency, was held liable when an employee sent to Germany to work on a construction site was injured due to lack of site safety. The employer also has the duty to employ competent fellow workers. So in *Hudson v Ridge Manufacturing Co Ltd* [1957] 2 QB 348 the employer was held liable for continuing to employ a man who was known to be prone to acts of horseplay and who by such an act injured the claimant. Equipment is not just the machinery the employee operates, but necessarily includes the maintenance of that machinery so that it operates safely and for the provision to the employee of any safety or protective equipment necessitated by the risks inherent in the employment duty. This includes safety gloves and shoes, goggles and boots/shoes.[2] Similarly, in respect of a safe system of work the employer does not fulfil its duty simply by providing it; it must also take reasonable steps to see that it is carried out.[3]

1   *Garcia v Harland & Woolf Ltd* [1943] 2 All ER 477.
2   *Crouch v British Rail Engineering Ltd* [1988] IRLR 404 at 408.
3   *Crookall v Vickers-Armstrong Ltd* [1955] 1 WLR 659 and more recently *Fraser v State Hospitals Board of Scotland* 2001 SLT 1051, para 129.

THE STANDARD OF CARE

2.50 The standard of care, and when that is not adhered to what consequently is negligent conduct, is determined by requirements of reasonableness. Taking reasonable care is always a question of fact. The classic citation is that of Alderson B in *Blyth v Birmingham Waterworks Co* (1856) 11 Exch 781 at 784:

> 'Negligence is the omission to do something which a reasonable man, guided upon those considerations which ordinarily regulate the conduct of human affairs, would do, or doing something which a prudent and reasonable man would not do.'

2.51 Thus all depends upon the conduct of a hypothetical 'reasonable man'—an imaginary being, sometimes bearing a remarkable resemblance to a judge. As Lord Radcliffe succinctly put it in *Davis Contractors Ltd v Fareham Urban District Council* [1956] AC 696: 'the spokesman of the fair and reasonable man, who represents after all no more than the anthropomorphic conception of justice, is and must be the court itself. This person, who is neither imprudent nor over-cautious, determines the standard of care. The outcome of this legal fiction is explained by Lord Macmillan in *Glasgow Corpn v Muir* [1943] AC 448 at 457:

> 'The standard of foresight of the reasonable man is in one sense an impersonal test. It eliminates the personal equation and is independent of the idiosyncrasies of the particular person whose conduct is in question. Some persons are unduly timorous and imagine every path beset with lions; others, of more robust temperament, fail to foresee or nonchalantly disregard even the most obvious dangers. The reasonable man is presumed to be free both from over-apprehension and from over-confidence.'

2.52 The standards of reasonableness are only partially determined by existing practice; to that extent the citation of Alderson B may be a little misleading. The standard of care sets norms rather than reflects them. Consequently, individual or even widespread shortcomings are generally ignored. It is no defence to argue that a failure, whether of knowledge or skill, was due to a personal lack of capacity or experience: see *eg Nettleship v Weston* [1971] 2 QB 691 at 699 (learner driver expected to meet standards of qualified driver).[1] Likewise, it is no defence to show that other employers were equally careless: see para 2.103.

1   An exception is made for children.

2.53 On the other hand, the reasonable person is not entirely abstract, but is expected to meet the standards required by his (or her) particular role. A person in a position calling for special knowledge or skill, such as a doctor, must match up to the standards of a person performing that duty or task.[1] Because the law protects the expectations of others who may be affected by persons in that position, relative inexperience (on the part of the defendant) is not a reason for a lower standard: see *Wilsher v Essex Area Health Authority* [1987] QB 730, CA. This applies with equal force to those who manage or control a business. An employer is expected both to meet the standards of reasonableness imposed on employers in general and to have the skilled knowledge special to its particular trade, including knowledge of the accompanying risks and safety precautions.[2] This is one reason why a higher standard of care is expected of employers than employees,[3] although an employee is required to meet the skills of his or her position— 'for example to use that degree of care which an ordinary, prudent crane-driver would have used': *Staveley Iron and Chemical Co Ltd v Jones* [1956] AC 627 at 638. Similarly an employer must allow for the fact that employees may be inadvertent or become heedless of the risks of their employment. So the employer has a duty to instruct employees in safety procedures and to see that the procedures are followed.

1   *Wilsher v Essex Area Health Authority* [1988] AC 1074.
2   Although an expert may be entitled to rely on a specialist with greater knowledge: *Investors in Industry Ltd v South Bedfordshire District Council* [1986] QB 1034, CA. Deemed knowledge of risks is now reinforced by the duty to conduct a risk assessment under the Management Regulations, see para 10.19, below.
3   Cf *General Cleaning Contractors Ltd v Christmas* [1953] AC 180.

2.54 The principles which determine what standard of care is expected of an employer are no more than guides, for the standard of care varies with the circumstances. The duty is owed to an individual employee so the individual circumstances will inform the standard of care. The classic example is that where an employee is known to have only one eye then a greater degree of care must be shown towards him than towards a man with two eyes, so goggles may be required for him but not the employee with both eyes.[1] Reasonableness is a flexible notion, very much dependent upon the particular circumstances, and not subject to strict rules of law: see *Brown v Rolls-Royce Ltd* [1960] 1 WLR 210, HL. What is reasonable depends upon what a person ought to know, and what actions are reasonable in the light of that deemed knowledge. This involves competing considerations. In particular, the risk of harm occurring and the likely seriousness of that harm should be balanced against the practicability and costs of measures to combat that harm and the importance of the activity concerned.

1   *Paris v Stepney Borough Council* [1951] AC 367.

Knowledge of the risk

2.55 The duty of the employer is to guard against risks and prevent exposure of the employee to risks which the employer knows of or ought to have known about. A failure to take measures to protect against a risk of which no-one was, or could have been, aware plainly cannot amount to negligence. Some risks may be so unusual that no reasonable person could realistically imagine their occurrence. An example of such 'fanciful' risk is to be found in the Scots case where a cow entered an open door, walked upstairs, turned on the taps and flooded the floor below: *Cameron v Hamilton's Auction Marts* 1955 SLT (Sh Ct) 74. Very few risks fall within this category, as exemplified by the asbestosis and vibration claims. However in *Armstrong v British Coal Corpn* [1997] 8 Med LR 259 the defendants denied knowledge of any risk of vibration white finger to British mineworkers. The Court of Appeal upheld the judge's findings that the defendants were on notice that there might have been a problem of significant incidence of vibration white finger from a very small survey conducted in 1968. In consequence the employer was then under a duty to conduct an epidemiological investigation amongst its workforce and evaluate its findings (which, on balance, would have shown an unacceptable incidence of vibration white finger consequent on use of vibratory hand tools).[1] Two recent decisions exemplify how the courts presently approach the issue of knowledge of risk. In *Brown v Corus (UK) Ltd* [2004] EWCA Civ 374, [2004] PIQR P 476, another equipment vibration case, the Court of Appeal held that since the risk of vibration injury was established the onus was on the employer to justify why the situation was allowed to continue and the failure to reduce vibration exposure was 'in plain breach of duty'. In *Doherty v Rugby Joinery (UK) Ltd* [2004] EWCA Civ 147, [2004] ICR 1272, the Court of Appeal held that once the employer should have been aware of the symptoms of vibration syndrome affecting some employees, its duty was not simply to restrict them to use of the tools for no longer than the maximum recommended period but to ensure that they did not use vibrating tools at all.

1   A finding borne out subsequently by the payment of some £2.5 billion in compensation to over 130,000 ex-mineworkers suffering from vibration white finger.

2.56 But some risks may be unknown owing to deficiencies in existing scientific or expert knowledge: there are many examples of industrial diseases whose causes or outbreak went unnoticed for many years. The principle that those who occupy a particular position must hold the expertise required for that role is equally applicable to employers: it is no defence for an employer to argue that it did not have the knowledge or experience deemed necessary for a particular kind of venture (see, inter alia, the obligations of the Framework Directive cited at para 10.04, below). Here, the relevant level of expertise is judged at the time the tort was committed, and later advances in knowledge are generally ignored: *Roe v Minister of Health* [1954] 2 QB 66. Although this must be considered carefully in the light of the decision in *Jeromson v Shell Tankers (UK) Ltd* [2001] EWCA Civ 101, [2001] ICR 1223 where it was held that since it was known that exposure to asbestos dust could produce lung disease it was irrelevant that the specific link between asbestos dust and mesothelioma was not known until a later date. But where an employer subjectively knows of risks of which others are ignorant, the reasonableness of its conduct should be judged in the light of its subjective knowledge—even if that exceeds what is deemed 'reasonable' to know: see the citation of Swanwick J in *Stokes v Guest, Keen and Nettlefold (Bolts and Nuts) Ltd* at para 2.61, below. That is, after all, consistent with imposing a higher standard of care when a defendant knows of a particular individual weakness of an employee.[1]

[1] Less clear is whether an employer will be judged by the standard of its own knowledge if it subjectively considers a risk to be serious, which in fact materialises, although informed opinion at the time is that this harm would not occur: see *Clerk and Lindsell on Torts* (19th edn, 2005) ch 13.

2.57 It will be more difficult for an employer to rely on ignorance of a risk in the context of an accident. In *Henderson v Henry E Jenkins & Sons and Evans* [1970] AC 282, for example, a lorry owned by the defendants killed a member of the public when its brakes failed as a result of a defect which could only have been detected by removing the brakes, something not recommended by the manufacturers. Although the brakes were regularly inspected without removal, the House of Lords held that the defendants had failed to displace the inference of negligence since they failed to show that there were no special circumstances in the past use of the vehicle indicating that the pipe might have been corroded, so requiring a fuller inspection. Similarly, in *Barkway v South Wales Transport Co Ltd* [1950] AC 185, the defendants were liable for failing to instruct its drivers to report incidents which might have caused an unusual kind of tyre fracture, although they too followed an established maintenance practice in all respects. The duty on the employer to be aware of risks is now strengthened by the obligation, originating in the Framework Directive 89/391/EEC, and implemented by reg 3 of the Management of Health and Safety at Work Regulations 1999, SI 1999/3242, to conduct a 'suitable and sufficient assessment' of the risks arising out of the conduct of the undertaking. This duty should inform the common law standard of care with the result, in the authors' view, that the courts will reject a defence of ignorance when a proper risk assessment would have revealed the kind of risk concerned: see, by analogy, *Barclays Bank plc v Fairclough Building Ltd (No 2)* (1995) Times, 15 February, CA.

2.58 The defence of ignorance of a risk is more likely to arise in the context of ill health, the onset of which is either gradual or not readily detectable, rather than accidents caused by work. In this regard, an employer is expected to keep reasonably abreast of current knowledge concerning dangers arising within its trade, and should be aware of pamphlets of the HSE and other safety organisations drawing attention to risks which have come to light (and the means of avoiding them): *Wright v Dunlop Rubber Co Ltd and ICI Ltd* (1972) 13 KIR 255 (substances added in processing rubber causing onset of bladder cancer after 20 years); *Cartwright v GKN Sankey Ltd* (1973) 14 KIR 349 (arc welder's lung disease: special risk of fumes at close quarters even though general ventilation good); and *Barclays Bank v Fairclough Building* (above). These cases show that large organisations, with their own medical and scientific research sections, may be expected to know considerably more than a small employer, and must ensure that information affecting safety is brought to the notice of executive authorities with power to decide. But an employer is not generally expected to be aware of scientific and medical matters known only in specialist circles: see *Wallhead v Ruston and Hornsby Ltd* (1973) 14 KIR 285. Thus a building firm was not expected to have medical knowledge of the risks of dermatitis from cement and brick dust: *Riddick v Weir Housing Corpn* 1971 SLT 24. The court added that, as knowledge diffused more widely, a point would come when it ought to know; the point at which knowledge ceases to be specialist but may not be generally known is a matter of fact. In *Ogden v Airedale Health Authority* [1996] 7 Med LR 153 at 159 it was held that it was 'incumbent upon an employer who requires employees to use chemicals in the course of their work to make enquiries as to the safety hazards which they present' (X-ray developing chemicals caused occupational asthma).

2.59 The general approach of the courts is that the employer must act reasonably and prudently taking positive thought for the safety of its employees in the context of what it knows or ought reasonably to know. This approach was specifically endorsed by the Court of Appeal in *Heyes v Pilkington Glass Ltd* [1998] PIQR P 303, where it was held that an employer was not liable for failing to prevent an employee from contracting 'vibration white finger' given the then general state of knowledge about the condition, since the defendant had not fallen below the standards of a reasonable and prudent employer (however, this is to be compared with the recent decisions on vibration white finger, eg *Doherty v Rugby Joinery (UK) Ltd* [2004] EWCA Civ 147, [2004] ICR 1272, where the date of knowledge was established, liability thereafter followed). Similarly, an employer was held not liable to its employee fisherman for failing to provide a single chamber life jacket, since the duty of care of the reasonable and prudent employer at the time of the accident did not demand this: *Gray v Stead* [1999] 2 Lloyd's Rep 559, CA. A further ground for allowing the appeal was that it was unreasonable to imagine that the fisherman would have departed from the standard practice of fishermen, which was not to wear buoyancy aids.

2.60 In each case of this kind the courts have reviewed the medical literature; the material available from industrial and state bodies; the material generated inside the defendants' organisation; and evidence from expert engineers, safety advisers and others as to the state of knowledge in the particular branch of industry (on evidence on this point, see *Gallon v Swan Hunter Shipbuilders* [1995] 23 LS Gaz R 33, CA). Often the existence of HSE pamphlets will be decisive, since *Cartwright,* above, makes clear that they should be read carefully by a person in authority. Depending upon the size of the employer, these may well fix the date from which liability arises: see eg *Thompson v Smiths Shiprepairers (North Shields) Ltd* [1984] QB 405. Thus, in *McSherry v British Telecommunications plc* [1992] 3 Med LR 129 it was held that an organisation like BT should have been aware by 1985 of the risks of upper limb injuries from repetitive keyboard use. However mere mention of the possibility of a risk in a HSE pamphlet will not necessarily be sufficient to found liability, see *Walker v Wabco Automotive UK Ltd* (11 May 1999, unreported), CA. Provided that an employer, having taken reasonable care to keep itself informed, would not be aware of a particular risk, there is no liability: *Graham v Co-operative Wholesale Society Ltd* [1957] 1 All ER 654 (mahogany dust cause of dermatitis); *Tremain v Pike* [1969] 3 All ER 1303 (farmer not expected to know of Weil's disease—leptospirosis—contractable from materials contaminated by rats' urine, no warning having been issued by health authorities).[1] This is now clear in respect of the dates of knowledge in vibration white finger cases following the decision in *Doherty v Rugby Joinery (UK) Ltd* [2004] EWCA Civ 147, [2004] ICR 1272 where the court relied on a report and medical literature to establish the earliest date of the employer's knowledge. Once a risk is known, however, it is no defence to argue that it was considered unlikely to occur: *Voller v Schweppes (Home) Ltd* (1969) 7 KIR 228 (unless the risk is entirely fanciful, see paras 2.24, above and 2.68, below).[2]

[1]   A difficult point is whether the health authorities themselves will sometimes owe a duty of care to warn.

[2]   This paragraph in the previous edition of this work (which did not include the reference to *Walker*) was cited with approval by Otton LJ in *Heyes v Pilkington Glass Ltd* [1998] PIQR P 303 at 309.

Knowledge of precautions

2.61   Even where an employer knows of a risk, it may not be aware of any means of protecting against it. Just as an employer should be aware of the risks associated with a particular sort of work, so it should know of HSE and other reasonably available information as to the appropriate steps to combat that risk. Both the Framework Directive and the Management Regulations 1999 require that an employer identify precautionary measures (see art 6(1) and reg 3(1), (2)); it is thought that the courts will probably recognise a common law duty of equivalent standard to identify precautionary measures appropriate to the risk.[1] It is unlikely that failure to carry out a risk assessment will of itself give rise to liability, see *Hawkes v London Borough of Southwark* (20 February 1998, unreported), CA, although see also *Swain v Denso Marston Ltd* [2000] ICR 1079, CA. Moreover the risk must be a real risk: see *Koonjul v Tameslink Healthcare Services* [2000] PIQR P 123. Greater knowledge of risks brings with it a higher duty to take precautions: see the citation of Swanwick J in *Stokes v Guest, Keen and Nettlefold (Bolts and Nuts) Ltd* [1968] 1 WLR 1776 at 1783 (see para 2.56, above).

[1]   The duty in the Directive, art 6(1), is almost a strict one: 'the employer *shall* take the measures *necessary* for the safety and health protection of workers' (author's emphasis).

2.62   An employer is not necessarily under a duty to invent means of prevention; but it must introduce known devices.[1] The test is what is feasible:

'The measures taken must be possible in the light of current knowledge and according to known means and resources … judged in the light of the state of the relevant knowledge at the time of the alleged breach. Thus, the fact that at some later date some method of production has been discovered which was not dreamed of at the date of the alleged breach, even though all individual materials thereof were known and available, will not suffice.' (per Evershed MR in *Richards v Highway Ironfounders (West Bromich) Ltd* [1955] 3 All ER 205, 210)

1   The Framework Directive may be relevant here. The Preamble recites that 'whereas
     employers shall be obliged to keep themselves informed of the latest advances in
     technology and scientific findings concerning workplace design, account being taken of the
     inherent dangers in their undertaking ...'. And art 6(1) requires employers to take the
     measures necessary for the safety and health protection of workers and states:

> 'The employer shall be alert to the need to adjust these measures to take account of
> circumstances and aims to improve existing situations.'

It is arguable that 'circumstances' includes 'advances in technology and scientific findings'.
Article 6(2)(e) imposes as a general principle of prevention, that of 'adapting to technical
progress'. Only the latter point is found in the Management of Health and Safety
Regulations 1999, Sch 1(e).

2.63 In *Thompson v Smiths Shiprepairers (North Shields) Ltd* [1984] QB
405, shipbuilders knew of the possible damage to hearing caused by excess
noise, but were unaware of an appropriate remedy; the issue arose as to when
they should have become aware that ear muffs of a satisfactory design would
provide protection. Mustill LJ said:

> 'The practice of leaving employees unprotected against excessive noise had
> never been followed "without mishap". Yet even the plaintiffs have not
> suggested that it was "clearly bad", in the sense of creating a potential liability
> in negligence, at any time before the mid-1930s. Between the two extremes is a
> type of risk which is regarded at any given time (although not necessarily later)
> as an inescapable feature of the industry. The employer is not liable for the
> consequences of such risks, although subsequent changes in social awareness,
> or improvements in knowledge and technology, may transfer the risk into the
> category of those against which the employer can and should take care. It is
> unnecessary, and perhaps impossible, to give a comprehensive formula for
> identifying the line between the acceptable and the unacceptable. Nevertheless,
> the line does exist, and was clearly recognised in *Morris v West Hartlepool
> Steam Navigation Co Ltd* [1956] AC 552. The speeches in that case show, not
> that one employer is exonerated simply by proving that other employers are just
> as negligent, but that the standards of what is negligent is influenced, although
> not decisively, by the practice in the industry as a whole. In my judgment, this
> principle applies not only where the breach of duty is said to consist of a failure
> to take precautions known to be available as a means of combating a known
> danger, but also where the omission involves an absence of initiative in seeking
> out knowledge of facts which are not in themselves obvious. The employer
> must keep up to date, but the court must be slow to blame him for not
> ploughing a lone furrow.'[1]

The test he adopted was as follows:

> 'From what date would a reasonable employer, with proper but not extraordi-
> nary solicitude for the welfare of his workers, have identified the problem of
> excessive noise in his yard, recognised that it was capable of solution, decided
> to adopt it, acquired a supply of the protectors, set in train the programme of
> education necessary to persuade the men and their representatives that the
> system was useful and not potentially deleterious, experimented with the
> system, and finally put it into full effect?'

1   Cited in turn in the vibration white finger case of *Smith v British Jeffrey Diamond* (10 June
     1991, unreported) HCJ, per Swinton-Thomas J at 22.

2.64 As Mustill LJ said, the evidence on the issue of the date does not admit
of a precise answer but is a matter of degree. This approach has been followed

in many cases: see eg, again in the context of deafness, *Baxter v Harland & Wolff plc* [1990] IRLR 516, NICA. In *Doherty v Rugby Joinery (UK) Ltd* [2004] EWCA Civ 147, [2004] ICR 1272 Hale LJ (as she then was) held that the relevant literature available to the employers identified that by 1991/92 employers in the woodworking industry should have been aware of the danger to its employees and imposed a duty from that time to assess and monitor its employees for vibration induced white finger from the texts in 1987 and 1990.

2.65 Although employers are expected to keep in touch with current improvements, they are not necessarily bound to adopt them until their advantages and practicability have been investigated. To fail to provide a barrier cream as protection against dermatitis is not negligent when there are doubts as to the value of such protection: *Brown v Rolls Royce Ltd* [1960] 1 All ER 577. But where an employer knows of a hazard, it is under a duty to take initiatives to seek out knowledge of facts which are not obvious (see Mustill LJ in *Thompson v Smiths Shiprepairers (North Shields) Ltd*, above), and to take initiatives, whether alone or with others in the same industry, to try and solve the problem: see *Baxter v Harland & Wolff plc*, above. In *Baxter*, MacDermott LJ said that the employers should have sought advice on reducing the risk of deafness, and pooled ideas with others in the industry. In *Brown v Corus (UK) Ltd* [2004] EWCA Civ 374, [2004] PIQR P 476 the Court of Appeal held that once the employer knew that the employees were subjected to excessive levels of vibration the burden shifted to the employers to show justification for the continuation of the situation where it was plain that there should have been and had not been a beneficial reduction in the level of vibration. Further, the employers failed to comply with their obligations to train their employees, thereby materially increasing the risk of vibration induced injury.

2.66 Where a method of protection is practicable and available, it would usually be negligent to delay in adopting it. It is now negligent, for instance, not to supply a window cleaner with a harness: *King v Smith* [1995] ICR 339, CA. If the new method is not necessarily practicable, safer or economically justified it will not be negligent not to adopt it: *Nilsson v Redditch Borough Council* [1995] PIQR P 199, CA (not negligent not to introduce wheelie-bins to supersede plastic bags so as to avert risk of cuts to refuse collectors). But an employer must act promptly, and not neglect reasonable precautions because of interferences with production or that 'turmoil' might be caused if the risk was the subject of further investigations or warnings: *Stokes v Guest, Keen and Nettlefold (Bolts and Nuts) Ltd* [1968] 1 WLR 1776 (scrotal cancer caused by overalls soaked with mineral oil). The failure to rig up a guard rail was negligent where a seaman who asked for it 'would probably be laughed at': *Morris v West Hartlepool Steam Navigation Co Ltd* [1956] AC 552. But in *Coates v Jaguar Cars Ltd* [2004] EWCA Civ 337, [2004] All ER (D) 87 (Mar) the Court of Appeal decided that steps without a guardrail posed no real risk to those using them with reasonable care and that it was wrong to equate 'foreseeability of risk with a finding of a duty to install a rail.' This practical decision must be contrasted with the importance of employers keeping up to date with the developing knowledge of the dangers to their employees and the necessity to act accordingly demonstrated in the recent vibration white finger decisions of *Brown v Corus (UK) Ltd* [2004] EWCA Civ 374, [2004] PIQR P 476 and *Doherty v Rugby Joinery (UK) Ltd* [2004] EWCA Civ 147, [2004] ICR 1272.[1]

1   And also *Brookes v South Yorkshire Passenger Transport Executive* [2005] EWCA Civ 452, [2005] All ER (D) 405 (Apr).

The magnitude of the risk

2.67 A further significant consideration is how great is the probability of the risk materialising and what would be the gravity of the harm if it does occur: see *Paris v Stepney Borough Council* [1951] AC 367. The duty is to take reasonable precautions: the greater the magnitude of the risk and the greater the gravity of harm should the event occur, the higher is the duty to take precautions, even if these are expensive or difficult to adopt. 'The law in all cases exacts a degree of care commensurate with the risk created': per Lord Macmillan in *Read v J Lyons & Co Ltd* [1947] AC 156 at 173. Whilst the more serious the consequences if an accident were to occur, the greater, other things being equal, the level of precautions which must be taken, it is also important to weigh in the scales the likelihood of the risk of an accident eventuating. The degree of likelihood of an accident occurring is an important element in determining what precautions are required.[1]

1   See, albeit in the context of duties under the HSWA 1974, *Austin Rover Ltd v Inspector of Factories* [1990] 1 AC 619 at 625D–627A.

2.68 Where a risk is a 'fantastic possibility', in the words of Lord Dunedin, no precautions may be necessary at all. But the risk of an incident occurring must be extremely slight for it to be ignored (see Lord Reid in *The Wagon Mound (No 2)* [1967] 1 AC 617) (and see para 2.22 above).[1] In *Bolton v Stone* [1951] AC 850, for instance, a batsman hit a ball out of a cricket ground, over a 17-foot fence, so that it struck a passer-by. The evidence was that cricket balls had only been hit into a road six times in 30 years and that no one apart from the claimant had ever suffered an injury. While accepting that the risk to those outside the ground was too small to require preventative action, the House of Lords considered the case to be a borderline one: see Lord Normand at 861, Lord Oaksey at 863, Lord Reid at 867.[2] If, however, the risk could easily have been avoided, then it would be negligent not to take such steps, regardless of how remote is the risk: see the *Wagon Mound (No 2)* [1967] 1 AC 617 (negligent to spill oil, even though chance of it catching fire was remote), applied in *Jolley v Sutton London Borough Council* [2000] 1 WLR 1082 (upturned rotten boat collapsed on 14-year-old boy playing under it).[3]

1   The risk must be more than a 'mere possibility' but plainly not need amount to a greater than even likelihood: see para 2.23 and *Lewis v Buckpool Golf Club* 1993 SLT (ShCt) 43 (risk of injury from inexperienced golfer easily avoided by waiting until other golfers were clear before playing).

2.68   The general principles of negligence

2   See also: *Voller v Schweppes (Home) Ltd* (1969) 7 KIR 228. For those who like cricketing cases: see *Miller v Jackson* [1977] QB 966 (eight or nine balls knocked out of the ground each season led to liability); footballers may prefer *Hilder v Associated Portland Cement Manufacturers Ltd* [1961] 1 WLR 1434 (football frequently kicked by boys over low wall into road: owners liable).

3   See at 1091H–1092B. This case which expands the category of injury for which a defendant is liable may put in doubt *Doughty v Turner Manufacturing Co Ltd* [1964] 1 QB 518 (no liability for burns caused by unforeseeable eruption of molten liquid) and *Crossley v Rawlinson* [1982] 1 WLR 369 (no liability for trip in concealed hole whilst running with extinguisher to fire).

2.69 The same principle applies with yet greater force to accidents the probability of which is remote but the consequences of which would be very serious. Where there is a risk to life, the exercise of reasonable care will justify great expense and trouble to prevent the event occurring: see *Henderson v Carron Co* (1889) 16 R 633 (dismantling of furnace in a dangerous condition).

2.70 In *Marshall v Gotham Co Ltd* [1954] AC 360 at 373, Lord Reid said:

> '... if a precaution is practicable it must be taken unless in the whole circumstances that would be unreasonable. And as men's lives may be at stake it should not lightly be held that to take a practicable precaution is unreasonable.'

However, as exemplified by the facts in *Thompson v Smith Shiprepairers (North Shields) Ltd* [1984] QB 405, employers are only liable when they have or could reasonably have had the relevant knowledge. In that case the employers were only liable for the injury to the hearing of their employees once there was an awareness of the danger to employees of excessive noise and the preventive measure of suitable protective equipment was available.

2.71 'The law in all cases exacts a degree of care commensurate with the risk created', held Lord MacMillan in *Read v J Lyons & Co Ltd* [1947] AC 156 at 173.[1] The point was exemplified by Lord Morton in *Paris v Stepney Borough Council* [1951] AC 367:

> 'In considering generally the precautions which an employer ought to take for the protection of his workmen it must, in my view, be right to take into account both elements, the likelihood of an accident happening and the gravity of the consequences. I take as an example two occupations in which the risk of an accident taking place is exactly equal; if an accident does occur in the one occupation, the consequences to the workman will be comparatively trivial; if an accident occurs in the other occupation the consequences to the workman will be death or mutilation. Can it be said that the precautions which it is the duty of an employer to take for the safety of his workmen are exactly the same in each of these occupations? My Lords, that is not my view. I think that the more serious the damage which will happen if an accident occurs, the more thorough are the precautions which an employer must take.'

This implies a high, though unquantified, value on human life and limb.

1   See also *Beckett v Newalls Insulation Co* [1953] 1 WLR 8 (appropriate care required from firm bringing gas containers onto ship under construction).

2.72 In *R v Board of Trustees of the Science Museum* [1993] ICR 876, Steyn LJ at 882, giving the judgment of the Court of Appeal, held that 'risk' (for the purposes of the HSWA 1974, s 3) means 'the possibility of danger' rather than actual danger. It is thus the possibility of danger which must be weighed against the possible precautions. In the case of an activity involving ultra-hazardous materials, such as explosives, an exacting standard of care is owed.

2.73 In *Paris v Stepney Borough Council* itself, the House of Lords found it negligent not to supply a man blind in one eye with goggles for the carrying out of tasks where particles might strike the eye, though for a normal workman the risk could be ignored: total blindness is a much graver injury than the loss of an eye. It is for precisely this reason that a higher standard of care is owed to persons who, as a result of individual differences, are more likely to suffer serious injuries.

Mistakes of others

2.74 In considering the likelihood of a risk occurring, the possibility of others making mistakes should be taken into account. It is foreseeable that a danger may be brought on or magnified owing to the negligence of others 'when experience shows such negligence to be common': *London Passenger Transport Board v Upson* [1949] AC 155 at 176. On the other hand, in *Grant v Sun Shipping Co Ltd* [1948] AC 549 at 567, Lord du Parcq said it was legitimate to infer that statutory codes will be observed, provided that in practice they are strictly enforced. Contrast the position where the employer knows or should know that employees are not complying with their statutory duties: see *Bux v Slough Metals Ltd* [1974] 1 All ER 262.

2.75 Clearly, an employer ought to expect that, when a dangerous process or operation is continually repeated, there will be mistakes or accidental slips due to wavering attention or the urgency of completing the work, and 'have in mind not only the careful man but also the man who is inattentive to such a degree as can normally be expected': *Smith (or Westwood) v National Coal Board* [1967] 2 All ER 593, per Lord Reid. Lord Oaksey said in *General Cleaning Contractors Ltd v Christmas* [1953] AC 180 at 189–190:

> 'It is ... well known to employers ... that their work-people are very frequently, if not habitually, careless about the risks which their work may involve.'[1]

So an employer is required to take steps to see that employees act on instructions issued for their welfare and where appropriate the employer's duty may extend to taking steps to enforce the use of safety equipment.[2]

---

[1] Cf *Baynes v Union Steamship Co of New Zealand Ltd* [1953] NZLR 617 (tarpaulin spread on top of uneven cargo with gaps—foreseeability of workmen walking over carelessly).

[2] *Bux v Slough Metals Ltd* [1973] 1 WLR 1358 where the failure to enforce the use of safety goggles led to liability of the employer.

2.76 An employer must also take into account the possibility that a worker may have a sudden attack of illness, eg that a scaffolder may have a sudden attack of giddiness when working at a height: *Holtum v WJ Cearns Ltd* (1953) Times, 23 July, CA.

Individual characteristics of the claimant

2.77 The standard of care varies in accordance with the characteristics of the individuals who are at risk. Thus, the fact that unaccompanied blind persons may walk along city streets is reasonably foreseeable, even though they are relatively few in number, so that account should be taken of them in protecting an excavation if undue expense is not involved: see *Haley v London Electricity Board* [1965] AC 778 (long hammer placed in front of trench not adequate). So, too, persons should in general exercise greater care towards children who they know may be injured by their actions.[1]

[1] See *Jolley v London Borough of Sutton* [2000] 1 WLR 1082 at 1093 and the numerous driving cases on this issue, such as *Gough v Thorne* [1966] 3 All ER 398. These cases establish that the younger the child, the less likely is a finding of contributory negligence.

2.78 By the same token, an employer should take account of individual weaknesses of its employees of which it knows or ought to know, see para 4.61. More care is owed to an employee who is inexperienced than one who is fully experienced. Greater care may need to be taken in warning employees who are illiterate: see para 2.54, *Hawkins v Ian Ross (Castings) Ltd* [1970] 1 All ER 180 or whose knowledge of English is imperfect: *Bux v Slough Metals Ltd* [1974] 1 All ER 262.

2.79 The individual focus of negligence is given further strength by the European Framework Directive 89/391/EEC, the significance of which must be understood in the wider context of an employer's statutory obligations to his employees. The Framework Directive provides for the adoption of subsequent 'daughter Directives' and outlines the broad principles of the legislation. The approach under the Framework Directive is similar in principle to that provided by the Health and Safety at Work Act 1974 but takes matters a very great deal further. The Regulations made under the Act are to be 'designed to maintain or improve the standards of health and safety'.[1] In compliance with its obligations to the European Union, the UK has sought to implement the Framework Directive and its daughter directions by making regulations under the HSWA 1974, s 15. These regulations are the means by which the pre-1992 legislation is being gradually revoked, setting in its place a system of statutory control over matters concerning health, safety and welfare at work, as required by the European directives. These were initially the Management of Health and Safety at Work Regulations 1992 which have since been revoked and re-enacted by the Management of Health and Safety at Work Regulations 1999, SI 1999/3242.[2] These require specific consideration of individual risks, risk assessments and safety steps specific to such tasks to safeguard the employees' health and safety.

1   HSWA 1974, s 1(2).
2   And see Approved Code of Guidance, para 10.15, below.

2.80 Where an employer is aware of a risk and has, after careful investigation, fixed a reasonable standard of exposure, it may be negligent to fail to give warning or arrange medical examinations or other special precautions for employees: see para 10.23. On the other hand, where an experienced employee should know of the risk of the job and has been provided with appropriate safety equipment but does not comply, then the employer will not be in breach of duty. This is evident from *Qualcast (Wolverhamptom) Ltd v Haynes* [1959] AC 743, where it was held that an experienced employee could be relied on to wear foot protection when ladling molten metal, so no warning was required.

Practicability of precautions

2.81 The costs and practicability of overcoming a risk are matters which should properly be considered in deciding whether the appropriate care has been used to discharge the duty of care owed by the employer. Consideration is given to the probability and seriousness of the risk, against which the courts will weigh the expense and effort involved in taking safety measures, and the necessity of carrying out the work or the end to be achieved by the activity: see *Watt v Hertfordshire County Council* [1954] 1 WLR 835 at 838. Lord Reid said, for example, in *Morris v West Hartlepool Steam Navigation Co Ltd* [1956] AC 552:

> 'It is the duty of the employer in considering whether some precaution should be taken against a foreseeable risk, to weigh, on the one hand, the magnitude of the risk, the likelihood of an accident occurring and the possible seriousness of the consequences if an accident does happen, and, on the other hand, the difficulty and expense and any other disadvantage of taking the precaution.'

Put more simply by Denning LJ in *Latimer v AEC Ltd* [1952] 2 QB 701 at 711, 'In every case of a foreseeable risk, it is a matter of balancing the risk against the resources necessary to eliminate it.'

2.82 Here the law, prior to the introduction of the Framework Directive and 'daughter Directives', proceeded on a utilitarian basis, assuming (for example) that economic profit or social utility can on occasions outweigh the protection of health and safety.[1] If, for instance, equipment is being used which (through no fault of the employer) is not entirely satisfactory from a safety viewpoint, it has not generally been seen as reasonable to stop all operations, however effective that would be as a precaution: see the comments of Asquith LJ in *Daborn v Bath Tramways Motor Co Ltd and Smithey* [1946] 2 All ER 333 at 336. Thus, an employer was not obliged to shut down a factory because, following a violent storm, oily cooling liquid had been washed out of ducts and had left the floor in an abnormally slippery and dangerous state: *Latimer v AEC Ltd* [1953] AC 643.[2] But it has also been recognised that there may be occasions when the danger is so great that work ought to be stopped altogether: Lord Tucker at 659. In *Wright v Dunlop Rubber Co* (1972) 13

KIR 255, the continued use of carcinogenic chemicals to produce rubber was held to be negligent; the duty required simply that they should not be used. More recently, the Court of Appeal considered the practicability of precautions against noise-induced deafness in *Harris v BRB (Residuary) Ltd* [2005] EWCA Civ 900.

1   Indeed this is still true in a non-employment context, as demonstrated by the decision of the House of Lords in *Tomlinson v Congleton Borough Council* [2003] UKHL 47, [2004] 1 AC 46.
2   The employer will, of course, be obliged to do what is reasonable within those constraints: compare *Johnson v Rea Ltd* [1962] 1 QB 373.

2.83 In *Nilsson v Redditch Borough Council* [1995] PIQR P 199, where a refuse collector was injured, the Court of Appeal found that the trial judge ought to have examined in greater detail the practicability and commercial viability of alternatives to the system of householders leaving black bags of rubbish outside their homes. In *Koonjul v Thameslink Healthcare Services NHS Trust* [2000] PIQR P 123, the Court of Appeal concluded that it would be impracticable to provide an experienced care assistant in a residential home with instruction in various everyday tasks.

2.84 It is notable that the well-established principles and tariffs for the valuation of human suffering and economic loss are never used by the courts as the counterweight to the cost of the precautions which would have avoided the danger, and it may be that the significantly tighter mandatory controls upon the assessment of the health and safety of employees after the Framework Directive and 'daughter' Directives are used to highlight that hitherto the scales have not been properly balanced.

Gross disproportion and reasonable practicability

2.85 The weighing of danger against precaution in negligence is paralleled by the assessment as to whether a precaution is or is not reasonably practicable under much of the health and safety legislation. This assessment is not done with a view to seeing whether the scales just tip. The words of Asquith LJ in *Edwards v National Coal Board* [1949] 1 KB 704, CA at 712 are familiar:

> '"Reasonably practicable" is a narrower term than "physically possible", and seems to me to imply that a computation must be made by the owner in which the quantum of risk is placed on one scale and the sacrifice involved in the measures necessary for averting the risk (whether in money, time or trouble) is placed in the other, and that, if it be shown that there is a gross disproportion between them—the risk being insignificant in relation to the sacrifice—the defendants discharge the onus on them.'

2.86 It has sometimes been argued that the test is mere *disproportion* rather than *gross disproportion*, in reliance on Lord Oaksey's words in *Marshall v Gotham Co Ltd* [1954] AC 360. The point is ill-founded. In that case Lord Oaksey (at 369) endorsed the speech of Lord Atkin in *Coltness Iron Co Ltd v Sharp* [1938] AC 90 at 93–94 in which the latter had stated, in relation to the facts of the case, that 'the time of non-protection is so short and the time, trouble and expense of any form of protection is *so* disproportionate that I think the defence is proved' [emphasis added]. In the following sentence Lord Oaksey in *Marshall* then paraphrased Lord Atkin's words in *Edwards:*

> 'That is to say, what is reasonably practicable depends upon a consideration whether the time trouble and expense of the precautions suggested are disproportionate to the risk involved.'

2.87 Lord Reid in his speech in *Marshall* expressly endorsed the words of Asquith LJ in *Edwards*. None other of their Lordships dealt with *Edwards,* none suggesting that the test of gross disproportion was not appropriate or that *Edwards* was wrong. It is thus the case that the House of Lords in *Marshall* endorsed a test of gross disproportion and not disproportion alone. On a proper analysis, then, the test is that reasonable practicability requires a precaution to be taken unless the time, effort and expense of taking it in relation to the risk averted, is grossly disproportionate.[1] It is not thought that the weighing of precaution against risk in negligence imports any lower standard.

[1] It is respectfully suggested that the HSE summary of the position in *Enforcement Policy Statement* (2000) is inaccurate. There it is stated that: 'If there is a significant risk, the duty holder must take measures unless the cost of taking particular actions is clearly excessive compared with the benefit of the risk reduction'. From this description the essential element of 'gross disproportion' is missing.

The employer's resources

2.88 Account can be taken of the resources available to the employer, so that a higher standard can be expected of those organisations of great wealth: see *British Railways Board v Herrington* [1972] AC 877 at 899 per Lord Reid. This means not only that such employers may be expected to incur more expensive precautions but also that they may be obliged to exercise initiative in devising or securing safety precautions not available to the smaller firm. In *Knox v Cammell Laird Shipbuilders Ltd* (30 July 1990, unreported), HC, Simon Brown J held (at p 105 of the transcript) that shipbuilding employers 'were no more careless of the health of their workforce than other such commercial employers up and down the country'. But that was no defence to them (see para 2.98ff, especially at para 2.103) for failure to protect the workforce from lung disease caused by fumes since:

> '[the defendant was] in the forefront of the industry, one of the two largest yards in the country and with an enormous workforce. It was for employers like them to take the initiative in these matters, to be ever alert to the problems of their men and resourceful as to their solution'.

In *Baxter v Harland & Wolff plc* [1990] IRLR 516, NI CA, McDermott LJ said that a large employer in the shipbuilding industry should have sought advice and pooled ideas with others in the industry.

2.89 In *Allen v British Rail Engineering Ltd* (7 October 1998, unreported), HC, Janet Smith J held that BREL 'were a large employer and might have been expected to bring considerable pressure to bear on manufacturers who valued their custom' so as to encourage them to manufacture tools which gave off less injurious vibration than those which had caused the plaintiff's vibration white finger. Likewise in *Hall v British Gas plc* (7 April 1998, unreported), CC, HHJ Ensor held (at p 28 of the transcript) in a vibration white finger case that 'the defendants with their vast resources and a monopoly could have compelled manufacturers to produce low vibration tools capable of working efficiently'. In *Armstrong v British Coal Corpn* [1998] JPIL 320, CA (affirming the unreported judgment of HHJ Stephenson sitting as a deputy QBD judge of 15 January 1996) another large employer with vast resources was held to be expected to research into conditions such as vibration white finger from which its employees might be suffering.

2.90   Limited resources cannot give rise to a lower standard of care, save perhaps in very limited circumstances where the authority is a public body acting under a legal duty: see *Walker v Northumberland County Council* [1995] ICR 702; *Knight v Home Office* [1990] 3 All ER 237. Where a public body provides a service voluntarily, it has been held in Australia (*Cekan v Haines* (1990) 21 NSWLR 296 (NSW CA, per Mahoney JA at 314), that it:

> 'must take all such precautions against the risk of injury which the provision of those services will create. And, in particular, it is prima facie not open to it to plead lack of resources if it does not do so. A plaintiff may say that, if it has not the resources to make provision against risk, it should not offer those services'.[1]

1   See also, in Canada, *Swanson Estate v Canada* (1991) 80 DLR (4th) 741, and the discussion in *Clerk and Lindsell on Torts* (19th edn, 2005) at paras 14–41.

2.91   This is surely a statement of general principle for both public and private enterprises.[1] Nonetheless, in *Koonjul v Thameslink Healthcare Services* [2000] PIQR P 123 (see para 2.83, above), the Court of Appeal took account of the fact that the residential home was small, and there were only a small number of employees. But in *PQ v Australian Red Cross Society* [1992] 1 VR 19, McGarvie J was faced with a defence based on lack of resources to detect HIV infection in blood administered to the claimant. After examining the English authorities, he said at 33:

> 'Whether [the defendant] fell short of the required standard of care is to be tested, not by reference to a reasonable person with the defendant's actual resources of staff facilities and finance, but by reference to a reasonable person with adequate resources available to conduct the operation in which the [defendant] was engaged.'

1   See *Clerk and Lindsell on Torts* (19th edn, 2005) para 13.23ff.

2.92   It is certainly the case in the past, in the context of the public sector, that issues of resources have been raised to justify the employer's actions. In *Watt v Hertfordshire County Council* [1954] 1 WLR 835 at 839 Mills LJ considered the fire station's lack of resources in terms of space and vehicles to be relevant. More recently Pill J in *Knight v Home Office* [1990] 3 All ER 237 held that in respect of the facilities of a prison hospital the limited resources available for the public service were relevant. In *Walker v Northumberland County Council* [1995] ICR 702, Coleman J stated:

'... there can be no basis for treating the public body differently in principle from any other commercial employer, although there would have to be taken into account considerations such as budgetary constraints and perhaps lack of fluidity of decision-making which might not arise with a commercial employer'

and then commented that:

'the practicability of remedial measures must clearly take into account the resources and facilities at the disposal of the person or body owing the duty of care and the purpose of the activity giving rise to the risk of injury.'

2.93 However, in *Bull v Devon Health Authority* [1993] 4 Med LR 117 Mustill LJ in a non-employment context held that:

'It is not necessarily an answer to unsafety that there were insufficient resources to enable administrators to do everything which they would like to do ... there is perhaps a danger in assuming ... that it is necessarily a complete answer to say that even if the system in any hospital was unsatisfactory it was no more unsatisfactory than those in force elsewhere.'

Effectiveness of precautions

2.94 Apart from the costs to the employer in economic terms, issues may arise as to how practicable it is to use the protective measures, which may include risks to health and safety from the precautions themselves. Here too the courts engage in a form of utilitarian calculus, weighing the advantages against the disadvantages. The small risk, for instance, to seamen engaged in erecting a rope round an open hatchway at sea may be outweighed by the risk to others if the hatchway were left unguarded in poor light: *Morris v West Hartlepool Steam Navigation Co Ltd* [1956] AC 552.

2.95 However, generally as part of the employer's obligation to provide a safe system of work the appropriate integration of the precautions into the working system will be often necessary to make the precautions effective. Similarly it is obvious that precautions such as the wearing of safety equipment will only be efficacious to the employee if it is enforced and a failure to enforce use may be a breach of duty: see *Nolan v Dental Manufacturing Co Ltd* [1958] 1 WLR 936.

Other factors

2.96 Lastly, in determining what is reasonable, the courts may have regard to what they see as the importance of the activity and whether the defendant was acting in an emergency. Precisely what is the social importance of an activity is very much a matter for judicial intuition, unsupported by empirical evidence. Some examples are obvious. The utility derived from car transport means that drivers are not expected to drive at very low speeds, despite the lives this would save.[1] So, too, importance is attached to the economic activities of employers and the performance by the state of public services. Elsewhere some judges have been very sympathetic to some kinds of sport, and cricket in particular: see *Bolton v Stone* [1951] AC 850 and *Miller v Jackson* [1977] QB 966.[2] The tide has turned in the field of contact sports, as exemplified by the decision against the amateur referee in *Smolden v Whitworth* [1997] PIQR P 133.

1   The disutility caused to others by cars—cyclists (and pedestrians) being obvious examples—has up to now been ignored.
2   Football has been viewed with more distaste: see *Hilder v Associated Portland Cement Manufacturers Ltd* [1961] 1 WLR 1434.

2.97 Finally, a lower standard is demanded of those acting in conditions of emergency. But the fire brigade were liable for damage caused by a fire engine crossing a red light: *Ward v LCC* [1938] 2 All ER 341 and an ambulance driver was 40% liable for an accident which occurred when he crossed a red light: *Griffin v Merseyside Regional Ambulance* [1998] PIQR P 34, CA. Similarly in *Kent v Griffiths* [2001] QB 36 an ambulance service was liable for the delay in arrival of an ambulance.

'General and approved practice' as a criterion

2.98 General practice has always been taken into account in determining the standard of care but, as noted above (paras 2.88 and 2.103), it is not conclusive, because 'no one can claim to be excused for want of care because others are as careless as himself': per Cockburn CJ in *Blenkiron v Great Central Gas Consumers' Co* (1860) 2 F & F 437. It is not so much the uniform factual behaviour in a particular field to which the law gives weight, as the standard of conduct, whether uniformly followed or not, which is generally accepted as correct by informed opinion. Thus, as in the field of medical negligence, conformity with existing practice is only a defence if there exists a range of reasonable views and the defendant's conduct is supported by a reputable body of reasonable opinion.[1] Such a recognised standard of conduct, for example, is contained in official guidance (see para 8.18) such as the Highway Code, or in the Regulations for Preventing Collisions at Sea (as provided by the Merchant Shipping (Distress Signals and Prevention of Collisions) Regulations 1996, SI 1996/75).[2] It is to be noted that the ACOP accompanying the Management of Health and Safety at Work Regulations 1999 provides (in para 9) that in making the risk assessment required by reg 3,

> 'Employers ... are expected to take reasonable steps, eg by reading HSE guidance, the trade press, company or supply manuals etc to familiarise themselves with the hazards and risks in their work.'

1   *Maynard v West Midlands Regional Health Authority* [1985] 1 All ER 635; *Bolitho v City and Hackney Health Authority* [1998] AC 232.
2   Cf *Thomas Stone Shipping Ltd v Admiralty, The Albion* [1953] P 117 (collisions at sea rules represent proper standard of care for naval vessels, which are not technically bound by them).

2.99 In one case it was said that, regarding omissions, it was necessary:

> 'either to show that the thing which he did not do was a thing which was commonly done by other persons in like circumstances, or to show that it was a thing which was so obviously wanted that it would be folly in anyone to neglect it' (per Lord Dunedin in *Morton v Dixon (William) Ltd* 1909 SC 807).

2.100 It has now become clear that this does not lay down any proposition of law: see *Brown v Rolls Royce Ltd* [1960] 1 All ER 577. Although cited in some subsequent cases, this test cannot be correct in light of the nature of the duty to take reasonable care. For example, Lord Tucker said in *General Cleaning Contractors Ltd v Christmas* [1953] AC 180 at 195, that the correct principle is simply this:

> 'long-established practice in the trade, although not necessarily conclusive, is generally regarded as strong evidence in support of reasonableness'.

2.101 The matter was finally settled by the majority decision of the House of Lords in *Morris v West Hartlepool Steam Navigation Co Ltd* [1956] AC 552, where it was held to be negligent to fail to fence hatchways left open between decks in a grain ship at sea, notwithstanding evidence of a general custom that hatches are never fenced at sea. And in *Cavanagh v Ulster Weaving Co Ltd* [1960] AC 145, the House of Lords held that a jury was entitled to find negligence in the method of carrying cement on a roof although this method was in accordance with normal building practice. Similarly, Mustill J in *Thompson v Smiths Shiprepairers (North Shields) Ltd* [1984] QB 405 made clear that a long general practice in that industry of inaction with regard to the possibility of deafness and high industrial noice was unacceptable and once the employer was aware of the risk it was mandated to act appropriately, as a reasonable but not exceptionable employer would do.

2.102 Recognised practice has greater force in specialised departments of knowledge or practice, such as medical practice, or the management of an engineering works or a coal mine and also now to school teachers: *Chittock v Woodbridge School* [2002] EWCA Civ 915, [2003] PIQR P 6. The reason is that expert knowledge and judgement are often required to assess (a) the magnitude of the risks involved, and (b) what safety measures are practicable. If informed opinion is in agreement, it is almost conclusive, although the court may still find that too little emphasis has been put on safety, and too much on the expense of ensuring it. In particular it has been said that evidence of general practice is of little value unless it is shown to have been followed in similar circumstances without mishap for a sufficiently long period: per Lord Reid in *Morris v West Hartlepool Steam Navigation Co Ltd* [1956] AC 552.

2.103 The current tendency is to be increasingly critical of accepted practice.[1] The courts have not hesitated to judge for themselves, with the aid of expert evidence, the acceptability of an established system: see eg *Lloyds Bank Ltd v Savory (E B) & Co* [1933] AC 201 (ordinary practice of banks in accepting cheques nonetheless negligent); *Thompson v Smiths Shiprepairers (North*

Shields) [1984] QB 405 (industry-wide general practice of inaction on deafness in shipbuilding was no defence—see the quotations at para 2.63); *Baxter v Harland & Wolff plc* [1990] IRLR 516 (same principle also in shipbuilding deafness case); *Knox v Cammell Laird Shipbuilders Ltd* (30 July 1990, unreported), HC, Simon Brown J (industry-wide inaction in shipbuilding on fumes leading to lung disease was no defence—quoted at para 2.88 above); *Armstrong v British Coal Corpn* (1996) Times, 6 December, CA (coal industry-wide practice of inaction on vibration white finger no defence after survey revealed possible incidence amongst miners). In *Markland v Manchester Corpn* [1934] 1 KB 566 a burst pipe had flooded a road, and the flood water had remained undetected for three days when it froze over and caused an accident. The authority were held liable, despite checking in accordance with general practice, because they 'failed to take reasonable precautions against an obvious and known danger': per Slesser LJ at 582. Nor was it necessary for the claimant to show what exact precautions ought to have been taken (approved by the House of Lords at [1936] AC 360 at 364). In *General Cleaning Contractors Ltd v Christmas* [1953] AC 180, the general practice in the window-cleaning trade was held to be negligent in that no precautions were taken to protect the men against loose window-sashes; the claimant was not required to show exactly what the correct practice should be. In *Barkway v South Wales Transport Co Ltd* [1950] 1 All ER 392, HL, although an omnibus company had followed the established practice in all respects, it was negligent because it had not instructed its drivers to report incidents which might cause an unusual type of tyre fracture (see too *Henderson v Henry E Jenkins & Sons*, cited at para 2.57 above). The general practice in shipbuilding of painting from the steep altar courses of a dry dock without some such precaution as a safety belt was found to be negligent in *Hurley v J Sanders & Co Ltd* [1955] 1 All ER 833 (see too *Ross v Tennant Caledonian Breweries Ltd* 1983 SLT 676n: system of lowering kegs of beer loosely roped though followed for 17 years without accident failed to allow for keg slipping out and striking someone).

1   Compare cases where the established practice has (after examination) been approved by the court: *Wright v Cheshire County Council* [1952] 2 All ER 789 (gymnastics in school); *Sexton v Scaffolding (Great Britain) Ltd* [1953] 1 QB 153 (dismantling of scaffold); *Hawes v Railway Executive* (1952) 96 Sol Jo 852 (electricity not switched off for minor repairs to rails); *Martin v Greater Glasgow Health Board* 1977 SLT (Notes) 66 (nurse at a nurses' home fell over banisters which (at 34 ½ inches high) were no lower than at similar institutions).

2.104 The courts have stressed that employers should initiate steps to consider ways of protecting against the risk once knowledge begins to emerge. In *King v Smith* [1995] ICR 339, for example, the court said time had moved on and it was no longer acceptable to let a window-cleaner clean windows by standing on a sill without a harness.[1] Large employers gave a higher duty in this regard: see paras 2.88–2.89 above. On the other hand, following an established practice fulfils the employer's duty unless it is shown that the alternative system is practicable, safer (taking into account risks introduced by the new system) and economically justified (see below): *Nilsson v Redditch Borough Council* [1995] PIQR P 199, CA (judge held to have had insufficient evidence to conclude that council were negligent in failing to introduce wheelie bins to supersede rubbish bags to avert risk of cuts to dustmen). The test is what is feasible: see paras 2.62–2.63. But again the words of Mustill J in *Thompson v Smiths Shiprepairers (North Shields) Ltd* are appropriate in identifying the necessity for an employer, once aware of the risk to the employee, to act to investigate means of avoiding or ameliorating the risk and then implementing a safe system of working.

1 *General Cleaning Contractors v Christmas*, above, not followed.

2.105 Conversely, the fact that an employer does not follow (good) general practice in some matter (eg in providing cream as a protection against dermatitis) does not show conclusively that it is negligent: *Brown v Rolls Royce Ltd* [1960] 1 All ER 577. But—as was said in that case—it may well be sufficient evidence of negligence unless there is evidence which throws in doubt the value of the protection.

2.106 The effect of the actual decisions can be summarised as follows. General and approved practice in an industry is the primary guide in determining the standard of care; but it is not inflexible and may be departed from when there is a failure to take account of a danger that necessitates action by the employer for the employee's welfare. This way of stating the law was approved by Edmund Davies LJ in *Brown v John Mills & Co (Llanidloes) Ltd* (1970) 8 KIR 702 (unsafe practice to polish, with emery paper held in hand, brass components revolving in lathe: no excuse that it was common practice condoned by most employers).[1] Following the duty on all employers, contained in the Management of Health and Safety at Work Regulations, to conduct a risk assessment and to adopt a rational strategy of combating those risks[2] it is still more likely that unquestioned acceptance of past methods will be critically examined.

1 In Scotland, too, it is now accepted that where a precaution is shown to be reasonably practicable, it is not necessary to prove a practice elsewhere: *Macdonald v Scottish Stamping and Engineering* Co 1972 SLT (Notes) 73.
2 See para 10.18, below.

Statutory codes and provisions, official leaflets and publications as guides to the standard of care

2.107 As will be clear from the detailed consideration elsewhere in this text of the statutes and regulations affecting employment and employees' safety, this is an area where there has been continued growth and there is now not only increased statutory (and secondary) regulation after the Framework and daughter Directives but also increased reference to publications such as approved or other guidance notes. Many recent regulations, for instance the Management of Health and Safety at Work Regulations 1999, SI 1999/3242 (reg 3) make reference to the health and safety publications. These health and safety publications, which provide guidance to employers generally and specific to individual industries, will be useful in demonstrating both whether a risk (and its extent) should have been known and what steps ought to have been taken to combat it: see *Clifford v Charles H Challen & Son Ltd* [1951] 1 KB 495 (dermatitis from handling synthetic glue); *Dickson v Flack* [1953]

2 QB 464 (woodworking machinery). International Labour Organisation and Department of Health guidance were held to establish that a health authority employer ought to have known and taken precautions against fumes from X-ray processing chemicals in *Ogden v Airedale Health Authority* [1996] 7 Med LR 153.

2.108 The HSWA 1974, s 16, authorises the issue of an approved code of practice (in this book an 'ACOP') for any matter affecting health and safety at work; these should be illustrative of what is approved practice. A failure to observe the provision of a code does not of itself amount to criminal liability, but it is admissible in evidence: s 17.[1] Approved codes of practice are often of similar relevance in civil proceedings, as evidence of approved practice and informed opinion. So too should be the codes of guidance which accompany some of the new regulations, even though they are not within s 17 for the purpose of criminal proceedings. (See further on ACOPs, para 8.18.)

[1]   Unless the employer shows that the statutory requirement was met in some other manner, the breach will mean an offence is committed: *West Cumberland By-Products v DPP* [1988] RTR 391.

2.109 Specific recommendations in codes of regulations—for example that a plank of over a certain height must be of a certain width—are less likely to crystallise the common law duty of care: see *Chipchase v British Titan Products Co Ltd* [1956] 1 QB 545. In *Ward v Ritz Hotel (London)* [1992] PIQR P 315, on the other hand, the Court of Appeal held that a balcony six inches lower than the requirement of the relevant British Standard from which the claimant fell did breach the duty of care. Although British Standards were not legally binding, they provided strong evidence as to the consensus of professional opinion and practical experience as to sensible safety precautions as at their date of issue. The standards of the British Standards Institute (BSI) and the International Standards Organisation (ISO) were heavily utilised in the miners' v WF judgment: *Armstrong v British Coal Corpn* (1996) Times, 6 December, CA. However breach of a British Standard will not necessarily amount to negligence. Thus in *Green v Building Scene Ltd* [1994] PIQR P 259 there was no liability, although the stairs on which the plaintiff fell failed to comply with the relevant British Standard and Building Regulations because no central handrail was provided. The court accepted that the British Standard and Building Regulations represented the current professional opinion as to what was desirable in order that accidents should be avoided, but found that in the circumstances the stairs were reasonably safe.

2.110 Statutory duties may influence the common law standard of care. Statutory duties may be evidence of good practice which a reasonable employer should adopt: *Franklin v Gramophone Co Ltd* [1948] 1 KB 542 per Somervell LJ; *National Coal Board v England* [1954] AC 403; *Hewett v Alf Brown's Transport Ltd* [1991] ICR 471, affd [1992] ICR 530, CA. In *Bux v Slough Metals Ltd* [1974] 1 All ER 262 at 273–274, Stephenson LJ, in considering the relevance of statutory regulations to liability in negligence, said:

'the employer ... should acquaint himself with the statutory provisions applicable which he employs men to do and do his best to make sure that the men he employs to do the work know of them and understand them and the duties they impose ... The employer must try to make the law of the land a rule of the factory.'

2.111 That approach is likely to be of particular importance to the duties in the Management of Health and Safety at Work Regulations 1999 (see para 10.14, below). In *Butt v Inner London Education Authority* (1968) 66 LGR 379 a student at a technical college was injured by an unfenced printing machine. Although the Factories Act was inapplicable, it was treated as analogous so as to establish the standard in negligence. In *Moffat v Atlas Hydraulic Loaders Ltd* 1992 SLT 1123, OH, the duty to fence machinery at common law was held to be the same as under s 14(1) of the Factories Act 1961, that Act doubtless influencing the standard in negligence. For similar reasons, it can be argued that the standards and procedures laid down in European Directives may be evidence of what is the practice of reasonable employers—particularly in the light of the duty on UK courts to seek to achieve the same result as Directives (see para 9.33, below).

2.112 In some cases a statutory code may be sufficiently detailed and exhaustive so that compliance with it does meet the duty in negligence: see *Franklin v Gramophone Co Ltd* [1948] 1 KB 542. Yet in principle the duties are distinct, so that compliance with a statutory duty in the same field does not absolve an employer from common law negligence: see Lord Reid in *Gill v Donald Humberstone & Co Ltd* [1963] 3 All ER 180 at 183. Even an exhaustive code, like that which regulates shot-firing in a coal mine, may not fully meet all the requirements of the duty of care: *Nicol v National Coal Board* (1952) 102 L Jo 357; *Matuszczyk v National Coal Board* 1953 SC 8. In every case the court must form an independent judgment of what the common law requires, as did the Court of Appeal in *Bux v Slough Metals Ltd* [1974] 1 All ER 262 in finding that compliance with a statutory duty to provide goggles did not satisfy the common law duty of care—in this case not merely to provide but to encourage the wearing of goggles.

2.113 Overall it is to be hoped that where the courts are considering the safety and welfare of employees, even where the statutory and regulatory provisions do not apply, they will look to these as of principal assistance as they will also in respect of both governmental guidance and other authoritative publications pertinent to the particular trade or operation in issue.

Chapter 3

CAUSATION, APPORTIONMENT AND CONTRIBUTION, REMOTENESS OF DAMAGE, EVIDENCE AND LIABILITY WITHOUT NEGLIGENCE

David Wilby QC

Daniel Bennett

GENERAL PRINCIPLES

3.01 Issues of causation in personal injury actions including those in the context of employment are inevitably bound up with remoteness of damage. As a matter of basic principle, a claimant is entitled to recover damages for personal injuries caused by the defendant's negligence. Lord Bingham explained this general principle in his dissenting speech in *Chester v Afshar* [2004] UKHL 41, [2005] 1 AC 134 where, at 134, he stated:

'It is trite law that damage is the gist of the action in the tort of negligence ... A claimant is entitled to be compensated for the damage which the negligence of another has caused to him or her. A defendant is bound to compensate the claimant for the damage which his or her negligence has caused the claimant. But the corollaries are also true: a claimant is not entitled to be compensated, and a defendant is not bound to compensate the claimant, for damage not caused by the negligence complained of.'

3.02 In the vast majority of cases, if any degree of injury is foreseeable the claimant will be able to recover the whole extent of it. As is developed later in this chapter, this broad approach is often reduced to a consideration of the so-called 'but for' test, helpfully explained by Lord Nicholls in *Fairchild v Glenhaven Funeral Services Ltd* [2002] UKHL 22, [2003] 1 AC 32 that:

'In the normal way, in order to recover damages for negligence, a plaintiff must prove that but for the defendant's wrongful conduct he would not have sustained the harm or loss in question. He must establish at least this degree of causal connection between his damage and the defendant's conduct before the defendant will be held responsible for the damage. Exceptionally this is not so ...'

The 'exceptionally' refers to cases where for policy reasons the courts relax these strict causation principles to enable damage to be attributable to the defendant's breach of duty with a different degree of causal connection. This is exemplified in employers' liability by the industrial diseases cases where issues of material contribution to the damage are considered differently, and in clinical negligence where the difference in approach in specific circumstances is apparent from the decision of the majority in the House of Lords in *Chester v Afshar* [2004] UKHL 41.

3.03 In *Fairchild* when considering the correct test for legal causation, Lord Hoffmann stated:

> 'The causal requirements for liability often vary, sometimes quite subtly, from case to case. And since the causal requirements for liability are always a matter of law, these variations represent legal differences, driven by the recognition that the just solution to different kinds of case may require different causal requirement rules.'

The principles of causation may be summarised that, where a claimant can establish that the injury or damage he sustained was foreseeable, it is still necessary for the claimant, on whom the burden of proof lies, to establish that the wrongful act of the defendant was a cause of it, or at least materially contributed to it. The correct test is a matter of law and varies depending on the circumstances of the case.

The 'but for' test

3.04 In *Clough v First Choice Holidays and Flights Ltd* [2006] EWCA Civ 15 Phillips LJ, in considering this test, identified that:

> 'in the context of causation, the two words "but for" are shorthand. They encapsulate a principle understood by lawyers, but applied literally, or as if the two words embody the entire principle, the words can mislead. They may convey the impression that the claimant's claim for damages for personal injuries must fail unless he can prove that the defendant's negligence was the only, or the single, or even chronologically the last cause of his injuries. The authorities demonstrate that such an impression would be incorrect. The claimant is required to establish a causal link between the negligence of the defendant and his injuries or, in short, that his injuries were indeed consequent on the negligence. Although on its own it is not enough for him to show that the defendant created an increased risk of injury, the necessary causal link would be established if, as a matter of inference from the evidence, the defendant's negligence made a material contribution to the claimant's injuries.'

The first and crucial point in establishing causation is to establish the relevant cause and thus to eliminate irrelevant causes. This is the purpose of the 'but for' test, since the court is concerned not to identify a variety of potential causes for the claimant's damage but to establish the effective cause in order to identify the party responsible for that damage. So although the issue of causation might simply be stated as 'Did the defendant's act cause the claimant's injury or loss?' in this more specific context the issue is 'Would the damage suffered by the claimant have occurred "but for" the negligence or breach of duty of the defendant?'[1] Put differently, it is for the claimant to establish that had the defendant not committed the breach of duty concerned, his injury would not have occurred.

1   See general consideration of causation/'but for' test in *Clough v First Choice Holidays & Flights Ltd* [2006] EWCA Civ 15.

No need for exclusive causation

3.05 Complicated situations arise when multiple events all contribute to damage occuring. In such circumstances, the claimant is not required to establish that the defendant's fault is the sole or only cause of his injury and damage.[1] It is enough for these purposes that the defendant's wrong is a cause of the claimant's injury or a particular part of it. As Lord Reid stated in *Stapley v Gypsum Mines* [1953] AC 663, HL:

> 'To determine who caused an accident from the point of view of legal liability is a most difficult task. If there is any valid logical or scientific theory of causation it is quite irrelevant in this connection ... The question must be determined by applying common sense to the facts of each particular case. One may find, as a matter of history, that several people have been at fault and that if any one of them had acted properly the accident would not have happened, but that does not mean that the accident must be regarded as having been caused by the faults of all of them. One must discriminate between those faults which must be discarded as too remote and those which must not.
>
> Sometimes it is proper to discard all but one [party's fault] and to regard that one as the sole cause, but in others it is proper to regard two or more as having jointly caused the accident.'

1 Lord Reid in *Stapley v Gypsum Mines* [1953] AC 663 at 681, HL.

3.06 Accordingly, in the manual handling case of *O'Neill v DSG Retail Ltd* [2002] EWCA Civ 1139, [2003] ICR 222 the test applied by the Court of Appeal on causation was whether the defendant's breach was *a* cause of the injury (see Chadwick LJ at para 89). This approach was expressly adopted in *Goodchild v Organon Laboratories Ltd* [2004] EWHC 2341 (QB) at para 47.[1] Similarly, it is not a complete defence for the defendant to show that some other, non-wrongful, factor was also responsible for the claimant's injury.[2]

1 These cases are both manual handling cases, see generally chapter 21, below.
2 *McGhee v National Coal Board* [1972] 3 All ER 1008.

Relevance of the employee's conduct to causation

3.07 Often in an employment context the application of the 'but for' test relates not only to the conduct of the employer who is the defendant but also to what the employee would have done. The hypothetical question is 'What would have happened if there had not been a breach of duty by the defendant?' This is best understood by example. In *McWilliams v Sir Williams Arol & Co* [1962] 1 WLR 295, HL a steelworker fell 70 feet to his death. The employers were found to be in breach of statutory duty in failing to provide him with a safety harness, but the evidence showed that the dead man had rarely if ever worn a safety harness even when one was provided. His widow's claim for breach of statutory duty failed because she could not show that 'but for' the defendant's wrongdoing her husband's death would have been avoided. This was because of the probability that even if he had been provided with the safety equipment he would not have worn it. This case is unlikely to be followed today, where the regulatory regime generally requires not simply provision of equipment but monitoring of its use and often enforcing its use.

3.08

In *Henser-Leather v Securicor Cash Services Ltd* [2002] EWCA Civ 816, [2002] All ER (D) 259 (May) Kennedy LJ found that a defendant (having failed to provide personal protective equipment in the first place) was also in breach of its duty to take steps to ensure than it was used. Having taken no such steps, it was not open to the defendant to argue that the claimant might not have worn the equipment if provided. Applying a similar argument in a different situation in *Toole v Bolton* [2002] EWCA Civ 588, a claimant could not be held at fault at all for failing to use the equipment provided when such equipment was unsuitable and would not have prevented the injury.[1]

1   These cases are both PPE at work cases and are considered in context below at para 20.76.

3.09 Where there is an established breach of duty on the part of the defendant, the question of the employee's conduct is normally a question of contributory negligence. For an employer to be exonerated from liability on the basis of the conduct of an employee, then the employer's breach of duty must be brought about wholly by the claimant. If it is not, then the employer will be liable and must seek apportionment for the contributory negligence of the employee (see *Boyle v Kodak Ltd* [1969] 2 All ER 439 and para 6.29).

Statistics and causation

3.10 Considerable care should be exercised when relying on statistics as a means of establishing causation. The court is concerned primarily with the claimant's individual circumstances and general statistics are only relevant insofar as they educate the court in respect of those circumstances. The issue of statistical probability and its relationship to the balance of probability standard in civil proceedings was recently considered in *Gregg v Scott* [2005] UKHL 2, [2005] 2 AC 196, where the House of Lords were not persuaded to depart from the balance of probability standard in proof of causation. The practitioner and the judge must be particularly careful of the problems of using statistics which derive from trends in general populations to prove what 'probably' happened in a particular case.[1] Nonetheless, since inevitably proof of causation is about the burden of persuading a court of the probability that an event occurred, statistics can be highly persuasive when used in the right context and in a way discrete to the specific claimant and issue.

1   *Gregg v Scott* [2005] UKHL 2, [2005] 2 WLR 268 per Lord Nicholls.

Proof of causation

3.11 The onus is on the claimant to prove causation on the balance of probabilities: *Bonnington Castings Ltd v Wardlaw* [1956] AC 613. Hints to the contrary in *McGhee v National Coal Board* [1973] 1 WLR 1 at 6 and 7 per Lord Wilberforce, were rejected by the House of Lords in *Wilsher v Essex Area Health Authority* [1988] AC 1074 (per Lord Bridge at 1087) and more recently in *Gregg v Scott* [2005] UKHL 2, [2005] 2 AC 196, per Lord Nicholls. What is not clear, however, is what evidence will be treated as sufficient to meet this burden.[1]

1   It was formerly held that in actions for breach of statutory duty, where the duty was imposed to prevent a particular type of accident or disease, and a breach was followed by that accident or disease, it was presumed to be caused by the breach. That line of authorities was overruled by *Bonnington Castings*.

3.12 Whilst the burden is upon the claimant, the claimant is not bound to prove every single aspect of the chain of causation. The Court of Appeal in *Armstrong v First York* [2005] EWCA Civ 277, [2005] 1 WLR 2751 supported the trial judge's finding that a low velocity impact had caused the claimant's injuries despite the medical evidence being unable to explain or support the cause of such injury. In *Whalley v Montracon Ltd* [2005] EWCA Civ 1383, [2005] All ER (D) 269 (Nov) the claimant's medical expert changed his opinion as a result of listening to the claimant's description of his symptoms. As a result both doctors agreed that the claimant did not have hand arm vibration syndrome. The judge at first instance believed the claimant's evidence and found that the claimant did suffer from the disease. The Court of Appeal upheld the judge's finding. The judge was entitled to find in favour of the claimant on the balance of probabilities on the totality of the evidence, even though that evidence contained an element which pointed against the judge's conclusion. Cases involving injury associated with psychogenic factors face particular problems of proof. In *Alexander v Midland Bank plc* [2000] ICR 464, it was common ground that the claimants were suffering from fibromyalgia related to repetitive work and were genuinely suffering pain and disability. The issue was whether the condition was as a result of a physical injury albeit that its precise aetiology was unknown or whether the cause was psychogenic. The Court of Appeal held that the claimants' failure to prove the precise pathology or physiological explanation for their work-related upper limb disorder was no bar to their establishing that they had suffered a physical injury and that it was caused by their work.

3.13 If there is a complete absence of evidence of any association between a particular breach of duty and a certain kind of injury, then causation has not been established and the claim will fail. The breach of duty may have preceded the onset of the injury, but there may be no evidence that a breach of that particular kind tends to be followed by a certain sort of injury. Thus, lack of any explanation how an overdose of penicillin could cause deafness meant there was no liability in *Kay's Tutor v Ayrshire and Arran Health Board* [1987] 2 All ER 417: it was an accepted 'fact' that the overdose was incapable of resulting in deafness, this never having occurred in the past. Claims were similarly rejected in *Reay v British Nuclear Fuels plc* [1994] PIQR P 171 owing to the virtual absence of any evidence that exposure to ionising radiation in parents could cause a form of lymphoma in offspring. In *Loveday v Renton* [1990] 1 Med LR 117, the court declined to find a causal link between whooping cough vaccine and brain damage, largely owing to the inadequacy of the biological explanations put forward.

3.14 But the courts do not require (and in certain circumstances the state of scientific or medical knowledge does not currently permit) a full scientific account of exactly how a particular exposure causes a particular injury. In *McGhee v National Coal Board* [1973] 1 WLR 1, for example, it was accepted that dust in hot conditions could cause dermatitis, even though the precise mechanisms by which it did so were unclear. A similar approach was adopted in *Fairchild v Glenhaven Funeral Services Ltd* [2002] UKHL 22, [2002] IRLR 533, where it was accepted that the claimants' exposure to asbestos had caused their mesothelioma, even though the precise mechanism was not understood. In *Gardiner v Motherwell Machinery and Scrap Co Ltd* [1961] 3 All ER 831n, a demolition worker, after three months' extremely dirty work with the defendants, contracted dermatitis. He recovered from the defendants. Lord Reid stated:

> 'When a man who has not previously suffered from a disease contracts that disease after being subjected to conditions *likely* to cause it, and when he shows that it starts in a way typical of disease caused by such conditions, he establishes a prima facie presumption that his disease was caused by those conditions.'

'Presumption' must here be read to mean a legitimate inference. However, epidemiological evidence on its own is often unhelpful, unless the evidence is overwhelming. Even where the causal mechanism is reasonably well understood in medical terms, so that it can be stated authoritatively that exposure to a particular toxin will lead to the increase in the number of cases of a disease, it may still not be impossible for a single individual affected by exposure of the toxin to prove his disease was caused by exposure to it where there are other factors that can also cause it. (For an example of an attempt to use epidemiology, see *XYZ v Schering Health Care Ltd* [2002] EWHC 1420 (QB).)

Increased exposure to risk

3.15 The courts have adopted a different less stringent test on causation in specific circumstances where a claimant has obviously been injured by a specific agent (eg brick dust, asbestos dust) but is unable to prove that the injury was caused by dust to which he was negligently exposed, as opposed to non negligent exposure. In such circumstances, the law is prepared to treat a material increase in the risk of injury as sufficient to satisfy the causal requirements for liability. Lord Hoffmann clarifies in *Barker v Corus (UK) plc* [2006] UKHL 20 that the two essential conditions for the operation of this exception are that: (a) it is impossible to prove any more stringent causation test other than increase in risk, and (b) the injury is caused by a sole causative agent.[1] Accordingly, the less stringent causation test is not available in clinical negligence cases where a negligent act by a doctor increased the risk of a poor outcome but in the context of many agents acting to cause that outcome.[2] Similarly, it would not apply when a claimant has developed cancer, the risk of which was increased by a defendant's negligent act but it cannot be proved that other agents were not the more likely cause.[3] It is also important not to confuse this causation test with the separate a different test applied in cases such as *Bonnington Castings v Wardlaw* [1956] AC 613.[4] The 'material increase in risk' test, applied in cases such as *McGhee v NCB* [1973] 1 WLR 1 and *Fairchild* (above), is expressed to apply only in very restricted circumstances. The exception was created because the alternative of leaving the claimant with no remedy was thought by the House of Lords in *Fairchild* (above) to be unjust. Prior to *Fairchild*, the courts did adopt a common sense attitude to situations where risks were increased by reason of the employer's breach of duty. Where, for example, regulations allow a gap between a fence and a circular saw, and the gap is rather greater than it should be, it is legitimate to infer that the increased exposure has contributed to the accident, as in *Lee v Nursery Furnishings Ltd* [1945] 1 All ER 387. So, too, with the absence of a guard rail on a scaffold: *Cork v Kirby Maclean Ltd* [1952] 2 All ER 402; similarly inferred in relation to a space below a rail on a working platform through which a man working in a squatting position might fall: *McClymont v Glasgow Corpn* 1971 SLT 45; likewise the absence of a fence on a machine, though it was possible that the workman might have removed it, for the presence of a fence would at least have been a 'warning or deterrent': *Hodkinson v Henry Wallwork & Co Ltd* [1955] 3 All ER 236; *Allen v Aeroplane and Motor Aluminium Castings Ltd* [1965] 3 All ER 377. It is not necessary to prove exactly how a man's hands got into an unfenced machine, when they could not have got in if it were fenced: *Johnson v F E Callow (Engineers) Ltd* [1970] 1 All ER 129 sub nom *Callow (F E) Engineers Ltd v Johnson* approved on appeal [1970] 3 All ER 639 at 645. In general, if there is a reasonable probability that some safety measure would have given extra protection, and was not taken, the causal connection is sufficiently shown.

1   See paras 24 and 33 and also Lord Hoffmann in *Fairchild v Glenhaven Funeral Services Ltd* [2002] UKHL 22, at para 65.
2   Eg see *Wilsher v Essex Area Health Authority* [1088] AC 1074 and *Gregg v Scott* [2005] 2 AC 176.
3   See Lord Hoffmann at para 24 in *Barker* (above).
4   See para 3.18 below.

Damage would have occurred in any event

3.16 A claimant will fail to establish causation if the evidence is that, even without the breach of duty, the damage would still have in fact occurred. In *Barnett v Chelsea and Kensington Hospital Management Committee* [1969] 1 QB 428, a person who had drunk arsenic was negligently treated in hospital. But the evidence was that, even with proper treatment, he would have died. In the context of employment, just such an argument may be raised in relation to training or warning employees of risks endemic to a particular occupation: see eg *Koonjul v Thameslink Healthcare Services* [2000] PIQR P 123 and other manual handling cases discussed in more detail in chapter 21, below.

3.17 Similarly, where a defendant can prove that a particular disability or loss *would* have arisen in any event even if the original tort had not occurred, a defendant is not liable for the disability or loss from the time when such would have arisen in any event. In *Jobling v Associated Dairies Ltd* [1982] AC 794 the defendant employers admitted their liability for the claimant's back injury. Three years after it was suffered the claimant suffered from a myelopathy unrelated to his work, which rendered him unfit for work. The House of Lords held that the defendants were only liable for the incapacity suffered until the subsequent illness rendered the claimant unfit for work.

Material contribution

3.18 The application of the 'but for' test in causation has proved particularly problematic in the field of disease cases where analysis of the genesis of the condition presents complexities which make the application of the 'but for' test difficult, if not impossible. Occupational diseases and mental injuries in particular have complex causes. The precise medical causes of many diseases are not properly understood by medical experts. Further, the evidence of the exposure and events that may have led to the injury are often unclear. Errors and omissions occurring during the course of work which is hazardous in any event, create further difficulties. Over time, claimants in such cases have succeeded when the complexities of the case rendered proof of the 'but for' test impossible. The judgments in such cases cannot be read together as providing a distinct rule of causation. The cases, instead, read as different rules of causation in different situations. Any attempt to try and maintain that there was a single rule of causation was dismissed by Lord Hoffmann in *Fairchild v Glenhaven Funeral Services Ltd* [2002] 3 WLR 89 at para 48 onwards when considering the correct test for legal causation, he noted that the causal requirements for liability vary from case to case.[1]

1 See para 3.03, above.

3.19 The starting point for any analysis of this issue remains *Bonnington Castings v Wardlaw* [1956] AC 613. The claimant, who suffered from pneumoconiosis, had been exposed to silica dust arising from pneumatic hammers and swing grinders. There was clear evidence that pneumoconiosis was caused by a gradual accumulation of silica dust. Although the only breach of duty was the failure to protect against dust from the grinders, and the hammers gave rise to 'much the greater proportion of the noxious dust', the defendants were still held liable. Lord Reid, at 621, considered that any contribution to the exposure caused by the defendant's fault which was not de minimis would be sufficient in establishing causation. Only if the 'guilty' dust had been released so infrequently or in such an insignificant quantity, that even over a long period it could not be regarded as a material factor would the claimant fail (see Lord Keith). See too *Nicholson v Atlas Steel Foundry and Engineering Co Ltd* [1957] 1 All ER 776 (insufficient ventilation to remove dust: see Lord Simonds at 779).

3.20 The above cases involve the claimant being able to show at most that the negligence exposure made a material contribution to the injury. However, in certain circumstances, all that can be shown is that the negligent conduct made a material contribution to the risk of injury (see *McGhee v National Coal Board* [1973] 1 WLR 1, HL, especially Lord Simon, Lord Kilbrandon and Lord Salmon). So evidence of a link of an increased risk of cancer of the larynx from exposure to asbestos was enough to establish causation in *McPherson v Alexander Stephens & Sons Ltd* (1990) 175 HSIB 19. In *McGhee v National Coal Board* [1973] 1 WLR 1, HL, the House of Lords considered the proper approach in relation to subsequent, not simultaneous, exposure to the same agent. The claimant contracted dermatitis through exposure to brick dust while working in a kiln. The defendant breached its duty of care in failing to provide him with washing facilities. None of the experts could say that had the claimant washed after work, he would on the balance of probabilities not have developed dermatitis. Despite the likelihood that exposure in the kilns (for which the defendant was not liable) was also a cause of dermatitis, the defendant was held to have caused the dermatitis because its failure to provide the washing facilities had increased the risk to the claimant.

3.21 Following *McGhee* (above), it was often stated that a material contribution to the risk of injury equated with a material contribution to the injury itself. This interpretation of equating contribution to risk with contribution to injury, was rejected by a majority of the House of Lords in *Fairchild v Glenhaven Funeral Services Ltd*. The position was clarified by Lord Hoffmann in *Barker v Corus (UK) plc* [2006] UKHL 20, [2006] 07 LS Gaz R 25 when he stated that this *McGhee* or *Fairchild* exception was simply a different and less stringent test on causation to that which applied in other circumstances. In *Barker* Lord Hoffmann stated that the two essential conditions for the operation of this *Fairchild* exception are that: (a) it is impossible to prove any more stringent causation test in the particular circumstances of the case (such as proving a material contribution to the injury itself), and (b) the injury is caused by a sole causative agent such as dust.[1] In *Fairchild*, where multiple defendants had exposed a claimant to asbestos fibre, but where it was thought that an asbestos fibre from only one of them could have caused the injury (ie only one of them had actually contributed to the injury but which one could not be established), each defendant was found liable as each, through its breach of duty, had contributed to the risk of injury. The decision in *Barker v Corus (UK) plc* [2006] UKHL 20 confirms that whilst each is liable, in these specific circumstances the liability is divisible and each defendant is liable according to its contribution to the risk of injury. *Barker* also clarified that the test still applies even if a claimant exposed himself to asbestos as a self-employed man and contributed to his own risk before working for the defendant. However, the overall liability will be reduced to take into account the claimant own contribution to his own risk of injury. In *Fairchild*, each of the five Law Lords set out slightly different rules concerning when *Fairchild* exception might apply. Lord Bingham considered that liability can only be established if the claimant can show:

(a)   the claimant was employed by the defendant(s);
(b)   the defendant(s) were subject to a duty to prevent him inhaling asbestos because of the known risk of mesothelioma;
(c)   the defendant(s) breached that duty causing the claimant to inhale excessive asbestos;
(d)   the claimant developed mesothelioma;
(e)   the mesothelioma was developed as a result of exposure at work; and

(f)   the risk of the claimant developing mesothelioma was increased by the breach of duty by the defendant(s).

Where exposure to a disease has been contracted through exposure over a number of years, some of which are outside the time limit for liability, the exposure within the limitation period may satisfy the 'material contribution' test: *Clarkson v Modern Foundries Ltd* [1958] 1 All ER 33.[2]

1   See paras 24 and 33 and also Lord Hoffmann in *Fairchild v Glenhaven Funeral Services Ltd* [2002] UKHL 22, at para 65]
2   But damages will be limited to the further deterioration caused in that period: *Thompson v Smiths Shiprepairers (North Shields) Ltd* [1984] QB 405. See too *Bowman v Harland and Wolff plc* [1992] IRLR 349.

3.22

There is an obvious tension between these cases and the clinical negligence cases of *Wilsher v Essex Area Health Authority* [1988] AC 1074, HL and *Hotson v East Berkshire Area Health Authority* [1987] AC 750. However, applying Lord Hoffmann's rule (para 3.18, above) and Lord Bingham's test (para 3.21, above) it is clear that these are particular causation rules for particular types of injury: ie workplace disease cases.

3.23   Other than in the *Fairchild* exception, the position, therefore, seems to be that so long as a judge accepts evidence of a 'material contribution' to the claimant's injuries from the breach, whether physical or psychiatric (see *Page v Smith (No 2)* [1996] 1 WLR 855), the claimant will succeed. It is clear from what Lord Bridge said in *Wilsher*[1] that the judge need not find, as a matter of statistics, that there was a greater than 50 per cent chance that without the breach the injury would not have occurred. In accordance with the common-sense approach, it is enough to find that the breach was a 'material contributory cause'.[2]

1   And per Lord Reid in *Bonnington Castings Ltd v Wardlaw* [1956] AC 613 (above, para 3.19) that any contribution which was not de minimis would be material.
2   See also *Graham v Rechem International* [1996] Env LR 158, HC. The fact that in general more than 50 per cent of persons in the position of the claimant would develop a particular condition absent a particular act of negligence does not necessarily mean that the claimant would have.

3.24   Prior to the decision of the House of Lords in *Gregg v Scott* [2005] UKHL 2, [2005] 2 AC 176 many thought that the principle of a loss of chance could be applied in particular types of case where establishing causation on a balance of probability was not provable, but proof of a high prospect chance less than a balance of probability could be established. In that case, involving survival of cancer, the loss of a chance argument was that the defendant's negligence had reduced the claimant's chances of survival from 42% to 25%, this reduction of prospects being of some value and the claimant was entitled to compensation. The appeal failed and the principle enumerated in *Hotson v East Berkshire Health Authority* [1987] AC 750 was affirmed. However, the individual speeches of the five Law Lords are of particular interest and it may be that there is still scope for further development of the principle. Lord Hoffmann rejected the loss of chance approach completely, whereas Baroness Hale, who rejected it in that case, did consider that in some cases there could be a modest claim in respect of 'lost years' and Lord Phillips, whilst agreeing that on the facts the appeal must be dismissed, also considered that in certain cases 'there may be a case for permitting a recovery of damages that is proportionate to the increase in the chance of the adverse instance'. Lord Nicholls and Lord Hope were both strongly supportive of such an approach.

Apportionment and material contribution

3.25 In *Allen v BREL* [2001] EWCA Civ 242, [2001] ICR 942 the Court of Appeal stated five points of principle as follows:

1   The employee will establish liability if he can prove that the employer's tortious conduct made a material contribution to the employee's disability.
2   There can be cases where the state of the evidence is such that it is just to recognise each of two separate tortfeasors as having caused the whole of the damage of which the claimant complains; for instance where a passenger is killed as the result of a head on collision between two cars, each of which was negligently driven and in one of which he was sitting.
3   However in principle the amount of the employer's liability will be limited to the extent of the contribution which his tortious conduct made to the employee's disability.
4   The court must do the best it can on the evidence to make the apportionment and should not be astute to deny the claimant relief on the basis that he cannot establish with demonstrable accuracy precisely what proportion of his injury is attributable to the defendant's tortious conduct.
5   The amount of evidence which should be called to enable a judge to make a just apportionment must be proportionate to the amount at stake and the uncertainties which are inherent in making any award of damages for personal injury.

3.26 Case law demonstrates four specific examples where judges have consistently found evidence to show a real and arguable separation between the injury caused by the defendant's breach of duty and some other factors. The four examples are:

—   exacerbation of pre-existing condition or disability;
—   pre-date of knowledge exposure—injury caused by exposure to substances before a defendant knows or should have known of the link;
—   injury caused by a different employer employing the claimant at a different time;
—   injury caused or contributed to by the claimant's own actions.

As a general principle, it is for the defendant to raise the question of apportionment (see Hale LJ in *Sutherland v Hatton* [2002] EWCA Civ 76, [2002] ICR 613).

Pre-existing condition or disability

3.27 This arises regularly in many injury cases, particularly orthopaedic injury. Many claimants suffer from pre-existing conditions which can be aggravated by workplace events. In many cases, the claimant is unaware of the pre-existence of the condition as it was not symptomatic at the time. In such cases, the events at work, although not the cause of the condition, can accelerate the onset of symptoms or aggravate or exacerbate the condition. In each of these examples, it is necessary for a medical expert to decide the extent to which injury is caused by the incident at work as opposed to other factors.

3.28 The treatment of a pre-existing injury was first dealt with by the Court of Appeal in *Fowler v AW Hawksley* (1951) 95 Sol Jo 788, CA, which involved pre-existing injuries to a hand. In this, Lord Goddard CJ stated:

'... [I]t seems to me that in order to estimate the prospective loss of earnings it is necessary to compare the situation of the man in the labour market as he was before the accident, taking into account all the disabilities which he then had, with the situation of the same man after the accident, taking into account all the disabilities which he by that time had, in order to see to what extent his earning power has been affected.'

The matter came before the Court of Appeal in the context of accelerated degeneration of the spine in *Dray v Schneider* [1966] CA No 30. The Court of Appeal accepted that a pre-existing scoliosis condition had been aggravated by the plaintiff's fall. However, the scoliosis was such that by the time of the fall, the plaintiff was likely to develop pain on any strain or stress that might occur. Given that the plaintiff's fall did not cause the degenerative condition, the plaintiff was only entitled to compensation for the 14 or 15 months that the court considered her injury would have caused symptoms for, but for the degenerative condition.

3.29 An alternative to the method adopted in *Dray*, is for the medical experts and the court to assess the period of acceleration of symptoms. That is, the period by which the degenerative condition would have caused symptoms in any event. In *Newman v Nederlandschamerikaansche Stoomvaart Maatschappij NV* [1966] 2 Lloyd's Rep 266, Neild J assessed compensation on the basis that in five years' time the plaintiff's congenital condition would prevent him from continuing as a stevedore in any event and accordingly, any claim must be limited to the symptoms and losses sustained in that period only.

Pre-date of knowledge injury

3.30 In *Thompson v Smiths Shiprepairers* [1984] 1 QB 405, the High Court recognised that the defendants should have acted to protect employees from the risk of hearing loss due to exposure to noise at work from 1963. Accordingly, claimants exposed before 1963 could not succeed. Those exposed after 1963 succeeded in full. However, the complication was for claimants exposed both before and after 1963. For such claimants, they would only recover for the proportion of their industrial deafness caused after the date of knowledge (1963), even where the court had to make an educated guess at the proper apportionment. Having considered the evidence, the trial judge apportioned the claims on a simple pro rata basis to exposure.

3.31 That approach was approved in the Court of Appeal in *Armstrong v British Coal Corp (No 2)* (31 July 1998, unreported) for vibration white finger cases for injury caused before 1975. However, a pro rata apportionment was not applied. In VWF cases, prompt action by the defendant could have avoided symptoms exacerbating post-1975. Further, reduced exposure generally post-1975 may have avoided symptoms developing at all. Accordingly, there was very little if any reduction for pre-1975 exposure where it could be shown that most if not all the injury was caused by the later exposure. Accordingly, in *Brookes v South Yorkshire Passenger Transport Executive* [2005] EWCA Civ 452 where the claimant developed his first symptoms 10 years after the date of knowledge of the defendant, there was no apportionment for the many years of pre-date of knowledge exposure.

3.32 When apportioning for pre-date of knowledge exposure, an understanding of the medical causes of injury and exacerbation of injury is essential.

Non-defendant exposure

3.33 In *Holtby v Brigham & Cowan (Hull) Ltd* [2000] ICR 1086, the Court of Appeal allowed a defendant to reduce the extent of liability by 25% in an asbestosis case on the grounds that another employer had exposed the claimant to a substantial amount of asbestos at an earlier time and must therefore have contributed to the asbestosis. The defendant was, in effect, found to be severally liable for the claimant's disease and not jointly liable for the whole disease. The defendant was liable in full under *McGhee* principles. But, if the defendant could then satisfy the court that on the burden of proof another party was partially responsible for part of the injury, then there would be a reduction. The fact that this was an asbestosis case allowed the defendant to apportion the loss as all exposure occurring more than 10–15 years before symptoms contributed equally to the injury and apportionment could be made on a pro rata basis to exposure. The Court of Appeal in *Barker v Saint Gobain Pipelines plc* [2004] EWCA Civ 545 allowed no apportionment in a mesothelioma case on the basis that the injury was indivisible and as all exposure contributed to the risk of injury (and not cumulatively to the injury itself) the defendant could not show that non-defendant exposure had caused any actual injury. Each defendant was found jointly liable for the whole. This aspect of the Court of Appeal's decision was overruled by the House of Lords in *Barker* [2006] UKHL 20. The House of Lords considered that the attribution of liability according to the relative contribution to the chance of the disease being contracted was a just solution in a case in which the medical and scientific position on causation was based solely on risk and probability, and that each defendant had only been found liable on the basis of that it may have caused harm (ie contributed to the risk of injury: see paras 3.15 and 3.21 above). As with pre-date of knowledge apportionment, the defendant must be able to prove that another defendant caused a part of the injury (or contributed to the risk of injury in the *Fairchild* exception cases). As above, when apportioning for non-defendant exposure, an understanding of the medical causes of injury and exacerbation of injury is essential.

Claimant's own actions

3.34 The apportionment applied in *Allen v BREL* (above) is much misunderstood. At first instance the trial judge had reasoned:

'In my view, if the first defendants had complied with their duty to him, Mr Allen would probably have changed jobs within BREL by 1975 or would soon afterwards have moved to a job which entailed less use of vibrating tools. The likelihood is that, whether he moved within BREL or away from it, he would still have used his manual skills and would have used some vibrating tools. Doing the best I can, and bearing in mind that Mr Allen's exposure during the last 11 years with BR was not in any event very high, I conclude that if the first defendants had complied with their duty of care towards him, he would, between 1976 and 1987, have been exposed to a reduced level of vibration, of the order of a half to two thirds of the level to which he was actually exposed.'

The court reduced the damages by 50%. The Court of Appeal, in supporting the above, stated:

'There was however no evidence that non-vibratory work was available for which Mr Allen was suitable. The judge found that there was vibratory work involving lower doses of vibration and that if this had been offered Mr Allen would have taken it; if it had not been offered he would have found such work elsewhere.'

3.35 In the very similar case of *Smith v Wright & Beyer* [2001] EWCA Civ 1069, the first instance judge had found:

'Had the defendants, whether in 1977 or 1980, issued warnings, then, no doubt, the claimant in the early 1980s would have realised what was happening and then, no doubt, the defendants would have reorganised work patterns so that Mr Smith could work without enduring further symptoms. Alternatively, if that were not possible, they would have, no doubt, dismissed him. As it was, the claimant continued until and after his symptoms had reached a stage where damage was irreversible.

Further, the defendants in 1977 or 1980, had they done their duty, would have reorganised their working practice so as to reduce exposure to vibration and hence the claimant may not ever have reached a stage when he would have experienced symptoms.

Put shortly, the pain and suffering and loss of amenity which this claimant feels is entirely, in my judgment, due to the fault of these defendants and if I am wrong in not deducting something for symptomless damage occurring before the date of knowledge then, in my judgment, the deduction must be miniscule. In other words, hardly worth deducting.'

The Court of Appeal then supported the above, stating:

'The judge was entitled to find that, in this particular case, had there been a proper discharge by the defendants of their duties as employers, white fingers would not have developed, notwithstanding the long earlier period of exposure. It was open to the judge to hold that, had the employers discharged their duties, there would have been no further significant exposure to the vibrating tools. As a matter of fact, on the evidence before him, the judge was entitled to reach that conclusion.'

3.36 The above shows that the decision of *Allen* is a decision on facts relating to the likely actions of the claimant and not on legal principle. As for contributory negligence in occupational disease cases, see para 6.35, below.

Apportionment for concurrent non-negligent exposure

3.37 The most controversial aspect of apportionment is argument based upon the concurrent but non-negligent exposure which takes place in many industrial disease cases. For instance, the daytime non-negligent exposure to brick kiln dust in *McGhee* (above) as opposed to the relatively short period of negligent exposure post-work. It is often argued that damages should be apportioned generally to take account of the fact that the defendant's breach of duty contributed to only part of the injury and the non-negligent exposure caused the remainder. There is limited case law to support such a proposition. In *Barker v Barker v Saint Gobain Pipelines plc* [2004] EWCA Civ 545 (a mesothelioma case), the Court of Appeal confirmed that when the injury is not capable of division there is no apportionment.[1] That is, where there is no basis rooted in scientific fact upon which an apportionment can be made, then none can be made. Other cases, notably *Milner v Humphreys* have held that where the causes are concurrent in time, then the likelihood is that the injury will be indivisible. Where they are sequential in time and the cause is a cumulative exposure, then they are likely to be divisible. The words of Longmore J in the asbestosis case of *Milner v Humphreys & Glasgow Ltd* (24 November 1998, unreported) remain, it is suggested, an accurate statement of the law:

'... the principle [is] that where an injury is indivisible, any tortfeasor whose act has been a proximate cause must compensate for the whole injury, leaving the tortfeasor to sort out with other possible tortfeasors any other appropriate claim for contribution ... Where there are causes concurrent in time, it is not likely that an injury will be truly divisible; but where causes are sequential in time, it is not likely that an injury will be truly indivisible especially if the injury is a disease which can get worse with cumulative exposure.

... the principle is that where it is proved that a wrongful act has made a material contribution to the plaintiff's injury, the law regards this as sufficient discharge of the plaintiff's burden of proof on causation to render the defendant liable for the injury in full. That does not mean that no question of apportionment can ever arise, but it does, in my judgment, mean that, unless the defendant pleads and proves facts which justify apportionment, the plaintiff can recover in full.'

1   Although this principle in the Court of Appeal's decision was upheld, the House of Lords in Barker found in fact that each of the defendants' sequential exposure and contribution to risk was divisible (see *Barker v Corus (UK) plc* [2006] UKHL 20 and paras 3.15 and 3.21 above).

Causation and apportionment in stress-related illness

3.38 The situation in stress-related illness cases may involve further complications.[1] As with many occupational disease cases, in stress at work cases it is the cumulative effect of that stress that causes the injury. As with the occupational disease cases, some of this stress may be negligent and some non-negligent. However, whilst it is unlikely that a claimant would be exposed to hazardous substances outside work, claimants in stress cases are often exposed to considerable non-work related stress, such as at home. Causation and apportionment of damage in stress cases was addressed by the Court of Appeal in *Sutherland v Hatton* [2002] EWCA Civ 76. Addressing the issue of causation, Hale LJ stated:[2]

'Having shown a breach of duty, it is still necessary to show that the particular breach of duty found caused the harm. It is not enough to show that occupational stress caused the harm. Where there are several different possible causes, as will often be the case with stress-related illness of any kind, the claimant may have difficulty proving that the employer's fault was one of them: see *Wilsher v Essex Area Health Authority* [1988] AC 1074. This will be a particular problem if, as in *Garrett*, the main cause was a vulnerable personality which the employer knew nothing about. However, the employee does not have to show that the breach of duty was the whole cause of his ill-health: it is enough to show that it made a material contribution: see *Bonnington Castings v Wardlaw* [1956] AC 613.'

Moving on to address the issue of apportionment, she stated:

'Many stress-related illnesses are likely to have a complex aetiology with several different causes. In principle a wrongdoer should pay only for that proportion of the harm suffered for which he by his wrongdoing is responsible.'[3]

'Hence if it is established that the constellation of symptoms suffered by the claimant stems from a number of different extrinsic causes then in our view a sensible attempt should be made to apportion liability accordingly. There is no reason to distinguish these conditions from the chronological development of industrial diseases or disabilities.'[4]

'Where the tortfeasor's breach of duty has exacerbated a pre-existing disorder or accelerated the effect of pre-existing vulnerability, the award of general damages for pain, suffering and loss of amenity will reflect only the exacerbation or acceleration. Further, the quantification of damages for financial losses must take some account of contingencies. In this context, one of those contingencies may well be the chance that the claimant would have succumbed to a stress-related disorder in any event. As it happens, all of these principles are exemplified by the decision of Otton J at first instance in *Page v Smith* [1993] PIQR Q55 (and not appealed by the claimant: see *Page v Smith (No 2)* [1996] 1 WLR 855). He reduced the multiplier for future loss of earnings (as it happens as a teacher) from 10 to 6 to reflect the many factors making it probable that the claimant would not have had a full and unbroken period of employment in any event and the real possibility that his employers would have terminated his employment because of his absences from work.'[5]

1   See generally chapter 14, below.
2   At para 35.
3   At para 36.
4   At para 41.
5   At para 42.

3.39 The above approach was approved by the Court of Appeal in *Hartman v South Essex Mental Health NHS Trust* [2005] EWCA Civ 06, including the expressed requirement that the defendant prove the justification of apportionment, but the defendant's argument for an apportionment was rejected.

Intervening actions: novus actus interveniens

3.40 The most difficult cases tend to be those involving the intervening intentional or negligent actions of human agents other than the defendant. One person's negligent act (or omission) may set up a dangerous and continuing state of affairs, and an accident arising out of that continuing danger may still be interpreted by the courts as due to the original causes of the damage. There is no precise or consistent test identifying precisely when the intervening action will break causation—when it is termed a novus actus interveniens. The question of the effect of a 'novus actus' can only be answered on a consideration of all the circumstances and, in particular, the quality of the later act or event.[1] The law assigns some factors to background conditions—the existing circumstances necessary to the accident—and others to active causes, principally in reliance on little more than judicial intuition. As much is implicit in the words of Lord Asquith in *Stapley v Gypsum Mines Ltd* [1953] AC 663 at 687:

> 'Two causes may both be necessary preconditions of a particular result ... yet the one may, if the facts justify that conclusion, be treated as the real, substantial, direct or effective cause, and the other dismissed as at best a *causa sine qua non* and ignored for the purpose of legal liability.'

1   *Hogan v Bentinck West Hartley Collieries (Owners) Ltd* [1949] 1 All ER 588 at 593 per Lord Simonds.

3.41 However, there are four definable issues which require consideration:

(1)   Was the intervening conduct of the third party such as to render the original wrongdoing merely a part of the history of events?
(2)   Was the third party's conduct either deliberate or wholly unreasonable?
(3)   Was the intervention foreseeable?
(4)   Is the conduct of the third party wholly independent of the defendant?

The impact of intervening conduct

3.42 In the context of personal injuries, a good example of where intervening conduct may negate liability is *Knightley v Johns* [1982] 1 WLR 349. The first defendant's admitted negligence caused the blockage of a tunnel. After considerable confusion the second defendant, a police inspector, took charge of the situation. He did not immediately close the tunnel, which should have been the proper practice after such an accident. Subsequently he instructed the claimant, a police motorcyclist, to ride the wrong way back through the tunnel, against the traffic, to ensure that the tunnel was closed. Whilst doing so, the claimant was hit and injured by the third defendant who was driving too fast in the tunnel. The Court of Appeal decided judgment for the claimant against the first defendant. The sequence of events subsequent to the original negligence eclipsed that defendant's wrongdoing. The Court of Appeal stated:

> 'Too much happened here, too much went wrong, the chapter of accidents was too long and varied to impose on the first defendant liability.'

Third party's deliberate or wholly unreasonable conduct

3.43 Generally it will be easiser to establish a novus actus when the intervention of the third party is deliberate and intended. In *Dominion Natural Gas Ltd v Collins and Perkins* [1909] AC 640 at 646 Lord Dunedin said the defendants will not be liable:

> 'If the proximate cause of the accident is not the negligence of the defendant but the conscious act of another's volition.'

3.44 Although there are many cases in which that has proved to be a novus actus, there are other cases where even a deliberate human act may not break causation: see *Philco Radio and Television Corpn of Great Britain Ltd v J Spurling Ltd* [1949] 2 All ER 882. The difficulty is revealed in the following from Lord Wright in *Lord v Pacific Steam Navigation Co Ltd, The Oropesa* [1943] P 32 at 39, which simply provides concepts of equal vagueness as a means of 'explaining' when intervening acts will break causation:

> 'It must always be shown that there is something which I will call ultraneous, something unwarrantable, a new cause coming in disturbing the sequence of events, something that can be described as either unreasonable or extraneous or extrinsic. I doubt very much whether the law can be stated more precisely than that.'

3.45 In that case the death of a seaman following the capsizing of a lifeboat was held to be caused by the collision damaging his ship. It is here above all that judicial intuition is to the fore. For that reason, what follow are little more than examples, since in every case establishing (or breaking) causation is very much a question of fact. While the authorities purport to lay down guidelines, it is very difficult to apply these to any concrete facts; there must be every likelihood that the result is justified by subsequent rationalisation.

3.46 The more unreasonable the conduct of the third party, the more likely it is that the conduct will constitute a novus actus. In situations similar to that in *Knightley v Johns* [1982] 1 WLR 349 where a defendant creates an obstruction on the road which is likely to cause further accidents that defendant will normally bear some responsibility for the later consequences of his initial negligence. However, if a subsequent collision is caused by outright reckless-ness (*Wright v Lodge* [1993] 4 All ER 1299), or by total bungling by those involved in dealing with the first incident, the chain of causation may be broken (eg *Knightley v Johns*).

Foreseeability of intervening conduct

3.47 This issue may be relevant but in many instances may not be conclusive to questions of novus actus. Considering again the decision of the Court of Appeal in *Knightley v Johns* [1982] 1 WLR 349 the fact that the first defendant would not readily have contemplated such a string of foolish errors by the police called to deal with the obstruction created by his negligence was significant in concluding that there had been a novus actus. But the absence of foreseeability of events does not necessarily render intervening conduct a novus actus, as is evident from the facts in *The Oropesa* [1943] P 32, where the captain's conduct in putting to sea was not readily foreseeable. A particularly notable instance of where conduct was not foreseeable but not a novus actus is in *Philco Radio and Television Corpn of Great Britain Ltd v J Spurling Ltd* [1949] 2 All ER 882. The defendants negligently delivered parcels of flammable foam scrap to the claimant's premises. A typist touched one of the parcels with a lighted cigarette to pass the time by making a 'small innocuous bonfire', having no idea that the parcel contained highly inflamma-ble material. The defendants were held liable for the explosion, which seriously damaged the claimant's premises. The typist's act, although almost certainly unforeseeable, was not a novus actus. The court held that it was not so unreasonable or of such overwhelming impact as to negate the risk created by the defendant's original negligence.

Third party's conduct

3.48 Clearly, if the sole cause of the injury is not a negligent act of the defendant—it may be due to the actions of a third party or of the claimant—the action will fail: see *Judson v British Transport Commission* [1954] 1 All ER 624. When the conduct of the claimant is not the sole cause of the accident so no liability is attributed to the defendant, the claimant may by his conduct contribute to the occurrence of the accident or the exacerbation of his injuries. In such situations where the actions of both the claimant and defendant are deemed both to be causes, then the claimant's damages may be reduced owing to contributory negligence under the Law Reform (Contribu-tory Negligence) Act 1945 (see chapter 6, below). If, on the other hand, two or more defendants are both causative of the damage, liability will be shared in accordance with the degree of responsibility of each: Civil Liability (Contribution) Act 1978. In such a case a claimant may nonetheless recover in full against *either* defendant.

Intervening acts generally

3.49 Where, as in industrial disease cases, the specific negligent conduct of an individual defendant can be assessed for instance by the period of exposure, then the courts can attribute part of the damage to individual defendants. Conversely, however, where different defendants' respective torts were the causes of distinct aspects of the claimant's overall psychiatric condition and neither had caused the whole of it, the Civil Liability (Contribution) Act 1978, s 1(1) had no application: see *Rahman v Arearose Ltd* [2001] QB 351.

3.50 Specific issues arise in respect of the safety of equipment provided by an employer to his employee to undertake his work. In many instances the issue of who is liable for the malfunction or inadequacy of the equipment that causes or contributes to the accident will be resolved by the Employers' Liability (Defective Equipment) Act 1969, s 1(1). That section provides that an employer is personally liable in negligence if:

'(a)   an employee suffers personal injury in the course of his employment in consequence of a defect in equipment provided by his employer for the purposes of the employer's business; and

(b)   the defect is attributable wholly or partly to the fault of a third party (whether identifiable or not).'[1]

1   A defect includes everything that renders the plant etc unfit for the use for which it is intended if used carefully and as intended.

3.51 In cases of breach of statutory duty the claimant must still prove on a balance of probability that the damage was caused by the defendant's breach. However, even where the claimant can show causation in fact, the court may still reject the defendant's breach of statutory duty as the legal cause of the damage in favour of some other more important factual cause with which the defendant's breach of duty interacted. So if the court finds that the cause of the accident was the employee's deliberate act of folly, the employer will not be liable.[1] Similarly, such a deliberate act by a fellow employee beyond the employer's vicarious liability may break the causal link to the employer's breach of statutory duty, as in *Horton v Taplin Contracts Ltd* [2002] EWCA Civ 1604, [2001] ICR 179 where a fellow employee deliberately overturned a scaffolding tower on which the claimant was standing.

1   *Rushton v Turner Bros Asbestos Co Ltd* [1960] 1 WLR 96; *Horne v Lec Refrigeration Ltd* [1965] 2 All ER 898; see generally para 5.71, below.

REMOTENESS OF DAMAGE

3.52 Assuming that there is sufficient foreseeability of damage for a defendant to owe a claimant a duty of care, and that the breach of the duty caused harm to the claimant, still a defendant is only liable to a claimant if it was foreseeable that there would be damage to *the claimant* of the *kind* which he or she suffers as a consequence of the breach; and that the damage must be of the sort for which the law permits recovery (see para 2.22, above). As elsewhere in negligence, what a defendant should foresee is determined, in theory at least, by objective standards. The concept of remoteness of damage has limited place in claims for breach of statutory duty (see *Larner v British Steel plc* [1993] ICR 551 and chapter 5 generally) since the extent of the statutory duty is set out expressly by the statute alone.

3.53 At one time, remoteness of damage was determined by a double test: recovery was allowed for damage which was either reasonably foreseeable or which was a 'direct consequence' of the act, even if unanticipated: see Lord Porter in *Morrison Steamship Co Ltd v SS Greystoke Castle* [1947] AC 265 at 295. The direct consequences rule had its historical origins in the action for trespass.[1]

1 See Blackstone (*Commentaries* (17th edn) vol III, p 122):

> 'And it is a settled distinction, that where an act is done which is in itself an immediate injury to another's person or property, there the remedy is usually by an action of trespass vi et armis; but where there is no act done, but only by a culpable omission; or where the act is not immediately injurious, but only by consequence and collaterally; there no action of trespass vi et armis will lie, but an action on the special case, for the damages consequent on such omission or act.'

Trespass also included the type of case where there was an automatic sequence of events without deliberate human intervention: see *Scott v Shepherd* (1773) 2 Wm Bl 892, when a lighted squib was thrown in a market-house and persons in danger threw it away from themselves, as an automatic reaction.

3.54 Now, though, whether or not consequences are treated as flowing from the negligent act is largely a question of causation; and remoteness is a separate, distinct question. But the vagueness of the foreseeability test—particularly as to the intuitive decision of whether damage is of a different kind—allows courts a further measure of discretion whether to allow or deny recovery in a particular case. Put simply, if the consequences were intended by the defendant then they will never be too remote, and they do not have to be foreseeable. However, in cases of negligence there are two broad approaches to this issue. First, that a defendant is responsible for all the direct consequences of his negligence no matter how unexpected. Second, that a person is responsible for consequences that could reasonably have been anticipated. Although it is accepted that foreseeability is the proper test, in practice decisions about what it is that must be foreseen, combined with the principle that a defendant must 'take his victim as he finds him' mean that the limits of what is actionable lies between these two approaches.

Must be foreseeable that claimant might be injured

3.55 The concept of foreseeability is of central relevance to claims in negligence but often has no place at all in claims for breach of statutory duty (see *Larner v British Steel plc* [1993] ICR 551), and only where the statute expressly reintreoduces the concept into the language of the statute. If the kind of accident which happened is within the scope of the foreseeable risk created by the defendant's negligence it will not be too remote, and if the harm suffered is also foreseeable liability will be established (see *Jolley v Sutton London Borough Council* [2000] 1 WLR 1082 HL). However, a defendant may be negligent yet harm to a particular category of victim may not be reasonably foreseeable, in which case the defendant is not liable. This overlaps with the question of which persons are owed a duty of care by the defendant. It is sufficient that harm to members of a certain group, such as road users or those in the vicinity of a danger, is reasonably foreseeable. How close the claimant is in time and space to the accident will be relevant to whether he or she is within such a group; but, ultimately, the matter is not subject to a definitive test. The decision is very much one of intuitive categorisation.

3.56 Just as with causation, so the nature of the reasonable foresight test means that the intervention of a third party will not provide a defence if that intervention was reasonably foreseeable and so, therefore, was damage to the claimant. It is clearly foreseeable, for example, that if a person is in danger, others may take risks in trying to rescue him: see *Baker v TE Hopkins & Son Ltd* [1959] 1 WLR 966 (doctor called to well to assist workers overcome by fumes). That principle may permit recovery to someone who attempts to preserve property which has negligently been put at risk: see, for example, *Salmon v Seafarers Restaurants Ltd* [1983] 1 WLR 1264 (fireman injured attending at premises). Likewise, it is foreseeable that a person in a position of danger may well make an error of judgement which leads to greater harm; or that an injury 'may affect a person's ability to cope with the vicissitudes of life and thereby be the cause of another injury': Eveleigh J in *Wieland v Cyril Lord Carpets Ltd* [1969] 3 All ER 1006 (claimant whose injury caused her to wear cervical collar fell downstairs).

Damage must be within scope of duty of care

3.57 The damage must be within the type of damage which, being reasonably foreseeable, gave rise to the duty of care: see *The Wagon Mound (No 1)* [1961] AC 388. This rule is the counterpart of that applied to damages for breach of statutory duty (see chapter 5, below) and it inevitably overlaps with the test below.

Damage of particular kind must be foreseeable

3.58 The concept of foreseeability is of central relevance to claims in negligence but often has no place at all in claims for breach of statutory duty (see *Larner v British Steel plc* [1993] ICR 551) and only where the statute expressly reintroduces the concept into the language of the statute. To foresee possible harm to persons such as the claimant is insufficient; the defendant must, in principle, reasonably foresee harm of the kind which in fact ensues:[1] see *The Wagon Mound (No 1)* [1961] AC 388. As Lord Macfadyen put it in *Cross v Highlands and Islands Enterprise* [2001] IRLR 336, OH:

> 'It is, in my view, clear that if the injured party suffers no loss of a reasonably foreseeable type (or, to put the matter another way, if the only loss suffered is of a type that was not reasonably foreseeable), damages will not be recoverable (*The Wagon Mound*). But if reasonably foreseeable injury is caused, the wrongdoer is liable not only for that reasonably foreseeable injury, but for any complication, development or result of that foreseeable injury, even if the complication, development or result is itself unforeseeable. That principle, the so-called "thin skull" rule, was stated by Lord President Clyde in *McKillen v Barclay Curle & Co Ltd* [1967] SLT 41 at 42 ...'

1 See paras 2.22–2.30, above.

3.59 A claimant can recover for all injuries caused by the negligence so long as some injury to such a class of person was foreseeable, no matter how serious the extent of the injury, even if unforeseeable: see, for example, *Smith v Leech Brain & Co Ltd* [1962] 2 QB 405 (defendants liable for unforeseeable cancer following a foreseeable burn on a worker's lip caused by splash of molten metal).

3.60 Since the decision in *Page v Smith* [1996] 1 AC 155,[1] the courts do not distinguish between physical and psychiatric injury. If physical injury is foreseeable to the claimant then the defendant is liable for any psychiatric damage which the claimant sustained as a result of the defendant's negligence, even though physical injury did not in the event occur and the psychiatric damage was itself unforeseeable:

> 'Once it is established that the defendant is under a duty of care to avoid causing personal injury to the [claimant] it matters not whether the injury in fact sustained is physical, psychiatric or both.'[2]

1   See also *Simmons v British Steel plc* [2004] UKHL 20, [2004] ICR 585.
2   *Page v Smith* [1996] 1 AC 155 per Lord Lloyd at 190.

3.61 The decision in *Smith v Leech Brain & Co Ltd* [1962] 2 QB 405 upheld the so-called 'eggshell skull' principle, that if the claimant is unusually susceptible the defendant remains liable for the full extent of injury since 'the tortfeasor takes his victim as he finds him': Lord Parker CJ in *The Wagon Mound (No 1)* [1961] AC 388 at 414. By the same token, in cases of nervous shock (or 'recognisable psychiatric injury', the preferred phrase of Lord Denning in *Hinz v Berry* [1970] 2 QB 40) if some physical injury to a primary victim is foreseeable, he or she can recover for psychiatric injury whose extent is unforeseeable: *Page v Smith* [1995] 2 All ER 736, HL (physically unhurt victim of a road accident could recover for recognisable psychiatric injury).[1]

1   'There is no difference between an egg-shell skull and an egg-shell personality' as the matter was somewhat harshly put in *Malcolm v Boardhurst* [1970] 3 All ER 508 at 511.

3.62 An extreme example which demonstrates how the rule may work in attributing damage between two defendants is *Singh v Aitken* [1998] PIQR Q 37, where the defendant's negligence caused the death of the deceased who at the time of his death had an outstanding personal injuries claim against the first tortfeasor. His death reduced the value of that claim and the defendant was held liable to compensate for the consequent reduction in value of the first claim. The defendant can only escape liability if the damage is regarded as differing in kind from that which was foreseeable: Lord Reid in *Hughes v Lord Advocate* [1963] AC 837 at 845.

3.63 In practice the courts will rarely regard injuries as differing in kind. Lord Denning in *Stewart v West African Terminals Ltd* [1964] 2 Lloyd's Rep 371 at 375, spoke of the consequence being within the 'general range which any person might foresee (and not of an entirely different kind which no-one would anticipate)'. The consequences of a physical injury are almost never viewed as different in kind, exemplified by *Smith v Leech Brain*, above. Thus, employers were liable for encephalitis following a minor wound in *Robinson v Post Office* [1974] 2 All ER 737; for pneumonia and death which followed a leg injury in *Oman v McIntyre* 1962 SLT 168; and for frostbite caused by being in a van without a heater in *Bradford v Robinson Rentals Ltd* [1967] 1 WLR 337.

3.64 In some tension with these authorities is *Tremain v Pike* [1969] 1 WLR 1556 where a farm worker contracted leptospirosis from handling hay contaminated by rats' urine; the court held that while injury from contamination of food from rats or rat bites was foreseeable, the possibility of leptospirosis was not one which the farming community (in the 1960s) foresaw or ought to have foreseen. This decision seems hard to reconcile with *Page v Smith,* above, and is unlikely to be followed today for two reasons. First, the case would be brought for breach of the Control of Substances Hazardous to Health Regulations which imposes strict liability without any reference to foresight of harm (see *Dugmore v Swansea NHS Trust* [2002] EWCA Civ 1689 and paras 5.33–5.39, below). Second, the wider approach to foreseeability in negligence as demonstrated by the speeches of the House of Lords in *Page v Smith*. It is to be expected that in future the courts will increasingly approach the determination of the type of damage in a broad way, probably going as far as to treat all forms of personal injury as foreseeable as a result of the occurrence of any form of foreseeable personal injury.[1]

[1]   The opinion of the authors of *Clerk and Lindsell on Torts* (19th edn, 2005) para 2–128.

3.65 Nor can a defendant claim that it could not have foreseen the precise *manner* in which the injury was inflicted (subject to proof of causation): *Wiszniewski v Central Manchester Health Authority* [1998] Lloyd's Rep Med 223; *Jolley v Sutton London Borough Council* [2000] 1 WLR 1082. In *Hughes v Lord Advocate* [1963] AC 837 a manhole cover was left unattended but surrounded by paraffin warning lamps. A child playing with a lamp fell into the manhole, causing an explosion which injured the claimant. It was enough that the defendants could contemplate that children might play with the lamp and cause burning injuries; the precise, and unusual, circumstances causing the explosion need not have been reasonably foreseeable (nor the extent of the injuries). As Lord Reid said at 847:

> 'This accident was caused by a known source of danger, but caused in a way which could not have been foreseen, and in my judgment that affords no defence.'[1]

[1]   A similar uncertain penumbra of doubt concerns damage to property. In the *Wagon Mound (No 1)* [1961] AC 388 the Privy Council found that, while pollution damage from oil spillage was foreseeable, fire damage was not. Turning upon the prior, unreasoned decision as to how the harm is categorised, this distinction is an elusive one.

EVIDENCE OF NEGLIGENCE

3.66 The onus of proving negligence always rests upon the claimant, though the temporary onus of producing evidence, eg to show why trade practice has not been followed, may shift from time to time during the trial: *Brown v Rolls Royce Ltd* [1960] 1 All ER 577. The situation is very different in statutory duty claims where, having established that an injury of the kind envisaged by the statute has occurred, the burden passes to the defendant to demonstrate either that it complied with the statute or that any non-compliance was not the cause of the injury.

3.67 With the disappearance of juries from negligence trials, the rules as to whether the claimant has adduced sufficient evidence for a finding in his or her favour have become increasingly irrelevant. In general, a claimant will be concerned with two main aspects of evidence. In statutory duty cases, only the first of these is the burden of the claimant. First, there must be evidence of how the accident happened. If there was an eye-witness to the accident, even if the claimant alone, this requirement is satisfied. It is in the case of fatal accidents which no one saw that a claimant's estate is faced with a difficulty— eg when a person has drowned in a dock basin, or is found dead on a line of rails: *Mersey Docks and Harbour Board v Procter* [1923] AC 253; *Jones v Great Western Rly Co* (1930) 144 LT 194. But still there may be facts of a circumstantial nature which point to the accident having occurred in one way rather than another. The court has no right to make a 'conjecture', that is to say, a guess unsupported by the facts; but it is entitled to make proper inferences from the proved facts. It is sufficient if there are proved facts from which a reasonable person could draw an inference in favour of the claimant—which need not be compelling. This, in effect, is the principle explained by the House of Lords in *Jones v Great Western Rly Co*, above, distinguishing between unsupported conjecture on the one hand and legitimate inference on the other. But inference, theoretical or inductive evidence should not 'be allowed to displace proven facts': *Graham v Rechem International* [1996] Env LR 158, HC following *Hanrahan v Merck Sharpe & Dhome (Ireland) Ltd* (1988) IRLM 629, Irish Supreme Ct.

3.68 Second, there must be some evidence from which it can be inferred that the defendant has fallen below the proper standard of care, particularly when it is within the control of the defendant. A good illustration of the minimum degree of proof necessary under this head is *Vella v Llanberis SS Co Ltd* (1950) 84 Ll L Rep 140, where shiprepairer's men had access to their staging by means of a Jacob's ladder, which they left at night in a safe position; but on coming back the next day they found that it had been moved, and the ladder came away from its support when one of the men started to go down it.[1] The Court of Appeal held that it could properly be inferred that the shipowners ought to have made a daily inspection of the safety of the means of access, and that they had failed to do so. It was pointed out that if the shipowners thought that this was impracticable, they should have called evidence to that effect. The failure of the defendant to provide evidence specific to a particular issue or at all may be regarded as strengthening the case: *Wisniewski v Central Manchester Health Authority* [1998] PIQR P 324 per Brooke LJ.

[1] Compare *Flaherty v AE Smith Coggins Ltd* [1951] 2 Lloyd's Rep 397 where a load fell and injured the claimant though it was handled according to a proper and safe system.

Res ipsa loquitur

3.69 There is a class of cases where, as the Latin maxim says 'the thing speaks for itself'—res ipsa loquitur—and the happening of the accident is *in itself evidence* of negligence. This doctrine is a rule of evidence and states no principle of law. It requires to be specifically pleaded. The doctrine applies when the cause of the occurrence is not known and the relevant equipment or activity was under the sole control of the defendant.[1] As Morris LJ stated in the clinical negligence case of *Roe v Ministry of Health* [1954] 2 QB 66 at 67:

> 'This convenient and succinct formula possesses no magic qualities; nor has it any added virtue, other than that of brevity, merely because it is expressed in Latin.'

1   *Bennett v Chemical Construction (GB) Ltd* [1971] 1 WLR 1571.

3.70

In the case of *Scott v London and St Katherine Docks Co* (1865) 3 H & C 596, where the claimant, a customs officer, was injured by bags of sugar which fell from a crane, Erle CJ said:

> 'There must be reasonable evidence of negligence. But where the thing is shown to be under the management of the defendant or his servants, and the accident is such as in the ordinary course of things does not happen if those who have the management use proper care, it affords reasonable evidence, in the absence of explanation by the defendant, that the accident arose from want of care.'

3.71 In respect of the cause of the occurrence being unknown to the defendant, in the much earlier and important *Macfarlane v Thompson* (1884) 12 R 232, Lord Moncrieff LJC said:

> 'provided that it is proved that some defect in the machinery or plant caused the accident, it is not necessary to show the precise nature of that defect, and an onus is thrown upon the master to show that the defect was one for which he was not to blame'.

That is, the employer must show that the defect could not have been discovered by the exercise of reasonable care (this statement was approved by Lord Dunedin in *Ballard v North British Rly Co* 1923 SC (HL) 43 at 53). The remarks of Lord Moncrieff were based on *Fraser v Fraser* (1882) 9 R 896 where a rope supporting a steeplejack broke and, on proof that there was probably a 'nip' or kink in the centre which might have been detected by feel, it was held that an employer who had not carried out any examination could not be allowed to say that it would not have been discovered; see too *Walker v Olsen* (1882) 9 R 946 (stevedore's tackle broke).[1] In *Macfarlane v Thompson*, above, the actual decision was that the occurrence of an accident does not in itself prove a defect in the manner of rigging up plant (metal casing fell from top of boiler); there does not seem to have been an actual breakage.

1   Both these cases may be regarded as examples of res ipsa loquitur, and it is doubtful whether Lord Moncrieff's statement of the law applies in other cases.

3.72 The significance of the doctrine is illustrated by *Henderson v Henry E Jenkins & Sons & Evans* [1970] AC 282, which concerned a disastrous lorry crash due to brake failure. A pipe had corroded at a place not accessible to normal inspection. Despite evidence that the pipe ought to last a long period without inspection, the House of Lords held the defendants liable in the absence of their adducing positive proof of due care. This would include evidence that there were no special circumstances in the past use of the vehicle indicating that the pipe might have been subjected to a corrosive agent. Res ipsa loquitur was not mentioned, but the case is best explained on that basis.[1]

[1]   Ie the brake failure and crash raised res ipsa loquitur: Lord Pearson used 'a prima facie inference' which is much the same. The defendants excused themselves by saying that the part was not one which should be opened up and inspected, but if this was correct then the corrosion was abnormal, and the defendants failed to explain it in a way which excluded negligence on their part.

3.73 Cases of res ipsa not involving defective equipment are *Byrne v Boadle* (1863) 2 H & C 722, where a barrel rolled out of the upper floor of a warehouse without warning; and *McPherson v Devon Area Health Authority* [1986] CLY 44, where a pot of boiling water fell off a tray as it was put down. In *McLaughlin v East and Midlothian NHS Trust* 2001 SLT 387, OH, Lord Hardie (following *Scott v London and St Katherine Docks Co* (above), *Ball v North British Rly Co* (below) and *Murray v Edinburgh District Council* 1981 SLT 253) encapsulated the elements of the doctrine:

'in any case in which the pursuer relies upon res ipsa loquitur it is essential for the pursuer to establish first that there has been negligence on someone's part and secondly that because of the exclusive management and control in the defenders at the relevant time when the negligence occured, it can be presumed that it was the defenders who were negligent'.[1]

[1]   In that case res ipsa loquitur failed in respect of a hospital bed rail curtain which fell on a nurse but she succeeded under the Provision and Use of Work Equipment Regulations 1992, reg 6 and the Workplace (Health, Safety and Welfare) Regulations 1992, reg 5.

3.74 A good example in the context of employment is illustrated by the facts in *Bennett v Chemical Construction (GB) Ltd* [1971] 1 WLR 1571 in which two heavy panels fell onto the claimant workman and the defendants called no evidence. Although the judge was unable to find precisely how the panels came to fall, he concluded that they can only have done so because of the negligence of those working on the panels and his decision was upheld by the Court of Appeal.

3.75 The maxim does not apply where the operation (or equipment) was not under the sole control of the employer: *Carrigan v Mavisbank Rigging Co Ltd* 1983 SLT 316n (ladder collapsed). 'Control' here does not refer to actual control. In accordance with the non-delegable nature of the employer's duty (see paras 5.59 onwards, below), a right to control rather than actual control is sufficient.[1] If the claimant himself took any part in the operation, there is always the possibility that his own negligence was one of the causes of the accident. Yet the maxim may continue to apply, provided that the claimant's own negligence is clearly excluded: *Moore v R Fox & Sons* [1956] 1 QB 596.

[1]   *Lloyde v West Midlands Gas Board* [1971] 2 All ER 1240 at 1246–1247 per Megaw LJ.

3.76 As already emphasised, it is important to appreciate that res ipsa loquitur is not a rule of law; it is no more than a rule of evidence, largely based on judicial common sense.[1] Where an accident does not ordinarily occur without negligence, it is legitimate to infer there was negligence. It raises a presumption of fact which, if not displaced by other evidence or explanation, means that the claimant has established his or her case: see, for instance, *Turner v National Coal Board* (1949) 65 TLR 580; *Cassidy v Ministry of Health* [1951] 2 KB 343; *Moore v R Fox & Sons* [1956] 1 QB 596; *Swan v Salisbury Construction Co Ltd* [1966] 2 All ER 138 (presumption raised by collapse of crane, rebutted by evidence and positive finding employers not negligent). If an alternate explanation is equally as plausible as that alleged by the claimant, the claimant will fail because he bears the burden of proof: *The Kite* [1933] P154. The alternative view is that the doctrine reverses the burden of proof so that if the defendant shows that his explanation is equally plausible but no more so, then he will lose.[2] However, in *Ng Cuan Pui v Lee Chuan Tat* [1988] RTR 298 the Privy Council reaffirmed the view that the burden of proof does not shift to the defendant and thus remains on the claimant throughout. Apart from simple issues of proof, there are three principal ways in which the presumption may be displaced or rebutted.

1   *Parker v Miller* (1926) 42 TLR 408. Compare the cases on conduct of an undertaking under the HSWA 1974, and especially *R v Associated Octel Co Ltd* [1994] IRLR 540, CA.
2   *Henderon's Case* [1970] AC 282 and also applied in this way in *Ward v Tesco Stores Ltd* [1976] IRLR 92.

Alternative explanation not involving negligence

3.77 The defendant may offer an alternative explanation—even without proving it—of a way in which it is equally probable the accident could have happened, not involving negligence on its part. 'If the defenders can show a way in which the accident may have occurred without negligence, the cogency of the fact of the accident by itself disappears, and the pursuer is left as he began, namely, that he has to show negligence': per Lord Dunedin in *Ballard v North British Rly Co* 1923 SC (HL) 43 at 54. For, unless the happening itself points to negligent management as the explanation more likely than any other, the maxim does not begin to apply.[1] Thus it does not apply on the occurrence of a fire for which there are many possible causes: *Flannigan v British Dyewood Co Ltd* 1970 SLT 285. But once the maxim applies, a defendant cannot exonerate himself by hypothetical suggestions as to detailed causes: *Moore v R Fox & Sons* [1956] 1 QB 596. By way of example see *Colvilles Ltd v Devine* [1969] 2 All ER 53 (explosion of oxygen fed to furnace probably due to impurities in pipe, but negligence was not excluded as defenders had not examined filters); *Pearce v Round Oak Steel Works Ltd* [1969] 3 All ER 680 (piece fell off old machine due to metal fatigue: no proof of reasonable examination on purchase of machine second-hand); *Mullen v Quinnsworth Ltd* [1990] IR 59 (customer in supermarket slipped on oil; evidence of system of cleaning did not displace inference). A simple denial of negligence is not an alternative explanation and permitted summary judgment against an employer in *Bergin v David Wickes Television Ltd* [1993] PIQR P 167, CA (sledge under sole control of employers overturned, injuring actor).

1   This statement of the law was questioned in *Moore v R Fox & Sons,* above, on the ground that it was contained in a dissenting opinion, where it was stated that the presumption can be displaced only by (a) proof that the defendant exercised all due care, or (b) proof that the accident was due to a cause not involving negligence on his part.

Positive disproof of negligence

3.78 Since the essential purpose of the doctrine is for the court to infer negligence from the circumstances and sole control of the defendant, if the defendant can prove he was not negligent the claim will fail. So the defendant may prove by positive evidence that it exercised all reasonable care, even though it cannot show how the accident happened: see *Woods v Duncan* [1946] AC 401 (unexplained sinking of submarine); *Walsh v Holst & Co Ltd* [1958] 3 All ER 33 (brick fell off scaffold, but proof that regular inspection carried out); and *Turner v National Coal Board* (1949) 65 TLR 580 (unexplained breaking of wire rope in colliery which had been inspected regularly and found to be in good order).

Complete evidence of facts

3.79 Finally, since the principle only applies where the full cause of the occurrence is unknown, if the full facts leading to the accident can be shown, the doctrine then has no application. The court has to decide, on the proved facts, whether the defendants were negligent. This is the effect of *Barkway v South Wales Transport Co Ltd* [1950] AC 185 where a bus crashed as the result of a tyre burst; the defendant gave evidence of its methods of inspecting and maintaining tyres, and, since the detailed facts were available, res ipsa loquitur ceased to have any application: see too *Hay v Grampian Health Board* [1995] 6 Med LR 128 at 132.

Liability without proof of negligence

3.80 There are many circumstances in which a worker who sustains injuries in the course of his or her work can claim damages, either against the employer or against a third party, without proof of negligence. In the employment context, principally amongst these are the many statutory duties relating to health and safety in the workplace considered in general at chapter 5 below and in detail at chapters 15–27. Other statutory duties which impose strict or quasi-strict liabilities include the Nuclear Installations Act 1965, the Marine Safety Act 2003, the Environmental Protection Act 1990 and the implementation of the European Community Directive on Product Liability in the Consumer Protection Act 1987. These are beyond the scope of this book, relating more to the protection of the general public and environment.

3.81 It is instructive to consider the type of situation where the common law recognises an absolute or strict liability. The most significant of these is the rule in *Rylands v Fletcher,* sub nom *Fletcher v Rylands* (1868) LR 3 HL 330, imposing liability for damage caused by the escape of things that the defendant has brought on to its land and which are likely to do mischief if they escape, either by reason of their inherent nature or because they have been accumulated in quantity. This liability does not arise unless the defendant has brought the dangerous thing on to its land in the course of an artificial change from its natural use; and the harm or injury must be foreseeable: see *Cambridge Water Co Ltd v Eastern Counties Leather plc* [1994] 2 AC 264, HL, adopting a wide test of non-natural user (applied in *Graham v Rechem International* [1996] Env LR 158, HC. The rule has rarely been the subject of successful actions. But in *Transco plc v Stockport Metropolitan Borough Council* [2003] UKHL 61, [2003] 3 WLR 1467 Lord Hoffmann rejected an invitation to 'kill off the rule' by absorbing it into the law of negligence.

3.82 The precise extent of the rule is explained in general textbooks on the law of tort.[1] It is a cause of action attached to land akin to the tort of nuisance where the thing that does damage 'escapes' from the place where the defendant has occupation or control of land to a place outside his occupation or control. While there is no need to show fault, the defendant may excuse himself by showing that the escape and consequent damage were caused by an act of God (ie some violent catastrophe of nature), by the act of a third party, or by the act of the claimant. Liability is dependent upon the 'escape' of something from the premises where it is kept: *Read v J Lyons & Co Ltd* [1947] AC 156; *Cambridge Water Co v Eastern Counties Leather plc* above. There remains some doubt, however, whether the action applies to personal injuries at all. In *Read* Lord Macmillan considered that it would not, but in other cases recovery has been allowed.[2]

1   *Clerk and Lindsell on Torts* (19th edn, 2005) para 21.02.
2   Actions for personal injuries under *Rylands v Fletcher* succeeded in *Shiffman v Grand Priory in British Realm of Venerable Order of the Hospital of St John of Jerusalem* [1936] 1 All ER 557; *Hale v Jennings Bros* [1938] 1 All ER 579; and *Miles v Forest Rock Granite Co (Leicestershire) Ltd* (1918) 34 TLR 500, CA, but failed in *Howard v Furness Houlder Argentine Lines Ltd* [1936] 2 All ER 781 (escape of steam on a ship) on the ground that the 'escape' was within the premises, not to a place outside. See also *Perry v Kendricks Transport Ltd* [1956] 1 All ER 154. A form of strict liability is also imposed at common law for the escape of fire, although the exact nature of this rule is open to doubt. See *Clerk and Lindsell on Torts* (19th edn, 2005) paras 20.47ff.

3.83 Finally, injuries caused by animals can give rise to liability without proof of fault. The English law has been codified in the Animals Act 1971 and thus this is now statutory strict liability. Liability (s 2) still depends on the mere keeping of the animal, and no more need be proved if it is of a 'dangerous species' (see s 6(2)). For animals not of a dangerous species, it has to be shown that the damage was of a kind natural to the species or due to characteristics (known to the animal's keeper) not normally found in animals of that species, or not normally found except at particular times or circumstances.[1] These would include the specially dangerous characteristics due to an animal being tethered as a guard dog: *Cummings v Granger* [1977] 1 All ER 104.[2] Under the 1971 Act, s 5(2), voluntary acceptance of a risk excludes liability but by s 6(5) an employee who 'incurs a risk incidental to his employment' is not 'treated as accepting it voluntarily'. Liability is also excluded under s 5(1) where injury is 'due wholly to the fault of the person who suffers it'.

1   Discussed in *Cockhill v Muff* [1987] Ind LR, 22 June.
2   Apart from this absolute liability, there could always be liability for negligence in controlling animals and this is not altered by the Act, which merely replaces the old absolute liability, see s 1.

3.84 The majority of controversy under the Act has turned on the interpretation of s 2(2)(b) in respect of characteristics 'not normally found in animals of the same species' except at particular times or in particular circumstances. The preferred interpretation is that the second part of the passage is to be interpreted independently of the facts as decided in *Cummings v Grainger* [1977] QB 397.[1] This interpretation was approved by the majority of the House of Lords in *Mirvahedy v Henley* [2003] UKHL 16, [2003] 2 AC 491.

1   The Court of Appeal concluded that an Alsatian dog which attacked a trespasser was acting as a characteristic arising in particular circumstances even though this was normal behaviour for such dogs in such circumstances.

3.85 In Scotland, the former rules about strict liability for animals were replaced (where the injury occurred after 8 June 1987) by the Animals (Scotland) Act 1987. Under the Act, liability is imposed on the person who was the 'keeper' at the time of the injury: s 1(1)(a). To fall within the Act, an animal must belong to a species, or subdivision of a species, which by its 'physical attributes' or 'habits' is likely, if not controlled, to 'injure severely or kill persons or animals': s 1(1)(b). Liability under the Act extends only to injury due to the 'physical attributes' or 'habits' which bring the animal within the Act. In particular, under s 1(4) there is no liability for transmitting disease unless (in substance) it is incidental to a type of injury within the Act. There are exceptions to liability based on the fault of the injured person, voluntary assumption of risk, and trespass: s 2(1). A vet's practice was liable to a receptionist bitten by a dog in the employer's private garden in *Hill v Lovett* 1992 SLT 994: the evidence was that the dogs were of a pugnacious character.

Chapter 4

THE EMPLOYER'S DUTY OF CARE

The Honourable Mr Justice Langstaff

EMPLOYERS AND EMPLOYEES

4.01 This chapter will discuss the bases upon which an employer may be found liable to others. At common law, liability may arise under either contract or tort: the original formulation of the duty of care which an employer was said to owe its employees arose out of, and was allied to, the contract of employment, and there is an increasing tendency to return to a contractual analysis. Thus in cases which involve allegations of psychiatric injury, or which are said to arise out of the pressures which working practices impose on employees (such as 'stress at work' claims) the contract analysis is to be found more frequently than the tortious[1] (see, for instance, *Johnstone v Bloomsbury Health Authority* [1991] ICR 269, CA; *Hatton v Sutherland* [2002] ICR 613, CA; *Barber v Somerset County Council* [2004] 1 WLR 1089, HL; *Gogay v Hertfordshire County Council* [2000] IRLR 703, CA). In his speech in *Barber*, Lord Rodger of Earlsferry explores the extent to which specific requirements of the contract under which an employee works may have an impact on whether he may claim successfully for a breach which has caused him ill-health). A modern development is that whereas the tortious duty is expressed as, and is limited to, a duty to take reasonable care for the health and safety of employees (and arguably those in a position analogous to employees[2]) a contractual claim may be founded not just on a contractual duty to the same effect but also on the (automatically) implied contractual term not so to act as without good reason to be likely to destroy or damage the relationship of trust and confidence between employer and employee.[3] Under legislation, the liability of the employer may be to criminal charges (eg under the Health and Safety at Work etc Act 1974, whose provisions do not give rise directly to civil liability), or to civil remedies (eg under health and safety Regulations, principally those made under the HSWA 1974, but now also those specifically implementing European Directives (eg the Working Time Regulations 1998, SI 1998/1833) and arguably to a direct claim if it can be established that the Directive concerned has 'direct horizontal effect' (see chapter 9 below).

---

[1] This is explored more fully below.

[2] See below at paras 4.72–4.82.

[3] A contractual term recognised authoritatively by the House of Lords in *Mahmud v Bank of Credit and Commerce International SA (in liquidation)* [1998] AC 20, and developed in many cases since which have emphasised its utility in cases of personal injury, such as *Gogay v Hertfordshire County Council* [2000] IRLR 703, CA; the objective nature of the approach to be taken: *Meikle v Nottingham County Council* [2004] EWCA Civ 859, [2005] ICR 1, CA; and the importance of the qualification 'without good reason': *Miller Bros & FP Butler Ltd v Johnston* [2002] ICR 744, EAT.

4.02 The liability of an employer in tort may be of two kinds, which are not necessarily mutually exclusive, but which must be kept distinct. The first is best referred to as the 'personal' liability of an employer,[1] sometimes also termed primary liability. This refers to those duties which are imposed directly upon an employer as such by common law.[2] The second is vicarious liability, sometimes also termed 'secondary' liability, by which an employer is liable for the torts committed by its employees which have a sufficiently close connection with the employees' employment.[3]

[1] Though an employer may be corporate, nonetheless it will have legal personality.
[2] The same is true of statute: for the vicarious liability of an employer for a breach of a statutory duty which is imposed upon an employee as such, see *Majrowski v Guy's & St Thomas's NHS Trust* [2005] EWCA Civ 251, [2005] QB 848.
[3] The traditional formulation that the liability extends to torts committed 'in the course of employment' has been superseded as a test by that stated in the text, but may remain a useful guide. It is uncertain whether 'in the course of employment' has been rejected as an appropriate test in all circumstances, or whether it has been given a particular meaning where a tort has been intentionally committed, contrary to the instructions or known wishes of the employer, which permits of liability in those circumstances: see the discussion in *Lister v Hesley Hall Ltd* [2001] UKHL 22, [2002] 1 AC 215, para 15; and that in *Majrowski* at paras 28–30, 35 and *Bernard v Attorney General of Jamaica* [2004] UKPC 47, [2005] IRLR 398 at paras 18, 19.

4.03 The personal (or primary) liability of an employer encompasses the general duty of an employer to take reasonable care for the health and safety of its workers, and this book is mainly concerned with exploring the nature and extent of that duty. It extends, however, to the duties which an employer owes (by virtue of being an employer) to others who are not necessarily its employees, though the precise scope of this must be considered as being presently in a state of flux.[1] It is important to note that actions taken by employees in accordance with their express or implicit instructions are actions for which an employer is liable under its personal or primary liability, and not (properly speaking) vicariously: thus, as Auld LJ put it in *Majrowksi v Guy's & St Thomas's NHS Trust* [2005] EWCA Civ 251, [2005] QB 848, CA at para 29:

> '[Vicarious liability]… has traditionally been regarded as taking two forms: first liability for an authorised or negligently permitted unlawful act of an employee in the course of employment; and second, liability for an employee's unauthorised or not negligently permitted unlawful mode of doing an authorised act in the course of employment. Only the latter is truly vicarious liability; the former is primary liability.'

[1] In the previous edition of this work the authors concluded that, in the past, this duty has been owed in the main to employees and not to other workers, but that this division was 'becoming less rigid'. Since then, it has narrowed to exclude the possibility of an 'activity duty' arising by virtue of an employer's operations at a particular site being a liability arising under the Occupier's Liability Act 1957, though leaving open the possibility there might be a breach of common law duty for those same operations (*Fairchild v Glenhaven Funeral Services* [2001] EWCA Civ 1881, [2002] ICR 412, a point not subject to appeal when the decision of the Court of Appeal was reversed on other grounds by the House of Lords at [2002] UKHL 22, [2003] 1 AC 32). Operations conducted by an employer through its employees may cause injury or loss to others, whether through negligence, nuisance, *Rylands v Fletcher*, or by any development of these torts to give any requisite force to European Directives. An example of such operations being held to have caused injury to others is *Margereson v JW Roberts Ltd* [1996] PIQR P 358, CA.

4.04 Although the principal field of personal (or primary) liability of an employer is to members of its own workforce, this is not so with vicarious liability. Although many an employee may be able to bring a claim against an employer alleging that it is vicariously liable for a wrong as a result of which that employee has been injured (eg as the victim of a negligent, unauthorised act by a co-employee), non-employees too may succeed under this head. A common example is that of a road traffic accident in which an employee drives negligently, causing injury or damage. His employer will be liable vicariously where the driving is sufficiently closely connected with the employee's employment.

4.05 Traditionally the law has drawn a sharp distinction between employees and others. As a general rule, an employer owes a specific duty at common law to take reasonable care for the health and safety of workers only to those who are its own employees, and it is only for the torts of its own employees that an employer is vicariously liable. This distinction is becoming increasingly anomalous in the light of changes to the labour market and, in particular, the growth in the numbers of 'atypical' workers—the self-employed, agency workers, those on casual and zero-hours contracts, those whose employment is so intermittent that they may be regarded as employees (if at all) only when working, and those who are 'workers' but not 'employees'—when set against the decline in number of those workers legally classified as employees.[1] It seems odd that persons doing the same kind of work as employees should not be owed the same, or similar, duties by the employer or the organising undertaking. By the same token, it would seem harsh to deny recovery to an employee or other worker injured through the act of another worker, not an employee and perhaps uninsured, because of a narrow view of vicarious liability.

[1]   The percentage of workers who were self-employed almost doubled between 1979 and 1990: see Anderton and Mayhew 'A Comparative Analysis of the UK Labour Market' in Barrell (ed) *The UK Labour Market* (1994). The pattern of growth of these categories continues: Cully (et al) *Britain at Work* (1999); Millward (et al) *All Change at Work* (2000). See also Mark Freedland *The Personal Employment Contract* (OUP, 2003); and Burchell, Deakin and Honey *The Employment Status of Individuals in Non-Standard Employment* (March 1999, available at www.dti.gov.uk/IR/inofrm.htm).

4.06 Perhaps in the light of the increasing casualisation of the workforce, and the development of more 'flexible' arrangements under which one individual does work for another, the traditional sharp distinction between employees and others is becoming blurred. This is particularly true of legislative regulation.

4.07 A number of European measures have had the effect of extending health and safety protection to classes of workers who may not have traditionally been regarded as employees. Thus the Working Time Directive 2003/88/EC (replacing and consolidating 93/104/EC), which has been implemented in the UK by means of the Working Time Regulations 1998, SI 1998/1833, provides protection against the health effects of overwork not just to employees, but to 'workers', which is plainly a wider category (as recognised by the EAT in *Byrne Brothers (Formwork) Ltd v Baird* [2002] ICR 667, and the Court of Appeal in *Redrow Homes (Yorkshire) Ltd v Wright* [2004] ICR 1126, CA). This was despite a challenge to the jurisprudential basis of the measure, asserting it was one which regulated employment, not health and safety, and hence was subject to a national opt-out provision. Nonetheless, the ECJ held that it indeed related to health and safety in *United Kingdom v Council of The European Union* [1997] ICR 443. Less controversial measures have extended protection in certain areas to agency workers and those working under fixed-term contracts: thus the Temporary Workers Directive 91/383/EC specifies that they are to be owed the same level of health and safety protection as other workers in the user undertaking (see art 2(1)). The Pregnant Workers etc Directive 92/85/EC; Young Workers Directive 94/33/EC; and Posted Workers' Directive 96/71/EC also provide health and safety protection and cover most forms of 'employment'.[1] The Framework Directive on Health and Safety (89/391/EEC) provides that for its purposes (and hence for the purposes of those measures to which it acts as the parent Directive) a worker is 'any person employed by an employer, including trainees and apprentices but excluding domestic servants' and 'employer' is 'any natural or legal person who has an employment relationship with the worker and has responsibility for the undertaking and/or establishment'. The concept of an 'employment relationship' may be wider than the concept in domestic legislation of a 'worker'. Thus, in Case 186/83 *Botzen v Rotterdamsche Droogdok Maatschappij BV* [1985] ECR 519, the ECJ held, at 528, para 15 that 'An employment relationship is essentially characterised by the link existing between the employee and the part of the undertaking or business to which he is assigned to carry out his duties'. Hence it may be arguable that domestic statutory instruments which are intended to implement European law in the UK may not confer a sufficiently wide protection. However, the Court of Appeal has significantly restricted the opportunities for argument in *Governing Body of Clifton Middle School v Askew* [2000] ICR 286. It was held that, in the context of the Acquired Rights Directive,[2] 'an employment relationship' must be a reference to a relationship under some arrangement which goes beyond that covered by the phrase 'contract of employment'. However, that did not lead to the conclusion that the other arrangement must be non-contractual. It led only to the conclusion that, if contractual, that other arrangement was not, or might not be, regarded by the national law as a contract of employment. Thus it seems essential both for the purposes of common law and statutory protection that there be at least a contract between an employer and the individual providing it with his work under or by virtue of which the employer has an obligation to safeguard his health and safety. Non-contractual arrangements are simply not covered.

[1] The European Directives extending employment protection to atypical work do not make such a distinction and apply to 'workers' generally, as do the Regulations made to implement them. See the Part-time Work Directive 97/81/EC and the Agreement annexed thereto (cl 2) and the Fixed-term Work Directive 99/70/EC and the Agreement annexed thereto (cl 2).

[2] EC Directive 2001/23. Implemented in domestic law as the Transfer of Undertakings (Protection of Employment) Regulations 1981 ('TUPE'), now replaced by the TUPE Regulations 2006, SI 2006/246.

4.08 Existing duties in negligence seem to be tending towards a similar position, and there are signs of the common law extending equivalent protection to workers who are not, strictly, employees. This would seem to be a natural development of the law of negligence, which has since the decision in

Caparo Industries plc v Dickman [1990] 2 AC 605 been prepared to advance
the frontiers of liability for negligence by analogising the situation it has to
consider with those in which it is already recognised that liability will be
incurred. Thus it is entirely predictable that an 'employer' will be liable at
common law to a non-employee working for it for its failure to provide a safe
place of work, to provide safe plant and equipment, and to ensure safe and
competent fellow staff where that non-employee occupies a position which is
in relevant respects indistinguishable from that of a true employee. (It would
not, of course, be a true analogy if the non-employee had accepted responsibility as between the 'employer' and himself for the safe state of the place of
work, which turns out to be unsafe, for providing the equipment which
happened to be faulty, or for recruiting or directing fellow-staff in such a way
as to cause him harm.) It is less predictable, however, that an employer would
be liable to a non-employee for a failure to provide that person with a safe
system of work, for the true employer is in a position qua employer of being
able to require the worker to adopt it, and may not be in such a position as far
as the non-employee goes. So too the law is increasingly recognising duties of
care owed to those subject to another's control, regardless of whether they are
its employees or not. Finally, vicarious liability is a flexible doctrine. An
employee may be able to hold his employer vicariously liable for a tort
committed against him by someone who is not strictly a co-employee: the
possibilities of this have in particular been enlarged by a recent trilogy of cases
in the Court of Appeal: *Majrowski v Guy's & St Thomas's NHS Trust* [2005]
QB 848; *Viasystems (Tyneside) Ltd v Thermal Transfer (Northern) Ltd* [2005]
EWCA Civ 1151, [2005] IRLR 983; and *Hawley v Luminar Leisure Ltd*
[2006] EWCA Civ 18, which are considered further below.

4.09 But the starting point in contract, and in tort, both for vicarious and
primary liability, is still to decide whether a worker is an employee or not.
Quite apart from the primary duties in negligence, many of the statutory
duties are owed exclusively to employees, and by employers.[1]

1   So too liability is only owed by an employer: a shareholder of a company employer does
not owe an employee a duty of care: see *Sweeney v Duggan* [1991] 2 IR 275. That
conclusion is in accordance with the doctrine of corporate personality: see *Salomon v A
Salomon & Co Ltd* [1897] AC 22. However, if a director (or shareholder) has as a matter
of fact given the directions which, being negligently given, caused injury or loss the fact
that he is also a director or shareholder is no defence to an action against him. Thus those
who are majority shareholders, or 'proprietors' of small incorporated businesses do not
escape personal liability because they give the careless orders in their capacity as such. The
test is one of substance, not form.

Who is an employee?

4.10 In *Lee Ting Sang v Chung Chi-Keung* [1990] 2 AC 374, Lord Griffiths,
when delivering the advice of the Privy Council, described the question of
what was the appropriate English common law standard by which to
determine whether a workman was working as an employee or as an
independent contractor as one which '... has proved to be a most elusive

question'. He added that '... despite a plethora of authorities the courts have not been able to devise a single test that will conclusively point to the distinction in all cases.'

4.11 Various tests have been described in a variety of cases, the perspective of each of which has differed. In some, the question has been whether a worker was liable for tax or national insurance. In others, it has been whether his principal was alleged to be in breach of an employer's duties in respect of health and safety, whether there was a succession of pieces of work which might arguably be linked to form one employment under an overall 'umbrella' arrangement, or indeed whether the simple choice presented as between employee or independent contractor masked the fact that the essential contract with which the case was concerned was not one of service or for services, but of a different character altogether. The perspective from which the question 'employee or not' has been addressed may have to be kept in mind in appreciating how far each case advanced the search for the decisive criteria which Lord Griffiths termed elusive.

4.12 It can, however, be stated that an employee is someone who works under a contract of service, in contrast to an independent contractor who works under a contract for service. For the purpose of most employment rights, an employee is defined by the Employment Rights Act 1996, s 230 as: '... an individual who has entered into or works under (or, where the employment has ceased, worked under) a contract of employment.' Section 230(2) goes on to provide that: '... in this Act "contract of employment" means a contract of service ... whether express or implied, and (if it is express) whether oral or in writing'. By defining a contract of employment as a contract of service the statute necessarily refers to the common law development or recognition of the essential requirements of such a contract. Those requirements were concisely stated by Stable J in one sentence, in *Chadwick v Pioneer Private Telephone Co Ltd* [1941] 1 All ER 522 at 523D:

> 'A contract of service implies an obligation to serve, and it comprises some degree of control by the master.'

4.13 Stable's statement was expanded by MacKenna J in *Ready Mixed Concrete (SE) Ltd v Minister of Pension and National Insurance* [1968] 2 QB 497 at 515 who said:

> 'A contract of service exists if these three conditions are fulfilled:
> (i)   the servant agrees that, in consideration of a wage or other remuneration, he will provide his own work and skill in the performance of some service for his master,
> (ii)   he agrees, expressly or impliedly, that in the performance of that service he will be subject to the other's control in a sufficient degree to make that other master,
> (iii)   the other provisions of the contract are consistent with its being a contract of service.'

In respect of the first two conditions, MacKenna J said this: 'There must be a wage or other remuneration. Otherwise there will be no consideration, and without consideration no contract of any kind. The servant must be obliged to provide his own work and skill.'

4.14 MacKenna J supported his view that the test of 'control' was not necessarily decisive, even though without it there would be no contract of service at all, by citing Lord Wright's opinion from *Montreal v Montreal Locomotive Works Ltd* [1947] 1 DLR 161, PC where he said 'In the more complex conditions of modern industry, more complicated tests' (than that of control) '... have to be applied. It has been suggested that a four-fold test will in some cases be more appropriate, a complex involving (1) control; (2) ownership of the tools; (3) chance of profit; (4) risk of loss. Control in itself is not always conclusive ...'.

4.15 Further support for his view was gleaned from a dictum of Denning LJ in *Bank voor Handel en Scheepvaart NV v Slatford* [1953] 1 QB 248: '... the test of being a servant does not rest nowadays on submission to orders. It depends on whether the person is part and parcel of the organisation'. Although in the view of MacKenna J this begged more questions than it gave answers, it at least supported his opinion that control was not everything (see [1968] 2 QB 524C).

4.16 Mackenna J's judgment as to the necessary conditions for a contract of employment has been referred to with approval by appellate courts ever since. Thus it was the citations from the judgments of Stable J and MacKenna J quoted above which led to Stephenson LJ in *Nethermere (St Neots) v Gardiner* [1984] ICR 612 recognising, for what may have been the first time, that 'there must, in my judgment, be an irreducible minimum of obligation[1] on each side to create a contract of service', words which in turn were approved in the speech of Lord Irvine of Lairg LC in *Carmichael v National Power plc* [1999] ICR 1226 (at 1230G–H). It follows that the necessary elements of a contract of employment can be restated as:

(1)   a *contract* by which:
    (a)   the employee is *obliged* to perform at least some work:
        (i)   *personally*
        (ii)   in return for pay or some other promise by the employer;
    (b)   the employee agrees that the employer has authority to exercise control over his work;
(2)   there are no sufficient contra-indications from the contract itself (or from the factual arrangements operated by the parties to the contract).

---

[1]   The nature of the irreducible minimum of obligation resting upon the employer has been variously stated in different cases. The judgments in *Ready Mixed Concrete, Nethermere,* and *Carmichael* (though there are parts of the judgment of Dillon LJ in the former (at 634G)) and Lord Irvine in the latter (see 1230G) which suggest the employers' obligation is to provide work) contemplate the obligation on the employer as being that of providing pay. In *Stevedoring and Haulage Services Ltd v Fuller* [2001] EWCA Civ 651, [2001] IRLR 627, the 'mutual obligations' recognised by the Court of Appeal appear to have been to offer work, on the employer's side, and to accept it, on the employee's (see para 6). It is

unnecessary, however, to approach the definition of the obligation which is required on the employer's side upon too narrow a basis: as Sir Christopher Slade observed in *Clark v Oxfordshire Health Authority* [1998] IRLR 125, at para 41:

> '... the mutual obligations required to found a global contract of employment need not necessarily and in every case consist of obligations to provide and perform the work. To take one obvious example, an obligation by the one party to accept and to do work if offered and an obligation of the other party to pay a retainer during such periods as work was not offered would in my opinion, be likely to suffice. In my judgment, however ... the authorities require us to hold that some mutuality of obligation is required to found a global contract of employment.'

(He went on to note that, in *Clark,* a case in which it had been contended by a nurse that whilst on the 'bank' and awaiting assignment to work she was employed under a contract of employment, he could find no mutuality of obligation in the sense he had just described '... subsisting during the periods when the applicant was not occupied in a "single engagement").'

In *Carmichael, Clark* and *Fuller* the central issue to which the question of mutual obligations was directed was whether or not there was a 'global', 'over-arching' or 'umbrella' contract of employment, such that periods when an individual did not do any remunerative work were nonetheless to be counted as periods of time when he or she was subject to a contract of employment. Thus Sir Christopher Slade expressly distinguished the position when the nurse was actually working during the course of an assignment. The issue in *Carmichael* was not directed to whether, when the power station guides were actually engaged in guiding visitors around the power station, they were acting as employees or not.

4.17 Each of these elements requires further consideration. It must be recognised that the courts have sometimes been equivocal as to the absolute necessity of some of them. Thus, although in *Montgomery v Johnson Underwood Ltd* [2001] EWCA Civ 318, [2001] ICR 819, CA, Longmore LJ said, at para 46 that: 'Whatever other developments this branch of the law may have seen over years, mutuality of obligation and the requirement of control on the part of the potential employer are the irreducible minimum for the existence of a contract of employment', Buckley J in the same case noted that '... as society and the nature and manner of carrying out employment continues to develop, so will the court's view of the nature and extent of "mutual obligations" concerning the work in question and 'control' of the individual carrying it out.', and Rix LJ in *Viasystems (Tyneside) Ltd v Thermal Transfer (Northern) Ltd* [2005] EWCA Civ 1151, [2005] IRLR 983 commented that '... the right to control the method of doing work, has long been an important and sometimes critical test of the master/servant relationship, although the inadequacy of the test as a necessary condition of such a relationship has also, over time, been demonstrated especially in cases concerning employees who have to exercise their own skill and judgment in their work (see *Clerk and Lindsell on Torts* (18th edn, 2000) paras 5–06–5–11)', and later added, at para 79; 'Even in the establishment of a formal employer/employee relationship, the right of control has not retained the critical significance it once did.' It is suggested that the comments of Longmore LJ are justified by authority, and that the views of Rix LJ are influenced by a tort work which does not fully appreciate the sense in which 'control' is meant: that it is not the fact of control over the precise manner of working which must be satisfied for control in the relevant sense to be established, but the acknowledgment between the contracting parties that the one has the authority to direct the other. As it was put in *Zuijs v Wirth Brothers Proprietary Ltd* (1955) 93 CLR 561 at 571: 'What matters is *lawful authority* to command *so far as there is scope for it*.[1] And there must always be some room for it, if only in incidental or collateral matters.'

1   Emphasis added.

4.18 The control test (the notion, inherent in the concept of master and servant, that a 'servant is a person subject to the command of his master as to the manner in which he shall do his work') was the first diagnostic test adopted by the courts: see *Yewens v Noakes* (1880) 6 QBD 530. With a growing sophistication in the division of labour and the emergence of workers employed by very reason of their highly-skilled autonomy, that test ceased to catch many workers who seemed, apart from legal niceties, to be employees. It was also inconsistent with a desire to expand the scope of liability. It could be pointed out that an airline pilot might plainly be an employee, or an architect be employed by a local authority, but neither the board of the airline nor the council of the authority could tell him how to do his work.[1] The courts however recognised that someone such as a consultant doctor could be an employee (see eg per Greene MR in *Gold v Essex County Council* [1942] 2 KB 293) if subject to a contract of service (a circular argument, perhaps), and that control could not be equated with giving precise orders as to how to do such as a medical job (see per Somervell LJ in *Cassidy v Ministry of Health* [1951] 2 KB 343). Until the re-emergence of the importance of control as a necessary condition (even if not sufficient in itself to establish a contract as one of employment), considerations such as these gave rise to other approaches to determining whether a contract was one of employment, or of some different character. It is important to appreciate when these alternative approaches were at their most popular.

1   The 13th edition of this work was in error in suggesting that the law's response was exemplified by a decision that a surgeon was an employee, despite the lack of any real control over how he worked, perhaps in part to ensure recovery to those injured through medical negligence, by reference to *Cassidy v Ministry of Health* [1951] 2 KB 343, for Denning LJ in that judgment made it plain that it did not matter whether the surgeon was an employee or independent contractor. The ground of liability was that the hospital, by inviting people in for treatment, undertook a responsibility to provide careful and responsible treatment by those who were on its permanent staff, whether under a contract of employment or not.

4.19 Thus in *Stevenson Jordan & Harrison Ltd v MacDonald and Evans* [1952] 1 TLR 101, CA, Lord Denning said that:

'It is often easy to recognise a contract of service when you see it, but difficult to say where the difference lies. A ship's master, a chauffeur, and a reporter on the staff of a newspaper are all employed under a contract of service, but a ship's pilot, a taxi-man and a newspaper contributor are employed under a contract for services. One feature which seems to run through the instances is that, under a contract of service, a man is employed as part of the business, and his work is done as an integral part of the business; whereas under a contract for services, his work, although done for the business, is not integrated into it but is only accessory to it.'

See also *Bank voor Handel en Scheepvaart NV v Slatford* [1953] 1 QB 248, quoted above. Although there are modern echoes of this test (see eg the judgment of Rix LJ) in the early 1950s, the Court of Appeal (and especially Denning LJ) emphasised the 'integration test': *Viasystems (Tyneside) Ltd v Thermal Transfer (Northern) Ltd* [2005] EWCA Civ 1151, [2005] IRLR 983. The test is open to the objection that it is imprecise, amounting to little more than saying that you can recognise an elephant when you see it—there is no test other than the impressionistic for the degree of integration which marks the dividing line. Many businesses nowadays contract out essential functions which were once integral to their business. Those functions remain integral to the operation. Yet instead of being performed by employees, they may be performed by third parties/independent contractors/the employees of a contractor.

4.20 The fact that the 'integration' test was in vogue at the start of the 1950s may however be important to explain decisions such as *Cassidy v Minister of Health* [1951] 2 KB 343, where the integration of medical staff in the functioning of a hospital was critical to the reasoning that the hospital (for whom the Minister had responsibility) was liable for the acts and omissions of the medical staff, and for over-turning what had previously thought to be the position since *Hillyer v The Governors of St Bartholomew's Hospital* [1909] 2 KB 820, CA. (In this turn of the century case, hospital governors were not liable for an error in treatment which might equally have been caused by nurses, who were undoubtedly employees of the hospital, or by a visiting consultant doctor, who was self-employed, because it could not on the facts be shown that the error was probably that of a servant of the hospital so as to render the hospital vicariously liable.)[1] The integration test, coupled with a finding that the hospital's liability for those working therein was not delegable, permitted liability to be established. However, this case is often mistakenly thought to represent authority that a hospital consultant is an employee: the reasoning as indicated above, is rather different.[2] Similarly, a case such as *Roe v Minister of Health* [1954] 2 QB 66 (concerning the liability of a hospital for an anaesthetist using ampoules with microscopic cracks stored in toxic phenol, which contaminated the contents of the ampoules) depended upon the liability of a hospital for services integral to its operation. Whatever the juridical basis may have been, the 'hospital' cases are now regarded as amongst that select band of cases in which the courts will recognise that a defendant owes a non-delegable duty to anyone injured by his operations.[3] Closely allied with the 'integration' test is that of 'organisational reality' (*Young & Woods Ltd v West* [1980] IRLR 201, CA) which is open to the same objections.

---

[1] Such a problem, where there is admitted negligence but no way of knowing which of two potential tortfeasors is responsible for it, would nowadays be approached by applying the principle in *Fairchild v Glenhaven Funeral Services* [2002] UKHL 22, [2002] ICR 789.

[2] Most consultants working in NHS hospitals are indeed employees: they have contracts of service. The reasoning however may be important to identify the position of the doctor working in a private hospital, part time, or the works medical doctor whose main practice

lies elsewhere. It is suggested that the hospital, or the works employer, is likely to be liable in both cases for any failure by the doctor, principally by application of the 'undertaking that you will have competent treatment' which the holding out of the hospital or works clinic provides to the would-be patient, and which was the critical factor in determining liability in *Gold, Cassidy* and probably *Roe.*

3   The others are extremely hazardous operations: liability for projections over or onto the highway, and cases of highway obstruction; possibly education cases; and the non-delegable duty of an employer, for which see paras 4.53ff, 4.99. See generally *A (A Child) v Ministry of Defence* [2004] EWCA Civ 641, [2005] QB 183, where the cases are reviewed.

4.21 A third approach—which links with the third condition proposed by MacKenna J in *Ready-Mixed Concrete*—is to regard the question as answered by a fundamental test (after considering all the relevant factors). This was proposed by Cooke J in *Market Investigations v Minister of Social Security* [1969] 2 QB 173, where he said:

'the fundamental test to be applied is this: "Is the person who has engaged himself to perform these services performing as a person in business on his own account?" ... No exhaustive list has been compiled and perhaps no exhaustive list can be compiled of the considerations which are relevant in determining that question, nor can strict rules be laid down as to the relative weight which the various considerations should carry in particular cases ... control will always have to be considered although it can no longer be regarded as the sole determining factor; and the factors which may be of importance are such matters as whether the man performing the services provides his own equipment, whether he hires his own helpers, what degree of financial risk he takes, what degree of responsibility for investment of management he has, and whether and how far he has an opportunity of profiting from sound management in the performance of his task.'

4.22 In *Hall (Inspector of Taxes) v Lorrimer* [1992] ICR 739 at 744F–H, Mummery J observed, in relation to Cooke J's test that:

'In order to decide whether a person carries on business on his own account it is necessary to consider many different aspects of that person's work activity. This is not a mechanical exercise of running through items on a checklist to see whether they are present in, or absent from, a given situation. The object of the exercise is to paint a picture from the accumulation of detail. The overall effect can only be appreciated by standing back from the detailed picture which has been painted, by viewing it from a distance and by making an informed, considered, qualitative appreciation of the whole. It is a matter of evaluation of the overall effect of the detail, which is not necessarily the same as the sum total of the individual details. Not all details are of equal weight or importance in any given situation. The details may also vary in importance from one situation to another ... The decided cases give clear guidance in identifying the detailed elements or aspects of a person's work which should be examined for this purpose. There is no complete exhaustive list of relevant elements. The list includes the express or implied rights and duties of the parties; the degree of control exercised over the person doing the work; whether the person doing the work provides his own equipment and the nature of the equipment involved in the work; whether the person doing the work hires any staff to help him; the degree of financial risk that he takes, for example, as a result of delays in the performance of the services agreed; the degree of responsibility for investment and management; how far the person providing the services has an opportunity

119

to profit from sound management in the performance of his task. It may be relevant to consider the understanding or intentions of the parties; whether the person performing the services has set up a business like organisation of his own; the degree of continuity in the relationship between the person performing the services and the person for whom he performs them; how many engagements he performs and whether they are performed mainly for one person or for a number of different people. It may also be relevant to ask whether the person performing the services is accessory to the business of the person to whom the services are provided or is "part and parcel" of the latter's organisation.'

4.23 In *Lee Ting Sang v Chung Chi-Keung* [1990] 2 AC 374, Lord Griffiths, for the Privy Council observed that the matter had never been better put than it had been by Cooke J in the passage cited above. The Privy Council adopted the test for the purposes of evaluating facts found by a District Judge in Hong Kong. That was a case in which a mason, working for a building sub-contractor, fell from a high stool and suffered injury. His claim for compensation was resisted on the ground that he was an independent contractor, not an employee. The evidence established that the mason had been told to work at the construction site by the sub-contractor; that the sub-contractor gave him a plan showing him where to chisel, but did not thereafter supervise his work, although the foreman of the main contractor did check it from time to time; that his tools were provided by the sub-contractor; that he had worked at the site some 20 days before his accident; that he was normally paid in accordance with the amount of concrete he chiselled but on occasions, when the concrete was difficult to chisel or the work involved only a small area, he received a wage for an 8am to 5pm day; that when he completed his work before 5pm he would assist the sub-contractor to sharpen chisels and would, after so doing, be paid for that work on an hourly basis, and that he worked from time to time for other contractors but would, when the work of the sub-contractor was urgent, give priority to him, telling any other employer, for whom he was then working to engage another to finish the work. The uncontradicted evidence of the mason was that he would be sacked if he disappeared from site.

4.24 The proper application of the fundamental test proposed by Cooke J in *Market Investigations Ltd v Minister of Social Security* [1969] 2 QB 173, and the individual indicia referred to in the passage cited above, compelled Lord Griffiths to observe (at 383) that:

'Upon these findings of fact their Lordships would have had no hesitation, in sitting as a court of first instance, in concluding that the applicant was working for the [sub-contractor] as an employee and not as an independent contractor. All the tests, or perhaps it is better to call them indicia, mentioned by Cooke J in *Market Investigations Limited* point towards the status of an employee rather than an independent contractor. The applicant did not provide his own equipment, the equipment was provided by his employer. He did not hire his own helpers; this emerged with clarity in this evidence when he explained that he gave priority to the first respondent's work and if asked by the first respondent to do an urgent job he would tell those he was working for that they would have to employ someone else: if he was an independent contractor in business on his own account, one would expect that he would attempt to keep both contracts by hiring others to fulfil the contract he had to leave. He had no responsibility for investment in, or management of, the work on the construction site, he simply turned up for work and chipped off concrete to a required depth upon the beams indicated to him on a plan by the first respondent. There is no suggestion in the evidence that he priced the job, which is normally a feature of the business approach of a sub-contractor; he was paid either a piece-work rate or a daily rate according to the nature of the work he was doing. It is true that he was not supervised in his work, but this is not surprising, he was a skilled man and he had been told that the beams upon which he was to work and the depth to which they were to be cut and his work was measured to see that he achieved that result. There is no question of him being called upon to exercise any skill or judgment as to which beams required chipping or as to the depths that they were to be cut. He was simply told what to do and left to get on with it as for example would a skilled turner on a lathe who was required to cut a piece of metal to certain dimensions.

Taking all the foregoing considerations into account the picture emerges of a skilled artisan earning his living by working for more than one employer as an employee and not as a small businessman venturing into business on his own account as an independent contractor with all its attendant risks. The applicant ran no risk whatever save that of being unable to find employment which is, of course, a risk faced by casual employees who move from one job to another ...'

Lord Griffiths went on to say that the case was so clearly one of an employee that the decision at first instance was plainly wrong, and could properly be reversed on appeal.

4.25 Subsequently, in *Lane v Shire Roofing Co (Oxford) Ltd* [1995] IRLR 493 the Court of Appeal came to a similar conclusion, although the authoritative judgment of the Privy Council in *Lee Ting Sang* does not appear to have been cited to them. The worker there was a builder/roofer/carpenter who had since 1982 traded as a one-man firm. He had obtained self-employed fiscal status, with a right to 714 tax exemption certificates issued by the [then] Inland Revenue. As a one-man firm he solicited work through advertisements, and when engaged by clients would of course be responsible for estimating, buying in materials, and matters of that kind. But that work dried up. His public liability insurance lapsed. He answered an advertisement issued by the respondent, seeking men to work on a large roofing sub-contract. When that job was nearly over, he left it at the respondent's request to carry out building works involving the re-tiling of a porch roof of a house in Sonning Common. While he was doing that work, alone, he fell and was injured. He claimed a breach of the statutory duties imposed upon an employer. The respondent denied employment.

4.26 The judge at first instance found that the appellant was an independent contractor, and not an employee. His reasons for doing so appear, from the extracts cited by Henry LJ in his judgment when the matter came to appeal, to have been that the appellant had his own genuine roofing business, so that he was a roofing specialist, and had the benefit of 714 certificates so that he could pay his own tax and was thus paid gross; that he had continued with that system whilst working for the respondents; that he could work without supervision and was relied upon to do so; that there was no guarantee of

121

continuing work, and that there was no provision for notice or dismissal. On this basis he was found to be an independent contractor.

4.27 Reviewing—and differing from—the judge's conclusions, Henry LJ (with whom Nourse and Auld LJJ agreed) said, in relation to the distinction between employees and independent contractors that:

'[it]... all depends on the facts of each individual case. Certain principles relevant to this case, however, emerge.

First, the element of control will be important: who lays down what is to be done, the way in which it is to be done, the means by which it is to be done, and the time when it is done? Who provides (ie hires and fires) the team by which it is done, and who provides the material, plant and machinery and tools used?

But it is recognised that the control test may not be decisive—for instance, in the case of skilled employees, with discretion to decide how their work should be done. In such cases the question is broadened to whose business was it? Was the workman carrying on his own business, or was he carrying on that of his employers? The American Supreme Court, in *United States of America v Silk* [1946] 331 US 704, asks the question whether the men were employees "as a matter of economic reality". The answer to this question may cover much of the same ground as the control test (such as whether he provides his own equipment and hires his own helpers) but may involve looking to see where the financial risk lies, and whether and how far he has an opportunity of profiting from sound management in the performance of his task (see *Market Investigations*).'

4.28 Henry LJ returned, against the background of those principles, to consider the reasons given by the judge. He noted that the reasons would apply equally to work being done under a short term single job contract of employment. It was argued that there was a distinction between a situation where an employer engaged men on 'the lump' to do labouring work—as to which Henry LJ observed that 'the men are clearly employees, whatever their tax status may be'—and that where a specialist sub-contractor was employed to perform some part of a general building contract. Henry LJ dealt with the argument, and the evaluation of the facts by the Court of Appeal by saying that he:

'... would put this case substantially nearer "the lump" than the specialist sub-contractor. Though the degree of control that Mr Whittaker would use would depend on the need he felt to supervise and direct the appellant (who was just someone answering the advertisement) the question "whose business was it?" in relation to the Sonning Common job could only in my judgment be answered by saying that it was the respondents' business and not the appellant's. In my judgment, therefore, they owed the duties of employers to the appellant.'

It is plain that each court regarded a 'lump' worker as an employee.

---

[1]   In practice, the courts have tended to decide what persons look like employees and then deduce the criteria for explaining whether he or she is from that appearance. The circularity of the exercise is clear.

4.29 The House of Lords confirmed that the determination of the question whether there is a contract of employment is one of fact in *Carmichael v National Power plc* [1999] ICR 1226. They held that the question was only an issue of law if all the terms of the contract were contained in documents which required to be construed.

4.30 The label attached to the relationship by the parties is given some weight, particularly where it appears to be the result of a genuine choice on the part of the worker: *Massey v Crown Life Insurance Co* [1978] ICR 590, CA; but less so if the worker has little choice: *Ferguson v John Dawson & Partners (Contractors) Ltd* [1976] 1 WLR 1213, CA.

4.31 A contract of employment is one of personal service. In *Express and Echo Publications Ltd v Tanton* [1999] ICR 693, CA, a contract contained a clause that provided that if the driver concerned was 'unable or unwilling to perform the services personally he shall arrange at his own expense entirely for another suitable person to perform the services'. He could not be an employee. However, a limited power of substitution is not necessarily inconsistent with employment status: *Macfarlane v Glasgow City Council* [2001] IRLR 7; *Kelly and Loughran v Northern Ireland Housing Executive* [1999] 1 AC 428, HL, a case which concerned the expression 'contract personally to execute any work or labour', and in which Lord Clyde commented (at 448) that:

> 'The engagement of a portrait painter personally to paint a portrait would fall within the definition even if it was contemplated that some minor work would be carried out by an assistant in his studio. The work need not be intended to be performed exclusively by the contracting party. But an arrangement with the painter that the portrait would be painted by one of assistants would not be a contract with the painter personally to paint a portrait.'

Perhaps surprisingly, the Court of Appeal in *Tanton* was not referred to this authority.

4.32 The courts have recently been concerned to determine whether the parties to the supposed contract of employment enjoy 'mutuality of obligation'. This phrase has a particular significance in considering whether claimants have been working for long enough as employees to claim those employment rights, such as that not to be unfairly dismissed, which may not be claimed unless first a sufficient qualifying period has been worked. It is unlikely to have any significance in considering the status of an individual for the purpose of asserting health and safety rights, which do not depend upon any such qualifying period. Once again, the perspective from which a court has asked whether an individual is, or is not, an employee needs to be borne in mind. Thus, in *Clark v Oxfordshire Health Authority* [1998] IRLR 125, a case in which it had been contended by a nurse that whilst on the 'bank' and awaiting assignment to work she was employed under a contract of employment, whilst Slade LJ could find no 'mutuality of obligation' covering such a period, he expressly exempted occasions when she was employed during a 'single engagement'. Thus, if she had been injured by the negligence of her employer during such an engagement, she would have had a claim as an employee, even though when viewed at a time between assignments she would not be regarded as such.

4.33 In *Stephenson v Delphi Diesel Systems Ltd* [2003] ICR 471, Elias J, giving the judgment of the EAT, drew these strands together in a useful passage:

> '11 The significance of mutuality is that it determines whether there is a contact in existence at all. The significance of control is that it determines whether, if there is a contract in place, it can properly be classified as a contract of service, rather than some other kind of contract.
>
> 12 The issue of whether there is a contract at all arises most frequently in situations where a person works for an employer, but only on a casual basis from time to time. It is often necessary then to show that the contract continues to exist in the gaps between the periods of employment. Cases frequently have had to decide whether there is an over-arching contract or what is sometimes called an "umbrella contract" which remains in existence even when the individual concerned is not working. It is in that context in particular that courts have emphasised the need to demonstrate some mutuality of obligation between the parties but, as I have indicated, all that is being done is to say that there must be something from which a contract can properly be inferred. Without some mutuality, amounting to what is sometimes called the "irreducible minimum of obligation", no contract exists.
>
> 13 The question of mutuality of obligation, however, poses no difficulties during the period when the individual is actually working. For the period of such employment a contract must, in our view, clearly exist.'

4.34 It must be emphasised that much depends on the perspective from which the court answers the question 'employee or not'? For instance, the mutuality cases are concerned with acquiring sufficient unbroken service to qualify for employment rights; and in cases such as *Lane v Shire Roofing Co (Oxford) Ltd* [1995] IRLR 493, the Court of Appeal recognised that in the context of safety at work, there was a real public interest in recognising the employer/employee relationship. Although the court should ask itself whether the worker was subject to control or, in the case of a skilled worker, whose business it was, these questions should be addressed in the context of who was responsible for overall safety of the work, which was a question of law.

4.35 A court will not conclude that an individual is an employee simply because he is not a self-employed person carrying on a business of his own: *Wickens v Champion Employment* [1984] ICR 365 at 371; *Ironmonger v Movefield Ltd (t/a Deering Appointments)* [1988] IRLR 461 at paras 19–21. If party to a contract under which he is not an employee, he may be in some other category: the contract might for instance be one of agency (see the discussion of the position of agency workers below), or of licence (see *Cheng Yuen v Royal Hong Kong Golf Club* [1998] ICR 131, PC; *Khan v Checkers Cars Ltd* [2006] All ER (D) 149 (Feb), EAT) and in *Ready-Mixed Concrete* it was held to be one of carriage of goods.

Agency workers

4.36 Many recent cases have considered the position of agency workers.[1] Agency workers usually have a contract with the agency through whom they secure work. This is unlikely to be a contract of employment. The person for whom they work, the 'end-user', usually has a contract with the agency for the supply of the services of the agency worker. This, too, is not a contract of employment, nor is the agency worker party to it. Thus in the usual case, the agency worker has no contract with the end-user. Because he has no contract, he cannot be an employee of the end-user (nor is he a 'worker' as defined by the Employment Rights Act 1996 or Working Time Regulations 1998, for that status too requires that the individual is obliged by contract to provide his services personally). Thus, on any conventional analysis, agency workers 'slip through the net', and are employees of no-one: see *Hewlett Packard v O'Murphy* [2002] IRLR 4, EAT; *Montgomery v Johnson Underwood Ltd* [2001] EWCA Civ 318, [2001] IRLR 269; *Franks v Reuters Ltd* [2003] EWCA Civ 417, [2003] ICR 1166, CA; *Stephenson v Delphi Diesel Systems Ltd* [2003] ICR 471; *Brook Street Bureau (UK) Ltd v Dacas* [2004] EWCA Civ 217, [2004] ICR 1437, CA. *Motorola Ltd v Davidson* [2001] IRLR 4, EAT is sometimes (wrongly) assumed to be an exception to this rule—but no argument relying on the fundamental analysis of a tri-partite agency/end-user/worker relationship: the only point raised on appeal was whether the end-user had sufficient control over the worker. He did: but the absence of contract between the worker and the end-user, and its correct categorisation, was not considered.

[1]   See also the Conduct of Employment Agencies and Employment Business Regulations 2003, SI 2003/3319, actionable in civil proceedings, para 10.30, below.

4.37 In both *Franks v Reuters Ltd* [2003] EWCA Civ 417, [2003] ICR 1166, CA and *Brook Street Bureau (UK) Ltd v Dacas* [2004] EWCA Civ 217, [2004] ICR 1437 the possibility that a contract might be implied between the agency worker and the end user, by virtue of having provided the services integrally for the organisation over a long period of time, was raised as a possible common law answer to the iniquity of the situation (which would otherwise demand legislation), as was the possibility (in *Dacas*, by Mummery LJ) that the agency and end-user might jointly be the employer.[1] In a powerfully reasoned dissent in *Dacas*, however, Munby J held out for the doctrinal purity of the *O'Murphy* and *Montgomery* approaches. The approach taken in *Dacas* was fully endorsed by the Court of Appeal in *Cable & Wireless plc v Muscat* [2006] EWCA Civ 220. In that case, M had been an employee of a firm whose employment was transferred to C&W under the provisions of the Transfer of Undertakings Regulations 1981. C&W understood M to be an independent contractor. M continued to submit invoices for his services (in the name of E-Nuff) but C&W did not pay them. In August 2002, M was told that C&W did not deal with contractors direct and that he must deal with them through an agency, Abraxas plc (Abraxas), with whom C&W had entered into an agreement under which Abraxas had agreed to provide contract personnel for C&W. E-Nuff entered a 'Contract for Services' with Abraxas by which E-Nuff agreed (in part retrospectively) to provide services to C&W.

An employment tribunal purported to apply the guidance in *Dacas* and, so doing, implied a contract of employment between C&W and M. The EAT upheld this. On further appeal, the Court of Appeal unanimously affirmed the reasoning of the majority in *Dacas*, and held that it was for a tribunal to consider, in the light of all the facts and circumstances, whether there was an implied contract or not.[2] Here, all that changed was the identity of the paying party, and that did not change what had previously been a contract of employment into one which was not (at least, where the new payer did so by arrangement with the original payer).

[1]   A suggestion adopted from that of Professor Freedland in *The Personal Contract of Employment* (2nd edn, 2003).

[2]   This, Smith LJ said' 'No doubt, if employment tribunals apply their minds to the possibility of an implied contract between the worker and end-user, there will be some cases in which they find that relationship, as in this present case. There will no doubt also be many cases in the future in which employment tribunals will conclude that a worker in the triangular relationship is not an employee of the end-user. That may be because they find that he or she is an independent contractor. It may be that the employment tribunal will conclude, on the particular facts of the case, that the worker was employed by the agency. Another possibility is that the worker may be found to have had a series of short employment contracts with different end-users but no continuing contract of employment such as will support employment rights. All will depend on the facts of the individual case. We find it hard to imagine a case in which a worker will be found to have no recognised status at all, either as an employee of someone or as a self-employed independent contractor. But that question must await another day'.

4.38 It is in this context in particular that it is important to recognise the perspective from which the court addresses the question of employment status. The 'agency' cases are all ones in which the agency worker has sought to assert employment rights of the kind protected or conferred by the Employment Rights Act 1996 and cognate legislation. Where the issue is health and safety, it is suggested that a court is unlikely to hold that an end-user's obligations to agency workers working for it are different from the obligations owed at one and the same time to direct employees of the business, for that would be to contemplate a difference in result in respect of the same factual circumstances, simply because one person was an agency worker and the other a direct employee. The degree of moral blame would seem to be the same, and the usual reason for not holding the self-employed person liable—that he is expected to protect his own safety—does not apply to the person who is to all intents and purposes (other than the formally contractual) indistinguishable from an employee. Similarly, one of the purposes of the law of tort—to encourage the maintenance of proper standards of behaviour—would be denied if the two classes of worker were to be treated differently, for this would permit poorer standards of protection for some. Where the issue is vicarious liability, there may today be a greater willingness to regard the end-user as a 'temporary deemed employer' and thus liable for the torts of the agency worker (see in particular *Hawley v Luminar Leisure Ltd* [2006] EWCA Civ 18 where a night-club bouncer, employed by a security firm to whom door-security functions were contracted out, was held to be a temporary deemed employee of the club such that the club were liable for an unprovoked assault by the bouncer in the street outside the club; and *Viasystems (Tyneside) Ltd v Thermal Transfers (Northern) Ltd* [2005] EWCA Civ 1151, [2006] ICR 327) thus answering Sedley LJ's concern expressed in

Dacas that a finding there was no contract of employment between the agency worker and end-user could have implications for vicarious liability. He, too, would have found it virtually inconceivable that any civil court would not hold an end-user liable vicariously for any torts committed by a (regular) agency worker (see para 72).

PRIMARY LIABILITY

4.39 Primary liability may be contractual, or tortious. An employer owes in either case a duty to take reasonable care for the safety of its employees. The fact that the employment relationship gives rise to a duty of care in tort today overshadows the existence of a parallel duty in contract.[1] Decided before the law of negligence was very developed, many of the earlier cases held that the duties rested on the contract of employment: see e g Lord Hershell in *Smith v Baker & Sons* [1891] AC 325 at 362. Though even before *Donoghue v Stevenson*, the view was expressed that the duties could alternatively be based on negligence: *Baker v James* [1921] 2 KB 674. The speeches in the case most often credited with identifying the nature of the duty which an employer owes an employee, by virtue of that relationship, *Wilsons & Clyde Coal Co Ltd v English* [1938] AC 57, indicate at least as much a contractual approach as a tortious one. *Matthews v Kuwait Bechtel Corpn* [1959] 2 QB 57 is Court of Appeal authority for the fact that liability co-exists in both (and the claimant may choose one or the other), and the contractual nature of the duty was influential in more recent Court of Appeal decisions in relation to transfers of undertaking such as *Wilson v West Cumbria Health Care NHS Trust* [1995] PIQR P 38 and *Bernadone v Pall Mall Services Group* [2001] ICR 197, CA (the issue being whether or not a transfer of liabilities under a contract of employment transferred liabilities for an employer's breach of duty to take reasonable care for the health and safety of its employees).

1   As to limitation of liability by contract, see paras 4.40, 4.41 and 4.84, below.

4.40 In *Davie v New Merton Board Mills Ltd* [1959] AC 604 liability to an employee was regarded as arising in tort, although Viscount Simonds held it might also be based in contract. A similar analysis was adopted by the House of Lords in *Lister v Romford Ice and Cold Storage Co Ltd* [1957] AC 555, Lord Radcliffe holding that 'the duty is as much contractual as tortious' and that an action could be brought at the claimant's election under either head. In *Spring v Guardian Assurance* [1994] ICR 596 Lord Woolf, at 635 and 646, accepted that a claim could be brought either in contract or in tort, following the approach of Lord Bridge in *Scally v Southern Health and Social Services Board* [1991] ICR 771. If there is a parallel contractual obligation, the question arises whether the implied term is one which can be excluded or modified by agreement. In *Johnstone v Bloomsbury Health Authority* [1992] QB 333, Browne-Wilkinson VC suggested that where the parties were in a contractual relationship that alone should determine their rights and liabilities, but this was not ratio. However, in *Barber v Somerset County Council* [2004] UKHL 13, [2004] ICR 457, Lord Rodger of Earlsferry was concerned about the interaction of the contract of employment with the duties of the employer: the contract specified the duties to which the employee agreed, such that a complaint that he was being asked to do too much (with consequential health effects upon him) solely by being asked to fulfil the requirements of his contract might cause a conflict of approach between contract and duty. This is always likely to be a tension in cases where occupational stress is alleged, though the extent of working hours in themselves may at least be regulated by the Working Time Regulations such that it would be unreasonable of an employer to rely upon an employee's contractual commitment to work in excess of such hours (even if that were legitimate, which it will not (generally) be once the revised Directive of 2003 is fully assimilated within domestic law). The pressure of the work in itself may not easily be susceptible to contractual definition, and so, again, the tensions may be capable of resolution. However, in *Johnstone v Bloomsbury Health Authority* [1992] QB 333 the issue was summarised in argument as whether 'contract trumped tort', or the other way round, and the latter was held by majority to be the case (see in particular the judgment of Stuart-Smith LJ).

4.41 But in general employees rely upon tortious remedies, perhaps because to do so avoids the uneasy interaction between express and implied terms of the contract of employment, as demonstrated by the conflicting approaches of the Court of Appeal in *Johnstone v Bloomsbury Health Authority* [1992] QB 333. Where the choice is unavailable, distinctions in the tortious and contractual rules as to limitation and remoteness of damage have to be taken into consideration: *see Johnson v Coventry Churchill International Ltd* [1992] 3 All ER 14. But usually either remedy will produce the same result. Even if an employer tried to limit the scope of the implied duty to take reasonable care of an employee's health and safety, that exclusion would probably be rendered void by the Unfair Contract Terms Act 1977, s 2(1), on the ground that it purported to restrict liability for personal injury. This was accepted by the Court of Appeal in *Johnstone v Bloomsbury*, above.[1]

[1] See para 4.40.

4.42 In the past the duty was often given the alternative formulation that an employer must not expose its employees to 'unnecessary' or 'unreasonable' risk: see e g *Hutchinson v York Newcastle and Berwick Rly Co* (1850) 5 Exch 343; *Street v British Electricity Authority* [1952] 2 QB 399 at 406. In *Wilsons & Clyde Coal Co Ltd v English* [1938] AC 57 at 84, the House of Lords articulated the principle underlying those earlier authorities, rejecting a narrow basis for liability. Lord Wright said at 64:

> 'The whole course of authority consistently recognises a duty which rests on the employer, and which is personal to the employer, to take reasonable care for the safety of his workmen, whether the employer be an individual, a firm or a company, and whether or not the employer takes any share in the conduct of the operations.'

4.43 Since then, the House of Lords have generally treated the duty as one 'to take reasonable care for his servant's safety in all the circumstances of the case' (per Lord Oaksey in *Paris v Stepney Borough Council* [1951] AC 367 at 384), adding, where appropriate, references to the more specific duties.[1] As Lord Keith said in *Cavanagh v Ulster Weaving Co Ltd* [1960] AC 145:

'The ruling principle is that an employer is bound to take reasonable care for the safety of his workmen, and all other rules and formulas must be taken subject to this principle.'

¹ Eg *Latimer v AEC Ltd* [1953] AC 643; *General Cleaning Contractors Ltd v Christmas* [1953] AC 180; *Richard Thomas & Baldwins Ltd v Cummings* [1955] AC 321; *Carroll v Andrew Barclay & Sons Ltd* [1948] AC 477; *Davie v New Merton Board Mills Ltd* [1959] AC 604; *Qualcast (Wolverhampton) Ltd v Haynes* [1959] AC 743.

4.44 The duty extends to health as well as safety: per Glyn-Jones J in *Crookall v Vickers-Armstrong Ltd* [1955] 2 All ER 12. It may include inquiring into the safety hazards presented by chemicals used in the course of work: *Ogden v Airedale Health Authority* [1996] 7 Med LR 153 (occupational asthma caused by sensitisation by X-ray chemicals); and monitoring the health of employees during employment, particularly where they are exposed to harmful substances or other agents. The duty to give protection against injury to hearing by noise, for example, is now well recognised at common law: *McCafferty v Metropolitan Police District Receiver* [1977] 2 All ER 756. It includes looking after injured workers by providing medical equipment or care to mitigate the effects of injury: see eg *Kasapis v Laimos Bros* [1959] 2 Lloyd's Rep 378; *Smith v Howdens Ltd* [1953] NI 131; *Barrett v Ministry of Defence* [1995] 3 All ER 87, CA (naval airman unconscious through drink). As to psychiatric injury, see chapter 14.

The main branches of the duty

4.45 Though it was the judges who had created the doctrine of common employment (which held sway between 1837 and 1948), they were eventually prompted, by the harshness of the rule, to develop primary, non-delegable duties owed by the employer to its employees. The specific duties were to provide competent staff, adequate plant and a safe system of work. As Lord Maugham said in *Wilsons & Clyde Coal*, above, at 86:

'there was a duty on the employer to take reasonable care, and to use reasonable skill, first, to provide and maintain proper machinery, plant, appliances and works; secondly, to select properly skilled persons to manage and superintend the business, and, thirdly, to provide a proper system of working'.

4.46 See similarly Scott LJ in *Vaughan v Ropner & Co Ltd* (1947) 80 Ll L Rep 119 at 121:

'The three main duties [of the employer] are (1) to provide proper premises in which, and proper plant and appliances by means of which, the workman's duty is to be performed; (2) to maintain premises, plant and apparatus in a proper condition; (3) to establish and enforce a proper system of working'.

4.47 These two dicta provide a useful guide to the scope and nature of the duty establishing four elements: plant, premises, staff, and system of work. However, precedent rather than the broad principle is now the most reliable guide.

4.48 It must be stressed that the duty is not confined to these matters. An employer may, for instance, be under a duty to warn an employee of the risks of employment, something which cannot be readily placed in any of the above categories; nor can the duty to provide medical care (*Kasapis v Laimos Bros* [1959] 2 Lloyd's Rep 378). Likewise, where employees work overseas and a war situation or other serious danger arises, the employer's duty may extend to evacuating them or advising them to leave, depending on how imminent and how serious the danger is: *Longworth v Coppas International (UK) Ltd* 1985 SLT 111. But an employer in general has no duty to protect the financial welfare of an employee, for instance by advising him to take out insurance in a country where road accidents are not compensated: *Reid v Rush & Tompkins Group plc* [1990] ICR 61, CA; nor does the duty to provide a safe system of work impose on the employer a duty to protect a worker's possessions: *Deyong v Shenburn* [1946] KB 227 (actor's theatrical equipment stolen from insecure dressing room whilst he was on stage as pantomime dame).[1]

---

[1] But a contractual duty can arise in some circumstances: see *Scally v Southern Health and Social Services Board* [1992] 1 AC 294, HL.

4.49 However, it may be a mistake to regard the duties as separate duties: see the judgment of Parker LJ in *Wilson v Tyneside Window Cleaning Co* [1958] 2 QB 110, CA, at 123–24: 'for myself, I prefer to consider the master's duty as one applicable in all circumstances, namely, to take reasonable care for the safety of his men, or … to take reasonable care so to carry out his operation as not to subject those employed by him to unnecessary risk.' Thus, where an employee was injured when he slipped on a raised tile that had been left unguarded on the floor of a computer room in Saudi Arabia, owned and managed by a reliable company which was not the employer, the employer was not liable for a breach of its (non-delegable) duty to take reasonable care for his health and safety. It was not permissible to focus on the duty to provide a safe place of work as being a separately non-delegable component of the overall duty: *Cook v Square D Ltd* [1992] ICR 262, CA.

Employer liable though performance of duty delegated

4.50 The primary duty arises just by virtue of the employment relationship and exists 'whether or not the employer takes any share in the conduct of the operations' (Lord Wright in *Wilsons and Clyde Coal Co Ltd v English* [1938] AC 57 at 84, and see para 5.71, below). Thus, if the employer delegates performance of this duty to another, the employer remains liable if the duty is breached since the duty itself is non-delegable. It is not sufficient for the employer merely to select a competent person to perform the duty: see Lord Tankerton in *Wilsons* at 64, Lord Wright at 78. In the words of Parker LJ in *Davie v New Merton Board Mills Ltd* [1958] 1 QB 210 at 237–238, CA (decision upheld in the House of Lords, see below):

'The duty owed by a master to his servant at common law can be stated in general terms as a duty to take reasonable care for the safety of his servants … if the master delegates … the performance of that duty to another he remains liable for the failure of that other to exercise reasonable care … this principle holds good whether the person employed [ie employed to carry out the duty] by the master is a servant, a full-time agent or an independent contractor.'

4.51 This principle was explained in *Wilsons & Clyde Coal Co Ltd v English* [1938] AC 57 and clarified in *McDermid v Nash Dredging and Reclamation Co Ltd* [1987] AC 906, HL. It covers the personal duties to provide a safe system of work, safe workplace, safe plant, and competent staff (on the latter, see *Hudson v Ridge Manufacturing Co Ltd* [1957] 2 QB 348); and any other of the duties which are inherent in the employer's duty to take reasonable care for the health and safety of its employees. Subject to the approach taken in *Cook v Square D Ltd* [1992] ICR 262,[1] only if the employer shows that both it *and* the person charged with the performance of the duty exercised reasonable care is the relevant duty not breached. As Lord Tucker said in *Davie v New Merton Board Mills Ltd* [1959] AC 604:

'the employer may delegate the performance of his obligations in this sphere to someone who is more properly described as a contractor than a servant, but this does not affect the liability of the employer, he will be just as much liable for his negligence as for that of his servant. Such a contractor is entrusted by the employer with the performance of the employer's personal duty'.[2]

1 See para 4.49, above.
2 Of course in *Davie* the employer's liability was held not to extend to cover the negligent manufacturer of a tool, this case leading to the Employer's Liability (Defective Equipment) Act 1969. Similarly, it is suggested that an employer would not be held liable if it instructed the employee to travel abroad, and in the course of the flight conducted by a reputable carrier pilot error caused injury or death: though if it provided works' transport home in a minibus, driven by a co-employee, it would be liable.

4.52 The contractor is, in effect, the employer's agent. The position is succinctly encapsulated by Kennedy LJ in *Nelhams v Sandells Maintenance Ltd and Gillespie (UK) Ltd* [1996] PIQR P 52[1] at 55 (painter fell from unfooted ladder whilst working under supervision of contractor to employer):

'Where the employee has been instructed, in the course of his employment, to go to a site which his employer does not control, and to work there under the directions of a supervisor or supervisors employed by others who thus become the agents through whom the general employer seeks to discharge his obligations to his employee, ... the employer remains liable if the agents themselves do not use due care and skill in carrying out the employer's duty (*Wilson & Clyde Coal Co v English* [1938] AC 57). As Lord Hailsham said in *McDermid v Nash Dredging Reclamation Co* [1987] AC 906 at 910, "the employer cannot escape liability if the duty has been delegated and then not properly performed".

Beldam LJ pointed out in *Morris* that if there is negligence on the part of the supervisor to whom the claimant has been entrusted, the employers of that supervisor may be vicariously liable for his negligence, so it is entirely possible that more than one defendant will be found liable.'

1 It may be thought there is a conflict in approach between this case and that of *Cook v Square D Ltd*, above, which was not cited to the court.

4.53 Hence the courts may find employers primarily liable for the negligence of those who are not their employees, if that negligence caused a breach of the duty which the employer owes to the employee. In *McDermid v Nash Dredging and Reclamation Co Ltd*, above, an employee of the defendants was working on a tug owned by a Dutch company under the control of a Dutch captain employed by that company. As part of his work the claimant would untie mooring lines and would give a double knock when the ropes were cast off. On one occasion, the captain pulled away without waiting for the signal, injuring the claimant in the process. The House of Lords recognised that the employers' duty extended to the *operation* as well as the *provision* of a safe system of work (see Lord Hailsham at 911, Lord Brandon at 919). Because the acts of the captain were 'central' to the system and not 'casual', the primary duty was breached. The case illustrates how strict the duty is. It is noteworthy that the liability was that of the employer personally: the employer would not have been vicariously liable for the captain's actions, for he was not an employee—though if he had been, the employer would have been liable in this way, too. This illustrates how vicarious and primary liability can overlap.

4.54 In the past the courts have held employers not liable for acts of 'casual' or 'collateral' negligence which did not arise in the course of the act which the contractor was employed to perform: *Pearson v Cox* (1877) 2 CPD 369; *Penny v Wimbledon Urban District Council* [1899] 2 QB 72; *Padbury v Holliday and Greenwood Ltd* (1912) 28 TLR 494. But the courts have viewed this exemption restrictively: *Holliday v National Telephone Co* [1899] 2 QB 392, CA; and in *Salsbury v Woodland* [1970] 1 QB 324 at 348, CA, Sachs LJ 'derived no assistance at all from any distinction between "collateral and casual" negligence and other negligence'. The exemption was given short shrift by the House of Lords in *McDermid*.

So it is that the employer remains liable for failure to impose a safe system of work even when the system (or lack of it) is in the hands of a third party.

4.55 So far as negligence in the supply of equipment by a third party is concerned, liability on the part of the employer appears to turn on whether the supply was in the course of work by the third party which was integral to the work of his employer (eg employer using ladder erected by its subcontractor or by site controller) in which case the employer is likely to be liable. The employer is not likely to be liable if the supply by a third party is done exclusively for itself without any interest in (or in ignorance of) the employer's work (eg tool manufacturer or hirer supplying equipment as its business), unless the circumstances are such that the employer had a duty to inspect the equipment or warn the employee.

4.56 So far as employees working at a place under the control of a third party are concerned, all depends on the particular facts: the fact that the employer may have no control, not even an opportunity to inspect, are factors to be taken into account.

Ultra-hazardous activities

4.57 An employer is primarily liable for damage caused by 'extra-hazardous or hazardous operations', acts which are 'inherently dangerous', whether that damage is caused to a third party or an employee: see *Honeywill and Stein v Larkin Bros (London's Commercial Photographers) Ltd* [1934] 1 KB 191, CA, per Slesser LJ at 200. This is a distinct head of liability from that arising in contract or the tort of negligence to an employee, and is distinct, too, from vicarious liability. Liability for such operations is not strict but the duty is high. This duty, too, cannot be delegated, so that an employer is liable for the negligently inflicted damage caused by an independent contractor it has engaged.[1] The precise scope of that which is classed as 'extra-hazardous' is uncertain. It was taken to include work likely to cause damage in *Alcock v Wraith* [1991] NPC 135 (re-roofing by an independent contractor of a house exposing neighbouring houses in terrace to risk of water penetration in joint between slates and tiles)—which seems rather too wide. It was said not to include scaffolding in *McTeare v Dooley* (1994) 228 HSIB 19. As Slesser LJ recognised, extra-hazardous acts will not cause damage if carefully and skilfully performed, whilst a low risk activity may cause damage if negligently performed. What are involved under this rubric are, per Slesser LJ in *Honeywill* at 197:

> 'acts which, in their very nature, involve in the eyes of the law special danger to others; of such acts the causing of fire and explosion are obvious and established instances'.[2]

Examples of especially hazardous activities might be explosive demolition, or entering into competitive motor rallies. Further examples might be supplied if jurisprudence develops in relation to the Working Time Regulations 1998 as to what constitutes work involving special hazards: such work must not be performed in shifts of longer than eight hours at night, though longer shifts are permissible where work does not involve such special hazards (reg 6).[3]

1 See *Honeywill*, above; *Holliday v National Telephone Co* [1899] 2 QB 392; *Brooke v Bool* [1928] 2 KB 578.
2 See *Clerk and Lindsell on Torts* (19th edn, 2005) para 6–63 for further discussion and examples.
3 It has been suggested in litigation that work as an underground shift supervisor or face worker in a deep mine involves such special hazards, but the suggestion has not yet come to trial.

Inherent risks of employment

4.58 At one time, as a variant of the doctrine of common employment (see para 1.13, above), the courts sometimes said that an employee accepts the risk of the inherent dangers of employment and must mainly rely upon his own skill and nerve for his safety: cf *Thomas v Quatermaine* (1887) 18 QBD 685. That view is now unsustainable, in so far as it means that the employee is obliged to excuse his employer for the latter's negligence: see para 1.35. The duty is always on the employer to take reasonable care to reduce the risks of employment to a level which is reasonable, by providing a system of work, which being designed at leisure for use in places of danger is for the employer

133

to prescribe: *General Cleaning Contractors Ltd v Christmas* [1953] AC 180; *Ellis v Ocean Steamship Co Ltd* [1958] 2 Lloyd's Rep 373, CA. It is thus never an answer to an employee's claim that his employer has been in breach of duty to ask the employee in pleadings how he suggests matters should have been organised. That is the employer's responsibility, and a sufficient answer is clear: 'safely'. The greater the danger of the employment, the higher the degree of care expected from the employer: *Paris v Stepney Borough Council* [1951] AC 367, per Lord Morton.

4.59 However, an employer's duty is not that of an insurer. It does not undertake that there will be no risk, merely that such risks as there are will be reduced so far as reasonable.[1] To the extent that this leaves an employee at risk, he will accept the inherent risks that cannot be avoided by the exercise of such reasonable care and skill on his employer's part. Thus, an employee engaged to play rugby football will accept the risk of injury in a legitimate tackle; a stuntman the risks inherent in the stunts he is employed to perform; the steel erector the risks of working at height (with proper precautions); and an employee who is aware that there are special risks to him or her which may make injury inevitable may undertake to run those risks without there being recourse to his employer should injury occur. Thus in *Withers v Perry Chain Co Ltd* [1961] 1 WLR 1314, CA an employee was specifically asked to do work which she knew would expose her to cutting oil, when such exposure was likely to cause her extensive dermatitis. The employer's precautions were reasonable so far as the general run of employees was concerned. It was held that the employer had no duty in such a case to refuse employment, and that when dermatitis arose the employee could not successfully claim for it. Devlin LJ said: 'The relationship between employer and employee is not that of schoolmaster and pupil ... the employee is free to decide for herself what risks she will run ... if the common law were to be otherwise it would be oppressive to the employee by limiting his ability to find work, rather than beneficial to him.' This was cited with approval in *Dugmore v Swansea NHS Trust* [2002] EWCA Civ 1689, and echoed in *Hatton v Sutherland* [2002] EWCA Civ 76, [2002] 2 All ER 1 (para 34): 'In principle the law should not be saying to an employer that it is his duty to sack an employee who wants to go on working for him for the employee's own good', but in *Coxall v Goodyear Great Britain Ltd* [2002] EWCA Civ 1010, [2003] ICR 152, Simon Brown LJ was inclined to accept that all must depend on the circumstances. He suggested that employers might remain liable (for injury from falls) if, for instance, they retained as spidermen employees whom they knew to suffer intermittently from vertigo or epileptic fits, and there is strong support for this approach from European legislation which stresses adapting the work to the individual. Indeed there must now be doubt as to whether the 'Withers principle' would survive analysis against the backcloth of general European legislation (see paras 6.63–6.69, below).

---

[1]   Whether the duty is based on tort or contract, the employer is not under an absolute duty to ensure safety: a lack of reasonable care must always be shown. The common law makes no contractual promise, for instance, that machinery, plant or the system of work is absolutely safe: *Weems v Mathieson* (1861) 4 Macq 215, 149 RR 322 per Lord Wensleydale; *Wilsons and Clyde Coal Co v English* [1938] AC 57 per Lord Wright; *General Cleaning Contractors Ltd v Christmas* [1953] AC 180 per Lord Tucker; *Davie v New Merton Board Mills Ltd* [1959] AC 604.

4.60 An employer will only escape liability in those increasingly exceptional cases where there was nothing which could reasonably be done to protect against the risk: see eg *Rands v McNeil* [1955] 1 QB 253 (farm worker injured by bull);[1] *Watt v Hertfordshire County Council* [1954] 2 All ER 368 (unsuitable lorry used by fire brigade in emergency). With increases in knowledge of prevention or reduction of risks, earlier cases often become an unreliable guide to what will be expected of employers today: see eg *King v Smith* [1995] ICR 339, CA (intensifying duty to warn window-cleaners).

1   Since the Animals Act 1971 it is no longer permissible to rely on volenti as a defence to strict liability for dangerous animals since, by s 6(5), an employee of an animal keeper incurring 'a risk incidental to his employment shall not be treated as accepting it voluntarily'.

Duty owed to each individual

4.61 The employer's duty of care is owed to each employee as an individual: *Paris v Stepney Borough Council* [1951] AC 367. Hence an employer must take into account any special weakness or peculiarity of the worker of which the employer knows or ought to know, such as having one eye: A higher standard of care is owed to an employee with an imperfect knowledge of English, or those with less experience. This individual focus is given further emphasis by the Framework Directive. Article 6(2) requires that work be adapted to the individual, including in the design of the workplace and choice of equipment and production methods; art 6(3)(b) requires that the individual's capabilities be taken into account as regards health and safety when entrusting tasks to the worker.[1] Both the Directive (art 7) and the Management of Health and Safety at Work Regulations 1999, SI 1999/3242 (reg 6) require the employer to institute health surveillance. It seems unlikely that the courts will hold that the duties at common law impose lower standards, and it is arguable that the Framework Directive should inform the content of the duty of care, notwithstanding *Cross v Highlands and Islands Enterprise* [2001] IRLR 336, OH. In *Hone v Six Continents Retail Ltd* [2005] ECA Civ 922, [2006] IRLR 49 the standard of what was reasonable was informed by the restriction to an average 48 hour week made by the Working Time Regulations 1998 (pub manager who said he was working 90 hours per week: court held entitled to find that his employers knew of an unreasonable risk to his health in doing so).

1   Council Directive 89/391/EEC.

Breach of duty responsive to the times

4.62 The fact that the duty is to take *reasonable* care inevitably means that the standard of care will fluctuate over time. In general, what might have been reasonable ten years ago may not be reasonable today. Thus, for instance, the noise produced by machinery which might have been thought reasonable 20 years ago may not be tolerated today; exposing employees to a smoky atmosphere is now undoubtedly unreasonable, whereas even ten years ago it was not necessarily regarded as untoward.

4.63 The standard is set by the courts, having regard to a general need to improve standards of protection from risks to health and safety (which is required by the HSWA 1974, s 1) and by European Directives (the Framework Directive 89/391/EEC is explicitly designed to encourage improvements in the safety and welfare of workers at work: see art 1(1)).

4.64 This approach was already that of the common law. Swanwick J in *Stokes v Guest, Keen and Nettlefold (Bolts and Nuts) Ltd* [1968] 1 WLR 1776, said (at 1783):

> '... the overall test is still the conduct of the reasonable and prudent employer, taking positive thought for the safety of his workers in the light of what he knows or ought to know; where there is a recognised and general practice which has been followed for a substantial period in similar circumstances without mishap, he is entitled to follow it, unless in the light of common sense or newer knowledge it is clearly bad; but, where there is developing knowledge, he must keep reasonably abreast of it and not be too slow to apply it; and where he has in fact greater than average knowledge of the risks, he may be thereby obliged to take more than the average or standard precautions. He must weigh up the risk in terms of the likelihood of injury occurring and the potential consequences if it does; and he must balance against this the probable effectiveness of the precautions that can be taken to meet it and the expense and inconvenience they involve. If he is found to have fallen below the standard to be properly expected of a reasonable and prudent employer in these respects, he is negligent.'

In the leading speech in *Barber v Somerset County Council* [2004] UKHL 13, [2004] ICR 457 Lord Walker of Gestingthorpe said that this well-known statement remained the best statement of general principle. It emphasises the need for employers (and hence, for the standards regarded by the courts as acceptable) to move with the times and with the increasing and developing knowledge they bring.

General approach to protection

4.65 Inspired by Europe, there has been increasing emphasis on the need to reduce risks to the lowest level reasonably practicable: the ALARP principle. This is sought to be achieved in the scheme indicated by the Framework Directive (89/391/EC) by avoiding risks altogether; if they cannot be avoided, evaluating them, and combating the risks at source; adapting the work to the individual; adapting to technical progress; replacing the dangerous by the less dangerous or non-dangerous; giving collective protection priority over individual protection, and by emphasising information, consultation and monitoring (see, in general, art 6).

4.66 This finds its reflection in English law in an approach which seeks to avoid risks altogether. If that cannot be done, to minimise risks at source (eg by process design); to provide collective, then personal protection (eg overalls, gloves, ear-protectors); to provide first-aid measures should the personal protection fail (eg washing facilities if cutting oil should touch the skin, etc); and to back up these measures by regular monitoring and advice and information. This scheme has been implicitly recognised by the House of Lords in *Fytche v Wincanton Logistics plc* [2004] UKHL 31, [2004] ICR 975, where the decision rested in part on the fact that personal protective equipment was low down in the hierarchy of measures to be introduced, and by the Court of Appeal in *Ball v Street* [2005] EWCA Civ 76 (piece of agricultural machinery flew off into eye of operator). What is reasonable, in the light of modern developments, is thus liable to depend on the court's examination of the facts against this template of measures which are requisite in any reasonable system of health and safety protection.

The limits of the employer's duty: the course of the employment

4.67 The employer's duty does not extend to every aspect of the worker's life, but neither is it restricted to the period when the worker is physically within the workplace. The employer must still take reasonable care for the worker's safety when working at the premises of other persons: see above. The employer's duty is 'to provide for the safety of his servant in the course of his employment', as was said by Lord Abinger CB in *Priestley v Fowler* (1837) 3 M & W 1.

4.68 The course of the employment has been used as a test for determining the vicarious liability of the employer (see para 4.85ff), and the phrase was also used and defined in numerous cases under the Workmen's Compensation Acts. For present purposes, a somewhat broader view is taken, and decisions in other branches of the law will not necessarily apply: see *National Coal Board v England* [1954] AC 403. Under the Employers' Liability (Defective Equipment) Act 1969, it is a condition of liability (by s 1(1)(a)) that the injury occurred in the course of the employee's employment. Lord Cranworth LC said in *Brydon v Stewart* (1855) 2 Macq 30:

> '[An employer] is only responsible while the servant is engaged in his employment: but whatever he does in the course of his employment, according to the fair interpretation of the words—eundo, morando et redeundo—for all that the master is responsible.'

4.69 There, an employer was held liable for the unsafe condition of the pit shaft which resulted in an accident when the workmen were leaving the pit. The Latin phrase *eundo, morando et redeundo* may be translated freely as meaning 'while at his place of employment, and while entering and leaving it'. The employer's duty therefore extends to matters arising while the workers are coming to the place of work, or leaving it, at any rate while they are on the employer's premises, for example on the stairs on the way out: *Bell v Blackwood Morton & Sons Ltd* 1960 SC 11; but it may not extend to the safety of transport arrangements to take workers home: *Ramsay v Wimpey & Co Ltd* 1951 SC 692 (accident due to disorganised rush of men for transport).

4.70 The duty is not confined to the actual performance of work, but also applies when the worker is doing something reasonably incidental to work:

137

see eg *Davidson v Handley Page Ltd* [1945] 1 All ER 235 (claimant washing
a tea-cup when she slipped on an oily duck-board and injured herself).

> 'The obligation of the employer extends to cover all such acts as are normally
> and reasonably incidental to a man's day's work ...' (per Lord Greene at 237.)

It covers events which happen after the end of a shift. Thus when a man cycled
home after working in hot and dusty conditions in a brick kiln, without being
afforded proper washing facilities before he began his journey but after he
finished his shift, the employers were liable for the dermatitis he developed:
McGhee v National Coal Board [1973] 1 WLR 1, HL.

4.71 Difficult questions may arise where an employee strays to a part of the
premises where his duties do not require him to be. If the worker is doing the
employer's work, he does not cease to be acting in the course of his
employment by the fact that he is working in a place where he is forbidden to
go, even by statutory orders: see *Rands v McNeil* [1955] 1 QB 253 (entry into
shed where dangerous bull was kept); *Stapley v Gypsum Mines Ltd* [1953] AC
663 (working under roof which was not secure); *Laszczyk v National Coal
Board* [1954] 3 All ER 205 (trainee miner at coal face contrary to regulations). Likewise, disobedience to orders does not necessarily mean that the
worker has moved out of the course of the employment: *National Coal Board
v England* [1954] AC 403 (miner coupled up cables, which should be done by
shotfirer personally).[1] All these cases have the common feature that the
claimant, however foolishly or misguidedly, could still be seen as doing the
employer's work. However, in *Westwood v Post Office* [1973] 1 All ER 283
the Court of Appeal regarded an employee who went to part of the roof where
he was forbidden to go, for a smoke, and fell because part of the roof had not
been kept safe, as a trespasser and thus not within the scope of the employer's
duty of care at common law (the case was subsequently reversed on appeal in
the result, on the basis that the Office Shops and Railway Premises Act 1963
had been broken, and the employee was entitled to claim within that Act
notwithstanding that he was a trespasser). The House of Lords thought it
unnecessary to consider the common law position, though Lord Salmon
observed that he should not necessarily be thought to differ from that adopted
by the Court of Appeal. It was, however, important that the employer did not
know that employees regularly used the roof for the purpose of short breaks.
Thus it was not surprising that an injury sustained by a police officer whilst
playing for the force football team was held to have arisen out of his work, it
did not arise in the course of it: *R v National Insurance Commissioner,
ex p Michael* [1977] ICR 121. Nonetheless the courts have taken a broad view
of the course of employment perhaps because the fault of the claimant can
nowadays be taken into account to reduce the damages.[2]

---

[1] The decision in *Bloor v Liverpool Derricking and Carrying Co Ltd* [1936] 3 All ER
399, CA, that a man who went to assist a fellow-workman doing a different job 'accepted
the risk', and that no duty was owed to him, is inconsistent with these decisions and clearly
obsolete.

[2] See also the cases on the course of employment at para 4.86ff, which to some extent cover
the same ground in connection with vicarious liability.

DUTIES TO OTHER WORKERS

4.72 The duties owed by an employer to an employee have traditionally not extended to independent contractors: see *Jones v Minton Construction Ltd* (1973) 15 KIR 309. But under the general law of negligence, duties perhaps similar to those owed to employees have in certain circumstances been found to be owed by an undertaking to persons not in its employment. The cases have often been viewed as exceptions. Yet they increasingly illustrate the readiness of the law to award damages where one person has assumed a responsibility for another—whether through contract or through the factual nature of their relationship. This approach has been developed by Lord Goff in particular (see his speeches in *Maloco v Littlewoods Organisation Ltd* [1987] AC 241 at 272; *White v Jones* [1995] 1 All ER 691) and is to be welcomed. In *Maloco* Lord Goff said that a person (A) could be liable to another (B) for the intentional acts of a third party (C) either where the relationship between A and B was such that responsibility was imposed or assumed by B or where A was responsible for controlling C. That reasoning should apply with greater force to circumstances not involving deliberate harm. An employer in charge of a site, for example, can be said to have assumed a responsibility to workers on the site: certainly, they will in practice rely on it having had due regard for their health and safety. To the extent that they are not its employees (as to which see para 4.05ff, above), they may nonetheless be owed similar duties. So, too, an employer should owe a duty to organise the work of those under its control to prevent harm to others. But much uncertainty remains. It is possible to draw out two, broad underlying categories: workers subject to another's factual control or supervision, and workers practically involved with another's activities. The existence of these duties will not affect, of course, the primary duties which continue to be owed by the employer.

Workers subject to control of someone not their employer

4.73 Duties analogous to those owed by employers to employees have been found to exist in relationships characterised by factual or legal control, such as the chief constable of a police force: *Robertson v Bell* 1969 SLT 119. The authorities at an educational establishment owe some similar duties to the students (*Butt v Inner London Education Authority* (1968) 66 LGR 379; *Carmarthenshire County Council v Lewis* [1955] AC 549, though this does not extend to duties when the student is outside the classroom: *Bradford-Smart v West Sussex County Council* [2002] EWCA Civ 07); as may prison supervisors to inmates (*Ellis v Home Office* [1953] 2 All ER 149; *Ferguson v Home Office* (1977) Times, 8 October) and youth centres to gymnasts (*Fowles v Bedfordshire County Council* [1996] ELR 51). The Australian courts have formulated a general principle, based upon the fact of control or supervision, by which a person can be deemed to assume a responsibility to another: see *Kondis v State Transport Authority* (1984) 154 CLR 672, HC. Liability is determined by ordinary principles of negligence: there is no reason why an employer should be any less liable than any other person who stands in a relationship of proximity to a claimant. However, there may be occasions to remind oneself that the fact of the employment relationship does not necessarily mean that a claim will succeed where for a non-employee in similar circumstances it will not: *White v Chief Constable of South Yorkshire* [1999] ICR 216, HL (police officers suffering psychiatric injury from witnessing the Hillsborough disaster to be subject to the same control tests as other 'secondary victims'). The same principle may be emerging in common law negligence: see eg *Kirkham v Chief Constable of Greater Manchester* [1990] 2 WLR 987 at 991, per Lloyd LJ and at 996, per Farquharson LJ.

4.74 There already exist cases where control over workers has been held, of itself, to give rise to a duty of care, analogous to that owed to employees.[1] Thus in *Morris v Breaveglen* [1997] EWCA Civ 1662 a dumper truck driver employed by A was subject to the instruction of a site foreman employed by S. When an instruction was negligently given, such that he drove the truck over an unguarded edge, A remained liable as his general employers for breach of its (non-delegable) duty of care, but it is plain from the judgments that S would also have been vicariously liable for the negligent instruction of the foreman. A similar result was reached in *Nelhams v Sandells Maintenance Ltd and Gillespie (UK) Ltd* [1996] PIQR P 52, CA, where both the employer and the contractor under whose supervision the employee was working were held liable (painter complained to contractor of absence of worker to foot ladder, was told no-one was available, ladder slipped).

1   For a discussion of these issues, see E McKendrick 'Vicarious Liability and Independent Contractors—A Re-examination' (1990) 43 MLR 770. On this issue in relation to vicarious liability see para 4.100, below.

4.75 Cases which examine the scope of temporary deemed employment usually do so in the face of a claim by a third party (as in *Hawley v Luminar Leisure Ltd* [2006] EWCA Civ 18) or in the event of a dispute as to contribution between the general employer and the alleged temporary deemed employer (as in *Mersey Docks and Harbour Board v Coggins and Griffith (Liverpool) Ltd* [1947] AC 1). They do not normally examine the responsibility of the deemed employer to the loaned servant. However, there have been some cases where liability has been established even on this basis: *Garrard v AE Southey & Co and Standard Telephones and Cables Ltd* [1952] 2 QB 174 (electrician lent by his employer to contractor which controlled his work, fell from defective trestle, contractor held solely liable); the temporary employer was found liable in *Sime v Sutcliffe Catering Scotland Ltd* [1990] IRLR 228, Ct Sess).

4.76 The reasons for imposing a duty of care on a non-employer analogous to those owed by an employer are stronger where an undertaking controls a worker and other workers or operations where he works. It has been held that a principal contractor directing operations on a site which engages sub-contractors and their employees to do work is under a duty, even when not strictly the occupier, to co-ordinate the work and to ensure that reasonable safety measures are taken for the benefit of workers on the site: *McArdle v Andmac Roofing Co* [1967] 1 All ER 583.[1] There, a person in the position of building owner or occupier, who (in the absence of a main contractor) was co-ordinating the activities of sub-contractors, was liable for failure to allocate safety responsibilities when the operations of one sub-contractor endangered the workmen of another.[2] In *Kealey v Heard* [1983] 1 WLR 573 a building owner of a small property accepted no responsibility to supervise, but simply employed separate contractors to do the various jobs, including erection of a scaffold. He was nevertheless held liable to a self-employed plasterer injured in the collapse of the scaffold on the ground that he had a duty to take care that the equipment to be used by those who came on to the land to work there was fit for the purpose, and he had failed to provide any superintendence at all. Similarly a farmer was held liable for supplying an unsuitable ladder to a self-employed 'labour only' bricklayer: *Wheeler v Copas* [1981] 3 All ER 405.[3] However, in *Makepeace v Evans Brothers (Reading) (a firm)* [2001] ICR 241 the Court of Appeal, while reasoning that a main contractor might owe a duty to workers distinct from occupiers' liability, held that a site contractor owed no duty of care to a sub-contractor's employee to ensure that a tower scaffold that it provided for use on a building site was safe, although it was relevant that it was an ordinary piece of equipment.

[1] Another sub-contractor, whose employees caused the hole, was also liable; but this could be explained by vicarious liability.

[2] Sellers and Davies LJJ treated the duty as one arising from the fact of supervision and control: Edmund Davies LJ (quoting from Lord Herschell's words in *Membery v Great Western Railway Co* (1889) 14 App Cas 179) treated it as a duty created by a dangerous activity initiated through sub-contractors; if they had instructed the sub-contractors to attend to safety matters and provided equipment (the sub-contractors being for labour only) it might have been sufficient, but they did nothing.

[3] The HSWA 1974 imposes a series of general safety duties on various persons, in addition to the duty imposed on an employer (s 2) to its own employees. Thus duties, variously defined, are owed: by employers and self-employed persons to others *not* in their employment (s 3); by persons in control of premises (s 4); by manufacturers and designers of articles and substances used at work (s 6) (see chapter 8, below). Duties to persons other than employees are also laid down in many of the regulations passed under that Act.

4.77 In Australia circumstances may place an employer under a primary duty to supervise other workers or to co-ordinate their activities (although not to supervise in fact), even if they are not its employees: see *Kondis v State Transport Authorities* (above); *Stevens v Brodribb Sawmilling Co Pty Ltd* (1986) 160 CLR 16, HC.[1] The duty should extend to selecting competent independent contractors to do the work: *Pinn v Rew* (1916) 32 TLR 451. Conversely, where a person does not supervise others the courts have declined to impose liability. Thus an architect not controlling or supervising work escaped liability in *Clayton v Woodman & Son (Builders) Ltd* [1962] 2 QB 533. But an architect will owe a duty of care when he or she plans a demolition operation, for instance: see *Clay v A J Crump & Sons Ltd* [1964] 1 QB 533 (employee of building contractors injured by collapse of wall). Since workers on a site will generally rely on the organising body to co-ordinate safety measures, it is sensible to treat that person as having assumed, in law, a responsibility to do so.[2]

[1] See also *Oceanic Crest Shipping Co v Pilbara Harbour Services Pty Ltd* (1986) 160 CLR 626.

[2] See now the duties of co-ordination under the Management of Health and Safety at Work Regulations 1999, SI 1999/3242, at para 10.14, below, and under the CONDAM Regulations for building sites at chapter 19, below. An alternative means of reading the same result is to deem the worker an employee of the user, at least for the purposes of health and safety: see *Lane v Shire Roofing Co (Oxford) Ltd* [1995] IRLR 493, CA.

4.78 As an illustration of the same rationale, it has been held that employees of one employer transferred to sites under the control of another may be owed equivalent duties by the user undertaking (see Parker LJ in *O'Reilly v ICI Ltd* [1955] 1 WLR 1155)—and it is clear following *Morris v Breaveglen* [1993] ICR 766 that those transferred persons do not become employees of the user undertaking (as to agency workers and their status, see paras 4.36–4.38, above). Duties were owed by user undertakings in *Garrard v AE Southey & Co and Standard Telephones and Cables Ltd* [1952] 2 QB 174 (temporary user liable for failure to supply proper plant and equipment); *Denham v Midland Employers' Mutual Assurance* [1955] 2 QB 437 (employer of farmer working for boring contractor); *O'Reilly v ICI* above; *Savory v Holland, Hannen and Cubitts (Southern) Ltd* [1964] 3 All ER 18, and see the cases cited above in paras 4.74 and 4.75: *Garrard, Sime* and *Nelhams*. In *Denham,* Lord Denning said that where a worker was controlled by someone not his employer:

> 'The [worker] becomes so much a part of the organisation to which he is seconded that the temporary employer [ie the user] is responsible for him and to him ... The right of control carries the burden of responsibility.'

4.79 In *McArdle v Andmac Roofing Co* [1967] 1 All ER 583, CA, Sellers LJ at 589, referring to *Mersey Docks and Harbour Board v Coggins and Griffiths (Liverpool) Ltd* [1947] AC 1, HL (where it was said to be difficult for an employee to transfer the employment relationship itself to another (user) undertaking) said this:

> 'It may be [that case] did not sufficiently recognise the advantages where there is "teamwork" where an employer's own servants and "borrowed" labour work together in a joint effort or, as here, where labour alone is hired, in having responsibility placed on the employer [ie the user] undertaking the process or operation.'

This approach has much to commend it in modern conditions of work.[1]

[1] See too *R v Swan Hunter Shipbuilders Ltd* [1982] 1 All ER 264, CA, where, on the assumption that the duties in the HSWA 1974 were modelled on the common law duties, the Court of Appeal held it to be a breach of s 3 of that Act not to provide instructions to employees of another, just as the system of work would be unsafe if instructions were not given to employees. That approach to the construction of the section was not adopted in *R v Associated Octel Co Ltd* [1994] IRLR 540, CA, but the assumption of what the common law duty required is unaffected.

Workers practically involved in employers' activities

4.80 The law also appears increasingly to recognise that a worker who is practically involved in the activities of another undertaking but not personally subject to its control—perhaps its employees or contractors work with him—is owed a duty of care by that undertaking, not confined to vicarious liability for their torts, but which depends on the extent that undertaking can be said to have assumed a responsibility towards him[1] (as to whether an agency worker becomes an employee of the user, see para 4.36ff, above). Here, it is control over property or others which gives rise to a duty owed: the fact that the worker will invariably have no choice but to rely on the organisation concerned conducting its operations with due regard for health and safety is a strong reason for finding such responsibility: *R v Swan Hunter Shipbuilders Ltd* [1982] 1 All ER 264, CA.[2] Although this category is vague, to say the least, some examples can be given (and see chapter 7, below). It is already well-established that an occupier owes duties to visitors, just by virtue of the fact of control over the building (see e g *Hartley v Mayoh & Co* [1954] 1 QB 383 (duty to firefighters), although it is now conclusively established that there is no 'activity' duty imposed upon an occupier by the Occupiers Liability Acts 1957 and 1984: *Fairchild v Glenhaven* [2002] ICR 412, CA—this point was not the subject of the appeal to the House of Lords).[3] Analogous to the duty owed to employees, a contractor may be under an obligation to take reasonable care for the safety of plant and equipment to be used by independent contractors: see e g *Kealey v Heard* [1983] ICR 484 and para 4.42, above and 20.16, below; and note that this may be covered by the Provision and Use of Work Equipment Regulations 1998, SI 1998/2306 (see *Ball v Street*, above). Just by virtue of the fact that an undertaking has control over others or the potential to exercise control, it can owe primary duties to others likely to be harmed by those persons' acts: see *Home Office v Dorset Yacht Co Ltd* [1970] AC 1004; *Maloco v Littlewoods Organisation Ltd* [1987] AC 241, HL.[4] In this regard, it should generally be sufficient that the claimant reasonably relies on the other party conducting its affairs with due regard for his health and safety; no deliberate, voluntary acceptance of responsibility ought to be required: see, eg *Smith v Eric S Bush (a firm)* [1990] 1 AC 831, HL at 862 per Lord Griffiths. Contractors working on premises may owe a duty to other visitors if their work makes the premises unsafe: see eg *AC Billings & Sons Ltd v Riden* [1958] AC 240.

1   A taxi firm, using self-employed drivers, owed a primary duty to a woman injured when a door flew open: *Rogers v Night Riders* [1983] RTR 324, but this appears to have been in part because of the degree to which the mini-cab firm made assurances to the woman concerned, and the head of liability resembles that applying to hospitals. By issuing an invitation to use the services concerned, the firm was giving a sufficient assurance of their quality to be relied upon.
2   To some extent the duty in the HSWA 1974, s 3 would crystallise that owed in negligence. Again, see *Kondis v State Transport Authority* (1984) 154 CLR 672 and *Lane v Shire Roofing* (at para 4.25, above).
3   A person not an occupier may owe duties, extending beyond a mere warning, when he or she creates a risk on premises: see *Johnson v Rea Ltd* [1961] 1 WLR 1400 (slippery floor).
4   See especially the speech of Lord Goff.

4.81 To the extent there is a general principle underpinning these cases, it will apply, often with stronger force, to employers whose activities are likely to affect other workers who are not their employees. If an undertaking can owe duties of care to others in respect of deliberate harmful acts of others, as in *Dorset Yacht*, so should it owe duties if it organises workers under its control to perform tasks which may affect others. An employer conducting extra-hazardous activities owes primary duties to those injured by them: see *Honeywill & Stein Ltd v Larkin Bros Ltd* [1934] 1 KB 191 and see para 4.57, above. So too an employer can owe similar duties to a rescuer as it owes to its employees: *Baker v TE Hopkins & Son Ltd* [1959] 3 All ER 225, and even to members of an employee's family: see *Hewett v Alf Brown's Transport Ltd* [1992] ICR 530, CA (lead on employee's clothes injured wife). In *McArdle* (see para 4.76, above), other sub-contractors were partly liable with the principal contractor; and in *Morris v Breaveglen* [1993] ICR 766, above, Beldam LJ accepted that 'if the work on which [the worker] is employed is so closely connected with work being done by another contractor that contractor too owes him a duty to take care for his safety' (at 773). The greater the practical involvement of the undertaking, the stronger is the justification for imposing such duties: see Sellers LJ in *McArdle*, above, para 4.79.

4.82 These cases—of employees subject to de facto control or closely involved with the activities of another undertaking—will become more significant in the context of a labour market increasingly characterised by workers who are not strictly employees or are not employed by the user undertaking, yet who are frequently exposed to just the same risks. The nature of this duty will vary with the circumstances. If a controlling undertaking does not supply labour or equipment, it is hard to see why it should owe duties akin to an employer in these respects, though it is liable for failures in overall organisation. A sensible approach was adopted by the Court of Appeal in *Spalding v Tarmac Civil Engineering Ltd* [1966] 1 WLR 156, CA, where a driver and excavator were supplied to the user undertaking: the user was held liable for the driver's negligence, the supplier for the faulty brakes, both of which caused an accident.[1] If a controlling undertaking occupies the site, fails to select competent co-workers or to adopt a safe overall system, it should be liable just as would be an employer in respect of such failing. The Management of Health and Safety at Work Regulations 1999, SI 1999/3242 lay down duties of co-operation between employers sharing a site and requires them to supply information when an employee works on another's site (see para 10.32, below).

[1] Reversed by the House of Lords but because of the terms of the contract between the user and supplier: *Arthur White (Contractors) Ltd v Tarmac Civil Engineering Ltd* [1967] 1 WLR 1508.

VICARIOUS LIABILITY

4.83 An employer always remains liable in respect of its primary duty of care. It may equally be liable for the torts of its employees or of those under its control. This will typically arise in relation to a casual (as opposed to systemic) act of negligence, where it cannot be said that the system of work of the employer is unsafe. The distinction between casual acts of negligence (giving rise to vicarious liability) and systemic failures, giving rise to breaches of primary duty, is often not straightforward.[1] This section considers for what acts an employer will be vicariously liable.

[1] Particularly following the decision in *McDermid*, see paras 4.51–4.53, above; but see e g *Lindsay v Connell & Co* 1951 SC 281 (worker accidentally hit another employee while hammering; cf *Baxter v Colvilles Ltd* 1959 SLT 325). For an example of a 'one-off' incident attracting vicarious but not primary liability, see *Marshall v William Sharp & Sons Ltd* 1991 SLT 114.

Exclusion of liability

4.84 Any agreement in a contract of service or apprenticeship is void in so far as it seeks to exclude liability for the negligence of an employee's colleagues:

see *Smith v British European Airways Corpn* [1951] 2 KB 893 (term in pension scheme restricting employers' liability void); *Brodin v A/R Seljan* 1973 SLT 198 (term making seaman's contract subject to Norwegian law void, because that law excluded liability for a fellow servant). Under s 2(1) of the Unfair Contract Terms Act 1977 (s 16 under Scottish law), liability for negligence causing injury or death cannot be excluded by any contract or notice, which probably extends to vicarious liability just as much as primary liability.

The test for vicarious liability

4.85 Lord Pearce observed in *ICI Ltd v Shatwell* [1965] AC 656 at 685: 'the doctrine of vicarious liability has not grown from any very clear, logical or legal principle but from social convenience and rough justice'. The central issues in cases of vicarious liability are whether a tort was committed by the employee and whether it was committed in the course (or scope) of his employment (or whether it was committed by an agent within the course of his agency). If it meets these tests the employer is liable: *Staveley Iron and Chemical Co Ltd v Jones* [1956] AC 627, per Lord Morton.[1]

[1]   The employer remains liable even though the employee is immune because, eg, he is the claimant's husband: *Broom v Morgan* [1953] 1 QB 597.

4.86 The test for determining what constitutes the course of employment is easily stated but less easily applied: an employer is liable for tortious acts which amount to an unauthorised mode of performing authorised acts but not for acts which are not sufficiently connected with the authorised act so as to be a mode of doing it. The question is whether there is a sufficient connection between the act of the employee and the employment: the act must be so closely connected with what the employee is authorised to do that it could rightly be regarded as a mode, even if an improper one, of doing it: see per Lord Steyn in *Lister v Hesley Hall Ltd* [2001] UKHL 22, [2002] 1 AC 215;[1] *Canadian Pacific Railway Co v Lockhart* [1942] AC 591 at 599; *Racz v Home Office* [1994] 2 AC 45 at 53; and *Dubai Aluminium v Salaam* [2003] 2 AC 366, paras 22–24, 122–131, and the recent adoption by the Canadian Supreme Court of the 'sufficiently related to' or 'close connection' test in *Bazley v Curry* (1999) 174 DLR (4th) 45 and *Jacobi v Griffiths* (1999) 174 DLR (4th) 7. In the former, McLachlin J, giving the judgment of the court, articulated (at paras 30–32) as two main policy considerations underlying the imposition of vicarious liability, the risk created for others by the employment and the need, by deterrence, to minimise that risk. The test of sufficiently close connection takes these two considerations into account, in effecting a 'a compromise between two conflicting policies: on the one hand, the social interest in furnishing an innocent tort victim with recourse against a financially responsible defendant; on the other, a hesitation to foist any undue burden on a business enterprise'.[2] In *Lister* Lord Clyde's approach, at paras 37–42, was to gauge the sufficiency of the connection by asking whether the wrongful acts, in a broad sense, should be regarded as within the sphere or scope of the employment so as to be ways of carrying out the work authorised by the employer. Lord Hobhouse of Woodborough focused on the notion of delegation or entrustment, namely that an employer is vicariously liable for the wrongful act of its employee where it has 'entrusted' a duty to an employee who, by his wrongful act, has failed to perform it. Lord Millett's approach was broader. He said that it was a species of strict liability, best understood as 'a loss distribution device'. He concluded, in paras 69–79, in line with the approach of the Canadian Supreme Court in *Bazley v Curry* and *Jacobi v Griffiths*: (1) that the critical matter is the closeness of the connection between an employee's duties and his wrong-doing, not some fiction based on implied authority; and (2) that, therefore, where there is such connection, it is immaterial whether the employee's act in question was unauthorised or expressly forbidden by the employer or civilly or criminally illegal.

1   At para 15, citing Salmond *Law of Torts* (1st edn, 1907) pp 83–84; *Salmond & Heuston on the Law of Torts* (21st edn) p 443.
2   Fleming in *The Law of Torts* (9th edn, 1988) pp 409–410.

4.87   In *Bernard v The Attorney General of Jamaica* [2004] UKPC 47 Lord Steyn summed up the effect of *Lister* and *Dubai Aluminium* as follows (at para 18):

> 'In the leading opinion [in *Lister*] a single ultimate question was posed, namely:
>
> "... whether the warden's torts were so closely connected with his employment that it would be fair and just to hold the employers vicariously liable." '

The fact that particular acts are prohibited by the employer or illegal does not preclude them being done in the course of employment. The insight of *Bazley v Curry*, which though a Canadian case was regarded by Lord Steyn as the starting point for any discussion in an English court of the principles of vicarious liability, was that 'close connection' with employment was a more appropriate test than asking whether the conduct in question was a mode of doing the work, even if unauthorised. *Bazley* and *Lister* concerned whether employers were liable vicariously for the abuse by their employees of children in care homes. No-one could sensibly suggest that buggery of children in care was part of taking care of them. Under the law as it had been applied before *Bazley* and *Lister* that might therefore have been thought to include vicarious liability since the torts of the employees were not within the course of their employment. Since these cases, however, no more can it be argued that the worse, or more criminal, the conduct of the employee the less likely it is that the employer will be liable for his torts. A test of sufficiently close connection addresses the principles of liability by applying the two main philosophies underlying it: that of the employer being in a position to control the employee, by definition of the employment relationship (which as we have seen necessarily involves authority to control the employee); and the responsibility for the effects of the undertaking on third parties which an employer has by virtue of bringing the undertaking into being and operating it.

Intentional acts

4.88   It can, therefore, no longer be said that, if the actions concerned were intentional, it is less likely that they were done in the course of employment (see *O'Reilly v National Rail and Tramway Appliances Ltd* [1966] 1 All ER 499; and *Aldred v Nacanco Ltd* [1987] IRLR 292, both of which might be decided differently today, and contrast *Century Insurance Co v Northern Ireland Road Transport Board* [1942] AC 509). An employer was not liable for overseas phone calls made by someone employed to clean phones: the fact that employment created the opportunity to perform the act was insufficient (*Heasmans v Clarity Cleaning Co Ltd* [1987] IRLR 286; see too *Irving v Post Office* [1987] IRLR 289).[1] But in *Nahhas v Pier House (Cheyne Walk) Management Ltd* (1984) 270 Estates Gazette 328, the management company of a block of flats was liable for the burglary by a night porter to whom keys were entrusted by a tenant; and in *Racz v Home Office* [1994] 2 AC 45 the House of Lords refused to strike out a claim based on the vicarious liability of the Home Office for assaults on a prisoner by prison officers: that would be a question of fact for the trial judge.[2] Lord Jauncey said that the action would only be struck out 'if the unauthorised acts of the prison officers were so unconnected with the prison officers' authorised duties as to be quite independent of and outside those duties'. Applying a wide view of 'acts', the fraud of a solicitor's clerk attracted vicarious liability in *Lloyd v Grace, Smith & Co* [1912] AC 716.[3] In *Bracebridge Engineering Ltd v Darby* [1990] IRLR 3 a sexual assault on a woman by a supervisor was held to be committed in the course of supervision. But in *Makanjuola v Comr of Police for the Metropolis* (1989) 2 Admin LR 214, CA, there was no vicarious liability for a police officer who demanded sexual favours for not reporting the claimant to the immigration authorities (he had no ostensible authority, and was clearly engaged in behaviour outside the scope of his employment).

[1] See too *Reilly v Ryan* [1991] 2 IR 247: employer not liable for acts of employee who used a member of the public as a shield against a robber.
[2] The claim was for misfeasance in public office, but the principles of vicarious liability are the same. See Simblet [1994] CLJ 430.
[3] See too *Alliance and Leicester Building Society v Hamptons* [1994] NPC 36.

4.89 A clear example of the new approach to intentional acts is given by the decision of the Court of appeal in *Mattis v Pollock (t/a Flamingos Nightclub)* [2003] EWCA Civ 887, [2003] IRLR 603, to the effect that an assault deliberately carried out by a doorman, off the premises, who had first gone home to arm himself, and then had attacked a person he believed to have been a customer of the club with whom he had an altercation was one for which the night club were liable. *Hawley v Luminar Leisure Ltd* [2006] EWCA Civ 18 is to the same effect.

Practical jokes

4.90 Other intentional acts concern practical jokes. In *Smith v Crossley Bros Ltd* (1951) 95 Sol Jo 655, two apprentices who, by way of a practical joke, injected compressed air into the body of a third apprentice were 'on a frolic of their own'.[1] An employer was not vicariously liable when one employee pushed a basin against the claimant to startle her (*Aldred v Nacanco* [1987] IRLR 292); nor when two employees played together on trolleys (*McReady v Securicor* [1991] NI 229). These authorities will have to be reassessed following the decisions in *Lister, Dubai Aluminium,* and *Bernard* (above). But men authorised to tell a boy what to do were acting in the course of their employment when they misused their authority to play a practical joke by telling him to put his hand in the aperture of a machine: *Chapman v Oakleigh Animal Products Ltd* (1970) 8 KIR 1063, and when a man pushed a truck just a little off course to knock the claimant's duck-board as a practical joke, it was not so divergent from his work (even before *Lister*) that it ceased to be part of it: *Harrison v Michelin Tyre Co Ltd* [1985] ICR 696.

1   Cf *O'Reilly v National Rail and Tramway Appliances Ltd* [1966] 1 All ER 499 (man tempted another to hit live shell among scrap metal); *Coddington v International Harvesters of Great Britain Ltd* (1969) 6 KIR 146 (men lit tin of paint thinners for warmth; man passing kicked it over as a joke); *Wood v Duttons Brewery* (1971) 115 Sol Jo 186 (fellow employee induced to drink caustic soda from cask in belief it was beer: employers not at fault for failing to label in anticipation of such an accident).

Negligent acts

4.91 In relation to negligent acts, on the other hand, the courts have tended to adopt a wider view of course of employment and the link between any act and the employment.[1] Thus in *Century Insurance Co Ltd v Northern Ireland Road Transport Board* [1942] AC 509 a driver, who was delivering petrol in bulk, stood by while the petrol was flowing from the lorry to the tank, began to smoke, and threw the match down, with the result that a fire was started. The employers were held liable on the ground that smoking while delivering petrol in bulk was negligence in the discharge of the duty of delivery. A storekeeper was acting in the course of employment when he exposed a naked light while in charge of a store where petrol was kept: *Dunk v Hawkes Sanders Ltd* (1953) Times, 27 October, CA; so too when a fork-lift driver, finding a lorry in his way, got in to move it although not authorised to drive a lorry: *Kay v ITW Ltd* [1968] 1 QB 140. Where it is the accepted practice that employees of different contractors will give one another occasional assistance, such assistance is in the course of their employment: *Park v Tractor Shovels* 1980 SLT 94.[2] In *Ilkiw v Samuels* [1963] 1 WLR 991 an employer was liable for a lorry driver who negligently allowed an incompetent workman to drive his lorry a short distance to reposition it, injuring another.

1   Employers are not relieved from liability for the negligence of an employee by the fact that they are not allowed to do the work themselves, but are compelled by statute to employ a qualified person: *Wilsons and Clyde Coal Co Ltd v English* [1938] AC 57 (manager of mine).
2   See too *O'Connor v State of South Australia* (1976) 14 SASR 187, where a judge opened the door into a brother judge's room and struck that judge's secretary in the back (she, remarkably, was 50 per cent to blame for standing in the 'danger zone').

Travel to work

4.92 Numerous cases concern travelling to work. The use, with permission, of an employer's van for refreshment during the lunch hour was outside the course of employment in *Hilton v Thomas Burton (Rhodes) Ltd* [1961] 1 All ER 74. But where a workman, having finished his work, cycled to another part of the premises to collect his pay, his cycling was in the course of his employment: *Staton v National Coal Board* [1957] 2 All ER 667; but not where the worker was cycling home to lunch: *Highbid RC v Hammett Ltd* (1932) 49 TLR 104.[1] Employers were vicariously liable when workmen stampeded down stairs at the end of work: *Bell v Blackwood Morton & Sons Ltd* 1960 SC 11 but not for injury in a disorganised rush for transport after work: *Ramsay v Wimpey & Co Ltd* 1951 SC 692. Where two men travelled to a distant work site in the car of one of them, and were paid wages for the time spent in doing so—and not just travelling allowances—the driving was in the course of their employment: *Smith v Stages* [1989] AC 928, HL.[2] Curiously, where a fire brigade operated a 'go-slow' and arrived too late to put out a fire, the employers were not liable because the men were not performing their ordinary duty to drive expeditiously to a fire: *General Engineering Services Ltd v Kingston and St Andrew Corpn* [1989] 1 WLR 69. Likewise if deviation from the route reasonable to carry out the employer's work effectively constitutes 'an entirely new journey' the employer will not be liable for the driver's negligence: *Storey v Ashton* (1869) LR 4 QB 476 at 480.[3]

1 See also *Nancollas v Insurance Officer* [1985] 1 All ER 833.
2 See also *Vandyke v Fender* [1970] 2 QB 292; *Buckley's Stores Ltd v National Employers Mutual General Insurance Association Ltd* [1978] IR 351.
3 But see *Hemphill (A&W) v Williams* [1966] 2 Lloyd's Rep 101 (substantial deviations at request of passengers driver was transporting meant employer liable).

4.93 Workers owe a duty to take reasonable care for one another's safety, and an employer may be vicariously liable even if workers agree with one another not to carry out orders (eg to make the roof of a mine safe) or decide to unload cargo by an unsafe method which saves trouble: *Stapley v Gypsum Mines Ltd* [1953] AC 663; *Williams v Port of Liverpool Stevedoring Co Ltd* [1956] 2 All ER 69.[1]

1 A worker who consents to such an agreement will, of course, have his damages reduced in proportion to his or her share of the blame, and in some cases the defence of volenti non fit injuria may succeed: see chapter 6.

The standard of care of workers

4.94 An employer is liable for an employee who is negligent in the course of employment. The standard of care required from an employee is that appropriate to his position and duties, eg to act as a reasonable and prudent crane-driver. Everyday acts of carelessness or inadvertence can amount to negligence, and a lenient standard is not applied where workers are working in a team: *Staveley Iron and Chemical Co Ltd v Jones* [1956] AC 627. An experienced building worker should know that a masonry nail is hard and brittle, and refrain from hitting it with a heavy hammer when another worker is nearby: *Bowden v Barbrooke Bros* (1973) 15 KIR 232.

4.95 In Scotland, somewhat surprisingly, it has in the past been held that where one workman accidentally hits another with a hammer, or lets go of a barrel which he and another are lifting, that is not in itself evidence of negligence: *Baxter v Colvilles Ltd* 1959 SLT 325; *Dillon v Clyde Stevedoring Co Ltd* 1967 SLT 103.[1] In New Zealand, more sensibly, where a man tripped and sent the garbage can he was carrying through a window, it was held that tripping calls for an explanation, and the maxim res ipsa loquitur applies in the absence of one: *Frederic Maeder Proprietary Ltd v Wellington City* [1969] NZLR 222. Here, the Court of Appeal applied that doctrine where a heavy panel fell while several men were moving it; in the absence of any rebutting evidence by the defendants, the claim succeeded: *Bennett v Chemical Construction (GB) Ltd* [1971] 3 All ER 822 (see too *McPherson v Devon Area Health Authority* [1986] CLY 44 (pot of hot water fell off tray)). This approach received further support from *McCann v J R McKeller (Alloys) Ltd* 1969 SC (HL) 1 where the House of Lords sustained the verdict of a Scottish jury that it was negligent for a fellow workman to drop his end of a heavy steel ingot, although he excused himself by saying that his hand was suddenly 'jagged' or 'pricked' by a sharp edge.[2] In *Hill v James Crowe (Cases) Ltd* [1978] 1 All ER 812, where a badly nailed packing case collapsed, the inference was drawn that one of the employees of the maker had been negligent.

[1]   Reference was made to English cases similarly decided on the facts: *Sowerby v Maltby* [1953] 1 Lloyd's Rep 462; *O'Leary v Glen Line Ltd* [1953] 1 Lloyd's Rep 601; *Sims v T and J Harrison* [1954] 1 Lloyd's Rep 354 (dropping, or letting go of, a bag of sugar, a bale of rubber, the tail of a tent). But at the very least, it might be thought, to hit another's hand with a hammer, or drop one end of a load without warning, calls for an explanation such as 'the hand was too close', 'it was too heavy', or even 'a wasp stung me'. Such explanations may well indicate an unsafe system of work or negligence by the employee.
[2]   He said that he was pricked suddenly by the sharp edge and dropped his end 'automatically' without time to give warning. Lord Guest said that the fact that an action was 'automatic and instinctive' did not mean it was not negligent—it was no more than saying 'he jerked his hand away without thinking'. Lord Denning said that the dropping of the ingot was 'some evidence of negligence'.

Vicarious liability for breach of statutory duty by employee

4.96 Breach of statutory duty imposed directly on the employee has given rise in the past to difficult questions in establishing vicarious liability on the employer's part. It was argued, that a statutory duty which is imposed on the employee personally does not flow from the employer's orders and so does not concern it. But Lord MacDermott said in *Harrison v National Coal Board* [1951] AC 639 at 671:

> 'To my mind this, as a general proposition, finds no support in principle or authority. Vicarious liability is not confined to negligence. It arises from the servant's tortious act in the scope of his employment.'

4.97 Nevertheless the House of Lords left the question open, both in *Harrison* and in two subsequent cases: see *Stapley v Gypsum Mines Ltd* [1953] AC 663; *National Coal Board v England* [1954] AC 403. Although Lord MacDermott said that there was no support 'in principle or authority' for the proposition that an employer could not be held vicariously liable for its employee's breach of statutory duty, he did not identify any specific authority that he had in mind. However, in the following year Lord Guthrie, in the

Scottish Court of Session, held in *Nicol v National Coal Board* (1952) 102 LJ 357, another shot-firing case, that there was such vicarious liability—the only direct UK authority for the proposition that an employer may be vicariously liable for breach of statutory duty. In so holding, he expressly followed Lord MacDermott's obiter reasoning in *Harrison v NCB*. In *National Coal Board v England* Lord Oaksey took the opportunity, at 421–422, to express his approval of Lord Guthrie's judgment in *Nicol v NCB*:

> '... I agree with the judgment of Lord Guthrie in *Nicol v National Coal Board* ... that it cannot be said to be necessarily outside the course of the employment of a workman that he performs his work in a manner which is in breach of a statutory regulation. Here it was within the shot-firer's employment to fire the shot electrically, but he did it without due care and in breach of the regulation. Unless there is something in the statute which creates the obligation indicating the intention that no action shall be brought at common law in respect of its breach, the ordinary rules of the common law of tort are applicable, including the doctrine of respondent superior.'

4.98 PS Atiyah, in his authoritative 1967 work, *Vicarious Liability in the Law of Torts*, at pp 280–284, supported the view that vicarious liability applied generally to statutory torts committed in the course of employment, save where the wording of the statute directed otherwise or there was a good policy reason not to apply it. The authors of *Clerk and Lindsell on Torts* (18th edn, 2000), at paras 5–46 and 5–47, followed by the authors of the previous edition of this work, expressed the same view. In *Majrowski v Guys & St Thomas's NHS Trust* [2005] EWCA Civ 251, [2005] QB 848 Auld LJ observed that the development of the jurisprudence underlying vicarious liability (in cases such as *Bazley, Lister,* and *Bernard*), '... strongly influenced by academic authority of great distinction, on this issue since Lord MacDermott's notable obiter contribution to it in *Harrison v NCB* in 1951 speaks for itself ...' and concluded that in principle an employer would be vicariously liable for a breach of statutory duty by its employee where that had a sufficiently close connection with his employment. At the time of writing, the case is due to be heard by the House of Lords, but the principal issue seems to be whether the Prevention of Harassment Act should be construed so as to be one of the rare exceptions to the general principle of liability established by the Court of Appeal.

Vicarious liability for those not employees

4.99 An employer is not in general liable for the negligence of an independent contractor. But, as noted above, where the employer is subject to a primary duty of care, it is no defence to argue that it was delegated to another. In effect this may make an employer liable for the acts of an independent contractor, as in *McDermid v Nash Dredging and Reclamation Co Ltd* [1987] AC 906, HL.[1] There are other circumstances in which an employer can be liable for the torts of someone not in its employment.

---

[1] Discussed in paras 4.53–4.56, above. Note, too, the 'extra-hazardous' exception: para 4.57, above.

4.100   A defendant is liable for the torts of an independent contractor if he authorised the latter to commit the tort: *Ellis v Sheffield Gas Consumers Co* (1853) 2 E & B 767. More significantly, a business may also be liable for the torts of others, not its employees, committed while under its control: see *Union Steamship Co Ltd v Claridge* [1894] AC 185. In *Morris v Breave-glen Ltd (t/a Anzac Construction Co)* [1993] ICR 766, CA, a building site employee was temporarily lent to main contractors, who supplied the plant to the site and told the employee what to do and how to do it. Beldam LJ distinguished the employer owing primary duties to the employee from the undertaking which would be vicariously liable for torts: if the employee committed a tort while under the control of the borrowing 'employer', then it generally would be vicariously liable; but the original employer remained liable as employer for breaches of the duty to provide a safe system of work and the like.[1] Beldam LJ considered that some of the cases subsequent to *Mersey Docks and Harbour Board v Coggins and Griffiths (Liverpool) Ltd* [1947] AC 1 seemed to have wrongly concentrated on the test of control as determining who was liable as an employer, this test having been laid down for the different purpose in *Mersey Docks*. See eg *Garrard v AE Southey & Co and Standard Telephones and Cables Ltd* [1952] 2 QB 174.[2] The test insofar as it focuses on control is, therefore, concerned with which employer is vicariously liable for a worker's torts, and not with who is the employer in the strict sense.

[1]   At 773. Otherwise an employee could be effectively transferred to another employer without his consent, contrary to accepted law: see *Mersey Docks and Harbour Board v Coggins and Griffiths (Liverpool) Ltd* [1947] AC 1 at 14, per Lord Macmillan, at 15, per Lord Porter; Lord Denning in *Denham v Midland Employers Mutual Association Ltd* [1955] 2 QB 437 at 443; Bedlam LJ in *Morris* at 774.

[2]   In *Johnson v Coventry Churchill International Ltd* [1992] 3 All ER 14, Kay QC similarly treated *Mersey Docks* as concerned with which of two employers is vicariously liable to an injured third party rather than who was the employer for other reasons.

4.101   When will a person, not employed by another, be treated as under that other's control so as to make it, and not any original employer, liable for the worker's torts? The starting point is that it is difficult to show that control has transferred to the user undertaking: *Mersey Docks and Harbour Board v Coggins and Griffiths (Liverpool) Ltd* [1947] AC 1, per Viscount Simon at 1; *John Young & Co (Kelvinhaugh) v O'Donnell* 1958 SLT (Notes) 46, HL (crane driver not transferred to hirer). A transfer is more readily inferred when an employee is lent without equipment: *Garrard v AE Southey & Co and Standard Telephones and Cables Ltd* [1952] 2 QB 174 (electrician under orders of user undertaking)[1] and less so when a worker is lent with valuable equipment: *Savory v Holland Hannen & Cubitts (Southern) Ltd* [1964] 3 All ER 18. It follows from the control test that the less skilled the worker, the more likely it is that he or she is under the control of the user: see eg *Denham v Midland Employer's Mutual Assurance Ltd* [1955] 2 QB 437 (labourer assisting on brickfield under contractors' orders). Hence a fitter not supervised by the user business remained under the control of his original employer in *Moir v Wide Arc Services Ltd* 1987 SLT 495. A driver lent on permanent loan with a lorry was not transferred in *O'Reilly v ICI Ltd* [1955] 3 All ER 382: the hirers could not tell him how to do his work. If the worker is lent with a supervisor or as part of a unit, control is unlikely to be transferred: *Johnson v AH Beaumont Ltd and Ford Motor Co* [1953] 2 QB 184; *Brogan v William Allan Smith & Co Ltd* 1965 SLT 175. In general, the manner of working and not just the tasks to be done must be directed by the user undertaking: compare *Gibb v United Steel Companies Ltd* [1957] 2 All ER 110 (dock labourers under control of stevedores for whom they had worked for many years) with *Bhoomidas v Port of Singapore Authority* [1978] 1 All ER 956.

[1] Cf *Johnson v A H Beaumont Ltd and Ford Motor Co* [1953] 2 QB 184.

4.102 While control is the principal test, other matters, such as whether the worker forms part of the employer's workforce are also relevant.[1] In *Marshall v William Sharp & Sons Ltd* 1991 SLT 114 a quarry operator was vicariously liable for the negligence of an electrician, who Lord Ross considered was an independent contractor, in part because he formed part of the defenders' workforce and was on call to the defenders. The terms of the contract between the employer and the contractor to whom he is transferred may be relevant to whether a transfer has occurred: see *McConkey v Amec plc* (1990) 27 Con LR 88 (no transfer of crane driver supplied with crane).

[1] See Lord Porter in *Mersey Docks and Harbour Board v Coggins and Griffiths (Liverpool) Ltd* [1947] AC 1.

4.103 Most of the above cases concern persons who were employees, albeit not of the undertaking who was using them. But the principles should be equally applicable to persons who are not, strictly, employees at all. The fact of control alone should be enough to make the user vicariously liable: see *Marshall v William Sharp*, above. A user undertaking may equally be liable as a joint tortfeasor if it gives a specific instruction, whether to a transferred employee or an independent contractor, which results in negligent injury to a third party: see Lord Simon in *Mersey Docks and Harbour Board v Coggins and Griffiths (Liverpool) Ltd* [1947] AC 1.

4.104 In *Denham v Midland Employers' Mutual Assurance Ltd* [1955] 2 QB 437, the issue was which of two mutually exclusive liability insurance policies covered damages which an employer was liable to pay to the widow of an employee who was killed while he was working under the specific direction of engineers engaged by the employer to do work on their land. Denning LJ said (at 443) that much of the difficulty arose out of the nineteenth century conception that a servant of a general employer may be transferred to a temporary employer so as to become for the time being the servant of the temporary employer. The conception was a very useful device to put liability on the shoulders of one who should properly bear it, but it did not affect the contract of service itself. No contract of service could be transferred without the servant's consent. In none of the transfer cases was the consent of the man sought or obtained. The general employer had simply told the employee to go and do some particular work for the temporary employer and he had gone. The supposed transfer was nothing more than a device.

4.105 In *Viasystems (Tyneside) Ltd v Thermal Transfer (Northern) Ltd* [2005] EWCA Civ 1151, [2005] 4 All ER 1181 May LJ held that there was, in a modern context, little intrinsic sense in, or justification for, an assumption that where one employer had loaned another employer the use of an employee, only one of the two would be vicariously liable, and not both. The underlying basis for the assumption appeared to be the notion, exposed as a device by Denning LJ in *Denham*, that, to find a temporary employer vicariously liable, one had to look for a transfer of employment. If, on the facts of a particular case, the core question was who was entitled, and in theory obliged, to control the employee's relevant negligent act so as to prevent it, there would be some cases in which the sensible answer would be each of two 'employers'. *Viasystems* itself was such a case. A man, Strang, was working as a fitter's mate to a fitter employed by one firm, under the supervision of another fitter contracted to a second firm. Returning from an errand he crawled through a section of ducting, which he should not have done, which then moved so as to activate the firm's sprinkler system, causing damage. Both the fitter to whom he was mate, and the supervising fitter, had the responsibility of controlling Strang's actions. Both were thought equally responsible.

4.106 This does not, however mean that it will be usual for two employers each to be held liable for the negligent act of someone who whilst an employee of one is working principally for the other. In *Hawley v Luminar Leisure Ltd* [2006] EWCA Civ 18 a nightclub door supervisor was employed by a contractor, yet worked under the close control of the nightclub management (so close that the manger said that if she said 'jump' the door staff would jump). A door steward assaulted a customer, causing serious brain damage. It was held that the nightclub was solely vicariously liable: the fact that the contractor was employer and owed a duty of care to the doorman which was non-delegable did not mean that it too was responsible for his actions where control was operated by the club.

4.107 It seems likely that the growth of agency work and the general casualisation of the workforce in the twenty-first century will lead to a greater willingness on the part of the courts to hold the temporary employer liable vicariously for the acts of someone working for it, even though he is not their actual employee. Indeed, without such a development, flexible and agency working could rapidly become a device used by many to escape potential liability, the need to insure against it, and the potential repercussions of it, to the detriment of both the corrective and the compensatory effects of the tort system.

Chapter 5

BREACH OF STATUTORY DUTY

Barry Cotter

Daniel Bennett

5.01 Actions for breach of statutory duty often have significant advantages from the claimant's viewpoint over actions in negligence, the most obvious of which is that is usually unnecessary to prove fault.[1] In addition, duties under the regulations may be stricter[2] and sometimes absolute with no defence available to an employer. Many statutory duties do not require any proof of reasonable foresight of harm.[3] In broad terms, to succeed in a claim based on breach of a provision in a statute or regulations a claimant must show that:

(1)   the statutory provision gave rise to civil liability;
(2)   the claimant suffered damage of the kind contemplated by the statute;
(3)   the defendant has breached the duty and the duty is owed to the claimant;
(4)   the breach of the duty was a cause of the damage to the claimant;

In addition, any defences to the action will have to be considered.

[1]   See para 5.31ff.
[2]   See e g *Spencer v Boots the Chemist* [2002] EWCA Civ 1691, [2002] All ER (D) 465 (Oct) which allows comparison of the effect of a failure to undertake a risk assessment before and after the removal of the exclusion of civil liability for breach of the Management of Health and Safety at Work Regulations 1999, SI 1999/3242; breach of the Regulations was held to be no more than evidence which might assist an argument that the employers had failed to use reasonable care to avoid the injury which resulted.
[3]   See para 5.33ff.

STATUTE/REGULATIONS GIVING RISE TO CIVIL LIABILITY

5.02 When duties are imposed by an Act or regulations passed under it, the Act (or the regulations) may expressly state whether or not a person who suffers damage as a result of the breach can or cannot bring a civil action, effectively resolving the matter. This is the position in the case of the HSWA 1974 (see below). But sometimes legislation, particularly older legislation, fails expressly to deal with the matter so that it becomes a question of construction of the Act to determine whether or not a civil claim of damages may be brought.

The Health and Safety at Work Act 1974 and regulations passed under it

5.03 Whether there is civil liability for breach of the HSWA 1974 and all the regulations promulgated under it is a clear and express issue. Breach of the

155

5.03 *Breach of statutory duty*

HSWA 1974 does not of itself give rise to civil liability.[1] However, unless they state otherwise, the regulations introduced under the HSWA 1974 do give rise to civil liability. Section 47(2) of that Act states that:

> 'Breach of a duty imposed by health and safety regulations shall, so far as it causes damage, be actionable except in so far as the regulations provide otherwise'.

[1] See para 8.08, below.

5.04 An exception to this general rule that these regulations impose civil liability was the Management of Health and Safety at Work Regulations 1999, which excluded civil liability by reg 22. However, this exclusion was repealed by SI 2003/2457 with effect from 27 October 2003 such that breach of the Management Regulations does now give rise to civil liability. For this purpose 'health and safety regulations' means regulations made under s 15 of the Act,[1] (see also s 53(1)) the method of introduction of almost all modern health and safety regulations. 'Damage' is widely defined in s 47(6) to include 'the death of, or injury to, any person (including any disease and any impairment of a person's physical or mental condition)'; no doubt it extends to financial loss caused by such death or injury.

[1] In *Polestar Jowetts Ltd v Komori UK Ltd* [2005] EWHC 1674 (QB), [2005] All ER (D) 480 (Jul) Field J held that it could not be inferred from the terms of the Supply of Machinery (Safety) Regulations 1992 (which had not been made pursuant to the HSWA 1974) that one of the purposes of the Regulations was to confer a right of civil action. If it had been intended to confer such a right, the Regulations would have clearly declared that they did or that they were being made under the HSWA 1974.

5.05 The regulations which formed the 'six pack' and implemented various European Directives were all passed under the HWSA 1974, s 15. Many of the other regulations referred to in this book were also passed under s 15[1] and this section will be the means of introducing most new health and safety regulations in the future, as regulations under the HSWA 1974 progressively replace the 'existing statutory provisions'.[2]

[1] See eg Control of Substances Hazardous to Health Regulations 2002, SI 2002/2677 and the Work at Height Regulations 2005, SI 2005/735.
[2] See para 5.07, below.

5.06 In contrast with the duties in regulations, the general duties contained in the body of the HSWA 1974, ss 2–8—for example, the duty on an employer to ensure so far as is reasonably practicable,[1] the health, safety and welfare of its employees—do not give rise to civil liability, again as the Act expressly states (see s 47(1)). Those duties can only be enforced by criminal prosecutions, which can only be brought by an inspector or by another person with the consent of the Director of Public Prosecutions.[2]

[1] Cf the action brought against the United Kingdom by the Commission in relation to this qualification: Case C-127/05.
[2] See ss 33 and 38. Breach of health and safety regulations also gives rise to potential criminal liability.

156

5.07 The existence or not of civil liability for breach of the 'existing statutory provisions' within the meaning of the HSWA 1974—that is, the various Acts and regulations listed in Sch 1 which regulations passed under the s 15 of the Act will progressively repeal, revoke and replace—is unaffected by the Act.[1] As the 'existing statutory provisions' are progressively replaced by regulations introduced under s 15, the relevance of the case law on construing whether or not a statute, silent on the matter, gives rise to civil liability (see below) will correspondingly diminish: increasingly s 47 of the Act will resolve the issue.

[1] See definition of 'existing statutory provisions' in s 53(1) and s 15(3).

Statutes silent on the matter

5.08 Although the position on civil liability under the HSWA 1974 is clearly spelt out, that is not the case in all other statutes. The issue is then one of construction of the Act.[1] In *Cutler v Wandsworth Stadium Ltd* [1949] AC 398 Lord Simonds said:

> 'The only rule which in all circumstances is valid is that the answer must depend on a consideration of the whole Act and the circumstances, including the pre-existing law, in which it was enacted. But that there are indications which point with more or less force to the one answer or the other is clear from authorities which, even where they do not bind, will have great weight … For instance, if a statutory duty is prescribed, but no remedy by way of penalty or otherwise for its breach is imposed, it can be assumed that a right of civil action accrues to a person who is damnified by the breach. For, if it were not so, that statute would be but a pious aspiration. But, as Lord Tenterden CH said ((1831) 1 B & Ad 847) in *Doe d Rochester (Bishop) v Bridges*:
>
> > "… where an Act creates an obligation, and enforces the performance in a specified manner, we take it to be a general rule that performance cannot be enforced in any other manner."
>
> … But this general rule is subject to exceptions. It may be that, though a specific remedy is provided by the Act, yet the person injured has a personal right of action in addition.'

[1] See *R v Deputy Governor of Parkhurst, ex p Hague* [1992] 1 AC 58 at 159 and also as a recent example *Godden v Kent & Medway* [2004] EWHC 1629 (QB); on its construction the National Health Service Act 1977 did not give rise to civil liability, through creation of a statutory duty or a common law duty.

5.09 But the position is often far from clear as Lord Steyn stated in *Gorringe v Calderdale Metropolitan Borough Council* [2004] UKHL 15, [2004] 2 All ER 326:

> '… (concerning) negligence and statutory duties and powers. This is a subject of great complexity and very much an evolving area of the law. No single decision is capable of providing a comprehensive analysis. It is a subject on which an intense focus on the particular facts and on the particular statutory back-ground, seen in the context of the contours of our social welfare state, is necessary. On the one hand the courts must not contribute to the creation of a society bent on litigation, which is premised on the illusion that for every misfortune there is a remedy. On the other hand, there are cases where the courts must recognise on principled grounds the compelling demands of

corrective justice or what has been called "the rule of public policy which has first claim on the loyalty of the law; that wrongs should be remedied": *M (A Minor) v Newham London Borough Council and X (Minors) v Bedfordshire County Council* [1995] 2 AC 633, at 663, per Sir Thomas Bingham MR. Sometimes cases may not obviously fall in one category or the other. Truly difficult cases arise.'

5.10 Following *Pepper (Inspector of Taxes) v Hart* [1993] AC 593 it may be permissible to refer to Hansard to discover if Parliament, through the promoter of the Bill, made its intention plain. Special rules apply to legislation implementing European Directives (see chapter 9).

5.11 In *Lonrho Ltd v Shell Petroleum Co Ltd (No 2)* [1982] AC 173 at 185, Lord Diplock clarified the exceptions referred to by Lord Simonds. He said that there were two in particular:

'The first is where upon the true construction of the Act it is apparent that the obligation or prohibition was passed for the benefit or protection of a particular class of individuals, as in the cases of the Factories Act and similar legislation ... The second exception is where the statute creates a public right (ie a right to be enjoyed by all those of Her Majesty's subjects who wish to avail themselves of it) and a particular member of the public suffers what Brett J in *Benjamin v Storr* (1874) LR 9 CP 400, 407 described as "particular, direct and substantial" damage "other and different from that which was common to all the rest of the public".'

5.12 The second exception gives rise to the greatest conceptual difficulty but is of limited relevance to employers' liability to their employees.[1] As Lord Diplock recognised in his reference to the Factories Act, it has long been established that an action lies for breach of the general statutes passed for the protection and safety of workers despite the existence of parallel criminal sanctions (see below).[2] They are treated as falling within a particular class of the public.

[1] Lord Diplock viewed few statutes as creating a public right and added that a 'mere prohibition on members of the public from doing what it would otherwise be lawful for them to do is not enough' ([1986] AC 173 at 186). This category was not referred to by Lord Browne-Wilkinson in *X v Bedfordshire County Council* [1995] 2 AC 633, so that its status may be somewhat uncertain.
[2] Lord Diplock in *Lonrho* at 185, citing Lord Kinnear in *Butler (or Black) v Fife Coal Co Ltd* [1912] AC 149 at 165.

5.13 In other areas or where it is not clear whether the statute was passed for the protection of workers' safety, the fact that a statute appears to fall within one of the exceptions of *Lonrho* is not of itself sufficient to confer a right of action. The question remains, as set out in *Cutler v Wandsworth* (above), did Parliament intend to confer a private right? Meeting Lord Diplock's 'class' test is a necessary but not sufficient condition.[1] Other considerations are also relevant. If no remedy is provided in a statute, for example, this is a factor counting in favour of a civil claim for breach.[2]

1   See *Pickering v Liverpool Daily Post and Echo Newspapers plc* [1991] 2 AC 370 at 420, per Lord Bridge; *R v Deputy Governor of Parkhurst Prison, ex p Hague* [1992] 1 AC 58, especially Lord Bridge at 159, Lord Jauncey at 170–171; Lord Browne-Wilkinson in *X v Bedfordshire County Council* [1995] 2 AC 633.
2   The same may apply if the remedy is inadequate: see *Groves v Lord Wimborne* [1898] 2 QB 402.

5.14 By way of illustration, no civil liability arose from breach of a statute which required a water company to maintain a certain pressure in their pipes for extinguishing fires: *Atkinson v Newcastle and Gateshead Waterworks Co* (1877) 2 Ex D 441. Under the Factories Act 1961, the duty under s 17(2) not to sell or hire machinery of which certain parts are not encased was not held to give rise to a civil claim against a supplier: *Biddle v Truvox Engineering Co Ltd (Greenwood and Batley Ltd, Third Party)* [1952] 1 KB 101. The Court of Appeal was divided on whether a civil action lay for a failure to maintain fire escapes in breach of Building Acts: *Solomons v R Gertzenstein Ltd* [1954] 2 QB 243. Applying Lord Jauncey's approach in *Hague*, in *X v Bedfordshire County Council* [1995] 2 AC 633 it was held that the statutory obligations on local authorities to protect children with special educational needs did not give rise to a private law action. Although the duties were owed to a definite class, the imposition of a civil law duty would be inconsistent with the administrative system put in place to promote social welfare.

5.15 In *Richardson v Pitt Stanley* [1995] QB 123, the Court of Appeal held that there was no civil liability on the part of the company or its directors for its failure to insure under the Employers' Liability (Compulsory Insurance) Act 1969, in part because of the existence of substantial criminal penalties. It is not easy to reconcile this decision with the numerous authorities holding that Acts passed for the protection of the health and safety of workers do give rise to civil liability (see below). The argument that the Act is also passed for the benefit of employers as well, to ensure that they have insurance, seems rather unconvincing. If that is a purpose it is hardly the principal purpose, which is to ensure recovery for a particular class, namely employees.

Legislation protecting workers

5.16 In *Groves v Lord Wimborne* [1898] 2 QB 402 the question fully argued before the Court of Appeal was whether an action lay against the occupier of a factory for failing to fence dangerous machinery as required by the Factory and Workshop Act 1878. Despite the presence of parallel criminal penalties, the Court of Appeal decided that an action did lie. Vaughan Williams LJ made the following general observations at 415:

> 'It cannot be doubted that where a statute provides for the performance by certain persons of a particular duty, and someone belonging to a class of persons for whose benefit and protection the statute imposes the duty is injured by failure to perform it, prima facie and if there be nothing to the contrary, an action by the person so injured will lie against the person who has so failed to perform the duty.'

AL Smith LJ said with regard to the Factory and Workshop Act 1878 (at 406):

5.17   Breach of statutory duty

'The Act in question, which followed numerous other Acts in pari materia, is not in the nature of a private legislative bargain between employers and workmen ... but is a public Act passed in favour of workers in factories and workshops to compel their employers to do certain things for their protection and benefit.'

5.17   This decision has been accepted as good law ever since[1] and approved in many subsequent cases (see eg *Phillips v Britannia Hygenic Laundry* [1923] 2 KB 832 per Atkin LJ at 841; *Lonrho Ltd v Shell Petroleum Co Ltd (No 2)* [1982] AC 173 per Lord Diplock at 185). In *X (Minors) v Bedfordshire County Council* [1995] 2 AC 633, Lord Browne-Wilkinson at 730 said:

'The principles applicable in determining whether such statutory cause of action exists are now well established, although the application of those principles in any particular case remains difficult. The basic proposition is that in the ordinary case a breach of statutory duty does not, by itself, give rise to any private law cause of action. However a private law cause of action will arise if it can be shown, as a matter of construction of the statute, that the statutory duty was imposed for the protection of a limited class of the public and that Parliament intended to confer on members of that class a private right of action for breach of statutory duty. There is no general rule by reference to which it can be decided whether a statute does create such a right of action but there are a number of indicators. If the statute provides no other remedy for its breach and the Parliamentary intention to protect a limited class is shown, that indicates that there may be a private right of action since otherwise there is no method of securing the protection the statute was intended to confer. If the statute does provide some other means of enforcing the duty that will normally indicate that the statutory right was intended to be enforceable by those means and not by private right of action ... However, the mere existence of some other statutory remedy is not necessarily decisive. It is still possible to show that on the true construction of the statute the protected class was intended by Parliament to have a private remedy. Thus the specific duties imposed on employers in relation to factory premises are enforceable by an action for damages, notwithstanding the imposition by the statutes of criminal penalties for any breach : see *Groves v Wimborne* ...'

1   See eg *Ziemniak v ETPM Deep Sea Ltd* [2003] EWCA Civ 636.

5.18   As regards the Coal Mines Acts, an action based on these had been allowed before 1898 in a number of cases, including *Baddeley v Earl of Granville* (1887) 19 QBD 423. In *David v Britannic Merthyr Coal Co* [1909] 2 KB 146 Fletcher Moulton LJ said:

'By embodying in the provisions of an Act, such as the one now under consideration, those precautions which it is advised should be observed in the management of these dangerous undertakings the Legislature erects a standard of carefulness and requires all who carry them on to come up to that standard ... non-compliance with the provisions of the statute carries with it the same civil consequences as a verdict of negligence would do.'

5.19   These remarks were approved by the House of Lords in *Butler (or Black) v Fife Coal Co Ltd* [1912] AC 149; and in that case Lord Kinnear further said with reference to the Coal Mines Regulation Act then in force:

'If the duty be established, I do not think there is any serious question as to the civil liability. There is no reasonable ground for maintaining that a proceeding by way of penalty is the only remedy allowed by the statute ... We are to consider the scope and purpose of the statute and in particular for whose benefit it is intended. Now the object of the present statute is plain. It was intended to compel mine-owners to make due provision for the safety of the men working in their mines, and the persons for whose benefit all these rules are to be enforced are the persons exposed to danger. But when a duty of this kind is imposed for the benefit of particular persons, there arises at common law a correlative right in those persons who may be injured by its contravention.'

5.20 Here again, as under the Factories Act, the right to bring an action clearly applied to every breach of the safety provisions of the Act. As Lord Atkin said in *Lochgelly Iron and Coal Co v M'Mullan* [1934] AC 1 at 8, referring to the duty under the Coal Mines Act 1911, ss 49 and 52, to support the roof of the working place:

'... if it were necessary to show that they are designed to secure the safety of persons employed in the mine, it is only necessary to refer to the terms of the sections themselves and to the fact that they are contained in Part II of the Act which is entitled "Provisions for Safety".'

5.21 By virtue of the repeated approval of the principle in *Groves* it might be thought that the same conclusion is likely to apply to the other Acts and regulations which are stated or appear to be intended to protect safety of workers but where the Act or regulations do not deal with the matter expressly. However, two recent Court of Appeal decisions, both in relation to subordinate legislation in operation under sections of the Merchant Shipping Act 1995 reveal that, just as Lord Steyn stated in *Gorringe*, difficult cases still arise.

5.22 In *Todd v Adams* [2002] EWCA Civ 509 the Court of Appeal was concerned with whether secondary legislation on the safety and regulation of fishing vessels (ie the Vessel (Safety Provisions) Rules 1975, SI 1975/330 and subsequent rules made pursuant to the Merchant Shipping Act 1995, s 121(1)) was a means of enforcing safety requirements through statutory regulation rather than through the creation of civil liability on an owner for non-compliance. The case involved the capsizing and sinking of a beam trawler at sea with the loss of all hands. It was held that a breach of the Rules could not of itself form the basis of a civil claim by a person who had suffered damage as a result. The court recognised that there were arguments the other way and in particular saw the strength of a comparison between the relevant part of the 1995 Act and the Factories Acts. Neuberger J considered the case of *Groves v Wimborne* but distinguished it by reason of a number of factors:

(a) the duty considered in *Groves v Wimborne*, namely a breach of the Factory and Workshops Act 1891, s 6(2) was a short and simple duty, which was to be contrasted 'with the multifarious and sometimes complex duties set out in subordinate legislation, which has not been specifically considered by the legislature';

161

(b)   there was no question of any power of exemption of a particular factory or type of factory premises;

(c)   there was no certification procedure under the Factories Acts;

(d)   a provision for a part of a fine imposed on a breach of s 6(2) to be paid over to an injured person or his family supported the view that the purpose of the legislation was to confer rights, or potential rights, on a class of person;

(e)   an employer could escape liability if he could show that another employee was responsible for the breach;

(f)   at the date when *Groves v Wimborne* was decided, there was a somewhat unattractive defence open to an employer of common employment that prevented many otherwise valid claims from succeeding. The Court of Appeal's decision had to be seen as providing a way around the defence of common employment.

5.23 A short while later in *Ziemniak v ETPM Deep Sea Ltd* [2003] EWCA Civ 636 the Court of Appeal was concerned with an action in which the claimant, who was injured when a suspension chain holding a lifeboat failed, had brought an action for breach of statutory duty under the Merchant Shipping (Life Saving Appliances) Regulations 1980, SI 1980/538. It was held (distinguishing *Todd*) that the approach of the courts for many years had been that breach of legislative provisions enacted for the safety and protection of workers on land would generally lead to civil liability. Legislative history indicated that Parliament intended to eliminate distinctions between seamen and on-shore workers in respect of safety considerations. There was no valid reason for distinguishing the regulations in this case from other similar provisions intended to protect many other types of workers.

5.24 The two cases can be somewhat uneasily reconciled by virtue of a distinction between fishermen and others at sea. However, there must be some doubt as to the validity of the distinction drawn in *Todd* between the Fishing Vessel Construction Rules and the Factories Acts, and the decision seems to cut across the principle enunciated in *Groves v Wimborne*. It is suggested that *Todd* should be treated as confined to its facts until it is the subject of consideration by a higher court.

5.25 While it is established that provisions protecting safety are usually actionable, the position is less clear regarding other provisions. In general, the courts lean towards conferring a right on workers to claim damages for breach of statutory duties imposed on their employers: see Somervell LJ in *Solomons v R Gertzenstein Ltd* [1954] 2 QB 243. However, the test in every case should be that of Lord Diplock in *Lonrho v Shell*, as amplified by Lord Jauncey in *Hague*. In most examples it is clear that even welfare provisions were passed just as much for the benefit or protection of workers as were safety precautions. If a dirty floor leads to a disease or infection, there is every reason for allowing a claim to proceed, as the court held in *Carroll v North British Locomotive Co Ltd* 1957 SLT (Sh Ct) 2. Moreover, it is increasingly clear that even provisions seemingly with comfort as their primary concern can lead to personal injury—witness the expanding application of ergonomics. It is known, for example, that the failure to supply suitable seating may lead to upper limb or back injuries; duties to supply such seats should, therefore, be actionable (such conditions are no doubt 'damage' within the meaning of the HSWA 1974, s 47).[1]

> [1]   In *Wray v Greater London Council* [1987] CLY 2560, Michael Ogden QC held that the now repealed requirement in the Offices Shops and Railway Premises Act 1963, s 14 that a 'seat must be adequately and properly supported whilst in use' gave rise to absolute liability. Cf *Reid v Westfield Paper Co Ltd* 1957 SC 218, in which Lord President Clyde left undecided whether a purely welfare provision, such as facilities for seating, should give rise to liability. See too *Barr v Cruickshank & Co* 1959 SLT (Sh Ct) 9.

5.26   What is a separate and more difficult question is whether the employee has suffered *damage* of the kind the statute is meant to remedy. In *Pickering v Liverpool Daily Post and Echo Newspapers Ltd* [1991] 2 AC 370 at 420, HL, Lord Bridge said that he knew of no statutory duty which had given rise to a cause of action where its breach was not likely to cause personal injury, injury to property or economic loss; and he went on to say that the publication of information about a person's application to a mental health review tribunal, while adverse to his interests, was 'incapable of causing him loss or injury of a kind for which the law awards damages'. But Lord Bridge appeared to accept that the ultimate test is whether the statute was intended to confer a cause of action. If a breach is likely to cause injury that is an *indication* that the intention is present, but the intention may be present even where injury is not a probable consequence of the breach.[1] In principle, then, provisions protecting against discomfort may be actionable, although the necessary intention may be more difficult to show. Breaches of regulations under the HSWA 1974 are actionable to the extent that they cause 'damage' (s 47(2)), defined to include death or injury, in turn defined as including 'any impairment of a person's physical or mental condition' in s 47(6). It is arguable that the inclusion of 'impairment' in the concept of injury goes beyond traditional understandings of what is an 'injury'.

> [1]   There are cases of damages for injury other than personal injury, property damage or economic loss, eg *Ashby v White* (1703) 2 Ld Raym 938 (not cited in *Pickering*): loss of right to vote.

Parallel common law duties

5.27   In the event that it is accepted that a statute cannot be construed so as to allow a private action in damages to be brought for breach of the statutory duty can its content nonetheless be used to create or strengthen a parallel common law duty of care? Again, much depends upon the nature and construction of the Act and the nature of any duty owed.

5.28   The effect of statutory powers and duties on the common law liability of a highway authority was considered by the House of Lords in *Stovin v Wise (Norfolk County Council, third party)* [1996] AC 923. In that case the council had statutory powers which would have enabled it to improve visibility at a junction, and there was evidence that the relevant officers had decided in principle that it should be done, but they had not got round to doing it. The decision of the majority of the House was that the council owed no private law duty to road users to do anything to improve the visibility at the intersection. The statutory power could not be converted into a common law duty. The issue was then revisited in *Gorringe v Calderdale Metropolitan Borough Council* [2004] UKHL 15, [2004] 2 All ER 326. The court considered the provisions of the Road Traffic Act 1988 and held that a local authority did not owe a duty of care to paint markings on the surface of the road or to erect signs warning motorists to slow down on the approach to the crest of a road. The court held that if a statutory duty did not give rise to a private right to sue for breach, the duty could not create a duty of care that would not have been owed at common law if the statute were not there. Lord Hoffmann stated:

> 'If the statute does not create a private right of action, it would be, to say the least, unusual if the mere existence of the statutory duty could generate a common law duty of care'

and after reference to *O'Rourke v Camden London Borough Council* [1998] AC 188 (in which a homeless person sued for damages on the ground that the council had failed in its statutory duty to provide him with accommodation):

> 'In the absence of a right to sue for breach of the statutory duty itself, it would in my opinion have been absurd to hold that the council was nevertheless under a common law duty to take reasonable care to provide accommodation for homeless persons whom it could reasonably foresee would otherwise be reduced to sleeping rough'.

And:

> 'I find it difficult to imagine a case in which a common law duty can be founded simply upon the failure (however irrational) to provide some benefit which a public authority has power (or a public law duty) to provide'.

5.29 Of course in the area of health and safety at work common law duties already exist and it would be rare for there to be the need to argue that the existence of a statutory duty not conferring a right of action nevertheless created a parallel common law duty. Once a duty exists it is a far more attractive argument that statutory control underlines or strengthens that duty. Examples include the breach of the Management of Health and Safety at Work Regulations 1999, reg 3, which previously did not give rise to civil liability. However, the failure by an employer to comply with the general duty to assess the risk of injury pursuant reg 3, has been used to support foresight of harm and breach of subsequent duties (eg see *Griffiths v Vauxhall Motors Ltd* [2003] EWCA Civ 412 and *Sherlock v Chester City Council* [2004] EWCA Civ 210 considered at para 20.35 below).

SCOPE OF THE DUTY

5.30 Once it has been established that breach of a provision in a statute or regulation potentially gives rise to civil liability, it must be determined what the scope of the duty is, on whom it is imposed and to whom it is owed.

The nature of the action for breach of statutory duty: its resemblance to negligence

5.31 It is not generally necessary to establish foresight of harm or fault on the employer's part to establish breach of statutory duty. In *Lochgelly Iron and Coat Co v M'Mullan* [1934] AC 1, the House of Lords rejected an argument that the Workmen's Compensation Act 1925, s 29 only gave rise to a right of action if the breach was negligent or wilful. Despite the close relation of breach of statutory duty to negligence—in that in both it must be shown there was a breach of duty causing harm to the claimant—the two are not equivalent. Lord Wright said in *Caswell v Powell Duffryn Associated Collieries Ltd* [1940] AC 152 at 178:

'I do not think that an action for breach of a statutory duty such as that in question is completely or accurately described as an action in negligence. It is a common law action based on the purpose of the statute to protect the workman, and belonging to the category often described as that of cases of strict or absolute liability. At the same time it resembles actions in negligence in that the claim is based on a breach of a duty to take care for the safety of the workman.'

5.32 The same learned Lord added in *London Passenger Transport Board v Upson* [1949] AC 155 at 168:

'I think that the authorities ... show clearly that a claim of damages for breach of a statutory duty intended to protect a person in the position of the particular plaintiff is a specific common law right which is not to be confused in essence with a claim for negligence. The statutory right has its origin in the statute, but the particular remedy of an action for damages is given by the common law in order to make effective for the benefit of the injured plaintiff his right to the performance by the defendant of the defendant's statutory duty. It is an effective sanction. It is not a claim in negligence in the strict or ordinary sense ... whatever the resemblances, it is essential to keep in mind the fundamental differences of the two classes of claim.'

5.33 Foreseeability of injury will be irrelevant to an action for breach of statutory duty unless the statute expressly introduces such a concept. The Court of Appeal in both *Stark v Post Office* [2000] ICR 1013 and more recently *Ball v Street* [2005] EWCA Civ 76 have made clear that unforeseeable events occurring following faultless conduct by a defendant will not avoid liability when on its face a regulation is breached. In *Larner v British Steel plc* [1993] ICR 551, the Court of Appeal refused to read a test of reasonable foreseeability into the duty to provide a safe workplace under the Factories Act 1961, s 29. Peter Gibson J observed that the words of s 29:

'contain no express reference to foreseeability, reasonable or otherwise. "Safe" is an ordinary English word and I cannot see any reason why the question whether a place of work is safe should not be decided purely as a question of fact, without putting any gloss on the word.'

5.34 Adopting the same approach to that section, in *Mains v Uniroyal Englebert Tyres Ltd* [1995] IRLR 544 Lord Sutherland in the Court of Session said:

'There is nothing whatever in the section to suggest that the obligation is only to prevent any risk arising if that risk is of a reasonably foreseeable nature. Had that been the intention of Parliament it would have been perfectly simple for Parliament to have said so. If the duty had only been to take reasonably practicable precautions against reasonably foreseeable risks it is difficult to see how this section would have added anything of substance to the common law. Where the statute is designed to protect the safety of workmen it is, in my view, not appropriate to read into the statute qualifications which derogate from the purpose.'

5.35 In *Bilton v Fastnet Highlands Ltd* 1998 SLT 1323 at 1326, Lord Nimmo applied the *Larner v British Steel plc* [1993] ICR 551 approach to the Control of Substances Hazardous to Health Regulations 1988, reg 7 and stated:

'the pursuer does not require to do more than aver, as she has done, that she has suffered loss, injury and damage as a result of exposure to certain substances in the course of her employment, that these are substances falling within the ambit of the 1988 Regulations, and that her loss, injury and damage were caused by the defenders' breach of the duties incumbent upon them in terms of these regulations. Regulation 7(1), which is perhaps the most important provision for present purposes, is comparable with the provisions of section 29(1) of the Factories Act 1961 in respect that it imposes an absolute duty, subject to a defence of reasonable practicability.'

5.36 In *Williams v Farne Salmon & Trout Ltd* 1998 SLT 1329 the pursuer alleged that he had developed occupational asthma as a result of exposure to micro-organisms in salmon. The question raised was whether, on a proper construction of the Regulations, employers were only bound to comply with them to the extent that they knew or ought reasonably to foresee that a substance to which an employee was exposed was a substance hazardous to health. The judge noted, at 1333, that the definition was:

'couched in factual terms which are unqualified by the existence of any state of knowledge or reasonable foreseeability ... I can see no difference, for present purposes, between a substance being in fact hazardous to health and a place being in fact unsafe, and in my opinion the 1988 Regulations impose the same kind of absolute duty as is imposed by section 29(1). A number of other provisions of the Regulations reinforce me in this view ... The absolute nature of this duty is, in my view, made abundantly clear by the provisions of regulation 7(1), which uses the word "ensure" in connection with the employer's duties, subject to a limited defence of reasonable practicability in respect of the duty to prevent the exposure of his employees to substances hazardous to health. The risk assessment provisions of regulation 6(1), the monitoring provisions of regulation 10(1) and (3), the surveillance provisions of regulation 11(1) and the information, instruction and training provisions of regulation 12(1) all seem to me to presuppose the actual or potential existence of an objectively verifiable state of affairs, and to place the onus on the employer to discover this, the better to ensure compliance with his absolute duty to protect his employees from exposure to substances hazardous to health.'

5.37 In *Dugmore v Swansea NHS Trust* [2002] EWCA Civ 1689, [2003] 1 All ER 333 the analysis in *Williams* was considered and approved. The Court of Appeal held that, under the Control of Substances Hazardous to

Health Regulations 1988, SI 1998/1657, reg 7,[1] a hospital trust owed a nurse an absolute duty to ensure that her exposure to latex protein was adequately controlled. The trust was in breach of that duty by not supplying the claimant with vinyl gloves instead of powdered latex gloves. The defence of reasonable practicability qualified only the duty of total prevention; 'adequately' was defined in reg 7 without any reference to reasonableness or to the foreseeability of risk: it was a purely practical matter depending upon the nature of the substance and the nature and degree of the exposure. Lady Justice Hale (as she then was) stated:

> 'In our view, that analysis is correct. The duty in regulation 7(1) is an absolute one: to ensure that exposure is prevented or controlled ... the defendant ... sought to persuade us that the words "so far as is reasonably practicable" should be moved from their current position qualifying the duty to prevent exposure so as to qualify the duty to ensure that exposure is either prevented or controlled. There is no warrant for us to rewrite the regulation in this way. Its wording is even stricter than that in section 29(1) of the Factories Act 1961, where the phrase "so far as is reasonably practicable" came between "shall" and "be made and kept safe". If that was an absolute duty, then so must this be'.

1 See now the Control of Substances Hazardous to Health Regulations 2002, SI 2002/2677, reg 7.

5.38 A number of regulations do contain express concepts of foresight of harm as a mechanism for controlling the circumstances covered by the regulation. The Manual Handling Operations Regulations 1992 do not apply to all manual handling operations but only to those imposing a 'risk' of injury. The courts have construed 'risk' in the context of the Regulations as meaning that before the Regulations can be considered to apply in the given circumstances, the employee must prove that the operation posed a foreseeable possibility of harm (see discussion at para 21.36). Other examples of phrases which do introduce a concept of foreseeability include a qualification that the duty is to take 'suitable' steps (see para 5.73, below).

5.39 The distinction between negligence and breach of statute is equally clear in the case of an action based on regulations passed under the HSWA 1974. The action derives from the Act itself.[1] It is a simple question of construction whether the duty is absolute so that safety must be ensured or is qualified by other terms such as 'reasonably practicable' or 'suitable'.[2] Many duties are qualified by such phrases 'reasonably practicable', the natural inference is that those which are not should not have a similar qualification read into them. Concepts derived from common law negligence are, therefore, of little relevance.

1 In particular, s 47(2).
2 Both considered below at paras 5.73–5.83.

Construction of legislation on health and safety

5.40 The construction of a statute is a question of law. The court has to determine what the words of a particular provision mean in a particular context—sometimes regardless of the factual circumstances of the case before it. Once the court has arrived at that meaning, it is legally binding. Without a definitive ruling on a particular word or phrase, it may be hard to predict how the courts will interpret the term. What follows is no more than an outline of the principles.

5.41 Once the court has determined the meaning of words in one context, the decision will generally be followed in interpreting words in other statutes with similar or analogous objects, particularly where statutes have common language, common subject-matter and common intent: see *Goldsmith's Co v Wyatt* [1907] 1 KB 95, CA; *Hamilton v National Coal Board* [1960] AC 633; *Stark v Post Office* [2000] PIQR P 105, CA. A decision on the meaning of a phrase, such as 'reasonably practicable' or 'suitable', in the Factories Act will doubtless apply, in general, to the HSWA 1974 or regulations passed under that Act,[1] unless the context indicates otherwise. In *Stark*, for instance, the Court of Appeal gave the same interpretation to the phrase 'maintained in an efficient state, in efficient working order and in good repair' in reg 6(1) of the Provision and Use of Work Equipment Regulations 1992, introduced under the HSWA 1974, s 15, as had been given to the same words in the Factories Acts.

[1]   Cf the action brought by the commission against the UK in respect of the phrase reasonably practicable in s 2(1); *Commission v United Kingdom* Case C-127/05.

5.42 But the rule is based on presumed Parliamentary intention to follow an already accepted meaning, and may in some circumstances give way to other rules of statutory interpretation. Two should be mentioned. First, in the case of legislation implementing European Directives, that legislation should be interpreted so far as is possible to achieve the same result as European law (see chapter 9, below). This obligation is an overriding one, so that the court should not follow constructions established in other statutes of a similar sort if this would result in a divergence from the relevant provisions of a European Directive. (A similar rule applies to interpretation of legislation in the area of the European Convention on Human Rights, following the Human Rights Act 1998.) Second, to assist in determining what is the object of an Act or the meaning of a particular phrase, the courts may now have regard to Parliamentary materials: see *Pepper (Inspector of Taxes) v Hart* [1993] AC 593.[1] But their use is confined to circumstances where: the terms used are ambiguous, obscure or lead to obscurity; the material consists of statements by a Minister or other promoter of the Bill; and the statement relied upon is clear (see Lord Browne-Wilkinson).[2] In most cases, the wording of the statute alone is the sole guide.

[1]   The courts may also refer to Law Commission papers, White Papers and the like: see *Fothergill v Monarch Airlines Ltd* [1981] AC 251 per Lord Diplock at 281.
[2]   And see *Practice Direction: References to Hansard* [1995] 1 All ER 234.

5.43 Words or phrases used in regulations passed under an Act should be interpreted, like all statutory instruments, in accordance with the meaning defined in the Act unless the contrary intention is plain: Interpretation Act 1978, s 11.[1] The HSWA 1974 defines many of the terms found in the regulations introduced under it, such as 'work', 'employee', 'plant', 'premises', 'substance' and 'supply', so that it should be referred to when considering the meaning of terms used in such regulations.

1 Similarly, in interpreting words which are not defined, the courts presume these to bear the same meaning: *Potts (or Riddell) v Reid* [1943] AC 1. But if subordinate legislation is kept in force by a repealing statute, it should continue to receive the same interpretation as it did before the repeal: *Garcia v Harland & Wolff Ltd* [1943] 1 KB 731. A consolidation Act does not change the law even if it includes a new definition: *Associated Newspapers v Wilson, Associated British Ports v Palmer* [1995] ICR 406, HL.

5.44 The established principles or 'canons' of construction do not call for more than a brief mention here. *Ordinary words* are taken to be used in their ordinary sense, for which the standard dictionaries are a valuable guide, although they are not accepted as conclusive. *Technical words* are understood in their technical sense, which may have to be explained by expert witnesses, but it has first to be shown that the expression is used in a technical sense: *London and North Eastern Rly Co v Berriman* [1946] AC 278 ('permanent way men'). *Sentences and phrases* are construed according to the ordinary rules of grammar, unless there is something in the context which necessitates a deviation from these rules. Weight must be given to the whole of the statute, so that an ambiguity in one section may vanish when other sections are taken into account. The meaning of words may be controlled by the context of many sections.[1] If a section can be read in two alternative ways, one of which will carry out the object of the statute and one of which will not, the section should be interpreted so that the statute will work: *Potts (or Riddell) v Reid* [1943] AC 1 at 16. Lastly, the whole *scheme* of the statute is important—the purpose for which it was passed, and the manner in which it is drawn up to effectuate this purpose. The HSWA 1974 was passed, among other matters, to secure the 'health, safety and welfare of persons at work': just like the earlier Factories Act, this intention should govern the approach to interpretation of individual sections.

1 Eg 'machinery' was interpreted in the context of the Factories Act to mean machinery used in the factory, as distinct from machines made there: *Parvin v Morton Machine Co Ltd* [1952] AC 515; and 'scaffold', in the Building Regulations, meant a scaffold 'in use', as distinct from under construction: *Sexton v Scaffolding (Great Britain) Ltd* [1953] 1 QB 153.

The construction of penal provisions

5.45 Breaches of many of the Acts and regulations in this book are criminal offences which render the offender liable to penalties.[1] In general statutes creating penalties must be construed strictly, so that the benefit of any doubt must be given to the alleged wrongdoer: *Tuck & Sons v Priester* (1887) 19 QBD 629. But this does not mean that the plain meaning of the statute can be cut down by artificial doubts: *A-G v Lockwood* (1842) 9 M & W 378; *Dyke v Elliott, The Gauntlet* (1872) LR 4 PC 184; *Stark v Post Office* [2000] PIQR P 105, CA per Waller LJ at 111. The rule is subject to qualification in the case of legislation protecting workers. According to Denning LJ in *McCarthy v Coldair Ltd* [1951] 2 TLR 1226:

'So far as the Factories Act is concerned, the rule is only to be applied when other rules fail. It is a rule of last resort.'

And in *Harrison v National Coal Board* [1951] AC 639 at 650 Lord Porter said:

'It was suggested ... that the Coal Mines Act 1911 is a measure imposing criminal liability, and, therefore, should be interpreted as throwing no greater burden on the employer than its words compel. It has, however, to be remembered that this Act is also a remedial measure passed for the protection of the workmen and must, therefore, be read so as to effect its object so far as the wording fairly and reasonably permits.'

1 See eg the HSWA 1974, s 33.

5.46 Indeed it is 'an illegitimate method of interpretation of a statute, whose dominant purpose is to protect the workman, to introduce by implication words of which the effect must be to reduce that protection',[1] for example by reading into the words 'securely fenced' the qualification 'so far as practicable': per Viscount Simonds in *John Summers & Sons Ltd v Frost* [1955] AC 740 at 751.[1] Likewise, Hodson LJ said in *Ebbs v James Whitson & Co Ltd* [1952] 2 QB 877 at 886:

'I do not think it is legitimate to import into the language of the statute words attributing knowledge, or a duty of knowledge, to the occupiers. The words *may be injurious* must be given their natural meaning, as opposed to *may possibly* or *may probably*.'

1 See also *R (on the application of Junttan Oy) v Bristol Magistrates' Court* [2003] UKHL 55, [2003] ICR 1475.

5.47 Similarly, the court declined to restrict the full and fair meaning of the Factories Act in *Thurogood v Van den Berghs & Jurgens Ltd* [1951] 2 KB 537, and declined in *Norris v Syndic Manufacturing Co Ltd* [1952] 2 QB 135 to give a lenient meaning to s 119 of the Factories Act 1937, which imposed duties on workers, because 'the Act is intended to prevent accidents to workmen', and for that purpose imposes strict duties on workers as well as on employers. In *Stark v Post Office* [2000] PIQR P 105 the Court of Appeal similarly rejected an argument that reg 6(1) of the Provision and Use of Work Equipment Regulations 1992 should be interpreted narrowly because the regulation gave rise to criminal sanctions as well as civil liability. It preferred the common sense meaning of the phrase 'maintained in an efficient state, in efficient working order and in good repair', based on the interpretation of the same phrase in earlier legislation.[1] This approach, of not construing duties narrowly, is equally applicable to regulations implementing European Directives: the Directives, and hence the regulations derived from them, are not intended to reduce existing standards of protection.[2]

1 See too *Swain v Denso Marston Ltd* [2000] PIQR P 129, CA at 133–134.
2 See *Stark v Post Office* [2000] PIQR P 105, CA, the citation from the third edition of *Redgrave's Health and Safety* at 109 and the judgment of Waller LJ at 112.

5.48 Nevertheless, there are two situations where the maxim as to strict construction of penal statutes has significant force. First, there may be an *ambiguity:* but, said Denning LJ in *McCarthy's* case, above, 'this ... does not mean every ambiguity which the ingenuity of counsel may suggest, but only an ambiguity which the settled rules of construction fail to solve'.[1] Such an ambiguity occurred in *London and North Eastern Rly Co v Berriman* [1946] AC 278, where a doubt arose whether 'repairs' to a railway line included the oiling of signals. Another example was *Richard Thomas & Baldwins Ltd v Cummings* [1955] AC 321, where the question was whether machinery is 'in motion' when the power is cut off and it is moved by hand. Second, the court may refuse to give an equitable or benevolent construction to a statute by stretching its meaning beyond what is fairly expressed. A court will not put 'a strained meaning on the words' merely because the general intention of the Act is to protect workers: *Haigh v Charles W Ireland Ltd* [1973] 3 All ER 1137.

[1] See too James LJ in *Dyke v Elliott, The Gauntlet* (1872) LR 4 PC 184 at 191, cited in *Stark v Post Office* [2000] PIQR P 105, CA per Waller LJ at 111.

Upon whom is the duty imposed?

5.49 It is generally clear from the wording of a statute or piece of legislation upon whom the duty is imposed. Regulations under the HSWA 1974, which may be made for a number of broad purposes including but not restricted to 'securing the health, safety and welfare of persons at work', specify whether they apply to employers, occupiers, the self-employed or others in control of the work or workplace.[1] The Workplace (Health, Safety and Welfare) Regulations 1992, SI 1992/3004, for example, apply to employers as well as those who have 'to any extent, control of a workplace, extension or conversion'.[2] The Provision and Use of Work Equipment Regulations 1998, SI 1998/2306 apply to all employers and also to all those who have control, to any extent, of work equipment, a person at work who uses or supervises that equipment or the way in which work equipment is used at work.[3] In recognition of the nature of construction sites, the Construction (Health, Safety and Welfare) Regulations 1996, SI 1996/1592 will often not apply to the employer of a worker but instead to the contractor who controls that worker's work and workplace.[4]

[1] See eg the consideration of 'control' under the Construction (Health, Safety and Welfare) Regulations 1996 at para 19.24ff.
[2] See reg 4(1), (2) and discussion in context at para 18.18ff, below.
[3] See reg 3 and discussion in context at para 20.16ff.
[4] See chapter 19.

To whom are duties owed?

5.50 This, too, is a matter of construing the particular provision. The general provisions of the Factories Act 1961 were held to apply to all persons working in the factory, whether employed by the owner or not[1] and even if they were not doing work they were employed to do[2] or were working in an area where the employer could not foresee they would be. The phrase 'any workman employed by him' in the Construction (General Provisions) Regulations 1961, SI 1961/1580 did not apply to an independent contractor,[3] though it was not

5.50 *Breach of statutory duty*

restricted to building workers.[4] It was held that the Offshore Installations (Operational Safety, Health and Welfare) Regulations 1976[5] were intended to protect workers at all times when they are near the installation, including when not working, or resting or even harmed by another employee acting outside the scope of his or her employment: see *Robb v Salamis* [2005] SLT 523 and *MacMillan v Wimpey Offshore Engineers and Construction Ltd* 1991 SLT 515. By contrast, the Offices, Shops and Railway Premises 1963 do not extend to protecting a shop customer: *Reid v Galbraith Stores* 1970 SLT (Notes) 83.

1 See *John Summers & Sons Ltd v Frost* [1955] AC 740, HL.
2 See eg *Uddin v Associated Portland Cement Manufactures Ltd* [1965] 2 QB 582 and, on the Offices, Shops and Railways Premises Act 1963, s 16, *Westwood v Post Office* [1974] AC 1.
3 See *Herbert v Harold Shaw Ltd* [1959] 2 QB 138, CA. See too *Jones v Minton Construction Ltd* (1973) 15 KIR 309; *Smith v George Wimpey & Co Ltd* [1972] 2 QB 329.
4 See *Field v Perrys (Ealing) Ltd* [1950] 2 All ER 521 (night watchman).
5 Now revoked and replaced by SI 1998/2307.

5.51 Duties under regulations introduced under the HSWA 1974 are almost always owed to employees: defined in s 53(1); but see s 48 (Crown servants) and s 51A (police). Section 47(2) simply states that 'breach of a duty imposed by health and safety regulations shall, so far as it causes damage, be actionable', so that regulations can permit non-employees to bring an action. The regulations sometimes make clear that the duties apply only to employees. On other occasions, the regulations expressly apply to others carrying out work but who are not employees.[1] On rare occasions the regulations expressly cover those not at work but who may nevertheless still be affected by the work.[2] The purpose of regulations introduced under the HSWA 1974 can extend to protecting 'persons other than persons at work against risks to health or safety arising out of or in connection with the activities of persons at work'[3] so that recovery by persons other than employees is possible, depending upon the wording of the particular regulations.

1 See eg the Manual Handling Operations Regulations 1992, SI 1992/2793, reg 4: see para 21.20ff.
2 See eg the Construction (Health, Safety and Welfare) Regulations 1996, SI 1996/1592, reg 4: see para 19.15ff.
3 See eg the Control of Substances Hazardous to Health Regulations 2002, SI 2002/2677, reg 3: see para 22.13.

5.52 There have been numerous first instance decisions concerning the issue of whether those not at work, such as visitors to shop premises, can claim for breach of the Workplace (Health, Safety and Welfare) Regulations 1992. The Inner House in *Donaldson v Hays Distribution Services Ltd* 2005 SLT 733 concluded that the protection of the Regulations was not afforded to non-workers present in the workplace. Giving the opinion of the court, Lord Macfadyen analysed the numerous decisions in Scotland and England and Wales, the previous legislation, the Regulations and the European Directives and concluded as follows:

'Drawing together the various considerations which we have reviewed, we conclude from:

i   the fact that the Workplace Regulations were enacted to give effect in the United Kingdom to the Workplace Directive, which applies exclusively for the protection of workers;

ii   the absence of any positive indication in the legislation that it was intended that the Workplace Regulations should afford protection to those coming onto premises as visitors and not workers; and

iii the extreme improbability that the legislative intention was to supersede much of the law of occupiers' liability tacitly by the mere use of general language which might be said in the abstract to be capable of having that effect;

that on a sound construction of the Workplace Regulations in the relevant context they afford no protection to persons present in a workplace as visitors but not as workers. That does not mean that such persons are left unprotected. They continue to have the protection afforded to visitors to premises by the antecedent, and subsisting, law relating to occupiers' liability'.[1]

This decision accords with the decision of the Court of Appeal in *Ricketts v Torbay County Council* [2003] EWCA Civ 613 but which, given that it was an application for permission to appeal, may not be cited as authority.[2] The only common regulation which expressly applies to non-workers on the premises remains the Control of Substances Hazardous to Health Regulations 2002, which arguably also applies to neighbours of the premises.[3]

1   *Donaldson v Hays Distribution Services* [2005] CSIH 48 per Lord Macfadyen at para 35.
2   See *Practice Direction (Citation of Authorities)* [2001] 1 WLR 1001.
3   SI 2002/2677; see para 22.13, below.

CAUSATION

5.53 Causation for breach of statutory duty is dealt with in accordance with the same principles as negligence: see *Bonnington Castings Ltd v Wardlaw* [1956] AC 613 at 620, 624. Just as in the case of liability in negligence, a breach of statutory duty followed by an injury of the kind contemplated by the statute does not entail liability: it must be shown, on the balance of probabilities, that the breach caused the damage: see Lord MacMillan in *Caswell v Powell Duffryn Associated Collieries Ltd* [1940] AC 152 at 168. Causation is dealt with above in chapter 3.

5.54 A claimant is not required to establish that the defendant's breach of statutory duty is the sole or only cause of his injury and damage.[1] Accordingly, in the manual handling case of *O'Neill v DSG Retail Ltd* [2002] EWCA Civ 1139 the test applied by the Court of Appeal on causation was whether the defendant's breach was *a* cause of the injury (see Chadwick LJ at para 89). This approach was expressly adopted in *Goodchild v Organon Laboratories Ltd* [2004] EWHC 2341 (QB) at para 47. Similarly, it is no defence for the defendant to show that some other, non-wrongful, factor was also responsible for the claimant's injury.[2]

1   Lord Reid in *Stapley v Gypsum Mines Ltd* [1953] AC 663 681, HL.
2   *McGhee v National Coal Board* [1972] 3 All ER 1008 or more recently *Nixon v Chanceoption Developments Ltd* [2002] EWCA Civ 558.

NATURE OF THE HARM

5.55 If the statute is designed to protect against specified harm, then an action will fail if the damage suffered is not of the kind of harm against which the statute is designed to protect: *Gorris v Scott* (1874) LR 9 Exch 125 (sheep washed off ship in breach of duty to fence to protect against disease). Harm could be defined, widely or narrowly, to refer to a type of *injury*; or it could implicitly refer to *how* the injury was caused (for example, by defining the harm as injury from falling objects). Most of the cases concern the second category; but in some cases it may be clear that injury at all or of a particular kind was outside the scope of the section.[1] In *Fytche v Wincanton Logistics plc* [2004] UKHL 31, the claimant was employed to drive a tanker, and was provided with boots to protect his feet against injury from heavy objects. When digging the tanker out of snow he was unaware of a hole in one of his boots and suffered frostbite. In relation to an allegation of breach of the Personal Protective Equipment at Work Regulations 1992, reg 7(1) it was held by a majority, that reg 4 of the 1992 Regulations required employers to provide equipment suitable to protect employees against an identified risk; that the duty under reg 7(1) was to maintain and repair the equipment so that it continued to provide protection against that identified risk (falling heavy objects) and did not extend to repairs or maintenance having no bearing on its function as personal protective equipment.

[1]   See *Peabody Donation Fund (Governors) v Sir Lindsay Parkinson & Co Ltd* [1985] AC 210, where the House of Lords held that statutory powers of inspection of buildings were intended to protect against health rather than economic loss: a decision which focuses on the kind of harm rather than its manner of infliction.

5.56 The Court of Appeal in *Ball v Street* [2005] EWCA Civ 76 rejected any attempt to make *Fytche* into a case having any wider relevance than interpretation of its own regulation. In *Ball* the claimant was injured by a broken spring when repairing a haybob. The defendant argued successfully (at first instance) that the Provision and Use of Work Equipment Regulations 1998, SI 1998/2306 dealt only with identified risks of injury under the Regulations. The Court of Appeal rejected the defendant's arguments and allowed the appeal. Potter LJ held that PUWER dealt with the general duty to maintain work equipment so as to prevent injury to the person using the equipment and there was no basis for seeking to limit the Regulations to identified or foreseeable risks. The focus of PUWER was not upon the identification and assessment of risk concerning particular identified hazards (as were the Personal Protective Equipment Regulations 1992, SI 1992/2966) but upon general considerations of safety against the broad risk of accidental injury inherent in the use of machinery. As such any and all harm suffered was covered by the Regulations. It is submitted that the approach of *Fytche* will be applicable to regulations concerning specific matters; for example the Control of Noise at Work Regulations 2005, SI 2005/1643, where impaired hearing caused by noise exposure must be proved before relevant breaches can be alleged.

5.57 It is not usually necessary that the damage must be sustained in the precise manner which the statute appears to contemplate.[1] The HSWA 1974 expressly defines what is meant by 'damage' giving rise to liability for a breach of regulations introduced under it, reducing the scope for nice arguments on this issue. However, occasionally the wording of a provision may indicate that only damage caused in a certain manner is actionable. For example, breach of a duty 'not to do anything to endanger the safety of himself or other persons on or near the installation' in reg 32(3)(a) (now repealed) of the Offshore Installations (Operational Safety) Regulations 1976 did not extend to protect a worker who suffered psychiatric injury through witnessing the Piper Alpha disaster but who was not personally in physical danger.[2] But illustrating the general tendency to construe provisions widely, in *Donaghey v Boulton & Paul Ltd* [1968] AC 1, HL a regulation requiring crawling boards above a fragile roof was held to give protection against any fall from the roof, although the fragile material was not broken. It was irrelevant that a worker's arm was drawn into a machine in an unexpected manner in *Millard v Serck Tubes Ltd* [1969] 1 All ER 598 and a worker who injured his back while attempting to remove an obstruction recovered under a regulation stating that walkways were to be kept free from obstruction in *McGovern v British Steel Corpn* [1986] ICR 608, CA.[3]

1   In *Grant v National Coal Board* [1956] AC 649 the House of Lords held that the object of the Coal Mines Act was to safeguard miners against accidents generally. Hence an action could be brought based on a provision under which a roof had to be kept secure where the pursuer was injured by the derailment of a bogie when it struck a stone previously fallen from the roof.
2   *McFarlane v Wilkinson* [1997] 2 Lloyd's Rep 259, CA.
3   See, too, *Callow (FE) (Engineers) Ltd v Johnson* [1971] AC 335 at 341 per Lord Hailsham LC.

STATUTORY DUTY: HOW FAR ABSOLUTE?

5.58 Where a statute lays down a particular duty, that duty must be met and it is no defence to argue that performance of that duty was delegated to another. Instead of this clear certainty, what often causes difficulty is ascertaining the precise nature of the duty, which is again a matter of construction and standards of reasonable practicability or suitability can qualify a duty. The duty will generally specify the steps or procedures to be taken rather than the end result to be met.

Liability unaffected by delegation

5.59 If a statute places duties on an employer, and the latter delegates them to a subordinate or to an independent contractor—however competent—the employer remains liable if the duties are not performed. It is, therefore, no defence to breach of statutory duty for an employer to engage an independent contractor to fulfill a duty imposed on the employer. Delegation is only a defence if on the true construction of a statute the duty can be met simply by delegation and the employer has in fact delegated the work.[1] It is rare that health and safety legislation is construed in this way. The basic principle is as articulated by Lord Atkin in *Lochgelly Iron and Coal Co v M'Mullan* [1934] AC 1 when he said, at 8–9:

'... the duty is imposed upon the employer, and it is irrelevant whether his servants had disregarded his instructions or whether he knew or not of the breach.'

1   See *Donaghey v Boulton & Paul Ltd* [1968] AC 1, HL: no delegation in fact.

5.60 In *R v Associated Octel Co Ltd* [1996] 4 All ER 846 the House of Lords rejected an argument that if an employer delegated cleaning work to independent contractors it was not criminally liable under s 3(1) of the HSWA 1974 because it had no right to control how the independent contractors did their work. The statutory wording imposes a duty on an employer 'to conduct his undertaking in such a way as to ensure, so far as is reasonably practicable, that persons not in his employment who may be affected thereby are not thereby exposed to risks to their health and safety'. Lord Hoffmann stated:

'Section 3 requires the employer to [conduct his undertaking] in a way which, subject to reasonably practicability, does not create risks to people's health and safety. If, therefore, the employer engages an independent contractor to do work which forms part of the conduct of the employer's undertaking, he must stipulate for whatever conditions are needed to avoid those risks and are reasonably practicable. He cannot, having omitted to do so, say that he was not in a position to exercise any control.'

He went on to state that the 'question, as it seems to me, is simply whether the activity in question can be described as part of the employer's undertaking'. Whether the activity was delegated to a person for whose actions the employer was vicariously liable was, therefore, not decisive.

5.61 Similar reasoning applies to duties under regulations which give rise to civil liability. Many of the regulations introduced under the HSWA 1974 expressly place the obligations on the employer or another. By way of example, the Workplace (Health, Safety and Welfare) Regulations 1992, reg 4 states that:

'every employer shall ensure that every workplace ... which is under his control and where any of his employees works complies with any requirement of these Regulations which ... applies to that workplace'.

Such express statements are clearly inconsistent with a defence of delegation: the relevant obligations are placed on the employer.

Liability not dependent on fault, negligence or practicability

5.62 It follows, too, that a statutory obligation must be met; it is not, as a rule, necessary to show that a defendant was negligent, or that it was not practicable to meet the duty: see eg Lord Browne-Wilkinson in *X v Bedfordshire County Council* [1995] 2 AC 633, HL. Where a statute said that lifts shall be properly maintained in efficient working order, and a workman was injured through the braking mechanism failing, the employer was liable even though no-one could account for the failure: *Galashiels Gas Co Ltd v O'Donnell (or Millar)* [1949] AC 275. Lord MacDermott said, at 286:

'My Lords, if this means that every lift shall be kept continuously—or at least while it is available for use as a lift—in efficient working order, the nature of the obligation is clear. It then falls into a category long recognised and firmly established by authority; it is a strict or absolute duty and neither intention nor lack of care need be shown in order to prove a breach of it ... There was abundant proof that the mechanism had failed and that that failure resulted in the death of the respondent's husband. Once the absolute nature of the duty imposed *by* the statute is established that is proof enough.'

5.63 In *Stark v Post Office* [2000] PIQR P 105 the Court of Appeal held that reg 6(1) of the Provision and Use of Work Equipment Regulations 1992 (see now reg 5 of the 1998 Regulations) imposed an absolute obligation to maintain equipment in efficient working order, so that it was breached when the brake stirrup on a postman's bike broke, stuck in the front wheel and caused him to fall, even though the defect in the brake could not have been discovered by a rigorous examination.[1]

1   See also *Lewis v Avidan Ltd* [2005] EWCA Civ 670.

5.64 If a duty is qualified by terms such as 'reasonably practicable' or 'suitable', as are the general duties in the HSWA 1974, ss 2–6[1] and many of the relevant duties in regulations passed under that Act, the standard of compliance is obviously qualified (the meaning of these terms is considered below). The terms 'effective' or 'suitable' equipment do not mean perfect equipment.

1   Cf the action brought by the Commission against the United Kingdom (Case C-127/05).

5.65 The court cannot decide that a statute imposes less than an absolute obligation where the word 'shall' is used in the absence of clear words to the contrary. Qualifications such as reasonable care or foreseeability will not generally be read into statutory provisions. Thus, in *Larner v British Steel plc* [1993] ICR 551, the Court of Appeal refused to apply a test of reasonable foresight into the statutory duty to maintain a safe place of work.

Contravention of statute automatically establishes liability

5.66 In summary, whatever an Act requires to be done must be done, although it is always a matter of construction precisely what is the nature of the obligation. It is in this sense that, subject to causation, every statutory duty is absolute. As Lord Atkin said in *Smith v Cammell Laird & Co Ltd* [1940] AC 242 at 258:

'It is precisely in the absolute obligation imposed by statute to perform or forbear from performing a specified activity that a breach of statutory duty differs from the obligation imposed by common law, which is to take reasonable care to avoid injuring another.'

5.67 In this sense, a statutory duty is absolute even though it is qualified by the words 'as far as is reasonably practicable': for it is a question of fact whether a thing is reasonably practicable or not, and unless, on the facts, it is not reasonably practicable, the requirement must be carried out.

DEFENCES TO AN ACTION FOR BREACH OF STATUTORY DUTY

5.68 Using the word 'defence' in its broadest sense, the defence to an action for breach of statutory duty may take the form of denying that the duty was imposed on the defendant, that it was not as wide or absolute as alleged, or that it was broken. Alternatively, the defendant may deny that the claimant was intended to benefit from the statute, that the injuries have been caused by the breach, or that the accident was the sort of occurrence which the statute was designed to prevent.[1] All these points are essential ingredients in the claimant's cause of action; but there are other defences which set up exceptions—complete or partial—to a prima facie liability.

1   Eg *Fytche v Wincanton Logistics plc* [2004] UKHL 31, [2004] ICR 975.

5.69 By virtue of the HSWA 1974, s 15(6)(b), regulations made under that Act may 'provide for any specified defence to be available in proceedings for any offence under the relevant statutory provisions either generally or in specified circumstances'.[1] But by s 47(3) such a defence is inapplicable to civil proceedings unless the regulations so provide. Many duties in regulations are, however, qualified by the standard of reasonable practicability, and the onus of proving that all reasonably practicable steps were taken lies on the defendant.[2]

1   'Relevant statutory provisions' mean the provisions of Part 1 of the Act, regulations made under it and the existing statutory provisions—see s 53(1).
2   *Nimmo v Alexander Cowan & Sons Ltd* [1968] AC 107.

5.70 It is established law that the defence of voluntary acceptance of the risk ('volenti non fit injuria') is not available in answer to a breach of the employer's statutory duty: *Baddeley v Earl of Granville* (1887) 19 QBD 423; *Wheeler v New Merton Board Mills Ltd* [1933] 2 KB 669;[1] (see paras 6.70 and 6.71, below).

1   Although the defence is not available if the employer is in breach of a duty imposed on it, volenti may be a defence to a breach of statutory duty imposed on fellow-workers, for which the employer would otherwise be vicariously liable: *ICI Ltd v Shatwell* [1965] AC 656; see paras 6.58–6.71, below.

5.71 In some cases an employee who solely brings about breach of his or her employer's statutory duty may be totally precluded from recovering damages.[1] But the courts have been rightly slow to find this to have been the case. In *Boyle v Kodak Ltd* [1969] 1 WLR 661 the House of Lords held that to escape a breach of a statutory duty, the defendant had to establish that the claimant was wholly to blame or that the defendant had done all that was reasonable to ensure compliance. *Boyle* is authority for the high standard required to shift the statutory duty from the defendant to the claimant. As Lord Reid stated:

'Employers are bound to know their statutory duty and take all reasonable steps to prevent their men from committing breaches. If an employer does not do that he cannot take advantage of this defence. On the respondents' admission there is a difference under this regulation between cases where there is another practicable means of access to the top of the ladder, and cases where there is none or where there is nothing to which the ladder can be lashed. In the former case the man must use the alternative means of access, here the stairway, to get to the top to lash the ladder, and then return that way before ascending the ladder; in the latter case he is permitted to ascend the ladder without lashing it. I think the evidence shows that a skilled practical man might easily fail to appreciate this and that the respondents ought to have realised that and instructed their men accordingly. So they have not proved that they did all they could reasonably be expected to do to ensure compliance and they cannot rely on this defence so as to avoid their absolute vicarious liability under the regulation'.

For a recent affirmation of this principle see the helpful analysis of Latham LJ in *Sherlock v Chester City Council* [2004] EWCA Civ 201. Where a shift of the blame for a breach is made onto the employee's shoulders, there should be no question of contributory negligence because there was no blame on the part of the defendant to be apportioned. Indeed whether a claim was in negligence or for breach of a statutory duty, if the evidence showed that the entirety of the blame fell on the claimant, there should be no liability on the defendant (as reaffirmed in *Anderson v Newham College of Further Education* [2002] EWCA Civ 505).

1   But note in relation to arguments of contributory negligence that the purpose of imposing absolute duties is to protect workmen against those very acts of inattention which are sometimes relied upon as constituting contributory negligence, so that too strict a standard would defeat the object of the statute: *Staveley Iron and Chemical Co Ltd v Jones* [1956] AC 627; as recently cited with approval in *Toole v Bolton Metropolitan Borough Council* [2002] EWCA Civ 588; see generally chapter 6 and in particular paras 6.27–6.34.

CONSTRUCTION OF KEY WORDS USED TO DEFINE THE NATURE AND EXTENT OF STATUTORY DUTIES

Shall

5.72 The word '*shall*' means must and imposes a mandatory obligation to comply. When unqualified by other words, the presence of the word '*shall*' imposes an absolute and continuing obligation. Qualifications such as reasonable care or foreseeability will not be read into statutory provisions. Thus, in *Larner v British Steel plc* [1993] 4 All ER 102, the Court of Appeal refused to apply a test of reasonable foresight into the statutory duty to maintain a safe place of work. As demonstrated in *Stark v Post Office* [2000] ICR 1013, even where it is impossible to anticipate a failure before the event or explain it afterwards and even where all reasonable steps have been taken by an employer to comply with a duty, the simple fact that a state of affairs exists which is contrary to the duty places the employer in breach. The court cannot decide that a statute imposes less than an absolute obligation where the word 'shall' is used in the absence of clear words to the contrary.

Suitable

5.73 The word 'suitable' introduces a concept of foresight of harm into the regulations. It is used widely throughout health and safety regulations and its meaning can vary according to the context in which it appears. The contexts in which it has been considered by the appellate courts to date are the Provision and Use of Work Equipment Regulations 1998, reg 4[1] and the Workplace (Health, Safety and Welfare) Regulations 1992, SI 1992/3004, reg 12(1). The interpretation of 'suitability' under PUWER reg 4 (the duty to ensure that work equipment is suitable) is expressly defined by reg 4(4) as meaning suitable in any respect of which it is reasonably foreseeable will affect the healthy and safety of any person. In *Robb v Salamis* 2005 SLT 523 the Inner House concluded that the meaning of 'reasonably foreseeable' was the same as the common law meaning. In *Horton v Taplin Contracts Ltd* [2002] EWCA Civ 1604, [2003] ICR 179 it was considered that the target of achieving suitability for purpose was to be measured by reference to such hazards to anyone's health or safety as are reasonably foreseeable. Bodey J (sitting in the Court of Appeal) considered that the risk that a colleague would deliberately topple a scaffold tower by intentionally applying force to do so, was not foreseeable and accordingly the scaffold was suitable despite it toppling in unforeseeable circumstances.

[1]   See para 20.20, below.

5.74 Many of the cases defining 'suitability' have concerned the Workplace (Health, Safety and Welfare) Regulations 1992, reg 12(1) regulating the construction of floor surfaces. In *Palmer v Marks & Spencer plc* [2001] EWCA Civ 1528, the claimant tripped on a marginally raised weather strip in a doorway by the top of a flight of stairs. The Court of Appeal held that whilst reg 12(1) imposed an absolute duty, the meaning of 'suitable' was to be found in the reference to 'risk to ... health and safety' in reg 12(2). Therefore, suitability must be examined from a health and safety point of view. The mere fact of an accident due to an anomaly in the floor surface was not sufficient to establish that the floor was not suitable. The question whether the floor surface posed a risk to health and safety involved consideration of all relevant factors including the likelihood of harm, the potential seriousness of resulting injury and importance of taking adequate precautions. These factors have to be considered from a point in time before the accident which gave rise to the claim. A similar conclusion was reached in the Scottish case of *McGhee v Strathclyde Fire Brigade* 2002 SLT 680, OH in which a fireman slipped on the surface of a corridor floor alleged to be not suitable because of its slipperiness. The Outer House (Lord Hamilton) considered that the test of whether the slipperiness of the floor surface was in breach of reg 12(1) was whether the floor was sufficiently slippery so as to expose a person to a risk to his health or safety as referred to in reg 12(2). The court considered that the regulation envisaged that a floor may, by its construction, be slippery so as to expose any person to a risk to his health or safety, or so as not to do so. It was only slipperiness of the first kind to which the regulation was directed.[1]

[1]   See also *Lowles v The Home Office* [2004] EWCA Civ 985 and chapter 18 below.

5.75 The test of suitability set out by Waller LJ in *Palmer v Marks & Spencer plc* [2001] EWCA Civ 1528 has been applied widely. Waller LJ considered that the test must be carried out as matters were at the time of the accident and without the benefit of hindsight. In *Yorkshire Traction Co Ltd v*

Searby [2003] EWCA Civ 1856 (a case concerning PUWER, reg 4) both Pill and Chadwick LJJ supported this approach stating that what is required is a qualitative assessment of the risk of injury.

5.76 Suitability does not include any reference to the cost of additional precautions. The question arose in *Skinner v Scottish Ambulance Service* [2004] SC 790, IH with regard to the suitability of equipment and, if one piece of equipment were safer than another, whether the increased cost of the safer equipment could be considered a factor so as to make the cheaper but less safe equipment suitable. The Inner House concluded that, in the absence of a qualification of reasonable practicability, no consideration of cost was admissible and it was not open to the court to take into account the increased cost of safer equipment.

Reasonably practicable

5.77 The expression 'reasonably practicable' has a long history in health and safety legislation. Formerly present in numerous sections of the Factories Act 1961 as a qualification of the statutory duties, the term reasonably practicable is now found in many provisions of regulations passed under the HSWA 1974. The leading case on the meaning of the words '*reasonably practicable*' has long been *Edwards v National Coal Board* [1949] 1 KB 704, CA, in which Asquith LJ, setting out a 'balancing test' said (at 712):

> '"Reasonably practicable" is a narrower term than "physically possible", and seems to me to imply that a computation must be made by the owner in which the quantum of risk is placed on one scale and the sacrifice involved in the measures necessary for averting the risk (whether in money, time or trouble) is placed in the other, and that, if it be shown that there is a gross disproportion between them—the risk being insignificant in relation to the sacrifice—the defendants discharge the onus on them.'

The primary consideration of the phrase by the appellate courts in recent years has been in relation to the Workplace (Health, Safety and Welfare) Regulations 1992, reg 12(3), which states that floors should be kept free from obstructions 'so far as is reasonably practicable' and the duties in the Manual Handling Regulations 1992, which are similarly qualified. The interpretation of 'reasonable practicability' set out in *Edwards* has been expressly and repeatedly adopted by the Court of Appeal, see by way of example *Hawkes v London Borough of Southwark* (20 February 1998, unreported) and *O'Neill v DSG Retail Ltd* [2002] EWCA Civ 1139.

5.78 The burden of proving that all reasonably practicable steps have been taken is on the defendant. Accordingly, once a claimant has established that he or she sustained injury and that a cause of that injury was a breach of statutory duty, the burden of proof switches to the defendant: *Larner v British Steel plc* [1993] ICR 551. This view is also set out clearly by Staughton LJ in *Hawkes v London Borough of Southwark* (20 February 1998, unreported), CA, although he himself doubted its application in *Koonjul v Thameslink Healthcare Services* [2000] PIQR P 123. It is submitted that the overwhelming weight of authority supports the proposition that the burden of pleading and proving that all reasonably practicable steps have been taken is upon the defendant both in the context of the Manual Handling Operations Regulations 1992, SI 1992/2793 (see *Hawkes, Cullen, Anderson v Lothian Health Board* [1996] SCLR 1068; *King v RCO Support Services Ltd* [2001] ICR 608; *Skinner v Aberdeen City Council* [2001] Rep LR 118; *O'Neill v DSG Retail Ltd* [2002] EWCA Civ 1139; *Wright v Romford Blinds and Shutters Ltd* [2003] EWHC 1165 (QB) *and Davidson v Lothian and Borders Fire Board* 2003 SLT 939) and in respect of other statutory duties containing the same words (eg the Factories Act 1961, s 29: *Larner v British Steel plc* [1993] ICR 551, and the Coal Mines Act 1922, s 102: *Edwards v National Coal Board* [1949] 1 KB 704. See also *Hall v City of Edinburgh Council* 1999 SLT 744) and in the criminal context: *Sheldrake v DPP* [2003] EWHC 273 (Admin).

5.79 *Larner v British Steel plc* [1993] ICR 551, decided in relation to the Factories Act 1961, s 29(1) has been applied extensively to the interpretation of the modern version of that duty; the Workplace (Health, Safety and Welfare) Regulations 1992, reg 12(3). Per Tuckey LJ in *Bassie v Merseyside Fire and Civil Defence Authority* [2005] EWCA Civ 1474 at para 11:

> 'No question of knowledge or foreseeability is involved at this stage. The mere presence of a substance which may cause a person to slip is enough to engage the obligation imposed by the Regulation, subject to the reasonably practicable defence, which it is for the employer to prove.'

5.80 However, the effect of failure to plead any defence of reasonable practicability should be viewed in the light of the dictum of May LJ in *Pratt v Intermet Refractories Ltd* (21 January 2000, unreported), CA, that a claimant's objection that the defence had not been pleaded had no place 'in modern litigation' if the claimant was not prejudiced and the matter could be fully argued before the court.

5.81 Regarding the interpretation of the reasonable practicability defence in reg 12(3) of the Workplace Regulations, courts have interpreted the defence of reasonable practicability very strictly against defendants and repeatedly found defendants unable to prove the defence: see *Robinson v Midland Bank* (27 October, 2000, unreported), CA; *Anderson v Newham College of Further Education* [2002] EWCA Civ 505; *Harper v Staffordshire County Council* [2003] EWHC 283 (QB); *Lowles v Home Office* [2004] EWCA Civ 985; *Burgess v Plymouth City Council* [2005] EWCA Civ 1659; *Bassie v Merseyside Fire and Civil Defence Authority* [2005] EWCA Civ 1474.

5.82 The strictness of the test and the reversal of the burden of proof was challenged by a defendant in the context of a criminal conviction under the HSWA 1974: *R v Davies* [2002] EWCA Crim 2949. The Court of Appeal held that the duty and the reversal of the burden of proof took into account the fact that the duty-holders have chosen to engage in work or commercial activity and are in charge of it. They are therefore not unengaged or disinterested members of the public and in choosing to operate in a regulated sphere of activity, they must be taken to have accepted the regulatory controls that go with it. Where the duty holder has been shown not to have achieved the safety standard required by the duty, it was not unjustifiable or unfair to ask that duty-holder to prove that it had taken all reasonably practicable steps.

5.83 There has also been criticism that use of the term 'reasonably practicable' in the HSWA 1974, s 2(1) restricts the duty on employers to ensure health and safety and as a result there has been failure to comply with the Framework Directive 89/391, and specifically the obligations under art 5(1) and 5(4) (the legislative history of the Directive revealing express rejection of a 'so far as reasonably practicable' clause).[1]

1 See *Commission v United Kingdom* Case C-127/05.

Practicable

5.84 To do what is practicable involves more than taking reasonable care. 'Practicable' means that which is feasible, that which can be done. Lord Goddard said in *Lee v Nursery Furnishings Ltd* [1945] 1 All ER 387:

'"Practicable" is defined in the *Oxford Dictionary* as "capable of being carried out in action" or "feasible".'

5.85 And Hallett J said in *Schwalb v H Fass & Son Ltd* (1946) 175 LT 345:

'Clearly, the fact that the use of the appliances would slow up production does not render their use impracticable; and I have no right to substitute for the word "impracticable" expressions such as "difficult", "not too easy" or "inconvenient" or any other word.'

5.86 In considering what is practicable, account must be taken of the state of knowledge at the time. A defendant cannot be held liable for failing to use a method which, at the material time, had not been invented: *Adsett v K & L Steelfounders and Engineers Ltd* [1953] 2 All ER 320; nor for failing to take measures against a danger which was not known to exist: *Richards v Highway Ironfounders (West Bromwich) Ltd* [1955] 3 All ER 205 (subsequent proceedings [1957] 2 All ER 162: invisible dust not known at the time to be the cause of silicosis, therefore not practicable to insist on masks where only advantage over others was protection against invisible dust). But commercial considerations are not relevant: see e g *TNT Express v Richmond upon Thames London Borough Council* (1995) Times, 27 June.

Reasonably practicable in legislation implementing European Directives

5.87 English courts are under a duty to interpret legislation intended to implement European Directives as far as possible to achieve the same result as the Directive, and that duty should override competing rules of statutory interpretation. The Directives do not use the phrase 'reasonably practicable', but it appears in many of the regulations implementing the Directives and, as mentioned above, has been used in UK legislation for many years. Comparison between Directions and regulations is complicated, as regulations do not enact Directives word for word and can impose higher standards than the minimum required by the Directive. As set out above there has been criticism from the Commission that use of the term 'reasonably practicable' in the HSWA 1974, s 2(1) restricts the duty on employers to ensure health and safety and as a result there has been failure to comply with the Framework Directive 89/391 and specifically the obligations under art 5(1) and 5(4) (the legislative history of the Directive revealing express rejection of a so far as reasonably practicable clause).[1] However, the true tension between interpretation of the Directives and domestic implementation may be less than many perceive.

[1] See *Commission v United Kingdom* Case C-127/05.

5.88 Under the Workplace Directive, the floors in a workplace 'must have no dangerous bumps, holes or slopes and must be fixed, stable and not slippery' (Annex I, para 9.1). This duty is clearly qualified by the word 'dangerous' (thus permits bumps, holes or slopes which are not dangerous) and appears adequately and appropriately enacted within reg 12(1) of the Workplace Regulations. Whilst no mention is made of any qualification to Annex 1, para 9.1 of the Directive on grounds of cost or practicability, the Directive contains no requirement at all that floors (other than emergency routes and exits) be kept free from obstructions, articles or substances which may cause a person to slip trip or fall. Further, it is far from clear that the Directive is concerned with substances dropped onto a floor which may make the floor slippery. Instead, it appears that the Directive is concerned that the construction of the floor surface should not be slippery. As such, it appears that the duty under Workplace (Health, Safety and Welfare) Regulations 1992, SI 1992/3004, reg 12(3)—that a floor must be kept free from obstructions, articles or substances and which may cause someone to slip, trip or fall but only to the extent this is 'reasonably practicable'—is in any event beyond the minimum standards required by the Directive and perhaps is contained within the Regulations to maintain the protection previously provided to workers by the Factories Act 1961, s 29(1).

5.89 Article 3 of the Manual Handling Directive states that an employer shall take *'appropriate measures'* to avoid the need for manual handling or to reduce the risks of manual handling and, in art 4, in relation to workstations, states that where 'manual handling cannot be avoided the employer shall organise workstations in such a way as to make such handling as safe and *as healthy as possible'*. The corresponding duties in the Manual Handling Operations Regulations 1992 are qualified by the standard of reasonable practicability.

5.90 It has been argued before the Court of Appeal, that the Manual Handling Operations Regulations 1992 failed to implement the Directive properly by qualifying the duty by reference to a standard of reasonable practicability. Following the comments of Hale LJ (as she then was) in *King v*

Sussex Ambulance NHS Trust [2002] EWCA Civ 953, it seems likely that interpretation alone will overcome any distinction. Hale LJ noted that the Directive itself did not impose a strict standard of care in any event. The Directive is qualified by the obligation to take '*appropriate measures*' and to make the workplace '*as healthy as possible*'. The Regulations are qualified by the phrase '*to the lowest level reasonably practicable*', words which are absent from art 3(2) of the Directive.[1] However, the Regulation is not limited only to '*appropriate measures*'.

1   See para 21.19 below.

5.91 The meaning of '*appropriate measures*' in art 3(2) of the Directive was considered by the Court of Appeal in the case of *King v Sussex Ambulance NHS Trust* [2002] EWCA Civ 953. In that case, the employee (by amendment at trial) alleged breach of the Manual Handling Directive and the Ambulance Service accepted that, as an emanation of the State, the Directive was directly effective to the employee's rights against them. The employee sought to argue that the Directive imposed a stricter duty since it was not qualified by the defence of '*reasonable practicability*'. Hale LJ noted that '*appropriate*' must mean something more than a theoretical possibility and it must be judged against the circumstances of the case.[1] She further noted that the Directive accepts that some manual handling cannot be avoided and requires employers to take appropriate steps to reduce the risk involved. Similarly to the Regulations, the Directive does not impose a strict liability or require the avoidance of all risk of injury from manual handling operations. She then further noted the defendant's argument that whilst the Directive did not limit the duty on the employer by requiring it to take only steps which were '*reasonably practicable*' (as did the Regulations), that by limiting the duty to take '*appropriate*' measures or using '*appropriate*' means to reduce the risk, the distinction which some had drawn between the Directions and the Regulations was a false one.[2]

1   Para 13.
2   Paras 16–18.

5.92 The Court of Appeal unanimously allowed the appeal, finding that the defendant could take no further '*appropriate*' or '*reasonably practicable*' measures or steps to avoid the risk of injury or reduce it. Accordingly, there was no breach of either the Directive or the Regulations. Hale LJ accepted that it was not necessary in that case to resolve the debate about whether there was any material difference between the Directive and the Regulations.

5.93 For future courts to resolve that there is no distinction between the Directive and the Regulation then it would be necessary to find that the taking of '*appropriate*' steps to reduce the risk of injury must involve those steps which reduce the risk to the '*lowest level reasonably practicable*'. It is submitted that it is difficult to envisage what step might still be '*appropriate*' even though the risk had already been reduced to the '*lowest level reasonably practicable*'. It is also submitted that it is possible to define the Directive as imposing a lower standard, as the appropriate steps to reduce a risk (required by the Directive) may not necessarily involve all the steps necessary to reduce the risk to the lowest level reasonably practicable (as required by the regulations).

5.94 Nevertheless, although recent case law has thrown up no obvious examples where a regulation implementing a Directive has been found to implement a lower standard that the minimum required by the Directive (the opposite being the case on at least two occasions[1]) it should not be overlooked that no diminution of pre-existing national standard is permissible by the introduction of national law intended to implement a European Health and Safety Directive made under art 137 (ex art 118A) EC. This is because art 137 provides:

> 'Member States shall pay particular attention to encouraging improvements, especially in the working environment, as regards the health and safety of workers and shall set as their objective the harmonisation of conditions in this area, while maintaining the improvements made.'

That article also provides that the standards which the Directives adopt are:

> 'minimum requirements ... having regard to the conditions and technical rules obtaining in each of the Member States.'

Indeed the preamble to the Framework Directive states explicitly that:

> 'this Directive does not justify any reduction in levels of protection already achieved in individual Member States.'

Although these words are not found in the daughter Directives, the fact that each of the latter are made in pursuance of the Framework Directive probably imports that principle.

[1] Eg *Stark v Post Office* [2000] PIQR P105 and *Dugmore v Swnasea NHS Trust* [2002] EWCA Civ 1689.

5.95 Thus, in construing the UK statutory provisions, courts should seek to place on them a construction which at least maintains pre-existing standards and which regards Directives as setting minimum, not optional, standards. Hence both the provisions of national law, under the ultra vires doctrine, and the rules of construction derived from the EC, lean heavily against the downgrading of existing standards. It follows that the circumstances in which a national court will find itself obliged to give effect to Regulations that do permit such a lowering of standards of protection are virtually inconceivable. This proposition, set out in *Redgrave's Health and Safety*,[1] was expressly approved by the Court of Appeal in *Stark v Post Office* [2000] ICR 1013 at 1018–1019.

[1] 3rd edn at pp 15–16.

Chapter 6

CONTRIBUTORY NEGLIGENCE, CONSENTING TO THE RISK OF INJURY AND UNPAID VOLUNTEERS

Barry Cotter

CONTRIBUTORY NEGLIGENCE

6.01 In this chapter the main principles of contributory negligence and those aspects which are of particular importance in employers' liability cases are dealt with. Whilst the doctrine formerly referred to as 'volenti non fit injuria', embracing those who voluntarily consent to the risk of injury, has some similarities with contributory negligence it is a complete bar to recovery of damages in negligence, a discrete topic and is dealt with at the end of this chapter.

The 1945 Act and historical perspective

6.02 The Law Reform (Contributory Negligence) Act 1945, s 1(1) provides:

'Where any person suffers damage as the result partly of his own fault and partly of the fault of any other person or persons, a claim in respect of that damage shall not be defeated by reason of the fault of the person suffering the damage, but the damages recoverable in respect thereof shall be reduced to such extent as the court thinks just and equitable having regard to the claimant's share in the responsibility for the damage.'

That provision abolished the old common law rule that contributory negligence and 'common employment' was a complete defence.

6.03 Lord Atkin in *Caswell v Powell Duffryn Associated Collieries Ltd* [1940] AC 152 explained the old common law rule as follows:

'The injury may ... be the result of two causes operating at the same time, a breach of duty by the defendant and the omission on the part of the plaintiff to use the ordinary care for the protection of himself or his property that is used by the ordinary reasonable man in those circumstances. In that case the plaintiff cannot recover because the injury is partly caused by what is imputed to him as his own default.'

6.04 Prior to the abolition of the doctrine there had developed an elaborate body of law relating to causation. The objective of much of that law was to circumvent the rule and enable the claimant to succeed notwithstanding that the claimant had himself been careless. The Act introduced the concept of apportionment better to address the justice of the situation. Since the passage of the Act, employers' negligence or breach of statutory duty which might have been only a partial cause of the claimant's injuries will not be disregarded where the claimant or another employee has been at fault. There may well be concurrent causes, one of which is the negligence of the claimant. In that case the court will find contributory negligence. Likewise where two or more defendants are at fault the court will, in contribution proceedings, order a contribution by one to the other.

6.05 The Law Reform (Contributory Negligence) Act 1945,[1] in sweeping aside the old law, did cause a shift in the practical application of the doctrine. Denning LJ in *Davies v Swan Motor Co (Swansea) Ltd* [1949] 2 KB 291 at 322 said:

> 'The legal effect of the Act of 1945 is simple enough. If the plaintiff's negligence was one of the causes of his damage, he is no longer defeated altogether. He gets reduced damages. The practical effect of the Act is, however, wider than its legal effect. Previously, to mitigate the harshness of the doctrine of contributory number of competing causes, which was the cause—the effect of a predominant cause—of the damage, and to reject the rest. Now the courts have regard to all the causes and apportion the damages accordingly.'

[1] In Northern Ireland The Law Reform (Miscellaneous Provisions) Act 1948.

6.06 For many years after the passage of the 1945 Act some courts still managed to achieve the same result as would have been achieved before the passage of the Act. Those courts, while finding that the employer had been negligent and in breach of statutory duty, nevertheless allowed the employer to escape liability by finding that the claimant was 100% to blame. That approach is no longer permissible. In *Pitts v Hunt* [1991] 1 QB 24 at 48 Beldam LJ said:

> 'Section 1 of the Law Reform (Contributory Negligence) Act 1945 ... begins with the premise that the person suffers damage as a result partly of his own fault and partly of the fault of any other person or persons. Thus before the section comes into operation, the court must be satisfied that there is fault on the part of both parties which has caused the damage. It is expressly provided that the claim should not be defeated by reason of the fault of the person suffering the damage. To hold that he is himself entirely responsible for the damage effectively defeats his claim. It is then provided that the damages recoverable in respect thereof (that is the damage suffered partly as a result of his own fault and partly the fault of any other person) shall be reduced. It therefore presupposes that the person suffering the damage would receive some damages. Finally reduction is to be to such extent that the court thinks just and equitable, having regard to the claimant's share in the responsibility for the damage. To hold that the claimant is 100 per cent responsible is not to hold that he shared in the responsibility for the damage.'

6.07 Since the introduction of the Civil Procedure Rules 1998 a defendant in his defence must state which of the allegations in the particulars of claim are denied, which allegations he is unable to admit or deny, but which he requires the claimant to prove, and which of the allegations he admits.[1] The defence must provide a comprehensive response to the claim. Since the defence must be comprehensive the defendant must plead the precise respects in which he alleges the claimant has been guilty of contributory negligence.[2] The burden of proving contributory negligence is on the defendant.

1 CPR 1998, r 16.5(1).
2 See also the pre-CPR procedure, see *Fookes v Slaytor* [1978] 1 WLR 1293 where the Court of Appeal held that contributory negligence should be specifically pleaded, cf *Biguzzi v Rank Leisure plc* [1999] 1 WLR 1926.

What is contributory negligence?

6.08 Contributory negligence means some act or omission by the injured person which constituted a fault, in that it was a blameworthy failure to take reasonable care for his/her own safety and which has materially contributed to the damage caused. In *Froom v Butcher* [1976] QB 286 at 291 Lord Denning MR said:

'Negligence depends on a breach of duty, whereas contributory negligence does not. Negligence is a man's carelessness and breach of duty to others. Contributory negligence is a man's carelessness in looking after his own safety. He is guilty of contributory negligence if he ought reasonably to have foreseen that, if he did not act as a reasonable prudent man, he might hurt himself.'

6.09 In *Jones v Livox Quarries Ltd* [1952] 2 QB 608 at 615 Denning LJ said:

'Although contributory negligence does not depend on a duty of care, it does depend on foreseeability. Just as actionable negligence requires the foreseeability of harm to others, so contributory negligence requires the foreseeability of harm to oneself. A person is guilty of contributory negligence if he ought reasonably to have foreseen that, if he did not act as a reasonable, prudent man, he might hurt himself; and in his reckonings he must take into account the possibility of others being careless.'

6.10 Provided that the claimant can foresee that his conduct may expose him to injury, it is not necessary that he should be able to foresee the precise manner in which the injury will occur: *Jones v Livox Quarries Ltd* (above) per Singleton LJ at 613–614:

'In so doing he was exposing himself to danger. It may well be that the chief danger was that he might fall off, or be thrown off, or that he might become entangled in some part of the machine on which he was riding; but those were not the only risks to which he subjected himself ...'

Causative negligence

6.11 In all cases where contributory negligence is alleged, the question to be answered is: Whose negligence (or breach of statutory duty) caused the accident? Was it that of the defendant alone, or of the claimant alone, or of both together or a combination of both and others? Lord Atkin in *Caswell v Powell Duffryn Associated Collieries Ltd* [1940] AC 152 at 165:

'I find it impossible to divorce any theory of contributory negligence from the concept of causation ... and whether you ask whose negligence was responsible for the injury, or from whose negligence did the injury result, or adopt any other phrase you please, you must in the ultimate analysis be asking who "caused" the injury.'

6.12 Whether the claimant failed to take such care as was reasonable in the circumstances falls to be judged in the light of all the circumstances. The court does not, usually, scrutinise in every last detail the circumstances of the accident in order to detect contributory negligence at the behest of a negligent employer: *Machray v Stewarts & Lloyds Ltd* [1965] 1 WLR 602. In some cases the courts have held that the phrase 'just and equitable' in s 1(1) of the Act enabled the court to refuse to make any reduction in the damages even where contributory negligence had been made out.[1] However that view was subsequently rejected by the Court of Appeal in *Boothman v British Northrop* (1972) 13 KIR 112.

[1]	See *Hawkins v Ian Ross (Castings) Ltd* [1970] 1 All ER 180 at 188 and *Stocker v Norprint Ltd* (1970) 10 KIR 10 at 14.

6.13 The real question in each case is whether the claimant's conduct caused or contributed to the damage. It is, thus, irrelevant that the claimant was guilty of some blameworthy conduct if that conduct did not cause the injury. In *Westwood v Post Office* [1974] AC 1 a man fell through a door in a room to which entry had been prohibited. The notice prohibiting entry contained no warning of the danger that lay on the other side and the House of Lords held that disobedience to orders not to enter the room was not, in itself, negligent. In *Toole v Bolton Metropolitan Borough Council* [2002] EWCA Civ 588 an employee failed to heed a note that he should use 'heavy duty' gloves when picking up litter and sustained a needle stick injury, however the gloves made available by the employer would not have prevented the injury and the Court of Appeal held that there was no contributory negligence in such circumstances.[1]

[1]	The judge at first instance found the claimant to have been 75% to blame, which the Court of Appeal stated was too high for a case of breach of statutory duty in any event.

6.14 If there is found to be some degree of contributory negligence it cannot be ignored. It must result in an appropriate reduction in the damages, however small. In practice the courts have favoured a series of conventional deductions in percentages, 10, 20, 25, 33, 50, 66, 75. Often the courts deal with contributory negligence which is less than one-fifth by a finding that the claimant was merely momentarily inadvertent or understandably disregarded what was not a gross and obvious risk. It is only where inadvertence is such as to amount to negligence that an apportionment is made: *Mullard v Ben Line Steamers Ltd* [1971] 2 All ER 424. As Sedley LJ stated in *Butcher v Cornwall County Council* [2002] EWCA Civ 1640:[1]

'10% is so nearly a token figure that ones first reaction is that it betokens an absence of significant fault on the claimant's part'.[2]

[1]	See also *Cooper v Carillion plc* [2003] EWCA Civ 1811: a successful appeal against a finding of 10% contributory negligence.

2   Cf *Goodchild v Organon Laboratories Ltd* [2004] EWHC 2341 (QB) where Forbes J
found 10% contributory negligence for an employee known to have a vulnerable back
problem lifting a heavy box.

6.15 Addressing awards at the other end of the scale in *Toole v Bolton Metropolitan Borough Council* [2002] EWCA Civ 588, Buxton LJ stated:

'It is not usual for there to be marked findings of contributory negligence in a breach of statutory duty case, and it is, I am bound to say in my experience, very unusual indeed for there to be a finding of contributory negligence at the level of 75%. If in a statutory duty case the judge finds himself driven in that direction, he should, in my judgment, seriously consider whether he is in fact not finding that there has been no causal connection at all between the breach of statutory duty and the injury'.

This reflected a long-established 'rule of thumb' that if a breach of statutory duty by the employer was established any finding of contributory negligence should not normally exceed 50%.

More than one defendant

6.16 Where there are several defendants, the claimant's share of responsibility against all of them must first be assessed and then the balance divided between them: *Fitzgerald v Lane* [1989] AC 328. In that case the claimant was seriously injured when struck by two cars when attempting to cross a pelican pedestrian crossing when the lights were red for pedestrians. The trial judge, having held that the claimant was equally to blame with the two motorists, then awarded the claimant two-thirds of the total damages. The Court of Appeal allowed an appeal against that decision. There was a further appeal to the House of Lords which confirmed the result reached by the Court of Appeal. The House of Lords held that the judge had confused the extent of the claimant's contribution to his own loss with the separate issue of the apportionment of the damages between the defendants. Given his finding that the claimant had been equally to blame with the motorists for the accident the judge should only have awarded the claimant one-half that of his loss and not two-thirds. Lord Ackner said:

'Apportionment of liability in the case of contributory negligence between plaintiff and defendants must be kept separate from apportionment of contribution between the defendants inter se. Although the defendants are liable to the plaintiff for the whole amount for which he has obtained judgment, the proportions in which, as between themselves, the defendants must meet the plaintiff's claim do not have any direct relationship to the extent to which the total damages have been reduced by the contributory negligence.'

6.17 In so doing the House of Lords pointed to a rigorous separation between the issues of the claimant's own contributory negligence and the apportionment of the damages as between the defendants themselves. Lord Ackner in *Fitzgerald*[1] said that the judge had gone wrong in:

'allowing his judgment of the issue of contributory negligence to be coloured by his decision as to the proper apportionment of the claim between the defendants. While stating in substance on the one hand that the plaintiff's responsibility was no more and no less than that of either of the defendants, his ultimate conclusion, as mirrored in this Order, was that each of the defendants was twice as much to blame as the plaintiff. This could not be right on the facts.'

1   [1989] AC 328 at 341.

6.18   As a result where a claimant successfully sues more than one defendant for damages and there is a claim between co-defendants for contribution, there are two distinct stages in the decision making process: first in the main action between the claimant on the one hand and the defendants on the other as to which side is to blame and in what proportions; and second in the contribution proceedings between the defendants only as to what proportion each defendant must bear.

Assessment

6.19   Assessment of the injured person's share in the responsibility is undertaken first through consideration of his/her relative blameworthiness and then of the causative potency of the relevant act/omission.[1] In *Stapley v Gypsum Mines Ltd* [1953] AC 663 at 682, Lord Reid stated:

'A court must deal broadly with the problem of apportionment and in considering what is just and equitable must have regard to the blameworthiness of each party, but the plaintiff's share in the responsibility for the damage cannot I think, be assessed without considering the relative importance of his acts in causing the damage apart from his blameworthiness.'

As to the general approach Stanley Burnton J stated in *Badger v MOD* [2005] EWHC 2941 (referring to the speech of Lord Reid in *Stapley v Gypsum Mines* and the approach of the Court of Appeal in *O'Connell v Jackson* [1972] 1 QB 270 at 277–78):

'Once contributory negligence has been established, the court must take into account both the extent of the claimant's responsibility for his injury and damage and the blameworthiness of his conduct as opposed to that of the defendant in deciding on the reduction in damages that is just and equitable. The decision as to the appropriate reduction in the claimant's damages is to be dealt with in a broad, jury like and common sense way'.

1   See *Davies v Swan Motors Co (Swansea) Ltd* [1949] 2 KB 291 at 236.

6.20   Looking at the apportionment of fault in particular cases, it must be remembered that this is always comparative. The fact that 75% fault is attributed to the claimant does not necessarily mean that he or she was grossly negligent; it may only mean that the defendant's fault was slight and technical, or played a minor part in causation.

Breach of the employer's statutory duties

6.21 In *Boyle v Kodak Ltd* [1969] 2 All ER 439 the House of Lords held that a defendant employer could not exonerate itself from liability for a breach of statutory duty unless it was wholly brought about by the claimant employee. If it was, there is no liability, so the question of contributory negligence does not arise. If it was not wholly brought about by the claimant, there is automatically fault on the part of the employer (whether negligent or not) from the mere fact of breach of the duty, and there must be an apportionment to the employer of some of the blame.[1]

1 This principle was applied by the Court of Appeal in *McCreesh v Courtaulds plc* [1997] PIQR P 421. Thorpe LJ 'So the real question is, was the practice of permitting the use of an unguarded blade also contributive to causation'.

6.22 In a breach of statutory duty case the court has to have very clearly in mind the reasons why the duties that go beyond best endeavours are provided in the particular statute. In *Staveley Iron and Chemical Co Ltd v Jones* [1956] AC 627, Lord Tucker stated at 648:

'In Factory Act cases the purpose of imposing the absolute obligation is to protect the workmen against those very acts of inattention which are sometimes relied upon as constituting contributory negligence so that too strict a standard would defeat the object of the statute.'

6.23 Lord Hoffmann commented on that passage in *Reeves v Commissioner of Metropolitan Police* [2000] 1 AC 360 at 371, where his Lordship pointed out that the Law Reform (Contributory Negligence) Act 1945 requires the court to apportion not degrees of carelessness but the relative responsibility of the two parties, and that an assessment of responsibility must take into account the policy of the rule, such as that of the Factories Act, by which the liability is imposed.

Breach of the employee's statutory duties

6.24 Section 1(1) of the Law Reform (Contributory Negligence) Act 1945 refers to damage 'as a result partly of his own fault and partly of the fault of any other person'. Therefore, a breach of the employee's statutory duty, if it is a cause of the accident, is equivalent to contributory negligence: *Norris v Syndic Manufacturing Co Ltd* [1952] 2 QB 135 at 142. However whether breach of statutory duty by the employee will amount to contributory negligence depends on the nature of the respective duties of the employee and employer. In *Arbuckle v AH McIntosh & Co Ltd* 1993 SLT 857n, OH, it was held that the employee's duty 'to use and keep in proper adjustment' guards in pursuance of the Woodworking Machines Regulations 1947 only arose when the employer had fulfilled its duty to provide a properly-guarded machine. Therefore there was no contributory negligence. In considering how far the breach by an employee of its statutory duty should reduce the consequential damages, regard must be had, it is suggested, to the publicity given to the order. In particular regard should be paid whether the employers had taken

193

adequate measures to bring the order to the employee's notice and to ensure that he complied with it. Another factor to be taken into account is the workman's knowledge, and whether he was properly instructed and had sufficient experience.

6.25 There is a general duty imposed on employees by the HSWA 1974, s 7, to take reasonable care for the safety of themselves and other people affected by their acts or omissions at work and to 'co-operate' with employers and others in carrying out the duties imposed upon his employers and others. Under the Management of Health and Safety at Work Regulations 1999, reg 14 there is a duty placed on employees to use equipment in accordance with training and instructions given by the employer in compliance with the latter's statutory duties and to report serious and immediate dangers to health and safety. Although s 7 of the 1974 Act is unenforceable in civil law, following the coming onto force of the Management of Health and Safety at Work and Fire Precautions (Workplace) (Amendment) Regulations 2003, breach of reg 14 is now actionable. Many other Regulations impose duties on employees, for example the Personal Protective Equipment at Work Regulations 1992, reg 10(2). In *Henser-Leather v Securicor Cash Services Ltd* [2002] EWCA Civ 816 Kennedy LJ found that a defendant (having failed to provide PPE in the first place) was also in breach of reg 10(1) for having taken no steps to ensure than the claimant wore PPE. Having taken no steps to comply with reg 10(1) it was not open to the defendant to argue that the claimant was contributorily negligent as he might not have worn the PPE in breach of reg 10(2).

6.26 As in all cases where contributory negligence is pleaded, it must be shown by the defendant that the default complained of was a cause of the accident. This is an illustration of the general principle that before damages can be recovered the loss or damage must be shown to be as a result of a breach of duty. Section 47(2) of the HSWA 1974 reflects this in providing that a breach of a health and safety regulation is only actionable 'insofar as it causes damage'. It is suggested that the proper approach is to consider whether the employer complied with his statutory duty and, if he did so, whether the employee's breach was causative of the damage. In considering the degree of contributory negligence the court should have regard to what steps, if any, the employer took to encourage a culture of compliance with statutory obligations and health and safety awareness in the work place.

Breach of employer's statutory duty caused by the claimant alone

6.27 Difficulty has arisen in the past where the defendant employer has been held to be in breach of its statutory duty but the reason why this has occurred has been solely because of the conduct of the claimant employee. Where the employer has taken all reasonable steps to ensure that its employees are safe and the employee then, nevertheless, undertakes a course of action which negates the employer's efforts, basic common law principles would dictate that the employee is responsible for any consequential damage. For example, where an employee removes a fence from a machine contrary to express orders and warnings, it would be unreasonable to attribute legal liability to his employer.[1]

1   If the employer has created the risk by a breach of statutory duty which the claimant has then failed to rectify or adopted; the claimant's fault will be seen as subsequent and separate and although there may be a finding of contributory negligence primary liability will attach to the acts or omissions of the employer: see *Boyce v Wyatt Engineering* [2001] EWCA Civ 692.

6.28 However, where a statutory duty is involved, the position is somewhat different and greater caution is needed before an employer can be absolved from blame. The reason for this is that Parliament has placed directly on the shoulders of the employer the responsibility for ensuring compliance with the duty. Non-compliance with that duty, if it is a contributory cause, normally establishes liability.

6.29 In *Boyle v Kodak Ltd* [1969] 2 All ER 439 the House of Lords held that an employer could not exonerate itself from liability for a breach of statutory duty unless the breach was wholly brought about by the claimant. If it was, no liability would arise, so the question of contributory negligence would equally not arise. The mere fact of breach by the employer gives rise to liability on its part and there must be an apportionment to it of some of the damages. The overriding principle is set out in the Law Reform (Contributory Negligence) Act 1945, s 1(1) where the court decides that the loss should be apportioned between the parties. The result is that the claimant's damages have to be 'reduced to such extent as the court thinks just and equitable having regard to the claimant's share in the responsibility for the damage'. It is notable that the Act of 1945 does not contain the word 'cause'.[1] Responsibility for the loss should not be equated with causation of the loss. This is because if there is no causation there is no tort. But if there is causation, and the claimant contributed to the causation, then clearly the consequential damages to the claimant should be reduced. The Act speaks of the damages being 'reduced'. It therefore follows that the court cannot refuse to make any reduction merely because it thinks it is just and equitable to do so.[2] It is necessary to consider not only the causation of a particular act but also its blameworthiness.[3] In road traffic cases, if a pedestrian is struck by a car when both had a clear view of each other, in one sense the factors are equal. However, the motorist may be held to be the greater part to blame because he was in charge of a potentially lethal weapon, whereas the pedestrian posed little danger to the motorist. In this context culpability means not so much moral blameworthiness as a departure from the standard of care to be expected from the reasonable man. The court must also consider in addition to breach and causation the question of what is 'just and equitable'.[4] It is for this reason that the precise percentage by which the award is reduced is a question of fact in each case for the judge. The respective faults are to be assessed by looking at the matter broadly.

1   'That Act, with which I had some slight connection as a Member of the Law Revision Committee, carefully avoided all references to the word 'causation'. While it was being finally prepared by Lord Simon, the then Lord Chancellor, I discussed with him, and he emphasised that he was not going to allow any idea of causation to confuse the issue': Goodhart, 'Appeals and Questions of Fact' (1955) 71 LQR 402, 413–414.

2   *Boothman v British Northrop Ltd* (1972) 13 KIR 112 at 122.
3   See *Keaney v British Railways Board* [1968] 1 WLR 879 at 893; *Froom v Butcher* [1976] QB 286 at 292.
4   *Turner v Ford Motor Co Ltd* [1965] 1 WLR 948 at 953–954.

6.30 In *Jayes v IMI (Kynoch) Ltd* [1985] ICR 155 the Court of Appeal held that it could assess the claimant's contributory negligence at 100% and thus defeat the claim. There were breaches of the Operations at Unfenced Machinery Regulations 1938, for which the claimant was not responsible, in that the mechanics attending the machine were not qualified 'machine attendants' and no barrier had been erected to keep other persons out. The claimant was a supervisor who had called in the fitters; he foolishly took a rag to stop oil running and his fingers were caught. In an ex tempore judgment the Court of Appeal upheld a finding by the judge that he was 100% negligent for 'an act of folly'. The court based its reasoning upon *Mitchell v W S Westin Ltd* [1965] 1 WLR 297. However, the decision of the House of Lords in *Boyle v Kodak Ltd* [1969] 2 All ER 439 was not brought to the attention of the Court of Appeal and criticism of *Jayes* in previous editions of this text were adopted and approved by the Court of Appeal in *Anderson v Newham College of Further Education* [2002] EWCA Civ 505 with the comments that this case should not be followed by judges of first instance and should not be relied upon by advocated in argument (as noted above, a finding of 100% contributory negligence is inconsistent with the Court of Appeal's decision in *Pitts v Hunt* [1991] 1 QB 24).

6.31 In *Boyle v Kodak Ltd* [1969] 1 WLR 661 the appellant, an experienced painter, was employed on the painting of an oil storage tank some 30 feet high. He used the ladder in order to paint the top of the tank. By virtue of the Building (Safety, Health and Welfare) Regulations 1948, both he and his employers were under a statutory duty to secure the ladder by lashing it at the top before using it. There was an iron staircase on the side of the storage tank which gave access to the top of the ladder. However the workman did not use that means of access to lash the top of the ladder. He had never been told by the respondents to do so. He climbed the ladder in order to lash it to the top but the ladder fell before he had accomplished his aim. The trial judge held that the workman was solely to blame for the accident in that he had failed to use the staircase. The trial judge held that whilst there had been a breach by the employer of reg 24(4), the workman was not entitled to recover because he was wholly responsible for the accident. The Court of Appeal affirmed the decision. On appeal to the House of Lords it was held that the employers owed a duty to instruct even a skilled workman, concerning the application of the Regulations in situations where no danger was apparent. The House held that the employer had not proven that it had done all that could reasonably be expected of it to ensure compliance with the Regulations. Lord Reid said at 667:

> '... that, once the plaintiff had established that there was a breach of an enactment which made the employer absolutely liable, and that breach caused the accident, he need do no more. But it is then open to the employer to set up a defence that in fact he was not in any way in fault, but that the plaintiff employee was alone to blame. That does not mean that the employer must lead

evidence, he may be able to prove this from the evidence for the plaintiff, but I do not think that I went too far in *Ross's* case by saying at page 775, that he "cannot complain if in those circumstances the most favourable inferences were drawn from the appellant's evidence of which it is reasonably capable".'

6.32 Lord Reid, in the same case, at 668 said:

'Employers are bound to know their statutory duty and take all steps to prevent their men from committing breaches. If an employer does not do that he cannot take advantage of this defence. On the respondent's admission there is a difference under this Regulation between cases where there is another practicable means of access to the top of the ladder, and cases where there is none or where there is nothing to which the ladder can be lashed. In the former case the man must use alternative means of access, here the stairway, to get to the top to lash the ladder and then return that way before ascending the ladder; in the latter case he is permitted to ascend the ladder without lashing it. I think the evidence shows that a skilled, practical man may easily fail to appreciate this and that the respondent ought to have realised that and instructed their men accordingly. So they have not proved that they did all they could reasonably be expected to do to ensure compliance and they cannot rely on this defence so as to avoid their absolute vicarious liability under the Regulations'.

6.33 Lord Diplock in the same case at 672 said:

'The employer's duty to comply with the requirements of the Regulation differs from that of his employees. The employer, at any rate when he is a corporation, must if needs perform his duty vicariously through his officers, servants, agents or contractors; but he does not thereby rid himself of his duty. He remains vicariously responsible for any failure by any one of them to do whatever was necessary to ensure that the requirements of the Regulations were complied with; and among those for whose failure he is prima facie vicariously liable is any employee who is himself under a concurrent statutory duty to comply with those requirements. The employee's duty, on the other hand, is in respect of and is limited to his own acts or omissions. He is not vicariously liable for those of anyone else'.

He went on to say:

'The plaintiff establishes a prima facie case of action against his employer by proving the fact of non-compliance with the requirement of the Regulation and that he suffered injury as a result. He need prove no more. No burden lies with him to prove what steps should have been taken to avert the non-compliance, nor to identify the employees whose acts or defaults contributed to it, for the employer is vicariously responsible for them all. But if the employer can prove that the only act or default of anyone which caused or contributed to the non-compliance was the act or default of the plaintiff himself, he establishes a good defence. For the legal concept of vicarious liability requires three parties; the injured person, a person whose act or default caused the injury and the person vicariously liable for the latter's act or default. To say "you are liable to me for my own wrongdoing" is neither good morals nor good law. But unless the employer can prove this he cannot escape liability. If he proves that it was partly the fault of the employee plaintiff, as ex hypothesi, it will be in the postulated case, for the employee's own breach of statutory duty is "fault" within the meaning of s 1 of the Law Reform (Contributory Negligence) Act 1945, this may reduce the damages recoverable but will not constitute a defence to the action'.

6.34 The Court of Appeal has recently reaffirmed the importance of the principle in *Boyle* in *Anderson v Newham College of Further Education* [2002] EWCA Civ 505, *O'Neill v DSG Retail Ltd* [2002] EWCA Civ 1139[1] and also in *Sherlock v Chester City Council* [2004] EWCA Civ 210 (although the claimant was sufficiently well trained and experienced to identify the need for either a run off table or a second man when using a circular saw; the failure of the employer to undertake an assessment and identify the need for such equipment amounted to a breach of statutory duty, meant that it could not be absolved from liability).

[1]   See also *Goodchild v Organon Laboratories Ltd* [2004] EWHC 2341 (QB).

Disease cases

6.35 In cases where injury has had a gradual onset, such as many forms of occupational disease (and stress-related illness) the employee's share in the responsibility for the damage and hence what reduction, if any, may be just and equitable may be very difficult to assess. The vulnerability and general circumstances of the employee at the relevant time have to be taken into account (there is also the issue of the employee's foreseeability of the harm[1]). In *Rowntree v Commissioner of Police for the Metropolis* (26 October 2001, unreported), QBD (Nelson J) the failure of the claimant to recognise the extent of and then act upon and/or report her developing psychiatric problems, although causative, was held not to be blameworthy.[2] In the absence of vulnerability at the time, matters although still difficult to assess with any precision, may be more easily determined in the conventional way. In *Barker v Saint Gobain Pipelines plc* [2006] UKHL 20 the deceased, who died of mesothelioma, and who had been exposed to asbestos during his employment with the defendant, had failed to take any precautions on just three known occasions when he was heavily exposed to asbestos dust as a self-employed man. Moses J found him to have been contributorily negligent and reduced the damages by 20% although it is difficult to determine upon what factors influenced this level of deduction, a decision supported by the House of Lords as correct. In *Badger v MOD* [2005] EWHC 2941 (QB), a wife's claim for damages, following the death of her husband through exposure to asbestos was reduced by 20%, as her husband had contributed to his own death by refusing to give up smoking, which also caused the lung cancer that killed him. Stanley Burnton J held that the deceased had been guilty of a fault that was partly responsible for his death. A reasonably prudent man, warned that there was a substantial risk that smoking would seriously damage his health, would stop smoking.

[1]   Foreseeability of harm being a requirement: see *Jones v Livox Quarries Ltd* [1952] 2 QB 608 at 615.
[2]   See also *Young v Post Office* [2002] EWCA Civ 661.

What conduct by a worker amounts to contributory negligence?

6.36 It is important to note at the outset that an employee is normally entitled to assume that his employer has complied with his statutory duties (see

Westwood v Post Office [1974] AC 1) and as a result where there has been a breach of such duties it is important to ensure that the statutory requirement placed on the employer is not emasculated by a willingness on the part of the courts to find that an employee has been guilty of contributory negligence. As Keene LJ stated in *Cooper v Carillion plc* [2003] EWCA Civ 1811:

> 'It is very easy for a judge with the advantage of hindsight to identify some act on the part of the employee which would have avoided the accident occurring. That in itself does not demonstrate negligence on the part of the employee. As Lord Tucker put it in *Staveley Iron and Chemical Co Ltd v Jones* [1956] AC 627 at 648, one must avoid treating every risky act by an employee due to familiarity with the work or some inattention resulting from noise or strain as contributory negligence'.[1]

1   In relation to the importance of not overlooking the employer's breaches of statutory duty, see *Nixon v Chanceoption Developments Ltd* [2002] EWCA Civ 558.

6.37 There are two points which are relevant in all cases of contributory negligence. The first is that all the circumstances must be considered, such as the fact that an employee may have to give his attention to more than one thing. The second is that, just as a defendant is entitled to balance the disadvantages of safety measures against the risk involved, so too the claimant may expose himself to some degree of risk rather than submit to the curtailment of his activities. The question in every case is whether the claimant acted reasonably in taking a risk: *AC Billings & Sons Ltd v Riden* [1958] AC 240 where an elderly person was held justified in attempting to cross a contractor's workplace to get home for the night.[1]

1   See also *Sayers v Harlow Urban District Council* [1958] 2 All ER 342 (an attempt to escape from a locked lavatory) and *McCreesh v Courtaulds plc* [1997] PIQR P 421 (experienced joiner using an unguarded machine saw, failure to instruct and supervise).

6.38 The fact that there may be disadvantages as well as advantages in any particular course of action by the employee is particularly important in connection with failure to use equipment. In *Gibson v British Insulated Callenders Construction Co Ltd* 1973 SLT 2 the House of Lords held that, on the evidence, there was no contributory negligence in failing to wear a safety belt on top of an electricity pylon 'for though it could prevent a fall to the ground, it could in some circumstances cause a fall and might not prevent serious injury'.

6.39 Similarly, it may be legitimate to take a risk for the protection of other persons put in danger by the defendants' negligence: *Ward v T E Hopkins & Sons Ltd* [1959] 3 All ER 225 where a doctor descended a well full of dangerous fumes in order to rescue workers; and the same principle may apply to a worker taking a risk for the protection of the employers' property, or otherwise in the employers' interests.[1] It is rare that a court will hold that the rescuer was acting unreasonably. In *McFarlane v EE Caledonian Ltd* [1994] 2 All ER 1 at 10 Stuart-Smith LJ referred to the case of a rescuer who came into the area of danger after the event. Cardozo J in *Wagner v International Rly Co* 232 NY Rep 176 (1921) said that 'danger invites rescue'. That was cited with approval by Lord Oliver in *Alcock v Chief Constable of South*

Yorkshire Police [1992] 1 AC 310. Thus, it is unlikely that workers such as policemen, firemen and others involved in emergency services will be held to be contributorily negligent when they deliberately enter an area of danger in order to rescue others.

¹ See also *Neil v Harland & Wolff Ltd* (1949) 82 Ll L Rep 515, referred to under 'volenti' at para 6.59, below; (workman working on electrical cables without removing fuses to avoid need to shut down production).

6.40 It is clear that mere inadvertence on the part of an employee is not sufficient to amount to contributory negligence. In *Flower v Ebbw Vale Steel, Iron and Coal Co Ltd* [1936] AC 206 Lawrence J said:

'The tribunal of fact has to take into account all the circumstances of work in a factory and it is not for every risky thing which a workman in the factory may do in his familiarity with the machinery that a plaintiff ought to be held guilty of contributory negligence.'

6.41 Lord Atkin in *Caswell v Powell Duffryn Associated Collieries Ltd* [1940] AC 152 expressed agreement with Lawrence J:

'I am of the opinion that the care to be expected of the plaintiff in the circumstances will vary with the circumstances; and that a different degree of care may well be expected from a workman in a factory or a mine from that which might be taken by an ordinary man not exposed continually to the noise, strain and manifold risks of factory or mine.'

Lord Wright said in the same case (at 176–178):

'The jury have to draw the line where mere thoughtlessness or inadvertence ceases, and where negligence begins—what is all important is to adapt the standard of what is negligence to the facts, and to give due regard to the actual conditions under which men work in a factory or mine, to the long hours and the fatigue, to the slackening of attention which naturally comes from constant repetition of the same operation, to the noise and confusion in which the man works, to his preoccupation in what he is actually doing at the cost perhaps of some inattention to his own safety.'

6.42 That may be particularly relevant, in the modern day context, particularly where the worker may have to work long hours in a repetitive task. In *Lawrence v Syndic Manufacturing Co Ltd* [1952] 1 All ER 935 employees were engaged on repetitive and monotonous work. The court held that they were likely to be 'foreseeably' inadvertent from time to time. In *Koonjul v Thameslink Healthcare Services NHS Trust* [2000] PIQR P 123, the Court of Appeal pointed out that in carrying out a risk assessment under the Manual Handling Regulations 1992 the employer was not entitled to assume that all its employees would on all occasions behave with full and proper concern for their own safety (however there is no basis for anticipating that an employee will 'press on regardless of a risk' when there is nothing to stop an alternative course of action¹).

¹ See eg *Betts v Tokley* [2002] EWCA Civ 52.

6.43 These authorities are to some extent an application of the ordinary rule that all the circumstances must be taken into account. However, so far as they excuse an injured worker for inadvertence, they establish a more lenient standard than that expected of the reasonable employer or the reasonable road user. The explanation of this lenient standard is that it was evolved at a time when contributory negligence was a complete defence to breach of statutory duty, especially in respect of cases of unfenced machinery, where the duty was plainly to protect against inadvertence.[1] Inadvertence is failing to give attention to what one is doing, and must imply some lack of due care. This has been described by Lord Read in *Staveley Iron and Chemical Co Ltd v Jones* [1956] AC 627 as 'excusable lapses'. The key may lie in understanding that it is foreseeable on the part of an employer that workmen may from time to time be inadvertent, all the more so when the work is repetitive or monotonous: *General Cleaning Contractors Ltd v Christmas* [1953] AC 180 at 189 per Lord Oaksey: 'It is ... well known to employers ... that [in] their work people very frequently, if not habitually, careless about the risks their work may involve'. Lord Tucker in *Staveley Iron and Chemical Co Ltd v Jones* [1956] AC 627 seemed to recognise this when he said:

> 'Whilst accepting without question this and other dicta to a similar effect ... in relation to cases under the Factories Acts and other statutes imposing an absolute obligation ... I doubt very much whether they were ever intended or could properly be applied to a simple case of common law negligence ... where there is no evidence of work people performing repetitive work under strain for long hours at dangerous machines'.

[1] *McNeil v Roche Products Ltd (No 2)* 1989 SLT 498. Lord McCluskey said 'The whole purpose of a provision such as section 14 of the Factories Act 1961 is to avoid the risk of accident to the inadvertent workman or passer-by'. And see *Mitchell v North British Rubber Co* 1946 SLT 129; *R v Sanyo Electrical Manufacturing (UK) Ltd* (1992) 13 Cr App Rep (S) 657, CA.

6.44 The experience and age of the worker involved are also relevant factors: *Gunter v John Nicholas & Sons (Port Talbot) Ltd* [1993] PIQR P 67 (skilled woodworking machinist, contribution increased from 25% to 75%); *McCreesh v Courtaulds plc* [1997] PIQR P 421 (experienced joiner aged 53 using an unguarded machine, 100% contribution replaced with a finding of 75%); *Wilson v Rolls Royce plc* 1998 SLT 247 (experienced worker choosing to walk over floor he knew to be covered in ice, 50% contribution); *Blanchflower v Chamberlain* [1996] CLY 2997 (worker with 20 years' experience fell while putting tarpaulin on lorry, 50% contribution); *Fraser v Winchester HA* (1999) Times, 12 July (21 year old resident support worker promoted solely so she could take residents on a trip, but who knew of the dangers of changing a gas cylinder too near a naked flame, one third contribution); *Griffiths v Vauxhall Motors Ltd* [2003] EWCA Civ 412 (experienced operator failed to hold a gun used to secure bolts with care when knew it was liable to kick back, 50% contribution); *Butcher v Cornwall County Council* [2002] EWCA Civ 1640 (experienced storeman failed secure a door which was blown open by the wind, one third contribution); *Sherlock v Chester City Council* [2004] EWCA Civ 210 (joiner with many years experience used bench saw without a run off table or additional support when cutting a long piece of wood, 60% contribution). In *Laszczyk v National Coal*

Board [1954] 3 All ER 205 a young trainee miner was found to be 5% contributorily negligent; but such a ' token' finding would now be unlikely to be made as the reality is that the decision made was that there was no significant fault on the part of the young employee. Special protection has been afforded to young workers both historically[1] and under the Young People at Work Directive and the Management of Health and Safety at Work Regulations 1999, SI 1999/3242.

[1]   Eg the Factories Act 1961, s 20, *Denyer v Charles Skipper and East Ltd* [1970] 2 All ER 382.

6.45 The obligation to adapt the work to the worker set out in the Framework Directive and the Management of Health and Safety at Work Regulations 1999 and since carried through in, for example, the Manual Handling Operations Regulations 1992 must affect the weight to be given to the employee's capacity as a factor in the apportionment of damages, so tending to diminish the degree of contributory negligence in cases where the employer appoints an insufficiently trained, inexperienced or immature worker to undertake the task.

Conduct which is not contributory negligence: illustrations

6.46 These cases are cited as illustrations of the principles to be applied. They are not 'precedents' in the true legal sense. The court's task in each case is to find the facts upon the evidence, identify the relevant legal principles and apply those to the facts as found. Lord Steyn in *Jolley v Sutton London Borough Council* [2000] 1 WLR 1082 at 1089 said:

'... in this corner of the law the results of decided cases are inevitably very fact-sensitive. Both counsel nevertheless at times invited your Lordships to compare the facts of the present case with the facts of other decided cases. This is a sterile exercise. Precedent is a valuable stabilising influence in our legal system. But, comparing the facts of and outcomes of cases in this branch of the law is a misuse of the only proper use of precedent, viz to identify the relevant rule to apply to the facts as found.'

6.47 Many of these cases are illustrations of situations which the court have recognised that the employee is not placed in the same circumstances as the employer. That principle was memorably articulated by Lord Oaksey in *General Cleaning Contractors Ltd v Christmas* [1953] AC 180 at 189–190:

'Employers are not exempted from this duty by the fact that the men are experienced and might, if they were in the position of an employer, be able to lay down a reasonably safe system of work themselves. Workmen are not in the position of employers. Their duties are not performed in the calm atmosphere of a boardroom with the advice of experts. They have to make their decisions on narrow sills and other places of danger and in circumstances where the dangers are obscured by repetition'.

6.48 It has to be recognised that the employer creates the circumstances and environment in which the employee has to take decisions as to precise modes of carrying out his duties and the court should be slow to be overly critical. In *Cross v UGC Ltd (t/a Oxford Automotive)* [2001] EWCA Civ 685 the claimant was an experienced employee who was cleaning a paint spray booth which involved spraying the booth with a solution of water and cleaning fluid from up a step ladder, as a result of which the floor would become slippery and wet. He went back up it to retrieve a piece of equipment and on descent slipped. The system employed to prevent slipping, the spreading of sawdust, was haphazard. A decision that the claimant, who had failed to move the ladder before ascending to get the equipment or to have cleaned the sole of his boots on the bottom rung before ascending, was found not to have been contributorily negligent was upheld on appeal.

6.49 It is not necessarily negligent for a worker to follow the method of work accepted by the employer, even if it involves obvious risk. It is not the duty of a worker to break way from the employer's methods and devise a safer system, although he may have as much skill and experience as the employer. In Ireland the Supreme Court in *Stewart v Killeen Paper Mills Ltd* [1959] IR 436 has held that where the injury could not have occurred but for the breach of statutory duty on the part of the employer the court, according to Kingsmill Moore J at 449:

> '… is entitled to take into account that the action was taken by the workman in furtherance of the interest of his master and that zeal may have dulled the edge of caution: that the action was one undertaken to meet a situation where if anything was to be done it had to be rapidly and without deliberation: and that, if the act was one which was customarily performed, the master ought to have been aware of the practice and its danger, and ought to have taken steps to forbid it. Where it can be shown that a regular practice exists unchecked it is difficult to convict of contributory negligence a workman who follows such practice …'.

6.50 By way of examples, in *McNeill v Roche Products Ltd (No 2)* 1988 SCLR 629 an employee was not negligent when he followed the established practice of manually cutting off the petrol supplied to a machine instead of electrically switching off. Likewise in *Moffatt v Atlas Hydraulic Loaders Ltd* 1992 SLT 1123, OH, where the employee followed an ongoing practice of cleaning the machine whilst in motion though it had been unguarded for at least four months. Similarly, it is not negligent to disregard personal danger because the worker is absorbed in work, nor to take a deliberate risk in the employer's interests: *Hutchinson v London North Eastern Rly Co* [1942] 1 KB 481 (men working on railway line failed to keep sharp look out for trains); *Neil v Harland & Wolff Ltd* (1949) 82 Ll L Rep 515, CA (man worked on cables without removing fuses, because removal of fuses would have stopped factory); *Woods v Durable Suites Ltd* [1953] 2 All ER 391 (workman provided his own makeshift staging); *Machray v Stewarts & Lloyds Ltd* [1964] 3 All ER 716 (rigger used makeshift tackle for urgent job, proper tackle not available).

6.51 However, deliberate disobedience of regulations which the employer expects to be obeyed and of the employer's own orders which it enforces is not to be excused by impatience to get on with the works: *ICI Ltd v Shatwell* [1965] AC 656.

6.52 It is not necessarily negligent if a worker takes things for granted, where there is nothing to put him on inquiry. In *Grant v Sun Shipping Co Ltd* [1948] AC 549 a workman went into an unlighted part of a ship, where repairers had been doing work, and stepped into an uncovered hatchway. The House of Lords held that, though this was not a case of inadvertence, the workman had acted 'without conscious thought', taking it for granted that the statutory duty to cover the hatchways had been complied with, and that in the circumstances this was not negligence. Lord du Parcq said, at 567:

> 'Almost every workman constantly, and justifiably, takes risk in the sense that he relies on others to do their duty, and trusts that they have done it. I am far from saying that everyone is entitled to assume, in all circumstances, that other persons will be careful. On the contrary, a prudent man will guard against the possible negligence of others, when experience shows such negligence to be common. Where, however, the negligence is a breach of regulations, made to secure the safety of workmen, which may be presumed to be strictly enforced in the ordinary course of a ship's discipline, I am not prepared to say that a workman has been careless if he assumes that there has been compliance with the law.'

In *Cooper v Carillion plc* [2003] EWCA Civ 1811 Keene LJ referred to the employee's legitimate expectation that his employer has complied with its statutory duties (not contributorily negligent to fail to look underneath a piece of plywood on a building site before placing feet on the area previously concealed by it).

6.53 Mere inadvertence has been excused in many cases, eg *Pringle v Grosvenor* (1894) 21 R 532 (machine fenced on three sides only, woman cleaning inadvertently moved round to unfenced side); *Hunter v Glenfield and Kennedy* 1947 SC 536 (workman on scaffold put hand through factory wall and was injured by crane); *McArdle v Andmac Roofing Co* [1967] 1 All ER 583 (walked backwards pouring bitumen on roof—man behind had gone without warning and left hole); *Ryan v Manbre Sugars Ltd* (1970) 114 Sol Jo 492 (man knew of slippery step but forgot to put foot down carefully); *Stocker v Norprint Ltd* (1970) 10 KIR 10 (man collecting tags from guillotine machine put hand too far in inadequately guarded opening); *John v Martin Simms (Cheltenham) Ltd* [1983] 1 All ER 127 (excavator driver looking for leak in engine put hand near unfenced radiator fan). In *Moffat v Atlas Hydraulic Loaders Ltd* 1992 SLT 1123, OH, an employee was injured whilst cleaning an unguarded machine in motion in accordance with usual practice. The pursuer was found to be 'a keen and willing employee who had been anxious to get on with his job, as best he could, and who had not, at the time, given any great deal of thought as to how or why he adopted a particular method of work ... Such employees must, of course, be protected against the consequences of their own zeal and enthusiasm ...' (per Lord Mainoch at 1124), hence no contributory negligence.

6.54 Indeed inadvertence has been excused even in the case of skilled workers carrying out their skilled work without any special hurry or fatigue. In *Richard Thomas & Baldwins Ltd v Cummings* [1955] AC 321 a skilled worker trapped his fingers by pulling on a belt at a point too near to the pulley; in *John Summers & Sons Ltd v Frost* [1955] AC 740 a skilled worker held a piece of metal too near to a grinding wheel. Both were exonerated from blame, and Lord Keith, in his speech in *Frost's* case, indicated that 'momentary inadvertence' is not enough, and something like 'disobedience to orders', or 'reckless disregard by a workman of his own safety', must be proved before he can be held negligent.[1]

> [1] See also *Stocker v Norprint Ltd* (1970) 10 KIR 10. *Thornton v Swan Hunter (Shipbuilders) Ltd* [1971] 1 WLR 1759, CA and *Gunter v John Nicholas & Sons (Port Talbot) Ltd* [1993] PIQR P 67 seem at first sight out of line. In the first case though the claimant's negligence seemed slight, the breach by the employer was even slighter (fence removed for repairs, finger crushed whilst testing the repairs: 75% contribution). In the second case neither *Frost* nor *Cummings* nor the earlier House of Lords cases of *Flower* or *Caswell* were cited in argument or judgment (skilled woodworking machinist familiar with unguarded cutter and with knowledge that it had no brake).

Disobedience of orders

6.55 In *Flower v Ebbw Vale Steel, Iron and Coal Co Ltd* [1936] AC 206 it was accepted by the House of Lords that disobedience of orders would, prima facie, be contributory negligence, but the defence failed on the facts. A case of long-standing authority on this point is *Senior v Ward* (1859) 1 E & E 385 where there had been a fire in a colliery, which might have affected the ropes suspending the cage. To the knowledge of the miners, there was an order in force requiring the ropes to be tested each day by raising and lowering the cage before passengers used it. The miners themselves disregarded this rule, by going down without any test being made: and it was held that their action failed by reason of contributory negligence. Other cases are *National Coal Board v England* [1954] AC 403 (shotfiring rules in coal mine); *Smith v Chesterfield and District Co-operative Society Ltd* [1953] 1 All ER 447 (worker put hand under guard of pastry machine); *Stapley v Gypsum Mines Ltd* [1953] AC 663 (miner disobeyed orders to make roof safe); *Tearle v Cheverton & Laidler Ltd* (1970) 7 KIR 364 (chief maintenance engineer, contrary to own instructions, switched off starter button only, not power switch, then accidentally caught button: two-thirds blame). In *Laszczyk v National Coal Board* [1954] 3 All ER 205 a trainee miner disobeyed statutory orders by working in a place where he ought not to have been, but as he had been told not to go there by his superior, his fault was held to be slight (5% reduction of damages). In *Storey v National Coal Board* [1983] ICR 156 there was 75% contributory negligence when an experienced miner rode on a conveyor (not a man-riding) belt though he knew this was prohibited and dangerous.[1] In *Williams v Port of Liverpool Stevedoring Co Ltd* [1956] 2 All ER 69 a gang of six disobeyed the foreman's orders as to the method of unloading bags from a hold: one of the dockers was injured by the fall of a bag and his damages were reduced by 50%.

> [1] See *Toole v Bolton Metropolitan Borough Council* [2002] EWCA Civ 588 in relation to the rarity of such a high finding in a case of breach of statutory duty.

Disregard of obvious dangers

6.56 Disregard of obvious dangers was held to be negligent in *Storey v National Coal Board* [1983] ICR 156 (riding on non-man-riding conveyor in coal mine contrary to orders and warning notices, 75% fault); *Gunter v John Nichols & Sons (Port Talbot) Ltd* [1993] PIQR P 67 (cleaning unguarded cutter without a brake, fully conversant with machine and the danger); *Quintas v National Smelting Co Ltd* [1961] 1 All ER 630 (on roof in track of aerial ropeway with back turned); *Johnson v J Stone & Co (Charlton) Ltd* [1961] 1 All ER 869 (putting work-piece too near moving pulley); *Uddin v Associated Portland Cement Manufacturers Ltd* [1965] 2 All ER 213 (climbing on top of machine, where he had no right to be, to catch pigeon, 80% blame); *Upton v Hipgrave Bros* [1965] 1 All ER 6 (carelessly aligning wheelbarrow on hoist so that it was caught by a ledge and tipped); *Lovelidge v Anselm Odling & Sons Ltd* [1967] 2 QB 351 (tie hanging over grinding tool with unfenced shaft, 50% to blame); *Leach v Standard Telephones and Cables Ltd* [1966] 2 All ER 523 (using machine without authority and not adjusting fence, 25% blame); *Kerry v Carter* [1969] 3 All ER 723 (youth falsely told farmer he knew how to use circular saw, two-thirds blame); *Smith v Supreme Wood Pulp Co Ltd* [1968] 3 All ER 753 (driver used circular saw without experience, 25% blame); *Foster v Flexible Metal Co Ltd* (1967) 4 KIR 49 (did not ask for assistance, which was available, in re-setting machine tool); *Ball v Richard Thomas & Baldwins Ltd* [1968] 1 All ER 389 (too near crane when lifting, 25% blame); *Bunker v Charles Brand & Son Ltd* [1969] 2 QB 480 (not keeping firm handhold when walking over rollers, 50% blame); *Mullard v Ben Line Steamers Ltd* [1970] 1 WLR 1414 (walked several paces in pitch dark, fell down hatch, one-third blame); *Jennings v Norman Collison (Contractors) Ltd* [1970] 1 All ER 1121 (building foreman overbalanced pulling key out of door without handle near steep drop; could have fixed temporary handle to door, or safety rail, two-thirds blame); *Field v E E Jeavons & Co Ltd* [1965] 2 All ER 162 (electrician wiring electric saw not yet attached to bed: switched on to test without asking foreman's permission as was customary, 25% blame); *Denyer v Charles Skipper and East Ltd* [1970] 2 All ER 382 (young man, properly instructed, supposed to clean rollers when stationary, put hand in before fully stopped, 50% blame); *F E Callow v Johnson* [1971] AC 335 (squeezed oil into machinery to avoid trouble of preparing for automatic system, one-third blame); *Rodway v P D Wharfage and Transport Ltd* [1973] 2 Lloyd's Rep 511 (guiding slow-moving crane where driver's view imperfect, too close in front, one-third blame); *Wheeler v Copas* [1981] 3 All ER 405 (builder used fruit-picking ladder for building work on farm though it was obviously too flimsy and both stiles gave way); *Allen v Avon Rubber Co Ltd* [1986] ICR 695 (drove forklift over unfenced edge of loading bay, 50% blame); *Boyes v Carnation Foods Ltd* 1986 SLT 145 (mechanic cleaning hands with towel after adjusting machine, crouched too near and towel drawn in, 50% blame); *Anderson v Thames Case Ltd* 1987 SLT 564n (tried to remove rag from machine in motion, 50% blame); *Fraser v Winchester HA* (1999) Times, 12 July (changing a gas cylinder too near to a naked flame, one third blame); *Parker v PFC Flooring Supplies Ltd* [2001] EWCA Civ 1533 (employee climbing on a roof which he knew to be slippery, 50% blame); *Betts v Tockley* [2002] EWCA Civ 52 (leaving premises via an unlit set of steps rather than the front door, 60% blame); *Anderson v Newham College of Further Education* [2002] EWCA Civ 505 (site supervisor tripped on protruding leg of white board in classroom, 50% blame); *Griffiths v Vauxhall Motors Ltd* [2003] EWCA Civ 412 (experienced operator failed to hold a gun used to secure bolts with care when knew it was liable to kick back, 50% blame); *Butcher v Cornwall County Council* [2002] EWCA Civ 1640 (experienced storeman failed secure a door which was blown open by the wind, one third blame); *Sherlock v Chester City Council* [2004] EWCA Civ 210 (failed to use a second work bench or additional support when using a bench saw to cut a long board, 60% blame).

Failure to be on the alert for dangers

6.57 Some of these cases are just over the border-line from 'excusable lapses': *Reilly v British Transport Commission* [1956] 3 All ER 857 (worker tightening bolts on railway line failed to watch signals); *McDonald v British Transport Commission* [1955] 3 All ER 789 (foreman stepped on railway truck, failed to see large hole in floor); *Simmons v Bovis Ltd* [1956] 1 All ER 736 (foreman stepped on 'trap ends' on scaffold, ie planks overlapping supports and liable to tip up: slight blame, only 10%[1]). It is to be noted that in two of these cases the claimant was a foreman, and the first case was working alone on a railway line. Such workers might be expected to keep their eyes open. In *Smith (or Westwood) v National Coal Board* [1967] 2 All ER 593 a majority of the House of Lords assessed 25% blame for scrambling up an awkward bank instead of stopping as a shunting train approached (Lords Hodson and Upjohn thought it was excusable misjudgment in emergency). Other examples are *Astell v London Transport Board* [1966] 2 All ER 748 (in manoeuvring long pipe round corner of stairs, crouched below level of safety rail, 25% blame); *Woollins v British Celanese Ltd* (1966) 1 KIR 438 (not testing fragility of flat roof before stepping on it, 50% blame); *Kendrick v Cozens & Sutcliffe Ltd* (1968) 4 KIR 469 (working from ladder, moved on to fragile roof to avoid sparks, 75% blame); *McDowell v FMC (Meat) Ltd* (1967) 3 KIR 595 (experienced manager failed to spot overhead power line at showground, one-fifth blame); *Wheat v E Lacon & Co Ltd* [1966] AC 552 (overconfident that bottom of unlit staircase reached); *Baron v B French Ltd* [1971] 3 All ER 1111 (tripped over rubble heap in poorly lit corridor, hospital under construction, 50% blame); *Cox v HCB Angus Ltd* [1981] ICR 683 (electrician working in cab of fire engine failed to see loose pipe lying there and tripped over it, 50% blame); *Sole v WJ Hallt Ltd* [1973] QB 574 (stepped back near unfenced drop, one-third blame); *Byrne v EH Smith Roofing Ltd* [1973] 1 All ER 490 (walked along roof gutter, one foot on fragile asbestos, 20% blame); *Boothman v British Northrop Ltd* (1972) 13 KIR 112 (tripped over cable of own welding torch, 25% blame); *McClymont v Glasgow Corpn* 1971 SLT 45 (mechanic squatting by bus on four foot high servicing platform slipped under single-rail fence, 75% blame, perhaps not because mechanic was seriously negligent but because employer's fault was small).

[1]   Cf *Butcher v Cornwall County Council* [2002] EWCA Civ 1640: 10% 'so nearly a token figure as to betoken an absence of significant fault'.

CONSENTING TO THE RISK OF INJURY

6.58 This concept has been long referred to by use of the latin maxim 'volenti non fit injuria' which literally means 'no injury is done to one who consents'.

6.58   *Contributory negligence, volenti etc*

A person who consents (expressly or by implication) to run the risk of injury created by another person cannot recover damages for injuries sustained as a result of such risks. This principle may afford a complete defence[1] to any personal injury action founded on common law negligence (as opposed to an action based on a breach of statutory duty). However, in practice, its success is exceptionally rare especially in employers' liability cases (there being no recent reported cases of the defence succeeding in this field). This is far from surprising, as the difficulty of mounting such a defence successfully in an employer/employee negligence action has long been acknowledged due to the very nature of the relationship and its inherent inequality. As was pointed out in *Merrington v Ironbridge Metalworks Ltd* [1952] 2 All ER 1101 per Hallett J at 1103:

> 'A real assent to the assumption of the risk without compensation must be shown by the circumstances ... If, however, a man acts under the compulsion of a duty, such consent should rarely, if ever, be inferred, because a man cannot be said to be "willing" unless he is in a position to choose freely.'

1   And as a result must be specifically set out in the defence.

6.59 Further, the mere fact that an employee is aware of a risk and then proceeds to run that risk cannot, in itself, be said to amount to full and free consent. In *Neil v Harland & Wolff Ltd* (1949) 82 Ll L Rep 515 a workman consciously took the risk of working with electrical cables without removing the fuses, so as to avoid the need for the factory to stop production. It was held that the defence of consent to the risk of injury was not available to the employer as the employee had taken the risk in the interests of his employer. It has to be shown that the employee made an implied agreement to take the risk of harm upon himself and bear the consequences. The courts are reluctant to find the existence of an implied agreement in this situation, unless the person who is alleged to have made the agreement had full knowledge of the nature and extent of the risk to be run.[1]

1   *Osborne v London and North Western Rly Co* (1888) 21 QBD 220, followed by the Court of Appeal in *White v Blackmore* [1972] 2 QB 651 and *Wooldridge v Sumner* [1963] 2 QB 43.

6.60 Certainly continuance at work in the presence of the risk does not, of itself, prove consent to run that risk or, more importantly, bear the consequence of the materialisation of that risk. The Court of Appeal in *Bowater v Rowley Regis Corpn* [1944] KB 476 expressed the view that there were very few cases in the employment relationship where the defence of consent to the risk of injury can succeed.

6.61 Whilst knowledge of the risk does not equate to consent to bear the consequence, it may, nevertheless, amount to contributory negligence because, on the face of it, disregard of an obvious danger can amount to contributory negligence.

6.62 In any event no question of the defence can arise unless the defendant owed the claimant a duty of care. Whilst such a duty is, by definition, present in an employer/employee situation, in other areas of activity the issues of the existence and limits of the duty of care has troubled the courts. Indeed much of the case law on the subject concerns activities where the participants or onlookers of the activity have obvious free choice to avoid any risk of injury created by another. One area where the issue of consent to risk has arisen (although not strictly considered as an application of this principle due to the lack of a breach of duty) is when a risk to health has arisen through no apparent fault on the part of the employer and cannot be removed, ie a continuing risk will remain if the employee continues with his/her duties.

6.63 In the employment situation there are risks which are incidental to the employment. In respect of those the employer must take reasonable care to protect its employee against all hazards of his employment including the inherent risks: *Ellis v Ocean Steamship Co Ltd* [1958] 2 Lloyd's Rep 373 (seaman falling overboard). A separate question is always antecedent: was the employer negligent?[1] If the duty of care has been discharged then there is no consideration of voluntary acceptance of risk. But what is the scope of the duty of care if a risk to health arises through no fault on the part of the employer? Can the employee 'consent' to work on, and accept the risk of injury, or has the employee a duty to act? For many years the clear position was that once the employer had taken all appropriate steps to minimise a risk incidental to the employment, which did not arise from negligence, and had warned the employee of it, the employer was not obliged to dismiss the employee or demote the employee to a lower paid job so as to prevent or lessen exposure. This meant that the employee could consent to the continued risk without liability on the part of the employer. In *Withers v Perry Chain Co Ltd* [1961] 1 WLR 1314 the claimant, who suffered from dermatitis, returned to work when it was known that his continuation of work would give rise to a small risk of the dermatitis recurring. Sellers LJ stated:

> 'I cannot believe that the common law requires employers to refuse to employ a person who is willing to work for them simply because they think that it is not in the person's best interests to work.'[2]

[1] The question posed by Sellers LJ in *Wooldridge v Sumner* [1963] 2 QB 43 at 56 '… there is no liability unless there is negligence …'.
[2] See para 4.59, above and *Hatton v Sutherland* [2002] 2 All ER 1, para 14.51, below.

6.64 This view was adopted and approved in *Kossinski v Chrysler (UK)* (1973) 15 KIR 225 and *Henderson v Wakefield Shirt Co Ltd* [1997] PIQR P413. However, in *Hatton v Sutherland* [2002] EWCA Civ 76 it was recognised that taking this principle to its logical conclusion would justify perpetuating the most unsafe practices on the basis that the employee can always leave. Thereafter, in *Coxall v Goodyear Great Britain Ltd* [2002] EWCA Civ 1010 the judge at first instance refused to follow this line of authority on the basis that its origins lay 40 years previously and the landscape of employer's liability had changed considerably in the interim with duties and obligations on employers now being much more stringent. The Court of Appeal wrestled with the conflict between what it referred to as the '*Withers* principle' (endorsing its continued validity) and the contention on behalf of the employers that there is now a duty upon employers to protect their employees against themselves. The conclusion reached was that the principal consideration in determining whether or not any particular case falls within the *Withers* principle must be the actual nature and extent of the known risk. On the facts in question, the court decided that the employer was negligent for not following advice that the employee should not continue in the relevant employment (ie he should have been moved or dismissed). The decision failed to fully address the impact of the range of 1992 regulations upon the duty (in some cases absolute duty) of employers to act in the face of potential risk to health, including through dismissal. In *Lane Group plc v Farmiloe* [2004] PIQR P22 the EAT was concerned with the dismissal of an employee who was unable to wear the necessary protective footwear due to a medical condition and whose employer would have been in breach of the Personal Protective Equipment at Work Regulations 1992 if he had been permitted to work on (as he was willing to do) wearing ordinary shoes. Judge Peter Clark stated:

> 'in so far as the employer's common law duty of care is relevant, the employment tribunal was wrong to direct itself solely in accordance with the general rule in *Withers*. The significance of *Coxall* is the holding that there may be cases where an employer is under a duty at law to dismiss the employee so as to protect him from danger. We would go further on the facts of this case, applying *Stark*[1], and conclude that where an employer cannot comply with the requirements of the Personal Protective Equipment Regulations, he will be in breach of his common law duty by continuing to employ that individual in breach of the regulations and in these circumstances, all other avenues having been properly explored, will be obliged to dismiss him'.

[1]   *Stark v Post Office* [2000] ICR 1013.

6.65 *Coxall* is unsatisfactory as a decision in that it recognised but failed to resolve a conflict of principle, as a result leaving the law in a state of some uncertainty. There must be considerable doubt whether the *Withers* principle has any place in the modern world of employers' liability. However, it is clear at the very least that the *Withers* principle is no longer to be slavishly applied, notwithstanding the nature and extent of the risk to the employee, regardless of the employee's wishes.

6.66 Returning to the established principle of consenting to a risk, it operates on two levels. On the first level it means that an act done to a claimant with his or her full and informed consent cannot be complained of as being a legal wrong. A boxer, for example, cannot claim damages for being knocked out by his opponent provided he kept within the strict rules of the sport. The position may be different if a competitor steps sufficiently outside the rules: see *Condon v Basi* [1985] 1 WLR 866 which involved a dangerous football tackle.[1] Sir John Donaldson MR approved the statement of the applicable law formulated by Kitto J in the Australian case of *Rootes v Shelton* [1968] ALR 33:

> 'in a case such as the present, it must always be a question of fact, what exoneration from a duty of care otherwise incumbent upon the defendant was implied by the act of the plaintiff in joining in the activity ... the conclusion to

be reached must necessarily depend, according to the concepts of the common law, upon the reasonableness, in relation to the special circumstances, of the conduct which caused the plaintiffs injury.'

In *Blake v Galloway* [2004] EWCA Civ 814 two teenagers had engaged in an informal game/form of playing whereby they were throwing pieces of bark chipping at each other. The Court of Appeal held that by participating in the game they had both impliedly consented to the risk of a blow to the body provided that the offending missile was thrown more or less in accordance with the tacit understandings or conventions of the game.

1   In *Elliott v Saunders and Liverpool FC Ltd* (10 June 1994, unreported), Drake J applied *Condon*: '... an intentional foul or a mistake, or an error of judgment, may be enough to give rise to liability.'

6.67 On the second level the principle is sometimes taken to refer to the situation which arises where a claimant has voluntarily taken the risk of injury inherent in some activity not arising from anyone's negligence. That may describe the factual position but it has no application in the legal situation since there is no negligence on the part of anyone else. This situation arises, for example, when a spectator is injured by some misadventure at an organised sport or occasion. There is no liability when the participant, doing his best to win, moves fast or makes some misjudgment, because these risks are inherent in the sport and there is no negligence: *Wooldridge v Sumner* [1963] 2 QB 43 (a photographer at a horse show was injured when a horse deviated from the course);[1] *Lawridge v Sumner* [1963] 2 QB 4 (a spectator at a horse show injured when an experienced rider lost control of his horse, on appeal held there was no negligence so 'volenti' held not to arise).[2] The duty of care still exists, but it takes into account the necessities of the event.

1   A competitor going all out to win must not, however, act in disregard of spectators: *Wilkes v Cheltenham Home Guard Motorcycle and Light Car Club* [1971] 1 WLR 668.
2   Sellers LJ at 56 '... a competitor or player cannot in the normal case at least of competition or game rely on the maxim volenti non fit injuria in answer to a spectator's claim.'

6.68 Similarly, it has been held both in Canada and in England that a spectator at an ice hockey match has no right of action if he is hit by the puck: *Elliott v Amphitheatre Ltd* [1934] 3 WWR 225, *Murray v Haringay Arena Ltd* [1951] 2 KB 529, though the situation may be different now, with greater emphasis on spectator safety, more safety measures and safety systems available at reasonable cost.

6.69 In any event, where consent to the risk of injury is mounted as a defence the true question is not whether the claimant consented to run the risk of being hurt but rather whether the claimant consented to run that risk at his own expense so that he, and not the party alleged to be negligent, should bear the loss in the event of injury.[1] The consent which is relevant is not the consent to the risk of injury but consent to the lack of reasonable care that may produce that risk.[2]

1   See Lord MacDermott in *Kelly v Farrans Ltd* [1954] NI 41.
2   *Kelly v Farrans Ltd* [1954] NI 41.

Consent and breach of statutory duty

6.70 Consent to the risk of injury is not a defence to a breach of the employer's own statutory duty: *Baddeley v Granville (Earl)* (1887) 19 QBD 423; *Wheeler v New Merton Boardmills Ltd* [1933] 2 KB 669. However it is a defence to an employer's vicarious liability for the breach of an employee's statutory duty, at any rate if the employee was not a person of superior rank whose orders the claimant was bound to obey: *ICI Ltd v Shatwell* [1965] AC 656. *Shatwell* was an extreme case where the claimant, one of two shot firers in a quarry, fully appreciating the risk of explosion, consented to and actually took part in a deviation from regulations, strictly enforced by the employers.

6.71 In *Olsen v Carry and Gravesend Aviation Ltd* [1936] 3 All ER 241 an aircraft apprentice was injured owing to a negligent system of starting aircraft engines; it was held that as an inexperienced apprentice could not appreciate the risk, the defence of consent to the risk of injury failed completely. So, too, the defence failed when a fireman was exposed to exceptional risk of explosion through the presence of aluminium dust of which he had not been told: *Merrington v Ironbridge Metalworks Ltd* [1952] 2 All ER 1101.

LIABILITY TO AN UNPAID VOLUNTEER WORKER

6.72 While the doctrine of 'common employment' was still in force, the extent of an employer's liability to a person who had volunteered, without pay, to assist employees with their work, was rather obscure. In *Degg v Midland Rly Co* (1857) 1 H & N 773 the claimant ran to assist some railway employees who were trying to move a turntable, and was injured by a railway engine. It was held that the claimant could not assert any greater rights than those of the workers he was assisting. His claim was also subject, strangely, to the defence of common employment. That principle was affirmed in *Potter v Faulkner* (1861) 1 B & S 800, *Bass v Hendon Urban District Council* (1912) 28 TLR 317, *Heasmer v Pickfords Ltd* (1920) 36 TLR 818 and *Bromiley v Collins* [1936] 2 All ER 1061. In that case a boy had volunteered to help in moving a heavily laden trailer, and it was held that he was either in common employment with the other men, or a trespasser. These cases, in so far as they depend upon the doctrine of common employment, have been obsolete since the Law Reform (Personal Injuries) Act 1948. That Act abolished the defence. Now there is no reason, in principle, why the relationship of employer and employee cannot arise between a volunteer and the person for whom he volunteers to work in such circumstances.

6.73 Further, a claimant could succeed, even under the old law, if he could show that he was present in some capacity which created a common law duty towards him. In *Hayward v Drury Lane Theatre Ltd and Moss' Empires Ltd* [1917] 2 KB 899 the claimant was injured at a theatre where she was attending rehearsals with a view to engagement as a dancer. It was held that she was entitled to recover damages as an invitee. In *Lomas v M Jones & Son* [1944] 1 KB 4 the defendants had delivered a cow to the claimant's farmyard, and the claimant was helping to close the doors of the van when he was injured owing to the driver's negligence. It was held that the defendants were liable, as the claimant was lawfully present in his own farmyard, and the defendants owed him a duty of care. Much more recently in *Bottomley v Todmorden Cricket Club* [2003] EWCA Civ 1575 the Court of Appeal held that the defendant club which allowed a dangerous pyrotechnic display to take place on its land owed a duty of care to the claimant who was lawfully on the land assisting the contractors conducting the display, and was liable to the claimant along with the contractors when he was injured in an explosion because they and the club had failed to take ordinary precautions.

6.74 The modern approach at common law, it is suggested, is to focus on the degree of control exercised by the 'user' or 'borrower' of the volunteer's services. And the consequential degree of reliance of the worker on the work being conducted safely. The real test may well be simply one of foreseeability: was it foreseeable that the volunteer might be injured? Liability may arise if the activities are conducted negligently in the knowledge that the claimant was present and maybe in danger, in accordance with general principles of negligence or as a result of vicarious liability: *Fitzgerald v Great Northern Rly* (Ireland) [1947] NI 50. In *Morris v Breaveglen Ltd* [1993] ICR 766 and *Nelhams v Sandells Maintenance Ltd and Gillespie (UK) Ltd* [1996] PIQR P 52 the Court of Appeal held that where the claimant had been 'lent' to another employer, his own employer remained liable to him when he was injured. The duty of care owed by an employer to its employee cannot be delegated. There is no reason in principle why the employer should not be said to owe the same duty of care to a volunteer as it does to its workers.

6.75 In relation to potential statutory duties owed to an unpaid volunteer, these are limited by the fact that the HSWA 1974, s 52 defines work as work as an employee or as a self-employed person.

Chapter 7

THE LIABILITY OF THIRD PARTIES TO AN INJURED EMPLOYEE

Barry Cotter

GENERAL

7.01 With increased use of subsidiary companies and a growth in the use of 'contracted-in' labour, it is common for several employers to be engaged on a common task, or to be working on the same premises or at any rate in the same vicinity. As a result in building or engineering operations there may be a principal contractor and several sub-contractors, and in addition there will be the occupiers of the site. Agency workers, such as nurses, may be working with, and on the premises of, someone who is not their employer. Just like the employer, those persons may owe duties to workers. Chapter 4 considered when an undertaking might owe primary duties to persons under its control or supervision who were not its employees (see paras 4.72–4.82); and it also explained when a business could be vicariously liable for torts committed by persons not in its employment.[1] This chapter will briefly consider other legal duties towards workers which may affect persons who are not their employers, or which arise independently of an employment relationship (such as occupiers' liability).

[1]   Note the consideration of the scope of vicarious liability in *Viasystems (Tyneside) Ltd v Thermal Transfer (Northern) Ltd* [2005] EWCA Civ 1151; the court should concentrate on the relevant negligent act and then ask whose responsibility it was to prevent it. Entire and absolute control is not a necessary pre-condition of vicarious liability; see paras 4.99–4.107, above.

7.02 In the past it was rare for third parties to stand in the same close factual relationship to a worker as the employer, who generally had power to control the work and workplace. Accordingly their legal duty towards the worker was rarely as high, particularly when compared with the non-delegable duty of care.[1]

[1]   See *McDermid v Nash Dredging and Reclamation Co Ltd* [1987] AC 906, HL.

7.03 The HSWA 1974 lays down a general duty on an employer to conduct its undertakings to ensure, so far as is reasonably practicable, that persons other than its employees are not exposed to risks to their health and safety (s 3). In addition, persons who have to any extent control of non-domestic premises, means of access or egress thereto or plant or substance in the premises owe a similar duty to take reasonably practicable measures for the safety of non-employees who use the premises as a place of work or as a place where they may use plant or substances (s 4). Designers, manufacturers and importers of articles for use at work, of fairground equipment and of

214

substances also owe duties in relation to the safety of those items and matters (s 6). But none of these duties gives rise to civil liability (s 47(1)(a)).

7.04 Some of the regulations introduced under the Act, which are actionable in civil proceedings, apply to non-employees: an example is the Control of Substances Hazardous to Health Regulations 2002, SI 2002/2677.[1] It is to be noted that the duty imposed by the Management of Health and Safety at Work Regulations 1999, SI 1999/3242, reg 3 upon an employer in relation to persons not in his employment is still not actionable in civil proceedings[2] (see generally the discussion of this topic at chapter 18 on the workplace regulations).

[1] See reg 3.
[2] See the Management of Health and Safety at Work and Fire Precautions (Workplace) (Amendment) Regulations 2003, SI 2003/2457, reg 6.

7.05 Under the Temporary Workers Directive (91/383/EC) an undertaking using workers assigned to it by an employment agency must afford them the same level of protection as other, directly employed workers in its undertaking, and the duties in the linked daughter Directives apply in full to agency workers (art 2). Regulations implementing those Directives and, perhaps, the common law must be interpreted or developed to meet these requirements. The Conduct of Employment Agencies and Employment Businesses Regulations 2003, SI 2003/3319, which by reg 30 are actionable in civil proceedings require by reg 20 that neither an agency nor an employment business introduce or supply a work-seeker to a hirer unless the agency or employment business has made all such enquiries, as are reasonably practicable, to ensure that it would not be detrimental to the interests of the work-seeker or the hirer for the work-seeker to work for the hirer in the position which the hirer seeks to fill.

7.06 No doubt in part as a reflection of these legislative developments and in order to keep pace with changes in the organisation of work, it is likely that the common law will increasingly recognise duties on the part of undertakings to workers not employed by them, duties which will which vary in accordance with the degree of risk and the extent of factual control.[1] As stated in *Viasystems (Tyneside) Ltd v Thermal Transfer (Northern) Ltd* [2005] EWCA Civ 1151, the correct question to consider is who is entitled to exercise control over the relevant act or operation.

[1] See eg *Waltons and Morse v Dorrington* [1997] IRLR 488, in which the EAT derived an implied contractual duty from the HSWA 1974, s 2.

7.07 Certainly, if a third party—such as a building owner, superior contractor, safety consultant or architect—intervenes in the control of operations, or assumes responsibility for the method of carrying them out, the common law is now likely to recognise a duty of care similar to that owed by an employer, dependent on the extent of intervention and/or control.

PRODUCT LIABILITY

7.08 This section considers the liability of third parties who supply products which injure or harm a worker. Where an employee suffers personal injury at work owing to defective equipment provided by an employer, the employer is liable just as much as a manufacturer by virtue of the Employers' Liability (Defective Equipment) Act 1969.[1] In such circumstances consideration should also be given to the duties under the Provision and Use of Work Equipment Regulations 1998, SI 1998/2306 (see generally chapter 20 below). As a result, an employee injured by equipment at work will rarely have to consider the liability of any third party (although this may be of very real interest to the employer in terms of contribution proceedings usually based upon the contract of supply or the Civil Liability (Contribution) Act 1978).

[1] This Act redressed the unsatisfactory common law position established by *Davie v New Merton Board Mills Ltd* [1959] AC 604. A very wide meaning is to be given to the term 'equipment' for the purposes of this Act: see Lord Oliver in *Coltman v Bibby Tankers Ltd, The Derbyshire* [1988] AC 276.

Consumer Protection Act 1987

7.09 The liability of a third party to an employee for injury caused by defective products supplied to an employee will, if relevant, usually depend on Part I (ss 1–9) of the Consumer Protection Act 1987, which was passed to give effect to the Product Liability Directive (85/374/EC) and which came into force on 1 March 1988. Under this Act a manufacturer or other supplier may be absolutely liable for personal injury and (within limits) damage to property if caused by a 'defective' product, subject to a number of statutory exceptions. Liability cannot be excluded by agreement, notice or otherwise (s 7). The Act does not affect liability under the existing law (s 2(6)).

7.10 The Act imposes liability on the 'producer' (see s 2(2)(a)). This term can extend to persons who processed, placed their name on or was the first importer of the goods into the EEC (see s 2(2)). A supplier can be liable if it fails to identify the producer on request by an injured person (s 2(3)). The Act applies to 'any goods', and also 'electricity' (s 1(2)). It includes a product comprised in another product as (a) a component, or (b) raw material, or (c) otherwise. 'Goods' include growing crops and things attached to land, also any ship, aircraft or vehicle (s 45(1)). But there is no liability for a defect in 'game or agricultural produce' (which includes fishery produce) unless it has been treated by an industrial process.

7.11 The defect must be related to 'safety'; and this in turn includes risks to property, as well risks of injury and death (s 3(1)). The standard of safety is such as 'persons generally' are 'entitled to expect': see *EC Commission v United Kingdom (re Product Liability Directive)* [1997] ECR I-2649, ECJ. In deciding what they are entitled to expect (s 3(2)) all the circumstances are taken into account, in particular the purpose for which the product has been marketed, its get-up and markings, and any instructions and warnings: see e g *Worsley v Tambrands Ltd* [2000] PIQR P 95; *Tesco Stores v Pollard* [2006] EWCA Civ 393. Also relevant is what might be expected to be done with or in relation to the product.

7.12 There are statutory defences to liability in s 4, the burden of proof being upon the defendant in the event that a defect is found to have been present and causative of injury. The most commonly relied upon is that the defect did not exist at the 'relevant time', which generally means the date of supply by the producer or importer (s 4(1)(a)). This usually involves an allegation that someone subsequent to the supply has created the defect in an otherwise safe product.

Statutory duties of manufacturers and suppliers

7.13 Section 6 of the HSWA 1974 imposes certain duties upon any person who designs, manufacturers, imports or supplies[1] any article for use at work. However, it confers no right of action in civil proceedings (s 47(1)(a)).

[1]   See the definition of supply at s 53(1).

7.14 Further, general duties are also placed on a responsible person, usually the manufacturer of machinery (or the first importer into the EEC), which is for use at work by the Supply of Machinery (Safety) Regulations 1992, SI 1992/3073[1] as amended. The principal duties owed are to ensure that relevant machinery or a relevant safety component is safe and complies with specified essential health and safety requirements (see regs 11 and 12). The Regulations, which were not made under the HSWA 1974, are silent as to whether a breach will give rise to civil liability but in *Polestar Jowetts Ltd v Komori UK Ltd* [2005] EWHC 1674 (QB), Field J held that it could not be inferred from the terms of the Regulations and the scheme of the HSWA 1974 that one of the purposes of the Regulations was to confer a right of civil action. If it had been intended to confer such a right, the Regulations would have clearly declared that they were being made under the 1974 Act.

[1]   Designed to implement Directive 91/368.

The duty of a manufacturer, supplier or repairer at common law

7.15 The final potential cause of action in relation to a product related injury, (ie if the Employer's Liability (Defective Equipment) Act 1969 and/or the Provision and Use of Work Equipment Regulations 1998 which relate to a cause of action against the employer or the Consumer Protection Act 1987 as against a manufacturer, or person deemed to be a manufacturer, do not provide a suitable cause of action) is the manufacturer/producer, supplier or repairer's liability in negligence.

7.16 It used to be thought that a manufacturer owed no duty to the persons who ultimately used the plant, machinery or materials which it had manufactured, except when it had entered into a contract with those persons.

7.17 The liability of third parties to an injured employee

Eventually, in *Donoghue v Stevenson* [1932] AC 562 it was held that the manufacturer does owe a duty to take care for the safety of the ultimate user of its products.

7.17 At first no duty was considered to arise when the manufactured article was to be examined by some intermediate person, or by the injured person himself: *Farr v Butters Bros & Co* [1932] 2 KB 606. The reasonable probability that an article will be used without examination was taken as the test in *Grant v Australian Knitting Mills Ltd* [1936] AC 85 (manufacturers of pants containing injurious chemicals liable to purchaser who sustained dermatitis through wearing them without washing them); *Herschthal v Stewart and Ardern Ltd* [1940] 1 KB 155 (sale of re-conditioned motor car for immediate use); and *Haseldine v CA Daw & Son Ltd* [1941] 2 KB 343 (lift in building).

7.18 In the case of an article which ought to be examined from time to time, though not necessarily at once, an injury after a lapse of time may be too remote: *Evans v Triplex Safety Glass Co Ltd* [1936] 1 All ER 283. But in *Mason v Williams & Williams Ltd and Thomas Turton & Sons Ltd* [1955] 1 All ER 808 manufacturers who had supplied a chisel to employers were held liable to a workman who used the chisel and was injured because the steel was too hard and a piece flew out, on the ground that it is not the duty of an employer to examine tools supplied by reputable manufacturers; this was approved by the House of Lords in *Davie v New Merton Board Mills Ltd* [1959] AC 604.[1] This led to action by Parliament and an employer now is liable for defects in goods supplied by third parties under the Employers' Liability (Defective Equipment) Act 1969. The manufacturer's liability at common law may cease in part or whole if the employer, after discovering the dangerous condition of such a tool, chooses to keep it in use: *Taylor v Rover Co Ltd* [1966] 2 All ER 181. However the existence of the 1969 Act and the Provision and Use of Work Equipment Regulations 1998 will usually render this an academic point.

[1] Strictly speaking, the maxim res ipsa loquitur does not apply in these cases: *Donoghue v Stevenson* [1932] AC 562 at 622; *Mason v Williams & Williams Ltd and Thomas Turton & Sons Ltd* [1955] 1 All ER 808. Since, however, the process of manufacture or repair is under the defendant's control, the presence of some substance or dangerous defect which ought not to be there may give rise to an inference of negligence, which will be sufficient evidence in the absence of a good explanation, and the claimant is not required to prove exactly what went wrong in the course of manufacture: *Lockhart v Barr* 1943 SC 1.

7.19 In fact these decisions are best regarded as decisions on causation, rather than inherent limitations of the manufacturer's liability. In some cases knowledge of a defect may not break the causal connection, or for other reasons both manufacturer and employer may be liable: eg *Hadley v Droitwich Construction Co Ltd (Joseph Pugsley & Sons Ltd, third party)* [1968] 1 WLR 37 (crane inaccurately adjusted by manufacturers, users failed to check and maintain, crane collapsed, both equally liable). In *Carroll v Fearon* [1998] PIQR P 416, the Court of Appeal held that the manufacturers of a defective tyre were liable for personal injuries which resulted from the tyre exploding, even though there was a dearth of evidence as to the origin of the defect.

7.20 Where a part of the process of manufacture is carried out by an independent contractor, it is that contractor who owes the duty of care so far as any defect arises in the course of the process; and the manufacturer is entitled to rely on a reputable contractor: *Taylor v Rover Co Ltd*, above (faulty hardening of chisel). Similarly, in *Haseldine v CA Daw & Son Ltd*, above (an accident due to improper repair of hydraulic lift) the Court of Appeal, approving earlier cases, held that a repairer, who does not contemplate a further examination of the repaired plant or article after it has left his hands, is under the same duty as a manufacturer to the ultimate user.

7.21 Suppliers of materials for use in a manufacturing process, so far as they are aware of the nature of the process, owe as high a duty of care as the employer in assessing and eliminating the risks: they should at least give warning of any risks, and if it becomes clear that the materials are too dangerous to be used at all they should stop supplying them: *Wright v Dunlop Rubber Co* (1972) 13 KIR 255 (chemicals added to rubber to prevent rotting caused cancer of the bladder).

7.22 A supplier of a product who knows that the product is dangerous can be negligent for a failure to warn: *Hobbs (E) (Farms) Ltd v Baxenden Chemical Co Ltd* [1992] 1 Lloyd's Rep 54. But the supplier may also be negligent in failing to inspect or investigate its safety or to warn that this should be done: see eg *Andrews v Hopkinson* [1957] 1 QB 229 (second-hand car dealer liable for failing to check car for defective steering mechanism). Such a duty is likely to arise where the user relies, or can reasonably be expected to rely, upon the supplier having made some investigation of the product's safety.

7.23 This principle can be extended to supply through merely making available for use. It has been held that shipowners are liable to stevedores' employees for failing to take reasonable care for the safety of the ship's winches, and other equipment used in loading and unloading: *Butler v Hogarth Shipping Co Ltd* (1947) 80 Ll L Rep 84; *Norwegian Shipping and Trading Mission v Behenna* (1943) 169 LT 191. And building owners who accept no responsibility for supervision nevertheless owe a duty to independent contractors engaged to do work for them to take reasonable care for the safety of plant and equipment which is on the land for their use: *Wheeler v Copas* [1981] 3 All ER 405 (farmer lent flimsy fruit ladder to 'labour only' bricklayer); *Kealey v Heard* [1983] 1 WLR 573 (scaffold erected by another contractor collapsed under self-employed plasterer: building owner did nothing at all to supervise or check safety). Of course these cases would now involve alleged breaches of the Provision and Use of Work Equipment Regulations 1998, SI 1998/2306.

7.24 In *Oliver v Saddler & Co* [1929] AC 584 employees of a stevedoring company were raising bags of grain from the hold of a ship to the deck, and at the deck a portage company took over and transferred the loads to the quayside by means of a crane. The stevedores provided rope slings which they fitted to the load down in the hold and provided a man to examine the slings and reject defective ropes: the portage company relied on the stevedores to do this. On these facts the House of Lords held the stevedores liable when a defective sling broke and the load fell on to an employee of the portage company.

7.25 In *Griffiths v Arch Engineering Co (Newport) Ltd* [1968] 3 All ER 217 where a grinding wheel not properly set up was hired out to a firm carrying out work on a dock, and they in turn lent it (without charge) to a man working for another firm of contractors, both the owners and the hirers were held liable (cf *Fraser v Jenkins* [1968] NZLR 816). But lack of reliance meant the supplier was not liable in *Marshall v Cellactite and British Uralite Ltd* (1947) 63 TLR 456, CA. There, contractors were carrying out work in a factory, and were given a general permission to use the factory plant. A defect in a ladder belonging to the factory caused injury to one of the contractor's men, but, as the contractors had used their own judgment in selecting the ladder, the owners of the factory were not liable.

7.26 The foregoing cases relate to the plant and equipment used in the course of work, but in *Denny v Supplies and Transport Co Ltd* [1950] 2 KB 374 the Court of Appeal extended the same principles of law to third parties who prepare loads to be discharged by the workmen of another employer. A firm of stevedores had unloaded timber from a ship and stacked it negligently on a barge, in such a manner that unloading would be dangerous. The claimant was a labourer employed by a second firm, who helped to unload the barge at the quayside and sustained injury in handling the timber. The Court of Appeal held the stevedores liable to the claimant, and Sir Raymond Evershed MR remarked that it was a matter of practical necessity to unload the timber as it stood, even though the risk might be apparent. *Denny's* case was distinguished in *Twiss v WH Rhodes & Son Ltd and Mersey Docks and Harbour Board* [1951] 1 Lloyd's Rep 333, which was also a case of cargo badly stowed on a barge, on the ground that it was the duty of the claimant's employer to inspect the load and decide upon a safe system of unloading. It must be supposed that in this latter case it was possible to devise a safe method of unloading, whereas in the former case it was not: even so, the line of distinction between the two cases is very slender. Similar in principle is *Samways v Westgate Engineers Ltd* (1962) 106 Sol Jo 937, CA (liability to dustman for leaving cardboard carton with sharp glass sticking out).

Things dangerous in themselves

7.27 At one time the law drew a distinction between things 'dangerous in themselves' and other products. The distinction was very much an intuitive one, and it no longer represents the law. But the nature of the duty of care will vary in accordance with the risks of the product. It may be negligent to deliver a dangerous product to a junior employee (see *Yachuk v Oliver Blais Co Ltd* [1949] AC 386); perhaps warnings should be given (*Philco Radio and Television Corpn of Great Britain Ltd v J Spurling Ltd* [1949] 2 All ER 882);

and it may be negligent to leave them unguarded. Thus in *Dominion Natural Gas Co Ltd v Collins and Perkins* [1909] AC 640 at 646 Lord Dunedin said:

> 'It has, however, again and again been held that in the case of things dangerous in themselves, such as loaded firearms, poisons, explosives, and other things *ejusdem generis,* there is a peculiar duty to take precautions imposed upon those who send forth or install such articles where it is necessarily the case that other persons will come within their proximity.'

7.28 The owner of an industrial establishment may be liable if dangerous substances like petrol, acids, explosives or injurious chemicals are left in an accessible place instead of being stored under proper control: *Smedley v Moira Colliery Ltd* [1948] WN 467. Contractors working on a ship have similarly been held liable for leaving a cylinder of gas in a place where it might be tampered with and endanger the workmen of other contractors: *Beckett v Newalls Insulation Co Ltd* [1953] 1 All ER 250 (see also the HSWA 1974, s 4, although this confers no civil right of action).

7.29 At one time liability for defects was wide, extending to those which affected the value of property without injuring anyone: see especially *Anns v Merton London Borough Council* [1978] AC 728.[1] In subsequent cases the House of Lords sought to restrict liability: *Peabody Donation Fund (Governors) v Sir Lindsay Parkinson & Co Ltd* [1985] AC 210; *D & F Estates Ltd v Church Comrs for England* [1989] AC 177, HL. Finally, in *Murphy v Brentwood District Council* [1991] 1 AC 398, the House of Lords placed further limitations on liability for defective housing. This line of authority was applied in *Bellefield Computer Services Ltd v E Turner & Sons Ltd* [2000] BLR 97, CA to limit the liability for damage to the structure of the building of a negligent builder to a subsequent owner. Unless the defect causes personal injury (see eg *Otto v Bolton and Norris* [1936] 2 KB 46) or damage to *other* property, a claimant will rarely recover. Where personal injury is caused, a person is not automatically denied damages because, knowing of the defect, she continues in residence: see *Targett v Torfaen Borough Council* [1992] 3 All ER 27. There may also be liability for negligent design or planning of a building: *Rimmer v Liverpool City Council* [1985] QB 1 (fragile glass in council flat).[2]

[1] See too the Defective Premises Act 1972, especially s 3.
[2] Exceptionally a builder or local authority may be liable if the building is a potential source of injury to persons on neighbouring land, even though no one has yet been injured: see Lord Bridge in *Murphy v Brentwood* at 475.

7.30 Liability for defective premises can additionally arise under the Defective Premises Act 1972. It imposes duties on those who undertake work on dwelling houses, but not on industrial or commercial premises: see s 1. It is therefore of little relevance to this book. Of greater significance to injured workers are the duties placed upon occupiers. These duties can be owed just as much by an employer towards employees on its premises as by a third party in control of premises to visitors, including workers. In England and Wales the law is contained in the Occupiers' Liability Act 1957, which codifies common law principles in a revised form and is extended to trespassers by the

Occupiers' Liability Act 1984. There is a similar Act in Northern Ireland. The Scottish counterpart—the Occupiers' Liability (Scotland) Act 1960—is different in some respects.

The Occupiers' Liability Act 1957

7.31 The Occupiers' Liability Act 1957 applies to England and Wales, and there is a similar Act in Northern Ireland. The Act abolished the previous distinction between invitees and licensees, and defined the duty which the occupier owes to all visitors who are on the premises by his invitation or permission. Trespassers, who enter without any permission, express or implied, did not come within the Act, but are now protected by the Occupiers' Liability Act 1984. Both an occupier and an employer may be liable in respect of an injury. In *Andrews v Initial Cleaning Services Ltd* [2000] ICR 166, for example, the Court of Appeal apportioned blame for an injury to a cleaner 75% to the employer and 25% to the occupier.

7.32 The Act regulates 'the duty which an occupier of premises owes to his visitors in respect of dangers due to the state of the premises or to things done or omitted to be done on them' (s 1(1)). This means 'the duty imposed by law in consequence of a person's occupation or control of premises and of any invitation or permission he gives (or is to be treated as giving) to another to enter or use the premises' and it is owed to the persons who would, at common law, be invitees or licensees: they are now combined in a single class (s 1(2)). The Act is not limited to domestic premises.

7.33 It is important to note that the Occupiers' Liability Act 1957 only replaced the common law rules relating to the occupancy duties of an occupier and not those relating to the activity duties of an occupier (see *Fairchild v Glenhaven Funeral Services Ltd* [2002] 1 WLR 1052 and *Bottomley v Todmorden Cricket Club* [2003] EWCA Civ 1575; both confirming that *Honeywill & Stein Ltd v Larkin Brothers (London's Commercial Photographers) Ltd* [1934] 1 KB 191, which was concerned with an occupier's activity duty, remained binding).

7.34 An occupier is a person who in fact has control over premises. This is a question of fact, and does not depend on the possession of a legal interest: thus brewers were the occupiers of the private part of an inn occupied by their manager who sometimes took in lodgers, the manager also being occupier: *Wheat v E Lacon & Co Ltd* [1966] AC 552[1] (in such a case, the care to be expected from the two occupiers may cover different matters, eg structure for one, day-to-day matters such as lighting for the other); where a club included a restaurant run by a licensee, he and the club were both occupiers: *Fisher v CHT Ltd (No 2)* [1966] 2 QB 475. The main contractors of a London underground tunnel under construction, who retained general control although at the weekend sub-contractors came in to overhaul plant, were held to be the occupiers: *Bunker v Charles Brand & Son Ltd* [1969] 2 QB 480. But in some circumstances a sub-contractor may be the sole occupier, eg of a scaffolding: *Kearney v Eric Waller Ltd* [1967] 1 QB 29; more dubiously, a self-employed man alone on a building site was said to be the occupier of the relevant part (ladder propped against scaffold) under the Scottish Act: *Poliskie v Lane* 1981 SLT 282. A company may, of course, occupy premises through its employees or agents; but it will continue to owe a duty in its capacity as occupier, to those persons. The duty owed by an occupier varies in accordance with the extent of control.

1 Applied in *Rhind v Astbury Water Park Ltd* [2003] EWHC 1029 (QB).

7.35 By s 2, the occupier owes to all visitors a 'common duty of care'. The duty extends to visitors who enter in the exercise of a right conferred by law (s 2(6)), such as firefighters[1] or other emergency services, and the purpose for which the right is given is treated as a purpose for which permission is given. However, a person who uses a right of way to reach a place where he or she is a lawful visitor is *not* a visitor to the land which he crosses and is not protected by the 1957 Act: *Holden v White* [1982] QB 679 (although he or she may be protected under the 1984 Act). An occupier owes a duty to take reasonable care 'to see that the visitor will be reasonably safe in using the premises for the purposes for which he is invited or permitted by the occupier to be there'. This is not a statutory duty in the technical sense, but sets out a revised principle of the common law: *Roles v Nathan* [1963] 2 All ER 908 per Lord Denning MR.

1 See generally *Ogwo v Taylor* [1987] 3 WLR 1145 and the liability of a householder who negligently starts a fire to the rescue services who subsequently attend.

7.36 All the factual circumstances are relevant. The general duty is to protect the visitor from any danger which he may encounter within the scope of his invitation or permission, including dangers (eg to a visiting worker) from the work being carried on: *Savory v Holland Hannen and Cubitts (Southern) Ltd* [1964] 3 All ER 18.[1] But no precautions may be required where a careful visitor should run no risk: *Wheat v E Lacon & Co Ltd*, above (back stair where hand-rail stopped before foot; even when unlit, stair was safe if not used imprudently); *Staples v Dorset District Council* [1995] 18 LS Gaz R 36, CA (no need to warn of obvious danger). It was held in *Whyte v Redland Aggregates Ltd* [1998] CLY 3989, CA, that the owner of a disused gravel pit who had put up a sign stating 'Danger, keep out' was under no duty to put up a further notice stating 'no swimming'.

1 But query whether, as this case suggested, the duty extends to telling a visiting worker how to carry out his *own* work. But it has been held to require provision of boards to cover a staircase well for self-employed workers working above it: *Sole v WJ Hallt Ltd* [1973] QB 574.

7.37 The scope of the duty under the 1957 and 1984 Acts was recently considered by the House of Lords in *Tomlinson v Congleton Borough Council* [2003] UKHL 47, a case which reversed what many commentators saw as a recent and worrying extension of the scope and nature of the duty to those visiting premises whether by invitation or not. In *Tomlinson* it was held by the House of Lords that there was no liability under the Occupiers' Liability Act 1984, s 1(3) for the claimant's injuries from diving into a shallow lake, as the risk was obvious. It did not arise from the state of the premises or anything done or not done on them and accordingly, no duty of care was owed. The risk of the claimant striking his head on the lake bottom was one arising from a natural feature of the lake which were obvious to him and he did not need to be warned against the risk. Further, the risk of striking the lake bottom from diving, in what the claimant knew to be shallow water, was not one against which the defendant might reasonably have been expected to have offered him some protection. It would be unreasonable to impose on public authorities a duty to protect persons from self-inflicted harm sustained when taking voluntary risks in the face of obvious dangers. Even if swimming had not been prohibited and even if the defendant had owed a duty of care, ie had the case been brought under the 1957 Act, that duty would not have required the defendant to prevent the claimant from diving or warn him against dangers which were perfectly obvious.

7.38 This decision has created something of a sea change with courts adopting a more robust attitude to the acts of visitors and the duty under the 1957 Act than has often previously been the case. In *Lewis v Six Continents plc* [2005] EWCA Civ 1805, when a hotel guest fell out of a bedroom window, it was held by the Court of Appeal that the window did not present any obvious danger to an adult, no accident had ever previously occurred and it was not therefore reasonably foreseeable that an adult would lean out of the window in such a way as to say the occupier should have limited the way the window opened; *Clare v Perry* [2005] EWCA Civ 39: a visitor leaving a hotel jumped down off a six foot wall: no liability under the Act.

7.39 But by s 2(3), a person who is present in the exercise of his calling may be expected to 'appreciate and guard against any special risks ordinarily incident to it, so far as the occupier leaves him free to do so'. Thus under the Scottish Act the occupier was not liable when a bar on a window came out when grasped by the window-cleaner: the occupier had no duty to inspect: *Kilbride v Scottish and Newcastle Breweries Ltd* 1986 SLT 642. Lord Denning MR said in *Woolins v British Celanese Ltd* (1966) 1 KIR 438 that s 2(3) applies to:

> 'special risks incident to the work, such as live wires to an electrician ... [Not] an ordinary risk incident to the premises themselves'.

In that case the risk of putting a foot through a fragile roof was not a special risk of this kind to a Post Office engineer. Where demolition contractors were employed on the premises, and one of their men was injured because of an unsafe method of work, his employers alone were liable: the occupier had no responsibility for supervising the work: *Ferguson v Welsh* [1987] 1 WLR 1553. However, in *Eden v West & Co* [2002] EWCA Civ 991 the Court of Appeal, when considering this section, held that it could not be inferred that a competent joiner, who was injured when brickwork collapsed, should have been aware of the possibility of the absence of a lintel.

7.40 Under the Scottish Act, the House of Lords has held that there is no duty to foresee and provide against the risks to firemen in case of fire, eg as to dangers in gaining access: *Bermingham v Sher Bros* 1980 SLT 122 (it was alleged there should have been a fire screen protecting the stairway of a warehouse). But if the occupier is in breach of duty to other visitors, for example by negligently starting the fire, the occupier will also be liable to a fireman: *Salmon v Seafarer Restaurants Ltd* [1983] 1 WLR 1264 and *Ogwu v Taylor* [1987] 3 WLR 1145.

7.41 It is expressly declared (s 2(4)) that a warning or notice[1] does not, in itself, absolve the occupier from liability, unless in all the circumstances it was sufficient to enable the visitor to be reasonably safe: this overrules *London Graving Dock Co Ltd v Horton* [1951] AC 737. In *Roles v Nathan*, above, the occupier was exonerated by a warning given by his expert to chimney-sweeps on the danger from fumes. But in *Bunker v Charles Brand & Son Ltd* [1969] 2 QB 480, knowledge or warning that the means of access to a machine was over precarious rollers did not exonerate the occupiers as there was no other way and something safer could have been provided. Failure to warn may be negligent although no other action is called for, *eg McDowell v FMC (Meat) Ltd* (1967) 3 KIR 595 (high voltage line crossing showground). These provisions, however, deal with the question whether a warning is sufficient performance of the duty, assuming it to exist. In some cases, a prominent notice or other warning may exclude the duty. Section 2(5) preserves the defence of volenti non fit injuria (voluntary acceptance of risk) if it would have been available at common law. For this purpose it has to be shown that the visitor knew of the risk, and consented to it in circumstances where he was free to decide. Agreement to, or awareness of, a warning does not of itself amount to acceptance of the risk: see the Unfair Contract Terms Act 1977, s 2(3). It does not apply to a worker who, being required to enter a place in the course of work, is not free to refuse: *Burnett v British Waterways Board* [1973] 2 All ER 631 (worker on barge entering dock injured by breaking rope: notice excluding dock's liability ineffective). In other cases a warning notice, if read, may be enough to establish voluntary acceptance of risk (eg 'cliff paths subject to landslips—visitors use at own risk').

[1] With regard to the adequacy and required effect of notices see *Tomlinson v Congelton Borough Council* [2003] UKHL 47; *Brioland Ltd v Searson* [2005] EWCA Civ 55.

7.42 Apart from this, s 2(1) says that the occupier owes the duty 'except in so far as he is free to and does extend, restrict, modify or exclude his duty ... by contract or otherwise'. At common law, an occupier could exclude or restrict liability by a contractual term: see *White v Blackmore* [1972] 2 QB 651. But under the Unfair Contract Terms Act 1977, s 2, exclusion of liability for death or injury due to negligence is not permissible by either a contract or a notice—and 'negligence' is defined by s 1(1)(c) to include liability under the Occupiers' Liability Act. By s 1(3), this restriction applies only to a 'business' liability— something which arises from the course of business. This is defined in s 14 so as to include professions, government departments and local authorities. Hence it would apply to any attempt by an employer or other undertaking to restrict the duties otherwise owed to workers.[1]

[1] Under an amendment in the Occupiers' Liability Act 1984, s 2, this restriction does not include liability to a person obtaining access 'for recreational or educational purposes' by reason of the 'dangerous state of the premises' unless access is given as part of a business.

So a person making a charge to see a waterfall or enjoy a woodland walk cannot restrict liability—unless it is proved that the charge is not intended to make a profit and so does not amount to carrying on a business.

7.43   Section 2(4)(b) of the 1957 Act sets up an involved and uncertain rule where a danger was due to faulty work by an independent contractor: the occupier is not vicariously liable for the faulty work if it acted reasonably in entrusting the work to an independent contractor and took such steps (if any) as were reasonable to satisfy itself that the contractor was competent (in appropriate circumstances insured[1]) and the work was properly done. An occupier may, however, be liable on other grounds, for example, if it became aware of the danger after the contractor had finished, and failed to have it put right. The occupier may owe a duty to check that the work has been properly done: *Woodward v Mayor of Hastings* [1945] KB 174 (school liable for failing to check independent contractor had cleared away snow). The duty may extend to employing a competent person to supervise the work: *AMF International Ltd v Magnet Bowling Ltd* [1968] 1 WLR 1028. Where the occupier breaches these duties, it may be liable to an employee of the independent contractor who is injured as a result of the danger: *Ferguson v Welsh* [1987] 1 WLR 1553.[2] In *Bottomley v Todmorden Cricket Club* [2003] EWCA Civ 1575 it was held that the defendant club which engaged an independent contractor and allowed a dangerous pyrotechnic display to take place on its land owed a duty of care to the claimant who was lawfully on the land assisting the contractors conducting the display, and was liable to the claimant along with the contractors when he was injured in an explosion because they and the club had failed to take ordinary precautions. It was reiterated that the Occupiers' Liability Act 1957 only replaced the common law rules relating to the occupancy duties of an occupier and not those relating to the activity duties of an occupier.

---

[1]   See *Gwilliam v West Hertfordshire Hospitals NHS Trust* [2002] EWCA Civ 1041; *Naylor v Payling* [2004] EWCA Civ 560.

[2]   The independent contractor might also be jointly liable as the employer.

7.44   The common duty of care is also owed to persons who enter the premises under the terms of a contract, unless the contract contains express terms on the subject (s 5). But where persons enter premises under the terms of a contract made by another person—eg when workers enter premises under a contract made by the occupier with their employer—the occupier's duty cannot be restricted or excluded by a term in that contract: s 3(1). (Nor can the occupier exclude liability by a notice to the workers: see above.) But if the occupier has undertaken additional obligations, for instance to make scaffolds safe, the duty of care is enlarged to incorporate those obligations (s 3(1)). This innovation may enable a worker to claim, in substance, upon the terms of a contract made with his or her employer (but in such a case the occupier's vicarious liability for independent contractors cannot be enlarged except by express words (s 3(2)).[1]

---

[1]   Subject to any lawful limitation of duty under the contract, a person entering premises under a contract who sustains injury does not need to sue for breach of contract: he or she can sue in tort under s 2, so that contributory negligence will reduce the damages instead of being a complete defence: *Sole v WJ Hallt Ltd* [1973] QB 574.

7.45 Under s 4 of the Defective Premises Act 1972 (which replaced in wider terms s 4 of the 1957 Act) a landlord who is responsible for repairs under the tenancy may be liable to a visitor endangered by defects for which the landlord is responsible, provided that the landlord knows or ought to know of the defect (see eg *Davies v Oxley Plumbers Merchants (SBG Felt Roofing, Pt 20 defendant)* [2002] EWCA Civ 540). There need not be a tenancy in the strict sense: occupation under a contract or a statutory right is sufficient. By s 4(4), a landlord who is entitled to enter the premises to do maintenance or repair is treated for the purpose of the section as if he were responsible for repairs within the scope of his right of entry. A landlord who retained possession of common parts was liable for an accident to a meter inspector, though (following disconnection of the electricity) the local authority had taken over payment for electricity and was collecting rents to reimburse itself: *Jordan v Achara* (1988) 20 HLR 607, CA. Under this section, a worker may sometimes be able to claim against the landlord of his own employer.

7.46 Formerly a trespasser could not establish liability against an occupier unless it could be shown that injury was caused wilfully or recklessly. Subsequently, in *British Railways Board v Herrington* [1972] AC 877 the House of Lords decided that while in general an intruder on another person's land is there at his or her own risk, an occupier must act according to standards of 'common humanity'. The duty is more likely to apply to young children than to adults: in *Herrington's* case the railway was held liable for failing to repair a gap in a fence near an electrified line. In *Southern Portland Cement Ltd v Cooper* [1974] AC 623 liability was established—again to a child—because a mound of rubble had piled up so as to bring within reach an overhead electric cable. This created a danger which could have been avoided without expense or trouble. Similarly, in *Pannett v P McGuinness & Co Ltd* [1972] 2 QB 599 demolition contractors were negligent for failing to keep children away from bonfires of debris.

7.47 These decisions have largely been superseded by the Occupiers' Liability Act 1984. By s 1, the duty of an occupier to a person other than 'his visitors', includes not only trespassers but also borderline cases such as persons using a right of way (who were held to be outside the 1957 Act). For the duty to arise the occupier must know of the risk, or have reasonable grounds to believe that it exists and that the person concerned is already in, or may come within, the vicinity of the danger. The occupier will be liable if 'the risk is one against which … he may reasonably be expected to offer the other some protection'. In *Higgs v Foster (t'a Avalon Coaches)* [2004] EWCA Civ 843 a policeman who was held to be a tresspasser fell into an uncovered pit; held occupier had no reason to believe that anyone would come into the vicinity of the pit. 'Reasonable grounds to believe' does not include constructive knowledge: *Swain v Natui Ram Puri* [1996] PIQR P 442, CA. In *Young v Kent County Council* [2005] EWHC 1342 (QB), [2005] All ER (D) 217 (Mar) it was held that a council had a duty of care under the 1984 Act to protect children from the known risk of them climbing onto the roof of a school building. There had been a breach of that duty where a council had failed to protect against that risk despite the existence of a low cost solution. However this duty was to children only and, in view of the decision in *Tomlinson v Congleton Borough Council* [2003] UKHL 47, [2004] 1 AC 46, if the claimant had not been a child he would have recovered nothing.

7.48 When the duty exists, it is to protect the person concerned against injury from the perceived danger (s 1 (4)); and in appropriate cases it may be discharged by giving a warning or deterring entry (s 1(5)).

The Occupiers' Liability (Scotland) Act 1960

7.49 This Act regulates the duty of the person 'occupying or having control of land or other premises' (the 'occupier') 'towards persons entering on the premises in respect of dangers due to the state of the premises[1] or to anything done or omitted to be done on them and for which he is in law responsible' (s 1(1)). The common law rules still decide who is 'the occupier' (s 1(2)). To remove previous doubts in Scottish law, premises include both fixed and movable structures, in particular 'any vessel, vehicle or aircraft' (s 1(3)(a)).

[1] Eg in *Nimmo v East Ayrshire Council* (1 April 2005, unreported), Sh Ct (Sheriff McKay) it was held that the use of a single pane of plate glass in a part of the front door of a house, that was liable to come into contact with a person's hand when opening or shutting the door, was a clear hazard and it was reasonably foreseeable that the glass might break on contact and cause injury. In failing to replace that glass, a local authority was in breach of its duty under 1960 Act to take reasonable care to guard against that hazard

7.50 As regards the conduct of third parties on the premises, the duty is restricted to things 'for which he is in law *responsible*'. This cannot be a reference to vicarious liability for agents and servants: it must mean that liability depends on the degree of *control*. The duty is (s 2(1)) to take reasonable care 'to see that person' (ie any person 'entering on the premises': s 1(1)) 'will not suffer injury or damage by reason of any such danger'. The occupier is not required to foresee and take measures against risks to a fireman in the event of a fire: *Bermingham v Sher Bros* 1980 SLT 122.

7.51 But this duty is without prejudice to, among others, cases where the occupier 'is *entitled* to and *does* extend, restrict, modify or exclude by *agreement* his obligations' (s 2(1)). The Unfair Contract Terms Act 1977, s 16 and s 15(2)(d), prohibits the exclusion of liability for 'breach of duty' causing injury or death; and the courts will critically examine a clause which seeks to restrict liability by the definitional trick of narrowly defining a duty.

7.52 By s 3 of the Act of 1960, a landlord (including the landlord of a subtenancy) who is responsible (either by agreement or by a statute such as the Housing Acts) for 'maintenance or repair' has the same liabilities as the occupier for dangers arising from his default.

7.53 Unlike the English Act, the Scottish Act contains no special provision relieving the occupier of his vicarious liability for independent contractors, under such authorities as *Thomson v Cremin* [1953] 2 All ER 1185. Again unlike the English Act, the duty is not confined to persons entering 'by invitation or permission', so trespassers are not as a matter of law excluded. But the fact that the visitor is a trespasser is one of the circumstances determining the degree of care: *McGlone v British Railways Board* 1966 SLT (Notes) 72; *Titchener v British Railways Board* [1983] 1 WLR 1427.

Duties of contractors and other persons using premises

7.54 Persons using the same premises—principal contractors, sub-contractors and the like—are naturally responsible to one another for damage caused by the negligent conduct of their activities: but they may in addition be responsible for dangers arising from the static condition of the premises, if due to their acts or omissions.[1] Again when considering potential liability in such circumstances first recourse will be to the duties imposed under the Workplace Regulations (see generally chapter 18 below). In *Grant v Sun Shipping Co Ltd* [1948] AC 549, ship-repairers' employees went away leaving a hatch uncovered and in darkness, and a stevedore, without any negligence on his part, fell into the hatch. The House of Lords held that the ship-repairers, having worked at the hatch and left it in an unsafe condition, were liable for the accident at common law quite apart from their duties under the Docks Regulations.[2]

[1] Note that contractors with a sufficient degree of control over premises may be occupiers for the purposes of the Occupiers' Liability Act 1957: see *Bunker v Charles Brand & Son Ltd* [1969] 2 QB 480, and *Kearney v Eric Waller Ltd* [1967] 1 QB 29.
[2] Cf *Baron v B French Ltd* [1971] 3 All ER 1111 (electrician sub-contractor's employee tripped over rubble heap left by head contractors in badly-lit corridor).

7.55 In the same way contractors working on premises may be liable to casual visitors. In *Kimber v Gas Light and Coke Co* [1918] 1 KB 439, the gas company's workmen had removed floorboards to alter the gas fittings in an unoccupied house: the claimant was admitted by the workmen, who saw her go upstairs where the boards had been removed, but gave no warning. The court held the company liable.

7.56 The House of Lords has held, in general terms:

'that a person executing works on premises ... is under a general duty to use reasonable care for the safety of those whom he knows or ought reasonably to know may be affected by or lawfully in the vicinity of his work': *AC Billings & Sons v Riden* [1958] AC 240 (per Lord Somervell).[1]

[1] Overruling *Malone v Laskey* [1907] 2 KB 141 and *Ball v LCC* [1949] 1 All ER 1056. See also *Christie v James Scott & Co Ltd* 1961 SLT (Notes) 5; *Johnson v Rea Ltd* [1962] 1 QB 373.

7.57 Anyone who starts a fire negligently on any premises is liable to those who are endangered, and this includes professional firemen who are at risk in spite of their skill: *Ogwo v Taylor* [1988] AC 431; see also *Langley v Dray and MT Motor Policies at Lloyd's* [1998] PIQR P 314, CA (criminal liable for injury to policeman in pursuit); *Johnson v BJW Property* [2002] EWHC 1131: an occupier may be vicariously liable for the acts of an independent contractor which lead to the spread of a fire.

7.58 However, in Scotland it has been held that where a building worker entered premises to investigate after a fire had been started by a sub-contractor, a fall into an unguarded drop was not within the scope of the fire risk: *Reid v Sir Robert McAlpine & Son Ltd* 1986 SLT 108.

Dangerous activities

7.59 At common law, persons who carry on activities which are likely to endanger other persons, owe a duty to those other persons to exercise reasonable care. This proposition is founded directly on the general principles of negligence. Of course there may be no duty when the defendants have no reason to expect that anyone is in the vicinity: *Batchelor v Fortescue* (1883) 11 QBD 474. Three obvious examples of such activities are as follows.

Handling objects liable to fall from a height

7.60 Illustrations are:

— barrels rolled along the upper floor of a warehouse: *Byrne v Boadle* (1863) 2 H & C 722;
— loads swung overhead on cranes: *Scott v London and St Katherine Docks Co* (1865) 3 H & C 596;
— the felling of trees: *Mourton v Poulter* [1930] 2 KB 183.

These cases have previously been described and relied upon as good examples of the maxim res ipsa loquitur (the thing speaks for itself) and, assuming that the operation was under the sole management of the defendant, there has traditionally been a presumption of negligence. However, in *Carroll v Fearon* [1999] PIQR P 416, CA, where it was held that res ipsa loquitur was of no relevant application, Judge LJ doubted (at P 421) whether the maxim was 'ever susceptible to refined argument and detailed analysis of authority.' Furthermore, the maxim was judicially disapproved in *Fryer v Pearson* (2000) Times, 4 April, CA, where May LJ opined that such Latin expressions are not readily comprehensible to those for whose benefit they are supposed to exist.

Control or operation of dangerous machinery

7.61 See *Excelsior Wire Rope Co Ltd v Callan* [1930] AC 404 (haulage machine started with children in the vicinity). In *Field v E E Jeavons & Co Ltd* [1965] 2 All ER 162 occupiers of a factory who left a circular saw in a position where it would move forward if switched on were held liable to an electrician who wired it and switched it on for testing, although he should first have asked the foreman's permission.

Manoeuvring or driving railway engines, trucks, cranes and other vehicles

7.62 On or near a highway, an injured worker has the same rights as any other member of the public. On private property a driver must exercise the same reasonable care as on the public highway: *Bowre v Shenkin* 1934 SC 459; but this is subject to the proviso that the driver must know, or have reason to suppose, that other persons may be in the vicinity: *Johnson v Elder Dempster Lines Ltd* (1948) 81 Ll L Rep 335 (a case of a crane on a dockside). A crane-driver may be held negligent for lifting the load without a preliminary test lift to check that it is correctly centred: *Staveley Iron and Chemical Co Ltd v Jones* [1956] AC 627. Whether such a check is necessary must depend, of course, on the nature of the load. In general, a crane-driver is in much the same position as a motor-driver, and cannot be held negligent if, while keeping a good look-out and with the crane well under control, someone moves without warning into the track of the load: *Smith v Port Line Ltd* [1955] 2 All ER 297.

Negligent instructions

7.63 Such a person as an architect may be liable if he or she intervenes personally in an operation and gives instruction for work to be done in an unsafe way. A firm selling a machine owed a duty, in demonstrating it, to give clear instructions to the customer's workmen as to safe operation: *William v Trim Rock Quarries Ltd* (1965) 109 Sol Jo 454, CA (machine toppling during demonstration in quarry).

Chapter 8

THE HEALTH AND SAFETY AT WORK ACT 1974

Barry Cotter

GENERAL

8.01 The HSWA 1974[1] was meant to be, and remains, an over-arching Act setting out general duties and provisions in relation to health and safety in employment. It brought together a disparate group of inspectorates under a single safety Commission (the HSC) which must do such things and make such arrangements as it thinks appropriate for the general purposes of Part 1 of the Act[2] (s 11) together with an Executive (the HSE) which, acting under the control of the Commission is the body responsible for enforcing the Act (s 18). Under the Act, there is a power to delegate enforcement to local authorities in specified matters. Such delegation of enforcement powers has taken place for most offices, shops and warehouses: Health and Safety (Enforcing Authority) Regulations 1998, SI 1998/494.

[1] Largely based upon the Report of the Robens Committee on Health and Safety at Work (1972, Cmnd 5034).
[2] In 2004 the Commission published 'A strategy for Workplace Health and Safety in Great Britain to 2010 and beyond'. This developed upon an earlier strategy statement in 2000 which had resulted in focus upon eight key activity areas: falls from height, workplace transport, musculoskeletal disorders, work-related stress, construction, agriculture, health services and slips and trips.

8.02 The Act sets out the objectives (at s 1) of securing the health and safety of persons at work; protecting persons other than persons at work against risks to health or safety arising out of or in connection with the activities of persons at work, and controlling the keeping and use of explosive or highly flammable or otherwise dangerous substances and generally preventing the unlawful acquisition, possession and use of such substances. This was to be achieved by replacing the then existing wide range of statutory provision by a streamlined system of the general duties under Part 1 (ss 1–54), linking in with regulations made under the powers contained in the Act and approved codes of practice. Although it was the original intention that the Act would steadily supersede all existing safely legislation and replace it by degrees with regulations and codes of practice, in fact this was slow in occurring and many of the principal Acts (Factories, Mines and Quarries, Offices, Shops and Railway Premises, Agriculture) still remained in force as the Act approached its twentieth anniversary and it took the European Directives of the 1990s and associated regulations to replace the old legislation.

8.03 At the core of the general duties under the Act are those in relation to the duty of an employer towards its employees (s 2) with regard to the duty in respect of the safety of persons other than employees (s 3), the duty upon

232

persons having control of non-domestic premises (s 4) and the duty upon those concerned with the production and supply of articles for use at work (s 6). Employees are also required to take reasonable care for their own health and safety, and that of others (s 7).

8.04 As for specific duties, regulations made under the HSWA 1974 have been passed to revise parts of the older statutes and regulations, and, most significantly, to deal with certain hazards across all (or nearly all) industries, occupations and processes (it has been widely acknowledged that the most change brought about by the Act was through the secondary legislation introduced under it).

8.05 Apart from the regulations made under it and the impact of the unified administration with its new and unified powers, the HSWA 1974 initially had little impact on civil liability, since the primary obligations in ss 2–8 are unenforceable in civil law (s 47(1)). Those primary obligations were, and remain, invaluable as providing the central pillars of the criminal liability. However, more recently health and safety law has been increasingly dominated by duties specifically enshrined in regulations made under the HSWA 1974, s 15, a breach of which does give rise to civil liability unless the regulations expressly state to the contrary (see s 47(2)). The relationship between criminal offences created by the general duties and those co-existing by virtue of duties under specific regulations was considered by the House of Lords in *Junttan Oy v Bristol Magistrates' Court* [2003] UKHL 55 (the majority holding that nothing in the Supply of Machinery (Safety) Regulations 1992, SI 1992/3073 prevented a prosecution in relation to the supply of machinery and therefore prima facie covered by those regulations being brought under s 6 which carried a greater maximum penalty). In practice the prosecution of health and safety matters usually reflects the view that the HSWA 1974 and regulations function in parallel at different levels of seriousness, with more serious breaches being reflected with charges relating to the general duties.

8.06 The Act applies to employment generally and not to specific categories of employee. An 'employee' is defined at s 53 as meaning an individual who works under a contract of employment. 'Work' has an extended definition set out at s 52 which applies, like other definitions in the Act, to regulations made under the Act (unless otherwise stated). It means work as an employee or a self-employed person and includes persons engaged on certain training schemes: Health and Safety (Training for Employment) Regulations 1990, SI 1990/1380, as well as persons in the public service of the Crown (s 48) and certain other categories. The protection of the Act was extended to the police (s 51A, added by the Police (Health and Safety) Act 1997). Under s 52(1)(b) an employee is at work throughout the time when he is in the course of his employment, but not otherwise.[1]

[1] In relation to the continuation of duties (in relation to plant) to employees outside those hours, see *Bolton Metropolitan Borough Council v Malrod Insulation Ltd* [1993] ICR 358.

ENFORCEMENT AND PROSECUTION

8.07 The Act also sets out powers and procedures in relation to enforcement (ss 18–26), including through the use of improvement and prohibition notices and also the bringing of prosecutions (ss 33–42). Importantly, there is a reverse burden of proof in any prosecution in that the onus of proving that something was not reasonably practicable is placed on the defendant (s 40).[1]

[1] The compatibility of this burden with art 6(2) of the European Convention on Human Rights was considered by the Court of Appeal in *Davies v Health and Safety Executive* [2002] EWCA Crim 2949. The court held that the imposition of the burden of proof on the defendant was justified, necessary and proportionate.

THE GENERAL SAFETY DUTIES

8.08 The general safety duties in the Act (ss 2–7) do not give rise to civil liability (s 47(1)(a)), but only to potential criminal prosecution and liability (s 33). As the functions of the civil law and the criminal law are different, with that of the criminal code being normative, to provide rules to be observed the infringement of which leads to sanction, there is no simple relationship between these duties and the overlapping common law duty of care.[1] Indeed it is clear that they require a different standard, for at least three reasons:

(1)   the statutory duties are there to prevent the risk of harm and so are not dependent on proof of damage *(R v Board of Trustees of the Science Museum* [1993] IRLR 853, CA), and are no longer to be viewed as merely criminalising existing common law duties;

(2)   the protective intent of the Act is paramount and is not to be necessarily defeated by arguments that liability would not have arisen in a civil action, so that for example a head employer may be liable under the Act for injuries to self-employed contractors and their employees: *R v Associated Octel Co Ltd* [1997] IRLR 123, HL;[2]

(3)   the tendency is to view the statutory duties (especially in ss 2 and 3) as imposing strict liability, 'subject only to the defence of' reasonable practicability: *R v British Steel plc* [1995] IRLR 310, CA.[3]

[1] See generally *Hampstead Heath Swimming Club v Corporation of London* [2005] EWHC 713 (Admin) (Stanley Burnton J).
[2] Cf *Hampstead Heath Winter Swimming Club v Corporation of London* (above) in which the court held that it would be anomalous if certain actions, liability for which in tort had been removed by the House of Lords when considering the Occupier Liability Acts, should infringe the HSWA 1974, s 3.
[3] See also *R v Gateway Foodmarkets Ltd* [1997] ICR 382.

SAFETY POLICIES, SAFETY REPRESENTATIVES AND CONSULTATION

8.09 An employer must (s 2(3)) put on record a statement of its general policy and organisation for safety and welfare, and publicise it to employees.[1] Guidance on the content of these policies has been given by the HSE,[2] and not surprisingly this stresses the importance of risk assessments. Although some have questioned the importance of these documents in light of the more detailed requirements under the Management of Health and Safety at Work Regulations, SI 1999/3242, they remain a useful starting point for analysis of an undertaking's approach to health and safety (and are viewed as such by the HSE's Inspectors).

1   A written statement is not required if there are no more than five employees; Employers' Health and Safety Policy Statement (Exception) Regulations 1975, SI 1975/1584. To determine whether an employer is within this exception, regard may only be had to employees present on the site at the same time: *Osborne v Bill Taylor* [1982] ICR 168.
2   See generally *An Introduction to Health and Safety; Health and Safety in Small Businesses* (2004).

8.10 The Act also introduced consultation with the workforce as a central support within the structure of the domestic health and safety law. Section 2(6) introduced the duty to consult with workers' representatives. The power to appoint representatives for the purposes of this section is now no longer restricted to trade unions which an employer has chosen to recognise (s 2(4)).[1] Section 2(7) makes provision in relation to safety committees.[2]

1   See the Safety Representatives and Safety Committees Regulations 1977, SI 1977/500 and, following as a result of the decision in *EC Commission v United Kingdom* [1994] ICR 664, ECJ, the Health and Safety (Consultation with Employees) Regulations 1996, SI 1996/1513.
2   See the Safety Representatives and Safety Committees Regulations 1977.

HEALTH AND SAFETY REGULATIONS

8.11 All health and safety at work regulations since 1974 have been made under the HSWA 1974 (ss 15,[1] 50, 80 and Sch 3). They are made by the Secretary of State, either on the proposal of the Commission, or on his or her own initiative (after consulting the Commission); in either case various government departments and other interested bodies must be consulted (s 50). Under amendments made by the Employment Protection Act 1975 (Sch 15, paras 6, 16) ss 15 and 50 also give a concurrent power to make regulations to the Minister responsible for agricultural matters. The Secretary of State also has power to repeal regulations and statutes on the grounds that they are a burden on business: Deregulation and Contracting Out Act 1994, s 37. (This power goes well beyond the existing powers of repeal under the HSWA 1974, s 80.)

1   The Regulations implementing the European Directives which came into force on 1 January 1993 were made under this section.

8.12 By s 1(2), the power to make regulations is to be exercised to replace, by degrees, existing safety and health legislation (listed in Sch 1 to the Act). This existing legislation is, together with the HSWA 1974 and its regulations, referred to in the Act as 'the relevant statutory provisions'.[1]

1   See s 53.

8.13 Section 1(2) requires that new regulations are 'designed to maintain or improve the standards of health, safety and welfare established by or under those enactments'. In *R v Secretary of State for Employment, ex p NACODS* (16 December 1993, unreported) the Divisional Court held that the question whether regulations were so designed or not was not one the courts were to decide; it was a matter for Parliament. The Secretary of State thus has, in addition to almost unfettered power to repeal under the Deregulation etc Act 1994 (since a health or safety regulation must be, almost by definition, a burden on some businesses), an unreviewable power to introduce new regulations altering pre-existing standards so long as he or she asserts that the former are designed to maintain or improve standards. However the courts (UK or ECJ) might be obliged to intervene to restrain ministerial dilution of legislation dealing with matters covered by the Framework Directive and its 'daughter' Directives, as the preamble to the Framework Directive states that 'this Directive does not justify any reduction in levels of protection already achieved in Member States'. Under the guise of purporting to comply with a Directive, the government should not be permitted to relax pre-existing legislative standards.

8.14 Regulations may be general, or apply to particular circumstances or even a particular case. They may specify the persons who have to comply with requirements, the persons liable to prosecution for contravention and (to some extent) the limits of a prosecution (eg whether summary only, restriction on penalties, special defences). They may also grant exemptions, exclude general duties, and (of course) repeal the existing legislation in Sch 1.

8.15 The subject matter for which regulations may be made—broadly covering every type of premises, plant, material, process and operation, also administrative matters such as registration, records, powers of search—is set out at length in Sch 3.

8.16 An action for damages will lie for breach of health and safety regulations made under s 15 unless the regulations themselves exclude such liability. 'Damage' in this context includes impairment of a person's mental or physical condition: s 47(6).

8.17 By s 47(1)(b), civil liability for breach of the pre-existing safety regulations or statutes is not affected in any way: nor is liability independently of the Act—ie common law liability for negligence is untouched: s 47(4). Any agreement excluding or limiting civil liability for contravention of health and safety regulations is void, unless allowed by the regulations: s 47(5). Where under the terms of any regulations a defence such as due diligence is available in a criminal prosecution for breach of regulations, it does not afford a defence in civil proceedings unless this is expressly provided by the regulations: s 47(3).

CODES OF PRACTICE

8.18 Section 16 enables the Commission (by virtue of s 12) to approve and issue codes of practice (now commonly referred to as 'Approved Codes of

Practice' or 'ACOPs') for giving practical guidance on health and safety duties (see s 53 for the definition of a code of practice). They have the advantage of giving simple explanations (without the necessity for legal precision) of established safety methods, often with illustrations. There has been a long running debate as to the extent to which such codes of practice trespass on what should properly be the remit of regulations. Further, there has recently been increased reference in the courts to HSE guidance notes on certain areas of health and safety, however these do not have an equivalent status to a code of practice.

8.19 By s 17, failure to comply with an ACOP raises a *presumption* in criminal proceedings that the related safety requirement has been contravened: this may be displaced only by proof that the duty was carried out in some other way.[1] Although the Act does not say so, ACOPs (and guidance notes) will clearly be admissible in civil actions as evidence of good practice and of what is 'reasonably practicable'. Indeed the comparison has been made between the special status given to codes of practice under the Act and that given to the Highway Code.

1   See generally *West Cumberland By-products v DPP* [1988] RTR 391.

Chapter 9

EUROPEAN LAW

Philip Mead

GENERAL

9.01 The traditional approach to the regulation of health and safety in the workplace, prior to 1974, was by a mixture of incremental development of the common law, and statutory regulation of particular types of industry. Thus factories were regulated under different statutory provisions from those relating to offices, shops and railway premises or to mines and quarries; and amongst factories, iron foundries were regulated comprehensively under regulations dedicated to them, as were non-ferrous metal foundries, lead works and so on. The Robens report, which was reflected in the HSWA 1974, anticipated a comprehensive scheme of legislation for health and safety affecting all work, with regulations relating to particular risks rather than particular products. In this respect, its intent echoed developments on the mainland of Europe.

9.02 Since 1974, homegrown legislation did not fulfil the Robens' anticipation of comprehensive legislation; it took the impact of EU legislation to achieve this objective. The trend since has been an increasing emphasis on the regulation of risks general to all industries rather than that of processes particular to a few only.

9.03 Both the common law and, especially, the statutory regulatory framework, have become influenced to an increasing degree by the developing law of the European Union. This law is based on underlying principles and concepts which are largely European. The European practice is to adopt a prescriptive rather than a flexible approach to regulation.[1]

[1] A number of European Directives appear to contemplate that the absolute duty may not be performed by the person on whom it is imposed, and provide for subsidiary duties/alternative modes of satisfying an employer's duty in such a case. It remains arguable that the UK legislation in this respect affords lesser rights to the worker than the parent Directive.

9.04 European law ('Community law' or 'EC law' is usually referred to in this book as 'European law') has effect in one of three ways in relation to health and safety: first, in interpreting the meaning to be given to domestic legislation in the same area as that covered by European law; second, in the case of Directives by direct effect (as against public authorities or 'emanations of the State'), and third by providing a right of action against the government, or possibly any public authority, for damages where there has been a failure properly to implement the requirements of European law. In what follows, these principles are explained, following a brief description of the structure of European law.

238

Background

9.05 European law arises from the various treaties which established the European Union, and in particular the Treaty of Rome, now formally called in its currently amended form, the 'Treaty Establishing the European Community' (the EC Treaty). These treaties gave birth to the institutions of the EU and, notably: the European Parliament; the Council of Ministers, the primary decision-making body and the source of most power; the European Commission, which is something akin to a civil service with some executive powers; and the European Court of Justice (the 'ECJ'), which is given the power to rule on the meaning of the various provisions of European law, including Directives. These institutions, Member States and individual nationals of those States are governed by European law.[1]

1   For European legislation and case law, see the EUR-Lex website (http://europa.eu.int/eur-lex/lex/en/index.htm), also see the ECJ website (http://www.curia.eu.int/). Both websites provide indices and digests covering general principles of European law.

9.06 The Council of Ministers, which consists of representatives of governments of the Member States, is the principal body with legislative power. To decide some matters it requires unanimity; but Directives relating to health and safety, passed under art 137 (ex art 118A) EC, can be adopted under a process which is known as co-decision under art 251 (ex art 189B) EC which does not require unanimity. This procedure involves significant consultation with and involvement of the European Parliament. The result has been a decreased capability on the part of any Member State (and in particular, the United Kingdom) to resist health and safety Directives.[1]

1   Thus, for example, the UK unsuccessfully sought to argue that the Working Time Directive (93/104/EC) should be annulled because its subject matter related to employment (where unanimity was necessary) and had not been validly adopted under what was then art 118A (which related to health and safety issues, and prescribed adoption by qualified majority vote). The Directive was then implemented by the Working Time Regulations 1988, SI 1998/1833: see *United Kingdom of Great Britain and Northern Ireland v Council of the European Union* [1997] ICR 443, ECJ. The UK's implementation was later found to be defective: *R (on the application of BECTU) v Secretary of State for Trade and Industry* [2001] IRLR 559, ECJ.

9.07 European law is 'a new order of international law for the benefit of which the States have limited their sovereign rights, albeit within limited fields': *NV Algemene Transport-en Expeditie Onderneming Van Gend en Loos and Nederlandse v Nederlandse Belastingadministratie* [1963] ECR 1 at 12). European law is binding on Member States by virtue of art 10 (ex art 5) EC, which states:

'Member States shall take all appropriate measures, whether general or particular, to ensure fulfilment of the obligations arising out of this Treaty or resulting from action taken by the institutions of the Community. They shall facilitate the achievement of the Community's task.'

9.08 The articles of the relevant Treaties are thus to be law in the Member States without any further domestic enactment. In the United Kingdom, this has largely been achieved by the European Communities Act 1972. This provides, by s 2, that:

'(1) All such rights, powers, liabilities, obligations and restrictions from time to time created or arising by or under the Treaties, and all such remedies and procedures from time to time provided for by or under the Treaties, as in accordance with the Treaties are without further enactment to be given legal effect or used in the United Kingdom shall be recognised and available in law, and be enforced, allowed and followed accordingly; and the expression "enforceable Community right" and similar expressions shall be read as referring to one to which this subsection applies.'

9.09 The reference in s 2 to 'obligations (which) ... are without further enactment to be given legal effect ...' is not only to articles of the Treaty itself, but also to EU *Regulations* (not to be confused with national regulations passed in order to implement a Directive: in this book, regulations emanating from Europe are termed 'EU Regulations'), and to *decisions* issued by the Council or Commission. These are made under art 249 (ex art 189) EC, which states that an EU Regulation 'shall be binding in its entirety and directly applicable in all Member States', and that a decision 'shall be binding in its entirety upon those to whom it is addressed'. As a matter of European law, EU Regulations 'render automatically inapplicable any conflicting provision of current national law': *Amministrazione delle Finanze dello Stato v Simmenthal SpA* [1978] ECR 629, ECJ at 643.

9.10 Apart from Treaty articles, Regulations and decisions there is one further primary source of European law, namely *Directives*. Much of the law relating to the implementation and enforceability of Directives can be understood by having regard to the wording of art 249(3) (ex art 189) EC, which states:

'A Directive shall be binding, as to the result to be achieved, upon each Member State to which it is directed but shall leave to the national authorities the choice of form and methods.'

9.11 It is thus addressed to the Member State itself, not directly to the citizens of that State. What has to be achieved by the Member State is the result intended by the Directive, but it is up to the Member State itself how precisely it should achieve that result. In general, therefore, it is envisaged that domestic legislation will be necessary in Member States if they do not already have provisions in force which achieve the result demanded by the Directive.[1]

---

[1] It may be noted that art 137(3) EC expressly permits Member States to entrust management and labour with implementation of Directives in the field of health and safety, provided that the Member State is in a position to guarantee the results required by the Directive.

9.12 Each Directive has a time limit within which it must be implemented. The implementing laws need not use the same terminology, but they must give full effect to the Directive in a clear and precise manner.[1] Although Directives relating to health and safety have been introduced under art 95 (ex art 100A) EC Treaty, it is the legal basis of art 137 (ex art 118A) EC upon which the Commission has relied when introducing the most recent legislative proposals.

¹ *EC Commission v Denmark* [1985] ECR 427, ECJ; see also Case C-217/97 *EC Commission v Germany* [1999] ECR I-5087, ECJ, para 31; and Case C-214/98 *EC Commission v Greece* [2000] ECR I-9601, ECJ, para 49.

9.13 If the time limit prescribed in the Directive has passed, then the result to be achieved by the Directive is binding upon the Member State. This has three consequences. First, any legislation introduced with the aim (or apparent aim) of achieving the result required by the Directive within the Member State must be interpreted so far as possible to achieve that aim. Second, whether or not domestic legislation achieves the effect intended by the Directive, the articles of the Directive remain binding upon the Member State (and each and every part of it: thus being in theory enforceable without the need for implementing legislation against any public authority, or 'emanation of the State', within the Member State). Third, if the Member State defaults on its obligation to introduce domestic legislation to achieve the result intended by the Directive, and a citizen of that State suffers consequential loss, he may be able to bring a claim against the State for compensation for that loss.

European law in the United Kingdom

9.14 The European Communities Act 1972 has the effect of transplanting, as it were, European principles into UK law. By virtue of s 2(1) it follows that where provisions (for example European Regulations) do not require any implementing measures before they take effect in national law (are 'directly applicable') the same result arises as a matter of UK law. Where European law requires implementation through the means of domestic law—typically Directives—then s 2(2) of the European Communities Act gives power to pass that legislation.¹ By virtue of s 3 of the European Communities Act, UK courts are bound to interpret European law in accordance with the principles and decisions of the ECJ.

¹ See *R v Secretary of State for Trade and Industry, ex p UNISON* [1996] ICR 1003 for the scope of s 2(2).

9.15 Section 3(1) of the European Communities Act 1972 states:

'For the purpose of all legal proceedings any question as to the meaning or effect of any of the Treaties, or as to the validity, meaning or effect of any Community instrument, shall be determined as a question of law (and, if not referred to the European Court, be for determination as such in accordance with the principles laid down by and any relevant decision of the European Court).'

9.16 The correct meaning to be given to European Directives is thus regarded as a question of law. English courts have long been accustomed to dealing with questions of statutory interpretation as questions of law. Yet European legislation hardly resembles that familiar to British lawyers: most notably, it is extremely brief, confining itself to general principles. As a result the techniques of interpretation differ from UK practice. Essentially, the approach is teleological, purposive, dynamic (such that interpretations may develop and even vary over time, in accordance with the state of development of the EU), and has regard to questions such as proportionality and effectiveness of remedy.

9.17 By virtue of art 220 (ex art 164) EC, the ultimate arbiter of the proper interpretation of European legislation is the ECJ, which usually sits in chambers, and hands down one collegiate judgment.[1] Most cases come before the ECJ under art 234 (ex art 177) EC, which gives the court jurisdiction to make preliminary rulings on questions of interpretation referred to it by national courts. Of importance, too, is the opinion of the Advocate General, which precedes the judgment of the court and usually gives a much fuller analysis of the law.[2] The analogy with a first instance decision of a UK court is less than perfect: the Advocate General's analysis is more of a submission in order to assist the court, albeit an impartial one.[3] But, particularly where the ECJ follows his or her reasoning, wider statements of the Advocate General provide useful indications of how the court came to its conclusions and how it may reason in future judgments.

1   See art 221 (ex art 165) EC. The judgments of the ECJ may suffer from their need to speak with one voice.
2   The opinion of the Advocate General is not part of the judgment of the ECJ.
3   See art 222 (ex art 166) EC.

9.18 The section below considers, first, the legislative framework and context for the proper interpretation of European Directives, with particular reference to the field of health and safety; second, the method of interpretation of national law in fields covered by European law; third, the circumstances in which a claimant can rely on provisions of a European Directive itself before national courts, including the remedies which should be available; fourth, the nature of the claim for compensation for a failure to implement a Directive in domestic law (known as a *Francovich* action); and lastly, the procedure in respect of preliminary references from national courts to the ECJ.

9.19 In most cases where a European issue arises involving obligations contained in a Directive, the courts will attempt first to interpret the provisions of national law in accordance with the European obligation; where that is not possible, in cases where a public authority (an 'emanation of the State') is concerned, the court may assess whether the European provision is directly effective; only if an individual has no remedy, where there has been a breach of European law, may an action for damages against the State arise.

Interpreting European Directives

9.20 The distinction between how the ECJ interprets legislation and the normal approach to statutory interpretation of the English courts should not be over-estimated. In both cases the wording of the legislation is of central importance.[1] However, the ECJ is more strongly influenced by the purpose of the legislation rather than the literal or conventional meaning of terms. In determining what is the objective of legislation, it will have regard to the preamble as well as to the main text, and to the general framework and objectives of European law as a whole, which may change over time.[2] As these underlying objectives change, so does the approach of the ECJ to particular provisions: the ECJ does not focus on a presumed intent of the legislature at the time a particular law was passed. Thus, provisions of the Treaty incapable of leading directly to legislation may nonetheless be aids to interpretation of other provisions in the same field. A good example is provided by *R v Secretary of State for Trade and Industry, ex p Broadcasting, Entertainment, Cinematographic and Theatre Union (BECTU)* [2001] IRLR 559, ECJ which concerned the lawfulness of the UK regulations implementing the Working Time Directive (93/104), which contained a restriction on access to rights under the Directive until a worker had been employed for a continuous period of 13 weeks. The ECJ examined the purpose of art 7 of the Directive by reference to art 137 (ex art 118A) EC, the recitals in the Directive, the Community Charter of the Fundamental Social Rights of Workers adopted by the European Council in 1989 (referred to in the recitals of the Directive) as well as the other provisions of the Directive itself.[3]

1   In the case of European legislation all the language versions are equally relevant as aids to interpretation: see *Srl CILFIT and Lanificio di Gavardo SpA v Ministry of Health* [1982] ECR 3415, ECJ.
2   See *Srl CILFIT and Lanificio di Gavardo SpA v Ministry of Health* at 3430.
3   The ECJ at para 39 referred to the Charter 'which declared, in point 8 and the first subparagraph of point 19, that every worker in the European Community must enjoy satisfactory health and safety conditions in his working environment and that he is, in particular, entitled to paid annual leave ...'. The Charter was also referred to by the ECJ in the following working time cases: Case C-151/02 *Landeshauptstaat Kiel v Jaeger* [2003] IRLR 804, ECJ; Joined Cases C-397/01–403/01 *Pfeiffer v Deutsches Rotes Kreuz v Kreisverband* [2004] ECR I-8835, ECJ; Case C-14/04 *Dellas Premier Ministre* [2006] IRLR 225, ECJ.

9.21 The most important provisions of the EU Treaty for the purposes of the health and safety Directives are those which permit the Council to adopt Directives. Prior to the entry into force of the Single European Act in 1987, most health and safety legislation had been passed under the general harmonisation power under art 100 EC, which required unanimity. The new legal basis of Community competence under art 137 (ex art 118A EC, inserted by the Single European Act in 1987), has permitted the adoption of health and safety Directives by majority voting. That article reflects the tension underlying the European social policy between the capacity of Member States to adopt their own standards in the field of social policy on the one hand, and the protection of Europe-wide standards on the other. Express reference is made in art 136 (ex art 117) EC to the European Social Charter of 1961 and the 1989 Community Charter of the Fundamental Social Rights of Workers.

9.22 The new text of art 137 EC (as amended by the Nice Treaty) dilutes the emphasis on worker protection to be found in the former art 118A,[1] but still retains the core of the earlier version when it states:

'With a view to achieving the objectives of article 136, the Community shall support and complement the activities of the Member States in the following fields:

(a) improvement in particular of the working environment to protect workers' health and safety; ...'

The revised text of art 137 EC also lists: working conditions, protection of workers where their employment is terminated and information and consultation of workers as falling within the sphere of legislative competence of the Community institutions.

[1] Former art 118A(1) EC stated as follows 'Member States shall pay particular attention to *encouraging improvements,* especially in the working environment, as regards the health and safety of workers and shall set as their objective the harmonisation of conditions in this area, *while maintaining the improvements made'.*

9.23 The interpretation of (former) art 118A EC Treaty was the subject of a significant challenge by the UK government in *United Kingdom v EU Council* [1997] ICR 443, ECJ where the UK argued that the Council of Ministers had acted outside its powers under the EC Treaty by adopting the Working Time Directive 93/104.[1] The ECJ held (at para 15):

'There is nothing in the wording of article 118A to indicate that the concepts of "working environment", "safety" and "health" as used in that provision should, in the absence of other indications, be interpreted restrictively, and not as embracing all factors, physical or otherwise, capable of affecting the health and safety of the worker in his working environment, including in particular certain aspects of the organisation of working time. On the contrary, the words "especially in the working environment" militate in favour of a broad interpretation of the powers which article 118A confers upon the Council for the protection of the health and safety of workers. Moreover, such an interpretation of the words "safety" and "health" derives support in particular from the preamble to the Constitution of the World Health Organisation to which all the Member States belong. Health is there defined as a state of complete physical, mental and social well-being that does not consist only in the absence of illness and infirmity.'

[1] 1993 OJ L307/18.

9.24 It is clear as a consequence of the ruling of the ECJ that a broad and purposive interpretation should be applied to the scope of the Treaty and secondary legislation adopted under art 137 EC (or its predecessor, art 118A) in the field of health and safety. Whereas art 137(2) EC provides that the Council, when adopting Directives, should avoid adopting measures which might hinder small and medium sized enterprises, as the ECJ held (at para 44), this power contemplates the adoption of special economic measures for such enterprises; the Treaty itself does not introduce general economic considerations into the field of health and safety.[1]

[1] Confirmed in *ex p BECTU,* above, at paras 59 and 60.

9.25 The aim of encouraging improvements in provision for health and safety amongst the Member States of the EU is expressed in Directive 89/391/EC ('the Framework Directive')[1] which provided a basis for 'daughter' Directives making provision for particular aspects of health and safety at work. The preamble states that the Directive 'does not justify any reduction in levels of protection already achieved in individual Member States'; '... the Member

States being committed under the Treaty to encouraging improvements and to harmonising conditions while maintaining the improvements made'; '... Member States' legislative systems covering safety and health at the workplace ... need to be improved ...'; 'preventative measures must be introduced or improved without delay in order to ... ensure a higher degree of protection'; the improvement of workers' safety, hygiene and health at work is an objective which should not be subordinated to purely economic considerations'.[2] Within an enterprise itself, the Framework Directive demands maintenance of improvements: see arts 1(1), 1(3) and 6(3)(a). These principles should, accordingly, inform the general approach to construing individual 'daughter' Directives and, it follows, the domestic implementing regulations.[3] In *Stark v Post Office* [2000] ICR 1013, CA Waller LJ noted that the Framework Directive and the Work Equipment Directive (89/655/EC) '... recognise that if Member States already impose obligations higher than those minimum obligations sought to be imposed by the Directives, those higher obligations should be maintained'.

1 Article 1.
2 On 21 March 2005, the Commission commenced an action against the United Kingdom seeking a declaration that the United Kingdom had failed to fulfil its obligations under art 5(1) and 5(4) of the Framework Directive: see case C-127/05.
3 See too *Opinion 2/91 Re ILO Convention No 170* [1994] IRLR 135, ECJ. The principle of 'non-regression' was recognised in Case C-144/04 *Mangold v Helm* [2006] IRLR 143, ECJ; see in particular paras 54–59 of the Opinion of Tizzano A-G.

9.26 A similar principle is contained in the HSWA 1974, s 1(2). Regulations made under that Act are to be 'designed to maintain or improve the standards of health and safety'. But in *R v Secretary of State for Employment, ex p NACODS* (16 December 1993, unreported, DC) the Divisional Court declined to reach a conclusion as to whether the MASHAM Regulations[1] met the criteria. It was not for the court to judge whether standards of health and safety would be maintained or improved, but for the Minister making subordinate legislation under the Act to do so. The only exception would be where no reasonable Minister could come to the conclusion he did as to the effect of the intended regulations upon standards of health and safety.

1 Management and Administration of Safety and Health at Mines Regulations 1993, SI 1993/1897.

9.27 Formal recommendations of the EC Commission do not have any binding force (see art 249(5) EC), but national courts are bound to consider them, in particular when they clarify the interpretation of national provisions implementing European Directives: see *Grimaldi v Fonds Des Maladies Professionnelles* [1990] IRLR 400, ECJ (Commission recommendation on compensation for certain occupational diseases not directly effective).

9.28 The ECJ may be less willing to consider the provisions of other international treaties, such as the ILO, as influencing the meaning of Directives: see the *Convention No 170 of the ILO* [1994] IRLR 135. The ECJ has, however, incorporated human rights into the general principles of EC law, in part because all the Member States are parties to the European Convention on Human Rights: see for example *Internationale Handelsgesellschaft mbH v*

Einfuhr und Varratstelle fur Getreide und Futtermittel [1970] ECR 1125, ECJ and *Kent Kirk* [1985] 3 All ER 453. In Case C-144/04 *Mangold v Helm* [2006] IRLR 143, however, the ECJ did refer to the preamble of Directive 2000/78 establishing a general framework for equal treatment in employment and occupation[1] which cites the European Convention on Human Rights, the Universal Declaration of Human Rights, the United Nations Convention on the Elimination of All Forms of Discrimination against Women, the United Nations Covenants on Civil and Political Rights and on Economic, Social and Cultural Rights and Convention No 111 of the ILO, as well as the Employment Guidelines for 2000 agreed by the European Council at Helsinki in December 1999. As a consequence, the ECJ held that there existed a general principle of non-discrimination on grounds of age which applies within the scope of the application of European law, the effect of which was to require the German referring court to disapply conflicting national provisions.

[1] OJ 2000 L 303/16.

9.29 The Charter of Fundamental Rights of the European Union, signed in Nice (2000 OJ C 364/01), is the most significant example of 'soft law' from which the ECJ and national courts are likely to draw assistance when interpreting particular legislative provisions. Tizzano A-G specifically referred to this Charter in his Opinion in the *ex p Bectu* case.[1] The principal purpose of the Nice Charter was to draw up for the institutions of the European Union a set of principles which are declaratory and not (yet) legally binding. The Charter fills a gap, since the Union is not party to the European Convention on Human Rights and Fundamental Freedoms. The Charter goes further than the Convention and includes social rights as well as civil and political rights in its identification of the rights and obligations which are necessary and pre-eminent in the European context. In relation to employer's liability, the two most relevant provisions of the Charter are art 31, giving a right to safe working conditions, and art 47 which establishes a right to an effective remedy and to a fair trial, including the right to public funding in so far as such aid is necessary to ensure effective access to justice. Article 31 states as follows:

'1   Every worker has the right to working conditions which respect his or her health, safety and dignity.

2   Every worker has the right to limitation of maximum working hours, to daily and weekly rest periods and to an annual period of paid leave.'

[1] At paras 26–28.

9.30 In the context of health and safety at work, reference should also be made to art 5 concerning the prohibition of slavery and forced labour, art 26 on the integration of persons with disabilities, art 27 on workers' right to information and consultation within the undertaking and art 32 on prohibition of child labour and protection of young people at work.

9.31 Further fundamental principles can be derived from the Framework Directive, which should be borne in mind when interpreting both other health and safety Directives, and domestic legislation made to implement them.

These include the following. First, none of the European obligations preclude Member States adopting higher standards of health and safety provision.[1] Second, employers' duties are not to be treated as reduced as a result of any obligations imposed on employees.[2] Third, work should be adapted to the individual.[3] Fourth, an employer should undertake a coherent strategy of combatting health and safety risks (see art 6(2)). Fifth, employers should consult with workers and/or their representatives 'on all questions relating to health and safety' (art 11). Very significantly, the Commission has now commenced an action against the United Kingdom seeking a declaration that the United Kingdom had failed to fulfil its obligations under art 5(1) and 5(4) of the Framework Directive. The complaint is based upon the HSWA 1974, s 2(1) and the qualification of the duty by the phrase 'so far as is reasonably practicable'. The Commission considers that this qualification is incompatible with the articles and permits an employer to escape responsibility if it can prove that the sacrifice involved in taking measures is grossly disproportionate to the risk whereas the legislative history of the Directive reveals express rejection of such a clause: see Case C-127/05.

1   See art 1(3) and art 137(5) (ex art 118A(3)) EC.
2   See art 5(3).
3   See art 6(2)(d) and (3)(b).

9.32 Another general principle emerges from the Temporary Workers Directive (see para 10.09, below) that workers who work under a fixed-term contract or who are assigned to another business 'are afforded, as regards safety and health at work, the same level of protection as that of other workers in the user undertaking and/or establishment' (art 2(1)).

The interpretative obligation

9.33 English legislation which has been introduced in order to implement European Directives should be construed in the light of the wording and purpose of the particular Directive, as reflected in the decisions of the ECJ. This duty of construction includes all provisions of Directives, and not merely those which are directly effective. It marks something of a break with the past attitude of English courts to statutory interpretation, see below: the courts are now under a duty to attempt to achieve the same result as a Directive. As part of this duty, as well as legislation intended to implement European law, in some circumstances courts may have to construe English law which pre-dates a Directive so as to give effect to the meaning of the Directive.

The approach of the ECJ

9.34 From the viewpoint of European law, national courts are under a duty by virtue of art 10 (ex art 5) EC to construe national legislation in accordance with European law: see *Von Colson and Kamann v Land Nordrhein-Westfalen* [1984] ECR 1891 at 1909. The nature of the interpretative obligation was elaborated in *Marleasing SA v La Comercial Internacional de Alimentacion SA* [1990] ECR I-4135 in which the ECJ, again basing itself on art 5 (now art 10 EC), stated that:

> '... in applying the national law, *whether the provisions in question were adopted before or after the Directive,* the national court called upon to interpret is required to do so, *as far as possible,* in the light of the wording and the purpose of the Directive in order to achieve the result pursued by the latter and thereby comply with the third paragraph of article 189 [now art 249 EC].' [emphasis added].

9.35 In relation to legislation not passed to implement a Directive, this duty arises once the date for implementation contained in the Directive has passed: see *Officier van Justitie v Kolpinghuis Nijmegen BV* [1987] ECR 3969.[1]

1   Legislation intended to implement a Directive should, by contrast, be interpreted in accordance with the Directive once that legislation is passed: see *Kolpinghuis Nijmegen.* This does not preclude the possibility of transitional provisions as part of the national implementation process, provided this does not seriously compromise the result to be achieved by the Directive: see Case C-129/96 *Inter-Environnement Wallonie ASBL v Region Wallonie* [1997] ECR I-7411, and Case C-144/04 *Mangold v Helm* [2006] IRLR 143, at para 67.

9.36 The ECJ has not elaborated on the meaning of the phrase 'as far as possible', but left the matter for the consideration of the national courts. Van Gerven A-G considered that the provisions of national law must be 'open to interpretation' and added that the national court 'must, having regard to the usual methods of interpretation in its legal system, give precedence to the method which enables it to construe the national provision concerned in a manner consistent with the Directive'.[1] Although the short judgment of the ECJ makes no reference to such methods, it has appeared to recognise some constraints on the duty. For, if the obligation was absolute, it would largely render irrelevant the distinction between 'vertical effect' (only available against emanations of the State) and 'horizontal effect' (available against a private body only where the European provisions have been incorporated into national law). Yet in *Marleasing*, and consistently thereafter, the ECJ has reaffirmed the position that 'a provision of a Directive may not be relied upon as such against an individual'.[2] Thus, Case C-160/01 *Mau v Bundesanstalt fur Arbeit* [2003] ECR I-4791, where the referring court stated that it would be 'impossible' to interpret national law in a certain manner may be contrasted with Case C-35/02 *Landeszahnartztekammer Hessen v Vogel (Markus)* [2003] ECR I-12229, where the national court seeking a preliminary ruling considered that it was 'possible' to interpret national law in a specific manner.

1   At I-4146, para 8. This was the view taken of the effect of *Marleasing* in *Porter v Cannon Hygiene Ltd* [1993] IRLR 329, NICA. In Joined Cases C-397/01–403/01 *Pfeiffer* [2004] ECR I-8835 the ECJ held at para 116 'In that context, if the application of interpretative methods recognised by national law enables, in certain circumstances, a provision of domestic law to be construed in such a way as to avoid conflict with another rule of domestic law or the scope of that provision to be restricted to that end by applying it only in so far as it is compatible with the rule concerned, the national court is bound to use those methods in order to achieve the result sought by the Directive.'
2   At I-4158, para 6. See too *Ministere Public et Direction du Travail et l'Emploi v Levy* [1994] IRLR 139. This was confirmed in *Faccini Dori v Recreb Srl* [1994] ECR I-3325, and more recently in Joined Cases C-397/01–403/01 *Pfeiffer* [2004] ECR I-8835.

9.37 The interpretation of national law not specifically introduced to implement European duties throws this issue into sharp focus. Some limitation on the scope of the interpretative obligation should follow from the recognition by the ECJ of the doctrine of legitimate expectation: see *Kolpinghuis Nijmegen* above.[1] That doctrine cannot affect the interpretation of particular *implementing* legislation: the plain expectation is that such provisions should meet the standards of the Directive. But the principle may limit the extent to which the courts will reinterpret existing provisions of national law, with settled meanings, to comply with European law. A defendant may reasonably argue that it had a legitimate expectation that the hitherto accepted meaning was the correct one. In the context of the interpretation of a pre-existing national provision the ECJ has held that there is a limit on the extent to which national law may be interpreted in a purposive manner, where such an interpretation leads to the imposition of an obligation laid down by a Directive which has not been transposed into national law or determining or aggravating a liability in criminal law.[2] Nevertheless, outside the criminal context, the position is hardly clear, since the claimant has a competing legitimate expectation that national law will be interpreted in accordance with Community obligations.[3]

[1]   In *Marleasing* the Advocate General stated that the interpretative obligation was restricted by the principles of legal certainty and non-retroactivity: see [1990] ECR I-4135 at 4147, para 8.
[2]   See Case C-168/95 *Arcaro (criminal proceedings against)* [1996] ECR I-4705, para 42. For that might equally breach the principle of non-retroactivity. And see Van Gerven A-G in *Marleasing* at 4147.
[3]   See *Burca* (1992) 55 MLR at 229–231. The ECJ has stated that the doctrine of non-retroactivity, outside the criminal sphere, is not an absolute one: see *R v Minister of Agriculture, Fisheries and Food and the Secretary of State for Health, ex p FEDESA* [1991] 1 CMLR 507. Note, however, that in *Marleasing* the Advocate General did say that reinterpretation could not permit a Directive to introduce a 'civil penalty' I-1447, para 8; see also the case of *Wells*, discussed below, para 9.58, fn 3. For the approach of the English courts, see below.

9.38 What is clear from *Marleasing*, however, is that courts are under a duty, in their capacity as organs of the State, to seek to bring English law into line with European law. This doctrine applies to the whole legal system of the Member State.[1] The national court may not, in other words, construe legislation or other law in accordance with European law only where it is clearly ambiguous: the duty is more extensive. Indeed, the duty to interpret national law in accordance with European law applies notwithstanding any contrary interpretation which may arise from Hansard.[2] Nor is it an exercise based on the imputed intent of the national legislative body: the interpretation of national law which pre-dates a Directive to give effect to that Directive cannot logically be referable to the intention of a legislative will. In the context of implementing legislation, the ECJ has said that the national court should assume that the national Parliament *did* intend fully to comply with its European obligations: see *Wagner Miret v Fondo de Garanatia Salarial* [1993] ECR I-6911.[3] The duty on the national court is to ensure, for matters within its jurisdiction, the full effectiveness of European law.[4] To that end, it is necessary not only to consider the transposing provisions, but national law as a whole.[5]

1   See, for example, at I-4159 where the court stated that 'It follows that the requirement that national law *must* be interpreted in conformity with Article 11 of Directive 68/151 *precludes* the interpretation otherwise than as set out in the Directive' (emphasis added). Similarly, at para 13, it stated that a national court was 'bound' to interpret national law in the required manner. See also Lenz A-G in *Faccini Dori v Recreb Srl* [1995] All ER (EC) 1 at 11. Perhaps the strongest indication that courts are under a duty to interpret national law in accordance with European law and principles is Case C-224/01 *Kobler v Austria* [2003] ECR I-10239, where the ECJ held in principle that a breach of European law by a national court of last instance could give rise to a claim for damages.

2   See for example Case C-371/02 *Bjornekulla Fruktindustrier AB v Procordia Food AB* [2004] ECR I-5791, para 13.

3   Followed and applied in Cases C-397/01–403/01 *Pfeiffer* [2004] ECR I-8835.

4   See e g Case C-144/04 *Mangold v Helm* [2006] IRLR 143, at para 77.

5   See the *Pfeiffer* case, at paras 115 and 119.

The approach of United Kingdom courts

9.39 The traditional approach of UK courts faced with legislation enacted to comply with Treaty obligations is to construe that legislation in accordance with the relevant Treaty where the legislation is ambiguous or unclear.[1] Initially the same approach was used in relation to European law, relying upon the European Communities Act 1972, s 2(4).

1   See *Rayner v Department of Trade and Industry* [1990] 2 AC 418; *R v Secretary of State for Home Department, ex p Brind* [1991] 1 AC 696, concerning the relevance of the European Convention on Human Rights to the interpretation of domestic law, now overtaken by the implementation of the Human Rights Act 1998.

9.40 But, after some hesitancy, the UK courts have recognised that they should adopt a bolder approach when construing a law enacted to give effect to a Directive. Already, in *Garland v British Rail Engineering Ltd* [1983] 2 AC 751, Lord Diplock said that implementing legislation should be construed if 'reasonably capable of bearing such a meaning, as intended to carry out the [Treaty] obligation' (at 771). Later, in accordance with the approach of the ECJ, in *Litster v Forth Dry Dock and Engineering Co Ltd* [1990] 1 AC 546 the House of Lords inserted words into the Transfer of Undertakings (Protection of Employment) Regulations 1981, SI 1981/1794 to bring their provisions into conformity with the Acquired Rights Directive 77/187/EEC, now 2001/23/EC.[1] The speech of Lord Oliver in particular recognised that the court had a greater latitude than under normal rules of construction, saying that the court should imply the words necessary to achieve the same result as the Directive 'even though ... it may involve some departure from the strict and literal application of the words'[2] and Lord Keith spoke of a duty to construe the regulations in accordance with the decisions of the ECJ.[3] In *Webb v EMO Air Cargo (UK) Ltd* [1993] ICR 175 Lord Keith accepted that it is sufficient if the national legislation is 'open to an interpretation consistent with the Directive', so long as that does not distort the meaning of the domestic legislation without requiring that it be ambiguous on its face. So too in *Porter v Cannon Hygiene Ltd* [1993] IRLR 329, the Northern Ireland Court of Appeal, having considered *Marleasing*, concluded that there had to be no more than a possible meaning which accorded with the Directive for the national court to be under a duty to adopt that interpretation (at para 19).

¹ This approach was cited with apparent approval by the Advocate General in *Marleasing* at I-4147, 13. See too *Pickstone v Freemans plc* [1988] ICR 697 at 722–723, 725, HL.
² At 125.
³ At 125.

9.41 More recently, in *Clarke v Kato, Smith and General Accident Fire and Life Assurance Corpn plc* [1999] PIQR P1 at 9, Lord Clyde considered that the:

'adoption of a construction which departs boldly from the ordinary meaning of the language of the statute is, however, particularly appropriate where the validity of legislation has to be tested against the provisions of European law. In that context it is proper to strain to give effect to the design and purpose behind the legislation, and to give weight to the spirit rather than the letter. In this way the court may implement the requirement formulated by the European Court of Justice in *Marleasing* [para 8 of the ECJ judgment is recited]. But even in this context the exercise must still be one of construction and it should not exceed the limits of what is reasonable.'

Provided that the 'distortion' exception is kept within narrow bounds, this approach appears fully to accord with that of the ECJ.

9.42 The first two decisions of the Court of Appeal subsequent to the implementation of the European health and safety Directives are indicative of the approach to the interpretation of English secondary legislation designed to implement European health and safety obligations: *Hawkes v London Borough of Southwark* (20 February 1998, unreported), CA¹ which concerned the interpretation of the words 'reasonably practicable' in reg 4 of the Manual Handling Operations Regulations 1992, and *Stark v Post Office* [2000] ICR 1013, which concerned regs 5 and 6 of the Provision and Use of Work Equipment Regulations 1992. In both cases, the Court of Appeal made reference to pre-existing case law of some antiquity to interpret the words in the implementing regulations, which jurisprudence had previously been applied in a purely domestic context, prior to the accession of the United Kingdom to the Community. In neither case was it contended that the European legislation required an interpretation which went further than that to be found in the earlier case law (in *Stark* the defendant even contended that European law required a less strict interpretation).

¹ Considered in the case of *Swain v Denso Marston Ltd* [2000] PIQR P 129.

9.43 The words 'maintained in an efficient state, in efficient working order and in good repair', the subject of interpretation in *Stark* by the Court of Appeal in respect of their application to work equipment, were the subject of further judicial scrutiny by the House of Lords in *Fytche v Wincanton Logistics plc* [2004] UKHL 31, [2004] ICR 975, but in the context of the Personal Protective Equipment at Work Regulations 1992. Again, in this case the minimum requirements of the Directive (89/656/EC) were met, and the controversy concerned the extent to which the national implementing regulations went beyond the European minimum standards. Their Lordships split

3–2 on the meaning of the domestic provisions; however, the substantive obligation to interpret the national provisions in light of the Directive was uncontroversial.[1]

¹ The meaning of the words in *Fytche* differed from that in *Stark* because the majority in the House of Lords held that the statutory context in which the words of the particular regulation fell to be considered differed. The Court of Appeal held that there was no discrepancy between the two cases in the subsequent case of *Ball v Street* [2005] EWCA Civ 76 where the interpretation of the words in *Stark* in relation to work equipment was re-affirmed; see para 20.27, below.

9.44 Where the implementing regulations use familiar words and phrases with a settled meaning, it is likely to be less easy to persuade an English judge to apply a new meaning, since it is presumed that the intention of Parliament was to adopt that standard which had previously applied. However, as stated above, if it is possible to interpret the national implementing legislation in the light of superior European norms in a purposive manner, the courts should do so, irrespective of the intention of Parliament.[1] It may be argued that the intention of Parliament, having enacted the European Communities Act 1972, is that European jurisprudence should apply rather than established English jurisprudence, where there is a potential conflict with the obligations in the Directive. One case where it was not possible to interpret national legislation in accordance with a European Directive was *Mann v Secretary of State for Employment* [1999] ICR 898, where the House of Lords refused to interpret implementing legislation creatively so as to apply to correct an acknowledged pre-existing breach of EC law, where to do so would (per Lord Hoffmann) deny citizens the protection of the presumption against retrospectivity (despite the fact that the case itself concerned the claiming of benefits from the respondent Minister).

¹ To that extent, it is considered that the observation of Aldous LJ at p 10 of the transcript in *Hawkes* is not correct, although it is not clear from the report the extent to which it was argued that a purposive interpretation required a meaning other than that set out in the pre-existing case law.

9.45 What approach should the UK courts adopt when faced with English law which clearly was *not* enacted to give effect to a Directive? In *Duke v Reliance Systems Ltd* [1988] AC 618 the House of Lords declined to construe the Equal Pay Act 1970 and the Sex Discrimination Act 1975 in accordance with the Equal Treatment Directive 76/207, in part because neither were intended to give effect to that Directive.[1] That decision, however, pre-dated *Marleasing*; as a result, it may not have adequately recognised the nature of the duty on national courts to construe national law so as to give effect to the Directive. Instead the House based itself on traditional principles of divining the intention of Parliament. In keeping with the duty approach of the ECJ, in *Webb v EMO Air Cargo (UK) Ltd* [1993] ICR 175 the House of Lords accepted that it was under an obligation to construe even legislation pre-dating a Directive in accordance with European law. Lord Keith said at 186 that:

'... it is for a United Kingdom court to construe domestic legislation in *any field* covered by a Community Directive so as to accord with the interpretation of the Directive was laid down by the European Court of Justice'. [emphasis added]

1 See too *Finnegan v Clowney Youth Training Programme Ltd* [1990] 2 AC 407, which also adopted an approach based on Parliamentary intention in relation to a provision which post-dated the Directive, but which used identical wording to a provision enacted prior to the Directive.

9.46 The intention of Parliament, however ascertained, is increasingly irrelevant to this exercise; the decision in *R v Secretary of State for Employment, ex p Equal Opportunities Commission* [1995] 1 AC 1 exemplifies this more confident judicial attitude.

9.47 Some uncertainty remains as to how far the national courts should go. Quite apart from the tension between this duty and the doctrine of legitimate expectation (see para 9.37, above), does the duty extend to the common law, as well as to legislation for example? Indeed, in *Marleasing* itself the ECJ was construing a provision of the Spanish Civil Code on the nullity of public companies to which the rules of contract were applied by analogy; an appropriate comparison for this in English law may well be the common law. To the extent that *Marleasing* imposes a duty on courts to achieve the result intended by Directives, it could be said that the courts may be under an obligation to approach the common law in this manner.[1] But, significantly, in *Marleasing* the Advocate General at least was prepared to treat reasoning by analogy as a method of interpretation, and he seemed to take a similar view as to the meaning of general concepts of contract.[2]

1 Of course, there is some difficulty in describing the application of the common law as 'interpretation'; the approach of the courts is typically one of reasoning by analogy, of a search for the deep principles embedded in the tradition, rather than an exercise in analysing the linguistic meanings of terms.
2 *Marleasing SA v La Comercial Internacional de Alimentacion SA* [1990] ECR I-4135, para 20.

9.48 This issue arose in *White v White and Motor Insurers Bureau* [2001] PIQR P281 in connection with the proper interpretation of the 1988 uninsured drivers agreement made between the Secretary of State for Transport and the MIB. Lord Nicholls, giving the leading speech, stated that the *Marleasing* principle, as such, could not apply to the interpretation of the MIB agreement. The MIB agreement was not legislation but a contract between citizens, even where one of the parties is an emanation of the State. However, it was the intention of the parties that the agreement should be construed in the light of the Second Motor Insurance Directive. By this method, the House of Lords achieved the same result as applying purposive canons of interpretation.[1] It is to be noted that a similar duty of interpretation 'so far as it is possible to do so' is contained in the Human Rights Act 1998, s 3(1). Even prior to the full implementation of that Act, the House of Lords expanded the common law duty of care in negligence, in the light of the jurisprudence of the European Court of Human Rights under the ECHR, art 6 (right to a fair trial) in *Osman v United Kingdom* (1998) 29 EHRR 245: see *Barrett v Enfield London Borough Council* [1999] PIQR P 272. Whilst the decision in *Barrett* was reached without direct consideration of art 6 ECHR, the conclusions of their Lordships were clearly compatible with the Strasbourg case law.

1 See paras 20–23.

9.49 Much remains to be resolved in this area. Already the courts considering common law claims have referred to statutory duties as evidence of what is good practice for an employer to adopt: see eg paras 4.62–4.64, above. On the other hand, given the discretion that Member States have in relation to the form of implementation into domestic law of obligations contained in Directives under art 249 (ex art 189) EC, it cannot be said that domestic regulation by means of the criminal law was an unreasonable option to choose when many other obligations under the HSWA 1974 give rise to obligations under criminal but not civil law.

9.50 In summary, the national court should, first, decide what the Directive itself means, in accordance with the approach of the ECJ. The correct approach for an English court is the radical approach taken in *Litster*, although the court may be somewhat more circumspect in approaching law not intended to implement a Directive. Provided that the UK legislation in the area covered by a Directive is capable of being construed in accordance with the Directive, a court should generally adopt that interpretation. Previous decisions on the meaning of the particular concept can, and should, be departed from if an alternative meaning better meets the aim of the Directive. Precisely this approach should be adopted, it has been suggested, in interpreting the phrase 'reasonably practicable' in the various regulations implementing Directives.[1] Various reasons point towards strengthening rather than relaxing this duty to ensure Directives are effective: one is the ECJ's retreat from horizontal direct effect; another is that *Francovich* actions, for compensation against the state, may prove to be restricted in scope (and these actions can *only* permit compensation and not other remedies).

[1] See paras 5.77–5.95, above, but note *Hawkes v London Borough of Southwark,* referred to in para 9.42, above.

Direct effect

9.51 Under art 249 (ex art 189) EC, a Directive is binding 'as to the result to be achieved ... but shall leave to the national authorities the choice of form and methods'. Thus, for example, the Framework Directive imposes an obligation on Member States themselves to introduce legal provisions to implement the Directive (see art 4). Where a Member State fails to meet this duty, the Commission may bring infringement proceedings under arts 226–228 (ex arts 169–171) EC—just as it did following the failure of the UK government to provide for consultation on collective redundancies and transfer of undertakings where no union is recognised in the workplace.[1] Despite an increased willingness on the part of the Commission to do this, such proceedings are extremely lengthy and Member States continue to be guilty of long delays in implementation or of failures to implement at all. Alternatively, an affected party can challenge the Member State's implementation in the domestic courts which, in turn, may refer the matter to the ECJ for a preliminary ruling, as happened with the UK's implementation of the Working Time Directive.[2]

[1] See *EC Commission v United Kingdom* [1994] ICR 664.
[2] *R v Secretary of State for Trade and Industry, ex p BECTU* [2001] IRLR 559, ECJ.

9.52 To ensure the effective implementation and application of European law, early in its history the ECJ recognised that some provisions of European law, whether in the Treaty, Community Regulations, decisions or Directives, could give rights to individuals of each Member State, which are to be recognised and enforced by the national courts of Member States: see for example *Van Gend en Loos* [1963] ECR 1 and art 10 (ex art 5) EC. Thus, art 141 (ex art 119) EC has been held to give rise to directly effective rights, which national courts must respect.[1] In *Van Duyn v Home Office (No 2)* [1974] ECR 1337, the ECJ extended the doctrine to the provision of a Directive stating that, despite the need for implementing legislation under art 189(3) (now art 249(3) EC), the effect of Directives would be weakened if individuals could not rely on them in this manner. In the case of articles of the Treaties, these can be relied on by an individual against another private person, whereas directly effective provisions of Directives can only be used against an emanation of the State.

[1] See *Defrenne v Sabena* [1976] ECR 455.

9.53 In the context of health and safety, however, the principal article of the Treaty, art 137 (ex art 118A) EC, is no doubt too vague to give rights of itself; here it is almost exclusively the Directives which are of interest, and so this book deals with direct effect in relation to them, below.[1]

[1] In Case C-144/04 *Mangold v Helm* [2006] IRLR 143, the ECJ held that a general principle of law common to the Member States, namely the duty not to discriminate on grounds of age, was capable of having direct effect such as to impose a duty on a national court to disapply conflicting domestic provisions introduced during the period for transposition of provisions of a Directive.

9.54 The consequence of directly effective rights is radical: within the sphere of application of such rights, Member States have effectively given up some of their sovereignty: see *Costa v ENEL* [1964] ECR 585. Directly effective provisions will override conflicting national law or permit actions in the absence of implementing legislation: see *Verbond van Nederlandse Ondernemingen v Inspecteur der Invoerrechten en Accijnzen* [1977] ECR 113; *Suffriti v Instituto Nazionale della Providenza Sociale* [1993] IRLR 289. Thus, the ECJ has stated that directly applicable Community laws 'by their entry into force render automatically inapplicable any conflicting provisions of current national law': *Amministrazione delle Finanze dello Stato v Simmenthal SpA* [1978] ECR 629. In *R v Secretary of State for Transport, ex p Factortame Ltd (No 2)* [1991] 1 AC 603 at 644, the ECJ viewed as 'automatically inapplicable' a rule of national law precluding the granting of injunctions against the Crown, with the consequence that it was eventually set aside.[1] A national procedural rule was likewise set aside in *Emmott v Minister for Social Welfare* [1993] ICR 8, ECJ.[2]

[1] On return to the House of Lords: see *Factortame* [1991] 1 AC 603. For discussions, see HWR Wade 'What has Happened to Parliamentary Sovereignty' [1991] 107 LQR 1 and P Allott 'Parliamentary Sovereignty—From Austin to Hart' [1990] 49 CLJ 377.
[2] The *Emmott* case has subsequently been confined to its particular facts, see further para 9.71, below. Compare *Ministere Public et Direction du Travail v Levy* [1994] IRLR 139.

9.55 In the UK this result is effected by the European Communities Act 1972, s 2(4), by which 'any enactment passed or to be passed ... shall be construed and have effect subject to [obligations and rights] under or by virtue of the Treaties'. In *Factortame Ltd v Secretary of State for Transport* [1990] 2 AC 85, HL, Lord Bridge, at 140, made clear that the effect of this section was that directly enforceable rights prevail over conflicting provisions of national law. The surrender of Parliamentary sovereignty which this entails was also explicitly recognised by Hoffmann J in *Stoke-on-Trent City Council v B and Q plc* [1990] 3 CMLR 31.[1]

[1]   See D Oliver 'Fishing with the Incoming Tide' (1991) 54 MLR 442. In this context the rule that the courts cannot overrule an Act of Parliament (*British Railways Board v Pickin* [1974] AC 765) has gone. In *R v Secretary of State for Employment, ex p Seymour-Smith* [1995] IRLR 464, CA a discriminatory qualifying period for unfair dismissal established by statutory instrument was overridden; decided differently in the House of Lords: [2000] IRLR 263.

9.56 Where a Directive has been fully implemented (with adequate remedies) into United Kingdom law a claimant can simply rely on the provisions of the implementing regulations, without specific reference to the European provisions. However, it is important to recognise that the adoption of national measures correctly implementing a Directive does not exhaust the full effects of the Directive. Member States remain bound to ensure the full application of the Directive even after the adoption of such measures, including in circumstances where a Directive has been correctly implemented but the national provisions are not being applied in such a manner as to achieve the results required by the Directive.[1]

[1]   See Case C-62/00 *Marks & Spencer plc v Commissioners of Customs and Excise* [2002] ECR I-6325.

9.57 The principles upon which it is determined whether such European legislation has direct effect are broadly the same, whatever the source of that law. In particular, the provision concerned must be sufficiently precise and unconditional so as to be capable of granting rights to an individual claimant. In the case of the provisions of a Directive, a further condition must be met: the action must be against an 'emanation of the State'. Each of these conditions is considered below. A claimant cannot bring an action until the date for implementation has passed: see *Becker v Finanzamt Münster-Innenstadt* [1982] ECR 53.

An emanation of the State

9.58 The principal reason why directly effective provisions of Directives should be enforceable only against an emanation of the State is estoppel—the State should not be permitted to rely on its own breach of European law.[1] Direct effect has also been justified on the ground that it ensures that the effectiveness of Directives is not diminished.[2] Although at one time it appeared that the ECJ might seek to give Directives 'horizontal effect'—that is, to permit their provisions to be enforced against private persons—it has since retreated from that position and required that the defendant is a State body:

see *Marshall v Southampton and South West Hampshire Area Health Authority (Teaching)* [1986] QB 401; *Officier Van Justitie v Kolpinghuis Nijmegen BV* [1987] ECR 3969 and *Faccini Dori v Recreb Srl* [1995] All ER (EC) 1.[3] Consistent with the effectiveness approach, the ECJ has adopted a broad view of what are State bodies.

1   See *Pubblico Ministero v Ratti* 148/78 [1979] ECR 1629; *Marshall* above.
2   See *Foster v British Gas plc* [1991] 1 QB 405 at 427, para 16 and the Advocate General at 411–413.
3   The previous uncertainty, illustrated by the statement of the ECJ in *Habermann-Beltermann v Arbeiterwohlfahrt, Bezirksverband Ndb/Opf eV* [1994] ECR I-1657, that it had 'not *so far* held that Directives have direct horizontal effect' [emphasis added], has effectively been resolved by *Faccini Dori v Recreb,* above; for discussion of this case, see N Bernard (1995) 24 ILJ 97. More recently, see Joined Cases C-397/01–403/01 *Pfeiffer v Deutsches Rotes Kreuz, Kreisverband Waldshut eV* [2004] ECR I-8835. See also Case C-201/02 *R (on the application of Wells) v Secretary of State for Transport, Local Government and the Regions* [2004] ECR I-723, paras 56–57 where the ECJ drew a distinction between cases where there was an entitlement to rely on a directly effective right (with potential adverse consequences on individual third parties) and a triangular situation where reliance on direct effect against an emanation of the State would affect a State obligation directly linked to the performance of another obligation falling pursuant to the Directive on another third party which would be contrary to legal certainty.

9.59   To ensure uniformity, whether or not a body is part of the State (often described as 'an emanation of the State') is determined in accordance with principles of European law, although these principles are to be applied by the national court to the particular body before it.[1] In accordance with the view that direct effect is aimed at ensuring the effectiveness of Directives (and in tension with the 'estoppel' justification), emanations of the State are not confined to those bodies which themselves decide whether to implement Directives. Rather, the State should be prevented from obtaining any advantage from its non-implementation of European law, so catching any body charged with a public function or under the control of the State.[2]

1   See *Foster v British Gas* [1991] 1 QB 405, ECJ, at 426, para 15.
2   See the Advocate General at 421–424 and Lord Templeman [1991] 2 AC 306 at 315, HL.

9.60   In the leading case of *Foster v British Gas plc* [1991] ICR 84, the ECJ held as follows:

'... the court has held in a series of cases that unconditional and sufficiently precise provisions of a Directive could be relied on against organisations or bodies which were subject to the authority or control of the state or had special powers beyond those which result from the normal rules applicable to relations between individuals. (para 18)

A body, whatever its legal form, which has been made responsible, pursuant to a measure adopted by the State, for providing a public service under the control of the State and has for that purpose special powers beyond those which result from the normal rules applicable in relations between individuals. (para 20)

The answer to the question referred by the House of Lords must therefore be that article 5(1) of Council Directive of 9 February 1976 (76/207/EEC) may be relied upon in a claim for damages against a body, whatever its legal form, which has been made responsible, pursuant to a measure adopted by the state, for providing a public service under the control of the state and has for that purpose special powers beyond those which result from the normal rules applicable in relations between individuals.' (para 22)

When the case returned to the UK courts, the House of Lords, applying the test, was in no doubt that prior to privatisation British Gas was an emanation of the State: *Foster v British Gas plc* [1991] 2 AC 306.

9.61 Other bodies which have been found to be emanations of the State against which directly effective rights may be relied include a constitutionally independent police authority responsible for public order and safety;[1] public health bodies;[2] local or regional authorities;[3] tax authorities;[4] a nationalised corporation under State control;[5] a privatised water company: *Griffin v South West Water Services Ltd* [1995] IRLR 15; the governing body of a voluntary aided school: *NUT v St Mary's Church of England (Aided) Junior School (Governing Body)* [1997] IRLR 242.[6]

1   *Johnston v Chief Constable of the Royal Ulster Constabulary* [1987] ICR 83.
2   *Marshall v Southampton and South West Area Health Authority* [1986] QB 401, ECJ.
3   *Fratelli Costanzo SpA v Comune di Milano* [1990] 3 CMLR 239, ECJ, also Case C-187/00 *Kutz-Bauer v Freie und Hansestadt Hamburg* [2003] ECR I-2741. In Case C-411/96 *Boyle v EOC* [1998] ECR I-6401, it was conceded that the EOC was an emanation of the State.
4   *Becker v Finanzamt Münster-Innenstadt* [1982] ECR 53, ECJ.
5   See *Foster; R v British Coal Corpn, ex p Vardy* [1993] IRLR 104; and more recently Case C-343/98 *Collino and Chiappero v Telecom Italia Spa* [2000] ECR I-6659; Case C-157/02 *Rieser Internationale Transporte GmbH v Autobahnen-und Schnellstrassen-Finanzierung-AG (Asfinag)* [2004] ECR I-1477.
6   Such bodies are, in UK law, akin to those bodies against which judicial review will be granted, although the latter is a wider category: see *Council of Civil Service Unions v Minister for Civil Service* [1985] AC 374 at 409; *R v Panel on Takeovers and Mergers, ex p Datafin* [1987] QB 815, CA.

9.62 The Advocate General in *Foster* considered that the concept of public service was broader than the 'classic' functions of security,[1] and this is implicit in the judgment of the House of Lords in *Foster*, since it was concerned with the supply of gas. In relation to the question of control, the Advocate General in *Foster* spoke of any capability of exercising decisive influence over the body, other than by general legislation ([1991] 1 QB 405 at 422–423) and the House of Lords rejected a narrow construction to control ([1991] 2 AC 306 at 315). On this approach, regulatory control, shareholder control or board control should suffice; even the potential to exercise de facto control through contractual influence may meet the test.[2]

1   [1991] 1 QB 405 at 416 where he stated that *Marshall and Johnston* showed that 'any public body charged with functions by the State' was caught.
2   Day-to-day control appears unnecessary: see *Griffin v South West Water Services Ltd* [1995] IRLR 15; also the NUT case, described below.

9.63 The decision of the ECJ in *Foster* is not without some uncertainty. First, it is not clear whether a body must meet all three criteria or only one to be an emanation of the State. Having stated that direct effect applied against bodies subject to State control *or* which had special powers, the court then simply went on to rule that a body with both features (like British Gas) must be an emanation of the State. The view of the Advocate General was that either bodies exercising authority over individuals *or* those subject to decisive influence by the State were State bodies: [1991] 1 QB 405 at 415–416. That view was, however, rejected by the Court of Appeal in *Doughty v Rolls-Royce plc* [1992] ICR 538, perhaps in part because Mustill LJ treated the matter as principally based on estoppel, contrary to the broader basis advanced above.

9.64 Purporting to apply *Foster,* the Court of Appeal excluded a State-owned corporation in *Doughty v Rolls Royce plc* [1992] ICR 538 on the grounds that the 'service' was provided to the State and not the public and because the body did not have special powers. In *Griffin v South West Water*, above, however, a privatised water company was found to be an emanation of the State. Blackburne J considered that it was sufficient that the service, rather than the company management, was under State control. In *NUT v St Mary's Church of England (Aided) Junior School,* [1997] IRLR 242, the Court of Appeal held that it was wrong to apply the tri-partite test in *Foster* as if it was a statutory definition of an emanation of the State. The court applied a broad definition to what constituted a public service, stating that the doctrine of direct effect applied to any public body charged with a particular duty by the Member State from which it derives its authority. It is arguable that the decision of the ECJ in *Kampelmann v Landschaftsverband Westfalen-Lippe* [1998] IRLR 333[1] gives renewed recognition to the 'alternative' rather than 'cumulative' test, and that *Doughty v Rolls-Royce* is inconsistent with it.[2]

[1] The ECJ repeated its formulation of the test from Kampelmann, without determining the issue, in Case C-196/02 *Nikoloudi v Orgsnismos Tilepikonion Ellados AE* [2005] ECR I-1789.
[2] For recent examples of private companies subject to State control, see the cases of *Collino and Chiappero* and *Rieser Internationale Transporte* above.

Unconditional and sufficiently precise

9.65 The second set of requirements concern what provisions of Directives can be directly enforced: each article must be examined individually, so that if its terms are insufficiently precise, or if the terms are conditional or leave too great a discretion to the Member State,[1] no action will lie: see *Van Duyn v Home Office (No 2)* [1974] ECR 1337. Even if some parts of a Directive are too imprecise to be directly effective, other articles may nonetheless give rise to individual rights: *see Johnston v Chief Constable of the Royal Ulster Constabulary* [1987] ICR 83. In *Francovich v Italy* [1992] IRLR 84, the ECJ ruled that the beneficiaries of the rights must be clearly identifiable, the persons subject to the obligation should be ascertainable and the content of the rights must be unconditional and sufficiently precise.[2] In the context of health and safety Directives, it is generally plain that the obligations are imposed on employers (or other defined bodies) for the benefit of employees (or other workers). While the duties in the Directives are for the most part confined to workers who are employed (see art 3(a) of the Framework Directive, defining 'worker'), it is likely that under European law this would extend to cover workers not technically employees under English law, such as Crown servants (note on this the HSWA 1974, s 48(3)). Only public servants whose duties *inevitably* conflict with the standards of the Directives appear to be excluded (see art 2 of the Framework Directive).

¹   Ignoring the general discretion implicit in all Directives as to what methods a Member State may use to pass implementing legislation.
²   For useful discussions of this case, see E Szyszczak (1992) 55 MLR 690 and D Curtin (1992) 21 ILJ 76.

9.66 The principal area of doubt is whether the rights given by particular articles are sufficiently clear. In *Francovich,* the ECJ accepted that a provision is not prevented from being directly effective despite considerable uncertainty as to the nature of the right. That case concerned a provision in a Directive (80/987/EEC) protecting employees' rights in an insolvency. Member States were required to guarantee payment of the employees' claims in these circumstances. Despite a discretion as to the length of the period for which such claims should be guaranteed and as to the amount of overall loss to be guaranteed, the ECJ decided that multiple options to achieve the result of a Directive did not preclude direct effect; deriving a 'minimum guarantee' was sufficient.¹ Reflecting the same generous approach, in *Faccini Dori v Recreb Srl* [1995] All ER (EC) 1, the failure to specify the legal consequences of cancelling a consumer contract under Directive 85/577/EEC did not prevent direct effect.² On the other hand, in *Griffin v South West Water Services Ltd* [1995] IRLR 15 Blackburne J considered that the obligation to consult workers representatives 'provided for by the laws or practices of Member States' was insufficiently precise, although the practice was ascertainable.

¹   See too *McDermott and Cotter v Minister for Social Welfare* [1987] ECR 1453 and *R v Secretary of State for the Home Department, ex p Flynn* [1997] 3 CMLR 888, CA. In *Francovich* the provision was not directly effective because the guaranteeing institution could not be ascertained from the Directive; this particular discretion meant the obligation was not unconditional, which was followed in *Wagner Miret v Fondo de Garanata Salaridl* [1993] ECR I-6911, and the English case of *Mighell v Reading and MIB* [1999] PIQR P 101. See also *Gibson v East Riding of Yorkshire Council* [2000] IRLR 598, CA, where a provision of the Working Time Directive was held not to have direct effect.
²   The Advocate General thought differently.

9.67 Consistent with *Francovich,* the majority of provisions in the various Directives which protect workers' health and safety should be directly effective. Even many of the more general duties contained in the Framework Directive are sufficiently precise: for instance, the duty to conduct a risk assessment. Less clear is whether the general duty to 'ensure the health and safety of workers in every aspect relating to work' (art 5) is directly effective. Probably the more concrete provisions which specify how that duty is to be met—by implementing measures on the basis of a clearly defined strategy—should give rise to directly effective rights (see art 6).

Procedures and remedies

9.68 Although Directives do not themselves provide for enforcement, this being a matter for the national implementing law, European law requires that any national law which provides a remedy must give 'effective legal protection' for the beneficiaries of directly effective rights: see *Von Colson and*

Kamman v Land Nordhein- Westfalen [1984] ECR 1891. This encompasses both procedure and remedies. In *Rewe Handelsgesellschaft Nord mbH v Hauptzollamt Kiel* [1981] ECR 1805 the ECJ stated that:

> '... it must be possible for every type of action provided by national law to be available before the national courts for the purpose of ensuring observance of Community provisions having direct effect, on the same conditions concerning enforceability and procedure as would apply were it a question of ensuring observance of national law.'

9.69 In *Amministrazione delle Finanze dello Stato v San Giorgio SpA* [1983] ECR 3595, the ECJ stated (at 3612, para 12) that:

> '... conditions both as to substance and form laid down by the various national laws ... may not be less favourable than those relating to similar claims regarding national laws and they must not be framed so as to render virtually impossible the exercise of rights conferred by national law.'

9.70 Hence, national rules of procedure must not make 'it impossible in practice to exercise the rights which the national courts have a duty to enforce': *Comet BV v Produktschap voor Siergewassen* [1976] ECR 2043. Member States must:

> '... fulfil their obligations under Community Directives and may not plead provisions practices or circumstances existing in their internal legal systems, in order to justify a failure to comply with those obligations'.[1]

1 *EC Commission v Belgium* [1985] 3 CMLR 624 at para 25.

9.71 The ECJ held in *Emmott v Minister for Social Welfare* [1993] ICR 8, that a Member State cannot rely on the expiry of national limitation periods until such time as a Directive has been properly implemented in national law. Nor could a Member State rely on a national rule, restricting unjust enrichment, to deprive an individual of her European rights: *Cotter and McDermott v Minister for Social Welfare and A-G* [1991] IRLR 380, ECJ. But more recent decisions have accorded Member States a greater liberty to use procedural devices to limit liability, and the ECJ may be seen to have stepped back from the significant consequences that the *Emmott* case could have created in practice. *Steenhorst-Neerings v Bestuur Van de Bedrijvereniging voor Detailhandel, Ambachten en Huisvrauwen* [1994] IRLR 244 concerned the failure to implement a Directive by 1984; a woman, in 1988, claimed benefits to which she would have been entitled from that date if the Directive had been correctly implemented. The ECJ, distinguishing *Emmott*, said that it was permissible to have a rule limiting recovery of social security benefits to a period of one year before the date of the claim (ie back to 1987 only): unlike rules on time limits, this rule merely limited the retroactive effect of claims. This is a rather nice distinction,[1] however: the effect of the ruling was to permit the State to gain advantage from its own non-implementation of the Directive. The same approach is illustrated by *Johnson v Chief Adjudication Officer (No 2)* [1995] ICR 375, ECJ (national law limiting period for which benefit payable permissible, provided that limit was no less favourable than that applicable to similar domestic actions). In *Fantask A/S v Industriminis-teriet (Erhvervsministeriet)* [1997] ECR I-6783 the ECJ confined the effect of *Emmott* to the particular circumstances of the case. Advocate General Jacobs considered that the consequences of *Emmott* should be restricted to cases where the Member State has both failed to implement a Directive and in some other way has obstructed exercise of a judicial remedy or in some other way has contributed to the delay in the individual bringing a claim.[2]

1   A distinction which Ward LJ found 'difficult to grasp' in *Walker-Fox v Secretary of State for Work and Pensions* [2005] EWCA Civ 1441, at para 29.
2   See para 87 of the opinion, followed and applied by the Court of Appeal in *Walker-Fox v Secretary of State for Work and Pensions* [2005] EWCA Civ 1441, at para 36.

9.72 Few Directives specify the remedies for breach, with the consequence that remedies themselves are rarely directly effective.[1] At one time the ECJ asserted that while every type of action provided by national law must be available to protect directly effective rights, the national court was not obliged to create new remedies: *Rewe Handselsgesellschaft Nord mbHv Hauptzollamt Kiel* [1981] ECR 1805. That position soon came under challenge. Subsequent cases emphasised the overriding requirement for national laws to provide effective and adequate remedies: see *Von Colson and Kamann v Land Nordrhein-Westfalen* [1984] ECR 1891.[2] In *EC Commission v Greece* [1989] ECR 2965 the ECJ said that, in order to comply with art 10 (ex art 5) EC, remedies for breach of European law must be, first, effective, in the sense of being a real deterrent; second, proportionate to the seriousness of the harm (and therefore adequate); and, third, at least comparable to the sanctions imposed for infringements of similar provisions of national law. This overriding obligation to impose effective and adequate sanctions has been emphasised in other cases, most notably in *Factortame* (below). In *EC Commission v United Kingdom* [1994] ICR 664, the ECJ held that a ceiling of two or four weeks' wages on compensation for failure to consult on redundancies was an inadequate remedy. It stressed that sanctions for breach of a Directive must '*in any* event make the penalty effective, proportionate and dissuasive'.[3]

1   Cf *Johnston v Chief Constable Chief Constable of Royal Ulster Constabulary* [1987] ICR 83.
2   In that case trivial compensation was held to be an inadequate remedy for breach of the Equal Treatment Directive. In *Francovich* the Advocate General said that the national court must create an appropriate national remedy if one does not exist.
3   See too *Belgium v Vandevenee* [1991] ECR I-4371; *Anklagemyndigheden v Hansen & Son I/S* [1992] ICR 277 at 286.

9.73 This may involve ignoring national restrictions or limitations on the sanctions which are available. Stating that the courts 'must ensure the legal protection which persons derive from direct effect', in *R v Secretary of State for Transport, ex p Factortame* [1991] 1 AC 603 the ECJ ruled that an injunction could be granted against the Crown to ensure the effective enforcement of European rights, although no such remedy would be available for the infringement of similar provisions of national law.[1] Similarly, in *Marshall v Southampton and South West Hampshire Area Health Authority (No 2)* [1993] IRLR 445 the ECJ ruled that if compensation is the chosen remedy, that must make full reparation for the loss and damage sustained through the infringement.² Hence employment tribunals could not confine themselves to the statutory limit on damages for sex discrimination. It also held that full compensation must include interest.³

1   On the return of the case, the House of Lords accepted this duty: see [1991] 1 AC 603. But cf *Bourgoin SA v Ministry of Agriculture, Fisheries and Food* [1986] QB 716, doubted in *Kirklees Metropolitan Borough Council v Wickes Building Supplies* [1993] AC 227, HL.
2   Cf *Steenhorst-Neerings* para 9.71, above.
3   In case C-63/01 *Evans v Secretary of State for the Environment, Transport and the Regions* [2003] ECR I-14447, the ECJ held that compensation awarded to road traffic accident victims who had suffered injuries caused by unidentified or uninsured vehicles must take account of the effluxion of time before payment of compensation is made, whether by way of the payment of interest or in the calculation of any lump sum; but that the reimbursement of costs was not required except to the extent to which such reimbursement is necessary to safeguard the rights of victims in conformity with the principles of effectiveness and equivalence.

9.74 Some ECJ decisions have displayed something of a retreat from this position, however. The ECJ has allowed Member States to rely on procedural rules effectively to override the requirement of effective sanctions, preferring an approach based on similarity of treatment to like provisions of national law: see *Steenhorst-Neerings* and *Johnson* in para 9.71, above; and *Fisscher v Voorhuis Hengelo BV* [1994] ECR I-4583.

9.75 A ruling from the ECJ illustrates the fine distinctions it draws in relation to questions of effectiveness and non-discrimination in relation to the availability of parallel remedies. *Preston v Wolverhampton Healthcare NHS Trust* [2000] ICR 961 was one of the lead cases in relation to various claims brought by women part-time workers who had been excluded from participating in occupational pension schemes and who sought to exercise their rights to equal pay under art 141 (ex art 119) EC. Several questions had been referred to the ECJ by the House of Lords in relation to national procedural rules which provided for: (1) a limitation period of six months within which proceedings were to be brought; (2) a limit of two years from the date proceedings were brought upon the exercise of the right to equal pension provision. The ECJ cited its now extensive case law on the procedural autonomy of the Member States, subject to the application of the two principles of EC law, namely the principle of equivalence and the principle of effectiveness. The ECJ held that a limitation period of six months did not in principle breach the principle of effectiveness. The ECJ did hold, however, following an earlier case *of Magorrian v Eastern Health and Social Services Board* [1998] ICR 979, that the two year limit contravened the principle of effectiveness. In relation to the issue of the application of the principle of equivalence, or non-discrimination, the ECJ ruled, following an earlier case of *Levez v TH Jennings (Harlow Pools) Ltd* C-326/96 [1998] ECR I-7835 that the national court must take into consideration both the purpose and the essential characteristics of similar domestic actions. The principle of equivalence would be breached where a claimant incurred greater costs or suffered delay in comparison with equivalent domestic causes of action. In conducting such an examination it was necessary objectively and in the abstract to examine any procedural rules as a whole and in their general context, taking into account the operation of the procedure and any special features.

9.76 However, in the recent Case C-537/03 *Candolin v Vahinkovakuutuso-sakeyntio Pohiola* [2005] All ER (D) 375 (Jun), the ECJ held that the ruling of a national court refusing an award of compensation to a drunk passenger injured in a vehicle driven by a drunk driver was contrary to the motor insurance Directives. Although European law did not harmonise national law in relation to claims for personal injury damages, the ECJ held that the autonomy of the national courts to award damages to persons injured in road traffic accidents was constrained by the Directives providing for the provision of compulsory motor insurance so as to preclude the limitation of the right to receive compensation in a disproportionate manner.

9.77 In the case of a worker injured through breach of a directly effective provision in a health and safety Directive, the action would probably resemble one for breach of statutory duty.[1] Compensation in damages on a tortious basis would usually be adequate for the damage sustained, in accordance with *Von Colson* and *Marshall (No 2)* (paras 9.72 and 9.73, above).

[1]   The House of Lords so ruled in relation to infringement of European competition law, in that case a breach of art 86 of the Treaty: *Garden Cottage Foods Ltd v Milk Marketing Board* [1984] AC 130. Cf *Bourgoin SA v Ministry of Agriculture, Fisheries and Food*, above, doubted in *Kirklees*, above.

9.78 But in some cases it may be necessary for courts to grant *other* kinds of remedy: *R v Secretary of State for Transport, ex p Factortame* confirmed that injunctions should be available in principle to enforce Community rights, and interlocutory injunctions to restrain a breach of the Treaty were granted in *Garden Cottage Foods Ltd v Milk Marketing Board* [1984] AC 130, above, and in *Cutsforth v Mansfield Inns Ltd* [1986] 1 WLR 558.

Francovich action

9.79 National law may not be capable of interpretation so as to give effect to European law, and an individual may be unable to rely on the corresponding provision of the Directive under the doctrine of direct effect, for example because the defendant is not an emanation of the State. Nevertheless, an individual who suffers damage as a result of the incorrect implementation of Community law, or the failure to implement altogether, may nonetheless have a claim in damages against the State for breach of European law. The leading case where this principle was first recognised is *Francovich and Bonifaci v Italy* [1992] IRLR 84 where Italy was sued for a total failure to implement Directive 80/987 relating to the protection of employees in the event of insolvency into national law.[1] Three requirements must be met in order to establish liability. First, the rule of European law which has been breached must have been intended to confer rights on individuals, although the provision concerned need not itself be directly effective. Second, the breach must be sufficiently serious. Third, the failure to implement the Directive must cause the loss to the individual.

[1]   For a discussion see E Szyszczak (1992) 55 MLR 690.

9.80 The seriousness of the breach will depend on the nature of the breach of EC law. In the case of Directives, a Member State has a limited margin of discretion in exercising any legislative function, since under art 249 (ex art 189) EC there is an obligation to take all necessary measures within a given period to achieve the result required. A failure to take any implementing measures within the time prescribed constitutes a serious breach of EC law: *Dillenkofer v Germany* [1997] QB 259. Where, on the other hand, the Member State wrongly implements a Directive, the State will be liable in damages where it has manifestly and gravely disregarded the limits on the exercise of its powers: *Brasserie du Pecheur v Germany; ex p Factortame* [1996] QB 404.[1] Where the State commits an error which is not manifestly wrong when implementing a Directive into national law, this is insufficient in itself to constitute a serious breach: *R v HM Treasury, ex p British Telecommunications plc* [1996] QB 615. If a State, however, implements provisions contrary to a Directive, such conduct is likely to be a serious breach: *Rechberger v Austria* [2000] 2 CMLR 1. When assessing whether a breach is sufficiently serious, a national court before which the claim for damages is brought shall take into account all the circumstances of the case, including the clarity and precision of the rule infringed, whether the infringement and the damage caused was intentional or involuntary, whether any error of law was excusable or inexcusable, and the fact that the position taken by a Community institution may have contributed towards the adoption or maintenance of national measures or practices contrary to European law: see Case C-424/97 *Haim v Kassenzahnarztliche Vereinigung Nordrhein* [2000] ECR I-5123. A breach is likely to be sufficiently serious where there is a failure to take into account the established case law of the ECJ. In this respect, the courts may be found to have committed a sufficiently serious breach of European law to found a claim for damages: see Case C-224/01 *Kobler v Austria* [2003] ECR I-10239.

[1]   Applied in *R v Secretary of State for Transport, ex p Factortame (No 5)* [2000] 1 AC 524.
       See also *R v Attorney General for Northern Ireland, ex p Burns* [1999] IRLR 315.

References under art 234 EC

9.81 To determine the meaning of European law is often a difficult exercise, depending on policy implications and subject to the different language versions of the legislation. Yet to guarantee uniformity throughout Member States, the different national courts must apply the same EU law. To this end, as well as giving the ECJ jurisdiction to decide on the meaning of European law, the EC Treaty also contains a mechanism by which it is able to give preliminary rulings when such questions are relevant to proceedings before national courts. Article 234 (ex art 177) EC states:

'The Court of Justice shall have jurisdiction to give preliminary rulings concerning:
(a)   the interpretation of this Treaty;
(b)   the validity and interpretation of acts of the institutions of the Community and of the ECJ;
(c)   the interpretation of the statutes of bodies established by an act of the Council, where those statutes so provide.

Where such a question is raised before any court or tribunal of a Member State, that court or tribunal may, if it considers that a decision on the question is necessary to enable it to give judgment, request the Court of Justice to give a ruling thereon.

Where any such question is raised in a case pending before a court or tribunal of a Member State against whose decisions there is no judicial remedy under national law, that court or tribunal shall bring the matter before the Court of Justice.'[1]

1   For fuller discussions of the art 234 procedure, see D Anderson *References to the European Court (2002)*; also F Jacobs and D Anderson in G Barling and M Brearley (eds) *Practitioners' Handbook of EC Law* (1998).

9.82 The jurisdiction to interpret the meaning of provisions of Directives, including whether these are directly effective, is found in art 234(b). The ECJ only rules on the legal meaning of the instrument; it does not apply that meaning to the facts: see *Kledingverkoopbedrijf De Geus en Vitdenbogerd v Robert Bosch GmbH* [1962] ECR 45. That latter task is left to the national court to which the proceedings are returned after the reference; but the ECJ ruling may effectively remove any discretion.

9.83 Article 234 draws a distinction between courts which may and those which must refer questions.[1] As to the latter, despite some ambiguity in the meaning of the phrase 'against whose decision there is no judicial remedy' in art 234, it seems that this phrase applies to the judgments of courts whose decisions can never be appealed: see *Costa v ENEL* [1964] ECR 585. The possibility of interlocutory proceedings being challenged in the subsequent trial of the issue means that at that stage there is no obligation to refer, although a national court may do so: *Hoffman-la Roche A-G v Centrafarm Vertriebsgesellschaft Pharmazeutischer Erzeugnisse mbH* [1977] ECR 957. Instead this is a matter of the general discretion courts have to refer questions even if they are not the final court in the proceedings under art 234. A court is not under an obligation to make a reference where the point has already been decided by the ECJ: *Da Costa en Schaake NV v Nederlandse Belastingadministratie* [1963] ECR 31. The same applies where the provision concerned is absolutely clear: *CILFIT Srl and Lanificio di Gavardo v Ministry of Health* [1982] ECR 3415, ECJ. No doubt prompted by awareness of the open-ended nature of texts—consider the difficult policy arguments which underlie interpretation—in *CILFIT*, the ECJ stated that it applies only where the law is 'so obvious as to leave no scope for reasonable doubt' for the court of any Member State. The House of Lords has applied a similar test: see *Henn and Darby v DPP* [1981] AC 850.

1   Whether a particular body is a 'court' is a matter of EU law: *Politi v Ministero delle Finanze* [1971] ECR 1039. A wide interpretation has been given to this term, catching many administrative tribunals: see eg *Vassen nee Gobbels v Management of the Beambtenfonds voor het Mijnbedriff* 61/65 [1966] ECR 261.

9.84 References may also be made by a court whose judgment can be appealed. English courts and tribunals are displaying a greater readiness to refer questions under this general discretion, despite the inevitable delay: see

R v International Stock Exchange of the United Kingdom and the Republic of Ireland, ex p Else (1982) Ltd [1993] QB 534, CA, in which Sir Thomas Bingham MR said that the matter should be referred unless the UK court could 'with complete confidence resolve the issue itself',[1] bearing in mind the difficulties of interpreting European law (described above). Ordinarily the court will decide the facts of the case first: see *Bulmer (HP) Ltd v Bollinger SA* [1974] Ch 401; *R v International Stock Exchange, ex p Else* [1993] QB 534. But that is only a matter to take into consideration, and it should be weighed against others, including the saving of costs and the wishes of the parties (see the guidelines of Lord Denning MR in *Bulmer,* above). Even where the point has already been decided by the ECJ in another judgment, a national court may in principle still refer a question under this discretion, since the ECJ may depart from its earlier rulings (see Lord Denning in *Bulmer* at 422–423).

[1] Compare the previous restrictive approach of *Bulmer v Bollinger,* above. See too *Society of Lloyds v Clements* (1994) Times, 16 November and D Walsh 'The Appeal of an Article 234 Referral' (1993) 56 MLR 881.

9.85 Whether a court may or must refer, in either case a reference can only be made if the question arises in proceedings before a national court and a decision on European law is 'necessary' for the judgment in the sense that it effectively should decide an issue in the proceedings.[1]

[1] Lord Denning in *Bulmer,* above, at 422. See too *Wellcome Foundation Ltd v Secretary of State for Social Services* [1988] 1 WLR 635, HL.

9.86 An art 234 reference may be made at any stage of proceedings, including in interlocutory proceedings. In *R v Secretary for Transport, ex p Factortame (No 2)* [1991] 1 AC 603, Spanish fishermen applied for an injunction against the Crown, requiring it to disapply national legislation, pending resolution by the ECJ of whether UK legislation on fishing quotas contravened Community law. The ECJ ruled that interim relief must be available in these circumstances, even those rights the existence or extent of which remains to be determined by the ECJ:

'... the full effectiveness of Community law would be just as much impaired if a rule of national law could prevent a court ... from granting interim relief in order to ensure the full effectiveness of a judgement to be given on the existence of rights claimed under Community law.'[1]

[1] At 644.

9.87 Interim relief can, therefore, take the radical step of disapplying the effect of national legislation or other national rules of law (such as the rule preventing injunctive relief against the Crown).

9.88 The granting of interim relief does not automatically follow from the referral of a question under art 234. In the context of applications to disapply legislation, the applicant must show a 'firmly based' case that the national legislation is in conflict with Community law.[1] After that threshold is overcome (and in other cases not dependent upon overruling existing national law), a similar test is applied as on the grant of interlocutory injunctions (usually *American Cyanamid Co v Ethicon Ltd* [1975] AC 396).[2] Following the decision of the ECJ, the House of Lords in *Factortame (No 2)* did grant an injunction against the Crown: Lord Goff, first, considered whether damages would be an adequate remedy to either party and, second, where the balance of convenience lay. The irrecoverable damage to the Spanish fishing fleet outweighed the competing loss to the UK fleet.[3] The ECJ has adopted a similar approach to applications for interim relief: see *Zuckerfabrik Suderdithmarschen A-G v Hauptzouamt Itzehoe* [1991] ECR I-415. However, the ECJ has no jurisdiction to rule on applications for interim relief in respect of national proceedings where a reference for a preliminary ruling is made under art 234 EC.[4]

[1]   Lord Goff in *Factortame (No 2)*, above, and *R v HM Treasury, ex p British Telecommunications plc* [1994] 1 CMLR 621.

[2]   For an earlier example of granting an interim injunction, see *EMI Records Ltd v CBS United Kingdom Ltd* [1975] 1 CMLR 285.

[3]   These criteria may not be particularly apt for the public issues at stake: the 'balance of convenience' test may not take sufficient account of those persons, like the UK fishermen, who may suffer loss by reason of the injunction yet do not have directly effective rights to compensation: see D Oliver 'Fishing with the Incoming Tide' (1991) 54 MLR 442.

[4]   See for example the order in Case C-186/01 *Dory v Bundesrepublik Deutschland* [2001] ECR I-7823.

Chapter 10

THE GENERAL LEGISLATION: THE FRAMEWORK DIRECTIVE, THE TEMPORARY WORKERS DIRECTIVES, THE MANAGEMENT OF HEALTH AND SAFETY AT WORK REGULATIONS AND WORKING TIME

Barry Cotter

Damian Brown

GENERAL

10.01 The Management of Health and Safety at Work Regulations 1999, SI 1999/3242, replaced and revoked the Management of Health and Safety at Work Regulations 1992, which were primarily intended to implement many of the provisions of the Framework Directive 98/391 (and also sought to implement two further Directives: 92/85 on the health and safety of pregnant workers and 94/33 on the protection of young people at work). They marked the beginning of a new regime in UK health and safety law, based on European Directives rather than domestic legislation. The central characteristic of the new European approach was the emergence of general duties applicable to all employers but which, unlike the very general duties in the HSWA 1974, ss 1–3, also set out relatively specific procedures to eliminate or reduce risks. These duties have been amplified in the other Directives and regulations considered in this book.

10.02 The Management of Health and Safety at Work and Fire Precautions (Workplace) (Amendment Regulations) 2003 (in force from 27 October 2003) introduced a very significant change to the 1999 Regulations in that they removed the majority of the exclusion for civil liability previously contained at reg 22 of the 1999 Regulations (there remains potential criminal liability for breach of the regulations). The amended reg 22 now states:

'Breach of a duty imposed on an employer by these Regulations shall not confer a right of action in any civil proceedings insofar as that duty applies for the protection of persons not in his employment.'

Hence the amendment still prevents third parties from instituting a civil action for damages against employers.

10.03 The 1999 Regulations were made in part by exercise of the powers under the Health and Safety at Work Act 1974, s 15 and when interpreted this should be taken into account. Further, whilst the regulations have replaced the duties specific to certain kinds of workplace in the Factories Act and the like, they do not detract from the common law duties set out in chapter 4 above.

THE FRAMEWORK DIRECTIVE

10.04 The regulations owe their origin to the Framework Directive (89/391/EEC), which also provided the basis for other, more specific, 'daughter' Directives; it also sets out the broad principles which influence how those Directives should be interpreted. The underlying philosophy of the Directive is of creating uniform levels of health and safety protection throughout Member States, so ensuring that competition does not take place at the expense of worker protection. But this process, to be implemented through domestic legislation (see art 4(2)), is not intended to affect those Member States with a higher level of protection than that guaranteed by the Directive (see art 1(3)). The envisaged result is of levelling upwards (see Preamble, and arts 1(1), 6(3)(a) which make clear that within the enterprise standards should improve). The same was an explicit goal of art 138 (ex art 118A) EC itself: 'Member States ... shall set as their objective the harmonisation of conditions in their area, while maintaining the improvements made'. This analysis, of levelling upwards, was supported in *Stark v Post Office* [2000] ICR 1013 at 1018–1019, CA. This underlying aim should be borne in mind whenever the individual provisions of other Directives are considered.

10.05 The Directive provides that all employers 'shall have a duty to ensure the safety and health of workers in every aspect related to work' (art 5(1)), and shall take all measures necessary to this end, which should be adjusted to take account of changing circumstances (art 6(1)). The definition of worker in art 3 includes all employees apart from domestic servants. The Directive excludes public service activities and civil protection activities, but only where their peculiar characteristics *inevitably* conflict with its provisions (art 2(2))—a narrow exception. The only (optional) qualifications to this apparently strict and extensive duty are:

> 'where occurrences are due to unusual or unforeseeable consequences beyond the employer's control, or to exceptional events, the consequences of which could not have been avoided despite the exercise of all due care'. (art 5(4))

Introducing a qualification of 'reasonably practicable' into implementing regulations may go beyond the scope of that exception.[1]

---
[1] See the Action brought by the Commission against the UK (Case C-127/05).

10.06 The duty on an employer is to 'take the measures necessary for the safety and health protection of workers' (art 6(1)). But art 6 goes further and sets out a general principle of preventative strategy, involving a hierarchy of measures. Thus, the primary aim should be to avoid risks altogether rather than reacting to existing risks, and unavoidable risks should be combated at source if possible (art 6(2)(a), (c)). As part of this strategy, the employer should evaluate the risks to workers, and this assessment should be in its possession (arts 6(3), 9).[1] Article 6(3)(a) requires employers to evaluate *all* risks, not just those on a specific list.[2] The preventative measures must ensure an improvement in the level of protection (art 6(3)). More specific duties include designating workers to assist in the prevention of and protection against risks (art 7); the introduction of measures to deal with fire and the evacuation of workers in the case of serious, imminent and unavoidable danger (art 8); and the provision to workers of information and training on health and safety matters (arts 10, 11). Where several undertakings share a workplace, they are under a duty to co-ordinate their activities in order to safeguard workers' health and safety (art 6(4)).

[1] See C-5/00 *Commission v Federal Republic of Germany* [2002] ECR 01305: Germany failed to fulfil its obligations under art 9.
[2] See C-49/00 *Commission v Italian Republic* [2001] ECR 08575.

10.07 Of great significance is the individual focus of the Directive. Most significantly, it states that work should be adapted to the individual, even regarding the choice of production methods (which should aim to avoid monotony or work at a pre-determined rate) (art 6(2)(d)). In addition, the individual's capabilities should be taken into consideration when tasks are entrusted to him or her (art 6(2)(d), (3)(b)).[1] Particularly sensitive groups of workers must be given special protection: art 15. This emphasis should be borne in mind when construing duties in the 'daughter' Directives and regulations meant to implement them.

[1] See C-302/03 *Commission v Republic of Austria* [2005] ECR 00935; prohibition of women workers in underground work; Directive 89/391 does not justify a breach of equal treatment.

10.08 Similarly important is the emphasis the Directive places on employee involvement in the sphere of health and safety: the Preamble refers to the need for developing 'information, dialogue and balanced participation on safety and health at work'. First, the employer is obliged to supply workers with information relating to the risks of work (see art 10) and this duty is not confined to its employees. Second, there are duties in relation to consultation. The employer is under a general duty to consult with workers or workers' representatives and to allow workers to take part in discussions 'on all questions relating to safety at work' (art 11). It must also consult with workers or their representatives on, among others, measures which may substantially affect safety and health (art 11(2)) and on the introduction of new technologies (art 6(3)(c)). An employer must appoint a competent person to assist in combating occupational risks (art 7).[1] Finally, workers' representatives must be allowed adequate time off with pay (art 11(4)). Worker consultation is discussed more fully in chapter 12 below, on industrial relations.

[1] This is a mandatory provision: see C-49/00 *Commission v Italian Republic* [2001] ECR 08575. While the standard of care under the Directive may be that of the competent person, that does not affect the standard under the common law, which remains that of the reasonable employer: *Cross v Highlands and Islands Enterprise* [2001] IRLR 336, OH at 352, paras 65 and 66.

THE TEMPORARY WORKERS DIRECTIVE

10.09 The 'daughter' Directives to which the Framework Directive gave birth, should also be read in the light of the Temporary Workers Directive 91/383 (full text in *Redgrave's Health and Safety* (4th edn) p 331). The Directive recognises the increased prevalence of temporary employment relationships and the vulnerability of such workers and seeks to ensure that temporary workers (as defined) receive the same level of health and safety protection as other workers. While it does lay down some concrete obligations of its own, its principal effect is on the application of the obligations in other Directives. All the obligations in the Framework and 'daughter' Directives are equally applicable to temporary workers (art 2(3)).

10.10 This Directive is of particular importance because, in numerous instances, the United Kingdom does not appear to have met its requirements in relation to temporary workers in its implementing regulations.[1] The United Kingdom has not passed legislation specifically implementing this Directive.[2] Hence, the obligations in each set of regulations implementing the 'daughter' Directives must be examined to see to what extent they do not comply with the Temporary Workers Directive. The consequences of non-compliance are complicated (see below).

[1]   See eg the Manual Handling Regulations 1992, which are confined to employees of the employer and the discussion of this issue below at para 21.22ff.
[2]   See now the very limited duties imposed under the Conduct of Employment Agencies and Employment Businesses Regulations 2003.

Workers covered

10.11 The Directive applies to employment relationships of a fixed duration and workers employed by an agency who work for another undertaking (see art 1). On its face, the Directive seems to be restricted to employees and not to extend to the self-employed. But it is possible that the Directive has in mind categories of worker wider than those defined in UK law as employees. Although the fixed duration category refers to workers whose relationship is governed by a 'contract of employment' (art 1(1)), if that was intended to be restricted to employees in a narrow sense it is hard to see why these workers would need to be referred to in the Directive at all. For they would, as employees, automatically be covered by all the Directives under which duties are owed to employees. It is accordingly suggested that the Directive may contemplate any workers who are employed, in the sense of 'used', under a contract of fixed duration. That interpretation would seem best to accord with its underlying purpose, of extending protection to vulnerable categories of worker: consider, for example, the prevalence of notional 'self-employment' in the building trade.

The duties

10.12 Article 2 sets out the broad underlying principle of the Temporary Workers Directive. Put simply, those workers to whom the Directive applies are to be afforded the same level of health and safety protection as other workers in the user undertaking (art 2(1), (2)), and the obligations in the Framework and 'daughter' Directives apply in full to them (art 2(3)). Presumably this means that the user undertaking must comply in full with those obligations.

10.13 The Directive goes on to set out more specific duties. The user undertaking must inform temporary workers of the risks they will face at work, including what qualifications or skills are needed (art 3). Those workers designated to protect against risks must be told of the presence of temporary workers. The user undertaking must tell the employer of agency workers of the qualifications needed for the job and the specific features of the job; the agency must pass this information on to its employees (art 7). Temporary workers must receive sufficient training for the job (art 4). It is not clear whether this obligation is to be imposed upon the user undertaking or, in the case of agency workers, the agency: Member States must take steps to ensure it is placed on one or the other, however. In relation to these requirements, the introduction of some limited duties under the Conduct of Employment Agencies and Employment Businesses Regulations 2003, SI 2003/3319 has merely begun the process of implementation.

THE MANAGEMENT OF HEALTH AND SAFETY AT WORK REGULATIONS 1999

10.14 The Management Regulations 1992 were intended largely to implement the Framework Directive in the United Kingdom. They were passed under the HSWA 1974, s 2(3), and were effective (in their original 1992 form) from 1 January 1993. In some cases it was considered that no amendments to the existing law were necessary.[1] The original 1992 Regulations were amended in 1994 to add risk assessment and suspension from work requirement in the case of women of child-bearing age and pregnant employees (to comply with the Pregnant Workers Directive 92/85/EC). Further amendments were made in 1997 to comply with the Protection of Young People at Work Directive 94/33/EC. They were then reissued in 1999 (SI 1999/3242), largely in similar form, but with the addition of a specific reference to the 'principles of prevention' in the Directive (reg 4), a requirement of contact with external services (reg 9) and a short but important provision increasing an employer's liability for the default of an employee (reg 21). The Management of Health and Safety at Work and Fire Precautions (Workplace) (Amendment) Regulations 2003, SI 2003/2457 (in force from 27 October 2003) then amended the 1999 Regulations including by way of the removal of the majority of the exclusion for civil liability.

[1] It seems, for example, that the Health and Safety (First-Aid) Regulations 1981, SI 1981/917 and duties on record-keeping in the Reporting of Injuries, Diseases and Dangerous Occurrences Regulations 1995, SI 1995/3163, were considered sufficient to meet the duties on first aid in art 8 and on reporting in art 9(1) of the Framework Directive.

The Code of Practice

10.15 The Regulations are accompanied by an Approved Code of Practice ('ACOP') and guidance. This Code is only specifically made admissible in criminal proceedings: see the HSWA 1974, s 17. Whilst the Approved Codes of Practice have no formal status in civil proceedings, courts will often give the ACOP significant consideration in considering the scope of the Regulations. The guidance notes, which accompany many of the new regulations, should have a similar effect, despite not falling within s 17. Where, on the other hand, a code or guidance note appears to treat a duty as being lower than that imposed by regulations or a Directive, the code cannot be relied upon to justify a breach.

The persons covered

10.16 The Management Regulations apply to all sectors of activity, except for ships.[1] The principal duties are those imposed on employers in respect of their employees; but duties are also owed by employers and the self-employed to employees of another who are working in the undertaking.

[1] See reg 2, as amended by SI 2003/2457, and the limitation of the exclusion to 'normal ship-board activities'.

The general duties on employers

10.17 Regulations 2–19 impose a range of duties on different persons. In keeping with all regulations under the HSWA 1974, a breach gives rise to the possibility of a criminal prosecution.

Risk assessment

10.18 Under reg 3, every employer must make a suitable and sufficient assessment of the risks to the health and safety of its employees to which they are exposed while at work. Where more specific regulations require a risk assessment, that will satisfy the employer's duty in respect of those particular risks. An assessment must also be made of the risks to other persons 'arising out of or in connection with the conduct by [the employer] of his undertaking'. What does amount to 'conduct of his undertaking' is likely to be determined in the same fashion as under the HSWA 1974, s 3, which does not require either actual control over the operations or a common law duty to exercise control: see *R v Associated Octel Co Ltd* [1997] IRLR 123, HL. Some explanation on 'suitable and sufficient' is provided in the ACOP (paras 9–26). Broadly, it requires a systematic examination of the workplace, examining the hazards present and the likelihood of their arising; the extent of this assessment will vary with the complexity of the operation.

10.19 The risk assessment is intended to identify the measures to be taken to comply with the employer's statutory duties (see reg 3). Because these duties include the very general ones to ensure the health, safety and welfare of employees and to minimise health and safety risks to others, the risk assessment should cover all risks other than the utterly trivial, taking account of relevant publications (see generally the guidance on risk assessment in the ACOP). By way of example, in *Bailey v Command Security Services Ltd* [2001] All ER (D) 352 (Oct), QBD at a time when there was no civil liability under the regulations, the defendant was held to be negligent in that it did not carry out any thorough risk assessment of the premises. If it had it would have recognised that the unguarded lift shaft posed a danger to its employees. The problems of the earlier exclusion of civil liability were amply highlighted in *Spencer v Boots the Chemist Ltd* [2002] EWCA Civ 1691 where the Court of Appeal held that a failure to undertake a risk assessment did not equate to, but was evidence of, a breach of the common law duty of care.[1] Thankfully the removal of the exclusion has made matters much more straightforward.

[1]   See also *Griffiths v Vauxhall Motors Ltd* [2003] EWCA Civ 412 and its discussion at para 20.19 below.

10.20 It should include, for example, risks of stress from the work. The duty should extend to consulting with employees as to how they actually perform tasks in practice and their perceptions or experience of risks; equally, advice from in-house or contracted experts, such as ergonomists, may well be necessary.[1] It is arguable that in keeping with the approach of the Directive, the assessment should take account of individual characteristics of employees.[2] The assessment should be kept under regular review in the light of changing knowledge or practice: see reg 3(3). There is a duty to record the risk assessment which, unlike the Directive, is limited to employers who employ five workers or more: reg 3(6).

[1]   See ACOP, paras 15–22.
[2]   Regulation 3 talks of a duty to record any 'group' of employees especially at risk, which does not seem to go quite as far. See reg 4 and Sch 1.

Preventive measures

10.21 The purpose of the assessment is to identify the measures an employer needs to take to comply with 'the relevant statutory provisions', which means, broadly, all health and safety duties, including those arising under these Regulations,[1] so as to protect against the risks. The Directive sets out a clear hierarchical approach to employer strategy, in particular requiring that work should be adapted to the individual as regards the very organisation of work itself (see art 6). This duty was missing from the original 1992 Regulations, appearing only in the ACOP accompanying them. However, reg 4 of the 1999 Regulations specifically states that where an employer implements any preventive and protective measures, he must do so on the basis of the 'principles of prevention' in art 6(2) of the Directive. These principles (set out in Sch 1 to the Regulations) are:

(a)   avoiding risks;
(b)   evaluating the risks which cannot be avoided;
(c)   combating the risks at source;

(d)   adapting the work to the individual, especially as regards the design of workplaces, the choice of work equipment and the choice of working and production methods, with a view, in particular, to alleviating monotonous work and work at a pre-determined work-rate and to reducing their effect on health;[2]

(e)   adapting to technical progress;

(f)   replacing the dangerous by the non-dangerous or the less dangerous;

(g)   developing a coherent overall prevention policy which covers technology, organisation of work, working conditions, social relationships and the influence of factors relating to the working environment; [3]

(h)   giving collective protective measures priority over individual protective measures; and

(i)   giving appropriate instructions to employees.

While some of these are obvious to the point of banality, they could be useful in a common law action for negligence in at least giving pegs on which to hang specific allegations, under the overall heading of the employer's duty to take reasonable care to provide a safe system of work. This could be another interesting informal cross-fertilisation between civil liability and those health and safety laws which are ostensibly restricted to administrative/criminal enforcement. Appropriate arrangements should be put in place to plan, organise, control, monitor and review these measures (reg 5).

[1]   See HSWA 1974, s 53.

[2]   This reference to monotonous work and work at a pre-determined rate could be argued to implement (in addition to art 6(2)(d) of the Framework Directive) art 13 of the Working Time Directive 93/104/EC which refers to the alleviation of such work and also to the general principle of adapting work to the worker (also referred to in head (d)). The Working Time Regulations 1998 do not specifically implement art 13; the nearest they come is in reg 8 (pattern of work) which only states that where the work pattern puts the worker at risk (in particular because the work is monotonous or the work-rate is pre-determined) the employer must ensure that the worker is given adequate rest breaks. Principle (d) goes much farther than that.

[3]   The reference to the 'working environment' (here, and in EC health and safety law generally) shows a significantly wide approach. It has been picked up in modern employment law, in the establishment of an implied term in contracts of employment that the employer will take reasonable care to provide a suitable working environment: *Waltons & Morse v Dorrington* [1997] IRLR 488, EAT.

10.22 Further duties are imposed by the regulations on employers in relation to their employees. Employees must be provided with comprehensible and relevant information on the risks at work shown by the assessment, together with the preventative measures and various other matters (reg 10). The employer should also provide the information given to it by anyone else who shares the same workplace as to the risks arising out of the conduct of that person's undertaking.[1] The existence of the more explicit duty in the regulations should, in future, inform the duty in negligence. To a large extent the common law duty to warn of risks and the like already matches this standard. But the individual focus of the Directive suggests that there should be a duty to ensure that the information can be understood by the employees, and hence the employer should take into account the individual level of knowledge, literacy and experience.[2] Some older common law cases do not appear to go quite as far, but they should now be viewed with caution.[3] Similarly, the presence of a duty to warn may mean that common law authorities suggesting that an employer need not do so where this could cause disruption to the workplace may have to be treated with caution.

1   See reg 11(1)(c).
2   See ACOP, para 64.
3   See *eg James v Hepworth and Grandage Ltd* [1968] 1 QB 94.

10.23   When allocating tasks among employees, the employer should similarly take into account individual capabilities (reg 13(1)).[1] The employer must ensure that all employees receive adequate health and safety training, both on recruitment and whenever they are given new tasks or responsibilities, and which should be repeated periodically and up-dated. The assessment should identify what training is necessary. Health surveillance should also be provided where appropriate (reg 6)—if, for example, employees were subject to a particular type of injury or disease which could be identified and thus prevented by regular checks. Depending on the type of workplace, this could extend from mere enquiries as to symptoms to detailed expert monitoring. It is unlikely, in the authors' view, that any lower standard is required in negligence.

1   See Framework Directive, art 6(2)(d)–(3)(b).

Competent assistance

10.24   To assist in undertaking these protective measures, the employer should appoint one or more 'competent persons' (reg 6(1))—defined as someone with a sufficient degree of training, experience or knowledge (reg 6(5)) and preferably in the employer's employment (reg 6(8))—who must be given adequate time to fulfil their functions (see earlier authorities on this expression such as *Gibson v Skibs A/S Marina* [1966] 2 All ER 476). In accordance with its emphasis on employee participation, the Framework Directive specifies that the employer shall designate one of its *employees* for these activities unless none have sufficient competence (art 7; see the definition of 'worker' in art 3); by contrast, the regulations permit the employer to appoint an outsider if there is no appropriate employee. In addition to appointing competent persons, the employer must also ensure that any necessary contracts with external services are arranged,[1] particularly as regards first-aid, emergency medical care and rescue work (reg 9).

1   Para 53 of the ACOP gives detailed guidance on this. Para 54 states that procedures should be written down (pursuant to reg 5(2)) and that this should clearly set out the limits of actions to be taken by employees.

Duties to pregnant workers

10.25   The original 1992 Regulations were amended by the Management of Health and Safety at Work (Amendment) Regulations 1994 to implement the Pregnancy Directive (92/85/EEC). These provisions, now in the 1999 Regulations, impose specific duties in relation to new or expectant mothers.[1] The risk assessment must consider risks arising to the woman or her baby from work conditions: reg 16.[2] Where risks cannot be avoided, the employer should 'if it is reasonable to do so' alter the working conditions or hours so worked (reg 16(2)). If such reasonable alteration is not possible, the pregnant employee should be suspended (reg 16(3)).[3] Similar duties to suspend arise in relation to pregnant women who do night work and who present a medical certificate showing that they should not be at work at that time (reg 17).

[1]   Note that each of the principal Directives and the other 'six-pack' regulations made under them make specific provision for these workers and nursing mothers.
[2]   These include the specific risks identified in the Pregnancy Directive, 92/85/EEC, Annexes I and II. See too *New and Expectant Mothers at Work—A Guide for Employers* (HSG 122; 2002; ISBN 0 7176 2583 4).
[3]   See *New Southern Railway v Quinn* (13 January 2006, unreported).

10.26 The duty to alter working hours or suspend the employee does not arise until the employee has notified the employer in writing that she is pregnant, has given birth within the previous six months or is breast-feeding (reg 18). However, if the employee has given a medical certificate arguably indicating pregnancy, the onus may pass to the employer to show that there was no notification.[1] The duty to conduct a pregnancy-related risk assessment is not conditional on notification, and is triggered simply by the employment of a woman of child-bearing age in work involving a risk to new or expectant mothers or to babies; the woman need not actually be pregnant.

[1]   *Day v T Pickles Farms Ltd* [1999] IRLR 217, EAT and *Hardman v Mallon (t/a Orchard Lodge Nursing Home)* [2002] IRLR 516, EAT. The EAT has held that failure to carry out the necessary risk assessment might constitute a 'detriment' under the Sex Discrimination Act 1975.

Duties to young persons

10.27 Regulation 3(4) and (5) make specific provision for young persons.[1] There is an obligation on an employer to ensure that young persons[2] employed by it are protected at work from any risks to their health and safety arising from their lack of experience, or absence of awareness of existing or potential risks or the fact that young persons have not yet fully matured (reg 19(1)). No employer may employ a young person for work:

(a)   beyond his physical or psychological capacity;
(b)   involving harmful exposure to certain agents;
(c)   involving harmful exposure to radiation;
(d)   involving a risk of accident particularly likely to affect the inexperienced, or
(e)   in which there is a risk to health from extreme cold or heat, noise or vibration (reg 19(2)).

The employer, on taking on a young worker, needs to undertake a risk assessment, considering these specified matters in particular.[3] There is an exception (for young persons but not children) where the work is necessary for his training, the young person will be supervised by a competent person and any risk will be reduced to the lowest level that is reasonably practicable (reg 19(3)).

1   The principal rules in the employment of children are contained in the Children and Young Persons Act 1933, ss 18–30, as amended by the Children (Protection at Work) Regulations 1998, SI 1998/276 in order to secure compliance with the Protection of Young Persons at Work Directive 94/33/EC.
2   'Young person' means any person who has not attained the age of 18; 'child' means a person not over compulsory school age: reg 1(2).
3   ACOP, para 98.

Duties to self-employed and outside workers

10.28 As stated above, the risk assessment should cover the risks to persons who are not employees of the employer, but whose health and safety is at risk owing to the conduct of the employer's undertaking; the measures so identified should also be directed towards such persons (and see serious and imminent dangers, below). To these duties should be added others.

Workers working in the undertaking

10.29 An employer who uses self-employed workers or employees from an outside undertaking is obliged to supply those persons with appropriate instructions and comprehensible information regarding risks to their health and safety if they are 'working in his undertaking' (reg 12(3)). Some difficulties surround 'working in his undertaking', particularly in the case of pure visitors. Is a visiting window-cleaner, for example, to be treated as working in the employer's undertaking and hence to be given information under reg 12(3)? In the context of this purpose of the regulations and the obligations in the Temporary Workers Directive, it is plausible that such temporary workers should be owed the relevant duties, unless it is impossible to say that they are working in the undertaking: the phrase is, after all, working 'in', not working 'for', the undertaking. If an employer knows or should know of a particular risk, even to a transitory visitor, such as a postman or postwoman, whose work takes him or her to the premises, a duty may well be owed to supply information to that person.[1] The relevant risks for these purposes would be those arising from the use of the employer's workplace, rather than any risk associated with the work of the worker. An employer is under a duty to provide similar information to any employer whose employees work in the former employer's undertaking (reg 12(1)) and to other employers who are sharing a particular workplace (reg 11(1)).

1   The ACOP expressly states that these Regulations would apply to contract cleaners or repairers: para 79. The wording of 'working in his undertaking' is potentially wider than the phrase 'conduct of his undertaking' under the HSWA 1974, s 3—the latter seems to involve work done by the employer. But that expression has been given a wide definition: see *R v Associated Octel Co Ltd* [1997] IRLR 123, HL.

Agency and fixed-term workers

10.30 An employer owes additional duties to employees who work under a fixed-term contract and employees of employment businesses—usually an employment agency.[1] When an employer uses either category of worker,[2] each worker must be supplied with information on special occupational qualifications or skills which are necessary for carrying out their work safely (reg 15(1), (2)). It must also provide the same information to the employment agency (reg 15(3)); see also the Conduct of Employment Agencies and Employment Business Regulations 2003, SI 2003/3319, reg 30 (which by reg 30 are actionable in civil proceedings).

1   These duties should be read in the light of the Temporary Workers Directive, which requires the same level of protection to be given to fixed-term or agency workers: see art 2.
2   Such persons will, of course, automatically be covered by the duties in reg 12(3) as well.

10.31 That obligation does not, of course, remove the duties from the employment business towards its employees under the 1999 Regulations, the Conduct of Employment Agencies and Employment Business Regulations 2003 and at common law. It should provide them with training and information, for example: see regs 10 and 13. Regulation 3(1) refers to the risk assessment covering the risks to employees 'while they are at work' without more. The 2003 Regulations (reg 20) specifically require an employment business or agency to make all such enquiries, as are reasonably practicable, to ensure that it would not be 'detrimental to the interests of the work-seeker or the hirer for the work-seeker to work for the hirer in the position which the hirer seeks to fill'. The limits to what measures such an employer needs to take to comply with the relevant legislation are not obvious. But the employment agency must nonetheless, take all the necessary steps to inform itself of the risk its workers will face, wherever they work, and to seek to ensure their protection accordingly.

Duties of co-operation

10.32 In addition to supplying information to employees who work in the undertaking of another employer (see above), where two or more employers (or self-employed persons) share a workplace, they are placed under a duty to co-operate and to co-ordinate their activities to ensure that they fulfil the relevant duties (reg 11). This provision relates to meeting all statutory obligations, so that duties are owed to outsiders as well as to employees. The ACOP recommends the appointment of a health and safety co-ordinator if no employer is in control of the site (para 71). Although the common law has in the past recognised duties of co-ordination and the like,[1] establishing liability has been difficult, since the precise scope of the duties on particular undertakings is uncertain.

1   See, for instance, *McArdle v Andmac Roofing Co* [1967] 1 All ER 583.

10.33 The Regulations do not define a workplace. It will not always be obvious when a workplace is in fact shared, particularly when the activities contain some interrelationship but are to a large extent spatially distinct. In the case of a multi-occupancy building, it is possible that some of the common parts may be treated as shared workplaces: the ACOP gives the example of a shared reception in an office building. Further, the distinction between sharing a workplace and an employee working in another employer's undertaking is unclear; yet these give rise to different obligations on the part of the employers towards each other: see regs 11(1) and 12(1). It is unclear whether a labour-only sub-contractor, for example, shares a workplace with the principal contractor.

Duties on the self-employed and employees

10.34 The self-employed are also under a duty to conduct a risk assessment, comprising the risks to their own safety and others from their business. And they, too, are subject to duties in respect of the employees of outside undertakings who work in their undertaking (reg 12). Employees are placed under a duty to use their equipment in accordance with their training and instruction (reg 14). This duty should be read together with the duty on employees to take reasonable care for the health and safety of others and to co-operate with the employer on the health and safety duties contained in the HSWA 1974, s 7.

Serious and imminent dangers

10.35 Regulation 8 sets out a duty to establish specific procedures in the event of serious and imminent danger to 'persons at work in the undertaking', so extending beyond employees. These duties comprise the provision of information of the risks and steps to be taken and of procedures for evacuation; instructions to persons to stop work immediately; and the nomination of competent persons to implement any measures for evacuation.[1] Uncertainty surrounds what is a 'serious and imminent danger' for these purposes.

[1] Again the Directive contemplates that these should be employees (art 8(2)), whereas reg 8(1)(b) talks only of 'competent persons'.

Liability for employees' actions

10.36 Regulation 21 states that nothing in the health and safety provisions is to 'operate so as to afford an employer a defence in any criminal proceedings for a contravention of those provisions by reason of any act or default of (a) an employee of his, or (b) a person appointed by him under regulation 7'. In most cases, the employer will be corporate and so only able to operate through employees (high and low); the modern tendency has been to increase corporate criminal liability, in particular and crucially by the policy decision by the courts that the 'identification doctrine' (ie that a company can only be liable for the acts of its 'guiding brains', ie effectively at board level) has no place in health and safety law.[1] Thus, at the very least, local managers can make the company liable for health and safety offences, and there is always the possibility of liability (direct or vicarious, depending on the statutory provision) for the acts of those lower in the chain. However, the decision in *R v Nelson Group Services (Maintenance) Ltd* [1999] IRLR 646, CA showed a glitch in that analysis, where there was a statutory duty to do something as far as reasonably practicable. One of the company's gas fitters had left a domestic appliance in a dangerous state. He had not done all that was reasonably practicable on that occasion, *but* the company could show that it had taken reasonable steps to train and instruct him. At which level was the reasonable practicability test to be applied? The Court of Appeal held that it was to apply at *corporate* level, and so the company had a defence. This had, in fact, been viewed by the HSE as an important test case, which they lost. The result was the incorporation into the new Management Regulations of reg 21 which aimed to reverse *Nelson,* so that the company can be liable for isolated lapses by individual employees. The ACOP (para 102) states that in practice enforcers will take into account all the circumstances of a case in deciding who to charge in such a case, and that the fact than the company has taken reasonable steps to ensure competency in the employee (or appointed person) will be taken into account. Ultimately, however, reg 21 shows that it cannot actually be a defence, thus tending more towards strict liability in the criminal enforcement sphere (see generally chapter 11).

[1]   *R v British Steel plc* [1995] IRLR 310, CA; *R v Gateway Foodmarkets Ltd* [1997] IRLR 189, CA.

WORKING TIME

General

10.37 The first step in the history of statutory health and safety law in Britain focused on restricting working time. The 1802 Act for the Preservation of the Health and Morals of apprentices and others employed in Cotton and other Mills and Cotton and other Factories restricted the young apprentices from more than 12 hours' labour in each day and prohibited them working between 9pm and 6am. Since that time there has been much UK legislation on working time, though little (except in relation to women and young people) of general application. The purpose of the legislation has always been the same: to prevent injury to health (and in many situations, safety) by excessive hours of work.[1]

[1]   As a recent example, see the Railways (Safety Critical Work) Regulations 1994, SI 1994/299.

10.38 As will be seen immediately below, most of the existing domestic law was repealed by various deregulatory measures, but this was soon trumped by EC law in the form of the Working Time Directive 93/104/EC (and the associated Protection of Young People at Work Directive 94/33/EC) which has been responsible for the introduction for the first time in this country of across-the- board rules on working time, night working, rest breaks and annual holidays. Although it is of fundamental importance that these matters are now treated as health and safety issues in EC law, they still represent a hybrid with employment law and sit uneasily in a book such as this. The approach adopted here is to consider first the repeal of the previous domestic provisions, then the two Directives, then the Working Time Regulations 1998, SI 1998/1833 (in outline only) and finally to consider the important issue of the potential liabilities on employers, including certain spin-offs which may be possible into mainstream personal injury law.

Previous UK law

10.39 Government policy in the 1980s and the early 1990s resulted in many of the previous legislative maximum limits on working time being repealed in accordance with the view that such protections imposed a burden on business from which the latter should be freed.[1] This policy ran at complete variance with EU policy as evidenced in the Working Time Directive.

> 1   See eg the White Papers *Lifting the Burden* (1985, Cmnd 9751); *Building Business ... Not Barriers* (1986, Cmnd 9794).

10.40 Section 7 of the Sex Discrimination Act 1986 and s 9 of the Employment Act 1989 repealed the long-standing restrictions on the hours of work, shift work, night work and provision for bank holidays etc for adult women in factories, mines, quarries and transport and other industries.[1] Section 10 of the Employment Act 1989 removed the restrictions on the hours of shift work, night work and provision for bank holidays etc for youngsters above school leaving age. The maximum underground shift for mineworkers of 7½ hours established by the Coal Mines Regulations Act 1908, as amended, was repealed by the Coal Industry Act 1992. The protection against Sunday working for shopworkers under the Shops Act 1950 was removed by the Sunday Trading Act 1994. The remaining limitations on shop workers—hours, provisions for meal breaks, their compulsory half day off per week under the Shops Act 1950—were repealed by the Deregulation and Contracting Out Act 1994. That Act permitted Sunday work for bookmakers (by amending the Betting, Gaming and Lotteries Act 1963). Wages Councils which regulated hours and holidays for some millions of workers were deprived of that jurisdiction by the Wages Act 1986 prior to their abolition by the Trade Union Reform and Employment Rights Act 1993. Only the Agricultural Wages Board[2] survives and still has the power to stipulate limits on agricultural hours of work and provide for minimum holidays.

> 1   Including similar provisions for particular industries, eg parts of the Hours of Employment (Conventions) Act 1936 (sheet glass workers) and the whole of the Bakery Industry (Hours of Work) Act 1954 (bakery workers).
> 2   Pursuant to the Agricultural Wages Act 1948.

10.41 In purely domestic law, this process left only certain provisions relating to the hours of work of road haulage workers, seafarers and railway workers,[1] and the employment of children.[2] Holidays have never been governed as such by law, with even the status of bank holidays being largely ambiguous and left, as with so many other matters, largely as a matter of contract, with or without the underpinning of collective bargaining. While certain abuses of the 'long-hours culture' so often spoken of in the UK could be attacked either in an employment law action based on implied terms of the contract of employment,[3] or in a common law damages claim for stress-related illness[4] (once the damage has been done), the lack of any overall, systematic statutory coverage of working hours has long been a characteristic of the UK labour market. It is this that makes the recent intervention of EC law so important, though its limitations (in the current form) have to be accepted.

1 See the Railway (Safety Critical Work) Regulations 1994, SI 1994/299.
2 Children and Young Persons Act 1963, s 18; Children and Young Persons Act 1963, ss 35–44.
3 *Johnstone v Bloomsbury Health Authority* [1992] QB 333, CA (junior doctor working a 40-hour basic week, on call for a further 48 hours and often working more, could bring an action for breach of the implied contractual duty to take reasonable care for his health and safety in order to recover for resultant damage to health).
4 *Walker v Northumberland County Council* [1995] 1 All ER 737.

Young People at Work Directive

10.42 The Protection of Young People at Work Directive 94/33/EC[1] prohibits work for those under 13 years of age, and regulates work for young persons under 18 years. There are restrictions on the kind of work which may be undertaken by young persons aged under 16 years. Those in full-time education are limited to 12 hours work per week outside school hours, and no more than two hours on a school day. Work in school holidays or by a young person not in full-time education must not be more than seven hours per day or 35 hours per week (eight per day and 40 per week for those over 15 years); must allow for two rest days per week; a rest period of 14 consecutive hours[2] every 24 hours; and a rest period of at least half an hour after 4½ hours work. Crucially these are absolute time limits and are not averaged over a reference period (reg 5A). At least four weeks' annual leave must be given to those young people not in full-time education. Night work is regulated and, in most cases, prohibited. There are exemptions from and variations on some provisions in respect of training; apprenticeship; work experience; cultural, artistic and sports activities; advertising; shipping; fishing; police and military service; hospitals; catering; domestic service and work in family undertakings. The Directive also makes provision for a number of health and safety measures.

1 Passed 22 June 1994.
2 12 for those over the age of compulsory education.

The Working Time Directive

10.43 The Working Time Directive 93/104/EC[1] was passed against the wishes of the government, by the device of categorising it as a health and safety matter (amenable to qualified majority voting under art 137 (ex art 118a) EC) rather than as an employment law matter (requiring unanimity). The British government challenged the legality of the use of this treaty base but eventually lost before the ECJ (except in relation to one minor aspect of Sunday working).[2] The upshot was that, with the change in government in 1997 and the time needed to consult on and produce implementing Regulations, the UK was almost two years late in implementing the Directive. An early attempt to rely directly on the Directive to enforce rights (to annual holiday) during this period of non-implementation failed, on the basis that the Directive is not sufficiently precise and unconditional to support direct effect.[3] On the other hand, it has been held that a *Francovich* action can lie against the government for damages for non-implementation.[4]

1   Passed 23 November 1993. On this Directive see Bercussen *Working Time in Britain: Towards a European Model* (Institute of Employment Rights, 1994).

2   *United Kingdom v EU Council* C-84/94 [1997] IRLR 30, ECJ.

3   *Gibson v East Riding of Yorkshire Council* [2000] IRLR 598, CA. Note, however, that in the context of non-implementation in Spain of the detailed provisions in the Directive on the reference power for averaging weekly working hours, the ECJ subsequently held that those provisions (art 16(2) and then art 17(2), (3) and (4) allowing derogations) can be interpreted as having direct effect: C-303/98 *Sindicato de Medicos de Asistencia Publica v Conselleria de Sanidad y Consumo de la Generalidad Valenciana* [2000] IRLR 845, ECJ.

4   *R v A-G for Northern Ireland, ex p Burns* [1999] IRLR 315. For the meaning of a *Francovich* action see para 9.79, above.

10.44 The Directive requires: 11 consecutive hours of rest per 24-hour period (art 3); rest breaks if the working day is longer than six hours; the details, duration and terms of rest periods to be established by collective agreement locally or nationally, failing which, to be established by national legislation (art 4); at least 35 hours continuous rest per seven-day period (art 5); maximum working time of 48 hours per seven-day period averaged over a period established by legislation at not more than four months (art 6); a minimum of four weeks' paid annual leave per annum (art 7); in any 24-hour period, no more than eight hours night work (art 8); health assessments and other protections for night workers (arts 9, 10, 11, 12); and patterns of work to be organised so as to adapt the work to the worker with the view, in particular, of alleviating monotonous work and work at a predetermined work rate (art 13). Member States are permitted (by arts 17 and 18) to make a wide variety of derogations from these provisions in respect of specified categories of work and by collective agreements. The 48-hour maximum week (art 6) may be disapplied by a Member State if it takes measures to ensure that no employer can require a longer week without the individual worker's agreement (the refusal of which may not be subject to a detriment),[1] and that employers maintain records (open to inspection) of workers working in excess of the 48-hour week.

1   Although it is unclear whether this can prevent the refusal of employment to a job applicant who refuses to agree to a contract of employment which expresses his consent to working in excess of 48 hours.

10.45 The role of collective bargaining in this legal structure is remarkable, not only for allowing variations and derogations from the law to be determined by collective agreement, but also by making collective agreements the primary means of determining rest breaks (art 4) in every workplace and enterprise.

The Working Time Regulations 1998

10.46 The detailed provisions of the Working Time Regulations are considered fully elsewhere. Two definitional matters must firstly be dealt with:

10.46   *The general legislation*

(1)   Workers
The use of the wider concept of 'worker' means that the Regulations apply not only to 'employees' in the strict sense, but also to persons under any other contract whereby the individual undertakes to do or perform personally any work or services for another party to the contract where status is not that of a client or customer of any profession or business undertaking carried on by the individual: reg 2(1). The DTI view is that this will include all except the 'genuinely self-employed'. The Court of Appeal in *Wright v Redrow Homes (Yorkshire) Ltd* [2004] EWCA Civ 469, [2004] IRLR 720 stated that in determining whether there was an obligation to work personally, the contract must be construed in light of the circumstances in which it was made. Just because the work was done personally, does not mean that there was an obligation to work personally. However on the facts it was found that the respondent bricklayers were workers under the Regulations. Children under compulsory school age are not workers for the purpose of the Regulations, though there is special provision for their inclusion under reg 2(1) (*Addison t/a Brayton News v Ashby* [2003] IRLR 211).

(2)   Working time
'Working time' is primarily defined as 'any period during which [the worker] is working, at his employer's disposal and carrying out his activities or duties': reg 2(1). This is taken from the Directive, art 2, under which the ECJ have held that time on call at the employer's premises is 'working time', but time on call elsewhere (ie being at home but contactable) is not (except when actually called on to work): *C-303/98 Sindicato de Medicos de Asistencia Publica v Consellaria de Sanidad y Consumo de la Generalided Valenciana* [2000] IRLR 845, ECJ. Similarly in *Landeshauptstadt Kiel v Jaeger* [2003] IRLR 804 the ECJ held that being present in a hospital while on call, though permitted to sleep, was working time under the Directive. The ECJ noted that the decisive factor was the requirement to be present and available to provide services immediately they were needed. Proposals were put to introduce 'on call time' and 'inactive on call time' into the Directive. The latter would not be working time, unless national law specifies differently, except insofar as duties or activities are carried out. These were rejected by the Council of Ministers but will be reconsidered at some stage.

10.47   The four principal areas covered are maximum weekly working time, rest periods, paid annual leave and night working.

Maximum weekly working time

10.48   A worker's working time, including overtime, is not to exceed an average of 48 hours for each seven days in any particular reference period (reg 4). Annual leave and sick pay may not be included or must be neutral in the calculation of the average weekly hours of work (reg 4(6) and (7)). The averaging process is vital here, allowing considerable fluctuations in actual weekly hours. The normal 'reference period' is 17 weeks but this is increased to 26 weeks in certain 'special cases' (set out in reg 21), and can be raised to 52 weeks by collective or workforce agreement. The extension must be justified by 'objective or technical reasons or reasons concerning the organisation of work'. The reference period is automatically 52 weeks for 'offshore work' (reg 25B). The European Parliament recently rejected a proposal to extend the reference period to one year upon agreement between the Member State and the relevant social partners.

10.49 An employer is under a duty to take all reasonable steps to ensure that workers comply with the 48-hour limit (reg 4(2)). In a recent tribunal-level case, it was held that the failure to monitor and regulate a worker's hours constituted a repudiatory breach entitling her to resign and claim constructive unfair dismissal (*Owen v Smith Walker* ET Case No 2702239/99). This duty is particularly difficult where a worker has two or more jobs and the total may exceed the 48-hour limit. The DTI Guidance therefore recommends that where the employer knows of the second job, an opt-out should be signed. The European Commission is proposing a specific limit on the aggregate hours of any worker, which already exists regarding young workers via art 8(4) of the Young Workers Directive.

10.50 Probably the widest 'derogation' permitted by the Regulations applies here, namely the ability of the individual worker to opt out of this protection by a simple written agreement (reg 5). Individual consent is needed and this cannot just be through the acceptance of a collective agreement (*Pfeiffer v Deutsches Rotes Kreuz Kreisverband Waldshurt eV* [2005] IRLR 137). To bring an opt-out to an end, a minimum of seven days notice must be given (reg 5(2)) and if the opt-out requires notice to be given, it cannot be more than three months (reg 5(3)). Records must be kept as to who has signed an opt-out, the terms on which they agreed and the number of hours worked. This is a considerably reduced recording requirement than previously. Employees are protected against detriment and dismissal due to refusing to sign an opt-out (ERA 1996, s 101A), however this opt-out does not extend to refusals of employment. Proposals for an amendment of the Directive were presented to the Council of Ministers in 2005, recommending, amongst other things requiring greater specificity for an individual opt-out to operate, a collective agreement or national law to allow art 6 of the Directive to apply and proposing an absolute maximum working week of 65 hours. However the process has been stalled, primarily due to disagreement over the use of the opt-out.

Rest periods

10.51 An adult worker is entitled to: (a) a daily rest period of not less that 11 hours in each 24-hour period (reg 10); (b) a weekly rest period of not less than 24 hours in each seven day working period (reg 11); and (c) a rest break of at least 20 minutes where daily working time is more than six hours (reg 12). In the case of young workers, these entitlements are raised to 12 hours daily rest,

48 hours weekly rest, and at least 30 minutes rest after 4½ hours' work. Rest breaks must be time which the worker can use as they please. They must also know when it will start, therefore downtime cannot retrospectively be a rest break just because it goes on for 20 minutes (*Gallagher v Alpha Catering Services Ltd (t/a Alpha Flight Services)* [2004] EWCA Civ 1559, [2005] IRLR 102). Special rules apply in relation to shift workers and workers whose work is split up over the day.

10.52 The 1998 Government Consultation Document on the Regulations stated that they provide entitlements and not obligations, therefore while the employee may insist upon taking the rest periods, it would not be unlawful for them to voluntarily forego them. In June 2000 Amicus raised a complaint with the European Commission that it was an obligation, so it was an employer's responsibility to ensure that rest periods were taken. The Commission upheld the complaint in April 2002 and commenced discussions with the UK government. However these subsequently broke down, and on 23 November 2004 the Commission commenced proceedings against the government about daily and weekly rest periods. It is unclear why proceedings have not been commenced regarding daily rest breaks.

Paid annual leave

10.53 A worker is entitled to a minimum of four weeks' paid leave in each leave year (reg 13 and reg 17). This applies to casual workers (after 13 weeks' continuous employment) and to part-time workers on a pro rata basis. After much urging by the TUC, it is understood that the government are now committed to adding an entitlement to the eight bank holidays. In *R v Secretary of State for Trade and Industry, ex p BECTU* [2001] IRLR 559, it was held by the ECJ that the imposition of the 13-week qualifying period was in breach of the Working Time Directive. Consequently the Regulations have been amended via the Working Time (Amendment) Regulations 2001. However the effects of this have been mitigated by the addition of accrual requirements in reg 15A. During the first year of employment, annual leave is deemed to accrued at 1/12th of the entitlement on the first day of each month and rounding of these figures is provided for in reg 15A(3). Moreover, the leave is actually to be taken during the leave year (not bought out or carried forward). 'Leave year' is left primarily to the agreement of the parties; in default it runs from the date of commencement of employment. Workers who are on long-term sick leave, and have run out of sick pay entitlement, are not entitled to annual leave. The Court of Appeal in *IRC v Ainsworth* [2005] EWCA Civ 441, [2005] IRLR 465 emphasised that annual leave was about 'leave' from work on a health and safety basis, which did not apply when one was on long term sick. The claimants in *Ainsworth* have leave to appeal to the House of Lords. This decision should be contrasted to that of the ECJ in *Gomez v Contintental Industrias del Caucho SA* [2004] IRLR 407 that where annual leave was fixed in time and that coincided with the claimant's maternity leave, she should be entitled to take the annual leave after her maternity leave ends.

10.54 Workers are entitled to the rate of one week's pay per week for leave (reg 13). In calculating a week's pay, reg 16 refers to the ERA 1996, ss 221–224. Overtime is not included in the calculation of holiday pay unless it is required by the employment contract (*Bamsey v Albon Engineering and Manufacturing plc* [2004] EWCA Civ 359, [2004] IRLR 457). Similarly the contractual entitlement must be used even where commission is paid on the basis of successful signing of contracts. Such commission relates to success achieved rather than work done and therefore falls outside of the ERA 1996, s 221 (*Evans v Malley Organisation Ltd (t/a First Business Support)* [2002] EWCA Civ 1834, [2003] IRLR 156). Another recent question relating to the validity of rolled up holiday pay has been referred to the ECJ, in *Marshalls Clay Products Ltd v Caulfield* [2004] EWCA Civ 422, [2004] IRLR 564. The Court of Appeal held that there was no obligation under art 7 of the Directive that holiday pay be paid at the time the leave is taken and the position was the same under the Regulations. Rolled up pay did not discourage workers from taking holidays in that there was not a substantial obstruction to the right. Furthermore, since the holiday pay was governed by a collective agreement, this pointed strongly to the system's legitimacy. The ECJ has held (C-131/04) that rolled up holiday pay is prima facie unlawful. However, if the holiday pay element of the rolled-up elements is sufficiently transparent, the employer can set off that payment against money due for the specific period when leave is actually taken.

10.55 There can be no payment in lieu of annual leave except upon termination (reg 13(9)(b)). Clawback where excess annual leave has been taken and employment terminated, is only possible where there is a 'relevant agreement' under reg 14(4) but the accrual provisions operate to mitigate the effects of this.

Limits on night working

10.56 A night worker's normal hours of work in any reference period are not to exceed an average of eight hours in each 24 hours (reg 6). Again, the reference period is 17 weeks. 'Night worker' means a worker who normally works at least three hours of his daily working time during night time, or such proportion of his annual working time as may be specified in a collective or workforce agreement (reg 2(1)). The reference period and the length of night work can be disapplied or modified by collective or workforce agreement (reg 23(a)). The health and safety aspect is particularly strong in relation to night working and its possible health effects (as can be seen in the recitals at the beginning of the Directive), and in addition to these hours limits, it is also provided in reg 7 that: (a) an adult worker must have the opportunity for a free health assessment before being assigned to night work, with regular re-assessments at later times (a young worker[1] must have the opportunity of such an assessment as to health and capacity whenever assigned to work between 10pm and 6am); and (b) the employer must transfer a night worker to non-night work if a registered medical practitioner so advises and suitable work is available.

¹ 'Young worker' means a worker who has attained the age of 15 but not the age of 18, and who is over school age (reg 2(1)).

10.57 The Regulations are as notable for their adoption in full of the 'derogations' permitted by the Directive as for the four principles above. We have already seen the simple opt-out procedure in the case of the maximum working week. In addition, certain activities were completely excluded but now have some protection.¹ There can also be very significant amendments or even disapplications of the major rights (except annual holidays) where there is agreement to that effect in a collective or workforce agreement.² There is also scope for moulding the application of the Regulations to individual circumstances (eg in defining 'working time' and 'night time') by such agreements or by contract.

¹ Until 1 August 2003 the transport, sea fishing and other sea sectors, the activities of doctors in training, and services such as the armed forces, police and civil protection services were completely excluded from the Regulations because their characteristics conflicted with the provisions of the Regulations: reg 18. Workers in these sectors are now offered some protection through five specific Directives: Horizontal Amending Directive (2000/34/EC); Road Transport Directive (2002/15/EC); Seafarers' Directive (1999/63/EC); Seafarers' Enforcement Directive (1999/95/EC); and Civil Aviation Directive (2000/79/EC).
² Regulation 23. The concept of a 'workforce agreement' is an important one under the Regulations, permitting consultation and agreement with a non-unionised workforce, through the medium of directly-elected worker representation (Sch 1).

10.58 In addition to all of this, there are two major statutory qualifications. The first is the category of 'special cases' in reg 21, where most of the nightworking and rest break provisions are disapplied. These cases are potentially broad, applying for example to security and surveillance activities, cases where there is a need for continuity of service (eg in hospitals, prisons, docks, airports, research and development activities and agriculture), cases where there is a foreseeable surge of activity (eg tourism and postal services), and cases involving emergencies (for the application of reg 21 see *Gallagher v Alpha Catering Services Ltd (t/a Alpha Flight Services)* [2004] EWCA Civ 1559, [2005] IRLR 102). The second, and most controversial, qualification is the disapplication of the maximum working week, night working and rest-break provisions in cases of 'unmeasured working time' in reg 20. The examples given in the Regulations are narrow (managing executives, family workers and priests), but on the other hand in a more flexible workforce many employees could be said to have at least an element of discretion and self-regulation in their work activities. Under pressure from employers to make the Regulations more business-friendly, the government amended reg 20 by adding a second paragraph, stating that where part of the working time is not measured or pre-determined, the provisions on the maximum working week and night working hours only apply to the rest of the work. There is the major qualification that the worker must be doing this extra, unmeasured, work 'without being required to do so by the employer' and therein lies the problem. The government state that the end result is still that no-one can be forced to work past (in particular) the 48-hour average,¹ but how much informal pressure can be exerted on the employee (eg in relation to promotion) before that is considered to be an employer 'requirement'? We can expect to see litigation over just these sorts of highly uncertain areas during the currency of this edition.

1 Your Guide to the Working Time Regulations (DTI, March 2000) at p 20. The Guide (which replaced the original DTI guidance, unfortunately in shortened and less helpful form) goes on to give worked examples of 'extra' work which may and may not come within the new rules.

Liability issues

10.59 The nature of the Regulations as a hybrid between health and safety law and employment law (with no direct involvement of civil liability for personal injury) is shown by the provisions on enforcement. The provisions on the maximum working week and night working (the 'limitations') are stated to be enforceable only by the HSE (with no individual complaint to a tribunal); the provisions on rest breaks and paid annual leave (the 'entitlements') are enforceable by such an individual complaint to an employment tribunal (see regs 29 and 30). A worker is also protected against any detriment, including dismissal, due to refusal to comply with an employer's requirement which is in contravention of the regulations, refusal to sign an opt-out and making an allegation that the employer has contravened the regulations (reg 31). The stark division between the HSE and employment remedies has already been softened by the adventurous decision of Gage J in *Barber v RJB Mining (UK) Ltd* [1999] IRLR 308 that observance of the 48-hour working week provisions is to be treated as being an implied obligation on an employer under the contract of employment, so that an employee made to work past the maximum (without opting out) would have a remedy for breach of contract. However, even here the emphasis is upon an employment law remedy. It is questionable now whether the decision of *Barber* has survived following *Commissioner of Inland Revenue v Ainsworth* [2005] IRLR 465. This stated that claims, in this case for holiday pay, must be brought under reg 30 and not as unlawful deduction of wages under the Employment Rights Act 1996, s 23. Finally, it should be noted that a grievance must be lodged under the Employment Act 2002 before a claim is brought in the tribunal.

Application to personal injury action

10.60 There is no express provision for the Regulations to be applicable, but there is no express prohibition. To be relevant, they would have to feed into an established cause of action, namely negligence or breach of statutory duty. Causation would, of course, be a major hurdle, but assuming that in a particular case a breach of the Regulations (eg excessive hours or no rest breaks) could be shown to have caused or contributed to an industrial accident, or for instance a stress-induced illness, it is suggested that there are two main possibilities. The first is that, given the high profile of the Regulations, a breach of them by the employer could be considered to be negligent, in particular through a failure to provide a safe system of work. Given the greater emphasis in modern law on systems and organisation of work, this could be a strong argument. The second possibility is that it could be argued that the Regulations support civil liability, so that an employer causing injury by failing to observe them could be liable for breach of statutory duty. Naturally, the normal elements of this tort would have to be made out, including Parliament's inferred intent that there should be a civil remedy (in addition to the means of enforcement specifically set out, see above). In *Pakenham-Walsh v Connell Residential* [2006] EWCA Civ 90, the Court of Appeal upheld a decision that a trial judge had been entitled to take into account the employer's ignorance of the regulations and the duty to keep records when concluding that a psychiatric injury had been reasonably foreseeable.

10.61 Two points are made in favour of inferring an intent to provide a civil remedy. The first is that, although the Court of Appeal have held that the Directive is not precise enough to support direct effect,[1] one basis for that was that certain key concepts were left to be fleshed out by domestic enacting legislation. That has now been done, and the Regulations themselves are fairly clear and unambiguous as to their requirements and as to those who are intended to benefit from them (and the Court of Appeal decision is open to question following a decision of the ECJ that provisions of arts 16 and 17 *are* directly effective[2]). Moreover, the health and safety provenance of this law should also point in the direction of civil liability. The second point is that, intriguingly, the original DTI consultation document on implementing the Directive actually raised the possibility that any resulting Regulations might well support civil liability.[3] Such liability would not be automatic under the HSWA 1974, s 47(2) because these Regulations were not passed under that Act, but under the European Communities Act 1972, and so a court in a novel case would have to go through the normal arguments in favour of and against civil enforceability (see chapter 9). The result is awaited with interest. Thus far the Regulations, though not fully argued, have been used in supporting a finding that psychiatric harm was foreseeable where the worker had not signed an opt-out and was working around 90 hours per week (*Mark Hone v Six Continents Retail Ltd* [2005] EWCA Civ 922), which may be the first step towards more extensive use of the Regulations in personal injury matters.

[1]   *Gibson v East Rising of Yorkshire Council* [2000] IRLR 598.
[2]   See *Sindicato de Medicos de Asistencia Publica (SIMAP) v Conselleria de Sanidad y Consumo de la Generalidad Valenciana* [2000] IRLR 845.
[3]   Consultation document URN: 98/645 at para 184. This passage did not appear in the eventual DTI guidance, and certainly does not appear in the current, truncated Guide.

Chapter 11

REPORTING AND ENFORCEMENT

Barry Cotter

REPORTING OF INJURIES, DISEASES AND DANGEROUS OCCURRENCES

11.01 A system of reporting injuries and dangerous events was first introduced in the Notification of Accidents and Dangerous Occurrences Regulations 1980, which were principally concerned with administering industrial injuries benefit. Employers are now under a duty to report injuries and dangerous occurrences by virtue of the Reporting of Injuries, Diseases and Dangerous Occurrences Regulations 1995, SI 1995/3163. The 1995 Regulations came into force on 1 April 1996. They revoke and replace the 1985 Regulations of the same name. They apply to all work activities in Great Britain and to offshore industry (see reg 12). The HSE has published a guide to the Regulations. The clear objective of the Regulations is the immediate supply of reports of relevant incidents to the HSE and to local authorities, in the process alerting the enforcement authorities to individual accidents and providing valuable data for statistical analysis. Like all regulations passed under the HSWA 1974, a breach of the Reporting of Injuries, Diseases and Dangerous Occurrences Regulations 1995 is a criminal offence.[1]

[1]   See the defence in reg 11.

11.02 The Reporting of Injuries, Diseases and Dangerous Occurrences Regulations 1995 impose a duty on the 'responsible person' to notify the enforcing authority—either the HSE or the local authority[1]—of certain events (see reg 3).[2] In the case of accidents of employees this person is the employer, although there are exceptions for mines, quarries, closed tips, offshore installations, pipelines, wells, diving projects and road vehicles, when the duty is generally imposed on the owner or operator. In the case of accidents involving persons other than employees, the duty is imposed on the person controlling the premises in connection with which the event arises.[3] The duty arises if there is an accident at work, which is broadly defined (see reg 2(2)(c)), resulting in death or certain, relatively serious, injuries or other conditions specified in reg 3(2); these include any injury which results in a person being taken from the site to hospital. The definition of 'accident' in reg 2(1) includes injuries caused through intentional assaults.

[1]   See the Health and Safety (Enforcing Authority) Regulations 1998, SI 1998/494.
[2]   The requirements of regs 3–5 are subject to reg 10.
[3]   See the definition of 'responsible person' in reg 2.

11.03 The enforcing authority must be told of the occurrence by the quickest practicable means and a report on an approved form must be submitted within ten days (reg 3(1)). If an employee is incapacitated from work owing to a work-related accident, then the reporting obligation (but not the notifying obligation) applies (see reg 3(2)). Should an employee die within one year as a result of a reportable event, the enforcing authority must be informed of this fact (reg 4). Additional obligations are imposed under reg 5, where workers in particular industries contract certain diseases, which are set out in Sch 3.

11.04 By reg 7 a duty is imposed on the responsible person to keep records of any event which must be reported under reg 3 or reg 5.

11.05 A duty also arises if there is a 'dangerous occurrence' (reg 3(1)(e)); these are events defined in Sch 2 and include such matters as explosions, collapses of building or incidents involving the carriage of dangerous substances by road.[1] This duty does not apply just by virtue of being an employer; instead it applies, broadly, to the person controlling the premises at which the dangerous occurrence arose.[2] Further obligations arise in relation to gas incidents under reg 6 and in relation to mines and quarries under reg 8 and Sch 5.

[1] Note that specific rules apply to dangerous occurrences in relation to mines, quarries, relevant transport systems and offshore workplaces: see reg 2.
[2] See the definition of 'responsible person' in reg 2.

ENFORCEMENT

General

11.06 Since the Framework Directive 89/391 (on the introduction of measures to encourage improvements in the safety and health of workers at work) there has been increased focus on guaranteeing a better level of protection for workers at work against risks that may be present in employment. The Directive introduced, amongst others, duties to avoid, evaluate and combat at source risks to health and safety and to develop a coherent overall prevention policy and in so doing set out the overarching strategy to which the subsequent Directives (most obviously the six numbered Directives that accompanied it) have added detail. However, by June 2000 it was necessary for the HSC and the DETR to jointly produce a strategy statement on revitalising health and safety, setting specific objectives including the reduction of the incidence of fatal and major injury claims. This was followed in February 2004 by a new strategy for workplace health and safety in Great Britain to 2010 and beyond. The need for the existence of such strategies when taken against a high level of direct regulation of the workplace reveals that the goal of self-regulation which the Robens report described as 'the most fundamental conclusion to which our investigations have led us' is nowhere near achievement. Hence an effective system of enforcement is as important as ever if workplaces are to become safer and accidents are to be prevented. Although much change for the good should have been achieved through the Directives, many have been disappointed at the rate of progress in reducing the incidence of accidents at work. It is a settled principle of European law that enforcement should be left to Member States so long as they provide effective measures. There is clearly an issue as to whether, in the absence of direct European stimulus, current domestic enforcement is in fact an effective driver for reform.

Enforcement policy

11.07 The enforcement of health and safety law is principally the responsibility of the Health and Safety Commission (which is responsible to the Secretary of State), the Health and Safety Executive (which enforces health and safety at work law on a day to day basis) and local authorities.[1] Of these the HSE is by far the most important in terms of actual enforcement practice. It is a multi-disciplinary body, the public face of which is most usually seen through its inspectors[2] and whose wide-ranging powers are set out in the HSWA 1974, s 20[3] (see below). Any action taken by an inspector should be based upon the Commission's Enforcement Policy Statement (2002 HSC 15) which sets out the principles and approach to be adopted and followed when enforcement authorities seek to enforce health and safety law. It also sets out a requirement that enforcing authorities publicise the decision-making process which has resulted in the HSE producing the enforcement management model, which outlines a step by step process to ensure that inspectors take account of all the factors in the enforcement policy statement. Both the policy statement and the management model are available on the HSE website.[4] By way of illustration of the content and effect of these documents, enforcing authorities should consider prosecution when:

(1) it is appropriate in the circumstances as a way to draw general attention to the need for compliance with the law and the maintenance standards required by law, especially where there would be a normal expectation that a prosecution would be taken or where, through the conviction of offences, others may be deterred from similar failures to comply with the law;

(2) there is judged to have been a potential for considerable harm arising from the breach or, of course, such harm (or indeed death) as been occasioned; or

(3) the gravity of the offence, taken together with the general record and approach of the offender warrants it, for example apparent reckless disregard for standards, repeated breaches, persistent poor records.

1   The general rule is that HSE is the enforcing authority except to the extent that Health and Safety (Enforcing Authority) Regulations 1998, SI 1998/494 (see Sch 1) specify that the local authority is the enforcing authority instead.
2   As at April 2005 there were over 1,400 inspectors out of a total staff exceeding 3,500.
3   The appointment of inspectors is governed by the HSWA 1974, s 19.
4   www.hse.gov.uk/enforce/index.htm.

Inspectors' powers—general

11.08 There are 13 general powers set out at the HSWA 1974, s 20(2). They include powers of entry (with a constable if 'serious obstruction' is apprehended); and, on entry, to examine, investigate, measure, photograph, record, take samples, dismantle, test and remove for testing. Inspectors can direct that things are left undisturbed pending investigation. They may require persons to give information[1] and answer questions, and to provide facilities and assistance. They may require documents to be produced and may keep copies. There are various procedural safeguards in s 20.[2] Obstructing an inspector is an offence (s 33(1)(h)).[3]

1   See *R (on the application of London Borough of Wandsworth) v South Western Magistrates' Court* [2003] EWHC 1158 (Admin).
2   See also *Skinner v John G McGregor (Contractors) Ltd* 1977 SLT (Sh Ct) 83 and *Laws v Keane* [1982] IRLR 500.
3   See s 33(1)(e) and (f).

11.09   Whilst it is clearly the aim that inspectors should principally exert their influence to maintain the legal standards by visiting premises, informing, advising and seeking to persuade, the threat of an inspection undoubtedly providing a powerful incentive to comply with relevant regulations. The demand for inspection significantly exceeds that possible with the current level of resources. In July 2004 the Department of Work and Pensions Select Committee report (which set out the view that both the HSC and the HSE were under-resourced) recommended that the number of inspectors in the Field Operations Directorate be doubled. In October 2004 the government published its response, which was to require the HSE to prioritise and target its activities using existing resources.

Inspectors' powers—notices

11.10   One of the really significant innovations of the HSWA 1974 was giving inspectors powers to serve improvement notices (s 21) and prohibition notices (s 22). It is an offence to contravene any requirement of such notices (s 33(1)(g)).

11.11   An inspector may serve an *improvement notice* if he is of the opinion that the person:

(a)   is contravening one or more of the relevant statutory provisions; or
(b)   has contravened one or more of those provisions in circumstances that make it likely that the contravention will continue and be repeated.

The notice will set out relevant provisions[1] and give particulars of reason and state a period within which a person is required to remedy the contravention.[2] This must be at least 21 days and is the period within which an appeal may be lodged with an employment tribunal (s 24) The procedure on appeal is governed by the Employment Tribunals (Constitution and Rules of Procedure) Regulations 2004, SI 2004/1861. The employment tribunal may rephrase a notice: *Chrysler (UK) Ltd v McCarthy* [1978] ICR 939, and extend time limits for remedying the breach: *Campion v Hughes (HM Inspector)* [1975] IRLR 291. The effect of lodging the appeal suspends the notice and in the past has been used to ensure a greater period of time within which to comply, if this could not be obtained by negotiation. Usually inspectors will give notice of their intention to issue an improvement notice.

1   *BT Fleet Ltd v Jason McKenna* [2005] EWHC 387 (Admin): an improvement notice must state what is said to be wrong and why; the notice has to be clear and easy to understand. Where a statute provided an option to prescribe how a recipient could comply with a notice, any directions given as to compliance formed part of the notice and, if confusing, could operate to make the notice invalid.
2   An improvement notice could require an 'anti-bandit screen' to protect building society staff: *West Bromwich Building Society v Townsend* [1983] ICR 257.

11.12 A *prohibition notice* may be served if the inspector forms the opinion that there is 'risk of serious personal injury'.[1] An inspector is entitled to issue a notice even though the prohibited activities have been temporarily suspended or interrupted: *Railtrack plc v Smallwood* [2001] EWHC 78 (Admin), [2001] ICR 714. The notice must state the opinion of risk of injury, the matters giving rise to the risk, and, if the risk arises from breach of statutory duty, the statutory provision. Reasons must be given in the notice. The notice, of course, specifies what activity is prohibited and when the prohibition is to come into effect.[2]

1   The risk need not be imminent: *Tesco v Kippax* (1990) 180 HSIB 8. In any appeal the burden is on the inspector to show on a balance of probabilities there was the relevant risk, whereupon the burden falls on the employer to show all that was reasonably practicable was done to avoid it: *Readmans v Leeds City Council* [1993] COD 419.
2   See *Otterburn Mill Ltd v Bulman* [1975] IRLR 223.

11.13 Argument on appeal (the procedure is the same as that for improvement notices) may turn on the question whether or not the safety measure was 'reasonably practicable' and so whether or not there was a breach of statutory duty.[1]

1   As examples, particularly in relation to cost as a factor, see: *Nico Manufacturing Co Ltd v Hendry* [1975] IRLR 225; *Belhaven Brewery Co Ltd v McLean* [1975] IRLR 370; *Harrison (TC) (Newcastle-Under-Lyme) Ltd v Ramsey (HM Inspector)* [1976] IRLR 135; also *Davis (AC) and Sons v Environmental Health Department of Leeds City Council* [1976] IRLR 282.

Prosecutions

11.14 Since this book is devoted to civil liability the reader is directed on criminal matters to more specialist texts. Nonetheless, a broad outline can be set out. On a conviction it is to be noted that the court has power (as well as imposing the appropriate penalty) of ordering that the breach of statutory duty be rectified: HSWA 1974, s 42.

Offences

11.15 Section 33 of the HSWA 1974 is the foundation stone of criminal liability under the Act, setting out the principal offences and preserving those created under earlier legislation. Sections 2–9 constitute the principal duties (along with other duties under other, more specific, legislation) for prosecution under s 33 and for improvement and prohibition notices under ss 21 and 22.

11.15 *Reporting and enforcement*

For the purpose of criminal prosecution failure to comply with a (s 16) code of practice raises a presumption that a related safety requirement was not complied with: s 17.[1]

[1] In *Tudhope v City of Glasgow District Council* 1986 SCCR 168 there was held to be no breach where in an emergency the employers had acted on specialist advice.

11.16 It is important to note that the general duties, those within ss 2–8, impose duties only so far 'as reasonably practicable'. Further, s 40 provides that the burden of proof in proving that the relevant precautions were not reasonably practicable falls on the defendant.[1] In *R v British Steel plc* [1995] IRLR 310, the Court of Appeal held that s 3(1) (and hence each of the other analogous duties):

'... creates an absolute prohibition. And the defence [of reasonable practicability] is a narrow one analogous to the defence under section 29(1) of the Factories Act 1961, which simply comprehends the idea of measures necessary to avert the risks to health and safety.'

[1] See *Davies v HSE* [2002] EWCA Crim 2949: the imposition of a legal burden of proof was justified, necessary and proportionate and therefore compatible with art 6 of the European Convention on Human Rights.

11.17 In *R v Sanyo Electrical Manufacturing (UK) Ltd* (1992) 156 JP 863, the Court of Appeal held that the purpose of this legislation was to protect employees against the consequences of doing things by reason of inadvertence or inattention which they would not normally do.

11.18 Section 2 of the HSWA 1974 provides that the employer must ensure 'the health, safety and welfare at work of all his employees', with particular regard to plant and system of work, handling of articles and substances, instruction,[1] training and supervision, place of work and access (where under his control), safe and healthy working environment. By s 52(1)(b), an employee is not 'at work' except 'during the course of his employment'.[2] The meaning of 'at work', however, extends to Crown servants and the police in the course of their duties, and certain trainees (see HSWA 1974, ss 48, 51A and 52(1)(bb)).

[1] See *Pope v Gould* (20 June 1996, unreported), QBD; the section is concerned not just with the giving of instructions but also ensuring that they are carried out.
[2] But those 'at work' are not confined to those engaged in the specific process for which the plant in question was made available: *Bolton Metropolitan Borough Council v Malrod Insulations Ltd* [1993] ICR 358, DC.

11.19 This general duty for the safety of the employer's own workforce may involve giving information and instructions to persons *not* in its employment, and supervising their system of work, if it might otherwise endanger its employees: *R v Swan Hunter Shipbuilders Ltd* [1981] ICR 831 (shipbuilders gave instructions to own employees for safe use of oxygen equipment but gave no instruction to sub-contractors).

11.20 Section 3 of the HSWA 1974 provides that the employer's duty is to conduct the undertaking in such a way that persons who are *not* employees are not exposed to risks[1] to health and safety.[2] This duty extends not only to other workers but to the general public.[3] A similar duty applies to self-employed workers, for their own safety and that of others. The word 'undertaking' means 'enterprise' or 'business' and it is not necessary to show that the employer has some actual control over how the work is done: *R v Associated Octel Co Ltd* [1997] IRLR 123, HL (employer liable for injury to a contractor's employee because cleaning the plant on which he was engaged was part of the employer's 'undertaking' as a simple question of fact, and the employer had not shown that there was nothing further that it could reasonably have done). The undertaking is being 'conducted' even when shut down for maintenance: *R v Mara* [1987] ICR 165, CA. 'Conduct' includes not only industrial processes but trading and selling to customers: *Sterling-Winthrop Group Ltd v Allan* 1987 SCCR 25. The general duty to ensure safety under s 3(1)[4] may require instructions and information to be given, to non-employees as well as employees, for instance about fire risks from the use of oxygen: it is irrelevant that s 3(3) specifically provides for giving 'information' in circumstances which have not yet been prescribed by regulations: *R v Swan Hunter Shipbuilders Ltd*, above; *Carmichael v Rosehall Engineering Works Ltd* [1983] IRLR 480.

1   Risk is sufficient; proof of harm is not necessary: *R v Board of Trustees of the Science Museum* [1993] 3 All ER 853.
2   There was a breach of this duty when a cleaning company left a machine with an electrical defect at the works of a customer who had permission to use it: *R v Mara* [1987] 1 WLR 87, CA. The defect was a breach of the duty to their own employees under s 2(2)(a), and leaving the machine was part of the conduct of their own undertaking which affected third parties.
3   See *R v Lightwater Valley* (1990) 12 Cr App Rep (S) 328.
4   The powers of inspectors under ss 20, 21 and 22 are an important contextual aid in construing s 3(1): *R v Board of Trustees of the Science Museum*, above.

11.21 Section 4 of the HSWA 1974 imposes duties on persons controlling (to any extent) premises. More than one person may be in control: *Austin Rover Group Ltd v HM Inspector of Factories* [1990] 1 AC 619. Where these are *non-domestic* and are used as a place of work (or a place of resort to use plant or substances) by persons who are *not* their employees, such persons have a duty to see that the premises, access to them, and plant and substances provided are safe for the persons using them. This has been held to include the lifts and other installations in private blocks of flats so as to require the protection of persons who came to repair or maintain them: *Westminster City Council v Select Management Ltd* [1985] ICR 353. The duty was also broad enough to cover children attending a play centre: *Moualem v Carlisle City Council* (1994) 158 JP 1110. The duty is to make the place safe for the purposes for which the visitors are expected to use them: *Austin Rover Group plc v HM Inspector of Factories*, above (no liability for unexpected risk taken by cleaners).

11.22 Section 6 of the HSWA 1974 imposes various detailed health and safety duties on designers, manufacturers, importers, suppliers, erectors and installers of articles and substances for use at work,[1] or any article of fairground equipment.

[1] A prototype mine undergoing trials when it exploded was not 'an article for use at work': *McKay v Unwin Pyrotechnics Ltd* [1991] Crim LR 547, DC. Contrast, however, the wide approach taken to 'work equipment' under the Employers' Liability (Defective Equipment) Act 1969, applying it to a whole sea-going ship *(Coltman v Bibby Tankers Ltd, The derbyshire* [1988] AC 276, HL) and to a flagstone being laid *(Knowles v Liverpool County Council* [1993] IRLR 588, HL).

11.23 Section 7 of the HSWA 1974 places a duty on employees to take reasonable care for the safety of themselves and all other persons affected by their acts and omissions at work; also to 'co-operate' with their employers and other persons on whom duties are imposed under any relevant health and safety legislation, so far as necessary to enable the duties to be performed.[1]

[1] The HSE failed in a prosecution against a college lecturer for failing to co-operate with a risk assessment. See HSIB 236 p 9.

11.24 Section 8 of the HSWA 1974 imposes a duty on all persons not to interfere with anything provided for health, safety or welfare under the statutory provisions.

11.25 Section 9 of the HSWA 1974 prohibits employers charging employees for anything done or provided under the statutory provisions.

11.26 These are the general duties established under the HSWA 1974 and by reason of the potential for a greater penalty to be imposed than in relation to contravention of any of the regulations covered by s 33 of the Act, consideration will usually be given to reference to alleged breaches of them within a prosecution even if there are also charges brought in relation to more specific offences under relevant regulations. As for specific regulations, there are general duties under the Management of Health and Safety at Work Regulations 1999, SI 1999/3242 and also under the Workplace Regulations 1992, SI 1992/3004, and also other regulations. The 1992 Regulations widen the range of offences for which the HSE can prosecute and provide more specific offences in many cases than those under the HSWA 1974, ss 2–9.[1]

[1] This may assist to overcome problems of particularisation of offences: see e g *Cleveland Structural Engineering Ltd v Hamilton* 1994 SLT 590.

Criminal responsibility of corporations

11.27 Up until 1944 all criminal cases of responsibility of corporate bodies were based on vicarious liability. However, since 1944 a company can be criminally liable on the basis that the acts of certain employees are regarded as being 'the acts of the company itself'. This is direct, personal, not vicarious liability and has been labelled 'the doctrine of identification' by reason of the need to identify the relevant individuals. See *DPP v Kent & Sussex Contractors Ltd; R v ICR Haulage Co Ltd* (1944) KB 551 and *Moore v I Brestler Ltd* [1944] 2 KB 515.

11.28 In the *Tesco Supermarkets Ltd v Nattrass* [1972] AC 153 it was established that the doctrine of identification applied, in principle, to all offences not based upon vicarious liability. The House of Lords held that a corporation could be convicted of a non-regulatory offence requiring proof of mens rea if the person who committed the actus reus of the offence could be identified with the corporation. This decision has been widely criticised but it confirms the trio of cases introducing the principle of identification (confirming that a corporation could in principle be personally liable for almost any non-regulatory criminal offence, however serious). It has been said that the identification principle makes conviction possible only within small companies and not large ones. Certainly, the HSE at one point stated that it had identified a trend on the part of many organisations to decentralise safety services. It has been said that the model of a 'ladder of responsibilities', referred to in *Tesco*, is a somewhat simplistic tool with which to analyse the decision-making in a large modern corporation let alone a multi-national enterprise.

11.29 The difficulties involved in convicting corporations for serious crimes (rather than regulatory offences) has ensured that such prosecutions have remained a rarity. The principle of identification was reaffirmed by the Court of Appeal in *Attorney General's Reference No 2 of 1999* (2002) 2 Cr App Rep 207, a prosecution for manslaughter brought against Great Western Trains as a result of the Southall rail disaster. Two questions were referred to the Court of Appeal by the Attorney General, the second of which was 'can a non-human defendant be convicted of the crime of manslaughter by gross negligence in the absence of evidence establishing the guilt of an identified human individual for the same crime?'

The answer was no:

> 'in our judgment, unless an identified individual's conduct, characterisable as gross criminal negligence, can be attributed to the company, the company is not, in the present state of the law, liable for manslaughter'.

11.30 As a result of this reaffirmation of principle and the continued criticism[1] of the near immunity from prosecution other than under the HSWA 1974 said to be created as a result,[2] the government repeatedly stated its intention to introduce relevant statutory offences. At the time of writing there is a Corporate Manslaughter Bill, potentially introducing new offences holding organisations to account for gross failings by their senior management that had fatal consequences.

[1] See generally the Law Commission's 1996 report 'Legislating the Criminal Code: Involuntary Manslaughter' Law Com No 237.
[2] Between 1992 and 2005 there were only 34 prosecution cases for work-related manslaughter, and only six small organisations convicted.

11.31 Currently, the starting point for consideration of manslaughter by gross negligence remains the decision of the House of Lords in *R v Adomacko* [1995] 1 AC 171. The ordinary principles in the law of negligence apply to determine whether the defendant was in breach of the duty of care towards the victim;[1] on the establishment of such breach of duty, the next question is whether it caused the death of the victim, and if so, whether it should be characterised as gross negligence and therefore a crime. It is 'eminently' a jury question to decide whether, having regard to the risk of the death involved, the defendant's conduct was so bad in all the circumstances as to amount to a criminal act or an omission.

1 In *R v Lidar* (2000) 4 Archibald News 3, CA, it was said in the case of conscious risk-taking that it was appropriate to direct the jury by reference to recklessness and that what has to be proved is an obvious risk of serious harm of the defendant's conduct, objectively assessed, and an indifference to that risk on the part of the defendant, or foresight thereof plus a determination nevertheless to run it.

Liability of a company for the acts of another

11.32 Section 36 of the HSWA 1974 provides that though the relevant obligations of the statutes may fall on one person, where the wrongful act or default[1] is that of 'another person', then that other person is criminally liable. This is particularly relevant in relation to employers which are companies and thus potentially able to shift criminal liability to individuals to whom the company (acting through its board of directors) has delegated the responsibility of ensuring compliance with the statutory duties. The case of *Tesco Supermarkets Ltd v Nattrass* [1972] AC 153, HL a consumer protection case, was formerly treated as amplifying this rule so that employers could easily evade criminal liability by delegation. However, in *R v British Steel plc* [1995] IRLR 310 the Court of Appeal blocked this escape route. Steyn LJ, giving the judgment of the court, distinguished *Nattrass* on the grounds that:

(1) it involved consumer protection which required less stringent protection than health and safety at work;

(2) *Nattrass* turned on the Trade Descriptions Act 1968 which provided a 'due diligence' defence which is not found in the HSWA 1974 (and was repealed long ago from the Factories Act 1961, s 161);

(3) s 3(1) of the HSWA 1974 created a duty of strict liability 'and the words "so far as reasonably practicable" are simply referable to measures necessary to avert the risk'.

1 See *Noss Farm Products Ltd v Lilico* [1945] 2 All ER 609; *Lamb v Sunderland and District Creamery Ltd* [1951] 1 All ER 923.

11.33 This rejection of the identification doctrine in health and safety cases brought under the HSWA 1974, essential in order to promote the protective intent of the statute, was then reaffirmed in *R v Gateway Foodmarkets Ltd* [1997] IRLR 189 where the company was held liable for a fatal accident to a member of its staff, caused by an unsafe practice adopted at one of its supermarkets, with the knowledge of the local management, but no involvement of any 'guiding brains' at company level. A new possible escape for the company appeared to be opened up in *R v Nelson Group Services (Maintenance) Ltd* [1999] IRLR 646 whenever the duty in question is to do something 'as far as reasonably practicable'. Where the company's gas fitter left an appliance in a dangerous state the Court of Appeal held that the question was not whether there was anything more that the fitter could reasonably have done, but whether there was anything more that the *company* could have done (ie the defence was applied at corporate level). As the company had had a good system of training and supervising its fitters, it was not liable for this individual failing. However, this was effectively reversed by reg 21 of the Management of Health and Safety at Work Regulations 1999, which provides:

> 'Nothing in the relevant statutory provisions shall operate so as to afford an employer a defence in any criminal proceedings for a contravention of those proceedings by any act or default of ... an employee of his ...'

The upshot is that delegation, whether to the most senior or most junior employee, of the duty under s 2(1) (and analogous duties) by an employer will not avoid criminal liability if such duty is breached. It would thus appear that in relation to the principal duties under ss 2–9 and similar duties elsewhere in the legislation, s 36 will not enable employers to escape conviction by pointing a finger at employees to whom they have delegated responsibility, though s 36, of course, also enables prosecution of the delegated employee.

Prosecution of individuals

11.34 Enforcing authorities should identify and prosecute or recommend prosecution of individuals under the HSWA 1974 if they consider that a conviction is warranted and can be secured under ss 7 or 37. Section 37 of the HSWA 1974 provides that where a corporation is guilty of an offence so also is any director, manager or similar officer[1] who consented or connived at the commission of the offence or who was guilty of neglect[2] to which the offence was attributable. They will actively consider the management chain and the role played by individual directors/managers and have to evaluate whether it can be shown that the offence was committed with their consent or guidance or to have been attributable to neglect on their part. Although most commonly there will be criminal proceedings against the company as well as against the director or manager, it is not necessary to prosecute both. Where appropriate, the enforcing authority should also seek the disqualification of directors (directors convicted under s 37 may also be disqualified for up to two years from being a company director: Company Directors Disqualification Act 1986, s 2(1)). Prosecutions of individual employees for breach of the general duty owed under s 7 are rare.

1   This does not include an employee standing in for the manager of a shop whilst the latter was away for a week's holiday: *R v Boal* [1992] QB 591; it does include a Council's Director of Roads: *Armour v Skeen* [1977] IRLR 310. *Boal* holds that only those responsible for deciding corporate policy and strategy were 'managers'.
2   See *Wotherspoon v HM Advocate* 1978 JC 74 at 78.

Procedure

11.35 The first step in the consideration of a prosecution under the HSWA 1974 is usually the enforcement report. The relevant inspector or officer produces a report which will normally encompass:

(i)   summary of the facts;
(ii) summary of the investigation;
(iii) the standards involved;

  (iv) the legal conclusions;
  (v) the enforcement recommendations;
  (vi) prosecution justification;
 (vii) evidence to be adduced;
(viii) liability of witnesses;
  (ix) response of the defendant.

The report then goes to an approving officer who has to give his/her reasons for approval/non approval of the investigating inspectors' reasons for proposing prosecution.[1] An inspector has the power to appear and prosecute any matter if it is tried in the magistrates court (s 39). If it is thought necessary 'to move to the Crown Court' then the head of operations may be required to authorise prosecution. In suitable cases the Crown Prosecution Service may also have been involved and they will have prepared an 'advice on case' report.

[1]   The approving officer also should consider alternative information, exacerbating/mitigating factors, possible offences, relevant case law and proposed venue.

11.36 The decision to prosecute is taken in light of the HSC's enforcement policy and with adherence to the management model. There are two different relevant categories:

  (i) circumstances where there would ordinarily be prosecution;
 (ii) circumstances where the enforcement authority is expected to consider prosecution.

11.37 Currently, the HSC expects that enforcing authorities will *normally prosecute*, or recommend prosecution where, following an investigation or other regulatory contact, the following circumstances apply:

  (i) death was a result of a breach of legislation;
 (ii) the gravity and alleged offence, taken together with the seriousness of any actual potential harm, or the general record and approach of the offender warrant it;
(iii) there has been a reckless disregard of health and safety requirements;
 (iv) there have been repeated breaches of persistent poor compliance;
  (v) work has been carried out without or in serious breach of an appropriate licence or safety case;
 (vi) there has been a failure to comply with a written warning or an improvement or prohibition notice;
(vii) inspectors have been intentionally obstructed in the lawful course of their duty.

11.38 The HSC also expects that enforcing authorities will *consider prosecution* or recommending prosecution where, following an investigation or other regulatory contact, the following circumstances apply (list in order of priority):

  (i) false information has been wilfully supplied, or there has been an attempt to deceive;
 (ii) there have been serious failures in the management of health and safety;

(iii)   it is appropriate in the circumstances as a way to draw general attention to the need for compliance with the law and the maintenance of standards required by law, and conviction may deter others from similar failures to comply with the law.

Sentencing

11.39 A serious breach under the HSWA 1974 may be tried on indictment, when the maximum penalty is two years' imprisonment, an unlimited fine, or both. On summary conviction the general maximum fine is £5,000, though an amendment in 1992 raised this to £20,000 for breach of the general duties in ss 2–6 of the Act, and to the same level and/or six months' imprisonment for breach of a prohibition or improvement notice or a court order to rectify a defect

11.40 In *R v F Howe & Son (Engineers) Ltd* [1999] IRLR 434 the Court of Appeal provided much-needed assistance in respect of sentencing guidelines for health and safety offences. Scott Baker J commented that the level of fines for such offences had generally been too low in the past and that fines should be sufficient to send out a message to companies and, notably, their shareholders. However, he acknowledged that a court will have to perform a delicate balancing exercise. The fine should reflect the gravity of the offence and the means of the offender and should not be so large as to imperil the position of other employees. Each case must be considered on its own facts and the Court of Appeal declined to lay down tariffs.

11.41 When considering the severity of a case the relevant aggravating factors include:[1]

(a)   the failure to heed warnings;
(b)   a deliberate attempt to gain financially from a failure to take necessary precautions; and
(c)   a deliberate attempt to run a risk so as to save money or cut corners.

Likewise, the mitigating factors include:

(a)   steps taken to remedy any deficiencies or dangers;
(b)   a prompt admission of responsibility and timely guilty plea; and
(c)   a good safety record.

As the *Howe* case dealt with the severity of an offence and hence the likely level of fine, it is carefully considered at sentencing hearings by magistrates when deciding whether to accept or decline jurisdiction.

1   This should be agreed between the parties if possible: see generally *R v Friskies Petcare (UK) Ltd* (March 2000, unreported), CA.

Employees' remedies

11.42 The rights to have safety representatives and safety committees, and their rights to be consulted, receive information and to make inspections are set out at chapter 8. These rights of safety representatives to be involved have received much support from the European Directives which place them centrally in European health and safety strategy and reflect the EU policy of 'social partnership'. However, employees have rights to take action themselves, the most significant of which is the right to stop work and immediately proceed to a place of safety in any situation where there is a serious and imminent danger: Management of Health and Safety at Work Regulations 1999, SI 1999/3242, reg 8.

Injunctions and declarations

11.43 The use of injunctions in health and safety law in the work sphere seems to be almost unknown. Some commentators have suggested that the injunction may be a remedy more readily available in consequence of the impact of the European Directives and the 'six pack' Regulations of 1992, but in seems clear that in principle injunctive relief was, in any event, potentially available under UK law. By the Supreme Court Act 1981, s 37(1) the court has jurisdiction to 'grant an injunction in all cases in which it appears to the court to be just and convenient to do so'; see now CPR 1998, r 25.1(1)(a). There must also be added force in the fact that the Directives require an effective remedy (see generally chapter 9, above).

11.44 In the apparent absence of authority on injunctions in employers' liability cases the exact requirements are uncertain. But it would seem that the claimant will have to show a clear breach of duty together with a real risk of injury if the injunction is not granted. Plainly the necessary degree of probability of harm occurring will vary according to the potential gravity of the harm if it does occur. Previous injuries arising from the breach will, of course, be telling matters. In *Khorasandjian v Bush* [1993] QB 727, the Court of Appeal granted an injunction to restrain threatening phone calls even though no psychiatric injury had as yet been caused to the claimant, but where there was an 'obvious risk' it would be (Dillon LJ at 736).

11.45 In order to obtain injunctive relief it is necessary to demonstrate the inadequacy of other remedies. The starting point must be that the claimant would have to show that he was obliged by his contract of employment to do whatever it was that exposed him to risk. The employee's right, where serious and imminent danger are believed to exist, to leave the workplace (Management of Health and Safety at Work Regulations 1999, SI 1999/3242, reg 8(2)(b)) would not seem to be an alternative remedy sufficient to debar injunctive relief, since the right is plainly a temporary and immediate response which does nothing to rectify the danger or protect against pressure (other than threat of detriment) to continue to work whilst exposed to it. Neither should the fact that the HSE inspectorate have powers to make improvement and prohibition notices of itself bar a claimant from injunctive relief. However, if the claimant had failed to take any step to draw the inspectorate's attention to the problem, that might weigh with a court exercising the discretion inherent in equitable relief. Had an inspector visited and declined to issue any notice, that would be likely to weigh heavily against the grant of an injunction. Conversely, had the inspectorate given advice or served a notice to rectify the danger which had not been heeded within a reasonable or specified time, that would count very strongly in favour of an injunction. Damages for any subsequent injury would not, it is thought, be an adequate remedy: the court should naturally incline to preventing injury occurring. Further, the court may have regard to the difficulties in pursuing litigation in respect of any injury. Although the HSWA 1974, s 47(2) only permits civil actions where a breach of regulations 'causes' damage (s 47(2)), this should not inevitably preclude an action for an injunction where no damage has yet occurred (just as no action in negligence arises until damage has been caused).

11.46 By virtue of the risk of injury and consequential need for speedy relief, an application for an interlocutory injunction may be appropriate on the basis of the principles enunciated in *American Cyanamid Co v Ethicon Ltd* [1975] AC 396 which continue to apply under CPR 1998, r 25.1(1)(a). In short: a serious issue to be tried, inadequacy of damages or other remedy, and a balance of convenience in favour of granting the injunction. It would be unlikely that a court would require an employer to install expensive and inconvenient precautions on an interlocutory basis and the claimant's cross-undertaking in damages might be difficult if this was the form of injunction sought. However, relatively cheap and easy innovations (which the claimant would have to spell out) might be ordered, as well as the simple expedient of putting the claimant onto other, safe, work.

11.47 In cases where there is no or little risk of injury (or at least no immediate risk of injury), a declaration may be a useful option. An interim declaration may be sought under CPR 1998, r 25.1(1)(b). There is a discretionary element to the grant of a declaration, though it merely states the rights and duties of the parties on the matter in dispute. A declaration also disposes of the problem of seeking a mandatory order requiring the employer to install some complex, expensive and disputed safety measures. A declaration that the employer is in breach of a statutory requirement (or even, though more difficult, a common law duty of care) would leave the remedy in the hands of the employer. An employer who failed to remedy a breach identified by a declaration would be open to further proceedings and there would be obvious pressure on the HSE to investigate and take appropriate action. A subsequent injunction would be easier to obtain and any claim for damages in respect of an accident or ill-health occurring by reason of the breach would be virtually unanswerable.

11.48 An interim (or final) declaration would seem a useful way of seeking to enforce welfare provisions such as seating, rest rooms, eating facilities, changing rooms and the like. This might be a particularly attractive option for a pregnant or nursing mother with a State employer who was not providing rest accommodation which allowed her to lie down as the Workplace Directive requires but the Workplace (Health, Safety and Welfare) Regulations 1992 do not.

Damages

11.49 The legal enforcement mechanism most used is the civil action for damages. The basis for such claims is the primary subject matter of this book. Since such actions must, to succeed, show a breach of legal standard, it is right to see damages claims as a means of upholding standards, and not merely as a means of compensating victims or (which is also true) of distributing the economic risk and consequence of injury. No doubt the risk of future claims has often prompted a change in employer practice, to the benefit of workers. The amount of damages payable (the 'quantum' of damages), the availability (or non-availability) of damages beyond compensation (exemplary[1] and aggravated damages), the compensatable heads of loss, and the approach of the courts to the various heads are all matters beyond the scope of this book.

[1] See *Kuddus v Chief Constable of Leicestershire Constabulary* [2001] UKHL 29, [2002] 2 AC 122 and the potential availability of such damages.

Chapter 12

INDUSTRIAL RELATIONS

Damian Brown

12.01 This chapter considers what might be loosely termed the law of industrial relations in relation to health and safety matters. It does not deal with the typical contractual, unfair dismissal or disability discrimination claims which may arise from the dismissal of sick or ill workers.[1] Nor does it consider wider aspects of industrial relations. It concentrates on the duties imposed on an employer to consult and to provide information; and the specific rights given to employees in connection with health and safety issues. All these matters have been the subject of recent legislation.

---

[1]   See *Harvey on Industrial Relations and Employment Law* for detailed consideration of these subjects

CONSULTATION AND INFORMATION

History

12.02 Workers are often the persons best placed to know the risks associated with their work and, recognising this, legal rights to guarantee the involvement of workers in health and safety are not a recent development: from 1872 miners had rights to inspect their workplace. The Robens report, which led to the HSWA 1974, considered that employee involvement in health and safety matters was central to securing high standards in the area. The empirical evidence confirms this view,[1] which is reflected in s 2 of that Act and the subsequent introduction of the Safety Representative and Safety Committee Regulations 1977, SI 1977/500 (see below). In keeping with the political and industrial relations climate of the times, those Regulations were and are restricted to consultation with recognised unions.

[1]   On the effectiveness of safety representatives, see Reilly, Paci and Holl 'Unions, Safety Committees and Workplace Injuries' (1995) 33 BJIR 275.

12.03 Subsequent developments have largely been driven by Europe. Drawing upon a European vision of workers' organisations as one side of a partnership in the setting of corporate policy—as one of the 'social' partners—the Directives on health and safety have imposed obligations on employers to consult with workers on the matters falling within their scope. Derived in the first place from the Framework Directive (89/391/EEC), this consultation is seen as a means of improving standards on health and safety: the Preamble to the Framework Directive states that 'in order to ensure an improved degree of protection' workers and/or their representatives should contribute to health and safety discussions'. These laws were initially met with hostility on the part of a Conservative government opposed to any form of worker rights.

12.04 But it soon became clear that the restriction of consultation rights to those workplaces in which an employer chose or was forced to recognise a union was in breach of European law. In *C-382/92, C-383/92 EC Commission v United Kingdom* [1994] ICR 664, ECJ the UK was found to be in breach of art 6 of the Acquired Rights Directive 77/187 and arts 2 and 3 of the Collective Redundancies Directive 75/129 because of the failure to provide for a mechanism of consultation in workplaces where the employer refused to recognise a union.[1] The same conclusion was, as predicted in the 12th edition of this book, inevitable in respect of the 1977 Regulations because the Framework Directive and its daughter Directives require consultation with 'workers and/or their representatives' regardless of whether a union happens to be recognised or not. As a consequence and without the need for proceedings before the ECJ, the Health and Safety (Consultation with Employees) Regulations 1996, SI 1996/1513, were introduced. These Regulations operate in parallel with the 1977 Regulations and only apply when the employees are not represented by union representatives under the 1977 Regulations.

[1] Although art 2(c) of the Acquired Rights Directive defined 'representatives of the employees' as 'representatives ... provided for by the laws or practice of the Member States' the ECJ said: '[That article] leaves to Member States only the task of determining the arrangement for designating the employee representatives who must be informed and consulted under art 6(1) and (2).' It added: 'The intention of the Community legislature was not therefore to allow the different national legal systems to accept a situation in which no employee representatives are designated, since such designation is necessary to ensure compliance with the obligations laid down in art 6 of the Directive.'

12.05 The relevant provisions of European law are considered below, first, because these have led to amendments to earlier regulations (e g the Safety Representative and Safety Committee Regulations 1977, see below) and because domestic legislation in the same area as European law must be interpreted to give effect to that law. This principle should be borne in mind when considering the United Kingdom legislation, which follows the European section.

Duties under European law

12.06 Worker participation occupies a central place in the European Directives on health and safety. The Preamble to the Framework Directive (89/391/EEC), for example, states that 'information, dialogue and balanced participation on safety and health at work must be developed between employers and workers and/or their representatives', and this principle is reflected in the articles of that Directive and its daughter Directives. The Management of Health and Safety at Work Regulations 1999, the Safety Representative and Safety Committee Regulations 1977 and the Health and Safety (Consultation with Employees) Regulations 1996 are intended collectively to implement these duties.

12.07 By way of background, it is likely that the Directives envisage a wide ambit to the concepts of health and safety. In *C-84/94 United Kingdom v EU Council* [1997] IRLR 30 the ECJ considered whether the Working Time Directive concerned health and safety for the purposes of art 137 (ex art 118) EC. Holding that it did, the ECJ referred to the Constitution of the World Health Organisation in which health is defined 'as a state of complete physical, mental and social well-being that does not consist only in the absence of illness or infirmity'. The same interpretation will no doubt apply to health and safety matters in the Directives.

12.08 Under art 10 of the Framework Directive the employer must ensure that workers and/or their representatives in the undertaking receive all necessary information on risks to health and safety, the preventive and protective measures, and the measures for designating workers to implement first aid, fire-fighting and evacuation measures (art 10(1)). On its face this obligation extends to all employees actually working in the undertaking, including those who are not strictly the undertaking's employees.[1] Each of the daughter Directives includes an obligation on the part of the employer to inform workers of the measures to be taken pursuant to that Directive, but this is stated to be without prejudice to the general obligation in art 10.

1   Including employees of other organisations having work at the enterprise, eg postal staff, firefighters: see eg paras 10.08 and 10.29, above.

12.09 The Directives also impose duties of consultation. Under art 11(1) of the Framework Directive an employer is obliged to consult with 'workers and/or their representatives ... on *all* questions relating to health and safety at work' (authors' emphasis). This general duty is supplemented by additional, more specific subjects of consultation in art 11(2); these include consulting on matters which substantially affect health and safety, on the planning and organisation of training, and on the introduction of new technologies in relation to the consequences for health and safety (art 6(3)(c)). In keeping with the approach of the Framework Directive, each of the daughter Directives impose obligations to provide information and to consult in relation to the matters which fall within them, referring to arts 10 and 11 of the Framework Directive.[1]

1   See eg Workplace Directive, arts 7, 8; Work Equipment Directive, arts 6, 8; Manual Handling Directive, arts 6, 7; Personal Protective Equipment Directive, arts 7, 8; Display Screen Directive arts 6, 8.

12.10 The employer's duty to consult is part of a spectrum of related duties. Article 11(1), as well as referring to the obligation to consult, also refers to the obligation to allow workers and their representatives to take part in discussions on all questions relating to health and safety at work. These two obligations do not amount to the same thing. Consultation, the soliciting of views, arises when the employer proposes to take an initiative. But the right to take part in discussions is, it seems, automatic: whenever the employer considers a health and safety matter, the workers and their representatives must have the opportunity to participate.

311

12.11 Article 11(1) goes on to state that those two duties on employers presuppose:

(1)   the consultation of workers;
(2)   the right of workers and/or the representatives to make proposals;
(3)   balanced participation in accordance with national laws or practice.

This is confusing. The three limbs appear to be conjunctive. The first limb, consultation, is a repetition of the statement of duty at the outset of art 11(1). The second limb is inherent in both consultation and participation in discussions. The third limb may be no more than a reiteration of the duty to allow the taking part in discussions, or it may be more, implying participation in decision-making.

12.12 Article 11(2) is yet more confusing, stating that workers or their representatives 'shall take part in a balanced way in accordance with national laws or practices, *or* shall be consulted' on various specific matters (see above). There is no clue as to whether the participation is to be in decision-making or merely discussions. The use of the word 'or' emphasises, however, that participation is a different concept to consultation. The use of that term also indicates that in relation to the matters specified in art 11(2) the employer's obligations would appear to be capable of being satisfied by consultation alone. The implication is therefore that on all other health and safety matters participation beyond mere consultation will be required. Yet few such health and safety matters can be envisaged outside those specified in art 11(2), in particular because one of the subjects of art 11(2) is 'any measure which may substantially affect safety and health'.[1] The general obligation in art 11(1) to ensure participation thus appears to be greatly diminished by the permission given under art 11(2) to consult instead over most health and safety matters.

[1]   It may be that the duty to consult on *all* questions in art 11(1) is of wider scope.

12.13 It remains unclear, then, whether the Directive establishes a right to participation beyond consultation. It may be that the rationale is that participation is only required in circumstances where, and to the extent that, national law or practice establishes it. If so, there is no such law in the UK. None is contained in the Management of Health and Safety at Work Regulations, the 1977 Regulations as amended or the 1996 Regulations, all of which are restricted to consultation, notwithstanding that the duties of consultation and of *participation* (by reference to art 11 of the Framework Directive) are found in all of the daughter Directives.[1] It also seems doubtful if any national practice of participation could be established on the evidence.[2] Yet absence of national law and practice cannot, under European law, permit evasion of a (relatively) explicit duty. Only litigation can resolve this conundrum. And this is not the end of the interpretation problems with art 11.[3]

[1]   See eg the Workplace Directive, art 8; the Work Equipment Directive art 8; the Personal Protective Equipment Directive, art 8; Manual Handling Directive, art 7; Display Screen Directive, art 8; Carcinogens at Work Directive, art 13.
[2]   Unlike the national practice in a different context established on the basis of expert evidence in *Griffin v Southwest Water Services Ltd* [1995] IRLR 15.

3   Another is that the duty to consult is in respect of workers *and/or their representatives* in art 11(1) (preamble) and art 11(2) (preamble). In contrast, the consultation on which the duties in art 11(1) are presupposed is a duty to consult only *workers*. This in turn must be contrasted with the two other presuppositions (above)—the rights to make proposals and of balanced participation—which are expressed to be in respect of workers *and/or their representatives*. The significance of the omission of the words 'and/or workers' representatives' in the first limb of the presuppositions is a mystery to the authors unless it is intended as a generalisation to include workers' representatives.

12.14 The Framework Directive also lays down certain worker roles relevant to the protection of health and safety. First, the employer must designate a worker to carry out activities relating to the prevention of occupational risk in the 'undertaking and/or establishment' (see art 7). This person is to be permitted time off, is to be given the necessary information on health and safety, and may not be placed at a disadvantage because of his or her activities (art 7(2), (3), (4)). Second, other provisions concern the clumsily defined 'workers' representative, with specific responsibility for health and safety' (see art 3(c)). This person is defined in art 3 as 'any person elected, chosen or designated in accordance with national laws and/or practices to represent the workers' in this area. The Directive does not specify the legal mechanisms by which these persons are to be appointed.[1] He or she has the right to ask the employer to take appropriate measures to mitigate hazards (art 11(3)); is entitled to appropriate training and time off with pay (arts 12(3), 11(5)); and may not be placed at a disadvantage because of his or her activities (art 11(4)). Third, the Directive also appears to contemplate other workers' representatives of a less formal kind (see art 11(1))—perhaps making representations on behalf of his or her colleagues in relation to a specific issue. Neither this person nor other workers may be placed at a disadvantage because they, for example, make proposals or engage in consultation (art 11(4)).

1   The approach is similar in the Collective Redundancy Directive 75/129, art 1(1)(b) and the Acquired Rights Directive 77/187, art 2(c).

The Safety Representative and Safety Committee Regulations 1977

12.15 Section 2(4) of the HSWA 1974 permitted the Secretary of State to make regulations providing for the appointment by 'recognised trade unions' of safety representatives to represent the employees in consultations with the employer on health and safety matters.[1] Section 2(6) of the HSWA imposes a duty on the employer:

'to consult any such representatives with a view to the making and maintenance of arrangements which will enable [the employer] and his employees to co-operate effectively in promoting and developing measures to ensure the health and safety at work of the employees'.

1   Originally, s 2(5) of the Act gave power to appoint representatives where unions were not recognised. That provision was repealed in 1975.

12.16 The relevant regulations are the Safety Representative and Safety Committee Regulations 1977, subsequently amended as a result of the Framework Directive by the Management of Health and Safety at Work

313

Regulations 1992 (now the 1999 Regulations of the same name). The Regulations are supplemented by Approved Codes of Practice issued under the HSWA 1974, s 16.[1]

1   See the HSC Codes of Practice on Safety Representatives and Safety Committees and on Time Off for the Training of Safety Representatives, now found in the HSE publication *Safety Representatives and Safety Committees* (1996).

12.17 By virtue of reg 3, a 'recognised trade union' is entitled to appoint safety representatives with whom the employer must consult under reg 4A and by virtue of the HSWA 1974, s 2(6). The representative must be an employee: *Costain Building and Civil Engineering Ltd v Smith* [2000] ICR 215, EAT (subject to exceptions in reg 8 for representatives of Equity or the Musician's Union). The Regulations have been amended by the Police (Health and Safety) Regulations 1999, SI 1999/860, so that constables are treated as employees and the various police representative organisations, such as the Police Federation, are deemed to be recognised unions.

12.18 The scope of consultation is wide, relating to the promotion and development of measures to ensure the health and safety of employees and the checking of the effectiveness of such measures as well as the more specific matters listed in reg 4A, including 'the introduction of any safety measure which may substantially affect the health and safety of the employees' and the health and safety consequences of introducing new technologies.[1] Reinforcing this wide duty is art 11(1) of the Framework Directive (89/391/EEC), requiring consultation on *all* questions relating to health and safety;[2] and the wide interpretation given to the concepts of 'health and safety' in art 137 (ex art 118) of the Treaty by the ECJ in *C-84/94 United Kingdom v EU Council* [1997] IRLR 30 (see para 12.07, above). The duty to consult in Regulations and in the HSWA 1974, s 2(6) should be interpreted to conform to these European standards.

1   See the HSWA 1974, s 2(6) and reg 4A(1).
2   More specific obligations, on which the reg 4A duties are based, are then set out in art 11(2).

12.19 Where the employer is subject to a duty to consult, implicit in that are duties to provide information as well as conscientiously taking representations into account.[1] The duty is explicit in the Regulations in any case, for the employer must supply the representatives with the information they need to exercise their functions, subject to some exceptions (reg 7(2)) and they are entitled to inspect and take copies of documents (reg 7). The Code of Practice gives examples of the sort of information which should be disclosed, including historical records of accidents, dangerous occurrences and notifiable diseases (see para 6). Safety representatives may inspect the workplace (regs 5–6).

1   See, on the nature of consultation generally: *R v Gwent County Council and Secretary of State for Wales, ex p Bryant* [1988] COD 19; *R v Warwickshire District Council, ex p Bailey* [1991] COD 284; and in the industrial relations context: *R v British Coal Corpn and Secretary of State for Trade and Industry, ex p Price* [1994] IRLR 72 (at paras 24–25); followed in *Rowell v Hubbard Group Services Ltd* [1995] IRLR 195 (at paras 15–16).

12.20 In addition to engaging their consultation rights, reg 4 confers specific functions on safety representatives to investigate potential hazards, to investigate complaints, to make representations to the employer and to represent employees before the HSE. If two or more representatives so request in writing the employer is obliged to establish a safety committee (s 2(7) of the Act and reg 9). Safety representatives are entitled to time off with pay during working hours as is necessary to perform their functions or to undergo training (reg 4(2)). A representative of a recognised union who has been refused paid time off can present a complaint to an employment tribunal (reg 11).[1]

1   For the scope of the right, see *Diamond v Courtaulds Hosiery Ltd* [1979] IRLR 449, *White v Pressed Steel Fisher* [1980] IRLR 176.

12.21 As to enforcement, a breach of s 2(6) of the Act would be a criminal offence (see the HSWA 1974, s 33(1)), but it would not give rise to a civil action (s 47(1)). Because the 1977 Regulations were introduced under s 2(4), they are not made actionable in civil proceedings by s 47(2).[1] It is arguable, however, that a right to bring a civil action should be read into the Regulations as part of the common law rules on breach of statutory duty (the Regulations are passed for the benefit of a particular class) reinforced by the requirements of effective sanctions under European law.

1   See the definition of 'health and safety regulations' in s 53(1).

12.22 As noted above, the duties in the Regulations are restricted to recognised unions alone. Following the repeal by the Employment Act 1980 of the compulsory recognition procedure contained in the Employment Act 1975, an employer who made it clear that it was refusing to recognise a union was able to achieve this result unilaterally: see *Associated Newspapers Ltd v Wilson* [1995] ICR 406, HL.[1] Although recognition could arise merely from an employer in fact engaging in collective bargaining with a trade union without expressly agreeing to recognise the union, this is not something which the courts will presume lightly.[2] There is, however, now a compulsory recognition procedure under the Trade Union and Labour Relations (Consolidation) Act 1992, s 70A and Sch Al, introduced by the Employment Relations Act 1999.

1   Recognition is defined in reg 2 of the Regulations by reference to what is now the Trade Union and Labour Relations (Consolidation) Act 1992, s 178.
2   See *Cleveland County Council v Springett* [1985] IRLR 131, EAT (a sustained course of conduct is normally required) and *National Union of Gold, Silver and Allied Trades v Albury Bros Ltd* [1978] ICR 62 (habitual negotiation over a period of time required).

The Health and Safety (Consultation with Employees) Regulations 1996

12.23 These Regulations were introduced to conform to European law, and to ensure that workers not represented by recognised trade unions are nonetheless consulted about health and safety. They only apply at workplaces where there are employees who are not represented under the 1977 Regulations (reg 3). Ships' crews and domestic staff in private households are excluded. The employer must then either consult with the employees directly

315

or with representatives elected by any group of employees (reg 4). It follows that the employer may have to consult under both the 1977 and 1996 Regulations.[1] The 1996 Regulations do not specify the means of election and nor do they define what is a 'group' of employees.[2] But it appears that the terminology of the Framework Directive ('workers and/or their representatives' (art 11)) presupposes that workers themselves should be free to decide who is to represent them, for an imposed representative is hardly a representative at all.[3] It seems equally consistent with the Framework Directive that workers should be able to insist on consultation through a representative, rather than direct with the workforce: only a representative may have the time and competence to ensure that health and safety standards are met. The HSC Codes of Practice do not apply to these Regulations (see para 12.16, above) but there is Guidance on the Regulations, published in 1997.

[1] Under reg 3(2) of the 1977 Regulations, the employer is informed in writing of which groups of employees are represented by union representatives.
[2] The editors *of Harvey on Industrial Relations and Employment Law* refer to Sch 1 to the Working Time Regulations 1998 which indicate that a group may be defined by the workers' function, workplace or work unit (see para N [4016]).
[3] On this see *Harvey on Industrial Relations and Employment Law* at para N [4017].

12.24 The employer is under a similar, but not identical duty, to consult with the employees or the elected representative as that in the 1977 Regulations (see reg 3 of the 1996 Regulations). The duty is not identical because in the 1996 Regulations there is no duty corresponding to that in the HSWA 1974, s 2(6), which in any case is confined to consultation with recognised union representatives. But reg 3 of the 1996 Regulations refers to the general duty to consult 'employees in good time on matters relating to their health and safety at work'. Provided that phrase is read as the general obligation, and the examples in reg 3(a)–(e) as non-exclusive components of the general duty, the wording is wide enough to encompass the duties of consultation required under European law (see above under the 1977 Regulations).

12.25 The 1996 Regulations give representatives or employees rights to information 'necessary to enable them to participate fully and effectively in the consultation' (reg 5(1), (2)), subject to exceptions as under the 1977 Regulations in reg 5(3). Representatives are entitled to make representations to the employer and to represent employees in consultation with health and safety inspectors (reg 6). Unlike the 1977 Regulations, which no doubt assumed that a union would provide training, the employer is under a specific duty to provide reasonable training for representatives (reg 7(1)(a)). Representatives must be allowed paid time off for that training and for the purpose of performing their other functions (reg 7(1)(b)). Candidates for election as employee representatives are entitled to paid time off to act as a candidate (reg 7(1)(b)). There is no parallel in the 1996 Regulations to the duty to establish a safety committee in reg 9 of the 1977 Regulations.

Management Regulations 1999

12.26 Under the Management of Health and Safety at Work Regulations 1999, considered at para 10.14, above, an employer is obliged to supply its employees with information on the risks to their health and safety (reg 10) and to supply information to others who work in its undertaking (reg 12(3)). Regulation 22 was amended by the Management of Health and Safety at Work and Fire Precautions (Workplace) (Amendment) Regulations 2003, SI 2003/2457 (in force from 27 October 2003) which provides for a civil sanction for breach by employers.

12.27 The Management Regulations impose additional obligations on the employer. It must appoint a 'competent person' to assist it in carrying out its statutory health and safety duties (see reg 7(1)). The Management Regulations do not say, unlike the Framework Directive (art 7(1)), that this person must be an employee, still less a union representative.

The Offshore Installations Regulations

12.28 Separate regulations, introduced following the Piper Alpha disaster, cover offshore activities (dealt with more fully at para 27.38, below). The Offshore Installations (Safety Representatives and Safety Committees) Regulations 1989, SI 1989/971, made under the Mineral Workings (Offshore Installations) Act 1971, provide for the whole workforce—that is, every person working on an offshore installation (reg 2)—to elect safety representatives (reg 4). They do not provide for representatives to be appointed by recognised unions, probably because of the hostility to union recognition in the offshore industry. The Regulations set out in detail the election procedure (regs 5–13). The representatives have similar entitlements and rights to those conferred on safely representatives under the 1977 Regulations (see regs 16, 17, 18, 24, 16, 27). Provision is made for the establishment of a safety committee (regs 19–22). A breach of these Regulations does not give rise to civil liability: see the Mineral Workings (Offshore Installations) Act 1971, s 11. Nor, curiously, is there protection against victimisation for participating in elections (see para 12.32, below).

Mines and quarries

12.29 The first safety representatives to be recognised by legislation were in coalmines. Section 123 of the Mines and Quarries Act 1954 sets out the current provision for their appointment and powers and is dealt with at para 24.156. In addition the Quarries Regulations 1999, SI 1999/2024, which came into force on 1 January 2000, place a duty on operators and those who regularly work at the quarry to co-operate effectively in promoting and developing measures for health, safety and welfare (reg 40). To further that end the Regulations provide that a committee of persons may—but not must—be appointed by a representative association (eg a union) or associations (reg 40(2)). If appointed, the committee members have rights of inspection (reg 40(3), (4)), to scrutinise documents (reg 40(5)), and to suggest improvements to the risk assessment (reg 40(5)). If the suggested improvements are rejected, the operator must give written reasons (reg 40(6)).

12.30 *Industrial relations*

The Construction (Design and Management) Regulations 1994

12.30 Under these Regulations, the principal contractor must ensure that both employees and self-employed persons at work on a construction project 'are able to discuss, and offer advice to him on, matters connected with the project which it can reasonably be foreseen will affect their health and safety' (reg 18(a)). That contractor must in addition ensure that there are arrangements for co-ordinating the views of employees or their representatives (reg 18(b)) and must ensure that contractors provide their employees with information required by reg 10 of the Management of Health and Safety at Work Regulations 1999 (reg 17). No mention is made of trade unions or the 1977 Regulations (see below) but the ACOP (para 104) does refer to them in relation to reg 18. The HSC has produced a consultation document from which it is anticipated there will be consolidating regulations and revisions to the provisions of Construction (Design and Management) Regulations 1994, SI 1994/3140.[1] The HSE website contains details of all projected legislation at http://www.hse.gov.uk/aboutus /regulations/index.htm.

[1] Amended by the Construction (Design and Management) (Amendment) Regulations 2000, SI 2000/2380 and the Construction (Health, Safety and Welfare) Regulations 1996, SI 1996/1592 which implemented the Temporary or Mobile Construction Sites Directive (1992/57/EEC).

The Railways (Safety Case) Regulations 2000

12.31 Regulation 14(8) of the Railway (Safety Case) Regulations 2000, SI 2000/2688, requires an employer who prepares a railway safety case to consult, in relation to the preparation of that safety case, union representatives under the 1977 Regulations and other employees he is required to consult under the 1996 Regulations; such duties may well be implicit in any event in the 1977 and 1996 Regulations. Railway regulation is discussed in chapter 25 below.

EMPLOYEE RIGHTS

Health and safety dismissals and detrimental treatment

12.32 Employees have various rights not to be unfairly treated as a result of exercising health and safety functions. As mentioned above, art 11(4) of the Framework Directive specifies that neither workers or workers' representatives should be placed at a disadvantage as a consequence of their exercising rights under that Directive. It also requires the employer to inform workers of the risks of serious and imminent danger and take action to enable workers to stop or leave work in the event of a 'serious, imminent and unavoidable danger' (see art 8). Any workers who do leave their workstation in such circumstances may not be placed at a disadvantage (art 8(4)).

12.33 These duties were principally enacted in the UK by the Trade Union Reform and Employment Rights Act 1993,[1] which introduced new rights not to be unfairly dismissed or suffer a detriment in certain circumstances connected with health and safety, and are now found in the Employment Rights Act 1996, ss 100 and 44.[2] No qualifying period of employment is needed, but the rights are restricted to employees.[3] The individual rights are not confined to trade union representatives but cover a variety of 'protected acts'. It is automatically unfair to dismiss, to select for redundancy[4] or to subject an employee to a detriment on the ground for certain specified reasons (see below). None of the actions is to be treated as industrial action so as potentially to deprive the workers of their rights to complain of unfair dismissal under the Trade Union and Labour Relations (Consolidation) Act 1992, ss 237–238.[5] They include the following 'protected acts', adopting the same letters as the Employment Rights Act 1996, ss 44 and 100:

(a)   where persons designated to carry out health and safety activities by the employer carry or propose to carry out these functions;

(b)   where a representative of workers on matters of health and safety or a member of a safety committee (whether under the relevant regulations or if so acknowledged by the employer) perform or propose to perform their health and safety functions;

(ba)   where an employee took part in consultation with an employer or participated in an election under the Health and Safety (Consultation with Employees) Regulations 1996;

(c)   where there are no representatives or where it is not reasonably practicable to use them and employees draw to an employer's attention matters reasonably believed to be harmful to health and safety (this ties in with the duty in reg 14(2) of the Management of Health and Safety Regulations on employees to report serious or imminent dangers or shortcomings in health and safety);[6]

(d)   where employees propose to leave, leave or refuse to work in circumstances of danger which he or she reasonably believed to be 'serious and imminent';

(e)   where employees take 'appropriate steps' to protect themselves or others against dangers reasonably believed to be serious and imminent.

1   Regulation 8 of the Management Regulations 1999 requires the employer to set up procedures for evacuation in the event of a serious and imminent danger.
2   For discussion of these rights, see Ewing 'Swimming with the Tide: Employment Protection and the Implementation of European Labour Law' (1993) 22 ILJ 170–171. These rights apply offshore, too.
3   This may breach the Temporary Workers' Directive, so long as these rights amount to protection of health and safety at work (art 2(1)): see para 10.09ff, above. On the qualifying period, see s 108. The protection does not extend to ex-employees: *Fadipe v Reed Nursing Personnel* [2005] ICR 1760, which concerned an ex-employee complaining about acts by his ex-employers after leaving employment. The Court of Appeal's judgment is less than satisfactory in distinguishing *Coote v Granada Hospitality Ltd* [1999] ICR 100, which provides for protection of ex-employees where the employer reacts to legal proceedings to their detriment.
4   See ERA 1996, s 105(3).
5   See s 237(1A) and s 238(1A).
6   This provision may extend to risks to persons *other* than co-workers; but cf *Brendon v BNFL Fleurochemicals Ltd* COIT No 59163/94.

12.34 In practice, the central issue in a claim will typically be what was the true reason for the dismissal or detrimental treatment. In *Shillito v Van Leer*

(UK) Ltd [1997] IRLR 495, EAT, concerned with category (b) above, the EAT emphasised that the proper question was not whether the representative was acting reasonably or not, so that it was no defence if he intended (for example) to embarrass the company or behaved in a way unacceptable to the employer. The issue was, rather, whether he was dismissed or subjected to a detriment because he was performing the functions of a safety representative.[1] But an action can never be divorced from its purpose. If a representative's sole reason for raising a health and safety matter were to embarrass, the action would not be protected.[2] The EAT adopted the same approach in *Goodwin v Cabletel UK Ltd* [1998] ICR 112 some eight months later. In relation to a complaint under category (b) it was a misdirection for a tribunal to take the view that s 100 did not apply when an employee was dismissed because of the way he carried out his health and safety duties.

[1] The EAT drew a parallel with the law on trade union victimisation: see *Bass Taverns Ltd v Burgess* [1995] IRLR 596, CA.
[2] See *Shillito* at para 19.

12.35 The first category is not confined to the functions of safety representatives under the 1977 or 1996 Regulations, but can extend to those employees who are in practice treated as such by the employer, provided that they are acting within the scope of the acknowledgement. In *Shillito v Van Leer* (above), for example, the representative was not protected in part because he made complaints in relation to an area of a chemical factory for which he was not acknowledged and because he acted outside agreed procedures. The second reason, with respect, seems more directed to the manner of his action rather than whether it was 'any function' of a representative. As the EAT stated:

> 'The protection afforded to the way in which a designated employee carries out his health and safety activities must not be too easily diluted by finding acts done for that purpose to be a justification for dismissal; on the other hand, not every act, however malicious or irrelevant to the task in hand, must necessarily be treated as a protected act in circumstances where dismissal would be justified on legitimate grounds.'

12.36 Category (e) is an important right, which may permit individual workers or union employees to refuse to work until the workplace is made safe. 'Other persons' are not restricted to work colleagues, according to the EAT in *Masiak v City Restaurants (UK) Ltd* [1999] IRLR 780 in which a chef in a restaurant refused to cook frozen chicken and phoned an environmental health officer because of his concerns about the risks to customers. In *Harris v Select Timberframe Ltd* (1994) 220 HSIB 2, IT, an employee who complained to a health and safety inspector of the use of lindane was held to be unfairly dismissed within s 100(1)(e). It seemed that he reasonably believed there was a serious and imminent danger, and calling the inspector was an appropriate step. Under category (e), the appropriateness of the steps is to be judged by reference to the employee's knowledge of the facts: see s 44(2) and s 100(2). But the employer has a defence if the employee's actions were so negligent that a reasonable employer 'might' have treated the employee as the employer in fact did (s 44(3), s 100(3)). Compared with other jurisdictions, a worker's right to stop unsafe work in the UK appears modest.[1] In Sweden and some Australian states, safety representatives have the 'right to stop the job'. In the Australian State of Victoria safety representatives have the right to issue provisional improvement notices with which it is an offence for the employer not to comply, though the latter may require an inspector to confirm or cancel the notice.[2]

[1] Other jurisdictions outside the EU provide for safety representatives and safety committees. In Sweden, for example, the Working Environment Act 1977 reaffirmed safety delegates appointed by the union at the place of work. Canadian provincial legislation requires safety representatives and in Australia all states bar two provide for safety representatives.

[2] Occupational Health and Safety Act 1985, s 83.

12.37 If as a result of any of these 'protected acts' an employee is subject to a detriment or is dismissed, he or she may present a complaint to an employment tribunal, which may award compensation (see ss 22C, 72, 75A). A dismissal for such a reason is automatically unfair, with no limit on the level of compensatory award (s 124(1A)) and a minimum basic award if the dismissal falls within s 100(1)(a) or (b) by virtue of the Employment Rights Act 1996, s 120(1). Just as with trade union dismissals, an employee dismissed for a reason within s 100(a) and (b)—that is, a designated person or a workers' representative—may apply for 'interim relief', which if granted has the effect of reinstating the employee or paying his or her wages pending a full hearing (see the Employment Rights Act 1996, ss 128–132). The Directive simply states that the relevant persons shall 'not be placed at a disadvantage' because of their activities or actions (see eg arts 8(4), 11(4)), and consequently it is arguable that tribunals should be more willing to grant reinstatement or re-engagement in this field than they are in 'normal' unfair dismissal claims. A job is worth much more than just pay so that its loss in itself is a 'disadvantage'.[1]

[1] As the unfair dismissal legislation originally seemed to give precedence to these remedies rather than compensation (see the Employment Rights Act 1996, ss 113–117), there can be little doubt that it is open to interpretation in accordance with this approach: the lack of enthusiasm for reinstatement has been generated by the tribunals and courts. Alternatively, and to the extent that there is a divergence between the protections given by the Directive and ERA 1996, employees of an emanation of the State may seek to bring actions under the Directive itself, relying on direct effect and arguing that only reinstatement is an adequate remedy for breach of the Directive.

12.38 Detrimental treatment or dismissal of an employee for raising health and safety concerns can sometimes, in addition, amount to victimisation on grounds of trade union membership under the Trade Union and Labour Relations (Consolidation) Act 1992, s 146 and ss 152–153. In *Dixon and Shaw v West Ella Developments Ltd* [1978] ICR 856, EAT, a complaint by a worker to a trade union safety representative was held to constitute participation in the activities of a trade union for these purposes. Again, this can result in awards of compensation and interim relief: see s 149 and ss 156–167 of that Act. The details of these rights are outside the scope of this book.[1]

[1] See generally *Harvey on Industrial Relations and Employment Law* Division N.

12.39 Workers and/or the representatives also have the right by art 11(6) of the Framework Directive to appeal to the health and safety authority (the HSE presumably) if they think measures taken by the employer are inadequate from the viewpoint of health and safety. Although not transposed into UK law at the time, workers and representatives are free to raise matters with the HSE although lack of resources may mean the HSE is not able in fact to intervene to consider whether the measures are adequate or not. Specific protection is now given to workers who complain to the HSE.

Whistleblowers

12.40 In addition to direct protection for an employee making health and safety complaints (above), employment legislation now gives specific protection for employees disclosing health and safety shortcomings of their employer to outside bodies, including the press. This question, involving what is colloquially knows as 'whistleblowing', has always caused problems in drawing the line between an employer's legitimate interest in preserving confidentiality and an employee's ability to act in the greater public interest.

12.41 Employer rights to confidentiality are primarily grounded in the contract of employment, either through express clauses or, failing that, through well-developed implied terms which will be read into all contracts of employment.[1] The question has always been to define those circumstances in which an employee can make a disclosure, without being in breach of contract, because it is in the public interest to do so. The leading case at common law is *Initial Services v Putterill* [1968] 1 QB 396 (disclosure of price cartel to press) where Lord Denning MR said that this employee defence was not confined to the disclosure of crimes, but extended to 'any misconduct of such a nature that it ought in the public interest to be disclosed to others'.[2] The potential width of this remained a matter for debate, and arguments grew that it was not enough to leave this matter to the common law, especially with the growth of express 'gagging' clauses in unambiguously wide terms, for example within the NHS.

[1] See Smith & Wood *Industrial Law* (8th edn, 2003) pp 136ff.
[2] Although generally adopting a narrower approach, Ungoed-Thomas J considered it could cover medical risks to the public in *Beloff v Pressdram Ltd* [1973] 1 All ER 241 at 260; a generally wider approach was again adopted by the Court of Appeal in *Lion Laboratories Ltd v Evans* [1985] QB 526. This case law would still apply in any breach of contract action brought against a whistleblowing employee, but a court might be expected now to construe it in the light of the new statutory rules, below.

12.42 The result was legislation, with the government eventually adopting a private member's Bill, which became the Public Interest Disclosure Act 1998. This operates by way of making amendments to the Employment Rights Act 1996, adding rights not to be subjected to detriment or dismissed by reason of making what is referred to as a 'protected disclosure'. The Act seeks to establish a fair balance—the whistleblowing employee has statutory protection in his or her employment *provided* the subject matter of the disclosure satisfies the tests for a protected disclosure *and* that disclosure is made in the way envisaged by the Act. Great emphasis is placed on the initial disclosure in most cases being to the employer itself, the aim being to achieve resolution primarily through proper workplace procedures. It is only in certain circumstances that the employee can make a disclosure outside the workplace; one of these is where it is made to a prescribed regulatory body, concerning a matter within the remit of that body. It is important to note that disclosure to the press is at the *end* of the process, not the beginning, and may not be for money.

12.43 Three elements need to be established in order to qualify for protection. First, there needs to be a disclosure within the meaning of the Act. Second, that disclosure must be a 'qualifying disclosure' and third, it must be made by the worker in a manner that accords with the scheme set out at ERA 1996, ss 43C–43H. The Act provides a very broad definition of what amounts to a disclosure and 'any disclosure of information' will qualify (ERA 1996, s 43B(1)). However it appears clear from the statutory language that an actual disclosure must have taken place and it is not sufficient for there merely to have been a threat of disclosure. Whether the disclosure is a qualifying disclosure depends upon the nature of the information revealed. The worker must have only a subjective *reasonable belief* and it is not necessary for the information itself to be actually true. It follows that a disclosure may nevertheless be a qualifying disclosure even if it subsequently transpires that the information disclosed was incorrect.[1]

[1]   See *Darnton v University of Surrey* [2003] IRLR 133.

12.44 The Act sets out situations to which the information must relate if the disclosure is to be one qualifying for protection (ERA 1996, s 43B(1)(a)–(f)):

(a)   that a criminal offence has been committed, is being committed or is likely to be committed;

(b)   that a person has failed, is failing or is likely to fail to comply with any legal obligation to which he is subject;[1]

(c)   that a miscarriage of justice has occurred, is occurring or is likely to occur;

(d)   that the health and safety of any individual has been, is being or is likely to be endangered;

(e)   that the environment has been, is being or is likely to be damaged; or

(f)   that information tending to show any matter falling within any one of the preceding paragraphs has been, or is likely to be deliberately concealed.

[1]   In *Parkins v Sodexho Ltd* [2002] IRLR 109 it was held that a breach of contract in instructing an employee to use an industrial buffing machine without supervision fell within 'failure to comply with any legal obligation'. However in *Kraus v Penna plc* [2004] IRLR 260 a reasonable belief that redundancy selection breached employment law did not fall within this or any category. The worker's reasonable belief relates only to the information that he is disclosing and not to the existence of the legal obligation. The employer was not, as a matter of law, actually subject to the relevant legal obligation so there was no protected disclosure even though the worker had a reasonable belief that the employer was subject to it.

12.45 While the protection is broad it is not without its limits. In *Street v Derbyshire Unemployed Workers' Centre* [2004] EWCA Civ 964, [2005] ICR 97 a disclosure concerning the misuse of funds was not in good faith because the employee also had personal motives of antagonism towards his manager. Good faith involves more than just a reasonable belief in the truth of the allegations, and an employment tribunal should inquire into the worker's motive. If those motives are mixed the tribunal must discover the dominant purpose.

1   Employment Rights Act 1996, ss 47B and 103A respectively.

12.46 This legislative scheme is of general application but has potential for use in the health and safety sphere for two reasons:

(1)   one of the categories of 'protected disclosure' is where, in the reasonable belief of the worker[1] making the disclosure, the disclosure is of information which tends to show that 'the health or safety of any individual has been, is being, or is likely to be endangered' (Employment Rights Act 1996, s 43B(1)(d));

(2)   the HSE is a prescribed body for the purposes of a protected disclosure, in relation to 'matters which may affect the health or safety of any individual at work' and 'matters which may affect the health or safety of any member of the public, arising out of or in connection with the activities of persons at work' (Public Interest Disclosure (Prescribed Persons) Order 1999, SI 1999/1549, Schedule).

1   The Act applies to 'workers', not just to 'employees'. 'Worker' is defined as a person under a contract of employment or under any other contract to do or perform personally any work or services for another, other than a client or customer of any profession or business undertaking carried out by the person: Employment Rights Act 1996, s 230(3). In addition, s 43K specifically includes agency workers, homeworkers, work trainees and certain specified NHS staff who might not otherwise have qualified.

12.47 If the person making the protected disclosure is dismissed for that reason, not only is that dismissal automatically unfair (Employment Rights Act 1996, s 103A), with no qualifying period or upper age limit applying (ss 108(1), (3)(ff), 109(1), (2)(ff)) but there is also the possibility of interim relief enforcing continued employment (s 128(1)) and, most significantly of all (as a matter of positive policy in the Employment Relations Act 1999), the normal statutory limit on the compensatory award of £50,000 does not apply, so that compensation is at large (s 124(1A)). For good measure, any agreement between worker and employer is declared to be void in so far as it purports to prevent the worker from making a protected disclosure.[1]

1   Section 43J. This includes a settlement of legal proceedings.

Chapter 13

MISCELLANEOUS: CROWN LIABILITY, TRANSFER OF UNDERTAKINGS, EMPLOYERS' LIABILITY INSURANCE

Toby Kempster

Damian Brown

Daniel Bennett

THE GENERAL LIABILITY OF THE CROWN

13.01 Before the Crown Proceedings Act 1947,[1] the Crown was not liable in tort. Therefore, a worker[2] engaged in service of the Crown could not sue for damages for personal injuries caused by the negligence of the Crown or of his fellow workers. Similarly, no action could be based on breach of statutory duty, even though the statute, like the Factories Act 1937, was binding on the Crown.

[1] 13 Halsbury's Statutes (4th edn) 9.
[2] A Crown servant is in a different position from workers in what might be termed the public sector, for example state education and local authorities, who are, subject to meeting the relevant criteria, employees. The traditional view was that a Crown worker was engaged at the good pleasure of the Crown and therefore had no contract of employment. But slowly shifting with the times, the law probably now recognises that Crown servants do have contracts of employment: see *R v Lord Chancellors Department, ex p Nangel* [1991] ICR 743. The police are in a special position: see below.

13.02 Section 2(1) of the Crown Proceedings Act 1947 provides as follows:

'Subject to the provisions of this Act, the Crown shall be subject to all those liabilities in tort to which, if it were a private person of full age and capacity, it would be subject:
(a)   in respect of torts committed by its servants or agents;
(b)   in respect of any breach of those duties which a person owes to his servants or agents at common law by reason of being their employer; and
(c)   in respect of any breach of the duties attaching at common law to the ownership, occupation, possession or control of property.'

13.03 Section 2(1)(b) clearly makes the Crown liable to persons in its service for negligence in failing to provide a safe system of work, a safe place of work and safe appliances, in the same way as other employers; and s 2(1)(a), in conjunction with the Law Reform (Personal Injuries) Act 1948, which binds the Crown, makes the Crown vicariously liable for the torts of persons in its service, whether harming workers or others. Under head (c), both the

Occupiers' Liability Act 1957 (by s 6) and the Occupiers' Liability (Scotland) Act 1960 (by s 4) are binding on the Crown. So, under head (b), is the Employers' Liability (Defective Equipment) Act 1969.

13.04 Breach of statutory duty is dealt with by s 2(2):

> 'Where the Crown is bound by a statutory duty which is binding also upon persons other than the Crown and its officers, then, subject to the provisions of this Act, the Crown shall, in respect of a failure to comply with that duty, be subject to all those liabilities in tort (if any) to which it would be so subject if it were a private person of full age and capacity.'

13.05 By s 4, the law on indemnity and contribution between tortfeasors, and on division of damages in cases of contributory negligence, is applied to the Crown. Crown immunity remains for judicial functions: s 2(5).

13.06 These provisions, broadly, place the Crown in the same position as a private employer, but care must be taken in bringing an action for breach of statutory duty to see that the statute is one which is binding on the Crown. Section 48(1) of the HSWA 1974 makes binding on the Crown the general duties of that Act, together with those set out in regulations passed under that Act. But the Crown cannot be prosecuted for non-compliance (s 48(1)). Significantly, persons 'in the service of the Crown' are deemed to be employees for the purposes of Part 1 of the Act and its regulations (s 48(3)). Consequently, those persons are able to bring civil actions based on regulations passed under that Act just like any other employee. The authors are unaware of any statutory duty in relation to health and safety at work from which the Crown would be exempted. Note that Crown immunity no longer applies at all to health authorities (National Health Service and Community Care Act 1990, s 60(1)). The Crown is no doubt an emanation of the State for the purposes of EC law, and hence European Directives are directly enforceable against it (see chapter 9).

The armed forces

13.07 The substance of the Crown Proceedings Act did not originally apply to the armed forces: their special position was dealt with in rather an elaborate manner in s 10. Section 10 was repealed by the Crown Proceedings (Armed Forces) Act 1987 except where a claim arises for an act or omission before 15 May 1987. But under s 2 of that Act the Secretary of State may make an order reviving s 10 either in case of national emergency or in the case of warlike operations outside the United Kingdom. Accordingly, for causes of action arising after 15 May 1987, a person serving in the armed forces can bring an employers' liability claim.

13.08 Prior to 15 May 1987, s 10(1) provided that a member of the armed forces could not in general sue the Crown for injuries caused by the negligence or other tort of a fellow-serviceman or woman, if he or she sustained the injuries while on duty, or while on land or premises, or on a ship, aircraft or vehicle, used for military purposes, provided that the accident was certified as attributable to service for the purposes of pension entitlement. In general, too, it was not possible to sue the fellow-service person, unless he or she was off duty at the time.[1]

---

1   Thus an airman being flown as a passenger from one place to another could not sue the pilot if he negligently crashed the aircraft, nor could he sue the Crown: nor could a soldier sue a medical officer for alleged negligent treatment in a military camp, though when a soldier was sent to a civil hospital without a note of explanation it was held that the resulting damage occurred outside the camp: *Bell v Secretary of State for Defence* [1986] QB 322 as explained in *Pearce v Secretary of State for Defence* [1988] AC 755.

13.09 Where negligence was alleged against the Atomic Energy Authority in the supervision of atomic bomb tests in the Pacific, s 10 did not afford a defence although the liabilities of the Authority were transferred to the Ministry of Defence: *Pearce v Secretary of State for Defence* [1988] AC 755.

13.10 Given the fact that s 10 only precludes causes of action arising before May 1987 it is in the context of industrial disease that it has been challenged in the courts in the last few years. In *Quinn v Ministry of Defence* [1998] PIQR P387 the claimant had been exposed to asbestos when serving in the Royal Navy prior to 1987 but developed injury after May 1987. In his attempt to recover damages from the Crown it was held that it was clear that Parliament had intended the Crown to be immune from liability both for the condition of any land or equipment and also for any omission by a Crown servant to protect the victim from that danger. The claim was dismissed. In *Matthews v Ministry of Defence* [2003] UKHL 4 a claimant who had similarly developed asbestos related disease succeeded at first instance in arguing that the Crown Proceedings Act 1947, s 10 infringed his rights as guaranteed by the Human Rights Act 1998, Sch 1, art 6. This success was overturned by the Court of Appeal, whose decision was upheld by the House of Lords. Section 10 of the 1947 Act was held not to infringe the right to a fair trial, as it formed part of the substantive law and was not a procedural bar.

13.11 Post-May 1987 the Ministry of Defence owes a duty of care similar to that owed by other employers to their employees, although the nature of the duty recognises the special nature of military service. A soldier does not, for example, owe a fellow soldier a duty of care in tort when engaging the enemy in battle conditions, nor is there any duty on the Ministry of Defence to maintain a safe place of work in these circumstances: *Mulcahy v Ministry of Defence* [1996] QB 732 (noise-induced hearing loss whilst operating an artillery gun). The Court of Appeal expressed the view that it would not be fair, just or reasonable to impose such a duty on a soldier or on the Ministry of Defence.

13.12 However, in more usual circumstances the Ministry of Defence will owe a duty of care to its armed services personnel. In *Jebson v Ministry of Defence* [2000] 1 WLR 2055 the claimant and his fellow soldiers (who were off-duty) were taken to a nightclub in an army vehicle which was being driven by an on-duty army driver. On their return journey the claimant, who was drunk, climbed onto the tailgate of the lorry and then fell onto the road. The Court of Appeal held that the MoD should have foreseen that the claimant and others would be drunk and that in such circumstances they owed him a duty of care to provide adequate supervision and a vehicle which would have been reasonably safe and prevented the accident.[1]

1   See too *Barrett v Ministry of Defence* [1995] 3 All ER 87, CA. Where a soldier alleges that he has suffered physical or psychological injury as a result of racial discrimination received from fellow soldiers the only claim available is under the Race Relations Act 1976: *Parchment v Secretary of State for Defence* (23 February 1998, unreported). The High Court rejected the submission that a claim could be brought on the basis that the MoD, by not preventing the discrimination, failed to provide a safe system or place of work.

13.13 In 1979 the MoD introduced the Civil Injuries Compensation (Overseas) Scheme, the aim of which was to provide compensation to victims (and relatives of victims) of crimes of violence whilst overseas. However, personal injury and death caused by an enemy during a state of war, or a war-like situation, is excluded from the scheme. In December 1994 Parliament decided that the scheme would not apply where personal injury or death occurred as a result of 'war operations or military activity by warring factions'. This alteration to the scheme was brought about to exclude injury and death caused to peacekeeping troops in Bosnia and similar UN peacekeeping activities. An argument that the activity which led to a person being injured or killed amounted to a criminal activity under international law, did not avoid the exclusion as defined by the scheme: *R v Ministry of Defence, ex p Walker* [2000] 1 WLR 806.

The police

13.14 Police officers holding the office of constable are vested with discretions which they must exercise independently. As a result they are not employees and nor are they Crown servants.[1] Reviewing the relevant authorities, in *Metropolitan Police Comr v Lowrey-Nesbit* [1999] ICR 401 the EAT held at 405D that:

> 'the case law is clear, as at 1998, that a police constable's status is governed by statute and he owes allegiance to the community at large, through his oath of office, rather than through private contractual rights and obligations.'

But the person responsible for directing police officers, in most cases the Chief Constable of the relevant police force, owes them a duty of care at common law similar in nature to that owed by an employer to its employees.

1   See *Fisher v Oldham Corpn* [1930] 2 KB 364; *A-G for New South Wales v Perpetual Trustee Co Ltd* [1955] AC 457.

13.15 In the past breaches of regulations passed under the HSWA 1974 were often pleaded against the police and, so far as the authors are aware, the point was never taken that the regulations were inapplicable because the police fell outside the scope of the Act on the ground that they were not employees.[1] The law now corresponds with practice. As a result of amendments introduced by the Police (Health and Safety) Act 1997, s 51A of the Act now treats persons holding the office of constable as employees for the purpose of the Act (and hence regulations passed under it) and s 52(1)(bb) deems such persons to be at work while on duty. Directly effective provisions of applicable European Directives can be relied upon by police officers: see *Peck v Chief Constable of Avon and Somerset* [2000] CLY 2971.

¹ See the definitions of 'employee' in s 53(1) and of 'work' in s 52.

TRANSFERS OF LIABILITY

The Transfer of Undertakings (Protection of Employment) Regulations

13.16 In some circumstances an employer may be liable for injury sustained at a time when it was not the employer of the person injured. Such transfers of liabilities occur principally by virtue of the Transfer of Undertakings (Protection of Employment) Regulations 1981 ('TUPE'), which were implemented to give effect to the Acquired Rights Directive 77/187/EEC, which has now been replaced by Directive 2001/23/EC.¹ Subsequent cases on the scope of the Directive suggested that TUPE did not correctly implement its provisions, and this led to amendments in the Trade Union Reform and Employment Rights Act 1993. Like all implementing domestic legislation, TUPE should be construed as far as possible to achieve the same result as the Directive. To the extent a divergence remains, employees of a State body may rely on directly effective provisions of the Directive itself (see chapter 9, above).

¹ The replacement regulations, the Transfer of Undertakings (Protection of Employment) Regulations 2006, SI 2006/246, came into force 6 April 2006.

13.17 The Regulations apply when there is a transfer of an undertaking or part of an undertaking from one person to another (reg 3). This apparently straightforward question has in practice given rise to a great deal of case law which is often difficult to reconcile and apply. Suffice it to note here that an 'undertaking' includes non-commercial ventures and that, probably, the decisive criterion for establishing the existence of a transfer is whether the entity before the transfer broadly retains its identity afterwards (and this is reflected in reg 3(1)(a)). A useful analysis of the relevant case law, and particularly the ECJ decisions, can be found in the EAT decision in *Cheesman v R Brewer Contracts Ltd* [2001] IRLR 144. This does not take account of some more recent ECJ decisions which appear to add clarification depending upon whether an undertaking can be classified as 'asset' or 'labour' intensive (see C-13/95 *Süzen v Zehnacker Gebäuderernigung GmbH Krankenhausservice* [1997] IRLR 255; C-172/99 *Oy Liikenne AB v Liskojärvi and Juntunen* [2001] IRLR 171, and C-340/01 *Abler v Sodexho MM Catering Gesellschaft GmbH* [2004] IRLR 168.

A full discussion of the many decisions and the difficulties of reconciling them can be found in *Harvey on Industrial Relations and Employment Law*.¹

¹ See Division F.

13.18 The effect of a transfer is that the contracts of employment of employees of the original employer (A) are not terminated but transfer automatically to the incoming employer (B): reg 4(1).[1] Anything done before the transfer by A 'in respect of ... a person employed in the undertaking [ie A] or a part shall be deemed to have been done ... by the transferee' (ie B) (reg 4(2)(b)). Further, all of A's 'rights, powers, duties or liabilities under or in connection with any such contract [of employment] shall be transferred to the transferee [B]' (reg 4(2)(a)). Put simply, employees of A automatically become employees of B.[2] TUPE only applies, though, to those employees of A who were employed immediately before the transfer or who would have been so employed but for the transfer: see *Litster v Forth Dry Dock and Engineering Co Ltd* [1989] ICR 341, HL.

[1]   Duties of consultation are imposed by TUPE and the Directive; these are not dealt with here.
[2]   Although they can choose not to transfer and resign instead: see *Katsikas v Konstantinidis* [1993] IRLR 179, ECJ and TUPE, reg 5(4A).

13.19 After some earlier uncertainty the courts have now accepted that the term 'in connection with' a contract of employment in reg 4(2)(a) is wide enough to apply to liabilities in tort. In *Bernadone v Pall Mall; Martin v Lancashire County Council* [2000] IRLR 487 the Court of Appeal, emphasising that the purpose of the Directive and therefore the Regulations is to safeguard the rights of employees, held that employers' tortious liabilities for personal injuries to their employees arose out of the relationship of employer and employee and hence were liabilities 'in connection' with contracts of employment. The decision was preceded by several first instance decisions to like effect.[1] A transfer clearly operates in relation to liability in negligence, for which a parallel action can be brought under the contract of employment.[2] The indications of Peter Gibson LJ, with whom the other Lords Justices agreed, is that liabilities for breach of statute and regulations should also transfer. In one of the cases a claimant sued for breach of the Occupiers Liability Act 1957. Peter Gibson LJ rejected an argument that because such a liability was imposed on occupiers, not employers, it should not transfer; rather it transferred because on the pleaded facts the duty had 'a sufficient connection with the contract of employment'.[3] The same conclusion is likely in the vast majority of cases in which employers are in breach of the duties laid down in health and safety regulations to protect their workers.

[1]   See *Wilson v West Cumbria Healthcare NHS Trust* [1995] PIQR P 38; *Taylor v Serviceteam Ltd and Waltham Forest Borough Council* [1998] PIQR P 201. But cf *Cramer v Watts Blake Bearne & Co* (31 December 1997, unreported).
[2]   See Peter Gibson LJ at paras 34–38.
[3]   At paras 38–39.

13.20 Because insurance protects both employers and employees, the Court of Appeal also held an insured employer's right to an indemnity under a policy of insurance in respect of injuries to its employees transferred under the Regulations to the transferee. For the court this right equally arose 'in connection' with the contract of employment, even though it was a right in a contract between the employer and a third party (the insurer).[1] Under the 2006 Regulations, where the transferor is exempt from the obligation to provide employers' compulsory liability insurance reg 12 makes the transferor and transferee jointly and severally liable for any personal injury suffered by an employee prior to the transfer of his employment. This is particularly useful for those transferring out of the public sector.

¹   See Peter Gibson LJ at para 48.

Transfers under other Acts

13.21 The transfer of liabilities has principally arisen in relation to TUPE transfers. But other Acts have similar effects. Thus, under the Further and Higher Education Act 1992, where a college previously controlled by a local education authority acquires independent status, it seems likely that tort liabilities transfer to that new, independent corporation (see s 23(2)(b)).¹ Other instances of transfers of liability are beyond the scope of this book, but readers should be aware of their potential existence.

¹   Although it may be that a tort liability is not acquired for the 'purpose' of a college within that subsection.

EMPLOYERS' LIABILITY INSURANCE

13.22 The Employers' Liability (Compulsory Insurance) Act 1969¹ requires employers carrying on any business in Great Britain to insure and maintain insurance against liability for bodily injury or disease sustained by employees, and arising out of and in the course of their employment in Great Britain in that business.² The obligation, therefore, is Great Britain specific, as a result of its restriction to employers carrying on any business in Great Britain. An employer not having a place of business in Great Britain shall be deemed not to carry on business there.³ Further, a relevant employer is not required to insure in respect of employees not ordinarily resident in Great Britain,⁴ and even where employees have residence in Great Britain, the relevant insurance is not required to extend to injury or disease suffered or contracted outside Great Britain.

¹   The Act was brought into force by the Employers' Liability (Compulsory Insurance) Act 1969 (Commencement) Order 1971, SI 1971/1116 on 1 January 1972.
²   Section 1(1).
³   Section 1(3)(d).
⁴   Section 2(2)(b) and the Employers' Liability (Compulsory Insurance) Regulations 1998, SI 1998/2573 (as amended) except where the employee is present in Great Britain in course of employment for at least 14 days, or where a non-resident employee has worked on an offshore installation for more than 7 days.

Extent of obligation to insure

13.23 For the purposes of the Act, the term 'employee' means any individual who has entered into or works under a contract of service or apprenticeship with an employer, whether by way of manual labour, clerical work or otherwise, whether such a contract is express or implied, oral or in writing.¹

¹   Section 2(1).

13.24 The obligation, therefore, does not extend to nor protect the self-employed working under a contract for services, and nor would it cover the situation where, for example, a contractor incurs liability in respect of injuries sustained by a sub-contractor or some other third party employee.[1] However, the position of, for example, agency workers and the existence of a contract of service 'by implication', requires some care as the courts have become increasingly prepared to recognise the existence of more than one contract of employment in such a situation, namely a general engagement with an agency and a specific engagement with the hirer.[2]

[1]   See *Denham v Midland Employees Mutual Assurance Ltd* [1955] 2 QB 437.
[2]   See for example *Motorola Ltd v Davidson* [2001] IRLR 4; *Franks v Reuters Ltd* [2003] EWCA Civ 417, [2003] ICR 1166; and *Dacas v Brook Street Bureau (UK) Ltd* [2004] EWCA Civ 217, [2004] ICR 1437.

13.25 The question of when an employee is and is not acting in the course of his employment has also been the subject of recent litigation and is dealt with in more detail in paras 4.83–4.87, above.[1] Particular difficulties have arisen over employees suffering injury while being driven to or from work. In *Stitt v Woolley* (1971) 115 Sol Jo 708, CA, the relevant employees were members of the local fire brigade and required to attend promptly at the fire station when an emergency arose. As such, the men were held to be on duty and therefore acting in the course of their employment when on their way to the station (and see also *Vendyke v Fender (Sun Insurance Office Ltd, third party)* [1970] 2 QB 292 and *Smith v Stages* [1989] AC 928).

[1]   See for example *Brown v Robinson* [2004] UKPC 56 and *Mattis v Pollock (t/a Flamingos Nightclub)* [2003] EWCA Civ 887, [2004] 4 All ER 85, CA.

13.26 Even if a qualifying employee, the Act contains a number of exclusions and exemptions. In addition to the 'non-residential' exclusion, the Act does not require an employer to insure in respect of certain family members.[1] Further, s 3 of the Act exempts a number of statutory bodies from the obligation to insure, most notably health service bodies and any body corporate under national ownership or control.

[1]   Section 2(2)(a).

13.27 The amount for which an employer is required to insure in respect of relevant employees must not be less that £5,000,000 in respect of a claim relating to any one (or more) employee arising out of any one occurrence, as well as any costs and expenses incurred in relation to any such claim.[1] A failure to insure is a criminal offence carrying with it a fine not exceeding £2,500.[2] A penalty can also be incurred in respect of a failure to display a relevant certificate of insurance (maximum £1,000). No civil liability arises in respect of such a failure (*Richardson v Pitt-Stanley* [1995] QB 123, CA).

[1]   Section 1(2).
[2]   Section 5 and see the Criminal Justice Act 1982 which categorises the offence as 'level 4 on the standard scale'.

13.28 There is no equivalent to the MIB Scheme (providing compensation in the absence of third party motor insurance) and therefore no protection in a situation of non-insurance. However, if an insured employer becomes insolvent, and having incurred a liability, the Third Parties (Rights Against Insurers) Act 1930 provides that the employer's rights under the policy as respects that liability are transferred to the claimant. Difficulties can arise where the company is dissolved, as no rights can pass to the injured person until liability is established.[1]

1   See *Bradley v Eagle Star Insurance Co Ltd* [1989] AC 957, but see also the Companies Act 1985, s 651 which enables the company to be restored to the register.

13.29 While it is common to find in an employer's liability policy a condition requiring the insured to take, for example, reasonable precautions to prevent accidents, the insurer clearly cannot negate the very protection that the policy is designed to affect, ie compensation in respect of breach of duty on the part of the employer. To this end, any condition within the contract of insurance which provides that no liability will arise if the employer fails to take reasonable care to protect the employee from injury or disease, or fails to comply with the requirements of any enactment for the protection of employees, is prohibited.[1]

1   Employers' Liability (Compulsory Insurance) Regulations 1998, SI 1998/2573, regs 1(2), 2(1).

13.30 There are a number of important limitations as to the obligation to insure, but there is no duty on an employer to advise an employee as to when or whether insurance is in place. In *Read v Rush & Tompkins Group plc* [1990] 1 WLR 212, CA, an employee was injured in a car accident in Ethiopia where there was no compulsory motor insurance and the employee was unable to recover any damages against the third party. It was held that there was no duty on an employer to advise an employee working abroad in these circumstances to take out insurance, or alternatively to provide appropriate insurance. The employer's duty of care to protect an employee's physical safety and wellbeing did not extend to protecting the employee from economic loss.[1]

1   But see some movement in this respect in *Scally v Southern Health and Social Services Board* [1991] IRLR 522, HL and *Spring v Guardian Assurance plc* [1994] IRLR 460, HL, in particular Lord Woolf's observation that 'in appropriate circumstances' the court will imply a duty to exercise due care in relation to the economic well-being of an employee (a case which related to the provision of references).

Chapter 14

PSYCHIATRIC INJURY, STRESS AND HARASSMENT

The Honourable Mr Justice Langstaff

GENERAL

14.01 There is now no doubt that an employer's duty of care extends to taking 'reasonable care not to subject the employee to working conditions which are reasonably likely to cause him psychiatric injury or illness': per Lord Macfadyen in *Cross v Highlands and Islands Enterprise* [2001] IRLR 336, OH, at 351, para 60. However, it has also become clear that the fact that a claimant is an employee of the person whose negligence may factually be causative of his psychiatric injury gives him no exemption from the rules which apply specially in the field of claims for compensation for the adverse psychiatric effects: *White v Chief Constable of South Yorkshire Police* [1999] 2 AC 455, HL. These particular rules limit recovery for injury to the mind: their rationale is rather obscure, but their effect has been to restrict liability. For this reason the matter is considered separately. At the outset it is important to distinguish different factual situations in which injury is caused by the fault of another:

(1)   a claimant suffers physical injury with accompanying psychiatric harm (see para 14.06ff); liability for the psychiatric harm will usually follow;

(2)   a claimant's participation in an event was such that he was a potential victim of physical harm (a 'primary' victim), but suffers psychiatric harm alone (see para 14.08ff); liability for the psychiatric harm will usually follow;

(3)   a claimant who was never exposed to events in which he was a potential victim of physical harm (a 'secondary' victim) sustains psychiatric injury by witnessing a shocking or horrific event (see para 14.20ff); liability for the psychiatric harm depends on control tests;

(4)   a claimant is an 'involuntary' participant in a shocking or horrific event and sustains psychiatric injury as a result of such participation (see para 14.29ff); liability for the psychiatric harm will usually follow;

(5)   a claimant who acts as a 'rescuer' sustains psychiatric injury as a result of his involvement in the rescue (see para 14.31ff); liability for the psychiatric harm may well follow;

(6)   a claimant suffers a psychiatric injury owing to continuing exposure to stress (see para 14.35ff); liability for the psychiatric harm will be determined by the normal application of the rules of occupational liability;

(7)   a claimant suffers harassment at the hands of other workers (see para 14.80ff): liability for any psychiatric harm (and, indeed, any physical harm) may well follow, though it might be vicarious, and the facts will need exploration.

The sixth category, in particular, is clearly of great empirical significance. British workers are reported as having the highest levels of stress in Europe; the HSE estimates that stress-related illnesses affect up to 5 million people, and were the cause of a loss of 12.8 million working days in 2004/05.[1] Probably both long hours and the widespread experience of job insecurity have contributed to this growth.[2] In response, the courts are increasingly recognising a duty on the employer to protect employees against this, illustrated by the decision in *Walker v Northumberland County Council* [1995] ICR 702.[3]

1   As reported by the HSE on their 'stress at work' website: www.hse.gov.uk/stress. Research by the Policy Studies Institute (1993) found that one-third of employees reported significant levels of stress. The union MSF found 60% of workers in a survey suffering from stress: (1995) Labour Research, July, p 15. See too HSE Contract Research Report No 61/1993 *Stress Research and Stress Management: Putting Theory to Work*, and the research cited in HSIB 215 at p 3 and the Labour Force Survey, cited in HSIB 217 at p 5, to the effect that stress was the second most frequently cited occupational illness. See also the international journal *Work and Stress*, especially volume 18, no 2.
2   See the research on workers facing redundancy in (1990) 301 BMJ 461, cited in *Stress at Work* (Labour Research Department, 1994).
3   Claims for work-related stress have been long recognised in Australia and the USA.

PSYCHIATRIC INJURY

14.02 To recover damages, the mental condition must amount to a recognisable psychiatric injury: sensations of fear or distress[1] alone are insufficient.[2] 'Anxiety and depression are normal human emotions' said Lord Bridge in *McLoughlin v O 'Brian* [1983] 1 AC 410 at 431. No damages were awarded to a road accident victim for a severe shock and shaking up in *Nicholls v Rushton* (1992) Times, 19 June. An employee who suffers no more than distress at work, not amounting to a psychiatric injury, will not recover damages in negligence. The employer's duty is not to prevent an employee suffering from unpleasant emotions such as grief, anger and resentment or normal human conditions, such as anxiety or stress: see *Fraser v State Hospitals Board for Scotland* (2000) Times, 12 September. However, the degree of distress may well have an impact on the amount of damages recovered, even if it does not of itself confer a basis for finding liability. Thus a person who is much more affected emotionally by an injury than another will receive greater compensation, even though the emotions do not amount to a recognised psychiatric illness. The level of damages for scarring in particular is heavily influenced by the claimant's reaction to the scar.

1   For damages for distress see the statutory tort of harassment and the Protection from Harassment Act 1997, s 3; para 14.92, below.
2   See *Hinz v Berry* [1970] 2 QB 40; *McLoughlin v O'Brian* [1983] 1 AC 410; *Alcock v Chief Constable of South Yorkshire Police* [1992] 1 AC 310; *Hicks v Chief Constable of South Yorkshire Police* [1992] 1 All ER 690, affd [1992] 2 All ER 65; *Reilly v Merseyside Regional Health Authority* [1995] 6 Med LR 246; *Page v Smith* [1995] 2 All ER 736, HL. In the field of criminal compensation, *R v Criminal Injuries Compensation Board, ex p Johnson* [1994] JPIL 311; *R v Chan-Fook* [1994] JPIL 332. See too *Mount Isa Mines Ltd v Pusey* (1970) 125 CLR 383 at 394.

14.03 Nor would an action for breach of the implied contractual duty to take reasonable care for the employee's health be likely to succeed in such a case.

Cases where the courts have allowed damages for distress tend to concern contracts which are, in some sense, aimed at positively conferring pleasure (such as a contract for an holiday) or the relief of mental distress[1] (or under a specific statutory provision, such as the Protection from Harassment Act 1997, s 3; para 14.92, below). By analogy with these authorities, if an employer specifically promised an employee that it would, say, supply a back-up worker to assist in relieving stress, then the employee might be able to recover for stress alone, subject to overcoming problems of contractual intent and consideration.[2] In *Gogay v Hertfordshire County Council* [2000] IRLR 703, CA a claimant was a care assistant employed by the defendant local authority. She suffered psychiatric damage as a result of her suspension following allegations of sexual abuse. The defendants failed to carry out any proper analysis of the need for the suspension. The Court of Appeal found that the test of whether the defendants' conduct amounted to a breach of the implied term of confidence and trust between employer and employee was a demanding one and the conduct must be such as liable to destroy or seriously damage the relationship. They ruled that although the duty was owed only in contract, as in other cases of breaches of an employer's duty, there was no reason to distinguish between physical and psychiatric injury.[3]

[1]   Claims have succeeded, for example, in relation to poor holidays (*Jarvis v Swans Tours Ltd* [1973] QB 233) and failures to obtain injunctions preventing molestations: *Heywood v Wellers* [1976] QB 446. A degrading or humiliating dismissal does not result in damages for breach of contract: *Addis v Gramophone Co Ltd* [1909] AC 488; recently reaffirmed in *O'Laoire v Jackel International Ltd (No 2)* [1991] ICR 718 and further considered in *Johnson v Unisys Ltd* 2003] 1 AC 518, HL. Damages cannot be awarded for depression, anxiety, frustration and illness arising out of unfair dismissal, despite the decision in *Cox v Philips Industries Ltd* [1976] ICR 138 that where caused by a demotion in breach of a contract of employment they might be claimed: *Dunnachie v Kingston upon Hull City Council* [2004] UKHL 36, [2005] 1 AC 226
[2]   Consider the facts of *Walker v Northumberland County Council*, see para 14.40, below.
[3]   Foreseeability of injury appears to have been assumed, rather than been the subject of detailed submission.

14.04 It is perhaps arguable that in an action for breach of statutory duty, damages could be recovered for distress or discomfort, although it is likely to be hard to show that Parliament intended such a remedy (see the HSWA 1974, s 47(2)). Much will depend upon the statute. If a claim is for discrimination, then it is likely to include damages for 'injury to feelings' since this is specified as possible in the discrimination statutes (Race Relations Act 1976, Sex Discrimination Act 1975, Disability Discrimination Act 1995), but even under the Protection from Harassment Act 1997 it was argued in *Majrowski v Guy's and St Thomas's NHS Trust* [2005] EWCA Civ 251, [2005] QB 848, CA for the successful claimant that one of the restrictions on a claimant free-for-all was the requirement that damages would be dependent on more than mere upset, distress and frustration. It is unclear whether an action could be brought to recover damages for distress under European health and safety Directives under the doctrine of direct effect (see para 9.51, above). The Working Time Directive (para 10.37, above), for example, regulates hours and rest, and abjures monotonous work. Such an action should succeed if it can be shown that the particular provision is sufficiently certain, no other national remedy is provided and it is intended to protect against the form of distress suffered, particularly since, under UK law, damages for distress alone are irrecoverable. However, damages would arguably be awarded here for the loss of the amenity which the Regulations are designed to provide, rather than for any distress caused by the fact of breach itself.

14.05 Despite the exclusion of pure distress, the boundaries of what are classified as psychiatric 'injuries' seem to be expanding. Damages are recoverable for a wide range of conditions such as clinical shock and post-traumatic stress disorder.[1] They include extreme 'pathological' grief[2] and there is no reason why the symptoms of a stress-related injury need to be acute.[3] Once some physical or psychiatric injury is foreseeable, and therefore recoverable, the claimant may recover for the full extent of his or her injuries, regardless of whether that extent is unforeseeable: *Brice v Brown* [1984] 1 All ER 997; *Page v Smith* [1995] 2 All ER 736, HL. The eggshell personality rule applies as forcefully as does the eggshell skull rule.

[1]   See the World Health Organisation guidelines *Classification of Mental and Behavioural Disorders* (Geneva, 1992).
[2]   See *North Glamorgan NHS Trust v Walters* [2002] EWCA Civ 1792.
[3]   See K Wheat 'Nervous Shock: The Present State of English Law' [1994] JPIL 131.

Physical injury with accompanying psychiatric injury

14.06 Turning then to the various different factual situations, the first is where a claimant suffers a physical injury that causes or is accompanied by psychiatric injury. Damages for the injury will include something for the pain and suffering, no doubt to some extent a mental phenomenon. Other heads of damage, such as loss of amenity, the enjoyment of life and of congenial employment, reflect the psychiatric effects of an injury as well as they do the physical. The approach is an holistic one. This applies even if some part of the psychiatric distress might have been expected in any event (at least where it cannot be said how far the upset would extend): thus in *Vernon v Bosley (No 1)* [1997] 1 All ER 577, CA it was recognised that although damages for normal grief and bereavement suffered as the result of another's negligence were not recoverable, a plaintiff in the position of secondary victim could recover damages for both post-traumatic stress disorder (ie the nervous shock of witnessing an accident or its immediate aftermath) and pathological grief disorder (ie grief which became so severe as to be regarded as abnormal and giving rise to psychiatric illness). No deduction was to be made for that degree of distress that would have been inevitable anyway.

14.07 Lord Steyn observed in *White v Chief Constable of South Yorkshire Police* [1999] 2 AC 455, HL, that it is a non-sequitur to say that because there is a duty not to cause physical injury there must be a duty not to cause psychiatric injury. However, it now appears established that the duty not to cause foreseeable physical harm and the duty not to cause psychiatric harm are two subcategories of a general duty not to cause foreseeable harm. There is no established principle limiting the duty in relation to psychiatric injury save in respect of claims by secondary victims (see para 14.20ff): see per Lord Macfadyen in *Cross v Highlands and Islands Enterprise* [2001] IRLR 336, OH, at

351, para 60 whose judgment appears consistent in this respect with *White v Chief Constable of South Yorkshire Police* [1999] 2 AC 455, HL, and *Page v Smith* [1995] 2 All ER 736, HL.

Participants in a dangerous event

14.08 A claimant who does not suffer any physical injury but, as a result of being, as a participant, put in a position of danger, suffers psychiatric harm has come to be known as a 'primary victim'. Such a person is one of the categories of 'shock' victims referred to by Lord Oliver in *Alcock v Chief Constable of South Yorkshire Police* [1992] 1 AC 310 at 407, where he made clear that, as a participant, the fact of participation alone makes their relationship to the defendant sufficiently proximate.

14.09 In these circumstances, a claimant can recover so long as physical injury was foreseeable to him or her even if none in fact occurred; there is no separate requirement that psychiatric injury is foreseeable: see *Page v Smith* [1995] 2 All ER 736, HL, especially per Lord Lloyd at 755 and 758. Just like other physical injury cases, foreseeability is judged in the light of what ought to have been foreseen before the relevant events and not in the light of the events that actually happened: Lord Lloyd in *Page* at 759.[1] It needs to be emphasised that what is foreseeable in the context of a tortious action is very different from that which is likely to happen: in *Bolton v Stone* [1951] AC 850 the chance of a cricket ball being hit over a perimeter fence so as to strike a passer-by in the road beyond was regarded as infinitesimally small, but it was none the less foreseeable: see *Overseas Tankship (UK) Ltd v The Miller Steamship Co Pty, The Wagon Mound (No 2)* [1967] 1 AC 617, per Lord Reid at 641–643, where he points out that the real question is whether the level of risk is such as to require measures to be taken to combat it. Thus, where oil on water was almost, but not quite, unknown ever to have caught alight, the party responsible for the spillage would be liable: it could not be said that it was impossible or unknown for such an event to happen, it was thus foreseeable, and it was accepted they already had a duty to prevent spillage, even if that duty was focussed upon the alternative and more obvious risk of fouling the slipway. A similar approach was taken in relation to personal injury in *Jolley v Sutton Borough Council* [2000] 3 All ER 409, HL.

[1]   Cf the dissenting remarks of Lord Keith at 741 and Lord Jauncey at 751. The requirement that psychiatric injury should be foreseeable to a person of ordinary fortitude necessarily disappears as a result of the decision in *Page v Smith*, if some injury was otherwise foreseeable.

14.10 In contrast, in non-participant, or secondary victim, cases it is now clear that a single unifying test for liability of foreseeability of recognisable psychiatric injury is not the present law. A secondary victim cannot recover damages for negligence unless he or she can satisfy three main requirements (developed in para 14.21ff):

(i)   that he had a close tie of love and affection with the person killed, injured or imperilled;

(ii)   that he was close to the 'accident' in time and space;

(iii)   that he directly perceived the 'accident' rather than, for example, hearing about it from a third person.[1]

See *Alcock* (above); *Page v Smith* (above) and *Frost v Chief Constable of South Yorkshire Police* [1999] 2 AC 455.

¹   This may helpfully be remembered, albeit in reverse order, as the criteria of 'nearness, hereness, and dearness'.

14.11 When is a person a participant or primary victim? Lord Lloyd in *Page* spoke of persons 'directly involved in the accident and well within the range of foreseeable physical injury' (at 755; see too Lord Oliver in *Alcock*, above, at 407). In *McFarlane v EE Caledonian Ltd* [1994] 2 All ER 1, CA, at 10 Stuart Smith LJ referred to three categories of participant: first, those who are in the actual area of danger but who escape physical injury; second, those who are not actually in danger but because of the sudden and unexpected nature of the event reasonably think they are; and, third, rescuers who come into the area of danger after the event. In *McFarlane* an oil worker who was in a boat close to the Piper Alpha disaster was held not to be a participant. The evidence was that he was never in actual danger and would have been able to take shelter if a risk arose.[1] So, a secondary victim is the unwilling witness who is shocked by events that physically endanger others; he is not himself physically endangered.

¹   In the light of the (reasonable) fear such a fire would be likely to prompt in those close to the scene, the decisions may appear harsh. The Court of Appeal may have been influenced by the fact that the claimant had not claimed to be in fear of his own safety until a late stage in the case: see Stuart Smith LJ at 12.

14.12 In *Frost v Chief Constable of South Yorkshire Police* [1999] 2 AC 455, HL the claimants were police officers on duty at the Hillsborough football stadium who suffered psychiatric injuries as a result of their involvement in the events at the stadium when 96 people died as a result of overcrowding, caused in part by bad policing by the defendants. None of the claimants had a tie of close love and affection with any of the victims. It was argued that by reason of the claimants' employment relationship with the defendants, they did not need to fulfil the three main requirements that a secondary victim claimant must ordinarily fulfil to recover, and, particularly relevant in the *Frost* case, the close tie of love and affection requirement. It was contended that the relationship put them in a different and altogether easier position when considering the question of duty to that of spectators at the match, even though what they saw and did at the match may have been the same. It was suggested that they were owed a duty of care by law, as employees: their employer owed them a duty to take reasonable care for their health and safety at work which it had broken. Moreover, as claimants who were directly involved in the incident caused by their employers' negligence which resulted in the injury or imperilment of another they were primary (or participant) victims.

14.13 This argument had earlier been made in the Scottish case of *Robertson v Forth Road Bridge Joint Board* 1995 SC 364. In that case the two claimants saw a workmate killed when the sheet of metal he was sitting on in a pick-up truck was blown over the side of the Forth Road Bridge in their sight. In rejecting the argument in *Frost* Lord Hoffmann said the argument really assumed what it needed to prove, noting, at 505G:

> 'The liability of an employer to his employees for negligence, either direct or vicarious, is not a separate tort with its own rules. It is an aspect of the general law of negligence. The relationship of employer and employee establishes the employee as a person to whom the employer owes a duty of care. But this tells one nothing about the circumstances in which he will be liable for a particular type of injury. For this one must look to the general law concerning the type of injury which has been suffered.'

14.14 He then considered whether the employment relationship should be a reason for allowing an employee to recover damages for psychiatric injury in circumstances in which he would otherwise be a secondary victim and not satisfy *the Alcock* control mechanisms asking, at 506E, the rhetorical question:

> 'Why should the policemen, simply by virtue of the employment analogy and irrespective of what they actually did be treated different [sic] from first aid workers or ambulance men?'

He concluded that, in line with authority, it would not be fair to permit recovery on such grounds, a decision supported by the majority.

14.15 It is now clearly established that the existence of the relationship of employment does not dispose of the need to satisfy the criteria the law has laid down that must be met in secondary victim cases. A distinction was recognised between the factual circumstances pertaining in *White* and those in cases such as *Walker v Northumberland County Council* [1995] ICR 702: Lord Hoffmann accepting, it appears, that as the victim of work pressures arising out of the system of work to which he was subject, Mr Walker was (and others in a similar position were) primary (or participant) victims. This position was made clear beyond doubt by the Court of Appeal in *Hatton v Sutherland* [2002] 2 All ER 1, which rejected any view that there were particular restrictions applying to claims for psychiatric injury which was allegedly suffered as a result of employment practices.

14.16 The decision in *White* is of considerable practical significance, for whilst horrific incidents such as Hillsborough are rare, and even rarer is the circumstance that those shocked in such an incident are the employees of the tortfeasor, horrific accidents at work that may shock fellow employees are not rare.

14.17 However, the distinction between primary and secondary victims remains debatable.[1] In Lord Oliver's speech in *Alcock v Chief Constable of South Yorkshire Police* two categories were identified: 'those cases in which the injured plaintiff was involved, either mediately or immediately, as a participant' (a primary victim) and 'those in which the plaintiff was no more than the passive and unwilling witness of injury caused to others' (a secondary victim). Three examples of primary victims were given: those who feared for their own safety, rescuers and involuntary participants. However, in *Page v Smith* Lord Lloyd referred to primary victims as being those who were 'directly involved in the accident and well within the range of foreseeable physical injury', and secondary victims as those who were 'in the position of a spectator or bystander'. The discrepancy between these two definitions has given rise to much discussion. In *Frost v Chief Constable of South Yorkshire Police* the House of Lords adopted Lord Lloyd's approach. Lord Griffiths said, 'In my view [the *Alcock* criteria] should apply to all those not directly imperilled or who reasonably believe themselves to be imperilled ...'. Lord Steyn regarded Lord Lloyd as having intended to narrow the range of primary victims. He remarked that 'Lord Lloyd said that a plaintiff who had been within the range of foreseeable [physical] injury was a primary victim. Mr Page fulfilled this requirement and could in principle recover compensation for psychiatric loss. In my view it follows that all other victims, who suffer pure psychiatric harm, are secondary victims and must satisfy the control mechanisms laid down in the *Alcock* case.' Lord Hoffmann, dealing with the argument for the police officer plaintiffs that they were primary victims as they had been akin to rescuers, said that there was no reason why 'they should be given special treatment as primary victims when they were not within the range of foreseeable physical injury and their psychiatric injury was caused by witnessing or participating in the aftermath of accidents which caused death or injury to others.' Lord Browne-Wilkinson agreed with Lord Steyn and Lord Hoffmann, but Lord Goff dissented on the basis that Lord Lloyd's remarks in *Page v Smith* could not have been intended to alter Lord Oliver's definition of primary victims in the earlier case of *Alcock*.

14.18 The precise demarcation between the two categories is further complicated by the suggestion of Lord Hoffmann in *Frost v Chief Constable of South Yorkshire Police* that the distinction between primary and secondary victims should depend on the cause of their psychiatric injury. A secondary victim would be an individual who suffers a psychiatric injury as a consequence of the death, injury or imperilment of another person that had been caused by the defendant's negligence.

14.19 Despite *Frost*, there are three situations where the courts have held people to be primary victims although they were not within the range of foreseeable physical injury. First, there is the case of the involuntary participant; second, the case of someone who suffers injury (whether psychiatric or physical) though not within the scope of foreseeable physical injury (occupational stress claims are a case in point); third the case of those who have suffered a wrong which would not foreseeably cause physical injury, but might foreseeably cause psychiatric injury. Each of these categories is dealt with below.

Non-participants ('secondary victims')

14.20 Suppose a claimant suffers a psychiatric injury owing to what has happened to someone else—typically, an injury to or death of a relative, or friend or work colleague—and the harm to that third party was caused by the negligence of the defendant. Historically, these cases have been known as cases of 'nervous shock' and such claimants have come to be known as 'secondary victims'. Here the courts have placed policy restrictions on recovery, see the summary at para 14.10. The three policy conditions imposed on recovery are constraints on whether there should be recovery at all. They have been put, in the early case of *Hay (or Bourhill) v Young* [1943] AC 92, HL, as resting on foreseeability (not foreseeable that a pregnant woman alighting from a tram would suffer a miscarriage there and then by hearing the sound of a collision involving a motor cycle on the far side of the tram, hidden from view) though also on the scope of the duty. Although foreseeability goes both to liability and to causation of damage (see *Overseas Tankship (UK) Ltd v Mort's Dock and Engineering Co Ltd, The Wagon Mound* [1961] AC 388), it seems to have been used here in the liability sense—there is no duty of care to someone who is not reasonably foreseeably at risk as a consequence of the relevant negligence. However, later cases have been frank in recognising the rule as one of policy. Each restrictive precondition to a successful claim must now be examined in greater depth.

14.21 'Close ties of love and affection' between the initial victim and the claimant will be (rebuttably) presumed in recognised cases, such as children and fiancés. They may also exist in close friendships, but the closeness must then be proved by evidence: *Alcock v Chief Constable of South Yorkshire Police* [1992] 1 AC 310, especially Lord Keith at 397, Lord Oliver at 415–416.[1] There is no judicial presumption of such a tie between work colleagues. Outside the presumed relationships it appears that the claimant must prove the requisite degree of closeness.

[1] Curiously, this presumption did not extend to brothers or grandsons. And Lord Keith recognised that affection between spouses could wane over the years (at 397).

14.22 What are not clear are the outer limits of this requirement. In *Alcock*, Lord Ackner (at 430), with whom Lord Oliver agreed, left open the possibility of recovery even by complete strangers in the context of a particularly horrific event, as did Lord Keith, who said that 'reasonable foreseeability should be the guide' (at 397). Yet recovery was denied to the claimant in *McFarlane v EE Caledonia Ltd* [1994] 2 All ER 1, CA, who witnessed an event just about as horrific as one could imagine and even though he knew his workmates were on board the burning oil rig.[1] If recovery to complete strangers may be allowed in particularly horrific circumstances, then why should recovery be denied to workmates in less traumatic circumstances, particularly if they are very close to the event? Certainly Lord Oliver envisaged a sliding rule of proximity of just this sort in *Alcock* (at 415–416); and it appears consistent with the outcome of *Dooley v Cammell Laird & Co Ltd* [1951] 1 Lloyd's Rep 271.[2] In Australia, recovery has been permitted to a colleague who found the body of his workmate after an explosion: see *Mount Isa Mines Ltd v Pusey* (1970) 125 CLR 383. Relationships formed at work are often long-lived and of great closeness; it seems inconsistent with a common law approach of protecting workers that they should be excluded in this fashion.[3]

1   For criticism, see Tan Keng Feng 'Nervous Shock: Bystander Witnessing a Catastrophe' [1995] CLJ 48.
2   See too Lord Ackner in *Alcock* at 404. The decisions appear particularly harsh in the light of a case where the courts did not strike out a claim by a woman who saw her house burning down: *Attia v British Gas plc* [1988] QB 304, CA. See too *Wigg v British Railways Board* [1986] NLJ Rep 446n (train driver recovered for injury following discovery of body on line).
3   For general criticism of the vagueness of the *Alcock* test, see Hedley 'Hillsborough: Morbid Musings of a Reasonable Chief Constable' [1992] CLJ 16.

14.23 In addition to witnessing a single horrific event, the claimant generally needs to be present at the accident itself or witness its 'immediate aftermath', usually stated as part of the test of proximity: see *McLoughlin v O 'Brian* [1983] 1 AC 410 as interpreted in *Alcock v Chief Constable of South Yorkshire Police* [1992] 1 AC 310, especially per Lord Ackner at 401, 404.[1] What constitutes the immediate aftermath is a matter of some difficulty. *In Alcock,* Lord Jauncey made plain that he thought it unwise to attempt a definition of what constituted the immediate aftermath. However, in that same case, Lord Ackner made clear that it should be narrowly construed (see 400H–401A), a proposition re-stated in the Court of Appeal decision in *Tranmore v TE Scuddder Ltd* (28 April 1998, unreported), CA. It is suggested that the concept is not one purely of elapsed time, but involves a qualitative as well as quantitative assessment. However, seeing bodies in a mortuary after a major disaster is too late (*Alcock*). Claims for damages for psychiatric injury failed the 'immediate aftermath' test in *Ravenscroft v Rederiaktiebølaget Transatlantic* [1992] 2 All ER 470n (a young man was crushed by machinery while working. He died in hospital two hours later: his mother went there 20 minutes after his death); in *Tranmore v T E Scudder Ltd,* also a fatal accident at work, where the father was told hours afterwards and saw his son's body the next day; in *Taylorson v Shieldness Produce Ltd* [1994] PIQR P329 where the father had a brief glimpse of his fatally injured son as he was transferred from the ambulance and was with him in intensive care after treatment; and in *Taylor v Somerset Health Authority* [1993] PIQR P262 where a woman who went to hospital within 20 minutes of being told that her husband had suffered a heart attack, was told he was dead and saw the body. On the other hand, in *Galli-Atkinson v Seghal* [2003] EWCA Civ 697 a mother was successful in her claim for damages for psychiatric injury when she went out looking for her daughter who had failed to return home from a ballet lesson, saw the scene of the accident about an hour after it had occurred and was taken to the hospital where she saw her daughter's terribly injured body in the mortuary. This was regarded as being part of the immediate aftermath. Also, in *Waller and Waller v Canterbury and Thanet Health Authority* [1993] CLY 1453 parents recovered for depressive illness after discovering their son's body, who committed suicide due to defendant's negligence.

1   See *Jaensch v Coffey* (1984) 155 CLR 549.

14.24 The following suggestions may be made to assist in the determination of what may constitute the 'immediate aftermath'. First, the immediate aftermath is always spoken of as the aftermath of the event; this is to be distinguished from the aftermath of the emergency created by the event. Stress caused by events subsequent to the immediate accident, such as inquests or criminal trials, does not permit recovery: see *Calascione v Dixon* [1994] JPIL 83, CA. Nor does shock caused to a woman on learning of her husband's death, and from identifying his body: *Taylor v Somerset Health Authority* [1993] PIQR P262. Nor does the effect of stress, whether physical or psychiatric, involved in caring for a spouse or relative who has been seriously injured by the negligence of another.[1]

1   Although if the injured relative is able to bring a claim for her or his injuries, the carer may benefit from the principle that (s)he must hold that part of the damages award which represents compensation for past care on trust for the carer.

14.25 Second, whilst there is no set time limit as to how much time may pass following the accident for the immediate aftermath itself to have passed, a period of two hours (allowed in *McLoughlin*) may indicate the degree to which the aftermath doctrine, insofar as it is temporal, can be stretched. Seeing a body eight hours after the Hillsborough disaster was outside the aftermath according to Lord Ackner in *Alcock*. However, an event need not be instantaneous: see *Walters v North Glamorgan NHS Trust* [2002] EWCA Civ 1792, [2003] PIQR P16: it may be difficult on occasion to distinguish the continuation of a single horrifying event from its aftermath (in that case, the parent of a brain-damaged child became only slowly aware over 36 hours of the extent of its injuries, but recovered as a secondary victim).

14.26 Third, in determining whether the immediate aftermath has passed, it is material to determine what stage after the accident itself had been reached when the claimant witnessed events—for example, were the emergency services present? Was some form of order being restored? Fourth, a distinction should be drawn between the shock of the news (which, subject to the exceptional cases below, is not to be compensated) and the shock of the experience of the primary event. Finally, it should be established what (if anything) the secondary victim saw of the primary victim and in what condition the latter was then found to be.

14.27 The precise means of witnessing the event or its aftermath are, curiously, accorded importance. In general it seems that the claimant must see or hear either of these directly with his or her eyes or ears (*McLoughlin v O'Brian* [1983] 1 AC 410) although in *Alcock* Lord Ackner considered that a television broadcast might permit recovery in some circumstances; everything turns upon how shocking it is deemed to be. Communication of shocking information by a third party does not in general permit recovery: *Ravenscroft v Rederiaktiebolaget* [1992] 2 All ER 470n; *Taylor v Somerset Health Authority*, above. Nor, it seems, does reading or hearing of the accident: *Alcock* per Lord Ackner at 400. However, claims for psychiatric injury arising out of the receipt of distressing news have sometimes been allowed. Apart from those cases in which the news itself is delivered as part of a practical joke or deliberate deceit: *Janvier v Sweeney* [1919] 2 KB 316; *Wilkinson v Downton* [1897] 2 QB 57: false news may give rise to a successful claim as in *Allin v City and Hackney Health Authority* [1996] 7 Med LR 167 where a mother was awarded damages for post-traumatic stress syndrome caused by her being told (falsely) that her new-born baby had died; and in *Farrell v Avon*

Health Authority [2001] Lloyd's Rep Med 458, where a father was falsely informed of the death of his child, was given a corpse of another baby to hold when he came to the hospital, and suffered psychiatric injury when the mistake was revealed. Claims may also arise where distressing but true information is imparted in an insensitive manner. For example, in *AB v Tameside and Glossop Health Authority* [1997] 8 Med LR 91 the authority, on learning that one of its health workers was HIV positive posted letters to former patients warning them that there was a very slight risk of infection: the authority conceded that a duty of care arose. On the facts, the information had been given in a reasonable way, and the Court of Appeal thus allowed the authority's appeal.[1]

[1] See also Mullany 'Liability for Careless Communication of Traumatic Information' (1998) 114 LQR 380.

14.28 The case law suggests that psychiatric injury caused by an extended exposure to distressing circumstances does not give rise to liability. Instead, the claimant must show the injury was attributable to his shock in reaction to a single horrific event: see *Alcock* (especially Lord Ackner at 400–401) and *Sion v Hampstead Health Authority* [1994] 5 Med LR 170. The uncertainty of this requirement is shown by *Tredget and Tredget v Bexley Health Authority* [1994] 5 Med LR 178, where a woman gave birth to a child who died two days later owing to the defendants' negligence; held that the chaos at the birth, coupled with her sense that something was wrong, was a sufficiently horrific event—despite the mother being sedated at the time, her not seeing the child at delivery and the death only occurring two days later. But in *Sion v Hampstead Health Authority*, above, the Court of Appeal reaffirmed that 'sudden awareness, violently agitating the mind, of what is occurring or what has occurred' is the crucial ingredient of shock in respect of which damages are recoverable. A grief reaction to the death of the claimant's son two weeks after the accident did not amount to a sudden and unexpected shock to the nervous system.[1] Thus in *Walters v North Glamorgan NHS Trust* [2002] EWCA Civ 1792, [2003] PIQR P16, a mother was awarded damages where she had been present from the time her baby son had a major epileptic seizure (due to acute hepatitis that the hospital had failed to diagnose) until his death 36 hours later. She was wrongly told that the seizure was not serious, when in fact it had caused major irreparable brain damage. Thomas J held that the mother had suffered a sudden appreciation of her son's injuries, and was in the category of true secondary victim. The Court of Appeal upheld this finding, rejecting an argument that a slow realisation over 36 hours prevented the episode being viewed as one single horrifying event.

[1] The curious assumptions of subjectivity underlying this approach may be vulnerable to similar criticisms as have been levelled at male bias in the defence of provocation in criminal law.

Involuntary participants

14.29 The 'involuntary participant' was identified as a category by Lord Oliver in *Alcock*. The authority taken as establishing the involuntary participant category is the decision of Donovan J in *Dooley v Cammel Laird*

& Co Ltd [1951] 1 Lloyd's Rep 271. The claimant, a crane driver, was the unwitting hand who caused an accident. A load from his crane fell into the hold of a ship where there were fellow workers employed and he feared for their safety. It was held that 'nervous shock' was a reasonably foreseeable consequence of witnessing an accident to another as it was proved that the claimant had been put in the position of thinking that he was about to be or had been the involuntary cause of another's death or injury. The phrase 'unwilling participant' is a synonym for the 'involuntary cause of ...'. Similarly, in *Salter v UB Frozen and Chilled Foods Ltd* 2003 SLT 1011, the pursuer was driving a hoist in the cage of which two of his colleagues were standing to carry out a stocktaking. The hoist jerked forward for some unexplained reason and one of the stocktakers was killed when he hit his head on a roof beam. The pursuer recovered. The distinction between this situation and such as that in *Robertson v Forth Road Bridge Joint Board* 1995 SC 364 (fellow workman blown over the edge of a bridge from a truck in which all were riding) where it is now established[1] that there should be no liability, seems a fine one, but must rest upon the involuntary participant's justified feeling of control over the process which unwittingly led to death, such that he not unreasonably considers himself the cause (or part of the cause) of it. This is indicated by the words of Lord Oliver who, in describing this category, spoke of the claimant as being 'mediately' involved, ie forming a connecting link or transitional stage, to act as an intermediary. For example, it covers the situation where a workman gives a scaffolding pole to a colleague, which he then raises and hits an electricity wire whereby he is electrocuted: see *Young v Charles Church (Southern) Ltd* (1997) 39 BMLR 146.

[1] *Frost v Chief Constable of South Yorkshire Police* [1999] 2 AC 455, HL.

14.30 A possible application of this principle in slightly different circumstances may be that of *W v Essex County Council* [2001] 2 AC 592, HL (a striking out application, arguing the claim disclosed no cause of action in negligence). A claim was made for psychiatric illness suffered by parents of children sexually abused by a child fostered by them through the agency of the defendant county council; the parents had specifically sought assurances that the fostered 15-year-old was not a known abuser. It was very hard to see how in the light of the *Frost* decision the parents could be primary victims in those circumstances but Lord Slynn said:

> 'As to being primary victims it is beyond doubt that they were not physically injured by the abuse and on the present allegations it does not seem reasonably foreseeable that there was a risk of abuse to the parents. But the categorisation of those claiming to be included as primary or secondary victims is not as I read the cases finally closed.'

He went on to allow the appeal against the striking out order.

Rescuers

14.31 Where, by breach of duty, an employer has created an emergency imperilling its employees, the employees (or others) may in some circumstances act as rescuers. The category of rescuer is established in the law of negligence generally, not just when considering liability for recognisable psychiatric illness. If a rescuer, the claimant is not concerned with arguments of contributory negligence, novus actus interveniens or volenti non fit injuria. Liability is based upon the view that 'Danger invites rescue'.[1]

1   Per Cardozo J.

14.32 Following the decision of the majority of the House of Lords in *Frost v Chief Constable of South Yorkshire Police* [1999] 2 AC 455, HL, it is clear that a rescuer is in no special position in relation to liability for psychiatric injury. In *Chadwick v British Railways Board* [1967] 1 WLR 912, Mr Chadwick had worked through the night tending to those injured in the Lewisham train disaster; that had involved him going into the carriages where the dead and injured were trapped. *Frost* establishes that *Chadwick* is to be interpreted not as a case where the claimant was held entitled to recover because of the horror of the whole event, but on the basis that liability was founded on the risk of personal injury to which the claimant submitted himself.

14.33 In *Duncan v British Coal Corpn* [1997] 1 All ER 540 it was held that a mining supervisor who gave mouth-to-mouth resuscitation to a colleague fatally injured in a mining accident for over two hours was not a rescuer because he had arrived some four minutes after the relevant accident. That decision and the decision in *McFarlane v EE Caledonia Ltd* [1994] 2 All ER 1, CA (para 14.11, above) emphasise that temporal and physical proximity is required where a victim is said to have functioned as a rescuer: the rescue is from present danger, not from the ensuing risk of death from injury suffered as a consequence of the materialisation of the danger.

14.34 The latter decision also emphasises that a 'function' test may usefully be applied when determining whether a given claimant is a rescuer. In *McFarlane*, merely handling some blankets was not enough to warrant the conclusion that the claimant was a rescuer.

OCCUPATIONAL STRESS

Introduction

14.35 The 'shock'[1] cases discussed above generally concern psychiatric injury caused by a single event or series of events. Claimants in stress cases have usually been the subject of a continuous causative process and are normally primary victims.[2] The 'control mechanisms' used for secondary victims[3] do not generally apply. Thus it is accepted at Court of Appeal level that the ordinary rules of occupational liability apply in respect of claims to have suffered psychiatric injury as a result of working conditions, and no special control mechanisms apply to claims for psychiatric (or physical) illness or injury arising from the stress of doing the work the employee is required to do: *Hatton v Sutherland* [2002] EWCA Civ 76, [2002] 2 All ER 1, at paras 20, 22, following *Garrett v Camden London Borough Council* [2001] EWCA Civ

395, CA and endorsed on this point by the House of Lords in *Barber v Somerset County Council* [2004] UKHL 13, [2004] ICR 457.

1   For a detailed discussion of the relevance of shock cases to stress cases see A Buchan 'Stress Cases, Foreseeability and Breach' (2001) 3 JPIL 7–9.
2   Lord Oliver in *Alcock* at 407A; *Alexander v Midland Bank plc* [1999] IRLR 723 per Stuart-Smith LJ at 732.
3   Summarised at para 14.10 and developed at para 14.20ff.

Definition

14.36 Claims for psychiatric injury arising from the extent of the work ('overwork') or its nature, or from the working conditions to which a person is subject, are often termed 'stress' claims. This is a misnomer, since stress is not an injury in itself, though (apart from beneficial effects, such as ensuring optimum performance or a sense of achievement in work) it may predispose to one, and it should always be remembered that everyone may be said to have a 'breaking point' no matter how robust they may normally seem to be. There are numerous definitions of stress which include engineering, physiological and psychological approaches. Stress is a normal part of life and work. It can be positive as well as negative. This part of this chapter is only concerned with liability for destructive occupational stress.[1] Destructive workplace stress includes an excess of demands beyond an individual's ability to cope.[2]

1   Stress (and injury caused by it) is multi-factorial, ie it can be caused for many reasons both occupational and non-occupational. It may be difficult to say that an occupational stressor has not contributed to a given psychiatric condition: a more useful forensic question is whether without it, there would probably have been the injury anyway, if not at the same time, then later. As Professor Simon Wessely has said: 'Stress is a subjective, not an objective, phenomenon. It is for that reason that it is incapable of scientific definition, and cannot be found in any major disease classifications. One person's stress is not another's. Whether or not the circumstances of a person's employment are objectively excessive or detrimental is essentially a matter of fact. It is for the court to determine the facts of the employment situation which is not a proper area for medical evidence. It is essentially a matter of fact and commonsense judgment'. For a useful list of the better known causes of stress see: Buchan 'Stress Cases, Foreseeability and Breach' (2001) 3 JPIL 10 and 11.
2   The definition adopted by the HSE.

Applicable principles: duty

14.37 The primary principle is that liability for injury caused by occupational stress should be treated no differently from liability for any other occupational injury. That demands the same approach as in any other occupational injury case as to whether there is a duty, whether there has been a breach of that duty, and whether the injury has been caused or contributed to by the breach (and not, it must be emphasised, by the work itself, unless the doing of work of the nature or to the extent performed itself constitutes a breach of duty). There may also be liability in contract, not simply for the breach of the contractual term which corresponds to the tortious duty to take reasonable care for the health and safety of employees, but also: (i) that which provides that an employer should not without good reason act in such a way as is liable to destroy or seriously damage the relationship of trust and confidence between employer and employee; and (ii) that which may amount to a term not to require an employee without his consent to work more than 48 hours in a week, averaged over 17 weeks as a running total (derived from the Working Time Regulations 1998 and the decision in *Barber v RJB Mining (UK) Ltd* [1999] ICR 679). These are discussed below at 14.77ff.

14.38 The existence of a duty of care in tort can be taken for granted.[1] In *Petch v Comrs of Customs and Excise* [1993] ICR 789, CA it was accepted that the ordinary principles of employers' liability applied to a claim for psychiatric illness arising from employment, although the claim failed. In that case the claimant joined the Civil Service in 1961 as a clerical officer, was highly regarded by his superior officers and by 1973 had risen to the rank of Assistant Secretary. In 1974, while working in the defendant's department, he had a mental breakdown. In 1975, after his return to work, he was transferred as Assistant Secretary to the Department of Health and Social Security. In 1983 he fell ill again but was able to return to work until 1986, when he was retired from the Civil Service on medical grounds. The trial judge held that, although the claimant would not have suffered a breakdown in 1974 if he had not been subject to heavy pressure of work, the defendants were not negligent in failing to take steps which would have prevented the claimant's illnesses. The appeal was dismissed on the ground that it had not been shown on the evidence that the defendant's senior management were aware, or ought to have been aware, in 1974 that the claimant was showing signs of impending breakdown or that his workload carried a real risk of breakdown. They had not acted negligently following his return to work, the defendants had not been in breach of their admitted duty to take reasonable care to ensure that the duties allocated to the claimant did not damage his health; and that, since on the facts the claimant's other claims had not been made out, the claimant's action failed. Dillon LJ endorsed a concession by counsel that:

'The defendants owe the plaintiff a duty to take reasonable care that the duties allocated to him should not damage his health ... that duty extended to mental as well as physical health, subject to a caveat that foreseeability and causation were likely to be more difficult issues in mental injury cases such as this.'

1   *Hatton v Sutherland*, para 19.

14.39 In relation to Mr Petch's first breakdown; Dillon LJ said:

'Unless senior management in the defendant's department were aware or ought to have been aware that the plaintiff was showing signs of impending breakdown, or were aware or ought to have been aware that his workload carried a risk that he would have a breakdown, then the defendants were not negligent in failing to avert the breakdown in October 1974.'

In relation to Mr Petch's second breakdown, Dillon LJ said:

'When the plaintiff returned to work at the beginning of January 1975 the admitted duty of care which the defendants owed him ... must have extended to taking reasonable care to ensure that the duties allocated to him did not bring about a repetition of his mental breakdown of October 1974.'

14.40 The first successful 'second breakdown' case to receive publicity was *Walker v Northumberland County Council* [1995] ICR 702. Mr Walker was employed by the council as an area social services officer and, against a background of an increasing workload, suffered a nervous breakdown in November 1986 attributed to the impact of his work on his personality. He went off work and during his absence it was agreed that he would receive additional help when he resumed. Within a month of his return to work in March 1987, the promised assistance had been withdrawn and the backlog of paperwork which had built up during his absence together with a continued increase in case load led to a second breakdown. In February 1988 his employment was terminated on grounds of permanent ill-health. The court held the council liable on the basis that they owed their employee a duty not to cause him psychiatric damage by the volume and/or character of the work he was required to undertake. The standard of care of a reasonable employer was dependant upon the magnitude of the risk of injury which was reasonably foreseeable, the seriousness of the consequences for the person to whom the duty was owed if the risk resulted in injury, and the cost and practicability of taking steps to avert the risk. On the facts of the case, there was no liability for the first breakdown, which was held not to be reasonably foreseeable, but its occurrence (and the causes for it) made it reasonably foreseeable that, unless proper steps were put in place to alleviate the circumstances leading to the initial breakdown, damage to the employee's health might re-occur. Thus the employer failed to provide a safe system of work prior to the second breakdown.[1] Colman J stated:

> 'Where it was reasonably foreseeable to an employer that an employee might suffer a nervous breakdown because of stress and pressures of his workload, the employer was under a duty of care as part of that duty to provide a safe system of work, not to cause the employee psychiatric damage by reason of the volume or character of the work which the employee was required to perform.'

14.41 The approach taken in *Walker* was approved by the Court of Appeal in *Leach v Chief Constable of Gloucestershire* [1999] 1 WLR 1421 at 1442D–E per Brooke LJ and Henry LJ at 1442D; *Beard v Jevans Furnishing Co Ltd* (6 October 1999, unreported), CA; *Alexander v Midland Bank plc* [1999] IRLR 723, per Stuart-Smith LJ at 732, paras 50–51, and *Garrett v Camden London Borough Council* [2001] EWCA Civ 395, [2001] All ER (D) 202 (Mar), before *Hatton* endorsed it further, and the House of Lords in turn approved much of the approach in *Hatton*, save only for restoring the traditional approach to an employer's duty (to be proactive, not reactive, when considering an employee's health and safety). It has also been followed in Scotland in the case of *Cross v Highland and Islands Enterprise* [2001] IRLR 336, OH per Lord Macfadyen at para 60, and in Ireland in *James Mcgrath v Trintech Technologies Ltd and Trintech Group plc* [2004] IEHC 342. The Law Commission in its consultation paper No 137 *Liability for Psychiatric Illness* at para 5.62 stated: '... the reasoning of Colman J appears to us to constitute a logical and just application of the law on safety at work to psychiatric illness'. This approach is consistent with and derives support from the comments of Windeyer J in *Mount Isa Mines Ltd v Pusey* (1970) 125 CLR 383 at 404:[1]

> '... Foreseeable harm caused by a master to the mind of his servant is just as much a breach of his duty of care for him as harm to his body would be.'

1   It also was that adopted in Australia with specific reference to occupational stress. In *Gillespie v Commonwealth of Australia* (1991) 104 ACTR 1 the claimant was a diplomat stationed in Caracas (Venezuela). He suffered panic attacks and anxiety attacks following the overseas posting. It was a new Embassy and his family was subject to intimidation by the local populace. It was held that the defendants had behaved unreasonably in withholding the information that he would experience difficulties greater than any other diplomatic post. However, only a general warning was required and as the claimant was an ambitious man it would have been unlikely to have deterred him. Therefore there was no breach. The judge found that considerable weight should be attached to the risk of psychiatric injury in this type of case.

Applicable principles: breach

14.42 Breach involves answering two central questions favourably to the employee: first, that the employer *knew or ought to have known of the risk* (often called 'foreseeability of injury') and second that, in the light of the magnitude of the risk which he should have or did appreciate, he *failed to take reasonable steps* to avert it. The magnitude of the risk is a combination of the severity of an injury if it should occur and the likelihood of its doing so—such that on normal employers' liability principles a small risk of a life-threatening injury is of great magnitude, yet a considerable risk of a slight injury is less so. On this last point, courts have treated the magnitude of the risk arising out of destructive occupational stress as relatively large: see *Gillespie v Commonwealth of Australia* (1991) 104 ACTR 1 per Miles CJ at 15 and Colman J in *Walker v Northumberland County Council* [1995] ICR 702 at 713F–G.

14.43 Knowledge of the risk ('foreseeability of injury') has been regarded as the threshold question. In *Hatton* the Court of Appeal set out what is now (post *Barber v Somerset County Council*) acknowledged to be practical guidance, though not of statutory force. At para 43 of the judgment, the court set out its conclusions as to this guidance, the threshold question being:

> '... whether this kind of harm to this particular employee was reasonably foreseeable: this has two components (a) an injury to health (as distinct from occupational stress) which (b) is attributable to stress at work (as distinct from other factors).'

The need for the injury to health to be attributable to 'stress at work' is questionable: the need to prove stress as an intermediate step is not necessary in logic, nor, it is suggested, in law. It must ultimately, however, be foreseeable that injury may result if the employer does, or fails to do, something which might cause or contribute to an injury occurring, and this is probably what the court meant in the context of that case, which was focussed upon 'stress at work'. 'Stress' is likely to be perceived subjectively: what matters for liability purposes is whether the employer has created, or failed to ameliorate, an unreasonable risk of injury of whatever type.

14.44 The court continued:

> 'Foreseeability depends upon what the employer knows (or ought reasonably to know) about the individual employee. Because of the nature of mental disorder, it is harder to foresee than physical injury, but may be easier to foresee in a

known individual than in the population at large. An employer is usually entitled to assume that the employee can withstand the normal pressures of the job unless he knows of some particular problem or vulnerability.'

This is open to the criticism that taken in isolation it focuses upon the individual's response[1] to workplace conditions, and does not ask whether the workplace conditions themselves are such as may give rise to an unreasonable risk to health. However, the guidance read as a whole remedies this, since it continues to make it plain that the working conditions and demands of the job are relevant considerations too.

The court added:

'Factors likely to be relevant in answering the threshold question include: (a) the nature and extent of the work done[2] by the employee. Is the workload much more than is normal for the particular job? Is the work particularly intellectually or emotionally demanding for this employee? Are demands being made of this employee unreasonable when compared with the demands made of others in the same or comparable jobs? Or are there signs that others doing this job are suffering harmful levels of stress? Is there an abnormal level of sickness or absenteeism in the same job or the same department? (b) Signs from the employee of impending harm to health. Has he a particular problem or vulnerability? Has he already suffered from illness attributable to stress at work? Have there recently been frequent or prolonged absences which are uncharacteristic of him? Is there reason to think that these are attributable to stress at work, for example because of complaints or warnings from him or others?'

[1] As stress is subjective, it is impossible to state with any certainty whether a given set of circumstances will cause injury rather than anxiety or even distress. Some recent cases, especially in Scotland (*Rorrison v West Lothian College* [1999] GWD 1296, OH and *Fraser v State Hospitals Board for Scotland* (2000) Times, 12 September) have sought to use this factor as a reason for denying liability. Even where the claimant alleged being humiliated by her line manager as part of a campaign to criticise her, it was held that injury was not foreseeable. It was held that to suffer emotions of anxiety and distress is a normal part of human experience, and that what has to be foreseen is suffering to a pathological degree. It is suggested that this may confuse the test of foreseeability with the question of whether what is foreseen is such as to require a particular response from an employer: surely, it must be foreseeable that the target of bullying *may* suffer distress which might shade into injury (and a risk, not a probability, is all that is needed: *Wagon Mound No 2* [1967] AC 619, at 641–643, per Lord Reid). What matters is how small the risk should have appeared such as to excuse an employer from not reacting to it, or reacting only to the factually insufficient degree it did). Certainly it is narrower than that adopted in recent cases in England and Wales: see *Cox v Phillips Industries Ltd* [1976] 1 WLR 638; *Leach v Chief Constable of Gloucestershire Police* [1999] 1 WLR 1421; *Attia v British Gas plc* [1988] QB 304; *W v Essex County Council* [2000] 2 All ER 237; *Waters v Comr of Police for the Metropolis* [2000] 1 WLR 1607, HL; and *Gogay v Hertfordshire County Council* [2000] IRLR 703.

[2] The court thought that no occupation should be regarded as intrinsically dangerous to mental health (para 24). If this dictum is applied too literally, however, it may obscure the fact that some occupations give rise to a more obvious risk than others. Thus those who work in the army, police, ambulance or fire service may be more exposed than most to the trauma of seeing the dead and newly bereaved, and this may demand particular measures, eg the availability of counselling if the particular risks to employees generally of those occupations are to be combated.

14.45 Controversially, the court observed (at general guideline (6)):

'The employer is generally entitled to take what he is told by his employee at face value, unless he has good reason to think to the contrary. He does not generally have to make searching inquiries of the employee or seek permission to make further inquiries of his medical advisers.'

This may be thought to excuse the employer of constructive knowledge—it is only what it knows, rather than what it ought to know, by which its conduct is to be judged. It was this 'reactive' approach which was attacked in argument in *Barber v Somerset County Council* [2004] UKHL 13, [1004] ICR 457. It was by reference to such an approach (as well as by suggesting that no precise point could be identified at which the employer's duty arose, on the facts) that the Court of Appeal allowed the employer's appeal in that case: and it was that which Lord Walker (with whom the majority agreed) rejected. He referred to the recognition by the Court of Appeal that the causes of mental illness will often be complex and depend upon the interaction between the patient's personality and a number of factors in a patient's life, and that it is not easy to predict who will fall victim, how, why or when. He stated that this uncertainty has two important consequences. First, overworked people have different capacities for absorbing stress, and different breaking points. Second, senior employees—especially professionals—will usually have quite strong inhibitions against complaining about overwork and stress, even if it is becoming a threat to their health. He noted (at para 65 of his speech) that the Court of Appeal had said:

'But when considering what the reasonable employer should make of the information which is available to him, from whatever source, what assumptions is he entitled to make about his employee and to what extent is he bound to probe further into what he is told? Unless he knows of some particular problem or vulnerability, an employer is usually entitled to assume that his employee is up to the normal pressures of the job. It is only if there is something specific about the job or the employee or the combination of the two that he has to think harder. But thinking harder does not necessarily mean that he has to make searching or intrusive inquiries. Generally he is entitled to take what he is told by or on behalf of the employee at face value. If he is concerned he may suggest that the employee consults his own doctor or an occupational health service. But he should not without a very good reason seek the employee's permission to obtain further information from his medical advisors. Otherwise he would risk unacceptable invasions of his employee's privacy.'

and commented:

'This is, I think, useful practical guidance, but it must be read as that, and not as having anything like statutory force. Every case will depend on its own facts and the well-known statement of Swanwick J in *Stokes v Guest, Keen and Nettlefold (Bolts and Nuts) Ltd* [1968] 1 WLR 1776 at 1783 remains the best statement of general principle:

"... the overall test is still the conduct of the reasonable and prudent employer, taking positive thought for the safety of his workers in the light of what he knows or ought to know; where there is a recognised and general practice which has been followed for a substantial period in similar circumstances without mishap, he is entitled to follow it, unless in the light of common sense or newer knowledge it is clearly bad; but, where there is developing knowledge, he must keep reasonably abreast of it and not be too slow to apply it; and where he has in fact greater than average knowledge of the risks, he may be thereby obliged to take more than the average or standard precautions. He must weigh up the risk in terms of the likelihood of injury occurring and the potential consequences if it does; and he must balance against this the probable effectiveness of the precautions that can be taken to meet it and the expense and inconvenience they involve. If he is found to have fallen below the standard to be properly expected of a reasonable and prudent employer in these respects, he is negligent".'

14.46 Guideline (7) propounded by the Court of Appeal was:

'To trigger a duty to take steps, the indications of impending harm to health arising from stress at work must be plain enough for any reasonable employer to realise that he should do something about it'.

The word 'any' may suggest a more stringent test than that which applies normally in occupational liability—it may be thought to invite the question 'Could any reasonable employer not take the steps the claimant suggests ...' (in which case no liability) rather than the question 'What should a reasonable employer do?'. However, as in *Barber*, the guideline must be treated as such and, it is suggested, its wording was intended more to emphasise that the law requires reasonable conduct, and not a counsel of perfection, from employers in responding to hazards of which they know or ought to know, rather than substituting an approach akin to judicial review or to that adopted in asking whether professional judgment has been negligent.

Further, in relation to both guidelines (6) and (7), where an employer foresaw that employees exposed to particular traumas might suffer psychiatric injury and a particular employee suffered such injury as a result of such trauma, having previously shown no impending signs of psychiatric injury, foreseeability will be established and it is not relevant additionally to ask whether the employer could reasonably have foreseen the risk of injury to the particular employee,: *Hartman v South Essex Mental Health and Community Care NHS Trust* [2005] EWCA Civ 6, [2005] ICR 782, paras 132–34.[1]

[1]   For cases illustrating the application of the foreseeability threshold requirement, see *Bonser v RJB Mining (UK) Ltd* [2004] IRLR 164, which was a case where the claimant had a pre-existing emotional vulnerability but this was not apparent to the defendants. The defendants did not have reason to apprehend the danger and accordingly were not liable when she broke down. Similarly, in *Croft v Broadstairs & St Peter's Town Council* [2003] EWCA Civ 676. Mrs Croft was the defendant's town clerk. Her initial shock and distress at the unexpected receipt of a warning letter about her conduct was so exacerbated that she was rendered incapable of work through depression. The triggering factor was not the work she was required to do but receipt of the letter (which the council accepted would not have been written had it known of her psychiatric problems). The fact that two town councillors knew that Mrs Croft had been undergoing counselling was not enough to establish that the council knew of her psychiatric vulnerability. Potter LJ said that left the council in a position of employers who were entitled to expect ordinary robustness in Mrs Croft in an employment context, including disciplinary matters in which she had never been involved before. Her breakdown was not reasonably foreseeable.

14.47 Guideline (8) is:

'The employer is only in breach of duty if he has failed to take the steps which are reasonable in the circumstances, bearing in mind the magnitude of the risk of harm occurring, the gravity of the harm which may occur, the costs and practicability of preventing it, and the justifications for running the risk.'

It follows that if an employer has taken steps to meet a risk then what is in issue is not the foreseeability of injury, but whether the employer's conduct meets the standard of reasonableness. Mere foreseeability alone does not determine liability. Thus, in *Vahidi v Fairstead House School Trust Ltd* [2005] EWCA Civ 765, the Court of Appeal rejected an attack on the judge's conclusion (see [2005] PIQR P9) that an employer was not liable where it had taken steps to support a teacher on return from absence with agitated depression, but it had failed to prevent a relapse—the steps being thought a reasonable response to the identified risk.

14.48 Guideline (9) is:

'The size and scope of the employer's operation, its resources and the demands it faces are relevant in deciding what is reasonable; these include the interests of other employees and the need to treat them fairly, for example, in any redistribution of duties.'

This is familiar law.

14.49 Guideline (10) is:

'An employer can only reasonably be expected to take steps which are likely to do some good: the court is likely to need expert evidence on this.'

This tenth guideline may be too starkly stated: all must depend on the facts. If an employee is complaining of the adverse effects of overwork, through working too many hours in a week, the step which might be taken is obvious: cutting the hours, or insisting on proper prioritisation of work. A standard already exists, in the 48 hours per week averaged over a running period of 17 weeks, provided for by the Working Time Regulations 1998, and it must be accepted by the courts that such a standard has been set with regard to risks to health in the general run of employees. Expert evidence of the need to reduce workload in such circumstances is not thought necessary, and its absence did not defeat the claim in *Hone v Six Continents Retail Ltd* [2005] EWCA Civ 922, [2006] IRLR 49.

14.50 Guideline (11) is:

'An employer who offers a confidential advice service, with referral to appropriate counselling or treatment services, is unlikely to be found in breach of duty (paras 17 and 33).'

This is controversial if by it the court meant to say that the mere presence of such a service operated as a defence to a claim. It is suggested that this could not be what the court had in mind (not least, given its starting point that ordinary occupational injury principles applied). Moreover, paying lip service to a policy is well recognised as insufficient, so what must be required is at the least such a service as is (a) relevant to the case in question and (b) operated properly. Even that has only the potential to operate as a defence, rather than a certainty of it, since all must depend on the particular facts of a particular case (occupational liability cases depend upon a breach to a given individual, and are not decided on general conduct towards a class of individuals). Further, employees will often consult an occupational service after negligent action or inaction has begun to affect them, and the presence of the service then can afford no defence if otherwise the (in)action was negligent.

14.51 Guideline (12) is:

'If the only reasonable and effective step would have been to dismiss or demote the employee, the employer will not be in breach of duty in allowing a willing employee to continue in the job'.

This echoes the decision in *Withers v Perry Chain Co Ltd* [1961] 1 WLR 1314, CA that in principle the law should not be saying to an employer that it is its duty to sack an employee who wants to go on working for it for the employee's own good, but must now be read subject to Simon Brown LJ's comments in *Coxall v Goodyear Great Britain Ltd* [2002] EWCA Civ 1010, [2003] ICR 152 (see paras 6.63–6.65, above) and to European legislation, which stresses adapting the work to the individual.

14.52 Guideline (13) is:

'In all cases, therefore, it is necessary to identify the steps which the employer both could and should have taken before finding him in breach of his duty of care'.

This is axiomatic. In many 'stress at work' cases it seems to have been argued that harm caused by the work itself is sufficient ground to bring a claim. It is not. The employer must be at fault, and will only be so if there is some aspect of the work which it is at fault for permitting to remain a feature of it, or some reasonable steps it could and should take to reduce the risk of injury. In the author's experience, the single most significant ground upon which 'stress at work' cases fail is an inability to show that the employer could or should have taken preventative steps which, if it had done so, would have averted the impending psychiatric disaster. The law was aptly summed up by Simon Brown LJ in *Garrett v Camden London Borough Council* [2001] EWCA Civ 395, para 63:

'Many, alas, suffer breakdowns and depressive illnesses and a significant proportion could doubtless ascribe some at least of their problems to the strains and stresses of their work situation: be it simply overworking, the tension of difficult relationships, career prospect and worries, fears or feeling of discrimination or harassment, to take just some examples. Unless, however, there was a real risk of breakdown which the claimant's employers ought reasonably to have foreseen and they ought properly to have averted there can be no liability'.

14.53 In *Barber v Somerset County Council* [2004] UKHL 13, [1004] ICR 457 there was broad acceptance of the propositions put forward by the Court of Appeal in *Hatton*, though as noted above the test to be applied is not that set out in para 29 of *Hatton* but the statement of general principle by Swanwick J. The test expounded by Swanwick J in *Stokes*, and accepted by some members of the House of Lords in *Barber* and by the Court of Appeal in *Hartman v South Essex Mental Health and Community Care NHS Trust* [2005] EWCA Civ 6, [2005] ICR 782, is not as restrictive on the issue of foreseeability as that adopted by the Court of Appeal in *Hatton*. It requires a more proactive approach by the employer, than the reactive approach that appears to be have been adopted in *Hatton*.[1]

1   The wording of this paragraph, which it is considered accurately states the law, is lifted directly from the judgment of Higgins J in *Michael Beattie v Ulster Television plc* [2005] NIQB 26 (21 April 2005) at paras 54, 78.

14.54 Moreover, in *Hartman* itself, it was emphasised that the general principles in *Hatton* needed care in their application to the particular facts under consideration. For instance, while each appeal in Hatton involved an employee who had suffered ongoing stress in day-to-day work, two of the cases amongst the *Hartman* six (*Melville*, and to some extent *Hartman*) involved stress caused by specific traumas; and in *Harding v The Pub Estate Co Ltd* [2005] EWCA Civ 553 the injury in fact suffered by the claimant was a heart attack rather than a psychiatric breakdown. No general principles were stated in *Hartman*, but the six cases are useful exemplars of the approach to be taken. Thus in *Hartman* it was held that foreseeability could not depend on knowledge of confidential medical information disclosed by the claimant to an employee within the defendant's occupational health department, since no other employee had any right of access to that information without the claimant's consent (employer's appeal allowed); in the second case, *Best v Staffordshire University*, an employer's appeal was allowed on the grounds that the judge stated the right test, but failed to apply it properly to the facts; in the third, *Wheeldon v HSBC*, the bank was held in breach of its duty of care when a line manager failed to discuss with a (part-time) employee who was complaining of stress due to overwork and understaffing, what could be done, but instead closed her file, taking the attitude that she should come to him, and not the other way round (cf *Hatton*, guideline 6); in the fourth, *Green v Grimsby & Scunthorpe Newspapers Ltd*, an employee whom all his colleagues thought was under less stress than anyone else, wrote a memo complaining of the effects of an inability to produce a specific magazine, which was causing him worry to the point of damaging his health. A meeting was called to discuss it, but before it could be held, he walked out and never returned to work: the defendant employer did not and could not reasonably have been expected to foresee the kind of injury to health suffered by the claimant. The fifth case, *Moore v Welwyn Components Ltd*, related to quantum, and the sixth, *Melville v Home Office* concerned a health care officer in prison who had to attend to cut down a suicide victim, remove a ligature and attempt revival, who developed nightmares and flashbacks, leading into a psychiatric illness. Although he had not complained himself of a pending risk of breakdown, general Home Office material demonstrated that the employer knew that employees who were exposed to particular traumatic incidents might suffer psychiatric injury. The risk of injury was thus in fact foreseen, and it could not therefore be said it was unforeseeable.

14.55 A foreseeable risk of injury in the long term but not a foreseeable risk of imminent injury from a related (but distinct) cause may need to be distinguished: in *Pratley v Surrey County Council* [2003] EWCA Civ 1067, [2004] ICR 159 Mrs Pratley, a social case-worker, agreed with her employer that a system would be introduced to prevent her from being flooded with new cases, before she had dealt with other ones and was in a position to take them on. Three weeks later, after a holiday she returned to find the system had not been introduced. In reaction to that failure (not the overwork itself) she suffered a psychiatric illness. The judge found there was a foreseeable risk of injury to her in the long term but not a foreseeable risk of imminent injury. It was argued on Mrs Pratley's behalf that as long as there was a foreseeable risk of injury from work that was sufficient. The Court of Appeal disagreed, though there is a divergence of approach between Ward, Mance and Buxton LJJ, and dismissed her appeal. This case may better be seen as one in which the risk which materialised was the risk to health caused by breaking a promise to introduce measures to reduce workload, which was a risk which was not foreseeable as producing an immediate breakdown. As Buxton LJ noted, at para 31, the claimant's problem was that whereas one type of injury, future damage if work overload was continued, was foreseen and foreseeable, it was another type of injury, immediate collapse, that in fact occurred.

Foreseeability in general: Management of Health and Safety at Work Regulations 1999

14.56 Foreseeability in respect of whether it is safe to ignore a risk, and insofar as it involves an inquiry into whether a risk exists, is to be determined in an individual case. It cannot be said that simply because a given percentage of the population as a whole will succumb to the ill-health effects of workplace stress, a given individual will. However, the starting point for the individual assessment will always be the general position. If in general (for instance) long hours are associated with increased ill-health, then (generally) long hours should be reduced by employers, and an individual working long hours should be seen as more credible if he should complain of overwork, or tiredness, or pressure from the amount of work he is doing. The extent to which employers should know (even if in fact they do not) of risks both in general and in particular must be assessed by the court, which should take into account the fact that since 1 January 1993 the Management of Health and Safety Work Regulations 1999 (originally 1992)[1] have required most employers to carry out a 'suitable and sufficient' assessment of the risks associated with the work of their employees.

[1] SI 1999/3242, which replaced the old Management of Health and Safety at Work Regulations 1992.

14.57 Regulation 3 of the 1999 Regulations, requiring a risk assessment, does give claimants an arguable[1] advantage in stress cases because of the rapid expansion in recent years of research into stress, its causes and methods of alleviation.[2] The risk assessment must be 'suitable and sufficient'. The approved code of practice (ACOP) accompanying the 1992 Regulations, para 9, gives guidance on the meaning of those words:

'9 A suitable and sufficient risk assessment:
(a)   should identify the significant risks arising out of work.

This means focusing on those risks that are liable to arise because of the work activity.

Trivial risks can usually be ignored as can risks arising from routine activities associated with life in general, unless the work activity compounds those risks, or there is evidence of significant relevance to the particular work activity.

Employers ... are expected to take reasonable steps, eg by reading HSE guidance, the trade press, company or supply manuals etc to familiarise themselves with the hazards and risks in their work.'

Thus expert evidence will be relevant and admissible in order to deal with the question of what a reasonable employer[3] should have known about the risks of occupational stress. The employer will be expected to have kept abreast of recent guidance (as *Stokes v Guest, Keen & Nettlefold* advises).[4] Employers are under a duty to appoint a competent person to assist them in compliance.[5]

1   How much has yet to be decided. But see the physical injury case of *Hawkes v London Borough of Southwark* [1998] EWCA Civ 310 and *Cross v Highland and Islands Enterprise* [2001] IRLR 336 at para 74.
2   Consideration should also be given to the other regulations depending upon the circumstances of the case, eg in particular regs 8, 10, 13 (capabilities and training) and 14 (employees' duties) and the HSWA 1974, s 7.
3   The Framework Directive 89/391/EEC, art 7 requires the employer to appoint a competent person to carry out activities related to the protection and prevention of occupational risks. It has been held in Scotland that this does not add to the previous common law standard of care: *Cross v Highland and Islands Enterprise* [2001] IRLR 336 at para 66. It was also decided that the Directive was not intended to apply to the mental as opposed to physical health of workers. It is submitted that this is too narrow and ignores the broader purposive approach of European legislation. Finally, it was decided that the Framework Directive was not directly applicable in the UK. This is a matter that may yet be considered at a higher level.
4   Primary sources recommended by ACAS in a guide to stress for employers published in November 2004 include: Earnshaw and Cooper 'Stress and employer liability' (CIPD, 2001); Ferrie 'Work, stress and health: the Whitehall II study' (CCSU/Cabinet Office, 2004); www.ucl.ac.uk/epidemiology/Whitehall/Whitehallbooklet.pdf; 'Real solutions, real people: a managers' guide to tackling work-related stress' (HSE, 2003); 'Working together to reduce stress at work—a guide for employees' (HSE); 'Managing stress' (IDS, 2004); 'Stress at work' (IDS, 2003); Jamdar and Byford 'Workplace stress: law and practice' (Law Society, 2003); Jordan (et al) 'Beacons of excellence in stress prevention' (HSE Books, 2003); 'Stress in the UK workplace' (Personnel Today, 2003); Tehrani 'Managing organisational stress: a CIPD guide to improving and maintaining employee well-being' (CIPD, 2003). Useful websites are listed as: The International Stress Management Association, www.isma.org.uk, which exists to promote sound knowledge and best practice in the prevention and reduction of human stress; The Health and Safety Executive (HSE), www.hse.gov.uk/stress/index.htm, for what the HSE are doing about stress at work, plus information, resources and further contacts; NHS plus, www.nhsplus.nhs.uk/your_health/stress.asp which has advice for individuals about workplace stress; The Stress Management Society, www.stress.org.uk which provides training to help manage stress; The UK National Work Stress Network, www.workstress.net which campaigns on the issue of stress at work; Centre for Stress Management, www.managingstress.com which offers training for HR professionals, stress audits and counselling services.
5   Regulation 7.

14.58 In May 1995 the HSE published guidelines[1] on stress at work. These acknowledged officially for the first time that office work can be stressful and give rise to injury. They give guidance on good practice. They are not compulsory. However, as with other HSE guidelines in the past, they will constitute a yardstick by which to measure the reasonableness of the system of work of employers:

'Ill health resulting from stress caused at work has to be treated the same way as ill health due to other, physical causes present in the workplace. This means that employers do have a legal duty to take reasonable care to ensure that health is not placed at risk through excessive and sustained levels of stress arising from the way work is organised, the way people deal with each other at their work or from the day to day demands placed on their work. Employers should bear stress in mind when assessing possible health hazards in their work places, keeping an eye out for developing problems and being prepared to act if a harm to health seems likely. In other words, stress should be treated like any other health hazard.'

1   *Stress at work, a guide for employers* (HS(G) 116). The HSE also published a useful booklet in 1993 called *Emergency Measures*. These set out some of the symptoms of an impending breakdown. The HSE have published a great deal of other material on occupational stress which it is not possible to deal with in this work. See also *Help on work-related stress: a short guide* (20 October 2000, INDG 281) and the HSE website www. hse.gov.uk. See also those sources cited in para 14.57 fn 4.

14.59 Courts have dismissed claims in *McCotter v McNally and McGeown* [2004] NIQB 59 (workload as a solicitor); *Campbell v The University of Edinburgh* [2004] Scot CS 114 (pursuer failed to identify any person within senior management as representative of the University throughout the period covered by his averments and as being the person who possessed knowledge of the events complained of and of their effects upon his mental state, or to whom knowledge of these events and their effects upon his mental state could reasonably be attributed); *James McGrath v Trintech Technologies Ltd and Trintech Group plc* [2004] IEHC 342 (not foreseeable); *Ringland v South Eastern Education and Library Board* [2004] NIQB 89 (McCollum J) (employer did not know); *Foumeny v University of Leeds* [2003] EWCA Civ 557 (claimant resigned: he never in fact expected his resignation to be accepted and, ultimately, his mental health problems which thereafter began to surface had their origins in the shock he felt at that result); *Beattie v Ulster Television* plc [2005] NIQB 36 (Higgins J) (television researcher); *Green v Argyll & Bute Council* [2002] ScotCS 56 (Lord Bonomy) (social worker who had suffered a major depressive disorder as a result of an excessive workload: no foreseeable risk of the pursuer suffering such a condition); *Rorrison v West Lothian College* [1999] Scot CS 177 (Lord Reed) (nurse); *Bonser v UK Coal Mining Ltd* [2003] EWCA Civ 1296; *Pakenham-Walsh v Connell Residential* [2006] EWCA Civ 90 (sales manager for estate agents).

Courts have permitted claims to proceed (upon an application to strike-out) in *Mather v British Telecommunications plc* [2000] ScotCS 141, OH; in *Eastwood v Magnox Electric plc* and *McCabe v Cornwall County Council* [2004] UKHL 35, [2005] 1 AC 503.

Successful claims have only rarely been reported.

Causation

14.60 If a failure to take reasonable care to meet foreseeable risk is identified, and hence a breach of duty is established, the question arises whether that breach has caused any damage. It is insufficient that 'the work' should have caused the injury, or 'the workload', or a failure to supervise: that establishes nothing about whether it is the fault of the employer that the work, or workload, or failure(s) that causes the injury, and it is this latter which is essential before a cause of action can be made out in respect of that breach. Since in tort and most contract claims it is necessary that there should be a recognised psychiatric injury or illness, medical evidence will normally be required to establish this.[1] Care should be taken that what is truly attributable to a breach, as opposed to work more generally, is identified. In a case where, for instance, the allegation is one of unreasonable workload, it must be established whether a breach of the employer in contributing to, or failing to relieve that workload at least to an extent, has made any difference. Contribution to a psychiatric injury which would have occurred anyway for reasons of non-negligent workload gives rise to no sustainable claim. The rule in *Bonnington Castings Ltd v Wardlaw* [1956] AC 613, reinforced by *Nicholson v Atlas Steel Foundry and Engineering Co Ltd* [1957] 1 WLR 613, HL, and *McGhee v National Coal Board* [1973] 1 WLR 1, HL (that it is sufficient to show that a breach contributes to an injury) does not assist a claimant where it appears that the injury would have been just as bad, just as early as happened irrespective of the contribution made by the consequences of the breach. However, it often transpires that medical experts will accept a degree of worsening, or acceleration, caused by the breach. This is sufficient for liability, but will have an impact when quantum is considered, since a contribution to exacerbating or accelerating the onset of an injury which would probably have occurred anyway demands much less compensation both for pecuniary and non-pecuniary loss.

1 But note that in an unreported overwork case where the trial judge did not expressly refer to the link between the reduction of the work and prevention of injury the Court of Appeal refused to interfere. Swinton Thomas LJ found that it was quite plain, and in accordance with common sense, that on the facts as found by the trial judge, if the weight of work had been substantially reduced then, as a matter of probability, the claimant would not have been injured: *Beard v Jevans Furnishings Co Ltd* (6 October 1999, unreported), CA.

14.61 In *Hatton* the last three guidelines related to causation. The first of these, guideline (14) expresses pithily the substance of the foregoing paragraph:

'(14) The claimant must show that that breach of duty has caused or materially contributed to the harm suffered. It is not enough to show that occupational stress has caused the harm.'

14.62 Guideline (15) is, however, more controversial:

'Where the harm suffered has more than one cause, the employer should only pay for that proportion of the harm suffered which is attributable to his wrongdoing, unless the harm is truly indivisible. It is for the defendant to raise the question of apportionment.'

The critical words here are 'unless the harm is truly indivisible'. It is well established that where there is one condition, to the inception of which a given causative factor cannot be said to have made a discrete contribution, either in its occurring or its extent when it does, there should be no reduction in damages.[1] The rule is different if it can be shown that the contribution was discrete, for a defendant should have to pay compensation for no more than the damage he has caused and in such a case the damage can be separately assessed: here, the claimant may be left to sue others for the balance of his injury, or accept that it is the product of factors for which no other is to blame: see *Thomson v Smith's Dock*. The same principles, it is suggested, apply where there is one psychiatric condition.[2] The author's experience is that medical evidence is often to the effect that a stress-related illness has been caused or contributed to by a number of different factors, some arising from the personality of the claimant, some from the workplace, some from his social and domestic (or financial) circumstances, all of which may have combined to cause the illness which can be identified. In such a case, apportionment can rarely be argued by a defendant—though he may take considerable advantage of guideline (16), which is considered in the next paragraph.

1 See paras 3.25ff.
2 The issue may yet be considered by the House of Lords. Argument on the apportionment issue was invited by their Lordships in *Barber v Somerset County Council*, and the parties considered the issue on paper: but at the hearing, when it became apparent that it had no bearing on the case before them, the House declined to hear any further argument. The House is due to hear an appeal in *Barker* but it is thought this will affect only those cases which depend for liability upon an application of the principle that liability may follow a material contribution not to an injury, but to the risk of that injury, as in *Fairchild v Glenhaven* [2001] EWCA Civ 1881, [2002] ICR 412 and *McGhee v National Coal Board* [1973] 1 WLR 1.

14.63 Guideline (16) is:

'The assessment of damages will take account of any pre-existing disorder or vulnerability and of the chance that the claimant would have succumbed to a stress-related disorder in any event.'

In particular, where it is plain that a number of factors have contributed to an illness, it can only be where a court can exclude the possibility of those having resulted in illness or loss that a 'full' award will be made.

14.64 If the claimant is an eggshell personality then provided he can show that the unsafe system of work materially contributed to his injury the fact that the particular type of injury was unforeseeable is irrelevant: see chapters 2 and 3 above, except as to quantum for the reasons given immediately above. There is no difference in principle between an eggshell skull and an eggshell personality: *Malcolm v Broadhurst* [1970] 3 All ER 508 and *Page v Smith* [1995] 2 All ER 736, per Lord Browne-Wilkinson at 754a.

14.65 In *Mather v British Telecommunications plc* [2000] Scot CS 141, OH it was pointed out that before a psychiatric illness could sound in damages, the illness must have been caused by the breach of duty concerned and not by what might have happened after the breach of duty had come to an end (per Lord Osborne, para 38).

Contributory negligence

14.66 In *Maurice Young v The Post Office* [2002] EWCA Civ 661, [2002] IRLR 660, CA, the Court of Appeal upheld a decision that (in a 'second breakdown' case) the Recorder was entitled on the facts to hold that the defendants were liable to Y, for failing adequately to support him on his return to work after illness. An argument that the judge should have allowed a discount for the contributory fault of the claimant in not complaining about his position was rejected in these terms by May LJ:

> 'I consider that the Recorder was entitled to take the view on the facts of this case that it was not negligent on Mr Young's part not to speak up. He was both conscientious and vulnerable and can scarcely be blamed for doing his best to undertake the tasks which he understood were expected of him, when he had made complaints in the past which had not been heeded. Although, as the case of (*Hatton v*) *Sutherland* indicates, in many circumstances an employer may not be expected to know that an employee who does not speak up is vulnerable, an employee who is known to be vulnerable is not necessarily to be regarded as responsible for a recurrent psychiatric illness if he fails to tell his employer that his job is again becoming too much for him. A finding of contributory negligence in a case of psychiatric illness, although no doubt theoretically possible in other circumstances, does not in my view sit happily with the facts of this case. I know of no case in which a claimant such as Mr Young, vulnerable to psychiatric illness which he successfully holds to his employers, has been held to be contributorily negligent, and counsel was unable to draw our attention to any such case.'

Although this decision turned on its own facts, the author is similarly unaware of a case in which contributory fault has been found to exist in such circumstances as May LJ described. Though the possibility should not be rejected out of hand, many of those who succumb to psychiatric illness are unaware of the immediacy of the risk to their mental health until it eventuates, and this dictum is powerful support for the view that usually it will be difficult for a defendant to establish contributory fault (see also para 6.35, above).

Duty in contract

14.67 The usual cause of action asserted in employers' liability cases is negligence, though liability can equally be founded on contract.[1] In the absence of express terms it ought to be immaterial whether the claim is based upon contract or tort. Unless there is an express term to the contrary[2] in both causes of action the duty is to take all reasonable care for the employee's safety and well-being, and this includes the employee's psychiatric well-being.[3] There may be cases where the express terms of the contract expose the employee to a riskier working environment in relation to stress than would be tolerated at common law. Equally the express terms may require more care from the employer than would be implied at common law. However, the duty is so well settled as a normal incident of any contract of employment that a court is unlikely to hold it excluded unless compelled to do so, and in any event would have to be satisfied that the Unfair Contract Terms Act 1977 did not render such an exclusion unenforceable. This applies to contracts of employment: see *Brigden v American Express Bank Ltd* [2000] IRLR 94. Liability for personal injury or death cannot be excluded by a notice: it seems unlikely that the courts would regard a diminution of the protection to be afforded an employee from duties of his employer which are non-delegable in tort as reasonable, especially given European emphasis on maintaining and improving levels of health and safety protection generally (see the Framework Directive 89/491 EEC).

1   See paras 4.39–4.41.
2   But see the discussion at paras 4.40, 4.41 and 4.84.
3   *Petch v Comrs of Customs and Excise* [1993] ICR 789; *Walker v Northumberland County Council* [1995] ICR 702; *Hatton v Sutherland* [2002] 2 All ER 1.

14.68 The relationship between claims in tort and those in contract was explored in *Johnstone v Bloomsbury Health Authority* [1992] QB 333, CA. Mr Johnstone could be required to work up to 88 hours per week under his contract as a junior hospital doctor. Things came to a head when he fell asleep at the wheel of his car and drove into a tree when on holiday, following an alleged 110-hour working week. He was not injured but he resigned from his job, and claimed to have been constructively dismissed. The question was whether the claim should be struck out, on the ground that the claimant could be obliged contractually to work so many hours in excess of his standard working week as foreseeably would injure his health (thus being contrary to the implied duty of care to provide a safe system of work). By a majority the court held the claim could proceed. The health authority had to exercise its contractual power in such a way as not to injure the claimant and accordingly it could not require the claimant to work so much overtime in any week that his health might reasonably foreseeably be damaged. The Court of Appeal held that it was arguable that the Unfair Contract Terms Act 1977, s 2(1) would prevent the health authority from relying on an express contractual term, as such long hours would breach the implied duty to take care for the safety of the claimant.

14.69 Lord Rodger in *Barber v Somerset County Council* [2004] UKHL 13, [2004] ICR 457, examined (obiter) the issues that might arise if the claim is not that a contractual power to require excess hours of work has been utilised, but the very contract which an employee has signed up to achieves that effect. It is (tentatively) suggested that if the provisions of a contract could have the effect that an employer was otherwise relieved of duties to take reasonable care of its employee's health and safety, those provisions would not obstruct a claim in tort. Systems of work have long been capable of being contractual, but so far as is known it has not been suggested that a system which creates risk for an individual employee should be regarded as non-negligent, because an employee has contracted to adopt it. It is difficult to see why it should constitute no defence to a claim in tort, yet be one to a claim in contract otherwise covering the same ground.

14.70 Contractual liability may, however, go beyond claims for breach of the duty to take reasonable care for the employee's health and safety. The House of Lords have held that there is a default term implied into every contract of employment that an employer will not act (without reasonable cause) in such a way as is liable to destroy or seriously damage the relationship of mutual trust and confidence between employer and employee: *Mahmud v Bank of Credit and Commerce International SA (in liq)* [1998] AC 20 per Lord Steyn.

The importance and closeness of the employment relationship led Lord Slynn to say in *Spring v Guardian Assurance plc* [1995] 2 AC 296 that there are now:

'... far greater duties imposed on the employer than in the past, whether by statute or by judicial decision, to care for the physical, financial and even psychological welfare of the employee ...'

The effect of the conduct is to be judged objectively: *Meikle v Nottinghamshire County Council* [2004] EWCA Civ 859, [2005] ICR 1. It needs to be emphasised that, if a breach is to be established, there must be no reasonable cause for the employer's conduct: see *Miller Bros and FP Butler Ltd v Johnston* [2002] ICR 744, EAT.

14.71 Recognition of this implied term, and that a breach of it may cause distress and lead to illness, gives a jurisprudential coherence to a number of cases in which an employer has been held liable to an employee, where there has been a breach of good industrial relations practices.[1] These include:

(i) failure to control bullying. Thus if an employer fails to protect an employee who has been 'sent to Coventry' by his fellow workers, the employee may treat the contract of employment as repudiated by the employer;[2]

(ii) making accusations against an employee falsely and without reasonable cause;[3]

(iii) subjecting an employee to unacceptable abuse;[4]

(iv) treating a longstanding employee without dignity and consideration;[5]

(v) imposing a disciplinary sanction out of all proportion to the offence;[6]

(vi) failing to give a reasonable opportunity to an employee to obtain redress for any grievance;[7]

(vii) running a corrupt business;[8]

(viii) damaging its employees' future employment prospects;[9]

(ix) suspending an employee for no sufficient reason;[10]

(ix) failing to provide and monitor for its employees, 'so far as is reasonably practicable, a working environment which is reasonably suitable for the performance by them of their contractual duties'.[11]

---

[1] See also Brodie 'Recent Cases, Commentary, the Heart of the Matter, Mutual Trust and Confidence' (1996) 25 ILJ 121.

[2] *Wigan Borough Council v Davies* [1979] ICR 411 per Arnold J at 419. More recently *Waters v Comr of Police for the Metropolis* [2000] 1 WLR 1607, HL.

[3] *Robinson v Crompton Parkinson Ltd* [1978] ICR 401.

[4] *Palmanour Ltd v Cedron* [1978] ICR 1008.

[5] *Garner v Grange Furnishing Ltd* [1977] IRLR 206.

[6] *BBC v Beckett* [1983] IRLR 43.

[7] *WA Goold (Pearmak) v McConnell* [1995] IRLR 516.

[8] *Malik v Bank of Credit and Commerce International SA* [1998] AC 20.

[9] *Malik v Bank of Credit and Commerce International SA* [1998] AC 20.

[10] *Gogay v Hertfordshire County Council* [2000] IRLR 703, CA.

[11] *Waltons and Morse v Dorrington* [1997] IRLR 488. Commenting on this judgment *Harvey on Industrial Relations and Employment Law* says (at para **DI[471]**) that the term may extend '... to creating a working environment which is not psychologically damaging to the welfare of employees, such as one where bullying or harassment occurs. These developments also mirror the increasing regulation of health and safety in the workplace which followed on from the UK's implementation of the various EC Directives promulgated under art 137 (ex art 118A) in 1992'.

14.72   A particular example, subsequently drawn on in the House of Lords by Lord Slynn in *Waters v Metropolitan Police Comr* [2000] 1 WLR 1607 as demonstrating that liability for psychiatric injury in employment had been recognised in a number of cases over the years, was that of *Wetherall (Bond St W1) Ltd v Lynn* [1978] 1 WLR 200. Mr Lynn was undermined and upbraided in the presence of his subordinates by the retail sales manageress. He had a breakdown when he received an unwarranted warning letter, and resigned. This led to his successfully arguing that he had been constructively unfairly dismissed. A breach of contract is necessary for constructive dismissal. Although damages for personal injury as such are not available before an employment tribunal, if the injury is within the contractual foreseeability test as a consequence of breach, there seems no reason why damages should not be recoverable at common law.

14.73   Where an employee has been dismissed in circumstances where the events leading up to dismissal are said to be those which cause him to suffer psychiatric illness, there may be a fine judgment to be made as to whether the loss is caused by the actual act of dismissal itself, or by an antecedent breach of contractual duty on the part of his (former) employer. In the former case, the consequence of *Johnson v Unisys Ltd* [2001] UKHL 13, [2001] ICR 480 and of *Dunnachie v Kingston-upon-Hull Council* [2004] UKHL 36, [2005] 1 AC 226, is that no claim for damages is available—the claimant must sue if at all before an employment tribunal, under the Employment Rights Act 1996, especially s 94 thereof (unfair dismissal). If the latter, he may sue: *Eastwood v Magnox Electric plc* and *McCabe v Cornwall County Council* heard together and reported at [2004] UKHL 35, [2005] 1 AC 503. There, the House of Lords held that although it would be desirable if the implied obligation on an employer at common law to act fairly towards its employee applied to a decision to dismiss him, such a development could not co-exist satisfactorily with the statutory code regarding unfair dismissal; that, however, where an employee had, prior to his unfair dismissal, whether actual or constructive, acquired a common law cause of action against his employer in respect of the employer's failure to act fairly towards him, and financial loss had flowed directly from that failure, he could, subject to the rule against double recovery, bring an action at law in respect of that loss and such action was not barred by the availability of a claim in the employment tribunal under the unfair dismissal legislation.

14.74   In a non-occupational context the courts have long since recognised that intentional conduct, even in the form of a practical joke, may give rise to a cause of action for psychiatric injury: *Wilkinson v Downton* [1897] 2 QB 57; and see *Janvier v Sweeney* [1919] 2 KB 316, CA.[1]

[1]   See para 4.90 on vicarious liability for practical jokes.

Statutory liabilities: (1) discrimination claims

14.75   The types of cases that give rise to personal injury claims for stress are multifarious. Harassment at work (employer/employee conflict) is one such situation dealt with below. But it should be borne in mind that in appropriate circumstances a claim for stress from harassment may form part of a claim to the employment tribunal in respect of race, sex or disability discrimination: *Sheriff v Klyne Tugs (Lowestoft) Ltd* [1999] ICR 1170.[1] The effect is that where a claimant has brought such a claim before an employment tribunal, relying upon one of the statutory torts created by the discrimination statutes, he may be precluded from advancing a common law injury claim where to do so would be to rely upon the self-same facts as gave rise to the complaint of discrimination (subject to overriding questions of justice: see *Johnson v Gore Wood & Co (a firm)* [2002] 2 AC 1, HL); or where a defendant has had findings adverse to it made by a decision of an employment tribunal, he may be subject to an issue estoppel against it in relation to that finding in any subsequent proceedings before a civil common law court. For reference to the detailed principles applicable to claims of discrimination see *Harvey on Industrial Relations and Employment Law.*

---

[1] It is not necessary in discrimination cases brought in the employment tribunal to prove foreseeability of injury. Stuart Smith LJ stated: 'The advantage of the statutory tort, from the claimant's point view, is that this requirement (foreseeability of injury) does not need to be established: all that needs to be established is the causal link.' See also *Essa v Laing* [2004] EWCA Civ 02, [2004] ICR 746.

Statutory liabilities: (2) Whistle blowers

14.76 Recent legislation, namely the Public Interest Disclosure Act 1998, has been enacted to protect the position of 'whistle blowers' who have hitherto been vulnerable to victimisation by their employers. In cases where a whistle blower claims that psychiatric injury has been caused to him by victimisation arising out of this conduct, the Act should be studied in detail: this work will not consider it further.

Statutory liabilities: (3) Working time

14.77 The ECJ has determined that working time is a health and safety issue: *United Kingdom v European Commission* [1996] ECR 1–5755. Excessive working hours may lead to stress and injury, and breach of the Working Time Regulations 1998, SI 1998/1833 may result in liability on the part of the employer for personal injury. Advocate-General Leger at para 103 of his opinion in *United Kingdom v European Commission* gave it as his view that without the guarantees of the Directive, workers are exposed:

> 'To the risk of frequently being required to work excessively long hours beyond their physical or psychological capabilities, thereby jeopardising their health and safety.'

As to the requirements of the Regulations, see para 10.46, above.

14.78 The Regulations may affect a claim for stress-related injury in one of three ways. First, if it can be shown that a person has been working excessive hours beyond an average of 48 per week (over a rolling period of 17 weeks) there may be a claim for breach of contract causing that injury. This assumes that *Barber v RJB Mining (UK) Ltd* [1999] ICR 679 was correctly decided in concluding that reg 4 of the 1998 Regulations imports a term into the contract of employment upon which an employee who has not opted-out of the maximum week may rely.

14.79 The second way in which they may affect a claim for stress-related injury is to indicate a standard by which to assess whether an employer is reasonable in adopting the system of work it does. Third, it may indicate to an employer that there is a general risk to members of its workforce (which it is unreasonable to run) in working beyond the average, such that where an employee does so it may be foreseeable that he will suffer injury. Thus in *Hone v Six Continents Retail Ltd* [2005] EWCA Civ 922, [2006] IRLR 49, CA there was no direct evidence of impending breakdown (so the trial judge found) from an employee who claimed to work in excess of 90 hours per week, and who had refused to sign an opt-out, yet these factors were significant in aiding the judge to his conclusion that injury was foreseeable as a consequence of the employer providing insufficient help to the employee so that his hours and the pressure of them on him might reduce. Thus the Court of Appeal refused to interfere with the findings.

HARASSMENT

Harassment and bullying at common law

14.80 This is treated separately, since (a) it is less likely to arise from a poor system of work than do other claims for damages for injury caused by stress at work; and (b) it is more likely to give rise to a claim that the employer is vicariously liable than that it is primarily liable. The latter liability will, however, arise where it can be shown that the employer was alerted to the risk of bullying or harassment (or should have been aware of it) and took insufficient steps in the light of the risk to obviate it. It is liability subject to the usual principles of employer's liability. Thus it is not an insurance liability, but one which depends on the fault of the employer. As Lord Hutton observed in *Waters v Comr of Police for the Metropolis* [2000] 1 WLR 1607, HL, 'It is not every course of victimisation or bullying by fellow employees which would give rise to a course of action against the employer, and an employee may have to accept some degree of unpleasantness from fellow workers. Moreover the employer will not be liable unless he knows or ought to know that the harassment is taking place and fails to take reasonable steps to prevent it.'

14.81 'Harassment' remains undefined in UK legislation: not even in the Prevention from Harassment Act 1997, although s 1 'defines' it as 'including' alarming persons or causing them distress. What is prohibited by that Act is a course of conduct that amounts to harassment: speech is covered, but a course of conduct involves at least two incidents. In EU law, the Framework Directive for Equal Treatment in Employment (2000/78/EC) defines harassment (art 2.3) as giving rise to the prohibitions against discrimination when: 'unwanted conduct related to [religion, belief, disability, age or sexual orientation] takes place with the purpose or effect of violating the dignity of a person and of creating an intimidating, hostile, degrading, humiliating or offensive environment.' It adds: 'In this context, the concept of harassment may be defined in accordance with the national laws and practice of the Member States.'

14.82 The definition introduced into the Race Relations Act 1976 by the Race Relations Act 1976 (Amendment) Regulations 2003, SI 2003/1626 may be wider than that in the Directive. It defines harassment not as violating dignity *and* creating an intimidating, hostile, degrading, humiliating or offensive environment, but instead uses the word '*or*' between the two limbs. It notes that conduct should be regarded as having the effect of violating dignity or creating an hostile environment if (and only if), having regard to all the circumstances including the perception of the victim, it should 'reasonably be considered as having that effect'. If sexual harassment is involved, this occurs (according to the EC Equal Treatment Amendment Directive) 'where any form of unwanted verbal, non-verbal or physical conduct of a sexual nature occurs, with the purpose or effect of violating the dignity of the person, in particular when creating an intimidating, hostile, degrading, humiliating or offensive environment'.

14.83 So far as primary liability is concerned, an employer will not be liable if it has no reason to suspect someone of being a risk to others by reason of his harassing them (*Coddington v International Harvesters of Great Britain* (1969) 6 KIR 146), but it may be under an obligation properly to check references, or to see whether a person had a criminal record: see, by way of analogy, *Nahhas v Pier House (Cheyne Walk) Managements Ltd* (1984) 270 Estates Gazette 328 (night porter burgled premises: employers should have checked reference). Failing to remove a worker who persistently harassed another could equally be in breach of the duty to provide a safe system of work: see *Veness v Dyson Bell & Co* (1965) Times, 25 May (bullying fellow employee). In *Long v Mercury Mobile* (HHJ Thompson, QC sitting as a Deputy High Court Judge, 4 May 2001, unreported) (a case which settled during trial), a successful telephone procurement manager without history of psychiatric injury was asked to provide a confidential report, which implicated his line manager in mismanagement. The report was disclosed to his line manager, who then immediately carried out a 'vendetta' against Mr Long with the probable intent of driving him out of the company. This vendetta involved wrongfully blaming him for the mismanagement, taking important procurement contracts from him, making unfounded allegations against him of abusing customers and breach of confidence resulting in suspension, and placing orders without authority. The claimant complained to the personnel manager about this conduct but not about the effect it was having upon him. The personnel manager in turn complained to the managing director who did nothing because he favoured the line manager. Eventually, the claimant was separated from the line manager by being demoted. He suffered an adjustment reaction. The defendants admitted liability on the third day of the trial and disputed causation and quantum. The judge expressed his agreement with the defendant's admission and awarded £327,500 damages with indemnity costs.

14.84 So far as vicarious liability is concerned, an assault or harassment committed by an employee with a sufficiently close connection to his employment will make his employer vicariously liable: see eg *Bracebridge Engineering v Darby Ltd* [1990] IRLR 3, and the cases considered under vicarious liability at para 4.83ff.

14.85 That both primary and vicarious liability might arise out of the same set of facts is illustrated by *Waters v Comr of Police for the Metropolis* [2000] 1 WLR 1607, HL. A WPC complained that the Commissioner was liable to her because the police 'caused and/or permitted officers to maliciously criticise, harass, victimise, threaten, and assault and otherwise oppress her'. Alternatively, she alleged that he was liable vicariously for the acts of officers under his command in the Metropolitan Police. There was no allegation of a conspiracy between the various police officers named to harm or to fail to look after the appellant. She did not rely simply on individual acts taken separately; she attached importance to the cumulative effect of the acts particularly in regard to the causation of psychiatric injury which she alleged. At the heart of her claim lay the belief that other officers reviled her and failed to take care of her because she had broken the team rules by complaining of sexual acts by a fellow police officer (she had been, she claimed, sexually assaulted by an off-duty PC, as to which no claim was brought directly). An application to strike out the claim as disclosing no cause of action or having no reasonable prospect of success was rejected by the House of Lords, since it was not plain and obvious that: (a) no duty analogous to an employer's duty can exist; (b) that the injury to the claimant was not foreseeable in the circumstances alleged; and (c) that the acts alleged could not be the cause of the damage. Though many of the individual items taken in isolation were, at the least, very unlikely to have caused the illness alleged, the appellant's case emphasised the cumulative effect of what happened under the system as it existed.[1]

[1]   For an early bullying case see *Veness v Dyson, Bell & Co* (1965) Times, 25 May. For a more detailed analysis of what constitutes bullying see: www.successunlimited.com.

Breach

14.86 The only known case before *Waters v Metropolitan Police Comr* [2000] 4 All ER 934 (see below) which specifically considered the scope of the duty not to bully in the workplace (as such)[1] was *Veness v Dyson, Bell & Co* (1965) Times, 25 May. Unfortunately no full law report of this case exists. Here Widgery J held that an action for damages in tort alleging that the claimant was '... so bullied and belittled by her colleagues that she came to the verge of a nervous breakdown and had to resign ...' should not be struck out.

[1]   Copious authority deals with such actions before employment tribunals, where they are taken on the grounds of the race, sex or disability of the victim.

14.87 Self-evidently, bullying will be a source of stress:[1] by its nature, it is targeted upon an individual and either designed to cause the victim of it distress, or the perpetrator is careless as to whether it does so or not, and it ought nowadays to be foreseeable that to deliberately cause someone distress at least risks that person suffering such a degree or nature of distress as to cause her or him a recognised psychiatric illness. A specific application of the duty on an employer to provide a safe system of work is a duty of care to protect an employee who it is foreseeable may suffer a stress related illness as a result of uncontrolled hostility at work. In *Waters v Chief Metropolitan Comr* [2000] 1 WLR 1607, HL, Lord Slynn stated:

'If an employer knows that acts being done by employees during their employment may cause physical or mental harm to a particular fellow employee and he does nothing to supervise or prevent such acts, when it is in his power to do so, it is clearly arguable that he may be in breach of his duty to that employee ... he may also be in breach if he can foresee that such acts may happen and if they do, that physical or mental harm may be caused to an individual. I would accept ... that if this sort of sexual assault is alleged ... and the officer persists in making complaints about it, it is arguable that it can be foreseen that some retaliatory steps may be taken against the woman and she may suffer harm as a result. Even if this is not necessarily foreseeable at the beginning it may become foreseeable or indeed obvious ... that there is a risk of harm and that some protective steps should be taken.'

1   But see the Scottish case *of Rorrison v West Lothian College* [1999] GWD 1296, OH. The claimant was a welfare auxiliary. She enjoyed her work. However she was subjected to a campaign of humiliation and criticism by her line manager. It was held that it was not foreseeable that this would cause injury.

14.88 Employees expect employers to secure for them a workplace in which they can do their work without fear or apprehension. Bullying, ostracism and lack of support are plainly susceptible to control by the employer.

14.89 Violence, threats of violence, bullying and abuse by one or more employees in the course of employment against another will render the employer vicariously liable (see paras 4.83 and 14.84, below). Vicarious liability is now understood as a liability of an employer for the torts (as opposed to being for the acts) of its employees (see e g *Majrowski*). A tort committed by the employee must therefore be established. Debate whether a cause of action in tort exists for harassment and, if so, whether it forms part of the tort of nuisance,[1] has been resolved by concluding that nuisance gives rise to no right to claim for personal injury, and that there is no separate common law tort of harassment as such: *Hunter v Canary Wharf Ltd* [1997] AC 655, and see *Wainwright v Home Office* [2003] UKHL 53. However, whether in assault or negligence, unreasonable harassment of a person while lawfully at work is liable to be tortious if it causes injury, and may (if it forms part of a series of acts) be a breach of statutory duty under the Prevention of Harassment Act 1997.[2]

1   Arising out of *Thomas v National Union of Mineworkers (South Wales Area)* [1985] ICR 886, in which Scott J held that during the miners strike the '... unreasonable harassment ...' of working miners exercising the right '... to use the highway for the purpose of entering and leaving their respective places of work ...' was tortious.
2   *Waters v Chief Metropolitan Comr* [2000] 1 WLR 1607 at 1611B–C; *Majrowski v Guys and St Thomas's NHS Trust* [2005] QB 848.

14.90 Outside the workplace it had been held that harassment not amounting to a threat but causing or likely to cause physical or psychiatric illness to the victim can be restrained by an injunction quia timet: *Khorasandjian v Bush* [1993] QB 727. While the House of Lords disapproved the reasoning of *that case* in *Hunter v Canary Wharf Ltd* [1997] AC 655, the grounds of that disapproval were not as to liability but as to the legal basis for it: the extension of the tort of nuisance to a situation in which the claimant did not hold an interest in land. That reservation is most obvious in the judgment of Lord Hoffmann at 707 where he said:

> '... The perceived gap in *Khorasandjian v Bush* was the absence of a tort of intentional harassment causing distress without actual bodily or psychiatric illness. This limitation is thought to arise out of cases like *Wilkinson v Downton* [1897] 2 QB 57 *and Janvier v Sweeney* [1919] 2 KB 316. The law of harassment has now been put on a statutory basis (see the Protection from Harassment Act 1997[1]) and it is unnecessary to consider how the common law might have developed. But as at present advised, I see no reason why a tort of intention should be subject to the rule which excludes compensation for mere distress, inconvenience or discomfort in actions based on negligence: see *Hicks v Chief Constable of the South Yorkshire Police* [1992] 2 All ER 65. The policy considerations are quite different. I do not therefore say that *Khorasandjian v Bush* was wrongly decided. But it must be seen as a case on intentional harassment, not nuisance ...'.

Lord Cooke said at 714D–E:

> '... I share the disposition to think that harassment by telephone calls or otherwise should also be actionable when it occurs outside the home ...'.

Lord Goff said at 691G:

> '... In truth, what the Court of Appeal appears to have been doing was to exploit the law of private nuisance in order to create by the back door a tort of harassment which was only partially effective in that it was artificially limited to harassment which takes place in her home.'[2]

1 Below at para 14.92ff. This Act is not retrospective.
2 This has been interpreted by some as deciding that no tort of harassment exists at common law. See Infield & Platford *The Law of Harassment and Stalking* (Butterworths, 2000) para 12.7.

14.91 After *Hunter*, two conclusions can be drawn. First, harassment forms no part of the law of nuisance, and second, whatever the common law basis of liability might be, there is no need to identify it, as the matter has now been placed upon a statutory footing. As Lord Hoffmann said it is 'unnecessary to consider how the tort might have developed'. However, harassment under the Protection from Harassment Act 1997 does not cover a one-off event. To deal with such a situation it may yet be necessary to revert to the question whether such an act may be one of trespass to the person or of negligence.

Statutory tort of harassment: Protection from Harassment Act 1997

14.92 A failure to prevent acts of bullying or harassment may constitute a breach of the employer's primary, or personal, duty to its employee. It is more likely however that a claimant will seek to establish vicarious liability,[1] for this involves showing only that torts involving bullying or harassing acts were committed against the claimant by a co-employee in the course of the latter's employment with their common employer, whereas primary liability involves showing not only that such acts have been committed, but that the employer knew or ought to have been aware of the risk that they might be and did insufficient to prevent them occurring (or, in a rare case, may have been instrumental in their happening) and that the employer was itself aware that there was a risk to the employee's health and safety of such a magnitude as to need protective or preventative measures to be taken against it.[2] Acts for which a fellow employee may be liable in tort may constitute acts to which the Protection from Harassment Act 1997 applies, in which case no issue of foreseeability of injury occurs. In such a case, therefore, the 'threshold issue', as the court described it *Hatton v Sutherland* [2002] 2 All ER 1, is avoided.

[1] See para 41 of the judgment of Auld LJ in *Majrowski v Guys and St Thomas's NHS Trust* [2005] EWCA Civ 251, [2005] QB 848, where he carefully distinguishes the two possible routes by which an employer may be liable to an employee for harassment of the latter.
[2] In *Banks v Ablex Ltd* [2005] EWCA Civ 173, [2005] ICR 819, a claim was dismissed where an employer did not know, prior to the day when acts of swearing and shouting took place (which caused the employee to leave employment the next day and to suffer depression), that the employee was in any way vulnerable or might suffer injury to her mental health as a consequence of aggressive behaviour toward her by a fellow-employee. It does not appear to have been argued that the employer was vicariously liable at common law for the tort of the co-employee, or, if argued, the Court of Appeal appear not to have dealt with the issue.

14.93 Harassment contrary to the Act is rendered both a criminal offence and a matter which exposes the perpetrator to civil liability. A person must not pursue a course of conduct which amounts to harassment of another and which he knows or ought to know amounts to harassment of the other: s 1. Thus an individual who bullies a fellow employee at work will be liable for doing so (assuming the other conditions of the Act are met: see below). It has currently been resolved, at Court of Appeal level, that his employer will be liable vicariously for the statutory tort of its employee in committing the bullying acts: *Majrowski v Guy's and St Thomas's NHS Trust* [2005] EWCA Civ 251, [2005] QB 848.

14.94 The Act prohibits a course of conduct which amounts to harassment of another and which the harasser knows, or ought to know, amounts to harassment of the other: s 1(1). The test is objective. A person whose course of conduct is in question ought to know that it amounts to harassment of another if a reasonable person in possession of the same information would think the course of conduct amounted to harassment of the other: s 1(2). If this is established the onus is put on the alleged harasser to prove that the conduct was for either the prevention or detection of crime, or was directly or indirectly authorised by statute, or was reasonable in the particular circumstances: s 1(3).

14.95 The Act therefore proscribes the pursuit of a course of conduct[1] which causes alarm or distress. A course of conduct involves more acts on more than one occasion. Those acts must be directed at the complainant on both occasions: it is not permissible to aggregate acts committed against others to a single act against the claimant: *Banks v Ablex Ltd* [2005] EWCA Civ 173, [2005] ICR 819. In the employment context the interpretation of s 1(2) and s 1(3) is crucial. Thus, a course of otherwise unlawful conduct may be reasonable in the circumstances as proved by the employer. On the face of it s 1(2) does not require proof of intent, or even a mental element, on the part of the perpetrator. It has to be seen in context. If the course of conduct was known to be unwelcome, that is certainly an important criterion.[2] This, together with the fact that the course of conduct has to occur on more than one occasion,[3] suggests that the harasser knows or ought to know that the conduct was unwelcome. Thus the reaction of the victim is important.

[1]   On two or more occasions, s 7(3).
[2]   HL Official Report (5th series) col 827 (17 December 1996), Lord Mackay LC.
[3]   Section 7(3).

14.96   In the employment context an employer may directly or through its employees cause an employee or a group of employees to be subject to a course of unwelcome conduct. It might for example be necessary to bring disciplinary proceedings against an employee. This will no doubt be perceived by the employee as unwelcome. However, in the context it may well be reasonable conduct, and hence would not amount to a breach of the statute. It is submitted that the type of course of conduct that may well fall foul of s 1(2) is such conduct as would not reasonably be expected as part of the particular job in question. Thus an employee would not expect to be shouted at, telephoned outside work unjustifiably and sworn at, still less beaten by his workmates (see eg the facts in *Jones v Tower Boot Co Ltd* [1997] ICR 254, CA). In less obvious cases where the interpretation of the conduct is a matter of perception of the employee, it is likely that the courts will require some evidence from the employee that the course of conduct was unwelcome: but it must be remembered that an act will not amount to harassment unless a reasonable person in possession of the same information as the perpetrator would think it so (s 1(2)).

14.97   The Act does not say that it applies to omissions as well commissions. Although it may seem difficult to 'pursue a course of conduct' by omission, a course of conduct consisting of deliberate omissions (such as 'sending some-one to Coventry ') would plainly be covered. Thus in the criminal case of *R v Ireland* [1998] AC 147, HL the accused made a large number of telephone calls to three women and remained silent when they answered, and as a result they suffered from psychiatric injury. The House of Lords rejected the argument that if speech could not constitute an assault then neither could silence. The case did not involve interpretation of s 1 of the 1997 Act. However, the conduct in question was that of making the telephone calls and the defendant's silence simply invested those calls with menace. The Act is more likely to apply in such a situation in the case of group rather than individual harassment. This is because a group are more likely to have, by agreement, put themselves in a position where the omission to speak or ignore manifests their conduct with menace. Each case will undoubtedly depend very much upon its own facts.

14.98 The Act specifically provides for a civil remedy.[1] It also gives the court power to grant an injunction in appropriate cases. Breach of the injunction can result in a warrant for the arrest of the defendant.[2] The limitation period for claims under the Protection from Harassment Act 1997, s 3 is specifically six years.[3] There is no provision for extension of this limitation period due to date of knowledge.[4]

[1]   Section 3(1).
[2]   Section 3(3)(ii).
[3]   See the Protection from Harassment Act 1997, s 6.
[4]   *Stubbings v Webb* [1993] AC 498.

Vicarious liability

14.99 Breach of statutory duty imposed directly on the employee has given rise in the past to difficult questions in establishing vicarious liability on the employer's part. It was argued that a statutory duty which is imposed on the employee personally does not flow from the employer's orders and so does not concern it. In *Majrowski v Guys & St Thomas's NHS Trust* [2005] EWCA Civ 251, [2005] QB 848 Auld LJ observed that the development of the jurisprudence underlying vicarious liability (in cases such as *Bazley v Curry* (1999) 174 DLR (4th) 45, *Lister v Hesley Hall Ltd* [2001] UKHL 22, [2002] 1 AC 215, and *Bernard v The Attorney General of Jamaica* [2004] UKPC 47, [2005] IRLR 398, PC), 'strongly influenced by academic authority of great distinction, on this issue since Lord MacDermott's notable obiter contribution to it in *Harrison v NCB* in 1951 speaks for itself ...' and concluded that in principle an employer would be vicariously liable for a breach of statutory duty by its employee where that had a sufficiently close connection with his employment. By a majority the Court of Appeal determined that the Protection from Harassment Act therefore gave rise to liability, and should not be so construed as to be one of the rare exceptions to the general principle of liability established by the Court of Appeal. At the time of writing, an appeal centring on this point is due to be heard by the House of Lords.

14.100 It has been decided that s 1 of the 1997 Act applies both to protect, or to render liable, a corporate body.[1] The court further concluded that 'another' in s 1 of the Act included a limited company. By virtue of s 1(2) of the Act, because intention is irrelevant, harassment by servants or agents of a company will be attributed to the company for the purposes of s 2, and the company will be vicariously liable for the statutory tort, if the conduct had a sufficiently close connection with the course of the harasser's employment by the company.[2]

[1]   For protection see *Huntingdon Life Sciences Ltd v British Union for the Abolition of Vivisection* (1998, unreported); for rendering liable see *Thomas v News Group Newspapers Ltd* [2001] EWCA Civ 1223; *Sharma v Jay* [2003] EWHC 1230 (QB) (Gray J), referred to at para 67 of *Majrowski*; and *Majrowski* itself.
[2]   The 'tight, but not always readily applicable, constraint of Salmond's traditional test of "in the course of employment" ' (as Auld LJ called it in *Majrowski*), has had substituted for it a test of fairness and justice, turning, in the circumstances of each case, on the sufficiency of the connection between the breach of duty and the employment and/or whether the risk of such breach was one reasonably incidental to it: see especially *Lister v Hesley Hall Ltd*

[2001] UKHL 22, [2002] 1 AC 215; *Dubai Aluminium Co Ltd v Salaam* [2002] UKHL 48, [2003] 2 AC 407; *Bazley v Curry* (1999) 174 DLR (4th) 45; *Jacobi v Griffiths* (1999) 174 DLR (4th) 71; and *Bernard v The Attorney General of Jamaica* [2004] UKPC 47, [2005] IRLR 398.

14.101 The categories giving rise to liability under the Act may be identified by reference to those which have been regarded as a breach of common law duties. They might involve the following in the employment context:[1] fear for personal safety;[2] overwork;[3] underwork;[4] character of the work;[5] if physical injury was foreseeable then so will be psychiatric injury;[6] if psychiatric injury has already been caused by the work then unless there is any material change further psychiatric injury will be foreseeable;[7] if conduct is calculated to cause injury;[8] bullying;[9] destruction of property or work valuable to the employee.[10]

1   For a detailed analysis of early reported and unreported stress cases see Buchan 'Stress Cases Foreseeability and Breach' (2001) 3 JPIL 5.
2   See *Dulieu v White & Sons* [1901] 2 KB 669.
3   *Walker v Northumberland County Council* [1995] ICR 702.
4   *Cox v Phillips Industries Ltd* [1976] 1 WLR 638.
5   *Walker v Northumberland County Council* [1995] ICR 702 per Colman J at 707B.
6   *Page v Smith* [1996] AC 155 see above under shock claims.
7   *Walker v Northumberland County Council* [1995] ICR 702 at 707B.
8   *Wilkinson v Downton* [1897] 2 QB 57.
9   *Long v Mercury Mobile* (4 May 2001, unreported). HHJ Thompson QC, sitting as a Deputy High Court Judge.
10   *Attia v British Gas* [1988] QB 304.

EMPLOYMENT TRIBUNAL CLAIMS

14.102 It is well recognised that it is possible to claim damages for personal injury in the employment tribunal in discrimination cases: *Sheriff v Klyne Tugs (Lowestoft) Ltd* [1999] ICR 1170. It is not, however, possible to litigate such a claim as part of other complaints under the Employment Rights Act 1996 such as unfair dismissal (including constructive dismissal): *Dunnachie v Kingston upon Hull City Council* [2004] UKHL 36, [2005] 1 AC 226.

14.103 In practice, the circumstances of a dismissal are often relevant to a personal injury claim in negligence. Therefore, for the sake of completeness, unfair dismissal, constructive dismissal, and health and safety dismissals are also dealt with briefly below: this is not the work for a detailed exposition of such heads of claim.

14.104 Practitioners must be aware that where there are circumstances which may give rise to psychiatric illness, claims are not restricted to the common law courts. Depending on the specific facts, they may be brought in the employment tribunal under one of the statutory heads of liability which such tribunals have jurisdiction to determine.

14.105 Bullying or harassment may, for instance, involve racial or sexual abuse, or comments targeted at an individual's physical disability. This might seem to invite a claim alleging discrimination on the ground of race, sex or disability. However, it is always possible that (for example) racist epithets are used as part of a course of conduct which has some other cause—a personal dislike of someone, because of their position, their behaviour, or their personality may owe nothing in itself to the race or sex of the individual, but may be expressed in part in terms of racist or sexist abuse, in order to further the campaign of vilification conducted by the perpetrator. There is always a risk that fastening upon the odd 'racist' phrase, or sexist remark, may lead a claimant to bring a claim in the employment tribunal, when one in the common law courts might be more appropriate. In *Chief Constable of the West Yorkshire Police v Khan* [2001] UKHL 48, [2001] ICR 1065, following *Nagarajan v London Regional Transport* [2000] 1 AC 501, HL, the House of Lords placed emphasis upon identifying the reason for the conduct (note: the reason, not the motive), which, coupled with the approach to antagonistic epithets taken by the House of Lords in *Pearce v Mayfield School* [2003] UKHL 34, [2003] ICR 937, at least leaves open the argument for respondents that racism which is incidental to other reprehensible conduct does not afford a claim in the tribunal.

14.106 However, these reservations aside, references to sex and race, where present, suggest that an employment tribunal might easily be convinced that there has been discrimination, which should be remedied where it has caused a detriment.

14.107 It may be important to determine which forum to proceed in, since such a choice has repercussions. If the tribunal is chosen, even for a claim of unfair dismissal arising out of alleged racial or sexual harassment, and the claim fails, then it may subsequently be impossible to litigate a claim for personal injury arising out of the same facts: *Sheriff v Klyne Tugs (Lowestoft) Ltd* [1999] IRLR 481, CA.[1] If a common law claim is to be launched, time limits may thereafter prevent a tribunal claim under one of the discrimination statutes, yet to run a case in both the common law courts and tribunal at one and the same time creates a duplication of expense and effort.

[1]   In this case, the claimant sustained a psychiatric injury as the result of bullying by the captain and crew of a tug upon which he worked. He made an employment tribunal claim which he settled for £3,000 'in full and final settlement of all claims over which the tribunal has jurisdiction'. A subsequent common law claim for damages for personal injury was struck out as an abuse of the process. The Court of Appeal dismissed his appeal and decided that genuine claims for personal injury damages can be made in the employment tribunal for cases involving discrimination (sex, race and disability) where they involve the same facts. It did not, however, decide that parallel protective proceedings brought at common law, just in case the discrimination claim failed, would be an abuse of the process. It did decide that if a claim for discrimination is made in the employment tribunal and injuries are known to have resulted from the discrimination, a claim must be made for those injuries and should not be left for a later common law claim. If employment tribunal proceedings are contemplated and discrimination allegations are being made it may well be advisable for the claimant to consider issuing protective proceedings at common law just in case the discrimination issues are unsuccessful: but this has cost implications: see para 14.108, item (f), below.

14.108 Factors likely to be important in determining the appropriate forum for a claim are:

(a)   at common law, there is a need to prove either intention (if it is said the harm was inflicted deliberately) or, more usually, a lack of care, which involves the need to prove that the defendant/respondent appreciated that the conduct impugned might be harmful to health and safety, whereas before the tribunal there is no need to do so, but instead a need to prove that the conduct impugned was 'on the grounds of' race, sex, or both, or disability;

(b)   there may be no need in a tribunal claim to prove that the damage claimed was 'reasonably foreseeable', at least in a race case. The same principles are to be applied, once the act of discrimination is proved, as would apply in civil proceedings concerning a breach of statutory duty (see, eg the Sex Discrimination Act 1975, ss 65(1)(b), 66; the Race Relations Act 1976, ss 56(1)(b), 57). In *Essa v Laing Ltd* [2004] EWCA Civ 02, [2004] ICR 746, the Court of Appeal decided that this meant that the test was not one of 'reasonable foreseeability' but whether harm was caused directly, even though unforeseeably;

(c)   vicarious liability may be easier to establish in a tribunal than it is in the common law courts where a common law claim is brought: the whole argument in *Jones v Tower Boot Co Ltd* [1997] ICR 254 was to the effect that the words 'course of employment' in the statutory clause imposing vicarious liability (s 32(1)): 'Anything done by a person in the course of his employment shall be treated for the purposes of this Act ... as done by his employer as well as by him' did not import the whole of the common law as to what 'course of employment' meant in the context of common law vicarious liability. Instead, the purpose of the Act was such that the phrase necessarily had a wider context. However, the common law itself has seen a repositioning, as noted above, which markedly reduces the difference this is liable to make;

(d)   the threshold requirement for successfully claiming compensation in a claim based upon the Race Relations Act or the Sex Discrimination Act is lower than a common law claim (even if part of the particulars of the allegation of negligence or breach of contract is a failure to observe the provisions of the Sex, Race or Disability Discrimination Acts). This is because an award under the discrimination statutes may include a sum in respect of 'injury to feelings' which, as has been seen, is not permitted in a common law claim. Compensation, therefore, is more likely to be easily obtained through the employment tribunal, although employment tribunals generally are likely to be discouraged from awarding a full loss in cases in which the calculation of that loss may involve the multiplier/multiplicand approach (see *Dunnachie v Kingston-upon-Hull City Council (No 3)* [2003] IRLR 843: EAT discouraged the use of multipliers calculated with the help of Ogden Tables in unfair dismissal claims);

(e)   employment tribunal claims are less expensive than common law claims to mount in the first place (though probably no less expensive to run);

(f)   costs are unlikely to be awarded by an employment tribunal, nor upon the first rung of appeal therefrom (though the costs regime of the employment tribunal is expanding: awards of five figure sums by way of costs are not entirely uncommon). Accordingly, if a claimant has a doubtful case, the costs balance favours him proceeding before a tribunal; if, however, he has a case in which he or she expects to succeed, he will never receive full and fair compensation from the employment tribunal—because his costs of taking proceedings will have to be paid for, and may be regarded as a deduction from his compensation. By contrast, if he should succeed in the civil courts, he will be paid at least the bulk of the costs he has incurred;

(g) there is no requirement for front-loading cost and expense in a tribunal as there is in a civil claim, where protocols have to be observed, medical evidence served with the statement of case, and the probable claim for damage set out in a schedule;

(h) time limits are unhelpful before the tribunal (generally, three months since the act complained of in cases of discrimination);

(i) hearings before a tribunal are less likely to be on a 'running list';

(j) tribunals have no well developed structure for dealing with expert medical evidence where the harassment has caused psychiatric damage (or, for that matter, in cases of disability where the tribunals have much yet to learn from the common law courts);

(k) a questionnaire procedure is available in tribunals, and widely used, for which the only civil court counterpart is the interrogatory, which is not;

(l) there are three rungs of appeal from a tribunal (EAT, CA, HL) but only two from the civil courts (CA, HL in unusual cases); but an appeal from a tribunal is on a point of law only.

14.109 A claim for damages for personal injury as such cannot be made in a claim for unfair dismissal before an employment tribunal: *Dunnachie v Kingston upon Hull City Council* [2004] UKHL 36, [2005] 1 AC 226. However, findings of fact made in such a claim may found an issue estoppel in a subsequent claim before the civil courts: *O'Laoire v Jackel International Ltd* [1990] ICR 197.

14.110 If an employer's conduct is such as to give rise to a right to terminate on the part of the employee he can claim constructive dismissal (as either a tribunal claim or before the common law court—but damages may be restricted in the latter to sums which would otherwise have been earned during a notice period: see *Lavarack v Woods of Colchester Ltd* [1967] 1 QB 278, CA).[1] To succeed:

> 'The employee must establish more than unreasonable or oppressive conduct on the part of the employer. Whether or not an employee is entitled to terminate the contract is a question of fact to be determined in accordance with contractual principles. Words "entitled" and "without notice" are contractual concepts. An employee is entitled to treat himself as constructively dismissed if the employer is guilty of conduct which is a significant breach going to the root of the contract of employment; or which shows that the employer no longer intends to be bound by one or more of the essential terms of the contract.'[2]

[1] Employment Rights Act 1996, s 95(1)(c).
[2] *Western Excavating (ECC) Ltd v Sharp* [1978] IRLR 27, CA.

14.111 A disabled employee who is faced with an employer who refuses to make reasonable adjustments pursuant to the Disability Discrimination

Act 1995 may resign and then claim constructive dismissal, entitling him to damages under the Disability Discrimination Act 1995: *Meikle v Nottinghamshire County Council* [2004] EWCA Civ 859, [2005] ICR 1.

Disability Discrimination Act 1995

14.112 The employment provisions of this Act came into force on 2 December 1996. It may provide alternative grounds upon which an employer might be liable for psychiatric injury at work.

The definition of a disability

14.113 Section 1(1) of the Disability Discrimination Act 1995 provides that:

> 'A disabled person is a person who has had a physical *or mental impairment* which has a *substantial* and *long term* effect on his or her ability to carry out *normal day-to-day activities.*'[1]

As one would expect, 'stress' is not a disability in itself: *Ishiguro v Financial Times Ltd* [1999] Case No 2301852.

[1]   Emphasis added. For a case involving questions of past and continuing treatment upon a disability and the evidential value of a Medical Appeal Tribunal assessment of disability see *Abadeh v British Telecommunications plc* [2001] IRLR 23. For a case involving the effect of clinical depression on normal day to day activities, treatment and substantial adverse effect, see *Leonard v Southern Derbyshire Chamber of Commerce* [2001] IRLR 19.

14.114 Physical impairment caused by stress can include many conditions, including those of the heart and bowel. For example in *Piquin v Abbey National plc* [1999] HSB 283 an employee was transferred to a new position that she found to be highly stressful, and this caused a recurrence of her irritable bowel syndrome. An employment tribunal found this condition amounted to a disability under the Disability Discrimination Act 1995, s 1. The impairment was the continuous threat to the employee's continence and, along with her other symptoms of stress and depression, this also affected her memory and concentration.

14.115 'Mental impairment' must amount to an illness that is clinically well-recognised,[1] ie one that is recognised by a respectable body of medical opinion. It is very likely that this would include those specifically mentioned in publications such as the International Classification of Diseases and the American Diagnostic and Statistical Manual.[2] The tribunal should not substitute its opinion for that of experts.[3]

[1]   Disability Discrimination Act 1995, Sch 1, para 1.
[2]   See also the Code of Practice prepared by the Disability Rights Commission under powers conferred by the Disability Discrimination Act 1995, s 53A. The current edition is 'Disability Rights Commission Code of Practice: Employment and Occupation' (2004), approved by Parliament (SI 2004/2302), especially at paras 3.2–3.6.
[3]   See *Kapadia v London Borough of Lambeth* [2000] IRLR 14. The sole issue before the tribunal was whether the appellant was disabled within the meaning of the Disability Discrimination Act 1995. The appellant, his GP and his counsellor gave evidence and were

cross-examined. The respondent called no evidence on the disability issue. Whilst the majority accepted the diagnosis of reactive depression, they were not satisfied that on all the evidence it had more than a trivial effect on his ability to carry out normal day-to-day activities. The EAT referred to the conclusions of the tribunal. There was uncontested medical evidence that the appellant was disabled within the meaning of the Act, and it was wholly impermissible for the majority to ignore it and to conclude, apparently on the basis of how he had appeared to them when giving this evidence, that there was no evidence that his impairment had any adverse effect at all on his day-to-day activities, and to wholly disregard the effects of it.

14.116 The tribunal is also required to discount the effects of medical treatment.[1] In *Kapadia v London Borough of Lambeth* [2000] IRLR 14 there was evidence that without counselling sessions Mr Kapadia would probably have suffered a mental breakdown and hospitalisation. The EAT held that the counselling sessions constituted 'medical treatment' within the meaning of the Disability Discrimination Act 1995, and the tribunal should therefore have considered 'induced effects' on Mr Kapadia's day-to-day activities without such treatment, ie he would have had a breakdown.

1   Disability Discrimination Act 1995, Sch 1, para 6.

14.117 'Substantial' means an effect which is more than minor or trivial[1] and which indicates a limitation going beyond the normal differences in ability that may exist amongst people. In deciding whether or not an effect is 'substantial' it is necessary to take into account the time taken to carry out an activity and the way in which the activity is carried out. The cumulative effect of individual minor impairments can be taken together to be sufficient to amount to a substantial adverse effect for the purposes of the definition. It is to be judged not by asking what an individual can do, but asking what he cannot now do by reason of his disability: see *Ekpe v Comr of Police for Metropolis* [2001] ICR 1084, EAT.

1   Guidance, para A1 and see *Goodwin v Patent Office* [1999] IRLR 4 and *Vicary v British Telecommunications plc* [1999] IRLR 680.

14.118 'Long term' means that the effect of the impairment must have lasted at least 12 months, or is likely to last at least 12 months or for the rest of the life of the person affected.[1]

1   Disability Discrimination Act 1995, Sch 1, para 2.

14.119 In determining whether it is likely that an event will happen, the test is whether it is more probable than not it will happen,[1] and in assessing the likelihood of an effect lasting for any period, account should be taken of the total period for which the effect exists, including time before and after the point when the discriminatory behaviour occurred.[2]

1   Guidance, para B10.
2   Guidance, para E8, see also *Greenwood v British Airways* [1999] IRLR 600, EAT.

14.120 'Normal day-to-day activities' are classed into the following categories: mobility; manual dexterity; physical co-ordination; incontinence; ability to lift, carry or otherwise move everyday objects; speech, hearing or eyesight, memory or ability to concentrate, learn or understand; or perception of the risk of physical danger.[1] Generally, stress cases will involve issues of memory, concentration, the ability to learn or to understand and perceive a risk of danger.[2]

1 Disability Discrimination Act 1995, Sch 1, para 4.
2 The guidance sets out examples of effects that are not substantially adverse. These include occasionally forgetting the name of a familiar person and inability to concentrate on a task requiring application over several hours, an inability to fill in a long, detailed, technical document without assistance, an inability to read at faster than normal speed or minor problems with writing or spelling.

Paragraph C20 of the Guidance gives examples of how memory or ability to concentrate, learn or understand may be adversely affected, eg considerable difficulty in following a short sequence such as a brief list of domestic tasks. Paragraph C7 of the Guidance states that where a person has a mental illness, such as depression, account should be taken of whether, although the person can physically perform the task, in practice he is able to sustain it over a reasonable period of time.

14.121 *Goodwin v Patent Office* [1999] IRLR 4 sets out guidelines for the proper approach to the question of disability under the Disability Discrimination Act 1995, s 1.

(1)   The employment tribunal should look carefully at what the parties had said in the originating application and the notice of appearance. Directions might be required for expert evidence. The tribunal should be prepared to adopt an interventionist role. Some disabled persons might be unable, or unwilling, to accept that they have suffered from any disability. Without the direct help of the tribunal, there might be cases, when the claim has been drafted with outside help, which the applicant was unwilling to support.

(2)   A purposive approach to construction should be adopted. Reference should be made expressly to any relevant provisions of the Guidance or Code of Practice.[1]

(3)   The employment tribunal has to look at the evidence by reference to four different conditions:
   (a)   impairment;
   (b)   adverse effect;[2]
   (c)   substantiality; and
   (d)   long-term effect.

In *Goodwin*, the EAT considered that there was sufficient evidence from the employer's own documents that the applicant's capacity to concentrate and communicate had been adversely affected in a significant manner.

1 Code of Practice: Disability Discrimination Act 1996.
2 If the employment tribunal is to conclude that there is no connection between the applicant's work behaviour and his disability it is necessary to explain why: *Edwards v Mid Suffolk District Council* [2001] IRLR 190.

Knowledge of disability

14.122 Section 5(1) of the Disability Discrimination Act 1995 provides that:

'... an employer discriminates against a disabled person ... for a reason which relates to the disabled person's disability, [if] he treats him less favourably than he treats or would treat others to whom that reason does not or would not apply.'

14.123 The question arises as to whether an employer can be said to have discriminated 'for a reason which relates to the disability' if the employer is unaware that the condition was a disability. Although in *O 'Neill v Symm & Co Ltd* [1998] IRLR 232, EAT the EAT (Kirkwood J presiding) ruled that knowledge of the disability, or at least the material features of it, was necessary in order to establish that the discrimination was for a reason related to the disability, in *Heinz (HJ) Co Ltd v Kenrick* [2000] IRLR 144, EAT the EAT (Lindsay J presiding) held that the correct test was an objective one of the relationship between the disability and the treatment, not whether the employer knew of it. This latter appears the correct position: see *Clark v TDG Ltd (t/a Novacold)* [1999] IRLR 318, CA.

Comparators

14.124 The question arises as to with whom the tribunal should compare the treatment of a disabled employee. In *Clark v TGD Ltd (t/a Novacold)* [1999] IRLR 318, CA, Mr Clark was employed by Novacold in a physically demanding manual job. He sustained a back injury at work which resulted in him being absent from work from September 1996 to the time of his dismissal in January 1997. Prior to his dismissal, the employer had obtained a medical report which was unable to give a date for his return to work. Both the employment tribunal and the EAT ruled that the comparison under the Disability Discrimination Act 1995, s 5(1) was between Mr Clark and someone who had been off work for the same amount of time but for a non-disablement reason.

14.125 The Court of Appeal held that the Disability Discrimination Act 1995 does not require a 'like for like' comparison between the treatment received by a disabled person and the way a non-disabled person would have been treated. It is simply a question of identifying others to whom the reason for the treatment does not apply (ie those who are capable of performing a job and are not dismissed).

14.126 As in the case of sex and race discrimination, there is rarely any overt evidence of discrimination on grounds of disability. It is therefore necessary for tribunals to draw inferences from the primary facts where appropriate.[1] In *Roberts v Warrington Borough Council* (1999, unreported), the EAT held that the same guidelines are equally valid when determining whether less favourable treatment on grounds of a person's disability has occurred.

[1] See *King v Great Britain-China Centre* [1991] IRLR 513, CA for the well-established position in relation to claims alleging race discrimination.

14.127   *Psychiatric injury, stress and harassment*

The duty to make reasonable adjustments

14.127 The Disability Discrimination Act 1995 provides two methods of establishing liability under s 3A

(1)   s 3A(1) prohibits less favourable treatment of a disabled person by an employer which the employer cannot show to be justified;
(2)   s 3A(2) provides that an employer also discriminates against a disabled person if it fails to comply with a duty to make 'reasonable adjustments', imposed upon it in relation to the disabled person.

The duty to make adjustments is provided for by s 4A(1). Where: (a) a provision, criterion or practice applied by or on behalf of an employer; or (b) any physical feature of the premises occupied by the employer, place the disabled person at a substantial disadvantage in comparison with persons who are not disabled, it is the duty of the employer to take such steps as it is reasonable, in all the circumstances of the case, for it to have to take in order to prevent the provision, criterion or practice, or feature, having that effect.

14.128 Harassment on the ground of disability is specifically proscribed by s 4(3). Harassment is defined (by s 3B(1)) as occurring where a person subjects a disabled person to harassment where, for a reason which relates to the disabled person's disability, he engages in unwanted conduct which has the purpose or effect[1] of: (a) violating the disabled person's dignity; or (b) creating an intimidating, hostile, degrading or offensive environment for him.

[1]   It will only have such an effect if 'having regard to all the circumstances, including in particular the perception of the disabled person, it should reasonably be considered as having that effect': s 3B(2).

14.129 In stress at work cases an employee may well be suffering from a mental impairment as a result of his workload. If he advises his employer that he has either suffered or (possibly) may suffer an injury as a result of the workload, unless it is reduced and the employer fails to reduce the workload without a material and substantial reason, that failure may (if all the other requirements such as the definition of disability, etc are satisfied) amount to unlawful discrimination under the Disability Discrimination Act 1995.[1]

[1]   See for example *Fu v London Borough of Camden* [2001] IRLR 186.

14.130 In the case of *London Borough of Hillingdon v Morgan* [1999] IDS 649 the EAT held that the failure by an employer to permit a staged return to work by somebody who had been off with ME was a failure to make a reasonable adjustment and therefore a breach of the Act. The provision of a short period of home working as a means of rehabilitation was a 'reasonable adjustment' in that the employer's financial and administrative resources rendered it a feasible option. See also *Archibald v Fife Council* [2004] UKHL 32, [2004] ICR 954, (Sc).

Justification

14.131 Section 3A(3) of the Disability Discrimination Act 1995 provides a defence to an employer where the less-favourable treatment can be justified as being both material to the circumstances of the particular case and substantial. A justification defence cannot be thought up after the event, when it has never been considered during the period of employment: *Quinn v Schwarzkopf Ltd* [2001] IRLR 67.

14.132 The Disability Discrimination Act Code of Practice requires that the reason for the treatment has to relate to the individual circumstances in question and not just be trivial and minor.[1] In *Baynton v Saurus General Engineers Ltd* [1999] IRLR 604, EAT it was decided that the test of justification requires the tribunal to carry out a balancing exercise between the interests of the disabled employee and those of the employer. Thus the tribunal has to take into account the circumstances of both the employer and the employee. The EAT, in the case of *Heinz (HJ) Co Ltd v Kenrick* [2000] IRLR 144, concluded that the threshold for justification under what was then the Disability Discrimination Act 1995, s 5(3) (now 3A(3)) was 'very low'. If the treatment relates to the individual circumstances in question and is not just trivial or minor, then justification must be held to exist. In *Heinz* the EAT was sceptical about the possible scope for the 'balancing exercise' between the interests of the disabled employee and the interests of the employer as suggested in *Baynton*. However it pointed out the more rigorous nature of the justification defence in cases where the applicant is able to show that the employer was under a duty to carry out a reasonable adjustment. The justification defence will not be held to apply unless the less favourable treatment would still have been justified even if the employer had carried out reasonable adjustments. In practice health and safety arguments will often form the basis of a justification defence.

[1]   Paragraph 4.6.

Sex Discrimination Act 1975 and Race Relations Act 1976

14.133 The principles of law for the determination and for the award of damages for distress are outside the scope of this book: reference should be made to works such as *Harvey on Industrial Relations and Employment Law*.

Chapter 15

DUST DISEASES

Andrew Hogarth QC

INTRODUCTION

15.01 The inhalation of dust of any kind has been recognised as being likely to result in injury for over 100 years. The combined result of the long latency periods for many forms of asbestos disease and the extreme toxicity of the material means that today most of the personal injury claims arising from the inhalation of dust are asbestos disease claims. However, there are other lung diseases which are the result of exposure to other dusts. Fibrosis of the lungs resulting from dust inhalation, which in the case of asbestos dust inhalation is known as asbestosis, can also result from inhalation of other dusts. Historically the most common forms were silicosis, from silica dust, and fibrosis from inhalation of coal dust. However, almost any non-organic dust can cause fibrosis if inhaled in sufficient quantity. In addition there are a number of diseases which are similar in effect to lung fibrosis, but which act by restricting the airways in the lungs. These diseases may be caused by the inhalation of a wide variety of organic dusts; of these, byssinosis, caused by cotton dust, and farmer's lung,[1] caused by the spores on mouldy hay or grain, are the most commonly encountered, although a wide variety of organic dusts can cause similar symptoms. Space prevents a detailed consideration of these individual diseases.

---

[1] A prescribed industrial disease since 21 June 1965: see the National Insurance (Industrial Injuries) (Prescribed Diseases) Amendment Regulations 1965.

15.02 The dusty atmosphere in factories was recognised as being likely to injure the workers in factories as long ago as 1864 when the Factories Acts Extension Act first required the occupier of a factory or workshop to provide ventilation to render harmless dust which 'may be injurious to health'. This provision was repeated in the Factories and Workshop Act 1901, s 74. Between 1900 and 1937 numerous statutory instruments dealing with health and safety in specific industries and processes contained regulations requiring dust to be removed. In the Factories Act 1937, s 47, a new and more onerous requirement was introduced, and the exposure of any worker in a factory to a 'substantial quantity of dust of any kind' was prohibited.

15.03 In his annual report for 1938, the Chief Inspector of Factories set out the understanding which he had of the reasons for the introduction in that year of the obligation under the Factories Act 1937, s 47 not to expose employees to a substantial quantity of dust of any kind. The report is often relied upon to show the state of general awareness of the dangers caused by all forms of dust and thus used against all employers as an allegation of negligence. He said:

'One of the greatest problems facing industry today is that of dust, and consideration is given later in this report to silicosis and asbestosis. We are but on the threshold of knowledge of the effects on the lungs of dust generally and I have referred in my reports from year to year to the enquiries made into cases of illness and deaths alleged to be due to the inhalation of dust. While section 47 of the Factories Act 1937 may be thought to be somewhat ambiguous in its reference to a substantial quantity of dust of any kind, it is, I consider, an admirable one in that it requests precautions even before it is possible to say specifically that the dust in question is harmful to a recognisable pathological extent. There can be no doubt that dust if inhaled is physiologically undesirable. Moreover, dust that is thought to be harmless today may, following further research be viewed in another light tomorrow. It is not many years ago when the dust of asbestos was regarded as innocuous, while today it is recognised as highly dangerous.'

This very clear warning given 67 years ago means that it is no longer necessary to consider whether or not an employer is in breach of its duty to its workers if the level of dust may be described as 'substantial'.

15.04 The long latency period of asbestos disease and the extreme toxicity of asbestos dust means that the majority of dust disease claims arise from exposure to asbestos dust. For this reason the remainder of this chapter deals with asbestos disease litigation. However, the legal principles described in this chapter are applicable to all dust disease claims, with some statutory modifications. The long latency periods for asbestos diseases means that this chapter deals with legislation which has long since been repealed. Modern legislation is dealt with elsewhere.

Liability at common law

15.05 The common law principles applicable in asbestos disease claims are the same as those applicable in any other type of personal injury action. Notwithstanding the universality of the principles involved, some aspects of the common law of negligence have a greater degree of prominence in asbestos disease litigation than in other types of personal injury action. The duty is, as always, a duty to take reasonable care to protect those affected by an activity against a foreseeable risk of injury to their health. The difficulty, as always, is in attempting to describe the circumstances in which a particular person will be found to be in breach of that duty, a difficulty made the more challenging by the fact that the events the court is considering invariably occurred many years before the trial.

15.06 Perhaps to avoid any suggestion that they are adopting standards which only seem to be appropriate with the benefit of hindsight, the courts have not devised a formulation of the circumstances in which a duty is owed, or in which it is likely to have been breached, which is unique to asbestos disease litigation. Instead, they have adopted the classic legal formulations of the circumstances in which a duty is owed and of the standard of care which is owed. However, the result is largely the same, as the statements of principle commonly utilised have the effect of imposing liability in circumstances which one cannot help feeling would have come as something of a surprise to the judges of earlier generations who formulated those tests. Previous generations seem to have regarded industrial disease as the inevitable lot of the working man, despite the fine sentiments contained in many of the legal tests used to determine liability. Today's generation do not perceive these same tests as just fine words. From the point of view of an insurer or defendant this different perspective is unfortunate. The enormous increase in the numbers who die from mesothelioma seems to have had the effect of making the judges less willing to excuse the shortcomings of an employer, and thus more likely to find in favour of claimants, than were the judges of a previous generation, when the number of deaths from mesothelioma was less than a tenth of the number it is today. In this section the aspects of the common law frequently encountered in asbestos disease litigation are selected for highlighting. The parallel, but similarly strict, approach to allegations of breach of statutory duty is dealt with in paras 15.21ff.

The need to keep up to date

15.07 Some of those using asbestos were genuinely ignorant of the dangers they were creating. That they were ignorant may be established by the evidence in a particular case, although that evidence will often reveal a degree of wilful blindness to the dangers being created. However, the ignorance established by the evidence is unlikely to provide a defence.

15.08 In his classic exposition of an employer's duty to keep himself up to date with the information available to him, Swanwick J said in *Stokes v Guest, Keen and Nettlefold (Bolts and Nuts) Ltd* [1968] 1 WLR 1776 at 1783:[1]

> '... the overall test is still the conduct of the reasonable and prudent employer, taking positive thought for the safety of his workers in the light of what he knows or ought to know; where there is a recognised and general practice which has been followed for a substantial period in similar circumstances without mishap, he is entitled to follow it, unless in the light of common sense or newer knowledge it is clearly bad; but, where there is developing knowledge, he must keep reasonably abreast of it and not be too slow to apply it; and where he has in fact greater than average knowledge of the risks, he may be thereby obliged to take more than the average or standard precautions. He must weigh up the risk in terms of the likelihood of injury occurring and the potential consequences if it does; and he must balance against this the probable effectiveness of the precautions that can be taken to meet it and the expense and inconvenience they involve. If he is found to have fallen below the standard to be properly expected of a reasonable and prudent employer in these respects, he is negligent.'

[1] A passage recently approved by the House of Lords in *Barber v Somerset County Council* [2004] UKHL 13, [2004] 2 All ER 385.

15.09 In *Thompson v Smiths Shiprepairers (North Shields) Ltd* [1984] QB 405, Mustill J considered Swanwick J's statement of principle in an industrial deafness action and adopted it. He did however point out:[1]

'The speeches in [*Morris v West Hartlepool Steam Navigation Co Ltd* [1956] AC 552] show, not that one employer is exonerated simply by proving that other employers are just as negligent, but that the standard of what is negligent is influenced, although not decisively, by the practice in the industry as a whole. In my judgment, this principle applies not only where the breach of duty is said to consist of a failure to take precautions known to be available as a means of combating a known danger, but also where the omission involves an absence of initiative in seeking out knowledge of facts which are not in themselves obvious. The employer must keep up to date, but the court must be slow to blame him for not ploughing a lone furrow.'

¹ [1984] QB 405 at 416.

15.10 This qualification, which is important in most other types of industrial disease litigation, is of less importance than might be expected in asbestos disease litigation. As Mustill J observed, there is a line to be drawn between collective negligence and common practice; the clearer the available information concerning the danger, the less likely the court is to regard the evidence as establishing anything more than widespread negligence. Typical of the robust manner in which courts have been unwilling to allow common malpractice to amount to a defence is the view expressed in *Dawson v Cherry Tree Manufacturing Ltd* [2001] EWCA Civ 101, [2001] ICR 1223 by Hale LJ when commenting on the contents of the Merewether and Price report, which was published in 1930. She said:

'The conclusion was that "the inhalation of asbestos dust over a period of years *results* in the development of a serious type of fibrosis of the lungs" ' (emphasis supplied by the judge).

'Incidence mounted rapidly after five years' exposure but the disease took longer to manifest itself in those engaged in the less dusty processes.'

15.11 If one adds to the contents of the Merewether and Price report, which dealt specifically with asbestos dust, the provisions of the Factories Act 1937, s 47 and its successor section, the Factories Act 1961, s 63, which contain clear warnings of the dangers caused by exposing a workman to a substantial quantity of dust of any kind, it soon becomes apparent why courts are seldom willing to accept that common practice amounts to a defence, and why courts have taken an increasingly strong view that an employer ought to have known of the dangers caused by exposure to a substantial quantity of dust of any kind.

15.12 In a pleading, the allegation by a claimant that 'The defendants failed to properly and sufficiently acquaint themselves with the danger likely to be caused to the claimant by the substances with which he was required to work (or to which he was likely to be exposed) in the course of his employment', will invariably prove to be very difficult to defeat.

15.13 Dust diseases

The injury which must be foreseeable

15.13 Of the six conditions commonly accepted as being caused by asbestos dust exposure, that is mesothelioma, lung cancer, asbestosis, pleural thickening, pleural plaques and psychiatric injury,[1] mesothelioma is the most recent to have come to light. Although cases of mesothelioma have been discovered among tissue samples of persons who died of lung disease as long ago as 1917,[2] it was not until about 1960 that the disease became recognised and related to asbestos exposure. The distinguishing feature of the disease in the context of establishing liability is that it may be caused by lower levels of exposure to asbestos than the other asbestos-induced diseases.

[1]   Following the decision of the Court of Appeal in *Rothwell v Chemical & Insulating Co Ltd* [2006] EWCA Civ 27 it is doubtful whether pleural plaques and freestanding psychiatric injury should be considered to be sufficient to give rise to a cause of action. Until the House of Lords have heard the pending appeals in these cases, neither should be regarded as giving rise to a cause of action.

[2]   An event recorded in the 1965 survey by Newhouse and Thompson.

15.14 That the disease was unknown, or that the fact that it resulted from asbestos exposure was unknown, does not provide a defence to a claim resulting from exposure in earlier periods. In *Page v Smith* [1996] AC 155 at 190, Lord Lloyd said:

> 'The test in every case ought to be whether the defendant can reasonably foresee that his conduct will expose the plaintiff to the risk of personal injury. If so, then he comes under a duty of care to that plaintiff. If a working definition of "Personal Injury" is needed, it can be found in section 38 (1) of the Limitation Act 1980. "Personal Injuries" includes any disease and any impairment of a person's physical or mental condition'.

15.15 In *Margereson and Hancock v J W Roberts Ltd* [1996] PIQR P358, Russell LJ, in delivering the judgment of the Court of Appeal, followed Lord Lloyd and said:

> 'We add only that in the context of this case we take the view that liability only attaches to these defendants if the evidence demonstrated that they should reasonably have foreseen a risk of some pulmonary injury, not necessarily mesothelioma.'

15.16

The reference in this passage to 'pulmonary injury' is perhaps surprising in the light of *Page v Smith*[1] and should perhaps be understood to mean any injury resulting from the inhalation of dust. In *Jeromson v Shell Tankers UK Ltd* [2001] EWCA Civ 101, [2001] ICR 1223 at [32], Hale LJ corrected this slip. She said:

> 'There was no dispute between the parties as to the relevant legal principles. It matters not that at the relevant time the diseases understood to be caused by exposure to asbestos did not include mesothelioma.'

The judge quoted Russell LJ in *Margereson v J W Roberts Ltd* [1996] PIQR P358 at 361:

'liability only attaches to these defendants if the evidence demonstrated that they should reasonably have foreseen a risk of some pulmonary injury, not necessarily mesothelioma ... Following the House of Lords decision in *Page v Smith* it is sufficient if any personal injury to a primary victim is foreseeable.'

1   The judgment was delivered in *Page v Smith* on 11 May 1995, almost 11 months earlier.

15.17 A claimant will therefore succeed in a mesothelioma action in the event that he is able to establish either:

(a)   that the defendant was in breach of a statutory duty owed to him and that he suffered disease of the type against which the statutory provision was intended to protect him, that is, respiratory disease; or

(b)   in a negligence action, that the exposure was sufficient to create a foreseeable risk of him suffering from some respiratory disease.

Prior to the date when the risk of mesothelioma became known, and therefore foreseeable, the risk to be foreseen will be that of some other respiratory disease caused by asbestos exposure.

15.18 The disease which a claimant will have to establish was foreseeable prior to the date of discovery of mesothelioma is asbestosis. It is correct that by this time the risk of lung cancer as a result of asbestos exposure was also well known. However, it was thought at that time that lung cancer was only attributable to asbestos exposure if the claimant was also suffering from asbestosis. It follows that the foreseeability of lung cancer is irrelevant for the purpose of establishing a foreseeable risk of injury. As it happens the level which gives rise to a foreseeable risk of lung cancer is about the same as that which gives rise to a foreseeable risk of asbestosis.

THE SETTING OF THE STANDARD OF CARE

15.19 The levels of dust to which workmen were subjected varied considerably from industry to industry and also from workman to workman. One workman might be subjected to considerably greater amounts of dust than his colleagues as he had, by chance, worked on more jobs in which he was exposed to asbestos than his colleagues. In *Jeromson v Shell Tankers UK Ltd* [2001] EWCA Civ 101, [2001] ICR 1223 the claimant had worked as an engineer aboard the defendant's tankers for some years between 1950 and 1960. In that time there were occasions when the engineers employed by the company would be exposed to dust in intense concentrations when aboard the vessels, but not every employee would be unfortunate enough to be subjected to such levels of dust exposure. The trial judge had concluded that the defendants should have taken into account the extent of the exposure to which an employee was potentially subjected, rather than that to which he was actually subjected when considering whether the defendants were in breach of the duty which they owed to the claimant. The Court of Appeal agreed, and concluded that the trial judge's direction was correct. They said:

'The judge had first to make findings of fact about that exposure. Before doing so he had to resolve a dispute between counsel as to whether he should be assessing the average or the potential exposure of marine engineers to asbestos dust. He concluded that, given the great variety of experience of individual engineers, a careful employer ought to be addressing his mind to the potential experience of any one of them in deciding what precautions he ought to take.'

To justify this conclusion, Hale LJ said:[1]

'However, where an employer cannot know the extent of any particular employee's exposure over the period of his employment, knows or ought to know that exposure is variable, and knows or ought to know the potential maximum as well as the potential minimum, a reasonable and prudent employer, taking positive thought for the safety of his workers, would have to take thought for the risks involved in the potential maximum exposure. Only if he could be reassured that none of these employees would be sufficiently exposed to be at risk could he safely ignore it.'

This conclusion of the Court of Appeal has important consequences for defendants, as many tasks involving asbestos gave rise to great variations in the amount of dust generated; unless precautions were taken, the claimant will establish a breach of duty.

1   [2001] ICR 1223 at [37].

THE STANDARDS IMPOSED BY STATUTORY DUTIES

15.20 The most onerous of the standards adopted by the various statutes and statutory instruments dealing with exposure to dust was probably that originally in the Factories Act 1937, s 47, and later in its successor section, the Factories Act 1961, s 63. Both prohibited the exposure of a workman to a substantial quantity of dust of any kind. This general duty was not qualified by the need for the dust to be 'likely to be injurious', but imposed a duty on an employer as long as the dust was present in a substantial quantity. Many occupations are outside the scope of the protection afforded by the Factories Acts and workmen in the building and civil engineering industry in particular are outside the scope of its protection. The issue raised is whether a standard of care set by statute in respect of a particular class of workman may be used by a workman who is outside that class as evidence that his employer was negligent, or, put another way, whether an employer who is under no statutory obligation to adopt a statutory standard, will be negligent if it fails to do so.

15.21 In recent years the courts have moved towards treating the duties imposed under a statutory regime as a form of warning to all employers, whether covered by the statutory provision or not, that a particular practice carries with it a foreseeable risk of injury. The more important the statute and the duty imposed by it, the more likely the court is to regard it as being evidence which shows that a defendant ought to have known that a particular precaution was required, or that a particular practice was unsafe.

15.22 In *Jeromson v Shell Tankers UK Ltd* [2001] EWCA Civ 101, [2001] ICR 1223 the claimant, who worked on one of the defendant's ships as an engineer, was unable to rely upon the breach of any statutory duty in his action against his employers. In an analysis of the state of knowledge which an employer should have had of the dangers of asbestos dust, Hale LJ regarded the provisions of the Asbestos Industry Regulations 1931 and of the Factories Act 1937 as being important elements in the knowledge which a reasonable employer should have had from the time the statutory provisions came into force, and as setting the standard of the care which the employer should have taken, notwithstanding that the employer was under no duty to comply with the particular statutory provision. There are many circumstances in which knowledge of particular dangers is capable of being proved by reference to the statutory framework, even when the statutory regime does not apply to the particular case.

15.23 The most obvious statutory duty for a claimant to rely upon as evidence of negligence is that contained in the Factories Act 1937, s 47 and the Factories Act 1961, s 63. However, there are many other examples of duties which can be utilised in the same manner. For instance, the Asbestos Industry Regulations 1931, reg 8(b) provides that: 'All sacks used as containers for the transport of asbestos within the factory shall be constructed of impermeable material and shall be kept in good repair'. It is not difficult to read this provision as a warning that asbestos dust will escape from hessian sacks and that its escape created a foreseeable risk of injury, with the result that a dock worker who unloads the hessian sacks may suggest that his employer was negligent in failing to adopt this statutory safety precaution.

DATES OF KNOWLEDGE

15.24 If some injury is a foreseeable consequence of the tortfeasor's actions, then the tortfeasor is liable for the damage which occurs, even if that damage is not of the precise type which he should have foreseen.[1] The first known asbestos disease was asbestosis and, if the level of exposure was sufficient to create a foreseeable risk of injury in the form of asbestosis when judged by the state of knowledge at the time, then a claimant does not have to establish that injury in the form of lung cancer or mesothelioma was foreseeable. For reasons already explained in para 15.18, the date by which an employer ought to have known that a given level of exposure to asbestos dust created a risk of lung cancer is never considered by the courts, and will probably never need to be considered. Expert evidence will determine whether the level of exposure at any given date was sufficiently high for asbestosis to be foreseeable.

1   The Court of Appeal in *Rothwell v Chemical & Insulating Co Ltd* [2006] EWCA Civ 27 distinguished the principle in *Page v Smith* that damages for a psychiatric injury were recoverable even if some physical injury was all that was foreseeable.

15.25 The level at which asbestosis is foreseeable has gradually declined over the years as it became apparent that it occurred at lower levels of exposure.

However, mesothelioma can occur as the result of exposure which is too low to create a foreseeable risk of asbestosis. It is therefore in mesothelioma claims that the date when an employer knew or ought to have known that low levels of exposure might cause injury is at its most critical. The decade in which it became apparent that mesothelioma could result from exposure to asbestos at levels too low to create a foreseeable risk of asbestosis, the 1960s, was also the decade in which the use of asbestos was at its most widespread. As a result there are a regrettably large number of deaths from mesothelioma as a result of exposure in this decade. The precise date by which different types of employer should have foreseen that there was a foreseeable risk of injury in the form of mesothelioma will be determined with the assistance of expert evidence, but is never prior to 1960 and never later than 1969.

15.26 The employer is under a duty to take steps to keep himself abreast of the current knowledge of the dangers caused to workmen by the substances with which they are required to work. In an often cited passage in *Stokes v Guest, Keen and Nettlefold (Bolts and Nuts) Ltd* [1968] 1 WLR 1776 at 1783, which was recently cited with approval by the House of Lords in *Barber v Somerset County Council* [2004] UKHL 13, [2004] 2 All ER 385, Swanwick J said of an employer's duty:

> 'where there is developing knowledge, he must keep reasonably abreast of it and not be too slow to apply it; and where he has in fact greater than average knowledge of the risks, he may be thereby obliged to take more than the average or standard precautions.'

15.27 There is no substitute for expert medical and engineering evidence to establish the date by which a particular employer should have known that low levels of exposure created a foreseeable risk of injury. Whether a particular person was exposed to a foreseeable risk of injury depends upon the assessment by the court of a combination of factors: the state of medical knowledge at the time, the accessibility of that knowledge to a particular defendant and the level of exposure to asbestos dust. The balance between these factors is unique in each case, but as an example of the approach of the courts, and perhaps as to a court's view of defendants who ignored their responsibilities, the recent decision of Morland J in *Maguire v Harland and Wolff* [2004] EWHC 577, [2004] All ER (D) 76 demonstrates the manner in which a court looks critically at the literature to which an employer should have regard. Although the actual result in that case was overturned on appeal to the Court of Appeal, Morland J's approach in *Maguire* is typical of the approach of judges when asked to determine when a foreseeable risk of injury was created. An attempt is made to assess the extent of exposure and this is then contrasted with the warnings contained in the literature which is examined and treated at face value. The fact that an employer did not bother to read it or to take any precautions does not provide a defence.

BREACH OF STATUTORY DUTY

Introduction

15.28 A survey of the relevant statutory provisions intended to protect employees from the dangers of inhaled dust often involves a journey through the history of legislation protecting the health and safety of workmen. Some of the statutory provisions protect workmen against particular forms of dust, some against all dusts. The long latency periods for dust diseases means that almost none of the of the relevant statutory provisions remain in force, many of the relevant definitions are no longer relevant to the current statutory arrangements for protection of workmen and may be unfamiliar. The statutory scheme for the protection of workmen imposed few relevant general duties prior to the introduction of the Asbestos Industry Regulations 1931 and the Factories Act 1937.

However, there were numerous statutory regulations requiring ventilation to protect against dust inhalation for individual industries or processes, some of which appear to us today to be rather bizarre.[1]

---

1   See for instance the rarely pleaded provisions of the Sorting, Willeying, Washing and Combing of Goat Hair, Camel Hair etc Regulations 1905, reg 2.

THE ASBESTOS INDUSTRY REGULATIONS 1931

15.29 The increasing numbers of asbestosis cases which were reported in the 1920s led to the Merewether and Price Report, which was published in 1930. The contents of the report resulted in the passing of the Asbestos Industry Regulations 1931, which, with the exception of regs 2(a) and 5, came into force on 1 March 1932. Regulations 2(a) and 5 came into force on 1 September 1932. These Regulations remained in force until 14 May 1970.

Premises to which the Asbestos Industry Regulations 1931 apply

15.30 The regulations were passed under the powers contained in the Factories and Workshop Act 1901 and initially applied to all factories and workshops to which that statute applied. Under the Factories Act 1937, s 159, the regulations were treated after 1 July 1938 as if they had been passed under the Factories Act 1937, with the result that from that date they adopted the definition of a factory in the Factories Act 1937, s 151, and later that in the Factories Act 1961, s 175. The definition of a factory under these statutes was wide and included 'any premises in which persons are employed in manual labour in the making of any article[1] ... the breaking up or demolition of any article ... the adapting for sale of any article'. It also expressly includes three types of premises in which asbestos exposure was frequent. The definition of factory included, 'any yard or dry dock (including the precincts thereof) in which ships or vessels are constructed, reconstructed, repaired, refitted, finished or broken up'. The definition of factory included ' any premises in which the construction, reconstruction or repair of locomotives, vehicles or other plant for use for transport purposes is carried on as ancillary to a transport undertaking or other industrial or commercial undertaking'. The definition of factory included 'any premises in which articles are made or prepared incidentally to the carrying on of building operations or works of engineering construction, not being premises in which such operations or works are being carried on'. Shipyards, railway engine works and premises in which asbestos materials for use in building operations were prepared were therefore all within the definition of a factory, and thus within the categories of premises potentially covered by the Asbestos Regulations 1931.

1   Factories Act 1937, s 151(1).

15.31 The reference in the title of the regulations to the 'Asbestos Industry' does not serve to limit the application of the regulations to asbestos factories. In *Dawson v Cherry Tree Machine Co Ltd* [2001] EWCA Civ 101, [2001] ICR 1223, the deceased had worked for the defendants who manufactured dry-cleaning presses. In the course of this work he mixed small quantities of asbestos fibre with water in order to create a paste with which he sealed a part of the equipment he was manufacturing. The Court of Appeal rejected the submission that the regulations did not apply if the use of asbestos in a factory was only an incidental part of the process of manufacture. They pointed out that the provision in the preamble to the regulations, exempting factories in which the specified processes were only carried on occasionally, envisaged that the regulations applied to all factories and not only to asbestos factories.[1]

1   See paras 20–25 of the judgment.

Processes to which the Asbestos Industry Regulations 1931 applied

15.32 The Asbestos Industry Regulations 1931 applied to all factories (and workshops) in which any of the following processes were carried on:

'(i)   breaking, crushing, disintegrating, opening and grinding of asbestos, and the mixing or sieving of asbestos, and all processes involving manipulation of asbestos incidental thereto;

(ii)   all processes in the manufacture of asbestos textiles, including preparatory and finishing processes;

(iii)   the making of insulation slabs or sections, composed wholly or partly of asbestos, and processes incidental thereto;

(iv)   the making or repairing of insulating mattresses, composed wholly or partly of asbestos, and processes incidental thereto;

(v)   sawing, grinding, turning, abrading and polishing, in the dry state, of articles composed wholly or partly of asbestos in the manufacture of such articles;

(vi)   the cleaning of any chambers, fixtures and appliances for the collection of asbestos dust produced in any of the foregoing processes'.[1]

1   As specified in the preamble to the regulations.

15.33 The mixing of asbestos, which was a common operation throughout industry as a preparatory stage in the use of asbestos insulation, was the most widespread of the operations described in the Asbestos Regulations 1931. In *Dawson v Cherry Tree Machine Co Ltd* [2001] EWCA Civ 101, [2001] ICR 1223, the Court of Appeal considered that mixing a 'couple of handfuls' of asbestos fibre with water amounted to the mixing of asbestos, and therefore that the Regulations applied to it. The court also expressed the view that the removal of old asbestos insulation was not a process to which the Regulations applied, but expressed the view that the mixing and application of new asbestos insulation was 'more likely' to be a process to which the Regulations applied.

15.34 However, the preamble to the Regulations provided that they did not apply to any:

> 'factory or workshop or part thereof in which the process of mixing of asbestos or repair of insulating mattresses or any process specified in [part (V) of the preamble][1] or any cleaning of machinery or other plant used in connection with any such process, is carried on, so long as:
> (a)   such process or work is carried on occasionally only and no person is employed therein for more than eight hours in any week, and
> (b)   no other process specified in the foregoing paragraphs is carried on.'

1   See para 15.33, above.

15.35 It may seem that this provision was sufficiently wide to exempt any premises in which one of the mixing processes was only carried on from time to time, perhaps for less than eight hours in a week. However, in *Dawson v Cherry Tree Machine Co Ltd*, the Court of Appeal agreed with the trial judge's conclusion that if the work involving asbestos was carried out on a regular basis, it could not be said to be carried on occasionally. Hale LJ said:

> 'But "occasional" describes something which happens casually or intermittently, or on a particular occasion, not something which happens regularly.'

15.36 This view of the exemption coincides well with the normal definition of what amounts to a process taken from the speech of Lord Griffiths in *Nurse v Morganite Crucible Ltd* [1989] ICR 15 at 21–22, with which the other members of the House of Lords agreed. He said:

> 'the word "process" is not used in the limited sense in which it was construed by the Court of Appeal, but in the broader sense of including any activity of a more than minimal duration involving the use of asbestos. ... Obviously the single act of knocking a nail into an asbestos panel cannot be considered a process. There has to be some degree of continuity and repetition of a series of acts in order to constitute a process ... where the word "process" is used in the Regulations it means any operation or series of operations being an activity of more than a minimal duration.'

These interpretations of the words 'process' and 'occasional' are perhaps wider than the drafter of the Asbestos Industry Regulations 1931 had in mind, but the result is that the regulations have been held to apply to a wide range of activities involving the use of asbestos if they are carried on on a regular basis, or if any person in the factory carries on one of the activities described for more than eight hours in a week.

The duties under the Asbestos Industry Regulations 1931

15.37 The duties under the Asbestos Industry Regulations 1931 are imposed upon the occupier of the factory. Regulation 1 imposed a duty on the occupier of any factory to which the regulations apply, to provide and maintain an exhaust draught effected by mechanical means which prevented the escape of asbestos dust into the air of any room in which persons work, for a number of different classes of machine. Most are machines likely only to be encountered in asbestos factories, but they included 'machines used for the sawing ... in the dry state ... of articles composed wholly or partly of asbestos'. Therefore, the use of power saws to cut asbestos board in a shipyard required a system of ventilation which complied with reg 1. The duty was apparently an unqualified one and there was no suggestion in the body of the regulations itself which specified any level of dust which may be created without a breach of this provision. The Factory Inspectorate did set 'dust datum' levels, which should be understood as being levels below which they did not consider that dust was present in the air.

15.38 Regulation 2(a) provided that the 'Mixing or blending by hand of asbestos shall not be carried on except with an exhaust draught effected by mechanical means so designed and maintained as to ensure as far as practicable the suppression of dust during the processes.' This regulation was considered by the Court of Appeal in *Dawson v Cherry Tree Machine Co Ltd* [2001] EWCA Civ 101, [2001] ICR 1223 and they concluded that it imposed a very far-reaching duty. In *Dawson*, Hale LJ pointed out that the obligation to provide an exhaust draught was an absolute one, it was the effectiveness of it that was qualified by the word 'practicable'.

15.39 The remaining regulations apply to machinery which is probably only ever encountered in asbestos factories. However reg 8(b) is of wider relevance as it required that: 'All sacks used as containers for the transport of asbestos within the factory shall be constructed of impermeable material and shall be kept in good repair'. It may therefore be said that this regulation carried with it a warning that there was a danger resulting from the use of permeable sacks to transport asbestos. If the use of permeable sacks created a danger within an asbestos factory sufficient to require a specific provision to prevent their use, the danger was also present if such sacks were used outside asbestos factories. Dockers unloading cargoes of asbestos in hessian sacks faced the same danger and may rely upon the warning contained in this regulation.

THE FACTORIES ACT 1937 AND THE FACTORIES ACT 1961

15.40 The Factories Act 1937 came into force on 1 July 1938. The Factories Act 1959 made one material addition to the duties under the 1937 Act, adding a new s 26 to the 1937 Act, which imposed for the first time a statutory duty on the occupier of the factory to provide a safe place of work. The Factories Act 1937 was re-enacted by the Factories Act 1961 with effect from 1 April 1962. The relevant provisions of the 1961 Act remained in force until they were repealed piecemeal by legislation imposing more onerous duties on occupiers of factories.

15.41 These statutes contained three important sets of provisions relevant to dust disease claims. The Factories Act 1937, s 4, and the Factories Act 1961, s 4, contained provisions dealing with the obligation to provide ventilation. The Factories Act 1937, s 47, and the Factories Act 1961, s 63 were directly concerned with the inhalation of all forms of dust. The Factories Act 1937, s 26, as introduced by the Factories Act 1959, s 5, and the Factories Act 1961, s 29, contained provisions requiring an occupier of a factory to provide a safe place of work.

The occupier of factory premises

15.42 The duty under the statutes was imposed upon the occupier of the factory by the Factories Act 1961, s 155, and Factories Act 1937, s 130. Thus the occupier of the factory has liability imposed upon him in respect of asbestos dust generated by contractors working inside his factory. In *Fairchild v Glenhaven Funeral Services Ltd* [2002] UKHL 22, [2003] 1 AC 32, the successful claim against Waddingtons plc was based upon their liability as occupiers of the factory to a workman employed by another who was working in the factory while renovation was being carried out at a time when the factory was in operation.

15.43 It is remarkable that the Factories Acts 1937 and 1961 contained no definition of the word 'occupier', although the word is widely used in both statutes and the 'occupier' was the person who was responsible for compliance with the provisions of the statute. In *Ramsay v Mackie* (1904) 7 F 106 Ct of Sess, at 109, a case under the Factories and Workshops Act 1901, Lord MacLaren gave the following definition:

> 'Occupier plainly means the person who runs the factory ... who regulates and controls the work that is done there, and who is responsible for the provisions of the Factory Act within it.'

15.44 In *Smith v Cammell Laird & Co Ltd* [1940] AC 242, a case dealing with the definition of the term occupier under the Factories and Workshop Act 1901 and the Shipbuilding Regulations 1931, the House of Lords accepted that the duty was imposed upon the person who was the occupier of the factory as a whole. In that case some staging on a ship under construction was in use by an insulation contractor, but the duty to comply with the provisions of the Shipbuilding Regulations 1931 remained on the person who had overall control of the factory.

Factories Act 1937, s 47 and Factories Act 1961, s 63

15.45 These provisions of the Factories Acts 1937 and 1961 were in identical terms and remained in force until 14 May 1970, when the provisions of the Asbestos Regulations 1969 were substituted for the Factories Act 1961, s 63(1), in respect of any process which involved the generation of asbestos dust.

15.46 Both statutes provided that:

'In every factory in which, in connection with any process carried on, there is given off any dust or fume or other impurity of such a character and to such extent as to be likely to be injurious or offensive to the persons employed, or any substantial quantity of dust of any kind, all practicable measures shall be taken to protect the persons employed against inhalation of the dust or fume or other impurity and to prevent its accumulating in any workroom, and in particular, where the nature of the process makes it practicable, exhaust appliances shall be provided and maintained, as near as possible to the point of origin of the dust or fume or other impurity, so as to prevent its entering the air of any workroom.'

'Process'

15.47 The definition of the term 'process' is common to the Asbestos Industry Regulations 1931 and the Factories Acts 1937 and 1961 and is dealt with at paras 15.35–15.36, above. In *Edgson v Vickers plc* [1994] ICR 510, a case under the similar wording of the Asbestos Regulations 1969, Geoffrey Burke QC, dealing with a case in which asbestos had been swept up at the end of the working day by the workmen in the factory, concluded that such a task fell within the definition of a process as described by Lord Griffiths in *Nurse v Morganite Crucible Ltd* [1989] ICR 15.

The nature of the statutory duties under ss 47 and 63

15.48 These statutory provisions created three distinct obligations, the first a duty not to expose a workman to a quantity of dust which was likely to be injurious to his health, the second a duty not to expose the workman to a quantity of dust which was likely to be offensive and the third a duty not to expose a workman to a substantial quantity of dust of any kind. It follows that if either a substantial quantity of dust or a sufficient quantity of dust to be offensive was present, there was a breach of the duty owed under these sections, even if the quantity present was not considered to be likely to cause injury when judged by the standards of the day.

15.49 In *Richards v Highway Ironfounders (West Bromwich) Ltd* [1955] 1 WLR 1049, CA, a case under the Factories Act 1937, s 47, Lord Evershed MR said:

'The first thing to notice about section 47(1) is the dichotomy, which the judge observed, between cases of the emission "of dust or fumes of such a character as to be likely to be injurious" on the one hand, and "substantial quantities of dust of any kind" on the other hand. In my judgment, the dichotomy was correctly noticed by the judge. Having regard to the state of knowledge, it may be taken that the dust, with which we are here concerned, was not at any material date dust within the first branch of the section, since it could not fairly be regarded then as likely to cause silicosis. On the other hand, there is no doubt that the dust was emitted in substantial quantities, so that it fell within the second branch of the language which I have read.'

15.50 This view that there are three separate duties within the section was one shared by the Chief Inspector of Factories. In his annual report for 1938 the Chief Inspector of Factories commented on the then new provision in the Factories Act 1937, s 47, which had come into force in that year. He said of it:[1]

> 'We are but on the threshold of knowledge of the effects on the lungs of dust generally … While section 47 of the Factories Act 1937 may be thought somewhat ambiguous in its reference to "a substantial quantity of dust of any kind", it is, I consider, an admirable one in that it requires precautions even before it is possible to say specifically that the dust in question is harmful to a recognisable pathological extent. There can be no doubt that dust if inhaled is physiologically undesirable. Moreover, dust that is thought today to be harmless may, following research, be viewed in another light tomorrow. It is not many years ago when the dust of asbestos was regarded as innocuous, while today it is recognised as highly dangerous.'

1 Chief Inspector of Factories, *Annual Report for 1938* (1939) (Cmd 6081) p 63.

15.51 The first of these three duties, the duty not to expose a workman to a quantity of dust which is likely to be injurious to him, adds nothing to the common law duty of care, although it may impose liability on the occupier of the factory if he is not the employer of the injured workman. The two remaining duties impose liability if the dust was offensive, or if the quantity present in the air was substantial, even if the circumstances were such that the quantity of dust involved was not considered at the time of exposure to be likely to cause injury to the workman. For this reason these statutory provisions commonly form the basis of the allegation that a defendant was in breach of a duty which he owed to the worker. As Jenkins LJ said in *Gregson v Hick Hargreaves & Co Ltd* [1955] 1 WLR 1252 at 1266:

> 'Cases of this sort may be said to bear to some extent heavily on employers … because it has only comparatively lately become known that the dust produced in an iron foundry contains this noxious constituent in the shape of free silica; but their duty is clearly set out in section 47. It is to take all practicable measures to protect their workpeople from the inhalation of dust, and their duty to do that does not depend on the question whether the dust is known or believed to be noxious or not.'

15.52 In claims which are based upon exposure before a standard was set for an acceptable level of exposure, claims are usually put forward on the basis that the level of dust present was substantial or that it was offensive. There is no decided case which assists with the meaning to be given to the words 'substantial' or 'offensive' used in the section. There are many cases in which judges have concluded that the atmosphere in a factory was offensive or contained substantial quantities of asbestos dust, but the assessment is always a matter of impression for a judge, rather than something on which expert evidence is appropriate. By way of example Boreham J in *Brooks v J & P Coates (UK) Ltd* [1984] ICR 158 at 174 said:

> 'Thus, in my judgment, during the relevant time there is really insufficient evidence for me to find that the defendants ought to have considered this dust in this fine count mill as likely to be injurious to the persons employed there.

> But that is not the end of the matter. The question remains, if it was not injurious to their health was it offensive to them or to take the second leg, was it given off in a substantial quantity? In my judgment there is no doubt—and I have done my best to describe the sort of conditions which prevailed—that the quantity of dust was sufficient to be offensive to people working in that mill and certainly was sufficient to be regarded, to use the words of the Act, as in substantial quantity. It follows, therefore, that it was the defendants' duty under section 63(1) to take all practicable measures to protect the persons employed from inhaling dust; (2) to take all practicable measures to prevent the dust accumulating, and (3)—and I quote—"where the nature of the process makes it practicable, to provide exhaust-carrying appliances as near as possible to the point of origin of the dust so as to prevent it entering the air of any workroom".'

15.53 In actions in which the exposure to asbestos dust occurred after standards had been set for acceptable levels of dust, the claimant will usually contend that the level was one which was 'likely to be injurious' to his health. In such a case an expert witness will be needed to prove or disprove that the quantity of dust from the operations carried out, as described by the witnesses, was considered by the standards of the day to be 'likely to be injurious'.

The extent of the duty owed

15.54 The duty owed under these sections was not an absolute one, but the occupier of a factory was under a duty to take 'all practicable measures' to prevent inhalation of asbestos dust, a standard which was none the less a very high one. In *Brooks v J & P Coates (UK) Ltd* [1984] ICR 158, Boreham J paraphrased the statutory standard set saying, 'I take practicable in this context to mean a precaution which could be taken or undertaken without practical difficulty'.

15.55 However, the duty was subject to the important qualification that the occupier of the dust must know that it was present in the air, either as a result of it being visible in the air or when it settled in the factory. In *Gregson v Hick Hargreaves & Co Ltd* [1955] 1 WLR 1252, Jenkins LJ commented:

> 'No one, I apprehend, would suggest that under section 47 employers such as the defendants are required to guard against elements the existence of which is unknown and the presence of which cannot be detected. The defendants' duty under the second branch of the section is to protect against dust so far as practicable. That, as it seems to me, means to protect against the ordinary, visible, dust arising in the course of the foundry operations'.

Factories Act 1937, s 4 and Factories Act 1961, s 4

15.56 The Factories Act 1937, s 47, and the Factories Act 1961, s 63 provided that: 'where the nature of the process makes it practicable, exhaust appliances shall be provided and maintained, as near as possible to the point of origin of the dust or fume or other impurity, so as to prevent its entering the air of any workroom'. The duty under ss 4 of the Factories Acts 1937 and 1961 was not to provide exhaust ventilation by the source of the dust, but rather to ensure that it was present to remove the dust throughout the whole of a workroom.[1] The Acts provided that:

> 'Effective and suitable provision shall be made for securing and maintaining by the circulation of fresh air in each workroom the adequate ventilation of the room, and for rendering harmless, so far as practicable, all such fumes, dust and other impurities generated in the course of any process or work carried on in the factory as may be injurious to health.'

The requirement that the dust must be known by the standards of the day to have been likely to be injurious to health, limits the practical effect of the statutory provisions and, except in circumstances in which it imposes a duty on the occupier of a factory who was not the employer of the injured workman, it adds nothing to the common law duty of care.

[1]   *Ebbs v James Whitson & Co Ltd* [1952] 2 QB 877; *Graham v Co-operative Wholesale Society Ltd* [1957] 1 WLR 511.

THE CONSTRUCTION (GENERAL PROVISIONS) REGULATIONS 1961

15.57 Workers engaged in the construction and civil engineering industries were not well protected by statutory health and safety provisions until 1970. It has already been pointed out that some processes, especially the sawing of asbestos board with a power saw, were within the range of processes to which the Asbestos Industry Regulations 1931 applied. The first statutory scheme specific to these industries was that in the Building (Safety, Health and Welfare) Regulations 1948 which were in force between 1 October 1948 and 1 March 1962, when they were replaced by the Construction (General Provisions) Regulations 1961. The 1961 Regulations remained in force until 14 May 1970, when the relevant Regulation was made redundant so far as asbestos exposure was concerned by the more onerous obligations imposed by the Asbestos Regulations 1969.

15.58 The duties imposed under Building (Safety, Health and Welfare) Regulations 1948, reg 82, and the Construction (General Provisions) Regulations 1961, reg 20, were in identical terms. The Regulations provided:

> 'Where in connection with any grinding, cleaning, spraying or manipulation of any material, there is given off any dust or fume of such a character and to such extent as to be likely to be injurious to the health of persons employed, all reasonably practicable measures shall be taken either by securing adequate ventilation or by the provision and use of suitable respirators or otherwise to prevent inhalation of such dust or fume.'

15.59 The requirement that the dust must be of such a character and present to such an extent as to be likely to be injurious adds nothing to the nature of the duty to take reasonable care at common law. The duty is owed to all workmen employed by the contractor, whether engaged in the building operations or not: see *Field v Perrys (Ealing) Ltd* [1950] 2 All ER 521 per

Devlin J. However, a duty under the Regulations is not owed by the contractor creating asbestos dust to persons who are not employed by him.[1]

[1]   See *Smith v George Wimpey & Co Ltd* [1972] 2 QB 329, a decision of the Court of Appeal. The judgment starts with one of Lord Denning's best opening lines: 'In the autumn of 1966, a great highway, the M1, was built near Chesterfield'.

REGULATIONS IN THE SHIPBUILDING INDUSTRY

15.60 The scheme for the protection of workmen in shipyards against asbestos dust is unique, as there was a period during which the statutory protection afforded to workmen in shipyards was reduced. Shipyards were factory premises under the Factories Acts 1937 and 1961. The beneficial provisions of the Factories Act 1937, s 47, and the Factories Act 1961, s 63, provided protection against exposure to a substantial quantity of dust of any kind for so long as they applied to shipyards. On 31 March 1961 the provisions of the Shipbuilding and Ship-repairing Regulations 1960 came into force. Regulations 53 and 76 of those regulations contained provisions dealing with dust exposure. These provisions remained in force until 14 May 1970 when reg 76 was repealed and reg 53 was made redundant in respect of asbestos dust by the Asbestos Regulations 1969.

15.61 The Shipbuilding and Ship-repairing Regulations 1960, reg 53, provided:

'Where in connection with any process carried on on board, in or on the outside of a vessel or part of a vessel there is given off any dust or fume or other impurity of such a character and to such extent as to be likely to be injurious to the persons employed, all practicable measures shall be taken to protect the persons employed against inhalation of the dust or fume or other impurity, and in particular, where practicable, exhaust appliances shall be provided and maintained, as near as possible to the point of origin of the dust or fume or other impurity, to protect such persons against such inhalation.'

15.62 The duty under this regulation, with its requirement that the dust must be 'likely to be injurious', was potentially less onerous than the duty under the Factories Act 1937. By reg 53(2), reg 53 'shall, as respects the operations carried on board, in or on the outside of a vessel or part of a vessel, be in substitution for the provisions of s 47 of the principal Act (which relates to the removal of dust or fumes)'. The shipyard was therefore divided into parts with the provisions of the Factories Acts applying to the workshops and the provisions of the Shipbuilding and Ship-Repairing Regulations 1960 applying to work on the vessels themselves.

15.63 Regulation 76 imposed an obligation to provide approved respiratory equipment for a number of processes carried in shipyards. The processes covered were:

'(a)   the application of asbestos by means of a spray;
(b)   the breaking down for removal of asbestos lagging;
(c)   the cleaning of sacks or other containers which have contained asbestos;

(d)   the cutting of material containing asbestos by means of portable power driven saws; and

(e)   the scaling, scurfing or cleaning of boilers, combustion chambers or smoke boxes, where his work exposes him to dust of such a character and to such an extent as to be likely to be injurious or offensive to persons employed in such work.'

15.64 This provision contained the first statutory references to two dusty processes, the spraying of asbestos and the removal of old asbestos insulation, both of which any shipbuilder should have recognised as being dangerous, as evidenced by the fact that they were specifically mentioned in the Regulations. It also contained a specific reference to the need for respiratory protective equipment when power saws were used to cut asbestos board, a common process in shipyards.

15.65 The duty differed from that under the Factories Act in that the requirement to provide protection when there is a substantial quantity of dust present was omitted. There is no authority which determines the meaning of the word 'offensive' and whether a quantity of dust which is 'substantial' is also 'offensive' remains for consideration by the courts. In *Brooks v J & P Coates (UK) Ltd* [1984] ICR 158, Boreham J, concluded on the basis of the evidence in the case before him that the dust was both offensive and present in substantial quantities.

15.66 The duty under reg 76 was owed to employees only. However, the duty under reg 53 was owed by the person who is carrying out the operation which generated the dust to any person affected by the operation, whether or not that person is an employee.[1] The Asbestos Industry Regulations 1931 applied to certain processes in shipyards, as did the provisions of the Factories Acts when in force.

1   By reg 4(1)(b)(i).

THE ASBESTOS REGULATIONS 1969

15.67 The Asbestos Regulations 1969 came into force on 14 May 1970. They remained in force until 1 March 1988 when they were replaced by the provisions of the Control of Asbestos at Work Regulations 1987, SI 1987/2115. They were in substitution for the relevant provisions of the Factories Act 1961 and repealed the less onerous provisions of the Ship-Building and Ship-repairing Regulations 1960 and of the Asbestos Industry Regulations 1931. Although, the less onerous provisions contained in the Construction (General Provisions) Regulations 1961 remained in force, the obligations under the Asbestos Regulations 1969 imposed a more onerous duty in respect of asbestos dust than was imposed by those regulations.

15.68 The Regulations were introduced following the realisation during the 1960s that low levels of asbestos dust were capable of causing injury. The duties imposed under the regulations were considerably wider and more onerous than those imposed under the statutory provisions which they replaced. They were stricter in terms of the levels of exposure tolerated, wider in terms of the premises and operations covered, the persons who owed the duties and the persons to whom the duties were owed.

Levels of dust

15.69 Under reg 2(3) all references in the Regulations to asbestos dust 'shall be taken to be references to dust consisting of or containing asbestos to such an extent as is liable to cause danger to the health of employed persons'. The Regulations were supported by an Approved Code of Practice and by hygiene standards which specified the levels of asbestos dust which were regarded as being acceptable, measured in terms of both level of exposure and duration of exposure. The hygiene standards become progressively stricter with time and varied according to the type of asbestos in question. The original standard was taken by the Factory Inspectorate from a report prepared by the British Occupational Hygiene Society and was set at 2 fibres per cc for chrysotile and amosite asbestos and 0.2 fibres per cc for crocidolite asbestos (1 fibre per cc is the same as 1,000,000 fibres per cubic metre). Whether these standards have been breached in any particular case will be a matter for expert as well as lay evidence.

The premises and operations covered

15.70 The Regulations imposed duties in respect of all premises and operations for which special regulations for safety and health could be passed under powers conferred by the Factories Act 1961. Those were, by s 123, electrical stations, by s 124, institutions, by s 125, warehouses other than warehouses within any dock or forming part of any wharf or quay, by s 126, work aboard ships while in a harbour or wet dock and by s 127, building operations and works of engineering construction.

15.71 The Regulations applied to every process involving asbestos or any article composed wholly or partly of asbestos, except to a process in connection with which asbestos dust cannot be given off. They did not apply to asbestos dust given off at an intensity which was not liable to cause danger.

The persons who owe the duties and those to whom the duties are owed

15.72 Regulation 5(2) dealt with building operations and works of engineering construction and reg 5(1) dealt with other situations. Under reg 5(2):

> 'it shall be the duty of every contractor and of every employer who is undertaking any process to which these Regulations apply to comply with the Regulations in relation to any person employed by him and any person employed there who is liable to be exposed to asbestos dust in connection with any process carried on by the contractor or employer (as the case may be), and

in relation to plant or materials under his control and any part of the site where he is carrying on the process or where asbestos dust in connection with that process is liable to escape'.

15.73 The duty was thus owed to all persons who were affected by any escaping asbestos dust. In *Edgson v Vickers plc* [1994] ICR 510, the contractor who carried out the removal of asbestos from the ceiling of a factory was held liable under reg 5(2) to the workmen working in the factory who inhaled the dust escaping from the area in which he was working.

15.74 Under reg 5(1), the occupier of the factory in which a process to which the Regulations applied was being carried on was under a duty to provide any person employed in the factory, whether employed by him or not, with approved respiratory protective equipment and protective clothing under reg 8. He was also under a duty to provide suitable accommodation for the respiratory protective equipment and protective clothing and for cleaning the clothing under regs 18 and 19. He owed a duty to the same classes of person to ensure that the cleaning and cleanliness requirements of regs 9–14 were complied with. However, he did not owe these duties to persons employed by the employer who was carrying out the asbestos process.

15.75 In addition, every employer, whether or not an occupier of the factory, who was undertaking in a factory any process to which the regulations applied owed a duty to comply with the requirements of the regulations in relation to any person employed by it, to any plant or material under its control, and any part of the factory in which it was carrying on the process or into which asbestos dust in connection with that process was liable to escape.

15.76 A single individual carrying out a process to which the regulations applied owed the same duties he would have owed if he was an employer, and he owed those duties to the same classes of person.

15.77 The wording of regs 5(1)(b) and 5(2) makes it clear that the duty under reg 18 was owed 'in relation' to persons employed. The duty under reg 18, which had the effect of requiring that the workman's asbestos-coated clothing remained in the factory, would seem to have been drafted to take account of the contents of the Newhouse and Thompson article of 1965,[1] which had noted a number of deaths from mesothelioma among the families of those working with asbestos as a result of inhalation of the dust from clothing brought home by the workman. If this was the danger against which this provision was intended to provide protection, then the words 'in relation' to persons employed would seem to have been drafted widely enough to provide the families of workmen who were exposed to dust brought home by the exposed workmen on his dirty clothing with a civil cause of action for breach of statutory duty. In *Hewett v Alf Brown's Transport Ltd* [1992] ICR 530, a case in which the statutory duty relied upon was a duty to provide uncontaminated clothing under the Control of Lead at Work Regulations 1980, the Court of Appeal had to consider a similar statutory provision. The claimant was the wife of a lorry driver and had become contaminated with lead as a result of cleaning her husband's overalls. Although the claim was dismissed on the ground that the employer was not in breach of the duty owed to the husband and had not exposed him to a prohibited amount of lead, the Court of Appeal seemed to accept the suggestion that Mrs Hewett was entitled to rely on this statutory duty, a statutory duty which was in very similar terms to that under the Asbestos Regulations 1969.

1   *British Journal of Industrial Medicine* (1965) Vol 22, p 261.

The precautions required by the Regulations

15.78 Regulation 7 dealt with ventilation. It provided that no process to which the Regulations applied was to be carried on in any factory unless equipment was provided, maintained and used, which produced an exhaust draught which prevented the entry into the air of any workplace of asbestos dust. Only if it was impracticable to comply with reg 7, did the duty become a duty to comply with reg 8. It was this provision which required, indirectly, the sheeting-off of the areas in which asbestos was being removed, in order to prevent the asbestos dust coming into contact with others present nearby.

15.79 Regulation 8 required the provision and use of approved respiratory protective equipment and protective clothing. The standard of the respiratory equipment required improved over time. A Martindale mask, a device which presses a pad of cloth against the mouth and nose, was never approved for use with asbestos and was ineffective to prevent asbestos dust from being inhaled.

15.80 Regulations 9–13 provided for the removal of asbestos dust and debris which had settled in the premises, by means of equipment which ensured that asbestos dust neither escaped nor was discharged into the air of any workplace.

Regulation 14 required that clothing not worn at work must be kept free of asbestos dust and reg 18 required that protective clothing must be kept at work.

MODERN ASBESTOS LEGISLATION

15.81 The provisions of the Asbestos Regulations 1969 remained in force until 1 March 1988 when they were replaced by the Control of Asbestos at Work Regulations 1987 and later by the Control of Asbestos in the Air Regulations 1990. Modern asbestos legislation is dealt with in chapter 22.

Table showing the statutory duties in force in respect of asbestos dust

	In force from	Repealed, or redundant after
Asbestos Industry Regulations 1931	1 March 1932 or 1 September 1932	14 May 1970
Factories Act 1937	1 March 1938	1 April 1962
Building (SHW) Regulations 1948	1 October1948	1 March 1962
Shipbuilding Regulations 1960	31 March 1961	Redundant after 14 May 1970
Construction (General Provisions) Regulations 1961	1 March 1962	Redundant after 14 May 1970
Factories Act 1961	1 April 1962	Redundant after 14 May 1970
Asbestos Regulations 1969	14 May 1970	1 March 1988

Chapter 16

HAND-ARM VIBRATION SYNDROME ('HAVS')

Ian Scott

16.01 The use of hand-held vibratory tools is a widespread phenomenon extending across numerous industries and occupations.[1] Their use ranges across manufacturing to agriculture and forestry, the public utilities and the building industry. The HSE[2] has recently drawn attention to a report[3] which indicates that about 5 million people are exposed to hand-arm vibration through their work activities. Of those it is estimated that as many as two million are risk of developing the disease. It is further estimated that around 800,000 people in Britain had some symptoms of vibration white finger linked to exposure to vibration at work and of these 300,000 were estimated to have advanced symptoms of the disease.

[1] See K Kyriakides *Survey of exposure to hand-arm vibration in Great Britain* (HSE Research Paper 26, 1988). For a detailed consideration of the medical factors associated with such injuries, we recommend *Hunter's Diseases of Occupations* (9th edn) at 307pp.
[2] HSE Consultation Document on Proposals for Control of Vibration at Work Regulations, November 2003, Preface to Annex 2.
[3] Contract Research Report 232/1999. Hand-transmitted vibration: Occupational exposures and their health effects in Great Britain (Medical Research Council Environmental Epidemiology Unit and the Institute of Sound and Vibration Research).

DIAGNOSIS AND ASSESSMENT

16.02 The syndrome is described in the HSE booklet *Hand-Arm Vibration HSG88*:

> '66. ... The term HAVS has been used to describe the effects of hand-transmitted vibration on the upper limb but is not clearly defined. In the United Kingdon, HAVS is considered to exist if, after prolonged exposure to hand-transmitted vibration, involvement of the vascular and/or peripheral nervous system occurs, with or without musculoskeletal involvement.

> 67. The symptoms result from pathological effects on the peripheral vascular system, peripheral nervous system, muscles, bones, tendons and soft tissues. Episodic finger blanching is the most widely known of these effects, but sensory changes are now being given greater importance. A particular worker who has signs or symptoms of one or more of the possible effects of hand-transmitted vibration on the upper limb may be considered as suffering from HAVS.'

16.03 Difficulties with diagnosis arise as the cause of the symptoms may be constitutional rather than work-related and there is no objective test which establishes the existence of the syndrome.[1] It is only when:

410

(a) other potential medical causes of the symptoms have been excluded;
(b) there is an appropriate work history involving regular exposure to hand-held vibratory tools; combined with
(c) an appropriate description by the claimant of symptoms which are recognised as being consistent with the disease that a diagnosis of HAVS can properly be made.

1 Between 4% and 6% of men suffer from 'Primary Raynaud's Disease' or 'constitutional white finger' a phenomenon through no known cause. The figure is higher for women.

16.04 The latent period between first exposure and development of symptoms can range from six months to more than 20 years (related to the intensity of the exposure and variable personal susceptibility). Inevitably, the reliance on the account given by the claimant as an essential part of the diagnostic process often leads to issues of credibility being pursued at trial. Examples of diagnostic indicators which point to a constitutional as opposed to a work-related cause include the claimant experiencing coldness in their feet or other extremities. Further, carpal tunnel syndrome ('CTS'), which can also be caused by exposure to vibration (and may also be caused constitutionally), can produce similar neurological symptoms in particular fingers. CTS is a separate prescribed disease (A12) and is actionable by a claimant. Other diseases which have been accepted as capable of being vibration induced include Palmer Arch Disease—damage to the artery in palm which supplies blood to fingers[1]—and Hypothenar Hammer Syndrome—damage of artery at base of thumb.

1 Eg *Griggs v Transco plc* [2003] EWCA Civ 564.

16.05 Whether or not a claimant is suffering from HAVS is a matter of fact for the judge. The Court of Appeal has recently confirmed that position in *Whalley v Montracon Ltd* [2005] EWCA Civ 1383. At first instance the claimant's medical expert changed his opinion as a result of listening to the claimant's description of his symptoms. As a result both doctors agreed that the claimant did not have HAVS. The judge at first instance believed the claimant's evidence and found that the claimant suffered from HAVS. The Court of Appeal upheld the judge's finding. The judge was entitled to find in favour of the claimant on the balance of probabilities on the totality of the evidence, even though that evidence contained an element which pointed against the judge's conclusion.

Classification of symptoms

16.06 The most widely respected and applied classification is now the Stockholm Workshop scale, developed in 1986, rather than the Taylor/Pelmear Scale. The Stockholm scale recognises the importance of neurological symptoms which are assessed separately to the vascular symptoms. It is accepted that vascular and neurological symptoms can (and often do) progress separately. A claimant may not suffer any vascular symptoms at all but display neurological damage. The HSE recommends application of the Stockholm Workshop scales which are conveniently set out in the HSE booklet *Hand-arm vibration* (HS(G)88) at Table 5.

16.07 For many years the consequences of such exposure to hand-held tools was not regarded as resulting in any particularly debilitating injury. However, over recent years the serious consequences of exposure to such tools, including permanent neurological damage, have become recognised and accepted. In particular, the outcome of multi-party litigation against British Coal in the 1990s increased awareness of the significant effect on an injured user: *Armstrong v British Coal Corpn* [1997] 8 Med LR 259, CA. Furthermore, the outcome of *Armstrong* raised the normal level of damages awards substantially and led to a significant upward revision in the Judicial Studies Board Guidelines for General Damages. The Court of Appeal did not disturb the general damages awarded at first instance: *Armstrong v British Coal Corpn* [1998] JPIL 320, CA.[1] The outcome of the multi-party litigation on behalf of the miners has been the agreement of a claims handling arrangement negotiated between the DTI and the group of solicitors representing the injured miners, under which 160,000 are being dealt with. Following *Armstrong* two further multi-party VWF judgments confirmed the seriousness with which the syndrome was treated: *Hall v British Gas plc* (7 April 1998, unreported) and *Allen v British Rail Engineering Ltd* (7 October 1998, unreported), QBD (see para 3.34, above).

[1]   The case went to the Court of Appeal twice, in 1996 and 1998.

16.08 The most widely familiar symptoms of HAVS are of cold-induced episodic blanching of the parts or the whole of fingers (vascular), which is generally known as vibration white finger. In fact the term is a misnomer as the condition normally affects a number of fingers on both hands (only in the most serious of cases thumbs) and is best regarded as a hand disability.[1] The onset of blanching and the return of the blood are often associated with intense pain. It should be noted however that it is now recognised that it is the permanent neurological damage resulting in symptoms of lack of sensitivity and clumsiness in the hands which is probably more serious and debilitating.

[1]   'The fact that the classifications themselves refer to the "fingers" or the "digits" and indeed that the name of the condition itself is vibration white finger may divert attention from the fact that in a severe case this injury should properly be regarded as damaging the hand or hands rather than being confined to the fingers' per Judge LJ in *Armstrong v British Coal Corpn* [1998] JPIL 320, CA.

Date of knowledge

16.09 Knowledge as to the possible damaging effects of operating hand-held power tools has been developing since as early as 1911.[1] Although there is no recognised universal date of knowledge applicable across all industries, in three recent multi-party group VWF judgments the date of knowledge in all of them was found to be the mid-1970s:

(1)   *Armstrong (British Coal):* the date from which the nationalised coal industry knew or ought to have known of a foreseeable risk of injury to underground and workshop workers was held to be 1 January 1973; the precautions of warnings and medical examination, 1 January 1975; job rotation, 1 January 1976;

(2) *Hall (British Gas)*: by the end of 1975 the nationalised gas industry should have been aware of the injury that vibrating tools were causing to their road workers and have implemented a comprehensive range of measures to minimise the risk;

(3) *Allen (BREL)*: by mid-1973, the surveys which should have been carried out would have revealed an incidence of VWF amongst riveters, platers and welders. The defendants should have warned these workers by the end of 1973, and by the end of 1974 a system of periodic medical examination for all exposed employees should have been instituted.

Further, in *Brown v Corus (UK) Ltd* [2004] PIQR P476, the defendant admitted that by the beginning of 1976 it ought to have been aware of the risk of injury from vibratory tools.

1   Eg 1911 Loriga 'Il Lavoro con Martelli pneumatic' Boll Ispett Lavoro 35–60.

16.10 In respect of fettling, Mr Justice Eastham in his judgment in *Musto v Saunders Safety Valve Co Ltd* (25 May 1979, unreported), stated:

'... In my view, on the totality of the evidence in this case by March 1969 seven facts were generally known in the industry, and I mean industry and not merely the medical profession:

1   It was known that operators of vibratory tools who were engaged in grinding work were at risk of developing VWF;

2   It was known that a significant percentage of such workers were likely to develop VWF to some extent ...'.

16.11 It is emphasised that the tools and work processes associated with the above judgments do not establish a date of knowledge across all industries. The importance of evidence at trial related to a particular employer's date of knowledge, and the triggering of an individual employer's duties to take precautions has been highlighted by two relatively recent Court of Appeal judgments: *Doherty v Rugby Joinery (UK) Ltd* [2004] EWCA Civ 147, [2004] ICR 1272 and *Brookes v (1) South Yorkshire Passenger Transport Executive (2) Mainline Group Ltd* [2005] EWCA Civ 452.

16.12 In *Doherty* as regards the defendants' constructive knowledge (the lack of actual knowledge was not in issue) the judge at first instance held that a reasonable employer would not have regarded warnings about dangers of exposing the human hand-arm system to vibration in a British Standards Institution draft for development published in 1975 (DD43) as applying to the woodworking industry. He also found that a guide which replaced the draft in 1987 (BS 6842) would not have alerted a reasonable employer in the defendants' position to the danger of using an orbital sander, as no employees had at that time complained of symptoms, finding instead constructive knowledge to run from 1991. The Court of Appeal dismissed the appeals of the four claimants whose only exposure pre-dated 1991 on the grounds that in the light of the expert evidence the judge at first instance had been entitled to conclude that, for the woodworking industry, neither the draft for development nor the guide was, by itself and in the absence of any complaint of symptoms by an employee, sufficient to trigger the defendants duties to take steps to protect the claimants from VWF. The judgment of Hale LJ in *Doherty* states:

> '40... The date of knowledge that hand-held vibratory tools might lead to VWF is generally put in the 1970s. There was nothing in the pleadings to suggest that the date of knowledge was in issue in these actions. The defence in all eight actions took issue with the level of exposure claimed by each claimant, but did not assert that at the date of their claimed exposure it was not reasonably foreseeable that the claimants might suffer VWF if over-exposed to vibration from the tools used at work.
>
> 53... If these employers had addressed their minds to the risks at an earlier stage and taken the step of having their tools examined they would not have been alerted to the risks except within the recommended levels.'

It should be noted however that both Hale LJ and Auld LJ emphasised that the case did not establish a general proposition that the date of knowledge of the risk of VWF in the woodworking industry is as late as 1991/92. It was the lack of evidence demonstrating that the particular employer should have known of the risk and taken precautions which was the cornerstone of the judgment.

16.13 In *Brookes* the judge at first instance held that the defendants had knowledge from 1975 and were liable to pay damages for their negligent exposure of the claimant (a fitter) to harmful vibration throughout his employment which began in 1982. At trial the defendants' position was that they had no actual knowledge of VWF. They had had no complaints from their workforce or the trade union about VWF. The first case of VWF of which they were aware within their workforce arose in the late 1990s. The defendants contended that they could not reasonably have been expected to be aware of the risks of VWF until 1994 when the HSE published guidance on VWF entitled 'Hand-Arm Vibration' (HSG88). The defendants averred that they knew nothing of DD43 or BS6842. The judge held that the defendants should have been aware of the potential risk of VWF in 1975 on the publication of DD43. The Court of Appeal upheld the defendants' appeal in respect of their constructive knowledge of DD43, as there was insufficient evidence to support the conclusion that the defendants ought to have been aware of DD43. Amongst other things, the Court of Appeal noted the absence of any evidence as to how and to what extent DD43 was publicised and discussed or written about in trade publications. In respect of BS6842 in 1987, however, the Court of Appeal held that it was of much greater significance for employers than DD43 had been and referred, amongst other things, to the fact that it was published against the background that VWF was by then a prescribed disease. The defendants were fixed with knowledge of BS6842 at or shortly after publication and should have taken remedial steps two years thereafter, in 1989.

16.14 Again in *Brookes* it should be noted that the Court of Appeal emphasised that it was not making a finding of general application that liability for VWF in fitters working in the transport industry arose in 1989:

'23 ... In another case, there may be evidence that would enable a judge to conclude that the particular employer was or should have been aware of the risk of harm to its employees much earlier than 1989, possibly because it was or should have been aware of DD43 ...'.

16.15 There are nonetheless a number of publications which are often referred to by engineering reports as the basis of constructive knowledge of the risks associated with the use of hand-held vibratory tools. The following paragraphs list some of them. However, it should be borne in mind that, applying the guidance from *Doherty* and *Brookes*, evidence is required as to how such documents came to or should have come to the attention of a particular employer. The most significant warrant detailed consideration.

16.16 *Draft for Development* (BSI DD43, February 1975): A guide to the evaluation of exposure of the human hand-arm system to vibration. The guide was:

'of a provisional nature because the present state of knowledge of the effects of exposure to vibration generated by hand-held tools or processes does not yet enable definite conclusions to be reached concerning the vibration levels to be specified for those tools or processes.'

DD43 is often misunderstood as regards exposure times referred to and whether or not they can be said to be safe.[1]

[1] Smith J (as she then was) explained the position clearly at first instance in *Allen* at para 20: '... The guide did not claim to be able to suggest safe levels of exposure to vibration. It comprised a graph of vibration levels plotted against frequencies on which vibration levels, thought to be unsafe, were given for two types of exposure; one for the man who used a vibrating tool for up to as much as 400 minutes per day; the other for a man who used a vibrating tool regularly but for not more than 150 minutes per day. For usage of 400 minutes, acceleration at the low frequencies, was not to exceed $1m/s^2$. For usage for 150 minutes, the maximum at low frequencies was $10m/s^2$. For the higher frequencies, the maxima could be read off the graph. The first defendants argued at trial that there was no exposure limit for men who used the vibrating tools for less than 150 minutes per day as these would not be classed as "regular users" and the guide only applied to "regular users". I cannot see how the guidance could sensibly have been so understood. The graph itself is marked "unacceptable vibration levels" above the 150 minute line and the guide contained explanatory notes which provided: "It is recommended that cumulative exposure time to vibration should never exceed 400 minutes; for intermediate periods between 150 and 400 minutes some interpolation should be made; the values given for 150 minutes apply for all shorter periods. These latter values should not be exceeded by regular users of hand held equipment". The confusion apparently arose because in an earlier paragraph the guide said: "It is expected that a regular user in industry will be subject to at least 150 minutes cumulative exposure per day." In my judgment there is no real difficulty about this as the advice is clear that the values given for 150 minutes apply to all shorter periods'.

16.17 *Vibration injuries—the conduct of the reasonable and prudent employer* (Southampton University, August 1978): A collection of notes to accompany a series of one-day seminars. In dealing with the topic of vibration injuries and the law this authoritative source, whose authors included the widely recognised expert Professor MJ Griffin, when dealing with negligence include the following comment:

'... The reasonable employer of the seventies will very rarely indeed be allowed to say "I never heard of it". It is difficult to set a date. The sixties show the reasonable employer perhaps a little more ignorant, the fifties more so again.'

Professor W Taylor, another leading authority, in 'Vibration White Finger in the Workplace' (1982) 32 Jnl Soc Occ Med 159–166 at 164, set out a number of steps which employers' medical departments are advised to take 'to avoid the stigma of negligence'. The advice included pre-employment warnings and medical surveillance of exposed employees.

16.18 By the Social Security (Industrial Injuries) (Prescribed Diseases) Regulations 1985, SI 1985/967, vibration white finger was prescribed for the following industries:

(a)   the use of hand-held chainsaws in forestry;

(b)   the use of hand-held rotary tools in grinding or in the sanding or polishing of metal, or the holding of materials being ground, or metal being sanded or polished, by rotary tools; or

(c)   the use of hand-held percussive metal-working tools, or the holding of metal being worked upon by percussive tools, in riveting, caulking, chipping, hammering, fettling or swaging; or

(d)   the use of hand-held powered percussive drills or hand-held powered percussive hammers in mining, quarrying, demolition, or on roads or footpaths, including road construction; or

(e)   the holding of material being worked upon by pounding machines in shoe manufacture.

It is difficult to see that many employers will be able to rely on a date of knowledge beyond the date of vibration white finger becoming a prescribed disease and reportable under the Reporting of Injuries, Diseases and Dangerous Occurrences Regulations 1985, SI 1985/2023 (see chapter 11 for more details on RIDDOR).

16.19 BS 6842 1987: British Standard Guide to measurement and evaluation of human exposure to vibration transmitted to the hand: The guide shows the frequency weighted vibration magnitudes expected to produce finger blanching in 10% of persons exposed for daily exposure times from 15 minutes to 8 hours. It is to be noted that the guide is not predictive for an individual, but only relates to exposed populations. The Standard also sets out guidelines on preventative measures.

16.20 HSE Hand-Arm Vibration HSG88 1994 (reprinted with limited amendments in 2001): The HSE gives guidance to the hazards and control programmes, technical ways to reduce vibration and clinical effects and the health surveillance programmes. It is the source of the HSE recommended action level of exposure at 2.8m/s squared. See the footnote to para 21 of HSG88 that the action level is not to be regarded as a completely 'safe' level. See now also the Control of Vibration at Work Regulations 2005, below at para 16.29.

BREACH OF DUTY

16.21 Having established a date of knowledge and the diagnosis of the condition it remains necessary for the claimant to establish breach of duty. What exposure to vibration (assuming that such exposure is later than the date of knowledge) is likely to be regarded as posing a foreseeable risk of injury?

16.22 The first step is to assess both the time per day that an employee is exposed to vibration, together with the intensity of exposure produced by the tool(s) being operated. Care is needed to assess the time that a tool is actually operating in the employee's hands, known as 'anger time'.

16.23 The magnitude of vibration given off differs from one tool to another. The usual measurement is frequency-weighted acceleration expressed in root mean square (rms) metres per second (m/s^2), eg pneumatic drills and picks (jackhammers) are recognised as generating about $20m/s^2$. The higher the value the greater is the risk associated with the tool. Vibration exposure from a tool is usually averaged on the basis of an 8-hour period (per day) known as an 'A8'. If (as is often the case) an employee uses a number of tools the A8 for each tool must be added to obtain a daily A8. Chapter 4 of the HSE booklet *Hand-arm vibration* (HS(G)88) describes the measurement process. Expert evidence will be required if the matter is to be of dispute. A nomogram used for calculating daily exposure to vibration appears in HS(G)88 (figure 10, p 43) and provides a useful initial assessment of the possible strength of a claim.

16.24 The HSE recommended that a programme of preventative measures and health surveillance should be instituted where exposure regularly exceeds an A8 of $2.8m/s^2$: HS(G)88, para 21. In the footnote to that paragraph there is guidance that the action level should not be regarded as safe. The action level is derived from BS6842 (see above) and reflects conditions which are expected to result in 10% of an exposed population developing blanching in eight years, but as the HSE put it:

'... this estimate is subject to considerable uncertainty. The action level should not therefore be regarded as a completely "safe" level'.

Applying, for example, the HSE action level of an A8 of $2.8m/s^2$ to the use of a rock drill whose frequency weighted acceleration is $20 m/s^2$ it will be seen via the nomogram (see HS(G)88, paras 122 to 126) that it would require less than 10 minutes operation per day to produce the action level of exposure.

16.25 In *Armstrong* the Court of Appeal considered the level of exposure which should have been reduced by job rotation. Judge LJ concluded:[1]

'... assuming that the defendants had been alert to the risk of VWF, I am satisfied that standards higher than those advised in the 1994 booklet should not be imposed upon them. This conclusion is not intended to lay down guidelines about appropriate levels of exposure in other employments. All it means is that when considering the reasonable safety of those employees exposed to vibrating tools the 1994 booklet provides a standard which it would have been reasonable for the defendants as prudent employers to apply when considering the appropriate level of permissible exposure. However, after January 1976 any level of exposure in excess of that advised by the handbook required job rotation, in addition to warnings, surveillance and other precautions identified at the first hearing.'

1   [1998] JPIL 320, CA at 20A–D.

16.26 Though the Court of Appeal did not finally decide the point, it thus appears clear that exposure above an A8 of 2.8m/s^2 is likely to be found to have been negligent and require the precaution of job rotation to lower it. Post the date of knowledge, where exposure is lower than an exposure of an A8 of 2.8m/s^2 the duty to warn and educate employees on the characteristic signs of first symptoms and the need to report such symptoms still exists and breach of such duty can provide the basis of establishing liability in appropriate circumstances.[1] The decision of Field J in *Billington v BREL* [2002] EWHC 105 is further authority for this point. The most specific statement on foreseeability within the published governmental guidance is in BS6842: 1987, which refers to exposure below 1m/s^2 as posing no foreseeable risk of injury.

1   See the lead case of *Stokoe v British Coal Corpn* as part of *Armstrong v British Coal Corpn* (September 1997, unreported) HHJ Stephenson at p 35, para (9): liability established with an A8 of 1.48. *Armstrong* also contains consideration of the nature of the warning.

16.27 Once the action level of 2.8m/s^2 has been exceeded, the the HSE 1994 guidance requires: (a) the implementation of medical surveillance; and (b) the introduction of control measures to reduce exposure to vibration, including: use of low vibration and damped tools; maintained equipment to ensure low vibration; consideration of the work process and methods to reduce use of vibrating tools (eg substitution with non-vibrating tools); rotation of jobs; education on techniques for holding tools. The Court of Appeal considered and approved a list of steps which a defendant should take in respect of the 2.8m/s^2 action level in *Brown v Corus* [2004] EWCA Civ 374.[1]

1   At paras 51–55, Scott Baker LJ.

Statutory duty

16.28 The Provision and Use of Work Equipment Regulations 1992, SI 1992/2932 (which were in force from 1 January 1993) and the Provision and Use of Work Equipment Regulations 1998, SI 1998/2306 (in force from 5 December 1998) are applicable to the vibratory tools associated with the risk of developing VWF. As yet there is no authority as to the effect of the Regulations upon the provision and use vibratory tools. See chapter 20 for a full consideration of these regulations.

The Control of Vibration at Work Regulations 2005

16.29 Following consultation on proposals for new Control of Vibration at Work Regulations to implement the Physical Agents (Vibration) Directive

(2002/44/EC) carried out by the HSE via a Consultative Document issued in November 2003 (CD 190), new Regulations controlling vibration at work came into force on 6 July 2005.[1] The Regulations are accompanied by HSE Guidance on the Regulations in respect of hand-arm vibration. It should be noted that the HSE Guidance to the 2005 Regulations replaces the previous HSE Guidance HSG88 originally published in 1994 (and reprinted in 2001).

1   The Control of Vibration at Work Regulations 2005, SI 2005/1093.

16.30 The Regulations set a daily exposure limit value of $5m/s^2$ and a daily exposure action value of $2.5m/s^2$. It should be noted that the exposure action value of 2.5 is reduced from the previous action level set in the previous HSE 1994 Guidance of $2.8m/s^2$. It is also to be noted that there is a transitional period for the commencement of the operation of limit values in the case of work equipment provided before 6 July 2007. For such work equipment, commencement is postponed until 6 July 2010. The transitional period applies only to the exposure limit value.

16.31 The other requirements of the Regulations came into force on 6 July 2005 and have to be complied with from that date. They include a duty to carry out a suitable and sufficient assessment of risk and identify the measures needed to meet the requirements of the Regulations (reg 5); elimination or, where elimination is not reasonably practicable, reduction of exposure to vibration to as low a level as is reasonably practicable (reg 6(1)); health surveillance (reg 7); the provision of suitable and sufficient information, instruction and training where risk assessment indicates there is a risk to health or where employees are likely to be exposed to vibration above the exposure action value (reg 8).

CAUSATION

16.32 Consideration of the application of the principles of causation in VWF cases has been considered by the Court of Appeal in *Brown v Corus (UK) Ltd* [2004] PIQR P476 and is based upon the classic consideration of causation in industrial disease law set out by *Bonnington Castings Ltd v Wardlaw* [1956] 1 All ER 615 and *McGhee v NCB* [1972] 3 All ER 1008.[1] The court held that the judge at first instance was wrong to find that the defendants were not in breach of duty in failing to reduce the vibration levels to which the claimants were exposed. In relation to causation, the claimants did not have to show to what extent reduction in vibration levels would have made a difference. The court concluded that:

> '48 ... once the position is reached that the respondents were in breach of duty in failing to reduce the vibration levels to which these three appellants were exposed, causation is established on the *McGhee* principle [ie *McGhee v National Coal Board* [1973] 1 WLR 1]. By not doing anything about vibration levels (and there were a number of things that could have been done) the respondents materially increased the risk that the appellants would suffer from HAVS. Had they taken such steps they would have materially reduced the risk

419

involved. Their failure to do so, in the words of Lord Simon in *McGhee*, made a substantial to the condition from which they suffer ...'.

1   See chapter 3, above for further consideration.

16.33 The court reached the same conclusion in respect of the effect of training where it again concluded that the judge was wrong to conclude that the causative link was not established:

'55 ... The court did not have to know the precise reduction in exposure that would have been brought about. It is enough that there would have been some reduction which, in our judgment on the evidence, there plainly would have been and this would have reduced the risk of injury to the appellants. Again the *McGhee* test applies'.

APPORTIONMENT

16.34 For a consideration of issues of apportionment in industrial disease generally, please see chapter 3, particularly para 3.25, above.

16.35 A discount is to be made from the full liability damages for the development of HAVS where symptoms have developed prior to the date of guilty knowledge of the employer. The discount concerned is related to the seriousness of the condition which has developed prior to the date of knowledge. In addition to the conventional discount made for symptoms which have developed prior to the date of knowledge, some complications have arisen related to apportionment of damages as a result of the accepted fact that the disease is caused by the cumulative exposure to vibration, ie it is dose-related. In particular, issues have arisen as to whether there should be a discount to damages to reflect non-negligent pre-date of guilty knowledge asymptomatic damage and whether there should be post date of guilty knowledge discount for non-negligent exposure, ie exposure which would have occurred in any event had the defendant complied with its duty.

16.36 As regards pre-date of knowledge discounts for asymptomatic damage, the judge at first instance in *Armstrong* made nominal reductions of £500–£700 for such damage. However, in *Hall* the judge did not make any such reductions as there was no evidential basis on which to make such a discount. There are thus conflicting first instance judgments as to whether such discounts are appropriate.

16.37 In respect of post-date of knowledge discounts, Smith J (as she then was) in *Allen v British Rail Engineering Ltd* at first instance made deductions from damages to reflect an assessment of what damage would have been caused by non-negligent exposure to vibration, ie that which would have occurred in any event even had the defendants complied with their duty. The judge did not apportion on a straight line basis, as she took the view that damages should reflect the onset and progress of the disability as well as actual damage. She gave greater weight to exposure after symptoms began than to early exposure (eg at para 126 of the judgment in respect of Mr Allen). The assessment of the stage to which the disease would have progressed under the influence of only non-negligent exposure was treated as a jury point. The Court of Appeal supported the judge's approach (see *Allen v British Rail Engineering Ltd* [2001] EWCA Civ 242, [2001] ICR 942).

16.38 Further consideration has recently been given to the approach which was adopted in *Allen*. In *Brookes v (1) South Yorkshire Passenger Transport Executive (2) Mainline Group Ltd* [2005] EWCA Civ 452 the Court of Appeal found (Smith LJ giving the court's judgment), in response to the defendants reliance on *Allen* for a submission that damages should be reduced to reflect non-negligent exposure, that there should be no discount from the claimant's damages for any such exposure. The claimant did not develop symptoms until 1999, about 17 years after his vibration exposure had commenced and ten years after the date by which remedial steps should have been taken. It was held that the claimant could properly argue that, but for the defendants' negligence, he would never have had any symptoms. The court held there was no evidential basis to justify any reduction in his damages. It was further held that the fact that damage is dose-related did not of itself lay the necessary evidential basis for any reduction. Arising from *Brookes* it can properly be argued:

(a)   *Allen* did not establish a principle that a defendant has a right to a discount for non-negligent exposure;

(b)   there has to be some evidential basis on which to make an assessment, and in the absence of such evidence the claimant should receive full damages because the negligence has made a material contribution to his condition; and

(c)   the fact that HAVS is dose-related is not of itself sufficient evidence to justify a discount.

16.39 The Court of Appeal's approach in *Brookes* is consistent with an earlier consideration of apportionment in *Smith v Wright & Beyer Ltd* [2001] EWCA Civ 1069. The central issue in the appeal was a submission that because a substantial amount of the claimant's exposure was before 1977, the judge ought to have made a discount from damages to allow for non-negligent exposure. The date of guilty knowledge was identified at first instance as 1975 with an allowance to 1977 for appropriate precautions to have been put in place. The claimant had been employed by the defendants since 1961. In the mid-1980s he experienced blanching of the fingers which by 1987 was affecting his sleep. The Court of Appeal upheld the judge's decision not to make any discount from full liability damages:

'He (the judge) was entitled to reach the conclusion that in 1977 it was open to the defendants, had they wished to discharge the duty on them as employers, to have "reorganised their working practice so as to reduce exposure to vibration and hence the claimant may not ever have reached the stage when he would have experienced symptoms".'

Chapter 17

OTHER OCCUPATIONAL DISEASES

Daniel Bennett

WORK-RELATED MUSCULO-SKELETAL DISORDERS

Introduction

17.01 This group of injuries (which can be known by many collective terms) are caused or aggravated by forceful, repetitive and awkward movements with insufficient rest or recovery time.[1] The term colloquially used to describe the group of injuries is 'repetitive strain injury' (RSI). This would be a useful portmanteau term for this group of known conditions that can be caused by work and it remains in use by the HSE. However its use in court is generally discouraged as it also used by medical practitioners to describe a non-specific diffuse pain to the forearm caused by work. It is to some extent discredited as a medical condition and following *Mughal v Reuters Ltd* [1993] IRLR 571, it is not recognised by the courts as a distinct injury (see para 17.04, below). The majority of this group of injuries are to the hands, wrists, elbows and shoulders and for that reason the term 'upper limb disorders' (ULDs) is commonly used. When these are caused occupationally, they are known as 'work-related upper limb disorders' (WRULDs). We have adopted the HSE's preferred terminology of musculo-skeletal disorders (MSDs) as this also covers neck, leg and low back pain caused by work. It is important to bear in mind that injuries to other parts of the body can and do fall within the general rubric of this chapter; eg injuries to the heel such as plantar faciitis (policeman's heel). Within the terminology of ULD or MSD conditions such as lateral and medial epicondylitis (tennis and golfer's elbow), tenosynovitis, peritendinitis and carpal tunnel syndrome are the most commonly diagnosed. Each describes a disease or injury which can be also caused by constitutional factors unrelated to work. The question of whether each condition is work-related is a factual matter resolved by expert (usually medical) evidence. Since most medical conditions considered in this chapter may be related to work but may also be related to other causes, causation will almost always be in issue. As a result it is often unhelpful to adopt a term that implies that it is not (such as WRULDs). Accordingly, this chapter adopts the term 'musculo-skeletal disorders' as appropriate. It is neutral, so far as causation is concerned, and covers injuries to all parts of the body.

[1] For a detailed consideration of the medical factors associated with such injuries, we recommend *Hunter's Diseases of Occupations* (9th edn) at 453pp.

17.02 The cases can usefully be split into two categories from a legal perspective: (a) injuries related to keyboard work and computers generally; and (b) all other injuries. The split is useful only because musculo-skeletal disorders arising out of work with keyboards and computers are dealt with by way of statutory duty in the Health and Safety (Display Screen Equipment)

Regulations 1992, SI 1992/2792.[1] As regards the remaining cases, these are very varied in circumstances. Cases can arise from office-based and manual jobs and examples include repetitive assembly line work, inspection and packing, meat and poultry preparation and laboratory work.[2] However, much of the earlier common law is defined by cases relating to typing and data entry, which would not be dealt with under the 1992 Regulations.

[1]   These Regulations are dealt with below in chapter 20 relating to work equipment at para 20.79 onwards.
[2]   See HSE Guidance 7/99 Upper Limb Disorders—Assessing the Risks.

Injuries

17.03 Musculo-skeletal disorders can be described as falling into two types: those conditions well-recognised as distinct pathological conditions, on the one hand, and those which do not show the pattern of a defined pathology. The latter can rarely amount to injuries in a legal context. Recognised pathological conditions include tenosynovitis (an inflammation of the tendon sheath), peritendinitis (an inflammation of the soft tissues surrounding a tendon), carpal tunnel syndrome (a condition caused by pressure on the median nerve as it passes through the carpal tunnel), cubital tunnel syndrome, median nerve compression in the forearm, lateral epicondylitis (tennis elbow), medial epicondylitis (golfer's elbow), de Quervain's disease (a tenovaginitis of the long abductor and short extensor tendons of the thumb), trigger finger, or trigger thumb, rupture of the long head of biceps, rotator cuff syndrome (a shoulder injury), capsulitis of the shoulder. To this list may also be added vibration white finger, characterised by intermittent blanching of the digits (the work-induced form of Raynaud's Phenomenon) involving damage to the nerves caused by the use of vibrating hand tools such as chainsaws, drills and air picks. Vibration white finger or hand-arm vibration syndrome (HAVS) as it is properly known, is dealt with above in chapter 16.

17.04 The term 'RSI,' has commonly been used to describe an unrecognised pathology, where the patient presents with diffuse symptoms such as aching, pain, weakness, or tenderness, often variable not just in intensity but in location in the upper limb, and showing a distribution which has no obvious anatomical explanation. The struggle for recognition of RSI as a distinct pathology was rejected by Judge Prosser in *Mughal v Reuters Ltd* [1993] IRLR 571 in a judgment which is often quoted out of context. In this, Judge Prosser stated:

'I have read and re-read many articles on the subject of RSI (Repetitive Strain Injury) and it is quite clear that there is a wide spectrum of debate and division about RSI. I believe that the mainstream view is that there is no pathology, no clinical symptoms that can be pointed to as confirming a patient having RSI[1]... [The defendant medical experts] are clear in their own minds that RSI is in reality meaningless, in that it has no pathology. Indeed, both take the view that RSI has no place in the medical books and, from my acquaintance with it in this case, I agree with them.'[2]

The above is often quoted as a judicial statement that there is no such thing as RSI. However, full reading of the judgment makes it clear that what the judge was stating is that: there is no distinct disease or condition known as RSI; no one managed to diagnose the claimant consistently with any known disease or condition;[3] in several places in the judgment, the judge accepts that there are well known conditions such as tenosynovitis, peritendinitis and carpal tunnel syndrome, which may be caused or aggravated by work[4] but that the claimant was not diagnosed with any such conditions.

1   At 576.
2   At 577; see also para 2.34, above.
3   See 578 at para 86.
4   See 576, para 55 and para 62.

17.05 The issue arose again in *Mountenay v Bernard Matthews plc* [1994] 5 Med LR 293 when nine claimants involved in poultry processing sought to allege that they had developed a specific condition known as RSI. HHJ Mellor rejected such a finding. However, the judge went on to confirm that each of the nine claimants had developed known conditions of tenosynovitis, peritendinitis and carpal tunnel syndrome, that such conditions were caused by work and as a consequence of a breach of duty by the defendant.

17.06 Following *Mountenay*, the approach to such cases reverted to one of establishing: (a) a known pathological condition; and (b) that such condition was caused by the work. In many ways this matches the approach to psychiatric injuries, where non-specific conditions are not recognised by the courts, but diagnosed mental disorders are.

Foreseeability

17.07 The variable nature of the work which can give rise to ULDs require an assessment of foreseeability in every case. Both the statutory requirements as to the suitability of seating, and the common law duty to take reasonable care for health and safety at work, require an assessment in the light of knowledge available at the time. An employer must have had actual or constructive knowledge that the work carried an inherent, specific and not insignificant risk of injury as a condition precedent to a finding that the employer breached its duty.

17.08 Assuming that the risk is defined broadly, in line with *Hughes v Lord Advocate* [1963] AC 837 and *Jolley v London Borough of Sutton* [2000] 3 All ER 409, the immediate question is whether it can be shown that the claimant's work should have been known to carry a risk of causing strains and pains to the forearm, hand and wrist. Neither the precise extent of the damage, nor the precise manner of its infliction need be foreseeable. If the consequence is one which was within the general range which any reasonable person might foresee (and was not of an entirely different kind which no-one would anticipate) then it is within the rule that a person who has been guilty of negligence is liable for the consequences. The cases decided on work related musculo-skeletal disorders have regarded strains and pains in the forearm, hand and wrist as belonging to the general class of injury that one might foresee from repetitive tasks involving the frequent use of the muscles of the hand and forearm, and often the application of force through the hand and fingers. As such, the precise definition of the injury (whether epicondylitis, peritendinitis, tenosynovitis, de Quervain's syndrome, carpal tunnel syndrome etc) is not a matter of critical importance so far as either knowledge or foreseeability is concerned. As Judge Byrt QC said in *McSherry v British Telecommunications plc* [1992] 3 Med LR 129 at 134:

> '... it is sufficient in law if the tortfeasor should reasonably have foreseen that his breach of duty was likely to cause injury within the broad category of injury that was in fact caused ... I am satisfied that the defendants should have been aware that bad posture could cause musculo-skeletal problems. The fact that the injuries sustained were more extensive than those they might have envisaged is of no consequence in law.'

17.09 A risk of injury to the forearm, hand and wrist from work has been appreciated for many years. The Workmen's Compensation (Industrial Diseases) Consolidation Order of 1929 recognised writers' cramp, telegraphists' cramp and inflammation of the synovial lining of the wrist joint and tendon sheaths, caused in mining, as industrial injuries for the purposes of the Workmen's Compensation Act 1925. In 1948, industrial injury benefit was extended to cover inflammation of the synovial lining of the wrist joint and tendon sheaths not just in mining but caused by 'any occupation ... involving manual labour, or frequent or repeated movements of the hand or wrist'.[1] The description of it alone should give rise to knowledge in any employer that an occupation involving frequent or repeated movements of the hand or wrist was liable to give rise to a hand injury, or to traumatic inflammation of the tendons. The 1948 Regulations were amended in 1958, but the nature of the occupation causative of tendon inflammation was the same. In addition, Prescribed Disease No 28 was 'cramp of the hand or forearm due to repetitive movements' which was said to be caused by 'prolonged periods of handwriting, typing or other repetitive movements of the fingers, hand or arm'.

1   National Insurance (Industrial Injuries) (Prescribed Diseases) Regulations 1948, SI 1948/1371, Sch 1, Pt 1.

17.10 Such cramp is now PD A4,[1] whereas traumatic inflammation of the tendons of the hand or forearm or of the associated tendon sheaths is now PD A8. The definition of prescribed disease A8 covers peritendinitis crepitans, tenosynovitis, and carpal tunnel syndrome secondary to tenosynovitis. Carpal tunnel syndrome is separately a prescribed disease when it is caused 'by the use of hand held vibrating tools'. HM Chief Inspector of Factories in his Annual Report of 1965 noted that: '(Tenosynovitis) is caused by the constant repetition of small quick movements. It may occur in a wide variety of jobs including the packeting of food, typing ...'. In 1972 the Chief Employment Medical Adviser published a Note of Guidance on Beat Conditions and Tenosynovitis. This guidance note was repeated in virtually identical terms in 1977, as Guidance Note MS10.

1   'PD': prescribed disease.

17.11 *Other occupational diseases*

17.11 In *Fade v Ross Poultry Ltd* (1 March 1978, unreported), Thomson J, the claimant suffered a condition that was not a 'true' tenosynovitis in the view of the judge, but her claim was not dismissed on these grounds. In *Presland v Padley* (29 January 1979, unreported), a decision at Lincoln before Tudor Evans J, the claimant suffered from tenosynovitis, but it was regarded as relevant that although tenosynovitis itself was relatively rare, there were a large number of cases of strain of the wrist, hand and forearm that had not been diagnosed as tenosynovitis but had undoubtedly occurred; and it was strain in general terms that founded the need for the employer to take steps to safeguard the employee. In *Pepall v Thorn Consumer Electronics Ltd* (20 December 1985, unreported), Woolf J identified injuries that could be 'loosely' described as tenosynovitis: tenosynovitis itself, de Quervain's syndrome, tennis elbow, trigger finger. That case involved a number of claimants: those employees with tenosynovitis, carpal tunnel syndrome, trigger finger, 'chronic non-specific irritative synovitis', de Quervain's, and even a sprain of the wrist and forearm were held to have suffered sufficiently to justify an award of damages. Those injuries were all regarded as falling within the area of risk that was foreseeable, and against which the employer should have taken precautions. In *Mountenay v Bernard Matthews plc* [1994] 5 Med LR 293 the judge was also satisfied that the fact that tenosynovitis, peritendinitis and carpal tunnel syndrome could be caused and/or aggravated by work was known generally by 1977[1] and by this particular defendant by 1972.

[1] See HSE Circular MS10 (1977).

17.12 In the Scottish case of *Cairns v Phillips Electronics and Associated Industries Ltd* (3 August 1984, unreported) carpal tunnel syndrome secondary to tenosynovitis, though aggravated by the menopause, was regarded as sufficient to justify a finding against the defendants. In *Ping v Esselte Letraset Ltd* [1991] 1 PIQR P74 conditions as varied as tennis elbow, golfer's elbow, carpal tunnel syndrome, true tenosynovitis, and trigger thumb were attributed to work in inspection and packaging which involved frequent repeated movement of the forearm, hand and wrists. However, In *McSherry v British Telecommunications plc* [1992] 3 Med LR 129, the county court felt that there was insufficient evidence to put even a large organisation such as BT on notice prior to 1985 of such a risk of musculo-skeletal disorder from keyboard operation as to warrant radical action before then. However, *Alexander v Midland Bank* [1999] IRLR 723 involved the Court of Appeal supporting a successful claim by five claimants who had developed fibromyalgia in their hands as a result of excessive work as encoders for the defendant bank. The Court of Appeal accepted that the risk of musculo-skeletal disorders generally was well known by the beginning of 1990.[1]

[1] See [1999] IRLR 723 at 729, para 34.

The duty of care

17.13 The duty to prevent or minimise musculo-skeletal disorders developing occupationally may arise by statute, under statutory instrument or at common law.

The duty of care: statutory provisions in primary legislation

17.14 Regulations relevant to the likely origin of upper limb disorders developing as a result of work relate to lifting, and other manual handling operations (see chapter 21 on manual handling); to the design and provision of workstations including seating (see chapter 18 on workplaces); and to keyboard work (see chapter 20 on work equipment: para 20.79 onwards). However, since it is thought that many muscular strains develop because of repetitive work of the same pattern, it is worth emphasising that the Working Time Regulations 1998 provide by reg 8 that an employer must ensure that a worker is given adequate rest breaks where the pattern according to which an employer organises work is such as to put the health and safety of a worker employed by it at risk, in particular because the work is monotonous or the work rate is pre-determined.

The duty of care: common law

Assessment

17.15 On the question of whether a work activity gives rise to a breach of duty, an engineering report is usually required but not always. An engineer's report is essentially an 'after the event' risk assessment. The defendant is under a general duty to assess the risk of injury by reason of the general duty to carry out risk assessments under reg 3 of the Management of Health and Safety at Work Regulations 1999. In the absence of such an assessment, or where the employers' assessment identified no risk, an engineer's report can identify both the risk and suggested measures for its abatement.

17.16 At common law many cases have been brought, covering a multitude of circumstances with mixed success. As stated above, although now subject to statutory regulation, keyboard cases to a large extent defined the common law. *The Gallagher v Bond Pearce* (9 February 2001, unreported) involved typing; *Ellis v Financial Times* (28 November 1995, unreported), HC and *Amosu v Financial Times* (unreported) were claims by newspaper sub-editors in respect of diffuse symptoms arising on typing); *Conaty v Barclays Bank plc* (6 April 2000, unreported) involved de Quervain's Syndrome arising out of keyboard use; *Gould v Shell UK Ltd* (22 September 1999, unreported) the pain suffered by use of a mouse in graphics work; *Alexander v Midland Bank plc* [2000] ICR 464, CA (information encoders suffering diffuse symptoms). The papermaking industry, the poultry processing industry, and the electronics industry have all featured successful claims for compensation since the late 1970s, from electrical harness assembly on a production line: *Sandra Boldstraw v Lucas Automotive Ltd* (20 September 2000, unreported); to power press operation: *Kaur v Priest Jackson Pressings* (13 March 2000, unreported) (de Quervain's Syndrome); meat processing: *Gill and Mainprize v Cranswick Country Foods Ltd* (April/May 1999, unreported); and food preparation: *Mility v FW Farnsworth* (22 December 1998, unreported) (cervical spondylosis aggravated by putting toppings on pizzas).

17.17 *Other occupational diseases*

17.17 In a factory or manual handling context, the HSE publication *Work-related upper limb disorders* (1990) identified the relevant factors as being:

(i)   force;
(ii) frequency and duration; and
(iii) awkward posture.

Any one or a combination of these factors could be a cause of musculo-skeletal disorder. Whether a particular job gives rise to such a foreseeable risk is an issue of fact to be determined after consideration of those three factors. However, this has to be seen in context. Millions of workers use a keyboard. Most do not suffer an injury. Although a risk may be foreseeable to all, it would not be so obvious as to require any preventative measure (beyond, perhaps, a warning) unless there were some aspect of the work such as the length of time spent, the posture at the workstation, or the pressure under which the job was done which made the risk greater than the norm.

Preventive measures

17.18 The duty to take reasonable steps to avoid or minimise a foreseeable risk of injury has been held to require warnings, rotation of tasks, better job design, mechanisation, a moderation of work rate, a response to the physical design of the workstation in line with ergonomic advice, and appropriate supervision, advice and training. Further, if a condition manifests itself when it is acute (perhaps after the first symptoms are reported) it may be incumbent upon an employer to ensure that there is rest from the task implicated to avoid that injury becoming chronic. Indeed, if a worker presents with physical complaints which may originate in working conditions, it is incumbent on the employer to review the system of work to see whether it is causative and, if so, remedy the situation.

Warnings

17.19 In *Presland v Padley* (29 January 1979, unreported) Tudor-Evans J held that there was a duty of care owed to applicants to tell them of the risks they would face in employment, at the stage of engaging staff, and held that:

> 'An employer is under a duty in cases where the nature of the work carries an inherent, specific and not insignificant risk of a servant developing an industrial disease or condition to tell the servant at the beginning of the employment about the risk in order to allow the servant the option whether to embark on the employment or not.'

17.20 The same approach has been adopted in *Burgess v Thorn Consumer Electronics Ltd* (1983) Times, 16 May in finding that a warning should have been given even though employment had started, and by Woolf J in *Pepall v Thorn Consumer Electronics* (20 December 1985, unreported). This approach was in turn adopted and applied in *Mountenay (Hazzard) v Bernard Matthews plc* [1994] 5 Med LR 293 where the court focused upon the requirement, identified by Woolf J, for there to be '... a relatively sophisticated programme of educating and warning employees ... [in the context of problems which] ... needed consideration and implementation by management at a high level'. In *Burgess v Thorne Consumer Electronics Ltd* (1983) Times, 16 May Bristow J held that a warning ought to have been given to assembly line workers that if they began to feel pains in their wrist or arm they must report it at once, and consult their GP, because the pain might indicate the presence of a condition which if dealt with promptly would resolve, but if not dealt with might become serious enough to require surgery.

Rotation

17.21 In *Mountenay v Bernard Matthews plc* [1994] 5 Med LR 293 a finding of liability was in part made because of a failure by the employer to provide for a proper rotation of tasks. The same was held in *Willis v Royal Doulton (UK) Ltd* (16 May 1997, unreported), CC where workmen were not adequately rotated away from a task which involved the loading of a conveyor with heavy moulds, occasioning them to suffer lateral epicondylitis.

Work rates

17.22 There is no accepted standard of work rate which may constitute too fast a rate of work. Much depends upon the individual, the posture, the force required and the other variables of the work environment. However, the length of time for which posture is maintained is likely to be of importance. In *Pickford v ICI plc* [1998] ICR 673, HL a trial judge found that a typist, suffering from cramp of the hand, had failed to satisfy him that it was caused by her typing work as opposed to being merely associated with it. The Court of Appeal reversed the trial judge. On appeal to the House of Lords, the judgment at first instance was restored, on the basis that the judge had made conclusions of fact which he was entitled to draw. The case suggests, obiter, that a typist spending most of the day typing should appropriately be warned of a need to adopt a proper posture, and the need to take breaks and rest pauses. However, the giving of warnings as to the risk of contracting PD A4, from which Ms Pickford claimed to suffer, was not compulsory. As Lord Hope of Craighead observed (at 692E–F), conditions which are associated with functional or psychogenic disorders present particular difficulty. The claimant's experience, responsibility and intelligence gave her the knowledge to appreciate the need to arrange work breaks and job variation. On the facts, in any event, she did not work for long periods without break or variation. It must, however, be remembered that the Health and Safety (Display Screen Equipment) Regulations 1992 were not relevant to the decision in *Pickford*, but would now be material (see para 20.79, below).

17.23 In the context of factory work, many ULD cases revolve upon work rates imposed by the machinery and process rather than the individual, such as conveyor belt work. The onset of injury amongst the workforce following an increase in the speed of the production line is a classic example.

Job design

17.24 In *Mughal v Reuters Ltd* [1993] IRLR 571, HHJ Prosser suggested that reasonable comfort in working position, where equipment complied with the relevant British Standards, was likely to be sufficient to discharge the employer's obligation. However, again, this case does not take into account the guidance referred to above given in connection with the Health and Safety (Display Screen Equipment) Regulations 1992 and the Workplace (Health, Safety and Welfare) Regulations 1992. In the context of factory work, the job design is likely to be a vital factor, eg a requirement that a worker work at an awkward height or uncomfortable position and the general layout of the work space. Much of the HSE's focus on the assessment of risks focuses on redesign of the job, the workstation or both.[1]

1   See HSE Guidance 7/99 Upper Limb Disorders—Assessing the Risks.

Supervision, advice and training

17.25 Where a risk of injury arises, employees should be advised on the risks they face from MSDs and the measures that they can take to protect themselves. This generally involves taking regular breaks and rests. Employees should also be advised on the typical signs and symptoms of MSDs so that they can be reported early. In that way, an employer can spot patterns of injury quickly. This common law duty as to the need for advice to an employee is supported by similar statutory duties in many contexts (eg Provision and Use of Work Equipment Regulations 1998, as well as the more obvious duties referred to in 17.14 above).

Causation

17.26 It is particularly important in cases of alleged musculo-skeletal disorder to relate the injury caused to the breach alleged, as opposed to the work in general or life in general. Each MSD's injury can be caused entirely by constitutional factors unrelated to work. Complex questions can arise on whether the work caused the onset of the condition, exacerbated a constitutionally caused condition or simply caused pain because the condition was present (eg like walking on a leg broken outside work). Where the claimant developed the constitutional condition first and this was aggravated or exacerbated at work, then it might have been very difficult for the defendant to foresee the injury. Complex questions of causation and breach of duty arise as to whether any injury arose out of the negligent work (ie from foreseeable risky work which could have been avoided or reduced). The questions here are common to many industrial diseases (eg *McGhee v NCB*, *Bonnington Castings* etc). Establishing that the injury was caused by work is not the same as establishing that it was caused by a breach of duty on the part of the defendant. If the absence of a warning is to be relied upon as a breach, then a claimant must be able to say that the warning would have made a difference.

The greatest factual hurdle to claims in respect of musculo-skeletal disorder succeeding is establishing the relationship between the injury, its cause and the breach of duty said to give rise to it.

ASTHMA AND DERMATITIS

Introduction

17.27 There are many similarities between asthma and dermatitis claims.[1] First, both have similar dual medical causes, capable of being caused by irritants or by allergic sensitisation. A number of substances can cause both asthma and dermatitis. Further, the allergenic nature of many of the substances results in an immunologist being the appropriate medical expert in many asthma and dermatitis cases. However, it is the norm in asthma cases for respiratory consultants to be instructed and for dermatologists to handle dermatitis cases. Second, both are typically (and by definition) caused by substances hazardous to health in the workplace and therefore subject to statutory duties imposed by the Control of Substances Hazardous to Health (COSHH) Regulations 2002, SI 2002/2677 (see chapter 22). By reason of the COSHH Regulations and the decision in *Dugmore v Swansea NHS Trust* [2002] EWCA Civ 1689 (applying the reasoning of *Larner v British Steel plc* [1993] ICR 551) issues such as knowledge and foreseeability have reduced relevance to both dermatitis and asthma claims.

[1]   For a detailed consideration of the medical factors associated with such injuries, we recommend *Hunter's Diseases of Occupations* (9th edn) at 633pp and 725pp.

17.28 Reported dermatitis cases go back much further in time than asthma cases, the most famous dermatitis case being *McGhee v National Coal Board* [1973] 1 WLR 1. The earliest successful reported asthma case is most probably *Ogden v Airedale Health Authority* [1996] 7 Med LR 153 or *Anderson v Crump* [1996] CLY 5657. However, as stated above, the precedent established by common law claims for asthma and dermatitis are now largely irrelevant, with cases brought instead pursuant to the COSHH Regulations 2002.

Allergic and irritant responses

17.29 Allergy (from the Greek 'allos' meaning changed or altered state and 'ergon' meaning reaction or reactivity) is used to describe an observed reaction due to the influence of external factors (ie the allergen) on the immune system. According to the Gell and Coombs' Classification of Hypersensitive Reactions, there are six types of allergic reaction. In the medico-legal context, only two types are of concern and these conform to a layperson's understanding of allergy. These two types of allergic reaction are known as Type I: immediate hypersensitivity and Type IV: delayed hypersensitivity.

17.30 An immediate hypersensitivity is an allergy which involves a response to an allergen within minutes of exposure. It is this type of allergy which is present in occupational asthma. It is this type of allergy which can also develop into a 'systemic allergy' as it can effect the whole of a person's system and can cause death by anaphylaxis. Nut allergies are Type I allergies. Some allergic dermatitis is Type I and it is characterised by hives and weals. Type IV delayed hypersensitivity concerns only dermatitis cases and is an allergy where the person reacts only at the site of the exposure some 24–48 hours after exposure. Contact allergic dermatitis is a Type IV allergy. It is characterised as a red rash at the point of exposure.

17.31 An allergen is a substance that can cause an allergic reaction. Allergens are substances that, in some people, the immune system recognises as 'foreign' or 'dangerous' but cause no response for most people. Allergies are acquired as a result of cumulative exposure. Whilst allergies only affect some of the exposed people and not others, the risk of any individual person developing an allergy is a combination of:

(a)   the individual's susceptibility to sensitisation to that substance—how atopic they are;[1] and

(b)   the exposure to the substance—duration, frequency and quantity.

Point (b) above is a vital issue on legal causation. A general reduction in the exposure of all individuals to known allergens will reduce the risk of susceptible people becoming allergic. Accordingly, applying the causation tests familiar in occupational disease cases, an increase in exposure to allergens will contribute to the development of an allergy and post-sensitisation, further exposure may exacerbate the allergy.

[1]   Atopy is the genetically determined state of hypersensitivity to environmental allergens. Ezcema, hayfever and other allergies are markers that a person is more susceptible to developing an allergic sensitisation.

17.32 An irritant is something which causes damage, inflammation or simply an excessive response to stimuli.

Asthma

17.33 Asthma is a breathing disorder involving the inflammation and narrowing of the airways. It is characterised by by reversible airway obstruction and attacks of breathlessness, wheezing and coughing. Originally a term used to mean 'difficult breathing', it is now used to denote bronchial asthma.[1] The airway's obstruction or narrowing can resolve spontaneously or as a result of treatment. The narrowing occurs not just in response to known allergens, but asthmatics demonstrate a generalised increased responsiveness to non-specific stimuli such as exercise or inhaled cold dry air, or to such matters as dust, smoke or fume.[2]

[1]   *Stedman's Medical Dictionary* (2000).
[2]   *Hunter's Diseases of Occupations* (9th edn) p 633.

Irritant asthma

17.34 Irritants such as volatile acids can cause wheezing and shortness of breath in anyone who inhales them. A single high exposure of a person to an irritant chemical by inhalation can cause a severe form of irritant-induced asthma, reactive airways disease syndrome, or RADS. RADS is a condition only characterised in the 1980s. In RADS the worker is exposed one time only to a high level of an airway irritant, such as hydrochloric acid, chlorine, acetic acid, ammonia fumes or glutaraldehyde. The result is a very severe, acute respiratory illness, often leading to emergency care and/or hospitalisation, and from which the patient eventually recovers. Initially the patient has shortness of breath, wheezing, cough and much respiratory distress. Gradually the symptoms improve, but the sequelae of that one-time intense exposure is continued 'reactive airways,' ie asthma that flare-ups around dust and fumes of almost any type. Thus, an intense, one-time exposure to an airway irritant can lead to asthma.

17.35 More recently, it has been suggested that lower levels of exposure to irritant substances repeatedly over time may also lead to the development of asthma. The general term 'Irritant Induced Asthma' (IIA) has been applied to this condition.[1]

[1]   John Ayres and Peter Baxter *Irritant Induced Asthma and RADS* (April 2004).

Allergic asthma

17.36 Allergic asthma is the classical definition of occupational asthma. In allergic asthma the inhaled material 'sensitises' the worker's airways so that later exposures to the same substance bring on cough and wheezing. As with irritant asthma, full-blown asthma often develops, with general exposure to dust and fume causing symptoms of breathlessness.

17.37 The most important issue to understand from a medico-legal perspective, is that allergies are acquired as a result of cumulative exposure. Whilst allergies only affect some of the exposed people and not others, the risk of any individual person developing an allergy is a combination of: (a) the individual's susceptibility to sensitisation to that substance—how atopic they are; and (b) the exposure to the substance—duration, frequency and quantity. A general reduction in the exposure of all individuals to known allergens will reduce the risk of susceptible people becoming allergic. Since asthma can be caused as a result of exposure to substances encountered in everyday life as well as from substances encountered at work, a worker will face the common problem associated with industrial disease litigation: proof of causation. Expert medical opinion will be required to establish whether, on the balance of probabilities, the cause of the asthma is occupational.

Dermatitis

17.38 Dermatitis is an inflammation of the upper layers of the skin, causing rash, blisters, scabbing, redness and swelling. Contact dermatitis is a reaction, which occurs when skin comes in contact with certain substances. Two common mechanisms exist by which substances can cause skin inflammation—irritation (irritant contact dermatitis) or allergic reaction (allergic contact dermatitis). Contact dermatitis is most often seen around the hands or areas that touched or were exposed to the irritant/allergen.

17.39 Common irritant causes of dermatitis include soap, detergents, acids, alkalis and organic solvents. Other causes include excessive wetness and sweating. Claims are often brought for those whose hands are often in the presence of such substances—nurses, cleaners, mechanics. Severe cases can leave the hands permanently damaged and incapable of any further contact, so causing the person to lose their job. Common causes of Type IV allergic contact dermatitis include nickel and cobalt. Claims for allergic contact dermatitis are rare. Avoidance of the allergen is relatively simple. The symptoms are rarely severe or long-lasting. Normally the work is unaffected if the substance is avoided.

17.40 Cases of Type I allergic dermatitis are much more serious matters. The reaction of hives and weals can occur all over the body and not just at the point of contact. Once sensitised, then the risk of inhaling or ingesting the allergen can lead to a risk of asthmatic reactions or anaphylaxis. Latex is the most common occupational cause.[1] Nuts and fish are others.[2]

1 See eg *Dugmore v Swansea NHS Trust* [2002] EWCA Civ 1689.
2 See eg *Bilto v Fastnet* 1997 SLT 1323, OH.

Incidence of asthma and dermatitis

Asthma

17.41 The HSE issued its first Guidance Note on the medical aspects of occupational asthma in 1991.[1] At that time, although unsure of the true levels of disease, the HSE was estimating the annual incidence in the hundreds.[2] By the time the HSE published its next guidance on occupational asthma,[3] it was reporting over 1,000 new cases of occupational asthma a year. This information was obtained from the Surveillance of Work-related and Occupational Respiratory Disease (SWORD) scheme. Initiated in 1988, the scheme was based on the voluntary submission of monthly reports of occupational respiratory illness by specialist respiratory and occupational physicians in the UK.

1 Medical Series 25 (December 1991).
2 In para 11.
3 *Preventing Asthma at Work: How to Control Respiratory Sensitisers* (1994).

17.42 In the last reporting year (1999), a total of 1,168 cases of occupational asthma were estimated from SWORD reports. In the period 1995–1997 the annual incidence of occupational asthma in all occupations was 38 cases per million workers. Those found to be most at risk were vehicle paint-sprayers, bakers, food processors, chemical processors, medical treatment workers and laboratory technicians. One-third of all cases of asthma were attributed to organic agents and one-third by exposure to chemicals.[1] The Shield 2004 survey (A Surveillance Scheme of Occupational Asthma in the Midlands) found the most common causes of occupational asthma were metal working fluid (44%), isocyanates (18%), chrome (13%), zinc (7%) and then flour, biocides, latex and cobalt. The HSE now publishes a list which is updated from time to time: *Asthmagens: Critical Assessments of the evidence for agents implicated in occupational asthma.*[2]

[1] McDonald, Keynes and Meredith 'Reported incidence of occupational asthma in the United Kingdom 1989–1997' (2000) 57 Occupational and Environmental Medicine, pp 823–829.
[2] (HSE Books, 1997).

Dermatitis

17.43 The Department of Employment Handbook 18 'Health & Safety at Work: Industrial Dermatitis; Precautionary Measures' (1972) stated that DHSS figures for the UK indicated that industrial dermatitis accounted for 13,000 spells of incapacity for men during a given year and 4,000 for women. It identified mineral oils, a range of chemicals, solvents and de-greasers as the most common causes of dermatitis at work. By the time the HSE issued Guidance Note EH26 'Occupational skin diseases: health and safety precautions' in January 1981, 65% of all industrial injury benefit was being paid for dermatitis. A similar range of causes was identified. The HSE Guidance Note MS24 'Health surveillance of occupational skin disease' (January 1991) noted a general reduction in levels of injury, but at that time 45% of industrial injury benefits remained dermatitis related. Appendix I to Guidance Note MS24 identified an extensive list of contact irritants and sensitisers. The Guidance also recognised the incidence of contact urticaria (hives and weals) caused by Type 1 allergic skin reactions. Updated in 1999, MS24 now contains a revised Appendix I which expressly states that it is in no way a comprehensive list of causative agents. The HSE's booklet 'Preventing Dermatitis at Work', the second edition of which was published in 2004, reported that 39,000 cases of occupational dermatitis had been diagnosed in 2002.

Diagnosis of injury

Asthma

17.44 Diagnosis of the cause of asthma is often the most problematic part of the case. Workers who allege that something at work is causing their asthma are generally unable to provide evidence to support the fact. Other than the acute period of injury, often lasting only 30 minutes with full recovery within a matter of hours, there is no ongoing sign of injury. The diagnosis of allergic

17.45 *Other occupational diseases*

asthma is complicated by the fact that asthma can be caused by many substances and, in many cases, asthma is believed to develop for no known reason at all. There are few cases where any test can be safely carried out to determine whether a person is sensitised to any substance. Latex is one of the few where blood tests are useful. The only foolproof way to determine if someone is sensitised is to hold the substance under their nose and see if they have an asthma attack. Few medico-legal experts will carry out such a test for risk of killing the patient.

17.45 Ideally, the worker will still be at work. In such cases, measurement of peak flow in work and away from work can provide good evidence. Lower peak flow levels at work will show that a substance at work is causing the asthma. If the worker has left work or the suspected substance has been removed from the workplace, then a detailed history will be needed. To support a workplace cause, the symptoms will be worse at work and when near the substance and much better away from work and best at weekends and on holiday. If the symptoms are much the same, then a constitutional or environmental cause is implicated. Ultimately this is a matter for medico-legal experts.

Dermatitis

17.46 Diagnosis of dermatitis is a much more simple matter. If the cause is an allergen, then skin prick tests combined with blood tests can provide a definitive diagnosis. But, beware cases where the worker arrives with a travelling diagnosis of allergy that has never been tested. If the cause of the dermatitis is irritants at work, then a thorough set of tests will still need to be undertaken to rule out any allergic cause. Diagnosis of an irritant dermatitis is usually by exclusion of other causes together with evidence of exposure to known irritants at work, worse symptoms at work and recovery away from work.

17.47 As with many other industrial diseases, claimants face potentially complicated issues of proof as a number of common non-occupationally caused types of dermatitis can look very like occupationally caused dermatitis. These include constitutional eczema and psoriasis. Skin disease is common in the population. It may be caused by items in everyday use outside of work such as detergents and bleaches. It is thus necessary to obtain medical evidence from an appropriately qualified expert (dermatologist) to establish occupational causation rather than constitutional or non-work exposure.

Knowledge and duties at common law

17.48 Substances that cause asthma and dermatitis will be substances hazardous to health within the meaning of the Control of Substances Hazardous to Health Regulations. The duties imposed by these Regulations are strict and without reference to issues of knowledge, foresight or reasonableness. Most, if not all, modern asthma and dermatitis injury cases will be brought under these Regulations, which are dealt with at chapter 22.

OCCUPATIONAL DEAFNESS[1]

Introduction

17.49 Hearing loss claims include claims for reduced hearing ability, tinnitus and hyperacusis.[2] Claims for damages for occupational hearing loss most commonly arise out of prolonged exposure to noise, although claims can arise for hearing loss caused by single traumatic events (eg explosions). This chapter deals with the first such type of claim. To succeed in a claim for noise-induced hearing loss, the claimant needs to prove: (1) he was, in the course of his employment by the defendant, exposed to noise levels above the acceptable limits (wrongful exposure); (2) he has suffered hearing loss; (3) his hearing loss is due to noise; and (4) the hearing loss is due to the defendant's wrongful exposure (ie the loss is caused by negligent noise and not non-negligent noise). Other issues that may arise are limitation and apportionment.

[1] Many thanks to Jonathan Clarke, whose papers on deafness formed the basis of much of this section and who considered and amended the text.
[2] For a detailed consideration of the medical factors associated with such injuries, we recommend *Hunter's Diseases of Occupations* (9th edn) at 283pp.

17.50 Hearing loss can be caused by a number of mechanisms, most importantly the normal ageing process (presbyacusis). To attribute the hearing loss to noise exposure, a medical expert (typically a consultant ear, nose and throat surgeon) needs to be satisfied that there has been exposure to sufficiently high levels of noise for sufficient periods of time to be likely to cause damage. For this the expert will need the employer's assessment of noise levels or, in the absence of such, an acoustic engineer's report evidencing the noise levels or, at the very least, a detailed statement from the claimant. A detailed work history from the claimant should include details of exposure to damaging levels of noise including details of the type of machinery operated and used in the vicinity, how close to that machinery the claimant was and for how long. He should also identify any periods in the armed services where guns were used.

17.51 Hearing is conventionally measured (tested) by pure tone audiometry (PTA). The subject is played a tone which starts inaudibly and gets gradually louder until he indicates he can hear it. The intensity (loudness) at which he can hear it (measured in decibels 'dB') is the threshold for that frequency, ie his 'hearing level'. The subject's ability to hear different pitches (frequencies) at different volumes (intensities) of sound is plotted on a graph, called an audiogram. The audiogram is an 'upside down' graph in that the 0 dB on the y axis is at the top of the chart. 'Perfect' human hearing is of noise in a range from about 0.05 kHz–20 kHz. The most important part of this range is that into which most human speech falls, which is 0.25 kHz–4 kHz. This is also the range most affected by damage to the hearing mechanism caused by exposure to excessive noise. Consequently it is this range of frequencies 0.25 kHz–4 kHz that is usually tested.

17.52 In a noise-induced hearing loss case, the audiogram should reveal a 'notch' (a dip on the graph) at around 4 kHz, showing the increased hearing thresholds at that frequency. The absence of a notch, although not helpful, is not necessarily fatal to a diagnosis of noise-induced hearing loss. Equally the presence of such a notch is not necessarily determinative, as it can be caused by ototoxic drugs or even ageing. However, the notch is a good indicator and can be used to demonstrate noise as a cause of the loss even if the total loss is no more than, or even less than, that which is to be expected if the claimant had statistically average age-related loss. In such a case, the notch serves to indicate that the claimant was peculiarly susceptible to noise damage. Without the notch, the characteristics of age and noise-related deafness are similar and often indistinguishable.

17.53 The extent of impairment is commonly assessed by averaging the decibel loss over a number of frequencies. The usual approach is to average at 1, 2 and 4KHz (the Benefits Agency averages at 1, 2 and 3kHz when assessing for industrial disease payments). The thresholds are usually expressed in averages. For example, the average thresholds at 1, 2, and 3 kHz (or at 1, 2 and 4 kHz) in each ear is the total of the thresholds at those frequencies in that ear divided by 3. Because we have two ears, one ear is nearly as good as two. Total deafness in one ear with the other unaffected does not mean that the total hearing loss is 50%. To work out the combined hearing threshold, one works out the 'binaural average' which is the average threshold (calculated as above) in the better ear multiplied by 4, then add the average threshold in the worse ear and then divide by 5.

17.54 Tinnitus is often associated with noise-related hearing loss. However, it is not unknown for individuals exposed to excessive noise levels to develop tinnitus without also incurring increased hearing thresholds. See eg *Dyer v Commissioner for the Police of the Metropolis* (26 October 1998, unreported), QB. Most commonly, tinnitus on its own is not noise-induced. One possible cause is cervical whiplash injuries, another is high blood pressure.

Apportionment

17.55 As exposure to industrial noise is likely to have taken place over a considerable number of years and will probably have involved a number of employers, the issue of apportionment often has to be dealt with: see chapter 3 for more detail. In both *Thompson v Smiths Shiprepairers (North Shields) Ltd* [1984] QB 405 (Mustill J) and *Kellett v BREL* (3 May 1984, unreported), QBD (Popplewell J), both judges considered the question of apportionment to be a jury question rather than a matter of law. The apportionment applied by Mustill J (in *Thompson*) broadly equated to a year by year basis. On the other hand, the apportionment of Popplewell J in *Kellett* reflected the effects that

438

the respective noise doses had on the quantum of damages appropriate to the total noise-induced loss. Despite these authorities, and in the absence of evidence to the contrary, the courts tend to treat years of equal noise exposure as having equally contributed to the loss. This method provides simplicity, as it avoids the difficulty in assessing the actual contribution which a particular period of noise exposure has made to the overall loss.

Knowledge and standards of care

17.56 It is generally accepted, following the judgment of Mustill J in *Thompson v Smiths Shiprepairers Ltd* [1984] QB 405, that the applicable date when employers in noisy industries ought to have foreseen and guarded against the risks from excessive noise by the provision of hearing protection is 1963, in view of the publication in 1962 of *Noise and the Worker* by the Ministry of Labour. Therefore 1963 is the commonly accepted start date for employers' liability for hearing loss caused by excessive noise, unless, on the evidence, a different date is shown to be appropriate for the particular defendant concerned.

17.57 A number of cases have established *earlier* dates of knowledge. In *Berry v Stone Manganese and Marine Ltd* [1971] 12 KIR 13, the fact that the employer introduced hearing protection before 1963 showed that it was aware of the risks. It was held liable as from 1956. In *Kellett v BREL* (3 May 1984, unreported), QB (Popplewell J), the defendant's own documents showed that it was aware of the risk earlier than 1963. It was held liable as from 1955. In *Baxter v Harland & Wolff plc* [1990] IRLR 516, (NI CA) it was found that the defendant, as large shipbuilders, ought to have been responding to the risks as from 1954.

17.58 A number of cases have established *later* dates of knowledge. In *Craven v Tonks* (14 November 1976, unreported), it was held that in the road haulage industry, the date of knowledge for the employer was 1972. In *Kill v Sussex Coastline Buses* [2000] CLY 2960, the employer's date of knowledge in relation to the risk to bus drivers was found to be 1972.

17.59 The common law duty is to take reasonable precautions to prevent the employee's exposure to dangerously high noise levels. '*Noise and the Worker*' (published by the Ministry of Labour in 1962) advised the provision of hearing protection where exposure was in excess of 85dB LEP,d which is broadly equivalent to 90dB(A) LEP,d[1] (this was also the limit later advised by the Department of Employment's *Code of Practice*, see below). This level of 90dB(A) LEP,d is generally taken to be the threshold for the common law duty before the statutory duties came into force, see below.[2]

---

[1] 'Noise and the Worker' referred to non-weighted decibels. 85dB is broadly equivalent to 90dB(A). The (A) refers to 'A weighting' which is an adjustment of the measurement of the total range of frequencies to which the ear is exposed to reflect those to which human hearing mechanism is particularly susceptible.

2   'The level of 90[dB(A) LEP,d] is generally recognised as the being a figure above which it is necessary for precautions to be taken': per Popplewell J in *Kellett v BREL* (3 May 1984, unreported), QB.

17.60 In 1972, the Department of Employment published its *Code of Practice for Reducing the Exposure of Employed Persons to Noise*. This gave employers guidance on limiting exposure of employees to noise. It indicated 'maximum acceptable levels' but pointed out that lower levels were 'desirable' and that lower levels should be achieved 'where it is reasonably practicable to do so'. It advised that exposure to noise should not exceed 90dB(A) averaged out over the course of an 8-hour day. Where it was not possible to calculate the 8-hour exposure, then hearing protection should be provided when at any time the exposure exceeds 90dB(A).

17.61 In *Dyer v Commissioner of Police for the Metropolis* (26 October 1998, unreported) (Garland J), the claimant was exposed to in excess of 90dB(A) for substantial periods of time (3–4 hours a day) although the 8-hour average was less. The defendant was found to have been negligent for its failure to heed the guidance provided by the 1972 *Code of Practice*.

17.62 The threshold of 90dB(A) is not fixed. The evidence may show that the employer was aware of the risks posed by exposure to lower levels. In *Cropper v Ford Motor Co* (17 November 1992, unreported), *Howells v British Leyland* (31 July 1992, unreported) and *Harris v BRB (Residuary) Ltd* [2005] EWCA Civ 900, the employer was found to have been under a duty to have protected against exposure that exceeded 85dB(A). The limit of acceptable average noise exposure of 90dB(A) was first given express statutory force by the Woodworking Machines Regulations 1974, reg 44.

Noise at Work Regulations

17.63 On 1 January 1990 the Noise at Work Regulations 1989 came into force. On 6 April 2005, they were revoked and replaced by the Control of Noise at Work Regulations 2005, SI 2005/1643 which are stricter.

The Noise at Work Regulations 1989[1]

17.64 The 1989 Regulations imposed a general duty in employers to reduce the risk of hearing damage to the lowest level reasonably practicable.[2] The Regulations also involve 'action levels' of noise exposure which, when reached, trigger specific duties upon the employer. The 'first action level' was a daily personal noise exposure of 85dB(A), the 'second action level' was a daily personal noise exposure of 90dB(A); 'the peak action level' was a level of sound pressure of 200 pascals.

1   The Noise at Work Regulations 1989, SI 1989/1790 were passed to comply with the European Directive 86/188/EEC.
2   See chapter 5 for an explanation of reasonable practicability in health and safety legislation.

17.65 Whatever the level of noise, the employer was under a duty to reduce the risks of hearing damage to the lowest level reasonably practicable (reg 6). Where an employee's exposure was likely to reach the first action level or the peak action level, the employer had to carry out noise assessments to see whether that employee's exposure did exceed those limits (reg 4) and had to keep copies of those assessments (reg 5). The employer was also required to provide the employee with adequate information, instruction and training on the risks of hearing damage from that exposure, the steps the employee could take to minimise those risks, how to request hearing protection[1] and the employee's own obligations under the Regulations (reg 11). The employer had to provide the employee with provide suitable and sufficient hearing protection if the employee requested it (reg 8(1)).

[1] As an employer was bound, under reg 8, to provide hearing protection if the employee asked for it, then the employer's failure to warn the employee (in breach of reg 11) can be causative of the absence of hearing protection and thus causative of the loss: *Harris v BRB (Residuary) Ltd* [2005] EWCA Civ 900.

17.66 Where an employee's exposure was likely to reach the second action level or the peak action level, the employer had to reduce, so far as reasonably practicable (by means other than hearing protection), that employee's exposure to noise (reg 7). The employer was also required to provide the employee with suitable hearing protection which, when properly worn, could reasonably be expected to reduce the risk of hearing damage to below that arising out of exposure to the second action level or as the case may be the peak action level (reg 8(2)). The employee was under a duty to wear the hearing protection provided where it was likely his exposure would otherwise reach the second action level or the peak action level (reg 10(2)). Every part of premises under the employer's control and in which an employee's exposure was likely to reach the second action level or the peak action level had to be demarcated by prescribed signs as an 'ear protection zone' into which the employer was to ensure that no employee would enter without wearing hearing protection (reg 9). The employer had to ensure, so far as reasonably practicable, that anything provided by it pursuant to the Regulations was maintained in an efficient state, in efficient working order and in good repair (reg 10(1)(b)).[1]

[1] As equipment provided under these Regulations is required to be provided to serve a specific function (noise reduction) then the test of whether it is 'maintained in an efficient state, in efficient working order and in good repair' is most probably to be judged in the context of whether it achieves that function. See *Fytche v Wincanton Logistics plc* [2004] UKHL 31, [2004] ICR 975 and para 20.78 below. Thus, if an employee develops frostbite in his ear due to a hole in his ear defenders, the employer is unlikely to be in breach of reg 10(1)(b).

The Control of Noise at Work Regulations 2005[1]

17.67 The 2005 Regulations introduced lower limits and more detailed requirements. They replace the former action levels with 'exposure values'. The 'lower exposure action values' are a daily or weekly average exposure of 80dB(A) and a peak sound pressure of 135dB(C). The 'upper exposure action values' are a daily or weekly average exposure of 85dB(A) and a peak sound pressure of 140dB(C). Daily averages are to be used unless the exposure levels vary markedly from day to day, in which case a 5-day weekly average may be used.

1   The Control of Noise Regulations 2005, SI 2005/1643, were passed to comply with the European Directive 2003/10/EC.

17.68   There is a general duty on employers to ensure that risk from exposure of its employees to noise is either eliminated at source or, where that is not reasonably practicable, reduced to as low a level as is reasonably practicable (reg 6(1)).[1] The employer must ensure that its employees are not exposed to noise above any exposure limit value (reg 6(4)).

1   See chapter 5 for an explanation of reasonable practicability in health and safety legislation.

17.69   Where an employer's work is likely to expose any employees to noise at or above any of the lower exposure action values, the employer must make a suitable and sufficient assessment of the risks and what measures need to be taken to combat them,[1] the employer must record the assessment and must involve the employees concerned, or their representatives (reg 5). The employer must provide the employees, and their representatives, with suitable and sufficient information, instruction and training.[2] The employer must make hearing protection available to employees who request it (reg 7). Where a risk assessment reveals an employee to be at risk from noise then the employer must place the employee under suitable health surveillance, including hearing tests. This surveillance must be recorded and the employee must have access to this record and must be told of any findings (reg 9).

1   Regulation 5(2)–(4) provides detailed requirements that the assessment must fulfil.
2   Regulation 10(2) provides detailed requirements as to what the suitable and sufficient information, instruction and training shall include.

17.70   Where an employer's work is likely to expose any employees to noise at or above any of the upper limit values, the employer shall reduce exposure to as low a level as is reasonably practicable by establishing and implementing a programme of organisational and technical measures, excluding the provision of personal hearing protectors, which is appropriate to the activity (reg 6(2)).[1] The employer must also provide hearing protection if the noise exposure cannot be reduced to below any upper exposure action value (reg 7(2)). Every area in the workplace under the employer's control where an employee's exposure is likely to reach an upper exposure action value must be demarcated by prescribed signs as a 'hearing protection zone' and the employer shall ensure, so far as is reasonably practicable, that no employee enters such a zone without wearing hearing protection (reg 7(3)).

1   Regulation 6(3) provides detailed requirements for the steps taken to comply with the duty under reg 6(1) and (2).

17.71   The employer must ensure, so far as is reasonably practicable, that anything provided by it pursuant to the Regulations is fully and properly used (reg 8(1)(a)). This duty does not apply to hearing protection. The duty is upon the employee to make full and proper use of hearing protectors which the employer is required to provide him and also to report any defect that he discovers in the hearing protectors (reg 8(2)). The employer must ensure that anything it provides pursuant to the Regulations is maintained in an efficient state, in efficient working order and in good repair (reg 8(1)(b)).[1]

1   As equipment provided under these Regulations is required to be provided to serve a specific function (noise reduction) then the test of whether it is 'maintained in an efficient state, in efficient working order and in good repair' is most probably to be judged in the context of whether it achieves that function. See *Fytche v Wincanton Logistics plc* [2004] UKHL 31, [2004] ICR 975 and para 20.78 below. Thus, if an employee develops frostbite in his ear due to a hole in his ear defenders, the employer is unlikely to be in breach of reg 8(1)(b).

Chapter 18

WORKPLACES

Jonathan Clarke

Daniel Bennett

INTRODUCTION

18.01 Safety of the workplace has long been protected by the common law. Over the last two centuries, legislation has steadily introduced specific duties in relation to specific workplaces.[1] These statutory duties have generally been stricter than the common law duty. By 1992, most workplaces were subject either to the Factories Act 1961 or to the Offices, Shops and Railway Premises Act 1963, though certain workplaces, such as dockyards, farms, mines and quarries and construction sites were, and to some extent remain, subject to their own specific legislation.[2]

---

[1] The earliest pieces of legislation specifically directed towards safety of the workplace (as opposed to welfare) were the Factories Act 1844 and Coals Mine Inspection Act 1850.

[2] See eg chapter 23 on shipbuilding yards and docks and chapter 24 on mines and quarries.

18.02 Most of the previous legislation relating to different types of workplaces has been revoked and replaced by the Workplace (Health, Safety and Welfare) Regulations 1992[1] which provide a uniform set of duties to a much wider range of workplaces. As a result of the duties imposed by the 1992 Regulations being wider and generally stricter than the duty imposed by the common law, employers' liability claims in the United Kingdom concerning the safety of the workplace now tend to focus on the statutory duties and there has been little, if any, development of the common law in relation to safety of the workplace since the previous edition of this work.[2]

---

[1] SI 1992/3004. The 1992 Regulations have, in part, been subsequently replaced by later legislation; see para 18.03, fn 1, below. The 1992 Regulations apply to Scotland, England and Wales. In Northern Ireland the similar Workplace (Health, Safety and Welfare) Regulations (Northern Ireland) 1993, SI 1993/37, apply.

[2] For those interested in the historical development of the common law, please see chapter 1 on history or the 13th edition of Munkman, chapter 5 on examples of common law negligence.

THE WORKPLACE (HEALTH, SAFETY AND WELFARE) REGULATIONS 1992

18.03 The Workplace (Health, Safety and Welfare) Regulations 1992, SI 1992/3004,[1] were made under the HSWA 1974, s 15 and implemented the European Workplace Directive 1989.[2] Breach of the Regulations is a criminal offence[3] and, if it causes damage, gives rise to a civil cause of action.[4] The Regulations are supplemented by the Workplace Health, Safety and Welfare

444

Approved Code of Practice approved by the Health and Safety Commission (HSC) under the HSWA 1974, s 16(1). The HSC has also published guidance on the Regulations.[5]

1   The Regulations have been subsequently amended by the Quarries Miscellaneous Health and Safety Provisions Regulations 1995, SI 1995/2036; the Construction (Health, Safety and Welfare) Regulations 1996, SI 1996/1592; the Quarries Regulations 1999, SI 1999/2024; the Health and Safety (Miscellaneous Amendments) Regulations 2002, SI 2002/2174; the Dangerous Substances and Explosive Atmospheres Regulations 2002, SI 2002/2776, and the Work at Height Regulations 2005, SI 2005/735.
2   89/654/EEC.
3   HSWA 1974, s 33(1)(c).
4   Civil liability is imposed by the HSWA 1974, s 47(2) and the absence of any exclusion of liability in the Regulations themselves.
5   The ACOP (L24) and the guidance are published together as *Workplace, health, safety and welfare* (ISBN 0 717 60413 6).

18.04 While the HSWA 1974 provides that an approved code of practice is admissible in criminal proceedings, it is silent with regard to civil proceedings. In practice, such codes and guidance are often cited and relied upon in civil proceedings.

Dates from which effective

18.05 The commencement provisions are set out in reg 1, which must be read along with the definitions of 'workplace' and 'a modification, an extension or a conversion' in reg 2 and its subsequent amendment. These are as follows:

'Regulation 1

(2) Subject to paragraph (3), these Regulations shall come into force on 1st January 1993.

(3) Regulations 5 to 27 and the Schedules shall come into force on 1st January 1996 with respect to any workplace or part of a workplace which is not:
(a)   a new workplace; or
(b)   a modification, an extension or a conversion.

Regulation 2

(1) In these Regulations, unless the context otherwise requires ...
"new workplace" means a workplace used for the first time as a workplace after 31st December 1992;
"workplace" ... , subject to paragraph (2), shall not include a modification, an extension or a conversion of any of the above until such modification, extension or conversion is completed.

(2) Any reference in these Regulations, except in paragraph (1), to a modification, an extension or a conversion is a reference, as the case may be, to a modification, an extension or a conversion of a workplace started after 31st December 1992.

The Health and Safety (Miscellaneous Amendments) Regulations 2002

Regulation 1

These Regulations ... shall come into force on 17th September 2002.

Regulation 6

The Workplace (Health, Safety and Welfare) Regulations 1992 shall be amended: ...
(b)   in the definition of "workplace" in regulation 2(1), by deleting the words "but shall not" to the end of the definition.'

18.06 Therefore the position is as follows. For a workplace already in use on 1 January 1993, regs 5–27 did not come into force until 1 January 1996.[1] A modification, an extension or a conversion of a workplace commenced before 1 January 1993 was not subject to regs 5–27 until 1 January 1996,[2] provided that the modification, extension or conversion had by that date been completed.[3] A workplace first used as a workplace after 31 December 1992 will always have been subject to the Regulations.[4] A modification, an extension or a conversion of a workplace started after 31 December 1992 became subject to the Regulations once the modification, extension or conversion was completed.[5] A modification, an extension or a conversion of a workplace started before 1 January 1993 and not completed prior to 1 January 1996 became subject to the Regulations as from the date it was completed,[6] or 17 September 2002 if not completed by that date.[7] A modification, extension or conversion not completed as of 17 September 2002, became subject to the Regulations as of that date, regardless of when it was started.[8]

[1]   Workplaces already in use on 1 January 1993 are not a 'new workplace' within the definition of that phrase in reg 2(1) and therefore are not excluded by reg 1(3)(a) from the start date afforded by reg 1(3), and thus are subject to regs 5–27 from 1 January 1996.

[2]   By the combination of reg 1(3) and reg 1(2), the Regulations came into force in relation to 'a modification, an extension or a conversion' on 1 January 1993. But as reg 2(2) defines 'a modification, an extension or a conversion' as meaning a modification, extension or conversion started after 31 December 1992, it therefore follows that a modification, extension or conversion started before 1 January 1993 is not a modification, extension or conversion which is, by reg 1(3)(b), excluded from the start date afforded reg 1(3) and, therefore, it is subject to Regulations as from 1 January 1996, provided it has been completed (see following note).

[3]   By reg 2(1) a workplace does not include a modification, an extension or conversion until completed and, because reg 2(2) does not apply to reg 2(1), this is so even if the modification, extension or conversion was started before 1 January 1993.

[4]   A workplace used for the first time as a workplace after 31 December 1992 is, by reg 2(1), a 'new workplace' and, by the combination of reg 1(2) and (3), the Regulations in respect of a new workplace reg 1(2), came into force on 1 January 1993.

[5]   A modification, extension or conversion started after 31 December 1992 is within the definition of 'modification, extension or conversion' which, by reg 2(2) is applied to reg 1(3)(b). Therefore, by reg 1(2) and the proviso to the definition of 'workplace' provided by reg 2(1), is subject to the Regulations when the modification, extension or conversion is completed.

[6]   By the combination of reg 1(3) and reg 1(2), the Regulations came into force in relation to 'a modification, an extension or a conversion' on 1 January 1993. But as reg 2(2) defines 'a modification, an extension or a conversion' as meaning a modification, extension or conversion started after 31 December 1992, it therefore follows that a modification, extension or conversion started before 1 January 1993 is not a modification, extension or conversion which is, by reg 1(3)(b), excluded from the start date afforded reg 1(3), in which case the Regulations would apply as from 1 January 1993. But by reg 2(1) a modification, an extension or conversion is not part of the workplace regardless of when the modification, extension or conversion was started because the reg 2(2) is expressed not to apply to reg 2(1).

[7]   As of 17 September 2002, the exclusion of incomplete modifications, extensions or conversions from the definition of workplace was removed by the Health and Safety (Miscellaneous Amendments) Regulations 2002, SI 2002/2174, reg 6(b).

[8]   See previous note.

What is a workplace?

18.07 For the purpose of the 1992 Regulations, 'workplace' is defined by reg 2(1) as:

'any premises or part of premises which are not domestic premises[1] and are made available to any person as a place of work,[2] and includes:

(a) any place within the premises to which such person has access while at work, and

(b) any, room, lobby, corridor, staircase, road or other place used as a means of access to or egress from that place of work or where facilities are provided for use in connection with the place of work other than a public road,'[3]

but, prior to 17 September 2002, did not include a modification, extension or conversion of any such place until that modification, extension or conversion was completed.[4]

1 By the HSWA 1974, s 53(1), 'domestic premises' means premises occupied as a private dwelling and includes any garden, yard, garage, outhouse or other appurtenance of such premises which is not used in common by the occupants of more than one such dwelling.
2 For the meaning of 'work' see below.
3 Regulation 2(1) defines public road as (in England and Wales) a highway maintainable at public expense within the meaning of the Highways Act 1980, s 329 and (in Scotland) a public road within the meaning assigned to that term by the Roads (Scotland) Act 1984, s 151.
4 Regulation 2(1), as amended by the Health and Safety (Miscellaneous Amendments) Regulations 2002, SI 2002/2174, reg 6(b).

18.08 The following are excluded:

— a workplace in or on a ship (as defined by the Docks Regulations 1988, SI 1988/1655, reg 2(1));[1]

— a workplace where the only activity being undertaken is construction work (as defined by the Construction (Health, Safety and Welfare) Regulations 1996, SI 1996/1592, reg 2(1)), unless it is a part of such a workplace set aside for purposes other than construction work (eg a portacabin office);[2]

— a workplace below ground at a mine;[3]

— a workplace in or on an aircraft, locomotive or rolling stock, trailer or semi trailer used as a means of transport or a vehicle requiring a licence (or exempted from the need for a licence) under the Vehicles (Excise) Act 1971,[4] (save that the Regulations *do* apply to a very limited extent if the aircraft etc is stationery in a workplace).[5]

1 Regulation 3(1)(a).
2 Regulation 3(1)(b) of the 1992 Regulations and reg 3(2) of the 1996 Regulations.
3 Regulation 3(1)(c).
4 See now the Vehicle Excise and Registration Act 1994.
5 Regulation 3(3). The limited extent is that, if the aircraft, locomotive etc is stationary inside a workplace, then it is subject to reg 13.

18.09 Uncompleted modifications, extensions or conversions of a workplace were, prior to 17 September 2002, excluded from the application of the Regulations but would, in all probability, have been construction sites and thus subject to the Construction (Health, Safety and Welfare) Regulations 1996. Since 17 September 2002, both sets of Regulations applied unless the *only* work carried out in the workplace is construction work, in which case only the 1996 Regulations apply.

18.10 For some types of workplaces, the 1992 Regulations apply only in part or to a lesser extent:

— for aircraft, locomotive or rolling stock, trailer or semi trailer used as a means of transport or a vehicle requiring a licence (or exempted from the need for a licence) under the Vehicles (Excise) Act 1971,[1] stationery in a workplace, only reg 13 applies;[2]

— for temporary work sites, all the Regulations apply, but regs 20–25 are subject to reasonable practicability;[3]

— in relation to any workplace in fields, woods or other land forming part of an agricultural or forestry undertaking but which is not inside a building and is situated away from the undertaking's main buildings, only regs 20–22 apply and are subject to reasonable practicability;[4]

— for a workplace at a quarry or above ground at a mine, all the Regulations apply save for reg 12 which applies only to floors or traffic routes inside a building.[5]

[1] See now the Vehicle Excise and Registration Act 1994.
[2] Regulation 3(3).
[3] Regulation 3(2). This is not in contravention of the Directive since the latter does not apply to temporary workplaces at all: art 1(2)(b).
[4] Regulation 3(4).
[5] Regulation 3(5) as inserted by the Quarries Miscellaneous Health and Safety Provisions Regulations 1995, SI 1999/2036, reg 11 as from 26 July 1998 in respect of workplaces used for the first time on or before 26 October 1995 or a modification, extension or conversion of a workplace carried out after 26 October 1995.

18.11 It is questionable whether this definition of workplace satisfies that given by art 2 of the Workplace Directive, which defines 'workplace' as 'the place intended to house workstations on the premises of the undertaking and/or establishment and any other place within the area of the undertaking and/or establishment to which the worker has access in the course of his employment.' The definition in the Directive does not, for instance, exclude domestic premises.

18.12 The essence of the definition of workplace is that it is a place made available for work or where facilities for use in conjunction with the workplace are provided. In *Parker v PFC Flooring Supplies* [2001] PIQR P115, QB, the roof of a workplace was considered to be part of the workplace when an employee fell through a skylight.

'Work'

18.13 A workplace is a place made available to a person as a place of work. The expressions 'work' and 'at work' are defined in the HSWA 1974, ss 52 and 53. These expressions are to be construed so that an employee[1] is at work throughout the time when he is in the course of his employment, but not otherwise; a person holding the office of constable is at work throughout the time when he is on duty, but not otherwise; and a self-employed person[2] is at work throughout such time as he devotes to work as a self-employed person.[3] Other Regulations have added to this definition of 'work'. As a result, the following are included: work experience on certain training schemes;[4] training which includes operations involving ionising radiations;[5] and activities involving genetic manipulation.[6]

[1]   By the HSWA 1974, s 53(1), 'employee' means an individual who works under a contract of employment or is treated by the HSWA 1974, s 51A as being an employee. Section 51A relates to police constables.
[2]   By the HSWA 1974, s 53(1) 'self-employed person' means an individual who works for gain or reward otherwise than under a contract of employment, whether or not he himself employs others.
[3]   HSWA 1974, s 52.
[4]   Health and Safety (Training for Employment) Regulations 1990, SI 1990/1380, reg 3.
[5]   Ionising Radiations Regulations 1999, SI 1999/3232, reg 2(3).
[6]   Genetically Modified Organisms Regulations 2000, SI 2000/2831, reg 4.

18.14 'At work' was defined by the Inner House in *Robb v Salamis (M & I)* 2005 SLT 523 (applying the meaning from the HSWA 1974, s 52(1)(b)) as being wider than 'carrying on work operations' and a person is at work the whole time when he is in the course of employment, which includes rest periods and when travelling between periods of work.[1]

[1]   A case concerning the Provision and Use of Work Equipment Regulations.

By whom the duty is owed

18.15 The duty to comply with the Regulations is placed upon:

(1)   an employer in control of the workplace, modification, extension or conversion where any of its employees work (reg 4(1));

(2)   any person who has, to any extent, control of a workplace, modification, extension or conversion (reg 4(2)); and

(3)   any person who is deemed to occupy factory premises by virtue of the Factories Act 1961, s 175(5) (reg 4(5)).

18.16 A person in control, to whom reg 4(2) applies, is under a duty to ensure that the workplace complies with any requirement of the Regulations which relates to matters within his control.[1] The control by the employer or other person of the workplace must be in connection with its carrying on of a trade, business or other undertaking, whether for profit or not.[2] No duty is imposed upon the self-employed in respect of their own work or that of any business partner.[3] The Crown is not exempted,[4] although, the Minister of Defence may exempt Her Majesty's Armed Forces or visiting armed forces from compliance on grounds of national security.[5]

[1]   Regulation 4(2).
[2]   Regulation 4(3).
[3]   Regulation 4(4).

⁴ HSWA 1974, s 48(1).
⁵ Regulation 26.

18.17 The duty owed, under reg 4(2), by a person who has control of a workplace where workers other than his employees work is limited only to 'matters within that person's control'.[1] As the Guidance to the ACOP states, a landlord who retains control over common parts of a workplace (such as the foyer and stairs in a multi-occupational office block) is responsible for ensuring that those common parts comply with the Regulations in so far as such compliance relates to matters under his control.[2] Therefore, such a landlord can be responsible for the suitable construction of the stairs but not for the slippery substance which has been spilt on them (unless he had undertaken to provide cleaning services).

1 Regulation 4(2)(c).
2 See para 16 of the Guidance.

18.18 Control is a question of fact.[1] In *Bailey v Command Security Services Ltd* [2001] All ER (D) 352 (Oct), QBD, the claimant was a night security guard who fell down an unfenced lift shaft while patrolling a warehouse. Geoffrey Burke QC (sitting as a High Court Judge) found that although the claimant's employer was an occupier of the warehouse and had power to report such dangers, these factors were not sufficient to establish control within the meaning of reg 4(1). It was the warehouse owner who had power to alter the workplace and the things in it so as to comply with the Regulations and who was therefore in control.

1 See *McCook v Lobo* [2002] EWCA Civ 1760 on the interpretation of 'control' in the similar context of the Construction (Health, Safety and Welfare) Regulations 1996.

18.19 In *Bailey* control had not passed; in *King v RCO Support Services Ltd* [2001] ICR 608, CA, the court found it had. In *King*, the claimant, who was employed by a contractor, slipped when gritting an icy yard in a bus garage. The court found that the bus company, which occupied the bus garage, was not in control (within the meaning of the 1992 Regulations) of the yard because it had contracted the task of removing ice to the claimant's employer and had retained no control over how the work was performed. Because the ice and the method of its being removed were not 'matters' within the bus company's control, the bus company was found to have had no duty under the Regulations in respect of the yard at that time.

18.20 *King* appears to be an exceptional case relating to the bringing in of specialist contractors and where the bus garage had no employees working in the vicinity. There is nothing in the Regulations which prevents one person being simultaneously in control of the workplace with another so as to be subject to the duties imposed by the Regulations.[1]

1 See eg *McCully v Farrans Ltd* [2003] NIQB 6 (Sheil J), decided under the identically worded provisions of the Workplace (Health, Safety and Welfare) Regulations (Northern Ireland) 1993.

To whom the duty is owed

18.21 The 1992 Regulations impose a duty on the person in control of the workplace to ensure that the workplace meets the standards required by the Regulations. The duty is owed by the person in control of the premises simply because it is a place of work regardless of whose employees are at work there. Consequently any worker in the workplace, regardless of whether he is employed by the person in control, may bring a claim against the person in control if the worker is injured as a result of that breach.[1]

[1] See e g *McCully v Farrans Ltd* [2003] NIQB 6 (Sheil J), decided under the identically worded provisions of the Workplace (Health, Safety and Welfare) Regulations (Northern Ireland) 1993.

18.22 The question of whether the workplace needs to be the injured person's place of work has been more vexed and has produced a number of conflicting decisions. In *Banna v Delicato* 1999 SLT (Sh Ct) 84, the pursuer was a customer in a shop who tripped over a bread basket on the floor. Sheriff Morrison QC held that the reference to 'a person' in reg 12(3) was not confined to persons working in the shop. Sheriff Herald in *O'Brien v Duke of Argyll's Trustees* 1999 SLT (Sh Ct) 88 came to the same conclusion. In *Layden v Aldi GmbH & Co KG* 2002 SLT (Sh Ct) 71, Sheriff Ross took a different view and held that the meaning of 'a person' in reg 12(3) was a person at work in the workplace. This decision was approved by the English Court of Appeal in *Ricketts v Torbay Council* [2003] EWCA Civ 613 in which the Recorder who tried the case held that the Regulations did not provide a right of action to a visiting member of the public injured in someone else's workplace. The Court of Appeal dismissed the claimant's application for permission to appeal.[1] Lord Drummond Young in the Outer House in *McCondichie v Mains Medical Centre* [2003] ScotCS 270, [2004] Rep LR 4 also held that the Regulations did not apply to persons who were not working in the workplace. The subsequent first instance decisions in *Mathieson v Aberdeenshire Council* 2003 SLT (Sh Ct) 91 (Sheriff Buchanan), *Fagg v Tesco Stores Ltd* (2004, unreported) (Sheriff Ireland) and *Pickett v Forbouys* [2004] CLY 1813 (HHJ Thompson QC) still went on to prefer the decisions in *Banna* and *O'Brien* over that in *Layden*. Finally, the Inner House in *Donaldson v Hays Distribution Services* [2005] Rep LR 92 held that the protection of the Regulations was not afforded to non-workers present in the workplace. Giving the opinion of the court, Lord Macfadyen analysed the decisions referred to above, the previous legislation, the Regulations and the European Directives and concluded as follows:

> 'Drawing together the various considerations which we have reviewed, we conclude from:
> i   the fact that the Workplace Regulations were enacted to give effect in the United Kingdom to the Workplace Directive, which applies exclusively for the protection of workers;
> ii   the absence of any positive indication in the legislation that it was intended that the Workplace Regulations should afford protection to those coming onto premises as visitors and not workers; and
> iii   the extreme improbability that the legislative intention was to supersede much of the law of occupiers' liability tacitly by the mere use of general language which might be said in the abstract to be capable of having that effect;

that on a sound construction of the Workplace Regulations in the relevant context they afford no protection to persons present in a workplace as visitors but not as workers. That does not mean that such persons are left unprotected. They continue to have the protection afforded to visitors to premises by the antecedent, and subsisting, law relating to occupiers' liability.'[2]

1   Although the Court of Appeal in *Ricketts* heard detailed oral submissions and gave a full and reasoned judgment, the effect of the *Practice Direction (Citation of Authorities)* [2001] 1 WLR 1001 is that this decision may not be cited before any court in England and Wales because it was only a decision as to whether to grant permission to appeal and the hearing was only attended by the applicant.
2   *Donaldson v Hays Distribution Services* [2005] CSIH 48 per Lord Macfadyen at para 35.

18.23   Therefore, because the Court of Appeal's decision in *Ricketts* is not citable before any court in England and Wales,[1] the only cases which presently may be cited in England and Wales are the Scottish cases and the county court decision in *Pickett*. In terms of binding authority, the matter therefore remains open in England and Wales. However, the decision of the Scots Outer House in *Donaldson* is binding in Scotland and commands great respect in England and Wales. It is persuasive both in terms of the status of the court and the power of Lord Macfaden's reasoning, which involved consideration of all the decided cases, including the Court of Appeal's decision in *Ricketts*.

1   See para 18.22 fn 1, above.

THE SPECIFIC DUTIES UNDER THE 1992 REGULATIONS

Stability and solidity of the building housing the workplace

18.24   As from 17 September 2002, reg 4A of the 1992 Regulations requires that where a workplace is in a building, the building shall have a stability and solidity appropriate to the nature of use of the workplace.[1] Although, the duty is strict, it is limited to what is 'appropriate', which is almost certainly to be construed to mean appropriate from the viewpoint of health and safety.[2]

1   Regulation 4A was added by the Health and Safety (Miscellaneous Amendments) Regulations 2002, SI 2002/2174, reg 6(c).
2   Such was the approach to the word 'suitable' in reg 12(1) in *Palmer v Marks & Spencer plc* [2001] EWCA Civ 1528, to the word 'efficient' in reg 5 in *Coates v Jaguar Cars Ltd* [2004] EWCA Civ 337, 'suitable' in reg 17(2) in *Pratt v Intermet Refractories* (21 January 2000, unreported), CA and to the word 'efficient' in reg 5 of the Provision and Use of Work Equipment Regulations 1998 in *Ball v Street* [2005] EWCA Civ 76.

Maintenance of the workplace, and certain equipment, devices and systems

18.25   Regulation 5 of the 1992 Regulations requires that the workplace, and certain equipment, devices and systems, shall be maintained (including cleaned as appropriate) in an efficient state, in efficient working order and in good repair. This parallels an identically worded obligation regarding work equipment imposed by the Provision and Use of Work Equipment Regulations.[1]

1   See the Provision and Use of Work Equipment Regulations 1992, reg 6 and the Provision and Use of Work Equipment Regulations 1998, reg 5.

'Maintain'

18.26 In *Coates v Jaguar Cars* [2004] EWCA Civ 337, the absence of a handrail from a flight of stairs was held not to be a failure of maintenance because the duty relates to maintenance and repair of what has been provided and not with what should be provided. Tuckey LJ said 'As its heading and content makes clear, reg 5 is concerned with maintenance. One must look elsewhere in the regulations to see what is required to be provided.'[1]

1 Per Tuckey LJ at para 12. Eg see reg 12(5) and duties in respect of handrails.

18.27 In *Malcolm v Commissioner of Police for the Metropolis* (24 February 1999, unreported), QBD, the claimant was injured by the doors of a lift closing on her. HHJ MacDuff QC found that the lift was not in an efficient state, in efficient working order and in good repair and therefore the Regulations were breached regardless of how good the maintenance operations had been or how unforeseeable was the defect. The duty is strict. In reaching this conclusion, the judge interpreted the phrase 'maintained in an efficient state, in efficient working order and in good repair' as meaning the same as it had been held to have meant in previous legislation.[1]

1 HHJ MacDuff relied upon the decision in *Galashiels Gas Co Ltd v Millar* [1949] AC 275 concerning the Factories Act 1937, ss 22(1) and 152(1). See also *Hamilton v National Coal Board* [1960] AC 633 in relation to the Mines and Quarries Act 1954, s 81(1). See also *Stark v The Post Office* [2000] PIQR P105 in respect of the Provision and Use of Work Equipment Regulations 1992, reg 6 (now replaced by the Provision and Use of Work Equipment Regulations 1998, reg 5).

'In an efficient state, in efficient working order and in good repair'

18.28 In *Malcolm v Metropolitan Police Comr* [1999] CLY 2880, QBD, the duty, under reg 5, to maintain equipment in an efficient state, in efficient working order and in good repair, was held to be a strict duty. In *Coates v Jaguar Cars* [2004] EWCA Civ 337, the court accepted the submission that 'efficient' in this context means efficient from the viewpoint of safety, not from the viewpoint of productivity or economy. *Ball v Street* [2005] EWCA Civ 76, involved the similarly worded duty under the Provision and Use of Work Equipment Regulations 1998, reg 5. The court found that equipment may not be in an efficient condition even though it still works. Potter LJ said:

'Where a defect renders the machine other than in good repair, consideration of overall efficiency loss in relation to the task in hand is not an exercise which the Regulation invites, or the court is required to follow. It would lead to varying and infinite arguments as to the percentage efficiency or other criteria of suitability in cases where, as pointed out in *Galashiels v Millar*, the imposition of an absolute duty is designed to render the task of an injured workman easier by simply requiring him to prove that the mechanism of the machine (which must mean any significant part of the machine) failed to work efficiently and/or was not in good repair and that such failure caused the accident (per Lord Morton).'

18.29 In *Lewis v Avidan Ltd* [2005] EWCA Civ 670, it was held that because a floor was wet and slippery from a burst pipe, it did not mean that the floor was not maintained in an efficient state, in efficient working order and in good repair. May LJ said:

> 'Perhaps it could be said that a flood could make the floor not in an efficient state; but those words have to be read in their context. The workplace, including the floor, has to be "maintained (including cleaned as appropriate) in an efficient state", and "efficient state" appears in conjunction with "efficient working order and good repair". The word "maintained" imports the concept of doing something to the floor itself, such as cleaning or repairing it. The mere fact of a flood does not mean that the floor is not maintained in an efficient state.

As Lord Oaksey said in *Latimer v AEC Limited* [1953] AC 643 at 656:

> "On the question of the construction of section 25(1) of the Factories Act, 1937, I am of the opinion that by virtue of that section and the interpretation section 152, the respondents were bound to maintain the floors and passages in an efficient state, but I do not consider that it was proved that they were not in an efficient state. A floor does not, in my opinion, cease to be in an efficient state because a piece of orange peel or a small pool of some slippery material is on it. Whilst I do not agree that the maintenance of the floors is confined to their construction, I think the obligation to maintain them in an efficient state introduces into what is an absolute duty a question of degree as to what is efficient."

> Mr Spencer Ley [counsel for the claimant] suggests that this could mean that a small amount of water would not be a breach of the regulation but that a flood might be. I disagree. This again veers away from "maintaining". The mere fact of an entirely unexpected and unpredictable flood does not mean that the floor is not maintained in an efficient state. There would, of course, be a breach of regulation 12(3) if the employer did not have the flood mopped up properly; but that is not the present case.'

Although May LJ sought to focus on the meaning of 'maintain', it is clear that his decision is based upon the meaning of 'an efficient state' in relation to a floor. Certainly that was the focus of the observations of Lord Oaksey in the passage quoted.

18.30 A similar conclusion had been reached in the earlier case of *Green v Yorkshire Traction Co Ltd* [2001] EWCA Civ 1952, in relation to the similarly worded Provision and Use of Work Equipment Regulations 1992, reg 6(1).[1] Because rainwater on the step of a bus was simply the result of the bus going about its ordinary everyday work, picking up passengers and transporting them in weather which was not in any way out of ordinary, the presence of the water, although creating a risk, was not such as to render the bus not in an efficient state, in efficient working order and in good repair. The decision in *Lewis* goes further, unless a leak from a burst water pipe is to be considered 'not in any way out of the ordinary'. However, in view of the House of Lords' decision in *Latimer v AEC Ltd* [1953] AC 643, this part of the decision in *Lewis* must be accepted as correctly decided.

---

[1]   Now replaced by the identically worded reg 5(1) of the Provision and Use of Work Equipment Regulations 1998, SI 1998/2306.

'Workplace'

18.31 The duty under reg 5 is to ensure that the workplace is maintained (including cleaned as appropriate) in an efficient state, in efficient working order and in good repair.

The Regulation draws a distinction between the workplace and equipment, devices and systems in it. The meaning of 'workplace' in this context has been considered in a number of cases.

18.32 In *Irvine v Commissioner of Police for the Metropolis* [2005] EWHC 1536 (QB), [2005] PIQR P11, HHJ Kirkham held that the workplace included both a staircase and the carpet laid upon it. He considered it to be an artificial approach to distinguish the carpet from the structure of the staircase in the context of the definition of workplace in reg 2(1). He rejected an argument that as reg 12 imposes specific duties in relation to stairs, stairs are therefore not covered by reg 5. He considered that the two regulations were not mutually exclusive. In *Coates v Jaguar Cars Ltd* [2004] EWCA Civ 337, the Court of Appeal upheld the decision that a flight of steps (although not a 'staircase' within the meaning of reg 12(5)) was part of the workplace within the meaning of reg 5.

18.33 On the other hand, in *Beck v United Closures and Plastics* 2001 SLT 1299, Lord McEwan considered that 'the interpretation of workplace in regulation 2 contemplates by definition things which are open spaces'.[1] Therefore doors which formed part of machinery were not part of the workplace.[2]

1 At para 25 of the opinion.
2 The doors were held to be governed by, reg 18 (doors and gates) and the Provision and Use of Work Equipment Regulations 1992, reg 6(1) (now replaced by the identically worded Provision and Use of Work Equipment Regulations 1998, reg 5).

18.34 In *Lewis v Avidan Ltd* [2005] EWCA Civ 670, a concealed water pipe in a nursing home burst causing water to be on the floor. Shortly afterwards, the claimant stepped in the water and slipped. May LJ accepted that the pipe was not maintained in good repair, but he found that the pipe was not the workplace. 'Workplace' is defined in reg 2(1) as 'premises or part of premises which are ... made available to any person as a place of work' and the concealed pipe was not considered by May LJ to be a place made available as a place of work. The floor was the workplace, but the concealed pipe was not. May LJ did however consider the pipe to be capable of being 'equipment, devices or systems' within reg 5 (see below).

18.35 The earlier decision in *Fox v Sherratt* (29 January 2005, unreported), Manchester County Court (Judge Holman), held that a roof of a building was part of the workplace such that a leak in the roof gave rise to a breach of the duty to maintain the workplace. This may be wrongly decided given the decision in *Lewis*. The first instance decision in *Parker v PFC Flooring Supplies* [2001] PIQR P115, QB, that a roof was a workplace or part of a workplace, is distinguishable because there the claimant had been permitted to climb onto the roof to remove debris and the roof was therefore his place of work at the time.

'Equipment, devices and systems'

18.36 The duty under reg 5 is also a duty to ensure that certain equipment, devices and systems are maintained (including cleaned as appropriate) in an efficient state, in efficient working order and in good repair. The equipment, devices and systems to which this Regulation applies are:

(a) equipment and devices a fault in which is liable to result in a failure to comply with any other of the Workplace Regulations (reg 5(3)(a));

(b) mechanical ventilation systems as required by reg 6 (reg 5(3)(b)); and

(c) equipment and devices intended to prevent or reduce hazards (reg 5(3)(c)).[1]

---

[1] Regulation 5(3)(c) was added as from 17 September 2002 by the Health and Safety (Miscellaneous Amendments) Regulations 2002, SI 2002/2174, reg 6(d).

18.37 In *Beck v United Closures & Plastics* 2001 SLT 1299, Lord McEwan found that the position of door handles on doors which made them difficult to open meant that the doors were not suitably constructed and therefore in breach of reg 18. However he found that there was no breach of reg 5 because the difficulty opening the doors affected their efficiency in terms of productivity, not health and safety, and so the doors were not equipment or a device to which reg 5(3)(a) applied.

18.38 In *Lewis v Avidan Ltd* [2005] EWCA Civ 670, May LJ stated that whilst he was prepared to assume that a leaking water pipe was equipment that was not in good repair, he considered that this would not of itself result in a breach of reg 5(3)(a). This was because the only other regulation which was alleged to have been breached as a result of the leak was reg 12(3) and, on the facts of the case, it was not reasonably practicable to have prevented the leak nor to have discovered and cleaned it up before the claimant slipped in it. Since there had been no breach of reg 12(3), there could be no breach of reg 5(3).

18.39 This approach to the interpretation of reg 5(3)(a) would mean that there can be no breach of the duty relating to equipment or devices unless there was also an existing breach of another of the Regulations. In terms of imposing a duty, the breach of which gives rise to an action in damages, this part of reg 5 is therefore superfluous. It is submitted that May LJ's interpretation requires reading the phrase 'is liable to' as meaning 'already has'. An alternate reading of 'is liable to' as meaning 'is likely to' or 'may' would appear a more appropriate interpretation. Such alternate reading would give the regulation a purpose consistent with the objective of both the Workplace Directive, the HSWA 1974, and other similar Regulations (eg PUWER 1998) as opposed to being superfluous.

Floors and traffic routes

18.40 Regulation 12 imposes a series of duties in respect of the floors and the surface of traffic routes in the workplace. Regulation 12(1) (supplemented by reg 12(2) and (4)) concerns the construction of the floor or of the surface of the traffic route. Regulation 12(3) concerns obstructions, substances and articles upon the floor or surface of the traffic route. Regulation 12(5) imposes a duty in respect of handrails or guards on staircases.

18.41 Traffic route is defined as 'a route for pedestrian traffic, vehicles or both and includes any stairs, staircase, fixed ladder, doorway, gateway, loading bay or ramp'.[1]

1   Regulation 12(1).

Construction of floors and traffic routes

18.42 Regulation 12(1) requires that every floor and the surface of every traffic route in a workplace shall be of a construction such that it is suitable for the purpose for which it is used. Regulation 12(2) requires that 'the floor, or surface of the traffic route, shall have no hole or slope, or be uneven or slippery so as, in each case, to expose any person to a risk to his health or safety and every such floor shall have effective means of drainage where necessary.[1] This is a strict duty. It is not subject to the limits of reasonable practicability.

1   Regulation 12(2)(a) and (b). Read literally this requires that the floor 'shall ... be uneven'. It is however clear, from the context, that the Regulation provides that 'the floor, or surface of the traffic route, shall not have any hole or slope, or be uneven or slippery so as, in each case, to expose any person to a risk to his health or safety'.

'Suitable'

18.43 Although the duty under reg 12(1) is strict, it is limited to ensuring the floor surface is suitable for the purpose for which it is used. This includes a requirement that it is suitable for any person using it for that purpose.[1] In *Palmer v Marks & Spencer plc* [2001] EWCA Civ 1528, the claimant tripped on a marginally raised weather strip in a doorway by the top of a flight of stairs. The Court of Appeal held that whilst reg 12(1) imposed an absolute duty, the meaning of 'suitable' was to be found in the reference to 'risk to ... health and safety' in reg 12(2). Therefore, suitability must be examined from a health and safety point of view. The mere fact of an accident due to an anomaly in the floor surface is not sufficient to establish that the floor was not suitable. The question whether the floor surface poses a risk to health and safety involves consideration of all relevant factors including the likelihood of harm, the potential seriousness of resulting injury and the importance of taking adequate precautions. These factors are to be considered from a point in time before the accident which gave rise to the claim. A similar conclusion was reached in the Scottish case of *McGhee v Strathclyde Fire Brigade* 2002 SLT 680, OH, in which a fireman slipped on the surface of a corridor floor alleged to be not suitable because of its slipperiness. The Outer House (Lord Hamilton) considered that the test of whether the slipperiness of the floor surface was in breach of reg 12(1) was whether the floor was sufficiently slippery so as to expose a person to a risk to his health or safety as referred to in reg 12(2). The court considered that the regulation envisaged that a floor may, by its construction, be slippery so as to expose any person to a risk to his health or safety, or so as not to do so. It is only slipperiness of the first kind to which the regulation is directed.

1 Regulation 2(3).

18.44 This approach to the meaning of 'suitable' in reg 12(1) was approved and followed by the Court of Appeal in *Lowles v Home Office* [2004] EWCA Civ 985. A step at the top of a ramp was held to be not suitable because it posed a risk of tripping, despite the fact that a warning sign was present saying 'please mind the step'. Applying all the factors identified in *Palmer*, a court must then step back and assess whether the floor was suitable. Of particular relevance in *Lowles* was that the step served no particular purpose. For no particular reason, the ramp failed to end flush with the floor.

18.45 The step in *Lowles* was also found to be an 'obstruction' contrary to reg 12(3). The Court of Appeal rejected the argument that the step could not be both an 'obstruction' and a feature of the floor's construction which rendered the floor not suitable. Regulations 12(1) and 12(3) were not mutually exclusive.

18.46 The ACOP states that where surfaces of floors and traffic routes are likely to get wet or to be subject to spillages, the surface should be of a type which does not become unduly slippery when wet.[1]

1 ACOP, para 93. Examples of where county courts have found that a floor's construction was sufficiently slippery to be unsuitable include *Drage v Grassroots* [2000] CLY 2967 and *Wenham v Bexley* [1999] CLY 2879.

Obstructions, articles and substances on floors and traffic routes

18.47 Regulation 12(3) requires that, so far as is reasonably practicable, every floor and the surface of every traffic route in the workplace shall be kept free from obstructions and from any article or substance which may cause a person to slip, trip or fall. This is in addition to the duty under reg 12(1). Therefore, a feature of the floor's construction can amount to an obstruction as well as rendering the floor's construction not suitable.[1] In both cases, the question is whether the feature gives rise to risk.

1 *Lowles v Home Office* [2004] EWCA Civ 985.

'Obstructions ... article or substance'

18.48 An obstruction can be a feature of the floor's surface, such as an unnecessary step.[1]

1   *Lowles v Home Office* [2004] EWCA Civ 985.

18.49 In *Jenkins v Allied Iron Founders Ltd* [1970] 1 WLR 304, the House of Lords considered the meaning of 'obstruction' in the Factories Act 1961, s 28(1).[1] Lord Reid said 'It is quite true that this word must be given a limited meaning. It is clearly not intended to include easily visible objects properly put on the floor in the course of a proper system of work.' In *Simmons v British Steel plc* 2002 SLT 711, OH, the pursuer tripped on tubing present on the floor. The tubing was in use and clearly visible. Lord Hardie accepted that the tubing was therefore not an obstruction but pointed out that reg 12(3) was wider than s 28(1) of the Factories Act because it also concerned 'articles'. The tubing was an article and it was reasonably practicable for it not to have been on the floor.

1   Section 28(1) of the Factories Act 1961 required that 'all floors ... shall, so far as is reasonably practicable, be kept free from any obstruction and from any substance likely to cause persons to slip'.

'Reasonably practicable'

18.50 Once a claimant has proved that he was injured as a result of an obstruction, or an article or substance which may cause a person to slip, trip or fall being present on the floor or the surface of the traffic route, the burden is then upon the defendant to plead and to prove that it was not reasonably practicable to prevent the presence of that obstruction, article or substance.[1] The claimant does not need to prove that the presence of the obstruction, article or substance, or the risks posed thereby, was known to, or reasonably foreseeable by, the defendant.[2] However, the lack of reasonable foresight is relevant to the question of reasonable practicability.[3]

1   See *Larner v British Steel plc* [1993] ICR 551, decided in relation to the Factories Act 1961, s 29(1), which required that, so far as reasonably practicable, every place of work shall be made and kept safe. The obligation on the defendant to plead any defence of reasonable practicability should be viewed subject to the dictum of May LJ in *Pratt v Intermet Refractories Ltd* (21 January 2000, unreported), that a claimant's objection that the defence had not been pleaded had no place 'in modern litigation' if the claimant was not prejudiced.

2   'No question of knowledge or foreseeability is involved at this stage. The mere presence of a substance which may cause a person to slip is enough to engage the obligation imposed by the Regulation, subject to the reasonably practicable defence, which it is for the employer to prove' per Tuckey LJ in *Bassie v Merseyside Fire and Civil Defence Authority* [2005] EWCA Civ 1474 at para 11.

3   *Larner v British Steel plc* [1993] ICR 551. See for instance *Furness v Midland Bank* (10 November 2000, unreported), CA, referred to below.

18.51 It is for the defendant to prove not only that it was not reasonably practicable to have removed the obstruction, article or substance but also that it was not reasonably practicable to have prevented it getting there in the first place.[1] Therefore the fact that the claimant tripped over an obstruction or article which she was employed as a cleaner to remove does not excuse the defendant from the duty, so far as reasonably practicable, to ensure that the obstruction or article was not there in the first place.[2]

[1]   *Johnston v Caddies Wainwright* [1983] ICR 407, CA, decided under the similarly worded Factories Act 1961, s 28(1).
[2]   *Burgess v Plymouth City Council* [2005] EWCA Civ 1659.

18.52 The expression 'reasonably practicable' has been used in legislation relating to health and safety for many years and the subject of a number of decisions.[1] Its application in workplace slipping and tripping cases is demonstrated by the following cases.

[1]   See e g *Nimmo v Alexander Cowan & Sons Ltd* [1968] AC 107; *Gibson v British Insulated Callendars Construction Co Ltd* 1973 SLT 2; *Bowes v Sedgefield District Council* [1981] ICR 234 and *Larner v British Steel plc* [1993] ICR 551.

18.53 In *Pratt v Intermet Refractories Ltd* (21 January 2000, unreported), CA, May LJ said that in straightforward tripping cases, 'what is reasonably practicable is a matter of common sense'. In *Jacob v Tesco Stores Ltd* (5 November 1998, unreported), CA,[1] the fact that the defendant had no reason to believe that its cleaning system was inadequate did not mean that it was not reasonably practicable for the obstruction, article or substance to have been removed. In *Pettie v Southampton University Hospitals NHS Trust* [2003] CLY 2974, a hospital administrative worker slipped on ice in the car park. The defendant argued that it was sufficient to grit the roadways but not the parking spaces. The court rejected this. It found that the additional resources required to grit the parking spaces were not disproportionate to the risk and it was reasonably practicable to have done so.

[1]   Decided under the similarly worded Offices Shops and Railway Premises Act 1963, s 16.

18.54 In *Robinson v Midland Bank* (27 October 2000, unreported), CA, the claimant tripped over a library kick stool which had not been present minutes earlier. The defendant had failed to show that it had taken all reasonably practicable measures to prevent its presence, therefore the defendant was in breach of the duty under reg 12(3). Similarly in *Anderson v Newham College of Further Education* [2002] EWCA Civ 505, the claimant tripped over the leg of a classroom whiteboard protruding into the passage between desks. The Court of Appeal allowed the claimant's appeal, as the defendant could have avoided the tripping hazard simply by ensuring that the board was turned round to face the other way.

18.55 In *Harper v Staffordshire County Council* [2003] EWHC 283 (QB), a teacher slipped on a discarded potato chip on a school staircase near the dining hall during lunch. The defendant was aware of the risks created by food being removed from the dining hall. The court found for the claimant, as the defendant had not shown that it was not reasonably practicable for the door to have been kept locked or to have inspected and cleaned the stairs sooner than waiting until after lunch. In *Burgess v Plymouth City Council*

[2005] EWCA Civ 1659, a school cleaner tripped on a box on a classroom floor. The school's routine was that such boxes were put away at the end of the day before the cleaners arrived, not least because of the risks associated with leaving them lying around. There was no evidence as to why it had not been reasonably practicable for the box to have been put away on this occasion. The claimant succeeded (subject to a finding of 50% contributory negligence).

18.56 Both *Harper* and *Burgess* involved items which were known would create a danger if their presence was not prevented. In *Furness v Midland Bank* (10 November 2000, unreported), CA, the claimant slipped in a minor spillage of water on stairs. There had been no reason to believe that water would be spilled on these stairs and a reasonable system of routine cleaning was in place. The Court of Appeal upheld the judge's finding that it was not reasonably practicable for the employer to have prevented, or detected the presence of a small drop of water.

18.57 In *Bassie v Merseyside Fire and Civil Defence Authority* [2005] EWCA Civ 1474, the claimant slipped and fell whilst performing exercises in a fire station's appliance room which was mopped once a week and swept before such exercises began. The sweeping failed to remove a fine layer of invisible dust, which an inspection after the accident revealed to be present. Mopping would have removed the dust. The gymnasium was mopped daily and there was no evidence showing that it had not been reasonably practicable also to have mopped the appliance room daily. The claimant succeeded and the Court of Appeal dismissed the defendant's appeal.

18.58 In *Lowles v Home Office* [2004] EWCA Civ 985, the top of a ramp did not end level with the portacabin floor but about two inches below it, therefore creating a step up from the ramp into the cabin. The claimant tripped on this step whilst entering the cabin. The court held that the step was an obstruction and that the defendant had not shown that it was not reasonably practicable to have ensured that the ramp ended flush with the cabin floor.

Slips, trips and falls caused by the arrangement of outdoor workstations

18.59 Regulation 11(3)(c) requires every workstation outdoors to be so arranged that it ensures that any person at work at the workstation is not likely to slip, trip or fall. Unlike the duty under reg 12(3), this is not subject to reasonable practicability.

Staircases

18.60 Regulation 12(5) requires all staircases to be fitted with suitable and sufficient handrails (unless this would obstruct a traffic route) and, if appropriate, guards. The duty is strict. In *Otaegui v Gledhill* (2 May 2003, unreported), QBD, where a staircase had no handrail and a handrail would have prevented the accident and could have been fitted without obstructing the traffic route, the defendant was held liable. In *Jaguar Cars Ltd v Coates* [2004] EWCA Civ 337, the court considered that a flight of four steps leading up to a building entrance was not a 'staircase' and therefore the failure to provide a handrail was not a breach of reg 12(5).

Organisation of traffic routes

18.61 Regulation 17 deals with the provision and layout of traffic routes. It requires that every workplace shall be organised in such a way that pedestrians and vehicles can circulate in a safe manner.[1] Suitable measures are to be taken to ensure that: (a) a traffic route may be used by pedestrians and/or vehicles without causing danger to the health or safety of persons at work near it; (b) there is sufficient separation of any vehicular traffic route from doors or gates or from traffic routes for pedestrians which lead onto it; and (c) where vehicles and pedestrians use the same traffic route, there is sufficient separation between them.[2] All traffic routes are to be suitably indicated where necessary for reasons of health or safety.[3] Traffic routes in a workplace shall be suitable for the persons or vehicles using them, sufficient in number, in suitable positions and of sufficient size.[4] These duties are all strict, save for the last which, in respect of workplaces already used as a workplace prior to 1 January 1993 or a modification, extension or conversion started prior to that date, is subject to reasonable practicability.[5] The ACOP advises marking of speed limits.[6]

[1] Regulation 17(1).
[2] Regulation 17(3).
[3] Regulation 17(4).
[4] Regulation 17(2).
[5] Regulation 17(3). Arguably this qualification in relation to the older workplaces is an inadequate implementation of the Workplace Directive. Article 4 and para 16 of Annex II of the Directive place an apparently absolute duty on the organisation of such workplaces such that 'pedestrians and vehicles can circulate in a safe manner'.
[6] ACOP, para 164.

18.62 A traffic route which is wide enough to allow safe passage and is well lit can still be suitable even though there is an obstruction intruding minimally across its edges: *Pratt v Intermet Refractories Ltd* (21 January 2000, unreported), CA. If a traffic route is locked by a gate which the claimant is unable to open, there is a breach of reg 17(2) as the traffic route is not 'suitable': *Wallis v Balfour Beatty Rail Maintenance* [2003] EWCA Civ 72.[1] In *Nichols v Beck Electronics Ltd* (30 June 2004, unreported), Norwich County Court (Recorder Wilson), a sliding door had been tied shut for safety reasons. The claimant was unaware of this and injured herself as a result of trying to pull it open. The failure to have warned her that the door was sealed shut amounted to a breach of the requirement, under reg 17(2), that traffic routes be suitable.

[1] However, despite the absence of a suitable traffic route, the claimant's claim failed because it was his decision, faced with the locked gate, to climb over a fence and proceed along a more dangerous route. The breach of reg 17 was therefore not causative of the accident.

Escalators and moving walkways

18.63 Regulation 19 requires that escalators and moving walkways shall function safely, be equipped with any necessary safety devices and be fitted with one or more emergency stop controls which are easily identifiable and readily accessible.

Falls and falling objects

18.64 Prior to being revoked[1] on 6 April 2005, reg 13(1) imposed a duty so far as reasonably practicable to take suitable and effective measures to prevent any person falling a distance likely to cause injury or being struck by a falling object likely to cause personal injury. So far as reasonably practicable, these measures were to be measures other than the provision of personal protective equipment, information, instruction, training or supervision.[2] Therefore the provision of personal protective equipment, information, instruction, training or supervision was to be no more than a second line of defence and the primary duty was to prevent the risk by other means, unless it was not reasonably practicable to do so. Any part of the workplace where there was such a risk was required to be clearly indicated where appropriate.[3] The obviousness of the danger is no defence.[4]

[1] By the Work at Height Regulations 2005, SI 2005/735, reg 19.
[2] Regulation 13(2), revoked as from 6 April 2005 by the Work at Height Regulations 2005, SI 2005/735, reg 19.
[3] Regulation 13(4), revoked as from 6 April 2005 by the Work at Height Regulations 2005, SI 2005/735, reg 19.
[4] See eg *Bailey v Command Security Services and TJX Incorporated* (25 October 2001, unreported), QB, unfenced lift shaft in warehouse.

18.65 In *Mathieson v Aberdeenshire Council* 2003 SLT 91, the pursuer stumbled against a low sagging chain fence around the edge of a raised platform. He was overbalanced by the top chain and fell over it to the ground below. The judge found that the risk of falling was obvious and this was why the chain fence had been provided. There was no evidence that it was not reasonably practicable to have fitted a rigid fence high enough to prevent the pursuer overbalancing it. The defender was found to be in breach of reg 13(1).

18.66 Where there is a risk of a person falling into a dangerous substance in a tank, pit or structure, then the tank, pit or structure shall so far as reasonably practicable be securely covered or fenced.[1] If the tank, pit or structure is not covered then any traffic route over or across it shall be securely fenced.[2]

[1] Regulation 13(5). This was not revoked by the Work at Height Regulations 2005.
[2] Regulation 13(6). This was not revoked by the Work at Height Regulations 2005.

18.67 The ACOP suggests that fixed ladders should not be provided in circumstances where it would be practical to install a staircase.[1] Where fixed ladders are to be used, the Code gives detailed recommendations including that the ladders be of sound construction, properly maintained and securely fixed but not depend solely upon nails, screws or similar fixings for their support. The rungs should be horizontal, and give an adequate foothold.[2]

1   ACOP, paras 119 and 126.
2   ACOP, paras 119–124.

18.68 In respect of roof work, the ACOP states that where regular access is needed to roofs, suitable permanent access should be provided and there should be fixed physical safeguards to prevent falls from edges and through fragile roofs.[1]

1   ACOP, para 192.

18.69 The ACOP suggests that the need to climb on top of vehicles should be avoided so far as possible and where it is unavoidable, fixed gantries or fencing should be provided.[1] In *Wright v Romford Blinds and Shutters Ltd* [2003] EWHC 1165 (QB), the employer was found liable under reg 13 for failing to prevent an employee falling from the roof of a transit van when he was loading the roof-rack and lost his footing. The court found that guardrails would have prevented the fall and so should have been provided.

1   ACOP, paras 138 and 139.

18.70 With effect from 6 April 2005, reg 13(1), (2), (3) and (4) of the 1992 Regulations was revoked and replaced by the Work at Height Regulations 2005, SI 2005/735, which imposed duties which are both wider and more specific than those it revoked. The 2005 Regulations are dealt with in the chapter on construction work from para 19.29 onwards.

Workstations

18.71 Regulation 11(1) requires every workstation to be arranged so that it is suitable for any person at work in the workplace who is likely to work at that workstation and so that it is suitable for any work of the undertaking which is likely to be done there.

18.72 'Workstation' is not defined in the Regulations or the Directive. In *Duncanson v South Ayrshire Council* 1999 SLT 519, a room in a children's nursery where the pursuer was working as a nursery nurse, was considered to be a workstation.[1]

1   However, on the facts of the case, there was nothing wrong with the workstation's arrangement.

18.73 'Suitable' probably means free from risk of injury.[1] The ACOP states that the workstation should be suitable for any special needs of the individual worker, including workers with disabilities. Spells of work which unavoidably have to be carried out in cramped conditions should be kept as short as possible because a static and awkward posture may lead to chronic injury. So too the use of undesirable force and an uncomfortable hand grip, often coupled with continuous repetitive work without sufficient rest and recovery.[2] The import of the Guidance is that the compliance with the Regulations should reduce the risk of work related upper limb disorders or other repetitive strain induced injuries.[3]

[1] Such was the approach to the word 'suitable' in reg 12(1) in *Palmer v Marks & Spencer plc* [2001] EWCA Civ 1528, to the word 'efficient' in reg 5 in *Coates v Jaguar Cars Ltd* [2004] EWCA Civ 337, 'suitable' in reg 17(2) in *Pratt v Intermet Refractories* (21 January 2000, unreported), CA and to the word 'efficient' in reg 5 of the Provision and Use of Work Equipment Regulations 1998 in *Ball v Street* [2005] EWCA Civ 76.

[2] Paras 82, 83 of the ACOP. Para 87 of the Guidance.

[3] Use of a computer at work is also covered by the wider and more specific provisions of the Health and Safety (Display Screen Equipment) Regulations 1992, see para 20.79 onwards.

Outdoor workstations

18.74 A workstation outdoors is required to be suitably arranged (as required under reg 11(1))[1] and also to be so arranged that so far as is reasonably practicable, it provides protection from adverse weather, it enables any person at the workstation to leave it swiftly or, as appropriate, to be assisted in the event of an emergency and so that it ensures that any person at the workstation is not likely to slip or fall.[2] The drafting of the Regulation affords the defence of reasonable practicability only to the requirement that the outdoor workstation provide protection from adverse weather. There is no reference to reasonable practicability in the paragraph dealing with the ability to leave quickly or receive emergency assistance nor in the paragraph dealing with prevention of slips, trips or falls. This would appear to impose strict liability for the presence of articles or substances likely to cause a person to slip, trip or fall if they are present on the floor of an outdoor workstation because of how the workstation is 'arranged'. This is to be compared with the duty under reg 12(3) to prevent the presence of such an article or substance so far as reasonably practicable.

[1] See para 18.71, above.

[2] Regulation 11(2).

Seating

18.75 Regulation 11(3), which should be read in conjunction with reg 11(4), requires the provision of a suitable seat for each person at work in the workplace whose work (or a substantial part of it) includes operations of a kind that can or must be done sitting.[1] The seat must be suitable for the person for whom it is provided as well as for the operations to be performed. A seat will not be suitable unless a suitable footrest is also provided where necessary.[2] There must be many workers who should now be provided with suitable seating since they *can* do 'a substantial part' of their work sitting down.[3] The words 'suitable' and 'necessary' are probably to be understood in terms of health and safety.[4] The Regulations also provide, since 17 September 2002, for the provision of suitable seating in restrooms.[5]

[1] Regulation 11(3).

[2] Regulation 11(4).

³   Use of a computer at work is also covered by the wider and more specific provisions of the
    Health and Safety (Display Screen Equipment) Regulations 1992, see para 20.79 onwards.
⁴   Such was the approach to the word 'suitable' in reg 12(1) in *Palmer v Marks & Spencer plc*
    [2001] EWCA Civ 1528, to the word 'efficient' in reg 5 in *Coates v Jaguar Cars Ltd* [2004]
    EWCA Civ 337, 'suitable' in reg 17(2) in *Pratt v Intermet Refractories* (21 January 2000,
    unreported), CA and to the word 'efficient' in reg 5 of the Provision and Use of Work
    Equipment Regulations 1998 in *Ball v Street* [2005] EWCA Civ 76.
⁵   Regulation 25 (see below).

Lighting

18.76 Regulation 8 requires that every workplace shall have suitable and
sufficient lighting which shall, so far as is reasonably practicable, be by
natural light. In addition, if persons are at work in a room where they are
specially exposed to danger if artificial lighting fails, then suitable and
sufficient emergency lighting shall be provided in that room. This is a strict
duty save for the provision of natural light which is subject to reasonable
practicability.

18.77 The duty is to ensure that the workplace has suitable and sufficient
lighting. This may be contrasted with s 5 of the Factories Act 1961 which
required that 'effective provision shall be made for securing and maintaining
suitable and sufficient lighting'. In *Lane v Gloucester Engineering Co Ltd*
[1967] 2 All ER 293, CA, in relation to s 5 of the 1961 Act, the plaintiff
tripped in an area of shadow. The Court of Appeal upheld the trial judge's
ruling that, as the lighting was adequate overall, the duty was not breached by
the particular point where the plaintiff tripped being in shadow. A different
conclusion was reached in *Miller v Perth and Kinross Council* [2002] Rep LR
22 (OH), which was decided under the 1992 Regulations. The pursuer lost her
footing on a sloping pavement as a result of it being in shadow from nearby
street lighting. The absence of sufficient illumination of the pavement was
found to be a breach of reg 8. There is no reference to *Lane* in Lord Hamilton's opinion in *Miller*. The reason for the difference is likely to be the wider
wording of the 1992 Regulations. Other cases decided in relation to s 5 of the
1961 Act illustrate that the duty is strict, such that lights which are provided
but are not turned on or are temporarily not working can constitute a breach
of the duty.¹

¹   *Thorton v Fisher & Ludlow Ltd* [1968] 2 All ER 241 and *Davies v Massey Ferguson
    Perkins Ltd* [1986] ICR 580.

Ventilation

18.78 Regulation 6 requires that effective and suitable provision shall be
made to ensure that every enclosed workplace is ventilated by a sufficient
quantity of fresh purified air.¹ Mechanical ventilation systems provided to
comply with this duty must be maintained (including cleaned as appropriate)
in an efficient state, in efficient working order and in good repair and, if
appropriate, be subject to a suitable system of maintenance.² There must be
visible or audible warning of any failure of ventilation plant.³

1   Regulation 6(1).
2   Regulation 5(1) and (2).
3   Regulation 6(2).

18.79 The ACOP states that the air which is introduced should, as far as possible, be free of any impurity which is likely to be offensive or cause ill health. Air taken from the outside can normally be considered 'fresh', but the air inlets of ventilation systems should not be sited where they may draw in excessively contaminated air. Where necessary, the inlet air should incorporate a filter to remove particulates.[1]

1   ACOP, para 29.

18.80 The duty to ensure that every enclosed workplace is ventilated by a 'sufficient quantity of fresh purified air' probably means sufficient in terms of avoiding risk to health and safety.[1] The requirement for ventilation under reg 6 is a general requirement and does not reduce the duties in relation to dangerous gases, fumes, dust etc (see e g chapter 22 on substances and phenomena at work).

1   Such was the approach to the word 'suitable' in reg 12(1) in *Palmer v Marks & Spencer plc* [2001] EWCA Civ 1528, to the word 'efficient' in reg 5 in *Coates v Jaguar Cars Ltd* [2004] EWCA Civ 337, 'suitable' in reg 17(2) in *Pratt v Intermet Refractories* (21 January 2000, unreported), CA and to the word 'efficient' in the Provision and Use of Work Equipment Regulations 1998, reg 5, in *Ball v Street* [2005] EWCA Civ 76.

Tobacco smoke

18.81 In *Rae v City of Glasgow Council* 1998 SLT 292, OH,[1] decided under the Offices, Shops and Railway Premises Act 1963, s 7,[2] Lord Bonomy accepted that s 7 was plainly directed at the mischief of foul air in the workplace and cigarette smoke fell within that mischief. However the duty under s 7 was not to extract impurities but to provide ventilation by the circulation of adequate supplies of air. Therefore how much the air should be freshened depends upon how much smoke is in the air. Breach of the duty would consist not of a failure to remove the smoke, but by a failure to introduce fresh air. In *Waltons and Morse v Dorringtons* [1997] IRLR 488, the EAT held that a failure to provide relief from cigarette smoke in the workplace amounted to a breach of an implied term in the contract of employment, based on the duty under the HSWA 1974, s 2(1).

1   See also *Rae v Strathclyde Joint Police Board* [1999] Scot CS 70 (9 March 1999).
2   The Offices, Shops and Railway Premises Act 1963, s 7(1) required that 'effective and suitable provision shall be made for securing and maintaining, by the circulation of adequate supplies of fresh or artificially purified air, the ventilation of every room comprised in, or constituting, premises to which this Act applies, being a room in which persons are employed to work'.

18.82 The 1992 Regulations do make specific provision for protection from discomfort from tobacco smoke, but this protection is limited to rest rooms and rest areas.[1]

1   Regulation 25(3) and, as from 17 September 2002, reg 25(3)(a).

Temperature

18.83 Regulation 7 requires that during working hours, the temperature in all workplaces inside buildings shall be reasonable.[1] Every workplace shall be adequately thermally insulated where necessary, having regard to the type of work carried out and the physical activity of the persons carrying out the work. Excessive effects of sunlight on temperature are to be avoided.[2] Any heating or cooling systems must not discharge into the workplace fumes, gas or vapour likely to be injurious or offensive.[3] A sufficient number of thermometers shall be provided to enable persons at work to determine the temperature in any workplace inside a building.[4] The requirement for a reasonable temperature is limited to workplaces inside buildings. On the other hand the requirements for insulation, avoidance of the heat effects of direct sunlight, safe and unoffensive temperature control systems and thermometers are not.

[1]   Regulation 7(1).
[2]   Regulation 7(1A) added from 17 September 2002 by the Health and Safety (Miscellaneous Amendment) Regulations 2002, SI 2002/2174, reg 6(f).
[3]   Regulation 7(2).
[4]   Regulation 7(3).

18.84 What is a 'reasonable' temperature or what fumes, gases or vapours are merely 'offensive' (as opposed to harmful) will be a matter for the court. 'Reasonable' probably means reasonable not only for the worker but in terms of the work, such that what temperature is reasonable in a refrigerated unit chiller must take account of the need for the unit to be chilled.[1]

[1]   ACOP, para 44 recognises this.

18.85 The ACOP states that the temperature in workrooms should provide reasonable comfort without the need for special clothing. If, because of the hot or cold processes of the work, that is impracticable, then the temperature should be as close as possible to comfortable. A minimum temperature of 16 degrees Celsius, or, where much of the work involves severe physical effort, at least 13 degrees Celsius, is recommended.[1] The Code gives no guidance as to the maximum temperature which may be said to be comfortable.

[1]   ACOP, paras 42 and 43.

Cleanliness and facilities

18.86 Regulation 9 requires that every workplace and the furniture, furnishings and fittings therein shall be kept sufficiently clean, the surfaces of the floors, walls and ceilings of all workplaces inside buildings shall be capable of being kept sufficiently clean and, so far as is reasonably practicable, waste materials shall not be allowed to accumulate in a workplace except in suitable receptacles.

18.87 The duty overlaps with the duties under regs 5, 12(3), 20(2)(b) and 21(2)(g).[1] The duties owed under regs 9 and 12(3) are subject to reasonable practicability. The duties under regs 5, 20(2)(b) and 21(2)(g) are not.

1   The duty under reg 5 is to keep clean certain equipment, devices and systems. The duty under reg 12(3) is to to keep the floors and surfaces of traffic routes free from obstructions and from any article or substance which may cause a person to slip, trip or fall. The duties under regs 20(2)(b) and 21(2)(g) are to keep sanitary conveniences and washrooms in a clean and orderly condition.

18.88 In *Pratt v Intermet Refractories Ltd* (21 January 2000, unreported), CA, pallets were stored overnight adjacent to a walkway. A broken piece of one of the pallets (an item of waste material) fell onto the edge of the walkway. The Court of Appeal upheld the finding that the system of storing the pallets overnight was not unreasonable because the pallets had to be stored somewhere, they were removed daily and the broken piece was not something normally stored in a receptacle (as required by reg 9(3)).

Room dimensions and space

18.89 Regulation 10 requires that every room where persons work shall have sufficient floor area, height and unoccupied space for purposes of health, safety and welfare.[1]

1   Regulation 10(1).

18.90 In respect of a workplace first used as a workplace prior to 1 January 1993 or a modification, an extension or a conversion commenced before that date, and which, in either case, was subject to the provisions of the Factories Act 1961 immediately before becoming subject to the 1992 Regulations,[1] this duty is complied with if the workplace does not contravene the provisions of the 1992 Regulations, Sch 1, Pt I.[2] This duty is strict. There is no defence of reasonable practicability.

1   The Regulations came into force on 1 January 1996 for workplaces already in use as a workplace prior to 1 January 1993 and on 1 January 1996 in respect of completed modifications, extensions started before 1 January 1993. (If not completed, then they became subject to the Regulations on 17 September 2002.)
2   Regulation 10(2). The requirements of Sch 1, Pt I are: (1) no room in the workplace shall be so overcrowded as to cause risk to health or safety of persons at work in it; (2) the number of persons employed at a time in any workroom shall not be such that the amount of cubic space allowed for each is less than 11 cubic metres; and (3) in calculating the amount of cubic space in any room no space more than 4.2 metres from the floor shall be taken into account and, where a room contains a gallery, the gallery shall be treated as if it were partitioned off from the remainder of the room and formed a separate room.

Confined spaces

18.91 Work in confined spaces is governed by the Confined Spaces Regulations 1997,[1] which came into force on 28 January 1998, revoking earlier relevant regulations and repealing the Factories Act 1961, s 30. A 'confined space' is any place (including any chamber, tank, vat, silo, pit, trench, pipe, sewer, flue, well or other similar space) in which, by virtue of its enclosed nature, there arises a reasonably foreseeable 'specified risk.'[2] A specified risk is a risk of: (a) serious injury to any person at work arising from a fire or explosion; (b) (i) the loss of consciousness of any person at work arising from an increase in body temperature; (ii) the loss of consciousness or asphyxiation of any person at work arising from gas, fume, vapour or the lack of oxygen; (c) the drowning of any person at work arising from an increase in the level of a liquid; or (d) the asphyxiation of any person at work arising from a free flowing solid or the inability to reach a respirable environment due to entrapment by a free flowing solid.[3] The Regulations do not apply to the work of the crew of a seagoing ship, or work below ground in a mine or diving work to which the Diving at Work Regulations 1997 apply.[4]

[1] SI 1997/1713. The Regulations are accompanied by ACOP L101 *Safe Work in Confined Spaces*.
[2] Confined Spaces Regulations 1997, reg 1(2).
[3] Confined Spaces Regulations 1997, reg 1(2).
[4] Confined Spaces Regulations 1997, reg 2(2). The exclusion relating to diving work was introduced from 1 April 1998 by the Diving at Work Regulations 1997, SI 1997/2776.

18.92 The duties under the Confined Spaces Regulations 1997 are imposed on an employer in respect of the work of its employees and in respect of the work of others in so far it relates to matters within the employer's control.[1] The duties are also imposed upon the self-employed in respect of their own work and in respect of the work of others in so far as relates to matters within the self-employed person's control.[2]

[1] Confined Spaces Regulations 1997, reg 3(1).
[2] Confined Spaces Regulations 1997, reg 3(2). By HSWA 1974, s 53(1), 'self-employed person' means an individual who works for gain or reward otherwise than under a contract of employment, whether or not he himself employs others.

18.93 The Regulations impose a hierarchy of measures. First, that no person shall enter a confined space to carry out work for any purpose unless it is not reasonably practicable to achieve that purpose without entering the confined space.[1] Second, so far as reasonably practicable, no person at work shall enter or carry out any work in or (other than as a result of an emergency) leave a confined space otherwise than in accordance with a system of work which, in relation to any relevant specified risks, renders that work safe and without risks to health.[2] In addition, before any work in a confined space begins, suitable and sufficient arrangements must be in place to rescue persons in the event of an emergency.[3]

[1] Confined Spaces Regulations 1997, reg 4(1).
[2] Confined Spaces Regulations 1997, reg 4(2).
[3] Confined Spaces Regulations 1997, reg 5.

Doors and gates

18.94 Regulation 18 of the Workplace, Health, Safety and Welfare Regulations 1992 requires doors and gates to be suitably constructed, including being fitted with any necessary safety devices. Every sliding door or gate must have a device to prevent it coming off its track during use. Every upward opening door or gate must have a device to prevent it falling back. Every powered door or gate must have suitable and effective features to prevent it causing injury by trapping any person. Where necessary for reasons of health or safety, every powered door or gate must be able to be operated manually unless it automatically opens in the event of a power failure. Every door or gate which is capable of opening by being pushed from either side must be of such a construction as to provide, when closed, a clear view of the space close to both sides.[1] Every transparent or translucent surface in a door or gate shall, where necessary for reasons of health or safety, be of safety material or be protected against breakage and be appropriately marked or incorporate features so as, in either case, to make it apparent.[2] The ACOP requires that doors and gates which swing in both directions should have a transparent panel and conventionally hinged doors on main traffic routes should similarly be so fitted.[3]

[1]   Regulation 18.
[2]   Regulation 14.
[3]   ACOP, para 183.

18.95 Subject to the proof that the doors were not suitable, liability is strict. *Beck v United Closures and Plastics* 2001 SLT 1299 involved an accident caused by two heavy doors in the workplace which formed part of functioning machinery. Despite the fact that the doors were found to be work equipment and not the workplace, Lord McEwan found that reg 18 applied and had been breached as the doors had to be opened and closed many times each day and the position of the handles on the door made this difficult and, therefore, the doors were not suitably constructed. In *Nichols v Beck Electronics Ltd* (30 June 2004, unreported), Norwich County Court (Recorder Wilson) a sliding door had been tied shut for safety reasons. The claimant was unaware of this and injured herself as a result of trying to pull it open. The failure to have warned her that the door was sealed shut amounted to a breach of the requirement, under reg 17(2), that traffic routes be suitable. The Court of Appeal in *Hurd v Stirling Group plc* (26 May 1999, unreported) upheld the first instance decision that the mere fact that a swing door swung closed on a person such as to trap their foot in the gap beneath it did not mean that the door was not 'suitably constructed'.

Windows, etc

18.96 Regulation 14 requires that every window or other transparent or translucent surface in a wall or partition, and every transparent or translucent surface in a door or gate, shall, where necessary for reasons of health or safety, be of safety material or be protected against breakage and be appropriately marked or incorporate features so as, in either case, to make it apparent.

18.97 Regulation 15 requires that no window, skylight or ventilator which is capable of being opened shall be likely to be opened, closed or adjusted in a manner which exposes any person performing such operation to a risk to his health or safety. Every window, skylight or ventilator which can be opened must be in a position such that when open it is not likely to expose any person in the workplace to a risk to his health or safety.

18.98 Regulation 16 requires that all windows and skylights in a workplace be of a design or be so constructed that they may be cleaned safely. Account may be taken of equipment used in conjunction with the window or skylight or of devices fitted to the building when considering whether a window or skylight is of the required design or construction.

All these Regulations are expressed in language which imposes a strict duty.

Drinking water

18.99 Regulation 22 requires that an adequate supply of wholesome drinking water shall be provided for all persons at work in the workplace. The supply shall be readily accessible at suitable places and conspicuously marked by an appropriate sign where necessary for reasons of health or safety. A sufficient number of suitable cups or other drinking vessels shall be provided unless the supply of drinking water is in a jet from which persons can drink easily.

Sanitary conveniences, washing facilities, changing rooms, restrooms and food

18.100 Regulation 20 requires that suitable and sufficient sanitary conveniences shall be provided at readily accessible places. Rooms containing sanitary conveniences must be adequately ventilated and lit. The sanitary conveniences and rooms containing them must be kept in a clean and orderly condition. Separate sanitary conveniences must be provided for men and women in separate rooms capable of being locked from the inside.

18.101 The requirement for cleanliness is in addition to that imposed by regs 5 and 9. The requirement that the sanitary convenience and the room containing it be kept in an orderly condition is in addition to that imposed by reg 5.

18.102 Regulation 21 requires that suitable and sufficient washing facilities (including showers if required by the nature of the work or for health reasons) be provided at readily accessible places. Washing facilities must be provided in the immediate vicinity of every sanitary convenience and also in the vicinity of any changing rooms required by reg 24 (see below). The washing facilities must include a supply of clean hot and cold, or warm, water (running water if practicable), soap or other suitable means of cleaning and towels or other suitable means of drying. The room containing the washing facilities must be sufficiently ventilated and kept in a clean and orderly condition. Separate washing facilities (other than for simply washing only hands, forearms and face) must be provided for men and women unless the washing facility is in a room which can be locked from the inside.

18.103 Regulation 23 requires that suitable and sufficient accommodation be provided for any person's non-work clothing and for special work clothing not taken home. The accommodation must be in a suitable location. Where facilities to change into and out of special work clothes are required (by reg 24, see below), suitable security for the non-work clothes must be provided. Separate accommodation must be provided for work clothes and for other clothing if necessary to avoid risks to health or damage to the clothing. The accommodation must, so far as is reasonably practicable, allow or include facilities for drying clothing.

18.104 Regulation 24 provides that where a worker has to wear special clothing in the workplace, sufficient facilities shall be provided to enable the worker to change clothing if he or she cannot, for reasons of health or propriety, be expected to change in another room. Separate changing facilities shall be provided for men and women where necessary for reasons of propriety. The facilities are to be easily accessible, of sufficient capacity and provided with seating.[1]

[1]   This requirement for accessibility, capacity and the provision of seating was added by the Health and Safety (Miscellaneous Amendments) Regulations 2002, SI 2002/2174, reg 6(g) as from 17 September 2002.

18.105 In *Post Office v Footitt* [2000] IRLR 243 postal workers were required to wear uniforms at work. There was a unisex changing area. The women changed into and out of their uniforms in the women's toilet. Upholding an employment tribunal's dismissal of the employer's appeal against an improvement notice, the High Court (Ognall J) held that 'special clothing' meant clothing which would not ordinarily be worn other than for work and which is designed to relate to work. This included the postal workers' uniforms even though many of the postal workers wore their uniforms when travelling to and from work. The changing facilities provided were unsuitable for reasons of propriety.

18.106 Regulation 25 requires suitable and sufficient rest facilities to be provided at readily accessible places. Suitable and sufficient facilities shall be provided for persons at work to eat meals where meals are regularly eaten in the workplace. If food would be likely to become contaminated if eaten in the workplace, then the rest facilities must include suitable facilities to eat meals. Rest rooms and rest areas shall include suitable arrangements to protect non-smokers from discomfort caused by tobacco smoke. Any pregnant woman or nursing mother at work must be provided with suitable facilities. Since 17 September 2002, rest rooms and rest areas must have an adequate number of tables, adequate seating with backs for the number of workers likely to use them at any one time and an adequate number of suitable seats for disabled workers. In the case of a workplace first used as a workplace after 31 December 1992 or an extension or a conversion started after that date, rest facilities shall include, where necessary for reasons of health or safety, rest facilities in one or more rest rooms. In the case of a workplace already in use as a workplace on 31 December 1992 or an extension or a conversion started before 1 January 1993, rest facilities shall include, where necessary for reasons of health or safety, rest facilities in rest rooms or rest areas.

Regulations 20–25 apply to temporary workplaces only so far as is reasonably practicable.[1]

1   Regulation 3(2). This is not in contravention of the Directive since the latter does not apply to temporary workplaces at all: art 1(2)(b).

Disabled persons

18.107 Regulation 25A requires that, where necessary, those parts of the workplace (including in particular doors, passageways, stairs, showers, wash-basins, lavatories and workstations) used or occupied directly by disabled persons shall be organised to take account of such persons. Any requirement under the Regulations that anything done or provided shall be suitable is to be construed to include a requirement that it is suitable for any person in respect of whom such thing is so done or provided.[1]

1   Regulation 2(3).

Chapter 19

CONSTRUCTION SITES

Daniel Bennett

INTRODUCTION

19.01 The construction industry is a major employer in the UK. It is also one of the most dangerous industries, with a fatality rate six times the national average. One of the features of the industry, and a contributor to its accident statistics, is the extent to which small firms operating as sub-contractors carry out the bulk of the work. Few of those at work on most construction sites are at places solely controlled by their own employers.

19.02 The Construction (Health, Safety and Welfare) Regulations 1996, SI 1996/1592, came into force on 2 September 1996. These Regulations amalgamated much of the pre-existing statutory regime and also provided codified replacement for much of the common law relating to construction sites.

19.03 The 1996 Regulations revoke and replace the Construction (Health and Welfare) Regulations 1966 and the Construction (Working Places) Regulations 1966, but they co-exist with the Construction (Design and Management) Regulations 1994, SI 1994/3140. The Construction (General Provisions) Regulations 1961 and the Construction (Lifting Operations) Regulations 1961 have also been revoked and replaced by a number of statutory instruments.

19.04 The Construction (Head Protection) Regulations 1989, SI 1989/2209 continue to apply to construction sites and are considered below. It is also important to recognise that other workplace regulations considered elsewhere in this book do still apply to construction sites, such as the Manual Handling Regulations 1992 (see chapter 21), the Provision and Use of Work Equipment Regulations 1998, and the Lifting Operations and Lifting Equipment Regulations 1998 (see chapter 20).

19.05 With effect from 6 April 2005, the Work at Height Regulations 2005 revoke and replace a significant proportion of the Construction (Health, Safety and Welfare) Regulations 1996. Regulation 6–8 and Sch 1–5 and all other parts dealing with falls and falling objects are revoked. Given that for all accidents prior to 6 April 2005 the old regulations apply, this edition will refer to both the 1996 and the 2005 Regulations in respect of falls and falling objects.

THE CONSTRUCTION (HEALTH, SAFETY AND WELFARE) REGULATIONS 1996

19.06 The Construction (Health, Safety and Welfare) Regulations 1996, SI 1996/1592 are concerned with maintaining a safe place of work and preventing accidents to those at work on constructions sites. The Regulations give effect to provisions similar to various aspects of the Management of Health and Safety at Work Regulations 1999 and the Workplace (Health, Safety and Welfare) Regulations 1992 but are adapted to the particular problems and hazards posed by work on construction sites. A breach of the Regulations can lead to civil liability (see HSWA 1974, s 47(2)).

Construction work

19.07 Regulation 2(1) defines a construction site as meaning any place where the principal work activity being carried out is construction work. Construction work is then defined as widely as possible, as the carrying out of any building, civil engineering or engineering construction work and includes:

(a)   the construction, alteration, conversion, fitting out, commissioning, renovation, repair, upkeep, redecoration or other maintenance, decommissioning, demolition or dismantling of a structure;

(b)   the preparation of an intended structure, including site clearance, exploration, investigation, excavation and laying the foundations of a structure;

(c)   the assembly of prefabricated elements to form a structure, or the dismantling of such a structure;

(d)   the removal of a structure or part of a structure or of any product or waste resulting from the demolition or dismantling of a structure or from disassembly of prefabricated elements which had formed a structure;

(e)   the installation, commissioning, maintenance, repair or removal of mechanical, electrical, gas, compressed air, hydraulic, telecommunications, computer or similar services which are normally fixed within or to a structure.

19.08 The term 'structure' is then given a far wider definition that its lay meaning. The full definition of structure is as follows:

'"structure" means:
(a)   any building, steel or reinforced concrete structure (not being a building), railway line or siding, tramway line, dock, harbour, inland navigation, tunnel, shaft, bridge, viaduct, waterworks, reservoir, pipe or pipe-line (whatever, in either case, it contains or is intended to contain), cable, aqueduct, sewer, sewage works, gasholder, road, airfield, sea defence works, river works, drainage works, earthworks, lagoon, dam, wall, caisson, mast, tower, pylon, underground tank, earth retaining structure, or structure designed to preserve or alter any natural feature, and any other structure similar to the foregoing,
(b)   any formwork, falsework, scaffold or other structure designed or used to provide support or means of access during construction work,

(c) any fixed plant in respect of work which is installation, commissioning , de-commissioning or dismantling and where any such work involves a risk of a person falling more than 2 metres.'

19.09 The definition of construction work is far wider that that used in the earlier regulations relating to construction, and any authorities limiting the meaning of construction work from earlier regulations are unlikely to be of use. The definition is drafted to be as inclusive as possible, covering all activities and operations ancillary to construction work.

19.10 The definition of structure is also intentionally very wide, ending with the catch all of 'and any other structure similar to the foregoing'. In an unreported decision (*Dawe v Carski* (7 September 2004, unreported), Bristol CC (Recorder Richie QC) a funeral pyre constructed to cremate infected cattle during the foot and mouth disease epidemic was a 'structure similar to the foregoing' such that work building it using heavy plant and machinery was construction work within the meaning of the Regulations.

19.11 Arguably, as with the previous statutory regime, low grade internal domestic cleaning and decoration may not covered by the Regulations (eg *O'Brien v Udec Ltd* (1968) 5 KIR 449, CA in relation to the earlier regulations). The decision of Sheriff Scott in *Matthews v Glasgow City Council* [2004] HLR 136 was that domestic redecoration work did not fall within the 1996 Regulations. However, the line between domestic redecoration and the redecoration of a structure (which is by definition 'construction work') is a difficult one to maintain.

Construction sites and workplaces

19.12 Ordinarily, a worker cannot be covered by both the Construction and the Workplaces (Health, Safety and Welfare) Regulations. The exclusions to the 1992 Workplace Regulations include work on a construction site (being a workplace where the only activity being undertaken is construction work, as defined by the Construction (Health, Safety and Welfare) Regulations 1996, reg 2(1)), unless it is a part of the workplace set aside for purposes other than construction work (eg a portacabin office). Regulation 3(2) of the 1996 Construction Regulations clarifies that the regulations shall not apply to any workplace on a construction site set aside for purposes other than construction work. Accordingly, if there is a place of work where both construction and non-construction work is being carried out, then both sets of Regulations may apply.

19.13 However, it is of note that the Work at Height Regulations 2005 apply to all falls and falling objects at work, regardless of where the work is taking place and that they revoke the equivalent sections of both regulations. Accordingly, from 6 April 2005, whether the place of work is a construction site or a workplace and whether or not the worker is carrying out construction work is irrelevant so far as the duties relating to falls and falling objects are concerned.

PERSONS UPON WHOM DUTIES ARE IMPOSED BY THE REGULATIONS

Construction Regulations 1996

19.14 Perhaps the major complication for labourers regarding the imposition of health and safety duties on construction sites is understanding upon whom the duty is placed. The complex nature of the contractual relationships often results in situations where the site and work upon it may be owned by one party, which contracts with a construction firm to carry out the work and that construction firm then sub-contracts many aspects of the work to other companies. Often the supply of labourers is itself sub-contracted to specialist employment agencies. Also, contracts for the provisions of equipment (such as cranes and JCBs) often include the provision for the supply of skilled operators, and such operators themselves may be self-employed or supplied pursuant to sub-contracts between the equipment supplier and an agency.

19.15 The Regulations make clear at reg 3(1) that they apply to and in relation to construction work carried out by a person at work. The contractual relationship of that labourer is irrelevant and this is supported by the definition of work within the HSWA 1974, s 52. Accordingly, any person carrying out construction at work has the benefit of the Regulations. The complication is knowing upon whom the duties are imposed.

19.16 Regulation 4 imposes the duties contained within the Regulations through the concept of 'control'. Whoever is in 'control' of the particular aspect of the work or the construction site is the one upon whom the duty is imposed. Control involves two concepts. First, there is control of people at work. This may be the employer or it may be a contractor. Second, there is control over the construction site and the work equipment itself.

19.17 Regulation 4(1) imposes the duty to comply with the Regulations on an employer whose employees are carrying out construction work and upon every self-employed person carrying out construction work to comply insofar as they affect him or any person at work under his control or relate to matters which are within his control.

19.18 Regulation 4(2) restates the obligation such that it is duty of every person who controls the way in which any construction work is carried out by a person at work to comply with the provisions of these Regulations insofar as they relate to matters which are within his control.

478

19.19 Regulation 4(3) additionally imposes the duty to comply with the Regulations upon an employee in so far as they relate to the performance of or the refraining from an act by him.

19.20 Regulation 4 does not apply to regs 22 (welfare facilities) and 29(2) (inspection of scaffold, excavation, cofferdam or caisson) which contain their own rules on control. Otherwise, these Regulations do not impose non-delegable duties on the employer (with the above stated exception of welfare facilities and inspection of scaffold, excavations, cofferdams or caissons).

19.21 The question of 'control' of a particular person or site is a question of fact (see *Makepeace v Evans Brothers (Reading) (a firm)* [2001] ICR 241). In many cases, contributory negligence may also be a potential issue, to the extent that a judge finds a person to be partially in 'control' of his or her own work.

19.22 The concept of 'control' was considered by the Court of Appeal in reference to claims under the Occupiers' Liability Act 1957 for accidents on construction sites on three occasions. Whilst the issue in these cases was who was the occupier of the site, the test for occupation is also control. In *Makepeace v Evans Brothers (Reading) (a firm)* [2001] ICR 241, the Court of Appeal accepted that under the Occupiers' Liability Act, main contractors did owe duties to employees of sub-contractors, but such duty did not extend to a duty to ensure that sub-contractors' employees were properly trained in the use of scaffolding. Accordingly, only the claimant's employer was liable for him falling off a scaffold tower. No claim was made under the Construction Regulations against the main contractor (the accident took place in 1990).

19.23 *Makepeace* was distinguished by the Court of Appeal in *McGarvey v Eve NCI Ltd* [2002] EWCA Civ 374 where the sub-contractor was found two-thirds liable for having failed to train the employee properly, but the contractor was one-third liable for requiring the claimant to use the wrong equipment. No allegation of breach of statutory duty appears to have been made under the Construction Regulations even though the accident occurred in 1999. In *Barr v CSW and Mitsui* (17 May 2001, unreported) the Court of Appeal found that the main contractor was wholly and solely responsible for the claimant injuring himself on a defective manhole cover. The sub-contractor and employer of the claimant had no knowledge or control over the safety or otherwise of the cover and therefore bore no liability. As above, liability was under the Occupiers' Liability Act 1957.

19.24 'Control' as used within reg 4 was first considered by the Court of Appeal in *McCook v Lobo* [2002] EWCA Civ 1760. The claimant was fitting a waste pipe to a ceiling when he fell. The ladder was unsupported and unsecured. The judge found that the employer in that case was in control of both the building work and the claimant. The employer was found 25% liable; the claimant 75% contributorily negligent. The two owners of the premises were found by the first instance judge to have no control over the work or the site, having delegated that to the employer. The Court of Appeal supported the finding as a finding of fact. Hale LJ stated (at para 28) that reg 4(2) depended entirely on the question of factual control. If a person has factual control and chooses not to exercise it, they cannot thereby escape liability. But, in the circumstances of an owner of premises who has contracted with a reputable contractor to conduct construction work in his premises, then in such circumstances an owner may have no control of the work on the premises.

19.25 Judge LJ at para 16 commented that the question of whether an owner had control was not answered affirmatively by demonstrating that an owner has some control over the site in a general sense as an occupier. The required control is related to control over the work of construction. Expressly applying that test, HHJ Playford QC found an occupier to owe no duty under the 1996 Regulations to an employee of a roofing contractor who fell through a fragile roof. Accordingly, the owner of the site was not liable to contribute to the roofing contractors' settlement of the employee's claim: *Hood v Mitie Property Services (Midlands) Ltd* [2005] All ER (D) 11 (Jul), QBD (Judge Playford QC). The views of Hale and Judge LLJ in *McCook* accord with the previous expressed view of the Court of Session, Outer House in *Rae v Scottish Power plc and Mitsui Babcock* (8 November 2001, unreported).

19.26 In *McCook* an argument was made that an owner retained some control of construction work by reason of that owners' potential liability pursuant to the Construction (Design and Management) Regulations 1994, reg 10: the duty to ensure that a health and safety plan has been prepared before construction work commences. This argument was rejected on the basis that the duty did not create the sort of control envisaged by reg 4(2) of the 1996 Regulations. A similar argument was rejected in *Hood*, where it was argued that an owner's potential criminal liability for breach of the Management of Health and Safety at Work Regulations 1999 suggested that it retained some control of construction work. *McCook* makes clear that the test is a factual test and not a legal one.

19.27 It is clear that more than one person can be in 'control' at the same time and more than one person can be found liable for breach of the same regulation. In *Humphreys v Nedcon UK Ltd* [2004] EWHC 1260 (QB) a claimant tripped over floor studs installed near a door by the second defendant. The first defendant was the head contractor who had sub-contracted that task to the second. The court found both to be in control of the work, apportioning responsibility two-thirds to the head contractor, one-third to the sub-contractor.

19.28 In *King v Farmer* (21 September 2004, unreported), QBD a self-employed decorator fell off his ladder, which was unfooted and unsecured. The judge recognised that a contractor remained liable to a sub-contractor for matters under his control pursuant to reg 4 (citing *McCook v Lobo* [2002] EWCA Civ 1760) but found that the claimant retained complete control over every aspect of his own work. Since the contractor had no control, it owed no duty under the Regulations. The claimant was held to be solely responsible for his own accident.

Work at Height Regulations 2005

19.29 The Work at Height Regulations 2005 apply a wider test for the imposition of duties than the Construction Regulations. Regulation 3 imposes on every employer a non-delegable duty in respect of all employees. Further, reg 3 imposes duties under the 2005 Regulations on employers, self-employed persons and any other person in respect of any other person under his control to the extent of his control (reg 3(2) and 3(3)). It is expected that the same case law on 'control', particularly the Court of Appeal's decision in *McCook*, will apply in respect of contractors and sub-contractors. However, the employer will always be subject to duties pursuant to reg 3(2)(a).

DUTIES IMPOSED BY THE CONSTRUCTION REGULATIONS

Safe place of work

19.30 Regulation 5 of the 1996 Regulations deals with the general safety of the site for work. Regulation 5(1) requires that there shall, so far as is reasonably practicable, be suitable and sufficient safe access to and egress from every place of work and to any other place provided for the use of any person while at work. Regulation 5(2) requires that every place of work shall, so far as is reasonably practicable, be made and kept safe. Regulation 5(3) requires suitable and sufficient steps to be taken to prevent any person gaining access to any place which is not safe, except (as clarified by reg 5(4)) to the extent that that person is there for the purposes of making it safe.

19.31 This duty covers slip and trip risks similar to those imposed in workplaces by reg 12 of the Workplace Regulations. However, it will also cover head injuries from low ceilings, falling masonry etc and every conceivable risk involved in access to, work at and exit from every conceivable construction site.

19.32 The wording is similar to that of the now repealed Factories Act 1961, s 29(1) and authorities on that section remain relevant. The Court of Appeal's judgment in *Larner v British Steel plc* [1993] 4 All ER 102 (dealing with s 29(1)) held that a statutory duty to ensure that the place of work is safe was not subject to any test of foreseeability of harm, unless the regulation expressly included such a requirement (which it did not). Further, where a duty is qualified by the requirement to take all reasonably practicable steps, the burden was on the person owing the duty to show that it had taken all such steps. A person at work need only prove that he or she was injured due to the place of work not being made or kept safe. The above approach was followed in *McFarlane v Scottish Borders Council* 2005 SLT 359. A sit-on roller fell down a hill, the claimant having driven too close to the edge of a single-track road on the hill. The defendant was in breach of reg 5(2), having failed to adduce any evidence on why reasonably practicable measures could not be taken to make the road wider.

19.33   The words 'sufficient safe means of access ...' were considered in *Trott v WE Smith (Erectors) Ltd* [1957] 3 All ER 500, CA. A 'means of access' is not sufficient if it is a possible cause of injury to anyone acting reasonably when using it. Therefore, where weather conditions might make a means of access slippery or otherwise dangerous, the employer who permits it to be used in such weather conditions will be in breach of reg 5: *Byrne v EH Smith (Roofing) Ltd* [1973] 1 All ER 490, CA.

19.34   In circumstances where both a safe and a potentially unsafe means of access are provided, the law is unclear. In *Manford v George Leslie Ltd* 1987 SCLR 684 the earlier Regulations were not said to be breached where the employee was injured using the unsafe route, notwithstanding the fact that he was discouraged by his employer from using the safe route. This would be consistent with the decision in *Wallis v Balfour Beatty Rail Maintenance* [2003] EWCA Civ 72 in respect of reg 17 of the 1992 Workplace Regulations.

19.35   In *Horton v Taplin Contracts Ltd* [2002] EWCA Civ 1604 a scaffold tower was not considered to be an unsafe place of work simply because a work colleague, following an altercation with the claimant, had toppled the tower deliberately. Even if the defendant had been in breach of the Regulations for failing to fit the tower with outriggers and stabilisers, the court found that such breach would have had no causative effect, as with sufficient force and pressure, the tower could still have been toppled.

19.36   A failure to erect barriers to cordon off a studded area of floor and warn of the presence of the studs on the floor was a breach of reg 5: *Humphreys v Nedcon UK Ltd* [2004] EWHC 1260 (QB). When a dumper truck tipped over when one of its wheels went into a depression just off a narrow ramp, the defendant was in breach of reg 5(2): *O'Gara v Paul John Construction Ltd* [2005] EWHC 2829 (QB) (Simon Brown QC).

Falls, fragile material and falling objects

Falls

19.37   Regulation 6(1) of the 1996 Regulations imposed a duty on the relevant person to ensure that '... suitable and sufficient steps are taken to prevent, so far as is reasonably practicable, any person falling ...'. Regulation 6(2) then provided that to the extent that the measures taken include the provision of guard rails, toe boards, barriers or other similar measures, then such measures should comply with Sch 1 to the Regulations. Where the measures include the provision of a working platform, then it must comply with Sch 2.

19.38 By reg 6(3), where any person is required to carry out work at a place from which he is liable to fall a distance of two metres or more, or where any person is to use a means of access to or egress from a place of work from which he is liable to fall such a distance, then a hierarchy of further measures shall be taken. The hierarchy is set out in reg 6(3)(a)–(d), with each sub-section requiring compliance with one of Schs1–4. The hierarchy is first for: (a) the provision for guard rails, toe boards, barriers and other similar means of protection in accordance with Sch 1, and/or (b) the use of working platforms in accordance with Sch 2. Where such measures are not practicable, (c) personal suspension equipment is required in accordance with Sch 3. If that is not practicable, then suitable and sufficient means of arresting the fall of any person in accordance with Sch 4.

19.39 With effect from 6 April 2005, reg 6 of, and Schs 1–4 to, the 1996 Regulations were revoked and replaced by the Work at Height Regulations 2005, regs 4–8 and Schs 1–5. The 2005 Regulations differ in some key respects. First, there is a mandatory obligation to ensure that all work at height is properly planned and appropriately supervised (reg 4). Such planning includes a mandatory obligation to ensure that the weather conditions do not jeopardise health and safety. Second, there is a mandatory obligation to ensure that work at height is restricted to those who are competent to do it, or are in the process of being trained by a competent person (reg 5). Third, so far as is reasonably practicable, work shall not be carried out at height at all (reg 6(2)).

19.40 Fourth, so far as the 1996 Regulations imposed additional measures when the distance a person is liable to fall exceed two metres, the measures set out in the 2005 Regulations have no such threshold. The 2005 Regulations apply regardless of the height, so long as the height is such that a fall is liable to cause injury.[1] Fifth, the 2005 Regulations set out a hierarchy of steps where work at height cannot be avoided. The hierarchy is similar to that set out in the 1996 Regulations at reg 6(3)(a)–(d) but expressed in different language. Suitable and sufficient measures first must be taken, so far as is reasonably practicable, to prevent any person falling a distance liable to cause personal injury (reg 6(3)). Next, where the risk of falling cannot be eliminated, measures shall be taken to minimise the distance and consequences of a fall (reg 6(5)).

[1] See reg 2(1): definition of 'work at height'. 'Liable' is thought to mean the same as 'likely' in this context.

19.41 Sixth, where work is carried out at height, the 2005 Regulations impose a series of general safety obligations in respect of both the place of work and the means of access to it, set out in Sch 1. The matters set out in that Schedule can most probably be implied into reg 5 of the 1996 Regulations. Schedule 1 to the 2005 Regulations requires the place of work at height to be:

(a)   stable and of sufficient strength;
(b)   rest on a stable and sufficiently strong surface;
(c)   be of sufficient dimension to permit safe passage of persons and plant;
(d)   posses suitable and sufficient means of preventing a fall;[1]
(e)   posses a surface which has no gap through which a person could fall or through which any material or object could fall and injure a person;
(f)   be so constructed so as to prevent, so far as is reasonably practicable, the risk of slipping, tripping or being caught on an adjacent structure;
(g)   where it has moving parts, be prevented by appropriate devices from moving inadvertently.

[1]   This is the same wording as reg 6 of the 1996 Regulations but is not limited by reasonable practicability.

Guard rails, toe boards, barriers and other suitable protection

19.42 The 1996 Regulations required, by reg 6(3)(a), that such means of protection were suitable and sufficient to prevent, so far as is reasonably practicable, the fall of any person from that place. Schedule 1 to the 1996 Regulations then set out that such means of protection shall be of suitable and sufficient strength and also set out the minimum sizes and gaps allowed. Schedule 2 to the 2005 Regulations imposes similar requirements, supplemented by the general requirements for work at height of Sch 1 referred to above.

Working platforms

19.43 The words 'working platform' are defined in reg 2(1) of the 1996 Regulations. Regulation 6(3)(b) required that where it is necessary in the interests of safety, suitable and sufficient working platforms shall be provided. Schedule 2 to the 1996 Regulations contained requirements that the surface upon which any supporting structure rests must be stable, of sufficient strength and of sufficient composition to support the supporting structure and working platform; any supporting structure of a working platform must be suitable and of sufficient strength and be securely attached to another structure (where necessary) to ensure its stability; any working platform must be suitable and of sufficient strength and rigidity for use, be so erected so as to prevent it being accidentally displaced and be dismantled in such a way as to prevent accidental displacement;

19.44 Further, the working platform must have sufficient space and a sufficient working area to permit persons to move freely and use equipment safely. It should also be not less than 600mm wide and should have no gap through which an object could fall or a person could otherwise be injured. The working platform should also be erected, used and maintained in such condition so as to prevent a person slipping or tripping, being caught between the platform and any adjacent structure and have footholds or handholds to prevent a person slipping from the structure.

19.45 Similar requirements are imposed by Sch 3 to the 2005 Regulations, to which the general obligations of Sch 1 must also apply. Schedule 3, Pt 2 provides additional requirements where the working platform is a scaffold.

Suspension equipment

19.46 Personal suspension equipment is defined in reg 2(1) of the 1996 Regulations. Regulation 6(3)(c) and Sch 3 provided that such equipment must be suitable and of sufficient strength in all the circumstances for the purpose(s) for which it was being used; must be securely attached to a structure or plant and the said means of attachment and structure or plant be suitable and of sufficient strength; must be installed or attached in such a way as to prevent uncontrolled movement of equipment.

Similar but more detailed requirements are imposed by Sch 5 to the 2005 Regulations.

Fall arresting

19.47 Suitable and sufficient means of arresting the fall of any person were required by reg 6(3)(d) of, and Sch 4 to, the 1996 Regulations. Schedule 4 provided that: the equipment (any equipment provided to arrest a fall of any person at work, including a net or harness) must be suitable and of sufficient strength to safely arrest the fall of any person who is liable to fall; the equipment must be securely attached to a structure or to plant and the means of attachment and the structure or plant shall be suitable and of sufficient strength to provide support; suitable and sufficient steps must be taken to prevent, so far as practicable, injury to a person in the event of a fall from the equipment itself. Competent supervision was required for the installation or erection of any personal suspension equipment or any other means of arresting a fall (reg 6(8)(b)).

Similar but more detailed requirements are imposed by Sch 4 to the 2005 Regulations.

Ladders

19.48 Regulation 6(5) of the 1996 Regulations provided that a ladder should not be used as a place of work or as a means of access to or egress from a place of work unless it is reasonable to do so having regard to (a) the nature of the work being carried out and its duration, and (b) the risks to the safety of any person arising from use of the ladder. However, where a ladder is being used, the provisions of reg 6(3) did not apply (reg 6(5)). Instead, Sch 5 was applicable.

19.49 Schedule 5 required that any surface upon which a ladder rests must be stable, level and firm, of sufficient strength and of suitable composition to safely support the ladder and any load to be placed on it; the ladder itself must be suitable and of sufficient strength, be so erected so as to ensure that it does not become displaced and when three metres or more in length be secured (so far as is practicable). Where it is not practicable to secure the ladder it should be footed by another person to prevent it slipping; all ladders used as a means of access between the places of work must be sufficiently secured so as to prevent the ladder slipping or falling; the top of any ladder which is used as a means of access to another level must unless a suitable alternative handhold is provided, extend to a sufficient height above the level to which it gives access; where a ladder or run of ladders rises a vertical distance of nine metres or more above its base there shall, where practicable, be provided at suitable intervals sufficient safe landing areas or rest platforms.

19.50 The case of *McCook v Lobo* [2002] EWCA Civ 1760 at first instance involved the employer being found 25% liable for an employee falling from an unsecured and unfooted ladder. Similarly in *Milstead v Wessex Roofline Ltd* [2005] EWHC 813 (QB), the defendant was found liable for an unfooted ladder in breach of Sch 5, para (2)(c) where a trainee had not been sufficiently trained and had failed to foot the ladder when instructed to do so by the claimant. In *King v Farmer* (21 September 2004, unreported), QBD, a self employed contractor was found entirely at fault for going up his own unfooted ladder.

19.51 The 2005 Regulations impose a mandatory obligation at Sch 6 that a ladder can only be used for work at height if a risk assessment under reg 3 of the 2005 Regulations has demonstrated that the use of more suitable work equipment is not justified because of the low risk, the short duration of use and the existing features on site. The remainder of the Schedule sets out similar but more detailed requirements than the 1996 Regulations.

Scaffolding

19.52 Pursuant to the 1996 Regulations, the installation of any scaffolding, whether for a working platform or other means of preventing a fall, and any substantial addition or alteration to such scaffold shall be carried out only under the supervision of a competent person (reg 6(8)(a)).

19.53 The provisions of both Schs 1 and 2 would apply to the construction of any scaffold. Further, by reason of reg 29(2), duties are imposed on all employers and on other persons who control the way in which construction work is carried out by persons using the scaffold to inspect the scaffold and ensure that it is of sound construction and that the safeguards required by the 1996 Regulations were in place before the scaffold is first used. Regulation 29(1) and Sch 7 additionally required that any working platform (including a scaffold) shall be inspected: (i) before being taken into use; (ii) after any substantial addition; (iii) after any event likely to have affected its strength or stability; and (iv) at regular intervals not exceeding seven days since the last inspection.

19.54 In *Nixon v Chanceoption Development Ltd* [2002] EWCA Civ 558, the Court of Appeal allowed an appeal against the dismissal of the claim where the first instance judge had found the labourer entirely at fault for having gone up a scaffold in windy conditions. The Court of Appeal found that from looking at the photographs of the scaffold it was clear that there was no guard rail and that the scaffold boards were loose, leaving a dangerous and unfenced drop through which the labourer had fallen. In such circumstances there could not be a clearer case of breach of statutory duty and this was the cause of the accident.

19.55 The 2005 Regulations provide a similar regime for scaffolding. These require by reg 5 that all work at height be carried out only by competent persons and there is no specific requirement of competency for constructing scaffold. Scaffolding is dealt with generally within the Regulations dealing with working platforms at reg 8(b) and Sch 3. The inspection requirements are contained within reg 12. The inspection obligation (as with the whole of the 2005 Regulations) impose non-delegatable duties upon the employer and upon any other person controlling work at height to inspect scaffolds and all work equipment used for work at height be inspected prior to use. Schedule 7 sets out the particulars to be included in the inspection report. Further, reg 13 requires that so far as is reasonably practicable, the surface, every parapet, permanent rail or other such fall protection measure of every place of work at height be checked on each occasion before the place is used.

Fragile material

19.56 Regulation 7 of the 1996 Regulations imposed a duty to take suitable and sufficient steps to prevent any person from falling through any fragile material (defined in reg 2(1)). The regulation also prohibited a person from being positioned on fragile material through which he would be liable to fall a distance of two metres or more unless:

(a) suitable and sufficient platforms, coverings or other similar means of support are provided and used to support that person's weight (reg 7(2)(a));
(b) suitable and sufficient guardrails, coverings or other similar means of preventing any person from falling through fragile material when passing across or working on it are provided (reg 7(2)(b)).

19.57 Where any person may pass across or work on or near fragile material through which, were it not for (a) or (b), he would be liable to fall two metres or more, prominent warning notices shall be placed at the approach to the place where the fragile material is situated. Under reg 36 of the 1966 Regulations it was held that 'approaches' meant something of such a character that, if a notice were affixed to it, would give a warning to a person about to work on or under it: *Harris v Bright's Asphalt Contractors Ltd* [1953] 1 All ER 395. In *R v Rhone-Poulenc Rover Ltd* [1996] ICR 1054, CA the phrase 'other suitable means' in reg 36 of the 1966 Regulations was said to require the provision of a physical preventative protective device and not merely a code of practice.

19.58 Regulation 9 of the 2005 Regulations revokes and replaces reg 7 of the 1996 Regulations. The language of the replacement regulation is very similar, the most significant difference being that the requirement for prominent warning notices shall not apply where members of the police, fire, ambulance or other emergency services are acting in an emergency.

Falling objects

19.59 Regulation 8(1) of the 1996 Regulations provided:

> 'Where necessary to prevent danger to any person, suitable and sufficient steps shall be taken to prevent, so far as is reasonably practicable, the fall of any material or object'.

19.60 Where the measures in reg 8(1), above, included the provision of: (a) a guardrail, toe board, barrier or other similar means of protection, or (b) any working platform, they had to comply with Schs 1 and 2 (see above). The regulation prohibited material or objects being thrown or tipped from a height in circumstances where it is liable to cause injury to any person (reg 8(4)). Likewise, materials and equipment had to be stored in such a way as to prevent danger to any person arising from the collapse, overturning or unintentional movement of such materials or equipment (reg 8(5)).

19.61 *Delaney v McGregor Construction Ltd* [2003] Rep LR 56, OH found the defendant liable when the claimant was struck by steel rods being unloaded from a truck by fork lift. The rods became stuck in the forks and the claimant tried to pull them free. They came free in an unexpected fashion and struck the claimant as they fell. Lady Paton considered that the rods were tipped from height in breach of reg 8(4).

19.62 Regulation 10 of the 2005 Regulations revoke and replace reg 8 of the 1996 Regulations. The regulations are very similar except that the 2005 Regulations do not include any equivalent of reg 8(2) of the 1996 Regulations, specifically referring to the provision of a guardrail, toe board, barrier or other similar means of protection, or any working platform.

Stability of structures

19.63 Regulation 9 of the 1996 Regulations imposes a duty to take all 'practicable' steps, where necessary to prevent danger to any person, to ensure that any new or existing structure or any part of such a structure which may become unstable due to the carrying out of construction work does not collapse. This requirement prohibits the loading of a structure in such a manner as to render it unsafe (reg 9(2)).

Demolition

19.64 Regulation 10(1) requires that suitable and sufficient steps shall be taken to ensure that the demolition or dismantling of any structure, or any part of any structure, being demolition or dismantling which gives rise to a risk of danger to any person, is planned and carried out in such a manner as to prevent, so far as is practicable, such danger.

19.65 In *Shaw v Young's Paraffin Light & Mineral Oil Co Ltd* 1962 SLT (Notes) 85, based on the Building (Safety, Health and Welfare) Regulations 1948, it was said that actual demolition is '... taking place when men engaged in the demolition operations are doing something to the wall or building that is to be demolished and that is not limited to occasions when a part of the structure is actually being brought down'. In *Fleming v Clarmac Engineering Co Ltd* 1969 SLT (Notes) 96 it was said that 'demolition' implied the destruction of an object and not merely its removal.

Excavations

19.66 An excavation includes any earthwork, trench, well, shaft, tunnel or underground workings (reg 2(1)). Regulation 12 is concerned with preventing accidents to persons caused by excavations or excavation work. In essence it requires the following:

(a)   all practicable steps to be taken to ensure that any new or existing excavation or any part of such excavation which may be in a temporary state of weakness or instability due to construction (including excavation) work does not collapse;

(b)   suitable and sufficient steps to prevent, so far as is reasonably practicable, any person from being buried or trapped by a fall or dislodgement of any material;

(c)   without prejudice to (b), above, where it is necessary for preventing any danger to any person from a fall or dislodgement of any material from a side or roof adjacent to any excavation, that excavation must as early as is practicable be sufficiently supported so as to prevent, so far as is reasonably practicable, the fall or dislodgement of such material.

19.67 Suitable and sufficient equipment for supporting an excavation shall be provided to ensure that the requirements of (a)–(c) above are complied with (reg 12(4)). The installation, alteration or dismantling of any support for an excavation pursuant to (a)–(c) above must only be carried out under the supervision of a competent person (reg 12(5)). Likewise, suitable and sufficient steps shall be taken to prevent any person, vehicle, plant, equipment or material from falling into an excavation (reg 12(6)). No person, vehicle, plant, equipment or material shall be placed or moved near to an excavation where it is likely to cause such a collapse (reg 12(7)).

19.68 Pursuant to reg 29(2), where the place of work is an excavation, any employer or any other person who controls the way in which the construction work is carried out shall ensure that the excavation is stable and of sound construction and that the safeguards imposed by reg 12 have been complied with prior to the first use of the place of work.

Cofferdams and caissons

19.69 A cofferdam is a waterproof wall, enclosing a construction area below the water level. Often an earthen dike, it provides a temporary watertight enclosure that is pumped dry to expose the bottom of a body of water so that construction, as of piers, a dam, and bridge footings, may be undertaken. It can also be a watertight chamber attached to the side of a ship to facilitate repairs below the water line.

19.70 'Caisson' is the French word for box. A caisson is a huge box made of steel-reinforced and waterproof concrete with an open central core. In a similar fashion to a cofferdam, a caisson is a watertight enclosure used to work under water level. Pilings for bridges are often built through the bottom of a caisson.

19.71 Regulation 13 requires that every cofferdam and caisson shall be of suitable design and construction and of sufficient strength and capacity for the purpose for which it is used and shall be properly maintained. Pursuant to reg 29(2) where the place of work is a cofferdam or caisson, any employer or any other person who controls the way in which the construction work is carried out shall ensure that it is stable and of sound construction and that the safeguards imposed by reg 13 have been complied with prior to the first use of the place of work.

Traffic routes

19.72 Regulation 15 creates duties in respect of traffic routes which are very similar to those set out in the Workplace (Health, Safety and Welfare) Regulations 1992. A 'traffic route' is defined in reg 2 as: '... any route the purpose of which is to permit the access to or egress from any part of a construction site for any pedestrians or vehicles, or both and includes any doorway, gateway or loading ramp'.

19.73 In essence, reg 15 provides that:

(a)   every construction site shall be organised in such a way that, so far as is reasonably practicable, pedestrians and vehicles can move safely and without risks to health (reg 15(1));

(b) traffic routes shall be suitable for the persons or vehicles using them, sufficient in number, in suitable positions and of sufficient size (reg 15(2)).

19.74 These are the basic and general requirements imposed by reg 15. However, reg 15(3) provides that a traffic route shall not satisfy (a) and (b), above, unless suitable and sufficient steps are taken to ensure that: pedestrians or vehicles may use a traffic route without causing danger to the health or safety of persons near to it; any door or gate used or intended to be used by pedestrians and which leads onto a traffic route for vehicles is sufficiently separated from that traffic route to enable pedestrians to see any approaching vehicle or plant from a place of safety; there is sufficient separation between vehicles and pedestrians to ensure safety or, where that is not practicable, other means of protection are made for pedestrians or a warning is given to any person who may be trapped or crushed by any vehicle; any loading bay has at least one exit point for the sole use of pedestrians; where it is unsafe for pedestrians to use any gate intended primarily for vehicles, one or more doors for pedestrians is provided in the immediate vicinity of any such gate and is clearly marked and kept free from obstruction.

19.75 Regulation 15(4) provides that no vehicle shall be driven on a traffic route unless, so far as is reasonably practicable, that traffic route is free from obstruction and permits sufficient clearance. However, where it is not reasonably practicable to comply with all or any of the requirements of 15(4), suitable and sufficient steps must be taken to warn the driver of the vehicle and any other person riding on it of any approaching obstruction or lack of clearance (reg 15(5)). Every traffic route shall be indicated by suitable signs, where necessary for reasons of health and safety (reg 15(6)).

Doors and gates

19.76 Regulation 16 imposes duties in respect of the safe operation and construction of doors and gates. However, reg 16 does not apply to any door, gate or hatch which forms part of any mobile plant or equipment (reg 16(3)). The Provision and Use of Work Equipment Regulations 1998 would apply to such plant and equipment.

19.77 A door or hatch must incorporate or be fitted with suitable safety devices where necessary to prevent the risk of injury to any person (reg 16(1)). Without prejudice to reg 16(1) further and more specific duties are created by reg 16(2):

(a) any sliding door, gate or hatch has a device to prevent it coming off its track during use;

(b) any upward opening door, gate or hatch has a device to prevent it falling back;

(c) any powered door, gate or hatch has suitable and effective features to prevent it causing injury by trapping any person;

(d)   any power door, gate or hatch can be opened manually unless it opens automatically if the power fails.

Vehicles

19.78 Regulation 17 imposes duties in respect of vehicles, defined in reg 2(1). It is intended to reduce to risk of accidents involving moving vehicles. Regulation 17(1) provides that suitable and sufficient steps shall be taken to prevent or control the unintended movement of any vehicle. This could involve anything from maintaining the brake system to placing blocks behind its wheel, depending on what is suitable and sufficient in the particular circumstances.

19.79 Where a person may be endangered by the movement of any vehicle, suitable and sufficient steps should be taken to ensure that the person having effective control of the vehicle shall give a warning to any such person at risk (reg 17(2)). When any vehicle, which is being used for construction work, is being driven, operated or towed, reg 17(3) provides that it must be driven, operated or towed in such a safe manner and be loaded in such a way that it can be driven, operated or towed safely.

19.80 A person should only ride on any vehicle which is being used for construction work at a place on the vehicle which is safe and provided for that purpose (reg 17(4)). Likewise, no person should remain or be required or permitted to remain on any vehicle during the loading or unloading of any loose material unless a safe location is provided and maintained (reg 17(5)).

19.81 In recognition of the number of accidents involving vehicles which overturn, reg 17(6) provides that in respect of any vehicle which is used for excavation or handling (including tipping) materials, suitable and sufficient measures shall be taken to prevent such a vehicle from falling into an excavation or a pit, or into water or overturning the edge of any embankment or earthwork.

Emergency routes and exits

19.82 Regulation 19 provides that a sufficient number of suitable emergency routes and exits shall be provided to enable any person to reach a place of safety as quickly as possible (reg 19(1)). The route shall lead as directly as possible to an identified safe area (reg 19(2)) and any traffic route or door shall be kept clear and free from obstructions and provided with emergency lighting (reg 19(3)).

19.83 The provision of emergency routes must be considered in light of factors such as the type of work for which the construction site is being used, the size and characteristics of the site, the plant and equipment being used, the number of persons likely to be present on the site and the physical and chemical properties of any substances on the site.

Fire

19.84 Regulation 18 imposes a duty on the relevant person to take suitable and sufficient steps to prevent, so far as is reasonably practicable, the risk of injury to any person arising from an explosion, flooding or from any substance likely to cause asphyxiation.

19.85 Likewise, reg 21 requires the provision of suitable and sufficient fire fighting equipment and fire detectors and alarm systems. Such detectors and alarms shall be properly maintained examined and rested (reg 21(3)) to ensure that they remain effective. Where work may give rise to a particular risk of fire a person shall not carry out such work unless he is suitably instructed so as to prevent that risk (reg 21(6)).

Lighting

19.86 Regulation 25 provides that there should be suitable and sufficient lighting at every place of work and approach thereto and on every traffic route. Such lighting should, so far as is reasonably practicable, be by natural light. If artificial lighting is provided it should not be of a colour which would adversely affect or change the perception of any sign or signal provided for purposes of health and safety (reg 25(2)). This regulation should be compared with reg 8 of the Workplace (Health, Safety and Welfare) Regulations 1992.

Good order

19.87 Every area of a construction site shall, so far as is reasonably practicable, be kept in good order and kept in a reasonable state of cleanliness (reg 26(1)). This provision is aimed at preventing all manner of accidents not covered by the Regulations, above, such as slipping and tripping accidents.

19.88 No timber or other material with projecting nails shall be used in any work in which the nails may be a source of danger or be allowed to remain in any place where the nails may be a source of danger to any person (reg 26(3)).

Plant and equipment

19.89 The duty in respect of plant and equipment used for construction work at reg 27 was revoked and replaced by the Provision and Use of Work Equipment Regulations 1998.

THE CONSTRUCTION (HEAD PROTECTION) REGULATIONS 1989

19.90 These Regulations (SI 1989/2209), amended by the Personal Protective Equipment Regulations 1992) apply to (a) building operations, and (b) works of engineering construction. Exemptions may be granted (reg 9).

Duties

19.91 The duty to provide head protection is a non-delegable duty imposed only upon an employer in respect of employees. However, contractors may be subject to duties in any event under reg 8 of the Construction (Health Safety and Welfare) Regulations 1996.

19.92 Every employer shall provide each employee at work on site with suitable head protection, maintain and replace it when necessary; and every self-employed person owes the same duty to himself (reg 3). Suitability of the headgear must be assessed (reg 3(4)). Each employer must ensure each employee wears the head protection unless there is no foreseeable risk.

19.93 The duty to ensure that head protection is worn falls jointly upon the employer and on any person who has control over people at work (reg 4). The duty to create hard hat zones and written rules on wearing hard hats falls primarily on the person in control of the construction site and second, jointly upon employers and persons in control of other people (reg 5). The site controller must make written rules for the wearing of head protection (reg 5). Every employee and self-employed person when required by the rules to do so must wear the head protection (reg 6). They must return the head protection after use (reg 6(4)) and, if it goes missing, report it (reg 7).

Chapter 20

EQUIPMENT AT WORK

Daniel Bennett

INTRODUCTION

20.01 The common law of negligence contained extensive case law on the duties of employers and others to provide workers with safe plant and machinery.[1] This common law was supplemented by specific legislation aimed at the safety of working with particular machinery. The prior common law and statutory regime has been almost entirely replaced by new general and specific statutory regulations. Most of the old regulations have been revoked.[2] The extent and generality of the new regulatory regime is such that the old common law is rarely of any relevance in modern case law.

1   See previous editions of this textbook.
2   See Provision and Use of Work Equipment Regulations 1998, Sch 4 for a list.

20.02 The principal general regulation relating to machinery and equipment used at work is the Provision and Use of Work Equipment Regulations 1998, SI 1998/2306, which revoked the 1992 Regulations of the same name. These Regulations, referred to in this chapter as 'PUWER 1998', are intended to implement the Work Equipment Directive 89/655/EEC and amendments to the Directive. In place of the old regulatory approach, characterised by regulations directed towards specific types of equipment, PUWER adopts a wide definition of 'equipment' and imposes general obligations in relation to its safety.

20.03 The focus of PUWER 1998 is upon general considerations of safety against the broad risk of accidental injury inherent on the use of machinery.[1] Regulations 4–10 of PUWER 1998 set out the general obligations in respect of machinery, described as Part II of the Regulations, Part I being the introduction. However, the latter parts of PUWER 1998 contain regulations on specific types of work equipment (mobile work equipment in Part III and power presses in Part IV). Further regulations deal with further specific types of work equipment, such as the Personal Protective Equipment at Work Regulations 1992, SI 1992/2966 (see below 20.51), Health and Safety (Display Screen Equipment) Regulations 1992, SI 1992/2792 (see below 20.79) and the Lifting Operations and Lifting Equipment Regulations 1998, SI 1998/2307 (see 20.93). The regulations generally should be read in conjunction with manufacturers' duties imposed by regulations such as the Supply of Machinery (Safety) Regulations 1992, SI 1992/3073 and the Electrical Equipment (Safety) Regulations 1994, SI 1994/3260.[2]

1   See dicta of Potter LJ in *Ball v Street* [2004] EWCA Civ 76 at para 57.
2   In relation to manufacturers' duties, see para 7.13, above.

PUWER

20.04 Both PUWER 1992 and 1998 were intended to implement the Work Equipment Directive 89/655/EEC (which sets out a few principal obligations in its body with the remainder in a detailed Annex—full text of both in *Redgrave's Health and Safety* (4th edn)). The advent of new legislation does not signify that the case law in relation to common law duties in relation to the provision of plant and equipment is no longer good law; however the breadth and strictness of PUWER has pushed the common law firmly into the background.

20.05 PUWER 1992 was neither an elaboration nor extension of the traditional legislative models. Both PUWER 1992 and 1998 provide a new format, a different philosophy, greater flexibility and almost universal application (there is provision for exemptions: reg 25). Save where the legislative language is identical, the Regulations should not be approached on the basis of, for example, the Factories Act: see *English v North Lanarkshire Council* 1999 SCLR 310. As under the old machinery and equipment legislation, the duties may be enforced by civil action as well as criminal penalty (see HSWA 1974, s 47(2) and s 33).

20.06 PUWER 1992 came into effect on 1 January 1993 except for equipment 'first provided for use in the premises or undertaking before 1 January 1993'.[1] PUWER 1992 applied to such equipment from 1 January 1997. PUWER 1998, which revokes in its entirety PUWER 1992, came into force on 5 December 1998 except that regs 25–30 (concerning mobile work equipment etc) do not apply to work equipment provided before 5 December 1998 until 5 December 2002 (reg 37). The Regulations are supplemented by Guidance and ACOP material in relation to regs 4, 7 and 9, entitled 'Safe Use of Work Equipment'. PUWER 1998 has been amended by numerous amendment statutory instruments, most recently SI 2005/1643 (see *Redgrave* 4th Edition, 3rd Supplement for the full wording).

[1] Paragraphs 31–34 of the accompanying Guidance elaborate on this phrase. It is important to note that the critical consideration is *not* when the equipment was purchased, nor whether it was bought as new.

20.07 PUWER applies to all work equipment at work with the exception of work equipment on board ship and where merchant shipping requirements are applicable (see reg 3(6)–(10)). The Regulations therefore apply to work equipment in offshore installations, in mines and quarries, on construction sites and in workplaces as well as in public places which cannot otherwise be described as a work place. The 1998 Regulations are wider in application in some significant ways than the 1992 Regulations they replaced and it is the 1998 Regulations only which are considered below.

Work equipment

20.08 'Work equipment' is defined as meaning 'any machinery, appliance, apparatus, tool or installation for use at work (whether exclusively or not)'

496

(reg 2(1)). 'Use' in relation to work equipment means 'any activity involving work equipment and includes starting, stopping, programming, setting, transporting, repairing, modifying, maintaining, servicing and cleaning, and related expressions shall be construed accordingly' (reg 2(1)). Regulation 3(1) clarifies that the requirements imposed by the Regulations shall apply to such equipment provided for use or used by an employee at work.[1] These are wide and comprehensive definitions and, as the accompanying Guidance suggests in its elaboration (paras 62–64), 'work equipment' covers 'almost any equipment used at work'. 'At work' is defined by the Inner House in *Robb v Salamis (M & I) Ltd* [2005] CSIH 28, applying the meaning from the HSWA 1974, s 52(1)(b), as being wider that 'carrying on work operations' and a person is at work the whole time when he is in the course of employment, which includes rest periods and when travelling between periods of work.

[1] This was added to PUWER 1998 and was not present in PUWER 1992.

20.09 Difficulty may arise where it is unclear if the object in question is work equipment under PUWER 1998 or part of the workplace, its equipment, systems and devices, under the Workplace (Health, Safety and Welfare) Regulations 1992. It is advisable that both be pleaded if there is any doubt. In *Beck v United Closures and Plastics Ltd* 2001 SLT 1299, two heavy doors which had to be closed to enable machinery to start up were considered by the Outer House to be work equipment rather than being part of the workplace. In *Irvine v Comr of Police for the Metropolis* a stair carpet was found to be part of the workplace and therefore within the Workplace Regulations 1992. In *Robb v Salamis (M & I)* 2005 SLT 523 a ladder to a bunk bed was found to be work equipment. Had it not been, then (but for it being on an offshore installation) the bunk bed ladder would probably have been part of the workplace.

20.10 The case law supports a very wide definition of work equipment. However, since *Hammond v Comr of Police for the Metropolis* [2004] EWCA Civ 830[1] (discussed below), a distinction must be made between equipment for use at work and equipment which can more properly be described as the work piece or work product. This is discussed further below following consideration of the relevant case law.

[1] A case concerning PUWER 1992.

20.11 In the case *of Stark v Post Office* [2000] PIQR P105, there was no challenge that a postman's bicycle amounted to work equipment. The radiator cap of a vehicle was similarly accepted as being work equipment in *Hislop v Lynx Express Parcels* 2003 SLT 785. The term 'apparatus' was held to include a bolt securing fish plates to railway track in *Kelly v First Engineering Ltd* 1999 SCLR 1025, OH, in which it was said that the terms in the definition of 'work equipment' in reg 2 should be given their ordinary meaning and Lord Abernethy considered that a bolt was apparatus and therefore work equipment. There seems no reason why the definition should not be construed consistently with that within the Employers' Liability (Defective Equipment) Act 1969, s 1(3). The courts have interpreted the word in a relatively unrestricted manner: *Coltman v Bibby Tankers* [1988] AC 276. Subsequently a flagstone being manually handled was held to be 'equipment': *Knowles v Liverpool City Council* [1993] ICR 21. In *Crane v Premier Prison Services Ltd* [2001] CLY 3298 a prison van used to escort prisoners was work equipment and in *Wright v Romford Blinds and Shutters Ltd* [2003] EWHC 1165 (QB), a van and roof rack were work equipment. Similarly, in *Green v Yorkshire Traction Co Ltd* [2001] EWCA Civ 1925 a step of a bus was considered work equipment. *Atkins v Connex South Eastern Ltd* [2003] CLY 1812 considered a signalling system on the railways to be work equipment. A dining hall table being moved by a caretaker was work equipment in *Mackie v Dundee City Council* [2001] Rep LR 62, as was a steel storage cabinet in *Duncanson v South Ayrshire Council* 1999 SLT 519 and a needle used by an ambulance man for an intravenous injection was work equipment in *Skinner v Scottish Ambulance Service* [2004] SC 790. In *Donachie v The Chief Constable of Greater Manchester Police* [2004] EWCA Civ 405 a tracking device to be fitted underneath a suspect's car was work equipment.

20.12 The above case law and general consensus on the wide definition of work equipment was put into doubt by the Court of Appeal's decision in *Hammond v Comr of Police for the Metropolis* [2004] EWCA Civ 830. Much of *Hammond* concerns the interpretation of PUWER 1992 and so is no longer relevant. In *Hammond*, the claimant was a police mechanic repairing a police car. When undoing a wheel bolt, the bolt sheered off and he sustained injury. A complication of the case was that whilst the mechanic was an employee of one police body, the police car was owned by another police body. The earlier law on non-employer liability under PUWER 1992 meant that the second defendant was found not to be subject to the Regulations. The Court of Appeal was generally concerned that if the wheel bolt was work equipment, then a garage might be liable for a defect in a customer's car, a matter over which they had no control.[1] Brooke LJ concluded that there was nothing in the Regulations of the Directive which suggested that the Regulations applied in relation to apparatus provided by third parties upon which employees are to work (ie the garage customer's car). However, the judgment of May LJ went significantly further stating that work equipment within the Regulations was concerned with what may loosely be described as the tools of the trade provided by an employer to an employee to enable the employee to carry out his work and might include a hoist. This definition would seem to exclude all machinery operated by workers, which is clearly work equipment, regulated extensively by PUWER. In any event, it is submitted that a distinction cannot be drawn between hand held work equipment (tools) and work equipment which sits on the floor (machinery).

1   See para 24 of May LJ's judgment.

20.13 May LJ stated that his definition of work equipment as being limited to tools of the trade was illustrative and not definitive (see para 24 of judgment) but he maintained the separation between what is worked with as opposed to worked upon. In that regard, he states at para 25(e) that although 'use' is defined by reg 2(1) to include 'any activity involving work equipment' you do not 'use' something you are working on or repairing. However, this contradicts the plain wording of reg 2(1) which defines 'use' expressly as including repairing, maintaining and servicing the equipment whilst further regulations expressly deal with the task of maintenance (eg reg 22). The dicta of May LJ does not appear to have been followed subsequently by the Court of Appeal in *Ball v Street* [2005] EWCA Civ 76 and by the Inner House of the Court of Session in *Robb v Salamis (M & I)* 2005 SLT 523. In the case of *Ball v Street* the claimant was in the process of repairing a haybob which belonged to a neighbouring farmer with whom the claimant had contracted to assist him. There appears to have been little dispute that the haybob upon which the claimant was working was work equipment.[1] See also *English v Lanarkshire* [1999] SCLR 310; cleaning machinery. In *Robb v Salamis* the pursuer was climbing out of a bunk bed when the ladder upon which he was standing gave way and fell to the floor. The defender sought to rely upon *Hammond* on the basis that the equipment was not used as a tool to carry out work and was therefore not work equipment. The Inner House preferred an approach based upon reg 2(1), looking at whether it was used at work. Since the ladder was used at work, it was work equipment.

[1] The dispute centred around (a) whether the defendant was subject to the regulations and (b) whether they were breached.

20.14 In *Robb v Salamis* the court did note that *Hammond* concerned a particular context where it was necessary to distinguish work equipment from the work piece on which work equipment was to be used. It is submitted that this distinction between work equipment (both tools and machinery) and the work piece or work product is a valid one but caution must be exercised in making such a distinction when one employee's work piece is another's work equipment. A recent consideration of the conflict was provided in *Spencer Franks v Kellog, Brown and Root Ltd* 2006 SLT (Sh Ct) 9, Sh Ct (Sheriff Tierney) where the claimant was employed by the first defendant to repair a door-closing device on the second defendant's oil platform. He was injured by a defect in the door-closing device when in the process of repairing it. Following *Hammond* the Sheriff found that the door-closing device was not the first defendant's work equipment as it had not been provided to any employee of the first defendant for use at work. However, he found that it was the second defendant's work equipment as the door and its closing device was provided for use by the second defendant by workers on the oil platform. The second defendant was therefore subject to PUWER in respect of the claimant's repair of the work equipment.

20.15 Much of the dicta of May LJ in *Hammond* on PUWER 1992 is not relevant to PUWER 1998. For instance, the police vehicle was provided for use and used by an employee of the first defendant's (ie the policeman whose vehicle it was) and May LJ noted that the police vehicle might well be the work equipment of the policeman driving it (para 24). Had *Hammond* been decided under the 1998 Regulations (and not the 1992 Regulations), then the car would have been work equipment within the meaning of reg 3(2),[1] as that defendant employed all the police. Regulation 3(2) clarifies that the Regulations are imposed on an employer whenever work equipment is used by any employee at work. The fact that that employee to whom the work equipment was provided was not the claimant is not a relevant factor under the 1998 Regulations. What is important is whether the equipment was used at work (within the definition at reg 2(1)). Further, the claimant in *Hammond* would have been 'using' such work equipment in any event by repairing it according to the definition of use within reg 2(1). Further, the fact that a police car or any car is work equipment is supported by Part III of PUWER which deals exclusively with mobile work equipment designed for carrying people.

1 Which is absent from PUWER 1992 but added to PUWER 1998.

Who is subject to the Regulations?

20.16 Regulation 3 of PUWER 1998 applies the regulations widely and significantly more widely than PUWER 1992. First, the requirements of the regulations are imposed upon employers in respect of all work equipment provided for use or used by an employee of its at work (reg 3(2)). There is no restriction upon by whom the equipment is provided, nor any 'control' test and it seems that an employer is subject to duties under the Regulations in respect of equipment provided to employees for their use at work by third parties.[1] Second, reg 3(3) imposes the obligations of the regulations upon any other person who has control to any extent of: (i) work equipment; (ii) a person at work who uses or supervises or manages the use of work equipment; or (iii) the way in which work equipment is used at work.

1 This differs from a possible situation in *Hammond* where the equipment provided by the third party was not provided for use to the claimant but for repair. This interpretation is queried in any event in paras 20.08–20.15.

20.17 This extended application of PUWER to those in 'control' of non-domestic premises imposes liability, for example, on the owner of a multi-occupied building in respect of the lifts, and on the main contractor (as well as possibly others) in relation to a scaffold on a building site. PUWER 1998 expressly excludes liability to the supplier of equipment for sale, agreement for sale or hire-purchase (reg 3(5)). However, the Regulations would apply to a hirer of equipment, such as a plant hire shop. The Court of Appeal in *Ball v Street* [2005] EWCA Civ 76 interpreted reg 3(3) widely when a claimant hired the services of a neighbouring farmer and his haybob machine. When the neighbour was not working on a Sunday, the claimant was injured when repairing the haybob machine. Potter LJ found the defendant to fall within reg 3(3) as a person who had control to any extent of work equipment and the way it was used and that such control was in connection with the carrying out of a trade or business (reg 3(4)). The court found the line to be between a person who sold work equipment (by hire-purchase or otherwise), in which case control may have unequivocally passed, and the situation where equipment is simply hired or loaned, in which case control has not passed.[1] See also *Spencer Franks v Kellog, Brown and Root Ltd* 2006 SLT (Sh Ct) 9, Sh Ct (Sheriff Tierney) where the operator of an oil platform was found to be in control of a door-closing device which was being repaired by an employee of another. Also, *Donaldson v Brighton District Council* [2001] CLY 02/2241 where an occupier had control of a defective ladder used by a contracted maintenance worker.

1   See judgment para 31.

Suitability of work equipment

20.18 Regulation 4(1) of PUWER 1998 (implementing art 3(1) of the Directive) requires the employer to ensure that work equipment is so constructed or adapted as to be suitable for the purpose for which it is used or provided. 'Suitable' means in all respects in which it is reasonably foreseeable that it will affect the health or safety of 'any person' (reg 4(4)). Article 3(1) may be of assistance in construing this, since it requires that the equipment may be used by workers without impairment to their safety or health. Article 3(2) adds that where it is not possible fully to ensure that work equipment can be used without risk, the employer shall take appropriate measures to minimise the risk. Article 3(2) is not expressly implemented within the Regulations. Regulation 4(3) (implementing para 2.12 of Annex I to the Directive) imposes the obligation that work equipment shall only be used for suitable operations and under suitable conditions. The ACOP says that the employer should take account of ergonomic risks in selecting equipment.

20.19 Regulation 4(2) (also implementing art 3(1) of the Directive) is a more specific aspect of the general duty to make risk assessments in that it requires that in selecting work equipment the employer shall have regard to the working conditions and risks posed by the premises, undertaking and use of the work equipment in turn. In *Yorkshire Traction Co Ltd v Searby* [2003] EWCA Civ 1856 Pill LJ held that the words 'working conditions' (also used in reg 4(3)) must require the taking into account of external forces, such as the likely behaviour of the public or weather conditions. In addition to a duty to assess the suitability under reg 4(2), *Griffiths v Vauxhall Motors Ltd* [2003] EWCA Civ 412 considered that the duties under PUWER must also be read in conjunction with the general duty to assess risks to the health and safety of employees pursuant to the Management of Health and Safety at Work Regulations 1999, reg 3.[1] Although that Regulation did not then impose civil liability, Clarke LJ upheld the decision of Recorder Hand QC that matters that would have been discovered by risk assessment can then be relevant to the identification of what an employer was obliged to do under PUWER. This approach was mirrored by the Inner House in *Robb v Salamis (M & I)* 2005 SLT 523, IH. Similarly, in *Sherlock v Chester City Council* [2004] EWCA Civ 210, it was argued that the general statutory duty to assess risks is important for defining the duty of care in any given situation. The conclusions are logical since an employer cannot ensure suitability without some assessment of the risks.

1   See chapter 10 for further detail.

20.20 The interpretation of 'suitability' under the Regulations is defined by reg 4(4) as meaning suitable in any respect of which it is reasonably foreseeable will affect the health and safety of any person.[1] The Directive does not contain any reference to 'reasonably foreseeable' in art 3 or otherwise define the term 'suitable'. However, art 3(2) makes plain that the Directive does not impose any absolute obligation to ensure that work equipment poses no risks to health and safety. Lord Cameron of Lochbroom in *McTigue v East and Midlothian NHS Trust* [1998] Rep LR 21, OH considered that the Directive would have to be worded differently if it did intend such an absolute guarantee of protection. In *Robb v Salamis (M & I)* 2005 SLT 523 the Inner House concluded that the meaning of 'reasonably foreseeable' was the same as the common law meaning and rejected an argument that it should be the same as the foreseeable possibility of injury test applied in manual handling cases.[2] In *Horton v Taplin Contracts Ltd* [2002] EWCA Civ 1604 it was considered that the target of achieving suitability for purpose was to be measured by reference to such hazards to anyone's health or safety as are reasonably foreseeable. Bodey J (sitting in the Court of Appeal) considered that the risk that a colleague would deliberately topple a scaffold tower by intentionally applying force to do so, was not foreseeable.

[1] See para 5.73.
[2] See para 21.36ff.

20.21 Regulation 4 of PUWER 1998 is thus a central plank of PUWER's scheme. Its obligations are broad and not constrained by the words 'as far as is reasonably practicable'. The question arose in *Skinner v Scottish Ambulance Service* 2004 SC 790, IH with regard to the suitability of equipment: if one piece of equipment were safer than another, whether the increased cost of the safer equipment could be considered a factor so as to make the cheaper but less safe equipment suitable. The Inner House considered the Directive and the Regulation and concluded that the absence of a qualification of reasonable practicability to reg 4 meant that no consideration of cost was admissible and it was not open to the court to take into account the increased cost of safer equipment.

20.22 The burden imposed by this regulation upon employers is a heavy one, but not as heavy as anticipated by the previous edition of this work. It was considered that wherever the use of a machine is capable of giving rise to a risk of injury it is deemed to be unsuitable and whenever injury arises out of such use the employer will be strictly liable. However, case law has found that to be too simplistic an approach. In *Griffiths v Vauxhall Motors Ltd* [2003] EWCA Civ 412 Clarke LJ held that reg 4 was concerned with the physical condition of the equipment and on the assumption that it was being properly operated by properly trained and instructed personnel. Judge LJ clarified that work equipment is not to be regarded as unsuitable when injury results from inadequate control or mishandling of the equipment which would otherwise have been safe for use. Accordingly, where a torque wrench kicked back and caused injury when this was a known propensity of the tool but it would not have done so had it been held more tightly, there was no proven breach of reg 4 but there was a breach of regs 8 and 9 for failing to provide adequate training and instruction to the operator.[1]

1   See paras 18.33–18.37 in respect of regs 8 and 9.

20.23 In *Yorkshire Traction Co Ltd v Searby* [2003] EWCA Civ 1856 the absence of a screen to separate a bus driver from passengers allowed a passenger to assault and injure the driver. The court accepted that this was a reasonably foreseeable risk for this bus on this route. However, the presence of the screen would create other risks and had been objected to by the drivers and their union. Pill LJ restated that reg 4 did not require complete and absolute protection from all foreseeable risks. He further applied the test of suitability set out by Waller LJ in *Palmer v Marks & Spencer plc* [2001] EWCA Civ 1528[1] considering that the test must be carried out as matters were at the time of the accident and without the benefit of hindsight. Both Pill and Chadwick LJJ supported this approach, stating that what is required is a qualitative assessment of the risk of injury. This involved a weighing of the risks created by the absence of the screen against the risks created by its presence. Having carried out the weighing process, the Court of Appeal found that the absence of the screen did not render the bus unsuitable within the meaning of the Regulations.

1   A case concerning the Workplace (Health, Safety and Welfare) Regulations 1992, reg 12(1). See chapter 18.

20.24 Examples of equipment found to be unsuitable include a meat slicing machine with no finger guard such that it could not be cleaned safely: *English v North Lanarkshire Council* [1999] SCLR 310; a prison van which did not have handholds where the employee was required to walk up and down the aisles whilst the van was in motion: *Crane v Premier Prison Services Ltd* [2001] CLY 3298; a vacuum cleaner unsuitable for short employees; *Watson v Warwickshire* [2001] CLY 3302. In *Fraser v Winchester Health Authority* (1999) Times, 12 July, CA sending a junior care worker camping with inadequate equipment was a provision of unsuitable equipment. In *Wallis v Balfour Beatty Rail Maintenance Ltd* [2003] EWCA Civ 72 a key provided to open one kind of lock was suitable even though it did not open another lock.

Maintenance of work equipment

20.25 Regulations 5, 22 and 7 of PUWER 1998 deal with maintenance. Regulation 5(1) requires every employer to ensure that work equipment is maintained in an efficient state, in efficient working order and in good repair. As elsewhere, efficiency relates the condition of the equipment to health and safety matters, and not productivity. The phraseology is taken from earlier legislation.

20.26 The ambit of reg 5(1) was considered by the court in *Stark v Post Office* [2000] ICR 1013. This case concerned an accident caused by a fault with a postman's bicycle (a problem with the brake stirrup) in which it was accepted that a perfectly rigorous examination would not have revealed the defect. The court however held that reg 5(1) imposed a strict obligation to ensure that the equipment was at all times maintained in an efficient state and that its failure amounted to a breach of such an obligation. The court was influenced by the House of Lords' interpretation of the Factories Act 1961, s 22 in *Galashiels Gas Co Ltd v Millar* [1949] AC 275, where at 286 Lord MacDermott said:

> 'To my mind they indicate conclusively that in section 22, subsection 1, "maintained" is employed to denote the continuance of a state of working efficiency. In the ordinary use of the language one cannot be said to maintain a piece of machinery in efficient working order over a given period if, on occasion within that period, the machinery, whatever the reason, is not in efficient working order. In short, the definition describes a result to be achieved rather than the means of achieving it.'

20.27 Thus it can be seen that the ambit of reg 5(1) is of very real significance in that it gives rise to strict liability if injury has been caused by malfunctioning equipment, irrespective of the system of maintenance and repair imposed by a conscientious employer. The Court of Appeal reconsidered the matter in *Ball v Street* [2005] EWCA Civ 76 following the House of Lords decision in *Fytche v Wincanton Logistics plc* [2004] UKHL 31 (a case concerning the Personal Protective Equipment at Work Regulations 1992).[1] In *Ball* the claimant was injured by a broken spring when repairing a haybob. The defendant argued successfully at first instance that the fact of the broken spring did not render the haybob in breach of reg 5 as, despite springs breaking from time to time, the machine continued to be in operational condition and therefore remained in an efficient state and in efficient working order. The defendant also argued successfully (at first instance) that reg 5 only dealt with identified risks of injury and not unforeseeable events. The Court of Appeal rejected the defendant's arguments and allowed the appeal. Potter LJ held that having found that the spring had broken it was no longer in good repair, nor was it in an efficient state or efficient working order. Given that this caused the claimant's injury, the claim succeeded. He continued that the regulation deals with the duty to maintain work equipment so as to prevent injury to the person using the equipment. The regulation was not concerned with the overall efficiency of the machine, of productivity or economy but with health and safety. Further, there was no basis for seeking to limit the regulation to identified or foreseeable risks. The focus of PUWER was not upon the identification and assessment of risk concerning particular identified hazards but upon general considerations of safety against the broad risk of accidental injury inherent in the use of machinery. The fact that an accident was not foreseeable was irrelevant. Longmore LJ added that ever since *Galashiels*, the employer has been held responsible pursuant to its maintenance obligations for the unexplained and indeed inexplicable accident. Any step back from that would be unfortunate and retrogressive.

1   See para 20.78.

20.28 Following *Stark*, in *Cadger v Vauxhall Motors* (2000) 6 CLD, reg 5 was breached when pneumatic work equipment malfunctioned; arguments about the reasonableness of the system of inspection and maintenance were irrelevant. In *Hislop v Lynx Express Parcels* 2003 SLT 785, IH the spontaneous projection of a radiator cap was itself sufficient proof of a breach of the regulation even in the absence of any identified defect. By reason of the cap flying off and landing on the ground without human intervention, a necessary inference was that the equipment was not maintained to the necessary standard. In *Hall v Jakto Transport Ltd* [2005] EWCA Civ 1327, the claimant sustained injury when using a torque wrench to tighten wheel nuts. Unlike *Stark, Cadger, Ball* and *Hislop*, the admissible evidence suggested that the accident was caused by either a defect in the wrench or an operator error by the claimant. In such circumstances, the case was not one where the happening of the accident itself gave rise to an inference of breach of duty and the claimant was under a burden to establish, on the balance of probabilities, that the accident was caused by a defect in the wrench. This the claimant did, despite the fact that the defect remained an unexplained one. In *Atkins v Connex South Eastern Ltd* [2004] CLY 1812 a railway signalling system developed a fault and in failsafe mode showed red, causing the driver to execute an emergency stop. The fact of the method used to mitigate the fault was irrelevant. The fact that a fault had developed meant that the signal was not in an efficient state or in efficient working order.

20.29 *Green v Yorkshire Traction Co Ltd* [2001] EWCA Civ 1925 adopted the reasoning of Factories Act 1961, s 29 cases such as *Latimer v AEC Ltd* [1953] AC 643 that the duty to maintain did not extend to eliminating transient or temporary conditions. As such, the presence of rainwater on the step of a bus rendering it slippery did not result in a conclusion that the step was not maintained in an efficient state. In *Griffiths v Vauxhall Motors Ltd* [2003] EWCA Civ 412 Clarke LJ confirmed that reg 5 (and reg 4) is concerned with the physical condition of the equipment. This included an assumption that it will be properly operated by properly trained and instructed personnel. Injuries caused by poorly trained and instructed personnel do not render the equipment in an inefficient state (although it might result in a breach of regs 8 and 9: see paras 20.33–20.37).

20.30 Regulation 22 of PUWER 1998 (implementing Annex to the Directive, para 2.13) provides that employers must take appropriate measures to ensure that maintenance operations can be carried out without exposing the person involved to risk or, if the risk cannot be avoided, measures must be taken to protect the person. These obligations are unqualified. The primary obligation, however, qualified by the phrase 'so far as is reasonably practicable', is to ensure that work equipment is constructed or adapted so that maintenance involving risk is done whilst the equipment is shut down. Paragraph 2.13 of Annex I to the Directive only permits alternative measures if it is 'not possible' to carry out maintenance whilst the equipment is shut down. Thus considerations of cost or production do not seem permissible. There appears to be a shortfall in the implementation of the Directive. In the Scottish case of *Callander (James) and Sons Ltd v Gallagher* [1999] GWD 32–1550, OH it was held that in considering whether reg 22 was satisfied it was necessary to have regard to the whole circumstances in which a machine was used—thus if it might be theoretically possible to stop the machine for maintenance but in reality this was never done, it could not be said that the employers had provided a machine that could be stopped within the meaning of reg 22(1).

20.31 Where equipment is likely to involve a specific risk, its use, maintenance, repair etc must be restricted to workers specifically allocated to it (reg 7 implementing art 5 of the Directive). The ACOP (para 167) says that wherever possible risks should be controlled by eliminating them altogether or, if not possible, using physical measures (eg guards).

Inspections

20.32 Regulation 6 of PUWER 1998 imposes an obligation upon employers to carry out inspections of machinery in specified circumstances. Regulation 6(1) provides for an inspection where machinery is placed for the first time in a position where the safety of the work equipment depends upon the installation conditions. Regulation 6(2) provides for regular inspections of work equipment that is exposed to conditions liable to cause deterioration giving rise to dangerous situations. Regulation 6(3) imposes an obligation to keep records. Regulation 6(4) imposes an obligation on the employer to ensure that no equipment can either leave its undertaking, or if obtained from another person, used in its undertaking, without physical evidence of the last inspection having been carried out pursuant to this regulation.

Instruction, warnings and training

20.33 By reg 8 of PUWER 1998 (implementing art 6 of the Directive) everyone using (or supervising or managing someone else using) work equipment must be provided with adequate health and safety information and, where appropriate, written instructions on its use, including:

'(a)   the conditions in which and the methods by which the work equipment may be used;
(b)   foreseeable abnormal situations and the action to be taken if such a situation were to occur; and
(c)   any conclusions to be drawn from experience in using the work equipment.'

20.34 Regulation 9 (implementing art 7 of the Directive) requires adequate training for those using (or supervising or managing someone else using) work equipment including: methods of use, risks of use, and precautions to be taken. This obligation reflects the more general duties in reg 13 of the Management Regulations 1999. PUWER 1998 replaces the specific training requirements of the Woodworking Machines Regulations 1974 and the Abrasive Wheels Regulations 1970 and reg 13 of the Woodworking Machines Regulations 1974. The ACOP sets out more detail on training drivers and chainsaw operators. Paragraph 181 of the accompanying Guidance states that it is the employer's responsibility to decide, in the circumstances, whether the instructions should be oral or in writing; such matters as the skill, experience and training of the operative and the complexity and duration of the job must be taken into account. The Guidance says that information should be easy to understand.

20.35 In *Fraser v Winchester Health Authority* (1999) 55 BHLR 122, CA there was a breach of this regulation where the defendant failed to provide a care worker with details as to how to change a cylinder in a camping stove. The circumstances of the accident were that the claimant sustained personal injuries when a tent which she was sharing with a severely handicapped client caught fire on a camping trip. In *Griffiths v Vauxhall Motors Ltd* [2003] EWCA Civ 412, having found that a torque wrench kicked back and caused injury when this was a known propensity of the tool, but it would not have done so had it been held more tightly, there was no proven breach of reg 4 but there was a breach of regs 8 and 9 for failing to provide adequate training and instruction to the operator. The need for such training should have been apparent from the risk assessment required by the Management Regulations, reg 3. Similarly in *Sherlock v Chester City Council* [2004] EWCA Civ 210 a risk assessment would have identified the need for the claimant to work with a run off bench to prevent kick backs on a saw cutting long fascia boards, and the failure to so instruct him was a breach of reg 8. In *Beelsey v MP Burke plc* (30 January 2001, unreported), (Preston CC) the failure to instruct an experienced driver on where to stand when operating a vehicle mounted crane was a breach of regs 8 and 9.

20.36 In *Tasci v Pelkalp of London Ltd* [2001] ICR 633, CA there was a breach of reg 13 of the Woodworking Machines Regulations 1974, SI 1974/903, which required the provision of sufficient training, when a Kurdish man who spoke little English was shown how to use a woodworking machine and thereafter was checked at half hourly intervals. In light of his background (among other matters) he should have been shown how to use the machine and have been given an explanation of why it was to be operated in that way and what dangers might arise if it was not. Although the relevant regulation referred to the provision of careful instruction on dangers, it is likely that the obligation in reg 9 and/or reg 8 of PUWER 1998 is at least as strict, particularly given the express duty to provide training on the risks from using equipment and the precautions to be taken (and see Guidance, para 182).

20.37 In addition to regs 8 and 9 requiring information and training, PUWER 1998, reg 24 (implementing paras 2.11 and 2.15 of the Annex to the Directive) requires work equipment to incorporate warnings or warning devices appropriate for health and safety. This may require permanent written warnings on or attached to the equipment, or temporary 'permit-to-work' warnings. Warning devices (lights, buzzers etc) will not be appropriate unless they are unambiguous, easily perceived, and easily understood (reg 24(2)). By reg 23, health and safety markings on work equipment must be clearly visible.

Dangerous parts

20.38 Regulations 11–24 of PUWER 1998 deal with the 'hardware' of work equipment. Regulation 11 deals with dangerous parts. Employers must ensure certain measures are taken to prevent access to any dangerous part (or rotating stock bar) or to stop movement before a person enters the danger zone. A danger zone is any zone in or around machinery' in which a person is exposed to contact with a dangerous part: reg 11(5). The measures to be taken in such circumstances are: fixed guards; or (to the extent those are not practicable) other guards or devices; or (to the extent those are not practicable) jigs, holders, push sticks or similar; or (to the extent those are not practicable) information, instruction, training, and supervision.

20.39 Under the now repealed provisions of the Factories Act 1961, s 14 the test as to whether a machine was dangerous was whether it might be a reasonably foreseeable cause of injury: see for example *Close v Steel Co of Wales Ltd* [1961] 2 All ER 953. It is suggested that this test is unlikely to be applied to these the Regulations in the absence of specific reference to the test of reasonable foreseeability (see eg *English v North Lanarkshire Council* 1999 SCLR 310, OH).

20.40 Regulation 11 seeks to implement para 2.8 of Annex I to the Directive. That paragraph requires provision of guards or devices to prevent access to danger zones, or to halt movement of dangerous parts before danger zones are reached. There is no provision for lesser measures if those alternatives are not 'practicable'; the obligation is absolute. To this extent there appears to be a shortfall in implementation of the Directive, thus allowing for the possibility of direct enforcement against a State employer. Furthermore, while PUWER extends to a multitude of workplaces not previously covered by the Offices, Shops and Railway Premises Act 1963, the Factories Act 1961 and the Mines and Quarries Act 1954, that legislation imposed absolute duties, in the requirements as to guarding dangerous parts (respectively: s 17, s 14, s 82)—without PUWER's qualification of practicability in relation to fencing. This provision of PUWER may therefore be in breach of the requirement of art 138 (ex art 118A) EC, the preamble to and art 1(1) of the Framework Directive 89/391/EEC, and the preamble and art 1(2) of the Work Equipment Directive in so far as those provisions preclude diminutions in pre-existing Member States' health and safety protection law. Yet further, since PUWER was implemented under the HSWA 1974, s 1(2) of that Act applies so that PUWER should be 'designed to maintain or improve the standards of the pre-existing legislation'. Unambiguous diminution of pre-existing statutory duties is difficult to contemplate as being so 'designed', though since *R v Secretary of State for Employment, ex p NACODS* it seems most unlikely that the UK courts would intervene on this ground.

20.41 Guards and protection devices are required by reg 11: to be suitable; to be of good construction, sound material and adequate strength; to be maintained in efficient working order and good repair; not to give rise to any increased risk; not to be easily bypassed or disabled; to be situated away from the danger zone; not to restrict necessary views; and to allow for safe maintenance.

Other risks

20.42 Regulation 12 of PUWER 1998 (expanding on paras 2.5, 2.7, 2.17, 2.18 of Annex I to the Directive) requires certain risks from the use of equipment to be prevented or, if that is not reasonably practicable, controlled both as to the likelihood of the hazard occurring and as to its effects if it did occur. The risks specified are: articles or substances falling or being ejected from work equipment; rupture or disintegration of parts of equipment; equipment catching fire or overheating; escape of articles or gas, dust, liquid, vapour etc produced, used or stored in the equipment; explosion. This regulation does not apply where stricter provisions of certain earlier regulations apply (reg 12(5)). By reg 13 (implementing Annex to the Directive, para 2.10) protection must be given against burns, scalds, or sears from high or low temperatures.

Controls

20.43 Provisions in regs 14–18 of PUWER 1998 (implementing and expanding para 2 of Annex I of the Directive) deal with controls. Regulation 14 requires controls to start, restart, or change the speed, pressure or other operating conditions of the equipment and to ensure that these activities can only occur by deliberate action on the control(s). Regulation 15 requires control(s) to stop the work equipment safely and in priority to other controls. 'If necessary' all energy sources must be switched off by the control after stopping the equipment. Also, if 'necessary for reasons of health and safety' the control shall bring the work equipment to a complete stop. The requirement of necessity is not found in the Directive: Annex I, para 2.3. By reg 16 there must be emergency stop control(s) unless unnecessary by reason of the nature of the hazard and time taken to come to a complete stop by a reg 15 stop control. Emergency stop controls must operate in priority to reg 15 stop controls. Regulation 17 deals with controls generally. They must be visible and identifiable, and where necessary, marked. They must be positioned so that the operator is not exposed to risk, and so far as is reasonably practicable, that the operator is able to ensure no one else is so exposed. If the latter is not reasonably practicable, there must be systems of work to make sure no one is in a dangerous position when equipment is about to start; and if that is not reasonably practicable, audible or visible warnings (see reg 24, below) must be given. The qualification of reasonable practicability is not found in the corresponding provisions of the Directive and it is possible that the phrase should therefore be narrowly interpreted.

20.44 Regulation 18 provides that control systems must not create any increased risk, and all systems must be, so far as is reasonably practicable, safe (cf para 2.1 of Annex I to the Directive). By reg 19, where appropriate, work equipment must be provided with suitable means of isolating it from all its energy sources which are clearly identifiable and readily accessible. This implements and expands para 2.14 of Annex I to the Directive but includes the qualification 'where appropriate' which is not found in the Directive which requires means of isolation for all work equipment.

Stability

20.45 Work equipment and any part of it must be stable by virtue of reg 20 of PUWER 1998 (implementing para 2.6, Annex I to the Directive). In *Horton v Taplin Contracts Ltd* [2002] EWCA Civ 1604 there was no breach of reg 20 when a work colleague of the claimant deliberately pushed over a scaffold tower upon which the claimant was working. The fact that outriggers would have stabilised the tower did not mean that they would have prevented the tower from being deliberately toppled. In *Sherlock v Chester City Council* [2004] EWCA Civ 210 there was a breach of reg 20 where a fascia board was not either clamped or supported by a run off bench such that it caused injury when sawed. In *Robb v Salamis (M & I)* 2005 SLT 523, IH there was not a breach of reg 20 when a ladder leading to a bunk bed was unstable not because of its mechanism (which would have secured it adequately) but because of the ladder being misplaced in its mechanism by another person.

Lighting

20.46 'Suitable and sufficient lighting which takes account of the operations to be carried out' is to be provided at any place where a person uses work equipment: reg 21 (implementing Annex I to the Directive, para 2.9). This appears at least as strict as the previous duty under s 5 of the Factories Act 1961 so that a failed light bulb would be in breach if the remaining lighting was not sufficient or suitable and work had to continue (see *Davies v Massey Ferguson Perkins Ltd* [1986] ICR 580). Reference should also be made in respect of the duty to provide lighting to reg 8 of the Workplace (Health, Safety and Welfare) Regulations 1992 (see chapter 18) and reg 25 of the Construction (Health, Safety and Welfare) Regulations 1996 (see chapter 19).

Mobile work equipment

20.47 Regulations 25–30 of PUWER 1998 introduce a number of provisions governing the use of mobile work equipment. Regulation 25 provides that all mobile work equipment in which employees are carried is suitable and that it incorporates features for reducing to as low as reasonably practicable risks to their safety, including risks from wheels or tracks. It is to be noted that the definition of 'suitable' in reg 4(4) applies only to that regulation but that any mobile equipment giving rise to an obvious risk to the safety of passengers is unlikely to be deemed suitable.

20.48 Regulation 26 obliges the employer to ensure that where there is a risk of mobile equipment rolling over specified steps are taken to stabilise it and protect the employee. Regulation 26(4) provides a number of exclusions to compliance, including where it would not be reasonably practicable to operate the equipment. This qualification is not found in the Directive (Annex I para 3.1.4) and further it is submitted that it cannot be read to permit the use of highly unstable machinery just because it could not be reasonably practicable to stabilise the same. It is also to be noted that the reg 26(4) provides more potential leeway to a employer than the previous, rather stark, PUWER 1992, reg 20.

20.49 Regulation 27 imposes a duty to reduce to the lowest level reasonably practicable the risks of a forklift truck overturning. Regulations 28 and 29 set out provisions for the safe running of self-propelled work equipment and remote controlled self-propelled work equipment. These provisions mirror exactly the minimum requirements of para 3.1.6 of Annex I to the Directive.

Power presses

20.50 Regulations 31–35 of PUWER 1998 replace the Power Presses Regulations 1965, which were revoked by PUWER 1998. Certain types of power press are exempted from the ambit of these Regulations by Sch 2, although obviously they will still be governed by the more general application of regs 4–11. Regulations 32–35 provide for a comprehensive system of examination, inspection and maintenance of power presses. In light of the Court of Appeal's analysis of the ambit of the obligation to maintain in *Stark v The Post Office* (see above) under reg 5(1) it is difficult to see how these specific provisions add a greater degree of protection to the worker in respect of establishing civil liability for a defective machine. Nevertheless they provide a rigorous framework for ensuring that machines and their guards are adequately installed, and maintained and that those who work upon them are sufficiently trained.

PERSONAL PROTECTIVE EQUIPMENT

General

20.51 The Personal Protective Equipment at Work Regulations 1992, SI 1992/2966, govern the provision of personal protective equipment (which is termed 'PPE' in this chapter). They were passed under the HSWA 1974, s 15, but owe their origin to the PPE Directive 89/656/EEC. Consequently the Regulations, which apply broadly to equipment worn or held by employees as protection against risks at work, should be read in the light of the broad hierarchical strategy laid down in the Framework Directive and the Management Regulations 1999. Thus, the provision of PPE should only be adopted as a last resort if other means of avoiding a risk cannot be adopted. That is explicit in the PPE Directive (art 3) and implicit in the Framework Directive, stating that collective protective measures should be given priority over individual protective measures (art 6(2)(h)). As with other European-based regulations, these Regulations set out a general rational strategy for the supply and monitoring of PPE, applicable to the vast majority of workplaces. Breach of the Regulations will give rise to civil liability under the HSWA 1974, s 47.

20.52 The application of the Regulations is expressly excluded where more detailed legislation governs a particular activity: see reg 3(3). At the same time, much previous legislation aimed at specific kinds of workplaces has been revoked (see Sch 3 to the Regulations); and other regulations, such as the Control of Lead at Work Regulations 1998, SI 1998/543[1] and the Construction (Head Protection) Regulations 1989, SI 1989/2209, have been modelled upon the approach of these Regulations.

[1]   Now revoked and replaced by the Control of Lead Regulations 2002, SI 2002/2676.

The Directive

20.53 The Directive states that PPE is only to be used when risks 'cannot be avoided or sufficiently limited by technical means of collective protection' (art 3). It specifies that PPE must be appropriate and comply with relevant EC provisions on design and manufacture (art 4). The employer must assess PPE before using it (art 5), and must inform and consult with workers and/or their representatives on all matters covered by the Directive (arts 7, 8). In art 6 it imposes an obligation on Member States to lay down in future general rules for the use of PPE, covering specific circumstances of risk. Annex III to the Directive lists some of the areas of work for which such rules may be appropriate, specifying in relation to each what kind of PPE may well be desirable. The amendments to some of the existing regulations made by these Regulations can be seen as part of this policy (see reg 14 and Sch 2). The HSE guidance notes, in Part 2, while hardly amounting to rules, provides further useful advice for specific types of work.

20.54 The Directive and Regulations tie in with other European regulations of the appropriate design and manufacturing standards of PPE. Already in force are the Personal Protective Equipment (EC Directive) Regulations 1992 (as amended by SI 1994/2326), which implement the PPE Product Directive 89/686/EEC, as amended by Directive 93/95/EEC. These amendments were in turn implemented in the UK by the Personal Protective Equipment (EC Directive) (Amendment) Regulations 1994, SI 1994/2326. This Directive, passed under art 94 (ex art 100A) EC, is principally aimed at harmonisation of the internal market. Only PPE that preserves the health and safety of the user may be placed on the market (art 2); but PPE bearing the 'CE' logo, granted following a certification procedure (arts 8–9), must be allowed to circulate freely (art 4). For various types of PPE it sets out basic health and safety requirements which must be met: see art 3 and Annex II. More specific European standardisation will occur in future through the publication of fixed standards, termed 'ENs', for particular kinds of PPE. The implementing regulations have established a statutory certification procedure to meet the

Directive. Although these obligations are aimed at manufacturers and importers, employers must ensure that the PPE provided to their employees complies with the standards laid down by this, and future, Directives (see reg 4(3)(e) and Sch 1 to the Regulations).

The Personal Protective Equipment at Work Regulations 1992

20.55 The Regulations came into force on 1 January 1993. All PPE must meet the standards of the regulations from the beginning of 1993, regardless of when a particular item was first purchased or supplied. They are accompanied not by an ACOP but by a guidance note. The guidance should, however, be relevant evidence of what is approved employer practice. According to art 4(6) of the Directive, an employer may not charge an employee for equipment supplied pursuant to these Regulations or for other matters done under these Regulations, such as training. Although the Regulations do not expressly state the same, any such charge would be contrary to the HSWA 1974, s 9.

Scope

20.56 In keeping with the European approach, the Regulations apply to all employers, including the Crown and those in its service (HSWA 1974, s 48) and the police (s 51A), subject to certain minor exceptions. The 'normal ship-board activities of a ship's crew' (reg 3(1)) are excluded. This exception would not apply to activities carried on by workers who were not members of the crew, or to activities which should not be categorised as 'normal ship-board' work, such as carrying out significant repairs while a ship is docked. Provision is also made for the Secretary of State to exclude certain categories of the armed forces, but only to the extent this is in the interests of national security (reg 12). Unlike the Directive (see art 2(2)), the Regulations do not exclude the emergency services or the police.

20.57 With the exception of reg 5 (compatibility of PPE) employers who are under a specific duty to supply PPE under other, more specific, legislation are not subject to the duties in the Regulations to the extent they meet that more specific standard. The Control of Lead at Work Regulations 2002, SI 2002/2676, the Noise at Work Regulations 2005, SI 2005/1643 and the Control of Substances Hazardous to Health Regulations 2002, SI 2002/2677 are just some examples (see reg 3(3)). An employer subject to one of these exemptions must nonetheless comply with the Regulations in relation to *other* kinds of risk not covered by the more detailed standard. An employer who is under a duty to supply PPE under legislation other than that listed in reg 3(3) must ensure that the supply of the PPE complies with the duties in both that legislation and the PPE Regulations.

20.58 The duties in the Regulations only arise in respect of the direct employees of an employer. An undertaking which uses agency workers, independent contractors or voluntary workers is not obliged to ensure that those workers are supplied with PPE under the Regulations. The different treatment of the two categories—employees and non-employees—may well be in breach of the Temporary Workers Directive (91/383/EEC). However, the employers of agency workers will be bound by the PPE Regulations in respect of their employees. Accordingly, an employment agency is bound by the Regulations in respect of its employees, regardless of the fact that the employees work under the control of a contractor.

Nature of PPE

20.59 A wide range of equipment potentially falls within the Regulations. The general definition is contained in reg 2(1) which states:

> '"personal protective equipment" means all equipment (including clothing affording protection against the weather) which is intended to be worn or held by a person at work and which protects him against one or more risks to his health and safety, and any addition or accessory designed to meet that objective.'

Typical examples of PPE would be safety helmets, harnesses, protective clothing, high visibility jackets, safety footwear, gloves, goggles or respiratory equipment.

20.60 Some equipment is expressly excluded from the Regulations under reg 3(2). Ordinary working clothes and uniforms fall outside the Regulations if they do not specifically protect the health and safety of the wearer. Difficulties may be encountered in some borderline cases: does a police helmet, for example, specifically protect against risks to health and safety? So long as protection against health and safety is *one* separate aim or function of the clothing, we suggest that should be sufficient for the Regulations to apply—even if an item, for example as part of a uniform, is also meant to fulfil other purposes. Only confusion can result from attempting to discern what is the primary purpose of the item. However, the HSE Guidance states at para 9 that uniforms provided for the primary purpose of presenting a corporate image are exempt. Clothing which protects against weather is expressly brought within the Regulations (reg 2(1)).

20.61 Regulation 3(2) also excludes offensive weapons used as self-defence or deterrence equipment. An employer is not obliged to supply the growing category of employees at risk of assaults at work with weapons. But there is no reason why an employer is not under an obligation to supply such employees with other kinds of PPE not amounting to weapons. For example, in *Henser-Leather v Securicor Cash Services Ltd* [2002] EWCA Civ 816, Kennedy LJ overturned the first instance judge, finding that the definition of PPE was clearly wide enough to include body armour where there is a risk of being shot. The Guidance, at para 12, states that as part of a general strategy of risk prevention an employer may be obliged to take other measures to protect employees against assault, such as providing security fences and the like. Equipment used during the playing of competitive sports is excluded. But sports equipment used in other circumstances—the HSE guidance notes give the example of life-jackets worn by professional canoeing instructors—is not exempt. Regulation 3 additionally excludes PPE used while travelling on a road (a crash helmet, for example) as well as portable devices for detecting and signalling risks and nuisances.

Duty to provide PPE

20.62 The Regulations provide general duties with which PPE must comply, relating to the selection and adequacy of equipment and the training of employees in its use. The overriding duty is contained in reg 4(1), by which every employer must ensure that 'suitable' PPE is provided to its employees who may be exposed to a risk to their health and safety while at work. Risk is not defined but it is expected that this will be construed identically to 'risk' within the Manual Handling Operations Regulations 1992. As such, there is no requirement that injury without PPE is reasonably foreseeable; a foreseeable possibility should warrant its provision (compare *Koonjul v Thameslink Healthcare Services* [2000] PIQR P123, CA).

20.63 The Police (Health and Safety) Regulations 1999, SI 1999/860 inserted a new reg 4(1A) by which where the characteristic of any policing activity is such that compliance with reg 4(1) would lead to a conflict with the exercise of police powers, then the requirement is complied with so far as is reasonably practicable. Such a circumstance would include undercover work. However, reg 4(1A) clarifies the strict nature of reg 4(1) otherwise and that the cost of PPE cannot be any defence to a failure to provide suitable equipment: see *Skinner v Scottish Ambulance Service* [2004] SC 790, IH in respect of PUWER.

20.64 An obvious requirement in practice is that PPE must be readily available. The Directive seems to contemplate that PPE should in general be supplied for each individual worker: see art 4(4). Implicit in the duty to provide is that PPE is available and ready to hand: see eg *Norris v Syndic Manufacturing Co Ltd* [1952] 2 QB 135. If PPE is available but this is unknown to the worker, PPE probably has not been provided: see *Finch v Telegraph Construction and Maintenance Co Ltd* [1949] 1 All ER 452. Further, reg 4(4) provides, added by amendment made by SI 2002/2174, that where there is a need for the PPE to fit correctly and/or there is a need for hygiene, an employer shall supply each individual employee with his own PPE. If items are used by more than one person, the Directive requires that appropriate measures are taken to ensure this does not give rise to health or hygiene problems (reg 4(4)).

20.65 The duty *to provide* does not extend to ensuring that PPE is in fact used, nor telling the worker to use the PPE. But this must be covered in any event by reg 9 and the requirement that where PPE is provided, the employer shall ensure that the employee is also provided with such information, instruction and training as is adequate and appropriate and by reg 10 to ensure that the PPE is properly used (see regs 9–10 at para 20.73). No significant restriction arises, either, from the use of the words 'at work' in reg 4(2), since that expression includes anything done in the course of employment (see HSWA 1974, s 52(1)), something which the courts have tended to construe widely. Where suitable PPE is available, but an employee substitutes his own equipment, that PPE is not, of course, provided by the employer so as to make it liable for deficiencies: see *Smith v British Aerospace* [1982] ICR 98.

20.66 One central principle is that PPE is to be used as a last resort. Article 3 of the Directive states that PPE should only be used where the risks 'cannot' be controlled by other means (of collective protection). The Regulations are more ambiguous. Regulation 4(1) says that PPE should be provided 'except where and to the extent that such risk has been adequately controlled by other means', without imposing a duty to use other means of control first. But the HSE guidance notes, drawing upon the general strategies of the Management Regulations, state that 'PPE should always be regarded as the "last resort" ' (para 20) that 'other means of protection should therefore be used whenever reasonably practicable'. This cost-benefit justification is absent from the Directive. An employer who relies upon PPE when other, more effective, means of protection are available, runs the risk of civil liability under other regulations or at common law negligence.

Suitable PPE

20.67 What is meant by suitable PPE is expanded in reg 4(3) (as amended by SI 2002/2174). First, the PPE should be appropriate for the risks involved, the conditions at the place where exposure to the risk may occur and the period for which it is work. Second, the PPE must take account of the ergonomic requirements and the state of health of the person or persons who may wear it and of the characteristics of the workstation of such person. Third, it must be capable of fitting the wearer correctly. Fourth, it must, so far as is reasonably practicable, be effective to prevent or adequately control the risks involved without increasing the overall risk. Finally, the employer must ensure that it complies with any relevant regulations implementing Directives concerned with health and safety standards in the design and manufacture of PPE.

20.68 The standard of suitability has now been considered in detail by the Court of Appeal in relation to other Regulations (see Waller LJ in *Palmer v Marks & Spencer plc* [2001] EWCA Civ 1528 and *Yorkshire Traction Co Ltd v Searby* [2003] EWCA Civ 1856). In addition to reading the duty in the context of the Regulation generally, the test of suitability: (a) must be carried out as matters were at the time of the accident and without the benefit of hindsight; and (b) require a qualitative assessment of the risk of injury, involving a weighing of the risks created by the absence of the PPE against the risks created by its presence. This last matter is expressly required by reg 4(3)(d). The case of *Rogers v George Blair & Co Ltd* (1971) 11 KIR 391 dealt with the question of whether goggles were suitable to protect the eyes of a plaintiff. Salmon LJ at 395 stated: 'The protection, to be suitable, need not make it impossible for the accident to happen, but it must make it highly unlikely.'

20.69 As at common law, and in accordance with the individual focus of the Framework Directive, an employer may be under a duty to supply PPE suitable to individual workers owing to their particular vulnerabilities: see eg *Paris v Stepney Borough Council* [1951] AC 367 (goggles for a one-eyed man where they would not be necessary in the ordinary course); *Pentney v Anglian Water Authority* [1983] ICR 464 (shatter-proof glasses for man who wore spectacles).

20.70 The initial duty on the employer is, of course, to select suitable equipment. Regulation 6 requires that the employer makes an assessment beforehand, assessing the risks and comparing the ideal characteristics of the PPE with its actual characteristics; this assessment is additional to the general risk assessment made under the Management Regulations. Because of the duty to review the assessment if it is suspected to be no longer valid (reg 6(3)(a)), one would expect the assessment to be recorded. An inadequate assessment may be relied upon in legal proceedings as evidence of why PPE was not suitable. Where the nature of the risks at work require workers to use more than one item of PPE, each item must be compatible (reg 5). Ensuring PPE is suitable may further require the inspection and, if necessary, testing of the PPE before it is issued to a worker (and see HSE guidance notes, para 46). In practice, employers should ensure that PPE complies with the relevant British Standards: many of these apply to specific kinds of PPE.

20.71 While there is no duty under the Regulations to consult with workers or their representatives as regards the characteristics of the PPE, individual or collective consultation will frequently be the best means of ensuring that the PPE is suitable. Matters of comfort and compatibility with work tasks—which clearly will affect to what extent PPE may not be used in practice—are very much within the sphere of individual workers' knowledge: see guidance notes, paras 29–32.

20.72 In *Henser-Leather v Securicor Cash Services Ltd* [2002] EWCA Civ 816, where the claimant's job involved collecting cash from commercial outlets, Kennedy LJ found there to be a clear duty under reg 6 to assess the risk of being shot, which the defendant did not do. Further, despite the fact that measures other than PPE were available to reduce the risk of injury, the risk could not be properly controlled without PPE such as body armour and was therefore in breach of reg 4. In *Toole v Bolton Metropolitan Borough Council* [2002] EWCA Civ 588 the defendant at first instance was found in breach of reg 4 for providing unsuitable gloves to an employee for the purposes of retrieving used syringes when the gloves were not impervious to a pin-prick injury.[1]

[1]   The Court of Appeal decision concerned contributory negligence and is commented upon at para 20.76.

Ensuring use of PPE

20.73 Having selected the PPE, an employer must determine its conditions of use. PPE which is awkward or uncomfortable to use may require the provision of breaks (see art 4(3) of the Directive). Employees should be provided with adequate information, instruction and training on the risks against which the PPE is to guard, together with the purpose for using the PPE: reg 9(1).

20.74 Regulation 9(1) can plainly be interpreted in accordance with the individual focus of the European Directives (see the Framework Directive, arts 6(2)(d) and (3)(b)): in particular, it states that the 'information, instruction and training must be "adequate and appropriate for the employee to know" '. The risks and the like, and the information and instruction must be comprehensible to the persons to whom it is provided. This suggests that individual characteristics must be taken into account. Not supplying illiterate workers with oral instructions, giving instructions in English to those who speak that as a second language, or not bothering to enquire whether workers understand the instructions are examples of possible breaches.[1] The HSE Guidance recommends refresher training (para 14). By SI 2002/2174, reg 9(3) has been added which requires an employer shall, where appropriate, and at suitable intervals, organise demonstrations in the wearing of PPE.

[1]   See also case of *Tasci* (above) at para 20.36.

20.75 The duties of an employer do not end once PPE has been selected and employees trained. The employer must provide appropriate accommodation for storing the PPE (reg 8). It must also monitor the actual use of PPE (reg 10), taking all reasonable steps to ensure that PPE is properly used. The Directive simply lists as one of the employer's obligations that PPE 'must be used in accordance with instructions' (art 4(9)). A duty properly to use PPE is also placed upon the employee, breach of which may amount to contributory negligence (reg 10). Employees must report losses of PPE or obvious defects (reg 11).

20.76 In *Henser-Leather v Securicor Cash Services Ltd* [2002] EWCA Civ 816 Kennedy LJ found that a defendant (having failed to provide PPE in the first place) was also in breach of reg 10(1) for having taken no steps to ensure than the claimant wore PPE. Further, having taken no steps to comply with reg 10(1) it was not open to the defendant to argue that the claimant might not have worn the PPE in breach of reg 10(2). Applying a similar argument in a different situation in *Toole v Bolton Metropolitan Borough Council* [2002] EWCA Civ 588, a claimant could not be held at fault at all for failing to use the PPE provided when such PPE provided was unsuitable and would not have prevented the injury.

Duty to maintain

20.77 A further component of the employer's continuing duties is to ensure that PPE is maintained in efficient working order and good repair (reg 7). Under other statutory duties, 'maintain' has been interpreted as meaning that the item must be kept in continuous good condition. Construing the same words 'properly maintained' under the Factories Act 1937, s 22(1) the House of Lords said that these words imposed an absolute obligation to keep the appliances in efficient working order and good repair and described the result to be met rather than the means of reaching it: *Galashiels Gas Co Ltd v O'Donnell* [1949] AC 275. A similar construction should be applied to the duties in reg 7 following *Stark v Post Office* [2000] ICR 1013, CA which adopted the previous case law in relation to language identical to reg 6 in the PUWER 1992 (now reg 5 of PUWER 1998).

20.78 However, in *Fytche v Wincanton Logistics plc* [2004] UKHL 31, the House of Lords (by a majority of three to two) found that the scope of reg 7 was narrower than that of PUWER 1998, reg 5. Lord Hoffmann stated that reg 7 of the PPE Regulations did not impose an absolute concept of repair, but must be construed in relation to what makes the equipment PPE. Regulation 7 extends in time the duty to provide suitable PPE under reg 4. However, reg 7 does not impose any duty which has nothing to do with its function as PPE. Accordingly, as clarified by Lord Nicholls, the existence of a small and inconspicuous hole in one of the claimant's steel toe capped boots, did not constitute a breach of the employer's obligations under the Regulations, as the boots continued to be adequate as PPE. Regulation 7 could not be read as imposing a wider obligation that reg 4. Since the claimant suffered frostbite, there was no breach of the duty (under reg 4 or 7) in respect of the provision of PPE to protect his toes from impact injury. Caution should be exercised against misunderstanding *Fytche* as having any application to wider more general regulations such as PUWER and Workplaces (Health, Safety and Welfare) Regulations (see *Ball v Street* [2004] EWCA Civ 76). *Fytche* may well be applicable to the duty to maintain equipment under the Noise at Work Regulations (see para 17.71, above).

DISPLAY SCREEN EQUIPMENT

20.79 The 1992 'six pack' Regulations and the Directives behind them are for the most part general and the consequent tendency has been to replace UK legislation devoted to specific equipment by regulations which apply to all equipment. This is particularly evident by PUWER and the multitude of particular regulations revoked by it. But one of the six pack Regulations, the Health and Safety (Display Screen Equipment) Regulations 1992, SI 1992/2792 (the 'VDU Regulations'; full text in *Redgrave's Health and Safety* (4th edn), bucks the trend by legislating for this particular type of equipment. This reflects the growing dominance of office-based work, including call centres, and the long hours that many spend working on computer equipment.

20.80 The VDU Regulations implement the Display Screen Equipment Directive 90/270/ EEC (full text in *Redgrave's Health and Safety* (4th edn)). The VDU Regulations came into force from 1 January 1993 with a period of grace until 1 January 1996 for workstations in use prior to 1 January 1993. A breach of the Regulations causing 'damage' gives rise to civil liability (see HSWA 1974, s 47(2)(b)).

20.81 The Regulations are not supported by an ACOP but there is a Guidance note called 'Display Screen Work Equipment' which has no formal status in any civil or criminal proceedings. However, the Guidance was given significant consideration and support for findings of breach of duty in both *Gallagher v Bond Pearce* (9 February 2001, unreported), Bournemouth CC (HHJ Tyzack QC) and in *Trotman v LB Tower Hamlets* (24 September 2002, unreported), Central London CC (HHJ Dean) and by the Court of Appeal in *Denton Hall v Fifield* [2006] EWCA Civ 169. The fact that there has been no previous legislation has meant that litigation prior to the coming into effect of the Regulations has turned on the common law requirements for the provision of a safe place and system of work, and safe plant and equipment. This litigation usually has been concerned with the foreseeability of 'work-related upper limb disorders' experienced by keyboard operators. Work-related upper limb disorders are now generally accepted as a risk arising from the use of these machines. However, other risks which have been associated with such use (eg eye damage, skin rashes, injury to foetus etc, cancers, Alzheimer's Disease etc) are not supported by scientific literature.

The equipment

20.82 The display screen equipment to which these Regulations apply is 'any alphanumeric or graphic display screen, regardless of the display process involved' (reg 1(2)(a)). The Directive employs the same language as the Regulations in this respect (art 2(1)). This appears considerably wider than the conventional notion of a VDU screen and the Guidance (para 6) acknowledges that non-electronic screens such as microfiche are included, though it claims that screens the main use of which is to show TV or film pictures are excluded, and adds that 'judgments about mixed media workstations will be needed to establish the main use of the screen'. Excluded from the Regulations are: display screens in drivers' and control cabs of vehicles and machinery, on board means of transport, intended mainly for public operation, in portable systems not in prolonged use, calculators, cash registers, window typewriters (and other small data displays required for direct use of the equipment): reg 1(4).

20.83 The Regulations impose duties in respect of workstations. These are defined in reg 1 as:

'an assembly comprising:
  (i)   display screen equipment (whether provided with software determining the interface between the equipment and its operator or user, a keyboard or any other input device),

(ii)   any optical accessories to the display screen equipment,

(iii)   any disk drive, telephone, modem, printer, document holder, work chair, work desk, work surface or other item peripheral to the display screen equipment, and

(iv)   the immediate work environment around the display screen equipment [reg 1(2)(e)].'

Employers' duties

20.84 The Regulations impose differing obligations on the employer in relation to three classes of worker, each of whom is defined as a person 'who habitually uses display screen equipment as a significant part of his normal work': reg 1(2)(b) and (c). There are 'operators' who are self-employed; and 'users' who are employees, in turn sub-divided into those employed by the employer and those employed by someone else. Whether display screen work is a habitual and significant part of normal work will be a question of fact. The Guidance suggests (paras 8–13) a number of indicative tests (eg usage of an hour or more a day, more or less daily) with examples (eg secretary, journalist, air traffic controller, graphic designer).

20.85 The principal duty under the Regulations (reg 2) is for employers to perform 'a suitable and sufficient analysis of ... workstations ... for the purpose of assessing the health and safety risks' for both classes of 'users' (in respect of workstations used for the employer's undertaking no matter who provided them) and 'operators' (in respect of workstations used for the employer's undertaking and provided by it). This is a particular application of the general duty to carry out risk assessments under the Management of Health and Safety at Work Regulations 1999, reg 3. In *Denton Hall v Fifield* [2006] EWCA Civ 169, the first instance judge and the Court of Appeal were particularly critical of 'tick box' assessments which are then filed away without any action being taken and such assessments are unlikely to be found to comply with the duty. Further, the Court of Appeal rejected the defendant's contention that the duty to assess was limited to the risks of injury arising from the use of the equipment but accepted that reg 2 also included an assessment of all known health problems that may be associated with the equipment (eg overuse of equipment properly set up), applying the Guidance to the Regulations. The risk assessment must be reviewed if there is reason to think it is no longer valid or if there are significant changes to the matters assessed. The Guidance adds detail to this regulation (paras 19–35). The application of this duty (and others under these Regulations) to 'users' shows the undertaking will owe obligations to temporary workers not necessarily employed by it, thus fulfilling the requirements of Temporary Workers Directive 91/383/EEC.

20.86 Following an amendment to reg 3 introduced in 2002, all workstations must comply with the requirements of the Schedule to the Regulations, to the extent specified in para 1 of the Schedule. This applies regardless of whether the equipment is used by users or operators. Paragraph 1 requires that an employer shall ensure that a workstation meets the requirements laid down in the Schedule to the extent that: (a) those requirements relate to a component which is present in the workstation concerned; (b) have effect with a view to securing the health, safety and welfare of persons at work; and (c) the inherent characteristics of a given task make compliance with those requirements appropriate as respects the workstation concerned. The Schedule contains a general duty at para 2(a) that the use of the equipment must not be a source of risk for operators or users. The combined impact of paras 1 and 2(a) impose a mandatory duty on employers. The remainder of the Schedule contains detailed provisions relating to the screen, keyboard, work surface, chair, space, lighting, reflections, glare, noise, heat, radiation, humidity and software.

20.87 Having conducted the risk assessment, the employer has a duty to 'reduce the risks identified to the lowest extent reasonably practicable': reg 2(3). The latter phrase is a qualification absent from the equivalent provision of the Directive (art 2(3)) which requires that 'Employers shall take appropriate measures to remedy the risks found'. It is arguable that 'appropriate' in the Directive is a stricter standard than 'reasonably practicable' (as traditionally interpreted) in the Regulations; to the extent interpretation cannot overcome this apparent shortfall in implementation a worker might be able directly to enforce the provision of the Directive as against a State employer (see chapter 9, above).

20.88 Daily work must be organised so as to provide breaks or changes of activity: reg 4. This duty is owed to both classes of user but not to operators. The Guidance elaborates (paras 44–48), suggesting that 5–10 minutes break after 50–60 minutes continuous screen or keyboard work is better than a 15 minute break every two hours (para 45). By reg 5, the employer must provide eye and eyesight tests. This duty is only owed to users employed by the particular employer. The duty to provide a test only arises when requested by the user; but for new users it must be performed before the worker becomes a 'user'. The tests should be repeated regularly (frequency to be as recommended by an optometrist or doctor: Guidance, para 56).

20.89 The employer must provide users it employs with training in the use of any workstation on which he or she may be required to work: reg 6(1). In apparent breach of the Temporary Workers Directive, that obligation does not extend to outside workers in the undertaking (although an employment agency would owe the duty to *its* employees). Training for both classes of user is required if the organisation of the workstation is to be substantially modified (reg 6(2)). Some indication of the essential matters to be covered by the training is to be found in para 65 of the Guidance.

20.90 While the duty to train is owed only to users, the employer's duty to provide information is owed both to users and operators who work in the undertaking under reg 7. The training provided by the employer must cover all aspects of health and safety relating to their workstations, including details of the employer's risk assessment under reg 2, the requirements of workstations under reg 3, the plan for breaks under reg 4 (information not required for operators), eye and eyesight tests under reg 5 (information only for users employed by it), the employer's initial training under reg 6(1) (information only required for users employed by it), and the employer's training prior to modification of workstation organisation under reg 6(2) (information not required for operators).

20.91 Article 8 of the Directive requires 'consultation and participation' of workers and/or their representatives. This is not provided for by the Regulations, probably on the basis that the Regulations on worker consultation adequately implement the function. The Guidance at para 29 does, however, state that safety representatives should be encouraged to play a full part in the performance of risk assessments and the reporting of any problems. No other role is mentioned for them, though it may be assumed that the Directive envisaged their involvement in other matters such as ways of ensuring compliance with the Schedule, the provision of information, and training.

20.92 In *McPherson v London Borough of Camden* (19 May 1999, unreported), QBD, HHJ Thornton QC found a breach of reg 2 and went on to find that had an assessment taken place, the defendant would have provided the claimant with a wrist rest and a flat keyboard, instructed her on appropriate posture, insisted she take regular breaks and reduce her keyboard use to no more than 50% of her working day. He therefore found breach of multiple regulations. In *Denton Hall v Fifield* [2006] EWCA Civ 169, the Court of Appeal supported the first instance judge's finding of breaches of the duty to assess and analyse a workstation under reg 2, to plan the daily work of its users under reg 4 and failure to provide adequate training in breach of reg 6. HHJ Reid QC had found that had the defendant complied with its duties, then the claimant's working practices would have been materially altered. Both Judge Reid and Appeal Court rejected the defendant's submission that if a claimant did not take sensible breaks and limit her periods of continuous typing, then she brought her own injury on herself. The Regulations do not allow a worker to be left to her own devices.

LIFTING EQUIPMENT

20.93 The Lifting Operations and Lifting Equipment Regulations 1998, SI 1998/2307, came into force on 5 December 1998 and revoke and replace a large number of pre-existing regulations including the Construction (Lifting Operations) Regulations 1961, SI 1961/1581 and the Offices, Shops and Railways Premises (Hoists and Lifts) Regulations 1968. Sections 22, 23 and 25–27 of the Factories Act are repealed, as is s 85 of the Mines and Quarries Act 1954. The Regulations provide for a comprehensive system for ensuring the strength and stability of all lifting equipment including rigorous testing and examinations. Lifting equipment is defined by reg 2(1) as meaning work equipment for lifting or lowering loads and includes its attachments used for anchoring, fixing or supporting it. The Regulations encompass a wide definition of lifting equipment, which would range from heavy equipment in ship-building to the patient lift on a hospital ward.

20.94 Regulation 3 applies the regulations widely and adopts the same language of application as PUWER 1998, substituting 'lifting equipment' for 'work equipment'. First, the requirements of the regulations are imposed upon employers to all lifting equipment provided for use or used by an employee of its at work (reg 3(2)). There is no restriction upon whom the equipment is provided by and it seems clear that an employer is subject to duties under the Regulations in respect of lifting equipment provided for use by employees by third parties. Second, reg 3(3) imposes the obligations of the regulations upon all other persons who have control to any extent of: (i) lifting equipment; (ii) a person at work who uses or supervises or manages the use of lifting equipment; or (iii) the way in which lifting equipment is used at work. Amendment by SI 2002/2174 clarifies that the person exercising control must be in connection with him carrying on a trade, business or other undertaking, whether for profit or not. This also mimics PUWER 1998.

20.95 By reg 4 every employer is required to ensure that the lifting equipment is of adequate strength and stability for each load having regard, in particular, to the stress induced at its mounting at fixed points and that every part of a load or anything attached to it and used for lifting is of adequate strength. The term 'adequate strength' was defined in *Milne v CF Wilson & Co* 1960 SLT 162 where Lord Cameron said:

> 'If this matter was free from authority, I should be inclined to say that "adequate strength" is to be construed in its ordinary and natural meaning and that so construed, the adjective "adequate" is not limited to adequacy in respect of the statutory safe working load, but that it must necessarily have regard to the load which in a particular case it is called upon to bear. Apart from authority, I should not be prepared to exclude this test of adequacy or to limit it to certified safe working load of the particular rope'.

Lord Cameron approved *Reilly v William Beardmore & Co Ltd* 1947 SLT 147 when he said:

> 'In my opinion, the case of *Reilly* is authority for the proposition that adequacy of strength may relevantly be judged by reference to the use by which the chain, rope or lifting tackle is being put on a particular occasion and that in those circumstances the main contention of the defenders is ill-founded'.

20.96 The Court of Appeal in *Ball v Richard Thomas & Baldwins Ltd* [1968] 1 All ER 389 approved that definition. The general rule is that if equipment is used for the wrong purpose, it does not fall within the statutory provision. However in any given case the line between the misuse of adequate equipment and the equipment itself being inadequate due to misuse is thin: *Beadsley v United Steel Cos Ltd* [1951] 1 KB 408. Further, if misuse is due to inadequate planning or inappropriate supervision, then reg 8 would be breached.

20.97 Regulation 5 imposes a mandatory duty to ensure that equipment used for lifting people is such as to prevent a person using it being crushed, trapped or struck or falling from the carrier. To the extent that there is a risk that the person is in the carrier, the duty is limited by reg 5(2) to reasonably practicable steps. Regulation 6 imposes a mandatory duty to position or install lifting equipment in such a way as to reduce to as low as is reasonably practicable the risk of the lifting equipment or a load (a) striking a person or (b) the load drifting, falling freely or being released unintentionally and that it is otherwise safe.[1] Regulation 7 provides that the employer has a duty to ensure that safe working loads are marked upon the equipment, accessories are marked with instructions for their safe use and, where the lifting equipment is not designed to lift people but might be so used in error, that the equipment carries clearly marked instructions that it is not designed for lifting people. Regulation 8 places on the employer a duty to ensure that the operation is planned by a competent person, is appropriately supervised and carried out in a safe manner. The duty under reg 8 is strict and, if an injury results, that would appear to be proof that the lifting operation was not carried out *'in a safe manner'*. However, such an interpretation would override the qualifications of the earlier duties. Regulation 9 requires a thorough examination and inspection before the equipment is put in place and thereafter at intervals of not greater than 12 months. Previously cranes and other lifting machines had, by virtue of the Factories Act 1961, s 27(2), to be thoroughly examined every 14 months. The Construction (Lifting Operations) Regulations 1961 required that the lifting tackle and gear should be thoroughly examined at least every six months. In place of those provisions, reg 9 of the 1998 Regulations permits a maximum gap between inspections of 12 months where the lifting equipment is not to be used for lifting people. If the equipment is to be used to lift people or as an accessory to such equipment, it is to be inspected every six months.

1   This duty will be complemented by duties under the Work at Height Regulations 2005: see chapter 19.

20.98 In *Delaney v McGregor Construction (Highlands) Ltd* [2003] Rep LR 56, in the absence of a crane or sling, the defendant used a fork lift truck to unload steel rods from a lorry. The rods fell on the claimant. Lady Paton found a breach of reg 8 in that the operation had not been properly planned by a competent person. She also found the defendant in breach of reg 6(1)(b)(ii) in that the defendant had failed to ensure that the risk of being hit by falling rods had been reduced to the lowest level reasonably practicable. In particular, the defendant had failed to explain why it had not been practicable to use a lift or hoist as opposed to a fork lift truck. In line with extensive authority on the issue in relation to other regulations, Lady Paton considered that the burden of showing compliance with the duty was upon the defendant (see para 92 of judgment).

Chapter 21

MANUAL HANDLING

Daniel Bennett

GENERAL

21.01 The HSE's survey of self-reported work-related illness estimated that in 2001/02 1.1 million people suffered musculoskeletal disorders caused or made worse by their work.[1] Further, of all work-related injuries causing three days or more work absence,[2] 38% (almost 2 in 5) are associated with manual handling.

[1] See the latest Guidance to the Regulations (3rd edn, 2004) at pp 1–3.
[2] Three days' absence being the point at which any work-related injury becomes reportable under RIDDOR: see chapter 11.

21.02 The common law and former (pre-1992) statutory position made it difficult for workers to hold employers liable for manual handling injuries. The law in relation to manual handling at work has been radically changed by the introduction of the Manual Handling Operations Regulations 1992, SI 1992/2793, introduced as a consequence of the Manual Handling Directive (90/269/EEC). The Regulations were amended by the Health and Safety (Miscellaneous Amendments) Regulations 2002, SI 2002/2174, which added a new reg 4(3).

21.03 Applying to all employers, the Manual Handling Operations Regulations, which are not confined to back injuries but cover all injuries arising out of manual handling operations, specify precisely what employers should do to prevent injuries caused by manual handling. The Regulations require an employer to adopt an ergonomic approach to manual handling at work, rather than focusing simply on the weight of the load.

21.04 It has to be emphasised however (adopting the words of Mr Justice Munby in *A & B v East Sussex County Council* [2003] EWHC 167 at para 126) that the intention of the Regulations is not to create a 'no risk' regime or even a 'risk elimination' regime. There is no absolute prohibition on hazardous lifting. The Regulations introduce a 'risk reduction' or 'risk minimisation' regime. There is no absolute requirement to make the situation absolutely safe for workers. The employer's obligation is to avoid or minimise the risk so far as is reasonably practicable.

THE FORMER STATUTORY LAW

21.05 Prior to the Regulations, the protection afforded to employees for injuries sustained through lifting was piecemeal and focused on the weight of the load rather than the nature of the operation. Section 72 of the Factories Act 1961 stated that an employee should not be required to 'lift, carry or move any load so heavy as to be likely to cause injury to him', and the Office, Shops and Railway Premises Act 1963, s 23 was similarly worded. Both sections were, of course, limited to particular types of workplace and they have been repealed.

21.06 It seemed, therefore, that where the injury was not caused by the weight of the load but by matters such as the repetitiveness of the task or the awkwardness of the position of the lifter, an employer was not liable: see *Chessum v Lesney UK Sales Ltd* (29 March 1989, unreported) CA, per O'Connor LJ. Further, the necessity of manually lifting the load as opposed to using equipment or reorganising the task, was not a matter considered. The courts' interpretation of the sections gave rise to particularly awkward questions of whether an employee had been 'employed' or 'required' to lift the particular load: difficulties arose over whether a person had stepped outside what he had been told to do: see *Brown v Allied Ironfounders Ltd* [1974] 2 All ER 135, HL; *Black v Carricks (Caterers)* [1980] IRLR 448. Neither of these restrictions is present in the 1992 Regulations.

Negligence

21.07 There is unlikely to be any circumstance now in which a claimant employee who has been injured by reason of a manual handling operation can succeed in negligence having failed to establish a breach of the Manual Handling Operations Regulations. The case law since the introduction of the Regulations shows no such case. However, the common law may remain of relevance for those at work wishing to proceed against a defendant who is not their employer. The nature of the duties imposed by the Manual Handling Operations Regulations may now inform the nature of the duty in negligence in any event.

21.08 The standard, nature and extent of the employer's duty in negligence was, and is, often unclear. The case law does little to establish any clear principles and is often inconsistent. A hospital, for instance, was not found to be obliged to warn a trained nurse against lifting patients with a method which caused her a back injury: see *Woolger v West Surrey and North East Hampshire Health Authority* (1993) 16 BMLR 120, CA.[1] By contrast, in *Colclough v Staffordshire County Council* [1994] CLY 2283, the defendants were held to be under an obligation to advise social workers of the risks of lifting clients, even though they would not be called upon to do so except in emergencies. But an experienced ambulance man need not be told exactly how to lift a patient out of an ambulance: *Parkes v Smethwick Corpn* (1957) 121 JP 415.

[1] See the section on lifting patients under the Regulations at para 21.62, below.

21.09 In *Devizes Reclamation Co v Chalk* (1999) Times, 2 April, CA it was held that there was no liability to a worker who, on his own initiative, tried to move a heavy piece of fallen lead. No system was involved, this was a one-off occasion, there were no instructions which could have appropriately been given. Nor was there a duty to give repeated instruction to an experienced worker who asked to return to full duties (after light work following a back injury) and injured his back again on lifting a 10kg box and turning to place it on a nearby shelf: *Rozario v Post Office* [1997] PIQR P15, CA. On the other hand in *Kinsella v Harris Lebus Ltd* (1963) 108 Sol Jo 14, CA it was not reasonable to leave a man to ask for help with an awkward load of 145 lbs when such help was not readily available and requests for help were discouraged. Though where help is readily available it is not unreasonable to leave a worker to ask for it: *Peat v NJ Muschamp & Co Ltd* (1969) 7 KIR 469.

21.10 The position at common law where the employer habitually allowed loads to be handled in a dangerous manner is different. In *Larmour v Belfast Corpn* [1945] NI 163, CA, it was held to be negligent to allow a workman at a gasworks to go up a vertical ladder with a heavy damper which caused him to overbalance. In *Ross v Tennent Caledonian Breweries Ltd* 1983 SLT 676n a system of lowering beer kegs in use for 17 years was held to be unsound when a keg escaped. However, in *Holmes v Tees & Hartlepool Port Authority* [1993] CLY 2020 it was not negligent to allow a stevedore to carry 2cwt bags using a system common in the trade. In *Mearns v Lothian Regional Council* 1991 SLT 338, liability was imposed for failing to instruct an employee not to lift an awkward weight without assistance (and see the following section). In *Fricker v Benjamin Perry & Sons* (1973) 16 KIR 356, though a load did not exceed the maximum safe weight for two men to lift, there was a foreseeable risk that the load would be shared unevenly if it jammed, for which no allowance had been made.

The Directive

21.11 Introduced pursuant to the Framework Directive, the Manual Handling Directive (90/269/EEC) adopts a broad definition of manual handling (art 2); states that the employer shall take appropriate measures 'in order to avoid the need for manual handling of loads by workers' (art 3(1)); and, to the extent these cannot be avoided, should take appropriate measures to reduce the risk (art 3(2)). The employer is required to have regard to numerous factors, including the type of load, the effort required, the characteristics of the work environment and the kind of activity. In accordance with the individual focus of the Framework Directive (see art 6(3)), the employer is under a duty to have regard to the particular characteristics of the individual worker, including whether he is 'physically unsuited to carry out the task' (art 5 and Annex II). The direct enforcement of the Directive by an employee against a State employer was accepted by the defendant in *King v Sussex Ambulance NHS Trust* [2002] EWCA Civ 953. Another case in which the Directive was enforced directly (and successfully) against a defendant was *Peck v Chief Constable of Avon and Somerset* [2000] CLY 2971.

THE MANUAL HANDLING OPERATIONS REGULATIONS 1992

21.12 The Regulations came into force on 1 January 1993, repealing prior statutory provisions including the Factories Act 1961, s 72. Regulation 4(3) was added by SI 2002/2174 with effect from 17 September 2002. Breach of the Regulations will give rise to civil liability to the extent damage is caused.[1] The Regulations are supplemented by guidance notes issued by the HSE (L23), which may serve as evidence of what is good and approved employer practice. The Guidance is currently in its third edition (2004).

[1] See the HSWA 1974, s 47.

21.13 The Regulations apply whenever an employee is engaged in a manual handling operation which involves a risk of injury. The Regulations are not restricted to back injuries or lifting injuries[1] and set no weight limit. Once the application of the Regulations has been established by the employee, the employer is subject to a hierarchy of measures under the Regulations. First, the employer must take all reasonably practicable steps to avoid the operation (reg 4(1)(a)). If that is not reasonably practicable, then the employer must assess the operation (reg 4(1)(b)(i)) and then take appropriate steps to reduce the risk of injury to the lowest level reasonably practicable (reg 4(1)(b)(ii)). Since 17 September 2002, the employer is also expressly obliged to take into account the individual employee's suitability for the operation (reg 4(3)). Employees are also subject to a duty to make use of any system of work provided by the employer to comply with the Regulations (reg 5).

[1] Eg see *King v RCO Support Services Ltd* [2001] ICR 608 when the claimant slipped. See para 21.30.

21.14 The Guidance to the Regulations contains a reminder that the Regulations should not be considered in isolation. In particular, reference is made to reg 3(1) of the Management Regulations (see chapter 10 for further detail), which requires employers to make a suitable and sufficient assessment of all risks to the health and safety of their employees while at work. The Guidance also states that the law requires employers to consult employees on matters that affect their health and safety under either the Health and Safety (Consultation with Employees) Regulations 1996, SI 1996/1513 or (for unionised workplaces) the Safety Representatives and Safety Committees Regulations 1977, SI 1977/500.[1]

[1] See Guidance Notes, para 18.

Conflict with the Directive

21.15 In the previous edition of this work, three matters were highlighted in respect of which it was argued that the Regulations did not properly implement the Directives. First, that the Regulations did not give proper effect to the Directive's requirement in Annex II that regard be given to the particular characteristics of the worker. These factors were mentioned in Sch 1 to the Regulations. This issue has been resolved by the amendment to reg 4(3) made by SI 2002/2174 which now requires that regard shall be had to the physical suitability of the employee to carry out the operations, his knowledge and training and whether the employee is within any group of employees identified as being specifically at risk.[1]

1   Amendment made by the Health and Safety (Miscellaneous Amendments) Regulations 2002, reg 4.

21.16 Second, art 6(2) of the Manual Handling Directive requires that employers must ensure that workers receive proper training and information on handling loads whilst the Regulations contain no such express provision. Whilst the Regulations continue to contain no such express provision, case law has considered the issue of training extensively in the context of reducing the risk of injury and its interpretation of reg 4(1)(b)(ii), a matter considered in detail below at paras 21.58–21.60. Further, the additional reg 4(3)(c) now requires an employer to take into account the employees' knowledge and training when assessing the appropriate steps necessary to reduce the risk of injury.

21.17 The third matter was that whilst the Directive did not qualify the duty in art 3 by reference to a standard of reasonable practicability, the Regulations did. It was suggested that interpretation alone could overcome that distinction. This remains a live issue but it appears more likely that interpretation alone will resolve it following the comments of Hale LJ in *King v Sussex Ambulance NHS Trust* [2002] EWCA Civ 953. Unlike other Regulations, the Directive itself does not impose a strict standard of care in any event and so the additional qualification does not make as much of a difference. Further, so far as the duty to reduce the risk of injury is concerned, reg 4(1)(b)(ii) also adds in the words '*to the lowest level*', words which are absent from art 3(2) of the Directive.[1]

1   See para 21.19 below.

21.18 The meaning of 'appropriate measures' in art 3(2) of the Directive was considered by the Court of Appeal in the case of *King v Sussex Ambulance NHS Trust* [2002] EWCA Civ 953. In that case, the employee (by amendment at trial) alleged breach of the Manual Handling Directive and the Ambulance Service accepted that, as an emanation of the State, the Directive was directly effective to the employee's rights against them.[1] The employee sought to argue that the Directive imposed a stricter duty since it was not qualified by the defence of 'reasonable practicability'. Hale LJ noted that 'appropriate' must mean something more than a theoretical possibility and it must be judged against the circumstances of the case.[2] She further noted that the Directive accepts that some manual handling cannot be avoided and requires employers to take appropriate steps to reduce the risk involved. Similarly to the Regulations, it does not impose a strict liability or require the avoidance of all risk of injury from manual handling operations. She then further noted the defendant's argument that whilst the Directive did not limit the duty on the employer by requiring it to take only appropriate steps which were 'reasonably practicable' (as did the Regulations), that by limiting the duty to take 'appropriate' measures or using 'appropriate' means to reduce the risk, the distinction which some had drawn between the Directions and the Regulations was a false one.[3]

1   Another case in which the Directive was enforced directly against a defendant was *Peck v Chief Constable of Avon and Somerset* [2000] CLY 2971.
2   Para 13.
3   Paras 16–18.

21.19 The Court of Appeal unanimously allowed the appeal, finding that the defendant could take no further 'appropriate' measures or steps to avoid the risk of injury or reduce it. Accordingly, there was no breach of either the Directive or the Regulations. Hale LJ accepted that it was not necessary in that case to resolve the debate about whether there was any material difference between the Directive and the Regulations. The Court of Appeal accordingly did not expressly consider the impact of any of the additional words in the Regulations. Regulation 4(1)(b)(ii), requires an employer '*to take appropriate steps to reduce the risk of injury ... to the lowest level reasonably practicable*'. The distinction between the Directive and the regulation is therefore the addition of the words '*to the lowest level*' as well as the words '*reasonably practicable*'. For future courts to resolve that there is no distinction between the Directive and the regulation then it would be necessary to find that the taking of '*appropriate*' steps to reduce the risk of injury must involve those steps which reduce the risk to the '*lowest level reasonably practicable*'. It is submitted that it is difficult to envisage what steps might still be '*appropriate*' even though the risk had already been reduced to the '*lowest level reasonably practicable*'. It is also submitted that it is possible to define the Directive as imposing a lower standard, as the appropriate steps to reduce a risk (required by the Directive) may not necessarily involve all the steps necessary to reduce the risk to the lowest level reasonably practicable (as required by the Regulations).

Persons subject to duties and to whom duties owed

21.20 The Regulations apply to all kinds of employer apart from an exception for seagoing ships (reg 3). There is provision for exemption of the home forces (reg 6). Offshore activities are covered (reg 7). Obligations are imposed on employees (reg 5). By the HSWA 1974, s 48(3), persons in the service of the Crown will be included as if employees of an employer and the police are similarly covered by virtue of s 51A.

21.21 One notable restriction is that the duty is only owed by an employer to its employees. This is narrower than most of the Regulations considered in this part of this book. However, the duty is owed by an employer to an employee regardless of the level of control the employer has over that employee. This is also unlike other regulations (such as the Workplace or Construction (Health, Safety and Welfare) Regulations) which restrict the duty upon the employer to situations in which the employer is in control of the worker's work.

21.22 *Manual handling*

21.22 It was argued in the previous editions of this work and in *Redgrave's Health & Safety* (4th edn) that the Regulations do not comply with art 2 of the Temporary Workers Directive, which requires that agency workers be given equivalent health and safety protection to other workers in the undertaking. Since the duties imposed by the Regulations do not extend to those contracting with agency workers, the Regulations appear to be in breach. The only way of construing the Regulations as not being in breach would be to interpret the Regulations such that an employer, (eg an employment agency), which exercises little or no control over the work of its employees, will remain liable for breaches of the Regulations in fact committed by others. The fact that the employer had no control would not appear to be a defence, as the application of the Regulations is not qualified by any concept of control.[1] However, if a court allowed an employer to argue that there were no reasonably practicable steps it could take when it had no control of the employees' work, then such an interpretation would result in the Regulations not complying with the Temporary Workers Directive.

[1] As many other regulations are, such as eg PUWER 1998, Construction (Health, Safety and Welfare) Regulations 1996.

21.23 Nurses and building workers are two obvious examples of persons often employed by an agency and sent to work for a contractor who, under UK law, is unlikely to be its employer (ie the agency remains the employer). In such cases, in the event of a manual handling injury, an agency worker must be careful to proceed in any allegation of breach of the Regulations against the employment agency and not the NHS Trust or construction site controller, who will owe no duty under the Regulations but may owe duties in common law of a similar nature. Additionally, if the contractor is an NHS Trust or other emanation of the State, then the worker can bring an action for breach of the Directive. Further, non-employers in charge of premises may well be subject to other statutory duties in respect of the agency worker, such as pursuant to the Workplace or Construction (Health, Safety and Welfare) Regulations, which impose duties on the person in control and not a non-delegable duty on the employer.[1]

[1] See chapters 18 and 19 for a more detailed consideration of the concept of control in the context of the Workplace and the Construction (Health, Safety and Welfare) Regulations.

What is a 'manual handling operation'

21.24 The Directive (art 2) and the Regulations contain a very wide definition of 'manual handling operations'. These are:

'any transporting or supporting of a load (including the lifting, putting down, pushing, pulling, carrying or moving thereof) by hand or by bodily force.' (reg 2(1))

A load expressly includes any person or animal, but is not otherwise defined: reg 2(1). The Guidance states that a load must be a discrete movable object and would include material supported on a shovel or fork. However, an implement, tool or machine such as a chainsaw, fire hose or breathing apparatus is not considered to be a load when in use for its intended purpose.[1] Such tools or machines will be loads when being transported or supported when not in use.

[1]   See Guidance Notes, para 23.

Transporting or supporting

21.25 The duties are not confined to lifting. The Regulations may apply whenever a load is either transported or supported. Hence the Regulations apply (as set out in reg 2(1)) to pushing objects at work as well as the dropping or throwing of an object. The Guidance clarifies that manual handling includes supporting a load in a static posture and also supporting a load on any part of the body.[1] In *Purves v Buckingham County Council* (20 November 1998, unreported), QBD it was accepted that a teacher grabbing an unruly child could fall within the Regulations. The case is also authority for the proposition that the Regulations applied to emergency operations as well as routine ones.

[1]   See Guidance Notes, para 25.

21.26 Some work operations plainly involve the risk of injury yet do not obviously involve the transporting or supporting of an object: the Guidance Notes give the example of turning a starting handle of an engine or lifting a control lever[1] where the aim of the operation is not to move an object from one place to another nor to support it. In *King v Carron Phoenix Ltd* [1999] Rep LR 51, the removing or fixing of bolts using a spanner was found not to involve the transport or support of a load and the Regulations did not therefore apply. Another example is keyboard work with a risk of upper limb injuries. This does not involve either the transporting or supporting of a load. Those injured by such activities should look to the Health and Safety (Display Screen) Regulations 1992.[2]

[1]   See Guidance Notes at para 26. Those injured by the pushing of a lever should look to the Provision and Use of Work Equipment Regulations 1998, dealt with in chapter 20.
[2]   Dealt with at para 20.79ff.

21.27 There is no requirement that the transporting or supporting of the load is performed exclusively by hand or bodily force. But there plainly will be operations where the role of mechanical assistance is so great that the movement can no longer accurately be described as one done by hand or bodily force. Driving a forklift truck to move pallets would be an example.[1] The Guidance clarifies that the Regulations do not apply when the loads are being transported entirely by mechanical handling as opposed to human effort.[2]

[1]   As above, this activity would be covered by the Provision and Use of Work Equipment Regulations 1998.
[2]   See Guidance Notes at para 24.

21.28 The Regulations are not limited to injuries arising from bearing excessive loads but cover all injuries sustained whilst in the act of either supporting or transporting a load. This interpretation of the Regulations was supported in the case of *Cullen v North Lanarkshire Council* 1998 SLT 847. An appeal was allowed after a Lord Ordinary had held that an accident caused by a person who tripped over a piece of fencing whilst loading debris was outside the Regulations as it was unconnected with the carrying of a load. The court looked at the Directive which the Regulations were intended to implement. Such consideration of the Directive:

'showed that the Directive was concerned with the risk of injury arising from manual handling of loads. It was not limited to the risk of back injury or strain injury or to risks arising out of loads which were heavy. It was on that basis that Article 3 imposed stringent requirements on employers to avoid the need for the manual handling of loads, or, where that could not be avoided, to reduce the risk involved in the manual handling of such loads. The Regulations were not qualified so as to apply only to the risk of injury happening in a particular way'.

Lord Justice Clerk Cullen at 850 said:

'We do not consider that, in order to establish a duty under reg 4(1), it is necessary for a pursuer to show that the risk of injury is a risk arising from the imposition of a load. Such a restriction is not required by the terms in which the Regulations are expressed and we are not persuaded that such an interpretation is required in view of the terms of the directive. ... For these reasons we consider that, assuming that an employee is undertaking a manual handling operation, it is enough if that operation involves a risk of that employee being injured, irrespective of whether it is to some extent due to the imposition of a load.'

21.29 In *Hawkes v London Borough of Southwark* (20 February 1998, unreported) damages were recovered for a claimant injured as he fell down stairs whilst carrying a door. In *Whitcombe v Baker* (9 February 2000, unreported), QBD the judge accepted that falling from the top of a stack of straw bales when building the stack as being within the Regulations (although he went on to find no breach). Similarly, in *Wright v Romford Blinds and Shutters Ltd* [2003] EWHC 1165 (QB) falling from the roof of a van whilst loading a roof rack gave rise to liability under the Regulations. The latter two cases would most probably be brought today under the Work at Height Regulations 2005.[1]

[1] See chapter 19.

21.30 In *King v RCO Support Services Ltd* [2001] ICR 608, CA Kay LJ accepted that the Regulations applied in circumstances in which the claimant sustained personal injuries when he slipped on ice whilst shovelling grit because the operation fell within the definition of 'manual handling operation' in reg 2. The fact that the primary cause of the accident was ice rather than the manual handling itself was irrelevant: the possibility of an icy surface was a factor that should have been considered when assessing the risk of the handling operation. Similarly, in *Purdie v Glasgow City Council* [2002] Rep LR 26, the pursuer slipped on a wet magazine which had fallen onto the floor when he was engaged in shovelling piles of wet magazines. The Regulations were held to apply. In *McIntosh v Edinborough City Council* 2003 SLT 827, the pursuer was dismantling his ladder. The ladder had become stuck in the grass and he lost his balance when it suddenly came free. Lord McEwan held this to be a manual handling operation. All three of these cases would probably sit more comfortably under either the Workplace or the Construction (Health, Safety and Welfare) Regulations. In *King* the claimant abandoned his claim for breach of the Workplace (Health, Safety and Welfare) Regulations, reg 12 against his employer and it is of note that Kay LJ stated that had the claim not been abandoned, he thought it very difficult to see what answer the employer might have to the claim.[1]

[1] At para 28.

21.31 In *Postle v Norfolk and Norwich NHS Healthcare Trust* [2000] 12 CL 283, a county court held that the Regulations applied in circumstances in which a nurse was hit by a trolley in the course of moving a patient, even though at the time the nurse was not actually holding or pulling the trolley. But on the facts the Regulations were not breached because a risk assessment would not have identified the risk of such injuries. In *Skinner v Aberdeen City Council* [2001] Rep LR 118, the pursuer was injured when lifting paving slabs with a crowbar. The slab broke, the crowbar slipped and he sustained injury when he jerked in response. The parties agreed that this was a manual handling operation within the Regulations. In *McBeath v Halliday* [2000] Rep LR 38, the fitting of electrical wiring to a floodlighting column was found to be a manual handling operation. In *Black v Wrangler (UK) Ltd* [2000] GWD 12–441, the pushing of a truck loaded with garments, where the injury was caused by loose threads being caught in the casters, was a manual handling operation within the Regulations. In *Wharf v Bildwell Insulations* (2 February 1999, unreported), QBD Kennedy J found the carrying of tools up a ladder where the injury was caused by the claimant slipping off the ladder, to be a manual handling operation. He went on to find (as might be found in all the cases in this paragraph) that there was also a breach of the Provision and Use of Work Equipment Regulations.

21.32 Finally, in *Fleming v Stirling Council* 2001 SLT 123, the Outer House held that the composite process of taking an elderly patient to the toilet was a manual handling operation within the meaning of the Regulations. The injury was caused when the patient got up from the toilet, stumbled and was caught by the employee.[1] In many cases more than one set of Regulations may be applicable. One of the advantages of the Manual Handling Operations Regulations is that they contain an express duty to assess the risks; something absent from most workplace regulations but present as a general duty under the Management Regulations.[2]

[1] The issues relating to the manual handling of people are dealt with at para 21.62, below.
[2] See chapter 10 for discussion of the Management Regulations.

A load

21.33 The Manual Handling Operations Regulations set no specific weight above which the Regulations first come into play and do not define 'load' as having any minimum weight. The Guidance[1] clarifies that any system based upon the weight of the load is too simple a view of the problem and an ergonomic approach requires consideration of a range of factors to determine the risk of injury and the steps for remedial action. When specific weights are mentioned in the Guidance to the Regulations, the expressed intention is to set out an approximate boundary below which the load is unlikely to create a risk of injury sufficient to warrant a detailed assessment.[2] There is no threshold below which manual handling operations may be regarded as safe.

[1]   At paras 17–20.
[2]   Appendix 2, para 3.

21.34 The county court decision of *Gissing v Walkers Smith Snack Foods Ltd* [1999] CLY 3983 is often quoted as authority for the proposition that the Regulations are inapplicable to repetitive packing of crisp bags as they were neither aimed nor directed at this type of work. It is possible that the transporting or supporting of crisps does not constitute 'a load' within the meaning of the Regulations. In *Spencer v Boots the Chemist Ltd* [2002] EWCA Civ 1691 the case involved a pharmacist whose job involved the repetitive transporting of 600g (when full) stock bottles. It appears from the Court of Appeal judgment that the case on the Regulations was dismissed at first instance on the basis that the weight of the load was only about one-third of the lowest guideline weight suggested by the Guidance to the Regulations for one handed lifting operations performed up to twice a minute. However, it also appears that the county court judge took into account a consideration that the Regulations were intended primarily at reducing back injury from handling significant loads, contrary to higher authority. The primary reason for the dismissal of the case was that the operations involved no risk of injury (see para 21.36).

21.35 Taking a purely mathematical approach to the guidance filter appended to the Guidance on the Regulations,[1] if a woman is transporting or supporting a load above shoulder height or below knee height, repeating such operation more than about 12 times per minute, then the Guidance recommends a risk assessment if the load exceeds 600 gms or (assuming a halving for one handed operations) 300gms. If the operation involves frequent twisting and turning, then the Guidance would suggest a risk assessment for loads below 300gms. *Given (a) the authority of Cullen v North Lanarkshire Council* 1998 SLT 847 followed repeatedly by the Court of Appeal that the Regulations are not limited to injury caused by the weight of the load but cover all manual handling operations involving a risk of injury, and (b) the fact that the Guidance to the Regulations suggests clearly that the Regulations apply to very light loads if the operation is sufficiently frequent, it is submitted that a repetitive strain type injury[2] may be covered by the Regulations when the manual handling operation is such as to create a risk of such injury.[3] In the context of the Regulations and taking the Guidance literally, such operation would have to be one involving frequent twisting and turning if the loads are very light, and such a case may face medical causation problems. Similarly, a person injured falling over when carrying out the transport of very light loads may be covered by the Regulations, where the operation involves a risk of

536

such injury. Whether the employer is in breach of the Regulations in such circumstances is a very different matter and it is of note that in both *Gissing* and *Spencer* there were findings that there was no breach of the Regulations in the event that they did apply. The claimant may be better served in such instances by relying on other more obviously applicable regulations.

1   Guidance Notes (3rd edn, 2004), App 3, p 54.
2   Now better known as musculo-skeletal disorders: see chapter 17.
3   See immediately below for consideration of 'risk'.

The risk of injury

21.36 Regulation 4 states that the duty to avoid manual handling operations arises only in respect of those operations which involve a '*risk*' of injury. There has accordingly been much judicial consideration of what might amount to a '*risk*' of injury within the meaning of the Regulations. The concern has been that by implying that the risk of injury must be a foreseeable risk, the protection provided by the Regulations may be reduced to the level of the common law. In *Anderson v Lothian Health Board* 1996 SCLR 1068, OH, Lord Macfadyen considered that a risk of injury was a foreseeable possibility which is something less than a likelihood of injury or a probability. In *Cullen* (above) Clerk LJ, concerned over setting too high a standard, concluded that the risk referred to 'no more than a foreseeable possibility; it need not be a probability', in *Hawkes* (above) Aldous LJ referred to the need to show a 'real risk' but that the same could be established even where the risk was 'slight'. The most quoted Court of Appeal judgment with consideration of the issue is that of Hale LJ in *Koonjul v Thameslink Healthcare Services* [2000] PIQR P123, CA. At 126 Hale LJ states that having considered both *Cullen* and *Hawkes* she was prepared to accept both those statements as to the level of risk which is required to bring the case within the obligations of the Regulations. She then went on to state that:

> 'There must be a real risk, a foreseeable possibility of injury; certainly nothing approaching a probability. I am also prepared to accept that, in making an assessment of whether there is such a risk of injury, the employer is not entitled to assume that all his employees will on all occasions behave with full and proper concern for their own safety. I accept that the purpose of regulations such as these is indeed to place upon employers obligations to look after their employees' safety which they might not otherwise have.

> However, in making such assessments there has to be an element of realism ... It also seems to me clear that what does involve a risk of injury must be context-based. One is therefore looking at this particular operation in the context of this particular place of employment and also the particular employees involved.'

21.37 The above passage has been quoted and approved repeatedly by the Court of Appeal in manual handling cases.[1] Perhaps the most detailed consideration of the meaning of 'risk' took place within the conflicting judgments of Lord Reed and Lord Carloway in *Taylor v Glasgow City Council* 2002 SC 364. Lord Carloway's view was that since *Nimmo v Alexander Cowan & Sons Ltd* [1968] AC 107,[2] it had been accepted law that the application of statutory duties was without regard to any concept of foreseeability of harm, unless the statute expressly provided for it. In that context, the use of the work 'risk' as opposed to 'foreseeable risk' required that the Regulations also applied to risks which were 'unforeseeable'. Accordingly, once an employee had proved that he had been injured by reason of a manual handling operation, the liability for the consequences could only be avoided if the defendant could prove that it could not take reasonably practicable steps to avoid or reduce the risk of injury. The additional test that the risk must have been foreseeable was not required by the statute. The very fact of injury was evidence of there being a 'risk' of injury. Lord Reed (who was supported by Lord Marnoch) considered that approach and recognised that it would give the word 'risk' its ordinary meaning. However, he rejected the approach and adopted the test of Hale LJ for the following reasons: (a) looking at the wider context of the Regulations, it was not possible to see how an employer could make an assessment of a risk which was not foreseeable. That suggests that the assessment could only be concerned with foreseeable risks; (b) further, what steps could be taken in any event to avoid or reduce an unforeseeable risk? The Regulations could not make any sense if they applied to unforeseeable risks. For those two reasons, by a majority, the Inner House adopted the same interpretation as the Court of Appeal. It is of note that the opposite conclusion was reached by Hale LJ in the Court of Appeal and the Scottish courts in the interpretation of the similarly worded Control of Substances Hazardous to Health Regulations[3] where the term 'hazard' is used as opposed to 'risk'.

[1] See eg *Alsop v Sheffield City Council* [2002] EWCA Civ 429, *O'Neill v DSG Retail Ltd* [2002] EWCA Civ 1139 and *Bennetts v Ministry of Defence* [2004] EWCA Civ 486 and by the majority in the Scottish courts in *Taylor v Glasgow City Council* 2002 SC 364, IH.

[2] Also see *Larner v British Steel plc* [1993] All ER 103.

[3] See paras 22.15 and 22.16 and in particular in *Dugmore v Swansea NHS Trust* [2002] EWCA Civ 1689.

21.38 Lord Reed in *Taylor* (above) remained concerned that, having adopted a 'foreseeable risk' test, the protection afforded by the statute might be reduced to the same level as the common law. However, having considered the hierarchy of measures imposed on an employer by the Regulations and the requirement that employers adopt an ergonomic approach to the operation and not one focusing simply on the weight of the load, he concluded that the Regulations provided better protection.

21.39 The decision in *Taylor* also considers the question of the *context* of foreseeability of risk. This cannot be assessed in too narrow a range of circumstances nor too wide a range of circumstances. A court must look at the general circumstances of the specific operation being carried out and ask whether that operation gave rise to a risk of injury. In *Taylor*, the pursuer was injured when moving a cupboard up two flights of stairs. It was that operation which must be considered when considering if a foreseeable risk of injury arose. A court would be wrong to address the general task of moving cupboards or the specific risk of not telling the claimant which side of the cupboard was the heaviest. This approach was followed in *McDougall v Spiers* [2002] Rep LR 80, in which the question was whether moving a piano down a set of curved steps posed a risk of the pursuer losing his footing and not whether him slipping on a particular foliage covered stone was a foreseeable risk. This matter was also given consideration by the Court of Appeal in *O'Neill v DSG Retail Ltd* [2002] EWCA Civ 1139 in which Nelson J adopted the common law reasoning of *Hughes v The Lord Advocate* [1963] AC 837 that it was not a necessary part of the test of foreseeability of injury that the precise circumstances in which an accident occurred must be foreseen. He went on to find that the risk of an employee twisting whilst carrying a load and sustaining injury was a foreseeable risk and it was incorrect to assess the foreseeability of him twisting in an instinctive response to hearing his name called from behind.

21.40 Examples of cases where no risk of injury had been found include *Alsop v Sheffield City Council* [2002] EWCA Civ 429, where the judge at first instance found that there was no risk of injury from wheeling wheelie bins up and down ramps. The Court of Appeal accepted that that was a finding she was entitled to make but went on to find that there had been no breach of the Regulations in any event. In *Warner v Huntingdonshire District Council* [2002] EWCA Civ 791 a refuse collector was injured from the lifting of approximately 500 bin bags a day. The judge at first instance concluded that this involved no risk of injury, although this appears to have been doubted on appeal, the Court of Appeal deciding the case on there being no breach of the Regulations. In *Bennetts v Ministry of Defence* [2004] EWCA Civ 486 the judge at first instance found that the operation out of which the injury occurred involved no risk of injury and this was similarly doubted on appeal, with the Court of Appeal preferring to find that there was no breach of the Regulations. The short judgment of Carnwath LJ in particular in *Bennetts* shows just how low a threshold 'risk' might be.

21.41 In the context of foreseeability, an employer will be deemed to know of any risks which would have been identified by a proper risk assessment under the Management of Health and Safety at Work Regulations (see chapter 10 above) and under these Regulations (see reg 4(1)(b)(i)).

Reasonable practicability and the burden of proof

21.42 Once the claimant has established that the task giving rise to the damage involved a risk of injury then the burden of proof switches to the defendant in respect of the various duties imposed by reg 4. This view is set out very clearly by Staughton LJ himself in *Hawkes* (above) although he has himself doubted its application (*Koonjul*). It is submitted that the overwhelming weight of authority supports the proposition that the burden of pleading and proving that all reasonably practicable steps have been taken is upon the defendant both in the context of the Regulations (see *Hawkes, Cullen, Anderson v Lothian Health Board* [1996] SCLR 1068; *King v RCO Support Services Ltd* [2001] ICR 608; *Skinner v Aberdeen City Council* [2001] Rep LR 118; *O'Neill v DSG Retail Ltd* [2002] EWCA Civ 1139; *Wright v Romford Blinds and Shutters Ltd* [2003] EWHC 1165 (QB) *and Davidson v Lothian* *and Borders Fire Board* 2003 SLT 939) and in respect of other statutory duties containing the same words (eg the Factories Act 1961, s 29: *Larner v British Steel* [1993] 4 All ER 102, and the Coal Mines Act 1922, s 102: *Edwards v National Coal Board* [1949] 1 KB 704. See also *Hall v City of Edinburgh Council* 1999 SLT 744 and *Bassie v Merseyside Fire and Civil Defence Authority* [2005] EWCA Civ 1474 in respect of the Workplace (Health, Safety and Welfare) Regulations 1996). The interpretation of 'reasonable practicability' is that set out in the judgment of Asquith LJ at p 712 of *Edwards v National Coal Board* (above) which was expressly adopted by the Court of Appal in respect of the Regulations in *Hawkes* (above) and see para 5.77ff.

Regulation 4(1)(a)

21.43 At the top of the hierarchy of measures which the employer must take is to avoid the need for its employees to undertake manual handling operations 'at work' so far as this is reasonably practicable. The burden on the employer in reg 4(1)(a) may be discharged by the employer demonstrating, by evidence, that there was no other way for the operation to be undertaken: *Brown v East and Midlothian Trust* 2000 SLT 342. The phrase 'at work' has a wide meaning.[1] 'At work' applies to anything done in, or reasonably incidental to, the course of employment.[2]

---

[1]   See the HSWA 1974, s 52. The phrase is absent from the Directive, which merely talks of avoiding the need for manual handling 'by workers' (art 3).

[2]   See the definition in the HSWA 1974, s 52(1). It includes training by virtue of the Health and Safety (Training for Employment) Regulations 1990, SI 1990/1380.

21.44 The duty under the Regulations is to avoid the need for manual handling 'so far as is reasonably practicable'. The corresponding provision of the Directive, art 3(1), is not so qualified by reasonable practicability but it is qualified by the requirement to take 'appropriate' steps. The question of whether there is any real difference between the two is considered in *King v Sussex Ambulance NHS Trust* [2002] EWCA Civ 953 and above at paras 21.18–21.19.

21.45 The Guidance to the Regulations recommends that an employer should consider as methods of avoiding manual handling the use of mechanisation, automation (eg piping or conveyor belts) and reorganisation of the system of work by bringing the work process to the object rather than transporting the object to the work process.

21.46 Despite the burden being on the defendant, there are few cases where courts have found that the manual handling operation could have been avoided. A rare example is *King v RCO Support Services Ltd* [2001] ICR 608, where Kay LJ found that the defendant had failed to prove that the gritting of the icy yard could not have been carried out by a mechanical gritter. In *Anderson v Lothian Health Board* 1996 SCLR 1068, OH, Lord Macfadyen found that the employer had failed to show that manual handling of laundry could not be avoided. In *Hall v Edinburgh City Council* 1999 SLT 744, the defendant was found in breach of reg 4(1)(a) on the basis that it had failed to bring any evidence to explain why the need for the employee to lift a 50kg bag of cement could not be avoided. Often, even in the absence of any pleaded case or evidence on avoidance, the courts have been prepared to recognise the obvious or common sense fact that many manual handling operations simply cannot be entirely avoided (see eg *O'Neill v DSG Retail Ltd* [2002] EWCA Civ 1139 *at paras 61–64). By further contrast, in an action for judicial review brought by patients against the local authority that employed their carers, the court found that a blanket ban on all manual lifting of patients was most unlikely to be lawful: A & B v East Sussex County Council* [2003] EWHC 167 (Admin).

Regulation 4(1)(b)

21.47 If it is not 'reasonably practicable' to avoid the need for manual handling operations, the employer is obliged to demonstrate compliance with the three separate duties under reg 4(1)(b).

Regulation 4(1)(b)(i)

21.48 Regulation 4(1)(b)(i) imposes a duty to undertake a 'suitable and sufficient' assessment of the risks to employees, which should be updated if it is believed to be no longer valid or if the nature of the operation changes (reg 4(2)). This is a more specific assessment than the general risk assessment required under the Management of Health and Safety at Work Regulations. At the very least it should 'look in a considered way at the totality of the manual handling operations', consulting with employees and drawing upon professional help if necessary. Guidance on the factors to be taken into account is provided in Sch 1 to the Regulations and in more detail within the Guidance.[1] These concentrate upon the nature of the task rather than adopting strict weight limits, entirely in keeping with ergonomic knowledge of the causes of injuries.

[1] See *HSE Guidance on the Regulations* (3rd edn, 2004).

21.49 The fact that an employer might have failed to have carried out a risk assessment does not act so to absolve it from the duty to reduce the risk of injury to the lowest level reasonably practicable under reg 4(1)(b)(ii) or from the duty to take other appropriate steps in reg 4(1)(b)(iii): see *Swain v Denso Martin Ltd* [2000] ICR 1079, CA. Walker LJ said that a proper risk assessment would have been a systematic assessment under the control of an outside consultant or an employer's health and safety officer. In *Swain* the Court of Appeal held that reg 4(1)(b)(i), (ii) and (iii) had to be read with the others. It rejected the contention that reg 4(1)(b) imposed three separate obligations. It rejected the suggestion that a failure to carry out a risk assessment relieved the employer of the obligation to provide an indication as to the weight of the load. In *Harvey v Northumberland County Council* [2003] EWCA Civ 338 the employer failed in its argument that it was not in breach for failing to assess, as it was awaiting guidance from the Government before advising social workers on how to restrain difficult and violent children.

21.50 A mere failure to carry out an assessment, whilst a prima facie breach, is of no causal value to an injured employee if the employer can still establish that a prudent employer, had it carried out its obligations, would not have done anything other than that which it did do and which could reasonably practicably have prevented/lessened the injury complained of: *Hawkes*; *Alsop v Sheffield City Council* [2002] EWCA Civ 429. This was in essence the conclusion of Hale LJ in *Koonjul v Thameslink Healthcare Services* [2000] PIQR P123, CA, that, if the employer had failed to assess the specific task of moving the bed which injured the employee's back, then such assessment would not have added anything to the existing manual handling training on moving numerous other everyday items (at P127). A further example is *Purvis v Buckinghamshire County Council* [1999] Ed CR 542, where the failure to undertake an assessment was found to be a technical breach only and was not causative in any way of the employee's accident.

21.51 In calculating what risks need to be assessed, employers are entitled to take a realistic assessment of risk; thus they need not examine every conceivable risk, no matter how small. Further, the assessment of risks should be context based, looking at the particular operation in the context of the particular place of employment and the particular employees involved: see *Koonjul* (again). Conversely, since the obligations in reg 4(1)(b)(i), (ii) and (iii) are *distinct* obligations and are not conjunctive, a defendant cannot rely on a failure to conduct a risk assessment to argue that it was under no obligation to take steps under regs 4(1)(b)(ii), (iii): *Swain* (above). The absence of an assessment may make it difficult for an employer to satisfy its continuing burden to prove that no reasonably practicable steps could have been taken to reduce the risk of injury.

Regulation 4(1)(b)(ii)

21.52 The most important of the three subordinate duties is reg 4(1)(b)(ii), namely the obligation to reduce the risk of injury to the lowest level reasonably practicable. It is upon an alleged breach of this regulation that most cases proceed. As above, the burden of proving that all reasonably practicable steps have been taken is upon the employer (see para 21.42, above). The Directive (see art 3(2)) imposes a duty to 'take the appropriate organisation measures or use the appropriate means ... in order to reduce the risk involved in the manual handling of such loads'. But the Directive does not require that those measures reduce the risk to '*the lowest level*' nor that the measures be qualified by those which are 'reasonably practicable'. The issue of whether there is any substantive difference between the Directive and the regulation is considered at paras 21.18–21.19 above.

21.53 In general, and following the duty to consult on all questions of health and safety contained in the Directive, employees should be consulted on the redesign of the work operations, as the Guidance Notes recognise. The introduction of mechanical assistance may be necessary. If it is introduced, that equipment must additionally satisfy the duties in the Provision of Work Equipment Regulations 1998 and the Lifting Operations and Lifting Equipment Regulations (see chapter 20). If, to assist in the safety of any manual handling, the employer provides personal protective equipment, such as gloves or non-slip shoes, additional duties will then arise under the Personal Protective Equipment at Work Regulations 1992 (see chapter 20). The examples of cases are numerous and most fit into one or more of the following categories:

(i)   a failure to provide equipment;
(ii)   a failure to reorganise the work;
(iii) a failure to provide more assistance;
(iii) a failure to provide training.

21.54 The above is by no means a comprehensive list of circumstances and is intended only to provide comparator cases for common circumstances. Any of the matters listed in Sch 1 to the Regulations are capable of giving rise to a cause of action for breach of the Regulations. The issue of lifting people raises separate consideration (see para 21.62, below) as the task of lifting a piano or cupboard down the stairs cannot be compared with lifting a person (see Hale LJ in *King v Sussex Ambulance NHS Trust* [2002] EWCA Civ 953). The issues relating to information concerning the weight of a load are dealt with below in the section on reg 4(1)(b)(iii) and the individual characteristics of the employee are dealt with below in the section on reg 4(3). Oddly, there are few reported cases where liability is established upon a simple failure to reduce the weight of the load.[1] It may be that such cases are too straightforward to reach court. Where tasks are frequent or strenuous, appropriate steps should extend to allowing and encouraging regular breaks, perhaps allowing each individual to choose when to take such breaks. This approach is also consistent with reg 4(3), ensuring that the work is matched to the physical suitability of the individual.

[1]   An example is the county court decision in *Watson v Warwickshire County Council* [2001] CLY 3302 (District Judge).

Equipment

21.55 In *Knott v Newham Healthcare NHS Trust* [2002] EWHC 2091 (QB), Simon J found the failure to provide a nurse with mechanical lifting aids for lifting long term brain injured patients several times each day, such that staff had to carry out the task entirely by hand, was in breach of reg 4(1)(b)(ii). In *Wright v Romford Blinds and Shutters Ltd* [2003] EWHC 1165 (QB) where the claimant fell from the roof of a van, the failure to provide guard rails, hand holds or raised edges to prevent slipping over the edge, was in breach of the regulation. In *Whitcombe v Baker* (9 February 2000, unreported), QB the judge found that no such steps were practicable where the claimant was working on top of a stack of straw bales.

Reorganisation or change of system

21.56 In *King v Sussex Ambulance NHS Trust* [2002] EWCA Civ 953 the failure to use the fire brigade to lift an elderly patient out of the upper story of a building was not a breach of duty as it was not reasonably practicable and failed to take into account the impact on the patient (considered below in more detail at para 21.62). In *Kerr v North Ayrshire Council* [2002] Rep LR 35 the school was not in breach of duty for requiring tables to be stacked vertically, which was what the manufacturer had intended. In *Anderson v Lothian Health Board* [1996] SCLR 1068 the introduction of a system of maximum loads was not sufficient where the defendant had failed to take reasonably practicable steps to ensure that the maximum load was not exceeded. In *Stone v Metropolitan Police Commissioner* (16 September 1999, unreported) the employer was found liable for failing to take a series of steps to ease the manual handling burden.

Assistance

21.57 In *Hawkes* (above) the Court of Appeal found the failure to prove why the claimant could not be provided with a colleague to assist him in carrying a heavy door up the stairs to be in breach of reg 4(1)(b)(ii). *Peck v Chief Constable of Avon & Somerset* [2000] CLY 2971, a case brought on the basis of the direct effect of the Directive, concluded that the failure to instruct officers to only lift protestors with assistance from others, was a breach of reg 4(1)(b)(ii). See also *Stone v Metropolitan Police Commissioner* (16 September 1999, unreported). *Wiles v Bedfordshire County Council* [2001] CL 3305 reached a similar conclusion regarding the toileting of an elderly patient, which should have been assessed (and subsequently was) as a two-person job. A failure to provide further assistance to an employee with a known health problem was found to be in breach of the Regulation in *Goodchild v Organon Laboratories Ltd* [2004] EWHC 2341 (QB).

Training and information

21.58 The provision of proper training is an express obligation under the Manual Handling Directive (art 6(2)). No express mention is made within the regulation, although reference to taking into account an employee's knowledge and training has been added in reg 4(3)(c). However, case law has considered extensively the need for training. The primary question in cases concerning the need for or lack of training and information is a causation one. The question was set out by Chadwick LJ in *O'Neill v DSG Retail Ltd* [2002] EWCA Civ 1139 as 'was the employer's failure to provide training a cause of the employee's injury?'.[1]

[1] See para 94 of the judgment.

21.59 In *Koonjul v Thameslink Healthcare Services* [2000] PIQR P123, CA, to the extent that there was any failure to train the claimant in the specific risks involved in pulling out a low wooden bed, such failure had no causative impact where the claimant had already received extensive manual handling training on lifting other everyday items such as a bed. A similar conclusion had been reached in *Brown v East and Midlothian NHS Trust* 2000 SLT 342 and in *Postle v Norfolk and Norwich NHS Healthcare Trust* [2000] 12 CL 283. In *Alsop v Sheffield City Council* [2002] EWCA Civ 429 on appeal, the court concluded that the failure to give refuse collectors more detailed instructions on how to wheel wheelie bins up and down ramps was not in breach of duty, since it amounted to no more than asking them to use common sense.[1] In *Warner v Huntingdonshire District Council* [2002] EWCA Civ 791 the refuse collector was injured from the lifting of approximately 500 bin bags a day. The claimant did not pursue a case based upon a failure to provide training and Latham LJ concluded that there was no evidence that any training would have made any difference. He does not appear to have considered the implication of it being the defendant's duty to prove that training would have made no difference. Had he found as a fact that the training would have made no difference, then that conclusion could not be challenged. That was the basis of the decision at first instance in *Bennetts v Ministry of Defence* [2004] EWCA Civ 486 supported as correct by the Court of Appeal, that there was no training or advice that could have been given which would have affected the mechanism of the injury.[2] In contrast, in *Smith v Notaro Ltd* (5 May 2006, unreported), the employer was held to be in breach of reg 4 for failing to give training in how to carry loads over uneven surfaces even though it might be seen to be training for something obvious.

[1]   The first instance judge rejected the case on there being no risk of injury and did not address reg 4(1)(b).
[2]   See para 26 of judgment.

21.60 Conversely, in *McBeath v Halliday* [2000] Rep LR 38, the failure to provide the pursuer with the written manufacturers' instructions had materially contributed to his accident. In *Peck v Chief Constable of Avon & Somerset* [2000] CLY 2971, the court found that the failure to instruct officers not to lift protestors on their own was a cause of the accident. In *Skinner v Aberdeen City Council* [2001] Rep LR 118, the employer's failure to train the employee in the correct methods for lifting large paving slabs had been the cause of the accident. A similar finding was made in respect of repetitive manual handling of large quantities of stationery supplies in *Stone v Metropolitan Police Commissioner* (16 September 1999, unreported). In *Harvey v Northumberland County Council* [2003] EWCA Civ 338, the failure to train residential social workers in methods and techniques for the restraint of violent children was a cause of the accident and in breach of duty. The Court of Appeal considered the issue extensively in *O'Neill v DSG Retail Ltd* [2002] EWCA Civ 1139, rejecting the argument that *Koonjul* (above) and *Alsop* (above) provided anything more than decisions on fact in those cases. The Court of Appeal found that the failure to provide the claimant with oral practical training, designed in part to train him out of the instinct to twist, to supplement his written training was in breach of reg 4(1)(b)(ii). However, the conclusion of Nelson J that the case differed from *Koonjul* was that DSG had recognised the need for training whereas in *Koonjul* the defendant had not, does not appear correct. First, a failure to recognise the need for training could arise by reason of a breach of the duty to assess under reg 4(1)(b)(i).

21.60 *Manual handling*

Second, in *Koonjul* and *Alsop* the conclusion of the courts was that additional training would have had no impact in the context of the job and the training which already existed. It is submitted that the correct question in these cases is that set out by Chadwick LJ in *O'Neill v DSG Retail Ltd* [2002] EWCA Civ 1139—was the employer's failure to provide training a cause of the employee's injury?[1] This is a question of fact which must be answered in every case.

[1]   See para 94 of judgment.

Other examples

21.61 In *Davidson v Lothian and Borders Fire Board* 2003 SLT 939, the failure to postpone a fire drill exercise due to poor weather conditions and a failure to assess what should be done in poor weather conditions generally, was a failure to reduce the risk of injury to the lowest level and a breach of reg 4(1)(b)(ii). This case would most likely be considered today under the Work at Height Regulations 2005.

Lifting people

21.62 The manual handling of people raises different issues. The Guidance recognises that the interests of the endangered or injured individual may often conflict with the interests of the manual handler and suggests that when lifting people, an employee may be required to accept a greater risk of injury than someone employed to lift inanimate objects.[1] This was emphasised by Hale LJ in *King v Sussex Ambulance NHS Trust* [2002] EWCA Civ 953 when she stated that whilst a removal firm can choose not to remove a piece of furniture if it cannot be done safely, that option was not always available to a rescuer such as an ambulance man. Further, various methods for moving furniture cannot necessarily be used for people. The matter came to stark attention when two patients sought judicial review of the local authorities' blanket ban on manual handling by their carers. When various parts of their care could not be carried out in any other way, the patients were subjected to long, embarrassing and uncomfortable delays whilst equipment was obtained: *A & B v East Sussex County Council* [2003] EWHC 167 (Admin). Mr Justice Munby concluded that a balance had to be struck between the health and safety of the carer and the human rights of the disabled person. Civil society cannot expect its nurses, care assistants and others to sacrifice their own health and safety for the care of the disabled. Equally, not every operation can and (even if it can) must be performed by hoist. The manual handling of disabled patients must maintain at all times the person's dignity, comfort and quality of life. As such, the assessment of what is a reasonably practicable method of avoiding or reducing the risk of injury must take into account the physical, emotional, psychological and social impact it will have upon the disabled person. As such, there will be circumstances where had the lift been of an object such as a piano, a hoist would be used, but due to the delay, discomfort or embarrassment which the disabled person might suffer, manual lifting is required. Specific examples where manual handling might be required where a hoist could theoretically be used include getting the disabled person out of the bath or off the toilet or off the floor when a hoist would take time to arrange.[2]

1   See Guidance at para 32.
2   See generally paras 125–155 of the judgment.

Regulation 4(1)(b)(iii)

21.63 Regulation 4(1)(b)(iii) requires the employer, where it is not reasonably practicable to avoid a manual handling operation, to provide the employee at risk with information as to the weight of the load and the heaviest side of any load. In *McBeath v Halliday* 2000 GWD 75 Lord MacFadyen held that the failure on the part of an employer to provide an employee with written instructions in circumstances where it was reasonably foreseeable that the employee would be exposed to injury resulted in liability because that failure had made a material contribution to the subsequent injury. In *Boyd v Lanarkshire Health Board* 2000 GWD 341 Lady Paton held, in the Outer House, that liability rested upon the employer of a laundry assistant who failed to provide her with a clear indication as to the weights involved in the lifting task and in circumstances where the evidence did not disclose that the safety audit carried out had taken into account the factors listed in Sch 1 to the 1992 Regulations.

21.64 The employer should additionally provide the employees engaged in such operations with information, including as to the precise weights of loads where this is reasonably practicable (reg 4(1)(b)(iii)). In *Kelly v Forticrete* (19 April 1999, unreported), CA Brooke LJ said that it was an insufficient discharge of duty for a defendant to 'place all its eggs in one basket' by simply providing information as to risk reduction without taking any other steps to reduce the risk of injury.

Regulation 4(3)

21.65 The original unamended 1992 Regulations arguably did not give proper effect to the Directive's requirement in Annex II that regard be given to the particular characteristics of the worker. This issue has been resolved by the amendment to reg 4(3) made by SI 2002/2174 which now requires that regard shall be had to the physical suitability of the employee to carry out the operations, his knowledge and training and whether the employee is within any group of employees identified as being specifically at risk.[1] However, Sch 1 to the Regulations always required an employer to consider whether the task requires unusual strength, special training or if an employee might be pregnant or have a health problem. Further, prior case law such as *Wells v West Hertfordshire Health Authority* (5 April 2000, unreported), HC interpreted a defendant's failure to take into account the claimant's individual capabilities as being in breach of reg 4(1) prior to the implementation of reg 4(3).

21.65 *Manual handling*

1   Amendment made by the Health and Safety (Miscellaneous Amendments) Regulations 2002, reg 4.

21.66 An employer should potentially be liable: (i) for individual weaknesses of which it has actual knowledge, and (ii) if it is aware of any objective characteristics, such as build or height, from which a reasonable employer would infer individual risk. This may extend to weaknesses it would have discovered had it engaged in proper training and to weaknesses which would have been revealed by proper health surveillance, as required by art 14 of the Framework Directive and the Management of Health and Safety at Work Regulations 1999, reg 6. In *Eastgate v Oxfordshire County Council* [2004] CL Oct, the fact of the claimant's known history of back problems was taken into account in establishing breach of reg 4, despite the fact that the claimant had failed to inform occupational health of his ongoing symptoms. In assessing risk an employer is also not entitled to assume that all employees will on all occasions act with full and proper concern for their own safety: see *Koonjul* (above). Thus assessments should take account of possible deviations from normal working practice and the steps taken to reduce injury should also be made with such an awareness.

Duties on employees, causation and contributory negligence

21.67 By virtue of reg 5 an employee is obliged properly to use any system of work provided by his employer for him. No duty should arise, however, where the employer fails altogether to introduce a system of work. Under the HSWA 1974, s 47(2), a breach of regulations is actionable 'so far as it causes damage'. That would make an employer vicariously liable for the actions of an employee which cause damage to another employee. However, the wording is with difficulty applicable to an employee who injures himself. In respect of the similarly worded duty in reg 10(2) of the PPE at Work Regulations, Kennedy LJ[1] held that a defendant, having taken no steps to ensure than a claimant wore PPE, was in no position to argue that even had it done so, the claimant might not have worn the PPE.

1   See *Henser-Leather v Securicor Cash Services Ltd* [2002] EWCA Civ 816; and para 20.76, above.

21.68 The conduct of the employee is often an issue raised in respect of both causation and contributory negligence.[1] Without repeating the contents of the chapters on these subjects, it is worth noting that an employer will not be able to escape liability for a breach of statutory duty, even though it had been brought about by the claimant, unless it could prove that its breach was no more than that created by the claimant (*Boyle v Kodak* [1969] 1 WLR 661). Further, a strict 'but for' test on causation does not work when the duty alleged to have been breached is reg 4(1)(b)(ii)—the duty to reduce the risk of injury. Accordingly, in *O'Neill v DSG* the test applied by the Court of Appeal on causation is whether the defendant's breach was *a* cause of the injury (see Chadwick LJ at para 89). This approach was expressly adopted in *Goodchild v Organon Laboratories Ltd* [2004] EWHC 2341 (QB) at para 47. If the claimant has contributed to the accident through conduct of his own, then contributory negligence must be assessed but with regard to the established case law discussed in chapter 6.

1   Chapters 3 and 6.

EXPERT EVIDENCE

21.69 Legal advisors should be cautious about the instruction of experts in cases involving manual handling injuries. The Court of Appeal has expressed its displeasure at evidence from experts who seek to give an opinion as to whether or not a task involved a risk of injury or as to whether the defendants were in breach of duty: see in particular the strident comment of Aldous LJ in *Hawkes* (above). The court will, however, require evidence of the weight of relevant objects and (subject to relevance) evidence of distances and changing centres of gravity. It is anticipated that most of the evidence of this kind is capable of presentation in a written report and that only in the most complicated of cases will experts be required to give oral evidence. The exceptions to the above situation will be cases involving complicated lifting and handling techniques, such as nursing care and restraint of violent individuals. In such cases, expert evidence is often required and regard should also be given to the Royal College of Nurses guide to manual handling. Other exceptions may involve cases where the methods necessary to avoid or reduce the risk of injury involve a technical complexity not obviously apparent to laypeople.

Chapter 22

STATUTORY CONTROL OF SUBSTANCES AND PHENOMENA HAZARDOUS TO HEALTH

Stuart Brittenden

Daniel Bennett

GENERAL

22.01 The common law duties to protect workers against dangerous substances and other phenomena such as asbestos, vibration and noise are considered above at chapters 14–16. This chapter deals with the statutory provisions in relation to other injurious substances and phenomena. Only the most commonly encountered regulations are dealt with. There are many others (see *Redgrave's Health and Safety*, 4th edn). Much of this legislation implements European Directives. The coverage of the Directives continues to expand. This chapter deals first with the general regulation of hazardous substances by the Control of Substances Hazardous to Health (COSHH) Regulations 2002, SI 2002/2677. Second, it addresses the more commonly encountered specific regulations dealing with genetically modified organisms (GMOs), lead, asbestos, ionising radiation, fire, electricity and gas. Whilst protection from lead, asbestos and ionising radiation are excepted from the COSHH Regulations,[1] GMOs are subject to both the general and specific regulations. Fire, electricity and gas are in most circumstances outside the definition of 'substance hazardous to health' (see below) and are phenomena. Finally, the chapter addresses the response of operators to major accidents involving the substances and phenomena addressed.

[1] See COSHH 2002, reg 5.

22.02 The UK regulations must be construed in the light of the Directives from which they derive (see chapter 9) and also the broader Directives (and implementing regulations) which form a backdrop to them, eg the Framework and Workplace Directives. The safety regulations in this chapter are made under the HSWA 1974, and, unlike previous regulations under the factories and mines legislation and other specific legislation, they apply to (nearly) all places of work. In general, the duty to comply with the regulations is imposed on the employers although the COSHH Regulations 2002 in particular are much wider; and the regulations are intended to operate not only for the protection of workers but also for the protection of others who may be endangered by their activities. A breach gives rise to civil liability (HSWA 1974, s 47(2)). Breach of the Regulations also involves liability to criminal prosecution.

550

22.03 The main effect of these Regulations is to require work with dangerous substances to be planned in advance and carried out in such a way as to either avoid risk, or if that cannot be attained, minimise risk. The use of some substances is prohibited entirely, others have to be notified in advance to the HSE, to enable them to exercise oversight, and the HSE also have to be informed of accidents and emergencies.

SUBSTANCES HAZARDOUS TO HEALTH

22.04 There have been four sequential Control of Substances Hazardous to Health (COSHH) Regulations:

Regulation	Came into force	Last day
1988 Regulations	1 October 1989	15 January 1995
1994 Regulations	16 January 1995	24 March 1999
1999 Regulations	25 March 1999	20 November 2002
2002 Regulations	21 November 2002	—

Since hazardous substances can cause injury through prolonged and persisted exposure, it is often the case that the causative period of exposure covers more than one set of regulations. Matters can be further complicated by amendments to the Regulations. The current 2002 Regulations, SI 2002/2677, have been amended by SIs 2003/978, 2004/698 and 2004/3386.

22.05 The Regulations implement numerous Directives addressing a range of specific substances. The COSHH Regulations provide a general regulation of substances hazardous to health, providing a uniform code for the control of almost any substance which may be harmful to health. The COSHH Regulations also contain some specific regulation of specific classes of substance. The first COSHH Regulations of 1988 replaced a large number of regulations under the Factories Act and other legislation which covered a wide range of particular substances as various as horse hair (which might carry anthrax germs), silica dust (causing silicosis), cyanide, chromium and agricultural pesticides. The 1994 Regulations (SI 1994/3246) consolidated a number of earlier statutory provisions, not only the COSHH Regulations of 1988 and the COSHH (Amendment) Regulations 1991 and 1992 but also the Health and Safety (Dangerous Pathogens) Regulations 1981. The 1994 Regulations also implemented the Biological Agents Directives of 1990 and 1993. The Regulations have been extended to cover the offshore oil and gas industry. There are three ACOPs (in one booklet): General, Carcinogens and Biological Agents. Further ACOPs have been issued in respect of Pesticides, Asthma at Work, the Pottery Industry, Vinyl Chloride and Fumigation. The COSHH Regulations 2002 make reference to the Chemicals (Hazard Information and Packaging for Supply) Regulations 2002, adopting definitions and lists of substances contained within those regulations.

'Substance hazardous to health'

22.06 'Substance' is defined in reg 2(1) as meaning a natural or artificial substance whether in solid or liquid form or in the form of a gas or vapour (including micro-organisms). Regulation 2(1) next defines 'substance hazardous to health'. The 1988, 1994 and 1999 Regulations defined 'substance hazardous to health' as follows:

> ' "substance hazardous to health" means any substance (including any preparation) which is—
>
> (a) a substance which is listed in Part 1 of the approved supply list as dangerous for supply within the meaning of [the Chemicals (Hazard Information and Packaging for Supply) Regulations 1994] and for which an indication of danger specified for the substance in Part V of that list is very toxic, toxic, harmful, corrosive or irritant;
>
> (b) a substance specified in Schedule 1 (which lists substances assigned maximum exposure limits) or for which the Health and Safety Commission has approved an occupational exposure standard;
>
> (c) a biological agent;
>
> (d) dust of any kind, when present at a substantial concentration in air;
>
> (e) a substance, not being a substance mentioned in sub-paragraphs (a) to (d) above, which creates a hazard to the health of any person which is comparable with the hazards created by substances mentioned in those sub-paragraphs.'

SI 2004/3386 amended the Regulations to replace the concepts of 'maximum exposure limits' and 'occupational exposure standards' with 'workplace exposure limits'. These are contained within the HSE publication EH40, which is regularly amended.

22.07 A 'biological agent' is defined by reg 2(1) as:

> 'a micro-organism, cell culture or human endoparasite, whether or not genetically modified, which may cause infection, allergy, toxicity or otherwise create a hazard to human health'.

The definition will certainly cover infectious harmful bacteria. It appears that viruses would also be covered by the definition.

22.08 The COSHH Regulations 2002 have amended the definition of substance above to refer to the Chemicals (Hazard Information and Packaging for Supply) Regulations 2002 (the 'CHIP' Regulations) and also to widen the catch-all sub-paragraph (e), stating:

> '(e) which not being a substance falling within sub-paragraphs (a) to (d) because of its chemical or toxicological properties and the way it is used or is present at the workplace creates a risk to health.'

22.09 When considering the earlier catch all sub-paragraph (e) from the 1994 Regulations, Lord Nimmo Smith rejected an argument that the pursuer must show that the substance alleged to have caused an injury shares the same characteristics as a substance listed within sub-category (a) or (b). He considered that the purpose of the definition was to bring within the ambit of the regulations any substance which creates a hazard to health and that the comparison was between hazards and not substances. As such, a substance which caused irritation was within the definition; see *Bilton v Fastnet Highlands Ltd* 1998 SLT 1323. Similarly, any substance which is very toxic,

toxic, harmful or corrosive would also be included. The current definition within the 2002 Regulations avoids the need for any comparison and simply requires that the substance creates a risk to health, whatever that risk might be.

22.10 A further widening of the 2002 definition is the addition of the phrase *'and the way it is used or is present at the workplace'*. This makes clear that the substance does not necessarily need to be used as part of the work process. It could be a by-product or waste product (eg animal faeces in a laboratory) or simply present by other reason (eg mould, pigeon faeces). This view is supported further by reg 2(2), which states that reference to exposure is reference to an employee being exposed to a substance hazardous to health arising out of or in connection with work at the workplace.

22.11 The burden is on the claimant to prove under the Regulations that he was exposed to a substance hazardous to health and that such exposure caused injury. In *Sayers v Loganair Ltd* (26 February 2004, unreported), Ct of Sess the defenders had bought an approved disinfectant and TG Coutts QC, sitting as a temporary judge, found that it was stretching inference too far to say they were 'using' dangerous substances simply because the disinfectant contained three chemicals/substances which had been listed as dangerous in terms of the CHIP Regulations. This was in the context of the pursuer being provided with the disinfectant diluted by at least 180 parts of water. Some claims will fail on causation grounds. Having established the presence of a substance hazardous to health, the claimant fails to prove that injury resulted from such exposure (see eg *Abbott v Rockware Glass Ltd* (30 July 1999, unreported), CA; *Evans v Volex Group plc* [2002] EWCA Civ 225 and *Moffat v AG for Scotland* [2006] CSOH 2).

22.12 Regulation 4 contains a list (by way of Sch 2 to the Regulations) of substances which are prohibited from use at work and sets out the relevant circumstances. Regulation 5 excepts certain hazardous substances from the application of the regulations. Respirable dust in coal mines, lead at work and asbestos at work are covered by other specific regulations (see below) and are excepted by reg 5(1). Substances which are hazardous solely by virtue of their radioactivity are excepted by reg 5(2). Substances administered in the course of medical treatment are also excepted by reg 5(3). However, substances with which a person comes into contact during the course of medical treatment, but which are not administered intentionally (eg latex or MRSA) will be covered by the Regulations.

To whom are duties owed

22.13 An employer owes duties under the COSHH Regulations to employers, contractors, visitors and anyone else who may be at risk of injury from hazardous substances. Regulation 3(1) states:

'Where a duty is placed by the Regulations on an employer in respect of his employees, he shall, so far as is reasonably practicable, be under a like duty in respect of *any other person, whether at work or not,* who may be affected by the work carried out by the employer ...'

The regulation continues to confirm that regs 10–13 only apply to employees, clarifying the application of regs 6–9 to others. In *Anderson v Crump* [1996] CLY 5657 a defendant was found liable under COSHH to a neighbour of a factory who developed asthma caused by fumes vented from the defendant's factory premises.

Assessment

22.14 Regulation 6(1) requires that an employer shall not carry out work which is liable to expose any employees to any substance hazardous to health unless: (a) it has first made a suitable and sufficient assessment of the risk created by that work to the health of those employees and of the steps that need to be taken to meet the requirements of the Regulations; and (b) it has implemented the steps identified. Regulation 6(2) provides a list of matters which the assessment must take into account. Regulation 6(3) provides the circumstances in which it must be reviewed. *Naylor v Volex Group plc* [2003] EWCA Civ 222 is an example of a case in which the defendant was found in breach of what is now reg 6(3)(a) for failing to review a risk assessment when it had information which suggested that an earlier assessment was no longer valid.

22.15 The duty to assess is expressed in strict terms. As such, it is no defence for an employer to rely upon the fact that the risk of harm was not foreseeable. The duty to assess requires both the assessment of foreseeable and unforeseeable hazards (see *Williams v Farne Salmon and Trout Ltd* 1997 SLT 1329). The fact that a risk assessment would not have revealed any hazard is irrelevant to the question of breach of reg 6 or the subsequent regulations (*Dugmore v Swansea NHS Trust* [2002] EWCA Civ 1689 judgment of Hale LJ at para 14).

Duties imposed by the Regulations

22.16 Once a claimant has established that he was exposed to a substance hazardous to health and sustained injury as a result, the burden in proving compliance with the Regulations is upon the defendant: see *Bilton v Fastnet Highlands Ltd* 1998 SLT 1323, OH and *Dugmore v Swansea NHS Trust* [2002] EWCA Civ 1689. The absence of any foreseeable risk is no defence under the Regulations (see *Williams v Farne Salmon and Trout Ltd* 1997 SLT 1329 and *Dugmore* (above)). Accordingly, it is not for the claimant to aver what the defendant should have done and did not do, but for the defendant to aver what they did and that this was sufficient to comply with the Regulations, following *Larner v British Steel plc* [1993] ICR 551 and see *Bilton* (above at 1326J). The purpose of the regulations is protective and preventive. In *Dugmore* (above) Hale LJ stated that it was not incompatible with the purpose of the Regulations that an employer who fails to discover a risk or rates it so low that it takes no precautions against it, should nevertheless be liable for the employee who suffers injury as a result.[1]

1   See para 27 of judgment.

22.17 The COSHH Regulations impose a hierarchy of measures in regs 7–12. The first step of the hierarchy is in reg 7(1), which requires that so far as is reasonably practicable, exposure to substances hazardous to health be prevented. The second step (also set out in reg 7(1)) is that, if total prevention is not reasonably practicable, then exposure shall be adequately controlled. Adequate is defined by reg 7(11) as having regard to the nature of the substance and the nature and degree of exposure to substances hazardous to health. The duty to adequately control exposure was not subject to any reasonable practicability defence: see *Dugmore v Swansea NHS Trust* [2002] EWCA Civ 1689.

22.18 However, by SI 2004/3386, reg 7(7) has been amended such that control of exposure shall only be treated as adequate if the principles of good practice set out in Sch 2A are applied and that any workplace exposure limit approved for the substance is not exceeded. Further, in respect of carcinogens and asthmagens, reg 7(7) adds that exposure shall only be treated as adequate if the exposure is reduced to as low a level as is reasonably practicable. Accordingly, in respect of carcinogens and asthmagens only, the words 'as low as reasonably practicable' must be read into the duty to adequately control within reg 7(1). In any event, the duty remains very strict. Hale LJ in *Dugmore* (at para 25) held that the duties under reg 7 are defined without any reference to reasonableness or the foreseeability of the risk: it is a purely practical matter depending on the nature of the substance and the nature and degree of the exposure and nothing else. In *Naylor v Volex Group plc* [2003] EWCA Civ 222 a breach of reg 7 was established as the defendant had failed to show why it was not reasonably practicable to avoid all exposure to the hazardous substance.

22.19 Regulation 7 continues to set out further steps in the hierarchy of steps. If avoidance is not possible, then substitution should be considered (reg 7(2)). By reg 7(3) the employer must then first make use of work processes, systems and controls to control exposure and, only to the extent that such measures do not provide adequate control, should personal protective equipment be provided (see reg 7(3)(c)).

22.20 Once a control measure is provided, the employer must ensure that it is properly used or applied (reg 8(1)), that any equipment is maintained (reg 9). Employees are under a duty to make full and proper use of any control measures by reg 8(2). Where indicated by the risk assessment or otherwise appropriate, the employer must monitor exposure at the workplace (reg 10 and Sch 5) and maintain health surveillance over the employees (reg 11 and Sch 6). Finally, there is a mandatory duty to provide employees with suitable and sufficient information, instruction and training (reg 12). The approach to the reduction of exposure is further spelled out in a series of ACOPs. Additional provisions relating to biological agents are dealt with in a separate schedule (Sch 3).

GENETICALLY MODIFIED ORGANISMS

22.21 The Genetically Modified Organisms (Contained Use) Regulations 2000, SI 2000/2831[1] came into effect on 5 November 2000, replacing the previous regulations of the same name (SI 1992/3217)[2] and should be mentioned here. They have since been amended by the Genetically Modified Organisms (Contained Use) (Amendment) Regulations 2005, SI 2005/2466.[3] They follow the structure of the COSHH Regulations and deal with processes involving the altering of genetic material in a way which does not occur naturally. The Regulations protect persons from risks to health whether immediate or delayed, arising out of activities involving the genetic modification of organisms as well as the protection of the environment from harm. A number of activities are outside the scope of the Regulations, and exemption certificates can also be obtained (reg 25). A person undertaking any activity involving genetic modification must ensure that the exposure to humans to such matter is reduced to the lowest level that is reasonably practicable (reg 17). Competent authorities have to be notified in advance in relation to any activity involving genetic modification (regs 9–11). The Regulations prohibit any activity involving genetic modification of micro and other organisms unless a suitable and sufficient risk assessment has been undertaken (regs 6, 7), and a safety committee has been established to advise in relation to the assessment (reg 16). Duties are also imposed in respect of devising and implementing containment measures (regs 18, 19). Where there is a reasonably foreseeable risk to the health and safety of any person outside the premises, or a risk of serious environmental damage, an emergency plan must be devised (reg 20).

1   The Regulations implement Directive 90/219 EC (as amended by Directive 94/51 EC and Directive 98/81 EC) on the contained use of genetically modified organisms.
2   Which in turn revoked the Genetic Manipulation Regulations 1989, SI 1989/1810.
3   The 2005 amendments implement Directive 2003/4/EC on public access to environmental information.

LEAD

22.22 The Control of Lead at Work Regulations 2002, SI 2002/2676 (replacing the previous Regulations of the same name, SI 1998/543) provide a uniform code for all places of work and to all work which exposes persons to lead. Prior to Control of Lead at Work Regulations 1980 (since repealed) there existed a number of old regulations which applied to particular types of work, such as manufacture of paint, enamelling, lead smelting, indiarubber and accumulators.

22.23 Under the 2002 Regulations the employer's duties extend not just to their employees, but in so far as is reasonably practicable, to any other person whether at work or not who may be affected by the work carried out by the employer (reg 3). The Regulations exclude operations carried out by a master or crew of a sea-going ship, or to the employer of such persons in relation to the normal shipboard activities of a crew under the direction of a master.

22.24 Regulation 4 sets out two prohibitions. First, a general prohibition on employers using a glaze other than a leadless glaze or a low solubility glaze in the manufacture of pottery. The second prohibition concerns the employment of a young person or a woman of 'reproductive capacity' in any specified activity listed in Sch 1 to the Regulations.

22.25 The core of the Regulations seeks to ensure that employers eliminate exposure of their employees to lead altogether, or where this is not reasonably practicable, to ensure that the exposure is adequately controlled (reg 6). This entails a requirement to consider product substitution in order to eliminate or reduce the health risks to employees. The degree of exposure to lead must be controlled where it is not reasonably practicable to prevent exposure altogether, using control measures (eg work processes, engineering controls, ventilation systems etc) in preference to personal protective equipment where this is reasonably practicable. Regulation 6(4) provides an illustrative list of control measures, including limiting the number of employees who may be exposed to lead, reducing the level and duration of exposure or the quantity of lead used, ventilation and hygiene measures, as well as the provision of washing facilities. Where, notwithstanding the control measures in place, the exposure of an employee to lead is likely to be 'significant', the employer shall provide suitable protective clothing (reg 6(5)). 'Significant' exposure is not defined but in *Hewett v Alf Brown's Transport Ltd* [1991] ICR 471; affd [1992] ICR 530, CA, it was held that intermittent exposures of no more than one hour per day were 'insignificant' even though the lead on the worker's clothing was sufficient to cause lead poisoning in his wife who cleaned his overalls but who was particularly susceptible. The exposure would have been 'relatively insignificant' for the average person. This approach appears to be inconsistent with risk-based approach of the Directives in this area: no reference appears to have been made at first instance or on appeal to the requirement that the Regulations should be purposively construed in the light of the Directives.

22.26 In so far as inhalation is concerned, any control measure is only regarded as being adequate where the occupational exposure limit is not exceeded. In circumstances where the exposure limit is exceeded, the employer must identify the reasons for this and take immediate steps to rectify the situation (reg 6(6)).

22.27 Any personal protective equipment supplied must comply with the Personal Protective Equipment Regulations 2002, SI 2002/1144. Such protective equipment is to be stored in a well-defined place, checked at suitable intervals and, where it is contaminated by lead, shall be removed on leaving the work area and kept apart from uncontaminated clothing and equipment.

22.28 In respect of any control measures implemented, these shall be maintained in an efficient state, in efficient working order and in good repair, and be in a clean condition (reg 8). Engineering controls and respiratory equipment must be examined and tested at suitable intervals.

22.29 An employer is not permitted to carry out work which is liable to expose any employee to lead unless a suitable and sufficient risk assessment has been undertaken which complies with the Regulations and that such assessment has been implemented (reg 5). The risk assessment must take into account the hazardous properties of lead, information as to the effect on health provided by the supplier, the level, type and duration of the exposure, the amount of lead involved in the particular work circumstances, any relevant occupational exposure limit, action and suspension levels, as well as the effect of preventative and control measures, medical surveillance, monitoring etc. Risk assessments should be reviewed regularly and where there has been a significant change in the work process.

22.30 Where a risk assessment indicates that any employee is liable to receive significant airborne exposure, the concentration of lead in the air must be measured in accordance with a suitable procedure and shall be carried out at least every three months (reg 9). In certain instances, the frequency of monitoring is extended to once every 12 months.

22.31 Employees should be provided with information, instruction and training which is to include information as to the health risks presented by exposure, the occupational exposure limit, safety data, significant findings as set out in the risk assessment, appropriate precautions to be taken, and the results of monitoring (reg 11).

22.32 Employers are required to ensure that employees do not eat, drink, or smoke in any place which is liable to be contaminated by lead, in so far as is reasonably practicable (reg 7). Provision is made for medical surveillance of employees who are liable to be exposed to lead where the exposure is likely to be significant or where blood-lead concentration levels exceed prescribed levels (reg 10).

ASBESTOS

22.33

Historic exposure causing asbestos related injuries is dealt with in chapter 15 above. This section deals solely with current asbestos exposure. The period between exposure and development of the disease is likely to be in the region of 20–30 years. Current exposure to asbestos will therefore not cause any injury for many years to come. According to latest statistics published by the HSE, historic asbestos exposure is responsible for at least 3,500 deaths in Great Britain each year from mesothelioma and asbestos-related lung cancer. Annual numbers of deaths are predicted to rise in the next decade. Analyses of mesothelioma deaths indicate that many deaths are due to heavy asbestos exposures in industries like shipbuilding and railway engineering in the past.

22.34 Control is now effected via the Control of Asbestos at Work Regulations 2002, SI 2002/2675 (repealing the previous 1987 Regulations, SI 1987/2115, which in turn had superseded the 1969 Regulations).

22.35 The 2002 Regulations impose obligations on 'dutyholders'. A 'dutyholder' is defined to include every person who has, by virtue of a contract or tenancy, an obligation of any extent in relation to the maintenance or repair of non-domestic premises or any means of access or egress to or from such premises. In relation to any part of non-domestic premises where there is no such contract or tenancy, duties are imposed upon any person who has to any extent control of that part of the premises or means of access or egress (reg 4).

22.36 Where a duty is placed upon an employer in respect of its employees, in so far as is reasonably practicable, it is also under a like duty in respect of any other person, whether at work or not, who may be affected by the work activity carried out by them (reg 3). Regulation 2(1) specifies control limits for concentrations of asbestos in the atmosphere: for chrysoltile: 0.3 fibres per mm of air averaged over a continuous period of four hours; 0.9 fibres per mm averaged over a continuous period of 10 hours; for any other form of asbestos either alone or in mixtures the control limits are: 0.2 fibres per mm of air averaged over a continuous period of four hours and 0.6 fibres per mm if averaged over a continuous period of 10 hours.[1]

[1] The 'control limits' under reg 2(1) have been the subject of some criticism from those experts who take the view that there is no level of exposure below which there can be safe exposure.

22.37 A dutyholder is required to ensure that a suitable and sufficient risk assessment is carried out as to whether asbestos is or is liable to be present in the premises. In making such assessment, they are required to take such steps as are reasonable in all of the circumstances, to assess the condition of any asbestos which is or has been assumed to be present in the premises, and to inspect those parts of the premises which are reasonably accessible (reg 4(4) and (5)). It is unlawful for an employer to carry out any work which is liable to expose its employees to asbestos unless such risk assessment has been undertaken and steps are identified so as to comply with the Regulations (reg 6). Where an assessment shows that asbestos is or is liable to be present in any part of the premises the dutyholder is required to ensure that a determination of the risk is made, a written plan should identify those parts of the premises concerned, and any measures which are to be taken for managing the risk are to be specified in a written plan (reg 4(8)). No work should be undertaken unless a suitable written 'plan of work' is drawn up detailing how the work is to be carried out (reg 7). The plan of work should specify the nature and probable duration of the work, the location of the place where the work is to be carried out, and the methods to be applied where the work involves the risk of handling asbestos, as well as the characteristics of any equipment to be used for the purposes of protection and decontamination of those carrying out the work. The written plan must include adequate measures for monitoring the condition of any asbestos or substances suspected of containing asbestos, and ensuring that any asbestos substance is properly maintained, or where necessary is safely removed (reg 4(9). The employer must then make—and review from time to time— both the risk assessment and written plan in advance of the risks involved in working with it and the measures required to reduce them. Information must be provided about the location and condition of any asbestos to any person who is liable to disturb it and should be made available to the emergency services. Before commencing work which exposes or is liable to expose employees to asbestos, an employer has to identify (by analysis or otherwise) the type of asbestos involved (reg 5).

22.38 Duties therefore arise where there is exposure to asbestos, even if this is quite small and incidental to other work. In *Edgson v Vickers plc* [1994] ICR 510 (a case under the predecessor 1969 Regulations) the Regulations were held to apply to a factory worker who swept asbestos from his workplace which fell frequently in dust and lump form from a deteriorating asbestos-coated roof. In *Barclays Bank plc v Fairclough Building Ltd (No 2)* [1995] PIQR P152, the Court of Appeal held that by 1988 at the latest, any contractor undertaking work on material containing asbestos should have been aware of the hazards (industrial cleaners using high pressure water to clean old asbestos roof).

22.39 An employer proposing to work with asbestos must notify the appropriate enforcing authority at least 14 days in advance in writing providing prescribed information (reg 8), unless of course the extent of the exposure neither exceeds nor is likely to exceed the action level as set out in reg 1 or the employer is licensed.

22.40 Employees who are liable to be exposed to asbestos or who supervise such employees must be given adequate information, instruction and training, and be aware of the significant findings of the risk assessment, the risks to health from asbestos, precautions which should be adhered to, and the relevant control limit and action level (reg 9). Information, instruction and training must be given at regular intervals and adapted where appropriate (reg 9(2)). There is a general duty (reg 10) to *prevent* exposure to asbestos where reasonably practicable. Where it is not reasonably practicable, the employer is required to reduce exposure to the lowest level reasonably practicable by measures other than the use of respiratory equipment. Where practicable, asbestos must be replaced with a substance which creates no risk or at least a lesser risk than asbestos (reg 10(2)). If asbestos is used, exposure must be reduced to the lowest reasonably practicable levels. An employer is therefore required to provide employees with suitable respiratory protective equipment which will reduce the concentration of asbestos in the air inhaled by the employee to a concentration which is as low as is reasonably practicable and in any event below the control limits (reg 10(4)). Personal protective equipment supplied must comply with the Personal Protective Equipment Regulations 2002 or otherwise conform to the standards approved by the HSE (reg 10(5)). Immediate steps must be taken to remedy the situation where the concentration of asbestos in the air inhaled by any employee exceeds the relevant control limit (reg 10(6)). Any control measures provided must be maintained in an efficient state, in efficient working order and be in good repair (reg 12). A number of duties apply to the provision of and cleaning of protective clothing (reg 13); air monitoring (reg 18); health surveillance (reg 21), the provision of storage facilities (reg 23); washing and changing facilities (reg 22); as well as arrangements to deal with accidents, incidents and emergencies (reg 14).

22.41 Wherever asbestos work is carried out, under reg 17 an area must be designated as an 'asbestos area' where exposure is below the 'action level' or a 'respirator zone' where the exposure would be liable to exceed the 'control limits' in reg 2. Only workers who are specifically 'authorised workers' may enter these zones, and no one must eat, drink or smoke there.

22.42 In addition to the detailed regulation of asbestos provided by the 2002 Regulations there are further particular Regulations. The Asbestos (Prohibitions) Regulations 1992, SI 1992/3067[1] totally forbid the importation, supply, spraying, or use (save for disposal) of crocidolite, amosite, fibrous actinolite, fibrous anthophyllite, fibrous tremolite and products containing them.

[1]   Replacing the Asbestos (Prohibitions) Regulations 1985.

22.43 Work with asbestos insulation or asbestos coating requires a licence from the HSE: the Asbestos (Licensing) Regulations 1983, SI 1983/1649 (amended several times). Any person working with asbestos or demolishing buildings etc containing asbestos must ensure that significant environmental pollution is not caused: Control of Asbestos in the Air Regulations 1990, SI 1990/556. Those Regulations also require that any emission of asbestos during its use shall not be greater than 0.1 mg of asbestos per cubic metre of air. These provisions are designed to protect the public; they also protect workers who may be affected on that or any other site.

IONISING RADIATION

22.44 'Ionising radiation' means radiation of such intensity that it can dislodge particles from atoms, and is therefore capable of damaging or distorting living cells. Alteration of a molecule in a cell, for instance, may result in disordered growth and in cancer, or may damage the hereditary genes in the reproductive organs. Since, however, the spaces within atoms are vast, a stream of radiation may pass through with no impact at all: so the risk of damage is to some extent statistical, depending on the chance of impact, and increases with frequency of exposure. But even one short exposure, for instance an X-ray of a tooth, could cause damage. Exposure to artificially produced radiation is exacerbated by reason of naturally occurring radiation which differs in intensity from one place to another and cannot be avoided.[1]

[1]   On causation, see *Reay v British Nuclear Fuels plc* [1994] PIQR P171.

22.45 The Ionising Radiations Regulations 1999, SI 1999/3232, largely revoke the previous 1985 Regulations of the same name (SI 1985/1333) and repeal the supplementary Ionising Radiations (Outside Workers) Regulations 1993. The 1999 Regulations apply to 'any work with ionising radiation' or 'practice' involving the production, processing, handling, use, storage, transport or disposal of radioactive substances which can increase an individual's exposure to radiation (regs 2, 3). The Regulations also cover the operation of certain electrical equipment and other prescribed circumstances. Various types of work with only mild exposure are excluded from the Regulations (eg medical exposures) and from the notification requirements contained in reg 6 (Schs 1 and 8), and so is work at licensed nuclear installations.[1] Exemptions may be given for the armed forces, including visiting forces (reg 40) and in other cases (reg 37). The duty of complying with the Regulations rests on the employer (or a self-employed person) undertaking work or practice involving ionising radiation, and the employer has to notify the HSE at least 28 days before commencing work with ionising radiation (reg 6). The employer owes the duty not only to its own employees but also to others who may be affected by its activities, and employers whose workers may be affected are expressly required to co-operate, for instance in providing information or checks as to the exposure of their workers, in order to ensure compliance with the Regulations (reg 15).

[1] Which are subject to the Nuclear Installations Act 1965 and see also the Radioactive Substances Act 1993.

22.46 'Ionising radiation' is defined to include the transfer of energy in the form of particles or electromagnetic waves which are capable of producing ions either directly or indirectly (reg 2).[1]

[1] The wavelength must be 100 nanometres or less or of a frequency of 3×10 hertz or more (reg 2).

22.47 The first duty of the employer is to assess in advance the risks of the particular work and the means of reducing them (reg 7), including contingency plans for an emergency (reg 12). The employer's main duty is then to restrict the exposure of employees and other persons to the fullest extent 'reasonably practicable' (reg 8). This is to be done in a number of ways which include using 'engineering controls' and 'design features' (a term which must include the lay-out of the site, as well as the equipment), as well as the provision of safety features, warning devices, systems of work as well as the provision and use of personal protective equipment (reg 8(2)). Where any system of work is specified or protective equipment supplied, the employer is under a duty to take all reasonable steps to ensure that the system is observed and equipment properly used (reg 8(4)). Any equipment provided must comply with the Personal Protective Equipment Regulations 2002, SI 2002/1144 (reg 9). Employers are also required to restrict the exposure of particulars persons, for instance by limiting entry into designated risk areas (regs 17, 18).

22.48 An important feature of the Regulations is the specified 'dose' limits to which employees and other persons may be subjected (reg 11). These dose limits are set out in Sch 4 to the Regulations, and there are separate limits for the whole body and for particular organs such as the eye or the female reproductive organs. The employer is under an important duty to 'ensure' that this limit is not exceeded for any person (reg 11). For this purpose dosimeters have to be worn by persons likely to receive a dose of more than three-tenths of the dose limit specified in Sch 1 ('classified persons'). Doses must be recorded, and classified persons are subject to health surveillance (regs 21–24).

22.49 Any area where it is necessary for any person to follow special procedures designed to restrict, prevent or limit significant exposure to ionising radiation, or where exposure is likely to exceed three-tenths of the dose limits—and more particularly the limits in Sch 4—must be set aside as a controlled area (reg 16). Controlled areas must be physically demarcated or otherwise suitably delineated where this is not reasonably practicable. Controlled areas should also be suitably signposted (reg 18(1)). In general only 'classified persons' specially authorised (and not under 18) are allowed in these areas, but there are exceptions if exposure is limited to a low dosage (reg 18(2), (3)). A less dangerous area—where exposure would exceed one-tenth of any dose limit contained in Sch 4 or where it is necessary to keep an area under review in order to decide whether or not it should be a designated controlled area, must be designated as a supervised area (reg 16(3)). There is no specific restriction in such an area, but the general duty to limit exposure requires persons to be kept out unless their presence is necessary. The radiation in both types of area must be checked regularly (reg 19).

22.50 Where a radioactive substance is used as a source of ionising radiation, employers must ensure that they are in the form of a 'sealed source' where reasonably practicable (reg 27(1)). The design, construction and maintenance of any article containing a radioactive substance must be such as to prevent leakage. Suitable tests must be carried out at appropriate intervals to detect leakage. Records of each test must be kept for at least two years. If transported, they must be in safe receptacles and labelled (reg 29).

22.51 Employees who are engaged in work with ionising radiation are under a duty not knowingly to expose themselves or others to ionising radiation to a greater extent than is necessary for carrying out their work. They must also make full use of any personal protective equipment provided, and must notify the employer immediately if any person has received an overexposure, or if any such substances have been released or otherwise lost or stolen (reg 34).

22.52 Employees must be given information and training as necessary to restrict their exposure to ionising radiation (reg 7(3)).[1] Manufacturers, suppliers and installers of equipment for use with ionising radiation are under specific duties to ensure that it is safe, and, in the case of those who install it, to make full tests after installation (reg 31). There is a similar duty for medical equipment (reg 32).

1   The High-activity Sealed Radioactive Sources and Orphan Sources Regulations 2005, SI 2005/2686 provides that such training and information shall include training and information requirements which comply with art 8(1) of Council Directive 2003/122/EURATOM ('the HASS Directive') (reg 19).

22.53 The Radiation (Emergency Preparedness and Public Information) Regulations 2001, SI 2001/2975[1] lay down basic safety standards for the protection of the health and safety of workers and the general public against the dangers arising from ionising radiation. Duties are imposed upon operators of premises where radioactive substances are present as well as specified carriers where quantities exceed specified thresholds. Operators and carriers are required to undertake a risk assessment in respect of hazard identification and risk evaluation. Where the assessment reveals a radiation risk, they are required to take all reasonably practicable steps to prevent a radiation accident, or to limit the consequences should such an accident occur (reg 4). Further assessments must be undertaken where there is a major change to the work involving ionising radiation, or within three years of the date of the last assessment unless there has been no material change (regs 5–6). A report must be sent to the HSE containing prescribed information. The HSE can demand a detailed assessment asking for further particulars (reg 6). Where the assessment reveals a reasonably foreseeable radiation emergency, emergency plans must be prepared. The emergency plans must be reviewed, tested and implemented at suitable intervals not exceeding three years (regs 7–10, 13). Where an emergency plan provides for the possibility of an employee receiving an emergency exposure, the employer is required to make provision such as dose assessments, medical surveillance, and to determine appropriate dose levels for employees who may be subject to such exposures (reg 14). Operators, carriers, employers and local authorities are required to consult and cooperate (reg 11).

1   Implementing Council Directive 96/29/EURATOM.

22.54 Further obligations are imposed under the Civil Contingencies Act (Contingency Planning) Regulations 2005, SI 2005/2042, which set out general duties in respect of assessing and planning for emergencies, as well as the provision of advice and assistance to business (which are outside the scope of this chapter).

22.55 The Carriage of Dangerous Goods and Transportable Pressure Equipment Regulations 2004, SI 2004/568 and the Radioactive Material (Road Transport) Regulations 2002, SI 2002/1093[1] are also worthy of mention. As regards the Carriage Regulations, these seek to consolidate a raft of 12 regulations which previously regulated the carriage of dangerous goods by road and rail within Great Britain.[2] The Regulations implement and expressly refer to the European Agreement concerning the International Carriage of Dangerous Goods by Road (ADR 2003) and also the International Carriage of Dangerous Goods by Rail (RID 2003). The detailed provisions of these regulations are outside the scope of this chapter.[3] The regulations aim to ensure that risks are reduced as far as possible and that incidents can be safely and effectively dealt with whilst simultaneously not impeding commerce. The main impact of the regulations is that commercial carriage of almost all dangerous goods in Britain must now be to the international standards. Duties are imposed upon everyone with a role in the carriage of dangerous goods, and specific duties are imposed on those involved in the transport chain (ie consignors, consignees, carriers, fillers, loaders, operators, packers etc). A few of the key provisions affecting road transport (ADR) include: new limited quantity and load thresholds for transporting dangerous goods; prohibition on carrying specified dangerous goods (reg 16), packaging requirements now based on ADR (reg 18); labelling obligations (reg 20), training (reg 9), driver training (reg 24), appointment of a safety advisor (reg 12), accident reporting (reg 13), and numerous provisions dealing with the construction, testing and use of tanks and other receptacles, carriage, loading and handling (reg 23).

The Road Transport Regulations impose a number of similar duties in respect of the transport of consignments of radioactive material (regs 14–23, and regs 31–46), as well as specifying radiation protection measures, safety information and programmes to the public (regs 14–27), packaging and labelling requirements (reg 50), as well as the process for obtaining approvals for design and shipment (regs 52–61).

1   Revoking the Radioactive Material (Road Transport) (Great Britain) Regulations 1996, SI 1996/1350 and implementing the regulations made by the International Atomic Energy Agency (IAEA) and its safety standards series for the Safe Transport of Radioactive Material (1996 edn), as well as Council Directive 96/29/EURATOM and Commission Directive 2001/7/EC.

2   Implementing Commission Directives 2003/28/EC, 2003/29/EC, Council Directive 96/49/EC on the approximation of the laws of Member States with regard to the transport of dangerous goods by rail (as amended by Directive 2000/62/EC and Commission Directive 2003/29/EC) and completing the implementation of Council Directive 1999/36/EC.

3   For a helpful analysis of the detailed regulations see Working with ADR: An introduction to the carriage of dangerous goods by road (HSE, 2004).

22.56 The Radioactive Material (Road Transport) Regulations 2002 impose a number of similar duties in respect of the transport of consignments of radioactive material (regs 14–23, and regs 31–46), as well as specifying radiation protection measures, safety information and programmes to the public (regs 14–27), packaging and labelling requirements (reg 50), as well as the process for obtaining approvals for design and shipment (regs 52–61).

22.57 The Ionising Radiation Regulations apply, of course, to hospital equipment and staff just as they do to any other place of work, but there are separate regulations for the protection of patients, the Ionising Radiation (Medical Exposure) Regulations 2000, SI 2000/1059 (which revoked the Ionising Radiation (Protection of Persons Undergoing Medical Examination or Treatment) Regulations 1988).

22.58 The Ionising Radiation Regulations impose duties on employers to persons other than its employees (reg 4). For instance, in relation to risk assessments (reg 7), measures to restrict exposure (reg 8); dose limitations (reg 11); the provision of information (reg 14); as well as the requirements for designated areas (reg 16). Outside workers are to be provided with a radiation passbook for the purposes of recording dose assessments (reg 21(3)(h)). As regards non-employees, the duty of co-operation between employers imposes obligations to provide information and such other co-operation so as to enable the employer to comply with its duties under the Regulations (reg 15). The Medicines for Human Use (Clinical Trials) Regulations 2004, SI 2004/1031 make a number of minor amendments to the 2000 Regulations and set out a number of responsibilities in respect of ethics committees in respect of clinical trials, clinical trial authorisations, the provision of ethics committee opinions, as well as pharmacovigilance (the recording and reporting of adverse events and reactions to medicinal products being used in clinical trials). The ambit of these Regulations is outside the scope of this chapter.

22.59 Liability for injury caused by radiation from nuclear installations is automatic under the Nuclear Installations Act 1965 so that there is no need to plead or prove a duty, only that the injury was caused by radiation at a nuclear installation.[1]

[1]   This liability derives from art 3 of Nuclear Energy Treaty (signed in Paris on 29 July 1960). The Act was the cause of action in *Mollinari v Ministry of Defence* [1994] PIQR Q 33, the first case to achieve an award of damages for leukaemia caused by exposure to radiation (fitter working on nuclear submarines, liability admitted).

FIRE

22.60 Flammable substances can be grouped into four categories: liquids, dusts, gases, and solids. Liquids such as fuel and solvents in industrial produces (such as paint, ink, adhesives and cleaning fluids) give off flammable vapour which, when mixed with air can ignite and explode. Flammable liquids fall into three categories: extremely flammable (eg liquids which have an initial boiling point lower to or equal 35 degrees); highly flammable (liquids which have a flash point below 21 degrees but which are not extremely flammable); and flammable. Dusts can be produced from many materials such as coal, wood, grain, sugar, and synthetic organic chemicals. A cloud of combustible dust can cause a violent explosion if ignited. Gases such as liquefied petroleum gas or methane are usually stored under pressure in cylinders and bulk containers. Solids include materials such as plastic foam, packaging and textiles, all of which may burn fiercely and give off dense and sometimes noxious black smoke.[1]

[1]   HSE website: About Fire and Explosion.

22.61 The Factories Act 1961 contained its own detailed code for safety in case of fire (ss 40–52: fire escapes, doors opening easily outwards to give quick exit, fire prevention, fire fighting, fire alarms). The Offices, Shops and Railway Premises Act 1963 followed similar lines, and the Mines and Quarries Act 1954 also had its own self-contained code.

22.62 The position was changed by the HSWA 1974, which brought all these different places of work under the Fire Precautions Act 1971. The Fire Precautions Act 1971 was passed after a series of fire disasters which showed that in many buildings fire precautions were non-existent. The scheme of the Act (s 1) was that premises could not be *used* for certain purposes unless a fire certificate was issued by the fire authority. These purposes were to be designated by the Secretary of State and are referred to as 'designated purposes': s 1(2) gave a list of uses which could be designated—mainly relating to such places as hotels, hostels, institutions, schools, places of entertainment, and places such as shops and offices open to the public. Under this scheme the fire authority had to carry out a thorough inspection of fire escapes, fire alarms, and fire precautions generally, before granting a certificate, and could insist on improvements to the premises: s 5. The 1971 Act was amended by the Fire Safety and Safety of Places of Sport Act 1987 and the Fire Precautions (Workplace) Regulations 1997, SI 1997/1840. These have since been repealed by the Regulatory Reform (Fire Safety) Order 2005, SI 2005/1541 which is now the primary source of fire regulation affecting employers.

22.63 The 2005 Order reforms the law relating to fire safety in non-domestic premises. It replaces fire certification under the 1971 Act with a general duty to ensure, so far as is reasonably practicable, the safety of employees, a general duty in respect of non-employees to take such fire precautions as may reasonably be required in the circumstances to ensure that premises are safe, and also detailed provisions regarding the need for risk assessments.[1]

1 The 2005 Order seeks to implement a host of EC Directives: Council Directive 89/391/EEC (the Framework Directive); 91/383/EEC (the Temporary Workers Directive); 94/33/EC (protection of young people at work); 98/24/EC (the Chemical Agents Directive); and 99/92/EC (the Explosives Atmospheres Directive).

22.64 Employers are required to comply with the 2005 Order. The main duties are imposed upon the 'responsible person'. Article 3 defines the 'responsible person' as an employer, provided that the workplace is 'to any extent' under their control, or the person who has the control of the premises (as occupier or otherwise) in connection with the carrying out of a trade, business or undertaking. In some instances, the owner of premises is caught by the Order where the person in control of the premises does not have control in connection with the carrying on of a trade, business or undertaking. In situations where two or more responsible persons simultaneously have duties in respect of the same premises (either on a temporary or permanent basis), they are required to co-operate with each other in so far as is necessary to comply with their obligations (art 22).

22.65 The Order applies to all non-domestic premises except for those specified under art 6. A number of premises are therefore excluded, including: domestic premises, offshore installations (as defined by the Offshore Installation and Pipeline Works (Management and Administration) Regulations 1995), ships in respect of the normal ship-board activities of a ship's crew which are carried out solely by the crew under the direction of the master, fields, woods or other land forming part of an agricultural or forestry undertaking, aircraft, locomotive or rolling stock, trailer or semi-trailers used as a means of certain transport, mines as defined by the Mines and Quarries

Act 1954, s 180 other than buildings on the surface of a mine, and boreholes. Where a person has by virtue of any contract or tenancy an obligation of any extent to maintain or repair any of the premises or otherwise to ensure the safety of the premises, they are also covered by the Order (art 5(4)).

22.66 The responsible person is required to take such general fire precautions as will ensure, so far as is reasonably practicable, the safety of any of their employees. As regards persons who are not employed, the responsible person is required to take such general fire precautions as may reasonably be required in the circumstances so as to ensure that the premises are safe (art 8).

22.67 A suitable and sufficient risk assessment must be undertaken for the purpose of identifying general fire precautions, and consideration must be given where a dangerous substance is or liable to be present in or on the premises (art 9). Schedule 1 sets out the matters which should be taken into account in carrying out the risk assessment. Employees must be provided with comprehensible and relevant information as to the risks highlighted by the assessment, preventative and protective measures, as well as the identity of a competent person who is responsible for assisting with preventative and protective measures (art 19). Adequate safety training must also be provided at the time when employees are first engaged or upon being exposed to new or increased risks (art 21). In cases where a dangerous substance is present, the responsible person must ensure that the risk to relevant persons is either eliminated or reduced so far as is reasonably practicable (art 12). This includes replacing the dangerous substance with an alternative one so as to eliminate or reduce such risk. Specific provision is made where a young person is employed, and in respect of recording of information where five or more employees are employed (art 10).

22.68 Where necessary, to the extent that it is appropriate to do so, premises should be equipped with appropriate fire-fighting equipment, fire detectors and alarms. Any non-automatic fire equipment provided should be easily accessible, simple to use and indicated by signs (art 13). Responsible persons are required to ensure that facilities, equipment and devices in connection with general fire precautions must be subject to a suitable system of maintenance and must be maintained in an efficient state and working order and in good repair (art 17). Emergency routes and exits must be kept clear at all times, be adequate in number, and must lead as directly as possible to a place of safety (art 14). A number of prescriptive obligations apply to dangerous substances and in respect of procedures for serious and imminent danger areas (arts 15 and 16).

22.69 It should be noted that the Order further imposes duties on employees to take reasonable care for their own safety, as well as co-operating with their employer in the discharge of their obligations under the Order, and to inform their employer of any work situation which would reasonably be considered to represent a serious and imminent danger to safety (art 23). Article 24 confers upon the Secretary of State the power to make further regulations concerning fire precautions. In the event of breach of the obligations imposed by the Order, this can give rise to civil liability (art 39) thereby reversing the effect of s 27A of the 1971 Act which precluded any civil action based on breach of any provision of the Act. Articles 29–31 provide for the service of alterations, enforcement and prohibition notices in prescribed circumstances. Part 4 of the Order provides for criminal liability for offences.

22.70 The Building Regulations 2000, SI 2000/2531 (as amended) repeal the previous regulations of the same name (SI 1991/2768) and impose a number of requirements in respect of certain building works. The main requirements are that building work and buildings extended to it falling within the Regulations must comply with a number of requirements set out in Sch 1 (reg 4). Where a person carries out building work or there is a material change in the use of the building, they are required to provide building plans and notices to the local authority (reg 12). The local authority can grant completion certificates once it has received notice of the building work and its completion, and that the relevant requirements have been complied with including aspects of fire safety (reg 17). The requirements contained in Sch 1 are of a general nature and provide for means of early warning of fire and escape, steps which should be taken to inhibit the spread of fire (including the materials used for lining, surfaces), as well as the design and construction of building works.

ELECTRICITY

22.71 According to provisional HSE figures, approximately 1,000 electrical accidents at work are reported each year, resulting in 30 fatalities. The principal causes of fatality and injury are attributable to the use of poorly maintained electrical equipment, working overhead or near to power lines, contact with underground cables during excavation work, or the use of unsuitable electrical equipment in explosive areas (eg car paint spraying booths).

22.72 The Electricity at Work Regulations 1989, SI 1989/635,[1] in force from 1 April 1990,[2] apply to all places of work within the HSWA 1974, including offshore installations (reg 31) and mines and quarries which formerly had special regulations. They do not apply to the seaboard activities of the master and crew of a seagoing ship, or to aircraft and hovercraft moving under their own power. A Guidance Note, and not an Approved Code of Practice, accompanies them. More recent guidance has been published,[3] and the HSE has issued booklets on specific areas.[4] Because faulty electrical components, especially portable equipment, may readily cause fire, these duties should be read in the light of those relating to fire (see para 22.60ff, above).

[1] Amended several times. See eg the Electrical Equipment for Explosive Atmospheres (Certification) (Amendment) Regulations 1999, SI 1999/2550.
[2] Replacing the Electricity Regulations 1908 and the Electricity (Factories Act) Special Regulations 1944.
[3] *Electricity at Work—Safe Working Practices* (HS(G)85, 1993).

⁴ See eg *Maintaining Portable Electrical Equipment in Offices and Other Low-Risk Environments* (HSE, 1994); *Maintaining Portable Electrical Equipment in Hotels and Tourist Accommodation* (HSE, 1994). The HSE website contains a number of sector specific publications providing guidance on electricity at work.

22.73 Employers and the self-employed are required by reg 3 to comply with the Regulations in all matters within their control, and so are the managers of mines and quarries. Employees are required to co-operate in the performance of these duties by employers, and to comply personally with the Regulations on matters within their control. Probably, just like the earlier regulations, a court would regard the regulations as intended to protect employees against inadvertence: see *R v Sanyo Electrical Manufacturing (UK) Ltd* (1992) 13 Cr App Rep (S) 657.

22.74 There are rather vague injunctions in reg 4 that electrical systems—which includes portable electrical equipment such as radios and irons—shall be so constructed and maintained, and work activities so carried out, as to avoid danger as 'far as reasonably practicable'. The HSE recommends regular inspection and testing by competent persons, together with record-keeping.¹ While record-keeping is not a strict obligation, clearly its absence would be prejudicial in litigation. Protective equipment is to be 'suitable', and maintained in that state.

¹ See Guidance Note and HSE *Maintaining Portable and Transportable Electrical Equipment* (HS(G)107, 1994). Contrast with the more relaxed approach of the HSE in the booklet on offices, referred to in para 22.72 fn 4.

22.75 The Regulations make a number of specific safety requirements. All conductors must be insulated or have equivalent protection (reg 7). Components which are potential conductors, though not part of the circuit, and may become live accidentally, must be earthed, and there must be no impediment in the earth connection (regs 8, 9). Joints and connections forming part of an electrical circuit must be suitable both electrically and mechanically (reg 10). Under the former regulation on this point, an action succeeded where a joint on a cable broke when pulled by an electrician and he lost his balance and fell to the ground: *Gatehouse v John Summers & Sons Ltd* [1953] 2 All ER 117. The use of components in excess of their 'strength and capability' is prohibited (reg 5). (The old regulation put it the other way round—components must be sufficient in power and size for their purpose.) There must be devices such as fuses and cut-outs to cut off the power if the current becomes excessive (reg 11). There must be means of cutting off the electricity to any piece of equipment and isolating it, such as switches and switchboards, with identifying signs or marks where necessary. This does not apply to a source of energy such as a generator, for which other 'reasonably practicable' precautions should be taken to prevent danger (reg 12(3)).

22.76 The Regulations aim to protect workers who are maintaining or repairing equipment, whether employees or independent contractors. Particular importance is accorded to shutting off the supply.

22.77 Where equipment is made dead to enable work to be done on or near it, precautions must be taken to prevent it becoming alive accidentally (reg 13). Work is prohibited on or near a live conductor which is not completely insulated unless:

(1)   it is positively 'unreasonable' to make it dead at the time;
(2)   it is nevertheless reasonable for the work to be done while it is live; and
(3)   suitable safety measures are taken (reg 14).

22.78 These would include, for example, using insulated tools, gloves and the like.[1] There must be adequate means of access, working space and lighting for work at or near any electrical equipment which is a source of danger (reg 15). Finally, no one is to be allowed to do any work unless he or she has all necessary technical knowledge and experience, or is working under adequate supervision (reg 16). The duties should extend to giving clear instructions to maintenance staff and to supervising their work. The Electricity (Supply) Regulations 1988[2] are a separate code for the construction, maintenance and operation of supply lines and installations from the generating station to the consumer, including overhead lines and underground cables, transformers and sub-stations. They are for the protection of the public rather than employees.

[1]   Note the duties under the Personal Protective Equipment Regulation 2002, SI 2002/1144.
[2]   Amended several times.

22.79 The dominant requirement is in reg 17, under which all suppliers' works have to be 'sufficient' for the purposes for which they are used, and 'so constructed, installed, protected (both electrically and mechanically), used and maintained as to prevent danger', as far as reasonably practicable. There must be protective devices to cut off excessive current and prevent leakage from high voltage lines; the maximum permitted voltage is 440,000 (regs 2, 22, 18).

22.80 Sub-stations in the open air must be fenced off and overhead lines made inaccessible: in both cases warning notices are required. Under previous regulations, it was held that 'efficient' fencing of a pylon did not require absolute exclusion of access. The fence was 'efficient' if it was carried up to a reasonable height and access prevented up to that height: *Craigie v North of Scotland Hydro Electricity Board* 1987 SLT 178.

22.81 Suppliers may refuse to give a supply to a consumer whose installation is unsafe: but under earlier regulations electricity suppliers were held to be under no duty to make inspections and tests: *Sellars v Best* [1954] 2 All ER 389.

22.82 Electrical stations and substations will be covered by the Workplace (Health, Safety and Welfare) Regulations 1992 for any person working there. It was expressly declared in s 103(5) of the Factories Act 1937 that electricity is not an article: consequently the generation of electricity was not the 'making of an article' so as to bring a generating station within the ordinary definition of a factory. For some reason s 103(5) was not repeated in the 1961 Act:

however, the matter is of no great importance since the Factories Act 1961, s 123 (re-enacting the Act of 1937, s 103) expressly brought generating stations and many other electrical stations within the Act and most of the Act is now repealed: the Act applies 'as if' electrical stations were factories; the employer is deemed to be the occupier.

22.83 Premises may fall outside the definition because, though electricity is generated, transformed or controlled there for one of the purposes mentioned, persons are not regularly employed there. These places, if large enough to admit a person, fall within s 123(2): the Act as a whole does not apply, but the places are subject to special regulations (now made under the HSWA 1974).[1]

1   Thus a small transformer kiosk where no one works is an electrical station within s 123(2): *Paine v Colne Valley Electricity Supply Co Ltd and British Insulated Cables Ltd* [1938] 4 All ER 803. Another example would be a generating shed attached to a private house or estate, which, however, is excluded by s 123(4). It is thought that a case would fall within s 123(2) if substantially the whole of a person's body could get in, as distinct from arms or head only.

22.84 Finally, by the Factories Act 1961, s 123(4) (and subject to any contrary direction in special regulations) neither s 123(1) nor s 123(2) applies to premises where electricity is generated, transformed or controlled, for the *immediate* purpose of driving an electric motor, or providing light or heat, or transmitting or receiving messages, or for other purposes. For instance, the section would not apply to an outbuilding where electricity is generated for use in a large house. Broadly speaking, s 123(4) excludes small private generating stations from the operation of the Act.

GAS

22.85 While there remains a very limited provision in the Factories Act 1961 (s 31(3)) dealing with gas energy, the majority of the very extensive provisions of the Gas Safety (Installation and Use) Regulations 1998, SI 1998/2451, replacing the former 1994 Regulations (SI 1994/1886)) do not apply to mines, quarries, factories as defined by the Factories Act, agricultural premises as well as temporary installations used in connection with construction work. The latter Regulations are intended to protect the public from dangers arising from the distribution, supply and use of gas and are therefore not particularly directed at the protection of workers (see also the Gas Safety (Management) Regulations 1996, SI 1996/551). Where an employer or self-employed person requires any work to be carried out in relation to a gas fitting at any workplace, they are responsible for ensuring that the person undertaking the work is approved (reg 4).

MAJOR ACCIDENTS

22.86 The Control of Major Accident Hazards Regulations 1999, SI 1999/743 (as amended by the Control of Major Accident Hazard (Amendment) Regulations 2005, SI 2005/1088), implement Council Directive

96/82/EC and replace the previous 1984 Regulations (SI 1984/1902). They apply to establishments where specified quantities of dangerous substances listed in the Regulations are kept. Operators are required to produce and implement a major accident prevention policy document setting out its policy in respect of such accidents (reg 5), and to devise a safety report which is to be reviewed with such frequency as prescribed by the Regulations. An operator is also required to produce an on-site emergency plan following consultation with a number of specified persons which must also be reviewed. Certain information must be provided to those likely to be in any area where persons are liable to be affected by a major accident, along with applicable safety measures at the site (reg 14).

22.87 The 2005 Amendment Regulations implement a few substantive changes making provision for: sending notifications by electronic means (reg 3); modifying the exclusions relating to mines, quarries, boreholes and waste landfill sites (reg 4); introducing a time limit for preparing a major accident prevention policy, and modifying existing time limits for the submission of a safety report and on-site emergency plan (regs 5–7 and 9); requiring the notification of certain modifications to an establishment (reg 6); notification requirements when a safety report is revised or where a review of an existing report does not lead to revision (reg 8); specific training requirements in respect of planning for emergencies for all persons working within the establishment (reg 15); and other measures regarding the preparation of an off-site emergency plan and consultation obligations (regs 10–12).

NOTIFICATION[1]

22.88 Many regulations require employers and operators to notify the HSE and/ or local authorities of their activities in varying degrees of detail. The Control of Major Accident Hazards Regulations 1999 (as amended), as noted, includes such an obligation. The primary purpose of many regulations is to require notification. The Notification of Cooling Towers and Evaporative Condensers Regulations 1992, SI 1992/2225, (intended to minimise the risk of legionella)[2] is one such. Other regulations require not merely notification but a licence as well, for example the Asbestos (Licensing) Regulations 1983, SI 1983/1649 and the Control of Explosives Regulations 1991, SI 1991/1531, as well as the Manufacture and Storage of Explosives Regulations 2005, SI 2005/1082, which sets out licensing provisions relating to the manufacture and storage of explosives and registration requirements (regs 9–12). The COSHH Regulations 2002 also require many activities and substances to be notified.

[1]   This passage deals with notification of activities. See para 11.01ff for the reporting of accidents.
[2]   Note *R v Board of Trustees of the Science Museum* [1993] 3 All ER 853.

22.89 In addition, the Notification of Installations Handling Hazardous Substances Regulations 1982, SI 1982/1357 (as amended by the Notification of Installations Handling Hazardous Substances (Amendment) Regulations 2002, SI 2002/2979, and the Manufacture and Storage of Explosives Regulations 2005, SI 2005/1082) prohibit activities involving more than the notifiable amount of listed hazardous substances, unless the HSE has been given three months prior notice in writing containing specified information.

22.90 The Dangerous Substances (Notification and Marking of Sites) Regulations 1990, SI 1990/304[1] also require sites containing 25 tonnes or more of substances classified under the CHIP 2002 Regulations to be notified to the HSE and the local fire authority. Such sites must be marked in accordance with a table of pictograms.

[1]   As amended many times. See also the Carriage of Dangerous Goods and Use of Transportable Pressure Equipment Regulations 2004, SI 2004/568.

EMISSIONS AND TRANSPORT

22.91 There is considerable statutory regulation of emissions of noxious substances into the atmosphere but the duties are directed to protecting the public rather than those exposed in their work. The rarity of situations in which people in their capacities as workers (rather than as, say, residents) might sustain injury through breach of such legislation has prompted the authors not to include even a brief description of: the Environmental Protection Act 1990; the Air Quality Limit Values Regulations 2003, SI 2003/2121 (revoking much of the Air Quality Standards Regulations 1989, SI 1989/317); and the Clean Air Act 1993.[1] Suffice to say that the Air Quality Limits Values Regulations 2003, SI 2003/1848, set out limit values for sulphur dioxide, nitrogen dioxide, nitrogen oxides, lead and other such substances found in ambient air ('relevant pollutants'), as well as setting out methods of assessing air quality, tolerance margins, action plans and other matters relevant to ozone protection.

[1]   See also the Smoke Control Areas (Authorised Fuels) (England) (Amendment) Regulations 2005, SI 2005/2895 and the Smoke Control Areas (Exempt Fireplaces) (Scotland) Order 2005, SI 2005/615 which are a few of a host of regulations passed in connection with the 1993 Act.

22.92 There is also considerable legislation now covering the transport of hazardous substances. Primarily designed to protect the public it also serves to protect transport workers (and also imposes certain duties on them). For reasons of space this body of law is not analysed here. The essential legislation on this area is the Carriage of Dangerous Goods and Use of Transportable Pressure Equipment Regulations 2004, SI 2004/568, and the Chemicals (Hazard Information and Packaging for Supply) Regulations 2002, SI 2002/1689.

Chapter 23

SHIPBUILDING YARDS AND DOCKS

Nadia Motraghi

Corinna Ferguson

SHIPBUILDING

23.01 Shipbuilding in the UK is a pale shadow of its former glory, so too the comprehensive code of Shipbuilding and Ship-Repairing Regulations 1960, SI 1960/1932, made under the Factories Act 1937, which more or less applied to all shipbuilding and ship-repairs wherever carried on. Large parts of the 1960 Regulations have been revoked in recent years and replaced by regulations which are not aimed solely at shipbuilding. Since the last edition of this work, the most significant changes have been first, the repeal of regs 7–10 (particular means of access) and regs 12–30 (staging) by the Work at Height Regulations 2005, SI 2005/735. The 2005 Regulations introduce a new scheme where the primary obligation is to ensure that work is not carried out at a height where it is reasonably practicable to carry out work otherwise than at height (see chapter 19). Second, Part V of the Regulations (regs 48–66) has been revoked by the Dangerous Substances and Explosive Atmosphere Regulations 2002, SI 2002/2776. The effect of this latest round of repeals is that only a few of the 1960 Regulations remain in force, viz obligations concerning safe access (reg 6); safe transport to vessels and floating platforms (reg 11); lighting, hatches, boilers and jumped up bolts (regs 69–72); young persons (reg 80) and safety supervision (reg 81). It remains important to note that most of the Workplace (Health, Safety and Welfare) Regulations 1992 do not apply to the crew of a sea-going ship or their employees in respect of the normal ship-board activities (cf reg 3(1)(a)).

Shipbuilding yards

23.02 The Factories Act 1961 has limited relevance now that it has largely been repealed and superseded by more recent regulation. Of the substantive sections in Part II of the Act, only s 39 (water-sealed gasholders) remains, for the moment. Sections 24 (teagle openings and similar doorways), 31 (explosive or inflammable dust, gas vapour or substance) and ss 34, 37 and 38 (on steam boilers) have been repealed.[1] As a consequence, the distinction (which remains[2]) between the definition of a shipbuilding yard (see s 175(2)(a)) as a factory, and a wet dock, to which only limited duties apply under the Factories Act 1961 (by s 126) is of much reduced significance.

---

[1] Section 24 repealed with effect from 6 April 2005 by the Work at Height Regulations 2005, SI 2005/735, reg 18; s 31 repealed with effect from 5 May 2003 by the Dangerous Substances and Explosive Atmospheres Regulations 2002, SI 2002/2776; ss 34, 37–38 repealed with effect from 21 February 2000 by the Pressure Systems Safety Regulations 2000, SI 2000/128, reg 18.

[2] See the 12th edn of *Munkman*, pp 358–360 for commentary and case law.

THE SHIPBUILDING AND SHIP-REPAIRING REGULATIONS 1960

The scope of the Regulations

23.03 The Regulations apply:

(1) by reg 2(1)(a), to work on 'operations' in 'shipyards' properly so-called; and
(2) by reg 2(1)(b), to work on 'operations in a harbour or wet dock', with important exceptions.

The second heading, therefore, brought work in docks and harbours, though not comprised in any shipyard, within the scope of the legislation. A number of important points have to be noted under both headings.

Work in shipyards

23.04 'Shipyard' is defined much as in the Factories Act 1961, s 175(2)(a) to mean 'any yard or dry dock (including the precincts thereof) in which ships or vessels are constructed, reconstructed, repaired, refitted or finished' (reg 3(2)). But (unlike the Act) it does not include a yard or dock where they are broken up. 'Dry dock' evidently includes a 'public dry dock', defined by reg 3 as one 'available for hire'.

Ships in docks and harbours

23.05 It is necessary to distinguish here between 'ship' and 'vessel' as defined in ss 255(1) and 313(1) of the Merchant Shipping Act 1995. 'Vessel' includes any ship or boat used in navigation; 'ship' includes only any vessel used in navigation—ie it is a powered sea-going (at any rate water-going) craft or sailing ship. In shipyards, work on all ships or vessels is subject to the Regulations—in docks and harbours only work on 'ships'. Work is excluded if done:

(1) by the master or crew of a ship; or
(2) by anyone on board during a trial run—these are the same exclusions as in s 126 of the Act of 1961; or
(3) to raise or remove a sunk or stranded ship; or
(4) on board a ship not 'under command' (ie not under control) to bring it 'under command': see reg 2(1)(b) for exact details.

Broadly speaking, (3) and (4) exclude salvage operations, but it may be noted that the Diving at Work Regulations 1997, SI 1997/2776 apply in these cases.

Operations to which the Regulations apply

23.06 The conditions which bring work within the Regulations are somewhat complex. There must be: (a) work; (b) either in a shipyard or on a ship in wet dock; and (c) it must be work 'carried out' in specified 'operations'. These are defined by reg 3(2) to mean, in relation to a ship or vessel:

(1) construction and reconstruction;
(2) repairing and refitting;
(3) painting and finishing;
(4) scaling, scurfing or cleaning of boilers (including combustion chambers or smoke boxes);
(5) cleaning of bilges, oil-fuel tanks last used for carrying oil of any kind.

Exclusions for small vessels

23.07 Many of the regulations are excluded in the case of small vessels. For shipyards all but regs 6 (safe access) and 80 (young persons) are excluded for work on vessels unless both: (a) the overall length exceeds 30 metres, and (b) the overall depth exceeds 2.9 metres: see reg 2(2)(a).

23.08 So far as ships in harbours and docks (reg 2(2)(b)) are concerned, the same limits of size apply, but, as in shipyards, reg 6 applies even to small ships. ('Vessels other than ships' are not within the Regulations at all when in harbours or docks not part of a shipyard.)

23.09 There are no longer any special exemptions for work carried out in a public dry dock (reg 2(2)(c)), where a vessel does not exceed the limits of size stated above for shipyards, and it follows that all regulations apply in a public dry dock even to small vessels and that, although strictly a public dry dock is only one kind of 'shipyard', for this purpose reg 2(2)(c) is an exhaustive statement of the position in such docks and reg 2(2)(a) in relation to shipyards does not apply.

Exemptions

23.10 The HSE has a sweeping power to grant exemptions: reg 2(3). By reg 2(4), the requirements of the Regulations are in addition to the (now reduced) requirements of the Factories Act.

Persons owing duties under the Regulations

Employers

23.11 Employers undertaking operations (reg 4(1)) are responsible to their own employees, broadly, for safe access, they are responsible for complying with regs 11(1) (safe transport to vessels), 70(1) and (4) (work on boilers), 80 (young persons) and 81 (safety supervision); also for regs 11(2), 69(1) (lighting), 70(2) and (3), except insofar as these duties devolve on persons in control of docks and ships.

23.12 *Shipbuilding yards and docks*

23.12 Employers are responsible to *all* persons for protection against insecure hatch beams and bolts for plates (regs 71, 72) but only in respect of things arising out of their own operations.

23.13 Lastly, by reg 4(9), an employer does not owe a duty to an employee who is not present in the place in the course of doing his employer's work, or with the express or implied permission of the employer. There is, no doubt, scope for permission to be 'implied' by the court when a worker strays in ignorance, eg looking for materials or a lavatory: see *Henaghan v Rederiet Forangirene* [1936] 2 All ER 1426 on rather different words in the Docks Regulations. Regulation 4(9) does *not* apply to reg 70 so in that case the duty is unqualified.

Shipyard managers

23.14 The persons having 'general management and control' of shipyards etc have duties under the following regulations (see reg 4(4)–(6)), except in certain cases where responsibility rests on the ship under reg 4(7), as follows.

(1)   public dry docks: regs 11(2)and 69(1): broadly, safety of floating platforms and lighting the approaches to the dock;
(2)   dock, wharf or quay where ship is lying: reg 69(1), lighting of approaches.

Shipowners and masters

23.15 The ship (ie the owners and the master or officer in charge) has, under reg 4(7), to comply with the duties under regs 69(2) and 70(2) and (3) regarding lighting, and work on boilers.

Persons employed

23.16 The employee must, by reg 4(8), carry out the requirements of those regulations—listed in reg 4(8)—which impose an express duty on them, namely ss 69(6), 70(4) and 72, and to report defects in plant and machinery promptly to his employer, foreman or safety representative.

To whom duties are owed

23.17 Like all duties imposed by regulations under the Factories Act 1961, s 76 these duties are for the benefit of 'persons employed' only, and do not, for example, include an independent contractor: *Herbert v Harold Shaw Ltd* [1959] 2 QB 138. However, the Regulations are for the protection of all 'persons employed', whether or not employed in shipbuilding processes; the expression 'persons employed', whatever its precise ambit, certainly includes 'a man who is ordinarily and regularly employed' in the area covered by the

Regulations, and therefore a member of the ship's crew may recover for damages for breach of the Regulations. There may be liability for breach of the Regulations in parts of the ship where an employee is not normally employed if it is foreseeable that he should go there: *Mullard v Ben Line Steamers Ltd* [1970] 2 Lloyd's Rep 121 (open unlighted hatch where man might go back to recover his tools, breach of regs 6, 26, 69, appeal as to contributory negligence only [1971] 2 All ER 424. Note, however, that reg 26 has been revoked).

The content of the Regulations

23.18 There are few Regulations which remain in force. The Regulations originally consisted of nine parts: Part I, which contains regs 1–5, deals with interpretation and general matters.

Means of access (Part II)

23.19 Regulation 6 sets out a comprehensive requirement for safe means of access, 'without prejudice' to the other regulations.

> 'There shall, so far as is reasonably practicable, be provided and maintained safe means of access to every place at which any person has at any time to work in connection with the operations, which means of access shall be sufficient having regard to the number of persons employed and shall, so far as is reasonably practicable, be kept clear of substances likely to make foothold or handhold insecure and of any obstruction.'

Under reg 6 it is the access to work, not the place of work itself, which is to be safe: cf *Lovell v Blundells and Crompton & Co Ltd* [1944] KB 502.

23.20 The precise requirements for particular means of access have now all been repealed by the Work at Height Regulations 2005, SI 2005/775 (in effect from 6 April 2005) with the exception of safe transport over water and sound construction and proper maintenance of floating platforms (both reg 11).[1]

1   See 13th edn of *Munkman* for commentary and case law prior to 2005.

Staging and precautions against fall of persons and materials

23.21 There is no longer any specific regulation under the 1960 Regulations concerning 'staging', the term used in shipbuilding for what would usually be called scaffolding in buildings on land. Nor does any section in Part III remain to regulate the precaution against fall of persons and materials; falls of persons would come within the ambit of the Work at Height Regulations 2005.

Ventilation, fumes and explosives (Part V)

23.22 Part V of the Regulations has been revoked by the Dangerous Substances and Explosive Atmospheres Regulations 2002, SI 2002/2776. The 2002 Regulations require that where a dangerous substance is liable to be present in the workplace an employer must make a risk assessment (reg 5); must ensure that the risk is eliminated or is reduced so far as is reasonably practicable (reg 6(1)) and if not reasonably practicable to eliminate the risk must apply measures consistent with the risk assessment to control the risks or mitigate harmful effects (regs 6(3), 6(4)).

Miscellaneous and general (Parts VI and IX)

Lighting

23.23 Parts of a vessel and other places where operations are carried on, together with all the approaches, must be sufficiently lighted (reg 69). In a wet dock or harbour where the shipowner retains control, the permanent lighting of the ship must be kept going to light the ship and access to it: but by reg 69(3) a failure of electric lighting is not a breach of the Regulations if other lighting is provided as soon as practicable. This overrules *Wilkinson v Rea Ltd* [1941] 1 KB 688. Petrol or other spirit with a high flash point is forbidden in portable lamps. The lighting is required to all approaches and places to which a person needs to get for the purposes of his work.[1]

1   See *Wenborn v Harland & Wolff Ltd* [1952] 1 Lloyd's Rep 255.

Miscellaneous

23.24 Work is not allowed in a boiler or associated furnace or flue until it is cool and entry into a steam boiler forming part of a range is forbidden unless steam and hot water are disconnected or sealed off (reg 70). Hatch beams taken off a hatch in use must be secured to prevent displacement (reg 71). Jumped-up bolts are not to be used for securing plates on the sides of vessels (reg 72). Young persons must not be employed where they may fall from a stage more than two metres, or into water, unless they have been in shipyards for at least six months (reg 80). In large shipyards, where the number of persons employed regularly or from time to time exceeds 500, there is be a full-time safety officer employed (reg 81).

DOCKS AND ASSORTED PREMISES, AND WAREHOUSES

23.25 Until the repeal of large parts of the Factories Act 1961, safety legislation in docks was a tangled story. It now consists mainly of the Docks Regulations 1988, SI 1988/1655, made under the HSWA 1974. The Workplace (Health, Safety and Welfare) Regulations 1992 apply to docks but not to ships (reg 3(1)(a)), and the Work at Height Regulations 2005, SI 2005/735, which came into force on 6 April 2005 also apply, subject to certain exceptions.[1] It is possible—in the ordinary docks—to have both the Shipbuilding Regulations 1960 and the Docks Regulations 1998 applying to a ship at the same time.

[1] Regulation 3(4) of the Work at Height Regulations 2005 excludes normal ship-board activities of a ship's crew, as well as any place specified in reg 7(6) of the Docks Regulations where persons are engaged in dock operations, and any place specified in reg 5(3) of the Loading and Unloading of Fishing Vessels Regulations 1988 where persons are engaged in fish loading processes.

23.26 The technical definitions contained in the Factories Act 1961, ss 175(2)(a) and 125 still remain in force, however the substantive rules have been largely swept away by the incoming tide of European regulation.[1] Section 125(1) and (2) continues to apply the following provisions to every dock, wharf and quay, and warehouses as defined: the power to make regulations under ss 50 and 51; the provisions in relation to general registers and the preservation of registers and records (ss 140 and 141); and in relation to offences (Part XII) and interpretation (Part XIV). Section 24 on teagle openings and similar doorways which applied to warehouses which are not on docks premises has been repealed by the Work at Height Regulations 2005 (warehouses on dock premises are regulated by the Docks Regulations 1988, regs 13 and 16).

[1] For the earlier legislation and case law, see the 12th edn *of Munkman* at p 371ff.

The Docks Regulations 1988

23.27 The Docks Regulations 1988, SI 1988/1655, came into force (with minor exceptions) on 1 January 1989. They were made under the HSWA 1974 and have a wider scope than the former Regulations of 1934 made under the Factories Act. All the case law under those Regulations is obsolete, though it is relevant because of the similar language employed in the current Regulations. The 1988 Regulations enter into great detail, especially in the definitions (reg 2) and can only be summarised in a general way, with particular attention to requirements likely to apply in injury cases. The Regulations are accompanied by an ACOP 'Safety in Docks' (1988), which is mainly an explanation of the Regulations but goes into detail on practical applications such as the standard of lighting.

23.28 The Regulations apply to 'dock operations' in Great Britain and within the 12 miles territorial limit (reg 3). These operations mean:

(1) loading and unloading of goods;
(2) embarkation and disembarkation of both passengers and crew, which was not within the old Regulations; and
(3) incidental activities such as supplies to a ship, transport on the dockside and preliminary handling of goods and passengers: provided that these various activities are carried on at 'dock premises', which means any dock, wharf or other place where ships land or take on goods or passengers, together with adjacent land and those parts of the ship involved in the operation (reg 2(1)).

23.29 But the definition excludes landing of fish, services to pleasure boats which do not carry fare-paying passengers—as in a yacht marina—and military beach landing operations (but not ordinary dock operations by the armed forces, for instance at a naval dockyard). Working from lighters in territorial waters is obviously included in reg 3.

23.30 There is a general requirement to plan and execute operations safely (reg 5). The duty to comply with the Regulations is normally imposed on employers, on self-employed persons, and on those in control of premises where others work, to the extent of their control (reg 4(1)).[1] Employees must comply with Regulations which apply to their own behaviour (reg 4(2)). Employees (and self-employed) must also report faults in any plant they are 'required to use' (reg 20). But the master and crew of a ship, and their employers, are excluded from the Regulations so far as regards the ship's own plant, and activities on the ship which involve only the master and crew (reg 4(4)). These general rules as to duties do not apply to regs 8(4), 11(5), 19(2)–(5) and 20 which impose duties on specific persons: these are mainly about keeping records.

1   See *Brown v Drake International Ltd* [2004] EWCA Civ 1629, a claim under the Fatal Accidents Act 1976, in which the Court of Appeal upheld the an equal apportionment of liability between Drake, the claimant's employer, and SCT, which had overall control of the work carried out at the dock. When considering 'somewhat technical' questions as to which of the defendants, if either, was liable for breaches of the Docks Regulations, the trial judge stressed that the real mischief in the case was the unsafe system of work. He apportioned liability equally 'in view of the close nature of the de facto joint control and supervision' exercised by the defendants.

23.31 The duties are not owed to employed persons only, as they were under the Factories Act Regulations of 1934: the HSWA 1974, under which they are now made, is for the protection of all persons at work and it seems that they may even extend to the protection of other persons such as passengers who may be endangered by working activities at the dock: see ss 1(1)(b) and (3) of the Act.

Access

23.32 Safe means of access must be provided and maintained to 'every part of dock premises which any person has to visit for the purpose of dock operations' (reg 7(1)). 'Has to visit' does not necessarily mean that he has been ordered to go there: it is sufficient that his work takes him to the place: *Smith (formerly Westwood) v National Coal Board* [1967] 2 All ER 593. The regulation goes on to forbid the use of various particular means of access— steps, stairs, floors, passages—unless of adequate strength, sound construction and properly maintained. In other words, if they are not in that condition, they must be put out of use. Regulation 7(2) requires floors, steps and other means of access to be kept free of slippery substances and 'obstacles', but this applies only so far as 'reasonably practicable'.

23.33 All this applies to access and other facilities on the ship, as well as on land. If safe access is provided, there is no liability if the employee uses unsafe access for his own purposes: *Lowe v Scruttons Ltd* [1953] 1 Lloyd's Rep 342.[1]

[1]   But see now *Kirkpatrick v Scott Lithgow Ltd* 1987 SCLR 567.

Ladders

23.34 Portable ladders are forbidden as a means of access to ships, or to holds and container stacks on ships: also to stacks of three or more on land (reg 7(3)); there is an exception if 'no other safer means of access' is reasonably practicable. Specific requirements as to the manner of use and positioning of ladders are set out in the Work at Height Regulations 2005, Sch 6, which came into force on 6 April 2005 and replace similar requirements formerly contained in the Docks Regulations, reg 7(5). The 2005 Regulations also repealed reg 7(4) of the Docks Regulations which required all ladders to be of 'good construction, sound material, adequate strength, free from patent defect and properly maintained'.

Fencing open places

23.35 Fencing is required at breaks, corners and other danger points on the dockside, and on open sides of gangways and footways over bridges, caissons and dock gates (reg 7(6)). There are exceptions where fencing is impracticable because of work actually going on. The fencing requirements originally also extended to any other place (except the dockside) where there is a drop of over two metres (reg 7(6)(c)). Although the 'two-metre rule' was abolished by the Work at Height Regulations 2005, these places are now likely to be covered by the 2005 Regulations, reg 19 of which repealed reg 7(6)(c).

Lighting

23.36 All parts of the premises used for dock operations must be adequately lit, with 'obstacles or hazards' made conspicuous by colouring or otherwise (reg 6). A temporary interruption of lighting was, under the former regulation, an automatic breach of the requirement: *Wilkinson v Rea Ltd* [1941] 1 KB 688; *Grant v Sun Shipping Co Ltd* [1948] AC 549.

Safety crossing water and on ships

23.37 Vessels used to transport dock workers must be safe, properly constructed and maintained, not overloaded or overcrowded, and under the charge of a competent person; they must also have a current safety certificate (reg 8).

23.38 By reg 10, hatch covers and beams are not to be used unless of sound construction and material, adequate strength, free from patent defect and properly maintained: they must be capable of removal and replacement without danger, and must be replaced in the correct position as shown by permanent marks. The hatch itself is not to be used unless the cover is completely off or securely replaced. Loads are not to be placed on hatch covers if this is likely to make them unsafe or endanger any person. Except in emergency, any power-operated hatch cover, or car-deck ramp (including one on the dockside) is to be operated only by an operator specifically authorised.

Lifting plant and lifting operations

23.39 There are particular rules in the Docks Regulations on lifting plant, and operations which apply to dock premises over and above the more general regime to be found in the Lifting Operations and Lifting Equipment Regulations 1998, SI 1998/2307, which came into force on 5 December 1998 (see chapter 20). 'Lifting plant' includes both lifting 'appliances' and lifting 'gear'. Lifting appliances means such things as cranes and other apparatus for raising or lowering loads or moving them, and includes 'lift trucks' such as the common forklift, but does not include such things as conveyors, pipes and moving walkways and escalators (reg 2(1)). Lifting gear means the device attaching the load to the lifting appliance but not forming part of it, with some exceptions such as 'one-way' slings which make one journey only and slings already on the load when it entered the dock.

23.40 Lifting plant (of both kinds) must not be used unless of 'good design and construction', 'adequate strength', 'sound material', 'free from patent defect', 'properly maintained' and 'properly installed' (reg 13(2)).[1] This regulation is more extensive than the former Factories Act and was revised to override some of the case law under that Act.

[1] On the meaning of 'properly maintained' see *Stark v Post Office* [2000] ICR 1013, CA: see chapter 20.

23.41 The excepted types of sling, also pallets and attachments integrated with the load, must be of 'good construction', 'adequate strength' for the purpose for which they are actually used, and 'free from patent defect' (reg 13(2)).

23.42 There is a general duty to operate lifting plant safely, and in particular not to exceed the safe working load which must be marked on or near it (regs 13(3) and (4), 16). The previous obligation to carry out periodic testing and examination (regs 14–16) was revoked by the Lifting Operations and Lifting Equipment Regulations 1998, SI 1998/2307, as from 5 December 1998.

23.43 Lifting appliances are to be operated only by competent persons[1] who are specifically authorised, and records of names and training must be kept (reg 11). Hoists and lifts are not within these Regulations.

¹   Ie one who is practical and reasonable, who knows what to look for and how to recognise it when he sees it: *Gibson v Skibs A/S Marina and Orkla Grobe A/B and Smith Coggins Ltd* [1966] 2 All ER 476.

Vehicles

23.44 Vehicles must be properly maintained, and driven only by authorised and competent persons: regs 11 and 12.

23.45 There must be arrangements for road and rail safety throughout the docks, including safety of re-fuelling facilities, security of loads (eg on cranes and lorries) and safe handling of containers: reg 11(2). With giant cranes operating and heavy traffic on the move, docks are much more dangerous than the highway but the Road Traffic Acts do not necessarily apply, so the dock authority is responsible for safe control of traffic.

Miscellaneous

23.46 Miscellaneous requirements include the provision of welfare facilities, safety helmets, and high visibility clothing in some situations: reg 19; equipment for rescue, fire-fighting and life-saving must be available round the docks: reg 9. There is power to grant exemptions from the Regulations, normally on conditions setting out alternative safety arrangements.

Other Regulations in docks

23.47 The Loading and Unloading of Fishing Vessels Regulations 1988, SI 1988/1656, are a parallel code to the Docks Regulations, but much shorter. They require a safe place of work and safe access to that and other places which any person has to visit for the purpose of loading or unloading processes or incidental activities such as mooring and supplying ships: reg 5(1). But so far as safety depends on keeping surfaces free from slippery substances, this applies only so far as reasonably practicable: reg 5(2). Danger spots have to be fenced as under the Docks Regulations: reg 5(3), as amended by the Work at Height Regulations 2005. Lighting must be adequate: reg 5(4). Rescue, life-saving and fire-fighting equipment must be provided: reg 5(5). Safe plant and equipment must (so far as reasonably practicable) be provided and maintained: reg 6(2). A further duty under reg 6(1) to plan and execute operations safely makes explicit an employer's common law duty.

23.48 The duty to comply with the Regulations is imposed (reg 4) on employers and the self-employed, on those who provide places of work and on skippers of fishing vessels, but in each case so far only as they have control. Exemptions may be granted: reg 7.

23.49 The Regulations extend to the 'handling' of wet fish at the dockside, including gutting, but not freezing or other processes: premises where these are carried on will be subject to the Workplace (Health, Safety and Welfare) Regulations 1992.

23.50 The Regulations do not apply to fishing vessels used only for sport or recreation, or to cargo and passenger vessels which carry fish only as an incidental activity: reg 2.

23.51 The Dangerous Substances in Harbour Areas Regulations 1987, SI 1987/37, in force 1 June 1987 as amended are for the protection of the public in general rather than dock workers as such. 'Dangerous substances' are defined very widely (reg 3) to include anything which creates a risk to health or safety when in a harbour; they include automatically anything listed in the Merchant Shipping (Dangerous Goods and Marine Pollutants) Regulations 1997, SI 1997/2367: but do not include food, feeding stuffs, cosmetics, medicines or drugs. Tanks which have contained a dangerous substance are within the Regulations until fumes and residues are cleared.

23.52 Vessels carrying such substances must give notice before entering the harbour and comply with the harbour master's directions. Warning flags and lights have to be displayed. The ship must be anchored or moored at a safe place and be ready to move at short notice (regs 6–15).

23.53 In the handling of dangerous substances, employers and others in control must plan the operations safely (reg 16), and ensure that workers have sufficient information and training, also safety equipment and protective clothing (reg 17). Where there is a risk of fire or explosion, preparations must be made in advance to prevent or minimise this if necessary (reg 18).

23.54 There is an elaborate code (regs 19–22) for liquid substances in bulk, such as petrol or liquefied gas, including control of cleaning operations. Other regulations deal with the marking of containers or tanks holding dangerous substances (regs 23–25), emergency plans (regs 26–27), storage on the docks (regs 29–32) and explosives (regs 33–42).

23.55 Under the Dangerous Vessels Act 1985, a harbour master may prohibit the entry into harbour of a ship if the ship or its cargo is a source of imminent danger, and may likewise require such a ship to leave the harbour area.

Chapter 24

MINES AND QUARRIES (INCLUDING MINES OF STRATIFIED IRONSTONE, SHALE AND FIRECLAY)

Stuart Brittenden

THE MINES AND QUARRIES ACT 1954 AND MASHAM REGULATIONS 1993

24.01 Mines are traditionally hazardous environments, with the possibility of fire, flood, explosion and collapse having the potential to injure a large number of people. At the beginning of the last century, one person in every 1,000 employees would die from a mining related accident each year. Historically, mine workers also suffered from higher incidences of ill-health than in other sectors of industry. Coal mining, for instance, has been associated with pneumoconiosis (dust-induced lung disease), work-related emphysema, noise-induced hearing loss as well as musculoskeletal disorders.

24.02 Currently there are in the region of 137 sites operating within Great Britain including 26 licensed underground coal mines (employing approximately 5,598 people) as well as 31 opencast coal sites. Fatal accidents in the mining sector have averaged at less than one death per annum in the last four years, whereas for the period 2003/2004 there were 492 reported injuries (48 of which were regarded as being major injuries).[1]

[1]   See *Coal Mines–Incident Statistical Digest* (provisional), produced by the HSE (2005).

24.03 All the previous legislation concerning safety in mines and quarries was brought up to date and replaced by the Mines and Quarries Act 1954. This Act was largely based on the Royal Commission on Safety in Mines (1938). It gave good service for nearly 50 years. In recent years the incentive of privatisation of the British Coal Corporation and proposed Directives from the European Union have changed and continue to alter the statutory regime. The most significant regulations[1] have been the Management and Administration of Safety and Health at Mines Regulations 1993, SI 1993/1897 (the 'MASHAM' Regulations). Other regulations are: the Mines (Safety of Exit) Regulations 1988, SI 1988/1729; the Coal and Other Safety-Lamp Mines (Explosives) Regulations 1993, SI 1993/ 208; the Mines (Shafts and Winding) Regulations 1993, SI 1993/302; the Coal Mines (Owner's Operating Rules) Regulations 1993, SI 1993/2331; the Mines Miscellaneous Health and Safety Provisions Regulations 1995, SI 1995/2005; the Escape and Rescue from Mines Regulations 1995, SI 1995/2870;[2] the Mines (Control of Ground

587

Movement) Regulations 1999, SI 1999/2463, and the Quarries Regulations 1999, SI 1999/2024. The Borehole Sites and Operations Regulations 1995, SI 1995/2038 deal with mineral extraction through drilling and correspond with the offshore drilling industries regulations (see chapter 26).[3]

1   The limit of working time underground to 7.5 hours plus one winding time imposed by the Coal Mines Regulation Act 1908 was removed by the Coal Industry Act 1992. The bar on women working underground originating from 1842 was removed by the Employment Act 1989.
2   Implementing in part Directive 92/104/EEC.
3   These Regulations implement the offshore requirements of Directive 92/91/EEC on mineral extraction through drilling.

24.04   The upshot today is a tortuous paperchase of sections, regulations and ACOPs with the need to check whether any peculiar provision is extant, and whether it has been limited in its application if it is extant. Widely differing philosophies underpin different parts of the legislative regime.

24.05   Previously, safety in coal mines depended upon the Coal Mines Act 1911: in other mines, and in quarries, it depended upon the Metalliferous Mines Regulations Act 1872 and the Mines and Quarries Act 1954. Although all mines and quarries are now governed by a single Act, the safety requirements are in many respects far more strict in the case of coal mines than they are in other cases. Accordingly, this chapter is primarily concerned with coal mines, and the application of the Act to other types of mines, and to quarries is dealt with separately at the end of this chapter. Mines of stratified ironstone, shale and fireclay were, however, included with coal mines in the Act of 1911 and for the most part the same requirements apply to them. These classes of mines, therefore, are treated as coal mines in this chapter, and not as 'miscellaneous mines' in the next section.

24.06 The Mines and Quarries Act 1954 took effect within the general framework of the HSWA 1974, and like other existing legislation is gradually being replaced by regulations under that Act. However, mines are so different from anything else, and safety underground is so paramount, that a previous author was able to state in the eleventh edition of *Munkman* that 'it is unlikely that the legislation built up over the years will be changed in anything but form'. That understandable misapprehension was made particularly evident by the Management and Administration of Safety and Health at Mines Regulations 1993, SI 1993/1897, known as 'MASHAM'. The mining unions bitterly opposed the MASHAM Regulations, which they perceived as a dilution of the Mines and Quarries Act. Having failed to make headway in discussions with the HSC over the ten editions of the draft regulations in the course of some five years, judicial review was sought of the regulations on the grounds that they were ultra vires, not being 'designed to maintain or improve the standards of health, safety and welfare established by or under those enactments' as required by the HSWA 1974, s 1(2) which included the Mines and Quarries Act. The Divisional Court in *R v Secretary of State for Employment, ex p NACODS* (16 December 1993, unreported) rejected the application, holding that it was for Parliament alone to determine whether or not the regulations maintained or improved pre-existing standards, and not for the courts.

24.07 In fact the alterations made by the MASHAM Regulations are profound and the unions' opposition was not without foundation: the words 'so far as is reasonably practicable' brought qualifications to many duties which were formerly absolute; the primary safety duties of the pit deputies have been emasculated and safety responsibility passed to the mine manager whose principal concern, in reality, must be production. It is significant that no audit of the workings of the Mines and Quarries Act 1954 seems to have preceded the MASHAM Regulations even though safety in British mines under the Act leads the world. On the other hand, the MASHAM Regulations promote flexibility, an objective much desired by mine operators. As Simon Brown LJ put it in the *NACODS* case: the conflict over the MASHAM Regulations:

'is a dispute between conflicting philosophies—between the respective benefits of certainty and flexibility, as to the proper relationship between the duties of inspection and supervision—deep-seated differences of that sort'.

In consequence, the Mines and Quarries Act 1954 and the MASHAM Regulations must now be read together.

24.08 Most of the administrative provisions of the Mines and Quarries Act 1954—the powers to make regulations and grant exemptions, appointment of inspectors, conduct of inquiries and prosecutions—have been repealed or modified by regulations under the HSWA 1974.[1] The HSE is now the authority responsible for enforcing the legislation.

[1] Mines and Quarries Acts 1954 to 1971 (Repeals and Modifications) Regulations 1974 and 1975, SI 1974/2013 and 1975/1102.

General scope of the legislation

24.09 By far the most important part of the Mines and Quarries Act 1954 for present purposes is Part III (ss 22–97) which is headed 'safety, health and welfare (mines)'.[1] Management and control of mines depends upon the MASHAM Regulations which largely replace Parts I and II save for quarries. (The corresponding provisions for safety and management in quarries are in Parts IV and V of the Act.) Notification of accidents and other dangerous occurrences is regulated by Part VI, and the inspection of mines on behalf of the workmen by Part VII.

[1] Most of these sections contain safety requirements of general application. Others, however, contained powers to require improvements in particular situations (e g roof support, roads, ventilation) or to make regulations; these have been repealed under the HSWA 1974 on the basis that they are covered by the powers under that Act. Sections 22–25, 33–35 and 70 have been replaced by the Mines (Safety of Exit) Regulations 1988, SI 1988/1729 as amended by the Reporting of Injuries, Diseases and Dangerous Occurrences Regulations 1995.

24.10 Restrictions on the employment of women and young persons (Part VIII) were largely abolished by the Employment Act 1989. The remainder of the Mines and Quarries Act 1954 is taken up with administrative matters, ie records (Part IX), certificates of mining qualifications (Part XII), offences and legal proceedings (Part XIV) and miscellaneous matters such as definitions (Part XV). Most of Parts X and XI (regulations and inspectors) and much of Part XIV (as to prosecutions) have been repealed and their place taken by the HSWA 1974 or regulations under it. Part XIII (fencing of abandoned and disused mines and quarries) is intended for the protection of the public at large.

24.11 The Mines and Quarries Act 1954 is binding upon the Crown, and applies to mines and quarries belonging to the Crown or a government department, or held in trust for the purpose of a government department.

24.12 The Mines and Quarries (Tips) Act 1969 regulates the safety of tips, whether still in use or disused.

Administration of the legislation

24.13 The HSWA 1974 now controls the making of regulations and the appointment and powers of inspectors. The HSE took over the former Mines Inspectorate, which continues as a specialist branch of the organisation.

Management of mines

24.14 The old scheme of mine management under the Mines and Quarries Act 1954 has been abolished and replaced by the MASHAM Regulations. There is provision for certified exemptions by the HSE (reg 38). The Regulations impose a duty on employers of employees at work at a mine to comply with the legislation; to co-operate with each other and with the mine manager (reg 4). The same duty falls on the self-employed (reg 3). The duties of employers under the MASHAM Regulations are in addition to the employer's duty to make its risk assessments under reg 3 of the Management of Health and Safety at Work Regulations 1999, SI 1999/3242 (see chapter 10) (which applies to mines and quarries).

24.15 Regulation 5 of the MASHAM Regulations imposes on employees the duty to: co-operate with the manager in fulfilling the latter's statutory safety obligations; leave the workplace safe at the end of a shift or fence it off; take steps to prevent blockage of ventilation; behave in an orderly fashion;[1] not to leave his workplace without lamp and self-rescuer; not to be intoxicated; not to sleep below ground or while in charge of equipment on the surface; not to pass a barrier or danger signal without authority; not to brush or waft out any flammable gas; to report any danger which he cannot suppress. Regulation 5 replaces various obligations of the 1954 Act which now only apply to quarries (see below) and much of the Coal and Other Mines (General Duties and Conduct) Regulations 1956, SI 1956/1761.

1   See eg *Hugh v National Coal Board* 1972 SC 252.

24.16 The principal duty under the MASHAM Regulations imposed on mine owners[1] is reg 6. It is 'to secure, so far as practicable, that the mine is managed and worked in accordance with the relevant statutory provisions' (reg 6(2)(b)) and planned and laid out accordingly. That duty reflects the duty under s 1 of the Mines and Quarries Act 1954 (which section no longer applies to mines) but with the added insertion of the qualifying words 'so far as is practicable'. That diminution of the s 1 duty has not been extended to quarries, which continue to be subject to s 1 of the 1954 Act. The owner's duty to secure conformity with the legislation applies not only to performance of its obligations but to securing the performance of the obligations of others (reg 6(5)). The owner can appoint agents to secure performance of its duty but such appointments must be notified to the HSE. The owner also has a duty to prepared and keep up to date a safety policy and bring it to the attention of all working at the mine (reg 6(4)). The owner must notify the HSE prior to working a mine or seam, or sinking a shaft or driving a new outlet (reg 7, Sch 2).

1   See Mines and Quarries Act 1954, s 181.

24.17 Part of the legislation with which the owner must ensure conformity is the Coal Mines (Owner's Operating Rules) Regulations 1993, SI 1993/2331. The HSE has issued Guidance on the Regulations. By reg 3 the owner must set down written Owners Operating Rules, bring them to the attention of all persons working at the mine (whether or not employed by the owner), send them to the HSE, and ensure, so far as is practicable, that all operations are conducted in conformity with them. The rules must deal with ventilation of blind ends, mine fires and frictional ignition (reg 4 and Sch). The HSE can require the owner to modify his rules (reg 3(3)). Annexed to the regulation are model rules drawn up by the HSE in respect of each of the three headings which extend over 30 pages in total. They deal with (amongst other things):

(1)   *auxiliary ventilation:* degassing operations; electrical power supplies, inspection, reports and reporting to the manager; management and regulation of airflow; co-ordination, battery powered free-steered vehicles;

(2)   *mine fires:* fire fighting; underground fire fighting; underground belt conveyors; winding engine houses; training in use of self-rescuers;

(3)   *frictional ignition:* assessment of ignition risk; ignition sources; fire damp; reports and rules; equipment and components.

24.18 Returning to the MASHAM Regulations, the owner is under an obligation to appoint a manager. No mine may be worked without there being a mine manager.

24.19 There must be a sole mine manager appointed by the owner, and the former must be 'suitably qualified and competent' (reg 8(1) and (2)). The qualifications required are not set out in the MASHAM Regulations, but are specified in Appendix 1 to the ACOP which accompanies them (and see paras 17–22). When the manager is unavailable there must be a substitute manager to act up (for a maximum of 72 days or longer if approved by the HSE). The appointment of manager and substitute must be notified to the HSE (reg 34).

24.20 The mine manager 'shall have the management, command and control of the mine exercisable subject to any instructions given to him by or on behalf of the owner' (reg 9(1)). The mine manager must exercise 'daily personal supervision' in the absence of which the mine may not be worked (reg 9(2)). His duty is ('so far as is reasonably practicable')[1] to ensure that all others (excluding the owner and the owner's agents) discharge their statutory obligations (reg 9(3)(d)). The mine manager also has the duty ('so far as is reasonably practicable') to manage and control the mine in accordance with the legislation (reg 9(3)(a)), and to ensure by the exercise of supervision and inspection the safety of persons and operations at the mine (reg 9(3)(b)).

[1]   Words not in the equivalent (now replaced) of the Mines and Quarries Act 1954, s 2(2).

24.21 This latter regulation, together with the duty (under reg 10) to appoint suitably qualified[1] and competent managers to a suitable management structure (set out in writing, defining the authority and responsibility of each person in it), institutes a new legislative scheme of management which, amongst other things, takes the place of the time honoured pit deputy.

[1]   The qualifications are not stipulated by regulation, but Appendix 1 of the accompanying ACOP sets out the HSE approved qualifications.

24.22 The deputy's function (under the repealed s 12 of the 1954 Act) was inspection of his district of the mine, in particular as to fire damp, ventilation, support for roof and sides, and general safety. The Coal and Other Mines (Managers and Officials) Regulations 1956 made extensive provision for such inspections but have been repealed by the MASHAM Regulations. In their place is the much more generalised reg 12 of the MASHAM Regulations together with the guidance of the ACOP, paras 96–115. Regulation 12 requires the manager to establish districts and assign suitable qualified and competent people (not employees of contractors) to inspect them. Inspections must be for firedamp (by use of an approved instrument), ventilation, support of roof and sides and general safety and be of such frequency to ensure safe entry and work. The inspector must assess the condition with respect to the health and safety of people, and prevent or report any dangers. At the end of a shift the inspector going off duty must communicate relevant information to the inspector coming on. The inspector must report on each inspection at shift's end and the report must be posted.

24.23 The detailed management structure required by reg 10 must provide that all persons below ground are 'under command' of managers with the duty to supervise them, and that where there is more than one such person on duty, the management structure makes arrangements for a suitable chain of command from the mine manager to the supervising managers (reg 10(2)).

24.24 Each manager must exercise due diligence, so far as is practicable to ensure compliance with the legislation, and 'so far as is practicable by the exercise of supervision ensure the safety of all persons below ground for whom he is responsible' (reg 10(4)). These duties are subject to any instruction from a more senior manager. While every manager must give precedence to health and safety duties over other duties, the old deputy's obligation under the repealed s 12 of the 1954 Act to devote 'the whole of [his] time' to the duties of inspection and supervision specified in regulations[1] has gone. The ACOP, paras 45–82 gives much guidance to the allocation and exercise of these management responsibilities.

[1]   The Coal and Other Mines (Managers and Officials) Regulations 1956 were repealed by the MASHAM Regulations.

24.25 The manager has a duty to ensure so far as is reasonably practicable that all plant and equipment is safely installed and systematically inspected, examined, tested and maintained (reg 11(1)). There must be a written scheme for these activities (reg 11(2)) and written and signed reports of each and of repairs which must set out defects and steps to remedy them (reg 11(4)). It is the manager's responsibility to appoint suitably qualified[1] and competent managers to direct and manage activities, supervisors to supervise them, persons to undertake them, and substitutes available for all the foregoing (reg 11(3)). This regulation, providing as it does for engineers, electricians, fitters and other technicians, their supervisors and managers, takes the place of the strict duty to appoint such persons and prescribe their duties by regulation[2] under s 13 of the 1954 Act, the latter being repealed by the MASHAM Regulations. The ACOP (paras 83–95) amplifies the inspection and maintenance scheme of the regulation.

[1]   Approved qualifications are set out in the ACOP at Appendix 1.
[2]   The Coal and Other Mines (Mechanics and Electricians) Regulations 1965, repealed by the MASHAM Regulations.

24.26 The mine manager is also obliged to ensure sufficient plant and equipment;[1] to record the names of those going underground and returning; to read and confirm the statutory reports or ensure someone suitably qualified and competent does; to arrange for barometric pressure readings (reg 13). A mine manager can only manage more than one mine if it is practicable to do so and the HSE has been notified (reg 14) though there can be more than one manager in a mine, if it can be divided and worked in separate parts (recorded on the plan) under each manager (reg 15). The mine owner can give instructions to the mine manager but to no one else at the mine without the manager's consent. If the manager thinks the instructions prejudicial to the manager's statutory duties 'or to the health or safety of persons employed at the mine' he may refuse to carry them out unless they are confirmed in writing by a person duly authorised by the owner who is qualified and competent to be a mine manager of that mine (reg 16).

[1]   Not an absolute duty so long as there is a reasonably adequate supply of (in this case) appropriate spanners: *Hills v National Coal Board* (1972) 13 KIR 486.

24.27 The approved qualifications for the various positions and functions specified in the Regulations are set out in Appendix 1 to the accompanying ACOP. The HSE can approve qualifications and issue certificates (regs 17–22). No person may do any work in a mine if not adequately instructed and trained unless supervised (reg 23) and the manager must appoint a training officer with suitable staff (regs 24 and 26) who must be consulted by the manager prior to the latter preparing a training scheme (reg 25 and ACOP, paras 141–167).

24.28 The manager must appoint a suitably qualified and competent surveyor for the mine (reg 27) who must be given all requisite information (reg 30), whose duties are to maintain proper plans (regs 28, 29, 31–33; ACOP, paras 177–206 and see the Mines and Quarries Act 1954, s 19 which remains unrepealed), and whose appointment must be notified to the HSE (reg 34). Plans are, of course, absolutely vital in a mine and the ACOP amplifies the Regulations in relation to plans in paras 172–206. The Mines (Precautions against Inrushes) Regulations 1979, SI 1979/318 require steps to be taken to prevent flooding by gas or water which rely on plans and the Prevention of Inrushes in Mines ACOP (effective from 1 October 1993) refers to the forgoing provisions of the MASHAM Regulations and ACOP and amplifies the need for and use of plans (Prevention of Inrushes in Mines ACOP, paras 18–25).

24.29 Plans are also required by the Mines (Safety of Exit) Regulations 1988, SI 1988/1729, reg 7(3) and para 28 of the accompanying ACOP (illustrated sketch plan to familiarise people with ways out of mine); the Escape and Rescue from Mines Regulations 1995, SI 1995/2870, reg 4 (emergency plans);[1] Electricity at Work Regulations 1989, SI 1989/635, reg 24 and ACOP (electrical distribution system); Coal Mines (Precautions against Inflammable Dust) Order 1956, SI 1956/1769, Sch 1, para 7(4) (plan for locating dust samples).

[1]   Replacing the Coal and Other Mines (Fire and Rescue) Regulations 1956.

Definition of 'mine'

24.30 Broadly speaking, the difference between a mine and quarry is that a mine is approached by underground workings while a quarry consists of open excavations: *Sims v Evans* (1875) 40 JP 199. Thus open-cast coal workings are quarries.

24.31 'Mine' is defined more precisely by s 180(1) of the Act[1] to mean:

> 'an excavation or system of excavations, including all such excavations to which a common system of ventilation is provided, made for the purpose of, or in connection with, the getting, wholly or substantially by means of involving the employment of persons below ground, of minerals (whether in their natural state or in solution or suspension) or products of minerals'.

[1]   As substituted by the MASHAM Regulations, Sch 3, Pt II.

24.32 Under s 180(3)(a), the mine is taken to include the surface workings, ie:

> 'so much of the surface (including buildings, structures and works thereon) surrounding or adjacent to the shafts or outlets of the mine as is occupied together with the mine for the purpose of, or in connection with, the working of the mine, the treatment, preparation for sale, consumption or use, storage or removal from the mine of the minerals or products thereof gotten from the mine or the removal from the mine of the refuse thereof'.

By a proviso, however, premises on the surface do not form part of the mine if 'a manufacturing process is carried on otherwise than for the purpose of the working of the mine ... or the preparation for sale of minerals gotten therefrom'.

24.33 By s 180(4) and (5), a mine also includes refuse dumps and railway lines serving it. If these serve more than one mine, the HSE has power to allocate them to one or other of the mines. Similarly, by s 180(6), a conveyor or aerial ropeway provided for the removal of minerals or refuse is part of the mine.

24.34 There is a corresponding definition of a quarry and its associated workings. All that need be said at this stage is that a quarry is defined as a system of excavations for minerals which is *not* a mine. As the definition of a mine involves, 'wholly or substantially', 'means involving the employment of persons below ground', it appears that a *limited* degree of underground working will not convert a quarry into a mine.

24.35 The whole of these complex definitions may be summed up simply and broadly as follows: a 'mine' means underground excavations for obtaining minerals and includes the surface workings and associated railway lines, conveyors, ropeways and refuse or spoil dumps; but it does not include premises at the surface where minerals are subject to a manufacturing process—such as the smelting of metals or the making of patent fuels from coal—as distinct from the mere preparation of the minerals for sale.

24.36 'Minerals' are defined by s 182 to include 'stone, slate, clay, gravel, sand and other natural deposits except peat'. This is obviously not a comprehensive definition, since it does not mention the main minerals such as coal and metallic ores: it is merely inserted to put one or two borderline cases beyond doubt.

24.37 There is no definition of a 'coal mine': but a number of the stricter requirements of the Act (eg those relating to the necessity for two shafts) are limited to mines of 'coal, stratified ironstone, shale or fireclay'; and the term coal mine will be used in this chapter (as it was used in the Act of 1922) to include all these cases.

24.38 The working of a mine includes the driving of a shaft or outlet as well as any time when persons are working underground or plant or equipment is in operation for safety reasons (s 182(3)(a)).

24.39 Excavations made for training purposes are deemed to be mines, but in this case the Secretary of State may make an order applying the Act with modifications (s 183).

24.40 Offices at mines and quarries and other workplaces above ground are subject to the Workplace (Health, Safety and Welfare) Regulations 1992; only underground workplaces at mines are excluded from those Regulations (see reg 3(1)(c)).

Liability to actions for damages for breach of statutory duty

24.41 Many sections of the Coal Mines Act 1911, such as s 49 with regard to the security of the roof, imposed a direct and personal duty upon the owners, who were therefore liable to an action for damages if the duty was not performed. Other duties under the Act and regulations, however, did not rest directly upon the owners, but were imposed specifically upon other persons: for example, the duties with regard to the use of explosives rested upon the shotfirer. In such cases the owners were not liable for the breach of duty, provided that they had taken all reasonable means to see that the Act and regulations were enforced: *Harrison v National Coal Board* [1951] AC 639. In the same case it was suggested that, even after the abolition of common employment, the owners would not become liable for the default of a shotfirer or other subordinate, because his statutory duty (it was said) was something independent of his employment. This point was left open by the House of Lords in that case[1] but was subsequently met by the Mines and Quarries Act 1954, s 159, which provides as follows:

> 'For the removal of doubts it is hereby declared that the owner of a mine is not absolved from liability to pay damages in respect of a contravention ... by a person employed by him of [a provision of the Act or of any order, regulation or notice under the Act] by reason only that the provision contravened was one which expressly imposed on that person or on persons of a class to which ... he belonged, a duty or requirement, or expressly prohibited that person or persons of such a class, or all persons, from doing a specified act ...'.

The wording of this section is far from ideal: but it clearly is intended to make the owners liable for a breach of statutory duty by their subordinates, provided that the breach arises in the course of the employment.

[1] And see *National Coal Board v England* [1954] AC 403.

24.42 Accordingly, under the Mines and Quarries Act 1954 it is possible to say in general terms that the owners are liable for all contraventions of the Act either by themselves or through the acts and omissions of their employees in the course of their work: and the difficulties which arose under the previous law may now be regarded as obsolete. So far as the MASHAM Regulations are concerned it has been noted that the specific duties on deputies and engineers have been removed so that the *Harrison* point could, in any event, no longer be raised in relation to persons exercising such functions. A breach of MASHAM gives rise to potential civil liability (see HSWA 1974, s 47).

24.43 However, under s 157 of the Act it is a defence in an action for damages, based on a contravention of the Act, or of any order or regulations or other requirement under the Act, if the defendant is able to prove:

'that it was impracticable to avoid or prevent the contravention'.

24.44 The word 'impracticable' should be noted. The corresponding expression in s 102(8) of the Act of 1911 was 'not *reasonably* practicable'. The change of wording implies that the standard of liability has been raised. Thus unless the regulations impose a weaker duty the issue is whether it was 'practicable' or not to comply with the Act: and questions of reasonableness—which involved considerations of expense, and loss of productive effect—are not in issue.[1] It has been noted above that many of the duties under the MASHAM Regulations revert to the 'reasonably practicable' standard instead of the s 157 standard. The onus of establishing this special defence under s 157 is clearly placed upon the defendant: *Gough v National Coal Board* [1959] AC 698. Even under the wording of the old section, it was a heavy burden. Tucker LJ said in *Edwards v National Coal Board* [1949] 1 KB 704 at 710:

'It was, I think, a heavy burden ... [the owners] start as insurers and have by evidence to divest themselves of this status. ...'

[1]   For a full discussion of practicability, see para 5.84, above.

24.45 In effect, as the above case shows, the owners must explain in every detail what they have done, and must establish that they have left no stone unturned in trying to comply with the Act: it is not enough to show that the accident *might* have happened without their negligence, in spite of all practicable steps being taken: *Sanderson v National Coal Board* [1961] 2 QB 244.

24.46 Comparisons with the law of negligence were discouraged even under the old wording by Lord Reid in *Marshall v Gotham Co Ltd* [1954] AC 360 at 373. Under the stricter test of 'impracticability', it can hardly ever be right to say, as was suggested obiter in *Jones v National Coal Board* [1957] 2 QB 55, that if there was no negligence the defence will be established.[1]

[1]   See also *Sanderson v National Coal Board* [1961] 2 All ER 796 and *Brown v National Coal Board* [1962] AC 574 (per Lord Denning), which show that the test for 'impracticability' is not the same as for absence of negligence, and that it is a stricter requirement than 'not reasonably practicable' under the 1911 Act.

24.47 Where the duty of complying with the Act rests on a subordinate, the owners must show that it was not reasonably practicable (under the Mines and Quarries Act 1954, 'impracticable') for the subordinate, their agent, to avoid or prevent the breach: *Yelland v Powell Duffryn Associated Collieries Ltd* [1941] 1 KB 154; *Crane v William Baird & Co* 1935 SC 715; for he is the person who is complying with the Act on their behalf.

24.48 Under the Mines (Safety of Exit) Regulations 1988, SI 1988/1729, the defence under s 157 is excluded (see reg 11): this is because the individual regulations are restricted to what is 'reasonably practicable' where this is appropriate.

Relationship between the Factories Act and the Mines and Quarries Act

24.49 The interplay between the Factories Act and the Mines and Quarries Act was somewhat difficult under the original Mines and Quarries Act 1954, s 184, but so far as mines are concerned is resolved by reg 40 of the MASHAM Regulations, which disapply the Factories Act 1961 from mines unless the mine is being used other than for getting minerals or ensuring the safety of another mine. In such a case there must be a certificate from the HSE excluding the application of the mines legislation.

24.50 So far as quarries are concerned, the position has been greatly simplified by the repeal of s 184 by the HSWA 1974 and the Quarries Regulations 1999, SI 1999/2024. By s 184(1), the Factories Act does not apply to premises which (under the definitions discussed above) form part of a quarry.

24.51 The exclusion of the Factories Act from mines and quarries is, however, subject to an exception by reg 40 of the MASHAM Regulations. The Mines and Quarries Act does not extend to works of building and engineering construction, which are regulated by s 127 of the Factories Act; but s 127 is not to apply to *any* work of engineering construction at a mine or quarry, whether above or below ground, or to building operations below ground. The Construction (Health, Safety and Welfare) Regulations 1996, SI 1996/1592 provide that s 127 applies in relation to premises forming part of a mine where building operations are undertaken above ground level: reg 40(3). This seems to be a roundabout way of saying that s 127 of the Factories Act (and the Construction Regulations made under the Act) applies to building operations on the surface, but otherwise has no application at a mine or quarry.

The security of the roof and sides

24.52 It has always been recognised that the security of the roof in a mine is a matter of great importance. Failure to make the roof safe might give rise to an action for negligence at common law, as in *Paterson v Wallace & Co* (1854) 1 Macq 748. Section 49 of the Coal Mines Act 1911 (replacing a similar section under the Act of 1887) imposed a simple and unqualified duty in the following terms:

'The roof and sides of every travelling road and working place shall be made secure ...'.

24.53 This was held in the earlier cases to create an absolute duty to keep the roof secure, subject to the defence of impracticability: *Lochgelly Iron and Coal Co v M'Mullan* [1934] AC 1 approving *Bett v Dalmeny Oil Co* (1905) 7 F 787. The old law was changed by the Mines and Quarries Act 1954. The relevant provisions of the 1954 Act were repealed by the Mines (Control of Ground Movement) Regulations 1999, SI 1999/2463. The Regulations apply to all mines within the meaning of the Mines and Quarries Act 1954 save where the Regulations state otherwise (reg 3). Exemptions may be granted (reg 15). The Regulations require managers of mines to ensure that ground control measures are implemented in order to keep secure every place where people work or pass in a mine. This duty only applies to foreseeable health and safety risks (reg 4).

24.54 An assessment of all factors likely to affect ground movement must be undertaken before any excavation work is carried out. This assessment has to be recorded in writing and reviewed where there has been a material change in circumstances (reg 5). Following an assessment, a 'design document' has to be prepared detailing the ground control measures which may need to be taken (reg 6). Ground control rules must be posted at the entrance to the mine so that they can be easily seen and read by persons who work there, and must generally be made available to all persons who have duties relating to ground control measures (reg 7(3)). A system for reviewing the adequacy of the ground control measures has to be established (reg 10). Where there is to be a significant change to any existing ground control measure in use at a coal mine, the HSE must be informed and provided with information, including the ground control assessment not less than 28 days before the change is introduced (reg 8). Mine officials are under a duty to take reasonable steps to ensure that ground support rules are implemented and that support material is installed even where not provided for in the rules if this is necessary for health and safety (reg 9).

24.55 The Regulations impose duties in respect of the provision and installation of materials. Managers have to ensure that a sufficient supply of suitable support materials is readily available at all times where these are required by any person whose duties include the installation of support materials (the 'installer') (reg 11(2)). Where a sufficient supply of support materials is not readily available, the installer must withdraw to a place of safety and immediately report this fact to a mine official (reg 11(3)). Officials are also under a duty to instruct the installer to withdraw where it is apparent that a sufficient supply of support material is not readily available (reg 11(5)). Installers must ensure that support materials are installed in accordance with the mine rules. Where any part of the roof or sides becomes exposed and support materials are needed to keep the exposed area safe, such materials must be installed immediately. If this is not possible, then the worker must withdraw to a place of safety, prevent access to the exposed area and report the matter to a mine official (reg 12(2)). Where support material becomes unsuitable or unstable, this must be replaced or stabilised as soon as possible, or if this is not possible, the regulations require the person to withdraw to a safe place, prevent access to the area and report the matter to an official (reg 12(3)). Officials are also required to prevent access to areas where support materials are deficient and to ensure that the situation is remedied as soon as possible. The Regulations prohibit the withdrawal of support material in a mine other than by a safe method and from a position of safety (reg 13). This echoes the content of the Mines and Quarries Act 1954, s 52(1).

24.56 The Regulations are accompanied by a Schedule containing detailed support system standards for face workings in coal mines where props, bars, powered supports, and packs are used (Part I), as well as for roadways where props, bars, steel arches and rockbolts are used (Part II).

Cases decided under the Mines and Quarries Act 1954

24.57 The former s 48(1) of the Mines and Quarries Act 1954 imposed similar obligations upon managers of mines and for this reason is considered below. It provided as follows:

> 'It shall be the duty of the manager of every mine to take with respect to every road and working place in the mine, such steps by way of controlling movement of the strata in the mine and supporting the roof and sides of the road or working place as may be necessary for keeping the road or working place secure.'

24.58 By a proviso, this did not apply to parts of the mine which are fenced off under reg 8 of the Mines (Safety of Exit) Regulations 1988 (formerly s 33 of the Act) as not being fit for use or entry.[1] By s 48(2), the manager had to ensure that he was in possession of all material information necessary for the discharge of his duty—for example, he had to study the geological plans of the mine, and keep himself informed on the condition of peat or other water-logged strata on the surface whose weight may cause the workings to collapse. The duty to keep informed is a duty to take all possible steps and not merely all reasonable steps, to discover what dangers are foreseeable, which involves making the use of the best and most up-to-date scientific knowledge: *Mettam v National Coal Board* (1988) Times, 23 July.

---

[1] As applied by the Mines (Control of Ground Movement) Regulations 1999, SI 1999/2463, reg 4.

24.59 The duty extended to watching and controlling the movements of the strata throughout the whole area of the mine workings. The duty had to be carried out not only by support measures but also by controlling the movement of the strata, which includes the bringing down of a dangerous mass of coal or other strata: *Robertson v William Crossen (Woodhall) Ltd* 1970 SLT 310; and bringing down stones in the roof such as balls of ironstone embedded in the strata, where the risk of falls is known to exist or ought to be known: *Davies v National Coal Board* (1974) 16 KIR 339.

24.60 On the other hand, the duty was not automatically broken by a fall of roof, and the onus lay with the claimant to prove a breach of the section: *Aitken v National Coal Board* 1982 SLT 545. It was not broken unless the manager (or those delegated by him) failed to take some step which was necessary in the light of the knowledge and information he has or ought to have: *Brown v National Coal Board* [1962] AC 574 (roof secure until girder dislodged by a tub; electrician hit by stone while removing light from girder preparatory to replacement—no breach of manager's duty). There was no liability, therefore, for an unforeseeable geological fault: *Tomlinson v Beckermet Mining Co Ltd* [1964] 3 All ER 1; or where girders were fixed and boarded over to a width which left only a negligible risk of a fall: *Soar v National Coal Board* [1965] 2 All ER 318. But where shotfiring involved foreseeable risk that the sides of a clay mine would be weakened, liability was established for failure to take steps in advance to maintain security, although supports for sides are not customary in a clay mine: *John G Stein Ltd v O'Hanlon* [1965] AC 890.

24.61 The duty of the manager was described in one case as a 'general long-term obligation': it was held that while he must keep himself informed from day to day, there was no breach of duty merely because a subordinate official knew that a steel strut had been placed without a wooden lid so that it bit into the roof: *Robson v National Coal Board* [1968] 3 All ER 159. This decision seems dubious. No doubt there is a long-term obligation, but that does not mean there is no short-term obligation. The decision went on the basis that the section was broken only by the acts or omissions of the manager, and not by the acts of deputies or other officials. This is clearly wrong. In *Brown v National Coal Board*, above, which the decision purported to follow, Lord Denning said (at 597, 90) that the manager has to act through overmen and deputies and is responsible for them. This principle must be fortified now by the manager's duties (para 24.16ff) imposed by the MASHAM Regulations. In Scotland there is a consistent line of authorities that performance of the manager's duty must be judged *as if* he had inspected the place before the accident (even if he never went there). If, on such a visit, there would have been no indication of insecurity, there is no liability: *Aitken v National Coal Board* 1973 SLT (Notes) 48. But if danger was foreseeable by a skilled and competent manager, it would be his duty to give instructions (eg to bring down the roof or improve the support), not to leave this to the decision of the deputy or other men on the spot: *O'Hara v National Coal Board* 1973 SLT (Notes) 25 (a considered decision of the Inner House on appeal: it was held that a projecting nose of coal liable to collapse should have been brought down; the manager never inspected it and said in evidence that he would have thought it dangerous but left those on the spot to decide). In *Hill v National Coal Board* 1976 SLT 261 the roof was supported by girders and wooden cladding; shotfiring in the night shift might have weakened the roof; the following morning a stone fell on a miner clearing dust. The Inner House held that in the absence of evidence that the manager had actually made an inspection after the shotfiring, the claim succeeded; the pursuer did not have to prove that some fault would have been discovered. Although a roof fall does not automatically establish a breach of duty, once it is shown that the risk of fall should have been known to a competent manager, there is a duty to make the roof secure either by support or bringing dangerous parts down, and non-performance can be excused only by the defence of 'impracticability' under s 157: *McFarlane v National Coal Board* 1974 SLT (Notes) 16 (the roof was brittle, there had been falls, the supports were too far apart: liability established); *Weir v National Coal Board* 1982 SLT 529 (deputy knew of dangerous cavity though manager personally did not).

24.62 Although, as stated above, the onus of proof that there has been a breach of the section was in the final balance on the claimant, it has been held that a fall of roof raised a prima facie case, which must be answered by at least some evidence of what steps have been taken: *Sinclair v National Coal Board* 1963 SC 586; *Beiscak v National Coal Board* [1965] 1 All ER 895. In *John G Stein v O'Hanlon,* above, the House of Lords left the point open. But in *Hill v National Coal Board* 1976 SLT 261 the Court of Session made it clear that the *Sinclair* decision had not been overruled.

24.63 There is a further noteworthy point in the former wording of the Mines and Quarries Act 1954. Under the old s 48 it was no longer the 'roof and sides' (as it was under the old Act) which had to be made 'secure'. It was the 'road or working place' itself which has to be secure, and not merely made secure but 'kept' secure, so that there was a continuing duty.

24.64 The expression 'working place' included 'any place where a miner is set to work': *Lochgelly Iron and Coal Co v M'Mullan* [1934] AC 1 at 19. The area of a 'working place' varies according to the nature of the work, and includes all places where a miner is properly working or may be expected to work, not necessarily excluding an area from which props are partly removed: *Venn v National Coal Board* [1967] 2 QB 557; *Hammond v National Coal Board* [1984] 3 All ER 321. In *Shevchuk v National Coal Board* 1982 SLT 557 the Court of Session decided that the roof newly exposed behind a coal cutter was not a 'working place' (and in particular that the manager could not be expected to know that a miner would go under the exposed roof without extending the canopy from the mechanical chock for protection). In *Hammond v National Coal Board,* above, the English Court of Appeal, by a majority, reluctantly followed this decision; accordingly there was no breach of s 48, although this part of the roof was known to be brittle from previous falls after the cutter had passed the same point, and could have been made secure in advance. There is much to be said for the dissenting view of Parker LJ that 'working place' should be interpreted in a broad sense to include 'the whole of the roof from the waste behind the chocks to the face, wherever the face might from time to time be', because otherwise 'a mine manager could deliberately allow cavities to develop, the repair of which would necessarily expose miners to danger'. In both these cases the accident was to a miner engaged in repairing a cavity.[1] 'Road' did not—by s 182(1)—include an 'unwalkable outlet', ie a vertical or steeply inclined shaft giving exit from the mine, but it appears to include every other track from one point to another in a mine.[2]

1   An appeal to the House of Lords was settled, leaving the question open at that level. It is difficult for an outsider to understand what is the best mining technology for roof support, but it seems that the *Hammond* decision is contrary to the common sense view of experienced mine deputies. It was a source of friction between NACODS (the deputies' union) and the NCB.

2   In *Wraith v National Coal Board* [1954] 1 All ER 231 it was held that the term 'road' did not include a disused roadway which was under reconstruction: and that the work of repair did not make it a 'working place'. Under the present Act this would still be the position provided that the place is in a part of the mine fenced off under s 33, but apparently not otherwise, as the wording of s 48 does not follow the material part of s 49 of the Act of 1911.

24.65 The word 'secure' means the same thing as 'safe', ie free from danger:[1] but the question has still to be asked, What dangers must it be free from? The answer appears to be that the structure of the roof must be free from danger of collapse through its own inherent weakness, and perhaps also from the danger of collapse under the impact of some external forces. Lord Tucker said in *Marshall v Gotham Co Ltd* [1954] AC 360 (a case decided under the Metalliferous Mines Regulations) at 374:

> 'I agree that the word "secure" does not involve security from the effects of an earthquake or an atom bomb, but I think that it must include security from all the known geological hazards inherent in mining operations.'

1   See *John Summers & Sons Ltd v Frost* [1955] AC 740; *Gough v National Coal Board* [1959] AC 698 and *Larner v British Steel plc* [1993] ICR 551.

24.66 On the other hand, it does not involve security from an abnormal explosion due to the fact that a large quantity of explosive is being carried in a manner prohibited by statute: *Jackson v National Coal Board* [1955] 1 All ER 145.[1]

1   This case contains a reference to an unreported case *of Hayes v National Coal Board*, which decided that there was no breach of s 49 of the Act of 1911 when a fall of roof occurred because a prop was accidentally knocked out. If this case is rightly decided, the protection of the section cannot extend to security against the shock of any external danger at all, and must be limited to collapse through inherent weakness. It must be said that the facts in *Hayes* bear some similarity to those in *Brown v National Coal Board* para 24.60, above, where no liability was found either.

24.67 In *Gough v National Coal Board* [1959] AC 698 where the question was whether the 'working face' is covered by the obligation to make secure, Lord Reid said:

> '"Secure" here means in such a state that there will be no danger from accidental falls. ... I can see nothing inconsistent in saying that a side or a roof shall be made secure against accidental falls at a time when steps are being taken to bring it down deliberately.'

24.68 It was held by the House of Lords under the old Act of 1911 (*Grant v National Coal Board* [1956] AC 649) that the protection given by the section is not confined to persons liable to be struck by a fall of roof; it also extends to consequential risks arising after the fall, such as the derailment of a bogie which struck fallen debris, as in *Grant's* case, or the blockage of a means of egress from the workings.

24.69 In *Hanks v National Coal Corpn* (1989) Times, 14 February, the Court of Appeal held that the fact that the mine manager had complied with s 49 (systematic support of roof and sides—see below) did not necessarily mean he had fulfilled his duty under s 48(1).

Other duties in relation to supports: managers, mineworkers, supervisors, inspectors

24.70 The manager of a mine is required to ensure so far as is practicable that all plant and equipment are safely installed and commissioned, and are systematically inspected, examined, tested and maintained: MASHAM, reg 11. Written reports have to be kept of such inspections or tests, recording any significant defects discovered as well as the steps taken to remedy them. Mine managers are also under a duty to ensure that adequate inspections of all parts of the mine below ground (other than shafts except in the course of being sunk) are carried out with sufficient frequency, including the support of the roof and sides of the mine (reg 12(5)).

24.71 By reg 5(3) of the MASHAM Regulations, it is the duty of every miner to deal with or to report any danger which comes to his knowledge. Duties of this kind do not, of course, mean that the whole duty of support passes to the mineworker: *Caulfield v P W Pickup Ltd* [1941] 2 All ER 510; but a breach of duty by him may amount to contributory negligence which will reduce the damages.

24.72 Those making inspections or supervising under, respectively, reg 12(1) or reg 10(2)(a) of the MASHAM Regulations (ie those performing the former deputies' functions), in carrying out inspections of their districts, are specially required to ensure 'to the best of his ability' that the Support Rules have been complied with and that all necessary additional supports are set (s 53).

Shafts and entrances to workings

24.73 An unsafe shaft, like an unsafe roof, might give rise to an action at common law, subject to negligence being proved or inferred: *Brydon v Stewart* (1855) 2 Macq 30. By s 30(1) of the Mines and Quarries Act 1954:

> 'Every mine shaft and staple-pit shall, save in so far as the natural conditions of the strata through which it passes render it unnecessary ... be made secure, and kept secure.'

24.74 It is a defence in a prosecution—but not in a civil action—to show that the insecure place was not in use and was not the site of shaft-driving operations (s 30(1), proviso). Security includes danger from things in the airspace of shafts, such as scaffolding and falling materials: *Coll v Cementation Co Ltd and National Coal Board* 1963 SLT 105. By s 30(2), the same requirements extend to an 'unwalkable outlet' at a mine, ie an outlet from the mine which is too steep to 'walk up with reasonable convenience' (see s 182(1)). A shaft is defined, by s 182(1), as a shaft of which the top 'is, or is intended to be, at the surface'; and a staple-pit includes a 'winze' (a ventilating shaft between two levels).[1]

---

1   A staple-pit is a shaft which does not come out on the surface, but at an underground level. The definition makes it clear that such shafts are included though not used for the movement of men or material. Of course a ventilating shaft may be an escape route.

24.75 The Mines (Shafts and Winding) Regulations 1993, SI 1993/302 replace (among other provisions) the former Mines and Quarries Act 1954, s 31 which dealt with mine entrances. They apply to all mines from 1 April 1993 save for tin mines, to which they apply from 1 January 1996. The owner has the duty, so far as is reasonably practicable, to ensure that the requirements and prohibitions of the regulations are complied with by those to whom they apply (reg 19). The owner also has the duty to plan and execute shaft sinking to be as safe as reasonably practicable (reg 4) (and detailed guidance in the accompanying ACOP, paras 13–40). The owner must ensure, so far as is reasonably practicable, that each shaft is equipped to be safe to use and provided with suitable winding apparatus; the manager must, so far as is reasonably practicable, maintain the shaft and appoint competent people to inspect, examine and report on it (reg 5). The manager must also ensure, so far as is reasonably practicable, that the shaft and fixtures are used safely (reg 6); that sufficient suitable safety harnesses with sufficient anchorages are available for people in the shaft and the latter must use them (reg 7); and that no one remains in uncovered space at the bottom of a shaft unless working with suitable safety precautions (reg 8).

24.76 By reg 9 the manager 'shall ensure' (*not* so far as is reasonably practicable, it is to be noted) that there is a suitable barrier at each shaft entrance. This provision is much less detailed then the former s 31 of the Mines and Quarries Act 1954 which provided, in summary, that the surface entrance to a mine shaft and all other entrances to it, and all entrances to a staple-pit, must be provided with an enclosure or barrier to prevent persons from accidentally falling down the shaft or coming into contact with a moving part of the winding apparatus. This also applies to the superstructure of the shaft, and to disused shafts, except at a mine which has been abandoned or not worked for 12 months (such mines have to be fenced under s 151). The enclosure or barrier is not to be removed or opened except as necessary for the proper use of the shaft or for doing work upon it (s 31(2)). Notwithstanding the judicial review decision *R v Secretary of State for Employment, ex p NACODS* (see para 24.06, above), it must be the case that, in accordance with the HSWA 1974, s 1(2), reg 9 of the regulations was 'designed to maintain or improve the standards of ... safety established by ... [s 31 of the 1954 Act]'. Accordingly reg 9 should, it is submitted, be so construed as to give effect to that design.[1] So the cases decided under s 31 should continue to apply. Thus it probably remains the law that to keep the barrier 'somewhat securely' in position is insufficient compliance: *Sowter v Steel Barrel Co Ltd* [1935] All ER Rep 231; *Chasteney v Michael Nairn & Co Ltd* [1937] 1 All ER 376; and see *John Summers & Sons Ltd v Frost* [1955] AC 740. Likewise, the regulation is unlikely to extend protection to a person falling from the cage since the purpose of the protection is to protect against falls from the shaft entrance: *Rodgers v National Coal Board* [1966] 3 All ER 124.

1   This view gains (some) support from the ACOP (paras 66, 67).

24.77 By reg 8 of the Mines (Safety of Exit) Regulations 1988 (replacing s 33 of the Mines and Quarries Act) there must be a barrier or enclosure to prevent access to any part of the mine where it is not for the time being safe to work, or pass through.

Second shaft and two exits in all mines

24.78 The Mines (Safety of Exit) Regulations 1988, SI 1988/1729, replaced various sections in the Mines and Quarries Act concerning safe exit from the mine and from the various underground workings. They came into force on 1 April 1989 for coal mines (including stratified ironstone, shale and fireclay) and for all *new* mines from that date; and to pre-existing miscellaneous mines from 1 April 1994. Regulation 9 (which relates to ventilation) also applies from that date, for all mines.

24.79 The Regulations apply underground at all types of mine: but the main requirements are (regs 3, 5, 7) that there shall be a minimum of two alternative shafts and two alternative ways of escape from every place of work do not apply to sinking a shaft or exploratory operations or the driving of an outlet other than a shaft if no more than 30 men are at risk (reg 2). A shaft is defined to include a staple-pit, raise, winze or similar excavation sunk or in the course of being sunk: and the vertical continuation of the shaft above ground is deemed to be underground so as to bring it within the regulations (reg 1(2)).

24.80 By reg 3(1), every mine must have a least two shafts, with two separate exits to the surface, and so situated that an accident to one shaft will not affect the other. If constructed after 1 April 1989, they must be at least 15 metres apart. By reg 3(2) the manager must ensure that so far as reasonably practicable at least two exits are *kept available* when anyone is below ground. If, due to planned maintenance, one exit only is in use, only safety and maintenance staff are allowed below ground (reg 3(6)). There must also be a plan for emergencies when only one exit becomes available, and in that event no one must be underground except safety and maintenance men and workers staying to finish their shift; an emergency has to be notified to the mines inspector who may require even safety and maintenance men to be withdrawn (reg 3(3)–(5)).

24.81 By reg 7 of the 1988 Regulations, the manager has to ensure that from 'every place where any person works' there are two different ways, each entirely separate and leading to different exits from the mine. These ways must be marked to show which shaft they lead to, and workers must be made familiar with both ways. Regulation 7(4) allows exceptions:

(1)
   (a)   at a heading or other place where not more than nine persons work (with up to three more temporarily);
   (b)   at a heading where not more than 18 work, if the working face is not wider than the approach;
(2)   if separate exits are 'not reasonably practicable';
(3)   where there are 'special' and 'suitable' arrangements for safe exit without relying on two escape routes.

Cross access between shafts

24.82 By reg 5, there must be access (by road, ladder or stairway) from every landing on a shaft or outlet to an alternative exit.

Winding apparatus

24.83 As noted above, reg 5(2) of the Mines (Shafts and Winding) Regulations 1993, SI 1993/302 requires the owner to provide suitable winding apparatus in shafts, reg 5(3) requires the manager to provide for its inspection and maintenance, and reg 6 requires the manager to ensure, so far as is reasonably practicable, safe usage of the shaft. These provisions substitute for s 28 of the Mines and Quarries Act 1954 in relation to inshafts but s 28 is left in place in relation to unwalkable outlets. As to the maintenance and operation of the winding gear, see para 24.120ff, below.

24.84 By s 28(1), every unwalkable outlet provided as a means of ingress or egress, at a mine of coal, stratified ironstone, shale or fireclay, must be provided with apparatus for carrying persons between the surface entrance and the various entrances to the workings. The apparatus must comply with requirements laid down in regulations. The regulations now in force are the Coal and Other Mines (Shafts, Outlets and Roads) Regulations 1960, SI 1960/69, Part XI, regs 65–70 and the Mines (Shafts and Winding) Regulations 1993, SI 1993/302.[1]

[1]   The Regulations provide inter alia for mechanically-operated apparatus where the vertical depth exceeds 150 feet, automatic precautions against overwinding, adequate brakes, and automatic indicator showing the position of each cage in the shaft, guides for the cage, regular maintenance of winding ropes, and covering the top of the cage where used for carrying persons; also regular examination and maintenance of both shaft and apparatus. 'Overwinding' means raising or lowering the cage too fast so that, for instance, it overturns at the top or lands at the bottom violently.

24.85 Section 28(2) similarly requires permanent apparatus to be provided in the unwalkable outlets at mines other than those mentioned above: but this does not apply unless the distance from the top of the outlet to the lowest entrance exceeds 45 metres[1] and in any case exemptions may be granted in the case of mines within this subsection.

[1]   Substituted by SI 1976/2063 unless shaft sunk before 1 February 1977.

24.86 By s 28(3), apparatus provided under both these subsections must 'be properly maintained, and, when not in use, kept constantly available for use'. This does not mean that workmen may go up and down whenever they please; they must conform to the rules of the mine: *Herd v Weardale Steel, Coal and Coke Co Ltd* [1915] AC 67.

24.87 Under reg 4 of the Mines (Safety of Exit) Regulations 1988, auxiliary apparatus and equipment must be provided and kept available to enable those below ground to reach the surface, and the miners must be trained to use such equipment. Auxiliary equipment, unlike the normal winding machinery, may be gravity-operated.

24.88 The manager is also under a specific duty to ensure the safety 'so far as reasonably practicable' of anyone who is endangered when the winding apparatus is put out of use or breaks down, particularly those travelling in a cage at the time of a breakdown.

These requirements replace s 29 of the Act and the Mines (Emergency Egress) Regulations 1973.[1]

[1] Except regs 5 and 6 of 1973 Regulations, which are re-worded by the 1988 Regulations and allow the use of gravity-operated apparatus when authorised by reg 4 of the 1988 Regulations.

Shafts in the course of being sunk

24.89 As noted above, reg 4 of the Mines (Shafts and Winding) Regulations 1993, SI 1993/302, imposes on the mine owner the duty to plan and execute the sinking of a shaft so as to be as safe as reasonably practicable (amplified in the accompanying ACOP, paras 13–40). These provisions are in substitution to Part XII of the Coal and Other Mines (Shafts, Outlets and Roads) Regulations 1960 which was revoked by the 1993 Regulations. As submitted earlier, since the HSWA 1974, s 1(2) requires substituting regulations to be 'designed to maintain or improve' the standards of the earlier legislation, the detailed requirements of the 1960 Regulations must be taken to be comprehended in the broad duty found in reg 4 of the 1993 Regulations. Thus reference must be made to the earlier provisions in an appropriate case, though space does not permit a summary of revoked provisions here. It is considered that *R v Secretary of State for Employment, ex p NACODS* (see para 24.06, above) does not contradict this approach since, in the context of a personal injury case, it will be the defendant who cannot be heard to argue that the 1993 Regulations were designed to diminish some obligation in the 1960 Regulations.

Ventilation

24.90 By s 55(1) it is the duty of the manager of every mine:

'to take such steps as are necessary for securing that there is constantly produced in all parts of the mine below ground ventilation adequate for the following purposes namely—
(a)   diluting gases that are inflammable or noxious so as to render them harmless and removing them; and
(b)   providing air containing a sufficiency of oxygen.'

The words 'necessary' and 'securing' make it clear that this is an absolute obligation which applies to all mines: and although the duty is imposed on the manager,[1] the owners are responsible in a civil action under s 159.

1   A personal and not merely a vicarious liability: *McCarthy v Lewis* [1957] 1 All ER 556 (a case under the earlier equivalent provision, the Coal Mines Act 1911, s 29(1)).

24.91 Without prejudice to the generality of s 55(1), there must not be a greater percentage of carbon dioxide in the air (by volume) than 1¼%, and the air must contain at least 19% of oxygen: see s 55(2). By s 55(3), the manager must aim, as far as possible, at reasonable working conditions as regards temperature, humidity and freedom from dust. By s 55(4), ventilation is not required in a part of the mine which is stopped up, or in any waste: but by s 56 precautions must be taken (by ventilation or other means) to prevent any dangerous emission of noxious or inflammable gas from any waste which has not been stopped off or stowed up.[1]

1   Since there is no duty to ventilate the waste itself, there was no liability when miners went into the waste to smoke and caused an explosion of firedamp gas: *Kirby v National Coal Board* 1959 SLT 7.

24.92 The obligation under the section is to keep up a continuous flow of ventilation, even on Sundays or other days when no work is in progress: *Knowles v Dickinson* (1860) 2 E & E 705. The main purpose is to disperse 'inflammable' gases, such as firedamp, with the consequent risk of explosion. But a further object is to keep down other 'noxious' gases, ie poisonous ones such as carbon monoxide.

24.93 By s 55(5), if the ventilation breaks down in any part of the mine, access must be restricted, and no one may enter except for restoring the ventilation or in case of emergency.

24.94 Section 58 requires mechanical apparatus to be maintained at the surface, capable of giving full ventilation to the mine, unless adequate ventilation is produced wholly by natural means, or unless the mine is exempted by regulations. The apparatus must be capable of reversing the direction of the air-flow. The use of a fire to assist ventilation in a mine is forbidden: so, too, is the use of compressed air to dilute gas, except with the consent of an inspector.

24.95 Where (in a mine of coal, stratified ironstone, shale or fireclay) there are two passages, of which one has been constructed after the commencement of the Act, it is not permissible to use one of the passages as an intake airway and the other as a return airway if there is any appreciable leakage of air between them: see s 59. This does not apply to parts of passages within a reasonable distance (usually 150 metres)[1] from the working face served by the airway.

1 Substituted by SI 1976/2063 which also substitutes metric measurements in the Coal and Other Mines (Ventilation) Regulations 1956.

24.96 Under reg 9 of the Mines (Safety of Exit) Regulations 1988 not more than 50 persons may be employed in any part of a mine (excluding those moving on a change of shift) unless there are two separate airways, such that fire and smoke cannot pass from one to the other, or one fire-resistant intake free as far as reasonably practicable from fire risk.

24.97 The Coal and Other Mines (Ventilation) Regulations 1956, SI 1956/1764, contain further detailed provisions with regard to keeping intake airways free from firedamp (inflammable gas), making regular checks of firedamp content in the air, and detection of firedamp by various means (including issue of safety lamps or other firedamp detectors to the miners), management of fans and other machinery for ventilation, and the prevention of air leakages by means of air-locks, ventilation doors and ventilation sheets. The ventilation doors and sheets are to prevent leakage of air between the intake and return airways which would short-circuit the ventilation flow.

24.98 The Coal Mines (Firedamp Drainage) Regulations 1960, SI 1960/1015, as amended regulate the precautions to be taken when firedamp gas is collected in an undiluted state by means of boreholes and pipes to be removed from the mine. The precautions laid down are intended to prevent accidental ignition of the gas and also contamination of the ventilation system of the mine.

Lighting, safety lamps and contraband

24.99 Under s 61, there is a general duty to provide 'suitable and sufficient lighting' in all parts of a mine (above or below ground) where 'persons work or normally pass', taking into account the lamps normally carried by those persons. This does not apply in places below ground where 'artificial lighting is inadvisable for reasons of safety'. All lighting installations must be 'properly maintained'. The use of electricity is now controlled by the Electricity at Work Regulations 1989.[1]

1 As amended by the Equipment and Protective Systems Intended for Use in Potentially Explosive Atmospheres Regulations 1996, SI 1996/192; the Quarries Regulations 1999, SI 1999/2024 and SI 1999/2550; and the Equipment and Protective Systems Intended for Use in Potentially Explosive Atmospheres (Amendment) Regulations 2005, SI 2005/830 which increased the level of penalties for breach of the Regulations.

24.100 There are certain mines (conveniently known as 'safety-lamp mines') where, under s 62, no lamps or lights must be used except 'permitted lights', ie as defined in s 182(1), locked safety lamps or other means of lighting which comply with the Electricity at Work Regulations 1989, reg 19(2)(a)–(d).

24.101 Section 62 applies to the following classes of mines:

(1)   coal mines (in the strict sense) opened on or after the date of commencement of the Act;

(2)   mines of any kind which were 'safety-lamp' mines—ie where safety lamps were obligatory in the absence of a special exemption—under the previous Acts;

(3)   mines of any kind where locked safety lamps were in fact in use— except as a temporary precaution—immediately before the commencement of the Act;

(4)   other mines opened before the Act and any mine opened after it, where an explosion or fire has been caused by inflammable gas naturally present, or locked safety lamps have been introduced except as a temporary measure.

Once a mine has become a safety-lamp mine, it does not lose its character unless special exemption is given by the inspector under s 62(5).

24.102 The construction and use of safety lamps is controlled by regulations (made under the now repealed s 63) and safety lamps must not be used unless provided by the owner and of a type which conforms to reg 19 of the Electricity at Work Regulations 1989 (s 64).[1] It is an offence under s 65 for a person to damage, destroy or lose a safety lamp issued to him, or to tamper with it.

1   The Coal and Other Mines (Ventilation) Order 1956, SI 1956/1764 and the Coal and Other Mines (Safety Lamps and Lighting) Order 1956, SI 1956/1765 (as amended by the Management and Administration of Safety and Health at Mines Regulations 1993) regulate the inspection and maintenance of safety lamps and other firedamp detectors (Sch 1, paras 2–6); the careful handling of safety lamps by the miners (Sch 1, paras 7–11); method of re-lighting safety lamps underground (Sch 1, paras 12–16); the lighting of entrances to shafts and other important points in the mine, especially where vehicles are handled (Sch 1, para 17); the use of electricity for lighting, subject to safeguards, in well-ventilated places at a safe distance from the working face (Sch 1, paras 18–20); the keeping of emergency lamps in places having general lighting (Sch 1, paras 21 and 22); and the whitening of the roof and sides at the places where general lighting is required by reg 17 (Sch 1, para 23). Paragraphs 4, 18, 18A and 19 were superseded and revoked by the Electricity at Work Regulations. Section 63 is repealed as being superseded by the general power to make regulations under the HSWA 1974.

24.103 It is also an offence to take or to have below ground, in a safety-lamp mine or a safety-lamp part of a mine, matches, lighters or smoking materials (s 66) or any article capable of producing an unprotected flame or spark (s 67).[1] In *Kirby v National Coal Board* 1959 SLT 7 the employers were held not liable for an explosion caused by employees who were smoking contrary to the Act of 1911. It is to be noted, however, that the smoking took place in a part of the waste where the men had gone for a quiet smoke, and the act was clearly outside the course of their employment.

1   See also the Mines (Manner of Search for Smoking Materials) Order 1956, SI 1956/2016.

Dust suppression

24.104 By s 74(1), it is the duty of the manager of every mine:

'to ensure that, in connection with the getting, dressing and transporting of minerals below ground in the mine, the giving off of—
(a)   any dust that is inflammable; and
(b)   in the case of a mine of coal dust of such character and in such quantity as to be likely to be injurious to the persons employed;

is minimised.'

This section is clearly directed against two distinct dangers: dust which may catch fire or explode, and dust which may cause injury or disease such as silicosis.

24.105 Section 74(2) deals with cases where an operation or process, either below ground or on the surface, gives rise to inflammable or injurious dust, and requires that measures shall be taken:

(1)   to intercept the dust as near as possible to its point of origin;
(2)   to trap or disperse dust which is not intercepted;
(3)   to clean up or render harmless accumulations of dust which cannot be prevented.

24.106 The Coal Mines (Precautions against Inflammable Dust) Order 1956, SI 1956/1769, and the Coal Mines (Respirable Dust) Regulations, below, contain a number of additional requirements which apply only to coal mines in a strict sense. Coal dust from the screens on the surface must be kept from entering downcast shafts (Sch 1, paras 2 and 3) unless the mine is naturally wet throughout (Sch 1, para 1). On underground roads, except within 30 feet of the working face or in anthracite workings, a proportion of incombustible matter, such as fine dust, must be added to the coal dust (Sch 1, paras 4–9). (There is an approved method of consolidating dust on the floor of a road by adding stone dust and calcium chloride and spraying the mixture.) Where a vehicle carries a load of coal dust along a road where there is electrical apparatus, the material must be enclosed to prevent the dust being thrown into the air if the vehicle is upset (Sch 1, para 10). By para 10A (added by the amending regulations) barriers of stone dust may have to be set up against the spread of fire in certain areas. The areas in question are those which include a length of road where coal conveyors are in use and which are exposed to the spread of flame by ignition of gas or coal dust at the coal face or some other point of danger.

24.107 The Coal Mines (Respirable Dust) Regulations 1975, SI 1975/1433, and the Mines (Substances Hazardous to Health) Regulations 1996, SI 1996/2001, require periodical samples to be taken in areas underground where harmful dust is likely to be present, also dust suppression schemes and medical checks of persons at risk. The risk visualised by these Regulations is, of course, damage to the lungs, in particular pneumoconiosis.[1]

---

[1]   Note the Control of Substances Hazardous to Health Regulations 2002 only apply to mines in so far as the 1975 Regulations do not apply: see reg 5.

Roads and transport

24.108 The main regulation on roads in a mine is now reg 6 of the Mines (Safety of Exit) Regulations 1988, SI 1988/1729. Under this, the manager must ensure that every road which persons walk along to or from a place of work must be: (a) suitably constructed and maintained as a walkway; (b) safe to walk along and normally not less than 1.7 metres high; and (c) kept free from obstructions. Exemptions may be granted under reg 10, subject to conditions to ensure safety.

24.109 Under the previous legislation—s 34 of the Act, repealed by the Regulations—a damaged tram, which was being taken along a haulage road and was involved in a collision, was held not to be an 'obstruction' under similar wording of the Act of 1911, collisions being more properly a matter for traffic rules: *Alexander v Tredegar Iron and Coal Co Ltd* [1945] AC 286. In general, things which form part of the equipment of the mine (and are in the place where they would normally be) are not 'obstructions' though out of use at the time: *Cook v National Coal Board* [1961] 3 All ER 220 (wire rope above rails, used for hauling tubs on other shifts); nor is material stacked in a reasonable position ready for use: *Jennings v National Coal Board* [1983] ICR 636. There is no 'obstruction' where a man is impeded in crossing from one side of a road to another as distinct from passing along: *Kerr v National Coal Board* 1968 SLT 49. As to the road itself, the essential requirement is a clear safe passage along some part of it. Given this, the old section was not contravened by unsatisfactory conditions in another part, such as uneven ballast between rails (*Wilson v National Coal Board* 1966 SLT 221) or a narrow and obstructed space on the opposite side of a conveyor: *Kerr v National Coal Board*, above. Where a transformer in a temporary position partly blocked the way, it was not an obstruction, but because the narrow passage left was uneven, with rails, cross-pieces and a sharp drop at the side, it was 'unsafe to tread' in breach of the section: *Malone v National Coal Board* 1972 SLT (Notes) 55.

24.110 Like the former s 48 (security of the roof), reg 6 specifically makes the manager responsible and if he has taken all possible measures to inspect and clear the road there is no liability, for instance if there is a stone on the road within one hour after inspection: *Connolly v National Coal Board* 1979 SLT 51.

24.111 References to height[1] in s 34 were held to relate only to the structure of the road itself and had nothing to do with the lay-out of conveyors or other equipment which may reduce height at particular points: *Lister v National Coal Board* [1970] 1 QB 228.

---

[1] Section 35 and the Coal and Other Mines (Height of Travelling Roads) Regulations 1956, which formerly regulated height, were repealed by the 1988 Regulations.

24.112 Regulation 6 also requires that all ladderways or stairways shall be so constructed, installed and maintained that they can be used safely.

24.113 Section 36(1) contains a general prohibition of the running of vehicles or conveyors in any length or road where they or their loads (or their haulage ropes, if any) may rub against the roof or sides or supports of anything else. Section 36(2) affords some special defences which apply only in a criminal prosecution.

24.114 In general, the safe operation of vehicles and conveyors in a mine is, under s 37, to be governed by special 'Transport Rules' made by the manager of the mine. It is the duty of the manager to see that the rules are complied with. This means that the rules must not only be publicised but effectively enforced, by penalties where necessary: so where there were merely trivial and occasional fines for riding on conveyors, and the practice continued, there was a breach of the section: *Storey v National Coal Board* [1983] ICR 156. The rules must, in particular, specify the standard height and width of roads used by vehicles and conveyors, specify maximum loads and speeds of vehicles, and restrict or control the carriage of persons on vehicles or conveyors.

24.115 Section 39 applies to every length of road used for the running of vehicles (unless moved by hand or by animals).[1] The use of these roads by persons on foot is forbidden, except when the movement of the vehicles is 'specially stopped' to allow such use: and where the road is used by not fewer than ten persons at the beginning and end of their shift, periods must be fixed when the traffic is stopped to allow them to move in safety. By s 39(3), certain 'authorised persons' are allowed to enter roads when vehicles are running, eg officials of the mine and persons engaged in running the vehicles or in repair or inspections. But no person must accompany, on foot, a vehicle moved by rope haulage apparatus, unless authorised by regulations or by the manager (in writing): instructions by a subordinate official will not do: *Puller v National Coal Board* 1969 SLT (Notes) 62. A further requirement for roads where vehicles run is that (subject to exemptions) refuge holes shall be provided at intervals and places prescribed by regulations, and shall be kept free from obstruction: see s 40.

1 Ie it applies—like s 43 of the Act of 1911—where vehicles are moved by mechanical power or by gravity.

24.116 By s 41, automatic safety devices must be provided to prevent accidents caused by vehicles running away: and precautions must be taken to protect persons at work against such accidents. This means vehicles running away by accident, and does not include trams running free as intended: *Jones v National Coal Board* [1965] 1 All ER 221. The section does not impose an absolute duty to provide brakes which will never fail: *Brandreth v John G Stein & Co Ltd* 1966 SLT (Notes) 87. Faulty construction or maintenance may be a breach of the Provision and Use of Work Equipment Regulations 1998.

24.117 Further rules for safe movement in transport roads are contained in Part X (regs 57–64) of the Coal and Other Mines (Shafts, Outlets and Roads)

Regulations 1960, SI 1960/69. Regulation 57 grants an exemption from s 39(1)(a)—and therefore allows persons to move on foot along transport roads—in the following cases:

(1)   where there is a continuous clearance of 600 mm between vehicles and the road side and the maximum speed does not exceed 4.5 metres per second;

(2)   on certain roads of low gradient in mines opened before the Act of 1911 came into force (1 July 1912) where maximum speed does not exceed 1.4 metres per second.

24.118 A clearance of 600 mm must be maintained between vehicles and road side at coupling places (reg 58).[1] Refuge holes must be at intervals varying from 30 feet to 60 feet (or, in the case of roads used by locomotives, 20 to 90 metres) according to the gradient and curve of the road and the nature and speed of the traffic. By regs 60–62, a train for carrying persons must be under the charge of a competent person; and no person is allowed to ride on a haulage rope, or to ride on vehicles moving faster than 1.4 metres per second for the purpose of attaching or detaching them from the rope. Except on a low gradient, a person moving a vehicle by hand down a slope is forbidden by reg 63 to go in front; and movement by hand down a slope is forbidden unless the vehicle can be properly controlled from behind. By reg 64, sprags, stop-blocks and similar contrivances must be provided to prevent accidents from runaway vehicles, especially on inclines, and means must be provided in certain cases to prevent accidental disconnection of vehicles from trains on which persons are carried. Regulation 64 does not affect the more general requirements of s 41 of the Act.

1   Details of clearances required at the sides of roads where conveyors or rail vehicles run are set out in the Coal Mines (Clearances in Transport Roads) Regulations 1959, SI 1959/1217. As might be expected, they vary according to the type of traffic in use, are wider at boarding points and working places, and may be narrower in unsettled ground near the working face. Regulation 58 of the Coal and Other Mines (Shafts, Outlets and Roads) Regulations 1960 does not apply where the Coal Mines (Clearances in Transport Roads) Regulations 1959 apply.

24.119 There is also the Coal and Other Mines (Sidings) Order 1956, SI 1956/1773, which was largely repealed by the Railway Safety (Miscellaneous Provisions) Regulations 1997, SI 1997/553 which applies to railways above ground deemed to be part of the mine with a gauge of not less than 1.432 metres.

Operation of winding and haulage apparatus[1]

24.120 'Winding apparatus' is used in a shaft, 'rope haulage apparatus' is used in an unwalkable outlet. The relevant sections of the Mines and Quarries Act 1954 have been modified in relation to shafts by the Mines (Shafts and Winding) Regulations 1993, SI 1993/302. Where winding or rope haulage apparatus is provided to carry persons, either through a mine shaft or elsewhere in a mine, and is operated by mechanical power or by gravity, it must be operated by a competent person of at least 22 years of age (s 42(1)).

A person appointed under this section must be in constant attendance so long as persons are employed below ground at a mine where access is gained through a shaft or unwalkable outlet by means of winding or rope haulage apparatus; and in the case of a coal mine such a person is not to be on duty for more than eight hours in a day. Where persons are not carried in winding or haulage apparatus, the apparatus must still, under s 43, be operated by a competent person not less than 18:[2] similarly, under s 44, a conveyor operated along a working face in a mine must be worked by a competent person of not less than 18.

[1]   In the earlier days of mining there were many serious accidents involving pit cages: *Bartonshill Coal Co v Reid* (1858) 3 Macq 266 where the cage was upset at the top due to over winding, is an example. The regulations are now strictly complied with, and accidents are rare. When they do occur, they are serious, and there is likely to be a public enquiry, after which liability may well be admitted. It is therefore unlikely that questions of liability in this type of case will come before the courts. In an accident in 1957, 28 men were injured when a cage landed too fast, and the inspector drew attention to the increased risks with bigger mines and deeper shafts. Yet in 1973 at Markham Colliery, Derbyshire, 18 men were killed when the cage plunged to the pit bottom; and more recent disasters in the South African gold mines demonstrate the need for strict legislation strictly enforced. Happily the use of other devices for taking miners below the surface, such as the extremely dangerous man-riding ladders of the West Cornwall tin mines, is a thing of the past.

[2]   Until 1 January 1996 the age limit was 21 for winding apparatus in the shaft of a tin mine.

24.121   There must be a proper signalling system in all shafts (reg 14: duty on owner to provide and manager to use) and unwalkable outlets (s 45) extending to the surface exits and underground entrances at all stages, unless the maximum distance involved is 15 metres or less. Regulation 14 is considerably less detailed than s 45[1] though it is amplified by the accompanying ACOP (paras 135–149). As in the replacement of the Act by recent regulations mentioned elsewhere in this book, it is submitted that the standards of the Regulations cannot be held to be designed to do other than maintain the standards of the Act as provided for by the HSWA 1974, s 1(2): *R v Secretary of State for Employment, ex p NACODS* (see para 24.06, above) is not a contrary authority. A signalling system is also required (s 46) for lengths of road exceeding 25 metres where rope haulage apparatus or conveyors may be operated.

[1]   Which continued to apply to tin mine shafts until 1 January 1996.

24.122   The Coal and Other Mines (Shafts, Outlets and Roads) Regulations 1960, SI 1960/69, contain extensive requirements for the construction, maintenance and operation of rope haulage apparatus in unwalkable outlets. In so far as these Regulations applied to shafts they are revoked by the Mines (Shafts and Winding) Regulations 1993 in relation to tin mines from 1 January 1996 and all other mines from 1 April 1993. The 1993 Regulations set out less detailed provision though amplified by the accompanying ACOP. The 1960 Regulations in relation to unwalkable outlets are dealt with first below.

24.123   The primary extant provisions of the Coal and Other Mines (Shafts, Outlets and Roads) Regulations 1960 in relation to haulage apparatus in unwalkable outlets are as follows. In general, where the depth exceeds 45 metres and more than 30 persons are employed underground, the apparatus must be mechanically operated (reg 6) from a fixed engine (reg 7) separated from any other engine or apparatus. Where the apparatus comprises a drum shaft, this must be bored longitudinally at the centre unless its diameter is less than 254mm (reg 8) and provided with flanges and other devices to prevent the rope slipping off (reg 10). There must be brakes on the drum, an indicator showing the position of each cage, and a locking device on the drum capable of holding a loaded cage in position (reg 9). There must be automatic protection against over winding, ie against the cage descending too fast and striking the bottom violently or ascending too fast with the risk of overturning (reg 11); and the automatic contrivance must be engaged before anyone is permitted to enter the cage (reg 53). Cages for carrying persons—except in the sinking, inspection or repair of an outlet—must be covered on top and at the two sides and have gates at the two ends (reg 12). Haulage ropes must not be spliced ropes, nor must they be used for more than three and a half years (reg 17) and there are special provisions for capping and re-capping of winding ropes (Part XI, regs 65–70). All the apparatus must be inspected regularly (reg 19).

24.124 There is also a signalling code in Part VIII (regs 46–50) for outlets and roads, which includes, in this context, unwalkable outlets.

24.125 In unwalkable outlets, the engineman must remain at the controls when the apparatus is in motion or where anyone is believed to be in a cage, carriage or kibble (reg 20). He must inspect the apparatus, see that it is cleaned and oiled, carry out periodical checks by raising and lowering it without passengers (regs 21, 22) and must not allow unauthorised persons to operate it (reg 23).

24.126 Other miscellaneous rules are as follows: minerals and other loads must not, in general, be carried through an unwalkable outlet while persons are being carried through it, unless the outlet is divided by a substantial partition (reg 51); the maximum number of persons to be carried in a cage or carriage must be fixed, and displayed on a notice (reg 52). A cage must not be signalled away till the gates are closed (reg 54) and barriers at an entrance must not be removed until the cage is stationary opposite the entrance (reg 55). Where a cage or carriage having more than one deck is to be raised, the top deck must be loaded first (reg 56).

24.127 So far as shafts are concerned, the above regulations are substituted by the Mines (Shafts and Winding) Regulations 1993, SI 1993/302.[1] The 1993 Regulations also revoke completely a number of the 1960 Regulations as well as revoking others only so far as they apply to shafts. In either case, as indicated above, it is submitted that since the HSWA 1974 (which is the authority for the 1993 Regulations) requires regulations (by s 1(2)) to be designed to maintain the standards of the previous legislation, the much less detailed provisions of the 1993 Regulations (though amplified in the accompanying ACOP) cannot be construed so as to diminish a (revoked) 1960 regulation so that those regulations (both those which are wholly and those which are partially revoked) must be borne in mind when considering the 1993 Regulations. *R v Secretary of State, ex p NACODS* (see para 24.06, above) is not, it is submitted, contrary authority.

¹ The Lifting Operations and Lifting Equipment Regulations 1998, SI 1998/2307 do not apply to mines: reg 9(5).

24.128 The primary provisions of the Mines (Shafts and Winding) Regulations 1993, SI 1993/302, in relation to winding apparatus in shafts are as follows. The owner must provide suitable winding apparatus with effective and suitable brakes, brake locking and interlocking devices, means of controlling power, means of preventing an overwind, means of preventing conveyance or counterweight excessive speed, means of stopping the conveyance or counterweight in event of overwind, means of monitoring conveyance movement (reg 10 and ACOP, paras 68–120). The owner must appoint competent persons to examine all aspects and make a report when winding apparatus is commissioned or modified, and the manager must not use such apparatus until the report says it is safe to do so (reg 11). Keps must not be installed or, if installed, not used when winding people (reg 12). The type of winding rope to be used must be specified, its life expectancy put in writing and kept in the mine office, and the winding rope must not be used after expiry of its life expectancy (reg 13 and ACOP, paras 124–134). The manager must ensure, so far as is reasonably practicable, that the winding apparatus is used safely, and must make rules for its use. The manager must also ensure that persons are not carried by winding apparatus operating automatically (reg 15). The manager must ensure (when persons are below ground) that there are sufficient competent winding engineers instructed in writing and in respect of whom maximum hours of work have been posted in the winding engine room. Winding enginemen must record their hours (reg 16, ACOP, paras 175–184). The manager must appoint sufficient competent persons regularly and adequately to examine, inspect, test and maintain the winding apparatus and report thereon (reg 17, ACOP, paras 185–210). The owner must provide suitable means of audible and visual signalling and means of communication by speech and the manager must ensure their use (reg 14 ACOP, paras 135–149) (which includes the standard code to be used). Radio must not be used except by suitable equipment and in a suitable manner (reg 15 ACOP, paras 165–166). In addition (as mentioned above), there is a signalling scheme in Part VIII, regs 46–50, of the 1960 Regulations for roads, which remains extant.

Use of engines and locomotives below ground

24.129 By s 83 of the Mines and Quarries Act 1954, internal combustion engines, steam boilers or locomotives cannot be used below ground except as authorised by regulations or with the consent of an inspector.

24.130 Where such consent has been given (see reg 34), the use of 'mechanically propelled vehicles running on rails and constructed or used for hauling other vehicles' is regulated by the Coal and Other Mines (Locomotive) Regulations 1956, SI 1956/1771.[1] They must be constructed as far as possible of non-inflammable material (inflammable components must have a metallic covering) and in such a manner that flames, sparks and hot exhaust gases are not emitted (Sch 1, reg 3).[2] They must have brakes, headlights, portable lamp, means of audible warning, speedometer and fire extinguisher (Sch 1, reg 4). There are regulations for rails, track and clearances (Sch 1, regs 6–8) and running is not allowed on a gradient exceeding 1.15 (Sch 1, reg 9). In a safety-lamp mine or part of a mine, there must be special checks of firedamp content (Sch 1, regs 11– 16). Locomotives must be driven by authorised persons only (Sch 1, reg 17) and not left unattended unless immobilised (Sch 1, reg 18). A red light must be attached at the back of the locomotive or train (Sch 1, reg 22). There are detailed provisions as to the filling of diesel engines, the handling of fuel oil and the control of exhaust gases (Sch 1, regs 25–31) and as to charging the batteries of locomotives which run on storage batteries (Sch 1, regs 32–33).

There are a number of variations in the regulations in their application to ironstone, shale and fireclay mines.

[1]   These Regulations have been partially revoked as from 1 July 2003.
[2]   By virtue of the Supply of Machinery (Safety) Regulations 1992, SI 1992/3073, reg 33, Sch 1, regs 3(1), (2)(a)–(c), (3), 4, 5(1)(a)–(g), (2), (3) of the 1956 Regulations do not apply to 'relevant machinery' within the meaning of reg 3 of the 1992 Regulations. So, in broad terms, the 1956 Regulations no longer apply to machinery first supplied or put into use after 1 January 1993, nor to machinery intended solely to carry passengers but which is being used to carry goods, nor to cableways for carriage of people.

Construction and fencing of machinery and apparatus

24.131 Sections 81 and 82 of the Mines and Quarries Act 1954 deal with the construction, maintenance and fencing of machinery and apparatus in mines and quarries. Those sections are repealed and replaced by the Provision and Use of Work Equipment Regulations 1998, SI 1998/2306 (formerly PUWER 1992) with effect from 5 December 1998. The 1998 Regulations are dealt with in chapter 20 above.

Cranes and other lifting machinery

24.132 The Lifting Operations and Lifting Equipment Regulations 1998, SI 1998/2307, repeal s 85 of the Mines and Quarries Act 1954 as regards their application to cranes and other lifting machinery. The 1998 Regulations are dealt with in chapter 20.

Steam and compressed air apparatus

24.133 By s 84(1):

'All apparatus used as, or forming, part of the equipment of a mine, being *apparatus which contains or produces air, gas or steam at a pressure greater* than atmospheric pressure shall be so constructed, installed, maintained and used as to obviate any risk from fire, bursting, explosion or collapse or the production of noxious gases.'

24.134 This, like s 81 (dealt with at para 24.131, above—though repealed—a section which applied to the air, gas and steam apparatus) is a remarkably wide and strict obligation. It includes, amongst other things, the increasingly rare steam boiler—the only apparatus of this kind mentioned in the Act of 1911—and compressed air apparatus. Under s 83, a steam boiler cannot be used below ground except with the consent of an inspector.

24.135 The Pressure Systems and Transportable Gas Containers Regulations 1989, SI 1989/2169, repealed the Coal and Other Mines (Steam Boilers) Regulations 1956 and made less comprehensive provision for regulating steam boilers. The 1989 Regulations have now been revoked by the Pressure Systems Safety Regulations 2000, SI 2000/128.

Electricity

24.136 The Electricity at Work Regulations 1989 apply to mines and quarries as well as to other places of work. The general part of these regulations is summarised at para 17.61, above. There is an ACOP specifically addressing duties in relation to mines. But there are in addition some further regulations (regs 17–28) which apply to mines alone. The defence under s 157 ('not reasonably practicable') has been in effect from 1 October 1993. The ACOP draws attention to the MASHAM Regulations (see para 24.14, above), in particular reg 6 (duty of owner to plan and lay out work), reg 7 (duty to notify HSE of mine working), and regs 27–33 (appointment of surveyor and requirements as to plans), and the MASHAM ACOP. See also the Electrical Equipment for Explosive Atmospheres (Certification) (Amendment) Regulations 1999, SI 1999/2550 which extends the reference to 'gassy mines' in order to implement Directive 98/65/EC.

24.137 First of all, under reg 3, the manager has a general duty to prevent any inrush into any working of the mine of either:

(1) gas from disused workings (which includes abandoned shafts and boreholes) whether they are mine workings or not (they could, for instance, be old canal or waterworks tunnels); or

(2) water, or material that flows or is likely to flow when wet (whatever the source).

24.138 Next, under reg 4, both the owner and manager are required to ensure that they have full information about disused workings in the vicinity, water-bearing strata and peat or other deposits liable to flow when wet.

24.139 In the particular case of workings carried on or proposed near the sea, a lake or river, or any other body of surface water, the owner and manager are both required by reg 5 to 'ascertain'—which means find out for 'certain'—the total thickness of strata between the workings and the surface water, and satisfy themselves that the strata are sufficiently reliable to prevent an inrush of water.

24.140 Special precautions are required by reg 6 before workings are carried out within 45 metres (measured in any direction) from the surface or water-bearing strata or peat or other substances likely to flow if wet, or disused workings (except mine workings). In the case of mine workings, the distance is reduced to 37 metres. In all these cases the manager must acquire sufficient information to form an opinion on whether an inrush may occur in the absence of precautionary measures. If he thinks it will not, he must notify the mines inspector 30 days in advance of working the place, but will still have to notify him again if there are signs of danger in the course of working. If he thinks special precautions are required, he must prepare a scheme for safe procedure to prevent inrushes, send a copy to the inspector and workers' representatives[1] 30 days in advance of working, and ensure that the scheme is complied with until working is completed.

[1]   The workers' representatives are, in a coal mine, those nominated by unions representing underground workers, and in other mines, s 123 inspectors, or safety representatives (under the Safety Representatives and Safety Committees' Regulations 1977, SI 1977/500); see chapter 12.

24.141 The ACOP amplifies the need for plans and recommends procedures and schemes of work to prevent inrushes. It gives particular guidance on undersea working and the appropriate use of longwall and pillar and stall working under the sea. The employer's duty to make a risk assessment is also governed by the Management of Health and Safety at Work Regulations 1999, reg 3.

The use of explosives: shotfiring

24.142 In all 'safety-lamp mines' (ie all coal mines and any other mine in which there has been a below ground fire damp explosion or more than 0.25% by volume firedamp has been found below ground: reg 2(1), below), shotfiring and explosives are governed by the Coal and Other Safety-Lamp Mines (Explosives) Regulations 1993, SI 1993/208, as amended, which revoke and replace the Coal Mines (Explosives) Regulations 1961 and the Coal Mines (Compressed Air Blasting Shells) Regulations 1960. The Stratified Ironstone, Shale and Fireclay Mines (Explosives) Regulations 1956, SI 1956/1943, as amended, now apply only to such of those mines which are not safety lamp mines and the Miscellaneous Mines (Explosives) Regulations 1959, SI 1959/2258, apply only to such mines as are neither safety lamp mines nor stratified ironstone, shale or fireclay mines.[1]

Only the 1993 Regulations can be dealt with here and then only their most salient features. An ACOP accompanies the 1993 Regulations.

1   These Regulations have been amended by the Manufacture and Storage of Explosives Regulations 2005, SI 2005/1082 which amend the definition of 'workshop' and 'explosives store'.

24.143 The manager must appoint suitably qualified and competent shotfirers and trainee shotfirers: reg 4. Approved qualifications are set out in Appendix 1 and appropriate education for shotfirers in Appendix 1, Part II. Wages must not depend on the number of shots fired or amount of mineral obtained by firing shots (reg 4(5)). Only approved materials and equipment, properly maintained, tested and stored may be used (reg 5). Appendix 2 sets out the currently approved materials and equipment. The manager must take all reasonable steps to ensure explosives and detonators are stored, handled and used safely and securely (reg 7). Persons handling explosives and detonators must handle them with care and keep them apart until used (reg 6). The manager must make rules for movement of explosives and detonators (reg 8). Explosives and detonators must be issued in a locked container (reg 9) and only a shotfirer (or other authorised person) may open such a container or have charge of it or its contents (regs 10 and 11), save that anyone finding explosives may take them to a competent person (reg 12). Regulations 13–17 deal with shotfiring procedure. Regulation 13 is particularly important in requiring the shotfirer to take all reasonable precautions to ensure the safety of persons at all stages of shotfiring. Regulations 18 and 19 require precautions to be taken against the presence of firedamp. Regulations 20–21 deal with the drilling and charging of shotholes and removal of charges. Only shotfirers may carry out shotfiring operations (reg 22). The shotfirer must identify a danger zone, so far as is reasonably practicable, examine all parts of it, and take all reasonable steps to prevent people entering it by sentries and fences (reg 23). *Jayne v National Coal Board* [1963] 2 All ER 220 is, it is submitted, still applicable (failure to make personal check was breach of reg 41 of the 1961 Regulations) even though the duty under the 1993 Regulations is the diminished 'so far as reasonably practicable'. A sentry posted under reg 23 must forbid people to enter the danger zone and stay at his post until the individual who posted him there withdraws him (reg 24) and no one shall pass such a sentry or a reg 23 fence (reg 25). Regulations 26–30 specify use of shotfiring cable, steps to be taken before shotfiring, operation of the exploder, maximum number of shots and prohibited shots. After firing, the shotfirer must examine the area after a specified minimum period of time (reg 31) and must take certain steps in the event of a misfire (reg 32).[1] The shotfirer must keep records (reg 33). It is the mine manager's duty to ensure, so far as is reasonably practicable, that everyone complies with their statutory duty (reg 38) and in respect of criminal proceedings the manager has the 'all due diligence' defence (reg 37). The HSE may grant exemptions from these Regulations.

1   There is no longer any prohibition for minimum periods in approaching misfires as under reg 62 of the 1961 Regulations and see *Costello v R Addie & Sons Collieries Ltd* [1922] 1 AC 164.

24.144 The 1993 Regulations, even with the guidance of the ACOP, are far less detailed and prescriptive than the 1961 Regulations they replaced. As argued earlier, since, by virtue of the HSWA 1974, s 1(2) it cannot be said that the later Regulations were other than 'designed to maintain or improve the standards' of the earlier Regulations, reliance may still be put on a specific provision of the earlier Regulations where the modern equivalent appears to impose a more general or weaker standard. It is submitted that *R v Secretary of State for Employment, ex p NACODS* (see para 24.06, above) is not contrary authority.

24.145 The Coal Mines (Cardrox and Hydrox) Regulations 1956, SI 1956/1942 regulate the use of cardox and hydrox shells for blasting.[1] These require special precautions in the filling of shells (normally above ground) and the provisions as to firing and taking shelter are broadly similar to those in the general regulations.

1 These are not strictly explosives but means of blasting by the expansion of gas from a liquid form. A cardox shell, for example, is a tube containing liquid carbon dioxide which, by an induced rise in temperature, is turned into gas of great expansive force.

Structures and means of access on the surface

24.146 Section 86 of the Act contains the following wide and general direction:

'All buildings and structures on the surface of a mine shall be kept in safe condition.'

24.147 Section 87(1), which is evidently based on the Factories Act 1937, s 26(1), provides as follows:

'There shall be provided and maintained safe means of access to every place in or on a building or structure on the surface of a mine, being a place at which any person has at any time to work.'

24.148 Section 87(2) similarly follows the former Factories Act, s 26(2):

'Where a person is to work at any such place as aforesaid from which he will be liable to fall a distance of more than two metres, then, unless the place is one which affords secure foothold and, where necessary, secure handhold, means shall be provided by fencing or otherwise for ensuring his safety.'

24.149 Some of the decisions under the Factories Act (now s 29 of 1961) will be material in applying these sections: but the wording of s 87 is different in material respects. For instance, it does not apply to a place which is neither 'in' nor 'on' a building or structure; and it is an absolute obligation, breach of which cannot be excused in a civil action except upon proof of 'impracticability' under s 157. Section 29 of the Factories Act 1961 has been repealed and replaced by the Workplace (Health, Safety and Welfare) Regulations 1992 (see chapter 18). Section 87 of the Mines and Quarries Act 1954 is not so affected and those Regulations do not apply to mines and quarries.

24.150   Mines and quarries

'Workmen's inspectors'

24.150 The provisions as to inspections of the mine are of fundamental importance; far more so than were the requirements in the Factories Act for the inspection of machinery, because of the changing conditions underground.

24.151 The Coal and Other Mines (Managers and Officials) Regulations 1956 provided for pre-shift and other inspections by deputies. The deputy's job is now history, reg 12 of the MASHAM Regulations having substituted for the extensive inspection duties of the deputy under the 1956 Regulations and the whole 1956 Regulations being revoked by reg 43(1) of, and Sch 5 to, the MASHAM Regulations, while reg 43(2) and Sch 6 remove the deputy's inspection role from all other legislation. The current inspection requirement under reg 12 of the MASHAM Regulations is dealt with at para 24.22, above.

24.152 The Mines and Quarries Act 1954 also provided by s 123 for inspections by workmen's inspectors, a provision with a long history. This section has not been repealed. The workmen's inspectors are popularly known as 's 123 inspectors'.

24.153 A trade union or other association or body representing the majority of the total number of persons employed at a mine or quarry may appoint a panel of persons of not less than five years' practical mining experience as s 123 inspectors. If no union or body has a majority then the panel is appointed jointly who together have the majority.

24.154 The owner must permit two s 123 inspectors (only one of whom must be employed at the mine or quarry) to inspect every part of the mine or quarry and all the equipment twice a month, and also the site of any accident or reportable occurrence (see the RIDDOR Regulations, above) and anything else for the purpose of ascertaining the cause. They may inspect documents and be accompanied by experts. They must be informed of occurrences tending to show a potential inrush: Mines (Precautions Against Inrushes) Regulations 1979, SI 1979/318, reg 6.

24.155 Section 123 does not preclude collective agreement being made between owner and union(s) but any such agreement may not abridge the rights conferred by the section.

24.156 When carrying out an inspection, s 123 inspectors are owed a duty by all persons employed at the mine or quarry to provide facilities and assistance within their responsibilities and the manager must provide all information in relation to workings proposed to be carried on.

24.157 After making an inspection the s 123 inspectors must make and sign a report in a book provided by the owner, a copy must be posted for 24 hours, and a copy sent to the HSE.

24.158 Section 123 inspectors whilst inspecting are not fulfilling obligations to the owner nor to the employees, they are simply exercising statutory functions: *Wild v John Brown & Co* [1919] 1 KB 134.

Withdrawal of workers

24.159 Under s 79 of the Mines and Quarries Act 1954, if inflammable gas is excessive in any part of the mine, or any other danger is found to be present, the person in charge of the area must withdraw all persons employed there. Persons who have been withdrawn must not be allowed to return—except for restoring safety in the area or for saving life—until the area is free from excessive gas and every other danger. Gas is normally excessive if the percentage amounts to 2% in a safety- lamp mine, or 1.25% in other cases.

24.160 In *Sneddon v Summerlee Iron Co Ltd* 1947 SC 555 at 567 Lord President Cooper said:

'Danger for the purposes of this section must not be tested by the opinion of uninstructed laymen. ... Mining is notoriously a dangerous trade ... from which some element of danger is rarely absent. The matter must be judged with the aid of evidence based on skilled experience of the industry.'

Accordingly there was no duty to withdraw the men because of the presence of ice in the shaft, when there was no reason to expect a dangerous fall.

24.161 If mineworkers are withdrawn under s 79 and re-admitted for fire-fighting, they must be withdrawn again if inflammable gas again reaches the dangerous percentage under s 79(5): *Wing v Pickering* [1925] 2 KB 777.

24.162 Under the Coal and Other Mines (Fire and Rescue) Order 1956, SI 1956/1768, Sch 1, reg 11[1] which applies only to safety-lamp mines, mineworkers may have to be withdrawn (from places which may be affected) if there is any smoke or other sign indicating that fire has broken out.

[1]   These Regulations have been partially repealed by the Escape and Rescue from Mines Regulations 1995, SI 1995/2870.

Miscellaneous: fire, rescue, medical examinations and training

24.163 The Mines Miscellaneous Health and Safety Provisions Regulations 1995, SI 1995/2005,[1] require the owner of a mine to ensure that no work is carried out unless a health and safety document has been prepared demonstrating that the risks to which persons working at the mine are exposed have been assessed and that adequate measures have and will be taken to safeguard their health and safety (reg 4). Where appropriate, specified plans should be set out in writing as regards fire, explosion, toxic gases, rock or gas outbursts (reg 4(2)). The owner is required to ensure that the measures set out in the health and safety document are taken and that any plans included in the document are followed (reg 4(4)), as well as co-ordinating the implementation of all measures relating to the health and safety of persons working at the mine (reg 5). Workers must be provided with appropriate health surveillance (reg 7). So far as is reasonably practicable, the manager must ensure that only hydraulic fluids which are difficult to ignite and which satisfy fire resistance and hygiene specifications approved by the HSE are used (reg 8). Where there is a risk of an unintended explosion above ground, the owner must take all necessary measures to prevent the occurrence and accumulation of explosive atmospheres and the ignition of such atmospheres. Where there is a particular risk of fire or explosion, smoking must be forbidden, and no open flame can be used or any work carried out which may cause an ignition unless safety precautions have been implemented (Sch 1, Part II paras 2, 3). Under the now repealed s 70 of the Mines and Quarries Act 1954, where workings in a coal mine are served by a single intake airway so that, if a fire occurred in that airway, the workmen might have difficulty in withdrawing, not more than 100 persons were to be employed below ground at any time. This did not apply where the airway is reasonably free from fire risk. This section was repealed and replaced from 1 April 1994 by reg 9 of the Mines (Safety of Exit) Regulations 1988 which apply to every kind of mine. This prohibits the employment of more than 50 persons below ground unless there are two airways, or a single airway which is fire resistant: see para 24.96, above.

1   Implementing in part Directive 92/104 concerning the minimum requirements for improving the safety and health protection of workers in surface and underground mineral extracting industries.

24.164 Means of escape (such as emergency exits) must be provided from places such as motor-rooms or other confined spaces where there is a special risk such as fire, steam or gas (s 73).[1] The Escape and Rescue from Mines Regulations 1995, SI 1995/2870,[2] impose a number of obligations including the necessity for emergency plans, equipment, accommodation as well as requirements for rescue and escape.

1   See also the Coal and Other Mines (Fire and Rescue) Order 1956, SI 1956/1768.
2   Implementing in part Directive 92/104 concerning the minimum requirements for improving safety and health protection of workers in surface and underground mineral extracting industries, and amended by reg 17 of the Mines (Control of Ground Movement) Regulations 1999, SI 1999/2463.

24.165 The HSWA 1974, s 78, extends the Fire Precautions Act 1971 to all places of work, which of course includes mines and quarries. Buildings on the surface of a mine, with certain exceptions, require a fire certificate from the HSE.

24.166 Medical examination of young persons entering the industry is compulsory pursuant to the Mines (Medical Examinations) Regulations 1964, SI 1964/209.[1]

1   Made under s 92 of the Act which was repealed under the HSWA 1974.

24.167 The Health and Safety (First-Aid) Regulations 1981, SI 1981/917, apply to mines and quarries.[1]

[1] Regulation 6 of the 1981 Regulations was revoked by the Management of Health and Safety at Work Regulations 1999, SI 1999/3242.

24.168 The Coal and Other Mines (Sanitary Conveniences) Order 1956, SI 1956/1776, requires the manager to ensure the provision of sanitary conveniences at various points on the surface and below ground. This Order amplifies the more general duty under s 94 to provide and maintain sanitary conveniences. Section 97 requires wholesome drinking water to be provided on the surface, and s 95 requires steps to be taken to keep the mine below ground free from rats and mice.

24.169 The Manual Handling Operations Regulations 1992, SI 1992/2793, apply to mines and quarries.[1]

[1] Repealing and replacing s 93 of the Mines and Quarries Act 1954.

24.170 The Coal and Other Mines (Horses) Order 1956, SI 1956/1777, makes provision for the welfare and care of horses underground, although this is doubtless of little (if any) application in current times.

Duties of workers

24.171 Statutory duties are imposed upon the workers by various sections. Breach of these duties may constitute contributory negligence or (under s 159) render the owners liable for injuries caused to other persons.

24.172 Most of these obligations are now found in the MASHAM Regulations, see para 24.14, above. There are also the provisions mentioned at para 24.99, above in relation to supports and with regard to safety lamps and contraband.

24.173 The extant parts of the Coal and Other Mines (General Duties and Conduct) Order 1956, SI 1956/1761 contain a code of behaviour for persons employed at a mine. They must enter the cage only when authorised, not interfere with the gates, and leave the cage only when it is stationary at a landing stage (Sch 1, para 3); travel only on authorised roads and keep out of unauthorised places, in particular engine houses (Sch 1, para 4) and refrain from interfering with machinery (Sch 1, para 6).

Fencing of abandoned mines and quarries

24.174 If a mine has been abandoned, or has not been worked for a period of 12 months, it is the duty of the owner to erect fences or barriers, or block up the shafts or other entrances, for the protection of the public. If a quarry is near a highway or otherwise dangerous to the public, it must be fenced whether it is still being worked or not. Details of these requirements are given in s 151 (as amended by the Environmental Protection Act 1990 and the Environment Act 1995). By regs 31 and 32 of the MASHAM Regulations, plans of abandoned mines and mine workings must be preserved.

24.175 Under the old law the owner of a disused mine shaft ceased to be responsible when it was taken over for another purpose, eg as a well: *Knuckey v Redruth Rural District Council* [1904] 1 KB 382.

Safety of tips

24.176 The Mines and Quarries (Tips) Act 1969, like the provisions about abandoned mines and quarries, is intended to protect the public rather than the worker and was passed in consequence of the Aberfan disaster where a tip collapsed because of heavy rain and overwhelmed a school. There is a general duty under Part I to make and keep secure all tips at a mine still in operation, whether the tip itself is in active use or not (ss 1, 2) and owners and manager must keep themselves informed (s 3). Part II (ss 11–36) contains provisions for making disused tips safe. The Mines and Quarries (Tips) Regulations 1971, SI 1971/1377, the associated Mines and Quarries (Tipping Plans) Rules 1971, SI 1971/1378, and the 1969 Act were amended by the Quarries Regulations 1999, SI 1999/2024, as regards their application to quarries. The 1969 Act only applies in respect of quarries to tips used for deposits prior to the implementation of the 1999 Regulations. Both of the 1971 Regulations provide for drainage of tips, regular supervision by a competent person, notification and a survey for suitability before a tip is taken into use (or fresh use after abandonment), and for plans showing underlying strata as well as surface features. Supervision and inspection are required for disused as well as active tips, and any abnormal or unusual feature must be reported.

Railway sidings at mines

24.177 See para 24.119, above.

MISCELLANEOUS MINES

24.178 Before the Mines and Quarries Act 1954, mines of coal, stratified ironstone, shale and fireclay were subject to the Coal Mines Act 1911 and all other mines were governed by the Metalliferous Mines Regulation Act 1872. The Metalliferous Mines General Regulations 1938 were made under the authority of the Act of 1872, but in substance they replaced it and formed a complete and self-contained safety code, based in many respects upon the Coal Mines Act 1911.

24.179 The Mines and Quarries Act 1954 applies to all mines without exception. But there are many differences in practice between coal mines and other classes of mines. Other mines are usually on a smaller scale, less deep, and less dangerous. They may be approached by underground tunnels instead of by shafts, and will not require the same elaborate winding apparatus as a coal mine. They are less mechanised and have fewer officials: and the special dangers of coal mines—inflammable firedamp gas and coal dust and poisonous gases—are not usually encountered.[1] On the other hand, small mines have some special dangers of their own, such as the use of ladders or open skips to descend shafts.[2]

[1] Foul air, of course, occurs in all mines, so that a ventilation system is always necessary.
[2] These remarks are, of course, limited to mines in the UK. Gold mines in South Africa are sometimes far deeper and are sunk through hard quartz rock so the technical problems are tremendous. Problems also arise with large-scale open cast workings in Australia. In third world countries copper, silver and other mines are appallingly dangerous.

24.180 In general, therefore, the requirements in coal mines and similar mines have been stricter than they are in other mines. The Act puts mines of coal, stratified ironstone, shale and fireclay into a class of their own. Some sections of the Act are restricted to these mines, and so are most of the codes of regulations. The remaining mines are now grouped together (in the regulations which apply to them) as 'miscellaneous mines'.

24.181 The MASHAM Regulations (see para 24.14, above) apply to all mines. So too, except where otherwise stated, all the safety requirements in the Mines and Quarries Act 1954 apply to mines of every class. In particular, all mines are subject to s 30 and the Mines (Shafts and Winding) Regulations 1993 (shafts and entrances to workings), s 28 (apparatus for unwalkable outlets),[1] ss 55, 56 and 58 (ventilation), ss 61, 62, 63–65 (lighting, safety lamps and contraband), s 74 (protection against dust), ss 34–41 (roads and traffic), ss 42–46 (operation of winding and rope haulage apparatus), s 83 (engines and locomotives), s 84 (steam and compressed air apparatus), s 69 (explosives), ss 86, 87 (structures on surface), s 79 and s 123 (inspections and withdrawal of workmen), and ss 73, 92 and 88 (fire and rescue precautions, medical examinations, and training). Section 151 (fencing of abandoned mines) also applies. All these sections, together with the relevant regulations which amplify them, are summarised earlier.

[1] Winding or haulage apparatus is not required in miscellaneous mines unless the length of the outlet exceeds 45 metres and in any case exemptions may be granted (s 28(2)).

24.182 On the other hand, the following requirements are restricted to mines of coal, stratified ironstone, shale and fireclay, ss 22–25 are expressly extended to other classes of mines by regulations:

— ventilation apparatus capable of reversing the direction of airflow (s 58(2)) (restricted to coal mines);
— no leakage allowed between intake and return airways (s 59).

24.183 The Mines (Safety of Exit) Regulations 1988 (summarised at para 24.77, above) require two separate shafts, two escape routes from every workplace, and (in some cases) two airways for ventilation. These came into force for existing 'miscellaneous' mines on 1 April 1994, but applied to new mines from 1 April 1989.

The Miscellaneous Mines Regulations

24.184 The Miscellaneous Mines Order 1956, SI 1956/1778, applies to all mines other than coal, stratified ironstone, shale and fireclay and came into force at the same time as the Act, ie 1 January 1957. The MASHAM Regulations revoke and replace much of this Order, and the Mines (Shafts and Winding) Regulations 1993, SI 1993/302, disapply the remaining relevant provisions from shafts leaving it to apply to unwalkable outlets only.[1]

1   It continued to apply to the shafts of tin mines until 1 January 1996.

Shafts and outlets

24.185 A fixed ladder in use below ground must not be vertical or overhanging, but must be inclined at the most convenient angle in the space available (reg 74(1)), there must be substantial platforms every 10 metres and unless there are strong handholds the tops of the ladders must project at least 1 metre above each platform or landing (reg 74(2)). The ladders in an outlet must be securely fastened to the lining or sides and each platform must be fenced (reg 7(2)).

Winding apparatus

24.186 Requirements for the construction and operation of winding apparatus in shafts (including staple-pits) and rope haulage apparatus in unwalkable outlets are similar to those in the coal mines regulations, but less strict. If the apparatus is mechanically operated—which does not appear to be obligatory in any case— there must be brakes, an indicator showing the position of cages, and devices to prevent the rope slipping off (reg 8). Cages or carriages used for carrying persons must be covered at the top, closed at two sides and have gates at the ends (reg 11), and the number of persons to be carried must be limited to a fixed maximum (reg 12). In a cage or carriage used to carry vehicles, there must be means to prevent them falling out (reg 13).

24.187 Generally, movement through both shafts and outlets is controlled by signals (reg 16) given by authorised persons only (reg 17) who must not give the 'away' signal if more than the maximum number are carried or the gates are not shut (reg 18). In general, loads are not allowed through a shaft or outlet while passengers are travelling through (reg 19). Winding and haulage apparatus must be examined at regular intervals (regs 39, 40).

Haulage ropes

24.188 Regulation 23 allows persons to travel on roads when vehicles are moving (notwithstanding s 39 of the Act) if there is a 600 mm clearance and speed is limited to 2.7 metres per second. Regulations 24–26 deal with the size and intervals of refuge holes, signals on roads, and the supply of sprags and other devices to hold vehicles on inclines.

Lighting, explosives, fire, floods etc

24.189 General lighting must be provided at underground entrances to shafts and outlets and at adjacent sidings (reg 27). Miners must carry their portable lamps with them (reg 29) and in safety lamp mines the manager must ensure that safety lamps taken below are in safe working order and locked (reg 28). Fire precautions (regs 31–35) include restrictions on inflammable material and oil below ground. The Mines Miscellaneous Health and Safety Provisions Regulations 1995, SI 1995/2005, provide that every place above ground at a mine where a person is likely to be exposed to risks in the event of the failure of artificial lighting are required to be provided with emergency lighting of adequate intensity, or where this is impractical, personal lamps should be provided (Sch 1, Part II, para 1). Precautions must be taken against inrushes of water, liquid matter or gas into the workings; these are now regulated by the Mines (Precautions against Inrushes) Regulations 1979, SI 1979/318 (para 24.158, above), which replace the former reg 36. Explosives were formerly (under reg 30) left to be regulated by the local rules of the mine. There are now general rules with regard to the use of explosives, which are summarised at para 24.142ff, along with the similar rules for quarries (and see too para 24.206).

Machinery

24.190 Section 82 of the Mines and Quarries Act 1954 (repealed by PUWER) is amplified by reg 37, which forbids the cleaning of machinery, and, with certain exceptions, oiling and greasing as well, while the machine is in motion. By reg 37(3) belts are not to be moved on and off, while machinery is in motion under mechanical power, except by means of a safety contrivance.

Fencing of certain places

24.191 By reg 75, the top of every hopper and kiln is to be kept securely fenced.

Duties of workers

24.192 Part X forbids unauthorised travel on aerial ropeways (reg 63) or underground roads, and entry into unauthorised parts of the mine (reg 64) and requires ventilation doors and screens to be kept shut (reg 65). Work on an unfenced ledge or similar place without a rope or safety appliance is forbidden (reg 68).

Electricity

24.193 Electricity, both at the surface and below ground, is now governed by the Electricity at Work Regulations 1989. The regulations for all places of work are summarised at chapter 18, above and the additional requirements for mines at para 24.136, above.

QUARRIES

24.194 Before the Mines and Quarries Act 1954, quarries were not governed by a separate Act. Various sections of the Metalliferous Mines Acts, the Coal Mines Acts, the Quarries Act 1894 and the Factories Act applied to them, and the net result of a complex network of legislation was that regulations could be made. Quarries were in fact governed by two self-contained codes of regulations, the Quarries General Regulations 1938 and the Quarries General (Electricity) Regulations 1938, as amended. The Mines and Quarries Act 1954 previously governed all quarries. The position has now changed. Quarries are now specifically governed by the Quarries Regulations 1999, SI 1999/2024. These replace the Quarries (General) Regulations 1956. The Regulations do not apply where there has been no extraction of minerals or where there has been no preparation for sale of any such minerals within the previous 12 months. Parts of quarries which are used exclusively for work activity unconnected with the extraction of minerals or for their preparation for sale are also excluded (reg 4). Exemptions can be granted (reg 46).

The Quarries Regulations 1999

24.195 So far as reasonably practicable, operators are under a duty to ensure that the quarry and its plant are designed, constructed, equipped commissioned, operated and maintained in such a way so that work can be undertaken without danger to health and safety. In relation to buildings, irrespective of whether or not they are intended to be permanent, the operator must also ensure that they are designed, adapted, constructed, maintained, operated, erected and supervised so as to withstand any foreseeable environmental conditions (reg 6(3)). Quarry operators are required to prepare a health and safety document demonstrating that the risks have been assessed, as well as setting out what measures as regards the design and maintenance of the quarry will be taken to ensure the safety of persons at the quarry and in the immediate vicinity (reg 7). Such measures must be reviewed on a regular basis, and whenever the circumstances so require (reg 11). The Regulations prohibit the operator from allowing anyone to carry out work at the quarry unless they are competent or otherwise work under the supervision and instruction of a competent person (reg 9).

24.196 Part III of the Regulations contains provisions concerning risk control. Operators have to devise and keep up to date a suitable written scheme for the inspection, maintenance and testing of all parts of the quarry, including all buildings and any plant (reg 12). Written records must be kept of such inspections, specifying the discovery of significant defects and what steps have been taken to remedy them. Benches and road hauls are required to be designed, constructed and maintained so as to allow plant and machinery to be used upon them safely (reg 13). Vehicles rules must be devised setting out measures designed to control the risks to persons arising out of their use at the quarry (reg 14). The Regulations require operators to ensure that adequate means of escape and rescue are provided and maintained as well as providing means of communication and warning to enable assistance and rescue operations to be prepared in the event of an emergency. Rescue equipment must be readily accessible and kept in an appropriate place ready for use (reg 15).

24.197 Before hazardous operations are carried out, or where the combination of operations may cause serious hazards, the operator is required to devise and implement a system to ensure that such work is not carried out without a permit specifying the conditions and precautions to be taken: reg 18. Safety drills must also be held at regular intervals (reg 19). Dangerous areas in a quarry have to be clearly marked and barriers put in place to prevent inadvertent entry (reg 22).

Dust precautions

24.198 Precautions against dust in quarry processes are now determined by the Control of Substances Hazardous to Health Regulations 2002. Dust is a 'hazardous substance' if it is either present in quantity, or, though there is not a great quantity, it is of a kind which is likely to endanger health.

Duties of workers

24.199 These duties are defined by the Quarries Regulations 1999. Every person working at a quarry must carry out their duties with reasonable care for their health and safety as well as others, and must comply with any rules or instructions pertaining to health and safety and the safe use of equipment set out under reg 10 (reg 42).

Electricity

24.200 Electricity at quarries, as at other places of work, is now regulated by the Electricity at Work Regulations 1989. An ACOP explains how the Regulations apply to mines (see chapter 22, above).

EXPLOSIVES IN QUARRIES AND MISCELLANEOUS MINES

24.201 Explosives in miscellaneous mines—all except coal, stratified iron-stone, shale or fireclay—are regulated by the Miscellaneous Mines (Explosives) Regulations 1959, SI 1959/2258, and the use of explosives in quarries is governed by the Quarries Regulations 1999.[1] Exemptions may be granted (Miscellaneous Mines Regulations, reg 3; Quarries Regulations 1999, reg 46).

[1] Both of which are amended by the Manufacture and Storage of Explosives Regulations 2005, SI 2005/1082.

24.202 There are strict requirements for the safe storage, handling and issue of explosives and detonators (Miscellaneous Mines Regulations, Part IV, regs 7–13). In mines, supplies must generally be stored in an explosives store at the surface, but issue points may be authorised near the top of the shaft (reg 7, mines). Schemes may be authorised at mines for conveying explosives in bulk (in locked canisters) to reserve stations below ground (reg 13, mines). Issue of detonators is the personal responsibility of the manager, and they must be carried when underground in a locked detonator case (regs 8, 9, mines). In general, explosives below ground must be in cartridge form and in a locked canister (regs 11, 12, mines). Detonators and explosives must not be taken out until required for immediate use (regs 10(1), 12(4), mines).

24.203 In a mine, shotfirers must be authorised persons not under 21, unless already appointed under previous regulations (reg 6, mines). Shotfiring must not be done by electrical apparatus, cable or fuse unless provided by the owner, and fuses must be safety fuses, detonating fuses or otherwise of an approved type (reg 14, mines). Detachable handles or keys for electrical firing must be held by the shotfirer and kept away from the apparatus except at the moment of firing (reg 15, mines). In a mine, electrical firing is only allowed by means of such a detachable handle, and shotfiring cable must not be used for any other purpose (regs 14, 17, mines). A defect in electrical apparatus must be reported at once and use of the apparatus suspended (reg 16, mines).

24.204 A regular procedure is laid down for general shotfiring in mines. The charging of shot-holes with cartridges and stemming must be done by the shotfirer or under his supervision: the jamming of explosives in too narrow a hole and the use of unauthorised tools are forbidden (regs 18–24, mines). Firing must not take place until surplus explosives have been cleared away (reg 25, mines). Warning must be given to neighbouring places where the shot may blow through, a danger zone fixed with sentries, and all persons required to withdraw to take proper shelter (regs 28–30, mines). The place must be examined for safety after firing (reg 31, mines). In shafts or similar places being sunk or deepened, there are further requirements. Electrical firing only is permitted (reg 35, mines); loose material must be cleared away in case there are old shot-holes (reg 32, mines). Explosives must not be taken in unless immediately required, and there is strict control of the taking in of a primer cartridge fitted with a detonator (regs 33, 34, mines). There is a procedure to be followed in case of misfires, involving a stated delay of 30 minutes after attempted firing (if by safety fuse) or five minutes after disconnecting the apparatus (if firing was electrical). The place may then be examined, and a further attempt made to fire: but a charge must not be removed unless it is a cartridge protruding from the hole (regs 36–38, mines).

24.205 In a safety lamp mine the Coal and Other Safety-Lamp (Explosives) Regulations 1993, SI 1993/208, apply—see para 24.142, above.

24.206 The Quarries Regulations require the operator to ensure that no person smokes or otherwise uses a naked flame or carries out any work which could give rise to a risk of unintended explosion by fire unless sufficient measures are taken to prevent explosion (reg 20). The presence and concentration of potentially explosive substances in the atmosphere must be measured. Automatic devices must be in place to monitor continuously the concentration of flammable or explosive gases and where the concentration reaches a dangerous level, trigger an alarm and cut off the power supply (reg 21). The other main provisions are contained in Part V. Operators are required to ensure so far as is reasonably practicable that all explosives are stored and transported safely and securely. Only authorised and competent persons are permitted to deal with the storage, transport or the use of explosives. Trainees must be under the close supervision of a duly authorised and competent person. An 'explosives supervisor' must be appointed to oversee all work in the quarry involving the use of explosives. Adequate written procedures must be devised for shotfiring, appointing shotfirers or trainees and storekeepers, and also for dealing with misfires.

24.207 Procedures are set out for the supervision of shotfiring operations (reg 26). All shotfiring operations must be carried out under the close personal supervision of the shotfirer, and must be fired from a safe place. A trainee is not permitted to fire shots except where he is under the close supervision of a shotfirer, and not until such time as the operator is satisfied that he has completed a suitable period of training and has attained appropriate experience. Before a shot is fired, the shotfirer must check the shotfiring system or circuit to see that it has been correctly connected. Where electrical detonators are used, the shotfirer must see that these have been correctly connected to the shotfiring system and have been tested with a suitable instrument from a position of safely. Where appropriate, the electrical integrity of the shotfiring system should be checked to make a misfire unlikely.

24.208 In the event of misfire, the operator (after consultation with the competent person appointed in charge of the operation of the quarry where appropriate), is required ensure so far as is reasonably practicable that no one other than himself and the explosives supervisor, shotfirer, trainee, or any other authorised person enters into the danger area until thirty minutes have elapsed since the misfire where the shot was fired by means of a safety fuse. Where the shot has misfired using other means, no other person is permitted to enter the danger area until after a period of five minutes has elapsed since the misfire and any shotfiring apparatus has been disconnected from the shot. Appropriate steps must be taken to ascertain the cause of the misfire and a suitable record kept (reg 28). Other miscellaneous procedures regarding the use of explosives are contained in reg 29, including a prohibition on anyone bringing any substance or article likely to cause an unintended explosion within ten metres of any explosives (except for the purpose of a lighting igniter or safety fuse) or taking a naked flame within ten metres of any explosives. Detonator leads, safety fuses, or other systems used for initiating shots must not be forcibly removed from a shothole after it has been charged and primed.

SAFETY OF TIPS

24.209 The Quarries Regulations 1999 impose obligations on quarry operators to ensure that all proposed and existing tips are appraised in order to determine whether or not they amount to a significant hazard. Where a significant hazard is identified, a geotechnical assessment must be carried out (regs 32(4), 33–34). The HSE has to be notified in respect of certain proposals (reg 37). Operators have to ensure that tips are be designed, constructed, operated and maintained so as to avoid instability or movement likely to give rise to a health and safety risk. The Regulations provide for operators to devise and implement tips rules so as to ensure the safe construction and operation of tips (reg 32). Sufficient records must be kept as to the nature, quantity and location of all substances accumulated or deposited in a tip so that an accurate assessment of the stability of the tip can be undertaken (reg 37).

Chapter 25

RAILWAYS AND OTHER GUIDED TRANSPORT SYSTEMS

Thomas Roe

INTRODUCTION

25.01 This chapter is concerned mainly with legislation about railways and other guided transport systems, where relevant to the liability of employers to their employees and other workers. In particular, it deals with the Railways and Other Guided Transport Systems (Safety) Regulations 2006, SI 2006/599.[1] It also considers other legislation in this area, the extent to which legislation of more general application may be relevant, and the continuing role of the common law.

[1] Which came into force on 10 April 2006, though many provisions do not take effect until 1 October 2006.

25.02 Two factors have shaped the current regime of railway safety legislation.[1] First, the denationalisation of the railways in 1994 and their consequent transition from a State monopoly to a number of competing private companies operating trains and stations with the infrastructure being owned by another body (initially Railtrack plc, also a private company; latterly the State-owned Network Rail). Second, and fundamentally, the Directive of the European Parliament and Council 2004/49 on safety on the Community's railways ('the Directive'). The Directive is part of a process which began in 1991 with Council Directive 91/440 and which is aimed at integrating the railways into a competitive European market and at affording to railway operators the 'status of independent operators behaving in a commercial manner and adapting to market needs'.[2] Further Directives in 1996 and 2001 dealt with 'interoperability', i e increasing compatibility between different European railway systems, and made provision for 'technical standards for interoperability' to be laid down.[3]

[1] For a summary of the history of safety regulation on the railways see the previous edition of this work at para **26.01**.
[2] Council Directive 91/440/EC, Preamble, paras 6 and 7. Articles 1 and 6 required Member States to separate the management of railway operation and infrastructure from the provision of railway transport services, though only the separation of accounts was compulsory, organisational or institutional separation being optional.
[3] Council Directive 96/48/EC on the interoperability of the trans-European high-speed rail system and Directive 2001/16/EC on the interoperability of the trans-European conventional rail system.

25.03 Before denationalisation, regulations concerned with railway safety had generally been made under various specific Acts dating back to 1839. However, the modern regime takes effect under the HSWA 1974, by virtue of the Railways Act 1993, s 117(2) which provides that ('[i]f to any extent they would not do so apart from this subsection') the general purposes of Part 1 of the HSWA 1974—and therefore the rule-making powers under s 15—include securing the proper construction and safe operation of railways, tramways, trolley vehicle systems and other guided transport systems and protecting the public (whether passengers or not) from personal injury and other risks arising from their construction and operation. The old enactments, together with the regulations made under them, were largely[1] repealed by the Railway Safety (Miscellaneous Provisions) Regulations 1997, SI 1997/553. The intent of the Directive is that '[t]he current situation, in which national safety rules continue to play a role, should be regarded as a transitional stage, leading ultimately to a situation in which European rules will apply' (Preamble, para 11).

[1]   But not entirely. So, for example, reg 3 of the Factory and Workshop Act 1901, use of locomotives and waggons on lines and sidings Regulations 1906, SI 1906/679, which requires lines of rails and points to be examined regularly and kept in efficient order, remains in force. See reg 12 of, and the Schedule to, the 1997 Regulations.

RAILWAYS AND OTHER GUIDED TRANSPORT SYSTEMS (SAFETY) REGULATIONS 2006

25.04 The Directive is given effect in Great Britain (along with some other provisions not derived from the Directive) by the Railways and Other Guided Transport Systems (Safety) Regulations 2006 ('the Regulations').[1] These are made under the HSWA 1974, s 15 and it follows that their breach is actionable by any person thereby caused damage: HSWA 1974, s 47(2). There is also a guidance note to which reference should be made. Four aspects of the Regulations are considered below: common safety methods and targets, safety certification and authorisation; general duties of transport operators; safety critical work; and safety verification.

[1]   Note that parts of the Regulations do not apply to the Channel Tunnel: see reg 2(3).

Common safety methods and targets, safety certification and authorisation

25.05 The heart of the Directive and consequently of the Regulations (which must be construed consistently with it to the extent that they seek to implement it—see chapter 9) is a system of European 'common safety methods' and 'common safety targets'. Common safety methods are methods developed pursuant to art 6 of the Directive to describe how safety levels, the achievement of safety targets and compliance with other safety requirements are assessed, revised and reissued from time to time (reg 2(1)). Common safety methods are to be prescribed from time to time at a European level by the European Railway Agency (art 6 of the Directive). The European Railway Agency was established by European Parliament and Council Regulation 881/2004. It is responsible for both safety and 'interoperability' (as to which see para 25.02 above). Common safety targets are the safety levels that must be reached by the different parts of the mainline railway system and the system as a whole expressed in 'risk assessment criteria' (reg 2(1)). They too are to be prescribed from time to time at a European level by the European Railway Agency (art 7 of the Directive).

25.06 Regulation 3(1) prohibits any person from operating a train in relation to any infrastructure on the mainline railway after 30 September 2006 unless, first, he has established and is maintaining a safety management system which meets the requirements of the Regulations and, second, he holds a current safety certificate in relation to the operation in question. A 'railway' is any railway with a gauge of at least 350mm and excludes a tramway (reg 2(1)). The 'mainline railway' is any railway or part of a railway except one whose infrastructure and rolling stock are reserved strictly for a local or 'heritage railway' use ('heritage railway' is itself a defined term), or for the purposes of tourism, or one which is functionally isolated from any other railway apart from a local, 'heritage' or touristic one (reg 2(1)). Regulation 3(1) does not apply to the extent that the person in question is operating a train in an engineering possession, ie a section of track closed to normal traffic for the purpose of carrying out maintenance, which includes any repair, alteration, reconditioning, examination or testing of infrastructure (reg 2(1)).

25.07 Regulation 3(2) prohibits any person responsible for developing or maintaining infrastructure other than a station or for managing and operating a station on the mainline railway from managing it and using it, or permitting it to be used, for the operation of trains after 30 September 2006 unless, first, he has established and is maintaining a safety management system which meets the requirements of the Regulations and, second, he or the person he permits to use it has a current safety authorisation.

25.08 Regulation 5(1) provides that the requirements for a safety management system on the mainline railway are: that it is established to ensure that the railway system can achieve the relevant common safety targets and is in conformity with relevant national safety rules and relevant safety regulations laid down in technical standards for interoperability; and that it applies the relevant parts of common safety methods, ensures the control of all categories of risk associated with the operation and takes into account, where appropriate and reasonable, the risks arising as a result of activities carried on by other persons. 'Risk', in this context, means risk to the safety of a person (reg 2(1)).

25.09 Regulation 5(1)(d)(iii) requires that a safety management system ensures the control of all categories of risk relating to the placing in service of infrastructure or vehicles which incorporate significant changes capable of significantly increasing an existing risk, or creating a 'significant safety risk'. Regulation 5(4) requires that '[i]n paragraph (1)(d)(iii) where such new or altered vehicles are intended to be placed in service, then before' doing so the transport operator shall ensure that he has an established safety verification scheme which meets the requirements and contains the elements set out in Sch 4, that he has appointed a competent person to undertake that safety verification, and that the competent person has done so. Since 'significant safety risk' is defined as a significant risk to the safety of passengers and members of the public (reg 2(1)), it may be doubtful whether any breach of reg 5(1)(d)(iii) which incidentally caused damage to a worker would be actionable as such by that worker (see by analogy *Fytche v Wincanton Logistics plc* [2004] UKHL 31). But it may arguably be negligent (depending, of course, on the precise facts) to permit or require a worker to work with or around any infrastructure or vehicle in respect of which the operator is in breach of these provisions.

25.10 Regulation 5(1) in addition requires the safety management system to meet the elements set out in Sch 1 to the Regulations, adapted to the character, extent and other characteristics of the operation in question. Schedule 1, which substantially reproduces the relevant part of the Directive verbatim, sets out prescriptively what the safety management system must contain: principally, it must describe the distribution of responsibilities for the safety management system within the operation, show how the control of the system is secured by the management on different levels, show how persons carrying out work directly in relation to the operation and their representatives at all levels are involved with the system and show how continuous improvement is ensured. There are further detailed provisions which are not reproduced here.

25.11 Regulation 5(7) adds further requirements for a person responsible for developing or maintaining infrastructure or for managing and operating a station on the mainline railway.

25.12 A 'safety certificate', which a train operator must have, is obtained by an application to the Office of Rail Regulation (reg 7). The applicant must set out the various matters prescribed in Sch 2: in essence, the applicant must show that there are systems in place to ensure that the operation is run in a way which meets the requirements of the Regulations. A 'safety authorisation', which a person developing or maintaining infrastructure or managing and operating a station must have, is likewise obtained by an application to the Office of Rail Regulation setting out how the person complies with the relevant requirements (reg 10).

25.13 Regulation 4 makes similar provision for any transport system which is not part of the mainline railway. 'Transport system' means a railway, tramway or any other system using guided transport (ie a system of transport guided automatically or by means external to the vehicle) where that system is used wholly or mainly for the carriage of passengers (reg 2(1)). The definition excludes, however, a guided bus system and a trolley vehicle system (reg 2(1)).[1]

[1] Also excluded by reg 2(1) are any part of a transport system within a harbour or harbour area or which is part of a factory, mine or quarry, any part of a transport system used solely for the purpose of carrying out a building operation or work of engineering construction or within a maintenance or goods depot or military establishment. So are fairground equipment, certain sorts of cableway installation and narrow gauge railways except (in the

last case) where they cross a carriageway. And so is any part of a transport system within a siding, except where the provisions as to safety critical work apply (see para 25.18 below).

25.14 The holder of a safety certificate or safety authorisation must notify the Office of Rail Regulation of any major changes to the means by which he meets the Regulations' requirements relating to the safety management system (reg 13). The Office of Rail Regulation must revoke a safety certificate or safety authorisation if satisfied that the holder is no longer satisfying its conditions and that there is significant risk as a result (regs 15 and 16).

General duties of transport operators

25.15 Regulation 19(1), which comes into force on 1 October 2006, places a general duty on any transport operator. A transport operator is any person who operates a vehicle in relation to any infrastructure (meaning fixed assets used for the operation of a transport system (as itself defined—see para 25.13)) or who is responsible for developing and maintaining infrastructure other than a station, or for managing and operating a station, and manages and uses that infrastructure or station, or permits it to be used, for the operation of a vehicle; but note that the definition provides that a person is not a transport operator solely on the basis that he carries out construction, maintenance repair or alteration of infrastructure or a station (reg 2(1)).

25.16 The duties are familiar from other European-derived regulations: (a) to make a suitable and sufficient assessment of the risks to the safety of any persons for the purpose of identifying the measures the operator needs to take to ensure safe operation of the transport system in question in so far as this is affected by his operation; and (b) to implement such measures. Where the operation is on the mainline railway, the operator must apply the common safety methods (reg 19(2)). Assessments must be recorded and reviewed and there must be appropriate arrangements for the effective planning, organisation, control, monitoring and review of the measures identified (reg 19(3)–(5)).

25.17 A duty of co-operation is imposed by reg 22.[1] Any transport operator whose operations may affect or be affected by the operations of another transport operator, and any employer or self-employed person carrying out work on or in relation to premises or plant owned or controlled by that other transport operator, must co-operate as far as necessary with that other transport operator to enable him to comply with the provisions of the Regulations.

[1]   The drafting is rather convoluted. Regulation 22 came into force on 10 April 2006.

Safety critical work

25.18 Particular provision is made in the Regulations for 'safety critical work' (in which respect the Regulations go beyond the scope of the Directive, which does not expressly address this matter). Safety critical work is work on or in relation to a transport system (as to which see para 25.13) which consists of a 'safety critical task'. Such tasks are defined in reg 23 as consisting of any of a list of tasks, where such task 'could significantly affect the health or safety of persons on a transport system.' The list, which is not reproduced in full here, includes driving, dispatching or otherwise controlling or affecting the movement of any vehicle, signalling, coupling or uncoupling and installation or maintenance of any part of a transport system. Regulation 24, which comes into force on 1 October 2006, requires that every controller of safety critical work shall, so far as reasonably practicable, ensure that a person under his management, supervision or control (other than a person is receiving practical training in a safety critical task) only carries out safety critical work: if he has been assessed as being competent and fit to carry out that work following assessment by an assessor; if there is an accurate and up to date record in writing of such competence and fitness which is available for inspection; and if there are in place arrangements for monitoring the competence and fitness of that person. Such assessments must be reviewed without unreasonable delay where the controller has reason to doubt the person's fitness or competence or there has been a significant change in the matters to which the assessment relates.

25.19 Every controller of safety critical work must have in place arrangements to ensure, so far as is reasonably practicable, that a safety critical worker under his management, supervision or control does not carry out safety critical work in circumstances where he is so fatigued that his health and safety or that of other persons on a transport system could be significantly affected (reg 25 (in force from 1 October 2006)). Every controller of safety critical work must co-operate with any other such controller, or any operator to enable that other controller of safety critical work to comply with these provisions (reg 26 (in force from 1 October 2006)).

25.20 The common law cases on the duty of an employer to select competent co-workers may be useful by way of analogy in considering this aspect of the Regulations (and see too *Gibson v Skibs A/S Marina* [1966] 2 All ER 476).

OTHER RAILWAY REGULATIONS STILL IN FORCE

25.21 As well as repealing or revoking much earlier legislation[1] the Railway Safety (Miscellaneous Provisions) Regulations 1997, SI 1997/553, which came into force on 10 May 1997, lay down important general safety duties relevant to railways and other systems of guided transport.[2]

1   See reg 12 and the Schedule.
2   See the definition of 'transport system' in reg 2. Note the amendments to the definitions in reg 2 made by the Railways and Other Guided Transport Systems (Safety) Regulations 2006, reg 33 and Sch 6, para 2.

25.22 By reg 3, a person in control of a transport system infrastructure must ensure, so far as is reasonably practicable and so far as is necessary for safety, that unauthorised access to the infrastructure is prevented.[1] This regulation, designed to protect against the deaths of trespassers, does not give rise to civil liability.[2] An infrastructure controller must also ensure, so far as is reasonably practicable, that appropriate procedures and equipment are in place to prevent collisions between vehicles or with buffer stops and to prevent derailments caused by excessive speed or incorrectly placed points (reg 5). Infrastructure controllers, vehicle operators, employers of those working on transport systems and self-employed persons so working are all under a duty to ensure, so far as is reasonably practicable, that appropriate procedures and equipment are in place, provided and maintained in order to prevent persons working on transport systems from being struck by or falling from a vehicle (reg 7). Vehicle operators must ensure that suitable and sufficient brakes are provided and maintained (reg 6).

[1] The regulation does not apply to a part of a transport system within a harbour or maintenance or goods depot or which is part of a factory, mine or quarry if access to the particular premises is adequately controlled (reg 3(3)).
[2] See reg 3(4).

25.23 The Railway Safety Regulations 1999, SI 1999/2244, came into force on 30 January 1999 and, broadly, require train operators and infrastructure controllers to ensure that after 1 January 2004 trains do not operate without a working train protection system designed to prevent or mitigate the effects of a signal being passed at danger.[1]

[1] Note the amendments made by the Railways and Other Guided Transport Systems (Safety) Regulations 2006, reg 33 and Sch 6, para 2.

25.24 The Carriage of Dangerous Goods and Use of Transportable Pressure Equipment Regulations 2004, SI 2004/568, which came into force on 10 May 2004, contain provisions about the transport of dangerous goods by rail. There are regulations on level crossings, which amend the Level Crossings Act 1983.[1]

[1] See the Level Crossings Regulations 1997, SI 1997/487. The Level Crossings Act 1983 is deemed by the Railways Act 1993, s 117 to have been made under the HSWA 1974.

RELEVANT GENERAL REGULATIONS

25.25 Many aspects of railways workers' work involve dangers which are not unique to railway work and lead to accidents which are similarly common-place. For example, 40% of major injuries to railway workers are caused by slips, trips and falls.[1] It should therefore be borne in mind that much legislation of more general application may also be relevant.

[1] *The Railway Strategic Safety Plan 2005* (Rail Safety and Standards Board, 2005).

25.26 Most of the so-called 'six pack' of European-derived regulations are capable of applying generally to work on railways and other guided transport

643

systems.[1] Likewise, the Control of Substances Hazardous to Health Regulations 2002. So are the Control of Noise at Work Regulations 2005, which came into force on 6 April 2006 (reg 1) and apply generally to noise at work (reg 3)[2] and the Control of Vibration at Work Regulations 2005, which came into force on 6 July 2005.[3] But not all legislation of general application applies to every aspect of work on railways. The Workplace (Health, Safety and Welfare) Regulations 1992 do not (with very limited exceptions) apply to work on or in a locomotive or rolling stock. Nor will they apply to any part of a workplace where the only activity being undertaken is construction work within the meaning of the Construction (Health, Safety and Welfare) Regulations 1996, ie 'the carrying out of any building, civil engineering or engineering construction work'.[4] However, the Work at Height Regulations 2005, which repeal the aspects of the Workplace and Construction Regulations dealing with falls and falling objects, will apply to work on railways.[5]

1   See the Management of Health and Safety at Work Regulations 1999, chapter 10, the Provision and Use of Work Equipment Regulations 1998, chapter 20, the Manual Handling Regulations 1992 chapter 21, the Health and Safety (Display Screen Equipment) Regulations 1992, chapter 20 and the Personal Protective Equipment at Work Regulations 1992, chapter 20.
2   See *Harris v BRB (Residuary) Ltd* [2005] EWCA Civ 900, [2005] ICR 1680: employer liable to train driver for breach of Noise at Work Regulations 1999 (the predecessor of the 2005 Regulations).
3   See chapter 16 for vibration at work and chapter 17 for noise at work.
4   Workplace (Health, Safety and Welfare) Regulations 1992, reg. 3; Construction (Health, Safety and Welfare) Regulations 1996, reg 2. Construction work includes the maintenance of any 'structure'; and 'structure' includes railway line or tramway line.
5   For convenience, the Work at Height Regulations are dealt with once only in chapter 19 on construction work.

25.27 Since 1 August 2003 the Working Time Regulations 1998, SI 1998/1833 have applied to workers in the rail sector (see the Working Time (Amendment) Regulations 2003, reg 4 removing the exclusion of such workers in the Regulations as originally made).[1]

1   See chapter 10.

SUMMARY OF THE FORMER REGIME

25.28 Since the Railways and Other Guided Transport Systems (Safety) Regulations 2006 do not come fully into effect until 1 October 2006, the former regulations which they revoke[1] will remain relevant for a period.[2] These are the Railways (Safety Case) Regulations 2000 and the Railways (Safety Critical Work) Regulations 1994. These Regulations are also relevant to the extent that certain steps taken under them when they were in force (eg assessments of competence and fitness under the 1994 Regulations) are deemed in many cases to amount to compliance with the 2006 Regulations until the time comes to take the step again under the 2006 Regulations.[3]

1   Regulation 34.
2   For a detailed account see chapter 24 of the previous edition of this work.
3   See eg reg 29.

25.29 The Railways (Safety Case) Regulations 2000 were in some ways similar to the provisions of the 2006 Regulations, though using different terminology and not imposed by European law. A 'safety case' was a document in which the relevant operator gave an account of the operation and the steps which were to be taken to ensure its safety (reg 2(2)). The document needed to be approved by the HSE and the operator was then under a duty to comply with its provisions (reg 10).[1]

> 1   Whereas the duty to put a safety case, once approved, into effect was spelled out expressly in the 2000 Regulations, it is not spelled out under the 2006 Regulations. The equivalent, which may come to the same thing in practice, would appear to be (in summary terms) the prohibition under reg 3 or 4 of operating at all unless one 'is maintaining' a safety management system which meets the relevant criteria.

25.30 The Railways (Safety Critical Work) Regulations 1994 were the predecessor to those parts of the 2006 Regulations which now deal with safety critical work. In addition, the HSE had issued a Code of Practice on hours of work for railway safety critical staff.

COMMON LAW

25.31 In practice there is a considerable overlap between duties in duties under regulations and duties at common law.

25.32 As regard the risks of collisions between trains, or of being run down, railway workers have similar rights at common law as members of the public would have in respect of the negligence of drivers, signal operators, shunters and other railway workers. It is recognised that a driver is in a difficult position and cannot readily be found negligent because he or she is on a fixed track, has to watch signals, cannot pull up quickly, and (though this will infrequently be of relevance in a modern case) cannot lean out all the time: *Trznadel v British Transport Commission* [1957] 3 All ER 196n. This does not mean, of course, that drivers and guards are excused from the duty of keeping a look-out: *Braithwaite v South Durham Steel Co Ltd* [1958] 3 All ER 161. It may also be negligent to give no warning, or insufficient warning, of one's approach: *Geddes v British Railways Board* (1968) 4 KIR 373 (long sustained whistle, not short blast only, should have been given at spot known to be dangerous).

25.33 Examples of successful claims in negligence against railway operators include *Harris v BRB (Residuary) Ltd* [2005] EWCA Civ 900, [2005] ICR 1680, where (in addition to the breach of statutory duty noted above at para 25.26 fn 2) the railway company was held liable in negligence to a train driver for damaging his hearing by failing to give him adequate protection against exposure to noise; and *Great Scottish & Western Railway Co Ltd v British Railways Board* (10 February 2000, unreported), CA where it was admitted that it had been negligent not to scotch (ie secure against rolling) a carriage which rolled down a hill and caused damage to another operator's train. Claims brought on behalf of dead or injured infrastructure maintenance workers often focus on the system of work adopted: for example, whether work should have been conducted with trains running on the track or under an engineering possession (see para 25.06).

Chapter 26

AGRICULTURE AND FORESTRY

Professor Andrew Watterson

GENERAL

26.01 Health and safety standards in agriculture and related industries have historically been poor. In 1998/99 there were over 200,000 agricultural holdings in England, Scotland and Wales with a workforce of over 530,000 people. Agriculture and forestry still have some of the highest fatal and serious workplace accident rates in the country. In the late 1990s, there was on average one death in agriculture each week and a fatal injury rate of 5.6 per 100,000 workers; accurate data on the numbers of cases of occupational caused or related ill-health do not exist for agriculture. In 2004/05, the HSE reported a rise in its agricultural fatal accident rate to 10.4 per 100,000 workers: almost double the figure of five years earlier (HSE Fatal Injuries in Farming, Forestry and Horticulture 2004/05). The poor health and safety record relates partly to the nature of the work, with many self-employed workers, families working on farms, vulnerable low paid workers on small units, linked sometimes to a lack of pressure to identify technological solutions to health and safety problems.

26.02 Perennial concerns about the role of gangmasters reached new heights in the twenty-first century with the death of at least 19 Chinese cocklers on Morecambe Bay in 2004, which followed the death of three migrant casual farm workers on their way to work on a road in July 2003, and two Polish workers on a fruit farm who became entangled in rope reeling machine (Hazards Magazine: www.hazards.org/migrants). This led to new gangmaster legislation. The Gangmasters (Licensing) Act 2004 was created by a Private Members Bill raised by James Sheridan MP and came into force in July 2004. The Act set up the Gangmasters Licensing Authority (GLA) that operates the licensing scheme for labour providers in the agriculture, shellfish gathering and associated processing and packaging sectors. The Act specifically failed to address health and safety issues directly, but did pick up wider labour law manifestations that impact upon occupational health and safety.

26.03 During the same period, diversification activities of farmers also led to health and safety prosecutions in relatively new activities and a number of these cases were settled outside court. For instance, fish farming, sometimes carried out inland and sometimes on sea lochs, saw exposure of workers to pesticides used to treat sea lice, especially on farmed salmon, and produced prosecutions for unsafe practices. In 2004, a successful prosecution occurred of the owner of a fish farm at sea under HSWA 1974, s 2(1). A worker drowned because of the owner's failure to provide and maintain plant and systems of work that were reasonably practical with regard to fish husbandry operations (*R v Lighthouse of Scotland Ltd* HSE Case No F200000613). The 'blue revolution' is likely to lead to more inland farmers pursing aquaculture interest beyond simply salmon and trout farming, possibly with a new or wider range of hazards linked to these activities.

26.04 The involvement of agricultural workers in the organisation of their own health and safety using roving health and safety representatives schemes, despite successfully evaluated pilots by the HSE, has been rejected by the government since 2001. In 2006, children aged 13 can still legally drive tractors on farms, thus perpetuating dangerous practices with fatal results for some children and blurring the line between home and workplace.[1] This is against a backdrop of reduced HSE enforcement activity since 2001 together with a declining number of HSE field and specialist staff, especially in the occupational health field. It is also linked to a reduction of labour input into the HSC Agriculture Industry Advisory Committee and other evidence of a decline in tripartism. In 2005 the government therefore continues to refuse to ratify 'ILO Convention 184 Health and Safety in Agriculture' for which it voted at the 2002 ILO Conference.

[1] Pursuant to the Prevention of Accidents to Children in Agriculture Regulations 1998, SI 1998/3262.

26.05 Agriculture has seen enormous increases in productivity, a significant decline in the workforce and often quite primitive technologies used to protect workers' health and safety in contrast to sophisticated technologies to achieve the production rates required by the farming industry. The industries also involve a range of construction tasks, machine hazards, electrical hazards—in 1998/99 six people were killed on farms by overhead power line contact—and exposure to a range of substances including pesticides covered by the COSHH Regulations (see chapter 22, above). Work-related mental health issues in agriculture also attracted serious attention in the 1990s and may fall within the scope of the HSWA 1974 if employees are affected. The HSWA 1974 is the controlling legislation and, although some existing regulations may continue in force, future regulations will be made under s 15 of that Act. The regulations were adapted to the metric system by the Agriculture (Metrication) Regulations 1981, SI 1981/1414.

26.06 Within agriculture, forestry and horticulture there are many potential causes of occupational ill-health linked to manual handling problems, respiratory diseases, skin diseases, vibration, extremes of temperature, and exposure to zoonoses.[1] Now all such problems are covered by the Management of Health and Safety at Work Regulations 1999 (as amended) in terms of employers assessing health and safety risk to employees. The Manual Handling Operations Regulations 1992, the Electricity at Work Regulations 1989 and the Noise at Work Regulations 1989 also apply to work in agriculture and forestry.[2]

[1] Cordes and Foster *Occupational Medicine: Health Hazards of Farming* (1991, Philadelphia); Donham, Rautianinen, Schuman, Lay *Agricultural Health and Safety: Recent Advances* (1997, New York).

2   The HSWA 1974, s 2 applied to a fatal electrocution of a farm worker in 1998 when a farmer was fined £15,000 because he knew that an overhead power line could be touched by a boom sprayer when the booms were folded vertically but he never enforced the safe system rigidly on his farm: *R v Foskett* (1999) HSE Case No F1500000315.

26.07 The Agriculture (Poisonous Substances) Act 1952 was passed to deal with pesticide hazards following a number of farm fatalities. In the 1970s further measures to control dangerous chemicals in agriculture were introduced and the 1980s saw the passage of the Food and Environment Protection Act in 1985 and then the Control of Pesticides Regulations 1986, SI 1986/1510. These provisions are supplemented by the COSHH Regulations 2002, which cover usage of chemicals in detail. Veterinary medicines such as sheep dip and antibiotics are authorised under the Veterinary Medicines Regulations 2005, SI 2005/2745, which implement EC single market legislation and the Medicines Act 1968. The use of such veterinary medicines is covered by the HSE and local authorities using COSHH and the HSWA 1974.

26.08 The general health and safety regulations considered elsewhere in this book, especially the Provision and Use of Work Equipment Regulations 1998, the Workplace (Health, Safety and Welfare) Regulations 1992, Management of Health and Safety at Work Regulations 1999, Supply of Machinery (Safety) Regulations 1992, SI 1992/3073, and Manual Handling Operations Regulations 1992, SI 1992/2793, together with COSHH, the Food and Environment Protection Act 1985 and the Control of Pesticides Regulations 1986 have replaced almost all the agricultural health and safety measures of the 1950s, 1960s and 1970s. The only specific regulations that still apply to machinery referred to below are the those relating to tractor cabs. As a result, this chapter is much shorter than its predecessors as, for the most part, agricultural workers are subject to the same regime as other workers.

THE FARM AS A WORKPLACE

26.09 It was always possible for a workshop on a farm (eg where a circular saw is in use) to be a workshop subject to the Factories Acts.[1] The Agriculture (Safety, Health and Welfare Provisions) Act 1956 was the first comprehensive Act for the protection of farm workers and provided a means to define 'agriculture' at some length in s 24(1) to include, in addition to farms in the ordinary sense, such things as orchards and nursery grounds. It also seems that the Act extended to forestry operations, because the definition included 'the use of land as ... woodland'. *Pottinger v Peterson* 1997 SLT 387, OH further clarified the meaning of employment in agriculture under what was then the Agriculture Field Machinery Regulations 1962, reg 3. This case arose from a claim by an employee for damages relating to serious leg injury in 1990 whilst operating a tractor-drawn peat cutter on a Scottish croft. The action was dismissed in so far as it was founded upon peat working being 'an agricultural activity' under the 1962 Regulations: a view not accepted by the court.

1   In *Longhurst v Guildford, Godalming and District Water Board* [1961] 1 QB 408
    Devlin LJ raised the somewhat strange argument that premises on a farm could not be
    within the definition of 'factory', because grain and similar things handled in bulk are not
    articles. If so, a flour mill cannot be a factory either.

26.10 The 1956 Act was replaced by provisions of the Workplace (Health,
Safety and Welfare) Regulations 1992, SI 1992/3004 covering basic welfare
and related issues on farms and other agricultural and forestry workplaces.
However reg 3(4) of those Regulations exempts 'workplaces in fields, woods
or other land forming part of an agricultural or forestry undertaking but
which is not inside a building and is situated away from the main buildings'
from: reg 5 (workplaces and equipment maintenance), reg 6 (ventilation),
reg 7 (temperature), reg 8 (lighting), reg 9 (cleanliness), reg 10 (space), reg 11
(workstations and seating), reg 12 (floors and traffic routes), reg 13 (falls),
reg 14 (translucent doors), regs 15 and 16 (windows), reg 17 (traffic routes),
reg 18 (doors), reg 19 (escalators), reg 23 (accommodation for clothing),
reg 24 (changing) and reg 25 (rest and meal facilities). Regulation 20 (toilets),
reg 21 (washing facilities), and reg 22 (drinking water) only apply as far as
reasonably practicable. These exemptions (including the 'reasonably practicable' qualification) are all consistent with the Workplace Directive which
(art 1(2)(e)) excludes the premises described entirely. The Provision and Use of
Equipment at Work Regulations 1992 (now 1998) made many revocations of
the various agricultural regulations, and replaced them with less specific duties
which came into effect in 1993 or 1997 (see below). The Personal Protective
Equipment Regulations 1992 and the Management of Health and Safety at
Work Regulations 1992 (now 1999) took effect on 1 January 1993 and both
apply to farm employees.

TRACTORS

26.11 The Agriculture (Tractor Cabs) Regulations 1974, SI 1974/2034,
which have remained in force, require tractors to have a safety cab or frame of
an approved pattern marked with an official sign (crown in triangle), with
exceptions for use in hop gardens and orchards or inside farm buildings where
use with the safety cab is not reasonably practicable. 'A safety cab' is one
which is rigid enough to protect the driver if the tractor overturns. Workers
must report overturning incidents or damage to the cab. Amendments in 1984
required official approval to be given where cabs conform to EC standards for
protection against noise and overturning. In 1999 the Agriculture (Tractor
Cabs) Regulations 1974 were used to prosecute a farmer when a worker was
seen using a tractor without roll-over protection when silage making: *R v JJ
How* (1999) HSE Case No F080000162. The Provision and Use of Work
Equipment Regulations 1998, reg 26 require seat restraints to be fitted in all
mobile machines used at work including tractors if there was a risk of
crushing between the machine and the ground. This was required for all
machines 'new' to a premises by 5 December 1998 and to all other machines
by 5 December 2002.

MACHINERY REGULATIONS

26.12 Almost all of the previous agriculture agricultural machinery regulations were revoked and replaced by PUWER 1998.[1] The detailed common European norms (CENs) that guide the design and manufacture of specific agricultural machinery are covered by the Supply of Machinery Regulations 1992. In 1998 a farmer was fined £1,250 when a general farm worker was fatally injured by rotating tine bars on a hay tedder when the power take off (PTO) mechanism failed on a tractor. There were no stand off guards, the PTO control was defective and the PTO was not properly enclosed and there was no risk assessment on the task thus breaching the HSWA 1974, s 2(1) and the Management Regulations, reg 3(1). In 1999, a wholesaler of agricultural machinery and accessories including implements for tractors was fined £75,000 (reduced to £20,000 on appeal) when a farm worker was killed by an unguarded shaft on an egg-collecting machine at a poultry farm, thus breaching the HSWA 1974, s 6(1): *R v RJ Patchett* HSE Case No FO80000158.

[1] For example the Agriculture (Threshers and Balers) Regulations 1960, the Agriculture (Stationery Machinery) Regulations 1959 and the Agriculture (Power Take off) Regulations 1957. For details of the previous regulations see the 12th edn of this work.

FARM TRANSPORT

26.13 This is covered by road traffic Acts and certain health and safety legislation. By 2000, the Supply of Machinery (Safety) Regulations 1992 were being used by enforcement agencies with the HSWA 1974, s 6 to ensure braking capacities on machines, operator visibility and audible warning signs were all being used on farm transport. PUWER 1998 and the Agriculture (Tractor Cab) Regulations 1974 cover tractors, farm dumpers and other farm transport in terms of maintenance of equipment. Such measures would also capture the design and use of all-terrain vehicles (ATVs) in agriculture and forestry. In 2001, a fatality occurred to a 14-year-old on part-time work placement from school when driving an ATV to feed pheasants. The prosecution that followed, under HSWA 1974, s 3(1), resulted in a £35,000 fine for the employer (*R v GAA Leisure Ltd* HSE Case No F120000521 (6 July 2005, unreported)).

ROOFING, LIFTING AND CONSTRUCTION WORK IN AGRICULTURE AND FORESTRY

26.14 Between 1989 and 1999, 23 deaths were recorded in agriculture from falls through roofs. By 2000 this hazard was a priority for enforcement agencies, who sought the compliance of farmers and others with the Construction (Health, Safety and Welfare) Regulations 1996, SI 1996/1592, in terms of risk assessments, use of working platforms, method statements and systems of work. These Regulations and the Construction (Design and Management) Regulations 1994, SI 1994/3140, cover most structural work activities on farms and related premises. With effect from 6 April 2005, the Work at

26.15 *Agriculture and forestry*

Height Regulations 2005 replace and revoke those aspects of the Construction (Health, Safety and Welfare) Regulations 1996 which relate to falls and falling objects.

26.15 In 1998 a farmer was fined £8,000 following an accident to an employee whose fingers were damaged in the chains of a lift truck while he stood on a home-made platform. Serious accidents have also occurred linked to lifting of agricultural produce and equipment on farms. The Lifting Operations and Lifting Equipment Regulations 1998, SI 1998/2307, require lifting operations involving lifting equipment to be properly planned by a competent person, supervised and carried out safely.

SAFETY OF CHILDREN AND YOUNG PEOPLE

26.16 In 1998 the Prevention of Accidents to Children in Agriculture Regulations were introduced, followed in 1999 by an Approved Code of Practice on Preventing Accidents to Children in Agriculture. The Regulations and ACOP applied all to children resident on and visitors to farms. Between 1987 and 1998, 66 children were killed as a result of agricultural and related work activities. The Prevention of Accidents to Children in Agriculture Regulations 1998, SI 1998/3262 replaced the Agriculture (Avoidance of Accidents to Children) Regulations 1958 under which children below the permitted age of employment (ie two years below school-leaving age, there-fore at present 14) must not be allowed to ride on or drive certain vehicles, machines and implements. The 1998 Regulations prohibit children under 13 years of age from riding in the cab of a tractor used in an agricultural operation where a known accident risk exists from farm machinery. Regula-tion 3(1) prohibits children from riding on tractors, self-propelled machinery, trailers, machine or agricultural implements mounted or towed on a trailer. Regulation 3(1) does not apply to a trailer when a child rides on its floor a load carried by it 'where it possesses adequate means for preventing the child falling from it' (reg 3(2)). Regulation 4 prohibits children driving a tractor or self-propelled vehicle while it is being used in the course of agricultural operations or is going to and from the site of such operations.

POISONOUS SPRAYINGS ETC

26.17 Prior to the 1985 legislation, a voluntary code existed for the approval of pesticides in the UK. The Agriculture (Poisonous Substances) Act 1952 (Repeals and Modification) Regulations 1975 regulated spraying and similar operations for specific chemicals. These Regulations were replaced by the Control of Substances Hazardous to Health Regulations 1988, and are now contained within the comprehensive COSHH Regulations 2002 and related ACOPs. These Regulations prohibit or restrict the use of some substances and impose general requirements for risk assessment, risk management, health surveillance, record keeping and safety and protective equipment on a much wider range of chemicals used in both agriculture and forestry. The Food and

652

Environment Protection Act 1985 and the Control of Pesticides Regulations 1986, SI 1986/1510, also apply to pesticide use, and successful prosecutions have been taken against farmers under the Food and Environment Protection Act 1985, Part III and the Control of Pesticides Regulations 1986 relating to storage of non-approved pesticides and storage of pesticides without taking precautions: *R v Wright* (2000) HSE Case No F130000205. The Control of Pesticides Regulations 1986 additionally require pesticide users, regardless of age, to obtain a certificate of competence in pesticide use if they provide commercial services and, if they are not providing a commercial service, to obtain a certificate if they were born later than 31 December 1964.

26.18 The Control of Pesticides Regulations 1986 cover toxicological and general health and safety data requirements for approval of pesticides, and procedures and safeguards for disclosure of information under the Regulations were introduced. They also require employers to control the risks associated with pesticides and to demonstrate that the use of pesticides is strictly monitored and controlled. A failure that resulted in a successful prosecution in 1999, when workers were exposed to sulphuric acid on a farm, was *R v Llewellin and Co* (2000) HSE Case No F110000535.[1] In 2003, offences relating to aerial spraying were committed under these Regulations. Helicopter sprayers failed to notify a chief environmental health officer of their activities when treating bracken with asulox herbicide (*R v MFH Helicopters* (2004) HSE Case No F110000820).

1   The largest fine for breaches of pesticide legislation came in 1999 for an offence committed in 1997 when a farmer was fined £222,000 for 11 separate charges relating to use of non-approved pesticides, lack of control over exposure of farm workers to such pesticides and falsification of spraying records. The offences included breaches of COSHH Regulations, the Management of Health and Safety at Work Regulations 1999, Control of Pesticides Regulations 1986: *R v Boswell* (1999) HSE Case No FO20000231. Additionally the HSWA 1974, s 3 applied when in 1999 a child fell into an uncovered sheep dip bath, where a cover to the sheep dip had not been fitted and where an enforcement notice had been served in the past to ensure the sheep dip was protected: *R v RD Harrison* HSE Case No F15000311.

26.19 The Control of Pesticides Regulations 1986 have raised complex legal questions with regard to the relationship between UK and European law and specifically EC Directive 91/414 dealing with plant protection products and markets which came into effect as the Plant Protection Products Regulations 1995.[1] In 2004, an appeal was allowed in the Court of Appeal and a retrial ordered in *R v Searby and RE Searby Ltd* [2003] EWCA Crim 1910 against their conviction under the Control of Pesticides Regulations 1986 of selling and storing pesticides without ministerial approval. The defence revolved around the extent to which EU law impacted on national pesticide approval systems and the defendants' belief that they did not need legal approval to sell or store particular pesticides and had therefore not applied for such approval.

1   Revoked and replaced by SI 2003/3241, since revoked and replaced by SI 2005/1435.

BIOCIDES

26.20 In 1998 the EC published the Biocidal Directive (1998/8/EC) for approval of these products. From May 2000 the Directive required all active substances currently marketed and used in biocidal products to be assessed across the EC and it is expected that the UK will progressively implement the Directive through the Biocidal Products Regulations 2001, SI 2001/880, covering approval, supply and the ramifications for use of biocides.[1]

[1] *A Guide to the Biocidal Products Regulations for Users of Biocidal Products* (HSG 209, 2001).

26.21 The Directive defines biocidal products as:

'active substances and preparations containing one or more active substances, put up in the form in which they are supplied to the user, intended to destroy, deter, render harmless, prevent the action of, or otherwise exert a controlling effect on any harmful organism by chemical or biological means.'

Hence the Directive and the UK Regulations cover a wide range of products used in agriculture, horticulture and forestry that do not currently require authorisation, such as disinfectants and preservatives as well as those non-agricultural pesticides such as wood preservatives, public hygiene insecticides, rodenticides and surface biocides widely used in agriculture and forestry and currently covered by the Control of Pesticides Regulations 1986.

Chapter 27

OFFSHORE OIL, GAS AND MINERAL INDUSTRIES AND DIVING OPERATIONS

Stuart Brittenden

OFFSHORE INSTALLATIONS AND SUBMARINE PIPELINES

27.01 Under the Territorial Sea Act 1987 the territorial sea of the United Kingdom was extended to 12 nautical miles, measured from official base lines and subject to modification in narrow waters such as the straits of Dover. Within this area the United Kingdom and its courts exercise full sovereignty.

27.02 Extra-territorial jurisdiction had already been assumed over a much wider area. Under the Continental Shelf Act 1964 the United Kingdom assumed jurisdiction, in pursuance of international agreement, over the mineral resources of the continental shelf adjacent to British shores. Offshore oil and gas exploration originally took place in the North Sea, but over the years it has extended and work is now being done in the Irish Sea.

27.03 The offshore oil and gas industry is one of the most dangerous occupations, as well as being one of the most unattractive in terms of working conditions, workers usually being taken by helicopter to live for two weeks on the rig working 12-hour shifts, away from family and home comforts amid particularly brutal seas and nasty weather. In 2005, an estimated 18,940 workers were based offshore. Provisional figures produced by the HSE confirm that in 2005 there were no offshore fatalities (compared with three in 2004). There were 48 'major injuries' reported in 2005, the largest proportion of which were attributable to workers being struck by moving objects.[1] 551 dangerous occurrences were officially reported which predominantly concerned hydrocarbon releases, failure of offshore and well equipment, and fire incidents.

[1] Offshore Safety Statistics Bulletin 2004/2005 (16 August 2005, HSE).

27.04

Section 10 of the Petroleum Act 1998[1] authorises the establishment of 500-metre safety zones around installations in respect of designated waters. The designated waters include any waters falling within the territorial sea adjacent to the United Kingdom, or those designated under the Continental Shelf Act 1964. The 1998 Act consists of five Parts and makes detailed provision for licensing requirements in respect of searching and boring for petroleum, the construction and use of submarine pipelines, and in respect of the 'bandonment' or withdrawal of offshore installations. Sections 10 and 11 of the 1998 Act authorise the exercise of criminal and civil jurisdiction within the 'designated areas' in respect of offshore activities, and orders have been made dividing the continental shelf for this purpose between the Scottish courts and the English courts.[2] These sections give jurisdiction over delicts or torts on offshore installations though the operator of the installation or other defendant is not resident in the United Kingdom: *Johnston v Heerema Offshore Contractors Ltd* 1987 SLT 407; but this does not apply to fishing vessels moving within the area: *Fraser v John N Ward & Son Ltd* 1987 SLT 513. Sections 22 and 23 make provision for criminal and civil liability in respect of submarine pipelines.

[1] Replacing the former Continental Shelf Act 1964 and the Oil and Gas (Enterprise) Act 1982.
[2] See the Continental Shelf (Designation of Areas) (Consolidation) Order 2000, SI 2000/3062 and SI 2001/3670.

Application of the legislation

27.05 The Mineral Workings (Offshore Installations) Act 1971[1] is the original foundation stone of the legislative provisions regulating offshore installations conducting activities on the continental shelf, a jurisdiction derived from the Continental Shelf Act 1964. The legislation was prompted by the development of natural gas and oil in the North Sea and by disasters such as that of the Sea Gem which killed 13 in 1965, but it may apply to any 'mineral resources', which are not defined, and could include almost any valuable substance.[2]

[1] Extensively amended and partially repealed by the Petroleum and Submarine Pipelines Act 1975, the Oil and Gas (Enterprise) Act 1982, and the Petroleum Act 1987. The Petroleum Act 1998 revoked and replaced much of the 1975 and 1987 Acts, and amended the 1982 Act.
[2] Pending future developments, the Deep Sea Mining (Temporary Provisions) Act 1981 (which is still in force) requires a licence for the exploration or exploitation of 'the hard mineral resources of the deep sea bed' and a licence will normally be subject to conditions for the safety of persons employed. For the form of licence see the Deep Sea Mining (Exploration Licences) Regulations 1984, SI 1984/1230.

27.06 The 1971 Act and the Regulations made under it, and the Petroleum Act 1998, now take effect within the general framework of the HSWA 1974. Most of that Act (ss 1–59 and 80–82) is extended to offshore installations and pipelines in territorial waters and areas designated under the Continental Shelf Act by the Health and Safety at Work Act 1974 (Application outside Great Britain) Order 2001, SI 2001/2127.

27.07 The 1971 Act has been greatly amended and rather relegated in prominence by the legislation which has flowed from the Cullen Report (1990, Cm 1310) into the Piper Alpha disaster, in particular the Offshore Safety Act 1992. Further Regulations have come into effect to implement European Directives, in particular 89/392/EEC and 92/91/EEC. The principal Regulations are the Offshore Installations and Pipeline Works (Management and Administration) Regulations 1995, SI 1995/738, the Offshore Installations and Wells (Design and Construction, etc) Regulations 1996, SI 1996/913 and the Offshore Installations (Safety Case) Regulations 2005, SI 2005/3117.

27.08 A number of definitions have to be considered to determine the precise activities to which the statutory provisions apply. Regulation 2 of the Offshore Installations and Pipeline Works (Management and Administration) Regulations 1995[1] contains a series of elaborate definitions.

1   As amended by the Offshore Installations (Safety Case) Regulations 2005, SI 2005/3117.

27.09 First of all 'relevant waters' are defined to mean:

(1)   tidal waters and parts of sea adjacent to Great Britain up to the seaward limits of the territorial waters; and
(2)   any area designated by the Continental Shelf Act 1964 (s 1(7)).

27.10 Under reg 3, the 1995 Regulations apply to the following:

(1)   any structure which is to be or has been used whilst standing or stationed in relevant waters, or on foreshore or land intermittently covered by water;
(2)   for exploitation, or exploration with a view to exploitation, of mineral resources by means of a well;
(3)   for storage of gas or the recovery of gas stored;
(4)   the conveyance of things by means of a pipeline;
(5)   premises used mainly for the provision of accommodation for persons who work on or from a structure which is not an excepted structure.

27.11 Although at present offshore installations are generally well out in the open sea, they can be quite close to land or on a tidal foreshore and they are covered by the legislation provided that there is no permanent link with land above the tidemark (so a seaside pier adapted for the purpose would be excluded).

27.12 An 'offshore installation' (which is the principal object to which the web of legislation outlined in this chapter applies) was originally (s 1(4)) an installation for the carrying on of one of the four activities above. It now includes wells, pipelines, 'flotels' and accommodation vessels (if that is their primary purpose) and activities including construction, repair, dismantling, loading, unloading and diving: Health and Safety at Work Act 1974 (Application outside Great Britain) Order 2001, SI 2001/2127.

27.13 Regulation 2 of the 1995 Regulations applies to a fixed offshore installation other than a mobile installation. A mobile installation is an offshore installation other than a floating platform which can be moved from place to place without major dismantling or modification.

27.14 Installations are in some ways analogous to ships, in others to mines, in others (the superstructure) to factories, and the legislation was of a hybrid character, related to the law on all three until the fundamental revisions after the Cullen Report (1990, Cm 1310) into the Piper Alpha disaster of 6 July 1988 when an explosion caused the death of 165 of the 226 workers aboard the oil rig. The subsequent legislation has adopted a different structure and one which is more consistent with that of European health and safety law. The basis for subsequent regulations has been the Offshore Safety Act 1992 which extends the jurisdiction of the HSWA 1974 and in particular the regulation-making power of the HSWA 1974, s 15, to the continental shelf and the offshore industry upon it. In *McFarlane v Wilkinson; Hegarty v EE Caledonia Ltd* [1997] 2 Lloyd's Rep 259, the Court of Appeal held that reg 32(3)(a) of the Offshore Installations (Operational Safety, Health and Welfare) Regulations 1976 (since revoked) did not apply to protect persons who suffered psychiatric injury as a result of witnessing the *Piper Alpha* fire from a ship nearby. Because the regulation imposed a duty 'not to do anything likely to endanger the safety or health' of persons on or near the installation, it would have to be shown that it was likely, and not merely reasonably foreseeable, that a breach of the duty would impair the mental health of someone on a vessel more than 100m away from the fire.

Registration and inspection

27.15 Under the Offshore Installations and Pipeline Works (Management and Administration) Regulations 1995, SI 1995/738, the owner or operator of a fixed or temporary offshore installation (the 'duty holder') is required to notify the HSE of the date of intended entry or departure of the installation from relevant waters. Notification is also required where there has been a change in duty holder (reg 5).

27.16 One of the recommendations of the Cullen Report was that responsibility for inspection as well as the health and safety authority for offshore installations, should be transferred from the Department of Energy to the HSE. This was effected by the Offshore Safety (Repeals and Modifications) Regulations 1993, SI 1993/1823. In consequence, the HSE has the powers of inspection and obtaining of information granted by the Offshore Installations (Inspectors and Casualties) Regulations 1973, SI 1973/1842. These Regulations also require the reporting of casualties in prescribed form by the installation manager.

Manager

27.17 Under reg 6 of the Offshore Installations and Pipeline Works (Management and Administration) Regulations 1995, SI 1995/738, introduced under the HSWA 1974, s 15, the duty-holder must appoint a competent person to take charge of the installation and persons on it, and must provide the manager with appropriate resources to be able to carry out their function effectively. The identity of the installation manager must be known to or readily ascertainable by every person on the installation.

Design and construction

27.18 Under reg 4 of the Offshore Installations and Wells (Design and Construction, etc) Regulations 1996, SI 1996/913, the duty-holder is under a general duty to ensure that an installation possesses 'such integrity as is reasonably practicable'. The Regulations impose a number of specific duties. Installations are to be designed, so far as is reasonably practicable, to ensure that they can withstand reasonably foreseeable forces of nature, and that their layout, fabrication, transportation, construction, operation, and any maintenance work can proceed without prejudicing their integrity (reg 5). This duty also extends to the choice of materials used for constructing the installation. Any work involving construction, modification, maintenance and repair has to be carried out in such a way as to ensure the integrity of the installation (reg 6). Duty-holders must also keep records of the operational limits of the installation, as well as the environmental conditions in which they may be safely operated, and ensure that such records are made available to any person involved in the operation of the installation (reg 7). Arrangements must be made for maintaining the integrity of the installation (reg 8), and the HSE must be notified within ten days of the appearance of a significant threat to the structural integrity of the installation (reg 9). Duty-holders are also required to ensure that additional requirements are complied with. These detailed requirements are set out in Sch 1 and cover matters such as the organisation of the installation, ventilation, room temperatures, roofing, heating, windows, doors, traffic routes and washing facilities. A number of specific regulations govern the design, construction and operation of wells (regs 13–21).

Safety case

27.19 The Offshore Installations (Safety Case) Regulations 2005, SI 2005/3117, came into force on 6 April 2006. The principal theme of the 2005 Regulations is to ensure the preparation of safety cases for offshore installations and to set out requirements for notification of prescribed activities to the HSE. The earlier 1992 Regulations (bearing the same name), sought to implement art 3(2) of Directive 92/91/EEC concerning the minimum requirements for improving safety and health protection of workers in the mineral extracting industries involving drilling. The 2005 Regulations are intended to make further provision in respect of minimum safety standards. Detailed provision is made for production and non-production installations, combined operations,[1] dismantling fixed installations, and in respect of well operations.

---

[1] Ie where there are two or more installations and an activity is carried out on, from or by one for a purpose related to another and where the activity could affect the health and safety of persons connected with any of the installations.

27.20 A 'safety case' is defined in the Regulations as a document containing prescribed information relating to the management of health and safety and the control of major accident hazards (see regs 2 and 12). The Schedules to the Regulations specify the prescribed information which should be included within a safety case. The procedures and arrangements set out in a safety case must be complied with on pain of criminal liability. Nothing is said about civil liability, so the Regulations will be actionable in accordance with the HSWA 1974, s 47(2).

27.21 The particulars which must be included within a safety case are too detailed for summary here but they include such matters as a description (with scale diagrams) of the structure of the installation, its materials, layout and connections to pipelines and wells.[1] A vital and noteworthy matter (after the Piper Alpha disaster) are the provisions protecting against fire, heat, smoke, toxic gas, or fumes by means of evacuation, temporary safe refuge and escape routes (including a statement of the performance standards achieved for them and a demonstration by quantitative risk assessment that the risks referred to are reduced to the lowest reasonably practicable level).

[1]   Schedule 1: contains particulars which must be included in a design or relocation notification; Sch 2: safety cases for production installations; Sch 3: safety cases for non-production installations; Sch 4: combined operations; Sch 5: dismantling operations; and Sch 6: well operations.

27.22 Particulars must also be given of the weather and sea conditions to which the installation may be subjected, and the measures taken to detect, prevent or minimise fire, explosion, leak of gas etc. In addition, the safety case must demonstrate that the operator or owner's management system is adequate (and is systematically audited) to ensure compliance with statutory requirements, identification of major accident hazards, evaluation of risks and their reduction to the lowest reasonably practicable level (reg 8).

27.23 An operator is required to ensure that a production installation is not operated unless a safety case has been prepared and sent to the HSE at least six months before commencing operations and that the HSE has accepted the safety case proposed (reg 7). A production installation includes one which extracts petroleum from the beneath the sea bed by means of a well; or stores gas in or under the shore or bed of relevant waters and recovers the gas which has been so stored; or installations which are used for the conveyance of petroleum by means of a pipe. The movement of a non-production installation in relevant waters with a view to it being operated is prohibited unless a safety case has been sent to and accepted by the HSE (reg 8). It is prohibited to dismantle a fixed installation unless a revised safety case has been submitted and accepted (reg 11). Safety cases have to be reviewed at five year intervals or when instructed to do so by the HSE (regs 13–14). The Regulations also give the HSE powers of access in respect of safety cases and related documentation.

27.24 Regulation 5 imposes duties upon licensees to ensure that the appointed operator is capable of satisfactorily carrying out functions and discharging duties under the relevant statutory provisions in force. The licensee is also required to 'take all reasonable steps' to ensure that any appointed operator carries out their functions and discharges all applicable statutory duties. Regulation 6(1) requires the operator of a 'production installation' to prepare a design notification containing particulars (specified in Sch 1) and send a copy to the HSE prior to submitting a field development programme to the Department of Trade and Industry. This is to enable the HSE to raise design matters affecting safety. Regulation 6(2) makes similar provision in circumstances where an operator of a production installation intends to move it to a new location (whether outside relevant waters or not). Where there is a material change in any of the relevant particulars to be provided, the operator must notify the HSE as soon as practicable.[1] Similarly, reg 9 makes detailed provision for instances where a non-production installation is intended to be converted to enable it to be operated as a production installation, the owner is required to submit a design notification to the HSE. The HSE must be notified prior to the commencement of well operations (reg 17). The Regulations require verification schemes to be in place, setting out monitoring procedures of safety critical elements by an independent and competent person (reg 19). Records must be retained for six months.[2]

[1]   Regulation 18(3).
[2]   A key recommendation of the Cullen Report (Cm 1310, 1990).

27.25 There are other complementary provisions contained in the Offshore Installations (Prevention of Fire and Explosion, and Emergency Response) Regulations 1995, SI 1995/743.[1] These make further provision for the prevention or minimisation of the risk of fire and explosion, detecting incidents requiring emergency response, protecting people in the event of fire or explosion, devising an emergency response plan, and other measures for securing effective emergency response in such event.

[1]   See also the Health and Safety (Safety Signs and Symbols) Regulations 1996, SI 1996/341, reg 4 and the Offshore Safety (Miscellaneous Amendments) Regulations 2002, SI 2002/2175, reg 2.

Other safety regulations

27.26 Many health and safety regulations apply offshore as well as onshore. It is to be noted that the Workplace (Health, Safety and Welfare) Regulations 1992 (see chapter 18) do not apply to offshore installations (though the other 'six pack' Regulations of 1992 do apply). The COSHH Regulations 2002 (see chapter 22) apply to the offshore industry. Regulations for safety on oil rigs include the Lifting Operations and Lifting Equipment Regulations 1998, SI 1998/2307, which impose specific duties on installation managers, owners and concession owners. They apply to all installations within Great Britain and those covered by the Health and Safety at Work Act 1974 (Application Outside Great Britain) Order 2001, SI 2001/2127. They apply to employers and also self-employed persons in respect of lifting equipment used by them. The provisions also extend to any person who has control to any extent over lifting equipment or how it is used, or of a person at work who uses, supervises or manages the use of lifting equipment. The scope of the 1998 Regulations (as amended) is dealt with in chapter 20. The

Manual Handling Regulations 1992 (see chapter 21) apply to work offshore (see reg 7) as do the Control of Lead at Work Regulations (reg 14), SI 2002/2676. Similarly, the Work at Height Regulations 2005, SI 2005/735 apply to work offshore (see reg 3). These Regulations impose duties relating to the organisation and planning of work at height (reg 4); require that persons at work be competent or at least are supervised by competent persons (reg 5); prescribe steps to be taken to avoid the risk of working at height (reg 6); impose duties in respect of the selection of work equipment (reg 7); as well as impose duties for the avoidance of risks from fragile work surfaces, falling objects and danger areas (reg 8) as well as inspection regimes (regs 12–13).

27.27 The Provision and Use of Work Equipment Regulations 1998, SI 1998/2306, also apply to offshore installations (these are dealt with in chapter 20). The Regulations impose requirements upon employers to ensure that work equipment provided is constructed or adapted so as to be suitable for the purpose for which it is used or provided (reg 4) as well as duties in respect of maintenance (reg 5); inspection (reg 6); the provision of information and instructions regarding the use of work equipment (reg 8); and the provision of adequate training (reg 9). Additional protection must be taken to either prevent or minimise exposure of persons using work equipment in respect of specified hazards (reg 12). Fencing of machinery and apparatus is dealt with by reg 11. The Personal Protective Equipment Regulations 2002, SI 2002/1144, apply offshore (see reg 7 and chapter 20). So do the Electricity at Work Regulations SI 1989/635, as well as the Control of Noise at Work Regulations 2005, SI 2005/1643, reg 14 (see Offshore Electricity and Noise Regulations 1997, SI 1997/1993) and more recently, the Control of Vibration at Work Regulations 2005 SI 2005/1093.

Drilling

27.28 The Offshore Installations and Wells (Design and Construction, etc) Regulations 1996, SI 1996/913,[1] require duty-holders or well-operators to ensure that no drilling is carried out until workers have been provided with such information, instruction, training and supervision so as to reduce the health and safety risks to the lowest level reasonably practicable (reg 21). Well operators are also required to provide reports to the HSE at weekly intervals unless otherwise agreed in respect of drilling operations (reg 19).

[1] Note the definition of 'installation' was amended by the Offshore Safety (Miscellaneous Amendments) Regulations 2002, SI 2002/2175.

Emergency requirements

27.29 The Offshore Installations (Prevention of Fire and Explosion, and Emergency Response) Regulations 1995, SI 1995/743, impose duties upon the operator or owner of an installation in addition to the protections afforded by the Offshore Installations (Safety Case) Regulations 2005, SI 2005/3117 and the Health and Safety (Signs and Symbols) Regulations 1996, SI 1996/341. The 1995 Regulations contain requirements for owners or operators of installations to take appropriate measures for the protection of persons on offshore oil and gas installations from fire and explosion (regs 4, 9) and to assess the risks of a major accident by fire or explosion, or any event which could give rise to the need for evacuation (reg 5). Arrangements must be in place for dealing with emergencies (reg 6), and the duty holder must prepare an emergency response plan following consultation with persons who are likely to be involved in an emergency response (reg 8), and for securing effective emergency response to safeguard the health and safety of persons in the event of an emergency. Among other things, there are arrangements for communicating emergency warnings to all persons on the installation by audible and visual alarm systems where necessary (reg 11), detecting emergency incidents (reg 10), as well as steps to mitigate the effects of fire and explosion (reg 13), and in respect of muster areas and facilities (reg 14). Regulations 15–17 provide for arrangements to be in place governing evacuation, escape, as well as for recovery and rescue by persons beyond the installation. Under reg 18, the duty-holder is required to provide personal protective equipment for use in an emergency against the risks to health caused by fire, heat, smoke, fumes or toxic gas, as well as immersion into the sea. Life saving appliances, including survival craft, life buoys and jackets, must be of such colour as to render them conspicuous, and must be suitably equipped and in sufficient numbers for immediate use (reg 20).

First aid

27.30 The Offshore Installations and Pipeline Works (First-Aid) Regulations 1989, SI 1989/1671 impose duties on the 'person in control' of the installation (ie the duty-holder or proposed owner of a pipeline), or person in whom the pipeline is vested (ie the installation manager or, if there is no manager, whoever has been made responsible by the owner for health and safety, as well as the owner and the person with the right to exploit or store the resources the installation is intended to exploit or store—reg 2).

27.31 The person in control must ensure that first aid is available to those employed and self-employed, whether on duty or not and the arrangements for it must be made known to them. The first aid arrangements required are: sufficient first aid facilities and equipment, sufficient trained and qualified first aiders (supervised by suitably qualified registered medical practitioners) to advise and who must be available to be present when needed (reg 5(1)).

Diving operations

27.32 These are no longer controlled by a special set of regulations, but are subject to the general safety code for diving operations which applies to all places of work: see para 27.46, below.

Submarine pipelines

27.33 It has already been noted that pipelines, as such, do not count as offshore installations, though apparatus and works connected with them may be brought within the definition by Order in Council. Pipelines have, however, their own statutory code, which is concerned with the safety of the pipeline itself and ships and persons in the vicinity rather than with employees in particular.

27.34 The Petroleum Act 1998 applies to a pipeline as defined by s 26, including a pipe or system of pipes (excluding drains or sewers), for the conveyance of anything together with any associated apparatus. Associated apparatus consists of the following: inducing, treating, cooling apparatus, valves, anything supplying energy, or the transmission information to the pipe system, as well as structures used solely to support the pipe or system of pipes.

27.35 Under the Petroleum Act 1998, ss 14–28, pipelines cannot be laid, used or altered in, under or over 'controlled waters' unless authorised by the Secretary of State (Department of Energy) who may make safety regulations under s 25. The Pipelines Safety Regulations 1996, SI 1996/825, require the operator to ensure that no fluid is conveyed in a pipeline unless it has been designed so far as reasonably practicable so that it can withstand: forces arising from its operation; fluids conveyed in it; external forces; chemical processes to which it may be subjected (reg 5).[1]

---

[1]   As amended by the Pipelines Safety (Amendment) Regulations 2002, SI 2002/2563 which makes special provision for iron pipelines, and decommissioning arrangements for iron pipes with HSE approval being sought.

27.36 No fluid is allowed to be conveyed unless safety systems have been provided as are necessary to protect against risks to health and safety (reg 6). Pipelines must be constructed of suitable materials (reg 8), and operators are required to ensure that no fluid is conveyed in a pipeline (save for testing· purposes) unless constructed or installed so that it is sound and fit for the purpose so designed (reg 9). No fluid is allowed to be conveyed in a pipeline unless safe operating limits have been established and provided that it is not operated beyond such safe operational limits. Before use, adequate arrangements dealing with accidental loss of fluid, discovery of a defect or damage, or other emergency in relation to the pipeline must be devised (reg 10). Operators are to ensure that pipelines are maintained in an efficient state, efficient working order, and in good repair (reg 13), and in order to prevent damage, operators are required to ensure that reasonable steps are taken to inform persons of the whereabouts of pipelines (reg 16). Where there are different operators for different parts of a pipeline, they are under a duty to co-operate as necessary in order to comply with the Regulations.

Action for breach of statutory duty

27.37 Section 11 of the Mineral Working (Offshore Installations) Act 1971 expressly provides that breach of any statutory duty imposed on any person by the Act, or by regulations which apply s 11, shall give rise to an action for damages for personal injuries (including disease or impairment) or death: but not for damage other than injuries or death. Defences available in criminal proceedings under s 9(3) ('due diligence' etc) or under regulations are not available in a civil action. The section binds the Crown in its official capacity. The general safety regulations all declare that there is civil liability for breach of these Regulations.

27.38 The Offshore Safety Act 1992 increased the penalties for criminal offences and extended the regulation-making powers of the HSWA 1974, s 15 to the continental shelf. The 1992 Act does not affect civil liability under the regulations in this chapter (see HSWA 1974, s 47).

Safety representatives

27.39 Although safety representatives and committees have been required by law onshore since the Safety Representatives and Safety Committees Regulations 1977, SI 1977/500, they were not required offshore until the 1988 Piper Alpha disaster caused the government hastily to introduce, even before the Cullen Inquiry had got underway, the Offshore Installations (Safety Representatives and Safety Committees) Regulations 1989, SI 1989/971.[1] Under the Offshore Regulations the entitlement to nominate and elect safety representatives is that of the workforce (reg 4) whereas under the 1977 Regulations the entitlement is that of recognised trade union(s). Thus it seems that on this point the Offshore Regulations conform to art 11(1) of the Framework Directive 89/391/EEC (and other Directives, eg art 8 of the Workplace Directive 89/654/EEC which provides that 'employers shall consult workers and/or their representatives ...').

[1]   For a discussion of the rather sordid history of this 12-year exclusion see Foster and Woolfson *Trade Unionism and Health and Safety Rights in Britain's Offshore Oil Industry* (ICTUR, 1992).

27.40 The Offshore Regulations provide that the workforce[1] are divided by the installation manager into constituencies created by the installation manager by reference to four criteria: installation areas, installation activities, employer, and other objective criteria of the installation manager (reg 5). There has to be consultation over the constituencies but it is to be wondered if the exclusivity of the installation manager's decision-making in this regard is consistent with the Directive and its purpose, which imply no such employer incursion into workforce representation.

[1]   Which includes employees, the self-employed, and indeed all workers other than the installation manager.

27.41 The Regulations specify the procedure for elections (regs 7–13). It is to be noted that the elections are conducted by the installation manager. Any member of the workforce can complain to the Secretary of State that the ballot has been conducted inconsistently with the regulations or unfairly.

27.42 Safety representatives can: investigate hazards, dangerous occurrences, accidents and complaints; make representations; inspect no more than once in three months any part or equipment (on written notice); inspect on notice (not necessarily in writing) the site and potential causes of notifiable incidents; approach the installation manager and/or any employer on health and safety matters; receive inspectors' reports; consult with HSE inspectors; consult members of the safety representative's own constituency; inspect statutorily required documents, including a summary of the safety case; and request the formation of and attend meetings of the safety committee (regs 16–20). It is notable that there is no power to stop any work being done: there is merely power to alert the HSE if any imminent risk of serious injury is believed to exist.

27.43 A safety committee can be requested where there are one or more safety representatives. It must be convened within six weeks of establishment and consists of all safety representatives, the installation manager as chairman, one other nominee of the installation manager or owner, together with unanimous co-options (reg 20). It must meet at least quarterly. The procedure and function of the safety committee are set out in regs 21 and 22.

27.44 The installation manager and owner have duties to facilitate the exercise of the safety representative's functions and provide him with the necessary information and documents. The duty to provide information and documents also falls on the relevant employer (regs 23–25).

27.45 The employer of the safety representative must also allow reasonable paid time off to carry out his other functions and paid training (regs 26 and 27). Exercise of the specified functions by a safety representative cannot give rise to criminal or civil liability (reg 16). Section 100 of the Employment Rights Act 1996 provides that an employee is unfairly dismissed if the reason or principal reason for dismissal is that the employee either carried out or proposed to carry out health and safety activities as designated by their employer, or performed such functions as a safety representative or member of a safety committee in accordance with arrangements under any Act. Curiously, however, there is no protection against victimisation falling short of dismissal for participating in elections (cf Employment Rights Act 1996, s 100(1)(ba)). Employees are also protected from being subjected to any detriment in respect of one of the circumstances specified above (s 44). It is significant that there is no such protection against detriment by the installation manager or owner.[1]

[1]   Neither was there under this section's predecessor, the Offshore Safety (Protection against Victimisation) Act 1992 repealed by the Trade Union Reform and Employment Rights Act 1993, s 51.

DIVING OPERATIONS AT WORK

27.46 Safety in diving operations is regulated by a single unified code, the Diving at Work Regulations 1997, SI 1997/2776. These came into force on

1 April 1998 and replaced the Diving Operations at Work Regulations 1981. There is a separate code for diving from ships, but this does not apply in United Kingdom waters (including the continental shelf) where the general code applies to ships as it does to any other 'installation'.

27.47 The summary which follows is of a general character, and is subject to many detailed qualifications. The HSE has power to grant exemptions (reg 16). The Regulations impose a duty on every person who to any extent is responsible for, has control over, or is engaged in a diving project, or whose acts or omissions could adversely affect the health and safety of persons engaged in a diving project. Such persons are required to take reasonable steps to ensure compliance with the Regulations (reg 4).

Appointment of diving contractors and their responsibilities

27.48 No person at work may dive in a diving project and no employer may employ any person to work in such a project unless there is only one person who is the diving contractor for that specific project (reg 5). There cannot be more than one diving contractor in respect of each project. In the event that there are potentially two diving contractors, they must jointly appoint one of themselves to act as the diving contractor before the commencement of the diving project (reg 5(3)). The diving contractor is under a duty to ensure so far as is reasonably practicable that the project is planned, managed, and conducted so as to protect the health and safety of all persons participating in the project. Before the commencement of a diving project, the diving contractor must prepare a diving plan and appoint a person to supervise the project. A written record must be kept of this appointment, and the supervisor must be provided with a copy of the relevant parts of the diving plan and a record of his appointment (reg 6). Records of the diving project must be kept for at least two years after the last entry on the record. No one is allowed to act as a diving contractor until the HSE has been notified of specified particulars contained in Sch 1 (reg 7). The diving project plan must be premised upon a risk assessment of the diving project, and must contain all information and instructions which are necessary to provide advice and to regulate the behaviour of those participating in the project to ensure their health and safety, so far as is reasonably practicable (reg 8). The diving contractor is responsible for ensuring that there are sufficient suitably qualified persons to participate in the diving project as well as sufficient plant. Such plant must be maintained, and all those taking part in the project must comply with the diving plan and regulations. Records must be kept of each diving operation.

Supervisors

27.49 Only one supervisor may be appointed to supervise the operation (reg 9). No one is allowed to be appointed or otherwise act as a supervisor unless they are competent and suitably qualified to supervise the project. They are expressly required to ensure so far as is practicable that the diving operation is carried out without risk to health and safety, and in accordance

667

with the regulations and diving project plan. Supervisors must ensure that all those participating in the diving project are familiar with the relevant provisions of the diving plan, and complete the necessary records (reg 10). Supervisors are generally prohibited from diving during diving operations except in specified instances, for instance where they are guiding or training, or are diving recreationally. They are empowered to give reasonable instructions and directions (reg 11).

Divers

27.50 The Regulations set out the duties and restrictions upon divers involved in diving projects. They must have approved qualifications, certificates of medical fitness to dive, and keep daily diving records (reg 12). Certain categories of diver are exempt from specified obligations. As regards others involved in the diving project, they are prohibited from diving unless they are competent, and provided that they are not aware of anything which renders them unfit to dive (reg 13). They are required to observe the directions given by the supervisor as well as the diving plan.

Approved qualifications

27.51 The HSE are empowered to approve such diving qualifications as they consider to be suitable for ensuring the adequate competence of divers, and can impose limitations and conditions upon obtaining such approval (reg 14).

Medical certificates

27.52 Appeals can be made to the HSE in respect of decisions to grant, refuse, revoke or otherwise impose conditions upon the granting of medical certificates (reg 15). The Regulations set out transitional and supplementary provisions in respect of training and medical certificates, diving operation log books and divers' log books (reg 17).

Chapter 28

FOREIGN ACCIDENTS AND ILL-HEALTH ABROAD[1]

Philip Mead

28.01 Workplace accidents which occur (or work illness that is caused) in another jurisdiction give rise to two legal questions which in normal circumstances are taken for granted: (1) do the domestic courts have jurisdiction (ie are they entitled as a matter of law) to determine the dispute? If the answer to that question is in the positive, (2) what law (or laws) applies to determine the dispute? These questions are pertinent not only in relation to foreign accidents, but also in connection with accidents which take place in one of the other jurisdictions within the UK (England and Wales, Scotland or Northern Ireland). The laws of each of the British jurisdictions have, directly and indirectly, been harmonised through Europe. Common rules now apply by virtue of the Brussels Regulation[2] and the Rome Convention, and the most recent legislative intervention provides uniform rules of private international law for tort and delict. In so far as this chapter describes conflicts of law rules, particularly procedural rules, which have not been harmonised, the law as described is from an English point of view.[3]

---

[1] For a more detailed analysis of the rules of private international law, see Collins (gen ed) *Dicey and Morris: The Conflict of Laws* (13th edn, 2000, with supplements); Plender and Wilderspin *The European Contracts Convention* (2nd edn, 2001); Layton and Mercer (eds) *European Civil Practice* (2nd edn, 2004); Briggs and Rees *Civil Jurisdiction and Judgments* (4th edn, 2005).

[2] Council Regulation (EC) No 44/2001 on jurisdiction and the recognition and enforcement of judgments in civil and commercial matters entered into force on and is directly applicable in the Member States from 1 March 2002 (referred to hereafter as the Brussels Regulation, see *Civil Court Practice 2006*, Volume 1, p 228) and supersedes the Brussels Convention, save that Denmark is not bound by the new regime and therefore the former Brussels Convention continues to apply in that regard.

[3] For Scottish reference works see 17 *Stair Memorial Encyclopaedia; Anton and Beaumont's Civil Jurisdiction in Scotland* (2nd edn, 1995); Aird and Jameson *The Scots Dimension to Cross-Border Litigation* (1996). Volume 2 of Layton and Mercer (eds) *European Civil Practice* (2nd edn, 2004) has separate chapters on Scotland and Northern Ireland.

JURISDICTION

28.02

There are two principal regimes which determine the entitlement of an injured claimant to sue in England and Wales: jurisdiction under the Brussels Regulation 44/2001 (which updates and revises the former regime contained in the 1968 Brussels Convention on Jurisdiction and the Enforcement of Judgments in Civil and Commercial Matters); alternatively, jurisdiction under

CPR 1998, Pt 6.20 (formerly RSC Ord 11). Until recently, there had been some controversy as to the capacity of the domestic courts to apply general principles of conflicts of law in cases which fall within the scope of the Brussels regime. Two judgments from the ECJ[1] make it clear that where a case falls within the scope of the European harmonised rules on jurisdiction there is now no entitlement to stay proceedings on the ground of forum non conveniens or for abuse of process.[2] Either a claim against a defendant falls exclusively within the scope of the Brussels Regulation or it does not. Most litigation concerning employers' liability with a transnational element is likely to involve either a UK-domiciled defendant or a European-domiciled defendant, in which case the Brussels regime applies. The circumstances in which the regime under CPR 1998, Pt 6.20 shall apply to allow proceedings to be brought in the UK courts against a non-European domiciled defendant in respect of an employers' liability claim is likely to be limited. The first part of this chapter describes: (1) the Brussels Regulation regime (which applies with equal effect in Scotland and Northern Ireland); (2) the rules applicable to determine jurisdiction as between jurisdictions within the UK (or in one UK jurisdiction); and (3) the rules applicable under CPR 1998, Pt 6.20, and the doctrine of forum non conveniens (whether England is the appropriate forum to hear the case).

1   Case C-159/02 *Turner v Grovit* [2005] 1 AC 101, and Case C-281/02 *Owusu v Jackson (t/a Villa Holidays Bal-Inn Villas)* [2005] QB 805, references respectively from the House of Lords and the Court of Appeal.
2   The boundary between the application of the Brussels Convention on the one hand, and domestic law conflicts of law principles on the other hand, had been unclear, in particular as to whether foreign-domiciled defendants and English defendants were subject exclusively to the Brussels Convention regime, where there is a more appropriate forum in a non-Contracting State. Previously, the Court of Appeal decision of *In Re Harrods (Buenos Aires) Ltd* [1992] Ch 72, which had held that the Brussels Convention did not preclude the application of the principle of forum non conveniens, had been followed in the cases of *Ace Insurance SA-NV v Zurich Insurance Co* [2001] EWCA Civ 173, [2001] 1 Lloyd's Rep 618, CA; *Eli Lilly and Co v Novo Nordisk A/S* [2000] IL Pr 73; *Haji-Ioannou v Frangos* [1999] 2 Lloyd's Rep 337; and *Sarrio SA v Kuwait Investment Authority* [1997] 1 Lloyd's Rep 113.

Jurisdiction under the Brussels Regulation

28.03 In order fully to understand the scheme of the Brussels Regulation, it is necessary to have regard to the provisions and case law decided under the previous regime under the 1968 Brussels Convention, as amended. The Brussels Convention was drafted under the auspices of the European Economic Community and was ratified by 12 EU Member States: Belgium; Denmark; France; Germany; Greece; Ireland; Italy; Luxembourg; Netherlands; Portugal; Spain and the UK. The three more recent EU Member States (Austria, Finland and Sweden) as well as Iceland, Norway, and Switzerland and the 12 EU Member States are parties to the 1988 Lugano Convention, which in very large measure replicates the Brussels Convention regime. These States are referred to as Contracting States in the Brussels and Lugano Conventions. The Brussels Convention has been implemented by the Civil Jurisdiction and Judgments Act 1982 and is annexed to the 1982 Act at Sch 1, the Lugano Convention is contained in Sch 3C.[1]

1   When interpreting the Conventions, it is also important to take into account the reports of
     the rapporteurs of the working parties which drafted the original 1968 Convention, the
     1971 Protocol granting jurisdiction to the ECJ and the Accession Convention of 1978 (the
     Jenard and Schlosser Reports in particular). These reports will continue to be of assistance
     in interpreting provisions of the Brussels Regulation.

28.04 The regime provided by the Brussels Regulation is prescriptive in that it defines those courts of the Member States which have jurisdiction under the Regulation in relation to European-domiciled defendants. Jurisdiction is established as of right, there is no discretion which resides in the domestic courts to apply national rules of procedure or conflicts of laws rules to stay proceedings in favour of another court, where that court is first seised of the issue in dispute. Provided that there are no other Member State courts seised of the dispute, where the defendant is domiciled in the UK the UK courts must accept jurisdiction over disputes of a civil or commercial character (which obviously includes actions for personal injury), where there is a choice between different jurisdictions of the Member States. Article 27 of the Brussels Regulation requires a court other than the court first seised of a dispute between the same parties and involving the same cause of action to stay proceedings of its own motion. The courts may also, under art 28, stay proceedings where there are parallel proceedings concerning related actions pending the outcome of the litigation at first instance in the court first seised.

28.05 The significance of this principle became apparent in Case C-281/02 *Owusu v Jackson* [2005] QB 801, where a claimant who had suffered catastrophic injury whilst on holiday in Jamaica brought proceedings in the High Court against an English-domiciled defendant and several Jamaican defendants. The defendants applied for the English proceedings to be stayed on the basis that the more appropriate forum for the litigation was Jamaica. The judge at first instance held that there was no power to stay proceedings against an English domiciled defendant by virtue of art 2 of the Brussels Convention (now art 2 of the Brussels Regulation), and that, accordingly, to prevent multiplicity of proceedings, the Jamaican defendants were also appropriately joined as necessary and proper parties to the action. On appeal to the Court of Appeal, a reference was made to the ECJ asking whether art 2 of the Brussels Convention precluded the exercise of a power to stay proceedings against an English-domiciled defendant in favour of the courts of a third non-EU State. The ECJ held that art 2 precluded the exercise of any discretion by the domestic court to stay proceedings, and that the claimant was entitled to bring proceedings against the English domiciled defendant in the English courts in accordance with the Brussels Convention. The claimant (and the defendants) were entitled to know with certainty which courts had jurisdiction to hear the claim. The consequence of the ruling in *Owusu* is that UK domiciled defendants are now answerable in their domestic courts for torts committed worldwide, whatever the proper law of the tort.

28.06 The Brussels Regulation provides for a hierarchy of rules in respect of jurisdiction. Where a claimant's claim falls within the scope of one rule, then that rule shall apply, rather than permitting the claimant to exercise a choice in respect of a rule lower in the hierarchy. The following provisions of the Brussels Regulation may be applicable in relation to an employers' liability claim:

(1)   art 22: claims which have as their object rights in rem in immovable property or tenancies of immovable property;
(2)   art 24: claims where the defendant has entered an appearance;
(3)   arts 8 to 14: claims arising out of a contract of insurance;
(4)   arts 18 to 21: claims arising out of a contract of employment;
(5)   art 2: claims in respect of defendants domiciled in the jurisdiction;
(6)   art 5(3): claims where the harmful event occurred within the jurisdiction;
(7)   art 6(1): claims in respect of more than one defendant, where a co-defendant is domiciled within the jurisdiction.

Exclusive jurisdiction: land

28.07 Article 22 of the Brussels Regulation (formerly Brussels Convention, art 16) is important, as should any dispute fall within its scope, then the courts of the Member State in which the property is situated shall have jurisdiction, regardless of the domicile of the parties. The rule concerns proceedings which have as their object rights in rem in immovable property or tenancies of immovable property.[1]

---

[1]   See *Dicey and Morris*, Rule 113. This rule may be of significance in relation to use, for example of holiday lets or time shares of property situated abroad, but is unlikely to be an issue in relation to employers' liability. For recent cases see: Case C-8/98 *Dansommer v Gotz* [2000] ECR I-393; Case C-73/04 *Klein v Rhodos Management Ltd* [2005] All ER (D) 148 (Oct), ECJ.

Claims where the defendant has entered an appearance

28.08 Article 24 of the Brussels Regulation (formerly Brussels Convention, art 18) provides jurisdiction to a court where a defendant enters an appearance. The rule does not apply where an appearance is entered to contest jurisdiction, or where jurisdiction is determined according to art 22.[1] The CPR, Part 11 provides a particular mechanism for disputing jurisdiction, upon filing an acknowledgment of service. By CPR Part 11(5) where a defendant files an acknowledgment of service and does not make an application to dispute the jurisdiction of the court within 14 days after filing the acknowledgment, the defendant is treated as having accepted that the court has jurisdiction to try the claim.

---

[1]   See *Dicey and Morris*, Rule 28(21), para 11R-346.

Claims arising out of a contract of insurance

28.09 Articles 8–14 of the Brussels Regulation provides a revised and expanded regime in relation to matters relating to insurance (formerly Brussels Convention, arts 7–12a). These provisions apply where a road traffic insurer is sued by a claimant relying on a direct cause of action granted under the Fourth Motor Insurance Directive.[1] The provisions are detailed and complex. A claim may be brought in the courts of the domicile of the insurer; in addition the injured claimant may sue in the courts of the domicile of the policyholder. Mention should also be made of the Fifth Motor Insurance Directive, which purports to amend the Fourth Motor Insurance Directive to provide that claimants may sue in the state of the claimant's domicile by the application of arts 9(1)(b) and 11(2) of the Brussels Regulation.[2] This author considers that this is an incorrect reading of the regime under the Brussels Regulation, in particular the wording of art 9(1)(b) in conjunction with art 11(2), which distinguishes between a beneficiary and an injured party. A claimant as an injured party cannot also constitute a beneficiary under a contract of insurance. The provisions of the Fifth Motor Insurance Directive amending the Fourth Motor Insurance Directive suggest that there is no such distinction.[3]

1   Directive 2000/26/EC on the approximation of the laws of the Member States relating to insurance against civil liability in respect of the use of motor vehicles and amending Council Directives 73/239/EEC and 88/357/EEC, OJ 2000 L 181/65.
2   See Article 5(1) of Directive 2005/14/EC amending Council Directives 72/166/EEC, 84/5/EEC, 88/357/EEC and 90/232/EEC and Directive 2000/26/EC relating to insurance against civil liability in respect of the use of motor vehicles (OJ 2005 L149/14).
3   Query how a Directive which requires implementation by the Member States can amend a directly applicable Regulation which has effect without any implementation. It is submitted that until the Brussels Regulation is amended, the result contended for by the Fifth Motor Insurance Directive is of no effect. For an analysis of the detailed provisions of the Regulation as it applies to road traffic claims, see Bona and Mead (eds) *Personal Injury Compensation in Europe* (2003) at 627pp.

Claims arising out of a contract of employment

28.10 The Brussels Regulation contains a new and discrete section in respect of disputes concerning individual contracts of employment, the Brussels Convention having dealt with the matter more generally in relation to contractual claims (under former art 5(1)):

'Section 5 — Jurisdiction over individual contracts of employment

Article 18

1. In matters relating to individual contracts of employment, jurisdiction shall be determined by this Section, without prejudice to Article 4 and point 5 of Article 5.

2. Where an employee enters into an individual contract of employment with an employer who is not domiciled in a Member State but has a branch, agency or other establishment in one of the Member States, the employer shall, in disputes arising out of the operations of the branch, agency or establishment, be deemed to be domiciled in that Member State.

Article 19

An employer domiciled in a Member State may be sued:
1   in the courts of the Member State where he is domiciled; or
2   in another Member State:
(a)   in the courts for the place where the employee habitually carries out his work or in the courts for the last place where he did so, or

(b)   if the employee does not or did not habitually carry out his work in any one country, in the courts for the place where the business which engaged the employee is or was situated.

Article 20

1. An employer may bring proceedings only in the courts of the Member State in which the employee is domiciled.

2. The provisions of this Section shall not affect the right to bring a counter-claim in the court in which, in accordance with this Section, the original claim is pending.

Article 21

The provisions of this section may be departed from only by an agreement on jurisdiction:

1   which is entered into after the dispute has arisen; or
2   which allows the employee to bring proceedings in courts other than those indicated in this Section.'

28.11   The provisions govern disputes which arise from an individual contract of employment. They do not concern other issues which arise in the course of the relationship of employer and employee, such as for example a dispute concerning the lawfulness of industrial action (see Case C-18/02 *Danmarks Rederiforening v LO Landsorganisationen i Sverige* [2004] ECR I-1417). Where an employee habitually carries out his work has been the subject of consideration by the ECJ (Case C-383/95 *Rutten v Cross Medical Ltd* [1997] ECR I-57; Case C-37/00, *Weber v Universal Ogden Services Ltd* [2002] ECR I-2013; and Case C-437/00 *Pugliese v Finmeccanica SpA* [2003] ECR I-3573). The habitual place of work will normally be the effective centre of the employee's working activities. Where there is no effective centre, then the court will assess whether there is a place from which the employee performed the essential part of his activities. An employee may be sued by an employer for breach of the contract of employment only in the courts of the State of domicile of the employee (save where the employers' claim is a counterclaim). Article 21 allows agreement between the parties in relation to the jurisdiction of the courts of another State only where such agreement is entered into after the dispute has arisen or the choice of forum is to the benefit of the employee. Article 23 of the Brussels Regulation specifies that such exclusive jurisdiction agreements shall be in writing or evidenced in writing (including communication by electronic means where there is a durable record of the agreement), or in a form which accords with practices which the parties have established between themselves.[1]

---

[1]   See art 23(1)(a) and (b); there is further provision in art 23(1)(c) in relation to jurisdiction agreements in international trade or commerce in a form which accords with a usage of which the parties are or ought to have been aware and which is widely known and observed by parties to contracts of the type involved in the particular trade or commerce concerned, which provision is unlikely to apply to individual contracts of employment.

Domicile of the defendant

28.12   Whereas the Brussels Regulation makes particular provision for claims in relation to insurance contracts and claims arising out of a contract of

674

employment, the principal basis under the Brussels Regulation by which the courts of a Contracting State may exercise jurisdiction over a civil or commercial dispute remains the domicile of the defendant (Brussels Regulation, art 2). The domicile of the defendant is to be determined at the date of issue of proceedings, and not at the date of service: *Canada Trust Co v Stolzenberg (No 2)* [2000] 3 WLR 1376. The nationality of the parties and the domicile of the claimant are irrelevant: Case C-412/98 *Universal General Insurance Co (UGIC) v Group Josi Reinsurance Co SA* [2000] 3 WLR 1625, at paras 34 and 43 in particular. The Brussels Regulation regime may apply therefore to a party domiciled in a Member State territory, in respect of acts or omissions which take place outside the EU, as occurred in the *Owusu* case.

28.13

Domicile was not defined in the Brussels Convention, but was defined in the Civil Jurisdiction and Judgments Act 1982, ss 41 (for individuals) and 42 (for corporations and associations). Under the new regime, the domicile of corporate bodies is regulated by art 60 of the Brussels Regulation, whilst art 59 provides that in order to determine whether a party is domiciled in a Member State, the court seised of the matter shall apply its internal law. To that end, the Civil Jurisdiction and Judgments Order 2001, SI 2001/3929, Sch 1, para 9[1] makes provision for the domicile of individuals. Paragraph 9(2) provides that an individual is domiciled in the UK if he is resident in the UK and the nature and circumstances of his residence indicate that he has a substantial connection with the UK. By para 9(6), where an individual has been resident in the UK for three months or more, it is presumed that he fulfils the requirement of substantial connection with the UK, unless the contrary is proved.[2] Residence connotes some degree of permanence or continuity, and is a mixed question of law and fact. Whether an individual is or is not resident will depend upon all the circumstances, and previous cases in relation to other areas, for example taxation, will not necessarily be decisive.

[1]   See *Civil Court Practice 2006*, Vol 1, pp 172–173.
[2]   Paragraph 9(3)–(6) determines in which part of the UK a person resides.

28.14

A corporation or association is domiciled where it has its statutory seat, or central administration, or principal place of business (see Brussels Regulation, art 60(1)). The statutory seat is defined for the purposes of the UK and the Republic of Ireland as meaning the registered office or, where there is no such office anywhere, the place of incorporation, or where there is no such place anywhere, the place under the law of which formation took place (art 60(2)).[1]

[1]   These provisions are similar to the provisions contained in the Civil Jurisdiction and Judgments Act 1982, s 42, which provide that a corporation or association has its seat in the UK if it was incorporated or formed under the law of a part of the UK and has its registered office or some other official address (ie an address which it is required by law to register, notify or maintain for the purpose of receiving notices or other communications: see s 42(8)) in the UK, or its central management and control is exercised in the UK (s 42(3)). Residence in a part of the UK arises where the activities described take place and where the corporation or association has a place of business (s 42(4)). Business is defined as including any activity carried on by a corporation or association.

Special jurisdiction and concurrent claims in tort and contract

28.15 For the purpose of establishing the jurisdiction of a UK court, where a claimant may have concurrent claims in contract and in tort against a European defendant, the regime under the Brussels Convention did not provide a choice of the basis of special jurisdiction under art 5. It was necessary to rely on, art 5(1) to the exclusion of art 5(3): *Source Ltd v TUV Rheinland Holding AG* [1998] QB 54. The general rule in relation to breaches of contract by a European defendant (repeated in the Brussels Regulation in respect of contracts other than individual contracts of employment) is that a person domiciled in one Contracting State may be sued in another Contracting State in the courts of the place of performance of the obligation in question, breach of which gives rise to the injury. It is to be noted that jurisdiction in such a case is dependent upon where the particular obligation is to be performed, and different breaches of contract could give rise to jurisdiction in different States.

Special jurisdiction: claims in tort

28.16 The European Court of Justice has held that 'tort' is defined as an independent, autonomous concept which is not dependent upon any definition under national law: Case 189/97 *Kalfelis v Schroder* [1988] ECR 5565; see also Case C-51/97 *Reunion Europeenne SA v Spliethoff's Bevrachtingskantoor* [2000] QB 690. The ECJ has ruled that tort is defined as covering 'all actions which seek to establish the liability of the defendant and which are not related to a contract within the meaning of Article 5(1)': see *Kalfelis* at 5585.[1] As noted above, where there are concurrent causes of action in contract and tort, the proper basis of special jurisdiction is under art 5(1), not art 5(3); in an employer's liability claim where there are concurrent claims for breach of the contract of employment and in tort, then the special provisions in arts 18–21, described above, apply.

---

[1] Thus, a consumer organisation taking proceedings against a trader cannot invoke the provisions in relation to consumer contracts but must rely on the provisions governing claims in tort: Case C-167/00 *Henkel* [2002] ECR I-8111.

28.17 Article 5(3) provides an additional basis of jurisdiction in an action in tort against a European defendant if the UK is the place where the harmful event occurred. The place where the harmful event occurred may be either the place where the damage occurred or the place where the event giving rise to the damage occurred. Thus, in *Handelskwekerij GJ Bier BV v Mines de Potasse D'Alsace* [1978] QB 708, which concerned a release of polluting chemicals into the river Rhine from a French factory, where damage was subsequently suffered by Dutch market gardeners in the Netherlands, the ECJ held that it was permissible to bring proceedings in either France or the Netherlands. The fact that a claimant who has sustained injury abroad continues to suffer the financial consequences of the injury in England does not permit the English courts to assume jurisdiction: see Case 220/88 *Dumez France v Hessische Landesbank* [1990] ECR I-49; Case C-364/93 *Marinari v Lloyds Bank plc (Zubadi Trading Co intervening)* [1995] ECR I-2719;

C-168/02 *Kronhofer v Maier* [2004] ECR I-6009. In *Henderson v Jaouen* [2002] EWCA Civ 75, the Court of Appeal confirmed that a deterioration of a personal injury did not give rise to a new cause of action.

28.18 There is an additional basis of special jurisdiction under art 5(4), which permits a European defendant to be sued in another Contracting State as regards a claim in damages which is based on an act giving rise to criminal proceedings, in the court seised of those proceedings, to the extent that that court has jurisdiction under its own law to entertain such proceedings.

Co-defendants

28.19 Article 6(1) of the Brussels Regulation permits a claimant to sue a European defendant in the UK where that defendant is domiciled in another State but a co-defendant is domiciled within the UK. The aim of art 6(1) is to prevent irreconcilable judgments in related actions in different courts seised of the respective disputes. Where there is a risk of conflicting decisions or findings of fact in connected disputes, it is appropriate to join the defendants in the same proceedings: Case 189/97 *Kalfelis v Schroder* [1988] ECR 5565. It is not necessary to serve the UK-domiciled defendant first in order to establish jurisdiction over the European defendant: see *Canada Trust Co v Stolzenberg (No 2)* [2000] 3 WLR 1376; also CPR 1998, Pt 6.20(3). The test to be applied as to whether a European defendant has been correctly joined is whether there is a good arguable case: *Canada Trust Co* at 1387B–D. Article 6 is likely to be a useful basis of special jurisdiction for obtaining jurisdiction within the UK over a European-domiciled defendant, where, for example, there is an English worker injured in a foreign road accident caused by either a foreign driver or an English-domiciled defendant, or the worker works abroad and is injured in circumstances where there is a claim against a contractor as well as the UK-domiciled employer.

Jurisdiction within the UK

28.20 Section 16 of, and Sch 4 to, the Civil Jurisdiction and Judgments Act 1982 prescribe the allocation of jurisdiction for civil and commercial disputes within the UK. The intra-UK regime mirrors the Brussels Convention regime which is restated in the Brussels Regulation, and applies whether or not the Regulation is also applicable. Rule 1 of Sch 4 repeats the principal rule that jurisdiction is based on the domicile of the defendant. Rules 3(a) and (c) and 5(a) of Sch 4 provide for special jurisdiction in relation to breaches of contract, tort and co-defendants. Rule 10 concerns jurisdiction over individual contracts of employment. Rule 3(c) of Sch 4 applies to provide jurisdiction to the courts of the place of a threatened wrong, as well as the place where the harmful event occurred. Rule 11 of Sch 4 reflects art 22(1) of the Brussels Regulation.

28.21 Rule 12(1) of Sch 4 permits parties to prescribe which courts within the UK shall have jurisdiction to settle a dispute. Rule 12 omits reference to the exclusive jurisdiction of the courts upon whom the parties have conferred jurisdiction, permitting those courts to decline jurisdiction where appropriate.

Jurisdiction under CPR Part 6.20 and the doctrine of forum non conveniens

28.22 A claimant may sue a European defendant in England and Wales in accordance with the Brussels Regulation without requiring the permission of a court (CPR Pt 6.19). Permission is required to serve proceedings on other foreign (non-European) domiciled defendants (hereafter 'foreign defendants') under CPR Pt 6.20 where the Brussels Regulation and the Brussels Convention have no application. Jurisdiction under CPR Pt 6.20 in relation to actions for damages concerning claims for personal injury at work over foreign defendants is likely to fall within one of the following categories:

(1)   a claim is made against a defendant (or proposed defendant) and there is between the claimant and that defendant a real issue which it is reasonable for the court to try, and the claimant wishes to serve the claim form on a foreign-domiciled defendant who is a necessary or proper party to that claim (CPR Pt 6.20(3));

(2)   the claim is for a breach of contract and the contract was made within the jurisdiction; or was made by or through an agent trading or residing in England and Wales; or the contract is governed expressly or by implication by English law;[1] or the contract contains a term granting jurisdiction to the court to hear and determine any action in respect of the contract (CPR Pt 6.20(5)); or a claim is made in respect of breach of contract committed within the jurisdiction (CPR Pt 6.20(6));

(3)   the claim is made in tort where the damage was sustained within the jurisdiction; or the damage sustained resulted from an act committed within the jurisdiction (CPR Pt 6.20(8)).[2]

[1]   See *Amin Rasheed Shipping Corpn v Kuwait Insurance Co, The Al Wahab* [1984] AC 50. This head of jurisdiction has been described as extraordinary. See commentary in *Dicey and Morris,* Rule 27.
[2]   See *Booth v Phillips* [2004] EWHC 1437 (Comm), [2004] 1 WLR 3292 where a claim as a dependent and for funeral expenses in a fatal accident claim was held to fall within the scope of the rule although the injury to the deceased was sustained abroad.

28.23 A contract is made where the letter of acceptance is posted. On the other hand, if acceptance is by some means of instantaneous communication, such as by fax or e-mail, the contract is made where the acceptance is communicated to the employer: *Entores Ltd v Miles Far East Corpn* [1955] 2 QB 327.

28.24 CPR Pt 6.21(2A) constrains the courts from granting permission to sue a foreign defendant unless the court considers that England and Wales is the proper place in which to bring the claim. CPR Pt 6.21 sets out the basis upon which an application for permission to serve a claim form out of the jurisdiction shall be made. The principles which the courts apply when granting permission are allied to those principles which the courts utilise when staying or striking out proceedings on the ground of forum non conveniens, namely that another foreign forum is more appropriate. The English courts have power to order a stay of proceedings on the basis that England is an inappropriate forum where:

(a)   the defendant shows there to be another court' with competent juris-diction which is clearly and distinctly more appropriate than England and Wales for the trial of the action; and

(b)   it is not unjust that the claimant is deprived of the right to trial in England.[1]

---

[1]   *Dicey and Morris,* Rule 31(2).

28.25 The leading House of Lords case which sets out this rule is *Spiliada Maritime Corpn v Cansulex Ltd, The Spillida* [1987] AC 460. When assessing which forum is appropriate, the court will consider which factors point in the direction of another forum, with which the action has the most real and substantial connection. Such factors may include: witness availability and availability of expert medical evidence, expense, and the extent of the documentary evidence. Where the defendant establishes that England is prima facie not the more appropriate forum, a stay will be granted unless the claimant can demonstrate that substantial justice would not be done in the more appropriate forum.

28.26 Two personal injury decisions of the House of Lords provide examples of the application of the *Spiliada* principles. Both cases concerned actions against defendants domiciled in England who were sued as of right by foreign claimants where the defendants sought a stay of the English proceedings in favour of more appropriate fora in Namibia and South Africa respectively. (It is to be noted, however, that since the ruling of the ECJ in Case C-281/02 *Owusu v Jackson (t/a Villa Holidays Bal-Inn Villas)* [2005] 1 QB 805 the cases would now not be decided under CPR Pt 6.20 because the English courts no longer have the power to stay proceedings brought as of right against English-domiciled companies.)

28.27 *Connelly v RTZ Corpn plc* [1998] AC 854 was an action by a Scottish expatriate worker against the English-domiciled parent company of his former Namibian employer and another English-domiciled subsidiary company for personal injury, namely cancer of the larynx, as a result of inhaling silica uranium at a uranium mine. The claimant's case was that the English companies had negligently devised the health and safety policy of the Namibian subsidiary company, alternatively had advised the Namibian sub-sidiary and had supervised the implementation of the health and safety policy. The claimant conceded that Namibia was prima facie the jurisdiction with which the claim had the most real and substantial connection. The House of Lords held that where there was a more appropriate forum, the claimant must take that forum as he finds it, even if that entails disadvantageous conditions, for example, lower damages or a less generous system of discovery: per Lord Goff at 872G. As a general rule, an English court will not refuse to grant a stay simply because the claimant has shown that no financial assistance (for example in the form of public funding) will be available in the appropriate forum but there is financial assistance available in England, although the presence or absence of such funding may be a relevant consideration in assessing whether substantial justice will be done if the claimant has to proceed in the appropriate forum: per Lord Goff at 873E–H. The House of Lords held (Lord Hoffmann dissenting) that in the light of the complexity of the case and the need for expert scientific witnesses the Namibian forum was not one in which the case could be tried more suitably (at 874E).

28.28 *Lubbe v Cape plc* [2000] 1 WLR 1545 concerned a multi-party action by predominantly South African-domiciled claimants against an English domiciled parent company of several South African subsidiaries which had carried out the mining and processing of asbestos. It was alleged that the parent company had failed to ensure that proper safety precautions had been observed throughout the group. During the complex interlocutory history of the action, which involved two hearings before the Court of Appeal and one in the House of Lords, it ceased to be contended that South Africa was not the more appropriate forum, under the first stage of the *Spiliada* test. The House of Lords held that the complexity of the proceedings, which required professional representation and expert evidence, in conjunction with the lack of means of the claimants in South Africa who would have the benefit of public funding in England, as well as the fact that there were no established procedures for conducting complicated group litigation in South Africa, lead to the conclusion that a stay of proceedings should be refused.

THE APPLICABLE LAW

28.29 Once it is established that the English courts have jurisdiction, it does not follow that English law applies. If the applicable substantive law is a foreign law, foreign limitation periods will also apply.[1] The English courts will apply the appropriate foreign law, where it is expressly pleaded, in relation to matters of substantive law, but will apply English law in relation to matters of procedure. The remainder of this chapter considers, first, from a conflicts of law point of view those matters which are characterised as procedural and those matters which are substantive. Then it analyses what is the applicable law, and finally sets out the particular rules concerning the pleading of foreign law, and the presumptions which apply where no party expressly relies upon foreign law.

[1] See the Foreign Limitation Periods Act 1984, s 1.

Substance and procedure

28.30 The question whether a matter is characterised as substantive (being governed by foreign law) or procedural (being governed by English law as the law of the forum) has involved some fine distinctions.[1] Listed below are the matters which have been characterised as substantive or procedural, which may be relevant to an action for personal injuries involving a foreign accident or ill-health contracted abroad.

1   See *Dicey and Morris,* Rule 17, discussed and considered in *Matthews v Ministry of Defence* [2003] UKHL 4, [2003] 1 AC 1163.

28.31 Substantive issues include:

(i)   remedies for breach of contract: Contracts (Applicable Law) Act 1990, s 2 and Sch 1, art 10(1);

(ii)   proof of a contract, including application of the burden of proof and presumptions of law: Contracts (Applicable Law) Act 1990, s 2 and Sch 1, art 14;

(iii) rules on the assessment of damages for breach of contract: Contracts (Applicable Law) Act 1990, s 2 and Sch 1, art 10(1)(c);[1]

(iv)   rules in tort governing the remoteness of damages, and recoverable heads of damage (including general damages): *Chaplin v Boys* [1971] AC 356; and the application of statutory caps and limitations on recoverable losses, the determination of the discount rate for future pecuniary loss and the applicable rate of interest, and the deduction of insurance monies: *Harding v Wealands* [2004] EWCA 1735, [2005] 1 WLR 1539.

(v)   existence and extent of any duty to mitigate loss: *D'Almeida Araujo Ltda v Sir Frederick Becker & Co Ltd* [1953] 2 QB 329.

1   This includes the assessment and award of interest: see *Lesotho Highlands Development Authority v Impreglio SpA* [2003] EWCA Civ 1159, [2004] 1 All ER (Comm) 97; the decision of the Court of Appeal was overturned on other grounds: see [2005] 3 WLR 129.

28.32 Procedural issues include:

(i)   rules determining actions against dissolved companies: *Banque Internationale de Commerce de Petrograd v Goukassow* [1923] 2 KB 682 (reversed on other grounds [1925] AC 150); *Deutsche Bank and Disconto Gesellschaft v Banque des Marchands de Moscou* (1932) 158 LT 364;

(ii)   rules governing entitlement of administrators of deceased persons: *Finnegan v Cementation Co Ltd* [1953] 1 QB 688; *Kamouh v Associated Electrical Industries International Ltd* [1980] QB 199;[1]

(iii) admissibility of evidence and competence of witnesses;[2]

(iv)   rules in tort governing the quantification or assessment of damages: *D'Almeida Araujo Ltda v Sir Frederick Becker & Co Ltd* [1953] 2 QB 329 at 338; *Coupland v Arabian Gulf Petroleum Co* [1983] 1 WLR 1136 at 1149; *Kohnke v Karger* [1951] 2 KB 670 at 676; *Chaplin v Boys* [1971] AC 356; *Roerig v Valiant Trawlers Ltd* [2002] EWCA Civ 21;

(v)   deduction of social security benefits: *Coupland v Arabian Gulf Petroleum Co* [1983] 1 WLR 1136; and the disregard of the deduction of benefits by virtue of the Fatal Accidents Act 1976, s 4: *Roerig v Valiant Trawlers Ltd* [2002] EWCA Civ 21.[3]

1   See also *Dicey and Morris,* Rule 127.
2   See *Dicey and Morris,* para 7–016ff.
     But see also Regulation (EEC) No 1408/71, art 93: OJ L 149/2, as amended; consolidated version 1997 OJ L 28/1. See also the updated consolidated version on the Eur-Lex website.

28.33 The distinction between what is substantive and what is procedural was the subject of a split decision in the Court of Appeal in the recent case of *Harding v Wealands* [2004] EWCA Civ 1735, [2005] 1 WLR 1539. At issue was the question whether particular provisions contained in the Motor Accidents Compensation Act 1999 of New South Wales were of a substantive character and to be applied as being part of the proper law of the tort, or whether English law being the law of the forum applied because the matters in question were of a procedural nature relating to the quantification of damage. The New South Wales provisions in issue prescribed limits on the amount of damages to be awarded for non-economic loss, the amount of damages recoverable for loss of earnings, when damages for gratuitous care may be awarded, and the amount of interest to be awarded, as well as restrictive provisions (from a claimant's point of view) in relation to the deduction of benefits received under an insurance policy and the applicable discount rate. Applying the reasoning of the High Court of Australia in *Pfeiffer Pty Ltd v Rogerson* (2003) 203 CLR 503, the majority in the Court of Appeal (Arden LJ and Sir William Aldous, with Waller LJ dissenting) held that the limitations in the New South Wales law bear on the existence, extent or enforceability of remedies, rights and obligations and should be characterised as substantive and not as procedural laws. Arden LJ considered that there is no bright line between questions of procedure and questions of substance in relation to damages, and that where the proper law of the tort is a foreign law, then reference to the law of the forum should be exceptional and justified by an imperative which has priority, for example where the court is unable to put itself into the shoes of the foreign court in that it cannot do justice unless it applies its own law.

The applicable law

28.34 Claimants who have suffered injury abroad will, in general, be entitled to sue in contract or tort. The substantive rules described below do not pre-empt any choice of cause of action which the injured claimant may have in framing his case: see *Matthews v Kuwait Bechtel Corpn* [1959] 2 QB 57; *Coupland v Arabian Gulf Petroleum Co* [1983] 1 WLR 1136 and 1151; *Johnson v Coventry Churchill International Ltd* [1992] 3 All ER 14.

Contract

28.35 The Contracts (Applicable Law) Act 1990 incorporates into UK law the Rome Convention on the law applicable to contractual obligations 1980 and the Brussels protocol on the interpretation of the Rome Convention by the ECJ, as well as the amending Conventions. The 1990 Act applies to contracts made after 1 April 1991.[1] The Rome Convention sets out harmonised rules on the proper law which applies to contractual obligations, whether the parties to the dispute are European or not. The Rome Convention applies to contractual obligations in any situation involving a choice between the laws of different countries (art 1(1)). The general scheme of the Rome Convention is to allow the parties to determine which law shall govern the terms and conditions of the contract (art 3(1)). There is scant authority on the interpretation of the Rome Convention. As with the Brussels Convention, assistance may be obtained from a report on the Rome Convention on the meaning and interpretation of the Convention.[2]

1   The protocol entered into force with effect from 1 March 2005: see the Contracts (Applicable Law) Act 1990 (Commencement No 2) Order 2004, SI 2004/3448.
2   The *Giuliano-Lagarde Report;* see s 3(3) of the 1990 Act.

28.36 Article 6 of the Rome Convention prescribes particular rules which apply to individual contracts of employment, as follows:

'(1) Notwithstanding the provisions of Article 3, in a contract of employment a choice of law made by the parties shall not have the result of depriving the employee of the protection afforded to him by the mandatory rules of the law which would be applicable under paragraph 2 in the absence of choice.

(2) Notwithstanding the provisions of Article 4, a contract of employment shall, in the absence of choice in accordance with Article 3, be governed
(a)   by the law of the country in which the employee habitually carries out his work in performance of the contract, even if he is temporarily employed in another country; or
(b)   if the employee does not habitually carry out his work in any one country, by the law of the country in which the place of business through which he was engaged is situated;
unless it appears from the circumstances as a whole that the contract is more closely connected with another country, in which case the contract shall be governed by the law of that country.'

28.37 Article 3 of the Rome Convention establishes the general choice of law rules where the parties have made a choice which is either express or can be demonstrated with reasonable certainty. Article 4 determines which law is applicable where no law has been chosen in accordance with art 3. Articles 3 and 4 will apply therefore to provisions establishing the governing law in both collective agreements and contracts of employment but provides a mechanism by which provisions are partly overridden but only where the agreement or arrangement containing them can be classed as a contract of employment: art 6.[1]

1   For a commentary on the application of the general conflicts of laws principles to contract, see *Dicey and Morris,* Chapter 32, Rule 172ff, and Plender and Wilderspin *The European Contracts Convention* (2nd edn, 2001).

28.38 Article 6(1) provides extra protection to employees whose contracts of employment specify expressly or by necessary and reasonable implication (eg by incorporation of a relevant collective agreement, works rule, employees' handbook or the like) which law governs the employment relationship. Article 6(1) does not determine who constitutes an employee for these purposes, nor which law should be applied to determine whether art 6(1) applies. Both *Dicey and Morris* and *Plender and Wilderspin* suggest that the putative applicable law under art 6 should be applied to determine the question whether under that law the contract is a contract of employment.[1] Article 6(1) would appear to give an employee a choice of protection under the law of the contract, or the provisions of the mandatory law. If the mandatory law is less generous than the chosen law, there would appear to be no reason why the more beneficial provisions cannot apply. Where there are alternative remedies available, depending on the applicable law, the employee would appear to have a choice as to which protection he prefers to rely upon.

1 See *Dicey and Morris*, paras 33–054 and 33–055; Plender and Wilderspin *The European Contracts Convention* (2nd edn, 2001), paras 8–06 to 8–10.

Article 6(2)—habitually works

28.39 Article 6(2) depends upon ascertaining where an employee 'habitually' carries out his work. This is not defined. Reference may be made to the case law of the ECJ under former art 5(1) of the Brussels Convention and the English courts in relation to the application of employment statutes to foreign workers for relevant factors in assessing where an employee works. As to the ECJ jurisprudence see C-383/95 *Rutten v Cross Medical Ltd* [1997] ECR I-57; also Case C-125/92 *Mulox IBC Ltd v Geels* [1993] ECR I-4075 (prior to the amendment of art 5(1)). As to the English authorities see: *Wilson v Maynard Shipbuilding Consultants AB* [1978] QB 665; *Todd v British Midland Airways* [1978] ICR 959; *Janata Bank v Ahmed* [1981] ICR 791; *Carver v Saudi Arabian Airlines* [1999] 3 All ER 61; *Lawson v Serco Ltd, Botham v Ministry of Defence, Crofts v Veta Ltd* [2006] UKHL 3, [2006] ICR 250.

28.40 The relevant factors are likely to include, in the absence of any express provision as to where the employee's place of work is, where the employee lives, where he travels from and to, who controls the employee and where that person is based, and where any headquarters may be. Article 6(2) makes reference to country, rather than State, and therefore the applicable law may be that of an individual region or state or part of a (federal) State.[1] If an employee does not habitually work in any one country, then the second limb of art 6(2) stipulates that the law of the country in which the place of business through which the employee was engaged is situated applies. This again is not defined, and may lead to problems of interpretation.[2]

1 For these purposes, England, Scotland and Northern Ireland are each countries, as are each of the states of the United States and Australia, and the provinces of Canada: see *Dicey and Morris*, para 1–060.
2 See *Dicey and Morris*, para 33–067; Plender and Wilderspin *The European Contracts Convention* (2nd edn, 2001), para 8–23.

Article 6(2)—more closely connected

28.41 The last element of art 6(2) gives a proviso, permitting the courts to apply the law of another country if it appears from all the circumstances that the contract is more closely connected with that country. Relevant factors may include the residence or domicile of the employer, or of the employee: *South African Breweries v King* [1899] 2 Ch 173; affd [1900] 1 Ch 273; *Re*

Anglo-Austrian Bank [1920] 1 Ch 69; *Sayers v International Drilling Co* [1971] 1 WLR 1176; *Coupland v Arabian Gulf Petroleum Co* [1983] 1 WLR 1136.

Article 6(2)—mandatory law

28.42 The benefit of this article to the qualifying employee is the entitlement to rely on the protections of the 'mandatory law' of the country in which he habitually works, notwithstanding that the contract of employment provides for some other law to apply.

28.43 What constitutes a mandatory law is likely to include most statutory provision in relation to health and safety.[1] It is probable that most statutory provision concerning employment protection will also be considered to be mandatory.[2] English authority on the Law Reform (Personal Injuries) Act 1948, s 1(3) suggests it is not a mandatory law, whereas more recent Scottish authority has held to the contrary: *Sayers v International Drilling Co* [1971] 1 WLR 1176; *Brodin v A/R Seljan* 1973 SC 213. It is considered that the non-delegable common law duties (see chapter 4) to take reasonable care for the safety of employees should be considered to be mandatory law in this context since they derive from contract as well as tort.

[1] The *Giuliano-Lagarde Report* refers to provisions concerning industrial safety and hygiene, at p 25.
[2] *Dicey and Morris* refers to the Employment Rights Act 1996; Equal Pay Act 1970; Patents Act 1977; Sex Discrimination Act 1975; Race Relations Act 1976; Trade Union and Labour Relations (Consolidation) Act 1992; National Minimum Wage Act 1998; Public Interest Disclosure Act 1998, see paras 33–070–33–082.

28.44 Article 7(2) of the Rome Convention should also be noted, since it permits the law of the forum to be applied in relation to rules which are mandatory irrespective of the law which otherwise is applicable to the contract. This final proviso will only permit, for example, English law to be applied where the courts have jurisdiction and the provisions of art 6 do not determine that English law otherwise applies because there has been a valid choice of law and any mandatory provisions applicable are foreign, or the employee habitually works abroad, or the place of business through which the employee was engaged was abroad.

Tort

28.45 The common law rule on the determination of the proper law of the tort in relation to personal injury actions[1] (known as the 'double actionability' rule) has been repealed and replaced by statute, by the Private International Law (Miscellaneous Provisions) Act 1995, which came into force on 1 May 1996.[2] The choice of law rules apply not only where an accident occurs outside the UK, but also where the injury was caused in one of the parts of the UK, and litigation occurs in another.[3]

1   The common law rules remain in relation to defamation actions: see the Private
     International Law (Miscellaneous Provisions) Act 1995, ss 9(3) and 13.
2   For a general commentary with reference to personal injury actions, see J Melville
     Williams QC and P Mead [1996] JPIL 112.
3   See s 9(7).

28.46 Section 11(1) of the 1995 Act establishes the general rule to determine
the proper law of the tort as the law of the country[1] in which the events
constituting the tort (or delict) in question occur. Section 11(2)(a) further
specifies that where elements of the events constituting the tort occur in
different countries, the applicable law under the general rule in relation to a
cause of action for personal injury[2] or death resulting from personal injury, is
the law of the country where the individual was when he sustained the injury.
Where a person suffers an injury in country A and subsequently dies in
country B, the applicable law which applies under the general rule in
accordance with s 11(2)(a) will be the law of country A. The consequence of
the application of the general rule is that for the first time foreign substantive
laws may apply which are unknown in the UK.[3] It is also important to note
that ss 10 and 12 of the Act expressly foresee the possibility that different
issues in a case may be governed by different laws.[4]

1   For these purposes, England, Scotland and Northern Ireland are each countries, as are each
     of the states of the United States and Australia, and the provinces of Canada: see *Dicey and
     Morris,* para 1–060.
2   Defined to include disease or any impairment of physical or mental condition: s 11(3).
3   For a survey of the domestic laws of 18 different European jurisdictions in respect of the
     law governing compensation for personal injury and in respect of fatal accidents and
     secondary victims, see Bona and Mead (eds) *Personal Injury Compensation in Europe*
     (2003), and Bona, Mead and Lindenbergh (eds) *Fatal Accidents and Secondary Victims*
     (2005).
4   The Private International Law (Miscellaneous Provisions) Act 1995 does not change the
     position in this respect; for the earlier case law, see *Chaplin v Boys* [1971] AC 356 at 391;
     Red Sea Insurance Co Ltd v Bouygues SA [1995] 1 AC 190; *Lubbe v Cape plc* [1999] IL Pr
     113 at 126, para 32, CA; *Pearce v Ove Arup Partnership Ltd* [1999] 1 All ER 769 at 803.

28.47 Section 12 provides an important exception to s 11, characterised as
the displacement of the general rule, as follows:

'(1) If it appears in all the circumstances, from a comparison of:
(a)   the significance of the factors which connect a tort or delict with the
       country whose law would be the applicable law under the general rule;
       and
(b)   the significance of any factors connecting the tort or delict with another
       country,
that it is substantially more appropriate for the applicable law for determining
the issues arising in the case, or any of those issues, to be the law of the other
country, the general rule is displaced and the applicable law for determining
those issues or that issue (as the case may be) is the law of that other country.

(2) The factors that may be taken into account as connecting a tort or delict
with a country for the purposes of this section include, in particular, factors
relating to the parties, to any events which constitute the tort or delict in
question or to any of the circumstances or consequences of those events.'

28.48 The circumstances in which s 12 may be invoked were considered in
the case of *Roerig v Valiant Trawlers Ltd* [2002] EWCA Civ 21. The case

concerned a claim under the Fatal Accidents Act 1976 brought by the Dutch claimant on behalf of herself and her children as dependents of a Dutch seaman who suffered fatal injury whilst working on an English registered trawler. The issue before the Court of Appeal was whether social security benefits paid to the claimant should be taken into account in computing the claimant's entitlement to damages, such benefits being taken into account under Dutch law but not English law. It was argued by the defendant that Dutch law should apply to the issue of quantification of loss, because the deceased was Dutch, employed by a Dutch company paying Dutch taxes and making contributions to obtain Dutch social security benefits and that the loss of dependency of the claimant and her children would occur in the Nether-lands. The Court of Appeal held that what was required under s 12 was a comparison of the significance of the factors which connect a tort (not an issue) with the country whose law would be applicable under the general rule, and the significance of the factors connecting the tort with another country. From that comparison, it was then necessary to determine whether it was substantially more appropriate for the law of that other country to determine the issue. To that end, it is necessary first to identify the issue in relation to which it is argued that the law under the general rule should not be applicable; second, those factors that connect the tort with the competing laws; third, to consider whether the significance of the factors under the alternative law argued for make it substantially more appropriate for the alternative law to apply.[1] In the *Roerig* case, the Court of Appeal held that the general rule is not to be dislodged easily, and that English law applied in accordance with the general rule.

[1] At para 12(iv) of the judgment at Q104, Waller LJ considered that where two English persons are in a foreign country on holiday and one tortiously injures the other, the significant factors in favour of England being the place by reference to which the damages should be assessed may make it substantially more appropriate that damages should be assessed by English law.

28.49 *Roerig* was followed and applied in *Harding v Wealands* [2004] EWCA Civ 1735, [2005] 1 WLR 1539, where the issue concerned whether the law under the general rule (the law of New South Wales, which contained various caps and substantive limitations on damages) should apply, or English law, being the law of the residence of the parties immediately prior to the accident. On the issue of the application of the proper law the Court of Appeal applied the test articulated in *Roerig* and found that English law was not the substantially more appropriate law. Waller LJ further stated[1] that where the general rule is also the national law of one of the parties, it will be very difficult to envisage circumstances that will render it substantially more appropriate that any issue could be tried by reference to some other law.

[1] See para 20.

28.50 The exception contained in s 12 is similar to the exception found in the earlier common law rule on the choice of the proper law of the tort (the rule on double actionability) which read as follows: 'But a particular issue between the parties may be governed by the law of the country which, with respect to that issue, has the most significant relationship with the occurrence and the parties'.[1] *Chaplin v Boys* [1971] AC 356 concerned a road traffic accident between two members of the armed forces stationed temporarily in Malta. Maltese law on heads of recoverable damages allowed the claimant to claim for special damages but not for general damages. The House of Lords ruled, applying the exception to the common law rule, that the claimant was entitled to rely on English heads of damages, given the normal residence of the parties in England, in particular that heads of damage is an issue strongly linked to the country where the claimant normally resided, which was the same as the defendant, in circumstances where there was no interest in Malta which would be infringed by applying English law. *Edmunds v Simmonds* [2001] 1 WLR 1003 concerned a claim governed by the Private International Law (Miscellaneous Provisions) Act 1995, and involved an English passenger who suffered injury in a car accident in Spain. The car in which the claimant was travelling was a Spanish hire car, the driver of the vehicle who was held liable for the accident was English, but the insurers of the vehicle were Spanish. Garland J, relying on *Chaplin v Boys*, applied English law under s 12 to the issue of what damages were recoverable.

1   Former Rule 203(2) of *Dicey and Morris* (12th edn) at pp 1487–1488, approved by the House of Lords in *Red Sea Insurance Co Ltd v Bouygues SA* [1995] 1 AC 190.

28.51 Connecting factors which were applied under the exception to the old double actionability rule which may be relevant in determining whether it is substantially more appropriate to displace the general rule on the proper law of the tort, include the fact that the parties are only temporarily or by chance in the jurisdiction where the accident occurred: *Chaplin v Boys* [1971] AC 356; *Coupland v Arabian Gulf Petroleum Co* [1983] 1 WLR 1136, or that there is a pre-existing relationship between the parties or a contract between the parties: *Coupland v Arabian Gulf Petroleum Co* [1983] 1 WLR 1136; *Johnson v Coventry Churchill International Ltd* [1992] 3 All ER 14.

Pleading and proof of foreign law

28.52 The consequences of ascertaining what is the proper law favours those seeking to rely on British law by reason of the strict rules on proof and pleading of foreign law. Foreign law must be pleaded in order to be part of a case, because it is characterised as a particular species of fact which must be proven by expert evidence.[1] If neither party formally pleads foreign law as part of their case, then there is no basis upon which a court will consider foreign law. The court will apply English law to the case instead.[2]

1   See *Dicey and Morris,* Rule 18, approved in *Bumper Development Corpn v Commissioner of Police of the Metropolis* [1991] 1 WLR 1362. An exception applies to laws of Commonwealth countries, where the court has a power under the British Law Ascertainment Act 1859 to order that the law be ascertained. Section 4(2) of the Civil Evidence Act 1972 permits findings or decisions on foreign law in previous proceedings of certain courts to be admissible in evidence as proof of that law. Reference to the presumption was made in *Roerig v Valiant Trawlers Ltd* [2002] EWCA Civ 21, at para 27.
2   Statutes (and statutory instruments) by their nature are of limited geographical application, and do not apply outside the UK, unless there is express provision. See 44(1) *Halsbury's Laws* (4th edn) para 1318. See eg *Lawson v Serco Ltd, Botham v Ministry of Defence, Crofts v Veta Ltd* [2006] ICR 250 for the application of the Employment Rights Act 1996, s 94(1) to employees who work abroad.

28.53 From a practical point of view, this will mean that many cases involving foreign accidents will proceed as if the action was based on English contract or tort principles without reference to foreign law. The claimant will not plead points of foreign law unless there is a particular advantage to be gained thereby, and defendants often take no point in this respect. Defendants will, however, no doubt be vigilant to ensure that proceedings are issued and served within time in accordance with the substantive law of the action since under some foreign laws time stops running only when the defendant has been properly served (which may require translation of pleadings and medical reports, and service by a particular process server). Issue of a claim form within the time stipulated by British law may therefore be insufficient for the purposes of foreign law.

Appendix 1

EXPLANATION OF LEGAL TERMS[1]

Act of Parliament. Law made by the House of Commons, House of Lords and assented to by the Crown. Prior to its passage into law referred to as a Bill. See also Legislation, Statute.

Action. Proceedings in a court, commenced usually by a Claim Form, to claim damages (or other relief).

A fortiori. Literally 'even more strongly'. A phrase used where the argument in favour of a point is stronger than for one which is apparently correct.

Aliter. 'Otherwise': often used to introduce the second of two cases where there have been conflicting decisions by different courts.

Case. (Early nineteenth century.) An old form of action where injuries had not been caused by a direct act of the defendant, but had resulted indirectly from his conduct (especially negligence). Formerly actions for direct interference with either person or property were started by a Writ of Trespass. This was extended by degrees to damage done indirectly by allowing a Writ of Trespass 'on the Case', which was abbreviated to an action of Case.

Cause of action. The set of facts which, if proved, will establish legal liability; Often, and less accurately, the basis of alleged legal liability (as in 'her cause of action was in negligence').

Claimant. The person who brings an action.

Common law. The law as made by the judges in deriving principles from, and reasoning by analogy with, earlier cases or precedents; to be contrasted with legislation, statutes, Acts of Parliament. The law of torts (and the right to damages for breach of a statute) is part of the common law.

Construction. Interpreting the meaning of (eg) an Act of Parliament.

Contributory negligence. Carelessness by an injured person which has contributed to cause his injuries.

Courts. In England and Wales, most personal injury actions are brought in the County Courts. Cases where the damages are expected to be in excess of £50,000 or a difficult issue of law or fact can be brought in the High Court or District Registries of the High Court at major provincial towns and cities. Depending on the level of court for the first instance hearing, Appeals go to either the High Court or the Court of Appeal.

In Scotland, actions are brought in the Sheriff court or the Outer House of the Court of Session. Appeals go to the Court of Session, Inner House. Ultimate appeals from both countries go to the Judicial Committee of the House of Lords (where they are heard by five of the Lords of Appeal).

Damages. Compensation in money for personal injuries and other loss or damage.

Defence. (a) Facts which, if proved, will free the defendant from liability or reduce the amount of damages; (b) a formal document in an action embodying the defence.

Defendant. The person against whom an action is brought (defender, in Scotland).

Ejusdem generis. 'Of the same kind'. A maxim used in interpretation where there is a list of particular things followed by general words—eg 'steamers, yachts and other craft'—the general words include only items within the same class, in this case 'sea-going' craft.

Forum conveniens. The convenient forum. Ie where litigation has connection with two or more countries, whichever country's courts are the most appropriate, taking into account the interests of all parties.

Forum non conveniens. The inappropriate forum for the litigation.

691

Appendix 1   Explanation of legal terms

Indemnity. A right (arising usually by agreement) to require another person to pay a debt or damages for which one is liable.

In pari materia. 'On equivalent subject-matter': used to refer to a previous decision on a similar point.

Legislation. Acts of Parliament and also laws made under the authority of Acts of Parliament such as the health and safety regulations.

Liability. An obligation to pay damages (or a debt) which can be enforced by an action.

Negligence. A form of legal action which, in essence, amounts to a failure to take reasonable care. It is necessary to show that the situation was one where the common law of negligence imposed a duty, that the duty was broken, and that damage was caused by the breach of duty.

Novus actus interveniens. A new intervening cause, typically of another human agent, so that any wrongful act by the defendant can no longer be held to be the act which caused the claimant's injury and damage.

Obiter dictum. 'Said in passing'. That part of a judge's judgement in a case which was not essential to the judge's reasoning in coming to a decision in the case. Such material does not constitute binding precedent, and therefore need not be followed by other judges: it is nevertheless treated with respect, especially if the judge had a high reputation.

Per incuriam. 'By an accidental oversight' (in giving judgment).

Pleadings. The formal documents (Particulars or Statement of Claim and Defence and Further and Better Particulars, Reply etc) in an action. *Not* the oral arguments in court.

Prima facie. 'On first impression'. A prima facie case is one which should succeed unless counteracted by contrary evidence.

Pursuer. The claimant in a Scottish action.

Quaere. Query. Used to express doubt about the accuracy of a decision or opinion.

Quia timet. A *quia timet* injunction is one granted to prevent feared wrongdoing.

Qui sentit commodum, sentire debet et onus. 'Whoever takes the benefit of a thing should also be subject to the burden.'

Res ipsa loquitur. 'The thing speaks for itself—the situation when the happening of an accident is in itself evidence of negligence.

Sine qua non. Literally, 'without which not'. A pre-condition without which an event could not happen, though not necessarily deemed an active cause, such as the fact that there is a road on which two cars are travelling when they collide.

Statement of Claim. A formal document in an action setting out the facts alleged to establish liability (*condescendence* in Scotland).

Statute. An Act of Parliament; a *statutory instrument* is a law made under the authority of an Act of Parliament.

Statutory duty. A duty imposed by a statute or statutory instrument.

Third party, (a) Colloquially, a person other than the injured person, the employer and fellow-employees; (b) in procedural law, a person who is brought into an action by the defendant on the ground that the former is liable to pay to the defendant the whole or a part of the damages awarded against the defendant.

Tort. A breach of the common law which includes various forms of legal action which give rise to an action for damages: eg negligence, breach of statutory duty, libel, etc.

Trespass. (Early nineteenth century.) A form of action where the defendant, by a direct and personal act, had injured the claimant or his property. Now usually limited to interference with land.

Vicarious liability. Liability for the conduct of another person, especially an employee.

Volenti non fit injuria. A phrase meaning that a claimant who deliberately takes the risk of injury, and who is injured, cannot subsequently succeed in an action for damages.

692

1   By special request from non-legal readers. Academic lawyers have thought this appendix should be omitted. It appears, however, that many readers have found it useful: a legal subject can be followed with surprising ease when a few elementary terms are explained. In the 10th edn it was amplified to include all Latin phrases. Use of Latin is now strongly discouraged by the courts and all but a few have been removed from the book.

ABBREVIATIONS

AC	Law Reports, Appeal Cases
ACOP	Approved Code of Practice
ACTR	Australian Capitals Territory Reports
AG	Attorney General
All ER	All England Law Reports
B & S	Best & Smith's Reports
BMLR	Butterworths Medico Legal Reports
BSI	British Standards Institution
CA	Court of Appeal
CD	Consultative Document
CHIP	Chemical (Hazard Information and Packaging for Supply) Regulations
CL	Current Law
CLJ	Cambridge Law Journal
CLR	Commonwealth Law Reports
CLY	Current Law Yearbook
COD	Crown Office Digest
COIT	Central Office of Industrial Tribunals
CONDAM	Construction (Design and Management) Regulations 1994
COSHH	Control of Substances Hazardous to Health Regulations 1988/1994/1999/2002
CPR	Civil Procedure Rules 1998
Cr App R	Criminal Appeal Reports
CTS	Carpal Tunnel Syndrome
D	Duxbury's Reports of the High Court of the South African Republic
dB	Decibel: measure of loudness
DC	Divisional Court
DEFRA	Department for Environment, Food and Rural Affairs
DETR	Department for Employment, Training and Rehabilitation
DG	Directorates General
DG Vd	Directorate General Vd
DLR	Dominion Law Reports
DPP	Director of Public Prosecutions
DSM-IV	Diagnostic and Statistical Manual of Mental Disorders – Fourth Edition

DTI	Department of Trade and Industry
EAT	Employment Appeal Tribunal
EC	European Community
ECJ	European Court of Justice
ECR	European Court Reports
EEC	European Economic Community
EU	European Union
EWCA Civ	England and Wales Court of Appeal – Civil
EWCA Crim	England and Wales Court of Appeal – Criminal
EWHC	England and Wales High Court
Ex p	Ex parte: 'in the absence of'
F & F	Foster & Finlason's Reports
FSR	Fleet Street [Patent Law] Reports
GLA	Gangmasters Licensing Authority
GWD	Green's Weekly Digest
H & N	Hurlstone & Norman's Reports
HAVS	Hand/Arm Vibration Syndrome
HHJ	His Honour Judge
HSC	Health and Safety Commission
HSE	Health and Safety Executive
HS(G)	HSE Guidance Booklets
HSIB	Health and Safety Information Bulletin
HSWA	Health and Safety at Work etc Act 1974
ICD-10	International Statistical Classification of Diseases and Related Health Problems: 10th revision
ICR	Industrial Cases Reports
ICTUR	International Centre for Trade Union Rights
IER	Institute of Employment Rights
IH or IHCS	Inner House, Court of Session (Scotland)
ILJ	Industrial Law Journal
IPMS	Institute of Personnel Management Services
IR	Irish Reports
IRLR	Industrial Relations Law Reports
J	Judge—High Court
JC	Justiciary Cases
JP	Justice of the Peace Reports
JPIL	Journal of Personal Injury Law
KB	Law Reports, King's Bench Division
KIR	Knight's Industrial Reports

L Jo	Law Journal Newspaper
Ld Raym	Lord Raymond's Reports
$L_{EP,d}$	Daily personal noise exposure
LGR	Local Government Reports
LJ	Lord Justice
LLJ	Lords Justice
Ll L Rep	Lloyd's List Law Reports (1919–1950)
Lloyd's Rep	Lloyd's List Law Reports
LOLER	Lifting Operations and Lifting Equipment Regulations 1998
LQR	Law Quarterly Review
LR PC	Law Reports, Privy Council
LT	Law Times
LT Jo	Law Times Journal
LTL	Lawtel
M/S	Metres per second squared: measure of acceleration
MASHAM	Management and Administration of Safety and Health at Mines Regulations 1993
Med LR	Medical Law Reports
MLR	Modern Law Review
MoD	Ministry of Defence
MR	Master of the Rolls
NCB	National Coal Board
NHS	National Health Service
NI	Northern Ireland Reports
NI CA	Northern Ireland Court of Appeal
NSWLR	New South Wales Law Reports
NZLR	New Zealand Law Reports
OH or OHCS	Outer House, Court of Session (Scotland)
OJ	Official Journal (EC)
P	Law Reports, Probate, Divorce and Admiralty Division
PD	Prescribed Disease
PIQR	Personal Injury & Quantum Reports
PMILL	Personal Injury and Medical Law Letter
PPE	Personal Protective Equipment
PUWER	Provision and Use of Work Equipment Regulations 1992 or 1998
QB	Law Reports, Queen's Bench Division
QC	Queen's Counsel
RADS	Reactive Airways Disease Syndrome: irritant asthma

RIDDOR	Reporting of Injuries, Diseases and Dangerous Occurrences Regulations 1995
RSI	Repetitive Strain Injury
RTR	Road Traffic Reports
SA	South Africa
SASR	South Australian State Reports
SCLR	Scottish Civil Law Reports/South Carolina Law Review
SCR	Canadian Law Reports (Supreme Court)
SI	Statutory Instrument
SLT	Scots Law Times
Sol Jo	Solicitors' Journal
SWORD	Surveillance of Work-related and Occupational Disease scheme
TLR	Times Law Reports
TUPE	Transfer of Undertakings (Protection of Employment) Regulations
ULDs	Upper Limb Disorders
UKHL	United Kingdom House of Lords
VDU	Video Display Unit
VWF	Vibration White Finger
WLR	Weekly Law Reports
WRULDs	Work-Related. Upper Limb Disorders
WWR	Western Weekly Reports

BIBLIOGRAPHY

Archbold *Criminal Pleadings, Evidence and Practice* (Sweet & Maxwell, 2001)

Atiyah's Accidents, Compensation and the Law (6th edn, 1999)

Atkins Court Forms Vol 20 (2nd edn, 2002)

Bennion *Statutory Interpretation* (Butterworths, 4th edn, 2002)

Bingham's Negligence Cases (5th edn, 2002)

Blackstone *Commentaries on the Laws of England* (17th edn) vol III

Brearley and Hoskins *Remedies in EC Law* (2nd edn, 1998)

BSI *Draft for Development* (DD 43, 1975)

Buchan 'Stress Cases, Foreseeability and Breach' (2001) 3 JPIL 7

Charlesworth and Percy on Negligence (10th edn)

Clerk and Lindsell on Torts (Sweet & Maxwell, 18th edn, 2000)

Cotter *Defective and Unsafe Products, Law and Practice* (Butterworths, 1996)

Dicey & Morris on The Conflict of Laws (Sweet & Maxwell, 13th edn, 2000)

Freedland *The Personal Contract of Employment* (2nd edn, 2003)

Hartley *The Foundations of European Community Law* (OUP, 5th edn, 2003)

Harvey on Industrial Relations and Employment Law (Butterworths, loose-leaf)

Hogarth, Walker, Burton & Gore *Asbestos Disease Claims* (Butterworths, 2004)

Hunter's Diseases of Occupation (9th Edn)

Kemp and Kemp *The Quantum of Damages* (Sweet & Maxwell, 1995)

Ladbroke Grove Rail Inquiry Reports 1 and 2 (HSE, 2001)

Langstaff 'Upper Limb Disorders: Work-related or Unrelated' (1994) JPIL 16

Occupational Illness Litigation (looseleaf)

Redgrave's Health and Safety (4th edn)

Salmond and Heuston on the Law of Torts (Sweet & Maxwell, 21st edn, 1996)

Southampton University *Vibration injuries—the conduct of the reasonable and prudent employer* (1978)

Taylor 'Vibration White Finger in the Workplace' (1982) 32 Jnl Soc Occ Med 159

Uff and Lord Cullen *The Joint Inquiry into Train Protection Systems* (HSE, 2001)

Winfield and Jolowicz on Tort (Sweet & Maxwell, 16th edn, 2002)

World Health Organisation 'Classification of Mental and Behavioural Disorders' ICD-10 (Geneva, 1993)

Index

Index

Index

Index

Index